MyBCommLab®: Improves Student Engagement Before, During, and After Class

Prep and Engagement

- **NEW! VIDEO LIBRARY –** Robust video library with over 100 new book-specific videos that include easy-to-assign assessments, the ability for instructors to add YouTube or other sources, the ability for students to upload video submissions, and the ability for polling and teamwork.

- **Decision-making simulations – NEW and improved feedback for students.** Place your students in the role of a key decision-maker! Simulations branch based on the decisions students make, providing a variation of scenario paths. Upon completion students receive a grade, as well as a detailed report of the choices and the associated consequences of those decisions.

- **Video exercises – UPDATED with new exercises.** Engaging videos that bring business concepts to life and explore business topics related to the theory students are learning in class. Quizzes then assess students' comprehension of the concepts covered in each video.

- **Learning Catalytics –** A "bring your own device" student engagement, assessment, and classroom intelligence system helps instructors analyze students' critical-thinking skills during lecture.

- **Dynamic Study Modules (DSMs) – UPDATED with additional questions.** Through adaptive learning, students get personalized guidance where and when they need it most, creating greater engagement, improving knowledge retention, and supporting subject-matter mastery. Also available on mobile devices.

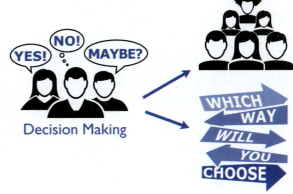

- **Writing Space – UPDATED with new commenting tabs, new prompts, and a new tool for students called Pearson Writer.** A single location to develop and assess concept mastery and critical thinking, the Writing Space offers automatic graded, assisted graded, and create your own writing assignments, allowing you to exchange personalized feedback with students quickly and easily.

  Writing Space can also check students' work for improper citation or plagiarism by comparing it against the world's most accurate text comparison database available from **Turnitin**.

- **Additional Features** – Included with the MyLab are a powerful homework and test manager, robust gradebook tracking, Reporting Dashboard, comprehensive online course content, and easily scalable and shareable content.

http://www.pearsonmylabandmastering.com

PEARSON

Today's students are holding the future of business communication in their hands

As another disruptive technology redefines business communication, Bovée and Thill are once again the first to respond with current, comprehensive, and fully integrated coverage.

Just as Bovée and Thill pioneered coverage of the social media revolution, they now lead the market with up-to-the-minute coverage of mobile business communication.

> "Mobile is the most disruptive technology that I have seen in 48 years in Silicon Valley."[1]
>
> —Venture capitalist Joe Schoendorf

The mobile revolution: key facts and figures

Smart business leaders know they must adapt and respond to the rise of mobile usage by consumers and employees:[2]

REAL-TIME UPDATES

LEARN MORE BY VISITING THIS WEBSITE

The mobile revolution by the numbers

Explore dozens of statistical measures that show the impact of mobile communication. Go to http://real-timeupdates.com/ebc12 and click on Learn More in the Students section.

- For millions of people, a mobile device is their primary way, if not their only way, to access the Internet.
- Globally, 80 percent of Internet users access the web at least some of the time with a mobile device.
- Mobile has become the primary communication tool for many business professionals, including a majority of executives under age 40.
- Email and web browsing rank first and second in terms of the most common nonvoice uses of smartphones.
- More email messages are now opened on mobile devices than on PCs.
- Roughly half of U.S. consumers use a mobile device exclusively for their online search needs.
- Many online activities that eventually migrate to a PC screen start out on a mobile screen.

Bovée and Thill's coverage of mobile business communication includes these important topics:

- *The Mobile Revolution*
- *The Rise of Mobile as a Communication Platform*
- *How Mobile Technologies Are Changing Business Communication*
- *Collaboration via Mobile Devices*
- *Business Etiquette Using Mobile Devices*
- *The Unique Challenges of Communication on Mobile Devices*
- *Writing Messages for Mobile Devices*
- *Designing Messages for Mobile Devices*
- *Optimizing Content for Mobile Devices*
- *Visual Media on Mobile Devices*
- *Creating Promotional Messages for Mobile Devices*
- *Integrating Mobile Devices in Presentations*

Integrated coverage and student activities

As with social media, the changes brought about by mobile run far deeper than the technology itself. Successful communication on mobile devices requires a new approach to planning, writing, and designing messages.

With in-depth, integrated coverage of the challenges and opportunities that mobile presents, *Excellence in Business Communication, 12th* Edition, helps students adapt their personal use of mobile devices to the unique demands of business communication. Through a variety of annotated model messages, questions, activities, and cases, students will gain valuable skills in the art of communicating via mobile devices.

Optimizing for mobile includes writing short headlines that get right to the point.

This introduction conveys only the information readers need in order to grasp the scope of the article.

All the key points of the documents appear here on the first screen.

Readers who want more detail can swipe down for background information on the five points.

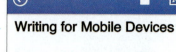

Writing for Mobile Devices

To write effectively for readers on mobile devices, use these five essential techniques:

- Use a linear flow
- Prioritize information for readers
- Create short, focused messages
- Use shorter subject lines and headings
- Use shorter paragraphs

Continue reading for background information on these guidelines.

EMAIL SKILLS / MOBILE SKILLS

7.33. Media Skills: Email [LO-5] The size limitations of smartphone screens call for a different approach to writing (see page 148) and formatting (see page 173) documents.

Your task: On th... find a news releas... leases) that annou... or any other writi... material in a way t...

WEB WRITING SKILLS/MOBILE SKILLS/ PORTFOLIO BUILDER

12.29. Message Strategies: Online Content [LO-2] Adapting conventional web content to make it mobile friendly can require rethinking the site's information architecture to simplify navigation and revising the content.

Your task: Choose the website of a company that makes products you find interesting. (Make it a conventional website, not one already optimized for mobile.) Analyze the section of the

MOBILE APPS
Pocket Letter Pro includes templates for a variety of letter types to simplify writing business letters on your mobile device.

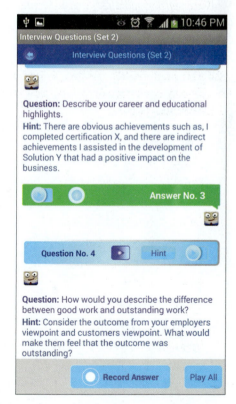

With realistic examples, pointers to dozens of business communication apps, and a full range of questions and projects, Excellence in Business Communication highlights the best current practices in mobile business communication.

1. "The Mobile Revolution Is Just Beginning," press release, Word Economic Forum, 13 September 2013, www.weforum.org.

2. "More Than Nine in 10 Internet Users Will Go Online via Phone," eMarketer, 6 January 2014, www.emarketer.com; Christina "CK" Kerley, *The Mobile Revolution & B2B*, white paper, 2011, www.b2bmobilerevolution.com; Jordie can Rijn, "The Ultimate Mobile Email Statistics Overview," Emailmonday.com, accessed 9 February 2014, www.emailmonday.com; Jessica Lee, "46% of Searchers Now Use Mobile Exclusively to Research [Study]," Search Engine Watch, 1 May 2013, http://searchenginewatch.com.

TWELFTH
EDITION

Excellence in Business Communication

John V. Thill

CHAIRMAN AND CHIEF EXECUTIVE OFFICER
GLOBAL COMMUNICATION STRATEGIES

Courtland L. Bovée

PROFESSOR OF BUSINESS COMMUNICATION
C. ALLEN PAUL DISTINGUISHED CHAIR
GROSSMONT COLLEGE

PEARSON

Boston   Columbus   Indianapolis   New York   San Francisco   Amsterdam   Cape Town
Dubai   London   Madrid   Milan   Munich   Paris   Montreal   Toronto   Delhi   Mexico City
São Paulo   Sydney   Hong Kong   Seoul   Singapore   Taipei   Tokyo

Vice President, Business Publishing: Donna Battista
Editor in Chief: Stephanie Wall
Acquisitions Editor: Emily Tamburri
Program Management Lead: Ashley Santora
Program Manager: Denise Weiss
Editorial Assistant: Olivia Vignone
Vice President, Product Marketing: Maggie Moylan
**Director of Marketing, Digital Services and
   Products:** Jeanette Koskinas
Field Marketing Manager: Lenny Ann Raper
Product Marketing Assistant: Jessica Quazza
Project Management Lead: Jeff Holcomb
Senior Project Manager: Nicole Suddeth
Operations Specialist: Carol Melville
Creative Director: Blair Brown
Art Director: Janet Slowik
VP, Director of Digital Strategy & Assessment:
   Paul Gentile

Manager of Learning Applications: Paul DeLuca
Digital Editor: Brian Surette
Director, Digital Studio: Sacha Laustsen
Digital Studio Manager: Diane Lombardo
Digital Studio Project Manager: Robin Lazrus
Digital Studio Project Manager: Alana Coles
Digital Studio Project Manager: Monique Lawrence
Digital Studio Project Manager: Regina DaSilva
Full-Service Project Management and Composition:
   Integra
Interior & Cover Designer: Integra Software Services
Cover Art: Rawpixel/Fotolia
Printer/Binder: LSC Communications
Cover Printer: LSC Communications
Text Font: 10.5/12 Albertina MT Pro

Acknowledgments of third-party content appear on the appropriate page within the text.

Microsoft and/or its respective suppliers make no representations about the suitability of the information contained in the documents and related graphics published as part of the services for any purpose. All such documents and related graphics are provided "as is" without warranty of any kind. Microsoft and/or its respective suppliers hereby disclaim all warranties and conditions with regard to this information, including all warranties and conditions of merchantability, whether express, implied or statutory, fitness for a particular purpose, title and non-infringement. In no event shall Microsoft and/or its respective suppliers be liable for any special, indirect or consequential damages or any damages whatsoever resulting from loss of use, data or profits, whether in an action of contract, negligence or other tortious action, arising out of or in connection with the use or performance of information available from the services.

The documents and related graphics contained herein could include technical inaccuracies or typographical errors. Changes are periodically added to the information herein. Microsoft and/or its respective suppliers may make improvements and/or changes in the product(s) and/or the program(s) described herein at any time. Partial screen shots may be viewed in full within the software version specified.

Microsoft® and Windows® are registered trademarks of the Microsoft Corporation in the U.S.A. and other countries. This book is not sponsored or endorsed by or affiliated with the Microsoft Corporation.

Library of Congress Cataloging-in-Publication Data
Thill, John V.
   Excellence in business communication / John V. Thill, Chairman and Chief Executive Officer, Global Communication
   Strategies, Courtland L. Bovee, Professor of Business Communication, C. Allen Paul Distinguished Chair, Grossmont
   College. — Twelfth Edition.
      pages cm.
   Includes bibliographical references and index.
   ISBN 978-0-13-431905-6
   1. Business communication—United States—Case studies.   I. Bovée, Courtland L.   II. Title.
   HF5718.2.U6T45 2016
   658.4'5—dc23

                                                          2015033275

5   18

ISBN 10:   0-13-431905-2
ISBN 13: 978-0-13-431905-6

Dedication

This book is dedicated to the many thousands of instructors and students who use Bovée and Thill texts to develop career-enhancing skills in business communication. We appreciate the opportunity to play a role in your education, and we wish you the very best with your careers.

John V. Thill
Courtland L. Bovée

Brief Contents

Preface **xix**
Prologue **xli**

PART 1 Understanding the Foundations of Business Communication **1**

 1 Professional Communication in a Digital, Social, Mobile World 2
 2 Collaboration, Interpersonal Communication, and Business Etiquette 36
 3 Communication Challenges in a Diverse, Global Marketplace 68

PART 2 Applying the Three-Step Writing Process **97**

 4 Planning Business Messages 98
 5 Writing Business Messages 127
 6 Completing Business Messages 158

PART 3 Crafting Brief Business **185**

 7 Crafting Messages for Digital Channels 186
 8 Writing Routine and Positive Messages 225
 9 Writing Negative Messages 251
 10 Writing Persuasive Messages 287

PART 4 Preparing Reports and Presentations **319**

 11 Planning Reports and Proposals 320
 12 Writing Reports and Proposals 360
 13 Completing Reports and Proposals 399
 14 Developing and Delivering Business Presentations 441

PART 5 Writing Employment Messages and Interviewing for Jobs **477**

 15 Building Careers and Writing Résumés 478
 16 Applying and Interviewing for Employment 512

Appendix **A** Format and Layout of Business Documents 547
Appendix **B** Documentation of Report Sources 562
Appendix **C** Correction Symbols 568

Handbook of Grammar, Mechanics, and Usage 571
Answer Keys 599
Brand, Organization, Name, and Website Index 603
Subject Index 606

Contents

Preface   xix
Prologue   xli

PART 1
Understanding the Foundations of Business Communication   1

1   Professional Communication in a Digital, Social, Mobile World   2

COMMUNICATING AT Jetblue   2

Understanding Why Communication Matters   3
  Communication Is Important to Your Career   3
  Communication Is Important to Your Company   5
  What Makes Business Communication Effective?   5
Communicating as a Professional   5
  Understanding What Employers Expect from You   7
  Communicating in an Organizational Context   8
  Adopting an Audience-Centered Approach   8
Exploring the Communication Process   9
  The Basic Communication Model   10
  The Social Communication Model   13
The Mobile Revolution   15
  The Rise of Mobile as a Communication Platform   15
  How Mobile Technologies Are Changing Business Communication   16
Using Technology to Improve Business Communication   18
  Keeping Technology in Perspective   18
  Guarding Against Information Overload   18
  Using Technological Tools Productively   18
  Reconnecting with People   24
Committing to Ethical and Legal Communication   24
  Distinguishing Ethical Dilemmas from Ethical Lapses   25
  Ensuring Ethical Communication   26
  Ensuring Legal Communication   27
Applying What You've Learned   28

SOLVING COMMUNICATION DILEMMAS AT Jetblue   28

Learning Objectives Checkup   29
Apply Your Knowledge   32
Practice Your Skills   32

Expand Your Skills   33
Improve Your Grammar, Mechanics, and Usage   34
THE ART OF PROFESSIONALISM Maintaining a Confident, Positive Outlook   8

2   Collaboration, Interpersonal Communication, and Business Etiquette   36

COMMUNICATING AT Cemex   36
Communicating Effectively in Teams   37
  Advantages and Disadvantages of Teams   37
  Characteristics of Effective Teams   38
  Group Dynamics   38
Collaborating on Communication Efforts   41
  Guidelines for Collaborative Writing   41
  Technologies for Collaborative Writing   42
  Giving—and Responding to—Constructive Feedback   44
Making Your Meetings More Productive   45
  Preparing for Meetings   45
  Conducting and Contributing to Efficient Meetings   45
  Putting Meeting Results to Productive Use   47
Using Meeting Technologies   48
Improving Your Listening Skills   49
  Recognizing Various Types of Listening   49
  Understanding the Listening Process   50
  Overcoming Barriers to Effective Listening   51
Improving Your Nonverbal Communication Skills   52
  Recognizing Nonverbal Communication   52
  Using Nonverbal Communication Effectively   53
Developing Your Business Etiquette   54
  Business Etiquette in the Workplace   54
  Business Etiquette in Social Settings   57
  Business Etiquette Online   57
  Business Etiquette Using Mobile Devices   58

SOLVING COMMUNICATION DILEMMAS AT Cemex   59

Learning Objectives Checkup   60
Apply Your Knowledge   63
Practice Your Skills   63
Expand Your Skills   64
Improve Your Grammar, Mechanics, and Usage   65
COMMUNICATING ACROSS CULTURES Whose Skin Is This, Anyway?   56

3 Communication Challenges in a Diverse, Global Marketplace 68

COMMUNICATING AT **EY** 68

Understanding the Opportunities and Challenges of Communication in a Diverse World 69
The Opportunities in a Global Marketplace 69
The Advantages of a Diverse Workforce 70
The Challenges of Intercultural Communication 70

Developing Cultural Competency 71
Understanding the Concept of Culture 71
Overcoming Ethnocentrism and Stereotyping 72

Recognizing Variations in a Diverse World 73
Contextual Differences 73
Legal and Ethical Differences 74
Social Differences 74
Nonverbal Differences 75
Age Differences 76
Gender Differences 76
Religious Differences 77
Ability Differences 78

Adapting to Other Business Cultures 78
Guidelines for Adapting to Any Business Culture 78
Guidelines for Adapting to U.S. Business Culture 79

Improving Intercultural Communication Skills 79
Studying Other Cultures 79
Studying Other Languages 80
Respecting Preferences for Communication Style 82
Writing Clearly 83
Speaking and Listening Carefully 86
Using Interpreters, Translators, and Translation Software 88
Helping Others Adapt to Your Culture 88

SOLVING COMMUNICATION DILEMMAS AT **EY** 89

Learning Objectives Checkup 90
Apply Your Knowledge 93
Practice Your Skills 93
Expand Your Skills 94
Improve Your Grammar, Mechanics, and Usage 94

COMMUNICATING ACROSS CULTURES Us Versus Them: Generational Conflict in the Workplace 77

PART 2
Applying the Three-Step Writing Process 97

4 Planning Business Messages 98

COMMUNICATING AT **H&R Block** 98

Understanding the Three-Step Writing Process 99
Optimizing Your Writing Time 100
Planning Effectively 100

Analyzing the Situation 100
Defining Your Purpose 101
Developing an Audience Profile 101

Gathering Information 103
Uncovering Audience Needs 103
Finding Your Focus 104
Providing Required Information 104

Selecting the Best Combination of Media and Channels 106
The Most Common Media and Channel Options 106
Factors to Consider When Choosing Media and Channels 112

Organizing Your Information 112
Defining Your Main Idea 113
Limiting Your Scope 114
Choosing Between Direct and Indirect Approaches 115
Outlining Your Content 115
Building Reader Interest with Storytelling Techniques 119

SOLVING COMMUNICATION DILEMMAS AT **H&R Block** 120

Learning Objectives Checkup 121
Apply Your Knowledge 124
Practice Your Skills 124
Expand Your Skills 125
Improve Your Grammar, Mechanics, and Usage 126

PRACTICING ETHICAL COMMUNICATION How Much Information Is Enough? 105

5 Writing Business Messages 127

COMMUNICATING AT **She Takes on the World** 127

Adapting to Your Audience: Being Sensitive to Audience Needs 128
Using the "You" Attitude 128
Maintaining Standards of Etiquette 129
Emphasizing the Positive 130
Using Bias-Free Language 131

Adapting to Your Audience: Building Strong Relationships 132
Establishing Your Credibility 132
Projecting Your Company's Image 134

Adapting to Your Audience: Controlling Your Style and Tone 134
Creating a Conversational Tone 135
Using Plain Language 136
Selecting the Active or Passive Voice 137

Composing Your Message: Choosing Powerful Words 138
Understanding Denotation and Connotation 140
Balancing Abstract and Concrete Words 140
Finding Words That Communicate Well 140

Composing Your Message: Creating Effective Sentences 142
Choosing from the Four Types of Sentences 142
Using Sentence Style to Emphasize Key Thoughts 143

Composing Your Message: Crafting Unified, Coherent Paragraphs 144
Creating the Elements of a Paragraph 144
Choosing the Best Way to Develop Each Paragraph 147

Writing Messages for Mobile Devices 148

SOLVING COMMUNICATION DILEMMAS AT **She Takes on the World** 150

Learning Objectives Checkup 151
Apply Your Knowledge 154
Practice Your Skills 154
Expand Your Skills 156
Improve Your Grammar, Mechanics, and Usage 156

THE ART OF PROFESSIONALISM Being Dependable and Accountable 134

6 Completing Business Messages 158

COMMUNICATING AT Jefferson Rabb Web Design 158

Revising Your Message: Evaluating the First Draft 159
Evaluating Your Content, Organization, Style, and Tone 159
Evaluating, Editing, and Revising the Work of Others 162
Revising to Improve Readability 162
Varying Your Sentence Length 163
Keeping Your Paragraphs Short 163
Using Lists to Clarify and Emphasize 164
Adding Headings and Subheadings 165
Editing for Clarity and Conciseness 166
Editing for Clarity 166
Editing for Conciseness 168
Producing Your Message 170
Designing for Readability 170
Formatting Formal Letters and Memos 173
Designing Messages for Mobile Devices 173
Proofreading Your Message 174
Distributing Your Message 175

SOLVING COMMUNICATION DILEMMAS AT Jefferson Rabb Web Design 176

Learning Objectives Checkup 177
Apply Your Knowledge 180
Practice Your Skills 180
Expand Your Skills 183
Improve Your Grammar, Mechanics, and Usage 183

PART 3

Crafting Brief Business 185

7 Crafting Messages for Digital Channels 186

COMMUNICATING AT GoPro 186
Digital Channels for Business Communication 187
Media Choices for Brief Messages 188
Compositional Modes for Digital Media 188
Creating Content for Social Media 189
Optimizing Content for Mobile Devices 191
Social Networks 191
Business Communication Uses of Social Networks 192
Strategies for Business Communication on Social Networks 194
Information and Content Sharing Sites 194
User-Generated Content Sites 195
Content Curation Sites 195
Community Q&A Sites 198

Email 198
Planning Email Messages 199
Writing Email Messages 199
Completing Email Messages 200
Instant Messaging and Text Messaging 202
Understanding the Benefits and Risks of IM 203
Adapting the Three-Step Process for Successful IM 203
Blogging and Microblogging 204
Understanding the Business Applications of Blogging 205
Adapting the Three-Step Process for Successful Blogging 206
Microblogging 209
Podcasting 210

SOLVING COMMUNICATION DILEMMAS AT GoPro 212

Learning Objectives Checkup 213
Apply Your Knowledge 217
Practice Your Skills 217
Expand Your Skills 219
Improve Your Grammar, Mechanics, and Usage 219
Cases 220

DIGITAL + SOCIAL + MOBILE: TODAY'S COMMUNICATION ENVIRONMENT Community Manager: One of the Hottest New Jobs in Business 192

DIGITAL + SOCIAL + MOBILE: TODAY'S COMMUNICATION ENVIRONMENT Will Emoticons Give Your Career a Frowny Face? 201

8 Writing Routine and Positive Messages 225

COMMUNICATING AT Get Satisfaction 225
Strategy for Routine Requests 226
Stating Your Request Up Front 226
Explaining and Justifying Your Request 226
Requesting Specific Action in a Courteous Close 227
Common Examples of Routine Requests 227
Asking for Information and Action 227
Asking for Recommendations 227
Making Claims and Requesting Adjustments 229
Strategy for Routine and Positive Messages 229
Starting with the Main Idea 232
Providing Necessary Details and Explanation 232
Ending with a Courteous Close 233
Common Examples of Routine and Positive Messages 233
Answering Requests for Information and Action 233
Granting Claims and Requests for Adjustment 233
Providing Recommendations and References 234
Sharing Routine Information 237
Announcing Good News 237
Fostering Goodwill 238

SOLVING COMMUNICATION DILEMMAS AT Get Satisfaction 240

Learning Objectives Checkup 241
Apply Your Knowledge 244
Practice Your Skills 244
Expand Your Skills 245
Improve Your Grammar, Mechanics, and Usage 246
Cases 246

9 Writing Negative Messages 251

COMMUNICATING AT Hailo 251

Using the Three-Step Writing Process for Negative Messages 252
Step 1: Planning a Negative Message 252
Step 2: Writing a Negative Message 254
Step 3: Completing a Negative Message 254

Using the Direct Approach for Negative Messages 255
Opening with a Clear Statement of the Bad News 255
Providing Reasons and Additional Information 255
Closing on a Respectful Note 257

Using the Indirect Approach for Negative Messages 257
Opening with a Buffer 258
Providing Reasons and Additional Information 258
Continuing with a Clear Statement of the Bad News 259
Closing on a Respectful Note 260

Maintaining High Standards of Ethics and Etiquette 261

Sending Negative Messages on Routine Business Matters 263
Making Negative Announcements on Routine Business Matters 263
Rejecting Suggestions and Proposals 263
Refusing Routine Requests 263
Handling Bad News About Transactions 264
Refusing Claims and Requests for Adjustment 265

Sending Negative Organizational News 267
Communicating Under Normal Circumstances 267
Responding to Negative Information in a Social Media Environment 267
Communicating in a Crisis 269

Sending Negative Employment Messages 270
Refusing Requests for Employee References and Recommendation Letters 270
Refusing Social Networking Recommendation Requests 271
Rejecting Job Applications 271
Giving Negative Performance Reviews 272
Terminating Employment 273

SOLVING COMMUNICATION DILEMMAS AT Hailo 274

Learning Objectives Checkup 275
Apply Your Knowledge 279
Practice Your Skills 279
Expand Your Skills 280
Improve Your Grammar, Mechanics, and Usage 281
Cases 281

PRACTICING ETHICAL COMMUNICATION The Deceptive Soft Sell 262

10 Writing Persuasive Messages 287

COMMUNICATING AT Red Ants Pants 287

Using the Three-Step Writing Process for Persuasive Messages 288
Step 1: Planning Persuasive Messages 288
Step 2: Writing Persuasive Messages 291
Step 3: Completing Persuasive Messages 292

Developing Persuasive Business Messages 292
Strategies for Persuasive Business Messages 292
Avoiding Common Mistakes in Persuasive Communication 297
Common Examples of Persuasive Business Messages 297

Developing Marketing and Sales Messages 301
Planning Marketing and Sales Messages 301
Writing Conventional Marketing and Sales Messages 302
Writing Promotional Messages for Social Media 302
Creating Promotional Messages for Mobile Devices 304

Maintaining High Standards of Ethics, Legal Compliance, and Etiquette 304

SOLVING COMMUNICATION DILEMMAS AT Red Ants Pants 305

Learning Objectives Checkup 306
Apply Your Knowledge 309
Practice Your Skills 309
Expand Your Skills 310
Improve Your Grammar, Mechanics, and Usage 311
Cases 311

PRACTICING ETHICAL COMMUNICATION Pushing the Limits of Credibility 292

PART 4
Preparing Reports and Presentations 319

11 Planning Reports and Proposals 320

COMMUNICATING AT MyCityWay 320

Applying the Three-Step Writing Process to Reports and Proposals 321
Analyzing the Situation 321
Gathering Information 323
Selecting the Best Combination of Media and Channels 323
Organizing Your Information 325

Supporting Your Messages with Reliable Information 327
Planning Your Research 328
Locating Data and Information 329
Evaluating Sources 329
Using Your Research Results 330

Conducting Secondary Research 332
Finding Information at a Library 334
Finding Information Online 334
Documenting Your Sources 336

Conducting Primary Research 337
Conducting Surveys 337
Conducting Interviews 339

Planning Informational Reports 340
Organizing Informational Reports 340
Creating Successful Business Plans 341
Organizing Website Content 342

Planning Analytical Reports   344
   Focusing on Conclusions   345
   Focusing on Recommendations   345
   Focusing on Logical Arguments   345
Planning Proposals   349

SOLVING COMMUNICATION DILEMMAS AT
MyCityWay   352

Learning Objectives Checkup   353
Apply Your Knowledge   356
Practice Your Skills   356
Expand Your Skills   358
Improve Your Grammar, Mechanics, and Usage   358

DIGITAL + SOCIAL + MOBILE: TODAY'S COMMUNICATION
ENVIRONMENT Research on the Go with Mobile
Devices   337

12 Writing Reports and Proposals 360

COMMUNICATING AT Warby Parker   360
Composing Reports and Proposals   361
   Adapting to Your Audience   361
   Drafting Report Content   363
   Drafting Proposal Content   367
   Helping Report Readers Find Their Way   370
   Using Technology to Craft Reports and Proposals   370
Writing for Websites and Wikis   371
   Drafting Website Content   371
   Collaborating on Wikis   371
Illustrating Your Reports with Effective
Visuals   373
   Understanding Visual Design Principles   373
   Understanding the Ethics of Visual
      Communication   374
   Identifying Points to Illustrate   375
   Selecting the Right Type of Visual   375
Producing and Integrating Visuals   383
   Creating Visuals   384
   Verifying the Quality of Your Visuals   385
   Visual Media on Mobile Devices   385

SOLVING COMMUNICATION DILEMMAS AT Warby
Parker   388

Learning Objectives Checkup   389
Apply Your Knowledge   392
Practice Your Skills   392
Expand Your Skills   394
Improve Your Grammar, Mechanics, and Usage   394
Cases   395

PRACTICING ETHICAL COMMUNICATION Distorting
the Data   386

13 Completing Reports and Proposals 399

COMMUNICATING AT Garage Technology
Ventures   399
Revising Reports and Proposals   400
Producing Formal Reports   401

   Prefatory Parts   403
   Text of the Report   408
   Supplementary Parts   409
Producing Formal Proposals   410
   Prefatory Parts   410
   Text of the Proposal   411
Proofreading Reports and Proposals   412
Distributing Reports and Proposals   412

SOLVING COMMUNICATION DILEMMAS AT Garage
Technology Ventures   429

Learning Objectives Checkup   430
Apply Your Knowledge   433
Practice Your Skills   433
Expand Your Skills   434
Improve Your Grammar, Mechanics, and Usage   434
Cases   435

REPORT WRITER'S NOTEBOOK Analyzing a Formal
Report   413

14 Developing and Delivering Business Presentations 441

COMMUNICATING AT Principato-Young
Entertainment   441
Planning a Presentation   442
   Analyzing the Situation   442
   Selecting the Best Media and Channels   444
   Organizing A Presentation   444
Developing a Presentation   449
   Adapting to Your Audience   449
   Crafting Presentation Content   450
Enhancing Your Presentation with Effective
Visuals   453
   Choosing Structured or Free-Form
      Slides   454
   Designing Effective Slides   455
   Integrating Mobile Devices in
      Presentations   459
Completing a Presentation   460
   Finalizing Your Slides   460
   Creating Effective Handouts   461
   Choosing Your Presentation Method   461
   Practicing Your Delivery   463
Delivering a Presentation   464
   Overcoming Anxiety   464
   Handling Questions Responsively   465
   Embracing the Backchannel   465
   Giving Presentations Online   466

SOLVING COMMUNICATION DILEMMAS AT Principato-Young
Entertainment   467

Learning Objectives Checkup   468
Apply Your Knowledge   472
Practice Your Skills   472
Expand Your Skills   473
Improve Your Grammar, Mechanics, and Usage   473
Cases   474

THE ART OF PROFESSIONALISM Being a Team
Player   453

PART 5
Writing Employment Messages and Interviewing for Jobs 477

15 Building Careers and Writing Résumés 478

COMMUNICATING AT VMWare 478

Finding the Ideal Opportunity in Today's Job Market 479
Writing the Story of You 479
Learning to Think Like an Employer 480
Researching Industries and Companies of Interest 481
Translating Your General Potential into a Specific Solution for Each Employer 482
Taking the Initiative to Find Opportunities 483
Building Your Network 484
Seeking Career Counseling 484
Avoiding Mistakes 484

Planning a Résumé 485
Analyzing Your Purpose and Audience 486
Gathering Pertinent Information 487
Selecting the Best Media and Channels 487
Organizing Your Résumé Around Your Strengths 487
Addressing Areas of Concern 488

Writing Your Résumé 489
Keeping Your Résumé Honest 489
Adapting Your Résumé to Your Audience 489
Composing Your Résumé 490

Completing Your Résumé 497
Revising Your Résumé 497
Producing Your Résumé 497
Proofreading Your Résumé 500
Distributing Your Résumé 500

SOLVING COMMUNICATION DILEMMAS AT VMWare 501

Learning Objectives Checkup 504
Apply Your Knowledge 507
Practice Your Skills 507
Expand Your Skills 508
Improve Your Grammar, Mechanics, and Usage 508
Cases 508

DIGITAL + SOCIAL + MOBILE: TODAY'S COMMUNICATION ENVIRONMENT Job Search Strategies: Maximize Your Mobile 482

THE ART OF PROFESSIONALISM Striving to Excel 485

16 Applying and Interviewing for Employment 512

COMMUNICATING AT Zappos 512

Submitting Your Résumé 513
Writing Application Letters 513
Following Up After Submitting a Résumé 518

Understanding the Interviewing Process 519
The Typical Sequence of Interviews 519
Common Types of Interviews 519
Interview Media 520
What Employers Look for in an Interview 521
Preemployment Testing and Background Checks 522

Preparing for a Job Interview 523
Learning About the Organization and Your Interviewers 523
Thinking Ahead About Questions 524
Bolstering Your Confidence 525
Polishing Your Interview Style 526
Presenting a Professional Image 526
Being Ready When You Arrive 529

Interviewing for Success 529
The Warm-Up 530
The Question-and-Answer Stage 530
The Close 531
Interview Notes 532

Following Up After the Interview 533
Follow-Up Message 533
Message of Inquiry 533
Request for a Time Extension 533
Letter of Acceptance 533
Letter Declining a Job Offer 535
Letter of Resignation 536

SOLVING COMMUNICATION DILEMMAS AT Zappos 537

Learning Objectives Checkup 538
Apply Your Knowledge 541
Practice Your Skills 541
Expand Your Skills 542
Improve Your Grammar, Mechanics, and Usage 542
Cases 543

COMMUNICATING ACROSS CULTURES Successfully Interviewing Across Borders 528

APPENDIX A
Format and Layout of Business Documents 547

First Impressions 547
Paper 547
Customization 547
Appearance 547

Letters 548
Standard Letter Parts 548
Additional Letter Parts 552
Letter Formats 554

Envelopes 556
Addressing the Envelope 556
Folding to Fit 557
International Mail 559

Memos 559
Reports 560
Margins 560
Headings 560
Page Numbers 561

APPENDIX B
Documentation of Report Sources 562

Chicago Humanities Style 562
In-Text Citation—Chicago Humanities Style 562
Bibliography—Chicago Humanities Style 563

APA Style 565
In-Text Citation—APA Style 565
List of References—APA Style 565

MLA Style 565
In-Text Citation—MLA Style 565
List of Works Cited—MLA Style 566

APPENDIX **C**

Correction Symbols   568

Content and Style   568
Grammar, Mechanics, and Usage   569
Proofreading Marks   570

Handbook of Grammar, Mechanics, and Usage   571

Diagnostic Test of English Skills   571
Assessment of English Skills   573
Essentials of Grammar, Mechanics, and Usage   573
1.0 Grammar   573
  1.1 Nouns   573
  1.2 Pronouns   575
  1.3 Verbs   576
  1.4 Adjectives   580
  1.5 Adverbs   581
  1.6 Other Parts of Speech   582
  1.7 Sentences   583
2.0 Punctuation   586
  2.1 Periods   586
  2.2 Question Marks   586
  2.3 Exclamation Points   587
  2.4 Semicolons   587
  2.5 Colons   587

  2.6 Commas   587
  2.7 Dashes   589
  2.8 Hyphens   589
  2.9 Apostrophes   589
  2.10 Quotation Marks   590
  2.11 Parentheses and Brackets   590
  2.12 Ellipses   590
3.0 Mechanics   591
  3.1 Capitalization   591
  3.2 Underscores and Italics   592
  3.3 Abbreviations   592
  3.4 Numbers   593
  3.5 Word Division   594
4.0 Vocabulary   594
  4.1 Frequently Confused Words   594
  4.2 Frequently Misused Words   595
  4.3 Frequently Misspelled Words   596
  4.4 Transitional Words and Phrases   597

Answer Keys   **599**

Brand, Organization, Name, and Website Index   **603**

Subject Index   **606**

Preface

Major Changes and Improvements in This Edition

Here are the major changes in the 12th edition of *Excellence in Business Communication*:

- Groundbreaking coverage of mobile business communication; see the next page for more information
- New text sections:
    Using All the Job-Search Tools at Your Disposal (Prologue)
    The Mobile Revolution (Chapter 1)
        The Rise of Mobile as a Communication Platform
        How Mobile Technologies Are Changing Business Communication
    Collaboration via Mobile Devices (Chapter 2)
    Putting Meeting Results to Productive Use (Chapter 2)
    Business Etiquette Using Mobile Devices (Chapter 2)
    Selecting the Best Combination of Media and Channels (Chapter 4)
    The Unique Challenges of Communication on Mobile Devices (Chapter 4)
    Writing Messages for Mobile Devices (Chapter 5)
    Designing Messages for Mobile Devices (Chapter 6)
    Optimizing Content for Mobile Devices (Chapter 7)
    Creating Promotional Messages for Mobile Devices (Chapter 10)
    Visual Media on Mobile Devices (Chapter 12)
    Organizing a Presentation (Chapter 14)
    Integrating Mobile Devices in Presentations (Chapter 14)
    Choosing a Design Strategy for Your Résumé (Chapter 15)
- Coverage of emerging issues that are reshaping business communication, including *digital information fluency* and the *bring your own device (BYOD)* phenomenon
- Coverage of *linear* and *nonlinear presentations*, discussing the relative strengths of slide-based presentations (linear) and Prezi-style presentations (nonlinear)
- Six new chapter-opening vignettes with accompanying end-of-chapter simulations, featuring JetBlue, GoPro, Hailo, Red Ants Pants, Warby Parker, and VMWare
- Revised treatment of media and channels to reflect the continuing evolution of digital formats; we now categorize media choices *oral, written,* and *visual,* each of which can be delivered through *digital* and *nondigital channels* to create six basic combinations
- A new highlight box theme, *Digital + Social + Mobile: Today's Communication Environment,* addressing such topics as gamification as way to engage audiences, the new careers available in social media community management, using mobile devices for business research, and using mobile devices in the job search process.
- More than 50 new business communication examples and figures—and the 12th edition includes nearly 30 mobile communication examples and more than two dozen social media examples
- New exercises and activities that focus on mobile communication
- A selection of communication cases that challenge students to craft messages for mobile devices

As Another Disruptive Technology Transforms Business Communication, Bovée and Thill Again Lead the Field with Innovative Coverage

The history of business communication over the past couple of decades has been one of almost constant change. The first major wave was the digital revolution, replacing much of the print communication of the past with email, instant messaging, web content, and other new forms. Then came social media, which fundamentally redefined the relationship between businesses and their stakeholders. And now comes the third wave, and it's proving to be every bit as disruptive—and full of exciting possibilities—as the first two.

Mobile communication, and mobile connectivity in the larger sense, is changing the way business communicators plan, create, and distribute messages. Mobile devices are overtaking PCs as the primary digital communication tool for millions of consumers, employees, and executives; businesses that don't get mobile-friendly in a hurry will fall behind.

For business communicators, the shift to mobile involves much more than the constraints of small screens and new input technologies. The ability to reach people anywhere at any time can be a huge advantage, but the mobile communication experience can also be a major challenge for senders and receivers alike. It requires new ways of thinking about information, message structures, and writing styles. With the notion of *radical connectivity* (see page 17), for example, many communication experiences are no longer about "batch processing" large, self-contained documents. Instead, communication is taking on the feel of an endless conversation, with recipients picking up smaller bits of information as needed, in real time, from multiple sources.

The fundamental skills of writing, listening, presenting, and so on will always be essential, of course, but those skills must be executed in a contemporary business context. That's why Bovée and Thill texts carefully blend technology awareness and skills with basic communication skills and practices. The new coverage of mobile communication is deeply integrated throughout the 12th edition, with major new sections in many chapters and important updates in other places, along with a variety of new questions, activities, and cases.

Welcome to the exciting new world of mobile business communication!

Why Business Communication Instructors Continue to Choose Bovée and Thill

- **Market-leading innovation.** The unique new coverage of mobile communication in this edition is just one example of how, for more than three decades, Bovée and Thill texts have pioneered coverage of emerging trends and their implications for business communication. Bovée and Thill were the first authors in the field to give in-depth coverage to digital media, then social media, and now mobile communication.
- **Up-to-date coverage that reflects today's business communication practices and employer expectations.** Technology, globalization, and other forces have dramatically changed the practice of business communication in recent years, even to the point of altering how people read and how messages should be constructed. To prepare students for today's workplace, the business communication course needs to address contemporary skills, issues, and concepts.
- **Practical advice informed by deep experience.** Beyond the research and presentation of new ideas and tools, Bovée and Thill are among the most active and widely followed users of social media in the entire field of business communication. They don't just write about new concepts; they have years of hands-on experience with social media, blogging, content curation, search technologies, and other important tools. They are active participants in more than 45 social media sites.

Scooped by Bovée & Thill's Online Magazines for Business Communication

Business Communication Instruction: How Students Can Learn More Through Online Media

Business Communication Instruction: How Student...

Bovée and Thill's extensive use of social media not only provides instructors and students with valuable content and resources—it has given the authors an unparalleled base of hands-on experience that is reflected in their coverage of contemporary media practices.

- **Engaging coverage of real companies and contemporary issues in business communication.** Bovée and Thill texts emphasize companies and issues students already know about or are likely to find intriguing. For example, cases in recent editions have addressed location-based social networking (the business communication implications of the FourSquare game app), employer restrictions on social media, and the use of Twitter in the job-search process.
- **Integrated learning.** In sharp contrast to texts that tack on coverage of social media and other new topics, Bovée and Thill continually revise their coverage to fully integrate the skills and issues that are important in today's workplace. This integration is carried through chapter-opening vignettes, chapter content, model documents, end-of-chapter questions, communication cases, and test banks to make sure students practice the skills they'll need, not just read about them in some anecdotal fashion.
- **Added value with unique, free resources for instructors and students.** From the groundbreaking Real-Time Updates to *Business Communication Headline News* to videos specially prepared for instructors, Bovée and Thill adopters can take advantage of an unmatched array of free resources to enhance the classroom experience and keep course content fresh. See page xxx for a complete list.

In-Depth Coverage of Digital, Social, and Mobile Media Topics in the 12th Edition

Excellence in Business Communication offers in-depth coverage of new and emerging media skills and concepts. These tables show where you can find major areas of coverage, figures, and communication cases that expose students to professional use of social media, mobile media, and other new technologies.

Major Coverage of Digital, Social, and Mobile Media

Topic	Page
Backchannel in presentations	465
Blogging and microblogging	204–210 (primary)
Collaboration technologies	42–44
Community Q&A websites	198
Compositional modes for digital media	188–189
Content curation	195, 198
Creating content for social media	189–191
Data visualization	380–381
Digital, social, and mobile media options	106–109 (primary)
Email	198-202
Infographics	383, 384
Instant messaging and text messaging	202–204
Interview media	520–521
Meeting technologies	48–49
Mobile devices in presentations	459–460
Mobile etiquette	58
Mobile media	15–18 (overview)
Online and social media résumés	499–500
Online etiquette	57–58
Podcasting	210–211
Social communication model	13–14
Social networking	191–194 (primary)
User-generated content	195
Web writing	342–344, 371–373
Wikis	371–373
Writing and designing messages for mobile devices	148–149, 173–174
Writing persuasive messages for mobile media	304
Writing persuasive messages for social media	302–303

Figures and Model Documents Highlighting Digital, Social, and Mobile Media (not including email, IM, or presentation slides)

Title	Figure	Page
Mobile Recruiting Apps	P1	xlvi
The Social Communication Model	1.7	14
Mobile Communication Tools	1.8	15
Wearable Technology	1.9	16
Mobile Communication: Opportunities and Challenges	1.10	17

(Continued)

Title	Figure	Page
Powerful Tools for Communicating Effectively	Feature	20–23
Unethical Communication	1.11	25
Ethical Communication	1.12	26
Shared Workspaces	2.2	43
Collaboration on Mobile Devices	2.3	44
Capturing Key Decisions and Discoveries from a Meeting	2.5	47
Virtual Meetings	2.6	48
Telepresence	2.7	49
Mobile Language Tools	3.3	82
Writing for Multilingual Audiences	3.5	87
Using Audience Analysis to Plan a Message	4.2	102
Media and Channel Choices: Written + Digital	4.4	108
Business Communicators Innovating with Mobile	Feature	110–111
Mind Mapping	4.5	114
Fostering a Positive Relationship with an Audience	5.1	129
Building Credibility	5.2	133
Plain Language at Creative Commons	5.3	137
Topic Sentences	5.5	145
Writing for Mobile Devices	5.6	149
Designing for Readability	6.3	171
Designing Messages for Mobile Devices	6.4	174
Compositional Modes: Status Updates and Announcements	7.1	190
Community Building via Social Media	7.2	195
Business Communicators Innovating with Social Media	Feature	196–197
Business Applications of Blogging	7.5	207
Business Applications of Microblogging	7.6	210
Mobile Podcasting Tools	7.7	212
Announcing Good News	8.6	237
Goodwill Messages	8.7	238
Internal Message Providing Bad News About Company Operations	9.6	268
Appealing to Audience Needs	10.1	289
Promotional Messages in Social Media	10.6	303
Executive Dashboards	11.3	325
Reader-Friendly Website Design	11.8	343
Writing for the Web	12.4	372
Data Visualization	12.11	381
Geographic Information Systems	12.13	382
Infographics	12.14	384
Visual Displays on Mobile Devices	12.15	387
Executive Summary	13.2	408
Nonlinear Presentations	14.3	445
Using Mobile Devices in Presentations	14.9	460
Mobile Job Search Tools	15.2	483
Job Task Simulations	16.3	521
Interview Simulators	16.4	527

Communication Cases Involving Digital, Social, or Mobile Media (not including email, IM, or presentations)

Case	Media	Page	Case	Media	Page
7.27	Social networking	220	9.47	Blogging	284
7.28	Social networking	220	9.48	Blogging	284
7.29	Social networking	220	9.49	Blogging	284
7.33	Mobile	221	9.50	Social networking	284
7.35	Blogging	221	9.51	Social networking	251
7.36	Blogging	221	10.37	Microblogging	311
7.37	Blogging	221	10.38	Blogging	311
7.38	Microblogging	221	10.44	Mobile	313
7.39	Microblogging	222	10.49	Web writing	314
7.40	Microblogging	222	10.50	Mobile	314
7.41	Podcasting	222	10.51	Podcasting	314
7.42	Podcasting	222	10.53	Web writing	315
7.43	Podcasting	222	10.54	Web writing	315
8.32	Blogging	246	10.55	Social networking	315
8.42	Podcasting	248	10.56	Microblogging	315
8.43	Blogging	248	12.29	Web writing, mobile	395
8.45	Microblogging	249	12.32	Wikis	395
8.47	Social networking	249	12.33	Web writing	396
8.48	Web writing	249	12.34	Web writing	396
8.49	Blogging	249	14.26	Social networking	474
8.50	Social networking	250	14.31	Mobile	475
9.36	Microblogging	281	15.33	Video	509
9.40	Microblogging	282	16.31	Video	543
9.41	Blogging	283	16.33	Microblogging	543
9.43	Podcasting	283	16.35	Blogging	544
9.46	Microblogging	284			

Extending the Value of Your Textbook with Free Multimedia Content

Excellence in Business Communication's unique Real-Time Updates system automatically provides weekly content updates, including interactive websites, infographics, podcasts, PowerPoint presentations, online videos, PDF files, and articles. You can subscribe to updates chapter by chapter, so you get only the material that applies to your current chapter. Visit http://real-timeupdates.com/ebc12 to subscribe.

1 Read messages from the authors and access over 175 media items avilable only to instructors. (Students have access to their own messages, assignments, and media items.)

2 Click on any chapter to see the updates and media items for that chapter.

3 Scan headlines and click on any item of interest to read the article or download the media item. Every item is personally selected by the authors to complement the text and support in-class activities.

4 Media items are categorized by type so you can quickly find podcasts, videos, infographics, PowerPoints, and more.

5 Subscribe via RSS to individual chapters to get updates automatically for the chapter you're currently teaching.

For Instructors: Features and Resources to Enhance the Course Experience

TARGET AUDIENCE

Everyone who teaches business communication is motivated to help students master the fundamentals of professional communication while also preparing them for the broader expectations they'll encounter in today's workplace. As the field of business communication continues to expand and get more complex, however, balancing those two objectives continues to get more difficult. Basing your course on a textbook that hasn't kept up with contemporary business media and professional practices puts both you and your students at a distinct disadvantage, and yet you obviously can't ignore basic writing skills.

The 12th edition of *Excellence in Business Communication* is optimized to provide that balance. Even in the context of social media, mobile, and other media innovations, every chapter gives students the opportunity to hone their foundational skills and improve their awareness of grammar, mechanics, and proper usage. The time-tested three-step writing process is integrated throughout the text, showing students how to adapt the skills they've acquired to every new challenge they encounter. Moreover, students also get a solid grounding in ethics, etiquette, listening, teamwork, and nonverbal communication.

Building on that platform of essential skills, *Excellence in Business Communication* introduces students to the tools they'll be expected to use when they enter the workforce over the next few years. We continuously monitor developments in electronic media and communication practices to choose the optimum time to introduce new topics.

With its comprehensive coverage of business communication concepts and up-to-the-minute treatment of contemporary practices and technologies, *Excellence in Business Communication* is ideal for business communication courses in any curriculum. While covering the full range of contemporary business media, *Excellence in Business Communication* maintains a strong emphasis on written communication and so is ideal for courses that feature report writing and similar activities. For business communication coverage in the broadest sense, you may find the authors' *Business Communication Today* to be the most effective text. Conversely, if you want a shorter text with strong emphasis on fundamental skills, consider *Essentials of Business Communication*.

Colleges and universities vary in the prerequisites established for the business communication course, but we advise at least one course in English composition. Some coursework in business studies will also give students a better perspective on communication challenges in the workplace. However, we have taken special care not to assume students have any in-depth business experience, so *Excellence in Business Communication* works quite well for those with limited work experience or business coursework.

A TOTAL TEACHING AND LEARNING SOLUTION

Excellence in Business Communication has helped more than 2 million students master essential skills for succeeding in the workplace. This 12th edition continues that tradition by offering an unmatched set of tools that simplify teaching, promote active learning, and stimulate critical thinking. These components work together at four levels to provide seamless coverage of vital knowledge and skills: previewing, developing, enhancing, and reinforcing.

PREVIEWING

Each chapter provides clear learning objectives that prepare students for the material to come and provide a framework for the chapter content. Each learning objective aligns with a major heading in the chapter, and this structure is carried on through to the end-of-chapter and online activities, making it easier for instructors and students to gauge learning progress.

After the learning objectives, a compelling On the Job vignette featuring a successful professional role model or company shows students how the material they will encounter in the chapter is put to use in actual business situations.

DEVELOPING

Chapter content develops, explains, and elaborates on concepts with a carefully organized presentation of textual and visual material. The three-step process of planning, writing, and completing is clearly explained and reinforced throughout the course. Some texts introduce a writing process model and then rarely, if ever, discuss it again, giving students few opportunities to practice it and leaving them to wonder just how important the process really is. *Excellence in Business Communication* adapts the three-step process to every category of messages in every medium, from traditional letters and reports to email, blogs, IM, podcasts, wikis, and online videos.

ENHANCING

Contemporary examples show students the specific elements that contribute to—or detract from—successful messages. *Excellence in Business Communication* has an unmatched portfolio of realistic examples for students to emulate, including 95 model documents and nearly 70 exhibits that feature communication efforts from real companies. In addition, the Real-Time Updates "Learn More" inserts connect students with dozens of carefully selected online media elements that provide examples and insights from successful professionals.

Excellence in Business Communication also extends students' awareness beyond the functional aspects of communication, with thorough and well-integrated coverage of business etiquette and ethics—vital issues that some texts raise briefly and then quickly forget. In light of employer concerns about the etiquette shortcomings of today's new-hires and the continuing struggles with business ethics, we integrate ethics and etiquette throughout the book and give students numerous opportunities to ponder ethical dilemmas and practice communication etiquette.

REINFORCING

Hundreds of realistic exercises and activities help students practice vital skills and put newfound knowledge to immediate use. Unique features include downloadable Word documents, podcasts, and PowerPoint presentations for students to analyze, and the innovative Bovée and Thill wiki simulator. Interactive Document Makeovers, pioneered by Bovée and Thill, let students experience firsthand the elements that make a document successful, giving them the insights they need in order to analyze and improve their own business messages. Nearly 130 communication cases, featuring dozens of real companies, encourage students to think about contemporary business issues as they put their skills to use in a variety of media, including blogging, social networking, and podcasting.

At every stage of the learning experience, *Excellence in Business Communication* provides the tools instructors and students need in order to succeed.

Features that Help Students Build Essential Knowledge and Skills	Previewing	Developing	Enhancing	Reinforcing
Learning objectives (beginning of chapter)	●			
On the Job communication vignette (beginning of chapter)	●			
Concise presentations of fundamentals (within chapter)		●		
Managerial and strategic perspectives on key topics (within chapter)		●		
Three-step writing process discussion and diagrams (within chapter)		●		
Real-life examples (within chapter)			●	
Annotated model documents (within chapter)			●	
Highlight boxes (within chapter)			●	
Handbook of Grammar, Mechanics, and Usage (end of book)			●	
Learn More media resources (online)			●	
MyBCommLab (online)			●	●
Real-Time Updates (online)			●	●

(Continued)

Features that Help Students Build Essential Knowledge and Skills	Previewing	Developing	Enhancing	Reinforcing
Marginal notes for quick review (within chapter)				●
Checklists (within chapter)				●
On the Job: Solving Communication Dilemmas (end of chapter)				●
Quick Learning Guide (end of chapter)				●
Apply Your Knowledge questions (end of chapter)				●
Practice Your Skills activities and exercises (end of chapter)				●
Expand Your Skills web activities (end of chapter/online)				●
Bovée and Thill wiki simulator (online)				●
Cases (following Chapters 7, 8, 9, 10, 12, 13, 14, 15, and 16)				●
Document Makeovers (online)				●

FULL SUPPORT FOR AACSB LEARNING STANDARDS

The American Association of Collegiate Schools of Business (AACSB) is a not-for-profit corporation of educational institutions, corporations, and other organizations devoted to the promotion and improvement of higher education in business administration and accounting. A collegiate institution offering degrees in business administration or accounting may volunteer for AACSB accreditation review. The AACSB makes initial accreditation decisions and conducts periodic reviews to promote continuous quality improvement in management education. Pearson Education is a proud member of the AACSB and is pleased to provide advice to help you apply AACSB Learning Standards.

Curriculum quality is one of the most important criteria for AACSB accreditation. Although no specific courses are required, the AACSB expects a curriculum to include learning experiences in the following areas:

- Written and oral communication
- Ethical understanding and reasoning
- Analytical thinking
- Information technology
- Interpersonal relations and teamwork
- Diverse and multicultural work environments
- Reflective thinking
- Application of knowledge

Throughout *Excellence in Business Communication*, you'll find student exercises and activities that support the achievement of these important goals, and the questions in the accompanying test bank are tagged with the appropriate AACSB category.

UNMATCHED COVERAGE OF ESSENTIAL COMMUNICATION TECHNOLOGIES

The Bovée and Thill series continues to lead the field with unmatched coverage of communication technologies, reflecting the expectations and opportunities in today's workplace:

- Applicant tracking systems
- Assistive technologies
- Automated reputation analysis
- Backchannel
- Blogs
- Cloud computing
- Community Q&A websites
- Computer animation
- Content curation
- Crowdsourcing
- Data visualization
- Digital documents (PDFs)
- Digital whiteboards
- Email
- Emoticons
- Enterprise instant messaging
- E-portfolios
- Extranets
- Gamification
- Geographic information systems
- Graphics software
- Groupware and shared online workspaces
- Infographics
- Information architecture
- Instant messaging
- Intellectual property rights

- Interactivity
- Internet telephony (Skype)
- Interview simulators
- Intranets
- Knowledge management systems
- Linked and embedded documents
- Location-based social networking
- Microblogs
- Mobile business apps
- Multimedia presentations
- Newsfeeds
- Online brainstorming systems
- Online research techniques
- Online survey tools
- Online video

- Podcasts
- PowerPoint animation
- Really Simple Syndication (RSS)
- Screencasts
- Search and metasearch engines
- Search engine optimization (SEO)
- Security and privacy concerns in electronic media
- Sentiment analysis
- Social bookmarking
- Social commerce
- Social media
- Social media résumés
- Social networking
- Tagging

- Teleconferencing and telepresence
- Text messaging
- Translation software
- User-generated content
- Video interviews
- Video résumés
- Videoconferencing
- Virtual communities
- Virtual meetings
- Virtual whiteboards
- Web content management systems
- Web directories
- Webcasts
- Website accessibility
- Wikis

COURSE PLANNING GUIDE

Although *Excellence in Business Communication* follows a conventional sequence of topics, it is structured so that you can address topics in whatever order best suits your needs. For instance, if you want to begin by reviewing grammar, sentence structure, and other writing fundamentals, you can ask students to read Chapter 5, "Writing Business Messages" and then the "Handbook of Grammar, Mechanics, and Usage." Conversely, if you want to begin with employment-related communication, you can start with the Prologue, "Building a Career with Your Communication Skills," followed by Chapters 15 and 16.

The following table suggests a sequence and a schedule for covering the chapters in the textbook, with time allocations based on the total number of class hours available.

	Chapter/Section	Hours Devoted to Each Chapter/Section		
		30-Hour Course	45-Hour Course	60-Hour Course
	Prologue: Building a Career with Your Communication Skills	0.5	1	1
1	Professional Communication in a Digital, Social, Mobile World	1	1	1
2	Collaboration, Interpersonal Communication, and Business Etiquette	1	1	2
3	Communication Challenges in a Diverse, Global Marketplace	1	2	3
4	Planning Business Messages	2	3	4
5	Writing Business Messages	2	3	4
6	Completing Business Messages	2	3	4
	Handbook of Grammar, Mechanics, and Usage	1	2	2
A	Format and Layout of Business Documents	1	1	1
7	Crafting Messages for Digital Channels	2	2	4
8	Writing Routine and Positive Messages	2	2	3
9	Writing Negative Messages	2	2	3
10	Writing Persuasive Messages	2	2	3
11	Planning Reports and Proposals	2	3	4
12	Writing Reports and Proposals	2	3	4
13	Completing Reports and Proposals	2	3	3
B	Documentation of Report Sources	1	1	2
14	Designing and Delivering Business Presentations	1	4	4
15	Building Careers and Writing Résumés	1.5	3	4
16	Applying and Interviewing for Employment	1	3	4

INSTRUCTOR RESOURCES AND SUPPORT OPTIONS

Excellence in Business Communication is backed by an unmatched selection of resources for instructors and students, many of which were pioneered by the authors and remain unique in the field.

Online Communities and Media Resources

Instructors are welcome to take advantage of the many free online resources provided by Bovée and Thill:

- Sponsorship of Teaching Business Communication instructors' communities (open to all) and Bovée and Thill's Inner Circle for Business Communication (for adopters only) on LinkedIn and Facebook
- Instructor tips and techniques in Bovée and Thill's Business Communication Blog and Twitter feed
- The Bovée and Thill channel on YouTube, with videos that offer advice on teaching the new elements of business communication
- The unique Real-Time Updates content-updating service (see page xxv)
- The popular Business Communication Headline News service (see below)
- A variety of videos and PowerPoint presentations on SlideShare
- More than 500 infographics, videos, articles, podcasts, and PowerPoints on Business Communication Pictorial Gallery on Pinterest
- The Ultimate Guide to Resources for Teaching Business Communication

We also invite you to peruse Bovée and Thill's Online Magazines for Business Communication on Scoop.it:

- Business Communication 2.0: Social Media and Electronic Communication
- Teaching a Modern Business Communication Course
- How the Mobile Revolution Is Changing Business Communication
- Teaching Business Communication and Workplace Issues
- Teaching Business Communication and Interpersonal Communication
- Teaching Oral Communication in a Business Communication Course
- Teaching Business Communication and Employment
- Teaching Visual Communication
- Exclusive Teaching Resources for Business Communication Instructors

Links to all these services and resources can be found at **http://blog.business communicationnetwork.com/resources**

Business Communication Headline News

Stay on top of hot topics, important trends, and new technologies with Business Communication Headline News (**http://bchn.businesscommunicationnetwork.com**), the most comprehensive business communication site on the Internet. Every weekday during the school year, we offer fresh lecture content and provide a wide range of research and teaching tools on the website, including a custom web search function that we created expressly for business communication research.

Take advantage of the newsfeeds to get late-breaking news in headlines with concise summaries. You can scan incoming items in a matter of seconds and simply click through to read the full articles that interest you. All articles and accompanying multimedia resources are categorized by topic and chapter for easy retrieval at any time.

This free service for adopters offers numerous ways to enhance lectures and student activities:

- Keep current with the latest information and trends in the field.
- Easily update your lecture notes with fresh material.

- Create visuals for your classroom presentations.
- Supplement your lectures with cutting-edge handouts.
- Gather podcasts, online video, and other new media examples to use in the classroom.
- Enhance your research projects with the newest data.
- Compare best practices from other instructors.
- Improve the quality and effectiveness of your teaching by reading about new teaching tips and techniques.

At the website, you also get free access to these powerful instructional resources:

- **Business Communication Web Search**, featuring a revolutionary approach to searching developed by the authors that lets you quickly access more than 325 search engines. The tool uses a simple and intuitive interface engineered to help business communication instructors find precisely what they want, whether it's PowerPoint files, PDF files, Microsoft Word documents, Excel files, videos, or podcasts.
- **Real-Time Updates** are newsfeeds and content updates tied directly to specific points throughout the text. Each content update is classified by the type of media featured: interactive website, infographic, article, video, podcast, PowerPoint, or PDF. Additional sections on the site include Instructor Messages and Instructor Media (both password protected), Student Messages, and Student Assignments.

You can subscribe to Business Communication Headline News and get delivery by email, RSS newsreader, mobile phone, instant messenger, MP3, Twitter, Facebook, and a host of other options.

Bovée and Thill Business Communication Blog

The Bovée and Thill Business Communication Blog (**http://blog.businesscommunica tionnetwork.com/**) offers original articles that help instructors focus their teaching to help students learn more efficiently and effectively. Articles discuss a wide variety of subjects, including new topics instructors should be teaching their students, resources instructors can use in their classes, solutions to common teaching challenges, and great examples and activities instructors can use in class.

Authors' Email Hotline for Faculty

Integrity, excellence, and responsiveness are our hallmarks. That means providing you with textbooks that are academically sound, creative, timely, and sensitive to instructor and student needs. As an adopter of *Excellence in Business Communication*, you are invited to use our Email Hotline (hotline@businesscommunicationblog.com) if you ever have a question or concern related to the text or its supplements.

Instructor's Resource Center

At the Instructor Resource Center, **www.pearsonhighered.com/irc**, instructors can easily register to gain access to a variety of instructor resources available with this text in downloadable format. If assistance is needed, our dedicated technical support team is ready to help with the media supplements that accompany this text. Visit **http://247pearsoned .custhelp.com/** for answers to frequently asked questions and toll-free user-support phone numbers.

The following supplements are available with this text

- Instructor's Resource Manual
- Test Bank
- TestGen® Computerized Test Bank (and various conversions)
- PowerPoint Presentation

For Students: How This Course Will Help You

No matter what profession you want to pursue, the ability to communicate will be an essential skill—and a skill that employers expect you to have when you enter the workforce. This course introduces you to the fundamental principles of business communication and gives you the opportunity to develop your communication skills. You'll discover how business communication differs from personal and social communication, and you'll see how today's companies are using blogs, social networks, podcasts, virtual worlds, wikis, and other technologies. You'll learn a simple three-step writing process that works for all types of writing and speaking projects, both in college and on the job. Along the way, you'll gain valuable insights into ethics, etiquette, listening, teamwork, and nonverbal communication. Plus, you'll learn effective strategies for the many types of communication challenges you'll face on the job, from routine messages about transactions to complex reports and websites.

Few courses can offer the three-for-the-price-of-one value you get from a business communication class. Check out these benefits:

- **In your other classes.** The communication skills you learn in this class can help you in every other course you take in college. From simple homework assignments to complicated team projects to class presentations, you'll be able to communicate more effectively with less time and effort.
- **During your job search.** You can reduce the stress of searching for a job and stand out from the competition. Every activity in the job-search process relies on communication. The better you can communicate, the more successful you'll be at landing interesting and rewarding work.
- **On the job.** After you get that great job, the time and energy you have invested in this course will continue to yield benefits year after year. As you tackle each project and every new challenge, influential company leaders—the people who decide how quickly you'll get promoted and how much you'll earn—will be paying close attention to how well you communicate. They will observe your interactions with colleagues, customers, and business partners. They'll take note of how well you can collect data, find the essential ideas buried under mountains of information, and convey those points to other people. They'll observe your ability to adapt to different audiences and circumstances. They'll be watching when you encounter tough situations that require careful attention to ethics and etiquette. The good news: Every insight you gain and every skill you develop in this course will help you shine in your career.

HOW TO SUCCEED IN THIS COURSE

Although this course explores a wide range of message types and appears to cover quite a lot of territory, the underlying structure of the course is actually rather simple. You'll learn a few basic concepts, identify some key skills to use and procedures to follow—and then practice, practice, practice. Whether you're writing a blog posting in response to one of the real-company cases or drafting your own résumé, you'll be practicing the same skills again and again. With feedback and reinforcement from your instructor and your classmates, your confidence will grow and the work will become easier and more enjoyable.

The following sections offer advice on approaching each assignment, using your textbook, and taking advantage of some other helpful resources.

Approaching Each Assignment

In the spirit of practice and improvement, you will have a number of writing (and possibly speaking) assignments throughout this course. These suggestions will help you produce better results with less effort:

- **First, don't panic!** If the thought of writing a report or giving a speech sends a chill up your spine, you're not alone. Everybody feels that way when first learning business communication skills, and even experienced professionals can feel nervous about major projects. Keeping three points in mind will help. First, every project can be broken down into a series of small, manageable tasks. Don't let a big project overwhelm you; it's nothing more than a bunch of smaller tasks. Second, remind yourself that you have the skills you need in order to accomplish each task. As you move through the course, the assignments are carefully designed to match the skills you've developed up to that point. Third, if you feel panic creeping up on you, take a break and regain your perspective.

- **Focus on one task at a time.** A common mistake writers make is trying to organize and express their ideas while simultaneously worrying about audience reactions, grammar, spelling, formatting, page design, and a dozen other factors. Fight the temptation to do everything at once; otherwise, your frustration will soar and your productivity will plummet. In particular, don't worry about grammar, spelling, and word choices during your first draft. Concentrate on the organization of your ideas first, then the way you express those ideas, and then the presentation and production of your messages. Following the three-step writing process is an ideal way to focus on one task at a time in a logical sequence.

- **Give yourself plenty of time.** As with every other school project, putting things off to the last minute creates unnecessary stress. Writing and speaking projects in particular are much easier if you tackle them in small stages with breaks in between, rather than trying to get everything done in one frantic blast. Moreover, there will be instances when you simply get stuck on a project, and the best thing to do is walk away and give your mind a break. If you allow room for breaks in your schedule, you'll minimize the frustration and spend less time overall on your homework, too.

- **Step back and assess each project before you start.** The writing and speaking projects you'll have in this course cover a wide range of communication scenarios, and it's essential that you adapt your approach to each new challenge. Resist the urge to dive in and start writing without a plan. Ponder the assignment for a while, consider the various approaches you might take, and think carefully about your objectives before you start writing. Nothing is more frustrating than getting stuck halfway through because you're not sure what you're trying to say or you've wandered off track. Spend a little time planning, and you'll spend a lot less time writing.

- **Use the three-step writing process.** Those essential planning tasks are the first step in the three-step writing process, which you'll learn about in Chapter 3 and use throughout the course. This process has been developed and refined by professional writers with decades of experience and thousands of projects ranging from short blog posts to 500-page textbooks. It works, so take advantage of it.

- **Learn from the examples and model documents.** This textbook offers dozens of realistic examples of business messages, many with notes along the sides that explain strong and weak points. Study these documents and any other examples that your instructor provides. Learn what works and what doesn't, then apply these lessons to your own writing.

- **Learn from experience.** Finally, learn from the feedback you get from your instructor and from other students. Don't take the criticism personally; your instructor and your classmates are commenting about the work, not about you. View every bit of feedback as an opportunity to improve.

Using This Textbook Package

This book and its accompanying online resources introduce you to the key concepts in business communication while helping you develop essential skills. As you read each chapter, start by studying the learning objectives. They will help you identify the most important concepts in the chapter and give you a feel for what you'll be learning. Following the learning objectives, the "On the Job" vignette features a successful professional role model who uses the same skills you will be learning in the chapter.

As you work your way through the chapter, compare the advice given with the various examples, both the brief in-text examples and the stand-alone model documents. Also, keep an eye out for the Real-Time Updates elements in each chapter. The authors have selected these videos, podcasts, presentations, and other online media to provide informative and entertaining enhancements to the text material.

At the end of each chapter, you'll revisit the "On the Job" story from the beginning of the chapter and imagine yourself in the role of a business professional solving four realistic communication dilemmas. Next, the "Learning Objectives Checkup" gives you the chance to quickly verify your grasp of important concepts. Each chapter includes a variety of questions and activities that help you gauge how well you've learned the material and are able to apply it to realistic business scenarios. Several chapters have activities with downloadable media such as presentations and podcasts or the use of the Bovée-Thill wiki simulator. If your instructor assigns these activities, follow the instructions in the text to locate the correct online files. And if you'd like some help getting started with Facebook, Twitter, or LinkedIn, we have created screencasts with helpful advice on these topics.

In addition to the 16 chapters of the text itself, here are some special features that will help you succeed in the course and on the job:

- **Prologue: Building a Career with Your Communication Skills.** This section (immediately following this Preface) helps you understand today's dynamic workplace, the steps you can take to adapt to the job market, and the importance of creating an employment portfolio and building your personal brand.
- **Handbook.** The Handbook of Grammar, Mechanics, and Usage (see page 571) is a convenient reference of essential business English.
- **Real-Time Updates.** You can use this unique newsfeed service to make sure you're always kept up to date on important topics. Plus, at strategic points in every chapter, you will be directed to the Real-Time Updates website to get the latest information about specific subjects. To sign up, visit http://real-timeupdates.com/ebc12.
- **Business Communication Web Search.** This unique web search tool formats more than 325 types of searches to help you find precisely what you want, whether it's PowerPoint files, PDF files, Microsoft Word documents, Excel files, videos, podcasts, videos, or social bookmarks. Check it out at http://websearch.businesscommunicationnetwork.com.

About the Authors

Courtland L. Bovée and John V. Thill have been leading textbook authors for more than two decades, introducing millions of students to the fields of business and business communication. Their award-winning texts are distinguished by proven pedagogical features, extensive selections of contemporary case studies, hundreds of real-life examples, engaging writing, thorough research, and the unique integration of print and electronic resources. Each new edition reflects the authors' commitment to continuous refinement and improvement, particularly in terms of modeling the latest practices in business and the use of technology.

Professor Bovée has 22 years of teaching experience at Grossmont College in San Diego, where he has received teaching honors and was accorded that institution's C. Allen Paul Distinguished Chair. Mr. Thill is a prominent communications consultant who has worked with organizations ranging from Fortune 500 multinationals to entrepreneurial start-ups. He formerly held positions with Pacific Bell and Texaco.

Both were recently awarded proclamations from the Governor of Massachusetts for their lifelong contributions to education and for their commitment to the summer youth baseball program that is sponsored by the Boston Red Sox.

Acknowledgments

The 12th Edition of *Excellence in Business Communication* reflects the professional experience of a large team of contributors and advisors. We express our thanks to the many individuals whose valuable suggestions and constructive comments influenced the success of this book.

REVIEWERS OF PREVIOUS EDITIONS

Thank you to the following professors: Lydia E. Anderson, Fresno City College; Victoria Austin, Las Positas College; Faridah Awang, Eastern Kentucky University; Jeanette Baldridge, University of Maine at Augusta; Diana Baran, Henry Ford Community College; JoAnne Barbieri, Atlantic Cape Community College; Kristina Beckman, John Jay College; Judy Bello, Lander University; Carol Bibly, Triton College; Nancy Bizal, University of Southern Indiana; Yvonne Block, College of Lake County; Edna Boroski, Trident Technical College; Nelvia M. Brady, Trinity Christian College; Arlene Broeker, Lincoln University; David Brooks, Indiana University Southeast; Carol Brown, South Puget Sound Community College; Domenic Bruni, University of Wisconsin; Jeff Bruns, Bacone College; Gertrude L. Burge, University of Nebraska; Sharon Burton, Brookhaven College; Robert Cabral, Oxnard College; Dorothy Campbell, Brevard Community College; Linda Carr, University of West Alabama; Alvaro Carreras Jr., Florida International University; Sharon Carson, St. Philip's College; Rick Carter, Seattle University; Dacia Charlesworth, Indiana University–Purdue University Fort Wayne; Jean Chenu, Genesee Community College; Connie Clark, Lane Community College; Alvin Clarke, Iowa State University; Jerrie Cleaver, Central Texas College; Clare Coleman, Temple University; Michael P. Collins, Northern Arizona University; M. Cotton, North Central Missouri College; Pat Cowherd, Campbellsville University; Pat Cuchens, University of Houston–Clear Lake; Walt Dabek, Post University; Cathy Daly, California State University–Sacramento; Linda Davis, Copiah–Lincoln Community College; Christine R. Day, Eastern Michigan University; Harjit Dosanjh, North Seattle Community College; Amy Drees, Defiance College; Cynthia Drexel, Western State College of Colorado; Lou Dunham, Spokane Falls Community College; Donna Everett, Morehead State University; Donna Falconer, Anoka–Ramsey Community College; Kate Ferguson Marsters, Gannon University; Darlynn Fink, Clarion University of Pennsylvania; Bobbi Fisher, University of Nebraska–Omaha; Laura Fitzwater, Community College of Philadelphia; Lynda K. Fuller, Wilmington University; Matthew Gainous, Ogeechee Technical College; Yolande Gardner, Lawson State Community College; Gina Genova, University of California–Santa Barbara; Lonny Gilbert, Central

State University; Camille Girardi-Levy, Siena College; Nancy Goehring, Monterey Peninsula College; Dawn Goellner, Bethel College; Robert Goldberg, Prince George's Community College; Jeffrey Goldberg, MassBay Community College; Helen Grattan, Des Moines Area Community College; Barbara Grayson, University of Arkansas at Pine Bluff; Deborah Griffin, University of Houston–Clear Lake; Alice Griswold, Clarke College; Bonnie Grossman, College of Charleston; Lisa Gueldenzoph, North Carolina A&T State University; Wally Guyot, Fort Hays State University; Valerie Harrison, Cuyamaca College; Tim Hartge, University of Michigan–Dearborn; Richard Heiens, University of South Carolina–Aiken; Maureece Heinert, Sinte Gleska University; Leighanne Heisel, University of Missouri–St. Louis; Gary Helfand, University of Hawaii–West Oahu; Cynthia Herrera, Orlando Culinary Academy; Kathy Hill, Sam Houston State University; Pashia Hogan, Northeast State Tech Community College; Sarah Holmes, New England Institute of Technology; Ruth Hopkins Zajdel, Ohio University–Chillicothe; Sheila Hostetler, Orange Coast College; Michael Hricik, Westmoreland County Community College; Rebecca Hsiao, East Los Angeles College; Mary Ann Hurd, Sauk Valley Community College; Pat Hurley, Leeward Community College; Harold Hurry, Sam Houston State University; Marcia James, University of Wisconsin–Whitewater; Frank Jaster, Tulane University; Jonatan Jelen, Parsons the New School For Design; Irene Joanette Gallio, Western Nevada Community College; Edgar Dunson Johnson III, Augusta State University; Mark Johnson, Rhodes State College; Joanne Kapp, Siena College; Jeanette A. Karjala, Winona State University; Christy L. Kinnion, Lenior Community College; Deborah Kitchin, City College of San Francisco; Lisa Kirby, North Carolina Wesleyan College; Claudia Kirkpatrick, Carnegie Mellon University; Betty Kleen, Nicholls State University; Fran Kranz, Oakland University; Jana Langemach, University of Nebraska–Lincoln; Joan Lantry, Jefferson Community College; Kim Laux, Saginaw Valley State University; Kathryn J. Lee, University of Cincinnati; Anita Leffel, University of Texas, San Antonio; Ruth Levy, Westchester Community College; Nancy Linger, Moraine Park Technical College; Jere Littlejohn, University of Mississippi; Dana Loewy, California State University–Fullerton; Jennifer Loney, Portland State University; Susan Long, Portland Community College; Sue Loomis, Maine Maritime Academy; Thomas Lowderbaugh, University of Maryland–College Park; Jayne Lowery, Jackson State Community College; Lloyd Matzner, University of Houston–Downtown; Ron McNeel, New Mexico State University at Alamogordo; Bill McPherson, Indiana University of Pennsylvania; Phyllis Mercer, Texas Woman's University; Donna Meyerholz, Trinidad State Junior College; Annie Laurie I. Meyers, Northampton Community College; Catherine "Kay" Michael, St. Edward's University; Kathleen Miller, University of Delaware; Gay Mills, Amarillo College; Julie Mullis, Wilkes Community College; Pamela Mulvey, Olney Central College; Jimidene Murphey, Clarendon College; Cindy Murphy, Southeastern Community College; Dipali Murti-Hali, California State University–Stanislaus; Shelley Myatt, University of Central Oklahoma; Cora Newcomb, Technical College of the Lowcountry; Ron Newman, Crafton Hills College; Linda Nitsch, Chadron State College; Leah Noonan, Laramie County Community College; Mabry O'Donnell, Marietta College; Diana Oltman, Central Washington University; Ranu Paik, Santa Monica College; Lauren Paisley, Genesee Community College; Patricia Palermo, Drew University; John Parrish, Tarrant County College; Diane Paul, TVI Community College; John T. Pauli, University of Alaska–Anchorage; Michael Pennell, University of Rhode Island; Sylvia Beaver Perez, Nyack College; Melinda Phillabaum, Indiana University; Ralph Phillips, Geneva College; Laura Pohopien, Cal Poly Pomona; Diane Powell, Utah Valley State College; Christine Pye, California Lutheran University; Norma Pygon, Triton College; Dave Rambow, Wayland Baptist University; Richard David Ramsey, Southeastern Louisiana University; Charles Riley, Tarrant County College–Northwest Campus; Jim Rucker, Fort Hays State University; Suzan Russell, Lehman College; Danielle Scane, Orange Coast College; Calvin Scheidt, Tidewater Community College; Nancy Schneider, University of Maine at Augusta; Brian Sheridan, Mercyhurst College; Melinda Shirey, Fresno City College; Bob Shirilla, Colorado State University; Joyce Simmons, Florida State University; Gordon J. Simpson, SUNY Cobleskill; Peggy Simpson, Dominican University; Eunice Smith, Bismarck State College; Jeff Smith, University of Southern California; Lorraine M. Smith, Fresno City College;

Harvey Solganick, LeTourneau University–Dallas; Stephen Soucy, Santa Monica College; Linda Spargo, University of Mississippi; W. Dees Stallings, Park University; Sally Stanton, University of Wisconsin–Milwaukee; Mark Steinbach, Austin Community College; Angelique Stevens, Monroe Community College; Steven Stovall, Wilmington College; Alden Talbot, Weber State University; Michele Taylor, Ogeechee Technical College; Wilma Thomason, Mid-South Community College; Ed Thompson, Jefferson Community College; Ann E. Tippett, Monroe Community College; Lori Townsend, Niagara County Community College; Lani Uyeno, Leeward Community College; Wendy Van Hatten, Western Iowa Tech Community College; Jay Wagers, Richmond Community College; John Waltman, Eastern Michigan University; Jie Wang, University of Illinois at Chicago; Chris Ward, University of Findlay; Dorothy Warren, Middle Tennessee State University; Glenda Waterman, Concordia University; Kellie Welch, Jefferson Community College; Bradley S. Wesner, Nova Southeastern University; Mathew Williams, Clover Park Technical College; Beth Williams, Stark State College of Technology; Brian Wilson, College of Marin; and Sandra D. Young, Orangeburg–Calhoun Technical College.

REVIEWERS OF DOCUMENT MAKEOVERS

We sincerely thank the following reviewers for their assistance with the Document Makeover feature: Lisa Barley, Eastern Michigan University; Marcia Bordman, Gallaudet University; Jean Bush-Bacelis, Eastern Michigan University; Bobbye Davis, Southern Louisiana University; Cynthia Drexel, Western State College of Colorado; Kenneth Gibbs, Worcester State College; Ellen Leathers, Bradley University; Diana McKowen, Indiana University; Bobbie Nicholson, Mars Hill College; Andrew Smith, Holyoke Community College; Jay Stubblefield, North Carolina Wesleyan College; and Dawn Wallace, Southeastern Louisiana University.

MYLAB CONTRIBUTORS

George Bernard, Seminole State; Gina L. Genova, University of California, Santa Barbara; Nancy Nygaard, University of Wisconsin Milwaukee; Storm Russo, Valencia College; and Susan C. Schanne, Eastern Michigan University.

PERSONAL ACKNOWLEDGMENTS

We wish to extend a heartfelt thanks to our many friends, acquaintances, and business associates who provided materials or agreed to be interviewed so that we could bring the real world into the classroom.

A very special acknowledgment goes to George Dovel, whose superb writing skills, distinguished background, and wealth of business experience assured this project of clarity and completeness. Also, recognition and thanks to Jackie Estrada for her outstanding skills and excellent attention to details. Her creation of the "Peak Performance Grammar and Mechanics" material is especially noteworthy.

We also feel it is important to acknowledge and thank the Association for Business Communication, an organization whose meetings and publications provide a valuable forum for the exchange of ideas and for professional growth.

In addition, we would like to thank Danielle Scane of Orange Coast College and Susan Schanne of Eastern Michigan University for their assistance in preparing supplements for this new edition.

We want to extend our warmest appreciation to the devoted professionals at Pearson Higher Education for their commitment to producing high-value, student-focused texts, including Tim Bozik, president; Stephanie Wall, editor-in-chief; Maggie Moylan, director of marketing; Emily Tamburri, acquisitions editor; Denise Weiss, program manager; Nicole Suddeth, project manager; and Jeff Holcomb, senior managing editor of production. We are also grateful to Heather Johnson of Integra.

John V. Thill
Courtland L. Bovée

Real-Time Updates—Learn More

Real-Time Updates—Learn More is a unique feature you will see strategically located throughout the text, connecting you with dozens of carefully selected online media items. These elements—categorized by the icons shown here representing interactive websites, online videos, infographics, PowerPoint presentations, podcasts, PDF files, and articles—complement the text's coverage by providing contemporary examples and valuable insights from successful professionals.

REAL-TIME UPDATES
LEARN MORE BY VISITING THIS WEBSITE

Check out the cutting edge of business communication   4
The mobile revolution by the numbers   16
Guidelines for trouble-free blogging   27
Looking for jobs at diversity-minded companies?   70
Expert advice on making technologies usable   148
See the newest designs from some of the brightest minds in typography   173
Learn from the best social media bloggers in the business   191
Insight into mobile strategies for routine communication   226
Asking for recommendations on LinkedIn   229
Get expert tips on writing (or requesting) a letter of recommendation   236
Best practices in mobile marketing   304
Try these 100 serious search tools   335
Learn to use Google more effectively   336
Step-by-step advice for developing a successful business plan   341
Crafting your "wow" statement   342
Effective examples of one-page web design   343
Ideas for using Instagram for business communication   383
Get practical advice on developing research reports   403
The latest tools and trends in presentations   452
Advice and free templates for more-effective slideuments   456
Converting your résumé to a CV   487
Find the keywords that will light up your résumé   491

REAL-TIME UPDATES
LEARN MORE BY WATCHING THIS VIDEO

The mobile business advantage   15
Positive ways to engage when you pick up negative social commentary   269
Persuasion skills for every business professional   291
Step up your search skills   335
Understand the basics of perception   373
Dealing with the difficult four   444
Nancy Duarte's five rules for presentations   444
How to establish an emotional connection with any audience   450
Learn to use LinkedIn's résumé builder   489
Video interviewing on Skype   521
Stay calm by pressing your "panic reset button"   531
Try these 100 serious search tools   335

Learn to use Google more effectively   336
Step-by-step advice for developing a successful business plan   341
Crafting your "wow" statement   342
Effective examples of one-page web design   343
Ideas for using Instagram for business communication   383

REAL-TIME UPDATES
LEARN MORE BY VISITING THIS WIKI

Get the latest news on gamification   19

REAL-TIME UPDATES
LEARN MORE BY READING THIS ARTICLE

Three factors that distinguish smart teams   38
The benefits of mobile collaboration   43
Turn listening into a competitive advantage   50
Improve your professional "curb appeal"   52
Simple steps to improve social media etiquette   58
Study the seven habits of effective intercultural communicators   88
Building credibility online   134
Take your communication skills from good to great   136
Practical tips for more-effective sentences   143
Improve your document designs by learning the fundamentals of typography   172
Should you email, text, or pick up the phone?   188
Telling compelling stories on social media   189
How social media have changed business communication   191
Etiquette guidelines for instant messaging   203
Ten years later, are business blogs still a good investment?   205
Twitter tips for beginners   209
Managing multiple Twitter accounts at Walmart   209
Simple rules for writing effective thank-you notes   239
Dissecting the apology letter from Target's CEO   257
Lessons in social media crisis communication from the air travel industry   260
Using stories to persuade   294
Fifty tips for being more persuasive   297
Inspire your presentations with advice from these bloggers   459
Two secrets to presenting like a pro   464
Smart strategies to explain gaps in your work history   488
Don't let these mistakes cost you an interview   500
The ultimate interview preparation checklist   523
Prepare your answers to these tough interview questions   524

REAL-TIME UPDATES

LEARN MORE BY LISTENING TO THIS PODCAST

How to keep small battles from escalating into big ones   41
Tips for proofing your papers   175
Expert tips for successful phone interviews   530

REAL-TIME UPDATES

LEARN MORE BY READING THIS INFOGRAPHIC

Whatever happened to live conversation?   58
See how expensive poor customer service really is   255
Decide how to respond to online reputation attacks   269
The color of persuasion   302
See how an applicant tracking system handles your résumé   490
Get a quick reminder of the key steps in preparing for an interview   526

REAL-TIME UPDATES

LEARN MORE BY EXPLORING THIS INTERACTIVE WEBSITE

Take a Closer Look at How the United States Is Changing   71
A business-focused model for identifying cultural differences   74

How are your global travel skills?   79
Grammar questions? Click here for help   138
How much are you worth?   518

REAL-TIME UPDATES

LEARN MORE BY READING THIS PDF

Dig deep into audience needs with this planning tool   103
Get detailed advice on using bias-free language   132

REAL-TIME UPDATES

LEARN MORE BY VIEWING THIS PRESENTATION

Smart advice for brainstorming sessions   113
Get helpful tips on creating an outline for any project   116
Exploring the potential of wearable technologies   16

Prologue

BUILDING A CAREER WITH YOUR COMMUNICATION SKILLS

Using This Course to Help Launch Your Career

This course will help you develop vital communication skills that you'll use throughout your career—and those skills can help you launch an interesting and rewarding career, too. This brief prologue sets the stage by helping you understand today's dynamic workplace, the steps you can take to adapt to the job market, and the importance of creating an employment portfolio and building your personal brand. Take a few minutes to read it while you think about the career you hope to create for yourself.

UNDERSTANDING THE CHANGING WORLD OF WORK

Even as the U.S. economy recovers from the Great Recession and employment levels improve, you're likely to encounter some challenges as you start or continue with your business career. As companies around the world try to gain competitive advantages and cost efficiencies, employment patterns will vary from industry to industry and region to region.

The ups and downs of the economic cycle are not the only dynamic elements that will affect your career, however. The nature of employment itself is changing, with a growing number of independent workers and loosely structured *virtual organizations* that engage these workers for individual projects or short-term contracts, rather than hiring employees. In fact, one recent study predicted that independent workers will outnumber conventional employees in the United States by 2020.[1]

Are you comfortable working on your own? Independent workers have become an important part of the global workforce.

xli

This new model of work offers some compelling advantages for workers and companies alike. Companies can lower their fixed costs, adapt more easily to economic fluctuations and competitive moves, and get access to specialized talent for specific project needs.[2] Workers can benefit from the freedom to choose the clients and projects that interest them the most, the flexibility to work as much or as little as they want, and (thanks to advances in communication technology) access to compelling work even if they live far from major employment centers such as New York City or California's Silicon Valley.[3]

On the other hand, this new approach also presents some significant challenges for all parties. These flexibilities and freedoms can create more complexity for workers and managers, diminished loyalties on both sides, uncertainty about the future, issues with skill development and training, and problems with accountability and liability.[4] Many of these challenges involve communication, making solid communication skills more important than ever.

These changes could affect you even if you pursue traditional employment throughout your career. Within organizations, you're likely to work with a combination of "inside" employees and "outside" contractors, which can affect the dynamics of the workplace. And the availability of more independent workers in the talent marketplace gives employers more options and more leverage, so full-time employees may find themselves competing against freelancers, at least indirectly.

As you navigate this uncertain future, keep two vital points in mind. First, don't wait for your career to just happen: Take charge of your career and stay in charge of it. Explore all your options and have a plan, but be prepared to change course as opportunities and threats appear on the horizon. Second, don't count on employers to take care of you. The era of lifetime employment, in which an employee committed to one company for life with the understanding it would return the loyalty, is long gone. From finding opportunities to developing the skills you need to succeed, it's up to you to manage your career and look out for your own best interests.

How Employers View Today's Job Market

From an employer's perspective, the employment process is always a question of balance. Maintaining a stable workforce can improve practically every aspect of business performance, yet many employers want the flexibility to shrink and expand payrolls as business conditions change. Employers obviously want to attract the best talent, but the best talent is more expensive and more vulnerable to offers from competitors, so there are always financial trade-offs to consider.

Employers also struggle with the ups and downs of the economy. When unemployment is low, the balance of power shifts to employees, and employers have to compete in order to attract and keep top talent. When unemployment is high, the power shifts back to employers, who can afford to be more selective and less accommodating. In other words, pay attention to the economy; at times you can be more aggressive in your demands, but at other times you need to be more accommodating.

Companies view employment as a complex business decision with lots of variables to consider. To make the most of your potential, regardless of the career path you pursue, you need to view employment in the same way.

What Employers Look for in Job Applicants

Given the complex forces in the contemporary workplace and the unrelenting pressure of global competition, what are employers looking for in the candidates they hire? The short answer: a lot. Like all "buyers," companies want to get as much as they can for the money they spend. The closer you can present yourself as the ideal candidate, the better your chances of getting a crack at the most exciting opportunities.

Communication skills will benefit your career, no matter what path or profession you pursue.

Specific expectations vary by profession and position, of course, but virtually all employers look for the following general skills and attributes:[5]

- **Communication skills.** The reason this item is listed first isn't that you're reading a business communication textbook. Communication is listed first because it is far and away the most commonly mentioned skill set when employers are asked about what they look for in employees. Improving your communication skills will help in every aspect of your professional life.

- **Interpersonal and team skills.** You will have many individual responsibilities on the job, but chances are you won't work alone very often. Learn to work with others and help them succeed as you succeed.

- **Intercultural and international awareness and sensitivity.** Successful employers tend to be responsive to diverse workforces, markets, and communities, and they look for employees with the same outlook.

- **Data collection, analysis, and decision-making skills.** Employers want people who know how to identify information needs, find the necessary data, convert the data into useful knowledge, and make sound decisions.

- **Digital, social, and mobile media skills.** Today's workers need to know how to use common office software and to communicate using a wide range of digital media and systems.

- **Time and resource management.** If you've had to juggle multiple priorities during college, consider that great training for the business world. Your ability to plan projects and manage the time and resources available to you will make a big difference on the job.

- **Flexibility and adaptability.** Stuff happens, as they say. Employees who can roll with the punches and adapt to changing business priorities and circumstances will go further (and be happier) than employees who resist change.

- **Professionalism.** Professionalism is the quality of performing at the highest possible level and conducting oneself with confidence, purpose, and pride. True professionals strive to excel, continue to hone their skills and build their knowledge, are dependable and accountable, demonstrate a sense of business etiquette, make ethical decisions, show loyalty and commitment, don't give up when things get tough, and maintain a positive outlook.

Adapting to Today's Job Market

Adapting to the workplace is a lifelong process of seeking the best fit between what you want to do and what employers (or clients, if you work independently) are willing to pay you to do. It's important to think about what you want to do during the many thousands of hours you will spend working, what you have to offer, and how to make yourself more attractive to employers.

WHAT DO YOU WANT TO DO?

Economic necessities and the vagaries of the marketplace will influence much of what happens in your career, of course, and you may not always have the opportunity to do the kind of work you would really like to do. Even if you can't get the job you want right now, though, start your job search by examining your values and interests. Doing so will give you a better idea of where you want to be eventually, and you can use those insights to learn and grow your way toward that ideal situation. Consider these questions:

- **What would you like to do every day?** Research occupations that interest you. Find out what people really do every day. Ask friends, relatives, alumni from your school, and contacts in your social networks. Read interviews with people in various professions to get a sense of what their careers are like.
- **How would you like to work?** Consider how much independence you want on the job, how much variety you like, and whether you prefer to work with products, machines, people, ideas, figures, or some combination thereof.
- **How do your financial goals fit with your other priorities?** For instance, many high-paying jobs involve a lot of stress, sacrifices of time with family and friends, and frequent travel or relocation. If location, lifestyle, intriguing work, or other factors are more important to you, you may well have to sacrifice some level of pay to achieve them.
- **Have you established some general career goals?** For example, do you want to pursue a career specialty such as finance or manufacturing, or do you want to gain experience in multiple areas with an eye toward upper management?
- **What sort of corporate culture are you most comfortable with?** Would you be happy in a formal hierarchy with clear reporting relationships? Or do you prefer less structure? Teamwork or individualism? Do you like a competitive environment?

You might need some time in the workforce to figure out what you really want to do or to work your way into the job you really want, but it's never too early to start thinking about where you want to be. Filling out the assessment in Table 1 might help you get a clearer picture of the nature of work you would like to pursue in your career.

WHAT DO YOU HAVE TO OFFER?

Knowing what you want to do is one thing. Knowing what a company is willing to pay you to do is another thing entirely. You may already have a good idea of what you can offer employers. If not, some brainstorming can help you identify your skills, interests, and characteristics. Start by jotting down achievements you're proud of and experiences that were satisfying, and think carefully about what specific skills these achievements demanded of you. For example, leadership skills, speaking ability, and artistic talent may have helped you coordinate a successful class project. As you analyze your achievements, you may well begin to recognize a pattern of skills. Which of them might be valuable to potential employers?

Next, look at your educational preparation, work experience, and extracurricular activities. What do your knowledge and experience qualify you to do? What have you learned from volunteer work or class projects that could benefit you on the job? Have you held any offices, won any awards or scholarships, mastered a second language? What skills have you developed in nonbusiness situations that could transfer to a business position?

TABLE 1 Career Self-Assessment				
Activity or Situation	**Strongly Agree**	**Agree**	**Disagree**	**No Preference**
1. I want to work independently.				
2. I want variety in my work.				
3. I want to work with people.				
4. I want to work with technology.				
5. I want physical work.				
6. I want mental work.				
7. I want to work for a large organization.				
8. I want to work for a nonprofit organization.				
9. I want to work for a small business.				
10. I want to work for a service business.				
11. I want to start or buy a business someday.				
12. I want regular, predictable work hours.				
13. I want to work in a city location.				
14. I want to work in a small town or suburb.				
15. I want to work in another country.				
16. I want to work outdoors.				
17. I want to work in a structured environment.				
18. I want to avoid risk as much as possible.				
19. I want to enjoy my work, even if that means making less money.				
20. I want to become a high-level corporate manager.				

Take stock of your personal characteristics. Are you aggressive, a born leader? Or would you rather follow? Are you outgoing, articulate, great with people? Or do you prefer working alone? Make a list of what you believe are your four or five most important qualities. Ask a relative or friend to rate your traits as well.

If you're having difficulty figuring out your interests, characteristics, or capabilities, consult your college career center. Many campuses administer a variety of tests that can help you identify interests, aptitudes, and personality traits. These tests won't reveal your "perfect" job, but they'll help you focus on the types of work best suited to your personality.

HOW CAN YOU MAKE YOURSELF MORE VALUABLE?

While you're figuring out what you want from a job and what you can offer an employer, you can take positive steps toward building your career. First, look for volunteer projects, temporary jobs, freelance work, or internships that will help expand your experience base and skill set.[6] You can look for freelance projects on Craigslist and numerous other websites; some of these jobs have only nominal pay, but they do provide an opportunity for you to display your skills. Also consider applying your talents to *crowdsourcing* projects, in which companies and nonprofit organizations invite the public to contribute solutions to various challenges.

These opportunities help you gain valuable experience and relevant contacts, provide you with important references and work samples for your *employment portfolio*, and help you establish your *personal brand* (see the following sections).

Second, learn more about the industry or industries in which you want to work and stay on top of new developments. Join networks of professional colleagues and friends who can help you keep up with trends and events. Many professional societies have student chapters or offer students discounted memberships. Take courses and pursue other educational or life experiences that would be difficult while working full time.

BUILDING AN EMPLOYMENT PORTFOLIO

Employers want proof that you have the skills to succeed on the job, but even if you don't have much relevant work experience, you can use your college classes to assemble that proof. Simply create and maintain an *employment portfolio*, which is a collection of projects that demonstrate your skills and knowledge. You can create a *print portfolio* and an *e-portfolio*; both can help with your career effort. A print portfolio gives you something tangible to bring to interviews, and it lets you collect project results that might not be easy to show online, such as a handsomely bound report. An e-portfolio is a multimedia presentation of your skills and experiences.[7] Think of it as a website that contains your résumé, work samples, letters of recommendation, relevant videos or podcasts you have recorded, any blog posts or articles you have written, and other information about you and your skills. If you have set up a *lifestream* (a real-time aggregation of your content creation, online interests, and social media interactions) that is professionally focused, consider adding that to your e-portfolio. The portfolio can be burned on a CD or DVD for physical distribution or, more commonly, it can be posted online—whether on a personal website, your college's site (if student pages are available), or a specialized portfolio hosting site such as Behance. To see a selection of student e-portfolios from colleges around the United States, go to http://real-timeupdates.com/ebc12, click on Student Assignments, and locate the link to student e-portfolios.

Throughout this course, pay close attention to the assignments marked "Portfolio Builder" (they start in Chapter 7). These items will make particularly good samples of not only your communication skills but also your ability to understand and solve business-related challenges. By combining these projects with samples from your other courses, you can create a compelling portfolio when you're ready to start interviewing. Your portfolio is also a great resource for writing your résumé because it reminds you of all the great work you've done over the years. Moreover, you can continue to refine and expand your portfolio throughout your career; many professionals use e-portfolios to advertise their services.

As you assemble your portfolio, collect anything that shows your ability to perform, whether it's in school, on the job, or in other venues. However, you *must* check with employers before including any items that you created while you were an employee, and check with clients before including any *work products* (anything you wrote, designed, programmed, and so on) they purchased from you. Many business documents contain confidential information that companies don't want distributed to outside audiences.

For each item you add to your portfolio, write a brief description that helps other people understand the meaning and significance of the project. Include such items as these:

- **Background.** Why did you undertake this project? Was it a school project, a work assignment, or something you did on your own initiative?
- **Project objectives.** Explain the project's goals, if relevant.
- **Collaborators.** If you worked with others, be sure to mention that and discuss team dynamics if appropriate. For instance, if you led the team or worked with others long distance as a virtual team, point that out.
- **Constraints.** Sometimes the most impressive thing about a project is the time or budget constraints under which it was created. If such constraints apply to a project, consider mentioning them in a way that doesn't sound like an excuse for poor quality. If you had only one week to create a website, for example, you might say that "One of the intriguing challenges of this project was the deadline; I had only one week to design, compose, test, and publish this material."

- **Outcomes.** If the project's goals were measurable, what was the result? For example, if you wrote a letter soliciting donations for a charitable cause, how much money did you raise?
- **Learning experience.** If appropriate, describe what you learned during the course of the project.

Keep in mind that the portfolio itself is a communication project, so be sure to apply everything you'll learn in this course about effective communication and good design. Assume that potential employers will find your e-portfolio site (even if you don't tell them about it), so don't include anything that could come back to haunt you. Also, if you have anything embarrassing on Facebook, Twitter, or any other social networking site, remove it immediately.

To get started, first check with the career center at your college; many schools offer e-portfolio systems for their students. (Some schools now require e-portfolios, so you may already be building one.) You can also find plenty of advice online; search for "e-portfolio," "student portfolio," or "professional portfolio."

BUILDING YOUR PERSONAL BRAND

Products and companies have brands that represent collections of certain attributes, such as the safety emphasis of Volvo cars, the performance emphasis of BMW, or the luxury emphasis of Cadillac. Similarly, when people who know you think about you, they have a particular set of qualities in mind based on your professionalism, your priorities, and the various skills and attributes you have developed over the years. Perhaps without even being conscious of it, you have created a **personal brand** for yourself.

As you plan the next stage of your career, start managing your personal brand deliberately. Branding specialist Mohammed Al-Taee defines personal branding succinctly as "a way of clarifying and communicating what makes you different and special."[8]

You can learn more about personal branding from the sources listed in Table 2, and you will have multiple opportunities to plan and refine your personal brand during this course. For example, Chapter 7 offers tips on business applications of social media, which are key to personal branding, and Chapters 15 and 16 guide you through the process of creating a résumé, building your network, and presenting yourself in interviews. To get you started, here are the basics of a successful personal branding strategy:[9]

- **Figure out the "story of you."** Simply put, where have you been in life, and where are you going? Every good story has dramatic tension that pulls readers in and makes them wonder what will happen next. Where is your story going next? Chapter 15 offers more on this personal brand-building approach.
- **Clarify your professional theme.** Volvos, BMWs, and Cadillacs can all get you from Point A to Point B in safety, comfort, and style, but each brand emphasizes some attributes more than others to create a specific image in the minds of potential buyers. Similarly, you want to be seen as something more than just an accountant, a supervisor, a salesperson. What will your theme be? Brilliant strategist? Hard-nosed, get-it-done tactician? Technical guru? Problem solver? Creative genius? Inspirational leader?

TABLE 2　Personal Branding Resources

Resource	URL
Personal Branding Blog	www.personalbrandingblog.com
Cube Rules	http://cuberules.com
Jibber Jobber	www.jibberjobber.com/blog

Courtesy of TheLadders.com.

Figure P1   Mobile Recruiting Apps
Make sure to explore the wide variety of mobile apps and online resources to help you during your career planning and job search.

- **Reach out and connect.** Major corporations spread the word about their brands with multimillion-dollar advertising campaigns. You can promote your brand for free or close to it. The secret is networking, which you'll learn more about in Chapter 15. You build your brand by connecting with like-minded people, sharing information, demonstrating skills and knowledge, and helping others succeed.
- **Deliver on your brand's promise—every time, all the time.** When you promote a brand, you make a promise—a promise that whoever buys that brand will get the benefits you are promoting. All of this planning and communication is of no value if you fail to deliver on the promises your branding efforts make. Conversely, when you deliver quality results time after time, your talents and professionalism will speak for you.

USING ALL THE JOB-SEARCH TOOLS AT YOUR DISPOSAL

As a final note, be sure to use all the job search tools and resources available to you. For example, many companies now offer mobile apps that give you a feel for what it's like to work there and let you search for job openings. A variety of apps and websites can help you find jobs, practice interviewing, and build your professional network (see Figure P1).

We wish you great success in this course and in your career!

ENDNOTES

1. Ryan Kim, "By 2020, Independent Workers Will Be the Majority," *GigaOm,* 8 December 2011, http://gigaom.com.

2. Darren Dahl, "Want a Job? Let the Bidding Begin," *Inc.,* March 2011, 93–96; Thomas W. Malone, Robert J. Laubacher, and Tammy Johns, "The Age of Hyperspecialization," *Harvard Business Review,* July–August 2011, 56–65; Jennifer Wang, "The Solution to the Innovator's Dilemma," *Entrepreneur,* August 2011, 24–32.

3. "LiveOps and Vision Perry Create New Work Opportunities for Rural Tennessee," LiveOps press release, 18 July 2011, www.liveops.com; Malone et al., "The Age of Hyperspecialization."

4. Adapted from Dahl, "Want a Job? Let the Bidding Begin"; Malone et al., "The Age of Hyperspecialization"; Wang, "The Solution to the Innovator's Dilemma"; Marjorie Derven, "Managing the Matrix in the New Normal," *T+D,* July 2010, 42–47.

5. Courtland L. Bovèe and John V. Thill, *Business in Action,* 5th ed. (Upper Saddle River, N.J.: Pearson Prentice Hall, 2010), 18–21; Randall S. Hansen and Katharine Hansen, "What Do Employers Really Want? Top Skills and Values Employers Seek from Job-Seekers," QuintCareers .com, accessed 17 August 2010, www.quintcareers.com.

6. Nancy M. Somerick, "Managing a Communication Internship Program," *Bulletin of the Association for Business Communication* 56, no. 3 (1993): 10–20.

7. Jeffrey R. Young, "'E-Portfolios' Could Give Students a New Sense of Their Accomplishments," *The Chronicle of Higher Education,* 8 March 2002, A31.

8. Mohammed Al-Taee, "Personal Branding," Al-Taee blog, accessed 17 August 2010, http://altaeeblog.com.

9. Pete Kistler, "Seth Godin's 7-Point Guide to Bootstrap Your Personal Brand," Personal Branding blog, 28 July 2010, www.personalbrandingblog; Kyle Lacy, "10 Ways to Building Your Personal Brand Story," Personal Branding blog, 5 August 2010, www.personalbrandingblog; Al-Taee, "Personal Branding"; Scot Herrick, "30 Career Management Tips—Marketing AND Delivery Support Our Personal Brand," Cube Rules blog, 8 September 2007, http://cuberules.com; Alina Tugend, "Putting Yourself Out There on a Shelf to Buy," *New York Times,* 27 March 2009, www.nytimes.com.

PART 1

Understanding the Foundations of Business Communication

CHAPTER **1** Professional Communication in a Digital, Social, Mobile World

CHAPTER **2** Collaboration, Interpersonal Communication, and Business Etiquette

CHAPTER **3** Communication Challenges in a Diverse, Global Marketplace

No other skill can help your career in as many ways as communication. Discover what business communication is all about, why communication skills are essential to your career, how social and mobile technologies are revolutionizing business communication, and how to adapt your communication experiences in life and college to the business world. Improve your skills in such vital areas as team interaction, etiquette, listening, and nonverbal communication. Explore the advantages and the challenges of a diverse workforce, and develop the skills that every communicator needs to succeed in today's global, multicultural business environment.

El Nariz/Shutterstock

1

Professional Communication in a Digital, Social, Mobile World

LEARNING OBJECTIVES

After studying this chapter, you will be able to

1 Explain the importance of effective communication to your career and to the companies where you will work.

2 Explain what it means to communicate as a professional in a business context.

3 Describe the communication process model and the ways social media are changing the nature of business communication.

4 Outline the challenges and opportunities of mobile communication in business.

5 List four general guidelines for using communication technology effectively.

6 Define *ethics*, explain the difference between an ethical dilemma and an ethical lapse, and list six guidelines for making ethical communication choices.

ON THE JOB: COMMUNICATING AT
JETBLUE

Socializing the Customer Service Experience

If you have ever worked in retail, customer service, or a similar job, you know what a challenge it can be to make sure each customer has a great experience with your company. Imagine the challenge of keeping 25 million customers happy. That's how many passengers JetBlue carries every year—an average of roughly 70,000 customers per day.

As a relatively new airline, taking its first flight in 2000, JetBlue has always tried to differentiate itself from the older carriers in the business. A great example is its pioneering use of Twitter as a customer service platform. JetBlue joined Twitter in 2007, only a year after the microblogging service launched and well before most companies were aware of its potential for business communication. The company views its website as the central hub of its online presence, but social media (the company is quite active on Facebook as well) provide a vital connection between customers and the website. In fact, digital communication of all forms is so important that the company considers itself a digital brand.

The airline was also one of the first companies to truly get the *social* part of social media—that Twitter and other systems were about more than just pushing information outward. Morgan Johnstone, the JetBlue communications staffer who got the

JetBlue's use of social media for customer support coincides perfectly with air travelers' use of mobile devices.

company started on Twitter, recognized early on the power of listening via social media. He wanted to hear what people were saying about the company, whether it was plea for help during travel, a compliment for a company employee, or even an unpleasant criticism. This interaction became so valuable to the company that it now has more than two dozen Twitter agents all ready to interact in real time with the nearly 2 million travelers who follow the company. They answer questions, resolve problems and complaints, and even rebook flights on the spot if needed. Travelers who need assistance don't have time to wait, and JetBlue boasts the fastest Twitter response time in the industry.

For a company that is all about moving people from point A to point B, it's no surprise that mobile communication has become an essential part of JetBlue's connection with its customers. Customers who ask for help or who post complaints on Twitter often do so on their mobile devices, whether they're on their way to catch a flight, stuck in an airport trying to rebook on a different flight, or even on board an aircraft waiting to take off. Mobile is now a core element in the company's communication strategy, with a mobile-friendly website and JetBlue smartphone apps. The company is considering adding such nifty features as augmented reality, which would let travelers hold up their smartphones in airports to see where restrooms, coffee shops, gates, and other vital facilities are located. However the company innovates as it moves forward, its focus will be on using digital, social, and mobile communication to make sure customers have the best possible experience.[1]

TWITTER.COM/JETBLUE

Understanding Why Communication Matters

1 LEARNING OBJECTIVE
Explain the importance of effective communication to your career and to the companies where you will work.

Whether it's as simple as a smile or as ambitious as a social media customer support program (see the chapter opener on JetBlue), **communication** is the process of transferring information and meaning between *senders* and *receivers*, using one or more written, oral, visual, or electronic media. The essence of communication is sharing—providing data, information, insights, and inspiration in an exchange that benefits both you and the people with whom you are communicating.[2] As Figure 1.1 on the next page indicates, this sharing can happen in a variety of ways, including simple and successful transfers of information, negotiations in which the sender and receiver arrive at an agreed-on meaning, and unsuccessful attempts in which the receiver creates a different message than the one the sender intended.

Communication is the process of transferring information and meaning between senders and receivers.

You will invest a lot of time and energy in this course developing your communication skills, so it's fair to ask whether the effort will be worthwhile. This section outlines the many ways in which good communication skills are critical for your career and for any company you join.

COMMUNICATION IS IMPORTANT TO YOUR CAREER

You can have the greatest ideas in the world, but they're no good to your company or your career if you can't express them clearly and persuasively. Some jobs, such as sales and customer support, are primarily about communicating. In fields such as engineering or finance, you often need to share complex ideas with executives, customers, and colleagues, and your ability to connect with people outside your field can be as important as your technical expertise. If you have the entrepreneurial urge, you will need to communicate with a wide range of audiences—from investors, bankers, and government regulators to employees, customers, and business partners.

Ambition and great ideas aren't enough; you need to be able to communicate with people in order to succeed in business.

The changing nature of employment is putting new pressure on communication skills, too. Many companies now supplement their permanent workforces with independent contractors who are brought on for a short period or even just a single project. Chances are you will spend some of your career as one of these independent freelancers, working without the support network that an established company environment provides. You will have to "sell yourself" into each new contract, communicate successfully in a wide range of work situations, and take full responsibility for your career growth and success.

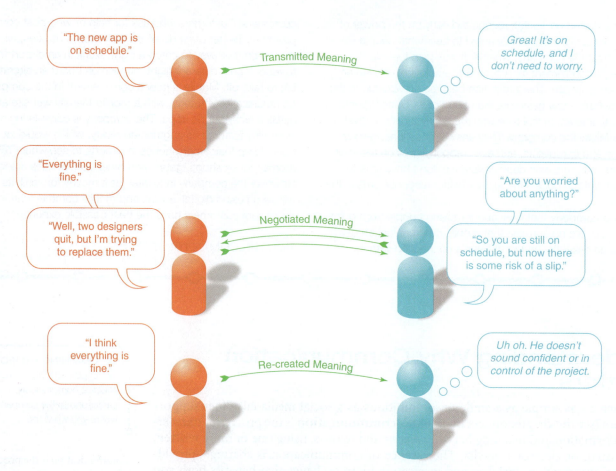

Figure 1.1 Sharing Information

These three exchanges between a software project manager (*left*) and his boss (*right*) illustrate the variety of ways in which information is shared between senders and receivers. In the top exchange, the sender's meaning is transmitted intact to the receiver, who accepts what the sender says at face value. In the middle exchange, the sender and receiver negotiate the meaning by discussing the situation. The negotiated meaning is that everything is fine so far, but the risk of a schedule slip is now higher than it was before. In the bottom exchange, the receiver has a negative emotional reaction to the word *think* and as a result creates her own meaning—that everything probably is not fine, despite what the sender says.

If you launch a company or move into an executive role in an existing organization, you can expect communication to consume the majority of your time. Top executives spend most of their workdays communicating, and businesspeople who can't communicate well don't stand much chance of reaching the top.

In fact, improving your communication skills may be the single most important step you can take in your career. The world is full of good marketing strategists, good accountants, good engineers, and good attorneys—but it is not full of good communicators. View this as an opportunity to stand out from your competition in the job market.

Employers sometimes express frustration at the poor communication skills of many employees—particularly recent college graduates who haven't yet learned how to adapt their communication styles to a professional business environment.[3] If you learn to write well, speak well, listen well, and recognize the appropriate way to communicate in any situation, you'll gain a major advantage that will serve you throughout your career.[4]

Strong communication skills give you an advantage in the job market.

REAL-TIME UPDATES

LEARN MORE BY VISITING THIS WEBSITE

Check out the cutting edge of business communication

This Pinterest board created by the authors highlights some of the most important changes taking place in the field of business communication. Go to http://real-timeupdates.com/ebc12 and click on *Learn More* in the Students section.

COMMUNICATION IS IMPORTANT TO YOUR COMPANY

Aside from the personal benefits, communication should be important to you because it is important to your company. Effective communication helps businesses in numerous ways. It provides[5]

- Closer ties with important communities in the marketplace
- Opportunities to influence conversations, perceptions, and trends
- Increased productivity and faster problem solving
- Better financial results and higher return for investors
- Earlier warning of potential problems, from rising business costs to critical safety issues
- Stronger decision making based on timely, reliable information
- Clearer and more persuasive marketing messages
- Greater employee engagement with their work, leading to higher employee satisfaction and lower employee turnover

Effective communication yields numerous business benefits.

WHAT MAKES BUSINESS COMMUNICATION EFFECTIVE?

Effective communication strengthens the connections between a company and all of its **stakeholders**—those groups affected in some way by the company's actions: customers, employees, shareholders, suppliers, neighbors, the community, the nation, and the world as a whole.[6] To make your communication efforts as effective as possible, focus on making them practical, factual, concise, clear, and persuasive:

- **Provide practical information.** Give recipients useful information, whether it's to help them perform a desired action or understand a new company policy.
- **Give facts rather than vague impressions.** Use concrete language, specific detail, and information that is clear, convincing, accurate, and ethical. Even when an opinion is called for, present compelling evidence to support your conclusion.
- **Present information in a concise, efficient manner.** Concise messages show respect for people's time, and they increase the chances of a positive response.
- **Clarify expectations and responsibilities.** Craft messages to generate a specific response from a specific audience. When appropriate, clearly state what you expect from audience members or what you can do for them.
- **Offer compelling, persuasive arguments and recommendations.** Show your readers precisely how they will benefit by responding the way you want them to respond to your message.

Effective messages are practical, factual, concise, clear, and persuasive.

Keep these five important characteristics in mind as you compare the ineffective and effective versions of the message in Figure 1.2 on the next page.

Communicating as a Professional

You've been communicating your entire life, of course, but if you don't have a lot of work experience yet, meeting the expectations of a professional environment might require some adjustment. A good place to start is to consider what it means to be a professional. **Professionalism** is the quality of performing at a high level and conducting oneself with purpose and pride. It means doing more than putting in the hours and collecting a paycheck: True professionals go beyond minimum expectations and commit to making meaningful contributions. Professionalism can be broken down into six distinct traits: striving to excel, being dependable and accountable, being a team player, demonstrating a sense of etiquette, making ethical decisions, and maintaining a positive outlook (see Figure 1.3 on page 7).

2 LEARNING OBJECTIVE
Explain what it means to communicate as a professional in a business context.

A key message to glean from Figure 1.3 is how much these elements of professionalism depend on effective communication. For example, to be a team player, you have to be able to collaborate, resolve conflicts, and interact with a wide variety of personalities. Without strong communication skills, you won't be able to perform to your potential, and others won't recognize you as the professional you'd like to be.

Communication is an essential part of being a successful professional.

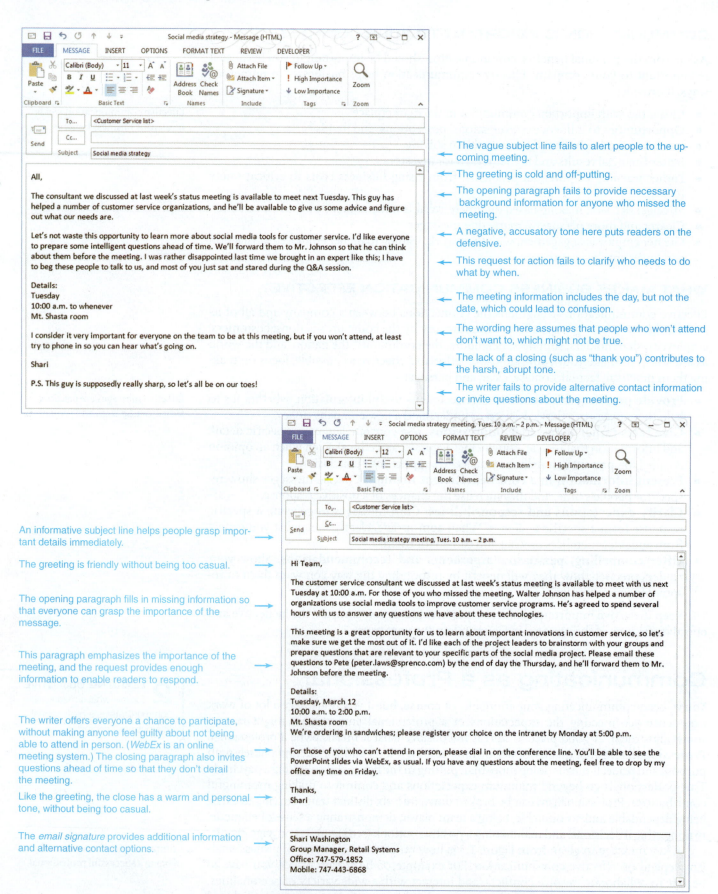

The vague subject line fails to alert people to the up-coming meeting.

The greeting is cold and off-putting.

The opening paragraph fails to provide necessary background information for anyone who missed the meeting.

A negative, accusatory tone here puts readers on the defensive.

This request for action fails to clarify who needs to do what by when.

The meeting information includes the day, but not the date, which could lead to confusion.

The wording here assumes that people who won't attend don't want to, which might not be true.

The lack of a closing (such as "thank you") contributes to the harsh, abrupt tone.

The writer fails to provide alternative contact information or invite questions about the meeting.

An informative subject line helps people grasp important details immediately.

The greeting is friendly without being too casual.

The opening paragraph fills in missing information so that everyone can grasp the importance of the message.

This paragraph emphasizes the importance of the meeting, and the request provides enough information to enable readers to respond.

The writer offers everyone a chance to participate, without making anyone feel guilty about not being able to attend in person. (*WebEx* is an online meeting system.) The closing paragraph also invites questions ahead of time so that they don't derail the meeting.

Like the greeting, the close has a warm and personal tone, without being too casual.

The *email signature* provides additional information and alternative contact options.

Figure 1.2   Effective Professional Communication

At first glance, this email message looks like a reasonable attempt at communicating with the members of a project team. However, review the blue annotations to see just how many problems the message really has.

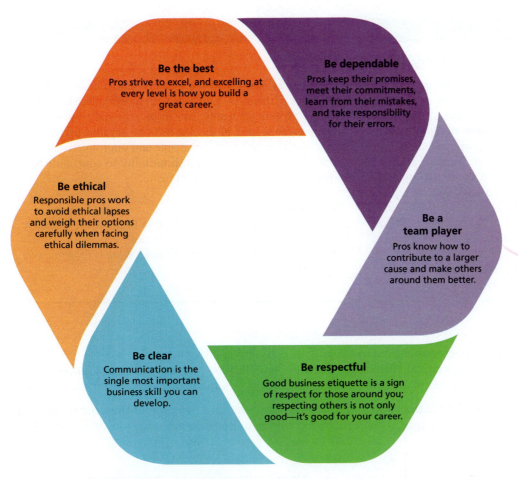

Figure 1.3   Elements of Professionalism
To be respected as a true professional, develop these six qualities.

This section offers a brief look at the skills employers will expect you to have, the nature of communication in an organizational environment, and the importance of adopting an audience-centered approach.

UNDERSTANDING WHAT EMPLOYERS EXPECT FROM YOU

Today's employers expect you to be competent at a wide range of communication tasks. Fortunately, the skills employers expect from you are the same skills that will help you advance in your career:[7]

- Recognizing information needs, using efficient search techniques to locate reliable sources of information, particularly from online sources, and using gathered information ethically; this collection of skills is often referred to as *digital information fluency*[8]
- Organizing ideas and information logically and completely
- Expressing ideas and information coherently and persuasively
- Actively listening to others
- Communicating effectively with people from diverse backgrounds and experiences
- Using communication technologies effectively and efficiently
- Following accepted standards of grammar, spelling, and other aspects of high-quality writing and speaking
- Communicating in a civilized manner that reflects contemporary expectations of business etiquette, even when dealing with indifferent or hostile audiences
- Communicating ethically, even when choices aren't crystal clear

Employers expect you to possess a wide range of communication skills.

THE ART OF PROFESSIONALISM

Maintaining a Confident, Positive Outlook

Spend a few minutes around successful people in any field, and chances are you'll notice how optimistic they are. They believe in what they're doing, and they believe in themselves and their ability to solve problems and overcome obstacles.

Being positive doesn't mean displaying mindless optimism or spewing happy talk all the time. It means acknowledging that things may be difficult but then buckling down and getting the job done anyway. It means no whining and no slacking off, even when the going gets tough. We live in an imperfect world, no question; jobs can be boring or difficult, customers can be unpleasant, and bosses can be unreasonable. But when you're a pro, you find a way to power through.

Your energy, positive or negative, is contagious. Both in person and online, you'll spend as much time with your colleagues as you spend with family and friends. Personal demeanor is, therefore, a vital element of workplace harmony. No one expects (or wants) you to be artificially upbeat and bubbly every second of the day, but one negative personality can make an entire office miserable and unproductive. Every person in a company has a responsibility to contribute to a positive, energetic work environment.

CAREER APPLICATIONS

1. Do you have an ethical obligation to maintain a positive outlook on the job? Why or why not?
2. How can you lift your spirits when work is dragging you down?

- Managing your time wisely and using resources efficiently
- Using **critical thinking**, which is the ability to evaluate evidence completely and objectively in order to form logical conclusions and make sound recommendations

You'll have the opportunity to practice these skills throughout this course, but don't stop there. Successful professionals continue to hone communication skills throughout their careers.

COMMUNICATING IN AN ORGANIZATIONAL CONTEXT

The formal communication network mirrors the company's organizational structure.

In addition to having the proper skills, you need to learn how to apply those skills in the business environment, which can be quite different from the social and scholastic environments you are accustomed to. Every organization has a **formal communication network**, in which ideas and information flow along the lines of command (the hierarchical levels) in the company's organization structure (see Figure 1.4). Throughout the formal network, information flows in three directions. *Downward communication* flows from executives to employees, conveying executive decisions and providing information that helps employees do their jobs. *Upward communication* flows from employees to executives, providing insight into problems, trends, opportunities, grievances, and performance, thus allowing executives to solve problems and make intelligent decisions. *Horizontal communication* flows between departments to help employees share information, coordinate tasks, and solve complex problems.[9]

Every organization also has an **informal communication network**, often referred to as the *grapevine* or the *rumor mill*, which encompasses all communication that occurs outside the formal network. Some of this informal communication takes place naturally as a result of employee interaction on the job and in social settings, and some of it takes place when the formal network doesn't provide information that employees want. In fact, the inherent limitations of formal communication networks helped spur the growth of social media in the business environment.

ADOPTING AN AUDIENCE-CENTERED APPROACH

An audience-centered approach involves understanding, respecting, and meeting the needs of your audience members.

An **audience-centered approach** involves understanding and respecting the members of your audience and making every effort to get your message across in a way that is meaningful to them. This approach is also known as adopting the **"you" attitude**, in contrast to messages that are about "me." Learn as much as possible about the biases, education, age, status, style, and personal and professional concerns of your receivers. If you're

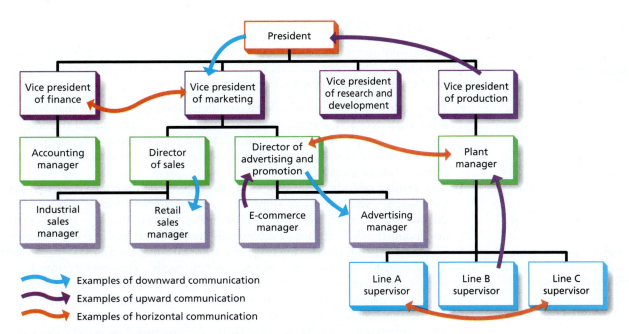

Figure 1.4   Formal Communication Network
The formal communication network is defined by the relationships between the various job positions in the organization. Messages can flow upward (from a lower-level employee to a higher-level employee), downward (from a higher-level employee to a lower-level employee), and horizontally (across the organization, between employees at the same or similar levels).

addressing people you don't know and you're unable to find out more about them, try to project yourself into their position by using common sense and imagination. This ability to relate to the needs of others is a key part of *emotional intelligence,* which is widely considered to be a vital characteristic of successful managers and leaders.[10] The more you know about the people you're communicating with, the easier it will be to concentrate on their needs—which, in turn, will make it easier for them to hear your message, understand it, and respond positively.

A vital element of audience-centered communication is **etiquette**, the expected norms of behavior in any particular situation. In today's hectic, competitive world, etiquette might seem a quaint and outdated notion. However, the way you conduct yourself and interact with others can have a profound influence on your company's success and your career. When executives hire and promote you, they expect your behavior to protect the company's reputation. The more you understand such expectations, the better chance you have of avoiding career-damaging mistakes. The principles of etiquette discussed in Chapter 2 will help you communicate with an audience-centered approach in a variety of business settings.

Etiquette, the expected norms of behavior in any particular situation, can have a profound influence on your company's success and your career.

Exploring the Communication Process

Even with the best intentions, communication efforts can fail. Messages can get lost or simply ignored. The receiver of a message can interpret it in ways the sender never imagined. In fact, two people receiving the same information can reach different conclusions about what it means.

Fortunately, by understanding communication as a process with distinct steps, you can improve the odds that your messages will reach their intended audiences and produce their intended effects. This section explores the communication process in two stages: first by following a message from one sender to one receiver in the basic communication model and then by expanding on that approach with multiple messages and participants in the social communication model.

3 LEARNING OBJECTIVE
Describe the communication process model and the ways social media are changing the nature of business communication.

Viewing communication as a process helps you identify steps you can take to improve your success as a communicator.

THE BASIC COMMUNICATION MODEL

By viewing communication as a process (Figure 1.5), you can identify and improve the skills you need to be more successful. Many variations on this process model exist, but these eight steps provide a practical overview:

- **The sender has an idea.** Whether a communication effort will ultimately be effective starts right here and depends on the nature of the idea and the motivation for sending it. For example, if your motivation is to offer a solution to a problem, you have a better chance of crafting a meaningful message than if your motivation is merely to complain about a problem.
- **The sender encodes the idea as a message.** When someone puts an idea into a **message**—which you can think of as the "container" for an idea—he or she is **encoding** it, or expressing it in words or images. Much of the focus of this course is on developing the skills needed to successfully encode your ideas into effective messages.

The medium is the *form* a message takes and the *channel* is the system used to deliver the message.

- **The sender produces the message in a transmittable medium.** With the appropriate message to express an idea, the sender now needs a **communication medium** to present that message to the intended audience. To update your boss on the status of a project, for instance, you might have a dozen or more media choices, from a phone call to an instant message to a slideshow presentation.
- **The sender transmits the message through a channel.** Just as technology continues to increase the number of media options at your disposal, it continues to provide new **communication channels** you can use to transmit your messages. The distinction between medium and channel can get a bit murky, but think of the medium as the *form* a message takes (such as a Twitter update) and the channel as the system used to *deliver* the message (such as a mobile phone).
- **The audience receives the message.** If the channel functions properly, the message reaches its intended audience. However, mere arrival at the destination is no guarantee that the message will be noticed or understood correctly. As "How Audiences Receive Messages" (page 12) explains, many messages are either ignored or misinterpreted as noise.
- **The audience decodes the message.** After a message is received, the receiver needs to extract the idea from the message, a step known as **decoding**. "How Audiences Decode Messages" (page 12) takes a closer look at this complex and subtle step in the process.
- **The audience responds to the message.** By crafting messages in ways that show the benefits of responding, senders can increase the chances that recipients will respond in positive ways. However, as "How Audiences Respond to Messages" (page 13) points out, whether a receiver responds as the sender hopes depends on the receiver (a) *remembering* the message long enough to act on it, (b) being *able* to act on it, and (c) being *motivated* to respond.

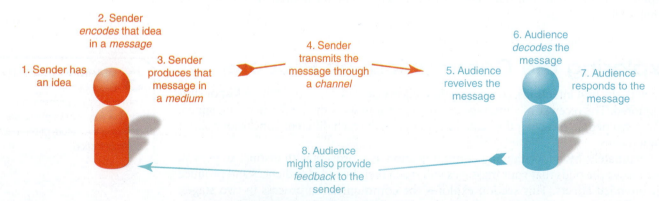

1. Sender has an idea

2. Sender *encodes* that idea in a *message*

3. Sender produces that message in a *medium*

4. Sender transmits the message through a *channel*

5. Audience reveives the message

6. Audience *decodes* the message

7. Audience responds to the message

8. Audience might also provide *feedback* to the sender

Figure 1.5 **The Basic Communication Process**
This eight-step model is a simplified view of how communication works in real life; understanding this basic model is vital to improving your communication skills.

- **The audience provides feedback to the sender.** In addition to responding (or not responding) to the message, audience members may give **feedback** that helps the sender evaluate the effectiveness of the communication effort. Feedback can be verbal (using written or spoken words), nonverbal (using gestures, facial expressions, or other signals), or both. Just like the original message, however, this feedback from the receiver also needs to be decoded carefully. A smile, for example, can have many meanings.

Considering the complexity of this process—and the barriers and distractions that often stand between sender and receiver—it should come as no surprise that communication efforts often fail to achieve the sender's objective. Fortunately, the better you understand the process, the more successful you'll be.

The following sections take a closer look at two important aspects of the process: environmental barriers that can block or distort messages and the steps audiences take to receive, decode, and respond to messages.

Barriers in the Communication Environment

Within any communication environment, messages can be disrupted by a variety of **communication barriers**. These barriers include noise and distractions, competing messages, filters, and channel breakdowns:

- **Noise and distractions.** External distractions range from uncomfortable meeting rooms to computer screens cluttered with instant messages and reminders popping up all over the place. Internal distractions are thoughts and emotions that prevent audiences from focusing on incoming messages. The common habit of *multitasking*—attempting more than one task at a time—is practically guaranteed to create communication distractions. Moreover, research suggests that "chronic multitasking" can reduce productivity and increase errors.[11] As more communication takes place on mobile devices, the need to insulate yourself from noise and distractions is going to keep growing.

  A number of barriers can block or distort messages before they reach the intended audience.

- **Competing messages.** Having your audience's undivided attention is a rare luxury. In most cases, you must compete with other messages that are trying to reach your audience at the same time.
- **Filters.** Messages can be blocked or distorted by *filters*, any human or technological interventions between the sender and the receiver. Filtering can be both intentional (such as automatically filing incoming messages based on sender or content) or unintentional (such as an overly aggressive spam filter that deletes legitimate emails). As mentioned previously, the structure and culture of an organization can also inhibit the flow of vital messages. And, in some cases, the people or companies you rely on to deliver your message can distort it or filter it to meet their own needs.
- **Channel breakdowns.** Sometimes the channel simply breaks down and fails to deliver your message at all. A colleague you were counting on to deliver a message to your boss might have forgotten to do so, or a computer server might have crashed and prevented your blog from updating.

Everyone in an organization can help minimize barriers and distractions. As a communicator, try to be aware of any barriers that could prevent your messages from reaching their intended audiences. As a manager, keep an eye out for any organizational barriers that could be inhibiting the flow of information. In any situation, a small dose of common sense and courtesy goes a long way. Turn off that mobile phone before you step into a meeting. Don't talk across the tops of other people's cubicles. Be sensitive to personal differences, too; for instance, some people enjoy working with music on, but music is a huge distraction for others.[12]

Minimizing barriers and distractions in the communication environment is everyone's responsibility.

Finally, take steps to insulate yourself from distractions. Don't let messages interrupt you every minute of the day. Instead, set aside time to attend to messages all at once so that you can focus the rest of the time.

Inside the Mind of Your Audience

After a message works its way through the communication channel and reaches the intended audience, it encounters a whole new set of challenges. Understanding how audiences receive, decode, and respond to messages will help you create more effective messages.

To actually receive a message, audience members need to sense it, select it, then perceive it as a message.

How Audiences Receive Messages   For an audience member to receive a message, three events need to occur: The receiver has to *sense* the presence of a message, *select* it from all the other messages clamoring for attention, and *perceive* it as an actual message (as opposed to random, pointless noise).[13] You can appreciate the magnitude of this challenge by driving down any busy street in a commercial section of town. You'll encounter hundreds of messages—billboards, posters, store window displays, car stereos, pedestrians waving or talking on mobile phones, car horns, street signs, traffic lights, and so on. However, you'll sense, select, and perceive only a small fraction of these messages.

Today's business audiences are much like drivers on busy streets. They are inundated with so many messages and so much noise that they can miss or ignore many of the messages intended for them. Through this course, you will learn a variety of techniques to craft messages that get noticed. In general, follow these five principles to increase your chances of success:

To improve the odds that your messages will be successfully perceived by your audience, pay close attention to expectations, ease of use, familiarity, empathy, and technical compatibility.

- **Consider audience expectations.** Deliver messages using the media and channels that the audience expects. If colleagues expect meeting notices to be delivered by email, don't suddenly switch gears and start delivering the notices via blog postings without telling anyone. Of course, sometimes going *against* expectations can stimulate audience attention, which is why advertisers sometimes do wacky and creative things to get noticed. However, for most business communication efforts, following the expectations of your audience is the most efficient way to get your message across.
- **Ensure ease of use.** Even if audiences are actively looking for your messages, they probably won't see the messages if you make them hard to find, hard to navigate, or hard to read.
- **Emphasize familiarity.** Use words, images, and designs that are familiar to your audience. For example, most visitors to company websites expect to see information about the company on a page called "About" or "About Us."
- **Practice empathy.** Make sure your messages speak to the audience by clearly addressing *their* wants and needs—not yours. People are inclined to notice messages that relate to their individual concerns.[14]
- **Design for compatibility.** For the many messages delivered electronically these days, be sure to verify technological compatibility with your audience. For instance, if your website requires visitors to have a particular video capability in their browsers, you won't reach those audience members who don't have that software installed or updated.

Decoding is a complex process; receivers often extract different meanings from messages than senders attempt to encode in their messages.

How Audiences Decode Messages   A received message doesn't "mean" anything until the recipient decodes it and assigns meaning to it, and there is no guarantee the receiver will assign the same meaning the sender intended. Even well-crafted, well-intentioned communication efforts can fail at this stage because assigning meaning through decoding is a highly personal process that is influenced by culture, individual experience, learning and thinking styles, hopes, fears, and even temporary moods. Moreover, audiences tend to extract the meaning they expect to get from a message, even if it's the opposite of what the sender intended.[15] In fact, rather than "extract" your meaning, it's more accurate to say that your audience members re-create their own meaning—or meanings—from the message.

Selective perception occurs when people ignore or distort incoming information to fit their preconceived notions of reality.

Cultural and personal beliefs and biases influence the meaning audiences get from messages. For instance, the human brain organizes incoming sensations into a mental "map" that represents the person's individual **perception** of reality. If an incoming detail doesn't fit into that perception, a message recipient may simply distort the information to make it fit rather than rearrange his or her mental map—a phenomenon known as **selective perception**.[16] For example, an executive who has staked her reputation on a particular business strategy might distort or ignore evidence that suggests the strategy is failing.

Differences in language and usage also influence received meaning. If you ask an employee to send you a report on sales figures "as soon as possible," does that mean within 10 seconds, 10 minutes, or 10 days? By clarifying expectations and resolving potential ambiguities in your messages, you can minimize such uncertainties. In general, the

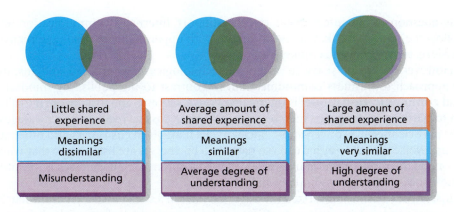

Figure 1.6 **How Shared Experience Affects Understanding**
The more two people or two groups of people share experiences—personal, professional, and cultural—
the more likely it is that receivers will extract the intended meanings senders encode into the messages.

more experiences you share with another person, the more likely you are to share perception and thus share meaning (see Figure 1.6).

Individual thinking styles are another important factor in message decoding. For example, someone who places a high value on objective analysis and clear logic might interpret a message differently than someone who values emotion or intuition (reaching conclusions without using rational processes).

How Audiences Respond to Messages Your message has been delivered, received, and correctly decoded. Now what? Will audience members respond in the way you'd like them to? Only if three events occur.

First, the recipient has to *remember* the message long enough to act on it. Simplifying greatly, memory works in several stages: *Sensory memory* momentarily captures incoming data from the senses; then, whatever the recipient pays attention to is transferred to *short-term memory*. Information in short-term memory will quickly disappear if it isn't transferred to *long-term memory*, which can be done either actively (such as when a person memorizes a list of items) or passively (such as when a new piece of information connects with something else the recipient already has stored in long-term memory). Finally, the information needs to be *retrieved* when the recipient wants to act on it.[17] In general, people find it easier to remember and retrieve information that is important to them personally or professionally. Consequently, by communicating in ways that are sensitive to your audience's wants and needs, you greatly increase the chance that your messages will be remembered and retrieved.

> Audiences will likely respond to a message if they remember it, if they're able to respond, and if they're properly motivated to respond.

Second, the recipient has to be *able* to respond as you wish. Obviously, if recipients simply cannot do what you want them to do, they will not respond according to your plan. By understanding your audience (you'll learn more about audience analysis in Chapter 4), you can work to minimize these unsuccessful outcomes.

Third, the recipient has to be *motivated* to respond. You'll encounter many situations in which your audience has the option of responding but isn't required to. For instance, a record company may or may not offer your band a contract, or your boss may or may not respond to your request for a raise. Throughout this course, you'll learn techniques for crafting messages that can help motivate readers to respond positively to your messages.

> By explaining how audiences will benefit by responding positively to your messages, you'll increase their motivation to respond.

THE SOCIAL COMMUNICATION MODEL

The basic model presented in Figure 1.5 illustrates how a single idea moves from one sender to one receiver. In a larger sense, it also helps represent the traditional nature of much business communication, which was primarily defined by a *publishing* or *broadcasting* mindset. Externally, a company issued carefully scripted messages to a mass audience that often had few options for responding to those messages or initiating messages of their own. Customers and other interested parties had few ways to connect with one another

The conversational and interactive *social communication model* is revolutionizing business communication.

to ask questions, share information, or offer support. Internally, communication tended to follow the same "we talk, you listen" model, with upper managers issuing directives to lower-level supervisors and employees.

However, in recent years, a variety of technologies have enabled and inspired a new approach to business communication. In contrast to the publishing mindset, this **social communication model** is interactive, conversational, and usually open to all who wish to participate. Audience members are no longer passive recipients of messages but active participants in a conversation. Social media have given customers and other stakeholders a voice they did not have in the past. And businesses are listening to that voice. In fact, one of the most common uses of social media among U.S. businesses is monitoring online discussions about a company and its brands.[18]

The social communication model can increase the speed of communication, lower cost, improve access to expertise, and boost employee satisfaction.

Instead of transmitting a fixed message, a sender in a social media environment initiates a conversation by asking a question or sharing valuable information. Information shared this way is often revised and reshaped by the web of participants as they forward it and comment on it. People can add to it or take pieces from it, depending on their needs and interests. Figure 1.7 lists some of the significant differences between the traditional and social models of business communication.

For all their advantages, social media tools also present a number of communication challenges.

The social communication model offers many advantages, but it has a number of disadvantages as well. Potential problems include information overload, fragmented attention, information security risks, distractions that hurt productivity, the need to monitor and respond to numerous conversational threads, and blurring of the line between personal and professional lives, which can make it difficult for people to disconnect from work.[19]

Of course, no company, no matter how enthusiastically it embraces the social communication model, is going to be run as a club in which everyone has a say in every business matter. Instead, a hybrid approach is emerging in which some communications (such as strategic plans and policy documents) follow the traditional approach, whereas others (such as project management updates and customer support messages) follow the social model.

You can learn more about business uses of social media in Chapter 7.

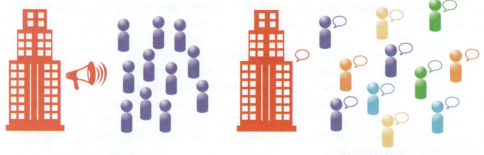

Conventional Promotion: "We Talk, You Listen"	The Social Model: "Let's Have a Conversation"
Tendencies	**Tendencies**
Publication, broadcast	Converstion
Lecture	Discussion
Intrusion	Permission
Unidirectinal	Bidirectional, multidirectional
One to many; mass audience	One to one; many to many
Control	Influence
Low message frequency	High message frequency
Few channels	Many channels
Information hoarding	Information sharing
Static	Dynamic
Hierarchical	Egalitarian
Structured	Amorphous
Isolated	Collaborative
Planned	Reactive
Resistive	Responsive

Figure 1.7   The Social Communication Model
The social communication model differs from conventional communication strategies and practices in a number of significant ways. You're probably already an accomplished user of many new-media tools, and this experience will help you on the job.

The Mobile Revolution

4 LEARNING OBJECTIVE
Outline the challenges and opportunities of mobile communication in business.

As much of a game-changer as social media have been, some experts predict that mobile communication will change the nature of business and business communication even more. Venture capitalist Joe Schoendorf says that "mobile is the most disruptive technology that I have seen in 48 years in Silicon Valley."[20] Researcher Maribel Lopez calls mobile "the biggest technology shift since the Internet."[21]

Companies recognize the value of integrating mobile technology, from communication platforms to banking to retail. Mobile apps and communication systems can boost employee productivity, help companies form closer relationships with customers and business partners, and spur innovation in products and services (see Figure 1.8). Given the advantages and the rising expectations of employees and customers, firms on the leading edge of the mobile revolution are working to integrate mobile technology throughout their organizations.[22]

This section offers a high-level view of the mobile revolution, and you'll see coverage of specific topics integrated throughout the book, in everything from collaborative writing and research to presentations and job search strategies.

REAL-TIME UPDATES
LEARN MORE BY WATCHING THIS VIDEO
The mobile business advantage

See how leading-edge companies are adapting to take advantage of mobile communication. Go to http://real-timeupdates.com/ebc12 and click on Learn More in the Students section.

THE RISE OF MOBILE AS A COMMUNICATION PLATFORM

Whether it's emailing, social networking, watching videos, or doing research, the percentage of communication and media consumption performed on mobile devices continues to grow. For millions of people around the world, a mobile device is their primary way, if not their only way, to access the Internet. Globally, roughly 80 percent of Internet users access the web at least some of the time with a mobile device.[23]

Mobile has become the primary communication tool for many business professionals, including a majority of executives under age 40.[24] Email and web browsing rank first and second in terms of the most common nonvoice uses of smartphones, and more

Mobile devices are rapidly taking over as the primary communication platform for many business professionals.

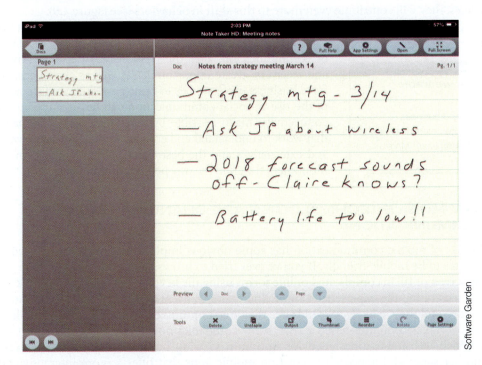

Software Garden

Figure 1.8   Mobile Communication Tools
Mobile technologies offer multiple ways to improve communication and other key business processes. For example, note-taking apps such as Note Taker HD offer an easy and unobtrusive way to take notes during meetings, site visits, and other business functions.

Used by permission of Uno Inc.

Figure 1.9 **Wearable Technology**
Smartwatches and other wearable mobile devices offer intriguing possibilities for business communication. The Uno Noteband incorporates Spritz speed-reading technology that makes it easier to read message content quickly.

email messages are now opened on mobile devices than on PCs.[25] Roughly half of U.S. consumers use a mobile device exclusively for their online search needs, and many online activities that eventually migrate to a PC screen start out on a mobile screen.[26] For many people, the fact that a smartphone can make phone calls is practically a secondary consideration; data traffic from mobile devices far outstrips voice traffic.[27]

Moreover, mobile phones—particularly smartphones—have become intensely personal devices in ways that PCs never did. For many users, the connection is so close they can feel a sense of panic when they don't have frequent access to their phones.[28] When people are closely attached to their phones, day and night, they are more closely connected to all the information sources, conversations, and networks that those phones can connect to. As a result, mobile connectivity can start to resemble a continuous stream of conversations that never quite end, which influences the way businesses need to interact with their stakeholders. If *wearable technologies* become mainstream devices, they will contribute even more to this shift in behaviors (see Figure 1.9).

The parallels between social media and mobile communication are striking: Both sets of technologies change the nature of communication, alter the relationships between senders and receivers, create opportunities as well as challenges, and force business professionals to hone new skills. In fact, much of the rise in social communication can be attributed to the connectivity made possible by mobile devices. Companies that work to understand and embrace mobile, both internally and externally, stand the best chance of capitalizing on this monumental shift in the way people communicate.

HOW MOBILE TECHNOLOGIES ARE CHANGING BUSINESS COMMUNICATION

The rise of mobile communication has some obvious implications, such as the need for websites to be mobile friendly. If you've ever tried to browse a conventional website on a tiny screen or fill in complicated online forms using the keypad on your phone, you know how frustrating the experience can be. Increasingly, users expect websites to be mobile friendly, and they're likely to avoid sites that aren't optimized for mobile.[29] As mobile access overtakes computer-based access, some companies now take a *mobile-first* approach, in which websites are designed for optimum viewing on smartphones and tablets.[30] Another successful approach is creating mobile apps that offer a more interactive and mobile-friendly experience than a conventional website can offer.

However, device size and portability are only the most obvious changes. Just as with social media, the changes brought about by mobile go far deeper than the technology itself. Mobile changes the way people communicate, which has profound implications for virtually every aspect of business communication.

Social media pioneer Nicco Mele coined the term *radical connectivity* to describe "the breathtaking ability to send vast amounts of data instantly, constantly, and globally."[31] Mobile plays a major and ever-expanding role in this phenomenon by keeping people connected 24/7, wherever they may be. People who've grown up with mobile communication technology expect to have immediate access to information and the ability to stay connected to their various social and business networks.[32]

People who grew up with mobile phones often expect to have the same level of connectivity as customers and as employees.

Here are the most significant ways mobile technology is changing the practice of business communication:

- Constant connectivity is a mixed blessing. As with social media, mobile connectivity can blur the boundaries between personal and professional time and space, preventing people from fully disengaging from work during personal and family time. On the other hand, it can give employees more flexibility to meet their personal and professional obligations.[33] In this regard, mobile plays an important role in efforts to reduce operating costs through telecommuting and other nontraditional work models.[34]

Constant connectivity is a mixed blessing; you can work from anywhere at any time, but it's more difficult to disconnect from work and recharge yourself.

- Small mobile displays and sometimes-awkward input technologies present challenges for creating and consuming content, whether it's typing an email message or watching a video. As you'll read in Chapter 6, for example, email messages need to be written and formatted differently to make them easier to read on mobile devices.

Collaboration and problem solving are two key areas where mobile connectivity can boost productivity by enabling real-time interaction and access to vital information.

- Mobile users are often multitasking—roughly half of mobile phone usage happens while people are walking, for instance—so they can't give full attention to the information on their screens.[35] Moreover, mobile use often occurs in environments with multiple distractions and barriers to successful communication.
- Mobile communication, particularly text messaging, has put pressure on traditional standards of grammar, punctuation, and writing in general. Chapter 4 has more on this topic.
- Mobile devices can serve as sensory and cognitive extensions.[36] For example, they can help people experience more of their environment (such as augmented reality apps that superimpose information on a live camera view) and have instant access to information without relying on faulty and limited human memory. The addition of *location-aware content*, such as facility maps and property information, enhances the mobile experience.
- Mobile devices create a host of security and privacy concerns, for end users and corporate technology managers alike.[37] Companies are wrestling with the "bring your own device" or "BYOD" phenomenon, in which employees want to be able to access company networks and files with their personal smartphones and tablets, both in the office and away from it. However, these devices don't always have the rigorous security controls that corporate networks need, and users don't always use the devices in secure ways.
- Mobile tools can enhance productivity and collaboration by making it easier for employees to stay connected and giving them access to information and work tasks during forced gaps in the workday or while traveling.[38]
- Mobile apps can assist in a wide variety of business tasks, from research to presentations (see Figure 1.10).[39]
- Mobile connectivity can accelerate decision making and problem solving by putting the right information in the hands of the right people at the right time. For example, if the people in a decision-making meeting need more information, they can do the necessary research on the spot.[40] Mobile communication also makes it easier to quickly tap into pockets of expertise within a company.[41] Customer service can be improved by making sure technicians and

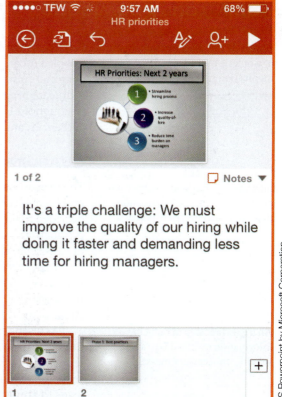

Figure 1.10 Mobile Communication: Opportunities and Challenges
From 24/7 connectivity to business-oriented apps that let professionals perform work tasks on the go (such as making notes for a presentation, as shown here on the mobile version of PowerPoint), mobile technology is revolutionizing business communication.

MS Powerpoint by Microsoft Corporation

other workers always have the information they need right at hand.[42] Companies can also respond and communicate faster during crises.[43]

- With interactivity designed to take advantage of the capabilities of mobile devices (including cameras, accelerometers, compasses, and GPS), companies can create more engaging experiences for customers and other users.[44]

The mobile revolution complicates business communication in some ways, but it can enhance communication in many ways if done thoughtfully. You'll read more about mobile in the chapters ahead.

Using Technology to Improve Business Communication

5 LEARNING OBJECTIVE
List four general guidelines for using communication technology effectively.

Today's businesses rely heavily on technology to enhance communication. In fact, many of the technologies you might use in your personal life, from microblogs to video games, are also used in business. You will find technology discussed extensively throughout this book, with specific advice on using both common and emerging tools. The four-page photo essay "Powerful Tools for Communicating Efficiently" (see pages 20–23) provides an overview of the technologies that connect people in offices, factories, and other business settings.

However, anyone who has used advanced technology knows the benefits are not automatic. Poorly designed or inappropriately used technology can hinder communication more than help. To communicate effectively, learn to keep technology in perspective, guard against information overload and information addiction, use technological tools productively, and disengage from the computer frequently to communicate in person.

MOBILE APP
Pocket collects content you'd like to read or view later and syncs it across your mobile devices.

KEEPING TECHNOLOGY IN PERSPECTIVE

Don't rely too much on technology or let it overwhelm the communication process.

Perhaps the single most important point to remember about technology is that it is simply a tool, a means by which you can accomplish certain tasks. Technology is an aid to interpersonal communication, not a replacement for it. Technology can't think for you or communicate for you, and if you lack some essential skills, technology can't fill in the gaps. Throughout the book, you'll see advice on keeping the focus on your messages and your audiences, and using technology to enhance the communication process.

GUARDING AGAINST INFORMATION OVERLOAD

Information overload results when people receive more information than they can effectively process.

The overuse or misuse of communication technology can lead to **information overload**, in which people receive more information than they can effectively process. Information overload makes it difficult to discriminate between useful and useless information, lowers productivity, and amplifies employee stress both on the job and at home, even to the point of causing health and relationship problems.[45]

You often have some level of control over the number and types of messages you choose to receive. Use the filtering features of your communication systems to isolate high-priority messages that deserve your attention. Also, be wary of subscribing to too many Twitter streams and other sources. Focus on the information you truly need in order to do your job.

An important step in reducing information overload is to avoid sending unnecessary messages.

As a sender, you can help reduce information overload by making sure you don't send unnecessary messages. In addition, when you send messages that aren't urgent or crucial, let people know so they can prioritize. Also, most communication systems let you mark messages as urgent; however, use this feature only when it is truly needed. Its overuse leads to annoyance and anxiety, not action.

USING TECHNOLOGICAL TOOLS PRODUCTIVELY

Facebook, Twitter, YouTube, and other technologies are key parts of what has been called the *information technology paradox*, in which information tools can waste as much time as they save. Concerns over inappropriate use of social networking sites, for example, have led many companies to ban employees from accessing them during work hours.[46]

DIGITAL + SOCIAL + MOBILE: TODAY'S COMMUNICATION ENVIRONMENT

It's All Fun and Games—and Effective Business Communication

The fact that millions of people spend billions of hours playing games on their mobile devices is not lost on companies looking for ways to enhance communication with employees and customers. Whether they feature skill, chance, or compelling storylines, successful games try to engage users intellectually and emotionally—just as successful business communicators try to do.

Gamification is the addition of game-playing aspects to an activity or a process with the goal of increasing user engagement, and it's a natural for social media and mobile devices. Foursquare's check-in competitions, in which the person who "checks in" using Foursquare the most times during a 60-day window is crowned the "mayor" of that location, are one of the best-known uses of gamification. Foursquare wasn't invented as a way for people to become imaginary mayors of places they shop or eat, of course. It is an advertising platform that relies on user activity and user-generated content, and the game element encourages people to use the app more frequently.

Foursquare is a simple example of gamification, but other companies are pushing the concept in new ways to engage and motivate employees and other stakeholders. For example, Bunchball's Nitro software applies gamification concepts to a number of business communication platforms. On a customer-service system, the software rewards employees for increasing their productivity, meeting their service commitments to customers, and sharing knowledge with their colleagues. On several collaboration and brainstorming systems, gamification encourages people to make more connections, share ideas, and boost their influence within a community.

Gamification is also a key strategy for many companies trying to improve customer loyalty. Badgeville's Reputation Mechanics system, for example, boosts the profile of knowledgeable customers who share expertise on social media sites and other online forums. By rewarding their *product champions* (see page 303) this way, companies encourage them to keep contributing their expertise, thereby helping other customers be successful and satisfied.

Incidentally, if you are in the Millennial generation, those born between 1981 and 1995, you're a special target of gamification in the workplace and the marketplace, given your generation's enthusiasm for video games. Don't be surprised to find more gamified apps and systems on the job and everywhere you turn as a consumer.

CAREER APPLICATIONS

1. Gamification is about influencing employee and customer behaviors in ways that benefit a company. Is this ethical? Explain your answer.

2. Assume a company provides a job-search game app that helps you navigate your way through applying for a job, explore various job openings, and understand what it would be like to work there. Would the app make you feel more positively about the company, or would you find that using a game for this purpose would trivialize something as important as your job search? Explain your answer.

Sources: Bunchball website, accessed 23 February 2014, www.bunchball.com; Badgeville website, accessed 23 February 2014, http://badgeville.com; Foursquare for Business website, accessed 23 February 2014, http://business.foursquare.com; Christopher Swan, "Gamification: A New Way to Shape Behavior," *Communication World*, May–June 2012, 13–14.

Inappropriate web use not only distracts employees from work responsibilities, it can leave employers open to lawsuits for sexual harassment if inappropriate images are displayed in or transmitted around the company.[47] Social media have created another set of managerial challenges, given the risk that employee blogs or social networking pages can expose confidential information or damage a firm's reputation in the marketplace. With all these technologies, the best solution lies in developing clear policies that are enforced evenly for all employees.[48]

Managers need to guide their employees in productive use of information tools because the speed and simplicity of these tools are also among their greatest weaknesses. The flood of messages from an expanding array of electronic sources can significantly affect employees' ability to focus on their work. In one study, workers exposed to a constant barrage of email, instant messages, and phone calls experienced an average 10-point drop in their functioning intelligence quotient (IQ).[49]

In addition to using your tools appropriately, knowing how to use them efficiently can make a big difference in your productivity. You don't have to become an expert in most cases, but you do need to be familiar with the basic features and functions of the tools you are expected to use on the job. As a manager, you also need to ensure that your employees have sufficient training to productively use the tools you expect them to use.

MOBILE APP

WhatsApp lets you send and receive messages, videos, and other content via your phone's Internet connection.

Communicating in today's business environment requires at least a basic level of technical competence.

REAL-TIME UPDATES

LEARN MORE BY VISITING THIS WIKI

Get the latest news on gamification

The Gamification Wiki offers information on gamification concepts and examples across a variety of industries. Go to http://real-timeupdates.com/ebc12 and click on Learn More in the Students section.

Powerful Tools for Communicating Effectively

The tools of business communication evolve with every advance in digital technology. The 20 technologies highlighted on the next four pages help businesses redefine the office, collaborate and share information, connect with stakeholders, and build communities of people with shared interests and needs. For more examples of business uses of social media tools in particular, see pages 191–198 in Chapter 7.

REDEFINING THE OFFICE

Thanks to advances in mobile and distributed communication, the "office" is no longer what it used to be. Technology lets today's professionals work on the move while staying in close contact with colleagues, customers, and suppliers. These technologies are also redefining the very nature of some companies, as they replace traditional hierarchies with highly adaptable, virtual networks.

Shared Online Workspaces

Microsoft Office 2013, copyright © 2013 Microsoft Corporation.

Online workspaces help teams work productively, even if they are on the move or spread out across the country. In addition to providing controlled access to shared files and other digital resources, some systems include such features as project management tools and real-time document sharing (letting two or more team members view and edit a document on screen at the same time).

Web-Based Meetings

Andrey Popov/Shutterstock

Web-based meetings allow team members from all over the world to interact in real time. Meetings can also be recorded for later playback and review. Various systems support instant messaging, video, collaborative editing tools, and more.

Videoconferencing and Telepresence

.shock/Fotolia

Videoconferencing provides many of the benefits of in-person meetings at a fraction of the cost. Advanced systems feature *telepresence*, in which the video images of meeting participants are life-sized and extremely realistic.

Antun Hirsman/Shutterstock

Voice Technologies

Fancy/Alamy

Speech recognition (converting human speech to computer commands) and *speech synthesis* (converting computer commands to human speech) can enhance communication in many ways, including simplifying mobile computing, assisting workers who are unwilling or unable to use keyboards, and allowing "one-sided" conversations with information systems. *Speech analytics software* can evaluate conversations to improve customer service and other interactions. *Mobile VoIP* lets people make voice calls on WiFi networks to save connection and roaming charges.

Mobile Business Apps

As the range of business software applications on smartphones and tablet computers continues to expand, almost anything that can be accomplished on a regular computer can be done on a mobile device (although not always as efficiently or with the same feature sets).

Instant Messaging

Microsoft Outlook, copyright © 2013 Microsoft Corporation.

Instant messaging (IM) is one of the most widely used digital communication tools in the business world, replacing many conversations and exchanges that once took place via email or phone calls. *Enterprise IM systems* are similar to consumer IM systems in many respects but have additional security and collaboration features.

Wikis

Screenshot "The Motley Fool" from The Motley Fool website. Copyright © by Erik Stadnik. Used by permission of Erik Stadnik.

Wikis promote collaboration by simplifying the process of creating and editing online content. Anyone with access (some wikis are private; some are public) can add and modify pages as new information becomes available.

Data Visualization

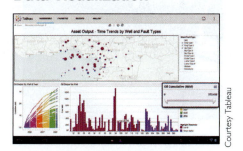

Courtesy Tableau

Data visualization is a powerful tool for presenting and exploring sets of data that are very large, complex, or dynamic. As more companies rely on "big data" to identify and capitalize on market opportunities, the ability to extract insights from these large data sets can be an important competitive advantage.

COLLABORATING AND SHARING INFORMATION

The need to work with and share information quickly and easily is a constant in business. A wide variety of tools have been developed to facilitate collaboration and sharing, from general purpose systems such as instant messaging to more specialized capabilities such as data visualization.

Crowdsourcing Platforms

Innocentive, Inc.

Crowdsourcing, inviting input from groups of people inside or outside the organization, can give companies access to a much wider range of ideas, solutions to problems, and insights into market trends.

Collaboration Platforms

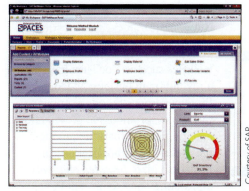

Courtesy of SAP.

From general-purpose communication systems to task-specific apps and programs, collaboration platforms help teams and business partners coordinate their work on projects.

CONNECTING WITH STAKEHOLDERS

Electronic media and social media in particular have redefined the relationships businesses have with internal and external stakeholders. Any groups affected by a company's decisions now have tools to give voice to their opinions and needs, and companies have many more conversational threads that need to be monitored and managed.

Content Curation

Content curation, selecting videos and other items of interest to followers of a website or blog, has become one of the most popular ways to connect with stakeholders. Pinterest and Scoop.it are among the leading technologies in this area.

Applicant Tracking Systems

Screenshot from Recruit by ZOHO Corporation. Copyright © by Mason Hering. Used by permission of Mason Hering.

Applicant tracking systems now play a huge role in employment-related communications. At virtually all large companies and many medium and small companies, your résumé and application information will be entered into one of these systems. Recruiters use various tools to identify promising candidates and manage the interview and selection process. After hiring, some firms use *talent management systems* to track employee development through workers' entire careers at the company.

Blogging

Courtesy of Xerox Corporation

Blogs let companies connect with customers and other audiences in a fast and informal way. Commenting features let readers participate in the conversation, too.

Podcasting

LearningStockImages/Alamy

With the portability and convenience of downloadable audio and video recordings, podcasts have become a popular means of delivering everything from college lectures to marketing messages. Podcasts are also used for internal communication, replacing conference calls, newsletters, and other media.

Online Video

Google and the Google logo are registered trademarks of Google Inc., used with permission.

The combination of low-cost digital video cameras and video-sharing websites such as YouTube has spurred a revolution in business video. Product demonstrations, company overviews, promotional presentations, and training seminars are among the most popular applications of business video. *Branded channels* allow companies to present their videos as an integrated collection in a customized user interface.

User-Generated Content Sites

User-generated content sites let businesses host photos, videos, software programs, technical solutions, and other valuable content for their customer communities.

Microblogging

Microblogging services (of which Twitter is by far the best known) are a great way to share ideas, solicit feedback, monitor market trends, and announce special deals and events.

One of the most significant benefits of new communication technologies is the ease with which companies can foster a sense of community among customers, enthusiasts, and other groups. In some instances, the company establishes and manages the online community, while in others the community is driven by *product champions* or other enthusiasts.

Gaming Technologies

Encouraging people to play games, even games as simple as "checking in" at various retail locations, can build interest in a company and its brands.

Social Networking

Community Q&A Sites

Many companies now rely heavily on communities of customers to help each other with product questions and other routine matters.

Businesses use a variety of social networks as specialized channels to engage customers, find new employees, attract investors, and share ideas and challenges with peers.

RECONNECTING WITH PEOPLE

No matter how much technology is involved, communication is still about people connecting with people.

Even the best technologies can hinder communication if they are overused. For instance, a common complaint among employees is that managers rely too heavily on email and don't communicate face to face often enough.[50] Speaking with people over the phone or in person can take more time and effort and can sometimes force you to confront unpleasant situations directly, but it is often essential for solving tough problems and maintaining productive relationships.[51]

Moreover, even the best communication technologies can't show people who you really are. Remember to step out from behind the technology frequently to learn more about the people you work with and to let them learn more about you.

Committing to Ethical and Legal Communication

6 LEARNING OBJECTIVE
Define *ethics*, explain the difference between an ethical dilemma and an ethical lapse, and list six guidelines for making ethical communication choices.

Ethics are the accepted principles of conduct that govern behavior within a society. Ethical behavior is a companywide concern, but because communication efforts are the public face of a company, they are subjected to particularly rigorous scrutiny from regulators, legislators, investors, consumer groups, environmental groups, labor organizations, and anyone else affected by business activities. **Ethical communication** includes all relevant information, is true in every sense, and is not deceptive in any way. In contrast, unethical communication can distort the truth or manipulate audiences in a variety of ways:[52]

Any time you try to mislead your audience, the result is unethical communication.

- **Plagiarizing.** Plagiarism is presenting someone else's words or other creative product as your own. Note that plagiarism can be illegal if it violates a **copyright**, which is a form of legal protection for the expression of creative ideas.[53]
- **Omitting essential information.** Information is essential if your audience needs it to make an intelligent, objective decision.
- **Selective misquoting.** Distorting or hiding the true intent of someone else's words is unethical.
- **Misrepresenting numbers.** Statistics and other data can be unethically manipulated by increasing or decreasing numbers, exaggerating, altering statistics, or omitting numeric data.
- **Distorting visuals.** Images can be manipulated in unethical ways, such as altering photos in order to deceive audiences or changing the scale of graphs and charts to exaggerate or conceal differences.
- **Failing to respect privacy or information security needs.** Failing to respect the privacy of others or failing to adequately protect information entrusted to your care can also be considered unethical (and is sometimes illegal).

Transparency gives audience members access to all the information they need in order to process messages accurately.

The widespread adoption of social media has increased the attention given to the issue of **transparency**, which in this context refers to a sense of openness, of giving all participants in a conversation access to the information they need in order to accurately process the messages they are receiving. In addition to the information itself, audiences deserve to know when they are being marketed to and who is behind the messages they read or hear. For example, with *stealth marketing*, companies recruit people to promote products to friends and other contacts in exchange for free samples or other rewards, without requiring them to disclose the true nature of the communication. Critics, including the Federal Trade Commission (FTC), assert that such techniques are deceptive because they don't give targets the opportunity to raise their instinctive defenses against the persuasive powers of marketing messages.[54]

Aside from ethical concerns, trying to fool the public is simply bad for business. As LaSalle University communication professor Michael Smith puts it, "The public backlash can be long, deep, and damaging to a company's reputation."[55]

DISTINGUISHING ETHICAL DILEMMAS FROM ETHICAL LAPSES

Some ethical questions are easy to recognize and resolve, but others are not. Deciding what is ethical can be a considerable challenge in complex business situations. An **ethical dilemma** involves choosing among alternatives that aren't clear-cut. Perhaps two conflicting alternatives are both ethical and valid, or perhaps the alternatives lie somewhere in the gray area between clearly right and clearly wrong. Every company has responsibilities to multiple groups of people inside and outside the firm, and those groups often have competing interests. For instance, employees naturally want higher wages and more benefits, but investors who have risked their money in the company want management to keep costs low so that profits are strong enough to drive up the stock price. Both sides have a valid ethical position.

In contrast, an **ethical lapse** is a clearly unethical choice. With both internal and external communication efforts, the pressure to produce results or justify decisions can make unethical communication a tempting choice. Telling a potential customer you can complete a project by a certain date when you know you can't is simply dishonest, even if you need the contract to save your career or your company. There is no ethical dilemma here.

Compare the messages in Figures 1.11 and 1.12 for examples of how business messages can be unethically manipulated.

An ethical dilemma is a choice between alternatives that may all be ethical and valid.

An ethical lapse is making a choice you know to be unethical.

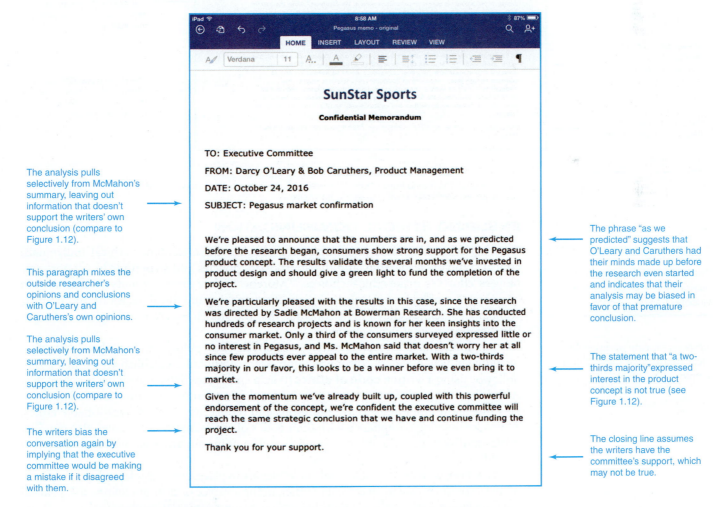

The analysis pulls selectively from McMahon's summary, leaving out information that doesn't support the writers' own conclusion (compare to Figure 1.12).

This paragraph mixes the outside researcher's opinions and conclusions with O'Leary and Caruthers's own opinions.

The analysis pulls selectively from McMahon's summary, leaving out information that doesn't support the writers' own conclusion (compare to Figure 1.12).

The writers bias the conversation again by implying that the executive committee would be making a mistake if it disagreed with them.

The phrase "as we predicted" suggests that O'Leary and Caruthers had their minds made up before the research even started and indicates that their analysis may be biased in favor of that premature conclusion.

The statement that "a two-thirds majority" expressed interest in the product concept is not true (see Figure 1.12).

The closing line assumes the writers have the committee's support, which may not be true.

SunStar Sports

Confidential Memorandum

TO: Executive Committee

FROM: Darcy O'Leary & Bob Caruthers, Product Management

DATE: October 24, 2016

SUBJECT: Pegasus market confirmation

We're pleased to announce that the numbers are in, and as we predicted before the research began, consumers show strong support for the Pegasus product concept. The results validate the several months we've invested in product design and should give a green light to fund the completion of the project.

We're particularly pleased with the results in this case, since the research was directed by Sadie McMahon at Bowerman Research. She has conducted hundreds of research projects and is known for her keen insights into the consumer market. Only a third of the consumers surveyed expressed little or no interest in Pegasus, and Ms. McMahon said that doesn't worry her at all since few products ever appeal to the entire market. With a two-thirds majority in our favor, this looks to be a winner before we even bring it to market.

Given the momentum we've already built up, coupled with this powerful endorsement of the concept, we're confident the executive committee will reach the same strategic conclusion that we have and continue funding the project.

Thank you for your support.

Figure 1.11   Unethical Communication

The writers of this memo clearly want the company to continue funding their pet project, even though the marketing research doesn't support such a decision. By comparing this memo with the version shown in Figure 1.12, you can see how the writers twisted the truth and omitted evidence in order to put a positive "spin" on the research.
Source: Screen shot reprinted with permission from Apple Inc.

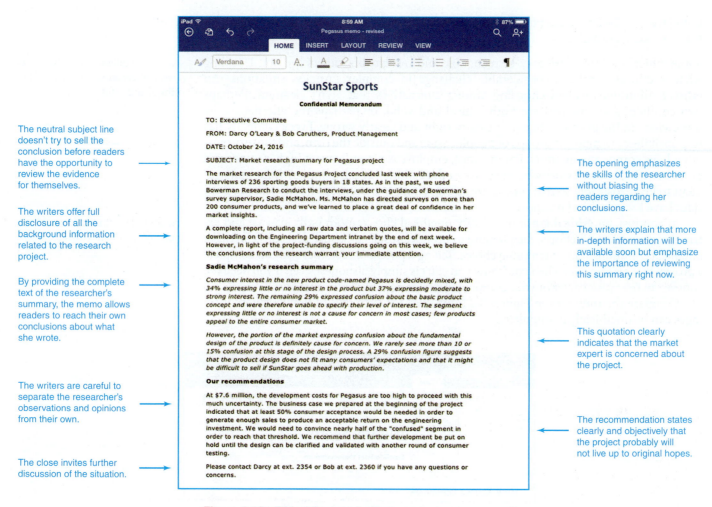

The neutral subject line doesn't try to sell the conclusion before readers have the opportunity to review the evidence for themselves.

The writers offer full disclosure of all the background information related to the research project.

By providing the complete text of the researcher's summary, the memo allows readers to reach their own conclusions about what she wrote.

The writers are careful to separate the researcher's observations and opinions from their own.

The close invites further discussion of the situation.

The opening emphasizes the skills of the researcher without biasing the readers regarding her conclusions.

The writers explain that more in-depth information will be available soon but emphasize the importance of reviewing this summary right now.

This quotation clearly indicates that the market expert is concerned about the project.

The recommendation states clearly and objectively that the project probably will not live up to original hopes.

Figure 1.12 **Ethical Communication**
This version of the memo from Figure 1.11 presents the evidence in a more honest and ethical manner.
Source: Screen shot reprinted with permission from Apple Inc.

ENSURING ETHICAL COMMUNICATION

Responsible employers establish clear ethical guidelines for their employees to follow.

If you can't decide whether a choice is ethical, picture yourself explaining your decision to someone whose opinion you value.

Ensuring ethical business communication requires three elements: ethical individuals, ethical company leadership, and the appropriate policies and structures to support employees' efforts to make ethical choices.[56] Moreover, these three elements need to work in harmony. If employees see company executives making unethical decisions and flouting company guidelines, they might conclude that the guidelines are meaningless and emulate their bosses' unethical behavior.

Employers have a responsibility to establish clear guidelines for ethical behavior, including ethical business communication. Many companies establish an explicit ethics policy by using a written **code of ethics** to help employees determine what is acceptable. A code is often part of a larger program of employee training and communication channels that allow employees to ask questions and report instances of questionable ethics. To ensure ongoing compliance with their codes of ethics, many companies also conduct **ethics audits** to monitor ethical progress and to point out any weaknesses that need to be addressed.

However, whether or not formal guidelines are in place, every employee has a responsibility to communicate in an ethical manner. In the absence of clear guidelines, ask yourself the following questions about your business communications:[57]

- Have you defined the situation fairly and accurately?
- What is your intention in communicating this message?
- What impact will this message have on the people who receive it or who might be affected by it?

- Will the message achieve the greatest possible good while doing the least possible harm?
- Will the assumptions you've made change over time? That is, will a decision that seems ethical now seem unethical in the future?
- Are you comfortable with your decision? Would you be embarrassed if it were printed in tomorrow's newspaper or spread across the Internet? Think about a person whom you admire and ask yourself what he or she would think of your decision.

ENSURING LEGAL COMMUNICATION

In addition to ethical guidelines, business communication is also bound by a wide variety of laws and regulations, including the following areas:

- **Promotional communication.** Marketing specialists need to be aware of the many laws that govern truth and accuracy in advertising. These laws address such issues as product reviews written by bloggers who receive compensation from the companies involved, false and deceptive advertising, misleading or inaccurate labels on product packages, and bait-and-switch tactics in which a store advertises a lower-priced product to lure consumers into a store but then tries to sell them a more expensive item.[58] Chapter 10 explores this area in more detail.

> Business communication is governed by a wide variety of laws designed to ensure accurate, complete messages.

- **Contracts.** A **contract** is a legally binding promise between two parties in which one party makes a specified offer and the other party accepts. Contracts are fundamental to virtually every aspect of business, from product sales to property rental to credit cards and loans to professional service agreements.[59]
- **Employment communication.** A variety of local, state, and federal laws govern communication between employers and both potential and current employees. For example, job descriptions must be written in a way that doesn't intentionally or unintentionally discriminate against women, minorities, or people with disabilities.[60]
- **Intellectual property.** In an age when instant global connectivity makes copying and retransmitting electronic files effortless, the protection of intellectual property has become a widespread concern. **Intellectual property (IP)** includes patents, copyrighted materials, trade secrets, and even Internet domain names.[61] Bloggers in particular need to be careful about IP protection, given the carefree way that some post the work of others without offering proper credit.

> **REAL-TIME UPDATES**
> LEARN MORE BY VISITING THIS WEBSITE
> **Guidelines for trouble-free blogging**
> The Electronic Frontier Foundation offers a free *Legal Guide for Bloggers*. Go to http://real-timeupdates.com/ebc12 and click on Learn More in the Students section.

- **Financial reporting.** Finance and accounting professionals who work for publicly traded companies (those that sell stock to the public) must adhere to stringent reporting laws. For instance, a number of corporations have recently been targets of both government investigations and shareholder lawsuits for offering misleading descriptions of financial results and revenue forecasts.
- **Defamation.** Negative comments about another party raise the possibility of **defamation**, the intentional communication of false statements that damage character or reputation.[62] (Written defamation is called *libel*; spoken defamation is called *slander*.) Someone suing for defamation must prove (1) that the statement is false, (2) that the language is injurious to the person's reputation, and (3) that the statement has been published.
- **Transparency requirements.** Governments around the world are taking steps to help ensure that consumers and other parties know who is behind the information they receive, particularly when it appears online. The European Union, for instance, outlaws a number of online marketing tactics, including "flogs," short for "fake blogs," in which an employee or a paid agent posing as an independent consumer posts positive stories about a company's products.[63] In the United States, the FTC requires product-review bloggers to disclose any relationship—such as receiving payments or free goods—they have with the companies whose products they discuss in their blogs.[64]

If you have any doubts about the legality of a message you intend to distribute, ask for advice from your company's legal department. A small dose of caution can prevent huge legal headaches and protect your company's reputation in the marketplace.

For the latest information on ethical and legal issues in business communication, visit http://real-timeupdates.com/ebc12 and click on Chapter 1.

Applying What You've Learned

At the beginning of this chapter, you read about JetBlue's experiences using social media to communicate with passengers. Each chapter opens with one of these slice-of-life vignettes. As you read through each chapter and become familiar with the concepts presented, imagine how they might apply to the company highlighted in the vignette.

At the end of each chapter, you'll take part in an innovative simulation called "On the Job: Solving Communication Dilemmas." You'll play the role of a person working in the highlighted organization, and you'll face situations you'd encounter on the job. You will be presented with several communication scenarios, each with several possible courses of action. It's up to you to recommend one course of action from each scenario as homework, as teamwork, as material for in-class discussion, or in a host of other ways. These scenarios let you explore various communication ideas and apply the concepts and techniques from the chapter.

Now you're ready for the first simulation. As you tackle each problem, think about the material you covered in this chapter and consider your own experience as a communicator. You'll probably be surprised to discover how much you already know about business communication.

ON THE JOB: SOLVING COMMUNICATION DILEMMAS AT JETBLUE

Imagine that you've joined the Twitter team at JetBlue, one of the more than two dozen communication specialists tasked with monitoring conversations about the company in the Twittersphere and responding to questions, requests, and complaints from passengers. Use what you've learned in this chapter to address the following challenges.

1. JetBlue emphasizes a friendly, open style of communication with its customers, even those occasional customers who make unrealistic demands or expect special treatment. Unfortunately, you've learned that some of the company's customer service representatives have been letting their emotions get in the way when dealing with these difficult customers. Several customers have complained about rude treatment. You're sensitive to the situation because you know customer service can be a difficult job, particularly in a social media environment where consumers are empowered to broadcast any disappointment they may feel. However, having a reputation for hostile customer service could spell doom for the company, so you need to communicate your concerns immediately. Which of the following sentences would be the best way to begin an email message to the customer service staff?

   a. "We must all work harder at serving customers in an efficient, timely manner."

   b. "The growing problem of abusive customers communications must stop immediately—after all,

without customers, we have no revenue; without revenue, you have no jobs."

   c. "Positive customer support is one of our most important competitive advantages, but it has come to management's attention that some of you are ruining the company's reputation by mistreating customers."

   d. "Thank you for your continued efforts at supporting our customers; I know this can be a challenging task at times."

2. The culture in your office is conscientious and professional but with a generally informal "vibe." However, as with any company, individual employees vary in how closely their own styles and personalities fit the corporate culture. For example, the new accounting manager in your organization tends to communicate in a formal, distant style that some company old-timers find off-putting and impersonal. Several of these people have expressed concerns that the new manager "doesn't fit in," even though she's doing a great job otherwise. How should you respond?

   a. Tell these people to stop complaining; the accounting manager is doing her job well, and that's what counts.

   b. In a private conversation with the accounting manager, explain the importance of fitting into the corporate culture and give her a four-week deadline to change her style.

   c. In a private conversation with the accounting manager, explain the reasoning behind the company's informal culture and its contribution to the company's success;

suggest that she might find her work here more enjoyable if she modifies her approach somewhat.

d. Allow the accounting manager to continue communicating in the same style; after all, that's her personal style, and it's not up to the company to change it.

3. A false rumor has begun circulating among JetBlue employees that the company plans to replace its social media team with an automated "bot" system that will answer tweets and email messages using artificial intelligence. Members of the social media team are worried about their jobs, and other employees are worried that customers will miss the human touch if customer service representatives are replaced by a computer. How should you respond to the rumor?

a. Try to spread a counter-rumor so that the employees who are worried about their jobs will get the right message the same way they got the wrong one.

b. Immediately schedule an in-person meeting to set the record straight, emphasizing to everyone in the company that JetBlue has no plans to replace its social media team with bots.

c. Post a message on an internal blog, setting the record straight and assuring the workforce that the social media jobs are safe; employees are accustomed to getting timely and essential information from this blog.

d. Ignore the rumor. Like all other false rumors, it will eventually die out.

4. A passenger whose luggage didn't arrive on his flight from Boston to San Francisco is sending a string of angry tweets from the baggage claim at the San Francisco airport, accusing JetBlue of everything from lying to stealing his luggage. He is including the @JetBlue handle in every tweet, so his rants are showing up in the timelines of the company's followers on Twitter—all 1.9 million of them. How should you respond?

a. Respond to every one of his tweets with a message that JetBlue is an honest company that would never steal luggage or lie to a passenger. In a situation like this, you have to fight fire with fire.

b. Ignore the passenger's rants; every time you respond, you increase the chance that more of your Twitter followers will see his complaints. He will eventually get tired of complaining, and the storm will blow over.

c. Get in touch with Twitter and ask the company to suspend the man's account. No one should be allowed to spread misinformation like that on social media.

d. Reply to one of his tweets with an apology for the trouble he was encountered and an offer to switch to direct messaging to work out a solution to his problem. As soon as you send this tweet, telephone your colleagues in San Francisco. Explain the situation, ask them to figure out which baggage carousel the man is likely to be near (based on his flight info), and ask them try to locate the man and talk to him in person. People are more prone to be abusive on social media than in person, and the employee in San Francisco might be able to convince him to stop tweeting and help reconnect him with his luggage.

Learning Objectives Checkup

Assess your understanding of the principles in this chapter by reading each learning objective and studying the accompanying exercises. You can check your responses against the answer key on page 599.

Objective 1.1: Explain the importance of effective communication to your career and to the companies where you will work.

1. Which of the following is the most accurate description of the role that communication will play in your career?
   a. Ideas matter more than anything, so as long as you are creative and have strong business sense, you can hire people to take care of communication tasks.
   b. No matter what other skills, connections, and attributes you have, your prospects will be limited if you don't have good communication skills.
   c. In today's tough business world, performance is the most important differentiator; everything else is a distant second.
   d. As a "soft skill," communication is important in some careers, such as sales and human resources, but not in technical, financial, or administrative careers.

2. Effective business messages are
   a. Entertaining, blunt, direct, opinionated, and persuasive

   b. Practical, objective, concise, clear, and persuasive
   c. Personal, clear, short, catchy, and challenging

3. Why is it important for a business message to clearly state expectations regarding who is responsible for doing what in response to the message?
   a. To make sure other employees don't avoid their responsibilities
   b. To make sure the person who sent the message isn't criticized if important tasks don't get completed
   c. To eliminate confusion by letting each affected person know his or her specific responsibilities

Objective 1.2: Explain what it means to communicate as a professional in a business context.

4. Which of the following is not a skill employers will expect you to have?
   a. Communicating effectively with people from diverse backgrounds and experiences
   b. Using communication technologies effectively and efficiently
   c. Managing your time wisely and using resources efficiently
   d. Commanding employees to follow orders

5. Which of the following is not one of the six traits of professionalism identified in the chapter?
   a. Striving to excel
   b. Being dependable

   c. Being ethical

   d. Being loyal to the company no matter what

6. An audience-centered approach to communication

   a. Starts with the assumption that the audience is always right

   b. Improves the effectiveness of communication by focusing on the information needs of the audience

   c. Is generally a waste of time because it doesn't accommodate the needs of the sender

   d. Always simplifies the tasks involved in planning and creating messages

7. Sensitivity to business etiquette

   a. Reduces the chance of interpersonal blunders that might negatively affect communication

   b. Is considered by most companies to be a waste of time in today's fast-paced markets

   c. Is now legally required in all 50 states

   d. Always increases the cost of business communication

Objective 1.3: Describe the communication process model and the ways that social media are changing the nature of business communication.

8. Communication style using the social communication model is best described as

   a. Conversational

   b. Multilingual

   c. Technical

   d. Playful

9. Which of the following pairs of attributes best describes the social communication model?

   a. Interactive and conversational

   b. Technical and instantaneous

   c. Electronic and print

   d. Relaxed and unrestricted

10. For audience members to successfully receive messages, they must first _____ the presence of the message, then _____ it from other sensory input, and then _____ it as a message.

11. For the receiver of a message to respond in the manner desired by the sender, the receiver needs to

    a. Remember the message

    b. Be able to respond to the message

    c. Have the motivation to respond to the message

    d. Do all of the above

Objective 1.4: Outline the challenges and opportunities of mobile communication in business.

12. Which of these is a potential disadvantage of the constant connectivity enabled by mobile communication devices?

    a. Blurring the lines between personal and professional time

    b. Losing contact with key business markets around the globe

    c. Making unethical choices more tempting

    d. Reducing employee access to corporate data

13. Which of these is not one of the advantages of mobile communication discussed in the chapter?

    a. Giving employees more flexibility to meet their personal and professional obligations

    b. Guaranteeing ethical treatment of message recipients

    c. Enhancing productivity and collaboration

    d. Creating more engaging experiences for customers and other users

Objective 1.5: List four general guidelines for using communication technology effectively.

14. Communication technology has value only if it helps deliver the right _____ to the right _____ at the right time.

15. The information technology paradox means that

    a. Communication tools can sometimes waste more time than they save

    b. Computers lose as much information as they save

    c. People are no longer needed to create messages

    d. Technology isn't as expensive as it used to be

16. Reconnecting frequently with colleagues and customers in person

    a. Is widely considered an inappropriate use of time, given all the electronic options now available

    b. Is frowned on by successful managers

    c. Is critical because it helps ensure that technology doesn't hinder human interaction

Objective 1.6: Define ethics, explain the difference between an ethical dilemma and an ethical lapse, and list six guidelines for making ethical communication choices

17. Ethical communication

    a. Is the same thing as legal communication

    b. Costs more because there are so many rules to consider

    c. Is important only for companies that sell to consumers rather than to other businesses

    d. Includes all relevant information, is true in every sense, and is not deceptive in any way

18. An ethical _____ exists when a person is faced with two conflicting but ethical choices or alternatives that are neither entirely right nor entirely wrong; an ethical _____ occurs when a person makes an unethical choice.

Quick Learning Guide

CHAPTER OUTLINE

Understanding Why Communication Matters
Communication Is Important to Your Career
Communication Is Important to Your Company
What Makes Business Communication Effective?

Communicating as a Professional
Understanding What Employers Expect from You
Communicating in an Organizational Context
Adopting an Audience-Centered Approach

Exploring the Communication Process
The Basic Communication Model
The Social Communication Model

The Mobile Revolution
The Rise of Mobile as a Communication Platform
How Mobile Technologies Are Changing Business Communication

Using Technology to Improve Business Communication
Keeping Technology in Perspective
Guarding Against Information Overload
Using Technological Tools Productively
Reconnecting with People

Committing to Ethical and Legal Communication
Distinguishing Ethical Dilemmas from Ethical Lapses
Ensuring Ethical Communication
Ensuring Legal Communication

Applying What You've Learned

LEARNING OBJECTIVES

1 Explain the importance of effective communication to your career and to the companies where you will work. (page 3)

2 Explain what it means to communicate as a professional in a business context. (page 5)

3 Describe the communication process model and the ways social media are changing the nature of business communication. (page 9)

4 Outline the challenges and opportunities of mobile communication in business. (page 15)

5 List four general guidelines for using communication technology effectively. (page 18)

6 Define *ethics*, explain the difference between an ethical dilemma and an ethical lapse, and list six guidelines for making ethical communication choices. (page 24)

KEY TERMS

audience-centered approach Understanding and respecting the members of your audience and making every effort to get your message across in a way that is meaningful to them

code of ethics A written set of ethical guidelines that companies expect their employees to follow

communication The process of transferring information and meaning using one or more written, oral, visual, or electronic media

communication barriers Forces or events that can disrupt communication, including noise and distractions, competing messages, filters, and channel breakdowns

communication channels Systems used to deliver messages

communication medium The form in which a message is presented; the four categories of media are oral, written, visual, and electronic

contract A legally binding promise between two parties, in which one party makes a specified offer and the other party accepts

copyright A form of legal protection for the expression of creative ideas

critical thinking The ability to evaluate evidence completely and objectively in order to form logical conclusions and make sound recommendations

decoding Extracting the idea from a message

defamation The intentional communication of false statements that damage character or reputation

encoding Putting an idea into a message (words, images, or a combination of both)

ethical communication Communication that includes all relevant information, is true in every sense, and is not deceptive in any way

ethical dilemma Situation that involves making a choice when the alternatives aren't completely wrong or completely right

ethical lapse A clearly unethical choice

ethics The accepted principles of conduct that govern behavior within a society

ethics audits Ongoing efforts to monitor ethical progress and to point out any weaknesses that need to be addressed

etiquette The expected norms of behavior in any particular situation

feedback Information from receivers regarding the quality and effectiveness of a message

formal communication network Communication channels that flow along the lines of command

informal communication network All communication that takes place outside the formal network; often referred to as the *grapevine* or the *rumor mill*

information overload Condition in which people receive more information than they can effectively process

intellectual property Assets including patents, copyrighted materials, trade secrets, and even Internet domain names

message The "container" for an idea to be transmitted from a sender to a receiver

perception A person's awareness or view of reality; also, the process of detecting incoming messages

professionalism The quality of performing at a high level and conducting oneself with purpose and pride

selective perception The inclination to distort or ignore incoming information rather than change one's beliefs

social communication model An interactive, conversational approach to communication in which formerly passive audience members are empowered to participate fully

stakeholders Groups affected by a company's actions: customers, employees, shareholders, suppliers, neighbors, the community, and the world at large

transparency Giving all participants in a conversation access to the information they need to accurately process the messages they are receiving

"you" attitude Communicating with an audience-centered approach; creating messages that are about "you," the receiver, rather than "me," the sender

Apply Your Knowledge

To review chapter content related to each question, refer to the indicated Learning Objective.

⭐ **1.1.** Why do you think communication is vital to the success of every business organization? Explain briefly. [LO-1]

⭐ **1.2.** How does the presence of a reader comments feature on a corporate blog reflect audience-centered communication? [LO-2]

1.3. What changes would you make to your email messages if you know your recipients are typically walking or riding on mass transit when they read your messages? [LO-4]

1.4. Is it possible for companies to be too dependent on communication technology? Explain briefly. [LO-5]

⭐ **1.5.** You're the CEO of a company whose sales are declining, and there is a 50/50 chance you will need to lay off some of your employees sometime in the next two to three months. You have to decide whether to tell them now so they can look for new jobs as soon as possible, even though you're not yet sure layoffs will be necessary, or wait until you are sure layoffs will occur. Explain why this is an ethical dilemma. Be sure to consider the effect a sudden exodus of valuable employees could have on the company's prospects. [LO-6]

Practice Your Skills

Message for Analysis: Analyzing Communication Effectiveness [LO-1]

Read the following blog posting, and then (a) analyze whether the message is effective or ineffective (be sure to explain why) and (b) revise the message so that it follows this chapter's guidelines.

> It has come to my attention that many of you are lying on your time cards. If you come in late, you should not put 8:00 on your card. If you take a long lunch, you should not put 1:00 on your time card. I will not stand for this type of cheating. I simply have no choice but to institute an employee monitoring system. Beginning next Monday, video cameras will be installed at all entrances to the building, and your entry and exit times will be logged each time you use electronic key cards to enter or leave.
>
> Anyone who is late for work or late coming back from lunch more than three times will have to answer to me. I don't care if you had to take a nap or if you girls had to shop. This is a place of business, and we do not want to be taken advantage of by slackers who are cheaters to boot.
>
> It is too bad that a few bad apples always have to spoil things for everyone.

Exercises

Each activity is labeled according to the primary skill or skills you will need to use. To review relevant chapter content, you can refer to the indicated Learning Objective. In some instances, supporting information will be found in another chapter, as indicated.

1.6. **Writing: Compositional Modes: Summaries, [LO-1] Chapter 4** Write a paragraph introducing yourself to your instructor and your class. Address such areas as your background, interests, achievements, and goals. Submit your paragraph using email, blog, or social network, as indicated by your instructor.

1.7. **Media Skills: Microblogging, [LO-1] Chapter 7** Write four effective messages of no more than 140 characters each (short enough to work as Twitter tweets, in other words) to persuade other college students to take the business communication course. Think of the first message as the "headline" of an advertisement that makes a bold promise regarding the value this course offers every aspiring business professional. The next three messages should be support points that provide evidence to back up the promise made in the first message.[65]

1.8. **Fundamentals: Analyzing Communication Effectiveness [LO-1]** Identify a video clip (on YouTube or another online source) that you believe represents an example of effective communication. It can be in any context, business or otherwise, but make sure it is something appropriate to discuss in class. Post a link to the video on your class blog, along with a brief written summary of why you think this example shows effective communication in action.

1.9. **Planning: Assessing Audience Needs, [LO-2] Chapter 4** Choose a business career that sounds interesting to you and imagine that you are getting ready to apply for jobs in that field. Naturally, you want to create a compelling, audience-focused résumé that answers the key questions a hiring manager is most likely to have. Identify three personal or professional qualities you have that would be important for someone in this career field. Write a brief statement (one or two sentences) regarding each quality, describing in audience-focused terms how you can contribute to a company in this respect. Submit your statements via email or class blog.

1.10. **Communication Etiquette: Communicating with Sensitivity and Tact [LO-2]** Potential customers frequently visit your production facility before making purchase decisions. You and the people who report to you in the sales department have received extensive training in etiquette issues because you deal with high-profile clients so often. However, the rest of the workforce has not received such training, and you worry that someone might inadvertently say or do something that would offend one of these potential customers. In a two-paragraph email, explain to the general manager why you think anyone who might come in contact with customers should receive basic etiquette training.

1.11. **Collaboration: Team Projects; Planning: Assessing Audience Needs, [LO-2] Chapter 2, Chapter 4** Your boss has asked your work group to research and report on corporate child-care facilities. Of course, you'll want to know who (besides your boss) will be reading your report. Working with two team members, list four or five other things you'll want to know about the situation and about your audience before starting your research. Briefly explain why each of the items on your list is important.

1.12. Planning: Constructing a Persuasive Argument, [LO-2] Chapter 10 Blogging has become a popular way for employees to communicate with customers and other parties outside the company. In some cases, employee blogs have been quite beneficial for both companies and their customers by providing helpful information and "putting a human face" on other formal and imposing corporations. However, in some other cases, employees have been fired for posting information that their employers said was inappropriate. One particular area of concern is criticism of the company or individual managers. Should employees be allowed to criticize their employers in a public forum such as a blog? In a brief email message, argue for or against company policies that prohibit critical information in employee blogs.

1.13. Fundamentals: Analyzing Communication Effectiveness [LO-3] Use the eight phases of the communication process to analyze a miscommunication you've recently had with a coworker, supervisor, classmate, teacher, friend, or family member. What idea were you trying to share? How did you encode and transmit it? Did the receiver get the message? Did the receiver correctly decode the message? How do you know? Based on your analysis, identify and explain the barriers that prevented your successful communication in this instance.

1.14. Fundamentals: Analyzing Communication Effectiveness [LO-4] Using a mobile device, visit the websites of five companies that make products or provide services you buy or might buy in the future. Which of the websites is the most user friendly? How does it differ from the other sites? Do any of the companies offer a mobile shopping app for your device?

1.15. Technology: Using Communication Tools [LO-5] Find a free online communication service that you have no experience using as a content creator or contributor. Services to consider include blogging (such as Blogger), microblogging (such as Twitter), community Q&A sites (such as Yahoo! Answers), and user-generated content sites (such as Flickr). Perform a basic task such as opening an account or setting up a blog. Was the task easy to perform? Were the instructions clear? Could you find help online if you needed it? Is there anything about the experience that could be improved? Summarize your conclusions in a brief email message to your instructor.

1.16. Communication Ethics: Distinguishing Ethical Dilemmas and Ethical Lapses [LO-6] Knowing that you have numerous friends throughout the company, your boss relies on you for feedback concerning employee morale and other issues affecting the staff. She recently asked you to start reporting any behavior that might violate company policies, from taking office supplies home to making personal long-distance calls. List the issues you'd like to discuss with her before you respond to her request.

1.17. Communication Ethics: Distinguishing Ethical Dilemmas and Ethical Lapses [LO-6] In less than a page, explain why you think each of the following is or is not ethical.

   a. Keeping quiet about a possible environmental hazard you've just discovered in your company's processing plant

   b. Overselling the benefits of instant messaging to your company's managers; they never seem to understand the benefits of technology, so you believe it's the only way to convince them to make the right choice

   c. Telling an associate and close friend that she needs to pay more attention to her work responsibilities, or management will fire her

   d. Recommending the purchase of equipment your department doesn't really need in order to use up your allocated funds before the end of the fiscal year so that your budget won't be cut next year, when you might have a real need for the money

1.18. Communication Ethics: Providing Ethical Leadership [LO-6] Cisco, a leading manufacturer of equipment for the Internet and corporate networks, has developed a code of ethics that it expects employees to abide by. Visit the company's website and find its *code of conduct*. In a brief paragraph, describe three specific examples of things you could do that would violate these provisions; then list at least three opportunities that Cisco provides its employees to report ethics violations or ask questions regarding ethical dilemmas.

Expand Your Skills

Critique the Professionals

Locate an example of professional communication from a reputable online source. It can reflect any aspect of business communication, from an advertisement or a press release to a company blog or website. Evaluate this communication effort in light of any aspect of this chapter that is relevant to the sample and interesting to you. For example, is the piece effective? Audience-centered? Ethical? Using whatever medium your instructor requests, write a brief analysis of the piece (no more than one page), citing specific elements from the piece and support from the chapter.

Sharpening Your Career Skills Online

Bovée and Thill's Business Communication Web Search, at http://websearch.businesscommunicationnetwork.com, is a unique research tool designed specifically for business communication research. Use the Web Search function to find an online video, a presentation, a website, or an article that describes an innovative use of mobile technology in business communication. Write a brief email message to your instructor or a post for your class blog, describing the item that you found and summarizing the information you found.

Improve Your Grammar, Mechanics, and Usage

The following exercises help you improve your knowledge of and power over English grammar, mechanics, and usage. Turn to the Handbook of Grammar, Mechanics, and Usage at the end of this book and review all of Section 1.1 (Nouns). Then look at the following 10 items. Underline the preferred choice within each set of parentheses. (Answers to these exercises appear on page 601.)

1.19. She remembered placing that report on her (*bosses, boss's*) desk.

1.20. We mustn't follow their investment advice like a lot of (*sheep, sheeps*).

1.21. Jones founded the company back in the early (*1990's, 1990s*).

1.22. Please send the (*Joneses, Jones'*) a dozen of the following: (*stopwatchs, stopwatches*), canteens, and headbands.

1.23. Our (*attorneys, attornies*) will talk to the group about incorporation.

1.24. Make sure that all (*copys, copies*) include the new addresses.

1.25. Ask Jennings to collect all (*employee's, employees'*) donations for the Red Cross drive.

1.26. Charlie now has two (*sons-in-law, son-in-laws*) to help him with his two online (*business's, businesses*).

1.27. Avoid using too many (*parentheses, parenthesis*) when writing your reports.

1.28. Follow President (*Nesses, Ness's*) rules about what constitutes a (*weeks, week's*) work.

For additional exercises focusing on nouns, visit MyBCommLab. Click on Chapter 1, click on Additional Exercises to Improve Your Grammar, Mechanics, and Usage, and then click on 1. Possessive nouns or 2. Antecedents.

MyBCommLab

Go to the Assignments section of your MyLab to complete these writing exercises.

1.29. How does the social communication model differ from traditional business communication practices? [LO-3]

1.30. How is mobile technology changing the practice of business communication? [LO-4]

Endnotes

1. JetBlue website, accessed 23 February 2014, www.jetblue.com; "5 Social Media All-Stars," *CNNMoney*, 29 August 2013, http://money.cnn.com; JetBlue Twitter account, accessed 22 February 2014, https://twitter.com/JetBlue; Todd Wasserman, "How JetBlue's Social Media Strategy Took Flight," *Mashable*, 1 June 2011, http://mashable.com; "A Day In The Life: Social Media," BlueTales blog, 19 January 2012, http://blog.jetblue.com, Chantal Tode, "JetBlue Exec: Mobile Is Discovery Piece for Travelers," *Mobile Marketer*, 22 January 2013, www.mobilemarketer.com.

2. Richard L. Daft, *Management*, 6th ed. (Cincinnati: Thomson South-Western, 2003), 580.

3. "Employers: 13 Common Complaints About Recent Grads," Youturn, 2 October 2012, www.youturn.com.

4. Julie Connelly, "Youthful Attitudes, Sobering Realities," *New York Times*, 28 October 2003, E1, E6; Nigel Andrews and Laura D'Andrea Tyson, "The Upwardly Global MBA," *Strategy + Business* 36 (Fall 2004): 60–69; Jim McKay, "Communication Skills Found Lacking," *Pittsburgh Post-Gazette*, 28 February 2005, www.delawareonline.com.

5. Brian Solis, *Engage!* (Hoboken, N.J.: John Wiley & Sons, 2010), 11–12; "Majority of Global Companies Face an Engagement Gap," Internal Comms Hub website, 23 October 2007, www.internalcommshub.com; Gary L. Neilson, Karla L. Martin, and Elizabeth Powers, "The Secrets to Successful Strategy Execution," *Harvard Business Review*, June 2008, 61–70; Nicholas Carr, "Lessons in Corporate Blogging," *BusinessWeek*, 18 July 2006, 9; Susan Meisinger, "To Keep Employees, Talk—and Listen—to Them!" *HR Magazine*, August 2006, 10.

6. Daft, *Management*, 147.

7. "CEOs to Communicators: 'Stick to Common Sense,'" Internal Comms Hub website, 23 October 2007, www.internalcommshub.com; "A Writing Competency Model for Business," BizCom101.com, 14 December 2007, www.business-writing-courses.com; Sue Dewhurst and Liam FitzPatrick, "What Should Be the Competency of Your IC Team?" white paper, 2007, http://competentcommunicators.com.

8. "Digital Information Fluency Model," 21cif.com, accessed 11 February 2014, http://21cif.com.

9. Philip C. Kolin, *Successful Writing at Work*, 6th ed. (Boston: Houghton Mifflin, 2001), 17–23.

10. Laura L. Myers and Mary L. Tucker, "Increasing Awareness of Emotional Intelligence in a Business Curriculum," *Business Communication Quarterly*, March 2005, 44–51.

11. Pete Cashmore, "10 Web Trends to Watch in 2010," CNN Tech, 3 December 2009, www.cnn.com.

12. Stephanie Armour, "Music Hath Charms for Some Workers—Others It Really Annoys," *USA Today*, 24 March 2006, B1–B2.

13. Paul Martin Lester, *Visual Communication: Images with Messages* (Belmont, Calif.: Thomson South-Western, 2006), 6–8.

14. Michael R. Solomon, *Consumer Behavior: Buying, Having, and Being*, 6th ed. (Upper Saddle River, N.J.: Pearson Prentice Hall, 2004), 65.

15. Anne Field, "What You Say, What They Hear," *Harvard Management Communication Letter*, Winter 2005, 3–5.

16. Chuck Williams, *Management*, 2nd ed. (Cincinnati: Thomson South-Western, 2002), 690.

17. Charles G. Morris and Albert A. Maisto, *Psychology: An Introduction*, 12th ed. (Upper Saddle River, N.J.: Pearson Prentice Hall, 2005),

226–239; Saundra K. Ciccarelli and Glenn E. Meyer, *Psychology* (Upper Saddle River, N.J.: Prentice Hall, 2006), 210–229; Mark H. Ashcraft, *Cognition*, 4th ed. (Upper Saddle River, N.J.: Prentice Hall, 2006), 44–54.

18. Ben Hanna, *2009 Business Social Media Benchmarking Study* (published by Business.com), 2 November 2009, 11.

19. Michael Killian, "The Communication Revolution—'Deep Impact' About to Strike," Avaya Insights blog, 4 December 2009, www.avayablog.com.

20. "The Mobile Revolution Is Just Beginning," press release, World Economic Forum, 13 September 2013, www.weforum.org.

21. Maribel Lopez, "Three Trends That Change Business: Mobile, Social and Cloud," *Forbes*, 28 January 2012, www.forbes.com.

22. Kevin Custis, "Three Ways Business Can Be Successful on Mobile," *Forbes*, 15 November 2013, www.forbes.com; "IBM Survey: Speed and Analytics Key Drivers in Mobile Adoption for Organizations," press release, IBM, 19 November 2013, www.ibm.com.

23. "More Than Nine in 10 Internet Users Will Go Online via Phone," eMarketer, 6 January 2014, www.emarketer.com.

24. Christina "CK" Kerley, *The Mobile Revolution & B2B*, white paper, 2011, www.b2bmobilerevolution.com.

25. Jordie can Rijn, "The Ultimate Mobile Email Statistics Overview," Emailmonday.com, accessed 9 February 2014, www.emailmonday.com.

26. Jessica Lee, "46% of Searchers Now Use Mobile Exclusively to Research [Study]," Search Engine Watch, 1 May 2013, http://searchenginewatch.com.

27. Dennis McCafferty, "10 Awesome Facts About the Mobile Revolution," *CIO Insight*, 6 December 2013, www.cioinsight.com.

28. Yun-Sen Chan, "Smartphones Are Changing Person-to-Person Communication," Modern Media Mix, 23 April 2013, http://modernmediamix.com.

29. "Mobile Facts and Market Stats," Mocapay, accessed 10 February 2014, www.mocapay.com.

30. *Mobile Revolution*, ebook, Extron, 2011.

31. Nicco Mele, *The End of Big: How the Internet Makes David the New Goliath* (New York: St. Martin's Press: 2013), 1–2.

32. "JWT's 13 Mobile Trends for 2013 and Beyond," J. Walter Thompson website, 2 April 2013, www.jwt.com.

33. *The Changing Role of Mobile Communications in the Workplace*, white paper, Frost & Sullivan, accessed 8 February 2014, www.frost.com.

34. *Top 10 Ways Successful Small Businesses Use Mobile Tech*, white paper, T-Mobile, 2012.

35. Armen Ghazarian, "How Do Users Interact with Mobile Devices," Medium.com, 29 November 2013, http://medium.com.

36. "JWT's 13 Mobile Trends for 2013 and Beyond."

37. "Bring Your Own Device: BYOD Is Here and You Can't Stop It," Garner, accessed 9 February 2014, www.garner.com.

38. Jessica Twentyman, "Deploying Smartphones, Tables, and Apps for a New Employee Communication Era," *SCM*, January/February 2013, 28–29; *The Changing Role of Mobile Communications in the Workplace*, Frost & Sullivan.

39. Aaref Hilaly, "The Biggest Opportunity in Mobile That No One Is Talking About," LinkedIn, 17 December 2013, www.linkedin.com.

40. Michael Saylor, *The Mobile Wave: How Mobile Intelligence Will Change Everything* (New York: Vanguard Press, 2012), 10.

41. *The Changing Role of Mobile Communications in the Workplace*, Frost & Sullivan.

42. *Top 10 Ways Successful Small Businesses Use Mobile Tech*, T-Mobile.

43. Milton Kazmeyer, "The Impact of Wireless Communication in the Workplace," *Houston Chronicle*, accessed 10 February 2014, http://smallbusiness.chron.com.

44. Gregg Hano, "The Power of Corporate Communications on Mobile Apps," Mag+, 1 August 2013, www.magplus.com.

45. Tara Craig, "How to Avoid Information Overload," *Personnel Today*, 10 June 2008, 31; Jeff Davidson, "Fighting Information Overload," *Canadian Manager*, Spring 2005, 16+.

46. "The Top Ten Ways Workers Waste Time Online," 24/7 Wall St., 30 September 2010, http://247wallst.com.

47. Eric J. Sinrod, "Perspective: It's My Internet—I Can Do What I Want," News.com, 29 March 2006, www.news.com.

48. Eric J. Sinrod, "Time to Crack Down on Tech at Work?" News.com, 14 June 2006, www.news.com.

49. Jack Trout, "Beware of 'Infomania,'" *Forbes*, 11 August 2006, www.forbes.com.

50. "Many Senior Managers Communicate Badly, Survey Says," Internal Comms Hub, 6 August 2007, www.internalcommshub.com.

51. Mike Schaffner, "Step Away from the Computer," *Forbes*, 7 August 2009, www.forbes.com.

52. Philip C. Kolin, *Successful Writing at Work*, 6th ed. (Boston: Houghton Mifflin, 2001), 24–30.

53. Nancy K. Kubasek, Bartley A. Brennan, and M. Neil Browne, *The Legal Environment of Business*, 3rd ed. (Upper Saddle River, N.J.: Prentice Hall, 2003), 172.

54. Word of Mouth Marketing Association, "WOM 101," accessed 2 June 2010, http://womma.org; Nate Anderson, "FTC Says Stealth Marketing Unethical," *Ars Technica*, 13 December 2006, http://-arstechnica.com; "Undercover Marketing Uncovered," CBSnews.com, 25 July 2004, www.cbsnews.com; Stephanie Dunnewind, "Teen Recruits Create Word-of-Mouth 'Buzz' to Hook Peers on Products," *Seattle Times*, 20 November 2004, www.seattletimes.com.

55. Linda Pophal, "Tweet Ethics: Trust and Transparency in a Web 2.0 World," *CW Bulletin*, September 2009.

56. Daft, *Management*, 155.

57. Based in part on Robert Kreitner, *Management*, 9th ed. (Boston: Houghton Mifflin, 2004), 163.

58. Henry R. Cheeseman, *Contemporary Business and E-Commerce Law*, 4th ed. (Upper Saddle River, N.J.: Prentice Hall, 2003), 841–843.

59. Cheeseman, *Contemporary Business and E-Commerce Law*, 201.

60. John Jude Moran, *Employment Law: New Challenges in the Business Environment*, 2nd ed. (Upper Saddle River, N.J.: Prentice Hall, 2002), 186–187; Kubasek et al., *The Legal Environment of Business*, 562.

61. Cheeseman, *Contemporary Business and E-Commerce Law*, 325.

62. Kubasek et al., *The Legal Environment of Business*, 306.

63. Robert Plummer, "Will Fake Business Blogs Crash and Burn?" *BBC News*, 22 May 2008, http://news.bbc.co.uk.

64. Tim Arango, "Soon, Bloggers Must Give Full Disclosure," *New York Times*, 5 October 2009, www.nytimes.com.

65. The concept of a four-tweet summary is from Cliff Atkinson, *The Backchannel* (Berkeley, Calif.: New Riders, 2010), 120–121.

Collaboration, Interpersonal Communication, and Business Etiquette

LEARNING OBJECTIVES

After studying this chapter, you will be able to

1 List the advantages and disadvantages of working in teams, describe the characteristics of effective teams, and highlight four key issues of group dynamics.

2 Offer guidelines for collaborative communication, identify major collaboration technologies, and explain how to give constructive feedback.

3 List the key steps needed to ensure productive team meetings.

4 Identify the major technologies used to enhance or replace in-person meetings.

5 Identify three major modes of listening, describe the listening process, and explain the problem of selective listening.

6 Explain the importance of nonverbal communication and identify six major categories of nonverbal expression.

7 Explain the importance of business etiquette, and identify four key areas in which good etiquette is essential.

ON THE JOB: COMMUNICATING AT
CEMEX

Social Communication "Makes a Big Company Look Like a Small Company"

You have probably been on a lab team or other project team that had trouble collaborating. Maybe you couldn't get everyone in the same room at the same time, or important messages got buried in long email threads, or good ideas were lost because the right information didn't get to the right people at the right time.

Imagine trying to collaborate when you have thousands of potential team members spread across dozens of countries. The Mexican company Cemex is one of the world's largest producers of concrete and its two primary components, cement and aggregates (crushed stone, sand, and gravel). Cemex faces teamwork challenges on a global scale, with 44,000 employees in more than 50 countries. After a period of worldwide expansion that began in the 1990s, the century-old company now operates quarries, cement plants, and other facilities on every continent except Antarctica.

Concrete and cement are two of the oldest products on earth and might not spring to mind when most people think of innovation. However, innovation is key to Cemex's long-term success, for several reasons. First, architects and builders continue to push the envelope by creating designs that require concrete with new performance and handling qualities. Second, Cemex's ability to operate profitably depends on running efficient

An innovative collaboration platform helps the global cement company Cemex operate with the agility and flexibility of a small company.

TABL

Dysfun

Controlli
superiorit

Withdrav
becoming
particular

Attention
and dema

Diverting
topics of i
those rele

likely to e
help ever
team reac

Allowin

Teams ty
A variety
productiv
problem-

1. Orie
   task
   barri
   team
   ings,
   vant

2. Conf
   in est

3. Brair
   cons.
   probl
   in too
   ideas
   bring

Figure 2.1
Groups gen
objectives.
Sources: B. A
McGraw-Hill,
Saddle River,
Western, 200

operations, from raw material extraction to processing to transportation. Third, the production and distribution of concrete-related products have significant environmental impacts, including the acquisition and consumption of heating fuels required by high-temperature cement kilns.

To stay competitive and profitable and to minimize the environmental effects of its operations, Cemex knew it needed to accelerate the pace of innovation. Company leaders figured the way to do that was to enable better collaboration, and the way to do *that* was to enable better communication.

The company's response to this multilayered challenge is a comprehensive online collaboration platform called *Shift*, which combines social networking, wikis, blogs, a Twitter-like microblogging system, social bookmarking, videoconferencing, a trend-spotting tool called *Shift Radar*, and more. A custom mobile app lets employees access the system wherever their work takes them.

By connecting people and information quickly and easily, Shift helps overcome the barriers of geography, time zones, and organizational boundaries. Employees and managers can tap into expertise anywhere in the company, workers with similar responsibilities can share ideas on improving operations, and problems and opportunities can be identified and brought to management attention in much less time.

Technology is only part of the solution, however. Many companies that have implemented social platforms struggle to get employees to change ingrained behaviors and use the new tools. By getting top-level executives on board early, Cemex achieved nearly universal adoption, with 95 percent of employees using Shift and forming more than 500 online communities based on technical specialties and shared interests. That level of engagement is paying off in numerous ways, such as launching a new global brand of ready-mix concrete in one-third the expected time, nearly tripling the company's use of renewable energy, and reducing carbon dioxide emissions by almost 2 million metric tons.

Perhaps most impressive, Shift has lived up to its name by shifting the entrenched hierarchical culture of a large, old-school company to a more agile and responsive social business that is better prepared to face the future in its highly competitive markets. As Gilberto Garcia, Cemex's innovation director puts it, social collaboration "can make a big company look like a small company" by connecting people and ensuring the free exchange of ideas.[1]

WWW.CEMEX.COM

Communicating Effectively in Teams

1 **LEARNING OBJECTIVE**
List the advantages and disadvantages of working in teams, describe the characteristics of effective teams, and highlight four key issues of group dynamics.

The interactions among the employees at Cemex (profiled in the chapter-opening On the Job) represent one of the most essential elements of interpersonal communication. **Collaboration**—working together to meet complex challenges—is a prime skill expected in a wide range of professions. No matter what career path you pursue, it's a virtual guarantee that you will need to collaborate in at least some of your work activities. Your communication skills will pay off handsomely in these interactions because the productivity and quality of collaborative efforts depend heavily on the communication skills of the professionals involved.

A **team** is a unit of two or more people who share a mission and the responsibility for working to achieve a common goal.[2] **Problem-solving teams** and **task forces** assemble to resolve specific issues and then disband when their goals have been accomplished. Such teams are often *cross-functional*, pulling together people from a variety of departments who have different areas of expertise and responsibility. The diversity of opinions and experiences can lead to better decisions, but competing interests can lead to tensions that highlight the need for effective communication. **Committees** are formal teams that usually have a long life span and can become a permanent part of the organizational structure. Committees typically deal with regularly recurring tasks, such as an executive committee that meets monthly to plan strategies and review results.

Collaboration, working together to solve complex problems, is an essential skill for workers in nearly every profession.

Team members have a shared mission and are collectively responsible for their work.

ADVANTAGES AND DISADVANTAGES OF TEAMS

When teams are successful, they can improve productivity, creativity, employee involvement, and even job security.[3] Teams are often at the core of **participative management**, the effort to involve employees in the company's decision making. A successful team can provide a number of advantages:[4]

- **Increased information and knowledge.** By pooling the experience of several individuals, a team has access to more information.
- **Increased diversity of views.** Team members can bring a variety of perspectives to the decision-making process—as long as these diverse viewpoints are guided by a shared goal.[5]

Effective teams can pool knowledge, take advantage of diverse viewpoints, and increase acceptance of solutions the team proposes.

4. **Emergence.** Consensus is reached when the team finds a solution that all members are willing to support (even if they have reservations).
5. **Reinforcement.** The team clarifies and summarizes the agreed-on solution. Members receive their assignments for carrying out the group's decision, and they make arrangements for following up on those assignments.

You may also hear the process defined as *forming, storming, norming, performing,* and *adjourning,* the phases identified by researcher Bruce Tuckman when he proposed one of the earliest models of group development.[17] Regardless of the model you consider, these stages are a general framework for team development. Some teams may move forward and backward through several stages before they become productive, and other teams may be productive right away, even though some or all members are in a state of conflict.[18]

Resolving Conflict

Conflict in team activities can arise for a number of reasons: competition for resources, disagreement over goals or responsibilities, poor communication, power struggles, or fundamental differences in values, attitudes, and personalities.[19] Although the term *conflict* sounds negative, conflict isn't necessarily bad. Conflict can be *constructive* if it forces important issues into the open, increases the involvement of team members, and generates creative ideas for solving a problem. Teamwork isn't necessarily about happiness and harmony; even teams that have some interpersonal friction can excel with effective leadership and team players committed to strong results. As teamwork experts Andy Boynton and Bill Fischer put it, "Virtuoso teams are not about getting polite results."[20]

In contrast, conflict is *destructive* if it diverts energy from more important issues, destroys the morale of teams or individual team members, or polarizes or divides the team.[21] Destructive conflict can lead to *win-lose* or *lose-lose* outcomes, in which one or both sides lose, to the detriment of the entire team. If you approach conflict with the idea that both sides can satisfy their goals to at least some extent (a *win-win* strategy), you can minimize losses for everyone. For a win-win strategy to work, everybody must believe that (1) it's possible to find a solution that both parties can accept, (2) cooperation is better for the organization than competition, (3) the other party can be trusted, and (4) greater power or status doesn't entitle one party to impose a solution.

The following seven measures can help team members successfully resolve conflict:

- **Proactive behavior.** Deal with minor conflict before it becomes major conflict.
- **Communication.** Get those directly involved in a conflict to participate in resolving it.
- **Openness.** Get feelings out in the open before dealing with the main issues.
- **Research.** Seek factual reasons for a problem before seeking solutions.
- **Flexibility.** Don't let anyone lock into a position before considering other solutions.
- **Fair play.** Insist on fair outcomes and don't let anyone avoid a fair solution by hiding behind the rules.
- **Alliance.** Get opponents to fight together against an "outside force" instead of against each other.

Overcoming Resistance

One particular type of conflict that can affect team progress is resistance to change. Sometimes this resistance is clearly irrational, such as when people resist any kind of change, whether the change makes sense or not. Sometimes, however, resistance is perfectly logical. A change may require someone to relinquish authority or give up comfortable ways of doing things. If someone is resisting change, you can be persuasive with calm, reasonable communication:

- **Express understanding.** You might say, "I understand that this change might be difficult, and if I were in your position, I might be reluctant myself." Help the other person relax and talk about his or her anxiety so that you have a chance to offer reassurance.[22]

Teams need to
impact of grou
agendas, and e

*Conflict in teams can be either
constructive or destructive.*

Effective teams
of purpose, ope
communication
decision makin
effective confli

Common sens
smarter team,
http://real-tir
the Students

*Destructive conflict can lead to
win-lose or lose-lose outcomes.*

Group dynamic
interactions and
take place in a te

Each member of
role that affects
the group's activ

*When you encounter resistance
or hostility, try to maintain your
composure and address the other
person's emotional needs.*

- **Bring resistance out into the open.** When people are noncommittal and silent, they may be tuning you out without even knowing why. Continuing with your argument is futile. Deal directly with the resistance, without accusing. You might say, "You seem to have reservations about this idea. Have I made some faulty assumptions?" Such questions force people to face and define their resistance.[23]
- **Evaluate others' objections fairly.** Use active listening to focus on what the other person is expressing, both the words and the feelings. Get the person to open up so that you can understand the basis for the resistance. Others' objections may raise legitimate points that you'll need to discuss, or they may reveal problems that you'll need to minimize.[24]

Hold your arguments until the other person is ready for them. Getting your point across depends as much on the other person's frame of mind as it does on your arguments. You can't assume that a strong argument will speak for itself. By becoming more audience centered, you will learn to address the other person's emotional needs first.

REAL-TIME UPDATES

LEARN MORE BY LISTENING TO THIS PODCAST

How to keep small battles from escalating into big ones

Use these insights to manage adversarial relationships in the workplace and keep them from getting destructive. Go to http://real-timeupdates.com/ebc12 and click on Learn More in the Students section.

Collaborating on Communication Efforts

When a team collaborates on reports, websites, presentations, and other communication projects, the collective energy and expertise of the various members can produce results that transcend what each individual could do alone.[25] However, collaborating on team messages requires special effort and planning.

2 LEARNING OBJECTIVE
Offer guidelines for collaborative communication, identify major collaboration technologies, and explain how to give constructive feedback.

GUIDELINES FOR COLLABORATIVE WRITING

In any collaborative effort, team members coming from different backgrounds may have different work habits or priorities: A technical expert may focus on accuracy and scientific standards, an editor may be more concerned about organization and coherence, and a manager may focus on schedules, cost, and corporate goals. In addition, team members differ in writing styles, work habits, and personality traits.

MOBILE APP
Freedcamp is a free collaboration and project management system.

To collaborate effectively, everyone must be flexible and open to other opinions, focusing on team objectives rather than on individual priorities.[26] Successful writers know that most ideas can be expressed in many ways, so they avoid the "my way is best" attitude. The following guidelines will help you collaborate more successfully:[27]

- **Select collaborators carefully.** Whenever possible, choose a combination of people who together have the experience, information, and talent needed for each project.
- **Agree on project goals before you start.** Starting without a clear idea of what the team hopes to accomplish inevitably leads to frustration and wasted time.
- **Give your team time to bond before diving in.** If people haven't had the opportunity to work together before, make sure they can get to know each other before being asked to collaborate.
- **Clarify individual responsibilities.** Because members will be depending on each other, make sure individual responsibilities are clear.
- **Establish clear processes.** Make sure everyone knows how the work will be managed from start to finish.
- **Avoid composing as a group.** The actual composition is the only part of developing team messages that does not usually benefit from group participation. Brainstorming the wording of short pieces of text, particularly headlines, slogans, and other high-visibility elements, can be an effective way to stimulate creative word choices. However, for longer projects, it is usually more efficient to plan, research, and outline together but assign the task of writing to one person or divide larger projects among multiple writers. If you divide the writing, try to have one person do a final revision pass to ensure a consistent style.

Successful collaboration on writing projects requires a number of steps, from selecting the right partners and agreeing on project goals to establishing clear processes and avoiding writing as a group.

- **Make sure tools and techniques are ready and compatible across the team.** Even minor details such as different versions of software can delay projects.
- **Check to see how things are going along the way.** Don't assume that everything is working just because you don't hear anything negative.

TECHNOLOGIES FOR COLLABORATIVE WRITING

A wide variety of collaboration tools now exist to help professionals work on reports, presentations, and other communication efforts.

A variety of tools and systems are available to help writers collaborate on everything from short documents to entire websites. The simplest tools are software features such as *commenting* (which lets colleagues write comments in a document without modifying the document text) and *change tracking* (which lets one or more writers propose changes to the text while keeping everyone's edits separate and reversible). The widely used Adobe Acrobat electronic document system (PDF files) also has group review and commenting features, including the option for live collaboration.

Collaboration Systems

Writing for websites often involves the use of a **content management system**, which organizes and controls website content and can include features that help team members work together on web pages and other documents. These tools range from simple blogging systems on up to *enterprise* systems that manage web content across an entire corporation. Many systems include *workflow* features that control how pages or documents can be created, edited, and published.

Wiki benefits include simple operation and the ability to post new or revised material instantly without a formal review process.

In contrast to the formal controls of a content management system, a **wiki**, from the Hawaiian word for *quick*, is a website that allows anyone with access to add new material and edit existing material. Public wikis (Wikipedia is the best known) allow any registered user to edit pages; private wikis are accessible only with permission. A key benefit of wikis is the freedom to post new or revised material without prior approval. Chapter 12 offers guidelines for effective wiki collaboration.

Teams and other work groups can also take advantage of a set of broader technologies often referred to as *groupware* or *collaboration platforms*. These technologies let people communicate, share files, review previous message threads, work on documents simultaneously, and connect using social networking tools. These systems help companies capture and share knowledge from multiple experts, bringing greater insights to bear on tough challenges.[28] Collaboration systems often take advantage of *cloud computing*, a somewhat vague term that refers to on-demand capabilities delivered over the Internet, rather than through conventional on-site software.[29]

Shared workspaces are online "virtual offices" that give everyone on a team access to the same set of resources and information (see Figure 2.2). You may see some of these workspaces referred to as *intranets* (restricted-access websites that are open to employees only) or *extranets* (restricted sites that are available to employees and to outside parties by invitation only). Many intranets have now evolved into social networking systems that include a variety of communication and collaboration tools, from microblogging to video clip libraries. For example, the performance troupe Blue Man Group uses a *social intranet* to help its 500 employees plan, stage, and promote shows all over the world.[30]

Social Networks and Virtual Communities

A *community of practice* links professionals with similar job interests; a key benefit is accumulating long-term organizational knowledge.

Social networking technologies are redefining teamwork and team communication by helping erase the constraints of geographic and organization boundaries. Some companies use social networks to form *virtual communities* or *communities of practice* that link employees with similar professional interests throughout the company and sometimes with customers and suppliers as well.

Internal social networks help companies assemble the best resources for a given task, regardless of where the employees are located.

The huge advantage that social networking brings to these team efforts is in identifying the best people to collaborate on each problem or project, no matter where they are around the world or what their official roles are in the organization. Such communities are similar to teams in many respects, but one major difference is in the responsibility for accumulating organizational knowledge over the long term. For example, the

Courtesy of SAP

Figure 2.2   Shared Workspaces
Shared workspaces give employees instant access to the all the files they need, from company reports to website content.

pharmaceutical company Pfizer has a number of permanent product-safety communities that provide specialized advice on drug safety issues to researchers throughout the organization.[31]

Social networking can also help a company maintain a sense of community even as it grows beyond the size that normally permits a lot of daily interaction. At the online retailer Zappos, fostering a supportive work environment is the company's top priority. To encourage the sense of community among its expanding workforce, Zappos uses social networking tools to track employee connections and encourage workers to reach out and build relationships.[32]

Collaboration via Mobile Devices

Mobile devices add another layer of options for collaborative writing and other communication projects, particularly when used with cloud computing. Today's mobile systems can do virtually everything that fixed-web collaboration systems can do, from writing on virtual whiteboards to sharing photos, videos, and other multimedia files.[33] Mobility lets workers participate in online brainstorming sessions, seminars, and other formal or informal events from wherever they happen to be at the time (see Figure 2.3 on the next page). This flexibility can be particularly helpful during the review and production stages of major projects, when deadlines are looming and decisions and revisions need to be made quickly.

An important aspect of mobile collaboration and mobile communication in general is **unified communication**, which integrates such capabilities as voice and video calling, voice and video conferencing, instant messaging, and real-time collaboration software into a single system. By minimizing or eliminating the need to manage multiple communication systems and devices, unified communication promises to improve response times, productivity, and collaboration efforts.[34]

Collaboration apps for mobile devices support nearly all the features of computer-based platforms.

REAL-TIME UPDATES

LEARN MORE BY READING THIS ARTICLE

The benefits of mobile collaboration

Going mobile helps teams get work faster and more effectively. Go to http://real-timeupdates.com/ebc12 and click on Learn More in the Students section.

Courtesy of Cafe Ria

Figure 2.3   Collaboration on Mobile Devices
Mobile connectivity is transforming collaboration activities, helping teams and work groups stay connected no matter where their work takes them. For example, this team was able to discuss and edit a press release using their tablets in different locations.

GIVING—AND RESPONDING TO—CONSTRUCTIVE FEEDBACK

When you give writing feedback, make it constructive by focusing on how the material can be improved.

Aside from processes and tools, collaborative communication often involves giving and receiving feedback about writing efforts. **Constructive feedback**, sometimes called *constructive criticism*, focuses on the process and outcomes of communication, not on the people involved (see Table 2.2). In contrast, **destructive feedback** delivers criticism with no guidance to stimulate improvement.[35] For example, "This proposal is a confusing mess, and you failed to convince me of anything" is destructive feedback. The goal is to be more constructive: "Your proposal could be more effective with a clearer description of the manufacturing process and a well-organized explanation of why the positives outweigh the negatives." When giving feedback, avoid personal attacks and give the person clear guidelines for improvement.

TABLE 2.2 Giving Constructive Feedback	
How to Be Constructive	**Explanation**
Think through your suggested changes carefully.	Many business documents must illustrate complex relationships between ideas and other information, so isolated and superficial edits can do more harm than good.
Discuss improvements rather than flaws.	Instead of saying "this is confusing," for instance, explain how the writing can be improved to make it clearer.
Focus on controllable behavior.	The writer may not have control over every variable that affected the quality of the message, so focus on those aspects the writer can control.
Be specific.	Comments such as "I don't get this" or "Make this clearer" don't give the writer much direction.
Keep feedback impersonal.	Focus comments on the message, not on the person who created it.
Verify understanding.	If in doubt, ask for confirmation from the recipient to make sure that the person understood your feedback.
Time your feedback carefully.	Respond in a timely fashion so that the writer will have sufficient time to implement the changes you suggest.
Highlight any limitations your feedback may have.	If you didn't have time to give the document a thorough edit, or if you're not an expert in some aspect of the content, let the writer know so that he or she can handle your comments appropriately.

When you receive constructive feedback, resist the understandable urge to defend your work or deny the validity of the feedback. Remaining open to criticism isn't easy when you've invested lots of time and energy in a project, but good feedback provides a valuable opportunity to learn and to improve the quality of your work.

> When you receive constructive feedback on your writing, keep your emotions in check and view it as an opportunity to improve.

Making Your Meetings More Productive

> **3 LEARNING OBJECTIVE**
> List the key steps needed to ensure productive team meetings.

Much of your workplace communication will occur during in-person or online meetings, so to a large degree, your ability to contribute to the company—and to be recognized for your contributions—will depend on your meeting skills. Well-run meetings can help companies solve problems, develop ideas, and identify opportunities. Meetings can also be a great way to promote team building through the experience of social interaction.[36] As useful as meetings can be, though, they can be a waste of time if they aren't planned and managed well. You can help ensure productive meetings by preparing carefully, conducting meetings efficiently, and using meeting technologies wisely.

PREPARING FOR MEETINGS

The first step in preparing for a meeting is to make sure the meeting is really necessary. Meetings can consume hundreds or thousands of dollars of productive time while taking people away from other work, so don't hold a meeting if some other form of communication (such as a blog post) can serve the purpose as effectively.[37] If a meeting is truly necessary, proceed with these four planning tasks:

- **Define your purpose.** Meetings can focus on exchanging information, reaching decisions, or collaborating to solve problems or identify opportunities. Whatever your purpose, define the best possible result of the meeting (such as "we carefully evaluated all three product ideas and decided which one to invest in"). Use this hoped-for result to shape the direction and content of the meeting.[38]
- **Select participants for the meeting.** The rule here is simple: Invite everyone who really needs to be involved, and don't invite anyone who doesn't. For decision-making meetings, for example, invite only those people who are in a direct position to help the meeting reach its objective. The more people you have, the longer it will take to reach consensus. Meetings with more than 10 or 12 people can become unmanageable if everyone is expected to participate in the discussion and decision making.
- **Choose the venue and the time.** Online meetings (see page 49) are often the best way and sometimes the only way to connect people in multiple locations or to reach large audiences. For in-person meetings, review the facility and the seating arrangements. Is theater-style seating suitable, or do you need a conference table or some other arrangement? Pay attention to room temperature, lighting, ventilation, acoustics, and refreshments; these details can make or break a meeting. If you have control over the timing, morning meetings are often more productive because people are generally more alert and not yet engaged with the work of the day.
- **Set the agenda.** The success of a meeting depends on the preparation of the participants. Distribute a carefully written agenda to participants, giving them enough time to prepare as needed (see Figure 2.4 on the next page). A productive agenda answers three key questions: (1) What do we need to do in this meeting to accomplish our goals? (2) What issues will be of greatest importance to all participants? (3) What information must be available to discuss these issues?[39]

> To ensure a successful meeting, decide on your purpose ahead of time, select the right participants, choose the venue and time, and set a clear agenda.

CONDUCTING AND CONTRIBUTING TO EFFICIENT MEETINGS

Everyone in a meeting shares the responsibility for making the meeting productive. If you're the leader, however, you have an extra degree of responsibility and accountability. The following guidelines will help leaders and participants contribute to more effective meetings:

> Everyone shares the responsibility for successful meetings.

The agenda title clearly identifies the scope of the meeting.

The clear and concise outline format identifies the topics that will be addressed and the order of discussion, which helps participants plan questions and suggestions.

Establishing a time limit for each section helps keep the meeting on track and ensures that time will be available for every topic.

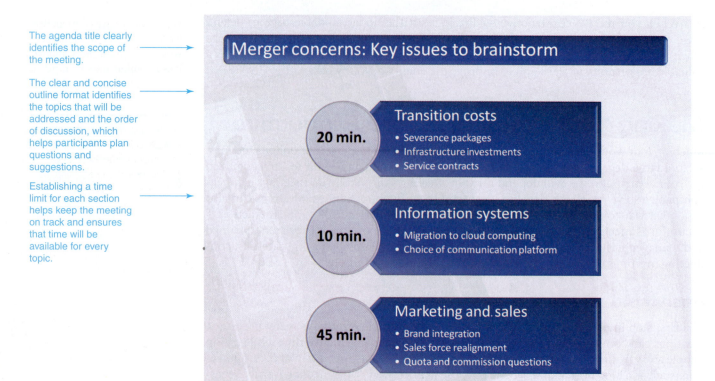

Figure 2.4   Typical Meeting Agenda

Agenda formats vary widely, depending on the complexity of the meeting and the presentation technologies that will be used. One good approach is to first distribute a detailed planning agenda so that presenters know what they need to prepare, then create a simpler display agenda such as this PowerPoint slide to guide the progress of the meeting. Note how the agenda includes the time limit for each topic.

- **Keep the discussion on track.** A good meeting draws out the best ideas and information the group has to offer. Good leaders occasionally need to guide, mediate, probe, stimulate, summarize, and redirect discussions that have gotten off track.
- **Follow agreed-on rules.** The larger the meeting, the more formal you need to be to maintain order. Formal meetings use **parliamentary procedure**, a time-tested method for planning and running effective meetings. The best-known guide to this procedure is *Robert's Rules of Order*.
- **Encourage participation.** You may discover that some participants are too quiet and others are too talkative. Draw out nonparticipants by asking for their input. For the overly talkative, you can say that time is limited and others need to be heard.
- **Participate actively.** Make a point to contribute to the progress of the meeting and the smooth interaction of participants. Use your listening skills and powers of observation to size up the interpersonal dynamics of the group, then adapt your behavior to help the group achieve its goals. Speak up if you have something useful to say, but don't talk or ask questions just to demonstrate how much you know about the subject at hand.
- **Use mobile devices respectfully.** Tweeting key points from a convention speech or using your phone or tablet to jot down essential ideas and follow-up questions can be productive and respectful ways to use a device during a meeting. Checking Facebook or working on unrelated tasks is not. If you intend to use your device to take notes during a meeting, consider letting the meeting leader know that's what you're doing.[40]
- **Close effectively.** At the conclusion of the meeting, verify that the objectives have been met or arrange for follow-up work, if needed. Either summarize the general conclusion of the discussion or the actions to be taken. Make sure all participants have a chance to clear up any misunderstandings.

PUTTING MEETING RESULTS TO PRODUCTIVE USE

In most cases, the value of a meeting doesn't end when the meeting ends. For example, problems or opportunities brought up during a meeting need to be addressed, any action items assigned during the meeting need to be acted on, and key decisions and announcements should be distributed to anyone who is affected but was unable to attend. Having a written, audio, or video record of a meeting also gives the participants a chance to verify their impressions and conclusions.

The conventional method of recording meetings is through written **minutes**, a summary of the important information presented and the decisions made. One person is usually assigned to keep notes as the meeting progresses and then to share them afterward. The specific format of the minutes is less important than making sure you record all the key information, particularly regarding responsibilities that were assigned during the meeting. Typical elements include a list of those present and a list of those who were invited but didn't attend, followed by the times the meeting started and ended, all major decisions reached at the meeting, all assignments of tasks to meeting participants, and all subjects that were deferred to a later meeting. In addition, the minutes objectively summarize important discussions, noting the names of those who contributed major points. Any handouts, electronic slides, or supporting documents can be attached to the minutes when they are distributed.

> Minutes are written summaries of important information presented and the decisions made in meetings.

Depending on the meeting technologies at your disposal, you may have software specifically designed to record, distribute, and store meeting minutes (see Figure 2.5). Some systems automatically forward action items to each employee, record audio discussions for future playback, and make all the relevant documents and files available in one convenient place.[41]

To review the tasks that contribute to productive meetings, refer to "Checklist: Improving Meeting Productivity" on the next page.

Courtesy of MeetingBooster

Figure 2.5   Capturing Key Decisions and Discoveries from a Meeting
Meeting technologies such as the MeetingBooster system help teams and other groups capture decisions and discoveries from meetings and put this information to productive use.

CHECKLIST ✔ Improving Meeting Productivity

A. Prepare carefully.
- Make sure the meeting is necessary.
- Decide on your purpose.
- Select participants carefully.
- Choose the venue and the time.
- Establish and distribute a clear agenda.

B. Lead effectively and participate fully.
- Keep the meeting on track.
- Follow agreed-on rules.
- Encourage participation.
- Participate actively.
- Close effectively.

C. Put the results to effective use.
- Distribute meeting minutes to participants and other interested parties.
- Make sure task assignments are clearly communicated.

---

4 LEARNING OBJECTIVE
Identify the major technologies used to enhance or replace in-person meetings.

Virtual meeting technologies connect people spread around the country or around the world.

MOBILE APP
WebEx Mobile gives you access to one of the world's most popular online meeting platforms.

Using Meeting Technologies

Today's companies use a number of technologies to enhance or even replace traditional in-person meetings. Holding **virtual meetings** can dramatically reduce costs and resource usage, reduce wear and tear on employees, and give teams access to a wider pool of expertise (see Figure 2.6).

Instant messaging (IM) and teleconferencing are the simplest forms of virtual meetings. Videoconferencing lets participants see and hear each other, demonstrate products, and transmit other visual information. *Telepresence* (see Figure 2.7) enables realistic conferences in which participants thousands of miles apart almost seem to be in the same room.[42] The ability to convey nonverbal subtleties such as facial expressions and hand gestures makes these systems particularly good for negotiations, collaborative problem solving, and other complex discussions.[43]

The most sophisticated web-based meeting systems combine the best of real-time communication, shared workspaces, and videoconferencing with other tools, such as *virtual whiteboards*, that let teams collaborate in real time. Such systems are used for everything from spontaneous discussions among small groups to carefully planned formal events such as press conferences, training sessions, sales presentations, and *webinars* (web-based seminars).[44] One of the newest virtual tools is online brainstorming, in which a company can conduct "idea campaigns" to generate new ideas from people across the organization.

Courtesy of Cisco Systems, Inc. Unauthorized use not permitted

Figure 2.6 Virtual Meetings
With broadband wireless connections, virtual meetings are easy to conduct using smartphones or tablets

Figure 2.7   Telepresence
How many people are actually in this conference room in Chicago? Only the two people in the foreground are in the room; the other six are in Atlanta and London. Virtual meeting technologies such as this telepresence system connect people spread across the country or around the world.

Conducting successful virtual meetings requires extra planning beforehand and more diligence during the meeting. Recognizing the limitations of the virtual meeting format is a key to using it successfully.[45] Because virtual meetings offer less visual contact and non-verbal communication than in-person meetings, leaders need to make sure everyone stays engaged and has the opportunity to contribute. Paying attention during online meetings takes greater effort as well. Participants need to stay committed to the meeting and resist the temptation to work on unrelated tasks.[46]

For the latest information on meeting technologies, visit **http://real-timeupdates .com/ebc12** and click on Chapter 2.

> Conducting successful virtual meetings requires extra planning and more diligence during the meeting.

Improving Your Listening Skills

Your long-term career prospects are closely tied to your ability to listen effectively. In fact, some 80 percent of top executives say listening is the most important skill needed to get things done in the workplace.[47] Plus, today's younger employees place a high premium on being heard, so listening is becoming even more vital for managers.[48]

Effective listening strengthens organizational relationships, alerts the organization to opportunities for innovation, and allows the organization to manage growing diversity both in the workforce and in the customers it serves.[49] Companies whose employees and managers listen effectively are able to stay informed, up to date, and out of trouble. Conversely, poor listening skills can cost companies millions of dollars per year as a result of lost opportunities, legal mistakes, and other errors. Effective listening is also vital to the process of building trust between organizations and between individuals.[50]

> **5** **LEARNING OBJECTIVE**
> Identify three major modes of listening, describe the listening process, and explain the problem of selective listening.

> Listening is one of the most important skills in the workplace.

RECOGNIZING VARIOUS TYPES OF LISTENING

Effective listeners adapt their listening approaches to different situations. The primary goal of **content listening** is to understand and retain the information in the speaker's message. Because you're not evaluating the information at this point, it doesn't matter whether you agree or disagree, approve or disapprove—only that you understand. Try to overlook the speaker's style and any limitations in the presentation; just focus on the information.[51]

> To be a good listener, adapt the way you listen to suit the situation.

REAL-TIME UPDATES

LEARN MORE BY READING THIS ARTICLE

Turn listening into a competitive advantage

See why companies that listen to their stakeholders have a competitive edge over those that don't. Go to http://real-timeupdates.com/ebc12 and click on Learn More in the Students section.

The goal of **critical listening** is to understand and evaluate the meaning of the speaker's message on several levels: the logic of the argument, the strength of the evidence, the validity of the conclusions, the implications of the message, the speaker's intentions and motives, and the omission of any important or relevant points. If you're skeptical, ask questions to explore the speaker's point of view and credibility. Be on the lookout for bias that could color the way the information is presented, and be careful to separate opinions from facts.[52]

The goal of **empathic listening** is to understand the speaker's feelings, needs, and wants so that you can appreciate his or her point of view, regardless of whether you share that perspective. By listening with empathy, you help the individual vent the emotions that prevent a calm, clear-headed approach to the subject. Avoid the temptation to jump in with advice unless the person specifically asks for it. Also, don't judge the speaker's feelings, and don't try to tell people they shouldn't feel this or that emotion. Instead, let the speaker know that you appreciate his or her feelings and understand the situation. After you establish that connection, you can help the speaker move on to search for a solution.[53]

No matter what mode they are using at any given time, effective listeners try to engage in **active listening**, making a conscious effort to turn off their own filters and biases to truly hear and understand what the other party is saying. They ask questions to verify key points and encourage the speaker through positive body language.[54]

> Listening actively means making the effort to turn off your internal "filters" and biases to truly hear and understand what the other person is saying.

UNDERSTANDING THE LISTENING PROCESS

Listening is a far more complex process than most people think—and most of us aren't very good at it. People typically listen at no better than a 25 percent efficiency rate, remember only about half of what's said during a 10-minute conversation, and forget half of that within 48 hours.[55] Furthermore, when questioned about material they've just heard, they are likely to get the facts mixed up.[56]

Why is such a seemingly simple activity so difficult? The reason is that listening is not a simple process, by any means. Listening follows the same sequence as the general communication process model described in Chapter 1 (page 10), with the added challenge that it happens in real time. To listen effectively, you need to successfully complete five steps:[57]

> Listening involves five steps: receiving, decoding, remembering, evaluating, and responding.

1. **Receiving.** You start by physically hearing the message and acknowledging it. Physical reception can be blocked by noise, impaired hearing, or inattention. Some experts also include nonverbal messages as part of this stage because these factors influence the listening process as well.
2. **Decoding.** Your next step is to assign meaning to sounds, which you do according to your own values, beliefs, ideas, expectations, roles, needs, and personal history.
3. **Remembering.** Before you can act on the information, you need to store it for future processing. As you learned in Chapter 1, incoming messages must first be captured in short-term memory before being transferred to long-term memory for more permanent storage.
4. **Evaluating.** The next step is to evaluate the message by applying critical thinking skills to separate fact from opinion and evaluate the quality of the evidence.
5. **Responding.** After you've evaluated the speaker's message, you react. If you're communicating one-on-one or in a small group, the initial response generally takes the form of verbal feedback. If you're one of many in an audience, your initial response may take the form of applause, laughter, or silence. Later on, you may act on what you have heard.

If any one of these steps breaks down, the listening process becomes less effective or may even fail entirely. As both a sender and a receiver, you can reduce the failure rate by recognizing and overcoming a variety of physical and mental barriers to effective listening.

OVERCOMING BARRIERS TO EFFECTIVE LISTENING

Good listeners look for ways to overcome potential barriers throughout the listening process (see Table 2.3). You may not be able to control some factors, such as conference room acoustics or poor phone reception. However, you can control other factors, such as not interrupting speakers and not creating distractions that make it difficult for others to pay attention. And don't think you're not interrupting just because you're not talking. Such actions as texting or checking your watch can interrupt a speaker and lead to communication breakdowns.

Good listeners actively try to overcome barriers to successful listening.

Selective listening is one of the most common barriers to effective listening. If your mind wanders, you may stay tuned out until you hear a word or phrase that gets your attention again. But by that time, you're unable to recall what the speaker *actually* said; instead, you remember what you think the speaker *probably* said.[58]

One reason listeners' minds tend to wander is that people think faster than they speak. Most people speak at about 120 to 150 words per minute, but listeners can process audio information at up to 500 words per minute or more.[59] Consequently, your brain has a lot of free time whenever you're listening, and if left unsupervised, it will find a thousand other things to think about. Make the effort to focus on the speaker and use the extra time to analyze and paraphrase what you hear or to take relevant notes.

Your mind can process information much faster than most speakers talk, so you need to focus to listen effectively.

Overcoming interpretation barriers can be difficult because you may not even be aware of them. As Chapter 1 notes, selective perception leads listeners to mold messages to fit their own conceptual frameworks. Listeners sometimes make up their minds before fully hearing the speaker's message, or they engage in *defensive listening*—protecting their egos by tuning out anything that doesn't confirm their beliefs or their view of themselves.

Even when your intentions are good, you can still misinterpret incoming messages if you and the speaker don't share enough language or experience. When listening to a speaker whose native language or life experience is different from yours, try to paraphrase that person's ideas. Give the speaker a chance to confirm what you think you heard or to correct any misinterpretation.

If the information you hear will be important to use later, write it down or otherwise record it. Don't rely on your memory. If you do need to memorize, you can hold information in short-term memory by repeating it silently or organizing a long list of items into several shorter lists. To store information in long-term memory, four techniques can help: (1) associate new information with something closely related (such as the restaurant in

TABLE 2.3   What Makes an Effective Listener?

Effective Listeners	Ineffective Listeners
Listen actively.	Listen passively.
Take careful and complete notes, when applicable.	Take no notes or ineffective notes.
Make frequent eye contact with the speaker (depends on culture to some extent).	Make little or no eye contact—or inappropriate eye contact.
Stay focused on the speaker and the content.	Allow their minds to wander, are easily distracted, work on unrelated tasks.
Mentally paraphrase key points to maintain attention level and ensure comprehension.	Fail to paraphrase.
Adjust listening style to the situation.	Listen with the same style, regardless of the situation.
Give the speaker nonverbal cues (such as nodding to show agreement or raising eyebrows to show surprise or skepticism).	Fail to give the speaker nonverbal feedback.
Save questions or points of disagreement until an appropriate time.	Interrupt whenever they disagree or don't understand.
Overlook stylistic differences and focus on the speaker's message.	Are distracted by or unduly influenced by stylistic differences; are judgmental.
Make distinctions between main points and supporting details.	Are unable to distinguish main points from details.
Look for opportunities to learn.	Assume they already know everything that's important to know.

Sources: Adapted from Madelyn Burley-Allen, *Listening: The Forgotten Skill* (New York: Wiley, 1995), 70–71, 119–120; Judi Brownell, *Listening: Attitudes, Principles, and Skills* (Boston: Allyn & Bacon, 2002), 3, 9, 83, 89, 125; Larry Barker and Kittie Watson, *Listen Up* (New York: St. Martin's, 2000), 8, 9, 64.

CHECKLIST ✔ Overcoming Barriers to Effective Listening

- Lower barriers to physical reception whenever you can (such as avoiding interrupting speakers by asking questions or by exhibiting disruptive nonverbal behaviors).
- Avoid selective listening by focusing on the speaker and carefully analyzing what you hear.
- Keep an open mind by avoiding any prejudgment and by not listening defensively.

- Don't count on your memory; write down or record important information.
- Improve your short-term memory by repeating information or breaking it into shorter lists.
- Improve your long-term memory by using association, categorization, visualization, and mnemonics.

---

which you met a new client), (2) categorize the new information into logical groups (such as alphabetizing a list of names), (3) visualize words and ideas as pictures, and (4) create mnemonics such as acronyms or rhymes.

For a reminder of the steps you can take to overcome listening barriers, see "Checklist: Overcoming Barriers to Effective Listening."

Improving Your Nonverbal Communication Skills

6 **LEARNING OBJECTIVE**
Explain the importance of nonverbal communication, and identify six major categories of nonverbal expression.

Nonverbal communication is the interpersonal process of sending and receiving information, both intentionally and unintentionally, without using written or spoken language. Nonverbal signals play a vital role in communication because they can strengthen a verbal message (when the nonverbal signals match the spoken words), weaken a verbal message (when nonverbal signals don't match the words), or replace words entirely. For example, you might tell a client that a project is coming along nicely, but your forced smile and nervous glances will send an entirely different message.

Nonverbal communication can supplement or even replace verbal messages (those that use words).

RECOGNIZING NONVERBAL COMMUNICATION

You've been tuned in to nonverbal communication since your first contact with other human beings. Paying special attention to nonverbal signals in the workplace will enhance your ability to communicate successfully. Moreover, as you work with a diverse range of people in the global marketplace, you'll also need to grasp the different meanings of common gestures, expressions, and other signals in various cultures. Six types of signals are particularly important:

Nonverbal signals include facial expression, gesture and posture, vocal characteristics, personal appearance, touch, and time and space.

- **Facial expression.** Your face is the primary vehicle for expressing your emotions; it reveals both the type and the intensity of your feelings.[60] Your eyes are especially effective for indicating attention and interest, influencing others, regulating interaction, and establishing dominance.[61]
- **Gesture and posture.** The way you position and move your body expresses both specific and general messages, some voluntary and some involuntary. Many gestures—a wave of the hand, for example—have specific and intentional meanings. Other types of body movement are unintentional and express more general messages. Slouching, leaning forward, fidgeting, and walking briskly are all unconscious signals that can reveal whether you feel confident or nervous, friendly or hostile, assertive or passive, powerful or powerless.
- **Vocal characteristics.** Voice carries both intentional and unintentional messages. A speaker can intentionally control pitch, pace, and stress to convey a specific message. For instance, compare "*What* are you doing?" and "What are *you* doing?" Unintentional vocal characteristics can convey happiness, surprise, fear, and other emotions (for example, fear often increases the pitch and pace of your speaking voice).

REAL-TIME UPDATES
LEARN MORE BY READING THIS ARTICLE

Improve your professional "curb appeal"

Send these nonverbal signals to build credibility in conversations. Go to http://real-timeupdates.com/ebc12 and click on Learn More in the Students section.

- **Personal appearance.** People respond to others on the basis of their physical appearance, sometimes fairly and other times unfairly. Although an individual's body type and facial features impose some limitations on appearance, you can control grooming, clothing, accessories, piercings, tattoos, and hairstyle. To make a good impression, adopt the style of the people you want to impress. Many employers also have guidelines concerning attire, body art, and other issues, so make sure you understand and follow them.[62]
- **Touch.** Touch is an important way to convey warmth, comfort, and reassurance—as well as control. Touch is so powerful, in fact, that it is governed by cultural customs that establish who can touch whom and how in various circumstances. Even within each culture's norms, however, individual attitudes toward touch vary widely. A manager might be comfortable using hugs to express support or congratulations, but his or her subordinates could interpret those hugs as a show of dominance or sexual interest.[63] Touch is a complex subject. The best advice: When in doubt, don't touch.
- **Time and space.** Like touch, time and space can be used to assert authority, imply intimacy, and send other nonverbal messages. For instance, some people try to demonstrate their own importance or disregard for others by making other people wait; others show respect by being on time. Similarly, taking care not to invade private space, such as standing too close when talking, is a way to show respect for others. Keep in mind that expectations regarding both time and space vary by culture.

USING NONVERBAL COMMUNICATION EFFECTIVELY

Paying attention to nonverbal cues will make you a better speaker and a better listener. When you're talking, be more conscious of the nonverbal cues you could be sending. Are they effective without being manipulative? Consider a situation in which an employee has come to you to talk about a raise. This situation is stressful for the employee, so don't say you're interested in what she has to tell you and then spend your time glancing at your computer or checking your watch. Conversely, if you already know you won't be able to give her the raise, be honest in your expression of emotions. Don't overcompensate for your own stress by smiling too broadly or shaking her hand too vigorously. Both nonverbal signals would raise her hopes without justification. In either case, match your nonverbal cues to the tone of the situation.

Also consider the nonverbal signals you send when you're not talking—the clothes you wear, the way you sit, the way you walk (see Figure 2.8). Are you talking like a serious

> Work to make sure your nonverbal signals match the tone and content of your spoken communication.

> What signals does your personal appearance send?

Radoslaw Korga/Shutterstock

Figure 2.8   Nonverbal Signals
The nonverbal signals you send in any business setting influence how others perceive you and your ideas.

CHECKLIST ✔ Improving Nonverbal Communication Skills

- Understand the roles that nonverbal signals play in communication, complementing verbal language by strengthening, weakening, or replacing words.
- Note that facial expressions (especially eye contact) reveal the type and intensity of a speaker's feelings.
- Watch for cues from gestures and posture.

- Listen for vocal characteristics that can signal the emotions underlying the speaker's words.
- Recognize that listeners are influenced by physical appearance.
- Be careful with physical contact; touch can convey positive attributes but can also be interpreted as dominance or sexual interest.
- Pay attention to the use of time and space.

---

business professional but dressing like you belong in a dance club or a frat house? Whether or not you think it is fair to be judged on superficial matters, the truth is that you are judged this way. Don't let careless choices or disrespectful habits undermine all the great work you're doing on the job.

When you listen, be sure to pay attention to the speaker's nonverbal cues. Do they amplify the spoken words or contradict them? Is the speaker intentionally using nonverbal signals to send you a message that he or she can't put into words? Be observant, but don't assume that you can "read someone like a book." Nonverbal signals are powerful, but they aren't infallible, particularly if you don't know a person's normal behavioral patterns.[64] For example, contrary to popular belief, avoiding eye contact and covering one's face while talking are not reliable clues that someone is lying. Even when telling the truth, most people don't make uninterrupted eye contact with the listeners, and various gestures such as touching one's face might be normal behavior for particular people.[65] Moreover, these and other behaviors may be influenced by culture (in some cultures, sustained eye contact can be interpreted as a sign of disrespect) or might just be ways of coping with stressful situations.[66]

If something doesn't feel right, ask the speaker an honest and respectful question; doing so may clear everything up, or it may uncover issues you need to explore further. See "Checklist: Improving Nonverbal Communication Skills" for a summary of key ideas regarding nonverbal skills.

7 LEARNING OBJECTIVE
Explain the importance of business etiquette, and identify four key areas in which good etiquette is essential.

Etiquette is an essential element of every aspect of business communication.

Developing Your Business Etiquette

You may have noticed a common thread running through the topics of successful teamwork, productive meetings, effective listening, and nonverbal communication: All these activities depend on mutual respect and consideration among all participants. Nobody wants to work with someone who is rude to colleagues or an embarrassment to the company. Moreover, shabby treatment of others in the workplace can be a huge drain on morale and productivity.[67] Poor etiquette can drive away customers, investors, and other critical audiences—and it can limit your career potential.

This section addresses some key etiquette points to remember when you're in the workplace, out in public, online, and using mobile devices. Long lists of etiquette rules can be difficult to remember, but you can get by in almost every situation by remembering to be aware of your effect on others, treating everyone with respect, and keeping in mind that the impressions you leave behind can have a lasting effect on you and your company. As etiquette expert Cindy Post Senning points out, "The principles of respect, consideration, and honesty are universal and timeless."[68]

BUSINESS ETIQUETTE IN THE WORKPLACE

Personal appearance can have considerable impact on your success in business.

Workplace etiquette includes a variety of behaviors, habits, and aspects of nonverbal communication. Although it isn't always thought of as an element of etiquette, your personal appearance in the workplace sends a strong signal to managers, colleagues, and customers (see Figure 2.9). Pay attention to the style of dress where you work and adjust your style

Paul Bradbury/OJO Images Ltd/Alamy

Figure 2.9   Showing Respect for Organizational Culture
Being aware of expectations for personal appearance in a business setting is not only a sign of respect, it will help keep you from making career-limiting mistakes.

to match. Expectations for specific jobs, companies, and industries can vary widely. The financial industries tend to be more formal than high-tech firms, for instance, and sales and executive positions usually involve more formal expectations than positions in engineering or manufacturing. Observe others, and don't be afraid to ask for advice. If you're not sure, dress modestly and simply—earn a reputation for what you can do, not for what you wear. Table 2.4 offers some general guidelines on assembling a business wardrobe that's cost-effective and flexible.

Grooming is as important as attire. Pay close attention to cleanliness, and avoid using products with powerful scents, such as perfumed soaps, colognes, shampoos, and after-shave lotions (many people are bothered by these products, and some are allergic to them).

TABLE 2.4 Assembling a Business Wardrobe			
1 **Smooth and Finished (Start with This)**	**2** **Elegant and Refined (To Column 1, Add This)**	**3** **Crisp and Starched (To Column 2, Add This)**	**4** **Up-to-the-Minute Trendy (To Column 3, Add This)**
• Choose well-tailored clothing that fits well; it doesn't have to be expensive, but it does have to fit and be appropriate for business. • Keep buttons, zippers, and hemlines in good repair. • Select shoes that are comfortable enough for long days but neither too casual nor too dressy for the office; keep shoes clean and in good condition. • Make sure the fabrics you wear are clean, are carefully pressed, and do not wrinkle easily. • Choose colors that flatter your height, weight, skin tone, and style; sales advisors in good clothing stores can help you choose.	• Choose form-fitting (but not skin-tight) clothing—not swinging or flowing fabrics, frills, or fussy trimmings. • Choose muted tones and soft colors or classics, such as a dark blue suit or a basic black dress. • If possible, select a few classic pieces of jewelry (such as a string of pearls or diamond cuff links) for formal occasions. • Wear jackets that complement an outfit and lend an air of formality to your appearance. Avoid jackets with more than two tones; one color should dominate.	• Wear blouses or shirts that are or appear starched. • Choose closed top-button shirts or button-down shirt collars, higher-neckline blouses, or long sleeves with French cuffs and cuff links. • Wear creased trousers or a longer skirt hemline.	• Supplement your foundation with pieces that reflect the latest styles. • Add a few pieces in bold colors but wear them sparingly to avoid a garish appearance. • Embellish your look with the latest jewelry and hairstyles but keep the overall effect looking professional.

COMMUNICATING ACROSS CULTURES

Whose Skin Is This, Anyway?

Generational differences abound in the workplace, but few are quite as visible as body art: tattoos, piercings (other than ear lobes), and hair dyes in unconventional colors. According to survey data from the Pew Research Center, people younger than 40 are much more inclined than those older than 40 to display some form of body art. For example, people 26 to 40 years old are four times more likely to have tattoos than people who are 41 to 64 years old.

With such profound differences, it's no surprise that body art has become a contentious issue in many workplaces, between employees wanting to express themselves and employers wanting to maintain particular standards of professional appearance. As employment law attorney Danielle S. Urban notes, the issue gets even more complicated when religious symbolism is involved.

Who is likely to win this battle? Will the body art aficionados who continue to join the workforce and who are now rising up the managerial ranks force a change in what is considered acceptable appearance in the workplace? Or will they be forced to cover up to meet traditional standards?

So far, most companies appear to be relying on the judgment of their employees and managers, rather than enforcing strict guidelines. Many seem to accept that tastes and norms are changing and that body art has become a widespread form of self-expression rather than a mode of rebellion. Starbucks, which used to require employees to hide tattoos under long sleeves, recently revised its policy to allow employees to display tattoos everywhere except on their faces. The semiconductor giant Intel even featured photos of employee tattoos in its online technology newsletter.

Job seekers are still advised to be discreet, however, particularly with facial piercings and large, visible tattoos. The nonverbal signals you think you are sending might not be the signals a hiring manager receives—or wants to receive.

CAREER APPLICATIONS

1. Should companies have stricter standards of appearance for "customer-facing" employees than for employees who do not interact with customers? Why or why not?
2. Should companies allow their employees the same freedom of expression and appearance latitude as their customers exhibit? For example, if a firm's clientele tends to be heavily tattooed, should employees be allowed the same freedom? Why or why not?

Sources: Micah Solomon, "Starbucks to Allow Tattoos, Piercings: Wise or Risky Customer Service, HR Move?" *Forbes,* 17 October 2014, www.forbes.com; "Intel Tattoos Speak Volumes," 17 March 2011, *Intel Free Press,* www.intelfreepress.com; Rita Pyrillis, "Body of Work," *Workforce Management,* November 2010, www.workforce.com; Danielle S. Urban, "What to Do About 'Body Art' at Work," *Workforce Management,* March 2010, www.workforce.com; "36%—Tattooed Gen Nexters," Pew Research Center, http://pewresearch.org.

Your telephone skills will be vital to your business success.

IM and other text-based tools have taken over many exchanges that used to take place over the phone, but phone skills are still essential. Because phone calls lack the visual richness of face-to-face conversations, you have to rely on your attitude and tone of voice to convey confidence and professionalism. Here are some important tips for using phones at work (for etiquette points specifically about mobile devices, see page 58):[69]

- **Be conscious of how your voice sounds.** Don't speak in a monotone; vary your pitch and inflections so people know you're interested. Slow down when conversing with people whose native language isn't the same as yours.

Basic courtesy on the phone makes communication more efficient and more pleasant for everyone involved.

- **Be courteous when you call someone.** Identify yourself and your organization, briefly describe why you're calling, and verify that you've called at a good time. Minimize the noise level in your environment as much as possible. For important or complicated conversations, plan what you want to say before calling.
- **Convey a positive, professional attitude when you answer the phone.** Answer promptly and with a smile so that you sound welcoming. Identify yourself and your company (some companies have specific instructions for what to say when you answer). Establish the needs of your caller by asking, "How may I help you?" If you know the caller's name, use it. If you can't answer the caller's questions, either forward the call to a colleague who can or advise the caller on how to get his or her questions resolved. If you do forward a call, put the caller on hold and call the next person yourself to verify that he or she is available.
- **End calls with courtesy and clarity.** Close in a friendly, positive manner and double-check all vital information such as meeting times and dates.
- **Use your own voicemail features to help callers.** Record a brief, professional-sounding outgoing message for regular use. When you will be away or unable to

answer the phone for an extended period, record a temporary greeting that tells callers when you will respond to their messages. If you don't check your messages regularly or at all, disable your voicemail. Letting messages pile up for days or weeks without answering them is extremely thoughtless.

- **Be considerate when leaving voicemail messages.** Retrieving voicemail messages can be a chore, so be thoughtful about leaving them. Unless voicemail is the best or only choice, consider leaving a message through other means, such as text messaging or email. If you do leave a voicemail message, make it as brief as possible. Leave your name, number (don't assume the recipient has caller ID), reason for calling, and times you can be reached. State your name and telephone number slowly so the other person can easily write them down; repeat both if the other person doesn't know you.

If you never or rarely check your voicemail, disable it or record an outgoing message advising callers to reach you another way.

BUSINESS ETIQUETTE IN SOCIAL SETTINGS

From business lunches to industry conferences, you may be asked to represent your company in public. Make sure your appearance and actions are appropriate to the situation. Get to know the customs of other cultures when it comes to meeting new people. For example, in North America, a firm handshake is expected when two people meet, whereas a respectful bow of the head is more appropriate in Japan. If you are expected to shake hands, be aware that the passive "dead fish" handshake creates an extremely negative impression. If you are physically able, always stand when shaking someone's hand.

When introducing yourself, include a brief description of your role in the company. When introducing two other people, speak their first and last names clearly and then try to offer some information (perhaps a shared professional interest) to help the two people ease into a conversation.[70] Generally speaking, the lower-ranking person is introduced to the senior-ranking person, without regard to gender.[71]

Business is often conducted over meals, and knowing the basics of dining etiquette will make you more effective in these situations.[72] Start by choosing foods that are easy to eat. Avoid alcoholic beverages in most instances, but if drinking one is appropriate, save it for the end of the meal. Leave business documents under your chair until entrée plates have been removed; the business aspect of the meal doesn't usually begin until then.

Remember that business meals are a forum for business. Don't discuss politics, religion, or any other topic that's likely to stir up emotions. Don't complain about work, don't ask deeply personal questions, avoid profanity, and be careful with humor—a joke that entertains some people could easily offend others.

Etiquette is particularly important when you represent your company out in public.

MOBILE APP
The Etiquette App helps you make appropriate choices in a variety of social and business situations.

BUSINESS ETIQUETTE ONLINE

Electronic media seem to be a breeding ground for poor etiquette. Learn the basics of professional online behavior to avoid mistakes that could hurt your company or your career. Here are some guidelines to follow whenever you are representing your company while using electronic media:[73]

- **Avoid personal attacks.** The anonymous and instantaneous nature of online communication can cause even level-headed people to strike out in blog postings, social networks, and other media.
- **Stay focused on the original topic.** If you want to change the subject of an email exchange, a forum discussion, or a blog comment thread, start a new message.
- **Don't present opinions as facts, and support facts with evidence.** This guideline applies to all communication, of course, but online venues in particular seem to tempt people into presenting their beliefs and opinions as unassailable truths.
- **Follow basic expectations of spelling, punctuation, and capitalization.** Sending careless, acronym-filled messages that look like you're texting your high school buddies makes you look like an amateur.
- **Use virus protection and keep it up to date.** Sending or posting a file that contains a computer virus puts others at risk.

When you represent your company online, you must adhere to a high standard of etiquette and respect for others.

REAL-TIME UPDATES

LEARN MORE BY READING THIS ARTICLE

Simple steps to improve social media etiquette

Follow these five tips for a more professional online presence. Go to http://real-timeupdates.com/ebc12 and click on Learn More in the Students section.

- **Use difficult-to-break passwords on email, Twitter, and other accounts.** If someone hacks your account, it can create spam headaches—or worse—for your contacts and followers.
- **Ask if this is a good time for an IM chat.** Don't assume that just because a person is showing as "available" on your IM system, he or she wants to chat at this moment.
- **Watch your language and keep your emotions under control.** A single indiscretion could haunt you forever.
- **Avoid multitasking while using IM and other tools.** You might think you're saving time by doing a dozen things at once, but you're probably making the other person wait while you bounce back and forth between IM and your other tasks.
- **Never assume privacy.** Assume that anything you type will be stored forever, could be forwarded to other people, and might be read by your boss or the company's security staff.
- **Don't use "Reply All" in email unless everyone can benefit from your reply.** If one or more recipients of an email message don't need the information in your reply, remove their addresses before you send.
- **Don't waste others' time with sloppy, confusing, or incomplete messages.** Doing so is disrespectful.
- **Respect boundaries of time and virtual space.** For instance, don't start using an employee's personal Facebook page for business messages unless you've discussed it beforehand, and don't assume people are available to discuss work matters around the clock, even if you do find them online in the middle of the night.
- **Be careful of online commenting mechanisms.** For example, many blogs and websites now use your Facebook login to let you comment on articles. If your Facebook profile includes your job title and company name, those could show up along with your comment.

Respect personal and professional boundaries when using Facebook and other social networking tools.

BUSINESS ETIQUETTE USING MOBILE DEVICES

Your mobile phone habits send a signal about the degree of respect you have for those around you.

Like every other aspect of communication, your mobile device habits say a lot about how much respect you have for the people around you. Selecting obnoxious ringtones, talking loudly in open offices or public places, using your phone right next to someone else, making excessive or unnecessary personal calls during work hours, invading someone's privacy by using your phone's camera without permission, taking or making calls in restrooms and other inappropriate places, texting during a meal or while someone is talking to you, allowing incoming calls to interrupt meetings or discussions—these are all disrespectful choices that will reflect negatively on you.[74] In general, older employees, managers, and customers are less tolerant of mobile device use than are younger people, so don't assume that your habits will be universally acceptable.[75]

MOBILE APP

Locale can "geofence" your smartphone, automatically changing settings based on your location—such as activating silent mode when you arrive at your office.

Virtual assistants and other mobile phone voice features can annoy and disrupt the workplace and social settings if not used with respect for others.

Virtual assistants, such as the Siri voice recognition system in Apple iPhones, raise another new etiquette dilemma. From doing simple web searches to dictating entire memos, these systems may be convenient for users, but they can create distractions and annoyances for other people.[76] As with other public behaviors, think about the effect you have on others before using these technologies.

Note that expectations and policies regarding mobile device use vary widely from company to company. At one extreme, venture capitalist Ben Horowitz fines his employees if they even look at a mobile device while an entrepreneur is making a business plan pitch, because he considers it disrespectful to people making presentations.[77] Not all bosses are quite so strict, but make sure you understand the situation in your workplace.

REAL-TIME UPDATES

LEARN MORE BY READING THIS INFOGRAPHIC

Whatever happened to live conversation?

See the impact of mobile devices on our conversational habits. Go to http://real-timeupdates.com/ebc12 and click on Learn More in the Students section.

ON THE JOB: SOLVING COMMUNICATION DILEMMAS AT **CEMEX**

You work as a customer account manager in Cemex's Houston office, where you're an enthusiastic user of the Shift collaboration platform. Even in the best work environments, conflicts and misunderstandings can arise. Study these scenarios and decide how to respond, based on what you learned in this chapter.

1. You rely heavily on CEMEXpedia, the wiki that contains technical and business information about the company's operations. As you've become more experienced in your job, you have also become a frequent contributor to the wiki. Lately you've noticed one particular employee from the Cemex office in Madrid, Spain, keeps editing the pages you create on the wiki, often making changes that appear to add no value, as far as you can see. She doesn't seem to be editing other employees' pages nearly so often, so you are beginning to wonder if she has a personal grudge against you, even though you have never met her. You want to address this uncomfortable situation without dragging your boss into it. How should you handle it?
   a. Edit some of her pages needlessly to help her understand how annoying this behavior is.
   b. Use the private messaging tools on Shift to ask her if there is something about your writing style that she finds unclear. That will open a conversation in a nonthreatening way.
   c. Post a notice on the wiki, emphasizing that all edits should be useful and that unnecessary edits waste everybody's time.
   d. Ignore her behavior; confronting her will get you nowhere.

2. You've been asked to take over leadership of a group of customer account managers that once had a reputation for being a tight-knit, supportive team, but you quickly figure out that this team is in danger of becoming dysfunctional. For example, minor issues that healthy teams routinely handle, from helping each other with computer questions to covering the phones when someone has an outside appointment, frequently generate conflict within this group. What steps should you take to help your crew return to positive behavior?
   a. Give the team the task of healing itself, without getting directly involved. Explain the steps necessary in forming an effective team and then let them figure out how to make it happen.
   b. Lead the "team restoration" project yourself so that you can mediate whatever conflicts arise, at least until the team is able to function on its own in a more positive manner.
   c. Don't try to interfere; the negative behaviors were probably caused by an ineffective manager in the past, but now that you're in charge, the team will return to positive behavior under your enlightened guidance.

   d. Your professional reputation is on the line, so you don't have time for the niceties of team building. Sit down with the group and demand that the negative, unprofessional behavior stop immediately.

3. After a few weeks with the account management team, you notice that team meetings often degenerate into little more than complaint sessions. Workers seem to gripe about everything from difficult customers to the temperature in the office. Some of these complaints sound like valid business issues that might require additional training or other employee support efforts; others are superficial issues you suspect are simply by-products of the negative atmosphere. How should you handle complaints during the meetings?
   a. Try to defuse each complaint with humor; after awhile, employees will begin to lighten up and stop complaining so much.
   b. Ask employees to refrain from complaining during meetings; after all, these are important business meetings, not random social gatherings.
   c. Set up a whiteboard and write down each issue that is raised. After you've compiled a list over the course of a week or so, add a problem-solving segment to each meeting, in which you and the team tackle one issue per meeting to determine the scope of each problem and identify possible solutions.
   d. Whenever a complaint is raised, stop the meeting and confront the person who raised the issue. Challenge him or her to prove that the problem is a real business issue and not just a personal complaint. By doing this, you will not only identify the real problems that need to be fixed but also discourage people from raising petty complaints that shouldn't be aired in the workplace.

4. You're in charge of hiring a replacement for a customer account manager who recently retired. Four job candidates are waiting outside your office, and you have a few moments to observe them before inviting them in for an initial interview (you can see them through the glass wall but can't hear them). Based on the following descriptions, which of these people seems like the best fit for the firm? Why?
   a. **Candidate A:** A woman who is dressed perfectly for an interview at Cemex. Her appearance is contemporary but business appropriate, which suggests that she appreciates and shows respect for the situation she finds herself in. However, you are slightly troubled by the fact that she's listening to music on her phone and has kicked off her shoes and tucked her feet under her while she waits in the chair.
   b. **Candidate B:** A man who has also dressed the part, although this candidate's behavior is nothing like the relaxed, carefree attitude that Candidate A is showing.

He seems to be juggling multiple tasks at once: checking notes on some sort of digital device, organizing a collection of papers he pulled from his briefcase, reattaching several sticky notes that keep falling loose, and fiddling with a mobile phone that he has answered at least twice in the few minutes you've been watching.

c. **Candidate C:** A woman who closed the notebook she was scanning in order to help Candidate B with some problem he was having with his mobile phone. (If you had to guess, he was having trouble figuring out how to silence the ringer.) After their interaction, they shake hands and appear to be introducing themselves with cordial smiles. Unfortunately, although the city is suffering through record high temperatures, her casual dress and sandals strike you as too informal for a job interview.

d. **Candidate D:** A man wearing what appears to be a finely tailored, conservative suit. His appearance is more dignified and businesslike than the other three, and he knows how to dress for success—carefully knotted tie, starched shirt, perfect posture, the works. He keeps to himself and avoids bothering the other candidates, although his facial expressions make it clear that he disapproves of the noise Candidate B is making with his mobile phone.

Learning Objectives Checkup

Assess your understanding of the principles in this chapter by reading each learning objective and studying the accompanying exercises. You can check your responses against the answer key on page 599.

Objective 2.1: List the advantages and disadvantages of working in teams, describe the characteristics of effective teams, and highlight four key issues of group dynamics.

1. Teams can achieve a higher level of performance than individuals alone because
   a. They combine the intelligence and energy of multiple individuals
   b. They can foster motivation and creativity
   c. They involve more input and a greater diversity of views, which tends to result in better decisions
   d. They do all of the above
2. Which of the following is a potential disadvantage of working in teams?
   a. Teams always stamp out creativity by forcing people to conform to existing ideas and practices.
   b. Teams increase a company's clerical workload because of the additional government paperwork required for administering workplace insurance.
   c. Team members are never held accountable for their individual performance.
   d. Social pressure within the group can lead to groupthink, in which people go along with a bad idea or poor decision even though they may not really believe in it.
3. Conflict in team settings can be _____ if it forces important issues into the open, increases the involvement of team members, and generates creative ideas for solving a problem.

Objective 2.2: Offer guidelines for collaborative communication, identify major collaboration technologies, and explain how to give constructive feedback.

4. Which of the following is the best way for a team of people to write a report?
   a. Each member should plan, research, and write his or her individual version and then the group can select the strongest report.
   b. The team should divide and conquer, with one person doing the planning, one doing the research, one doing the writing, and so on.
   c. To ensure a true group effort, every task from planning through final production should be done as a team, preferably with everyone in the same room at the same time.
   d. Research and plan as a group but assign the actual writing to one person, or at least assign separate sections to individual writers and have one person edit them all to achieve a consistent style.
5. Which of the following steps should be completed before anyone from the team does any planning, researching, or writing?
   a. The team should agree on the project's goals.
   b. The team should agree on the report's title.
   c. To avoid compatibility problems, the team should agree on which word processor or other software will be used.
   d. The team should always step away from the work environment and enjoy some social time in order to bond effectively before starting work.
6. Which of the following is not a benefit of using social media for business communication?
   a. Social media are "out in the open," so messages are easier for managers to monitor and control.
   b. Social media help erase geographic and organization boundaries.
   c. Social media give customers an easy way to voice their opinions and concerns.
   d. Social media can help "faceless" companies adopt a more human, conversational tone.

Objective 2.3: List the key steps needed to ensure productive team meetings.

7. What are the three key steps to making sure meetings are productive?
   a. Planning, planning, and more planning
   b. Preparing carefully, conducting meetings efficiently, and putting meeting results to productive use
   c. Preparing carefully, conducting meetings using true democratic participation, and using meeting technologies wisely
   d. Preparing carefully, using meeting technologies wisely, and distributing in-depth minutes to everyone in the company
8. *Robert's Rules of Order* is a guide to _____ procedure.

Objective 2.4: Identify the major technologies used to enhance or replace in-person meetings.

9. ____ teams are teams whose members work in different locations and interact electronically.

10. ____ technologies enable realistic conferences in which participants thousands of miles apart almost seem to be in the same room.

Objective 2.5: Identify three major modes of listening, describe the listening process, and explain the problem of selective listening.

11. After receiving messages, listeners ____ what they've heard by assigning meaning to the sounds.

12. If you're giving an important presentation and notice that many of the audience members look away when you try to make momentary eye contact, which of the following is most likely going on?
    a. These audience members don't want to challenge your authority by making direct eye contact.
    b. You work with a lot of shy people.
    c. The information you're presenting is making your audience uncomfortable in some way.
    d. The audience is taking time to carefully think about the information you're presenting.

13. If you don't agree with something the speaker says in a large, formal meeting, the best response is to
    a. Signal your disagreement by folding your arms across your chest and staring defiantly back at the speaker.
    b. Use your mobile phone to begin sending text messages to other people in the room, explaining why the speaker is wrong.
    c. Immediately challenge the speaker so that the misinformation is caught and corrected.
    d. Quietly make a note of your objections and wait until a question-and-answer period to raise your hand.

Objective 2.6: Explain the importance of nonverbal communication, and identify six major categories of nonverbal expression.

14. Nonverbal signals can be more influential than spoken language because
    a. Body language is difficult to control and therefore difficult to fake, so listeners often put more trust in nonverbal cues than in the words a speaker uses.
    b. Nonverbal signals communicate faster than spoken language, and most people are impatient.
    c. Body language saves listeners from the trouble of paying attention to what a speaker is saying.

15. Which of the following is true about nonverbal signals?
    a. They can strengthen a spoken message.
    b. They can weaken a spoken message.
    c. They can replace spoken messages.
    d. All of the above are true.

Objective 2.7: Explain the importance of business etiquette, and identify four key areas in which good etiquette is essential.

16. Which of the following is the best characterization of etiquette in today's business environment?

a. Business etiquette is impossible to generalize because every company has its own culture; you have to make it up as you go along.
b. With ferocious international competition and constant financial pressure, etiquette is an old-fashioned luxury that businesses simply can't afford today.
c. Ethical businesspeople don't need to worry directly about etiquette because ethical behavior automatically leads to good etiquette.
d. Etiquette plays an important part in the process of forming and maintaining successful business relationships.

17. If you forgot to shut off your mobile phone before stepping into a business meeting and you receive a call during the meeting, the most appropriate thing to do is to
    a. Lower your voice to protect the privacy of your phone conversation.
    b. Answer the phone and then quickly hang it up to minimize the disruption to the meeting.
    c. Excuse yourself from the meeting and find a quiet place to talk.
    d. Continue to participate in the meeting while taking the call; this shows everyone that you're an effective multitasker.

18. Your company has established a designated "quiet time" from 1:00 to 3:00 every afternoon, during which office phones, IM, and email are disabled so that people can concentrate on planning, researching, writing, and other intensive tasks without being interrupted. However, a number of people continue to flout the guidelines by leaving their mobile phones on, saying their families and friends need to able to reach them. With all the various ringtones going off at random, the office is just as noisy as it was before. What is the best response?
    a. Agree to reactivate the office phone system if everyone will shut off their mobile phones, but have all incoming calls routed through a receptionist who will take messages for all routine calls and deliver a note if an employee truly is needed in an emergency.
    b. Give up on quiet time; with so many electronic gadgets in the workplace today, you'll never achieve peace and quiet.
    c. Get tough on the offenders by confiscating mobile phones whenever they ring during quiet time.
    d. Without telling anyone, simply install one of the available mobile phone jamming products that block incoming and outgoing mobile phone calls.

19. Constantly testing the limits of your company's dress and grooming standards sends a strong signal that you
    a. Don't understand or don't respect your company's culture.
    b. Are a strong advocate for worker's rights.
    c. Are a creative and independent thinker who is likely to generate lots of successful business ideas.
    d. Represent the leading edge of a new generation of enlightened workers who will redefine the workplace according to contemporary standards.

Quick Learning Guide

CHAPTER OUTLINE

Communicating Effectively in Teams
Advantages and Disadvantages of Teams
Characteristics of Effective Teams
Group Dynamics

Collaborating on Communication Efforts
Guidelines for Collaborative Writing
Technologies for Collaborative Writing
Giving—and Responding to—Constructive Feedback

Making Your Meetings More Productive
Preparing for Meetings
Conducting and Contributing to Efficient Meetings
Putting Meeting Results to Productive Use

Using Meeting Technologies

Improving Your Listening Skills
Recognizing Various Types of Listening
Understanding the Listening Process
Overcoming Barriers to Effective Listening

Improving Your Nonverbal Communication Skills
Recognizing Nonverbal Communication
Using Nonverbal Communication Effectively

Developing Your Business Etiquette
Business Etiquette in the Workplace
Business Etiquette in Social Settings
Business Etiquette Online
Business Etiquette Using Mobile Devices

LEARNING OBJECTIVES

1 List the advantages and disadvantages of working in teams, describe the characteristics of effective teams, and highlight four key issues of group dynamics. (page 37)

2 Offer guidelines for collaborative communication, identify major collaboration technologies, and explain how to give constructive feedback. (page 41)

3 List the key steps needed to ensure productive team meetings. (page 45)

4 Identify the major technologies used to enhance or replace in-person meetings. (page 48)

5 Identify three major modes of listening, describe the listening process, and explain the problem of selective listening. (page 49)

6 Explain the importance of nonverbal communication, and identify six major categories of nonverbal expression. (page 52)

7 Explain the importance of business etiquette, and identify four key areas in which good etiquette is essential. (page 54)

KEY TERMS

active listening Making a conscious effort to turn off filters and biases to truly hear and understand what someone is saying

collaboration Working together to meet complex challenges

committees Formal teams that usually have a long life span and can become a permanent part of the organizational structure

constructive feedback Focuses on the process and outcomes of communication, not on the people involved

content listening Listening to understand and retain the speaker's message

content management systems Computer systems that organize and control the content for websites

critical listening Listening to understand and evaluate the meaning of the speaker's message

destructive feedback Delivers criticism with no guidance to stimulate improvement

empathic listening Listening to understand the speaker's feelings, needs, and wants so that you can appreciate his or her point of view

group dynamics The interactions and processes that take place among the members of a team

groupthink Situation in which peer pressure causes individual team members to withhold contrary or unpopular opinions

hidden agenda Private, counterproductive motives, such as a desire to take control of the group

minutes Written summary of the important information presented and the decisions made during a meeting

nonverbal communication Sending and receiving information, both intentionally and unintentionally, without using written or spoken language

norms Informal standards of conduct that members share and that guide member behavior

parliamentary procedure A time-tested method for planning and running effective meetings; the best-known guide to this procedure is *Robert's Rules of Order*

participative management The effort to involve employees in the company's decision making

problem-solving teams Teams that assemble to resolve specific issues and then disband when their goals have been accomplished

selective listening Listening to only part of what a speaker is saying; ignoring the parts one doesn't agree with or find interesting

self-oriented roles Unproductive team roles in which people are motivated mainly to fulfill personal needs

shared workspaces Online "virtual offices" that give everyone on a team access to the same set of resources and information

task forces Another form of problem-solving teams, often with members from more than one organization

task-oriented roles Productive team roles directed toward helping the team reach its goals

team A unit of two or more people who share a mission and the responsibility for working to achieve a common goal

team-maintenance roles Productive team roles directed toward helping everyone work well together

unified communication Integrates voice and video calling, voice and video conferencing, instant messaging, real-time collaboration software, and other capabilities into a single system

virtual meetings Meetings that take place online rather than in person

wiki Special type of website that allows anyone with access to add new material and edit existing material

Apply Your Knowledge

To review chapter content related to each question, refer to the indicated Learning Objective.

⭐ **2.1.** You head up the interdepartmental design review team for a manufacturer of high-performance motorcycles, and things are not going well at the moment. The design engineers and marketing strategists keep arguing about which should be a higher priority, performance or aesthetics, and the accountants say both groups are driving up the cost of the new model by adding too many new features. Everyone has valid points to make, but the team is bogging down in conflict. Explain how you could go about resolving the stalemate. [LO-1]

⭐ **2.2.** You and another manager in your company disagree about whether employees should be encouraged to create online profiles on LinkedIn and other business-oriented social networking websites. You say these connections can be valuable to employees by helping them meet their peers throughout the industry and valuable to the company by identifying potential sales leads and business partners. The other manager says that encouraging employees to become better known in the industry will only make it easier for competitors to lure them away with enticing job offers. Write a brief email message that outlines your argument. (Make up any information you need about the company and its industry.) [LO-2]

2.3. How can nonverbal communication help you run a meeting? How can it help you call a meeting to order, emphasize important topics, show approval, express reservations, regulate the flow of conversation, and invite a colleague to continue with a comment? [LO-3], [LO-6]

⭐ **2.4.** Why do you think people are more likely to engage in rude behaviors during online communication than during in-person communication? [LO-7]

⭐ **2.5.** You're giving your first major presentation at your new job and you notice at least half the people in the small conference room are looking at their mobile devices more than they are looking at you. How should you handle the situation? [LO-7]

Practice Your Skills

Message for Analysis: Planning Meetings [LO-3]

A project leader has made notes about covering the following items at the quarterly budget meeting. Prepare a formal agenda by putting these items into a logical order and rewriting, where necessary, to give phrases a more consistent sound.

- Budget Committee Meeting to be held on December 12, 2016, at 9:30 a.m., and we have allotted one hour for the meeting.
- I will call the meeting to order.

- Real estate director's report: A closer look at cost overruns on Greentree site. (10 minutes)
- The group will review and approve the minutes from last quarter's meeting. (5 minutes)
- I will ask the finance director to report on actual versus projected quarterly revenues and expenses. (15 minutes)
- I will distribute copies of the overall divisional budget and announce the date of the next budget meeting.
- Discussion: How can we do a better job of anticipating and preventing cost overruns? (20 minutes)
- Meeting will take place in Conference Room 3, with WebEx active for remote employees.
- What additional budget issues must be considered during this quarter?

Exercises

Each activity is labeled according to the primary skill or skills you will need to use. To review relevant chapter content, you can refer to the indicated Learning Objective. In some instances, supporting information will be found in another chapter, as indicated.

2.6. **Collaboration: Working in Teams [LO-1], [LO-2]** In teams assigned by your instructor, prepare a 10-minute presentation on the potential disadvantages of using social media for business communication. When the presentation is ready, discuss how effective the team was using the criteria of (a) having a clear objective and a shared sense of purpose, (b) communicating openly and honestly, (c) reaching decisions by consensus, (d) thinking creatively, and (e) knowing how to resolve conflict. Be prepared to discuss your findings with the rest of the class.

2.7. **Negotiation and Conflict Resolution: Resolving Conflicts; Communication Ethics: Providing Ethical Leadership [LO-1], Chapter 1** During team meetings, one member constantly calls for votes or decisions before all the members have voiced their views. As the leader, you asked this member privately about his behavior. He replied that he is trying to move the team toward its goals, but you are concerned that he is really trying to take control. How can you deal with this situation without removing the member from the group?

2.8. **Collaboration: Collaborating on Writing Projects; Media Skills: Blogging [LO-2]** In this project, you will conduct research on your own and then merge your results with those of the rest of your team. Search Twitter for messages on the subject of workplace safety. (You can use Twitter's advanced search function or use the site "twitter. com" qualifier on a regular search engine.) Compile at least five general safety tips that apply to any office setting, and then meet with your team to select the five best tips from all those the team has collected. Collaborate on a blog post that lists the team's top five tips.

2.9. **Communication Etiquette: Etiquette in the Workplace, Participating in Meetings [LO-3], [LO-7]** In group meetings, some of your colleagues have a habit of interrupting and arguing with the speaker, taking credit for ideas that aren't theirs, and shooting down ideas they don't agree with. As the newest person in the group, you're not sure if this is accepted behavior in this company, but it concerns you both personally and professionally. Should you go with the flow and adopt their behavior or stick with your own communication style, even though you might get lost in the noise? In a two-paragraph email message or post for your class blog, explain the pros and cons of both approaches.

2.10. Collaboration: Participating in Meetings [LO-3] With a classmate, attend a local community or campus meeting where you can observe a group discussion, vote, or take other group action. During the meeting, take notes individually and, afterward, work together to answer the following questions.

   a. What is your evaluation of this meeting? In your answer, consider (1) the leader's ability to articulate the meeting's goals clearly, (2) the leader's ability to engage members in a meaningful discussion, (3) the group's dynamics, and (4) the group's listening skills.

   b. How did group members make decisions? Did they vote? Did they reach decisions by consensus? Did those with dissenting opinions get an opportunity to voice their objections?

   c. How well did the individual participants listen? How could you tell?

   d. Did any participants change their expressed views or their votes during the meeting? Why might that have happened?

   e. Did you observe any of the communication barriers discussed in Chapter 1? Identify them.

   f. Compare the notes you took during the meeting with those of your classmate. What differences do you notice? How do you account for these differences?

2.11. Collaboration: Leading Meetings [LO-3], Chapter 3 Every month, each employee in your department is expected to give a brief oral presentation on the status of his or her project. However, your department has recently hired an employee who has a severe speech impediment that prevents people from understanding most of what he has to say. As department manager, how will you resolve this dilemma? Please explain.

2.12. Collaboration: Using Collaboration Technologies [LO-4] In a team assigned by your instructor, use Zoho (free for personal use) or a comparable system to collaborate on a set of directions that out-of-town visitors could use to reach a specific point on your campus, such as a stadium or dorm. The team should choose the location and the mode(s) of transportation involved. Be creative—brainstorm the best ways to guide first-time visitors to the selected location using all the media at your disposal.

2.13. Interpersonal Communication: Listening Actively [LO-5] For the next several days, take notes on your listening performance during at least a half-dozen situations in class, during social activities, and at work, if applicable. Referring to the traits of effective listeners in Table 2.3, rate yourself using *always, frequently, occasionally,* or *never* on these positive listening habits. In a report no longer than one page, summarize your analysis and identify specific areas in which you can improve your listening skills.

2.14. Nonverbal Communication: Analyzing Nonverbal Signals [LO-6] Select a business letter and envelope you

have received at work or home. Analyze their appearance. What nonverbal messages do they send? Are these messages consistent with the content of the letter? If not, what could the sender have done to make the nonverbal communication consistent with the verbal communication? Summarize your findings in a post on your class blog or in an email message to your instructor.

2.15. Communication Etiquette: Etiquette in the Workplace [LO-7] As the regional manager of an international accounting firm, you place high priority on professional etiquette. Not only does it communicate respect to your clients, it also instills confidence in your firm by showing that you and your staff are aware of and able to meet the expectations of almost any audience. Earlier today, you took four recently hired college graduates to lunch with an important client. You've done this for years, and it's usually an upbeat experience for everyone, but today's lunch was a disaster. One of the new employees made not one, not two, but three calls on his mobile phone during lunch. Another interrupted the client several times and even got into a mild argument. The third employee kept making sarcastic jokes about politics, making everyone at the table uncomfortable. And the fourth showed up dressed like she was expecting to bale hay or work in a coal mine, not have a business lunch in a posh restaurant. You've already called the client to apologize, but now you need to coach these employees on proper business etiquette. Draft a brief memo to these employees, explaining why etiquette is so important to the company's success—and to their individual careers.

Expand Your Skills

Critique the Professionals

Celebrities can learn from successful businesses when it comes to managing their careers, but businesses can learn from successful celebrities, too—particularly when it comes to building communities online using social media. For instance, social media guru Dan Schawbel cites Vin Diesel, Ashton Kutcher, Lady Gaga, Lenny Kravitz, and Michael Phelps as celebrities who have used Facebook to build their personal brands.[78] Locate three celebrities (musicians, actors, authors, or athletes) who have sizable fan bases on Facebook and analyze how they use the social network. Using whatever medium your instructor requests, write a brief analysis (no more than one page) of the lessons, positive or negative, that a business could learn from these celebrities. Be sure to cite specific elements from the Facebook pages you've chosen, and if you think any of the celebrities have made mistakes in their use of Facebook, describe those as well.

Sharpening Your Career Skills Online

Bovée and Thill's Business Communication Web Search, at http://websearch.businesscommunicationnetwork.com, is a unique research tool designed specifically for business communication research. Use the Web Search function to find a website, video, PDF document, podcast, or presentation that offers advice on improving your active listening skills in business situations. Write a brief email message to your instructor, describing the item you found and summarizing the career skills information you learned from it.

Improve Your Grammar, Mechanics, and Usage

The following exercises help you improve your knowledge of and power over English grammar, mechanics, and usage. Turn to the Handbook of Grammar, Mechanics, and Usage at the end of this book and review all of Section 1.2 (Pronouns). Then look at the following 10 items. Underline the preferred choice within each set of parentheses. (Answers to these exercises appear on page 601.)

2.16. The sales staff is preparing guidelines for (*their, its*) clients.

2.17. Few of the sales representatives turn in (*their, its*) reports on time.

2.18. The board of directors has chosen (*their, its*) officers.

2.19. Gomez and Archer have told (*his, their*) clients about the new program.

2.20. Each manager plans to expand (*his, their, his or her*) sphere of control next year.

2.21. Has everyone supplied (*his, their, his or her*) Social Security number?

2.22. After giving every employee (*his, their, a*) raise, George told (*them, they, all*) about the increased work load.

2.23. Bob and Tim have opposite ideas about how to achieve company goals. (*Who, Whom*) do you think will win the debate?

2.24. City Securities has just announced (*who, whom*) it will hire as CEO.

2.25. Either of the new products would readily find (*their, its*) niche in the marketplace.

For additional exercises focusing on pronouns, visit MyBCommLab. Click on Chapter 2, click on Additional Exercises to Improve Your Grammar, Mechanics, and Usage, and then click on 3. Case of pronouns and 4. Possessive pronouns.

MyBCommLab

Go to the Assignments section of your MyLab to complete these writing exercises.

2.26 As a team or department leader, what steps can you take to ensure that your meetings are successful and efficient? [LO-3]

2.27 Considering what you've learned about nonverbal communication, what are some of the ways in which communication might break down during an online meeting in which the participants can see video images of only the person presenting at any given time—and then only his or her head? [LO-6]

Endnotes

1. "Company Profile," Cemex website, accessed 8 February 2015, www.cemex.com; "What Is Shift," Cemex website, accessed 8 February 2015, www.cemex.com; *Cemex: Building the Future*, accessed 11 May 2013, www.cemex.com; Cemex Shift Twitter account, https://twitter.com/CX_Shift, accessed 11 May 2013; Dion Hinchcliffe, "Social Business Success: CEMEX," *ZDNet*, 1 February 2012, www.zdnet.com; "Cemex and Becoming a Social Business with IBM Software," video embedded in Jesus Gilberto Garcia, Miguel Angel Lozano Martinez, and Arturo San Vicente, "Shift Changes the Way Cemex Works," *Management Exchange*, 15 July 2011, www.managementexchange.com; Debra Donston-Miller, "Social Business Leader Cemex Keeps Ideas Flowing," *InformationWeek*, 6 November 2012, www.informationweek.co.uk.

2. Courtland L. Bovée and John V. Thill, *Business in Action*, 5th ed. (Upper Saddle River, N.J.: Pearson Prentice Hall, 2011), 172.

3. "Five Case Studies on Successful Teams," *HR Focus*, April 2002, 18+.

4. Stephen R. Robbins, *Essentials of Organizational Behavior*, 6th ed. (Upper Saddle River, N.J.: Prentice Hall, 2000), 98.

5. Max Landsberg and Madeline Pfau, "Developing Diversity: Lessons from Top Teams," *Strategy + Business*, Winter 2005, 10–12.

6. "Groups Best at Complex Problems," *Industrial Engineer*, June 2006, 14.

7. Nicola A. Nelson, "Leading Teams," *Defense AT&L*, July–August 2006, 26–29; Larry Cole and Michael Cole, "Why Is the Teamwork Buzz Word Not Working?" *Communication World*, February–March 1999, 29; Patricia Buhler, "Managing in the 90s: Creating Flexibility in Today's Workplace," *Supervision*, January 1997, 241; Allison W. Amason, Allen C. Hochwarter, Wayne A. Thompson, and Kenneth R. Harrison, "Conflict: An Important Dimension in Successful Management Teams," *Organizational Dynamics*, Autumn 1995, 201.

8. Geoffrey Colvin, "Why Dream Teams Fail," *Fortune*, 12 June 2006, 87–92.

9. Vijay Govindarajan and Anil K. Gupta, "Building an Effective Global Business Team," *MIT Sloan Management Review*, Summer 2001, 631.

10. Colvin, "Why Dream Teams Fail," 87–92.

11. Tiziana Casciaro and Miguel Sousa Lobo, "Competent Jerks, Lovable Fools, and the Formation of Social Networks," *Harvard Business Review*, June 2005, 92–99.

12. Stephen P. Robbins and David A. DeCenzo, *Fundamentals of Management*, 4th ed. (Upper Saddle River, N.J.: Prentice Hall, 2004), 266–267; Jerald Greenberg and Robert A. Baron, *Behavior in Organizations*, 8th ed. (Upper Saddle River, N.J.: Prentice Hall, 2003), 279–280.

13. B. Aubrey Fisher, *Small Group Decision Making: Communication and the Group Process*, 2nd ed. (New York: McGraw-Hill, 1980), 145–149; Robbins and De Cenzo, *Fundamentals of Management*, 334–335; Richard L. Daft, *Management*, 6th ed. (Cincinnati: Thomson South-Western, 2003), 602–603.

14. Michael Laff, "Effective Team Building: More Than Just Fun at Work," *Training + Development*, August 2006, 24–35.

15. Claire Sookman, "Building Your Virtual Team," *Network World*, 21 June 2004, 91.

16. Jared Sandberg, "Brainstorming Works Best if People Scramble for Ideas on Their Own," *Wall Street Journal*, 13 June 2006, B1.

17. Mark K. Smith, "Bruce W. Tuckman—Forming, Storming, Norming, and Performing in Groups," Infed.org, accessed 5 July 2005, www.infed.org.

18. Robbins and DeCenzo, *Fundamentals of Management*, 258–259.

19. Daft, *Management*, 609–612.

20. Andy Boynton and Bill Fischer, *Virtuoso Teams: Lessons from Teams That Changed Their Worlds* (Harrow, UK: FT Prentice Hall, 2005), 10.

21. Thomas K. Capozzoli, "Conflict Resolution—A Key Ingredient in Successful Teams," *Supervision*, November 1999, 14–16.

22. Jesse S. Nirenberg, *Getting Through to People* (Paramus, N.J.: Prentice Hall, 1973), 134–142.

23. Nirenberg, *Getting Through to People*, 134–142.

24. Nirenberg, *Getting Through to People*, 134–142.

25. Jon Hanke, "Presenting as a Team," *Presentations*, January 1998, 74–82.

26. William P. Galle Jr., Beverly H. Nelson, Donna W. Luse, and Maurice F. Villere, *Business Communication: A Technology-Based Approach* (Chicago: Irwin, 1996), 260.

27. Mary Beth Debs, "Recent Research on Collaborative Writing in Industry," *Technical Communication*, November 1991, 476–484.

28. Rob Koplowitz, "Building a Collaboration Strategy," *KM World*, November/December 2009, 14–15.

29. Eric Knorr and Galen Gruman, "What Cloud Computing Really Means," *InfoWorld*, 3 May 2012, www.infoworld.com; Lamont Wood, "Cloud Computing Poised to Transform Communication," *LiveScience*, 8 December 2009, www.livescience.com.

30. "How Blue Man Group Gets Creative with Its Social Intranet," Socialtext website, accessed 1 May 2012, www.socialtext.com.

31. Richard McDermott and Douglas Archibald, "Harnessing Your Staff's Informal Networks," *Harvard Business Review*, March 2010, 82–89.

32. Tony Hsieh, "Why I Sold Zappos," *Inc.*, 1 June 2010, www.inc.com.

33. "Adobe Connect Mobile," Adobe website, accessed 27 February 2014, www.adobe.com.

34. Parks Associates, "Mobile Collaborative Communications for Business," white paper, accessed 27 February 2014, www.parksassociates.com.

35. Chuck Williams, *Management*, 2nd ed. (Cincinnati: Thomson South-Western, 2002), 706–707.

36. Ron Ashkenas, "Why We Secretly Love Meetings," *Harvard Business Review* blogs, 5 October 2010, http://blogs.hbr.org.

37. Douglas Kimberly, "Ten Pitfalls of Pitiful Meetings," *Payroll Manager's Report*, January 2010, 1, 11; "Making the Most of Meetings," *Journal of Accountancy*, March 2009, 22.

38. Cyrus Farivar, "How to Run an Effective Meeting," BNET website, accessed 12 August 2008, www.bnet.com.

39. "Better Meetings Benefit Everyone: How to Make Yours More Productive," *Working Communicator Bonus Report*, July 1998, 1.

40. Janine Popick, "Business Meeting Etiquette: 8 Pet Peeves," *Inc.*, 9 April 2012, www.inc.com.

41. "Features Overview," MeetingSense website, accessed 11 May 2013, www.meetingsense.com.

42. Roger O. Crockett, "The 21st Century Meeting," *BusinessWeek*, 26 February 2007, 72–79.

43. Steve Lohr, "As Travel Costs Rise, More Meetings Go Virtual," *New York Times*, 22 July 2008, www.nytimes.com.

44. GoToMeeting website, accessed 3 May 2012, www.gotogmeeting.com; "Unlock the Full Power of the Web Conferencing," CEOworld.biz, 20 November 2007, www.ceoworld.biz.

45. Nick Morgan, "How to Conduct a Virtual Meeting," *Harvard Business Review* blogs, 1 March 2011, http://blogs.hbr.org.

46. "17 Tips for More Productive Conference Calls," AccuConference, accessed 30 January 2008, www.accuconference.com.

47. Judi Brownell, *Listening*, 2nd ed. (Boston: Allyn & Bacon, 2002), 9, 10.

48. Carmine Gallo, "Why Leadership Means Listening," *BusinessWeek*, 31 January 2007, www.businessweek.com.

49. Augusta M. Simon, "Effective Listening: Barriers to Listening in a Diverse Business Environment," *Bulletin of the Association for Business Communication* 54, no. 3 (September 1991): 73–74.

50. Robyn D. Clarke, "Do You Hear What I Hear?" *Black Enterprise*, May 1998, 129.

51. Dennis M. Kratz and Abby Robinson Kratz, *Effective Listening Skills* (New York: McGraw-Hill, 1995), 45–53; J. Michael Sproule, *Communication Today* (Glenview, Ill.: Scott Foresman, 1981), 69.

52. Brownell, *Listening*, 230–231.

53. Kratz and Kratz, *Effective Listening Skills*, 78–79; Sproule, *Communication Today*, 69.

54. Bill Brooks, "The Power of Active Listening," *American Salesman*, June 2003, 12; "Active Listening," Study Guides and Strategies website, accessed 5 February 2005, www.studygs.net.

55. Bob Lamons, "Good Listeners Are Better Communicators," *Marketing News*, 11 September 1995, 13+; Phillip Morgan and H. Kent Baker, "Building a Professional Image: Improving Listening Behavior," *Supervisory Management*, November 1985, 35–36.

56. Clarke, "Do You Hear What I Hear?"; Dot Yandle, "Listening to Understand," *Pryor Report Management Newsletter Supplement* 15, no. 8 (August 1998): 13.

57. Brownell, *Listening*, 14; Kratz and Kratz, *Effective Listening Skills*, 8–9; Sherwyn P. Morreale and Courtland L. Bovée, *Excellence in Public Speaking* (Orlando, Fla.: Harcourt Brace, 1998), 72–76; Lyman K. Steil, Larry L. Barker, and Kittie W. Watson, *Effective Listening: Key to Your Success* (Reading, Mass.: Addison Wesley, 1983), 21–22.

58. Patrick J. Collins, *Say It with Power and Confidence* (Upper Saddle River, N.J.: Prentice Hall, 1997), 40–45.

59. Morreale and Bovée, *Excellence in Public Speaking*, 296.

60. Dale G. Leathers, *Successful Nonverbal Communication: Principles and Applications* (New York: Macmillan, 1986), 19.

61. Gerald H. Graham, Jeanne Unrue, and Paul Jennings, "The Impact of Nonverbal Communication in Organizations: A Survey of Perceptions," *Journal of Business Communication* 28, no. 1 (Winter 1991): 45–62.

62. Danielle S. Urban, "What to Do About 'Body Art' at Work," *Workforce Management*, March 2010, www.workforce.com.

63. Virginia P. Richmond and James C. McCroskey, *Nonverbal Behavior in Interpersonal Relations* (Boston: Allyn & Bacon, 2000), 153–157.

64. Mary Ellen Slayter, "Pamela Meyer on the Science Behind 'Liespotting,'" SmartBlog on Workforce, 14 September 2010, http://smartblogs.com.

65. Slayter, "Pamela Meyer on the Science Behind 'Liespotting.'"

66. Joe Navarro, "Body Language Myths," *Psychology Today*, 25 October 2009, www.psychologytoday.com; Richmond and McCroskey, *Nonverbal Behavior in Interpersonal Relations*, 2–3.

67. John Hollon, "No Tolerance for Jerks," *Workforce Management*, 12 February 2007, 34.

68. Linton Weeks, "Please Read This Story, Thank You," NPR, 14 March 2012, www.npr.org.

69. Alan Cole, "Telephone Etiquette at Work," Work Etiquette website, 14 March 2012, www.worketiquette.co.uk; Alf Nucifora, "Voice Mail Demands Good Etiquette from Both Sides," *Puget Sound Business Journal*, 5–11 September 2003, 24; Ruth Davidhizar and Ruth Shearer, "The Effective Voice Mail Message," *Hospital Material Management Quarterly*, 45–49; "How to Get the Most Out of Voice Mail," *The CPA Journal*, February 2000, 11; Jo Ind, "Hanging on the Telephone," *Birmingham Post*, 28 July 1999, PS10; Larry Barker and Kittie Watson, *Listen Up* (New York: St. Martin's Press, 2000), 64–65; Lin Walker, *Telephone Techniques*, (New York: Amacom, 1998), 46–47; Dorothy Neal, *Telephone Techniques*, 2nd ed. (New York: Glencoe McGraw-Hill, 1998), 31; Jeannie Davis, *Beyond "Hello"* (Aurora, Col.: Now Hear This Inc., 2000), 2–3; "Ten Steps to Caller-Friendly Voice Mail," *Managing Office Technology*, January 1995, 25; Rhonda Finniss, "Voice Mail: Tips for a Positive Impression," *Administrative Assistant's Update*, August 2001, 5.

70. Dana May Casperson, *Power Etiquette: What You Don't Know Can Kill Your Career* (New York: AMACOM, 1999), 10–14; Ellyn Spragins, "Introducing Politeness," *Fortune Small Business*, November 2001, 30.

71. Tanya Mohn, "The Social Graces as a Business Tool," *New York Times*, 10 November 2002, sec. 3, 12.

72. Casperson, *Power Etiquette*, 44–46.

73. "Are You Practicing Proper Social Networking Etiquette?" *Forbes*, 9 October 2009, www.forbes.com; Pete Babb, "The Ten Commandments of Blog and Wiki Etiquette," *InfoWorld*, 28 May 2007, www.infoworld.com; Judith Kallos, "Instant Messaging Etiquette," NetM@nners blog, accessed 3 August 2008, www.netmanners.com; Michael S. Hyatt, "E-Mail Etiquette 101," From Where I Sit blog, 1 July 2007, www.michaelhyatt.com.

74. J. J. McCorvey, "How to Create a Cell Phone Policy," *Inc.*, 10 February 2010, www.inc.com.

75. Chad Brooks, "Poor Mobile Manners Not Lost on Bosses," Fox Business, 29 October 2013, http://smallbusiness.foxbusiness.com.

76. Nick Wingfield, "Oh, for the Good Old Days of Rude Cellphone Gabbers," *New York Times*, 2 December 2011, www.nytimes.com.

77. Cromwell Schubarth, "VC Ben Horowitz on What He Wants in a Startup and Why Rap Genius Is It," *Silicon Valley Business Journal*, 4 February 2014, www.bizjournals.com.

78. Dan Schawbel, "5 Lessons Celebrities Can Teach Us About Facebook Pages," Mashable, 15 May 2009, http://mashable.com.

LEARNING OBJECTIVES

After studying this chapter, you will be able to

1 Discuss the opportunities and challenges of intercultural communication.

2 Define *culture*, explain how culture is learned, and define *ethnocentrism* and *stereotyping*.

3 Explain the importance of recognizing cultural variations, and list eight categories of cultural differences.

4 List four general guidelines for adapting to any business culture.

5 Identify seven steps you can take to improve your intercultural communication skills.

ON THE JOB: COMMUNICATING AT

EY

Listening, Learning, and Leveraging the Power of Diversity

With 167,000 employees spread across 140 countries, the member firms of the global professional services organization EY have deep experience with the rewards and challenges of intercultural communication. With business operations in virtually every corner of the world, the organization's ability to communicate across cultures is vital to its success.

Huntstock/Disability Images/Alamy

Working with colleagues and customers from diverse backgrounds and life experiences can present new communication challenges.

As you'll read in this chapter, cultural background influences almost every aspect of communication, and cultural differences are among the most common barriers to successful communication. However, those differences can also enrich communication, decision making, and other aspects of business by bringing a broader range of perspectives and experiences to the table. Guiding the communication process in ways that minimize the barriers and maximize the benefits is one of the most important tasks for every business manager.

The keys are recognizing and appreciating the diversity of today's workforces and making sure all those diverse voices have the opportunity to be heard. Karyn Twaronite, Americas Inclusive Officer, who oversees the EY organization's diversity and inclusiveness strategies in North and South America, puts it this way: "Diversity and inclusiveness are not an appendage to our business strategy—both are central to the success of our people and our markets. All of our people bring diverse talents we can leverage, so we expect, reinforce, and reward inclusive leadership. Differences matter in our business and make us better."

EY has taken numerous steps to make its member firm leaders understand their diverse workforces and incorporate EY viewpoints into strategic planning and day-to-day business operations. Soon after she moved into her current role, for example, Twaronite went on a "listening tour" of EY member firm offices in nearly 20 cities, from São Paulo to Mexico City, to hear what made the EY employees feel included or excluded, how their team leaders factored into their feelings, and if they felt they could bring their "whole selves" to work.

In addition to giving employees a voice, Ernst & Young LLP, the U.S. unit of the global EY organization, also encourages collaboration and support through a variety of professional networks throughout the company. These include networks for women; working parents; veterans; people with differing abilities; lesbian, gay, bisexual, and transgender (LGBT) professionals; and members of specific ethnic groups. In addition to offering employees a sense of belonging, the networks aid in mentoring, recruiting, and fostering positive relationships with various external stakeholder groups, as well as helping the U.S. firm's people connect with their colleagues, clients, and communities. And in the spirit of inclusiveness, these networks are open to any employee or manager with an interest in the needs and perspectives of a particular employee community.

EY's proactive approach to diversity and inclusiveness pays off in multiple ways, from bottom-line profits to high levels of employee satisfaction and engagement. For example, Ernst & Young LLP was among *Fortune* magazine's "100 Best Companies to Work For" for the 15th consecutive year in 2013, and *DiversityInc* ranked the firm fourth on the "2013 DiversityInc Top 50 Companies for Diversity" list, marking the fifth consecutive year the firm appeared in the top 10. *DiversityInc* also frequently spotlights Ernst & Young LLP as one of the best places to work for women, people with disabilities, and LGBT employees.[1]

WWW.EY.COM

Understanding the Opportunities and Challenges of Communication in a Diverse World

1 LEARNING OBJECTIVE
Discuss the opportunities and challenges of intercultural communication.

EY (profiled in the chapter-opening On the Job) illustrates the opportunities and the challenges for business professionals who know how to communicate with diverse audiences. Although the concept is often framed in terms of ethnic background, a broader and more useful definition of **diversity** includes "all the characteristics and experiences that define each of us as individuals."[2] As one example, the pharmaceutical company Merck identifies 19 separate dimensions of diversity, including race, age, military experience, parental status, marital status, and thinking style.[3] As you'll learn in this chapter, these characteristics and experiences can have a profound effect on the way businesspeople communicate.

Diversity includes all the characteristics that define people as individuals.

Intercultural communication is the process of sending and receiving messages between people whose cultural backgrounds could lead them to interpret verbal and nonverbal signs differently. Every attempt to send and receive messages is influenced by culture, so to communicate successfully, you need a basic grasp of the cultural differences you may encounter and how you should handle them. Your efforts to recognize and bridge cultural differences will open up business opportunities throughout the world and maximize the contributions of all the employees in a diverse workforce.

MOBILE APP
The Diversity Now app serves up the latest news and insights in the field of diversity.

THE OPPORTUNITIES IN A GLOBAL MARKETPLACE

Chances are good that you'll be working across international borders sometime in your career. Thanks to communication and transportation technologies, natural boundaries and national borders are no longer the impassable barriers they once were. Local markets

You will communicate with people from other cultures throughout your career.

are opening to worldwide competition as businesses of all sizes look for new growth opportunities outside their own countries. Thousands of U.S. businesses depend on exports for significant portions of their revenues. Every year, these companies export hundreds of billions of dollars worth of materials and merchandise, along with billions more in personal and professional services. If you work in one of these companies, you may well be called on to visit or at least communicate with a wide variety of people who speak languages other than English and who live in cultures quite different from what you're used to. Of the top 10 export markets for U.S. products, only Canada and Great Britain have English as an official language; Canada also has French as an official language.[4]

Not surprisingly, effective communication is important to cross-cultural and global business. In a recent survey, nearly 90 percent of executives said their companies' profits, revenue, and market share would all improve with better international communication skills. In addition, half of these executives said communication or collaboration breakdowns had affected major international business efforts in their companies.[5] The good news here is that improving your cultural communication skills could make you a more valuable job candidate at every stage of your career.

THE ADVANTAGES OF A DIVERSE WORKFORCE

The diversity of today's workforce brings distinct advantages to businesses:

- *A broader range of views and ideas*
- *A better understanding of diverse, fragmented markets*
- *A broader pool of talent from which to recruit*

Even if you never visit another country or transact business on a global scale, you will interact with colleagues from a variety of cultures, with a wide range of characteristics and life experiences. Over the past few decades, many innovative companies have changed the way they approach diversity, from seeing it as a legal requirement (providing equal opportunities for all) to seeing it as a strategic opportunity to connect with customers and take advantage of the broadest possible pool of talent.[6] Smart business leaders recognize the competitive advantages of a diverse workforce that offers a broader spectrum of viewpoints and ideas, helps businesses understand and identify with diverse markets, and enables companies to benefit from a wider range of employee talents. "It just makes good business sense," says Gord Nixon, CEO of Royal Bank of Canada.[7]

Diversity is simply a fact of life for all companies. The United States has been a nation of immigrants from the beginning, and that trend continues today. The western and northern Europeans who made up the bulk of immigrants during the nation's early years now share space with people from across Asia, Africa, Eastern Europe, and other parts of the world. Across the United States, the term *minority*, as it is traditionally applied to nonwhite residents, makes less and less sense every year. Caucasian Americans make up less than half the population in a growing number of cities and counties and in two or three decades will make up less than half of the overall U.S. population.[8]

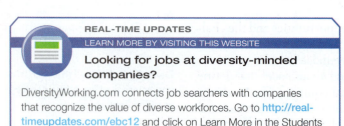

REAL-TIME UPDATES

LEARN MORE BY VISITING THIS WEBSITE

Looking for jobs at diversity-minded companies?

DiversityWorking.com connects job searchers with companies that recognize the value of diverse workforces. Go to http://real-timeupdates.com/ebc12 and click on Learn More in the Students section.

However, you and your colleagues don't need to be recent immigrants to constitute a diverse workforce. Differences in everything from age and gender to religion and ethnic heritage to geography and military experience enrich the workplace. Immigration and workforce diversity create advantages—and challenges—for business communicators throughout the world.

THE CHALLENGES OF INTERCULTURAL COMMUNICATION

Today's increasingly diverse workforce encompasses a wide range of skills, traditions, backgrounds, experiences, outlooks, and attitudes toward work—all of which can affect communication in the workplace. Supervisors face the challenge of connecting with these diverse employees, motivating them, and fostering cooperation and harmony among them. Teams face the challenge of working together closely, and companies are challenged to coexist peacefully with business partners and with the community as a whole.

A company's cultural diversity affects how its business messages are conceived, composed, delivered, received, and interpreted.

The interaction of culture and communication is so pervasive that separating the two is virtually impossible. The way you communicate is deeply influenced by the culture in which you were raised. The meaning of words, the significance of gestures, the importance of time and space, the rules of human relationships—these and many other aspects of communication are defined by culture. To a large degree, your culture influences the way you think, which naturally affects the way you communicate as both a sender and a receiver.[9] Intercultural communication is much more complicated than simply matching language between sender and receiver; it goes beyond mere words to beliefs, values, and emotions.

Elements of human diversity can affect communication at every stage of the communication process, from the ideas a person deems important enough to share to the habits and expectations of giving feedback. In particular, your instinct is to encode your message using the assumptions of *your* culture. However, members of your audience decode your message according to the assumptions of *their* culture. The greater the difference between cultures, the greater the chance for misunderstanding.[10]

Throughout this chapter, you'll see examples of how communication styles and habits vary from one culture to another. These examples are intended to illustrate the major themes of intercultural communication, not to give an exhaustive list of styles and habits of any particular culture. With an understanding of these major themes, you'll be prepared to explore the specifics of any culture.

Culture influences everything about communication, including
- Language
- Nonverbal signals
- Word meaning
- Time and space issues
- Rules of human relationships

REAL-TIME UPDATES
LEARN MORE BY EXPLORING THIS INTERACTIVE WEBSITE
Take a closer look at how the United States is changing

The U.S. population is aging and becoming more diverse; dive into the details with this interactive presentation. Go to http://real-timeupdates.com/ebc12 and click on Learn More in the Students section.

Developing Cultural Competency

Cultural competency includes an appreciation for cultural differences that affect communication and the ability to adjust one's communication style to ensure that efforts to send and receive messages across cultural boundaries are successful. In other words, it requires a combination of attitude, knowledge, and skills.[11]

The good news is that you're already an expert in culture, at least in the culture in which you grew up. You understand how your society works, how people are expected to communicate, what common gestures and facial expressions mean, and so on. The bad news is that because you're such an expert in your own culture, your communication is largely automatic; that is, you rarely stop to think about the communication rules you're following. An important step toward successful intercultural communication is becoming more aware of these rules and of the way they influence your communication.

2 LEARNING OBJECTIVE
Define *culture*, explain how culture is learned, and define *ethnocentrism* and *stereotyping*.

Cultural competency requires a combination of attitude, knowledge, and skills.

UNDERSTANDING THE CONCEPT OF CULTURE

Culture is a shared system of symbols, beliefs, attitudes, values, expectations, and norms for behavior. Your cultural background influences the way you prioritize what is important in life, helps define your attitude toward what is appropriate in a situation, and establishes rules of behavior.[12]

Actually, you belong to several cultures. In addition to the culture you share with all the people who live in your own country, you belong to other cultural groups, including an ethnic group, possibly a religious group, and perhaps a profession that has its own special language and customs. With its large population and long history of immigration, the United States is home to a vast array of cultures. As one indication of this diversity, the inhabitants of this country now speak more than 170 languages (see Figure 3.1 on the following page).[13] In contrast, Japan is much more homogeneous, having only a few distinct cultural groups.[14]

Members of a given culture tend to have similar assumptions about how people should think, behave, and communicate, and they all tend to act on those assumptions in much the same way. Cultures can vary in their rate of change, degree of complexity, and tolerance toward outsiders. These differences affect the level of trust and openness you can achieve when communicating with people of other cultures.

People learn culture directly and indirectly from other members of their group. As you grow up in a culture, you are taught by the group's members who you are and how best to function in that culture. Sometimes you are explicitly told which behaviors are acceptable;

Culture is a shared system of symbols, beliefs, attitudes, values, expectations, and behavior norms.

You belong to several cultures, each of which affects the way you communicate.

You learn culture both directly (by being instructed) and indirectly (by observing others).

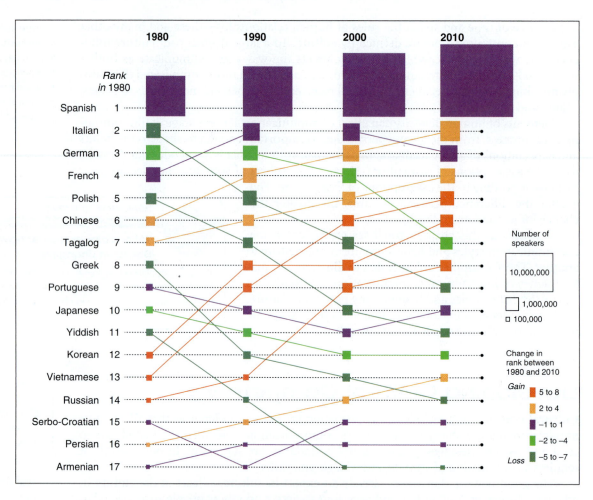

Figure 3.1   Language Diversity in the United States
Language is one of the distinguishing factors of population diversity. This chart shows the trend in relative ranking of languages other than English spoken in the United States since 1980.
Source: "Top Languages Other than English Spoken in 1980 and Changes in Relative Rank, 1990-2010," U.S. Census Bureau, accessed 17 March 2014, www.census.gov.

Cultures tend to offer views of life that are both coherent (internally logical) and complete (able to answer all of life's big questions).

at other times you learn by observing which values work best in a particular group. In these ways, culture is passed on from person to person and from generation to generation.[15]

In addition to being automatic, culture tends to be *coherent*; that is, a culture appears to be fairly logical and consistent when viewed from the inside. Certain norms within a culture may not make sense to someone outside the culture, but they probably make sense to those inside. Such coherence generally helps a culture function more smoothly internally, but it can create disharmony between cultures that don't view the world in the same way.

Finally, cultures tend to be complete; that is, they provide their members with most of the answers to life's big questions. This idea of completeness dulls or even suppresses curiosity about life in other cultures. Not surprisingly, such completeness can complicate communication with other cultures.[16]

OVERCOMING ETHNOCENTRISM AND STEREOTYPING

Ethnocentrism is the tendency to judge all other groups according to the standards, behaviors, and customs of one's own group.

Ethnocentrism is the tendency to judge other groups according to the standards, behaviors, and customs of one's own group. Given the automatic influence of one's own culture, when people compare their culture to others, they often conclude that their own is superior.[17] An even more extreme reaction is **xenophobia**, a fear of strangers and foreigners. Clearly, businesspeople who take these views are not likely to communicate successfully across cultures.

Distorted views of other cultures or groups also result from **stereotyping**, assigning a wide range of generalized attributes to an individual on the basis of membership in a particular culture or social group. For instance, assuming that an older colleague will be out of touch with the youth market or that a younger colleague can't be an inspiring leader would be stereotyping age groups.

Those who want to show respect for others and to communicate effectively in business need to adopt a more positive viewpoint, in the form of **cultural pluralism**—the practice of accepting multiple cultures on their own terms. When crossing cultural boundaries, you'll be even more effective if you move beyond simple acceptance and adapt your communication style to that of the new cultures you encounter—even integrating aspects of those cultures into your own.[18] A few simple habits can help:

- **Avoid assumptions.** Don't assume that others will act the same way you do, use language and symbols the same way you do, or even operate from the same values and beliefs. For instance, in a comparison of the 10 most important values in three cultures, people from the United States had *no* values in common with people from Japanese or Arab cultures.[19]
- **Avoid judgments.** When people act differently, don't conclude that they are in error or that their way is invalid or inferior.
- **Acknowledge distinctions.** Don't ignore the differences between another person's culture and your own.

Unfortunately, overcoming ethnocentrism and stereotyping is not a simple task, even for people who are highly motivated to do so. Moreover, research suggests that people often have beliefs and biases that they're not even aware of—and that may even conflict with the beliefs they *think* they have.[20]

Recognizing Variations in a Diverse World

You can begin to learn how people in other cultures want to be treated by recognizing and accommodating eight main types of cultural differences: contextual, legal and ethical, social, nonverbal, age, gender, religious, and ability.

CONTEXTUAL DIFFERENCES

Every attempt at communication occurs within a **cultural context**, which is the pattern of physical cues, environmental stimuli, and implicit understanding that convey meaning between two members of the same culture. However, cultures around the world vary widely in the role that context plays in communication.

In a **high-context culture**, people rely less on verbal communication and more on the context of nonverbal actions and environmental setting to convey meaning. For instance, a Chinese speaker expects the receiver to discover the essence of a message and uses indirectness and metaphor to provide a web of meaning.[21] The indirect style can be a source of confusion during discussions with people from low-context cultures, who are more accustomed to receiving direct answers. Also, in high-context cultures, the rules of everyday life are rarely explicit; instead, as individuals grow up, they learn how to recognize situational cues (such as gestures and tone of voice) and how to respond as expected.[22] The primary role of communication in high-context cultures is building relationships, not exchanging information.[23]

In a **low-context culture** such as the United States, people rely more on verbal communication and less on circumstances and cues to convey meaning. In such cultures, rules and expectations are usually spelled out through explicit statements such as "Please wait until I'm finished" or "You're welcome to browse."[24] The primary task of communication in low-context cultures is exchanging information.[25]

Contextual differences are apparent in the way businesspeople approach situations such as decision making, problem solving, negotiating, interacting among levels in the organizational hierarchy, and socializing outside the workplace.[26] For instance, in low-context

---

Margin notes:

Stereotyping is assigning generalized attributes to an individual on the basis of membership in a particular group.

Cultural pluralism is the acceptance of multiple cultures on their own terms.

You can avoid ethnocentrism and stereotyping by avoiding assumptions and judgments and by accepting differences.

3 LEARNING OBJECTIVE Explain the importance of recognizing cultural variations, and list eight categories of cultural differences.

Cultural context is the pattern of physical cues, environmental stimuli, and implicit understanding that conveys meaning between members of the same culture.

High-context cultures rely heavily on nonverbal actions and environmental setting to convey meaning; low-context cultures rely more on explicit verbal communication.

cultures, businesspeople tend to focus on the results of the decisions they face, a reflection of the cultural emphasis on logic and progress (for example, "Will this be good for our company? For my career?"). In comparison, higher-context cultures emphasize the means or the method by which a decision will be made. Building or protecting relationships can be as important as the facts and information used in making the decisions.[27] Consequently, negotiators working on business deals in such cultures may spend most of their time together building relationships rather than hammering out contractual details.

The distinctions between high and low context are generalizations, of course, but they are important to keep in mind as guidelines. Communication tactics that work well in a high-context culture may backfire in a low-context culture, and vice versa.

LEGAL AND ETHICAL DIFFERENCES

Cultural context influences legal and ethical behavior, which in turn can affect communication. For example, the meaning of business contracts can vary from culture to culture. Whereas a manager from a U.S. company would tend to view a signed contract as the end of the negotiating process, with all the details resolved, his or her counterpart in many Asian cultures might view the signed contract as an agreement to do business—and only then begin to negotiate the details of the deal.[28]

As you conduct business around the world, you'll find that both legal systems and ethical standards differ from culture to culture. Making ethical choices across cultures can seem complicated, but you can keep your messages ethical by applying four basic principles:[29]

Honesty and respect are cornerstones of ethical communication, regardless of culture.

- **Actively seek mutual ground.** To allow the clearest possible exchange of information, both parties must be flexible and avoid insisting that an interaction take place strictly in terms of one culture or another.
- **Send and receive messages without judgment.** To allow information to flow freely, both parties must recognize that values vary from culture to culture, and they must trust each other.
- **Send messages that are honest.** To ensure that information is true, both parties must see things as they are—not as they would like them to be. Both parties must be fully aware of their personal and cultural biases.
- **Show respect for cultural differences.** To protect the basic human rights of both parties, each must understand and acknowledge the other's needs and preserve each other's dignity by communicating without deception.

SOCIAL DIFFERENCES

Formal rules of etiquette are explicit and well defined, but informal rules are learned through observation and imitation.

The nature of social behavior varies among cultures, sometimes dramatically. Some behavioral rules are formal and specifically articulated (table manners are a good example), whereas others are informal and learned over time (such as the comfortable distance to stand from a colleague during a discussion). The combination of formal and informal rules influences the overall behavior of most people in a society most of the time. In addition to the factors already discussed, social norms can vary from culture to culture in the following areas:

- **Attitudes toward work and success.** In the United States, for instance, a widespread view is that material comfort earned by individual effort is a sign of superiority and that people who work hard are better than those who don't.
- **Roles and status.** Culture influences the roles people play, including who communicates with whom, what they communicate, and in what way. For example, in some

countries women still don't play a prominent role in business, so women executives who visit these countries may find they're not taken seriously as businesspeople.[30] Culture also dictates how people show respect and signify rank. For example, people in the United States show respect by addressing top managers as "Mr. Roberts" or "Ms. Gutierrez." However, people in China are addressed according to their official titles, such as "President" or "Manager."[31]

> Respect and rank are reflected differently from culture to culture in the way people are addressed and in their working environment.

- **Use of manners.** What is polite in one culture may be considered rude in another. For instance, asking a colleague "How was your weekend?" is a common way of making small talk in the United States, but the question sounds intrusive to people in cultures in which business and private lives are seen as separate spheres.

> The rules of polite behavior vary from country to country.

- **Concepts of time.** People in low-context cultures see time as a way to plan the business day efficiently, often focusing on only one task during each scheduled period and viewing time as a limited resource. However, executives from high-context cultures often see time as more flexible. Meeting a deadline is less important than building a business relationship.[32]

> Attitudes toward time, such as strict adherence to meeting schedules, can vary throughout the world.

- **Future orientation.** Successful companies tend to have a strong *future orientation*, planning for and investing in the future, but national cultures around the world vary widely in this viewpoint. Some societies encourage a long-term outlook that emphasizes planning and investing—making sacrifices in the short term for the promise of better outcomes in the future. Others are oriented more toward the present, even to the point of viewing the future as hopelessly remote and not worth planning for.[33]

- **Openness and inclusiveness.** At the national level as well as within smaller groups, cultures vary on how open they are to accepting people from other cultures and people who don't necessarily fit the prevailing norms within the culture. An unwillingness to accommodate others can range from outright exclusion to subtle pressures to conform to majority expectations.

> Cultures around the world exhibit varying degrees of openness toward both outsiders and people whose personal identities don't align with prevailing social norms.

- **Use of communication technologies.** Don't assume that colleagues and customers around the world use the same communication tools you use. For example, although mobile phone usage is high in most countries around the world, the percentage of users with smartphones and the broadband service required for communication services such as video varies widely.[34]

NONVERBAL DIFFERENCES

As discussed in Chapter 2, nonverbal communication can be a helpful guide to determining the meaning of a message—but this situation holds true only if the sender and receiver assign the same meaning to nonverbal signals. For instance, the simplest hand gestures have different meanings in different cultures. A gesture that communicates good luck in Brazil is the equivalent of giving someone "the finger" in Colombia.[35] Don't assume that the gestures you grew up with will translate to another culture; doing so could lead to embarrassing mistakes.

> The meaning of nonverbal signals can vary widely from culture to culture, so you can't rely on assumptions.

When you have the opportunity to interact with people in another culture, the best advice is to study the culture in advance and then observe the way people behave in the following areas:

- **Greetings.** Do people shake hands, bow, or kiss lightly (on one side of the face or both)? Do people shake hands only when first introduced or every time they say hello or goodbye?

- **Personal space.** When people are conversing, do they stand closer together or farther away than you are accustomed to?

- **Touching.** Do people touch each other on the arm to emphasize a point or slap each other on the back to show congratulations? Or do they refrain from touching altogether?

REAL-TIME UPDATES

LEARN MORE BY VIEWING THIS INFOGRAPHIC

Seven common hand gestures that will stir up trouble in other cultures

Find out what gestures that have positive meanings in the United States can have intensively negative meanings in other cultures. Go to http://real-timeupdates.com/ebc12 and click on Learn More in the Students section.

- **Facial expressions.** Do people shake their heads to indicate "no" and nod them to indicate "yes"? This is what people are accustomed to in the United States, but it is not universal.
- **Eye contact.** Do people make frequent eye contact or avoid it? Frequent eye contact is often taken as a sign of honesty and openness in the United States, but in other cultures it can be a sign of aggressiveness or disrespect.
- **Posture.** Do people slouch and relax in the office and in public, or do they sit up and stand up straight?
- **Formality.** In general, does the culture seem more or less formal than yours?

Following the lead of people who grew up in the culture is not only a great way to learn but a good way to show respect as well.

AGE DIFFERENCES

A culture's views on youth and aging affect how people communicate with one another.

In U.S. culture, youth is often associated with strength, energy, possibilities, and freedom, and age is sometimes associated with declining powers and the inability to keep pace. However, older workers can offer broader experience, the benefits of important business relationships nurtured over many years, and high degrees of "practical intelligence"—the ability to solve complex, poorly defined problems.[36]

In contrast, in cultures that value age and seniority, longevity earns respect and increasing power and freedom. For instance, in many Asian societies, the oldest employees hold the most powerful jobs, the most impressive titles, and the greatest degrees of freedom and decision-making authority. If a younger employee disagrees with one of these senior executives, the discussion is never conducted in public. The notion of "saving face"—avoiding public embarrassment—is too strong. Instead, if a senior person seems to be in error about something, other employees will find a quiet, private way to communicate whatever information they feel is necessary.[37]

The multiple generations within a culture present another dimension of diversity. Today's workplaces can have three or even four generations working side by side. Each has been shaped by dramatically different world events, social trends, and technological advances, so it is not surprising that they often have different values, expectations, and communication habits. For instance, Generation Y workers (see "Us Versus Them: Generational Conflict in the Workplace") have a strong preference for communicating via short electronic messages, but Baby Boomers and Generation Xers sometimes find these brief messages abrupt and impersonal.[38]

GENDER DIFFERENCES

Gender influences workplace communication in several important ways. First, the perception of men and women in business varies from culture to culture, and gender bias can range from overt discrimination to subtle and even unconscious beliefs.

Second, although the ratio of men and women in entry-level professional positions is roughly equal, the percentage of management roles held by men increases steadily the further one looks up the corporate ladder. This imbalance can significantly affect communication in such areas as mentoring, which is a vital development opportunity for lower and middle managers who want to move into senior positions. In one recent survey, for example, some men in executive positions expressed reluctance to mentor women, partly because they find it easier to bond with other men and partly out of concerns over developing relationships that might look inappropriate.[39]

Broadly speaking, men tend to emphasize content in their messages, whereas women tend to emphasize relationship maintenance.

Third, evidence suggests that men and women tend to have somewhat different communication styles. Broadly speaking, men emphasize content and outcomes in their communication efforts, whereas women place a higher premium on relationship maintenance.[40] As one example, men are more likely than women to try to negotiate a pay raise. Moreover, according to research by Linda Babcock of Carnegie Mellon University, both men and women tend to accept this disparity, viewing assertiveness as a positive quality in men but a negative quality in women. Changing these perceptions could go a long way toward improving communication and equity in the workplace.[41]

COMMUNICATING ACROSS CULTURES

Us Versus Them: Generational Conflict in the Workplace

The way people view the world as adults is profoundly shaped by the social and technological trends they experienced while growing up, so it's no surprise that each generation entering the workforce has a different perspective than the generations already at work. Throw in the human tendencies to resist change and to assume that whatever way one is doing something must be the best way to do it, and you have a recipe for conflict. Moreover, generations in a workplace sometimes feel themselves competing for jobs, resources, influence, and control. The result can be tension, mistrust, and communication breakdowns.

Lumping people into generations is an imprecise science at best, but it helps to know the labels commonly applied to various age groups and to have some idea of their broad characteristics. These labels are not official, and there is no general agreement on when some generations start and end, but you will see and hear references to the following groups (approximate years of birth shown in parentheses):

- **The Radio Generation (1925 to 1945).** People in this group are beyond what was once considered the traditional retirement age of 65, but some want or need to continue working.
- **Baby Boomers (1946 to 1964).** This large segment of the workforce, which now occupies many mid- and upper-level managerial positions, got its name from the population boom in the years following World War II. The older members of this generation are now reaching retirement age, but many will continue to work beyond age 65—meaning that younger workers waiting for some of these management spots to open up might have to wait a while longer.
- **Generation X (1965 to 1980).** This relatively smaller "MTV generation" is responsible for many of the innovations that have shaped communication habits today but sometimes feels caught between the large mass of baby boomers ahead of them and the younger Generation Y employees entering the workforce. When Generation X does finally get the chance to take over starting in 2015 or 2020, it will be managing in a vastly different business

landscape, one in which virtual organizations and networks of independent contractors replace much of the hierarchy inherited from the baby boomers.
- **Generation Y (1981 to 1995).** Also known as *millennials*, this youngest generation currently in the workforce is noted for its entrepreneurial instincts and technological savvy. This generation's comfort level with social media and other communication technologies is helping to change business communication practices but is also a source of concern for managers worried about information leaks and employee productivity.
- **Generation Z (after 1996).** If you're a member of Generation Y, those footsteps you hear behind you are coming from Generation Z, also known as *Generation I* (for Internet) or the *Net Generation*. The first full generation to be born after the World Wide Web was invented will be entering the workforce soon.

These brief summaries can hardly do justice to entire generations of workers, but they give you some idea of the different generational perspectives and the potential for communication problems. As with all cultural conflicts, successful communication starts with recognizing and understanding these differences.

CAREER APPLICATIONS

1. How would you resolve a conflict between a Baby Boomer manager who worries about the privacy and productivity aspects of social networking and a Generation Y employee who wants to use these tools on the job?
2. Consider the range of labels from the Radio Generation to the Net Generation. What does this tell you about the possible influence of technology on business communication habits?

Sources: Anne Fisher, "When Gen X Runs the Show," *Time*, 14 May 2009, www .time.com; Deloitte, "Generation Y: Powerhouse of the Global Economy," research report, 2009, www.deloitte.com; "Generation Y," Nightly Business Report website, 30 June 2010, www.pbs.org; Sherry Posnick-Goodwin, "Meet Generation Z," *California Educator*, February 2010, www.cta.org; Ernie Stark, "Lost in a Time Warp," *People & Strategy* 32 no. 4 (2009): 58–64.

RELIGIOUS DIFFERENCES

As one of the most personal and influential aspects of life, religion brings potential for controversy and conflict in the workplace setting—as evidenced by a significant rise in the number of religious discrimination lawsuits in recent years.[42] Many employees believe they should be able to follow and express the tenets of their faith in the workplace. However, companies may need to accommodate employee behaviors that can conflict with each other and with the demands of operating the business. The situation is complicated, with no simple answers that apply to every situation. As more companies work to establish inclusive workplaces, you can expect to see this issue being discussed more often in the coming years.

U.S. law requires employers to accommodate employees' religious beliefs to a reasonable degree.

ABILITY DIFFERENCES

Colleagues and customers with disabilities that affect communication represent an important aspect of the diversity picture. People whose hearing, vision, cognitive ability, or physical ability to operate electronic devices is impaired can be at a significant disadvantage in today's workplace. As with other elements of diversity, success starts with respect for individuals and sensitivity to differences.

Employers can also invest in a variety of *assistive technologies* that help people with disabilities perform activities that might otherwise be difficult or impossible. These technologies include devices and systems that help workers communicate orally and visually, interact with computers and other equipment, and enjoy greater mobility in the workplace. For example, designers can emphasize *web accessibility*, taking steps to make websites more accessible to people whose vision is limited. Assistive technologies create a vital link for thousands of employees with disabilities, giving them opportunities to pursue a greater range of career paths and giving employers access to a broader base of talent.[43]

> *Assistive technologies help employers create more inclusive workplaces and benefit from the contribution of people with physical or cognitive impairments.*

Adapting to Other Business Cultures

> **4 LEARNING OBJECTIVE**
> List four general guidelines for adapting to any business culture.

Whether you're trying to work productively with members of another generation in your own office or with a business partner on the other side of the world, adapting your approach is essential to successful communication. This section offers general advice on adapting to any business culture and specific advice for professionals from other cultures on adapting to U.S. business culture.

GUIDELINES FOR ADAPTING TO ANY BUSINESS CULTURE

You'll find a variety of specific tips in "Improving Intercultural Communication Skills," on page 79, but here are four general guidelines that can help all business communicators improve their cultural competency:

> *An important step in understanding and adapting to other cultures is to recognize the influences that your own culture has on your communication habits.*

- **Become aware of your own biases.** Successful intercultural communication requires more than just an understanding of the other party's culture; you need to understand your own culture and the way it shapes your communication habits.[44] For instance, knowing that you value independence and individual accomplishment will help you communicate more successfully in a culture that values consensus and group harmony.
- **Be careful about applying the "Golden Rule."** You probably heard this growing up: "Treat people the way you want to be treated." The problem with the Golden Rule is that other people don't always want to be treated the same way you want to be treated, particularly across cultural boundaries. The best approach: Treat people the way *they* want to be treated.
- **Exercise tolerance, flexibility, and respect.** As IBM's Ron Glover puts it, "To the greatest extent possible, we try to manage our people and our practices in ways that are respectful of the core principles of any given country or organization or culture."[45]
- **Practice patience and maintain a sense of humor.** Even the most committed and attuned business professionals can make mistakes in intercultural communication, so it is vital for all parties to be patient with one another. As business becomes ever more global, even people in the most tradition-bound cultures are learning to deal with outsiders more patiently and overlook occasional cultural blunders.[46] A sense of humor is a helpful asset as well, allowing people to move past awkward and embarrassing moments. When you make a mistake, simply apologize and, if appropriate, ask the other person to explain the accepted way; then move on.

REAL-TIME UPDATES
LEARN MORE BY WATCHING THESE VIDEOS
See what Google employees have to say about diversity
The search giant's YouTube channel features employees talking about their experiences working at Google. Go to http://real-timeupdates.com/ebc12 and click on Learn More in the Students section.

GUIDELINES FOR ADAPTING TO U.S. BUSINESS CULTURE

If you are a recent immigrant to the United States or grew up in a culture outside the U.S. mainstream, you can apply all the concepts and skills in this chapter to help adapt to U.S. business culture. Here are some key points to remember as you become accustomed to business communication in this country:[47]

- **Individualism,** In contrast to cultures that value group harmony and group success, U.S. culture generally expects individuals to succeed by their own efforts, and it rewards individual success. Even though teamwork is emphasized in many companies, competition between individuals is expected and even encouraged in many cases.
- **Equality.** Although the country's historical record on equality has not always been positive and some inequalities still exist, equality is considered a core American value. This principle applies to race, gender, social background, and even age. To a greater degree than people in many other cultures, Americans believe that every person should be given the opportunity to pursue whatever dreams and goals he or she has in life.
- **Privacy and personal space.** Although this appears to be changing somewhat with the popularity of social networking and other personal media, people in the United States are accustomed to a fair amount of privacy. That also applies to their "personal space" at work. For example, they expect you to knock before entering a closed office and to avoid asking questions about personal beliefs or activities until they get to know you well.
- **Time and schedules.** U.S. businesses value punctuality and the efficient use of time. For instance, meetings are expected to start and end at designated times.
- **Religion.** The United States does not have an official state religion. Many religions are practiced throughout the country, and people are expected to respect each other's beliefs.
- **Communication style.** Communication tends to be direct and focused more on content and transactions than on relationships or group harmony.

As with all observations about culture, these are generalizations, of course. Any nation of more than 300 million people will exhibit a wide variety of behaviors. However, following these guidelines will help you succeed in most business communication situations.

The values espoused by American culture include individualism, equality, and privacy.

Improving Intercultural Communication Skills

Communicating successfully between cultures requires a variety of skills (see Figure 3.2 on the next page). You can improve your intercultural skills throughout your career by studying other cultures and languages, respecting preferences for communication styles, learning to write and speak clearly, listening carefully, knowing when to use interpreters and translators, and helping others adapt to your culture.

5 LEARNING OBJECTIVE
Identify seven steps you can take to improve your intercultural communication skills.

STUDYING OTHER CULTURES

Effectively adapting your communication efforts to another culture requires not only knowledge about the culture but also the ability and motivation to change your personal habits as needed.[48] Fortunately, you don't need to learn about the whole world all at once. Many companies appoint specialists for countries or regions, giving employees a chance to focus on just one culture at a time. And if your employer conducts business internationally, it may offer training and support for employees who need to more about specific cultures.

REAL-TIME UPDATES
LEARN MORE BY EXPLORING THIS INTERACTIVE WEBSITE
How are your global travel skills?

Take this quiz to see if you have the knowledge to travel like a pro. Go to http://real-timeupdates.com/ebc12 and click on Learn More in the Students section.

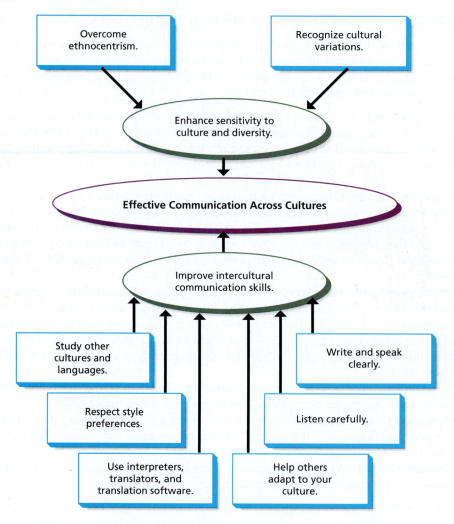

Figure 3.2   Components of Successful Intercultural Communication
Communicating in a diverse business environment is not always an easy task, but you can continue to improve your sensitivity and build your skills as you progress in your career.

Even a small amount of research and practice will help you get through many business situations. In addition, most people respond positively to honest effort and good intentions, and many business associates will help you along if you show an interest in learning more about their cultures. Don't be afraid to ask questions. People will respect your concern and curiosity. You will gradually accumulate considerable knowledge, which will help you feel comfortable and be effective in a wide range of business situations.

Numerous websites and books offer advice on traveling to and working in specific cultures. Also try to sample newspapers, magazines, and even the music and movies of another country. For instance, a movie can demonstrate nonverbal customs even if you don't grasp the language. (However, be careful not to rely solely on entertainment products. If people in other countries based their opinions of U.S. culture only on the silly teen flicks and violent action movies that the United States exports around the globe, what sort of impression do you imagine they'd get?) For some of the key issues to research before doing business in another country, refer to Table 3.1.

STUDYING OTHER LANGUAGES

As commerce continues to become more globalized and many countries become more linguistically diverse, the demand for multilingual communicators continues to grow as

Successful intercultural communication can require the modification of personal communication habits.

TABLE 3.1   Doing Business in Other Cultures

Action	Details to Consider
Understand social customs	• How do people react to strangers? Are they friendly? Hostile? Reserved? • How do people greet each other? Should you bow? Nod? Shake hands? • How do you express appreciation for an invitation to lunch, dinner, or someone's home? Should you bring a gift? Send flowers? Write a thank-you note? • Are any phrases, facial expressions, or hand gestures considered rude? • How do you attract the attention of a waiter? Do you tip the waiter? • When is it rude to refuse an invitation? How do you refuse politely? • What topics may or may not be discussed in a social setting? In a business setting? • How do social customs dictate interaction between men and women? Between younger people and older people?
Learn about clothing and food preferences	• What occasions require special attire? • What colors are associated with mourning? Love? Joy? • Are some types of clothing considered taboo for one gender or the other? • How many times a day do people eat? • How are hands or utensils used when eating? • Where is the seat of honor at a table?
Assess political patterns	• How stable is the political situation? • Does the political situation affect businesses in and out of the country? • Is it appropriate to talk politics in social or business situations?
Understand religious and social beliefs	• To which religious groups do people belong? • Which places, objects, actions, and events are sacred? • Do religious beliefs affect communication between men and women or between any other groups? • Is there a tolerance for minority religions? • How do religious holidays affect business and government activities? • Does religion require or prohibit eating specific foods? At specific times?
Learn about economic and business institutions	• Is the society homogeneous or heterogeneous? • What languages are spoken? • What are the primary resources and principal products? • Are businesses generally large? Family controlled? Government controlled? • What are the generally accepted working hours? • How do people view scheduled appointments? • Are people expected to socialize before conducting business?
Appraise the nature of ethics, values, and laws	• Is money or a gift expected in exchange for arranging business transactions? • Do people value competitiveness or cooperation? • What are the attitudes toward work? Toward money? • Is politeness more important than factual honesty?

well. The ability to communicate in more than one language can make you a more competitive job candidate and open up a wider variety of career opportunities.

Even if your colleagues or customers in another country speak your language, it's worth the time and energy to learn common phrases in theirs. Doing so not only helps you get through everyday business and social situations but also demonstrates your commitment to the business relationship. After all, the other person probably spent years learning your language.

Mobile devices can be a huge help in learning another language and in communicating with someone in another language. A wide variety of apps and websites are available that help with essentials words and phrases, grammar, pronunciation, text translation, and even real-time audio translation (see Figure 3.3 on the next page).

Finally, don't assume that people from two countries who speak the same language speak it the same way. The French spoken in Quebec and other parts of Canada is often noticeably different from the French spoken in France. Similarly, it's often said that the United States and the United Kingdom are two countries divided by a common language. For instance, *period* (punctuation), *elevator,* and *gasoline* in the United States are *full stop, lift,* and *petrol* in the United Kingdom.

Making an effort to learn about another person's culture is a sign of respect.

MOBILE APP

iTranslate translates more than 80 languages and features voice input and output.

English is the most prevalent language in international business, but don't assume that everyone understands it or speaks it the same way.

iTranslateapp.com

Figure 3.3 **Mobile Language Tools**
Translation apps are handy tools for working in multilingual business settings. Even if you don't speak a word of a particular language, you can get fast translations of essential phrases.

RESPECTING PREFERENCES FOR COMMUNICATION STYLE

Communication style—including the level of directness, the degree of formality, media preferences, and other factors—varies widely from culture to culture (see Figures 3.4a through 3.4d). Knowing what your communication partners expect can help you adapt to their particular style. Once again, watching and learning are the best ways to improve your skills. However, you can infer some generalities by learning more about the culture. For instance, U.S. workers typically prefer an open and direct communication style; they find other styles frustrating or suspect. Directness is also valued in Sweden as a sign of efficiency, but heated debates and confrontations are unusual. Italian, German, and French executives usually don't put colleagues at ease with praise before they criticize; doing so seems manipulative to them. Meanwhile, professionals from high-context cultures, such as Japan or China, tend to be less direct.[49] Finally, in general, business correspondence in other countries is often more formal than the style used by U.S. businesspeople.

UpdraftRC
4308 Preston Highway
Louisville, KY 40213
Toll Free: 1.800.FLY.RITE
Fax: (502) 555-1324
www.updraftrc.com

Zhejiang Shan Tou Manufacturing Company, Ltd.
Guoliwei Industry Park
Libang Road, Longgang District
Shenzhen, Guangdong, China

Dear Mr. Li,

My company, Updraft RC, has designed a cool new line of radio-control toys that use smartphones as the controller. We are looking for a manufacturing partner, and your firm is one of the candidates we're having a look at.

> Language such as "cool" and "having a look at" is too informal for external business communication, particularly for international correspondence.

Before we discuss technical details, I must say I have two sets of concerns about working with a foreign manufacturer. The first involves all the usual—transportation costs, delays, quality control, and risk of intellectual property theft. I'll need some assurances on how you address these issues to make sure they don't become problems in our relationship.

> The tone of this paragraph is too demanding.

Second, companies here in the States that use foreign manufacturers often have to deal with heavy news coverage and activist publicity on such matters as workplace safety, worker rights, and environmentally sensitive manufacturing. Even though the U.S. company doesn't directly control what happens in the overseas contract manufacturer, the U.S. company takes the heat when the media uncovers abuse, neglect, pollution, etc. I know that Nike and other U.S. companies have spent millions and worked for years to promote positive conditions in overseas factories, but even these major corporations haven't been able to completely avoid problems and bad press. How can I be sure that a small company such as ours will? I do not want our product launch to get caught up in some scandal over "sweatshops."

> "Here in the States" is too informal, and referring to the reader as "foreign" is potentially insulting.
>
> Inflammatory language as *bad press, scandal,* and *sweatshops* will put the reader on the defensive and discourage a positive response.

I look forward to seeing your comprehensive response as soon as possible.

> The request for a response sounds too demanding, and it lacks a specific deadline.

All the best,

Henry Gatlin

Henry Gatlin
Founder, CEO
Updraft RC

5 August 2016

> The closing is too informal.

Figure 3.4a   Intercultural Business Letter: Ineffective Original Draft
This letter (from a Kentucky company that designs radio-controlled airplanes) exhibits a number of problems that would create difficulties for its intended reader (the manager of a contract manufacturing company in China). Follow the changes in Figures 3.4b, 3.4c, and 3.4d to see how the letter was adapted and then translated for its target audience.

WRITING CLEARLY

Writing clearly is always important, of course, but it is essential when you are writing to people whose first language is not English. Follow these recommendations to make sure your message can be understood:[50]

- **Choose words carefully.** Use precise words that don't have the potential to confuse with multiple meanings. For instance, the word *right* has several dozen different meanings and usages, so look for a synonym that conveys the specific meaning you intend, such as *correct, appropriate, desirable, moral, authentic,* or *privilege.*[51]

> Clarity and simplicity are essential when writing to or speaking with people who don't share your native language.

The salutation should use a colon, not a comma.

The language is still too informal in the opening paragraph.

"Overseas" avoids the negative connotations of "foreign."

Idiomatic phrases such as "come into play" and "minimize the downsides" are vulnerable to mistranslation.

The vaguely accusatory tone of this paragraph assumes that problems will occur, which is likely to offend the reader.

"Mitigating" can be replaced by a more common word.

The request now has a helpful timeline, but the phrasing is still somewhat demanding.

The closing is still too informal.

Zhejiang Shan Tou Manufacturing Company, Ltd.
Guoliwei Industry Park
Libang Road, Longgang District
Shenzhen, Guangdong, China

Dear Mr. Li,

My company, Updraft RC, has designed a cool new line of radio-control toys that use smartphones as the controller. We are looking for a manufacturing partner, and your firm is one of the candidates we're having a look at.

This will be our first experience of partnering with an overseas manufacturer, and before we discuss specific technical details, I'd like to explore two sets of general concerns. The first set of concerns are the issues that might come into play with any manufacturing partnership, but particularly one located at quite some distance from our offices. The particular questions here are transportation costs, delays, quality control, and the risk of intellectual property theft. Can you let me know what practices and policies you have in place to minimize the downsides here?

Second, U.S. companies that work with overseas production partners face an increasing amount of scrutiny from the news media and activist groups regarding such matters as workplace safety, worker rights, and environmentally sensitive manufacturing. We can't directly control what takes place in your factories, of course, but we would have to deal with the public relations fallout if any problems are uncovered in the factories that make our products. The fact that that Nike and other major U.S. companies have spent millions and worked for years to promote positive conditions in overseas factories and still haven't been able to avoid all problems raises concerns for a small company such as ours.

Please share your company's philosophy and strategies for mitigating these concerns.

We would like to commence production in the second quarter of 2017, so a quick reply on your part would be great.

All the best,

Henry Gatlin

Henry Gatlin
Founder, CEO
Updraft RC

5 August 2016

Figure 3.4b   Intercultural Business Letter: First Revision
This version eliminates most of the problems with overly informal phrases and potentially offensive language. With these revisions, it would function well as a message between native speakers of English, but it still has some wording and formatting issues that could create difficulties for a Chinese reader. Compare with Figure 3.4c.

- **Be brief.** Use simple sentences and short paragraphs, breaking information into smaller chunks that are easier for readers to process.
- **Use plenty of transitions.** Help readers follow your train of thought by using transitional words and phrases. For example, tie related points together with expressions such as *in addition* and *first, second,* and *third.*
- **Address international correspondence properly.** Refer to Appendix A for more information.
- **Cite numbers and dates carefully.** In the United States, 12-05-15 means December 5, 2015, but in many other countries, it means May 12, 2015. Dates in Japan and China are usually expressed with the year first, followed by the month and then the day; therefore, to write December 5, 2015, in Japan, write it as 2015-12-05. Similarly, in

UpdraftRC
4308 Preston Highway
Louisville, KY 40213
Toll Free: 1.800.FLY.RITE
Fax: (502) 555-1324
www.updraftrc.com

Dear Mr. Li:

With the widespread adoption of mobile phones, more and more accessories and associated products are being developed to meet new market demands. My company, Updraft RC, has designed a new line of radio-controlled toys that use smartphones as the controller. Our market tests show strong potential for demand among younger consumers, who are often eager to try new products. We are now l ooking for a manufacturing partner, and we are very willing to collaborate with you.

This will be our first experience of partnering with an overseas manufacturer, and before we discuss specific technical details, I would like you to know two of our general concerns. The first concern involves all the general challenges of a long-distance manufacturing partnership, including transportation costs, shipping delays, quality control, and the risk of intellectual property theft.

Second, U.S. companies that work with overseas production partners face an increasing amount of scrutiny from the news media and activist groups regarding such matters as workplace safety, worker rights, and environmentally sensitive manufacturing. Nike and other major U.S. companies have spent millions of dollars and worked for years to improve conditions in overseas factories, but even they have not be able to avoid all problems. As a small company with no ability to monitor factories, we are worried about any manufacturing-related problems that could affect our public image.

Please share your company's philosophy and strategies for minimizing these two concerns.

We would like to commence production in the second quarter of 2017, so we would like to hear your reply as soon as possible.

Thank you,

Henry Gatlin

Henry Gatlin
Founder, CEO
Updraft RC

5 August 2016

An inside address is typically not used in Chinese correspondence.

The salutation uses a colon rather than a comma.

The revised opening gives the reader some helpful context and the assurance that this is a meaningful business opportunity.

The phrase "we are very willing to collaborate with you" shows respect for the reader and suggests the interest in forming a partnership.

This paragraph has been shortened to eliminate the redundant request for information.

This revised paragraph still conveys the seriousness of the writer's concerns without offending the reader.

"Minimizing" is easier for a non-native speaker to understand than "mitigating."

"Thank you" is a simple and adequately formal closing.

Figure 3.4c Intercultural Business Letter: Final Revision
Here is the final English version, revised to ensure more successful translation into Chinese and to conform to standard practices in Chinese business communication (including removing the inside address).

---

the United States and Great Britain, 1.000 means one with three decimal places, but it means one thousand in many European countries.

- **Avoid slang, idiomatic phrases, and business jargon.** Everyday speech and writing are full of slang and **idiomatic phrases**—phrases that mean more than the sum of their literal parts. Examples from U.S. English include "Knocked one out of the park" and "More bang for the buck." Your audience may have no idea what you're talking about when you use such phrases.
- **Avoid humor and references to popular culture.** Jokes and references to popular entertainment usually rely on culture-specific information that might be completely unknown to your audience.

Humor does not "travel well" because it usually relies on intimate knowledge of a particular culture.

李华先生：

随着智能手机的普及，越来越多的配件和周边产品正在被研发以满足市场的需求。我们的公司，Updraft RC,已经设计了一种新型的用智能手机控制的遥控玩具。我们的市场测试表明年轻客户，一个愿意尝试新产品的群体，（对我们的产品）有巨大的潜在需求。我们现在正在寻找制造伙伴，所以我们非常愿意与你们合作。

这是我们第一次与海外制造伙伴合作，在我们讨论具细节之前，我非常愿意让你们知道我们的两个问题。第一个问题对远距制造商合作关系来说都是一个挑战，这个挑战包括运输费用，运输延迟，质量控制和知识产权盗窃。

第二，与大洋对岸合作的美国公司面临着越来越高的来自新媒体和活跃组织的审查。这些审查包括工作场所安全性，劳工权益和可能对环境产生损害的制造。耐克和其他主要的美国公司已经花费了数百万美元，工作了几十年用来提升海外工厂的情况，但是他们仍然不能避免所有的问题。对于没有能力监控（海外）工厂的小公司来说，我们比较当心与制造相关的一系列问题可能影响到我们公司的形象。

所以请让我们知道你们公司解决这两个问题的策略和方法。

我们计划在 2017 年的第二个季度投入产品的生产。所以我们希望尽快得到你们公司的回应。

亨利 加特林
创始人，首席执行官
2016年8月5日

Figure 3.4d **Intercultural Business Letter: Translated Version**
Here is the translated version, formatted in accordance with Chinese business communication practice.

Although some of these differences may seem trivial, meeting the expectations of an international audience illustrates both knowledge of and respect for the other cultures (see Figure 3.5).

SPEAKING AND LISTENING CAREFULLY

Languages vary considerably in the significance of tone, pitch, speed, and volume, which can create challenges for people trying to interpret the explicit meaning of words themselves as well as the overall nuance of a message. The English word *progress* can be a noun or a verb, depending on which syllable you emphasize. In Chinese, the meaning of the word *mà* changes depending on the speaker's tone; it can mean *mother, pileup, horse,* or *scold.* And routine Arabic speech can sound excited or angry to an English-speaking U.S. listener.[52]

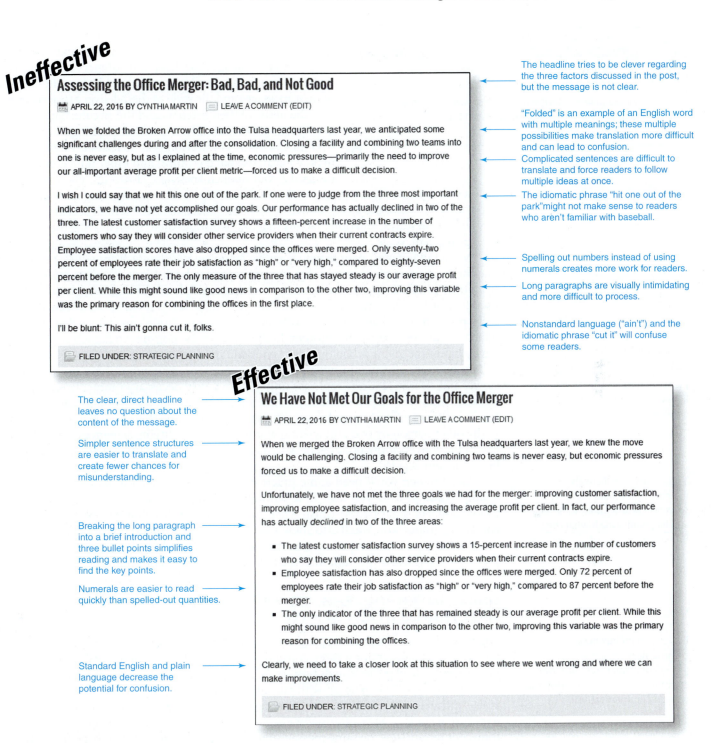

Ineffective

Assessing the Office Merger: Bad, Bad, and Not Good

📅 APRIL 22, 2016 BY CYNTHIA MARTIN   🗨 LEAVE A COMMENT (EDIT)

When we folded the Broken Arrow office into the Tulsa headquarters last year, we anticipated some significant challenges during and after the consolidation. Closing a facility and combining two teams into one is never easy, but as I explained at the time, economic pressures—primarily the need to improve our all-important average profit per client metric—forced us to make a difficult decision.

I wish I could say that we hit this one out of the park. If one were to judge from the three most important indicators, we have not yet accomplished our goals. Our performance has actually declined in two of the three. The latest customer satisfaction survey shows a fifteen-percent increase in the number of customers who say they will consider other service providers when their current contracts expire. Employee satisfaction scores have also dropped since the offices were merged. Only seventy-two percent of employees rate their job satisfaction as "high" or "very high," compared to eighty-seven percent before the merger. The only measure of the three that has stayed steady is our average profit per client. While this might sound like good news in comparison to the other two, improving this variable was the primary reason for combining the offices in the first place.

I'll be blunt: This ain't gonna cut it, folks.

📄 FILED UNDER: STRATEGIC PLANNING

The headline tries to be clever regarding the three factors discussed in the post, but the message is not clear.

"Folded" is an example of an English word with multiple meanings; these multiple possibilities make translation more difficult and can lead to confusion.

Complicated sentences are difficult to translate and force readers to follow multiple ideas at once.

The idiomatic phrase "hit one out of the park" might not make sense to readers who aren't familiar with baseball.

Spelling out numbers instead of using numerals creates more work for readers.

Long paragraphs are visually intimidating and more difficult to process.

Nonstandard language ("ain't") and the idiomatic phrase "cut it" will confuse some readers.

Effective

The clear, direct headline leaves no question about the content of the message.

Simpler sentence structures are easier to translate and create fewer chances for misunderstanding.

Breaking the long paragraph into a brief introduction and three bullet points simplifies reading and makes it easy to find the key points.

Numerals are easier to read quickly than spelled-out quantities.

Standard English and plain language decrease the potential for confusion.

We Have Not Met Our Goals for the Office Merger

📅 APRIL 22, 2016 BY CYNTHIA MARTIN   🗨 LEAVE A COMMENT (EDIT)

When we merged the Broken Arrow office with the Tulsa headquarters last year, we knew the move would be challenging. Closing a facility and combining two teams is never easy, but economic pressures forced us to make a difficult decision.

Unfortunately, we have not met the three goals we had for the merger: improving customer satisfaction, improving employee satisfaction, and increasing the average profit per client. In fact, our performance has actually *declined* in two of the three areas:

- The latest customer satisfaction survey shows a 15-percent increase in the number of customers who say they will consider other service providers when their current contracts expire.
- Employee satisfaction has also dropped since the offices were merged. Only 72 percent of employees rate their job satisfaction as "high" or "very high," compared to 87 percent before the merger.
- The only indicator of the three that has remained steady is our average profit per client. While this might sound like good news in comparison to the other two, improving this variable was the primary reason for combining the offices.

Clearly, we need to take a closer look at this situation to see where we went wrong and where we can make improvements.

📄 FILED UNDER: STRATEGIC PLANNING

Figure 3.5   Writing for Multilingual Audiences
In today's global and diversified work environment, chances are that many of your messages will be read by people whose native language is not English. Follow the guidelines on pages 83–85 to help ensure successful communication. (Notice how following these guidelines makes the message easier for *everybody* to read, including native English speakers.)

REAL-TIME UPDATES

LEARN MORE BY READING THIS ARTICLE

Study the seven habits of effective intercultural communicators

The willingness to take risks is a key habit; see what the other six are. Go to http://real-timeupdates.com/ebc12 and click on Learn More in the Students section.

To ensure successful conversations between parties who speak different native languages or even regional variations of the same language, speakers and listeners alike need to make accommodations.[53] Speakers should adjust the content of their messages and the style of their delivery to accommodate the needs of their listeners and the circumstances of the conversation. For example, if you are speaking in person or over an electronic connection that includes a video component, you can use hand gestures and other nonverbal signals to clarify your spoken message. However, when you don't have a visual connection, you must take extra care to convey your meaning through words and vocal characteristics alone. Conversely, listeners need to be tolerant of accents, vocabulary choices, gestures, and other factors that might distract them from hearing the meaning of a speaker's message.

When talking with people whose native language is different from yours, remember that the processing of even everyday conversations can be difficult. For instance, speakers from the United States sometimes string together multiple words into a single, mystifying pseudo-word, such as turning "Did you eat yet?" into "Jeetyet?" In spoken French, many word pairs are joined as a matter of rule, and the pronunciation can change depending on which words are next to one another. In these instances, non-native French speakers can have a hard time telling when one word ends and the next one begins.

To be more effective in intercultural conversations, remember these tips: (1) Speak slowly and clearly; (2) don't rephrase until it's obviously necessary (immediately rephrasing something you've just said doubles the translation workload for the listener); (3) look for and ask for feedback to make sure your message is getting through; (4) don't talk down to the other person by overenunciating words or oversimplifying sentences; and (5) at the end of the conversation, double-check to make sure you and the listener agree on what has been said and decided.

As a listener, you'll need some practice to get a sense of vocal patterns. The key is simply to accept what you hear first, without jumping to conclusions about meaning or motivation. Let other people finish what they have to say. If you interrupt, you may miss something important. You'll also show a lack of respect. If you do not understand a comment, ask the person to repeat it. Any momentary awkwardness you might feel in asking for extra help is less important than the risk of unsuccessful communication.

Speaking clearly and getting plenty of feedback are two of the keys to successful intercultural conversations.

To listen more effectively in intercultural situations, accept what you hear without judgment and let people finish what they have to say.

USING INTERPRETERS, TRANSLATORS, AND TRANSLATION SOFTWARE

You may encounter business situations that require using an *interpreter* (for spoken communication) or a *translator* (for written communication). Interpreters and translators can be expensive, but skilled professionals provide invaluable assistance for communicating in other cultural contexts.[54] Keeping up with current language usage in a given country or culture is also critical in order to avoid embarrassing blunders. Some companies use *back-translation* to ensure accuracy. Once a translator encodes a message into another language, a different translator retranslates the same message into the original language. This back-translation is then compared with the original message to discover any errors or discrepancies.

The time and cost required for professional translation has encouraged the development of computerized translation tools. Dedicated software tools, mobile apps, and online services such as WorldLingo offer various forms of automated translation. Major search engines let you request translated versions of the websites you find. Although none of these tools can translate as well as human translators, they are getting better all the time.

For important business communication, use a professional interpreter (for oral communication) or translator (for written communication).

HELPING OTHERS ADAPT TO YOUR CULTURE

Everyone can contribute to successful intercultural communication. Whether a younger person is unaccustomed to the formalities of a large corporation or a colleague from another country is working on a team with you, look for opportunities to help people fit in

Help others adapt to your culture; it will create a more productive workplace and teach you about their cultures as well.

CHECKLIST ✔ Improving Intercultural Communication Skills

- Understand your own culture so that you can recognize its influences on your communication habits.
- Study other cultures so that you can appreciate cultural variations.
- Study the languages of people with whom you communicate, even if you can learn only a few basic words and phrases.
- Help non-native speakers learn your language.
- Respect cultural preferences for communication style.
- Write clearly, using brief messages, simple language, generous transitions, and appropriate international conventions.

- Avoid slang, humor, and references to popular culture.
- Speak clearly and slowly, giving listeners time to translate your words.
- Ask for feedback to verify that communication was successful.
- Listen carefully and ask speakers to repeat anything you don't understand.
- Use interpreters and translators for important messages.

---

and adapt their communication style. For example, if a non-native English speaker is making mistakes that could hurt his or her credibility, you can offer advice on the appropriate words and phrases to use. Most language learners truly appreciate this sort of assistance, as long as it is offered in a respectful manner. Moreover, chances are that while you're helping, you'll learn something about the other person's culture and language, too.

You can also take steps to simplify the communication process. For instance, oral communication in a second language is usually more difficult than written forms of communication, so instead of asking a foreign colleague to provide information in a conference call, you could ask for a written response instead of or in addition to the live conversation.

For a brief summary of ideas to improve intercultural communication in the workplace, see "Checklist: Improving Intercultural Communication Skills." For additional information on communicating in a world of diversity, visit http://real-timeupdates.com/ebc12 and click on Chapter 3.

ON THE JOB: SOLVING COMMUNICATION DILEMMAS AT EY

Karyn Twaronite is responsible for workforce diversity and inclusiveness across EY's Americas region, but every manager throughout the company is expected to foster a climate of inclusion and support for employees of every cultural background. As a team leader in one of EY's U.S. offices, you're learning to exercise sound business judgment and use good listening skills to help resolve situations that arise within your diverse group of employees. How would you address these challenges?

1. Joo Mi Kang, a recent immigrant from South Korea, is a brilliant analyst who continues to impress with her knowledge of international taxation. Unfortunately, she usually doesn't do a good job of explaining tax matters to your corporate clients. You suspect from seeing some of her emails that she has trouble writing in English. What should your first step be?
   a. Send her an email reminding her of the need to communicate with clients; attach a copy of her job description.
   b. Suggest that she find a tutor to help her develop her English skills.

   c. Visit her in her office and discuss the situation; ask if she understands the importance of communicating with clients and whether she has encountered any difficulty in doing so.
   d. Assign several other analysts the task of pitching in to take care of her communication chores.

2. Your employees are breaking into ethnically based cliques. Members of ethnic groups eat together, socialize together, and often chat in their native languages while they work. You appreciate how these groups give their members a sense of community, but you worry that these informal communication channels are alienating nonmembers and fragmenting the flow of information. How do you encourage a stronger sense of community and teamwork across your department?
   a. Ban the use of languages other than English at work.
   b. Do nothing. This is normal behavior, and any attempt to disrupt it will only generate resentment.
   c. Structure work assignments and other activities (such as volunteer projects) in ways that bring people from the

various cultural groups into regular contact with one another and make them more dependent on one another as well.

   d. Send all your employees to diversity training classes.

3. Fabio Silva joined your office after immigrating from Brazil three years ago. He is a competent business strategist, but he resists working with other employees, even in team settings where collaboration is expected. Given the importance that you place on teamwork, how should you handle the situation?

   a. Stay out of the way and let the situation resolve itself. Silva has to learn how to get along with the other team members.

   b. Tell the rest of the team to work harder at getting along with Silva.

   c. Tell Silva he must work with others or he will not progress in the company.

   d. Talk privately with Silva and help him understand the importance of working together as a team. During the conversation, try to uncover why he doesn't participate more in team efforts.

4. You've been surprised at the confusion that some of your memos and other written messages have generated lately. You suspect your casual and often humorous writing style might be the culprit and decide to "test drive" a different writing style. You've drafted four versions of a blog post that explains a new policy aimed at keeping client projects on schedule as they near completion. Which of these do you choose and why?

   a. "As each new project nears completion, I recognize how hard you all try to keep projects on schedule, even with the last-minute problems that are always part of client projects. To lighten your workload during the hectic final phase, you'll no longer be expected to attend routine department meetings or tend to other nonessential tasks during the final four weeks of each project."

   b. "As each new project races toward the finish line, I appreciate that all of you work like dogs to keep projects on schedule, even with the inevitable glitches and gremlins that always seem to attack projects at the last minute. Good news: During the last four weeks of every project, you'll be excused from nonessential tasks such as routine department meetings so that you can focus on your programming work (admit it—I know you hate coming to these meetings anyway!)."

   c. "As usual, the solution to all of life's problems can be found on television! While watching the Raiders–Chiefs game yesterday, I realized that we need to have our own version of the two-minute drill. To help avoid schedule slippage during the crazy final few weeks of each project, team members will be excused from routine meetings and other nonessential tasks not directly related to their project responsibilities."

   d. "As you should all be aware, numerous entities both internal and external to the corporation rely on us for timely project completion. While the inherent nature of complex consulting projects presents unexpected difficulties during the final stages of a project, it is incumbent upon us to employ every tactic possible to avoid significant completion delays. Henceforth, team members will be excused from nonessential tasks during the final four weeks of every development project."

Learning Objectives Checkup

Assess your understanding of the principles in this chapter by reading each learning objective and studying the accompanying exercises. You can check your responses against the answer key on page 599.

Objective 3.1: Discuss the opportunities and challenges of intercultural communication.

1. Which of the following factors is a significant reason U.S. business professionals often need to understand the cultures of other countries?

   a. Recent changes to government regulations require cultural education before companies are granted export licenses.

   b. The U.S. economy has been shrinking for the past 20 years, forcing companies to look overseas.

   c. Many countries require business executives to be fluent in at least two languages.

   d. Thousands of U.S. companies, including many of the largest corporations in the country, rely on markets in other countries for a significant portion of their sales.

2. Which of the following is a benefit of a multicultural workforce?

   a. Providing a broader range of viewpoints and ideas

   b. Giving companies a better understanding of diverse markets

   c. Enabling companies to recruit workers from the broadest possible pool of talent

   d. All of the above

3. A culturally rich workforce, composed of employees representing a wide range of ethnicities, religions, ages, physical abilities, languages, and other factors,

   a. Always slows down the decision-making process.

   b. Can be more challenging to manage but can pay off in a variety of important ways.

   c. Is easier to manage because so many new ideas are present.

   d. Is a concern only for companies that do business outside the United States.

Objective 3.2: Define *culture*, explain how culture is learned, and define *ethnocentrism* and *stereotyping*.

4. Culture is defined as

   a. A distinct group that exists within a country.

   b. A shared system of symbols, beliefs, attitudes, values, expectations, and norms for behavior.

   c. The pattern of cues and stimuli that convey meaning between two or more people.

   d. Serious art forms such as classical music, painting, sculpture, drama, and poetry.

5. Which of the following is *not* an example of a cultural group?

   a. Hindus

   b. Wrestling fans

c. Television viewers
d. Members of a fraternity

6. Culture is learned from
  a. Family members.
  b. Explicit teaching by others in the culture.
  c. Observations of the behavior of others in the culture.
  d. All of the above.

7. _____ is the tendency to judge all other groups according to the standards, behaviors, and customs of one's own group.

8. _____ is the mistake of assigning a wide range of generalized attributes to individuals on the basis of their membership in a particular culture or social group, without considering an individual's unique characteristics.

9. Which of the following is one of several techniques you can use to make sure you don't fall into the traps of ethnocentrism and stereotyping?
  a. Minimize interactions with people whose cultures you don't understand.
  b. Make sure that the people you work with clearly understand your culture.
  c. Insist that every employee who works for you strictly follows the company's guidelines for intercultural communication.
  d. Avoiding making assumptions about people in other cultures.

Objective 3.3: Explain the importance of recognizing cultural variations, and list eight categories of cultural differences.

10. In business, recognizing cultural differences is important because
  a. Doing so helps reduce the chances for misunderstanding.
  b. Someone from another culture may try to take advantage of your ignorance.
  c. If you don't, you'll be accused of being politically incorrect.
  d. Doing so helps you become more ethnocentric.

11. An example of low-context cultural communication would be
  a. Someone using metaphors to convey meaning.
  b. Someone insisting that the details of an agreement can be worked out later.
  c. Someone vigorously arguing his point of view in a problem-solving situation.
  d. Someone encouraging socializing before entering into official negotiations.

12. Which of the following is generally true about high-context cultures?
  a. Employees work shorter hours in such cultures because context allows them to communicate less often.
  b. People rely less on verbal communication and more on the context of nonverbal actions and environmental setting to convey meaning.
  c. People rely more on verbal communication and less on the context of nonverbal actions and environmental setting to convey meaning.
  d. The rules of everyday life are explicitly taught to all people within the culture.

13. Differing attitudes toward greeting gestures, personal space, touching, facial expression, eye contact, posture, and formality are common examples of _____ differences between cultures.

Objective 3.4: List four general guidelines for adapting to any business culture.

14. Why is understanding your own culture an important step in learning to relate well with other cultures?
  a. Understanding your own culture is important because it helps you recognize personal biases that shape your communication habits.
  b. Understanding your own culture is important because it helps you identify the ways that other cultures are inferior (or at least might be inferior) to your own.
  c. Understanding your own culture is important because it helps you identify the ways that other cultures are superior (or at least might be superior) to your own.
  d. Understanding your own culture is not important when you are trying to reach out to other cultures.

Objective 3.5: Identify seven steps you can take to improve your intercultural communication skills.

15. When communicating orally to those who speak English as a second language, you should make a habit to always
  a. Immediately rephrase every important point you make to give your listeners two options to choose from.
  b. Speak louder if listeners don't seem to understand you.
  c. Ignore the other person's body language.
  d. Rephrase your key points if you observe body language that suggests a lack of understanding.

16. Understanding the nuances of a culture can take years to learn, so the best approach when preparing to communicate with people in a culture that you don't know well is to
  a. Learn as much as you can from websites, travel guides, and other resources and not be afraid to ask for help while you are communicating in that new culture.
  b. Learn as much as you can from websites, travel guides, and other resources but never ask for help because doing so will only show everyone how ignorant you are.
  c. Learn as much as you can from television shows and movies that feature the other culture; the combination of spoken words, visuals, and music is the best way to learn a culture.
  d. Not worry about cultural variations; you'll never have time to understand them all, so your energy is better spent on other business issues.

17. When writing for audiences who don't speak the same native language as you speak, you can improve communication by
  a. Spelling out numbers rather than writing them as figures.
  b. Using simple sentences and careful word choices.
  c. Using long paragraphs to reduce the number of visual breaks on the page.
  d. Doing all of the above.

18. When you are writing for multilanguage audiences, humor
  a. Should be used often because it makes your audience feel welcome on a personal level.
  b. Should rarely, if ever, be used because humor is one of the most difficult elements of communication to encode or decode in a second language.
  c. Should never be used because movies and other entertainment products rarely cross over national boundaries.
  d. Should be used at least once per letter to show that you appreciate your audience as human beings.

Quick Learning Guide

CHAPTER OUTLINE

Understanding the Opportunities and Challenges of Communication in a Diverse World
- The Opportunities in a Global Marketplace
- The Advantages of a Diverse Workforce
- The Challenges of Intercultural Communication

Developing Cultural Competency
- Understanding the Concept of Culture
- Overcoming Ethnocentrism and Stereotyping

Recognizing Variations in a Diverse World
- Contextual Differences
- Legal and Ethical Differences
- Social Differences
- Nonverbal Differences
- Age Differences
- Gender Differences
- Religious Differences
- Ability Differences

Adapting to Other Business Cultures
- Guidelines for Adapting to Any Business Culture
- Guidelines for Adapting to U.S. Business Culture

Improving Intercultural Communication Skills
- Studying Other Cultures
- Studying Other Languages
- Respecting Preferences for Communication Style
- Writing Clearly
- Speaking and Listening Carefully
- Using Interpreters, Translators, and Translation Software
- Helping Others Adapt to Your Culture

LEARNING OBJECTIVES

1 Discuss the opportunities and challenges of intercultural communication. (page 69)

2 Define *culture*, explain how culture is learned, and define *ethnocentrism* and *stereotyping*. (page 71)

3 Explain the importance of recognizing cultural variations, and list eight categories of cultural differences. (page 73)

4 List four general guidelines for adapting to any business culture. (page 78)

5 Identify seven steps you can take to improve your intercultural communication skills. (page 79)

KEY TERMS

cultural competency An appreciation for cultural differences that affect communication and the ability to adjust one's communication style to ensure that efforts to send and receive messages across cultural boundaries are successful

cultural context The pattern of physical cues, environmental stimuli, and implicit understanding that convey meaning between two members of the same culture

cultural pluralism The practice of accepting multiple cultures on their own terms

culture A shared system of symbols, beliefs, attitudes, values, expectations, and norms for behavior

diversity All the characteristics and experiences that define each of us as individuals

ethnocentrism The tendency to judge other groups according to the standards, behaviors, and customs of one's own group

high-context culture Culture in which people rely less on verbal communication and more on the context of nonverbal actions and environmental setting to convey meaning

idiomatic phrases Phrases that mean more than the sum of their literal parts; such phrases can be difficult for nonnative speakers to understand

intercultural communication The process of sending and receiving messages between people whose cultural backgrounds could lead them to interpret verbal and nonverbal signs differently

low-context culture Culture in which people rely more on verbal communication and less on circumstances and nonverbal cues to convey meaning

stereotyping Assigning a wide range of generalized attributes to an individual on the basis of membership in a particular culture or social group

xenophobia Fear of strangers and foreigners

CHECKLIST ✔

Improving Intercultural Communication Skills

- Understand your own culture so that you can recognize its influences on your communication habits.
- Study other cultures so that you can appreciate cultural variations.
- Study the languages of people with whom you communicate, even if you can learn only a few basic words and phrases.
- Help non-native speakers learn your language.
- Respect cultural preferences for communication style.
- Write clearly, using brief messages, simple language, generous transitions, and appropriate international conventions.
- Avoid slang, humor, and references to popular culture.
- Speak clearly and slowly, giving listeners time to translate your words.
- Ask for feedback to verify that communication was successful.
- Listen carefully and ask speakers to repeat anything you don't understand.
- Use interpreters and translators for important messages.

Apply Your Knowledge

To review chapter content related to each question, refer to the indicated Learning Objective.

3.1. Make a list of the top five priorities in your life (for example, fame, wealth, family, spirituality, peace of mind, individuality, artistic expression). Compare your list with the priorities that appear to be valued in the culture in which you are currently living. (You can be as broad or as narrow as you like in defining *culture* for this exercise, such as overall U.S. culture or the culture in your college or university.) [LO-2]

3.2. Do the priorities in your list align with the culture's priorities? If not, how might this disparity affect your communication with other members of the culture? [LO-2]

3.3. How does making an effort to avoid assumptions contribute to the practice of cultural pluralism? [LO-3]

3.4. Think about the last three movies or television shows set in the United States that you've watched. In what ways would these entertainment products be helpful or unhelpful for people from other countries trying to learn about U.S. culture? [LO-5]

⭐ **3.5.** How can helping someone adapt to your culture help you gain a better understand of it yourself?

Practice Your Skills

Message for Analysis: Adapting to Cultural Differences [LO-5]

Your boss wants to send a brief email message welcoming employees recently transferred to your department from the company's Hong Kong branch. These employees, all of whom are Hong Kong natives, speak English, but your boss asks you to review his message for clarity. What would you suggest your boss change in the following email message, and why? Would you consider this message to be audience centered? Why or why not? (Hint: Do some quick research on Hong Kong to identify the style of English that people in Hong Kong are likely to speak.)

> I wanted to welcome you ASAP to our little family here in the States. It's high time we shook hands in person and not just across the sea. I'm pleased as punch about getting to know you all, and I for one will do my level best to sell you on America.

Exercises

Each activity is labeled according to the primary skill or skills you will need to use. To review relevant chapter content, you can refer to the indicated Learning Objective. In some instances, supporting information will be found in another chapter, as indicated.

3.6. **Intercultural Communication: Recognizing Cultural Variations [LO-1], [LO-3], [LO-4]** Review the definitions of the generations on page 77. Based on your year of birth, in which generation do you belong? Do you feel a part of this generation? Why or why not? If you were born outside the United States, do the generational boundaries seem accurate to you? Now consider the biases that you might have regarding other generations. For example, if you are a member of Generation Y, what do you think about the baby boomers and their willingness to embrace new ideas? Identify several of your generational biases that could create friction in the workplace. Summarize your responses to these questions in a post on your class blog or an email message to your instructor.

3.7. **Intercultural Communication: Adapting to Cultural Variations [LO-2]** You are a new manager at K & J Brick, a masonry products company that is now run by the two sons of the man who founded it 50 years ago. For years, the co-owners have invited the management team to a wilderness lodge for a combination of outdoor sports and annual business planning meetings. You don't want to miss the event, but you know that the outdoor activities weren't designed for someone like you, whose physical impairments prevent participation in the sporting events. Draft a short email message to the rest of the management team, suggesting changes to the annual event that will allow all managers to participate.

3.8. **Intercultural Communication: Writing for Multiple-Language Audiences [LO-5]** Reading English-language content written by non-native speakers of English can be a good reminder of the challenges of communicating in another language. The writing can be confusing or even amusing at first glance, but the key to remember here is that your writing might sound just as confusing or amusing to someone else if your roles were reversed.

Identify a company that is based in a non-English speaking country but that includes English-language text on its website. (The "advanced" search capabilities of your favorite search engine can help you locate websites from a particular country.) Study the language on this site. Does it sound as though it was written by someone adept at English? If the first site you've found does have writing that sounds natural to a native U.S. English speaker, find another company whose website doesn't. Select a section of text, at least several sentences long, and rewrite it to sound more "American." Submit the original text and your rewritten version to your instructor.

3.9. **Intercultural Communication: Writing for Multiple-Language Audiences; Collaboration: Team Projects [LO-5] Chapter 2** With a team assigned by your instructor, review the Facebook pages of five companies, looking for words and phrases that might be confusing to a non-native speaker of English. If you (or someone on the team) are a non-native speaker, explain to the team why those word choices could be confusing. Choose three sentences, headlines, company slogans, or other pieces of text that contain potentially confusing words and rewrite them to minimize the chances of misinterpretation. As much as possible, try to retain the tone of the original—although you may find that this is impossible in some instances. Use Google Docs to compile the original selections and your revised versions, then email the documents to your instructor.

3.10. **Intercultural Communication: Speaking with Multiple-Language Audiences; Collaboration: Team Projects [LO-5], Chapter 2** Working with two other students, prepare a list of 10 examples of slang (in your own language) that might be misinterpreted or misunderstood during a business conversation with someone from another culture. Next to each example, suggest other words you might use to convey the same message. Do the alternatives mean *exactly* the same as the original slang or idiom? Submit your list of original words and suggested replacements, with an explanation of why each replacement is better than the original.

3.11. **Intercultural Communication: Writing for Multiple-Language Audiences [LO-5]** Explore the powers and limitations of free online translation services such as Google Translate. Enter a sentence from this chapter, such as "Local markets are opening to worldwide competition as businesses of all sizes look for new growth opportunities outside their own countries." First, translate the sentence from English to Spanish and click to complete the translation. Next, copy the Spanish version and paste it into the translation entry box and back-translate it from Spanish to English. Now repeat this test for German, French, Italian, or another language. Did the sentence survive the round trip? Does it still sound like normal business writing when translated back into English?

(1) What are the implications for the use of automated translation services for international correspondence? (2) Would you feel comfortable using an online tool such as this to translate an important business message? (3) How might you use this website to sharpen your intercultural communication skills? Summarize your findings in a brief report.

3.12. **Intercultural Communication: Speaking with Multiple-Language Audiences; Media Skills: Podcasting [LO-5], Chapter 7** Your company was one of the first to use podcasting as a business communication tool. Executives frequently record messages (such as monthly sales summaries) and post them on the company's intranet site; employees from the 14 offices in Europe, Asia, and North America then download the files to their music players or other devices and listen to the messages while riding the train to work, eating lunch at their desks, and so on. Your boss asks you to draft the opening statement for a podcast that will announce a revenue drop caused by intensive competitive pressure. She reviews your script and hands it back with a gentle explanation that it needs to be revised for international listeners. Improve the following statement in as many ways as you can:

Howdy, comrades. Shouldn't surprise anyone that we took a beating this year, given the insane pricing moves our knucklehead competitors have been making. I mean, how those clowns can keep turning a profit is beyond me, what with steel costs still going through the roof and labor costs heating up—even in countries where everybody goes to find cheap labor—and hazardous waste disposal regs adding to operating costs, too.

Expand Your Skills

Critique the Professionals

Find an online business document—such as a company webpage, blog post, Facebook Info tab, or LinkedIn profile—that you believe commits an intercultural communication blunder by failing to consider the needs of at least some of its target readers. For example, a website might use slang or idiomatic language that could confuse some readers, or it might use language that offends some readers. In a post on your class blog, share the text you found and explain why you think it does not succeed as effective intercultural communication. Be sure to include a link back to the original material.

Sharpening Your Career Skills Online

Bovée and Thill's Business Communication Web Search, at http://websearch.businesscommunicationnetwork.com, is a unique research tool designed specifically for business communication research. Use the Web Search function to find a website, video, PDF document, podcast, or presentation that offers advice on communicating with business contacts in another country or culture. Write a brief email message to your instructor, describing the item you found and summarizing the career skills information you learned from it.

Improve Your Grammar, Mechanics, and Usage

The following exercises help you improve your knowledge of and power over English grammar, mechanics, and usage. Turn to the Handbook of Grammar, Mechanics, and Usage at the end of this book and review all of Section 1.3 (Verbs). Then look at the following 10 items. Indicate the letter of the preferred choice in the following groups of sentences. (Answers to these exercises appear on page 601.)

3.13. Which sentence contains a verb in the present perfect form?

   a. I became the resident expert on repairing the copy machine.

   b. I have become the resident expert on repairing the copy machine.

3.14. Which sentence contains a verb in the simple past form?

   a. She knows how to conduct an audit when she came to work for us.

   b. She knew how to conduct an audit when she came to work for us.

3.15. Which sentence contains a verb in the simple future form?

   a. Next week, call John to tell him what you will do to help him set up the seminar.

b. Next week, call John to tell him what you will be doing to help him set up the seminar.

3.16. Which sentence is in the active voice?

   a. The report will be written by Leslie Cartwright.

   b. Leslie Cartwright will write the report.

3.17. Which sentence is in the passive voice?

   a. The failure to record the transaction was mine.

   b. I failed to record the transaction.

3.18. Which sentence contains the correct verb form?

   a. Everyone upstairs receives mail before we do.

   b. Everyone upstairs receive mail before we do.

3.19. Which sentence contains the correct verb form?

   a. Neither the main office nor the branches is blameless.

   b. Neither the main office nor the branches are blameless.

3.20. Which sentence contains the correct verb form?

   a. C&B Sales are listed in the directory.

   b. C&B Sales is listed in the directory.

3.21. Which sentence contains the correct verb form?

   a. When measuring shelves, 7 inches is significant.

   b. When measuring shelves, 7 inches are significant.

3.22. Which sentence contains the correct verb form?

   a. About 90 percent of the employees plans to come to the company picnic.

   b. About 90 percent of the employees plan to come to the company picnic.

For additional exercises focusing on verbs, visit MyBCommLab. Click on Chapter 3, click on Additional Exercises to Improve Grammar, Mechanics, and Usage, and then click on 5. Verb tenses, 6. Transitive and intransitive verbs, or 7. Voice of verbs.

MyBCommLab

Go to the Assignments section of your MyLab to complete these writing exercises.

3.23   How have market globalization and cultural diversity contributed to the increased importance of intercultural communication? [LO-1]

3.24   What four principles apply to ethical intercultural communication? [LO-3]

Endnotes

1. Karyn Twaronite LinkedIn profile, accessed 9 February 2015, www.linkedin.com; Ernst & Young website, accessed 9 February 2015, www.ey.com; "8 CEOs Whose Inclusive Styles Change Corporate Cultures," *DiversityInc*, accessed 21 January 2013, www.diversityinc.com; "E&Y's Karyn Twaronite Interviewed by HBA's Marianne Fray," Healthcare Businesswomen's Association, accessed 21 January 2013, www.youtube.com; "No. 6: Ernst & Young," *DiversityInc*, accessed 21 January 2013, www.diversityinc.com; "How Ernst & Young Improved Engagement, Innovation for 167,000 Employees," *DiversityInc*, accessed 21 January 2013, www.diversityinc.com; "HR & Communications: How Ernst & Young Gets Its Diversity Message to 50,000 Employees Every Day," *DiversityInc*, accessed 21 January 2013.

2. Michael R. Carrell, Everett E. Mann, and Tracey Honeycutt-Sigler, "Defining Workforce Diversity Programs and Practices in Organizations: A Longitudinal Study," *Labor Law Journal*, Spring 2006, 5–12.

3. "Dimensions of Diversity—Workforce," Merck website, accessed 4 January 2011, www.merck.com.

4. "Top Ten Countries with Which the U.S. Trades," U.S. Census Bureau website, accessed 29 December 2010, www.census.gov.

5. *Competing Across Borders: How Cultural and Communication Barriers Affect Business*, Economist Intelligence Unit Ltd., 2012, 4.

6. Nancy R. Lockwood, "Workplace Diversity: Leveraging the Power of Difference for Competitive Advantage," *HR Magazine*, June 2005, special section, 1–10.

7. Alan Kline, "The Business Case for Diversity," *USBanker*, May 2010, 10–11.

8. Paul Taylor, "The Next America," Pew Research Center, 10 April 2014, www.pewressarch.com; "More Than 300 Counties Now 'Majority–Minority,'" press release, U.S. Census Bureau website, 9 August 2007, www.census.gov; Robert Kreitner, *Management*, 9th ed. (Boston: Houghton Mifflin, 2004), 84.

9. Tracy Novinger, *Intercultural Communication, A Practical Guide* (Austin: University of Texas Press, 2001), 15.

10. Larry A. Samovar and Richard E. Porter, "Basic Principles of Intercultural Communication," in *Intercultural Communication: A Reader*, 6th ed., edited by Larry A. Samovar and Richard E. Porter (Belmont, Calif.: Wadsworth, 1991), 12.

11. Arthur Chin, "Understanding Cultural Competency," *New Zealand Business*, December 2010/January 2011, 34–35; Sanjeeta R. Gupta, "Achieve Cultural Competency," *Training*, February 2009, 16–17; Diane Shannon, "Cultural Competency in Health Care Organizations: Why and How," *Physician Executive*, September–October 2010, 15–22.

12. Linda Beamer and Iris Varner, *Intercultural Communication in the Workplace*, 2nd ed. (New York: McGraw-Hill Irwin, 2001), 3.

13. "Languages of the United States," Ethnologue website, accessed 29 December 2010, www.ethnologue.com.

14. Philip R. Harris and Robert T. Moran, *Managing Cultural Differences*, 3rd ed. (Houston: Gulf, 1991), 394–397, 429–430.

15. Lillian H. Chaney and Jeanette S. Martin, *Intercultural Business Communication*, 2nd ed. (Upper Saddle River, N.J.: Prentice Hall, 2000), 6.

16. Beamer and Varner, *Intercultural Communication in the Workplace*, 4.

17. Chaney and Martin, *Intercultural Business Communication*, 2nd ed., 9.

18. Richard L. Daft, *Management*, 6th ed. (Cincinnati: Thomson South-Western, 2003), 455.

19. Lillian H. Chaney and Jeanette S. Martin, *Intercultural Business Communication*, 4th ed. (Upper Saddle River, N.J.: Pearson Prentice Hall, 2007), 53.

20. Project Implicit website, accessed 29 December 2010, http:// implicit.harvard.edu/implicit.

21. Linda Beamer, "Teaching English Business Writing to Chinese-Speaking Business Students," *Bulletin of the Association for Business Communication* 57, no. 1 (1994): 12–18.

22. Edward T. Hall, "Context and Meaning," in *Intercultural Communication*, 6th ed., edited by Larry A. Samovar and Richard E. Porter (Belmont, Calif.: Wadsworth, 1991), 46–55.

23. Daft, *Management*, 459.

24. Charley H. Dodd, *Dynamics of Intercultural Communication*, 3rd ed. (Dubuque, Ia.: Brown, 1991), 69–70.

25. Daft, *Management*, 459.

26. Hannah Seligson, "For American Workers in China, a Culture Clash," *New York Times*, 23 December 2009, www.nytimes.com.

27. Beamer and Varner, *Intercultural Communication in the Workplace*, 230–233.

28. Ed Marcum, "More U.S. Businesses Abandon Outsourcing Overseas," *Seattle Times*, 28 August 2010, www.seattletimes.com.

29. Guo-Ming Chen and William J. Starosta, *Foundations of Intercultural Communication* (Boston: Allyn & Bacon, 1998), 288–289.

30. Mary A. DeVries, *Internationally Yours* (New York: Houghton Mifflin, 1994), 194.

31. Robert O. Joy, "Cultural and Procedural Differences That Influence Business Strategies and Operations in the People's Republic of China," *SAM Advanced Management Journal*, Summer 1989, 29–33.

32. Chaney and Martin, *Intercultural Business Communication*, 2nd ed., 122–123.

33. Mansour Javidan, "Forward-Thinking Cultures," *Harvard Business Review*, July–August 2007, 20.

34. "The 100 Million Club 2013: The Top 14 Mobile Markets by Number of Mobile Subscriptions And 3G/4G Subscribers," *MobiThinking*, 26 November 2013, www.mobithinking.com.

35. Tracy Novinger, *Intercultural Communication, A Practical Guide* (Austin: University of Texas Press, 2001), 54.

36. Peter Coy, "Old. Smart. Productive." *BusinessWeek*, 27 June 2005, www.businessweek.com; Beamer and Varner, *Intercultural Communication in the Workplace*, 107–108.

37. Beamer and Varner, *Intercultural Communication in the Workplace*, 107–108.

38. Steff Gelston, "Gen Y, Gen X and the Baby Boomers: Workplace Generation Wars," *CIO*, 30 January 2008, www.cio.com.

39. Joanna Barsh and Lareina Yee, "Changing Companies' Minds About Women," *McKinsey Quarterly*, 2011, Issue 4, 48–59.

40. John Gray, *Mars and Venus in the Workplace* (New York: Harper Collins, 2002), 10, 25–27, 61–63.

41. Jennifer Luden, "Ask for a Raise? Most Women Hesitate," *NPR*, 14 February 2011, www.npr.org.

42. "Religious Bias a Growing Issue," *Business Insurance*, 13 February 2012, 8; Mark D. Downey, "Keeping the Faith," *HR Magazine*, January 2008, 85–88.

43. IBM Accessibility Center, accessed 24 August 2006, www.03 .ibm.com/able; AssistiveTech.net, accessed 24 August 2006, www .assistivetech.net; Business Leadership Network website, accessed 24 August 2006, www.usbln.org; National Institute on Disability and Rehabilitation Research website, accessed 24 August 2006, www .ed.gov/about/offices/list/osers/nidrr; Rehabilitation Engineering & Assistive Technology Society of North America website, accessed 24 August 2006, www.resna.org.

44. Daphne A. Jameson, "Reconceptualizing Cultural Identity and Its Role in Intercultural Business Communication," *Journal of Business Communication*, July 2007, 199–235.

45. Leslie Knudson, "Diversity on a Global Scale," *HR Management*, accessed 17 August 2008, www.hrmreport.com.

46. Craig S. Smith, "Beware of Green Hats in China and Other Cross-Cultural Faux Pas," *New York Times*, 30 April 2002, C11.

47. Sana Reynolds and Deborah Valentine, *Guide for Internationals: Culture, Communication, and ESL* (Upper Saddle River, N.J.: Pearson Prentice Hall, 2006), 3–11, 14–19, 25.

48. P. Christopher Earley and Elaine Mosakowsi, "Cultural Intelligence," *Harvard Business Review*, October 2004, 139–146.

49. Bob Nelson, "Motivating Workers Worldwide," *Global Workforce*, November 1998, 25–27.

50. Mona Casady and Lynn Wasson, "Written Communication Skills of International Business Persons," *Bulletin of the Association for Business Communication* 57, no. 4 (1994): 36–40.

51. Lynn Gaertner-Johnston, "Found in Translation," Business Writing blog, 25 November 2005, www.businesswritingblog.com.

52. Myron W. Lustig and Jolene Koester, *Intercultural Competence*, 4th ed. (Boston: Allyn & Bacon, 2003), 196.

53. "'Can You Spell That for Us Nonnative Speakers?' Accommodation Strategies in International Business Meetings," Pamela Rogerson-Revell, *Journal of Business Communication* 47, no. 4 (October 2010): 432–454.

54. James Wilfong and Toni Seger, *Taking Your Business Global* (Franklin Lakes, N.J.: Career Press, 1997), 232.

Applying the Three-Step Writing Process

CHAPTER 4 Planning Business Messages

CHAPTER 5 Writing Business Messages

CHAPTER 6 Completing Business Messages

Every professional can learn to write more effectively while spending less time and energy in creating effective messages. Discover a proven writing process that divides the challenge of communicating into three simple steps: planning, writing, and completing messages. The process works for everything from blog posts to formal reports to your résumé. With a bit of practice, you'll be using the process to write more effectively without even thinking about it.

Photobee/Fotolia

4

Planning Business Messages

LEARNING OBJECTIVES

After studying this chapter, you will be able to

1 Describe the three-step writing process.

2 Explain why it's important to analyze a communication situation in order to define your purpose and profile your audience before writing a message.

3 Discuss information-gathering options for simple messages, and identify three attributes of quality information.

4 List the factors to consider when choosing the most appropriate medium for a message.

5 Explain why good organization is important to both you and your audience, and list the tasks involved in organizing a message.

ON THE JOB: COMMUNICATING AT
H&R BLOCK

Adding Some Excitement to a Most Unexciting Task

Many taxpayers don't think about their taxes until they absolutely have to and even then they want to think about taxes as little as possible. Knowing this makes communicating about tax preparation products and services a challenge, but one H&R Block has addressed with creative use of new communication media.

H&R Block is the leading tax-preparation firm in the United States, with a range of options for taxpayers. Those who want assistance with tax preparation can hand the job over to one of the company's 90,000 tax professionals. Those who prefer to do the work themselves can choose from the company's do-it-yourself alternatives, which include PC software and online solutions.

Although tax preparation isn't typically considered exciting, H&R Block has developed a reputation for a fresh approach to communication and innovative social media efforts. Through partnerships with social influencers, video series, sweepstakes, bilingual social channels, and more, the company takes a straightforward and often lighthearted approach to an otherwise daunting topic.

In the spirit of the social communication model (see Chapter 1), H&R Block emphasizes a conversational, two-way approach, in which it listens as carefully as it speaks. During tax season, the company's social media team is available almost round-the-clock, interacting with clients across social

H&R Block makes extensive use of social media to connect with customers and simplify the chore of filing tax returns.

networks and providing information and resources. The team often refers clients to the Block Talk Blog, which has a wealth of tax-related resources in an easy-to-read format. They also regularly surprise clients who post positive comments and reviews with fun prizes such as gift cards and H&R Block bow ties as a "thank you" for the social media praise, further cementing the two-way relationship.

For a business that has been operating since 1955 in a somewhat stodgy field, this cutting-edge communication has helped H&R Block bring tax preparation into the 21st century and positioned the firm as an innovator in the eyes of today's digital natives.[1]

WWW.HRBLOCK.COM

Understanding the Three-Step Writing Process

1 LEARNING OBJECTIVE
Describe the three-step writing process.

The emphasis that H&R Block (profiled in the chapter-opening On the Job) puts on connecting with customers is a lesson that applies to business messages for all stakeholders. By following the process introduced in this chapter, you can create successful messages that meet audience needs and highlight your skills as a perceptive business professional.

The three-step writing process (see Figure 4.1) helps ensure that your messages are both *effective* (meeting your audience's needs and getting your points across) and *efficient* (making the best use of your time and your audience's time):

The three-step writing process consists of *planning, writing,* and *completing* your messages.

- **Step 1: Planning business messages.** To plan any message, first *analyze the situation* by defining your purpose and developing a profile of your audience. When you're sure what you need to accomplish with your message, *gather the information* that will meet your audience's needs. Next, *select the best combination of medium and channel* to deliver your message. Then *organize the information* by defining your main

1 Plan →	**2** Write →	**3** Complete
Analyze the Situation Define your purpose and develop an audience profile.	**Adapt to Your Audience** Be sensitive to audience needs by using a "you" attitude, politeness, positive emphasis, and unbiased language. Build a strong relationship with your audience by establishing your credibility and projecting your company's preferred image. Control your style with a conversational tone, plain English, and appropriate voice.	**Revise the Message** Evaluate content and review readability, edit and rewrite for conciseness and clarity.
Gather Information Determine audience needs and obtain the information necessary to satisfy those needs.		**Produce the Message** Use effective design elements and suitable layout for a clean, professional appearance.
Choose Medium and Channel Identify the best combination for the situation, message, and audience.	**Compose the Message** Choose strong words that will help you create effective sentences and coherent paragraphs.	**Proofread the Message** Review for errors in layout, spelling, and mechanics.
Organize the Information Define your main idea, limit your scope, select a direct or an indirect approach, and outline your content.		**Distribute the Message** Deliver your message using the chosen medium; make sure all documents and all relevant files are distributed successfully.

Figure 4.1   The Three-Step Writing Process
This three-step process will help you create more effective messages in any medium. As you get more practice with the process, it will become easier and more automatic.
Sources: Kevin J. Harty and John Keenan, *Writing for Business and Industry: Process and Product* (New York: Macmillan Publishing Company, 1987), 3–4; Richard Hatch, *Business Writing* (Chicago: Science Research Associates, 1983), 88–89; Richard Hatch, *Business Communication Theory and Technique* (Chicago: Science Research Associates, 1983), 74–75; Center for Humanities, *Writing as a Process: A Step-by-Step Guide* (Mount Kisco, N.Y.: Center for Humanities, 1987); Michael L. Keene, *Effective Professional Writing* (New York: D. C. Heath, 1987), 28–34.

idea, limiting your scope, selecting the direct or indirect approach, and outlining your content. Planning messages is the focus of this chapter.

- **Step 2: Writing business messages.** After you've planned your message, *adapt to your audience* by using sensitivity, relationship skills, and an appropriate writing style. Then you're ready to *compose your message* by choosing strong words, creating effective sentences, and developing coherent paragraphs. Writing business messages is discussed in Chapter 5.
- **Step 3: Completing business messages.** After writing your first draft, *revise your message* by evaluating the content, reviewing readability, and editing and rewriting until your message comes across concisely and clearly, with correct grammar, proper punctuation, and effective format. Next, *produce your message.* Put it into the form that your audience will receive and review all design and layout decisions for an attractive, professional appearance. *Proofread* the final product to ensure high quality and then *distribute your message.* Completing business messages is discussed in Chapter 6.

Throughout this book, you'll learn how to apply these steps to a wide variety of business messages.

OPTIMIZING YOUR WRITING TIME

As a starting point, allot roughly half your available time for planning, one quarter for writing, and one quarter for completing a message.

The more you use the three-step writing process, the more intuitive and automatic it will become. You'll also get better at allotting time for each task during a writing project. Start by figuring out how much time you have to spend. Then, as a general rule, set aside roughly 50 percent of that time for planning, 25 percent for writing, and 25 percent for completing.

Reserving half your time for planning might seem excessive, but as the next section explains, careful planning usually saves time overall by focusing your writing and reducing rework. Of course, the ideal time allocation varies from project to project. Simpler and shorter messages require less planning than long reports, websites, and other complex projects. Also, the time required to produce and distribute messages can vary widely, depending on the media, the size of the audience, and other factors. However, start with the 50-25-25 split as a guideline, and use your best judgment for each project.

PLANNING EFFECTIVELY

For everything beyond brief and simple messages, resist the urge to skip the planning step.

As soon as the need to create a message appears, inexperienced communicators are often tempted to dive directly into writing. However, skipping or shortchanging the planning stage often creates extra work and stress later in the process. First, thoughtful planning is necessary to make sure you provide the right information in the right format to the right people. Taking the time to understand your audience members and their needs helps you find and assemble the facts they're looking for and deliver that information in a concise and compelling way. Second, with careful planning, the writing stage is faster, easier, and a lot less stressful. Third, planning can save you from embarrassing blunders that could hurt your company or your career.

2 LEARNING OBJECTIVE
Explain why it's important to analyze a communication situation in order to define your purpose and profile your audience before writing a message.

Analyzing the Situation

Every communication effort takes place in a particular situation, meaning you have a specific message to send to a specific audience under a specific set of circumstances. For example, describing your professional qualifications in an email message to an executive in your own company differs significantly from describing your qualifications in your LinkedIn profile. The email message is likely to be focused on a single goal, such as explaining why you would be a good choice to head up a major project, and you have the luxury of focusing on the needs of a single, personally identifiable reader. In contrast, your social networking profile could have multiple goals, such as connecting with your peers in other companies and presenting your qualifications to potential employers, and it might be viewed by hundreds or thousands of readers, each with his or her own needs.

The underlying information for these two messages could be roughly the same, but the level of detail to include, the tone of the writing, the specific word choices—these and other choices you need to make will differ from one situation to another. Making the right choices starts with defining your purpose clearly and understanding your audience's needs.

DEFINING YOUR PURPOSE

All business messages have a **general purpose**: to inform, to persuade, or to collaborate with the audience. This purpose helps define the overall approach you'll need to take, from gathering information to organizing your message. Within the scope of its general purpose, each message also has a **specific purpose**, which identifies what you hope to accomplish with your message and what your audience should do or think after receiving your message. For instance, is your goal simply to update your audience about some upcoming event, or do you want people to take immediate action? State your specific purpose as precisely as possible, even to the point of identifying which audience members should respond, how they should respond, and when.

Business messages have both a general purpose and a specific purpose.

After you have defined your specific purpose, take a moment for a reality check. Decide whether that purpose merits the time and effort required for you to prepare and send the message—and for your audience to spend the time required to read it, view it, or listen to it. Test your purpose by asking these four questions:

After defining your purpose, verify that the message will be worth the time and effort required to create, send, and receive it.

- **Will anything change as a result of your message?** Don't contribute to information overload by sending messages that won't change anything. For instance, if you don't like your company's latest advertising campaign but you're not in a position to influence it, sending a critical message to your colleagues won't change anything and won't benefit anyone.
- **Is your purpose realistic?** Recognizing whether a goal is realistic is an important part of having good business sense. For example, if you request a raise while the company is struggling, you might send the message that you're not tuned into the situation around you.
- **Is the time right?** People who are busy or distracted when they receive your message are less likely to pay attention to it. Many professions and departments have recurring cycles in their workloads, for instance, and messages sent during peak times may be ignored.
- **Is your purpose acceptable to your organization?** Your company's business objectives and policies, and even laws that apply to your particular industry, may dictate whether a particular purpose is acceptable.

When you are satisfied that you have a clear and meaningful purpose and that this is a smart time to proceed, your next step is to understand the members of your audience and their needs.

DEVELOPING AN AUDIENCE PROFILE

Before audience members will take the time to read or listen to your messages, they have to be interested in what you're saying. They need to know the message is relevant to their needs—even if they don't necessarily want to read or see it. The more you know about your audience members, their needs, and their expectations, the more effectively you'll be able to communicate with them. Follow these steps to conduct a thorough audience analysis (see Figure 4.2 on the next page):

Ask yourself some key questions about your audience:
- Who are they?
- How many people do you need to reach?
- How much do they already know about the subject?
- What is their probable reaction to your message?

If audience members have different levels of understanding of the topic, aim your message at the most influential decision makers.

- **Identify your primary audience.** For some messages, certain audience members may be more important than others. Don't ignore the needs of less influential members, but make sure you address the concerns of the key decision makers.
- **Determine audience size and geographic distribution.** A message aimed at 10,000 people spread around the globe will probably require a different approach than one aimed at a dozen people down the hall.
- **Determine audience composition.** Look for similarities and differences in culture, language, age, education, organizational rank and status, attitudes, experience, motivations, biases, beliefs, and any other factors that might affect the success of your message (see Figure 4.3 on the next page).

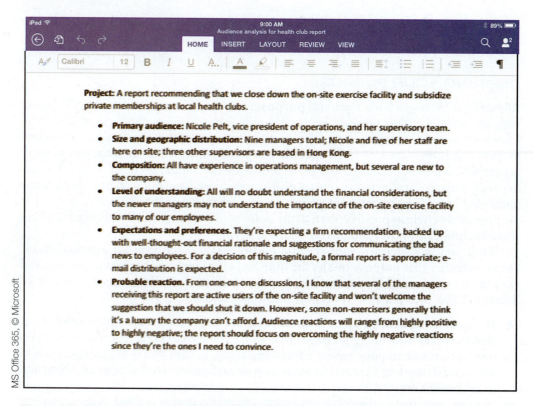

Figure 4.2 Using Audience Analysis to Plan a Message

For simple, routine messages, you usually don't need to analyze your audience in depth. However, for complex messages or messages for indifferent or hostile audiences, take the time to study their information needs and potential reactions to your message.

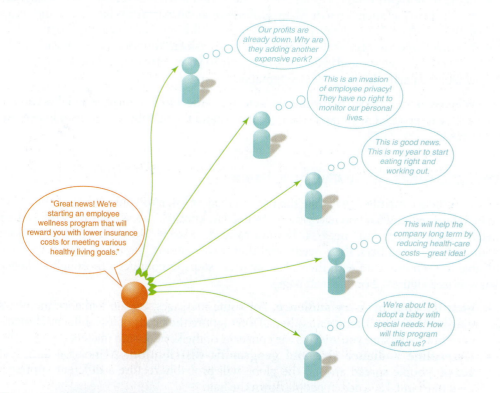

Figure 4.3 Predicting the Effects of Audience Composition

As just one example of why it's important to analyze the composition of your audience, the attitudes and beliefs of individual audience members can have a significant impact on the success of a message. In this scenario, for instance, a seemingly positive message about employee benefits can generate a wide range of responses from employees with different beliefs and concerns.

- **Gauge audience members' level of understanding.** If audience members share your general background, they'll probably understand your material without difficulty. If not, your message will need an element of education to help people understand your message.
- **Understand audience expectations and preferences.** For example, will members of your audience expect complete details or just a summary of the main points? In general, for internal communication, the higher up the organization your message goes, the fewer details people want to see.
- **Forecast probable audience reaction.** As you'll read later in the chapter, potential audience reaction affects message organization. If you expect a favorable response, you can state conclusions and recommendations up front and offer minimal supporting evidence. If you expect skepticism, you can introduce conclusions gradually and with more proof.

REAL-TIME UPDATES
LEARN MORE BY READING THIS PDF
Dig deep into audience needs with this planning tool
This in-depth tool can help you analyze audiences for even the most complex communication scenarios. Go to http://real-timeupdates .com/ebc12 and click on Learn More in the Students section.

Gathering Information

When you have a clear picture of your audience, your next step is to assemble the information to include in your message. For simple messages, you may already have all the information at hand, but for more complex messages, you may need to do considerable research and analysis before you're ready to begin writing. Chapter 11 explores formal techniques for finding, evaluating, and processing information, but you can often use a variety of informal techniques to gather insights and guide your research efforts:

3 LEARNING OBJECTIVE
Discuss information-gathering options for simple messages, and identify three attributes of quality information.

- **Consider the audience's perspective.** Put yourself in the audience's position. What are these people thinking, feeling, or planning? What information do they need in order to move forward? If you are initiating a conversation in a social media context, what information will stimulate discussion in your target communities?
- **Listen to the community.** For almost any subject related to business these days, chances are there is a community of customers, product enthusiasts, or other people who engage in online discussions. Find them and listen to what they have to say.
- **Read reports and other company documents.** Annual reports, financial statements, news releases, blogs by industry experts, marketing reports, and customer surveys are just a few of the many potential sources. Find out whether your company has a *knowledge management system*, a centralized database that collects the experiences and insights of employees throughout the organization.
- **Talk with supervisors, colleagues, or customers.** Fellow workers and customers may have information you need, or they may have good insights into the needs of your target audience.
- **Ask your audience for input.** If you're unsure what audience members need from your message, ask them, if at all possible. Admitting you don't know but want to meet their needs will impress an audience more than guessing and getting it wrong.

If a project doesn't require formal research techniques, or you need answers in a hurry, you can use a variety of informal techniques to gather the information your audience needs.

MOBILE APP
The note-taking apps Evernote and Notebook help you collect, organize, and retrieve the information for planning writing projects.

UNCOVERING AUDIENCE NEEDS

In many situations, your audience's information needs will be obvious, or readers will be able to tell you what they need. In other situations, though, people may be unable to articulate exactly what they want. If someone makes a vague or broad request, ask questions to narrow the focus. If your boss says, "Find out everything you can about Interscope Records," narrow the investigation by asking which aspect of the company and its business is most important. Asking a question or two often forces the person to think through the request and define more precisely what is required.

In addition, try to think of relevant information needs that your audience may not have expressed. Suppose you've been asked to compare two health insurance plans for your firm's employees, but your research has uncovered a third alternative that might be even

Audience members might not be able to describe all the information they need, or you might not have the opportunity to ask them, so you may have to engage in some detective work.

better. You could then expand your report to include a brief explanation of why the third plan should be considered and compare it to the two original plans. Use judgment, however; in some situations you need to provide only what the audience expects and nothing more.

FINDING YOUR FOCUS

Use free writing and other discovery techniques if you need to the find the focus of a new writing project.

You may encounter situations in which the assignment or objective is so vague that you have no idea how to get started in determining what the audience needs to know. In such cases, you can use some *discovery techniques* to help generate ideas and uncover possible avenues to research. One popular technique is **free writing**, in which you write whatever comes to mind, without stopping to make any corrections, for a set period of time. The big advantage of free writing is that you silence your "inner critic" and just express ideas as they come to you. You might end up with a rambling mess by any conventional measure, but that's not important. Within that tangle of expressions, you might also find some useful ideas and angles that hadn't occurred to you yet—perhaps the crucial idea that will jumpstart the entire project.

The best discovery option in some cases might not be writing at all, but rather *sketching*. If you're unable to come up with any words, grab a sketchpad and start drawing. While you're thinking visually, your brain might release some great ideas that were trapped behind words.

The techniques listed under "Defining Your Main Idea" on page 113 can also be helpful if you don't know where to start.

PROVIDING REQUIRED INFORMATION

The journalistic approach asks who, what, when, where, why, *and* how.

After you have defined your audience's information needs, your next step is to satisfy those needs completely. One good way to test the thoroughness of your message is to use the **journalistic approach**: Check to see whether your message answers *who, what, when, where, why,* and *how*. Using this method, you can quickly tell whether a message fails to deliver. For example, consider this message requesting information from employees:

> We are exploring ways to reduce our office space leasing costs and would like your input on a proposed plan in which employees who telecommute on alternate days could share offices. Please let me know what you think of this proposal.

The message fails to tell employees everything they need to know in order to provide meaningful responses. The *what* could be improved by identifying the specific information points the writer needs from employees (such as whether individual telecommuting patterns are predictable enough to allow scheduling of shared offices). The writer also doesn't specify *when* the responses are needed or *how* the employees should respond. By failing to address such points, the request is likely to generate a variety of responses, some possibly helpful but some probably not.

Be Sure the Information Is Accurate

You have a responsibility to provide quality information to your readers.

The *quality* of the information you provide is every bit as important as the *quantity*. Inaccurate information in business messages can cause a host of problems, from embarrassment and lost productivity to serious safety and legal issues. You may commit the organization to promises it can't keep—and the error could harm your reputation as a reliable businessperson. Thanks to the Internet, inaccurate information may persist for years after you distribute it.

You can minimize mistakes by double-checking every piece of information you collect. If you are consulting sources outside the organization, ask yourself whether the information is current and reliable. As Chapter 11 notes, you must be particularly careful when using sources you find online. Be sure to review any mathematical or financial calculations. Check all dates and schedules and examine your own assumptions and conclusions to be certain they are valid.

Be Sure the Information Is Ethical

By working hard to ensure the accuracy of the information you gather, you'll also avoid many ethical problems in your messages. If you do make an honest mistake, such as delivering information you initially thought to be true but later found to be false, contact the recipients of the message immediately and correct the error. No one can reasonably fault you in such circumstances, and people will respect your honesty.

Messages can also be unethical if important information is omitted (see "Practicing Ethical Communication: How Much Information Is Enough?"). Of course, as a business professional, you may have legal or other sound business reasons for not including every detail about every matter. Just how much detail should you include? Make sure you include enough to avoid misleading your audience. If you're unsure how much information your audience needs, offer as much as you believe best fits your definition of complete and then offer to provide more upon request.

Omitting important information can be an unethical decision.

Be Sure the Information Is Pertinent

When gathering information for your message, remember that some points will be more important to your audience than others. Audience members will appreciate your efforts to prioritize the information they need and filter out the information they don't. Moreover, by focusing on the information that concerns your audience the most, you increase your chances of accomplishing your own communication goals.

Select the information you include based on how pertinent it is to your readers.

If you don't know your audience or if you're communicating with a large group of people who have diverse interests, use common sense to identify points of interest. Audience factors such as age, job, location, income, and education can give you clues. If you're trying to sell memberships in a health club, you might adjust your message for athletes, busy professionals, families, and people in different locations or in different income brackets. The comprehensive facilities and professional trainers would appeal to athletes, whereas the low monthly rates would appeal to college students on tight budgets.

Some messages necessarily reach audiences with a diverse mix of educational levels, subject awareness, and other variables. If possible, provide each audience segment with its own targeted information, such as by using sections in a brochure or links on a webpage.

PRACTICING ETHICAL COMMUNICATION

How Much Information Is Enough?

Your company, Furniture Formations, creates a variety of home furniture products, with extensive use of fine woods. To preserve the look and feel of the wood, your craftspeople use a linseed oil–based finish that you purchase from a local wholesaler. The workers apply the finish with rags, which are thrown away after each project. After a news report about spontaneous combustion of waste rags occurring in other furniture shops, you grow concerned enough to contact the wholesaler and ask for verification of the product's safety. The wholesaler knows you've been considering a nonflammable, water-based alternative from another source but tries to assure you with the following message:

> Seal the rags in an approved container and dispose of it according to local regulations. As you probably already know, county regulations require all commercial users of oil-based materials to dispose of leftover finishes at the county's hazardous waste facility.

You're still not satisfied. You visit the website of the oil's manufacturer and find the following cautionary statement about the product you're currently using:

Finishes that contain linseed oil or tung oil require specific safety precautions to minimize the risk of fire. Oil-soaked rags and other materials such as steel wool must be sealed in water-filled metal containers and then disposed of in accordance with local waste management regulations. Failure to do so can lead to spontaneous combustion that results from the heat-producing chemical reaction that takes place as the finish dries. In particular, DO NOT leave wet, oil-soaked rags in a pile or discard them with other waste.

CAREER APPLICATIONS

1. Was the wholesaler guilty of an ethical lapse in this case? If yes, explain what you think the lapse is and why you believe it is unethical. If no, explain why you think the statement qualifies as ethical.
2. Would the manufacturer's warning be as effective without the explanation of spontaneous combustion? Why or why not?

4 LEARNING OBJECTIVE
List the factors to consider when choosing the most appropriate medium for a message.

Selecting the Best Combination of Media and Channels

With the necessary information in hand, your next decision involves the best combination of media and channels to reach your target audience. As you recall from Chapter 1, the medium is the *form* a message takes and the channel is the *system* used to deliver the message. The distinction between the two isn't always crystal clear, and some people use the terms in different ways, but these definitions are a useful way to think about the possibilities for business communication.

Most media can be distributed through more than one channel, so whenever you have a choice, think through your options to select the optimum combination. For example, a brief written message could be distributed as a printed letter or memo, or it could be distributed through a variety of digital channels, from email to blogging to social networking.

THE MOST COMMON MEDIA AND CHANNEL OPTIONS

Media can be divided into *oral, written,* and *visual* forms, and all three can be distributed through *digital* and *nondigital* channels.

The simplest way to categorize media choices is to divide them into *oral* (spoken), *written,* and *visual.* Each of these media can be delivered through *digital* and *nondigital channels,* which creates six basic combinations, discussed in the following sections. Table 4.1 summarizes the general advantages and disadvantages of the six medium/channel combinations. Specific options within these categories have their own strengths and weaknesses to consider as well. (For simplicity's sake, subsequent chapters occasionally use "digital media" to indicate any of the three media types delivered through digital channels.)

Oral Medium, In-Person Channel

The nonverbal and interactive aspects of in-person communication are difficult to replicate in most other media/channel combinations.

The oral medium, in-person combo involves talking with people who are in the same location, whether it's a one-on-one conversation over lunch or a more formal speech or presentation. Being in the same physical space is a key distinction because it enables the nuances of nonverbal communication more than any other media-channel combo. As Chapter 2 points out, these nonverbal signals can carry as much weight in the conversation as the words being spoken.

By giving people the ability to see, hear, and react to each other, in-person communication is useful for encouraging people to ask questions, make comments, and work together to reach a consensus or decision. Face-to-face interaction is particularly helpful in complex, emotionally charged situations in which establishing or fostering a business relationship is important.[2] Managers who engage in frequent "walk-arounds," chatting with employees face-to-face, can get input, answer questions, and interpret important business events and trends.[3]

Oral Medium, Digital Channel

Oral media via digital channels include any transmission of voice via electronic means, both live and recorded, including telephone calls, podcasts, and voicemail messages. Live phone conversations offer the give-and-take of in-person conversations and can be the best alternative to talking in person. However, without a video component, they can't provide the nuances of nonverbal communication. Podcasts can be a good way to share lectures, commentary, and other spoken content. You can read about podcasting in Chapter 7.

Written Medium, Print Channel

Written, printed documents are the classic format of business communication. **Memos** are brief printed documents traditionally used for the routine, day-to-day exchange of information within an organization. **Letters** are brief written messages sent to customers and other recipients outside the organization. Reports and proposals are usually longer than memos and letters, although both can be created in memo or letter format. These documents come in a variety of lengths, ranging from a few pages to several hundred, and are usually fairly formal in tone.

TABLE 4.1   Medium/Channel Combinations: Advantages and Disadvantages

Medium/ Channel	Advantages	Disadvantages
Oral, in-person	<ul><li>Provide opportunity for immediate feedback</li><li>Easily resolve misunderstandings and negotiate meanings</li><li>Involve rich nonverbal cues (both physical gesture and vocal inflection)</li><li>Allow you to express the emotion behind your message</li></ul>	<ul><li>Restrict participation to those physically present</li><li>Unless recorded, provide no permanent, verifiable record of the communication</li><li>Reduces communicator's control over the message</li></ul>
Oral, digital	<ul><li>Can provide opportunity for immediate feedback (live phone or online conversations)</li><li>Not restricted to participants in the same location</li><li>Allow time-shifted consumption (e.g., podcasts)</li></ul>	<ul><li>Lack nonverbal cues other than voice inflections</li><li>Can be tedious to listen to if not audience focused (recorded messages)</li></ul>
Written, printed	<ul><li>Allow writers to plan and control their messages</li><li>Can reach geographically dispersed audiences</li><li>Offer a permanent, verifiable record</li><li>Minimize the distortion that can accompany oral messages</li><li>Can be used to avoid immediate interactions</li><li>Deemphasize any inappropriate emotional components</li><li>Give recipients time to process messages before responding (compared to oral communication)</li></ul>	<ul><li>Offer limited opportunities for timely feedback</li><li>Lack the rich nonverbal cues provided by oral media</li><li>Often take more time and more resources to create and distribute</li><li>Can require special skills in preparation and production if document is elaborate</li></ul>
Written, digital	<ul><li>Generally, all the advantages of written printed documents plus:</li><li>Fast delivery</li><li>Can reach geographically dispersed audiences</li><li>Flexibility of multiple formats and channels, from microblogs to wikis</li><li>Flexibility to structure messages in creative ways, such as writing a headline on Twitter and linking to the full message on a blog</li><li>Ability to link to related and more in-depth information</li><li>Can increase accessibility and openness in an organization through broader sharing</li><li>Enable audience interaction through social media features Ease of integrating with other media types, such as embedded videos or photos</li></ul>	<ul><li>Can be limited in terms of reach and capability (e.g., on Twitter you can reach only those people who follow you or search for you)</li><li>Require Internet or mobile phone connectivity</li><li>Vulnerable to security and privacy problems</li><li>Are easy to overuse (sending too many messages to too many recipients)</li><li>Create privacy risks and concerns (exposing confidential data; employer monitoring; accidental forwarding)</li><li>Entail security risks (viruses, spyware; network breaches)</li><li>Create productivity concerns (frequent interruptions; nonbusiness usage)</li></ul>
Visual, printed	<ul><li>Can convey complex ideas and relationships quickly</li><li>Often less intimidating than long blocks of text</li><li>Can reduce the burden on the audience to figure out how the pieces of a message or concept fit</li><li>Can be easy to create in spreadsheets and other software (simple charts and graphs), then integrate with reports</li></ul>	<ul><li>Can require artistic skills to design</li><li>Require some technical skills to create</li><li>Can require more time to create than equivalent amount of text</li><li>Can be expensive to print</li></ul>
Visual, digital	<ul><li>Generally, all the advantages of visual printed documents and all the advantages of written digital formats plus:</li><li>Can personalize and enhance the experience for audience members</li><li>Offer the persuasive power of multimedia formats, particularly video</li></ul>	<ul><li>Potential time, cost, and skills needed to create</li><li>Can require large amounts of bandwidth</li></ul>

Although still a useful format, printed documents have been replaced by digital alternatives in many instances. However, here are several situations in which you should consider a printed message over electronic alternatives:

- When you want to make a formal impression
- When you are legally required to provide information in printed form
- When you want to stand out from the flood of electronic messages
- When you need a permanent, unchangeable, or secure record

Digital media/channel formats have replaced printed documents in many instances, but print is still the best choice for some messages and situations.

Obviously, if you can't reach a particular audience electronically, you'll need to use a printed message. Appendix A offers guidelines on formatting printed memos and letters.

Written Medium, Digital Channel

Most of your business communication efforts will involve the combination of written medium and digital channel.

Most of your business communication efforts will involve written digital messages, with everything from 140-character tweets to website content to book-length reports distributed as portable document format (PDF) files (see Figure 4.4). Business uses of written, digital messages keeps evolving as companies look for ways to communicate more effectively. For example, email has been a primary business medium for the past decade or two, but it is being replaced in many cases by a variety of other digital formats.[4] Chapter 7 takes a closer look at various written-digital combinations, from email to instant messaging (IM) to social networks.

Visual Medium, Print Channel

Photographs and diagrams can be effective communication tools for conveying emotional content, spatial relationships, technical processes, and other content that can be difficult to describe using words alone. You may occasionally create visual, printed messages as stand-alone items, but most will be used as supporting material in printed documents.

Visual Medium, Digital Channel

The combination of the visual medium and a digital channel can be the most compelling and engaging choice for many messages, although it is not always the easiest or cheapest format.

Business messages can really come alive when conveyed by visual media in digital channels. Infographics, interactive diagrams, animation, and digital video have the potential to

Courtesy Harley-Davidson

Figure 4.4   Media and Channel Choices: Written + Digital
Harley-Davidson could've chosen a variety of media/channel combinations to share this information Harley fans taking a cross-country ride on vintage motorcycles. Facebook was an appealing choice because the company's huge fan base (more than 7 million people) and the ease of sharing the message on the social network.

engage audiences in ways that other formats can't, which is why the use of visual elements in business communication continues to grow.

Traditional business messages rely primarily on text, with occasional support from graphics such as charts, graphs, or diagrams to help illustrate points discussed in the text. However, many business communicators are discovering the power of messages in which the visual element is dominant and supported by small amounts of text. For the purposes of this discussion, you can think of visual media as formats in which one or more visual elements play a central role in conveying the message content.

Messages that combine powerful visuals with supporting text can be effective for a number of reasons. Today's audiences are pressed for time and bombarded with messages, so anything that communicates quickly is welcome. Visuals are also effective at describing complex ideas and processes because they can reduce the work required for an audience to identify the parts and relationships that make up the whole. Also, in a multilingual business world, diagrams, symbols, and other images can lower communication barriers by requiring less language processing. Finally, visual images can be easier to remember than purely textual descriptions or explanations.

The Unique Challenges of Communication on Mobile Devices

Mobile devices can be used to create and consume virtually every digital form of oral, written, and visual media. Thanks to the combination of portability and the flexibility enabled by a wide array of business-focused apps, mobile devices have become a primary tool in business communication. In addition to the factors discussed on pages 16–18 in Chapter 1, consider these issues whenever your messages are likely to be viewed on mobile devices:

- **Screen size and resolution.** The screen resolution of phones and tablets has improved considerably in recent years, but the limited size of these screens still presents a challenge simply because many messages are significantly larger than the screens they will be viewed on. The result is a dilemma that pits clarity again context. Readers can zoom in to make text readable and visuals understandable, but particularly on phone screens, the inability to see an entire document page or visual at once can limit a reader's ability to grasp its full meaning. This can be particularly troublesome if you are collaborating on writing or presentation projects and team members need to review documents or slides.

- **Input technologies.** Even for accomplished texters, typing on mobile keyboards can be a challenge. Voice recognition is one way around the keyboard limitation, but anyone using it in public areas or shared offices runs the risk of sharing private message content and annoying anyone within earshot. In addition, even with a stylus, selecting items on a touch screen can be more difficult than doing so on a PC screen using a mouse. If your website content or other messages and materials require a significant amount of input activity from recipients, try to make it as easy as possible for them. Even simple steps such as increasing the size of buttons and text-entry fields can help.

- **Bandwidth, speed, and connectivity limitations.** The speed and quality of mobile connectivity varies widely by device, carrier, service plan, and geographic location. Even users with higher bandwidth service don't always enjoy the advertised transfer speeds they are paying for. Moreover, mobile users can lose connectivity while traveling, passing through network "dead spots," or during peak-demand hours or events (trade shows and conventions are notorious for this). Don't assume that your mobile recipients will be able to satisfactorily consume the content that you might be creating on a fast, reliable, in-office network.

- **Data usage and operational costs.** As the amount of video traffic in particular increases (video requires much higher bandwidth than text or audio), data consumption is becoming a key concern for mobile carriers and customers alike. Many mobile users do not have unlimited data-usage plans and have to manage their data consumption carefully to avoid excess fees. Some carriers offer unlimited data plans, but even those can come with restrictions such as bandwidth throttling that reduces the speed of a user's connection.[5] Given these factors, be careful about expecting or requiring mobile users to consume a lot of video or other data-intensive content.

The mobile digital channel has become significant in business communication of all types, but it presents some challenges that must be considered.

FACTORS TO CONSIDER WHEN CHOOSING MEDIA AND CHANNELS

You don't always have the option of choosing which medium or channel to use for a particular message. For example, many companies have internal IM or social networking systems that you are expected to use for certain types of communication, such as project updates. However, when you do have a choice, consider these factors:

Media vary widely in terms of *richness*, which encompasses the number of information cues, feedback mechanisms, and opportunities for personalization.

- **Richness.** *Richness* is a medium's ability to (1) convey a message through more than one informational cue (visual, verbal, vocal), (2) facilitate feedback, and (3) establish personal focus.[6] Face-to-face communication is a rich medium because it delivers information both verbally and nonverbally, it allows immediate feedback through both verbal and nonverbal responses, and it has the potential to be intimate and personal, at least in one-on-one and small-group settings. In contrast, lean media are limited in one or more of these three aspects. For example, texting and IM allow rapid feedback and can easily be personalized. However, they usually deliver information through only one informational cue (words), which can lead to misinterpretation. Emoticons (see page 201), which attempt to add emotional nuances that might otherwise be convey through visual means such as facial expressions, are a response to the one-dimensional leanness of text-only messages. In general, use richer media to send nonroutine or complex messages, to humanize your presence throughout the organization, to communicate caring to employees, and to gain employee commitment to company goals. Use leaner media to send routine messages or to transfer information that doesn't require significant explanation.[7]
- **Formality.** Your media choice is a nonverbal signal that affects the style and tone of your message. For example, a printed memo or letter is likely to be perceived as a more formal gesture than an IM or email message.
- **Media and channel limitations.** Every medium and channel has limitations. For instance, IM is perfect for communicating simple, straightforward messages between two people, but it is less effective for complex messages or conversations that involve three or more people.

Many types of media/channel combinations offer instantaneous delivery, but take care not to interrupt people unnecessarily (e.g., with IM or phone calls) if you don't need an immediate answer.

- **Urgency.** Some media establish a connection with the audience faster than others, so choose wisely if your message is urgent. However, be sure to respect audience members' time and workloads. If a message isn't urgent and doesn't require immediate feedback, choose a medium such as email or blogging that allows people to respond at their convenience.

Remember that media and channel choices can also send a nonverbal signal regarding costs; make sure your choices are financially appropriate.

- **Cost.** Cost is both a real financial factor and a perceived nonverbal signal. For example, depending on the context, extravagant (and expensive) video or multimedia presentations can send a nonverbal signal of sophistication and professionalism—or careless disregard for company budgets.

When choosing media and channels, don't forget to consider your audience's expectations and preferences.

- **Audience preferences.** If you know that your audience prefers a particular media and channel combination, use that format if it works well for the message and the situation. Otherwise you risk annoying the audience or having your message missed or ignored.
- **Security and privacy.** Your company may have restrictions on the media and channels that can be used for certain types of messages, but even if it doesn't think carefully whenever your messages include sensitive information. Never assume that your email, IM, and other digital communications are private. Many companies monitor these channels, and there is always the risk that networks could get hacked or that messages will be forwarded beyond their original recipients.

5 **LEARNING OBJECTIVE**
Explain why good organization is important to both you and your audience, and list the tasks involved in organizing a message.

Organizing Your Information

Organization can make the difference between success and failure. Good organization helps your readers or listeners in three key ways. First, it helps them understand your message. In a well-organized message, you make the main point clear at the outset, present additional points to support that main idea, and satisfy all the information needs of the audience. But if your message is poorly organized, your meaning can be obscured, and your audiences may form inaccurate conclusions about what you've written or said.

Second, good organization helps receivers accept your message. If your writing appears confused and disorganized, people will likely conclude that the *thinking* behind the writing is also confused and disorganized. Moreover, effective messages often require a bit more than simple, clear logic. A diplomatic approach helps receivers accept your message, even if it's not exactly what they want to hear. In contrast, a poorly organized message on an emotionally charged topic can alienate the audience before you have the chance to get your point across.

> Good organization benefits your audiences by helping them understand and accept your message in less time.

Third, good organization saves your audience time. Well-organized messages are efficient. They contain only relevant ideas, and they are brief. Moreover, each piece of information is located in a logical place in the overall flow; each section builds on the one before to create a coherent whole, without forcing people to look for missing pieces.

> Good organization helps you by reducing the time and creative energy needed to create effective messages.

In addition to saving time and energy for your readers, good organization saves *you* time and consumes less of your creative energy. Writing moves more quickly because you don't waste time putting ideas in the wrong places or composing material that you don't need. You spend far less time rewriting, trying to extract sensible meaning from disorganized rambling. Last but far from least, organizational skills are good for your career because they help you develop a reputation as a clear thinker who cares about your readers.

REAL-TIME UPDATES
LEARN MORE BY VIEWING THIS PRESENTATION

Smart advice for brainstorming sessions

Generate better ideas in less time with these helpful tips. Go to http://real-timeupdates.com/ebc12 and click on Learn More in the Students section.

DEFINING YOUR MAIN IDEA

The **topic** of your message is the overall subject, and your **main idea** is a specific statement about that topic (see Table 4.2). For example, if you believe that the current system of using paper forms for filing employee insurance claims is expensive and slow, you might craft a message in which the topic is employee insurance claims and the main idea is that a new web-based system would reduce costs for the company and reduce reimbursement delays for employees.

> The topic is the broad subject; the main idea makes a statement about the topic.

In longer documents and presentations, you often need to unify a mass of material with a main idea that encompasses all the individual points you want to make. Finding a common thread through all these points can be a challenge. Sometimes you won't even be sure what your main idea is until you sort through the information. For tough assignments like these, consider a variety of techniques to generate creative ideas:

- **Brainstorming.** Working alone or with others, generate as many ideas and questions as you can, without stopping to criticize or organize. After you capture all these pieces, look for patterns and connections to help identify the main idea and the groups of supporting ideas. For example, if your main idea concerns whether

TABLE 4.2	**Defining Topic and Main Idea**		
General Purpose	Example of Specific Purpose	Example of Topic	Example of Main Idea
To inform	Teach customer service representatives how to edit and expand the technical support wiki	Technical support wiki	Careful, thorough edits and additions to the wiki help the entire department provide better customer support.
To persuade	Convince top managers to increase spending on research and development	Funding for research and development	Competitors spend more than we do on research and development, enabling them to create more innovative products.
To collaborate	Solicit ideas for a companywide incentive system that ties wages to profits	Incentive pay	Tying wages to profits motivates employees and reduces compensation costs in tough years.

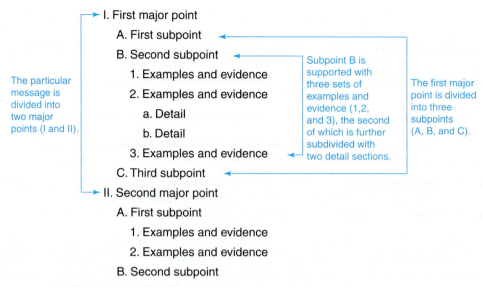

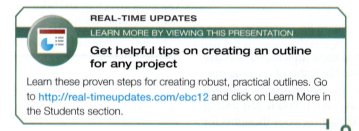

Figure 4.7   **Organizing Your Thoughts with a Clear Outline**
No matter what outlining format you use, think through your major supporting points and the examples and evidence that can support each point.

REAL-TIME UPDATES

LEARN MORE BY VIEWING THIS PRESENTATION

Get helpful tips on creating an outline for any project

Learn these proven steps for creating robust, practical outlines. Go to http://real-timeupdates.com/ebc12 and click on Learn More in the Students section.

faster writing. When you're preparing a longer, more complex message, an outline is indispensable because it helps you visualize the relationships among the various parts.

You're no doubt familiar with the basic outline formats that identify each point with a number or letter and that indent certain points to show which ones are of equal status. A good outline divides a topic into at least two parts, restricts each subdivision to one category, and ensures that each subdivision is separate and distinct (see Figure 4.7).

Another way to visualize the outline of your message is to create an organization chart similar to the charts used to show a company's management structure. Put the main idea in the highest-level box to establish the big picture. The lower-level ideas, like lower-level employees, provide the details. All the ideas should be logically organized into divisions of thought, just as a company is organized into divisions and departments.[8] Using a visual chart instead of a traditional outline has many benefits. Charts help you (1) see the various levels of ideas and how the parts fit together, (2) develop new ideas, and (3) restructure your information flow. The mind-mapping technique used to generate ideas works in a similar way.

Whichever outlining or organizing scheme you use, start your message with the main idea, follow that with major supporting points, and then illustrate these points with evidence.

Start with the Main Idea

The main idea establishes what you want your readers to do or think and why they should do so.

The main idea helps you establish the goals and general strategy of the message, and it summarizes two vital considerations: (1) *what* you want your audience members to do or think and (2) *why* they should do so. Everything in your message should either support the main idea or explain its implications. As discussed earlier, the direct approach states the main idea quickly and directly, whereas the indirect approach delays the main idea until after the evidence is presented.

State the Major Points

Choose supporting points, evidence, and examples carefully; a few strong points will make your case better than a large collection of weaker points.

You need to support your main idea with major points that clarify and explain the main idea in concrete terms. If your purpose is to inform and the material is factual, your major points may be based on something physical or financial—something you can visualize or measure, such as activities to be performed, functional units, spatial or chronological relationships, or parts of a whole. When you're describing a process, the major points are almost inevitably steps in the process. When you're describing an object, the major points often correspond to the parts of the object. When you're giving a historical account, major points represent events in the chronological chain of events. If your purpose is to persuade or to collaborate, select major points that develop a line of reasoning or a logical argument that proves your central message and motivates your audience to act.

Provide Examples and Evidence

After you've defined the main idea and identified major supporting points, think about examples and evidence that can confirm, illuminate, or expand on your supporting points. Choose examples and evidence carefully so that these elements support your overall message without distracting or overwhelming your audience. One good example, particularly if it is conveyed through a compelling story (see the next section), is usually more powerful than several weaker examples. Similarly, a few strong points of evidence are usually more persuasive than a large collection of minor details. Keep in mind that you can back up your major supporting points in a variety of ways, depending on the subject material and the available examples and evidence (see Table 4.3).

If your schedule permits, put your outline aside for a day or two before you begin composing your first draft. Then review it with a fresh eye, looking for opportunities to improve the flow of ideas.

Figure 4.8 on the next page illustrates several of the key themes about organizing a message: helping readers get the information they need quickly, defining and conveying the main idea, limiting the scope of the message, choosing the approach, and outlining your information.

TABLE 4.3 Six Types of Detail		
Type of Detail	**Example**	**Comment**
Facts and figures	Sales are strong this month. We have two new contracts worth $5 million and a good chance of winning another worth $2.5 million.	Enhances credibility more than any other type, but can become boring if used excessively.
Example or illustration	We've spent four months trying to hire recent accounting graduates, but so far, only one person has joined our firm. One candidate told me that she would love to work for us, but she can get $10,000 more a year elsewhere.	Adds life to a message, but one example does not prove a point. Idea must be supported by other evidence as well.
Description	Upscale hamburger restaurants target burger lovers who want more than the convenience and low prices of a McDonald's burger. These places feature wine and beer, half-pound burgers, and generous side dishes (nachos, potato skins). Atmosphere is key.	Helps audience visualize the subject by creating a sensory impression. Does not prove a point but clarifies it and makes it memorable. Begins with an overview of the function, defines its purpose, lists major parts, and explains how it operates.
Narration (storytelling)	When Rita Longworth took over as CEO, she faced a tough choice: shut down the tablet PC division entirely or outsource manufacturing as a way to lower costs while keeping the division alive. As her first step, she convened a meeting with all the managers in the division to get their input on the two options. (Story continues from there.)	Stimulates audience interest through the use of dramatic tension. In many instances, must be supplemented with statistical data in order to prove a point convincingly.
Reference to authority	I discussed this idea with Jackie Loman in the Chicago plant, and she was very supportive. As you know, Jackie has been in charge of that plant for the past six years. She is confident that we can speed up the number 2 line by 150 units an hour if we add another worker.	Bolsters a case while adding variety and credibility. Works only if authority is recognized and respected by audience.
Visual aids	Graphs, charts, tables, infographics, data visualization, photos, video	Helps audience grasp the key points about sets of data or visualize connections between ideas.

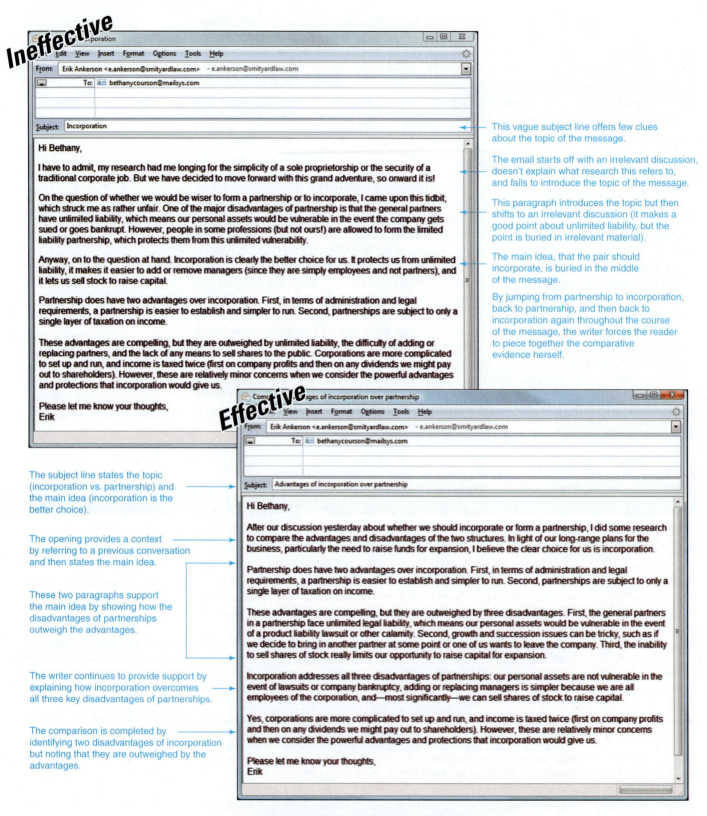

Figure 4.8 Improving the Organization of a Message

This writer is following up on a conversation from the previous day, in which he and the recipient discussed which of two forms of ownership, a partnership or a corporation, they should use for their new company. (*Partnership* has a specific legal meaning in this context.) That question is the topic of the message; the main idea is the recommendation that they incorporate, rather than form a partnership. Notice how the Improved version uses the direct approach to quickly get to the main idea and then supports that by comparing the advantages and disadvantages of both forms of ownership. In contrast, the Poor version contains irrelevant information, makes the comparison difficult to follow, and buries the main idea in the middle of the message.

BUILDING READER INTEREST WITH STORYTELLING TECHNIQUES

Storytelling might seem like an odd subject for a business communication course, but narrative techniques can be an effective way to organize messages in a surprising number of business situations, from recruiting and training employees to enticing investors and customers. Storytelling is such a vital means of communicating that, in the words of management consultant Steve Tobak, "It's hard to imagine your career going anywhere if you can't tell a story."[9] Fortunately, you've been telling stories all your life, so narrative techniques already come naturally to you; now it's just a matter of adapting those techniques to business situations.

You've already been on the receiving end of thousands of business stories: Storytelling is one of the most common structures used in television commercials and other advertisements. People love to share stories about themselves and others, too, which makes social media ideal for storytelling.[10]

Career-related stories, such as how someone sought and found the opportunity to work on projects he or she is passionate about, can entice skilled employees to consider joining a firm. Entrepreneurs use stories to help investors see how their new ideas have the potential to affect people's lives (and therefore generate lots of sales). Stories can be cautionary tales as well, dramatizing the consequences of career blunders, ethical mistakes, and strategic missteps.

A key reason storytelling can be so effective is that stories help readers and listeners imagine themselves living through the experience of the person in the story. Chip Heath of Stanford University and his brother, Dan Heath of Duke University, have spent years exploring the question of why some ideas "stick" and others disappear. One of their conclusions is that ideas conveyed through storytelling tend to thrive because stories "put knowledge into a framework that is more lifelike, more true to our day-to-day existence."[11]

In addition, stories can demonstrate cause-and-effect relationships in a compelling fashion.[12] Imagine attending a new employee orientation and listening to the trainer read off a list of ethics rules and guidelines. Now imagine the trainer telling the story of someone who sounded a lot like you in the near future, fresh out of college, and full of energy and ambition. Desperate to hit demanding sales targets, the person in the story began entering transactions before customers had actually agreed to purchase, hoping the sales would eventually come through and no one would be the wiser. However, the scheme was exposed during a routine audit, and the rising star was booted out of the company with an ethical stain that would haunt him for years. You may not remember all the rules and guidelines, but chances are you will remember what happened to that person who sounded a lot like you. This ability to share organizational values is one of the major benefits of using storytelling in business communication, particularly across diverse workforces.[13]

A classic story has three basic parts. The beginning of the story presents someone whom the audience can identify with in some way, and this person has a dream to pursue or a problem to solve. (Think of how movies and novels often start by introducing a likable character who immediately gets into danger, for example.) The middle of the story shows this character taking action and making decisions as he or she pursues the goal or tries to solve the problem. The storyteller's objective here is to build the audience's interest by increasing the tension: Will the "hero" overcome the obstacles in his or her path and defeat whatever adversary is keeping him or her away from her goal?[14] The end of the story answers that question and usually offers a lesson to be learned about the outcome as well.

By the way, even though these are "stories," they must not be made-up tales. Telling stories that didn't happen to people who don't exist while presenting them as real-life events is a serious breach of ethics that damages a company's credibility.[15]

Consider adding an element of storytelling whenever your main idea involves the opportunity to inspire, to persuade, to teach, or to warn readers or listeners about the potential outcomes of a particular course of action.

For fresh ideas and media materials on planning messages, visit **http://real-time updates.com/ebc12** and click on Chapter 4. For a quick refresher on message-planning tasks, see "Checklist: Planning Business Messages" on the next page.

Storytelling is an effective way to organize many business messages because it helps readers personalize the message and understand causes and consequences.

Organize stories in three parts: a beginning that introduces a sympathetic person with a dream or a challenge, a middle that shows the obstacles to be overcome, and an ending that resolves the situation and shows the moral or message of the story.

CHECKLIST ✔ Planning Business Messages

A. Analyze the situation.
- Determine whether the purpose of your message is to inform, persuade, or collaborate.
- Identify what you want your audience to think or do after receiving the message.
- Make sure your purpose is worthwhile and realistic.
- Make sure the time is right for your message.
- Make sure your purpose is acceptable to your organization.
- Identify the primary audience.
- Determine the size and composition of your audience.
- Estimate your audience's level of understanding and probable reaction to your message.

B. Gather information.
- Decide whether to use formal or informal techniques for gathering information.
- Find out what your audience needs to know.

- Provide all required information and make sure it's accurate, ethical, and pertinent.

C. Select the best combination of medium and channel for your message.
- Understand the advantages and disadvantages of oral, written, and visual medium distributed through both digital and nondigital channels.
- Consider media richness, formality, media limitations, urgency, cost, and audience preference.

D. Organize your information.
- Define your main idea.
- Limit your scope.
- Choose the direct or indirect approach.
- Outline content by starting with the main idea, adding major points, and illustrating with evidence.
- Look for opportunities to use storytelling to build audience interest.

ON THE JOB: SOLVING COMMUNICATION DILEMMAS AT **H&R BLOCK**

Robert Turtledove, H&R Block's chief marketing officer, was impressed enough with your communication skills and social media experience to add you to the team that markets H&R Block's digital tax-preparation solutions. Using the insights you gained in this chapter, address these internal and external communication challenges.

1. A carefully defined purpose is essential for every message, but particularly so with marketing messages. These persuasive messages can accomplish any number of different tasks, from changing perceptions about an overall category of products to encouraging shoppers to visit a retail store to enticing people to place an order for a specific product right away. Any confusion about purpose will result in a message that either doesn't know what it's trying to accomplish or tries to accomplish too much. Turtledove has asked you to plan a promotional campaign that encourages people who do their own taxes but have never used tax preparation software to at least consider these products. Which of the following statements does the best job of defining the specific purpose of this message?
   a. To persuade everyone who visits the H&R Block website to order a copy of H&R Block tax software within two hours of landing on the website.
   b. To persuade people who do their own taxes but have never used tax software to visit the H&R Block website and order a copy of H&R Block software.
   c. To persuade at least 75 percent of all visitors to the H&R Block website to learn more about the advantages of using software to prepare their taxes.

   d. To persuade people who do their own taxes but have never used tax software to visit the H&R Block website to learn more about the advantages of using software to prepare their taxes.

2. You've just learned that the company's software developers are going to redesign the H&R Block tax software to make it easier to use, and they have asked for feedback from Turtledove's department to help prioritize their work. Unfortunately, they actually made the request about a month ago, but the message fell through the cracks somehow and no one in marketing has prepared any information. The design team needs the information first thing tomorrow morning, and it's already 3:00 PM. You have a couple of hours to gather as much information as possible, then you can write a brief report this evening and email it to the development manager. Which of these is the best way to gather useful information?
   a. Interview the customer service manager to find out which features and functions have generated the most calls from frustrated customers.
   b. Use the software yourself for two hours, analyzing its usability and taking note of functions that are difficult to use.
   c. Do an extensive Internet search using several search engines. Look for negative reviews in software and financial magazines, negative comments from bloggers and Twitter users, and other feedback.
   d. Recruit a dozen people in your office for a panel discussion, asking them to share their own experiences with learning the software and to pass along any feedback they've heard from family, friends, and customers.

3. After submitting the emergency report on usability frustrations, you realize the company could benefit from a more systematic way of collecting feedback from customers. Which of the following media choices would you recommend and why?
   a. Publish the software development manager's email address and invite customers to write to that address whenever they get frustrated with any aspect of the software.
   b. Publish a toll-free telephone number that users can call whenever they are frustrated with the software. Operators can record the information and then email the results of each call to the software development manager.
   c. Build an Internet link into the software that gives users access to a feedback form whenever they get frustrated or confused. They can instantly record their grievances, and the information will then be transmitted to H&R Block and automatically fed into a searchable database.
   d. Create the same form and database described in choice (c) but put the form on the H&R Block website, rather than embedding it in the software.

4. You think you've spotted a potential business opportunity for H&R Block: a mobile app for personal financial planning. The company already has a mobile app for tax preparation, but a general-purpose financial app would let users track expenses, balance their checking accounts, and perform other routine tasks. You know that such a product would be a strategic departure for H&R Block, which has always been all about taxes, so your proposal will surely encounter some resistance and skepticism. Which of the following approaches should you take in organizing a proposal that recommends the company explore the possibility of creating this new app?

   a. Launching a new product is a serious business decision, so be direct. Come right out and say what you propose in the opening paragraph of your proposal and then back that up with details in the body of the message. Your readers will study the supporting details and then evaluate your idea on its merits alone.
   b. The fact that H&R Block doesn't already have a financial planning app is mystifying to you. After all, the company is one of the best-known firms in the financial services sector. Your proposal needs to be not only direct but also blunt: Without exactly saying so, you need to convey the message that only a fool would ignore an opportunity like this.
   c. Your proposal should take an indirect approach because your readers will initially be resistant to the idea. Moreover, it would be bad form to dictate precisely what the solution should be, so write only in general terms (such as "the opportunity for smartphone software apps is significant") and let the readers reach a conclusion on their own (as in, deciding specifically to create a personal finance manager for smartphones).
   d. If the proposal doesn't quickly address the audience's reservations regarding moving beyond tax preparation tools into general-purpose financial tools, audience members won't bother to read the details or consider the proposal. Consequently, an indirect approach is best. Start by announcing that you've identified a business opportunity that is ideal for H&R Block but needs to be acted on soon or a competitor will get there first. After you've captured the audience's attention with that intriguing opening, continue with your persuasive argument in favor of the financial planning app.

Learning Objectives Checkup

Assess your understanding of the principles in this chapter by reading each learning objective and studying the accompanying exercises. You can check your responses against the answer key on page 599.

Objective 4.1: Describe the three-step writing process.

1. The three major steps in the three-step writing process are
   a. Writing, editing, and producing.
   b. Planning, writing, and completing.
   c. Writing, editing, and distributing.
   d. Organizing, defining your purpose, and writing.
2. The first step of the three-step writing process is
   a. Writing the first draft.
   b. Organizing your information.
   c. Planning your message.
   d. Preparing an outline.
3. Which of the following tasks should you do when you're planning a writing project?
   a. Define your purpose.
   b. Revise carefully to make sure you haven't made any embarrassing mistakes.
   c. Choose words and sentences carefully to make sure the audience understands your main idea.
   d. Do all of the above.

Objective 4.2: Explain why it's important to analyze a communication situation in order to define your purpose and profile your audience before writing a message.

4. The _____ _____ of a message indicates whether you intend to use the message to inform, to persuade, or to collaborate.
5. If you were to write a letter to a manufacturer complaining about a defective product and asking for a refund, your general purpose would be
   a. To inform
   b. To persuade
   c. To collaborate
   d. To entertain
6. No matter what the message is or the audience you want to reach, you should always
   a. Determine the information your audience needs in order to grasp your main idea
   b. Learn the names of everyone in the target audience
   c. Estimate the percentage of audience members who are likely to agree with your message

   d. Determine a complete demographic profile of your audience

7. If audience members will vary in terms of the amount of information they already know about your topic, your best approach is to
   a. Provide as much extra information as possible to make sure everyone gets every detail
   b. Provide just the basic information; if your audience needs to know more, they can find out for themselves
   c. Gear your coverage to your primary audience and provide the information most relevant to them
   d. Include lots of graphics

Objective 4.3: Discuss information-gathering options for simple messages, and identify three attributes of quality information.

8. To make sure you have provided all the necessary information, use the journalistic approach, which is to
   a. Interview your audience about its needs
   b. Check the accuracy of your information
   c. Verify whether your message answers the questions of *who, what, when, where, why,* and *how*
   d. Make sure your information is ethical

9. To determine whether the information you've gathered is good enough, verify that it is
   a. Accurate
   b. Ethical
   c. Pertinent to the audience's needs
   d. All of the above

10. If you realize you have given your audience incorrect information, the most ethical action would be to
    a. Say nothing and hope no one notices
    b. Wait until someone points out the error and then acknowledge the mistake
    c. Post a correction on your website
    d. Contact the audience immediately and correct the error

Objective 4.4: List the factors to consider when choosing the most appropriate medium for a message.

11. The media choices of oral, written, and visual can be delivered through _____ and _____ channels.

12. Which of the following choices would be best for communicating a complex policy change to employees in a company with offices all over the world?
    a. A teleconference followed by an email message
    b. Instant messaging
    c. A traditional typed memo sent via regular postal mail
    d. A posting on an internal website with an email message alerting employees to the change and directing them to the website for more information

13. Media richness is a measure of
    a. A medium's ability to use more than one informational cue, facilitate feedback, and establish personal focus
    b. A medium's ability to use more than one informational cue, limit destructive feedback, and establish personal focus
    c. How expensive the delivery options are likely to be, particularly for large or geographically dispersed audiences
    d. How much total employee cost is involved in creating messages using a particular medium

Objective 4.5: Explain why good organization is important to both you and your audience, and list the tasks involved in organizing a message.

14. Which of the following is an important benefit of taking time to organize your business messages?
    a. You can delay the actual writing.
    b. You save time and conserve creative energy because the writing process is quicker.
    c. Organizing your thoughts and information saves you the trouble of asking colleagues for input.
    d. In many cases, you can simply send a detailed outline and save the trouble of writing the document.

15. The purpose of limiting your scope when planning a writing project is to
    a. Make your job easier
    b. Reduce the number of things you need to think about
    c. Make sure your memos are never longer than one page
    d. Make sure that your message stays focused on the main idea and any necessary supporting details

16. Starting with the main idea and then offering supporting evidence is known as the _____ approach.

17. Starting with evidence first and building toward your main idea is known as the _____ approach.

18. When your audience is likely to have a skeptical or even hostile reaction to your main idea, you should generally use
    a. The indirect approach
    b. The direct approach
    c. The open-ended approach
    d. The closed approach

19. Which of the following is one of the reasons storytelling can be effective in business communication?
    a. Stories help readers and listeners imagine themselves living through the experience of the person in story.
    b. Stories are entertaining, so they offer some diversion from the daily grind of work.
    c. Readers and listeners are overloaded with data, so avoiding facts and figures is a proven way to get their attention.
    d. Stories are inherently funny, and people are more receptive to new ideas when they are in a good mood.

Quick Learning Guide

CHAPTER OUTLINE

Understanding the Three-Step Writing Process
Optimizing Your Writing Time
Planning Effectively

Analyzing the Situation
Defining Your Purpose
Developing an Audience Profile

Gathering Information
Uncovering Audience Needs
Finding Your Focus
Providing Required Information

Selecting the Best Combination of Media and Channels
The Most Common Media and Channel Options
Factors to Consider When Choosing Media and Channels

Organizing Your Information
Defining Your Main Idea
Limiting Your Scope
Choosing Between Direct and Indirect Approaches
Outlining Your Content

Building Reader Interest with Storytelling Techniques

LEARNING OBJECTIVES

1 Describe the three-step writing process. (page 99)

2 Explain why it's important to analyze a communication situation in order to define your purpose and profile your audience before writing a message. (page 100)

3 Discuss information-gathering options for simple messages, and identify three attributes of quality information. (page 103)

4 List the factors to consider when choosing the most appropriate medium for a message. (page 106)

5 Explain why good organization is important to both you and your audience, and list the tasks involved in organizing a message. (page 112)

KEY TERMS

direct approach Message organization that starts with the main idea (such as a recommendation, a conclusion, or a request) and follows that with your supporting evidence

free writing An exploratory technique in which you write whatever comes to mind, without stopping to make any corrections, for a set period of time

general purpose The broad intent of a message—to inform, to persuade, or to collaborate with the audience

indirect approach Message organization that starts with the evidence and builds your case before presenting the main idea

journalistic approach Verifying the completeness of a message by making sure it answers the *who, what, when, where, why,* and *how* questions

letters Brief written messages sent to customers and other recipients outside the organization

main idea A specific statement about the topic

memos Brief printed documents traditionally used for the routine, day-to-day exchange of information within an organization

scope The range of information presented in a message, its overall length, and the level of detail provided

specific purpose Identifies what you hope to accomplish with your message and what your audience should do or think after receiving your message

topic The overall subject of a message

CHECKLIST ✓

Planning Business Messages

A. Analyze the situation.
- Determine whether the purpose of your message is to inform, persuade, or collaborate.
- Identify what you want your audience to think or do after receiving the message.
- Make sure your purpose is worthwhile and realistic.
- Make sure the time is right for your message.
- Make sure your purpose is acceptable to your organization.
- Identify the primary audience.
- Determine the size and composition of your audience.
- Estimate your audience's level of understanding and probable reaction to your message.

B. Gather information.
- Decide whether to use formal or informal techniques for gathering information.
- Find out what your audience needs to know.
- Provide all required information and make sure it's accurate, ethical, and pertinent.

C. Select the best combination of medium and channel for your message.
- Understand the advantages and disadvantages of oral, written, and visual medium distributed through both digital and nondigital channels.
- Consider media richness, formality, media limitations, urgency, cost, and audience preference.

D. Organize your information.
- Define your main idea.
- Limit your scope.
- Choose the direct or indirect approach.
- Outline content by starting with the main idea, adding major points, and illustrating with evidence.
- Look for opportunities to use storytelling to build audience interest.

Apply Your Knowledge

To review chapter content related to each question, refer to the indicated Learning Objective.

⭐ **4.1.** Some writers argue that planning messages wastes time because they inevitably change their plans as they proceed. How would you respond to this argument? Briefly explain. [LO-1]

⭐ **4.2.** A day after sending an email to all 1,800 employees in your company regarding income tax implications of the company's retirement plan, you discover that one of the sources you relied on for your information plagiarized from other sources. You quickly double-check all the information in your message and confirm that it is accurate. However, you are concerned about using plagiarized information, even though you did nothing wrong. Write a brief email message to your instructor, explaining how you would handle the situation. [LO-3]

⭐ **4.3.** You are organizing an exploratory in-person meeting with engineering representatives from a dozen manufacturers around the world to discuss updates to a technical standard that all the companies' products must adhere to. The representatives have a wide range of firmly held opinions on the subject, because the changes could help some companies and hurt others. They can't even agree on what should be addressed in the first meeting, so you need to develop a minimum level of consensus on what should be on the agenda. Which combination of media and channels would you use to move the conversation forward and finalize the agenda? Each company has one representative, and any discussions need to be kept confidential. [LO-4]

4.4. How might the inability to view an entire document at once on a mobile screen hinder a reader's ability to grasp the full meaning of the message? [LO-4]

4.5. You have been invited to speak at an annual industry conference. After preparing the outline for your presentation, you see that you've identified 14 different points to support your main idea. Should you move ahead with creating the slides for your presentation or move back and rethink your outline? Why? [LO-5]

Practice Your Skills

Message for Analysis: Outlining Your Content [LO-5]

A writer is working on an insurance information brochure and is having trouble grouping the ideas logically into an outline. Using the following information, prepare the outline, paying attention to the appropriate hierarchy of ideas. If necessary, rewrite phrases to make them all consistent.

Accident Protection Insurance Plan

- Coverage is only pennies a day
- Benefit is $100,000 for accidental death on common carrier

- Benefit is $100 a day for hospitalization as result of motor vehicle or common carrier accident
- Benefit is $20,000 for accidental death in motor vehicle accident
- Individual coverage is only $17.85 per quarter; family coverage is just $26.85 per quarter
- No physical exam or health questions
- Convenient payment—billed quarterly
- Guaranteed acceptance for all applicants
- No individual rate increases
- Free, no-obligation examination period
- Cash paid in addition to any other insurance carried
- Covers accidental death when riding as fare-paying passenger on public transportation, including buses, trains, jets, ships, trolleys, subways, or any other common carrier
- Covers accidental death in motor vehicle accidents occurring while driving or riding in or on automobile, truck, camper, motor home, or nonmotorized bicycle

Exercises

Each activity is labeled according to the primary skill or skills you will need to use. To review relevant chapter content, you can refer to the indicated Learning Objective. In some instances, supporting information will be found in another chapter, as indicated.

4.6. **Planning: Identifying Your Purpose [LO-2]** For each of the following communication tasks, state a specific purpose (if you have trouble, try beginning with "I want to . . .").
   a. A report to your boss, the store manager, about the outdated items in the warehouse
   b. A memo to clients about your booth at the upcoming trade show
   c. A letter to a customer who hasn't made a payment for three months
   d. A memo to employees about the department's high phone bills
   e. A phone call to a supplier, checking on an overdue parts shipment
   f. A report to future users of the computer program you have chosen to handle the company's mailing list

4.7. **Planning: Assessing Audience Needs [LO-2]** For each communication task that follows, write brief answers to three questions: Who is the audience? What is the audience's general attitude toward my subject? What does the audience need to know?
   - A final-notice collection letter from an appliance manufacturer to an appliance dealer that is 3 months behind on payments, sent 10 days before initiating legal collection procedures
   - An advertisement for smartphones
   - A proposal to top management, suggesting that the four sales regions in the United States be combined into just two regions
   - Fliers to be attached to doorknobs in the neighborhood, announcing reduced rates for chimney cleaning or repairs
   - A cover letter sent along with your résumé to a potential employer

- A website that describes the services offered by a consulting firm that helps accounting managers comply with government regulations

4.8. **Planning: Assessing Audience Needs [LO-2]** Choose a fairly simple electronic device (such as a digital music player) that you know how to operate well. Write two sets of instructions for operating the device: one set for a reader who has never used that type of device and one set for someone who is generally familiar with that type of machine but has never operated the specific model. Briefly explain how your two audiences affect your instructions.

4.9. **Planning: Analyzing the Situation; Collaboration: Planning Meetings [LO-2], Chapter 2** How can the material discussed in this chapter also apply to meetings, as discussed in Chapter 2? Outline your ideas in a brief presentation or a post for your class blog.

4.10. **Planning: Creating an Audience Profile; Collaboration: Team Projects [LO-2], [LO-3], Chapter 2** With a team assigned by your instructor, compare the Facebook pages of three companies in the same industry. Analyze the content on all the available tabs. What can you surmise about the intended audience for each company? Which of the three does the best job of presenting the information its target audience is likely to need? Prepare a brief presentation, including slides that show samples of the Facebook content from each company.

4.11. **Planning: Analyzing the Situation, Selecting Media; Media Skills: Email [LO-2], [LO-4], Chapter 9** You are the head of public relations for a cruise line that operates out of Miami. You are shocked to read a letter in a local newspaper from a disgruntled passenger, complaining about the service and entertainment on a recent cruise. You need to respond to these publicized criticisms in some way. What audiences will you need to consider in your response? What medium or media should you choose? If the letter had been published in a travel publication widely read by travel agents and cruise travelers, how might your course of action have differed? In an email message to your instructor, explain how you will respond.

4.12. **Planning: Assessing Audience Needs; Media Skills: Blogging; Communication Ethics: Making Ethical Choices [LO-3], Chapter 1** Your supervisor has asked you to withhold important information that you think should be included in a report you are preparing. Disobeying him could be disastrous for your working relationship and your career. Obeying him could violate your personal code of ethics. What should you do? On the basis of the discussion in Chapter 1, would you consider this situation to be an ethical dilemma or an ethical lapse? Explain your analysis in a brief email message to your instructor.

4.13. **Planning: Limiting Your Scope [LO-5]** Suppose you are preparing to recommend that top management install a new heating system that uses the cogeneration process. The following information is in your files. Eliminate topics that aren't essential and then arrange the other topics so that your report will give top managers a clear understanding of the heating system and a balanced, concise justification for installing it.

- History of the development of the cogeneration heating process
- Scientific credentials of the developers of the process
- Risks assumed in using this process
- Your plan for installing the equipment in the headquarters building
- Stories about the successful use of cogeneration technology in comparable facilities
- Specifications of the equipment that would be installed
- Plans for disposing of the old heating equipment
- Costs of installing and running the new equipment
- Advantages and disadvantages of using the new process
- Detailed 10-year cost projections
- Estimates of the time needed to phase in the new system
- Alternative systems that management might want to consider

4.14. **Planning: Choosing the Direct or Indirect Approach [LO-5]** Indicate whether the direct or indirect approach would be best in each of the following situations and briefly explain why. Would any of these messages be inappropriate for email? Explain.

- A message to the owner of an automobile dealership, complaining about poor service work
- A message from a recent college graduate, requesting a letter of recommendation from a former instructor
- A message turning down a job applicant
- A message announcing that because of high air-conditioning costs, the plant temperature will be held at 78° F during the summer
- A message from an advertising agency to a troublesome long-term client, explaining that the agency will no longer be able to work on the client's account

4.15. **Planning: Using Storytelling Techniques; Communication Ethics: Providing Ethical Leadership; Media Skills: Podcasting [LO-5], Chapter 1** Research recent incidents of ethical lapses by a business professional or executive in any industry. Choose one example that has a clear story "arc" from beginning to end. Outline a cautionary tale that explains the context of the ethical lapse, the choice the person made, and the consequences of the ethical lapse. Script a podcast (aim for roughly 3 to 5 minutes) that tells the story. If your instructor directs, record your podcast and post to your class blog.

Expand Your Skills

Critique the Professionals

Locate an example of professional communication in any medium-channel that you think would work equally well—or perhaps better—in another medium. Using the information in this chapter and your understanding of the communication process, write a brief analysis (no more than one page) of the company's media-channel choice and explain why your choice would be at least as effective. Use whatever medium your instructor requests for your report and be sure to cite specific elements from the piece and support from the chapter.

Sharpening Your Career Skills Online

Bovée and Thill's Business Communication Web Search, at http://websearch.businesscommunicationnetwork.com, is a unique research tool designed specifically for business communication research. Use the Web Search function to find a website, video, PDF document, podcast, or presentation that offers advice on planning a report, speech, or other business message. Write a brief email message to your instructor, describing the item you found and summarizing the career skills information you learned from it.

Improve Your Grammar, Mechanics, and Usage

The following exercises help you improve your knowledge of and power over English grammar, mechanics, and usage. Turn to the Handbook of Grammar, Mechanics, and Usage at the end of this book and review all of Section 1.4 (Adjectives). Then look at the following 10 items and identify the preferred choice within each set of parentheses. (Answers to these exercises appear on page 601.)

4.16. Of the two products, this one has the (*greater, greatest*) potential.

4.17. The (*most perfect, perfect*) solution is *d*.

4.18. Here is the (*interesting, most interesting*) of all the ideas I have heard so far.

4.19. The (*hardest, harder*) part of my job is firing people.

4.20. A (*highly placed, highly-placed*) source revealed Dotson's (*last ditch, last-ditch*) efforts to cover up the mistake.

4.21. A (*top secret, top-secret*) document was taken from the president's office last night.

4.22. A (*30 year old, 30-year-old*) person should know better.

4.23. The two companies are engaged in an (*all-out no-holds-barred; all-out, no-holds-barred*) struggle for dominance.

4.24. A (*tiny metal; tiny, metal*) shaving is responsible for the problem.

4.25. You'll receive our (*usual cheerful prompt; usual, cheerful, prompt; usual cheerful, prompt*) service.

For additional exercises focusing on adjectives, visit MyB CommLab. Click on Chapter 4, click on Additional Exercises to Improve Your Grammar, Mechanics, and Usage, and then click on 8. Adjectives.

MyBCommLab

Go to the Assignments section of your MyLab to complete these writing exercises.

4.26. Email lacks both the visual element and the instantaneous connection of some other media. Could these supposed shortcomings actually help some employees communicate more comfortably and effectively? Explain your answer. [LO-5]

4.27. Would you use the direct or indirect approach to ask employees to work overtime to meet an important deadline? Please explain. [LO-5]

Endnotes

1. H&R Block website, accessed 10 February 2015, www.hrblock.com; Paula Drum, "I Got People (Online): How H&R Block Connects by Using Social Media," presentation at BlogWell conference, 22 January 2009, www.socialmedia.org; Shel Israel, "Twitterville Notebook: H&R Block's Paula Drum," Global Neighbourhoods blog, 22 December 2008, http://redcouch.typepad.com/weblog; "H&R Block's Paula Drum Talks Up Value of Online 'Presence,'" The Deal website, video interview, 6 June 2008, www.thedeal.com; Shel Israel, "SAP Global Survey: H&R Block's Paula Drum," Global Neighbourhoods blog, 4 April 2008, http://redcouch.typepad.com/weblog; "Tango in Plain English," video, accessed 27 August 2008, www.youtube.com; "H&R Block, Inc.," *Hoovers*, accessed 27 August 2008, www.hoovers.com; Linda Zimmer, "H&R Block Tangoes into Second Life," Business Communicators of Second Life blog, 17 March 2007, http://freshtakes.typepad.com/sl_communicators; "H&R Block Launches First Virtual Tax Experience in Second Life," press release, 27 August 2008, www.hrblock.com.

2. Carol Kinsey Gorman, "What's So Great About Face-to-Face?" *Communication World*, May–June 2011, 38–39.

3. Linda Duyle, "Get Out of Your Office," *HR Magazine*, July 2006, 99–101.

4. Caroline McCarthy, "The Future of Web Apps Will See the Death of Email," Webware blog, 29 February 2008, http://news.cnet.com; Kris Maher, "The Jungle," *Wall Street Journal*, 5 October 2004, B10; Kevin Maney, "Surge in Text Messaging Makes Cell Operators," *USA Today*, 28 July 2005, B1–B2.

5. Roger Cheng, "Verizon CEO: Unlimited Data Plans Just Aren't Sustainable," *CNET*, 24 September 2013, http://news.cnet.com; Brian Bennet, "Sprint Officially Outs New Unlimited Plans," *CNET*, 11 July 2013, http://reviews.cnet.com; footnotes on Sprint website, accessed 2 March 2014, http://shop.sprint.com.

6. Laurey Berk and Phillip G. Clampitt, "Finding the Right Path in the Communication Maze," *IABC Communication World*, October 1991, 28–32.

7. Samantha R. Murray and Joseph Peyrefitte, "Knowledge Type and Communication Media Choice in the Knowledge Transfer Process," *Journal of Managerial Issues*, Spring 2007, 111–133.

8. Holly Weeks, "The Best Memo You'll Ever Write," *Harvard Management Communication Letter*, Spring 2005, 3–5.

9. Steve Tobak, "How to Be a Great Storyteller and Win Over Any Audience," *BNET*, 12 January 2011, www.bnet.com.

10. Debra Askanase, "10 Trends in Sustainable Social Media," Community Organizer 2.0 blog, 13 May 2010, www.communityorganizer20.com.

11. Chip Heath and Dan Heath, *Made to Stick: Why Some Ideas Survive and Others Die* (New York: Random House, 2008), 214.

12. Heath and Heath, *Made to Stick*, 206, 214.

13. Randolph T. Barker and Kim Gower, "Strategic Application of Storytelling in Organizations," *Journal of Business Communication* 47, no. 3 (July 2010): 295–312.

14. David Meerman Scott, "Effective Storytelling for Business," WebInkNow blog, 18 February 2013, www.webinknow.com.

15. Jennifer Aaker and Andy Smith, "7 Deadly Sins of Business Storytelling," American Express Open Forum, accessed 21 March 2011, www.openforum.com.

5

Writing Business Messages

LEARNING OBJECTIVES

After studying this chapter, you will be able to

1 Identify the four aspects of being sensitive to audience needs when writing business messages.

2 Explain how establishing your credibility and projecting your company's image are vital aspects of building strong relationships with your audience.

3 Explain how to achieve a tone that is conversational but businesslike, explain the value of using plain language, and define active and passive voice.

4 Describe how to select words that are both correct and effective.

5 Define the four types of sentences, and explain how sentence style affects emphasis within a message.

6 Define the three key elements of a paragraph, and list five ways to develop unified, coherent paragraphs.

7 List five techniques for writing effective messages for mobile readers.

ON THE JOB: COMMUNICATING AT
SHE TAKES ON THE WORLD

Natalie MacNeil Writes Her Way to a Better World

Natalie MacNeil is not a dreamer of small dreams. Here's how she introduces herself on one of her online profiles: "My name is Natalie MacNeil, and I want to change the world." For MacNeil, that change means inspiring and helping women launch their own businesses and take more control over their careers. As she puts it, "I want to see more women leading companies, organizations, and countries."

MacNeil knows a thing or two about launching a business. She started her first when she was 18 and by her mid-20s had founded or cofounded a small portfolio of companies, including an Emmy-winning digital media production company, a collaborative workspace for entrepreneurs in the early startup phase, and She Takes on the World, which MacNeil describes as "a training platform and community for women entrepreneurs."

Communication is at the heart of MacNeil's world-changing quest. On the She Takes on the World site and in a book by the same name, MacNeil shares firsthand knowledge on everything from finding investors to expanding a company internationally. Her writing has appeared in a variety of other popular forums as well, including AllBusiness, American Express OPEN Forum, Mashable, *Forbes*, Entrepreneur.com, and *The Wall Street Journal*.

Image by Ashley Wessel

Women who run or aspire to run their own businesses are the target audience for Natalie MacNeil's She Takes on the World, a training and community platform that offers advice on all aspects of launching and managing a company.

Plenty of entrepreneurs, executives, and other experts offer advice on launching businesses, so what sets MacNeil apart? One key element is a clear idea of who her audience is and the type of information these readers are likely to need. When promoting her book, for example, she emphasizes that no business book can appeal to every reader, and she lists the specific types of readers who can benefit from her book. She also does something that many business "how-to" writers don't: She addresses the personal side of being a successful entrepreneur.

Another key element is her positive writing style. The editor of *ForbesWoman* calls MacNeil's blog and book "smart, upbeat, inspirational, and full of practical advice for women who want to own their dream careers." As someone who came of age in the postdigital economy, MacNeil is also tuned into the new world of work, where individuals must manage their personal brands and take control of their careers. In fact, one of her target audiences is college students who might want to create their own companies right out of college, without ever pursuing traditional employment.

The content and style of her messages is clearly connecting with readers. She Takes on the World has grown to include several dozen bloggers who cover every aspect of managing an entrepreneurial career in the new economy. The site was named one of *Forbes* magazine's top 10 entrepreneurial websites for women, among numerous other awards and recognitions it has received. MacNeil shows no signs of slowing down, either, with new investors behind her and ambitious expansion plans.[1]

HTTP://SHETAKESONTHEWORLD.COM/

1 **LEARNING OBJECTIVE**
Identify the four aspects of being sensitive to audience needs when writing business messages.

Adapting to Your Audience: Being Sensitive to Audience Needs

Natalie MacNeil (profiled in the chapter-opening On the Job) knows it takes more than just a great idea to change the way people think. Expressing ideas clearly and persuasively starts with adapting to one's audience.

Whether consciously or not, audiences greet most incoming messages with a selfish question: "What's in this for me?" If your readers or listeners don't think you understand or care about their needs, they won't pay attention, plain and simple. You can improve your audience sensitivity by adopting the "you" attitude, maintaining good standards of etiquette, emphasizing the positive, and using bias-free language.

Readers and listeners are more likely to respond positively when they believe messages address their concerns.

USING THE "YOU" ATTITUDE

Chapter 1 introduced the notion of audience-centered communication and the "you" attitude—speaking and writing in terms of your audience's wishes, interests, hopes, and preferences. On the simplest level, you can adopt the "you" attitude by replacing terms such as *I, me, mine, we, us,* and *ours* with *you* and *yours*:

Adopting the "you" attitude means speaking and writing in terms of your audience's wishes, interests, hopes, and preferences.

Instead of This	Write This
Tuesday is the only day that we can promise quick response to purchase order requests; we are swamped the rest of the week.	If you need a quick response, please submit your purchase order requests on Tuesday.
We offer MP3 players with 50, 75, or 100 gigabytes of storage capacity.	You can choose an MP3 player with 50, 75, or 100 gigabytes of storage.

However, the "you" attitude is more than simply using particular pronouns. It's a matter of demonstrating genuine interest in your readers and concern for their needs (see Figure 5.1). You can use *you* 25 times in a single page and still offend your audience or ignore readers' true concerns. If you're writing to a retailer, try to think like a retailer; if you're dealing with a production supervisor, put yourself in that position; if you're writing to a dissatisfied customer, imagine how you would feel at the other end of the transaction.

Be aware that on some occasions, it's better to avoid using *you*, particularly if doing so will sound overly authoritative or accusing:

Avoid using you *and* your *when doing so*
- *Makes you sound dictatorial*
- *Makes someone else feel guilty*
- *Goes against your organization's style*

Instead of This	Write This
You failed to deliver the customer's order on time.	The customer didn't receive the order on time.
You must correct all five copies by noon.	All five copies must be corrected by noon.

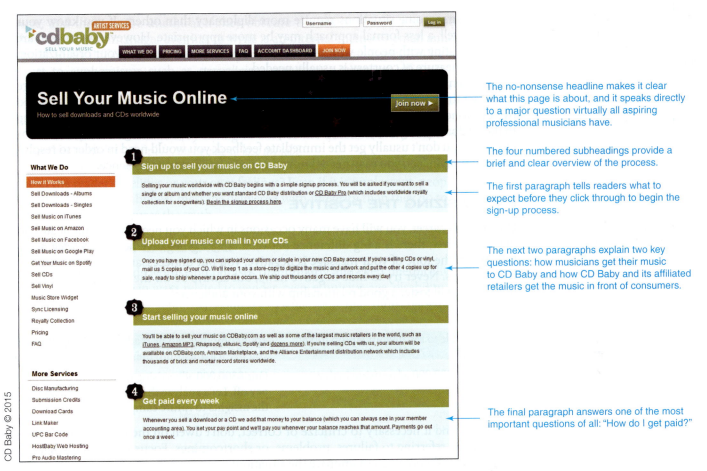

Figure 5.1   Fostering a Positive Relationship with an Audience
CD Baby, the world's largest retailer of independent music, uses clear, positive language to help musicians understand the process of selling their music through the company and its affiliates. By making the effort to communicate clearly and succinctly, the company encourages a positive response from its target readers.

As you practice using the "you" attitude, be sure to consider the attitudes of other cultures and the policies of your organization. In some cultures, it is improper to single out one person's achievements, because the whole team is responsible for the outcome; in that case, using the pronoun *we* or *our* (when you and your audience are part of the same team) would be more appropriate. Similarly, some companies have a tradition of avoiding references to *you* and *I* in most messages and reports.

MAINTAINING STANDARDS OF ETIQUETTE

Good etiquette not only indicates respect for your audience but also helps foster a more successful environment for communication by minimizing negative emotional reaction:

Even if a situation calls for you to be brutally honest, express the facts of the matter in a kind and thoughtful manner.

Instead of This	**Write This**
Once again, you've managed to bring down the entire website through your incompetent programming.	Let's review the last website update to explore ways to improve the process.
You've been sitting on our order for two weeks, and we need it now!	Our production schedules depend on timely delivery of parts and supplies, but we have not yet received the order you promised to deliver two weeks ago. Please respond today with a firm delivery commitment.

REAL-TIME UPDATES

LEARN MORE BY READING THIS PDF

Get detailed advice on using bias-free language

This in-depth guide offers practical tips for avoiding many types of cultural bias in your writing and speaking. Go to http://real-timeupdates.com/ebc12 and click on Learn More in the Students section.

is not simply about "labels." To a significant degree, language reflects the way we think and what we believe, and biased language may well perpetuate the underlying stereotypes and prejudices it represents.[4] Moreover, because communication is all about perception, simply *being* fair and objective isn't enough. To establish a good relationship with your audience, you must also *appear* to be fair.[5] Good communicators make every effort to change biased language. Bias can come in a variety of forms:

- **Gender bias.** Avoid sexist language by using the same labels for everyone, regardless of gender. Don't refer to a woman as *chairperson* and then to a man as *chairman*. Use chair, chairperson, or chairman consistently. (Note that it is not uncommon to use chairman when referring to a woman who heads a board of directors. Archer Daniels Midland's Patricia Woertz and Xerox's Ursula Burns, for example, both refer to themselves as "chairman."[6]) Reword sentences to use *they* or to use no pronoun at all rather than refer to all individuals as *he*. Note that the preferred title for women in business is *Ms.* unless the individual asks to be addressed as *Miss* or *Mrs.* or has some other title, such as *Dr.*

- **Racial and ethnic bias.** Avoid identifying people by race or ethnic origin unless such a label is relevant to the matter at hand—and it rarely is.

- **Age bias.** Mention the age of a person only when it is relevant. Moreover, be careful of the context in which you use words that refer to age; such words carry a variety of positive and negative connotations. For example, *young* can imply energy, youthfulness, inexperience, or even immaturity, depending on how it's used.

- **Disability bias.** Physical, mental, sensory, or emotional impairments should never be mentioned in business messages unless those conditions are directly relevant to the subject. If you must refer to someone's disability, put the person first and the disability second.[7] For example, by saying "employees with physical handicaps," not "handicapped employees," you focus on the whole person, not the disability. Finally, never use outdated terminology such as *crippled* or *retarded*.

Adapting to Your Audience: Building Strong Relationships

2 **LEARNING OBJECTIVE**
Explain how establishing your credibility and projecting your company's image are vital aspects of building strong relationships with your audience.

Successful communication relies on a positive relationship between sender and receiver. Establishing your credibility and projecting your company's image are two vital steps in building and fostering positive business relationships.

ESTABLISHING YOUR CREDIBILITY

People are more likely to react positively to your message when they have confidence in you.

Audience responses to your messages depend heavily on your **credibility**, a measure of your believability based on how reliable you are and how much trust you evoke in others. With audiences who don't know you and trust you already, you need to establish credibility before they'll accept your messages (see Figure 5.2). On the other hand, when you do establish credibility, communication becomes much easier because you no longer have to spend time and energy convincing people that you are a trustworthy source of information and ideas. To build, maintain, or repair your credibility, emphasize the following characteristics:

To enhance your credibility, emphasize such factors as honesty, objectivity, and awareness of audience needs.

- **Honesty.** Demonstrating honesty and integrity will earn you the respect of your audiences, even if they don't always agree with or welcome your messages.

- **Objectivity.** Show that you can distance yourself from emotional situations and look at all sides of an issue.

- **Awareness of audience needs.** Directly or indirectly, let your audience members know that you understand what's important to them.

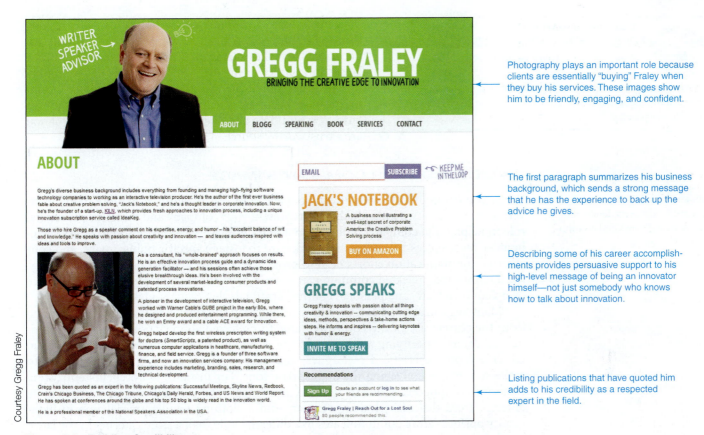

Photography plays an important role because clients are essentially "buying" Fraley when they buy his services. These images show him to be friendly, engaging, and confident.

The first paragraph summarizes his business background, which sends a strong message that he has the experience to back up the advice he gives.

Describing some of his career accomplishments provides persuasive support to his high-level message of being an innovator himself—not just somebody who knows how to talk about innovation.

Listing publications that have quoted him adds to his credibility as a respected expert in the field.

Figure 5.2 Building Credibility
Gregg Fraley is a highly regarded expert in the field of creativity and business innovation, but because his services are intangible, potential clients can't "test drive" those services before making a purchase decision. He therefore takes special care to build credibility as part of his communication efforts.

- **Credentials, knowledge, and expertise.** Audiences need to know that you have whatever it takes to back up your message, whether it's education, professional certification, special training, past successes, or simply the fact that you've done your research.
- **Endorsements.** An *endorsement* is a statement on your behalf by someone who is accepted by your audience as an expert.
- **Performance.** Demonstrating impressive communication skills is not enough; people need to know they can count on you to get the job done.
- **Sincerity.** When you offer praise, don't use *hyperbole*, such as "you are the most fantastic employee I could ever imagine." Instead, point out specific qualities that warrant praise.

In addition, audiences need to know that you believe in yourself and your message. If you lack faith in yourself, you're likely to communicate an uncertain attitude that undermines your credibility. In contrast, if you are convinced that your message is sound, you can state your case with authority. Look out for phrases containing words such as *hope* and *trust*, which can drain the audience's confidence in your message:

Instead of This	**Write This**
We hope this recommendation will be helpful.	We're pleased to make this recommendation.
We trust that you'll want to extend your service contract.	By extending your service contract, you can continue to enjoy top-notch performance from your equipment.

Finally, keep in mind that credibility can take a long time to establish—and it can be wiped out in an instant. An occasional mistake or letdown is usually forgiven, but major lapses in honesty or integrity can destroy your reputation. On the other hand, when you do establish credibility, communication becomes much easier because you no longer have to spend time and energy convincing people that you are a trustworthy source of information and ideas.

PROJECTING YOUR COMPANY'S IMAGE

Your company's interests and reputation take precedence over your personal views and communication style.

When you communicate with anyone outside your organization, it is more than a conversation between two individuals. You represent your company and therefore play a vital role in helping the company build and maintain positive relationships with all its stakeholders. Most successful companies work hard to foster a specific public image, and your external communication efforts need to project that image. As part of this responsibility, the interests and preferred communication style of your company must take precedence over your own views and personal communication style.

Many organizations have specific communication guidelines that show everything from the correct use of the company name to preferred abbreviations and other grammatical details. Specifying a desired style of communication is more difficult, however. Observe more experienced colleagues, and never hesitate to ask for editorial help to make sure you're conveying the appropriate tone. For instance, with clients entrusting thousands or millions of dollars to it, an investment firm communicates in a style quite different from that of a clothing retailer. And a clothing retailer specializing in high-quality business attire communicates in a different style than a store catering to the latest trends in casual wear.

3 LEARNING OBJECTIVE
Explain how to achieve a tone that is conversational but businesslike, explain the value of using plain language, and define active and passive voice.

Adapting to Your Audience: Controlling Your Style and Tone

Your communication **style** involves the choices you make to express yourself: the words you select, the manner in which you use those words in sentences, and the way you build paragraphs from individual sentences. Your style creates a certain **tone**, or overall

THE ART OF PROFESSIONALISM

Being Dependable and Accountable

By any definition, a "pro" is somebody who gets the job done. Develop a reputation as somebody people can count on. This means meeting your commitments, including keeping on schedule and staying within budgets. These are skills that take some time to develop as you discover how much time and money are required to accomplish various tasks and projects. With experience, you'll learn to be conservative with your commitments. You don't want to be known as someone who overpromises and underdelivers.

If you can't confidently predict how long a project will take or how much it will cost, be sure to let your client, colleagues, or supervisor know that. And if changing circumstances threaten your ability to meet a previous commitment, be sure to share that information with anyone who might be affected by your performance.

Being accountable also means owning up to your mistakes and learning from failure so that you can continue to improve. Pros don't make excuses or blame others. When they make mistakes—and everybody does—they face the situation head on, make amends, and move on.

CAREER APPLICATIONS

1. What steps could you take to make realistic commitments on tasks and projects in which you have little or no experience?
2. Does being accountable mean you never make mistakes? Explain your answer.

impression, in your messages. The right tone depends on the nature of your message and your relationship with the reader.

CREATING A CONVERSATIONAL TONE

The tone of your business messages can range from informal to conversational to formal. When you're communicating with your superiors or with customers, your tone may tend to be more formal and respectful.[8] However, that formal tone might sound distant and cold if used with close colleagues.

Compare the three versions of the message in Table 5.2. The first is too formal and stuffy for today's audiences, whereas the third is inappropriately casual for business. The second message demonstrates the **conversational tone** used in most business communication—plain language that sounds businesslike without being stuffy at one extreme or too laid-back and informal at the other extreme. You can achieve a tone that is conversational but still businesslike by following these guidelines:

- **Understand the difference between texting and writing.** Texting can be an efficient way to communicate quickly, particularly on mobile devices with cramped keyboards. However, it's best to view texting as a mode of *conversation*, rather than as a mode of *writing*—and to keep the two modes clear in your mind when you are writing. Communication effectiveness and your personal credibility can suffer if you let texting habits (such as using sentence fragments, sloppy punctuation, and lots of acronyms) creep into your business writing.

> Most business messages aim for a conversational style that is warm but businesslike.

TABLE 5.2   Finding the Right Tone

Tone	Example
Stuffy: too formal for today's audiences	Dear Ms. Navarro: Enclosed please find the information that was requested during our telephone communication of May 14. As was mentioned at that time, Midville Hospital has significantly more doctors of exceptional quality than any other health facility in the state. As you were also informed, our organization has quite an impressive network of doctors and other health-care professionals with offices located throughout the state. In the event that you should need a specialist, our professionals will be able to make an appropriate recommendation. In the event that you have questions or would like additional information, you may certainly contact me during regular business hours. Most sincerely yours, Samuel G. Berenz
Conversational: just right for most business communication	Dear Ms. Navarro: Here's the information you requested during our phone conversation on Friday. As I mentioned, Midville Hospital has the highest-rated doctors and more of them than any other hospital in the state. In addition, we have a vast network of doctors and other health professionals with offices throughout the state. If you need a specialist, they can refer you to the right one. If you would like more information, please call any time between 9:00 and 5:00, Monday through Friday. Sincerely, Samuel G. Berenz
Unprofessional: too casual for business communication	Here's the 411 you requested. IMHO, we have more and better doctors than any other hospital in the state. FYI, we also have a large group of doctors and other health professionals w/offices close to U at work/home. If U need a specialist, they'll refer U to the right one. Any ? just ring or msg. L8R, S

- **Avoid stale and pompous language.** Most companies now shy away from such dated phrases as "attached please find" and "please be advised that." Similarly, avoid using obscure words, stale or clichéd expressions, and overly complicated sentences designed only to impress others (see Table 5.3).
- **Avoid preaching and bragging.** Readers tend to get irritated by know-it-alls who like to preach or brag. However, if you need to remind your audience of something that should be obvious, try to work in the information casually, perhaps in the middle of a paragraph, where it will sound like a secondary comment rather than a major revelation.
- **Be careful with intimacy.** Business messages should generally avoid intimacy, such as sharing personal details or adopting a casual, unprofessional tone. However, when you have a close relationship with audience members, such as among the members of a close-knit team, a more intimate tone is sometimes appropriate and even expected.
- **Be careful with humor.** Humor can easily backfire and divert attention from your message. If you don't know your audience well or you're not skilled at using humor in a business setting, don't use it at all. Avoid humor in formal messages and when you're communicating across cultural boundaries.

USING PLAIN LANGUAGE

Audiences can understand and act on plain language without reading it over and over.

An important aspect of creating a conversational tone is using *plain language* (or *plain English* specifically when English is involved). Plain language presents information in a simple, unadorned style that allows your audience to easily grasp your meaning—language that recipients "can read, understand and act upon the first time they read it."[9]

You can see how this definition supports using the "you" attitude and shows respect for your audience. In addition, plain language can make companies more productive and more profitable because people spend less time trying to figure out messages that are confusing or aren't written to meet their needs.[10] Finally, plain language helps nonnative speakers read your messages.

Creative Commons, a not-for-profit organization that provides content creators with an alternative to traditional copyright law, offers a great example of adapting

REAL-TIME UPDATES

LEARN MORE BY READING THIS ARTICLE

Take your communication skills from good to great

These seven tips can help you transform your business writing from merely ordinary to powerful and persuasive. Go to http://real-timeupdates.com/ebc12 and click on Learn More in the Students section.

TABLE 5.3 Weeding Out Obsolete Phrases

Obsolete Phrase	Up-to-Date Replacement
we are in receipt of	we received
kindly advise	please let me/us know
attached please find	enclosed is or I/we have enclosed
it has come to my attention	I have just learned or [someone] has just informed me
the undersigned	I/we
in due course	(specify a time or date)
permit me to say that	(omit; just say whatever you need to say)
pursuant to	(omit; just say whatever you need to say)
in closing, I'd like to say	(omit; just say whatever you need to say)
we wish to inform you that	(omit; just say whatever you need to say)
please be advised that	(omit; just say whatever you need to say)

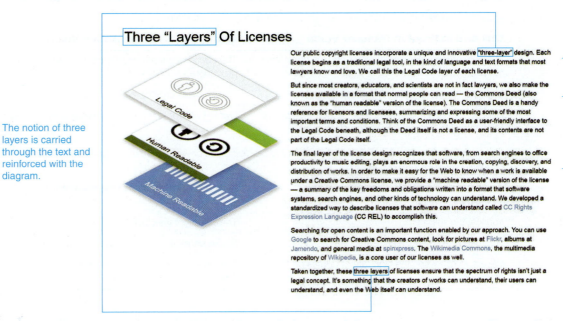

The notion of three layers is carried through the text and reinforced with the diagram.

The introductory sentence expresses the main idea, that the licenses are built in three layers (note that "use" would be a simpler alternative to "incorporate").

The paragraph on the "human readable" version explains why it exists and whom it benefits.

The purpose and function of the "machine readable" version are less obvious than in the other two versions, so this paragraph offers a more extensive explanation.

Figure 5.3　Plain Language at Creative Commons
Creative Commons uses this diagram and text to explain the differences among its three versions of content licenses.
Source: Creative Commons, Inc.

to readers with plain language. Its licensing terms are available in three versions: a complete "legal code" document that spells out contractual details in specific legal terms that meet the needs of legal professionals, a "human readable" version that explains the licensing terms in nontechnical language that anyone can understand, and a "machine readable" version fine-tuned for search engines and other systems (see Figure 5.3).[11]

SELECTING THE ACTIVE OR PASSIVE VOICE

Your choice of the active or passive voice affects the tone of your message. In **active voice**, the subject performs the action and the object receives the action: "Jodi sent the email message." In **passive voice**, the subject receives the action: "The email message was sent by Jodi." As you can see, the passive voice combines the helping verb *to be* with a form of the verb that is usually similar to the past tense.

Using the active voice helps make your writing more direct, livelier, and easier to read (see Table 5.4 on the next page). In contrast, the passive voice is often cumbersome, can be unnecessarily vague, and can make sentences overly long. In most cases, the active voice is your best choice.[12] Nevertheless, using the passive voice can help you demonstrate the "you" attitude in some situations:

- When you want to be diplomatic about pointing out a problem or an error of some kind (the passive version seems less like an accusation)
- When you want to point out what's being done without taking or attributing either the credit or the blame (the passive version shifts the spotlight away from the person or persons involved)
- When you want to avoid personal pronouns in order to create an objective tone (the passive version may be used in a formal report, for example)

The second half of Table 5.4 illustrates several other situations in which the passive voice helps you focus your message on your audience.

Active sentences are usually stronger than passive ones.

Use passive sentences to soften bad news, to put yourself in the background, or to create an impersonal tone when needed.

TABLE 5.4   Choosing Active or Passive Voice

In general, avoid passive voice in order to make your writing lively and direct.

Dull and Indirect in Passive Voice	Lively and Direct in Active Voice
The new procedure was developed by the operations team.	The operations team developed the new procedure.
Legal problems are created by this contract.	This contract creates legal problems.
Reception preparations have been undertaken by our PR people for the new CEO's arrival.	Our PR people have begun planning a reception for the new CEO.

However, passive voice is helpful when you need to be diplomatic or want to focus attention on problems or solutions rather than on people.

Accusatory or Self-Congratulatory in Active Voice	More Diplomatic in Passive Voice
You lost the shipment.	The shipment was lost.
I recruited seven engineers last month.	Seven engineers were recruited last month.
We are investigating the high rate of failures on the final assembly line.	The high rate of failures on the final assembly line is being investigated.

4 **LEARNING OBJECTIVE**
Describe how to select words that are both correct and effective.

Correctness is the first consideration when choosing words.

MOBILE APP
Dragon Dictation uses voice recognition to convert speech to text at up to five times faster than typing.

REAL-TIME UPDATES
LEARN MORE BY EXPLORING THIS INTERACTIVE WEBSITE

Grammar questions? Click here for help

This comprehensive online guide can help you out of just about any grammar dilemma. Go to http://real-timeupdates.com/ebc12 and click on Learn More in the Students section.

Composing Your Message: Choosing Powerful Words

After you have decided how to adapt to your audience, you're ready to begin composing your message. As you write your first draft, let your creativity flow. Don't try to write and edit at the same time or worry about getting everything perfect. Make up words if you can't think of the right word, draw pictures, talk out loud—do whatever it takes to get the ideas out of your head and onto screen or paper. If you've scheduled carefully, you should have time to revise and refine the material later. In fact, many writers find it helpful to establish a personal rule of never showing a first draft to anyone. By working in this "safe zone," away from the critical eyes of others, your mind will stay free to think clearly and creatively.

If you get stuck and feel unable to write, try to overcome writer's block by jogging your brain in creative ways. The introduction is often the hardest part to write, so put it aside and work on whichever parts of the document you're most comfortable with at any given moment. In most cases, you don't need to write the sections in any particular order.[13] Work on nontext elements such as graphics or your cover page. Revisit your purpose and confirm your intent in writing the message. Give yourself a mental break by switching to a different project. Sometimes all you need to do is start writing without worrying about the words you're using or how they will sound to the audience. Words will start flowing, your mind will engage, and the writing will come easier.

You may find it helpful to hone your craft by viewing your writing at three levels: strong words, effective sentences, and coherent paragraphs. Starting at the word level, successful writers pay close attention to the correct use of words.[14] If you make errors of grammar or usage, you lose credibility with your audience—even if your message is otherwise correct. Poor grammar suggests to readers that you're unprofessional, and they may choose not to trust you as a result. Moreover, poor grammar may imply that you don't respect your audience enough to get things right.

The rules of grammar and usage can be a source of worry for writers because some of them are complex and some evolve over time. Even professional editors and grammarians occasionally have questions about correct usage, and they may disagree about the answers. For example, the word *data* is the plural form of *datum*, yet some experts now prefer to treat *data* as a singular noun when it's used in nonscientific material to refer to a body of facts or figures.

With practice, you'll become more skilled in making correct choices over time. If you have doubts about what is correct, you have many ways to find the answer. Check the Handbook of Grammar, Mechanics, and Usage at the end of this book, or consult the many special reference books and resources available in libraries, in bookstores, and on the Internet.

In addition to using words correctly, successful writers and speakers take care to use the most effective words and phrases. Selecting and using words effectively is often more challenging than using words correctly because doing so is a matter of judgment and experience. Careful writers continue to work at their craft to find words that communicate with power (see Figure 5.4).

Effectiveness is the second consideration when choosing words.

In many cases, *global* is an absolute term and doesn't benefit from a modifier such as *truly*. However, economic globalization is occurring in stages, so *truly* here suggests the point at which globalization is nearly complete.

Two Sides of the Story

Growing interest in the global acceptance of a single set of robust accounting standards comes from all participants in the capital markets. Many multinational companies and national regulators and users support it because they believe that the use of common standards in the preparation of public company financial statements will make it easier to compare the financial results of reporting entities from different countries. They believe it will help investors understand opportunities better. Large public companies with subsidiaries in multiple jurisdictions would be able to use one accounting language company-wide and present their financial statements in the same language as their competitors.

Another benefit some believe is that in a truly global economy, financial professionals including CPAs will be more mobile, and companies will more easily be able to respond to the human capital needs of their subsidiaries around the world.

Nevertheless, many people also believe that U.S. GAAP is the gold standard, and something will be lost with full acceptance of IFRS. However, recent SEC actions and global trends have increased awareness of the need to address possible adoption. According to a survey conducted in the first half of 2008 by Deloitte & Touche among chief financial officers and other financial professionals, U.S. companies have an interest in adopting IFRS and this interest is steadily growing. Thirty percent would consider adopting IFRS now, another 28 percent are unsure or do not have sufficient knowledge to decide, while 42 percent said they would not. Still, an AICPA survey conducted in Fall 2008 among its CPA members shows a significant and positive shift in the number of firms and companies that are starting to prepare for eventual adoption of IFRS. A 55 percent majority of CPAs at firms and companies nationwide said they are preparing in a variety of ways for IFRS adoption, an increase of 14 percentage points over the 41 percent who were preparing for change, according to an April 2008 AICPA survey.

Claim is a powerful word here because it suggests a strong element of doubt.

Another concern is that worldwide many countries that claim to be converging to international standards may never get 100 percent compliance. Most reserve the right to carve out selectively or modify standards they do not consider in their national interest, an action that could lead to incompatibility—the very issue that IFRS seek to address.

GAAP and IFRS, Still Differences

The diplomatic use of passive voice keeps the focus on the issue at hand, rather than on the organizations that are involved.

Great strides have been made by the FASB and the IASB to converge the content of IFRS and U.S. GAAP. The goal is that by the time the SEC allows or mandates the use of IFRS for U.S. publicly traded companies, most or all of the key differences will have been resolved.

Because of these ongoing convergence projects, the extent of the specific differences between IFRS and U.S. GAAP is shrinking. Yet significant differences do remain. For example:

- IFRS does not permit Last In First Out (LIFO) as an inventory costing method.
- IFRS uses a single-step method for impairment write-downs rather than the two-step method used in U.S. GAAP, making write-downs more likely.
- IFRS has a different probability threshold and measurement objective for contingencies.
- IFRS does not permit curing debt covenant violations after year-end.
- IFRS guidance regarding revenue recognition is less extensive than GAAP and contains relatively little industry-specific instructions.

5

Robust goes beyond simply *strong* to suggest *resilient* and *comprehensive* as well.

Gold standard (a term borrowed from economics) refers to something against which all similar entities are compared, an unsurpassed model of excellence.

In the context of a survey *significant* means more than just *important*; it indicates a statistical observation that is large enough to be more than mere chance. *Positive* indicates the direction of the change and suggests *affirmation* and *progress*.

Carve out is much stronger than *remove* because it could suggest surgical precision if done well or perhaps violent destruction if not done with finesse. In this context, *carve out* is meant to express a concern about countries weakening the international financial standards by modifying them to meet their own needs.

Figure 5.4   Choosing Powerful Words

Notice how careful word choices help this excerpt from a report published by the American Institute of Certified Public Accountants make a number of important points. The tone is formal, which is appropriate for a report with global, public readership. (GAAP refers to accounting standards currently used in the United States; IFRS refers to international standards.)

UNDERSTANDING DENOTATION AND CONNOTATION

A word may have both a denotative and a connotative meaning. The **denotative meaning** is the literal, or dictionary, meaning. The **connotative meaning** includes all the associations and feelings evoked by the word.

The denotative meaning of *desk* is "a piece of furniture with a flat work surface and various drawers for storage." The connotative meaning of desk may include thoughts associated with work or study, but the word *desk* has fairly neutral connotations—neither strong nor emotional. However, some words have much stronger connotations than others and should be used with care. For example, the connotations of the word *fail* are negative and can have a dramatic emotional impact. If you say the sales department *failed* to meet its annual quota, the connotative meaning suggests that the group is inferior, incompetent, or below some standard of performance. However, the reason for not achieving 100 percent might be an inferior product, incorrect pricing, or some other factor outside the control of the sales department. In contrast, by saying the sales department achieved 85 percent of its quota, you clearly communicate that the results were less than expected without triggering all the negative emotions associated with *failure*.

BALANCING ABSTRACT AND CONCRETE WORDS

The more abstract a word is, the more it is removed from the tangible, objective world of things that can be perceived with the senses.

Words vary dramatically in their degree of abstraction or concreteness. An **abstract word** expresses a concept, quality, or characteristic. Abstractions are usually broad, encompassing a category of ideas, and they are often intellectual, academic, or philosophical. *Love, honor, progress, tradition,* and *beauty* are abstractions, as are such important business concepts as *productivity, profits, quality,* and *motivation*. In contrast, a **concrete word** stands for something you can touch, see, or visualize. Most concrete terms are anchored in the tangible, material world. *Chair, table, horse, rose, kick, kiss, red, green,* and *two* are concrete words; they are direct, clear, and exact. Incidentally, technology continues to generate new words and new meanings that describe things that don't have a physical presence but are nonetheless concrete: *software, database,* and *website* are all concrete terms as well.

As you can imagine, abstractions tend to cause more trouble for writers and readers than concrete words. Abstractions tend to be "fuzzy" and can be interpreted differently, depending on the audience and the circumstances. The best way to minimize such problems is to blend abstract terms with concrete ones, the general with the specific. State the concept, and then pin it down with details expressed in more concrete terms. Save the abstractions for ideas that cannot be expressed any other way. In addition, abstract words such as *small, numerous, sizable, near, soon, good,* and *fine* are imprecise, so try to replace them with terms that are more accurate. Instead of referring to a *sizable* loss, give an exact number.

FINDING WORDS THAT COMMUNICATE WELL

Try to use words that are powerful and familiar.

By practicing your writing, learning from experienced writers and editors, and reading extensively, you'll find it easier to choose words that communicate exactly what you want to say. When you compose your business messages, think carefully to find the most powerful words for each situation and to avoid obscure words, clichés, and buzzwords that are turning into clichés (see Table 5.5):

- **Choose strong, precise words.** Choose words that express your thoughts clearly, specifically, and dynamically. If you find yourself using a lot of adjectives and adverbs, you're probably trying to compensate for weak nouns and verbs. Saying that *sales plummeted* is stronger and more efficient than saying sales *dropped dramatically* or sales *experienced a dramatic drop*.
- **Choose familiar words.** You'll communicate best with words that are familiar to both you and your readers. Efforts to improve a situation certainly can be *ameliorative*, but saying they are *helpful* is a lot more effective. Moreover, trying to use an unfamiliar word for the first time in an important document can lead to embarrassing mistakes.

Avoid clichés, be extremely careful with trendy buzzwords, and use jargon only when your audience is completely familiar with it.

- **Avoid clichés and be careful with buzzwords.** Although familiar words are generally the best choice, avoid *clichés*—terms and phrases so common that they have lost some of their power to communicate. *Buzzwords*, newly coined terms often associated

TABLE 5.5 Selected Examples of Finding Powerful Words	
Potentially Weak Words and Phrases	**Stronger Alternatives (Effective Usage Depends on the Situation)**
Increase (as a verb)	Accelerate, amplify, augment, enlarge, escalate, expand, extend, magnify, multiply, soar, swell
Decrease (as a verb)	Curb, cut back, depreciate, dwindle, shrink, slacken
Large, small	(Use a specific number, such as $100 million)
Good	Admirable, beneficial, desirable, flawless, pleasant, sound, superior, worthy
Bad	Abysmal, corrupt, deficient, flawed, inadequate, inferior, poor, substandard, worthless
We are committed to providing. . .	We provide . . .
It is in our best interest to. . .	We should . . .
Unfamiliar Words	**Familiar Words**
Ascertain	Find out, learn
Consummate	Close, bring about
Peruse	Read, study
Circumvent	Avoid
Unequivocal	Certain
Clichés and Buzzwords	**Plain Language**
An uphill battle	A challenge
Writing on the wall	Prediction
Call the shots	Lead
Take by storm	Attack
Costs an arm and a leg	Expensive
A new ball game	Fresh start
Fall through the cracks	Be overlooked
Think outside the box	Be creative
Run it up the flagpole	Find out what people think about it
Eat our own dog food	Use our own products
Mission-critical	Vital
Disintermediate	Get rid of
Green light (as a verb)	Approve
Architect (as a verb)	Design
Space (as in, "we compete in the XYZ space")	Market or industry
Blocking and tackling	Basic skills
Trying to boil the ocean	Working frantically but without focus
Human capital	People, employees, workforce
Low-hanging fruit	Tasks that are easy to complete or sales that are easy to close
Pushback	Resistance

with technology, business, or cultural changes, are slightly more difficult to handle than clichés, but in small doses and in the right situation, they can be useful. The careful use of a buzzword can signal that you're an insider, someone in the know.[15] However, buzzwords quickly become clichés, and using them too late in their "life cycle" can mark you as an outsider desperately trying to look like an insider. When people use clichés and overuse buzzwords, they often sound as though they don't know how to express themselves otherwise and don't invest the energy required for original writing.[16]

- **Use jargon carefully.** *Jargon*, the specialized language of a particular profession or industry, has a bad reputation, but it's not always bad. Using jargon is usually an efficient way to communicate within the specific groups that understand these terms. After all, that's how jargon develops in the first place, as people with similar interests devise ways to communicate complex ideas quickly. For instance, when a recording engineer wants to communicate that a particular piece of music is devoid of reverberation and other sound effects, it's a lot easier to simply describe the track as "dry." Of course, to people who aren't familiar with such insider terms, jargon is meaningless and intimidating—one more reason it's important to understand your audience before you start writing.

MOBILE APP
The Advanced English Dictionary and Thesaurus helps you find the right word by organizing words according to their relationship with other words.

Composing Your Message: Creating Effective Sentences

5 LEARNING OBJECTIVE
Define the four types of sentences, and explain how sentence style affects emphasis within a message.

Arranging your carefully chosen words in effective sentences is the next step in creating powerful messages. Start by selecting the best type of sentence to communicate each point you want to make.

CHOOSING FROM THE FOUR TYPES OF SENTENCES

A simple sentence has one main clause.

Sentences come in four basic varieties: simple, compound, complex, and compound-complex. A **simple sentence** has one main *clause* (a single subject and a single predicate), although it may be expanded by nouns and pronouns that serve as objects of the action and by modifying phrases. Here's an example with the subject noun underlined once and the predicate verb underlined twice:

> <u>Profits</u> <u>increased</u> in the past year.

A compound sentence has two main clauses.

A **compound sentence** has two main clauses that express two or more independent but related thoughts of equal importance, usually joined by *and, but*, or *or*. In effect, a compound sentence is a merger of two or more simple sentences (independent clauses) that are related. For example:

> Wage <u>rates</u> <u>have declined</u> by 5 percent, and employee <u>turnover</u> <u>has been</u> high.

The independent clauses in a compound sentence are always separated by a comma or by a semicolon (in which case the conjunction—*and, but, or*—is dropped).

A complex sentence has one main clause and one subordinate clause.

A **complex sentence** expresses one main thought (the independent clause) and one or more subordinate, related thoughts (dependent clauses that cannot stand alone as valid sentences). Independent and dependent clauses are usually separated by a comma. In this example, "Although you may question Gerald's conclusions" is a subordinate thought expressed in a dependent clause:

> Although you may question Gerald's conclusions, <u>you</u> <u>must admit</u> that his research is thorough.

A compound-complex sentence has two main clauses and at least one dependent clause.

A **compound-complex sentence** has two main clauses, at least one of which contains a subordinate clause:

> <u>Profits</u> <u>increased</u> 35 percent in the past year, so although the company faces long-term challenges, I <u>agree</u> that its short-term prospects look quite positive.

When constructing sentences, choose the form that matches the relationship of the ideas you want to express. If you have two ideas of equal importance, express them as two simple sentences or as one compound sentence. However, if one of the ideas is less important than the other, place it in a dependent clause to form a complex sentence. For example, although the following compound sentence uses a conjunction to join two ideas, they aren't truly equal:

REAL-TIME UPDATES

LEARN MORE BY READING THIS ARTICLE

Practical tips for more-effective sentences

The Writer's Handbook from the University of Wisconsin offers tips on writing clear, concise sentences. Go to http://real-timeupdates .com/ebc12 and click on Learn More in the Students section.

> The chemical products division is the strongest in the company, and its management techniques should be adopted by the other divisions.

By making the first thought subordinate to the second, you establish a cause-and-effect relationship and emphasize the more important idea (that the other divisions should adopt the chemical division's management techniques):

> Because the chemical products division is the strongest in the company, its management techniques should be adopted by the other divisions.

In addition to selecting the best type for each thought you want to express, using a variety of sentence types throughout a document can make your writing more interesting and effective. For example, if you use too many simple sentences in a row, you may struggle to properly express the relationships among your ideas, and your writing will sound choppy and abrupt. At the other extreme, a long series of compound, complex, or compound-complex sentences can be tiring to read.

Maintain some variety among the four sentence types to keep your writing from getting choppy (too many short, simple sentences) or exhausting (too many long sentences).

USING SENTENCE STYLE TO EMPHASIZE KEY THOUGHTS

In every message of any length, some ideas are more important than others. You can emphasize these key ideas through your sentence style. One obvious technique is to give important points the most space. When you want to call attention to a thought, use extra words to describe it. Consider this sentence:

Emphasize specific parts of sentences by
- Devoting more words to them
- Putting them at the beginning or at the end of the sentence
- Making them the subject of the sentence

> The chairperson called for a vote of the shareholders.

To emphasize the importance of the chairperson, you might describe her more fully:

> Having considerable experience in corporate takeover battles, the chairperson called for a vote of the shareholders.

You can increase the emphasis even more by adding a separate, short sentence to augment the first:

> The chairperson called for a vote of the shareholders. She has considerable experience in corporate takeover battles.

You can also call attention to a thought by making it the subject of the sentence. In the following example, the emphasis is on the person:

> I can write letters much more quickly by using voice dictation.

However, by changing the subject, the voice dictation capability takes center stage:

> Using voice dictation enables me to write letters much more quickly.

Another way to emphasize an idea (in this instance, the idea of stimulating demand) is to place it either at the beginning or at the end of a sentence:

> **Less emphatic:** We are cutting the price to stimulate demand.
> **More emphatic:** To stimulate demand, we are cutting the price.

The best placement of the dependent clause depends on the relationship between the ideas in the sentence.

In complex sentences, the placement of the dependent clause hinges on the relationship between the ideas expressed. If you want to emphasize the subordinate idea, put the dependent clause at the end of the sentence (the most emphatic position) or at the beginning (the second most emphatic position). If you want to downplay the idea, put the dependent clause within the sentence:

> **Most emphatic:** The electronic parts are manufactured in Mexico, <u>which has lower wage rates than the United States</u>.
> **Emphatic:** <u>Because wage rates are lower in Mexico than in the United States</u>, the electronic parts are manufactured there.
> **Least emphatic:** Mexico, <u>which has lower wage rates than the United States</u>, was selected as the production site for the electronic parts.

Techniques such as these give you a great deal of control over the way your audience interprets what you have to say.

Composing Your Message: Crafting Unified, Coherent Paragraphs

6 LEARNING OBJECTIVE Define the three key elements of a paragraph, and list five ways to develop unified, coherent paragraphs.

Paragraphs organize sentences related to the same general topic. Readers expect every paragraph to be *unified*—focusing on a single topic—and *coherent*—presenting ideas in a logically connected way. By carefully arranging the elements of each paragraph, you help your readers grasp the main idea of your document and understand how the specific pieces of support material back up that idea.

MOBILE APP
Pages is a full-featured word processing app for iOS devices.

CREATING THE ELEMENTS OF A PARAGRAPH

Paragraphs vary widely in length and form, but a typical paragraph contains three basic elements: a topic sentence, support sentences that develop the topic, and transitional words and phrases.

Most paragraphs consist of
- A topic sentence that reveals the subject of the paragraph
- Related sentences that support and expand the topic
- Transitions that help readers move between sentences and paragraphs

Topic Sentence

An effective paragraph deals with a single topic, and the sentence that introduces that topic is called the **topic sentence** (see Figure 5.5). In informal and creative writing, the topic sentence may be implied rather than stated. In business writing, the topic sentence is generally explicit and is often the first sentence in the paragraph. The topic sentence gives

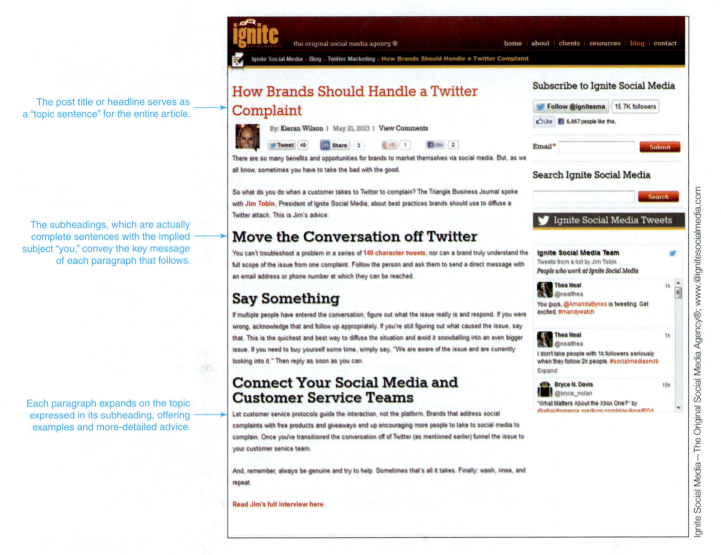

The post title or headline serves as a "topic sentence" for the entire article.

The subheadings, which are actually complete sentences with the implied subject "you," convey the key message of each paragraph that follows.

Each paragraph expands on the topic expressed in its subheading, offering examples and more-detailed advice.

Figure 5.5 Topic Sentences
In this blog post, informative subheadings function as topic sentences for the paragraphs that follow.

readers a summary of the general idea that will be covered in the rest of the paragraph. The following examples show how a topic sentence can introduce the subject and suggest the way the subject will be developed:

> The medical products division has been troubled for many years by public relations problems. [In the rest of the paragraph, readers will learn the details of the problems.]
>
> To get a refund, please supply us with the following information. [The details of the necessary information will be described in the rest of the paragraph.]

In addition to helping your readers, topic sentences help you as a writer because they remind you of the purpose of each paragraph and thereby encourage you to stay focused. In fact, a good way to test the effectiveness of your writing is to prepare a summary version that consists of only the first sentences of all your paragraphs. If this summary communicates the essence of your message in a sensible, compelling way, you've probably done a good job of presenting your information.[17]

Support Sentences

In most paragraphs, the topic sentence needs to be explained, justified, or extended with one or more support sentences. These related sentences must all have a bearing on the general subject and must provide enough specific details to make the topic clear:

> The medical products division has been troubled for many years by public relations problems. Since 2014, the local newspaper has published 15 articles that portray the division in a negative light. We have been accused of everything from mistreating laboratory animals to polluting the local groundwater. Our facility has been described as a health hazard. Our scientists are referred to as "Frankensteins," and our profits are considered "obscene."

The support sentences are all more specific than the topic sentence. Each one provides another piece of evidence to demonstrate the general truth of the main thought. Also, each sentence is clearly related to the general idea being developed, which gives the paragraph unity. A paragraph is well developed if it contains enough information to make the topic sentence understood and convincing, and if it doesn't contain any extraneous, unrelated sentences.

Transitions

Transitional elements include
- Connecting words (conjunctions)
- Repeated words or phrases
- Pronouns
- Words that are frequently paired

Transitions connect ideas by showing how one thought is related to another. They also help alert the reader to what lies ahead so that shifts and changes don't cause confusion. In addition to helping readers understand the connections you're trying to make, transitions give your writing a smooth, even flow.

Depending on the specific need within a document, transitional elements can range in length from a single word to an entire paragraph or more. You can establish transitions in a variety of ways:

- **Use connecting words.** Use conjunctions such as *and, but, or, nevertheless, however, in addition,* and so on.
- **Echo a word or phrase from a previous paragraph or sentence.** "A system should be established for monitoring inventory levels. *This system* will provide . . ."
- **Use a pronoun that refers to a noun used previously.** "Ms. Arthur is the leading candidate for the president's position. *She* has excellent qualifications."
- **Use words that are frequently paired.** "The machine has a *minimum* output of . . . Its *maximum* output is . . ."

Some transitions serve as mood changers, alerting the reader to a change in mood from the previous material. Some announce a total contrast with what's gone on before, some announce a causal relationship, and some signal a change in time. Here is a list of transitions frequently used to move readers smoothly between clauses, sentences, and paragraphs:

> **Additional detail:** moreover, furthermore, in addition, besides, first, second, third, finally
> **Cause-and-effect relationship:** therefore, because, accordingly, thus, consequently, hence, as a result, so
> **Comparison:** similarly, here again, likewise, in comparison, still
> **Contrast:** yet, conversely, whereas, nevertheless, on the other hand, however, but, nonetheless
> **Condition:** although, if
> **Illustration:** for example, in particular, in this case, for instance
> **Time sequence:** formerly, after, when, meanwhile, sometimes
> **Intensification:** indeed, in fact, in any event
> **Summary:** in brief, in short, to sum up
> **Repetition:** that is, in other words, as mentioned previously

Consider using a transition whenever it could help the reader understand your ideas and follow you from point to point. You can use transitions inside paragraphs to tie related points together and between paragraphs to ease the shift from one distinct thought to another. In longer reports, a transition that links major sections or chapters may be a complete paragraph that serves as a mini-introduction to the next section or as a summary of the ideas presented in the section just ending. Here's an example:

> Given the nature of this product, our alternatives are limited. As the previous section indicates, we can stop making it altogether, improve it, or continue with the current model. Each of these alternatives has advantages and disadvantages, which are discussed in the following section.

This paragraph makes it clear to the reader that the analysis of the problem (offered in the previous section) is now over and that the document is making a transition to an analysis of the possible solutions (to be offered in the next section).

CHOOSING THE BEST WAY TO DEVELOP EACH PARAGRAPH

You have a variety of options for developing paragraphs, each of which can convey a specific type of idea. Five of the most common approaches are illustration, comparison or contrast, cause and effect, classification, and problem and solution (see Table 5.6).

In some instances, combining approaches in a single paragraph is an effective strategy. Notice how the example provided for "Problem and solution" in Table 5.6 also includes an element of illustration by listing some of the unique products that could be part of the proposed solution. However, when combining approaches, do so carefully so that you don't lose readers partway through the paragraph.

In addition, before settling for the first approach that comes to mind, consider the alternatives. Think through various methods before committing yourself, or even write several test paragraphs to see which method works best. By avoiding the easy habit of repeating the same old paragraph pattern time after time, you can keep your writing fresh and interesting.

Five ways to develop paragraphs:
- Illustration
- Comparison or contrast
- Cause and effect
- Classification
- Problem and solution

TABLE 5.6   Five Techniques for Developing Paragraphs

Technique	Description	Example
Illustration	Giving examples that demonstrate the general idea	Some of our most popular products are available through local distributors. For example, Everett & Lemmings carries our frozen soups and entrees. The J. B. Green Company carries our complete line of seasonings, as well as the frozen soups. Wilmont Foods, also a major distributor, now carries our new line of frozen desserts.
Comparison or contrast	Using similarities or differences to develop the topic	When the company was small, the recruiting function could be handled informally. The need for new employees was limited, and each manager could comfortably screen and hire her or his own staff. However, our successful bid on the Owens contract means that we will be doubling our labor force over the next six months. To hire that many people without disrupting our ongoing activities, we will create a separate recruiting group within the human resources department.
Cause and effect	Focusing on the reasons for something	The heavy-duty fabric of your Wanderer tent probably broke down for one of two reasons: (1) a sharp object punctured the fabric, and without reinforcement, the hole was enlarged by the stress of pitching the tent daily for a week or (2) the fibers gradually rotted because the tent was folded and stored while still wet.
Classification	Showing how a general idea is broken into specific categories	Successful candidates for our supervisor trainee program generally come from one of several groups. The largest group by far consists of recent graduates of accredited business management programs. The next largest group comes from within our own company, as we try to promote promising staff workers to positions of greater responsibility. Finally, we occasionally accept candidates with outstanding supervisory experience in related industries.
Problem and solution	Presenting a problem and then discussing the solution	Selling handmade toys online is a challenge because consumers are accustomed to buying heavily advertised toys from major chain stores or well-known websites such as Amazon. However, if we develop an appealing website, we can compete on the basis of product novelty and quality. In addition, we can provide unusual crafts at a competitive price: a rocking horse of birch, with a hand-knit tail and mane; a music box with the child's name painted on the top; and a real teepee, made by Native American artisans.

7 **LEARNING OBJECTIVE**
List five techniques for writing effective messages for mobile readers.

Writing Messages for Mobile Devices

One obvious adaptation to make for audiences using mobile devices is to modify the design and layout of your messages to fit smaller screen sizes and different user interface features (see Chapter 6). However, modifying your approach to writing is also an important step. Reading is more difficult on small screens, and consequently users' ability to comprehend what they read on mobile devices is lower than it is on larger screens.[18] In fact, research shows that comprehension can drop by 50 percent when users move from reading on a full-size screen to reading on a smartphone, and they can scroll right past vital information without noticing it.[19] Use these five techniques to make your mobile messages more effective:

To write effectively for mobile devices
- Use a linear organization
- Prioritize information
- Write short, focused messages
- Use short subject lines and headings
- Use short paragraphs

- **Use a linear organization.** In a printed document or on a larger screen, readers can easily take in multiple elements on a page, such as preview or summary boxes, tables and other supporting visuals, and sidebars with related information. All these elements are in view at the same time, so readers can jump around the page to read various parts without feeling lost. However, with small mobile device screens, a complicated organization requires readers to zoom in and out and pan around to see all these elements at readable text sizes. This makes reading slower and raises the odds that readers will get disoriented and lose the thread of the message because they can't see the big picture. In addition, using a touch screen momentarily obscures some of the information, so the more users have to hunt and scroll, the more likely they will miss something.[20] To simplify reading, organize with a linear flow from the top to the bottom of the message or article.

- **Prioritize information.** Small screens make it difficult for readers to scan the page to find the information they want most. Prioritize the information based on what you know about their needs and put that information first.[21] Use the *inverted pyramid* style favored by journalists, in which you reveal the most important information briefly at first and then provide successive layers of detail that readers can consume if they want. Note that you may need to avoid using the indirect approach (see page 115) if your message is complicated, because it will be more difficult for readers to follow your chain of reasoning.

- **Write shorter and more-focused messages and documents.** Mobile users often lack the patience or opportunity to read lengthy messages or documents, so keep it short.[22] In some cases, this could require you to write two documents, a shorter *executive summary* (see page 407) for mobile use and a longer supporting document that readers can access with their PCs if they want more details.

- **Use shorter subject lines and headings.** Mobile devices, particularly phones, can't display as many characters in a single line of text as the typical computer screen can. Depending on the app or website, email subject lines and page headings will be truncated or will wrap around to take up multiple lines. Both formats make reading more difficult. A good rule of thumb is to keep subject lines and headlines to around 25 characters.[23] This doesn't give you much text to work with, so make every word count and make sure you start with the key words so readers can instantly see what the subject line or heading is about.[24]

- **Use shorter paragraphs.** In addition to structuring a message according to discrete blocks of information, paragraphs have a visual role in written communication as well. Shorter paragraphs are less intimidating and let readers take frequent "micro rests" as they move through a document. Because far less text is displayed at once on a mobile screen, keep paragraphs as short as possible so readers don't have to swipe through screen after screen before getting to paragraph breaks.

Compare the two messages in Figure 5.6 to get a sense of how to write reader-friendly mobile content.

For a reminder of the tasks involved in writing messages, see "Checklist: Writing Business Messages" on page 150.

REAL-TIME UPDATES
LEARN MORE BY VISITING THIS WEBSITE

Expert advice on making technologies usable

Usability experts at Nielsen Norman Group offer dozens of research-based articles on effective communication using mobile devices and other technologies. Go to http://real-timeupdates.com/ebc12 and click on Learn More in the Students section.

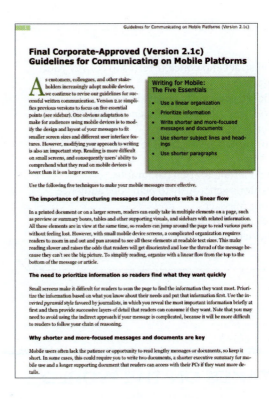

The text from this conventional report page is too small to read on a phone screen.

However, zooming in to read forces the reader to lose context and repeatedly move around to find all the pieces of the page.

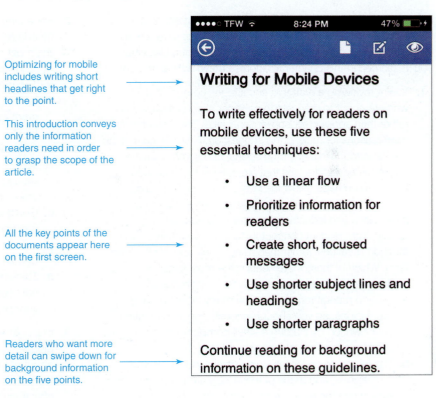

Optimizing for mobile includes writing short headlines that get right to the point.

This introduction conveys only the information readers need in order to grasp the scope of the article.

All the key points of the documents appear here on the first screen.

Readers who want more detail can swipe down for background information on the five points.

Figure 5.6 **Writing for Mobile Devices**

Messages and documents created for printed pages and full-sized screen can be difficult and frustrating on mobile devices (Figures 5.6a and 5.6b). For mobile audiences, rewrite with short headlines and concise, linear content (Figure 5.6c).

CHECKLIST: Writing Business Messages

A. Adapt to your audience.
- Use the "you" attitude.
- Maintain good etiquette through polite communication.
- Emphasize the positive whenever possible.
- Use bias-free language.
- Establish credibility in the eyes of your audience.
- Project your company's preferred image.
- Use a conversational but still professional and respectful tone.
- Use plain language for clarity.

B. Compose your message.
- Choose strong words that communicate efficiently.
- Pay attention to the connotative meaning of your words.

- Balance abstract and concrete terms to convey your meaning accurately.
- Avoid clichés and trendy buzzwords.
- Use jargon only when your audience understands it and prefers it.
- Vary your sentence structure for impact and interest.
- Develop coherent, unified paragraphs.
- Use transitions generously to help your audience follow your message.
- As needed adapt your writing for the limitations of mobile devices.

ON THE JOB: SOLVING COMMUNICATION DILEMMAS AT SHE TAKES ON THE WORLD

Natalie MacNeil recently hired you as an assistant editor at She Takes on the World. One of your responsibilities is to review the work of guest bloggers and suggest improvements. Use what you've learned in this chapter to address these writing challenges.

1. You're reviewing a draft that encourages college students who are about to graduate to consider starting a business rather than applying for conventional jobs. The writer has two main reasons for making this suggestion. First, the current job market is tough in many professions, and some graduates will be forced to take jobs that are outside their intended fields and perhaps below the level of their qualifications. Second, the nature of employment is changing in many professions and industries, and many companies now engage independent contractors (also known as freelancers) for short durations, rather than hiring employees for the long term. Which of these statements is the most sensitive to the audience's needs as they relate to this specific topic?
   a. The job market remains slow in many industries and professions, so you should seriously consider creating your own job by starting a small company and setting up shop as an independent contractor.
   b. The job market remains slow in many industries and professions, and many of those jobs aren't coming back even when the economy fully recovers. Chances are you'll end up working as an independent contractor at some point anyway, so you might as well do it now.
   c. What could be more fun than creating your own job the minute you graduate?
   d. Chances are you'll be facing a tough job market when you graduate, and many traditional jobs are converting to contract work. Why not convert a challenge into opportunity and create your own job?

2. For a blog post on the risks of going into business with friends or family members, which of these sentences has the most appropriate tone and demonstrates the best use of plain language?
   a. The attraction of entering into strategic partnerships with known personalities notwithstanding, one must exercise great caution when considering working with friends and family members.
   b. Going into business with friends or family members can sound appealing, but just because a relationship works on a personal level doesn't automatically mean it will work on a business level.
   c. Going into business with friends or family members can sound appealing, but you need to remember that managing a business is not the same as interacting with people in a social or personal sphere.
   d. Think about how even your best friends can drive you nuts sometimes—do you really want that kind of crazy in your business, too?

3. In a post about pitching a business plan to investors, a guest blogger wants to give entrepreneurs a realistic expectation about getting funding from venture capitalists. Which of the following sentence structures conveys this idea most effectively?
   a. Venture capitalists can provide valuable management expertise and industry connections in addition to startup funds, but they fund only a tiny percentage of all new companies.
   b. Venture capitalists, who fund only a tiny percentage of all new companies, can provide valuable management expertise and industry connections in addition to start-up funds.

c. Venture capitalists can provide valuable management expertise and industry connections in addition to start-up funds. However, they fund only a tiny percentage of all new companies.

d. They fund only a tiny percentage of all new companies, but venture capitalists can provide valuable management expertise and industry connections in addition to start-up funds.

4. The following paragraphs all have the same topic sentence; which has the most effective set of support sentences?

a. First-line supervisors, those on the lowest rung of the managerial ladder, face several unique challenges. As the interface between management and nonmanagerial employees, they have the most immediate responsibility for ensuring that necessary work is done according to agreed-on performance standards. They must also deal directly with any friction that exists between labor and management. Supervisors are also deeply involved in recruiting, hiring, and training of employees.

b. First-line supervisors, those on the lowest rung of the managerial ladder, face several unique challenges. These managers have a good feel for the concerns and activities of employees, given their close day-to-day contact with them. Plus, when supervisors are newly promoted into management, the experience of being an employee is still fresh in their minds—a perspective that is often lost as managers move higher up the corporate ladder.

c. First-line supervisors, those on the lowest rung of the managerial ladder, face several unique challenges. As the interface between management and nonmanagerial employees, they are the ones who must deal with any friction that exists between labor and management. Even if they are sympathetic to employees' concerns or complaints, they represent management and so must take management's side in any disputes.

Learning Objectives Checkup

Assess your understanding of the principles in this chapter by reading each learning objective and studying the accompanying exercises. You can check your responses against the answer key on page 599.

Objective 5.1: Identify the four aspects of being sensitive to audience needs when writing business messages.

1. Why should you take the time to adapt your messages to your audience?
   a. People are more inclined to read and respond to messages that they believe apply to them and their concerns.
   b. Adapting messages to audiences is corporate policy in nearly all large companies.
   c. Adapting your message saves time during planning and writing.
   d. You can manipulate audience responses more easily by adapting your messages.

2. How is your audience likely to respond to a message that doesn't seem to be about their concerns or that is written in language they don't understand?
   a. They will ignore the message.
   b. If they read the message, they will be less inclined to respond in a positive way.
   c. They will assume the writer doesn't respect them enough to adapt the message.
   d. All of the above could occur.

Objective 5.2: Explain how establishing your credibility and projecting your company's image are vital aspects of building strong relationships with your audience.

3. Credibility is a measure of
   a. Your power within the organization
   b. The length of time the audience has known you
   c. Your confidence
   d. The audience's perception of your believability

4. If you have developed a reputation for missing deadlines on projects you manage, which of the following statements would do the best job of helping to rebuild your credibility? (You have previously committed to a project completion date of April 1.)
   a. No April foolin' this time; we'll be finished by April 1.
   b. After analyzing past projects, I now realize that a failure to clarify project objectives up front created significant delays down the line. In order to meet the April 1 deadline, I will make sure to clarify the objective as soon as the team assembles.
   c. I plan to work extra hard this time to make sure we will be finished by April 1.
   d. I hope that we will be finished by April 1.

Objective 5.3: Explain how to achieve a tone that is conversational but businesslike, explain the value of using plain language, and define active and passive voice.

5. A good way to achieve a businesslike tone in your messages is to
   a. Use formal business terminology, such as "In re your letter of the 18th"
   b. Brag about your company
   c. Use a conversational style that is not intimate or chatty
   d. Use plenty of humor

6. Plain English is
   a. Never recommended when speaking with people for whom English is a second language
   b. A movement toward using "English only" in U.S. businesses
   c. A way of writing and arranging content to make it more readily understandable
   d. An attempt to keep writing at a fourth- or fifth-grade level

7. If you want to avoid attributing blame or otherwise calling attention to a specific person, the ____ voice is a more diplomatic approach.

8. The _____ voice usually makes sentences shorter, more direct, and livelier.

Objective 5.4: Describe how to select words that are both correct and effective.

9. Which of the following defines the connotative meaning of the word *flag*?
   a. A flag is a piece of material with a symbol of some kind sewn on it.
   b. A flag is a symbol of everything that a nation stands for.
   c. A flag is fabric on a pole used to mark a geographic spot.
   d. A flag is an object used to draw attention.
10. Which of the following is a concrete word?
    a. Little
    b. Mouse
    c. Species
    d. Kingdom
11. If you're not sure about the meaning of a word you'd like to use, which of the following is the most appropriate way to handle the situation?
    a. Your readers probably have instant access to online dictionaries these days, so go ahead and use the word.
    b. Use the word but include a humorous comment in parentheses saying that you're not really sure what this big, important word means.
    c. Either verify the meaning of the word or rewrite the sentence so that you don't need to use it.
    d. Find a synonym in a thesaurus and use that word instead.
12. Using jargon is
    a. Often a good idea when discussing complex subjects with people who are intimately familiar with the subject and common jargon relating to it
    b. Never a good idea
    c. A good way to build credibility, no matter what the purpose of the message
    d. A sign of being an "insider"

Objective 5.5: Define the four types of sentences and explain how sentence style affects emphasis within a message.

13. Where is the most emphatic place to put a dependent clause?
    a. At the end of the sentence
    b. At the beginning of the sentence
    c. In the middle of the sentence
    d. Anywhere in the sentence

14. Devoting a lot of words to a particular idea shows your audience that
    a. The idea is complicated
    b. The idea is the topic sentence
    c. The idea is important
    d. The idea is new and therefore requires more explanation

Objective 5.6: Define the three key elements of a paragraph and list five ways to develop unified, coherent paragraphs.

15. When developing a paragraph, keep in mind
    a. That you should stick to one method of development within a single paragraph
    b. That once you use one method of development, you should use that same method for all the paragraphs in a section
    c. That your choice of technique should take into account your subject, your intended audience, and your purpose
    d. All of the above
16. To develop a paragraph by illustration, give your audience enough _____ to help them grasp the main idea.
17. Paragraphs organized by comparison and contrast point out the _____ or _____ between two or more items.
18. To explain the reasons something happened, which of these paragraph designs should you use?
    a. Cause-effect
    b. Opposition and argument
    c. Classification
    d. Prioritization

Objective 5.7: List five techniques for writing effective messages for mobile readers.

19. What is meant by using a linear organization to craft messages for mobile devices?
    a. Using only ethically proven information
    b. Organizing all the information in a single topical thread from start to finish
    c. Putting each paragraph on its own line
    d. Using line art to convey key message points
20. The _____ _____ style recommended for mobile messages means you reveal the most important information briefly at first and then provide successive layers of detail that readers can consume if they want.
21. What is a good rule of thumb for the length of subject lines and headlines intended for mobile readers?
    a. Two words, three at a most
    b. As long as the device's screen is wide in landscape mode
    c. Around 25 characters
    d. Around 25 words

Quick Learning Guide

CHAPTER OUTLINE

Adapting to Your Audience: Being Sensitive to Audience Needs

Using the "You" Attitude
Maintaining Standards of Etiquette
Emphasizing the Positive
Using Bias-Free Language

Adapting to Your Audience: Building Strong Relationships

Establishing Your Credibility
Projecting Your Company's Image

Adapting to Your Audience: Controlling Your Style and Tone

Creating a Conversational Tone
Using Plain Language
Selecting the Active or Passive Voice

Composing Your Message: Choosing Powerful Words

Understanding Denotation and Connotation
Balancing Abstract and Concrete Words
Finding Words That Communicate Well

Composing Your Message: Creating Effective Sentences

Choosing from the Four Types of Sentences
Using Sentence Style to Emphasize Key Thoughts

Composing Your Message: Crafting Unified, Coherent Paragraphs

Creating the Elements of a Paragraph
Choosing the Best Way to Develop Each Paragraph

Writing Messages for Mobile Devices

LEARNING OBJECTIVES

1 Identify the four aspects of being sensitive to audience needs when writing business messages. (page 128)

2 Explain how establishing your credibility and projecting your company's image are vital aspects of building strong relationships with your audience. (page 132)

3 Explain how to achieve a tone that is conversational but businesslike, explain the value of using plain language, and define active and passive voice. (page 134)

4 Describe how to select words that are both correct and effective. (page 138)

5 Define the four types of sentences, and explain how sentence style affects emphasis within a message. (page 142)

6 Define the three key elements of a paragraph, and list five ways to develop unified, coherent paragraphs. (page 144)

7 List five techniques for writing effective messages for mobile readers. (page 148)

KEY TERMS

abstract word Word that expresses a concept, quality, or characteristic; abstractions are usually broad

active voice Sentence structure in which the subject performs the action and the object receives the action

bias-free language Language that avoids words and phrases that categorize or stigmatize people in ways related to gender, race, ethnicity, age, or disability

complex sentence Sentence that expresses one main thought (the independent clause) and one or more subordinate, related thoughts (dependent clauses that cannot stand alone as valid sentences)

compound sentence Sentence with two main clauses that express two or more independent but related thoughts of equal importance, usually joined by *and, but,* or *or*

compound-complex sentence Sentence with two main clauses, at least one of which contains a subordinate clause

concrete word Word that represents something you can touch, see, or visualize; most concrete terms related to the tangible, material world

connotative meaning All the associations and feelings evoked by a word

conversational tone The tone used in most business communication; it uses plain language that sounds businesslike without being stuffy at one extreme or too laid-back and informal at the other extreme

credibility A measure of your believability, based on how reliable you are and how much trust you evoke in others

denotative meaning The literal, or dictionary, meaning of a word

euphemisms Words or phrases that express a thought in milder terms

passive voice Sentence structure in which the subject receives the action

simple sentence Sentence with one main clause (a single subject and a single predicate)

style The choices you make to express yourself: the words you select, the manner in which you use those words in sentences, and the way you build paragraphs from individual sentences

tone The overall impression in your messages, created by the style you use

topic sentence Sentence that introduces that topic of a paragraph

transitions Words or phrases that tie together ideas by showing how one thought is related to another

CHECKLIST:

Writing Business Messages

A. Adapt to your audience.
- Use the "you" attitude.
- Maintain good etiquette through polite communication.
- Emphasize the positive whenever possible.
- Use bias-free language.
- Establish credibility in the eyes of your audience.
- Project your company's preferred image.
- Use a conversational but still professional and respectful tone.
- Use plain language for clarity.

B. Compose your message.
- Choose strong words that communicate efficiently.
- Pay attention to the connotative meaning of your words.
- Balance abstract and concrete terms to convey your meaning accurately.
- Avoid clichés and trendy buzzwords.
- Use jargon only when your audience understands it and prefers it.
- Vary your sentence structure for impact and interest.
- Develop coherent, unified paragraphs.
- Use transitions generously to help your audience follow your message.
- As needed adapt your writing for the limitations of mobile devices.

Apply Your Knowledge

To review chapter content related to each question, refer to the indicated Learning Objective.

⭐ **5.1.** Millions of people in the United States are allergic to one or more food ingredients. Each year, thousands of these people end up in the emergency room after suffering allergic reactions, and hundreds of them die. Many of these tragic events are tied to poorly written food labels that either fail to identify dangerous allergens or use scientific terms that most consumers don't recognize.[25] Do food manufacturers have a responsibility to ensure that consumers read, understand, and follow warnings on food products? Explain your answer. [LO-1]

⭐ **5.2.** When composing business messages, how can you communicate with an authentic voice and project your company's image at the same time? [LO-2]

5.3. Does using plain language make you come across as less of an expert? Explain your answer. [LO-3]

⭐ **5.4.** Should you bother using transitions if the logical sequence of your message is obvious? Why or why not? [LO-6]

5.5. Why can it be difficult to use the indirect approach for a complex message that will be read on mobile devices? [LO-7]

Practice Your Skills

5.6. Messages for Analysis: Creating a Businesslike Tone [LO-1], [LO-3]

Read the following email draft and then (a) analyze the strengths and weaknesses of each sentence and (b) revise the document so that it follows this chapter's guidelines. The message was written by the marketing manager of an online retailer of baby-related products in the hope of becoming a retail outlet for Inglesina strollers and high chairs. As a manufacturer of stylish, top-quality products, Inglesina (based in Italy) is extremely selective about the retail outlets through which it allows its products to be sold.

> Our e-tailing site, **www.BestBabyGear.com**, specializes in only the very best products for parents of newborns, infants, and toddlers. We constantly scour the world looking for products that are good enough and well-built enough and classy enough—good enough to take their place alongside the hundreds of other carefully selected products that adorn the pages of our award-winning website, **www.bestbabygear .com**. We aim for the fences every time we select a product to join this portfolio; we don't want to waste our time with onesey-twosey products that might sell a half dozen units per annum—no, we want every product to be a top-drawer success, selling at least one hundred units per specific model per year in order to justify our expense and hassle factor in adding it to the above mentioned portfolio. After careful consideration, we thusly concluded that your Inglesina lines meet our needs and would therefore like to add it.

Exercises

Each activity is labeled according to the primary skill or skills you will need to use. To review relevant chapter content, you can refer to the indicated Learning Objective. In some instances, supporting information will be found in another chapter, as indicated.

Writing: Communicating with Sensitivity and Tact [LO-1]
Substitute a better phrase for each of the following:

5.7. You claim that

5.8. You must update

5.9. It is not our policy to

5.10. You neglected to

5.11. In which you assert

5.12. We are sorry you are dissatisfied

5.13. You failed to enclose

5.14. We request that you send us

5.15. Apparently you overlooked our terms

5.16. We have been very patient

5.17. We are at a loss to understand

Writing: Demonstrating the "You" Attitude [LO-1] Rewrite these sentences to reflect your audience's viewpoint:

5.18. Your email order cannot be processed; we request that you use the order form on our website instead.

5.19. We insist that you always bring your credit card to the store.

5.20. We want to get rid of all our 15-inch LCD screens to make room in our warehouse for the new 19-, 23-, and 35-inch monitors. Thus, we are offering a 25 percent discount on all sales of 15-inch models this week.

5.21. I am applying for the position of bookkeeper in your office. I feel my grades prove that I am bright and capable, and I think I can do a good job for you.

5.22. As requested, we are sending the refund for $25.

5.23. If you cared about doing a good job, you would've made the extra effort required to learn how to use the machinery properly.

5.24. Your strategy presentation this morning absolutely blew me away; there's no way we can fail with all the brilliant ideas you've pulled together—I'm so glad you're running the company now!

5.25. Regarding your email message from September 28 regarding the slow payment of your invoice, it's important for you to realize that we've just undergone a massive upgrade of our accounts payable system and payments have been delayed for everybody, not just you.

5.26. I know I'm late with the asset valuation report, but I haven't been feeling well and I just haven't had the energy needed to work through the numbers yet.

5.27. With all the online news sources available today, I can't believe you didn't know that MyTravel and Thomas Cook were in merger talks—I mean, you don't even have to get up from your computer to learn this!

Writing: Emphasizing the Positive [LO-1] Revise these sentences to be positive rather than negative:

5.28. To avoid damage to your credit rating, please remit payment within 10 days.

5.29. We don't offer refunds on returned merchandise that is soiled.

5.30. Because we are temporarily out of Baby Cry dolls, we won't be able to ship your order for 10 days.

5.31. You failed to specify the color of the blouse that you ordered.

5.32. You should have realized that waterbeds will freeze in unheated houses during winter. Therefore, our guarantee does not cover the valve damage, and you must pay the **$9.50** valve-replacement fee (plus postage).

Writing: Using Unbiased Language [LO-1] Rewrite each of the following to eliminate bias:

5.33. For an Indian, Maggie certainly is outgoing.

5.34. He needs a wheelchair, but he doesn't let his handicap affect his job performance.

5.35. A pilot must have the ability to stay calm under pressure, and then he must be trained to cope with any problem that arises.

5.36. Renata Parsons, married and the mother of a teenager, is a top candidate for CEO.

5.37. Even at his age, Sam Nugent is still an active salesman.

5.38. **Writing: Establishing Your Credibility; Microblogging Skills, [LO-2], Chapter 7** Search LinkedIn for the profile of an expert in any industry or profession. Now imagine that you are going to introduce this person as a speaker at a convention. You will make an in-person introduction at the time of the speech, but you decide to introduce him or her the day before on Twitter. Write four tweets: one that introduces the expert and three that cover three key supporting points that will enhance the speaker's credibility in the minds of potential listeners. Make up any information you need to complete this assignment, and then email the text of your proposed tweets to your instructor.

5.39. **Writing: Using Plain Language; Communication Ethics: Making Ethical Choices, [LO-3], Chapter 1** Your company has been a major employer in the local community for years, but shifts in the global marketplace have forced some changes in the company's long-term direction. In fact, the company plans to reduce local staffing by as much as 50 percent over the next 5 to 10 years, starting with a small layoff next month. The size and timing of future layoffs have not been decided, although there is little doubt that more layoffs will happen at some point. In the first draft of a letter aimed at community leaders, you write that "this first layoff is part of a continuing series of staff reductions anticipated over the next several years." However, your boss is concerned about the vagueness and negative tone of the language and asks you to rewrite that sentence to read "this layoff is part of the company's ongoing efforts to continually align its resources with global market conditions." Do you think this suggested wording is ethical, given the company's economic influence in the community? Explain your answer in an email message to your instructor.

5.40. **Writing: Creating Effective Sentences: Media Skills: Social Networking, [LO-4], Chapter 7** If you are interested in business, chances are you've had an idea or two for starting a company. If you haven't yet, go ahead and dream up an idea now. Make it something you are passionate about, something you could really throw yourself into. Now write a four-sentence summary that could appear on the Info tab on a Facebook profile. Make sure the first sentence is a solid topic sentence, and make sure the next three sentences offer relevant evidence and examples. Feel free to make up any details you need. Email your summary to your instructor or post it on your class blog.

Writing: Choosing Powerful Words [LO-4], Write a concrete phrase for each of these vague phrases:

5.41. Sometime this spring

5.42. A substantial savings

5.43. A large number attended

5.44. Increased efficiency

5.45. Expanded the work area

5.46. Flatten the website structure

Writing: Choosing Powerful Words [LO-4], List terms that are stronger than the following:

5.47. Ran after

5.48. Seasonal ups and downs

5.49. Bright

5.50. Suddenly rises

5.51. Moves forward

Writing: Choosing Powerful Words [LO-4], As you rewrite these sentences, replace the clichés and buzzwords with plain language (for any terms you don't recognize, you can find definitions online):

5.52. Being a jack-of-all-trades, Dave worked well in his new general manager job.

5.53. Moving Leslie into the accounting department, where she was literally a fish out of water, was like putting a square peg into a round hole, if you get my drift.

5.54. My only takeaway from the offsite was that Laird threw his entire department under the bus for missing the deadline.

5.55. I'd love to help with that project, but I'm bandwidth-constrained.

5.56. The board green-lighted our initiative to repurpose our consumer products for the commercial space.

Writing: Choosing Powerful Words [LO-4], Suggest short, simple words to replace each of the following:

5.57. Inaugurate

5.58. Terminate

5.59. Utilize

5.60. Anticipate

5.61. Assistance

5.62. Endeavor

5.63. Ascertain

5.64. Procure

5.65. Consummate

5.66. Advise

5.67. Alteration

5.68. Forwarded

5.69. Fabricate

5.70. Nevertheless

5.71. Substantial

Writing: Choosing Powerful Words [LO-4], Write up-to-date, less-stuffy versions of these phrases; write "none" if you think there is no appropriate substitute or "delete" if the phrase should simply be deleted:

5.72. As per your instructions

5.73. Attached herewith

5.74. In lieu of

5.75. In reply I wish to state

5.76. Please be advised that

Writing: Creating Effective Sentences [LO-5] Rewrite each sentence so that it is active rather than passive:

5.77. The raw data are entered into the customer relationship management system by the sales representative each Friday.

5.78. High profits are publicized by management.

5.79. The policies announced in the directive were implemented by the staff.

5.80. Our computers are serviced by the Santee Company.

5.81. The employees were represented by Janet Hogan.

5.82. **Writing: Crafting Unified, Coherent Paragraphs; Collaboration: Evaluating the Work of Others, [LO-6] Chapter 6** Working with four other students, divide the following five topics among yourselves and each write one paragraph on your selected topic. Be sure each student uses a different technique when writing his or her paragraph: One student should use the illustration technique, one the comparison or contrast technique, one a discussion of cause and effect, one the classification technique, and one a discussion of problem and solution. Then exchange paragraphs within the team and pick out the main idea and general purpose of the paragraph one of your teammates wrote. Was everyone able to correctly identify the main idea and purpose? If not, suggest how the paragraph could be rewritten for clarity.

- Types of *phablets* available for sale
- Advantages and disadvantages of eating at fast-food restaurants
- Finding that first full-time job
- Good qualities of my car (or house, or apartment, or neighborhood)
- How to make a dessert (or barbecue a steak or make coffee)

Writing: Using Transitions [LO-6] Add transitional elements to the following sentences to improve the flow of ideas. (Note: You may need to eliminate or add some words to smooth out your sentences.)

5.83. Facing some of the toughest competitors in the world, Harley-Davidson had to make some changes. The company introduced new products. Harley's management team set out to rebuild the company's production process. New products were coming to market and the company was turning a profit. Harley's quality standards were not on par with those of its foreign competitors. Harley's costs were still among the highest in the industry. Harley made a U-turn and restructured the company's organizational structure. Harley's efforts have paid off.

5.84. Whether you're indulging in a doughnut in New York or California, Krispy Kreme wants you to enjoy the same delicious taste with every bite. The company maintains consistent product quality by carefully controlling every step of the production process. Krispy Kreme tests all raw ingredients against established quality standards. Every delivery of wheat flour is sampled and measured for its moisture content and protein levels. Krispy Kreme blends the ingredients. Krispy Kreme tests the doughnut mix for quality. Krispy Kreme delivers the mix to its stores. Financial critics are not as kind to the company as food critics have been. Allegations of improper financial reporting have left the company's future in doubt.

5.85. **Media Skills: Writing for Mobile Devices [LO-7]** Find an interesting website article on any business topic. Write a three-paragraph summary that would be easy to read on a phone screen.

Expand Your Skills

Critique the Professionals

Locate an example of professional communication from a reputable online source. Choose a paragraph that has at least three sentences. Evaluate the effectiveness of this paragraph at three levels, starting with the paragraph structure. Is the paragraph unified and cohesive? Does it have a clear topic sentence and sufficient support to clarify and expand on that topic? Second, evaluate each sentence. Are the sentences easy to read and easy to understand? Did the writer vary the types and lengths of sentences to produce a smooth flow and rhythm? Is the most important idea presented prominently in each sentence? Third, evaluate at least six word choices. Did the writer use these words correctly and effectively? Using whatever medium your instructor requests, write a brief analysis of the piece (no more than one page), citing specific elements from the piece and support from the chapter.

Sharpening Your Career Skills Online

Bovée and Thill's Business Communication Web Search, at http://websearch.businesscommunicationnetwork.com, is a unique research tool designed specifically for business communication research. Use the Web Search function to find a website, video, PDF document, podcast, or presentation that offers advice on writing effective sentences. Write a brief email message to your instructor, describing the item that you found and summarizing the career skills information you learned from it.

Improve Your Grammar, Mechanics, and Usage

The following exercises help you improve your knowledge of and power over English grammar, mechanics, and usage. Turn to the Handbook of Grammar, Mechanics, and Usage at the end of this book and review all of Section 1.5 (Adverbs). Then look at the following 10 items and indicate the preferred choice within each set of parentheses. (Answers to these exercises appear on page 601.)

5.86. Their performance has been (*good, well*).

5.87. I (*sure, surely*) do not know how to help you.

5.88. He feels (*sick, sickly*) again today.

5.89. Customs dogs are chosen because they smell (*good, well*).

5.90. The redecorated offices look (*good, well*).

5.91. Which of the two programs computes (*more fast, faster*)?

5.92. Of the two we have in stock, this model is the (*best, better*) designed.

5.93. He doesn't seem to have (*any, none*).

5.94. That machine is scarcely (*never, ever*) used.

5.95. They (*can, can't*) hardly get replacement parts for this equipment (*any, no*) more.

For additional exercises focusing on adverbs, visit MyBCommLab. Click on Chapter 5; click on Additional Exercises to Improve Your Grammar, Mechanics, and Usage; and then click on 9. Adverbs.

MyBCommLab

Go to the Assignments section of your MyLab to complete these writing exercises.

5.96 Why are email, texting, and other forms of digital communication so prone to inadvertent etiquette breakdowns, in which even well-intentioned writers insult or confuse readers? [LO-1]

5.97 What steps can you take to make abstract concepts such as opportunity feel more concrete in your messages? [LO-4]

Endnotes

1. Personal communication, Natalie MacNeil, 10 February 2015; She Takes on the World website, accessed 11 February 2015, http://shetakesontheworld.com; Prashanth Gopalan, "Natalie MacNeil Vs. the World," *TechVibes*, 29 September 2010, www.techvibes.com; Natalie MacNeil website, accessed 9 June 2013, http://nataliemacneil.com; product page for *She Takes on the World: A Guide to Being Your Own Boss, Working Happy, and Living on Purpose*, accessed 9 June 2013, www.amazon.com; Natalie MacNeil bio, *Huffington Post*, accessed 9 June 2013, http://www.huffingtonpost.com/natalie-macneil.

2. Annette N. Shelby and N. Lamar Reinsch Jr., "Positive Emphasis and You Attitude: An Empirical Study," *Journal of Business Communication* 32, no. 4 (1995): 303–322.

3. Quinn Warnick, "A Close Textual Analysis of Corporate Layoff Memos," *Business Communication Quarterly* 73, no. 3 (September 2010): 322–326.

4. Sherryl Kleinman, "Why Sexist Language Matters," *Qualitative Sociology* 25, no. 2 (Summer 2002): 299–304.

5. Judy E. Pickens, "Terms of Equality: A Guide to Bias-Free Language," *Personnel Journal*, August 1985, 24.

6. Xerox website, accessed 12 March 2014, www.xerox.com; ADM website, accessed 12 March 2014, www.adm.com.

7. Lisa Taylor, "Communicating About People with Disabilities: Does the Language We Use Make a Difference?" *Bulletin of the Association for Business Communication* 53, no. 3 (September 1990): 65–67.

8. Susan Benjamin, *Words at Work* (Reading, Mass.: Addison Wesley, 1997), 136–137.

9. Plain English Campaign website, accessed 28 June 2010, www.plainenglish.co.uk.

10. Plain Language website; Irene Etzkorn, "Amazingly Simple Stuff," presentation 7 November 2008, www.slideshare.net.

11. Creative Commons website, accessed 16 January 2011, www.creativecommons.org.

12. Susan Jaderstrom and Joanne Miller, "Active Writing," *Office Pro*, November/December 2003, 29.

13. Mary Munter, *Guide to Managerial Communication*, 7th ed. (Upper Saddle River, N.J.: Pearson Prentice Hall, 2006), 41.

14. Portions of this section are adapted from Courtland L. Bovée, *Techniques of Writing Business Letters, Memos, and Reports* (Sherman Oaks, Calif.: Banner Books International, 1978), 13–90.

15. Catherine Quinn, "Lose the Office Jargon; It May Sunset Your Career," *The Age* (Australia), 1 September 2007, www.theage.com.au.

16. Robert Hartwell Fiske, *The Dimwit's Dictionary* (Oak Park, Ill.: Marion Street Press, 2002), 16–20.

17. Beverly Ballaro and Christina Bielaszka-DuVernay, "Building a Bridge over the River Boredom," *Harvard Management Communication Letter*, Winter 2005, 3–5.

18. Jakob Nielsen, "Mobile Content Is Twice as Difficult," NN/g, 28 February 2011, www.nngroup.com.

19. Jakob Nielsen and Raluca Budiu, *Mobile Usability*, (Berkeley: New Riders, 2013), 10, 102.

20. Nielsen and Budiu, *Mobile Usability*, 23.

21. "Mobile Web Best Practices," W3C website, accessed 12 March 2014, www.w3.org.

22. "Mobile Message Mayhem," Verne Ordman & Associates, accessed 12 March 2014, www.businesswriting.biz.

23. "Mobile Message Mayhem."

24. Marieke McCloskey, "Writing Hyperlinks: Salient, Descriptive, Start with Keyword," NN/g, 9 March 2014, www.nngroup.com.

25. Food Allergy Initiative website, accessed 5 September 2008, www.foodallergyinitiative.org; Diana Keough, "Snacks That Can Kill; Schools Take Steps to Protect Kids Who Have Severe Allergies to Nuts," *Plain Dealer*, 15 July 2003, E1; "Dawdling over Food Labels," *New York Times*, 2 June 2003, A16; Sheila McNulty, "A Matter of Life and Death," *Financial Times*, 10 September 2003, 14.

6

Completing Business Messages

LEARNING OBJECTIVES

After studying this chapter, you will be able to

1 Discuss the value of careful revision, and describe the tasks involved in evaluating your first drafts and the work of other writers.

2 List four techniques you can use to improve the readability of your messages.

3 Describe eight steps you can take to improve the clarity of your writing, and give four tips on making your writing more concise.

4 List four principles of effective design, and explain the role of major design elements in document readability.

5 Explain the importance of proofreading, and give eight tips for successful proofreading.

6 Discuss the most important issues to consider when distributing your messages.

ON THE JOB: COMMUNICATING AT

JEFFERSON RABB WEB DESIGN

Using Leading-Edge Digital Media to Reach Today's Book Audience

As a composer, game designer, photographer, programmer, and website developer, Jefferson Rabb epitomizes the "multi" in multimedia. For all the technical and creative skills he brings, however, Rabb's work never loses sight of audiences and their desire to be informed and entertained when they visit a website.

Rabb's career history includes stints at MTV.com and Sephora.com, but most of his current work as an independent designer involves projects in the publishing industry. The best-selling authors he has helped bring to the web include Dan Brown, Gary Shteyngart, Jhumpa Lahiri, Laura Hillenbrand, and Anita Shreve.

Kathy deWitt/Alamy

Authors such as Monica Ali still rely on personal contact with readers to promote books, but websites and other digital media have become an increasingly important element in book promotion.

For every project, Rabb starts his design work with an in-depth analysis of the audience. The questions he asks about site visitors include their familiarity with the author's work, the range of their reading interests, and their general demographics. He also wants to know whether a site needs to serve book reviewers, bookstore buyers, and other industry professionals in addition to readers.

With some insight into who the target visitors are, Rabb puts himself in their place and imagines the knowledge and experiences they hope to gain during their visits. These needs can vary from biographical information about the author to multimedia exhibits (such as video interviews and photographs depicting locations mentioned in a book) to complex games that extend a novel's storylines. Rabb makes a point of finding compelling visual connections between a book and a website, too, such as basing the design of the site for Shteyngart's *Super Sad True Love Story* on the portable communication device featured in the story. Completing the multimedia experience, he often composes music to create a specific mood that reflects the themes of a book.[1]

Your business communication efforts may not always be as elaborate as Rabb's, but you can always apply his strategy of combining methodical analysis with creative design and implementation. This chapter addresses the third step in the three-step writing process, completing your messages—which includes the important tasks of revising, producing, proofreading, and distributing your messages.

WWW.JEFFERSONRABB.COM

Revising Your Message: Evaluating the First Draft

1 LEARNING OBJECTIVE
Discuss the value of careful revision, and describe the tasks involved in evaluating your first drafts and the work of other writers.

Successful communicators like Jefferson Rabb (profiled in the chapter opening On the Job) recognize that the first draft is rarely as tight, clear, and compelling as it needs to be. Careful revision can mean the difference between a rambling, unfocused message and a lively, direct message that gets results.

The revision task can vary somewhat, depending on the medium and the nature of your message. For informal messages to internal audiences, particularly when using instant messaging, text messaging, email, or blogging, the revision process is often as simple as quickly looking over your message to correct any mistakes before sending or posting it. However, don't fall into the common trap of thinking that you don't need to worry about grammar, spelling, clarity, and other fundamentals of good writing when you use such media. These qualities can be *especially* important in digital media, particularly if these messages are the only contact your audience has with you. Audiences are likely to equate the quality of your writing with the quality of your thinking. Poor-quality messages create an impression of poor-quality thinking and can cause confusion, frustration, and costly delays.

With more complex messages, try to put your draft aside for a day or two before you begin the revision process so that you can approach the material with a fresh eye. Then start with the "big picture," making sure that the document accomplishes your overall goals before moving to finer points, such as readability, clarity, and conciseness. Compare the letters in Figures 6.1 and 6.2 on the next two pages for an example of how careful revision improves a customer letter.

For important messages, schedule time to put your draft aside for a day or two before you begin the revision process.

EVALUATING YOUR CONTENT, ORGANIZATION, STYLE, AND TONE

When you begin the revision process, focus your attention on content, organization, style, and tone. To evaluate the content of your message, answer these questions:

- Is the information accurate?
- Is the information relevant to the audience?
- Is there enough information to satisfy the readers' needs?
- Is there a good balance between general information (giving readers enough background information to appreciate the message) and specific information (giving readers the details they need to understand the message)?

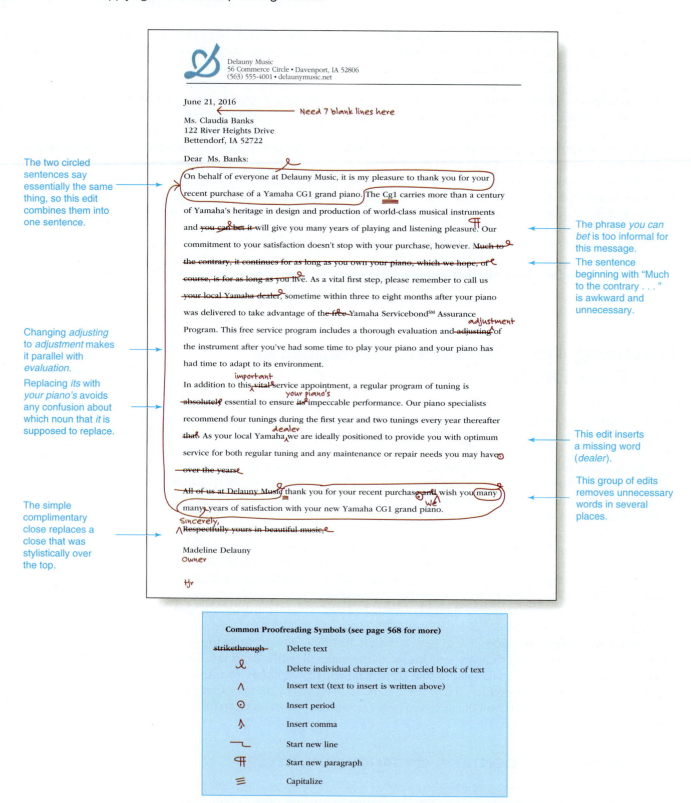

Figure 6.1 **Improving a Customer Letter Through Careful Revision**
Careful revision makes this draft shorter, clearer, and more focused. The proofreading symbols you see here are still widely used whenever printed documents are edited and revised; you can find a complete list of symbols in Appendix C. Note that many business documents are now "marked up" using such technological tools as revision marks in Microsoft Word and comments in Adobe Acrobat. No matter what the medium, however, careful revision is key to more effective messages.

Delauny Music
56 Commerce Circle• Davenport, IA 52806
(563) 555-4001 • delaunymusic.net

June 21, 2016

Ms. Claudia Banks
122 River Heights Drive
Bettendorf, IA 52722

Dear Ms. Banks:

Thank you for your recent purchase. We wish you many years of satisfaction with your new Yamaha CG1 grand piano. The CG1 carries more than a century of Yamaha's heritage in design and production of world-class musical instruments and will give you many years of playing and listening pleasure.

Our commitment to your satisfaction doesn't stop with your purchase, however. As a vital first step, please remember to call us sometime within three to eight months after your piano was delivered to take advantage of the Yamaha Servicebond℠ Assurance Program. This free service program includes a thorough evaluation and adjustment of the instrument after you've had some time to play your piano and your piano has had time to adapt to its environment.

In addition to this important service appointment, a regular program of tuning is essential to ensure your piano's impeccable performance. Our piano specialists recommend four tunings during the first year and two tunings every year thereafter. As your local Yamaha dealer, we are ideally positioned to provide you with optimum service for both regular tuning and any maintenance or repair needs you may have.

Sincerely,

Madeline Delauny

Madeline Delauny
Owner

tjr

The letter is now properly formatted.

The content is now organized in three coherent paragraphs, each with a distinct message.

The tone is friendly and engaging without being flowery.

Figure 6.2 Professional Business Letter
Here is the revised and finished version of the edited letter from Figure 6.1. Note that the *block format* used here is just one of several layout options; Appendix A also describes the *modified block format* and the *simplified format*.

When you are satisfied with the content of your message, you can review its organization. Answer another set of questions:

- Are all the points covered in the most logical order?
- Do the most important ideas receive the most space, and are they placed in the most prominent positions?
- Would the message be more convincing if it were arranged in a different sequence?
- Are any points repeated unnecessarily?
- Are details grouped together logically, or are some still scattered through the document?

Next, consider whether you have achieved the right tone for your audience. Is your writing formal enough to meet the audience's expectations without being too formal or academic? Is it too casual for a serious subject?

Spend a few extra moments on the beginning and end of your message; these sections usually have the greatest impact on the audience. Be sure that the opening is relevant, interesting, and geared to the reader's probable reaction. In longer messages, ensure that the first few paragraphs establish the subject, purpose, and organization of the material. Review the conclusion to be sure that it summarizes the main idea and leaves the audience with a positive impression.

EVALUATING, EDITING, AND REVISING THE WORK OF OTHERS

When you evaluate, edit, or revise someone else's work, remember that your job is to help that person succeed, not to impose your own style.

At many points in your career, you will be asked to evaluate, edit, or revise the work of others. Whether you're suggesting improvements or actually making the improvements yourself (as you might on a wiki site, for example), you can make a contribution by using all the skills you are learning in Chapters 4 through 6.

Before you dive into someone else's work, recognize the dual responsibility that doing so entails. First, unless you've been specifically asked to rewrite something in your own style or to change the emphasis of the message, remember that your job is to help the other writer succeed at his or her task, not to impose your writing style or pursue your own agenda. In other words, make sure your input focuses on making the piece more effective, not on making it more like something you would've written. Second, make sure you understand the writer's intent before you begin suggesting or making changes. If you try to edit or revise without knowing what the writer hoped to accomplish, you run the risk of making the piece less effective, not more. With those thoughts in mind, answer the following questions as you evaluate someone else's writing:

- What is the purpose of this document or message?
- Who is the target audience?
- What information does the audience need?
- Does the document provide this information in a well-organized way?
- Does the writing demonstrate the "you" attitude toward the audience?
- Is the tone of the writing appropriate for the audience?
- Can the readability be improved?
- Is the writing clear? If not, how can it be improved?
- Is the writing as concise as it could be?
- Does the design support the intended message?

You can read more about using these skills in the context of wiki writing in Chapter 12.

2 LEARNING OBJECTIVE
List four techniques you can use to improve the readability of your messages.

Revising to Improve Readability

After confirming the content, organization, style, and tone of your message, make a second pass to improve *readability*. Most professionals are inundated with more reading material than they can ever hope to consume, and they'll appreciate your efforts to make your documents easier to read. You'll benefit from this effort, too: If you earn a reputation for creating well-crafted documents that respect the audience's time, people will pay more attention to your work.

You may be familiar with one of the many indexes that have been developed over the years in an attempt to measure readability. For example, the Flesch-Kincaid Grade Level score computes reading difficulty relative to grade-level achievement, with, for instance, a score of 10 suggesting that a document can be read and understood by the average 10th grader. Most business documents score in the 8–11 range. Technical documents often score in the 12–14 range. A similar scoring system, the Flesch Reading Ease score, ranks documents on a 100-point scale; the higher the score, the easier the document is to read. If these measurements aren't built into your word processing software, you can find a number of calculators for various indexes online.

Readability indexes offer a useful reference point, but they are limited by what they are able to measure: word length, number of syllables, sentence length, and paragraph length. They can't measure any of the other factors that affect readability, such as document design, the "you" attitude, clear sentence structure, smooth transitions, and proper word usage. Compare these two paragraphs:

> Readability indexes offer a useful reference point, but they are all limited by what they are able to measure: word length, number of syllables, sentence length, and paragraph length. They can't measure any of the other factors that affect readability, from "you" orientation to writing clarity to document design.
>
> Readability indexes can help. But they don't measure everything. They don't measure whether your writing clarity is good. They don't measure whether your document design is good or not. Reading indexes are based on word length, syllables, sentences, and paragraphs.

The second paragraph scores much better on both grade level and reading ease, but it is choppy, unsophisticated, and poorly organized. As a general rule, then, don't assume that a piece of text is readable if it scores well on a readability index—or that it is difficult to read if it doesn't score well.

Beyond using shorter words and simpler sentences, you can improve the readability of a message by making the document interesting and easy to skim. Most business audiences—particularly influential senior managers—tend to skim documents, looking for key ideas, conclusions, and recommendations. If they determine that a document contains valuable information or requires a response, they will read it more carefully when time permits. Four techniques will make your message easier to read and easier to skim: varying sentence length, using shorter paragraphs, using lists and bullets instead of narrative, and adding effective headings and subheadings.

VARYING YOUR SENTENCE LENGTH

Varying the length of your sentences is a creative way to make your messages interesting and readable. By choosing words and sentence structure with care, you can create a rhythm that emphasizes important points, enlivens your writing style, and makes information more appealing to your reader. For example, a short sentence that highlights a conclusion at the end of a substantial paragraph of evidence makes your key message stand out. Try for a mixture of sentences that are short (up to 15 words or so), medium (15–25 words), and long (more than 25 words).

Each sentence length has its advantages. Short sentences can be processed quickly and are easier for nonnative speakers and translators to interpret. Medium-length sentences are useful for showing the relationships among ideas. Long sentences are often the best for conveying complex ideas, listing multiple related points, or summarizing or previewing information.

Of course, each sentence length also has disadvantages. Too many short sentences in a row can make your writing choppy. Medium sentences can lack the punch of short sentences and the informative power of longer sentences. Long sentences can be difficult to understand because they contain more information and usually have a more complicated structure. Because readers can absorb only a few words per glance, longer sentences are also more difficult to skim. By choosing the best sentence length for each communication need and remembering to mix sentence lengths for variety, you'll get your points across while keeping your messages lively and interesting.

To keep readers' interest, look for ways to combine a variety of short, medium, and long sentences.

KEEPING YOUR PARAGRAPHS SHORT

Large blocks of text can be visually daunting, particularly on screen, so the optimum paragraph length is short to medium in most cases. Unless you break up your thoughts somehow, you'll end up with lengthy paragraphs that are guaranteed to intimidate

Short paragraphs have the major advantage of being easy to read.

even the most dedicated reader. Short paragraphs, generally 100 words or fewer (this paragraph has 84 words), are easier to read than long ones, and they make your writing look inviting. You can also emphasize ideas by isolating them in short, forceful paragraphs.

However, don't go overboard with short paragraphs. In particular, be careful to use one-sentence paragraphs only occasionally and only for emphasis. Also, if you need to divide a subject into several pieces to keep paragraphs short, be sure to help your readers keep the ideas connected by guiding them with plenty of transitional elements.

USING LISTS TO CLARIFY AND EMPHASIZE

Lists are effective tools for highlighting and simplifying material.

An effective alternative to using conventional sentences is to set off important ideas in a list—a series of words, names, or other items. Lists can show the sequence of your ideas, heighten their impact visually, and increase the likelihood that a reader will find key points. In addition, lists help simplify complex subjects, highlight main points, break up a page or screen visually, ease the skimming process for busy readers, and give readers a breather. Compare these two treatments of the same information:

Narrative	**List**
Owning your own business has many potential advantages. One is the opportunity to pursue your own personal passion. Another advantage is the satisfaction of working for yourself. As a sole proprietor, you also have the advantage of privacy because you do not have to reveal your financial information or plans to anyone.	Owning your own business has three advantages: • Opportunity to pursue personal passion • Satisfaction of working for yourself • Financial privacy

You can separate list items with numbers, letters, or bullets (a general term for any kind of graphical element that precedes each item). Bullets are generally preferred over numbers, unless the list is in some logical sequence or ranking or you need to refer to specific list items elsewhere in the document.

Lists are easier to locate and read if the entire numbered or bulleted section is set off by a blank line before and after, as the preceding examples demonstrate. Furthermore, make sure to introduce lists clearly so that people know what they're about to read. One way to introduce lists is to make them a part of the introductory sentence:

> The board of directors met to discuss the revised annual budget. To keep expenses in line with declining sales, the directors voted to
>
> • Cut everyone's salary by 10 percent
> • Close the employee cafeteria
> • Reduce travel expenses

Another way to introduce a list is to precede it with a complete introductory sentence, followed by a colon:

> The decline in company profit is attributable to four factors:
>
> • Slower holiday sales
> • Increased transportation and fuel costs
> • Higher employee wages
> • Slower inventory turnover

TABLE 6.1	Achieving Parallelism
Method	**Example**
Parallel words	The letter was approved by Clausen, Whittaker, Merlin, and Carlucci.
Parallel phrases	We are gaining market share in supermarkets, in department stores, and in specialty stores.
Parallel clauses	I'd like to discuss the issue after Vicki gives her presentation but before Marvin shows his slides.
Parallel sentences	In 2014 we exported 30 percent of our production. In 2015 we exported 50 percent.

Regardless of the format you choose, the items in a list should be parallel; that is, they should all use the same grammatical pattern. For example, if one list item begins with a verb, every item should begin with a verb. If one item is a noun phrase, every one should be a noun phrase:

Nonparallel List Items (a mix of verb and noun phrases)

- Improve our bottom line
- Identification of new foreign markets for our products
- Global market strategies
- Issues regarding pricing and packaging size

Parallel List Items (all verb phrases)

- Improving our bottom line
- Identifying new foreign markets for our products
- Developing our global market strategies
- Resolving pricing and packaging issues

Parallel forms are easier to read and skim. You can create parallelism by repeating the pattern in words, phrases, clauses, or entire sentences (see Table 6.1).

ADDING HEADINGS AND SUBHEADINGS

A **heading** is a brief title that tells readers about the content of the section that follows. **Subheadings** are subordinate to headings, indicating subsections with a major section. Headings and subheadings serve these important functions:

- **Organization.** Headings show your reader at a glance how the document is organized. They act as labels to group related paragraphs and organize lengthy material into shorter sections.
- **Attention.** Informative, inviting, and in some cases intriguing headings grab the reader's attention, make the text easier to read, and help the reader find the parts he or she needs to read—or skip.
- **Connection.** Using headings and subheadings together helps readers see the relationship between main ideas and subordinate ones so that they can understand your message more easily. Moreover, headings and subheadings visually indicate shifts from one idea to the next.

Headings and subheadings fall into two categories. **Descriptive headings**, such as "Cost Considerations," identify a topic but do little more. **Informative headings**, such as "Redesigning Material Flow to Cut Production Costs," guide readers to think in a certain way about the topic. They are also helpful in guiding your work as a writer, especially if cast as questions you plan to address in your document. Well-written informative headings are self-contained, which means readers can read just the headings and subheadings and understand them without reading the rest of the document. For example, "Introduction" conveys little information, whereas the heading "Staffing Shortages Cost the Company $150,000 Last Year" provides a key piece of information and captures the reader's attention. Whatever types of headings you choose, keep them brief and use parallel construction throughout the document.

Use headings to grab the reader's attention and organize material into short sections.

Informative headings are generally more helpful than descriptive ones.

Editing for Clarity and Conciseness

After you've reviewed and revised your message for readability, your next step is to make sure your message is as clear and as concise as possible.

EDITING FOR CLARITY

Make sure every sentence conveys the message you intend and that readers can extract that meaning without needing to read it more than once. To ensure clarity, look closely at your paragraph organization, sentence structure, and word choices. Can readers make sense of the related sentences in a paragraph? Is the meaning of each sentence easy to grasp? Is each word clear and unambiguous (meaning it doesn't have any risk of being interpreted in more than one way)?

See Table 6.2 for examples of the following tips:

- **Break up overly long sentences.** If you find yourself stuck in a long sentence, you're probably trying to make the sentence do more than it can reasonably do, such

3 LEARNING OBJECTIVE Describe eight steps you can take to improve the clarity of your writing, and give four tips on making your writing more concise.

Clarity is essential to getting your message across accurately and efficiently.

TABLE 6.2   Revising for Clarity

Issues to Review	Ineffective	Effective
Overly Long Sentences Taking compound sentences too far	The magazine will be published January 1, and I'd better meet the deadline if I want my article included because we want the article to appear before the trade show.	The magazine will be published January 1. I'd better meet the deadline because we want the article to appear before the trade show.
Hedging Sentences Overqualifying sentences	I believe that Mr. Johnson's employment record seems to show that he may be capable of handling the position.	Mr. Johnson's employment record shows that he is capable of handling the position.
Unparallel Sentences Using dissimilar construction for similar ideas	Mr. Simms had been drenched with rain, bombarded with telephone calls, and his boss shouted at him. To waste time and missing deadlines are bad habits.	Mr. Sims had been drenched with rain, bombarded with telephone calls, and shouted at by his boss. Wasting time and missing deadlines are bad habits.
Dangling Modifiers Placing modifiers close to the wrong nouns and verbs	Walking to the office, a red sports car passed her. [suggests that the car was walking to the office] Reduced by 25 percent, Europe had its lowest semiconductor output in a decade. [suggests that Europe shrank by 25 percent]	A red sports car passed her while she was walking to the office. Europe reduced semiconductor output by 25 percent, its lowest output in a decade.
Long Noun Sequences Stringing too many nouns together	The window sash installation company will give us an estimate on Friday.	The company that installs window sashes will give us an estimate on Friday.
Camouflaged Verbs Changing verbs into nouns	The manager undertook implementation of the rules. Verification of the shipments occurs weekly. reach a conclusion about give consideration to	The manager implemented the rules. We verify shipment weekly. conclude consider
Sentence Structure Separating subject and predicate Separating adjectives, adverbs, or prepositional phrases from the words they modify	A 10% decline in market share, which resulted from quality problems and an aggressive sales campaign by Armitage, the market leader in the Northeast, was the major problem in 2010. Our antique desk lends an air of strength and substance with thick legs and large drawers.	The major problem in 2010 was a 10% loss of market share, which resulted from quality problems and an aggressive sales campaign by Armitage, the market leader in the Northeast. With its thick legs and large drawers, our antique desk lends an air of strength and substance.
Awkward References	The Law Office and the Accounting Office distribute computer supplies for legal secretaries and beginning accountants, respectively.	The Law Office distributes computer supplies for legal secretaries; the Accounting Office distributes those for beginning accountants.

as expressing two dissimilar thoughts or peppering the reader with too many pieces of supporting evidence at once. (Did you notice how difficult this long sentence was to read?)

- **Rewrite hedging sentences.** *Hedging* means pulling back from making a confident, definitive statement about a topic. Granted, sometimes you have to write *may* or *seems* to avoid stating a judgment or prediction as a fact. However, when you hedge too often or without good reason, you come across as being unsure of what you're saying.

- **Impose parallelism.** When you have two or more similar ideas to express, make them parallel by using the same grammatical construction. Parallelism shows that the ideas are related, of similar importance, and on the same level of generality.

- **Correct dangling modifiers.** Sometimes a modifier is not just an adjective or an adverb but an entire phrase modifying a noun or a verb. Be careful not to leave this type of modifier *dangling*, with no connection to the subject of the sentence.

- **Reword long noun sequences.** When multiple nouns are strung together as modifiers, the resulting sentence can be hard to read. See if a single well-chosen word will do the job. If the nouns are all necessary, consider moving one or more to a modifying phrase, as shown in Table 6.2.

- **Replace camouflaged verbs.** Watch for words that end in *-ion, -tion, -ing, -ment, -ant, -ent, -ence, -ance,* and *-ency*. These endings often change verbs into nouns and adjectives, requiring you to add a verb to get your point across.

- **Clarify sentence structure.** Keep the subject and predicate of a sentence as close together as possible. When the subject and predicate are far apart, readers may need

> Hedging is appropriate when you can't be absolutely sure of a statement, but excessive hedging undermines your authority.

> When you use parallel grammatical patterns to express two or more ideas, you show that they are comparable thoughts.

> Subject and predicate should be placed as close together as possible, as should modifiers and the words they modify.

DIGITAL + SOCIAL + MOBILE: TODAY'S COMMUNICATION ENVIRONMENT

Help! I'm Drowning in Social Media!

Anyone who has sampled today's social media offerings has probably experienced this situation: You find a few fascinating blogs, a few interesting people to follow on Twitter, a couple of podcast channels with helpful business tips, and then *wham*—within a few hours of signing up, your computer is overflowing with updates. Even if every new item is useful (which is unlikely), you receive so many that you can't stay ahead of the incoming flood. With Twitter, newsfeeds, email, instant messaging, and social networks—not to mention a desk phone and a mobile phone—today's business professionals could easily spend their entire days just trying to keep up with incoming messages and never get any work done.

To keep social media from turning into a source of stress and information anxiety, consider these tips:

- **Understand what information you really need in order to excel in your current projects and along your intended career path.** Unfortunately, taking this advice is even trickier than it sounds because you can't always know what you need to know, so you can't always predict which sources will be helpful. However, don't gather information simply because it is interesting or entertaining; collect information that is useful or at least potentially useful.

- **Face the fact that you cannot possibly handle every update from every potentially interesting and helpful source.** You have to set priorities and make tough choices to protect yourself from information overload.

- **Add new information sources slowly.** Give yourself a chance to adjust to the flow and judge the usefulness of each new source.

- **Prune your sources vigorously and frequently.** Bloggers run out of things to say; your needs and interests change; higher-priority sources appear.

- **Remember that information is an enabler, a means to an end.** Collecting vast amounts of information won't get you a sweet promotion with a big raise. *Using* information creatively and intelligently will.

CAREER APPLICATIONS

1. How can you determine whether a social media source is worth paying attention to?

2. Should you allow any information source to interrupt your work flow during the day (even just to signal that a new message is available)? Why or why not?

to read the sentence twice to figure out who did what. Similarly, adjectives, adverbs, and prepositional phrases usually make the most sense when they're placed as close as possible to the words they modify.

- **Clarify awkward references.** If you want readers to refer to a specific point in a document, avoid vague references such as the *above-mentioned, as mentioned above, the aforementioned, the former, the latter,* and *respectively.* Use a specific pointer such as "as described in the second paragraph on page 22."

EDITING FOR CONCISENESS

Many of the changes you make to improve clarity also shorten your message by removing unnecessary words. The next step is to examine the text with the specific goal of reducing the number of words. Readers appreciate conciseness and are more likely to read your documents if you have a reputation for efficient writing. See Table 6.3 for examples of the following tips:

Make your documents tighter by removing unnecessary words, phrases, and sentences.

- **Delete unnecessary words and phrases.** To test whether a word or phrase is essential, try the sentence without it. If the meaning doesn't change, leave it out.
- **Shorten long words and phrases.** Short words and phrases are generally more vivid and easier to read than long ones. Also, by using infinitives (the "to" form of a verb) in place of some phrases, you can often shorten sentences while making them clearer.
- **Eliminate redundancies.** In some word combinations, the words say the same thing. For instance, "visible to the eye" is redundant because *visible* is enough without further clarification; "to the eye" adds nothing.
- **Rewrite "It is/There are" starters.** If you start a sentence with an indefinite pronoun such as *it* or *there*, chances are the sentence could be shorter and more active. For instance, "We believe . . ." is a stronger opening than "It is believed that . . ." because it is shorter and because it identifies who is doing the believing.

As you rewrite, concentrate on how each word contributes to an effective sentence and on how each sentence helps build a coherent paragraph. For a reminder of the tasks involved in revision, see "Checklist: Revising Business Messages."

CHECKLIST ✔ Revising Business Messages

A. Evaluate content, organization, style, and tone.
- Make sure the information is accurate, relevant, and sufficient.
- Check that all necessary points appear in logical order.
- Verify that you present enough support to make the main idea convincing and compelling.
- Be sure the beginning and ending of the message are effective.
- Make sure you've achieved the right tone for the audience and the situation.

B. Review for readability.
- Consider using a readability index, but be sure to interpret the answer carefully.
- Use a mix of short, medium, and long sentences.
- Keep paragraphs short.

- Use bulleted and numbered lists to emphasize key points.
- Make the document easy to skim with headings and subheadings.

C. Edit for clarity.
- Break up overly long sentences and rewrite hedging sentences.
- Impose parallelism to simplify reading.
- Correct dangling modifiers.
- Reword long noun sequences and replace camouflaged verbs.
- Clarify sentence structure and awkward references.

D. Edit for conciseness.
- Delete unnecessary words and phrases.
- Shorten long words and phrases.
- Eliminate redundancies.
- Rewrite sentences that start with "It is" or "There are."

TABLE 6.3   Revising for Conciseness

Issues to Review	Ineffective	Effective
Unnecessary Words and Phrases		
Using wordy phrases	for the sum of	for
	in the event that	if
	prior to the start of	before
	in the near future	soon
	at this point in time	now
	due to the fact that	because
	in view of the fact that	because
	until such time as	when
	with reference to	about
Using too many relative pronouns	Cars that are sold after January will not have a six-month warranty.	Cars sold after January will not have a six-month warranty.
	Employees who are driving to work should park in the underground garage.	Employees driving to work should park in the underground garage. OR Employees should park in the underground garage.
Using too few relative pronouns	The project manager told the engineers last week the specifications were changed.	The project manager told the engineers last week that the specifications were changed. The project manager told the engineers that last week the specifications were changed.
Long Words and Phrases		
Using overly long words	During the preceding year, the company accelerated productive operations.	Last year the company sped up operations.
	The action was predicated on the assumption that the company was operating at a financial deficit.	The action was based on the belief that the company was losing money.
Using wordy phrases rather than infinitives	If you want success as a writer, you must work hard.	To succeed as a writer, you must work hard.
	He went to the library for the purpose of studying.	He went to the library to study.
	The employer increased salaries so that she could improve morale.	The employer increased salaries to improve morale.
Redundancies		
Repeating meanings	absolutely complete	complete
	basic fundamentals	fundamentals
	follows after	follows
	free and clear	free
	refer back	refer
	repeat again	repeat
	collect together	collect
	future plans	plans
	return back	return
	important essentials	essentials
	end result	result
	actual truth	truth
	final outcome	outcome
	uniquely unusual	unique
	surrounded on all sides	surrounded
Using double modifiers	modern, up-to-date equipment	modern equipment
It Is/There Are Starters	It would be appreciated if you would sign the lease today.	Please sign the lease today.
Starting sentences with *It* or *There*	There are five employees in this division who were late to work today.	Five employees in this division were late to work today.

4 **LEARNING OBJECTIVE**
List four principles of effective design, and explain the role of major design elements in document readability.

The quality of your document design, both on paper and on screen, affects readability and audience perceptions.

Good design enhances the readability of your material.

MOBILE APP
Genius Scan lets you scan documents with your phone and create PDFs on the go.

For effective design, pay attention to
• Consistency
• Balance
• Restraint
• Detail

White space separates elements in a document and helps guide the reader's eye.

Most business documents use a flush left margin and a ragged right margin.

Producing Your Message

Now it's time to put your hard work on display. The *production quality* of your message—the total effect of page or screen design, graphical elements, typography, and so on—plays an important role in the effectiveness of your message. A polished, inviting design not only makes your material easier to read but also conveys a sense of professionalism and importance.[2]

DESIGNING FOR READABILITY

Design affects readability in two important ways. First, if used carefully, design elements can improve the effectiveness of your message. In contrast, poor design decisions, such as using distracting background images behind text, pointless animations, or tiny typefaces, act as barriers to communication. Second, the visual design sends a nonverbal message to your readers, influencing their perceptions of the communication before they read a single word.

Effective design helps you establish the tone of your document and helps guide your readers through your message (see Figure 6.3). To achieve an effective design, pay careful attention to the following design elements:

- **Consistency.** Throughout each message, be consistent in your use of margins, typeface, type size, and space. Also be consistent when using recurring design elements, such as vertical lines, columns, and borders. In many cases, you'll want to be consistent from message to message as well; that way, audiences who receive multiple messages from you recognize your documents and know what to expect.
- **Balance.** Balance is an important but subjective issue. One document may have a formal, rigid design in which the various elements are placed in a grid pattern, whereas another may have a less formal design in which elements flow more freely across the page—and both could be in balance. Like the tone of your language, visual balance can be too formal, just right, or too informal for a given message.
- **Restraint.** Strive for simplicity in design. Don't clutter your message with too many design elements, too many typeface treatments, too many colors, or too many decorative touches. Let "simpler" and "fewer" be your guiding concepts.
- **Detail.** Pay attention to details that affect your design and thus your message. For instance, extremely wide columns of text can be difficult to read; in many cases a better solution is to split the text into two narrower columns.

Even without special training in graphic design, you can make your printed and electronic messages more effective by understanding the use of white space, margins and line justification, typefaces, and type styles.

White Space

Any space that doesn't contain text or artwork, both in print and online, is considered **white space**. (Note that "white space" isn't necessarily white; it is simply blank.) These unused areas provide visual contrast and important resting points for your readers. White space includes the open area surrounding headings, margins, paragraph indents, space around images, vertical space between columns, and horizontal space between paragraphs or lines of text. To increase the chance that readers will read your messages, be generous with white space; it makes pages and screens feel less intimidating and easier to read.[3]

Margins and Justification

Margins define the space around text and between text columns. In addition to their width, the look and feel of margins is influenced by the way you arrange lines of text, which can be set (1) *justified* (which means they are *flush*, or aligned vertically, on both the left and the right), (2) flush left with a *ragged-right* margin, (3) flush right with a *ragged-left* margin, or (4) centered. This paragraph is justified, whereas the paragraphs in Figure 6.2 on page 161 are flush left with a ragged-right margin.

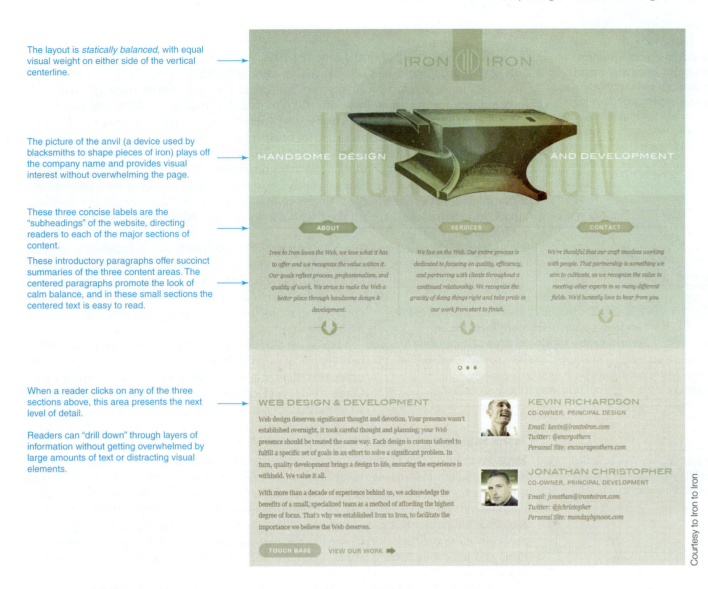

The layout is *statically balanced*, with equal visual weight on either side of the vertical centerline.

The picture of the anvil (a device used by blacksmiths to shape pieces of iron) plays off the company name and provides visual interest without overwhelming the page.

These three concise labels are the "subheadings" of the website, directing readers to each of the major sections of content.

These introductory paragraphs offer succinct summaries of the three content areas. The centered paragraphs promote the look of calm balance, and in these small sections the centered text is easy to read.

When a reader clicks on any of the three sections above, this area presents the next level of detail.

Readers can "drill down" through layers of information without getting overwhelmed by large amounts of text or distracting visual elements.

Courtesy to Iron to Iron

Figure 6.3   Designing for Readability
The website of the web development firm Iron to Iron is a model of elegant design that promotes easy reading.

Magazines, newspapers, and books often use justified type because it can accommodate more text in a given space. However, justified type needs to be used with care. First, it creates a denser look because the uniform line lengths decrease the amount of white space along the right margin. Second, it produces a more formal and less personalized look. Third, unless it is used with some skill and attention, justified type can be more difficult to read because it can produce large gaps between words and excessive hyphenation at the ends of lines. The publishing specialists who create magazines, newspapers, and books have the time and skill needed to carefully adjust character and word spacing to eliminate these problems. (In some cases, sentences are even rewritten in order to improve the appearance of the printed page.) Because most business communicators don't have that time or skill, it's best to avoid justified type in routine business documents.

In contrast to justified type, flush-left, ragged-right type creates a more open appearance on the page, producing a less formal and more contemporary look. Spacing between words is consistent, and only long words that fall at the ends of lines are hyphenated.

Centered type is rarely used for text paragraphs but is commonly used for headings and subheadings. Flush-right, ragged-left type is rarely used in business documents.

Typefaces

The classic style of document design uses a sans serif typeface for headings and a serif typeface for regular paragraph text; however, many contemporary documents and webpages now use all sans serif.

Typeface refers to the physical design of letters, numbers, and other text characters. (*Font* and *typeface* are often used interchangeably, although strictly speaking, a font is a set of characters in a given typeface.) Typeface influences the tone of your message, making it look authoritative or friendly, businesslike or casual, classic or modern, and so on (see Table 6.4). Be sure to choose fonts that are appropriate for your message; many of the fonts on your computer are not appropriate for business use.

Serif typefaces have small crosslines (called serifs) at the ends of each letter stroke. **Sans serif typefaces**, in contrast, lack these serifs. For years, the conventional wisdom in typography was that serif faces were easier to read in long blocks of text, because the serifs made it easier for the eye to pick out individual letters. Accordingly, the standard advice was to use serif faces for the body of a document and sans serif for headings and subheadings.

However, the research behind the conventional wisdom is not as conclusive as once thought.[4] In fact, many sans serif typefaces work as well or better for body text than some serif typefaces. This seems to be particularly true on screens, which often have lower resolution than printed text. Many contemporary documents and webpages now use sans serif for body text.

For most documents, you shouldn't need more than two typefaces, although if you want to make captions or other text elements stand out, you can use another font.[5] Using more typefaces can clutter a document and produce an amateurish look.

REAL-TIME UPDATES

LEARN MORE BY READING THIS ARTICLE

Improve your document designs by learning the fundamentals of typography

Knowing the basics of type usage will help you create more effective page and screen layouts. Go to http://real-timeupdates.com/ebc12 and click on Learn More in the Students section.

Type Styles

Avoid using any type style that inhibits your audience's ability to read your messages.

Type style refers to any modification that lends contrast or emphasis to type, including boldface, italic, underlining, color, and other highlighting and decorative styles. Using boldface type for subheads breaks up long expanses of text. You can also boldface individual words or phrases to draw more attention to them. For example, the key terms in each chapter in this book are set in bold. Italic type also creates emphasis, although not as pronounced as boldface. Italic type has specific uses as well, such as highlighting quotations and indicating foreign words, irony, humor, book and movie titles, and unconventional usage.

As a general rule, avoid using any style in a way that slows your audience's progress through the message. For instance, underlining or using all-uppercase letters can interfere with a reader's ability to recognize the shapes of words, and shadowed or outlined type can seriously hinder legibility. Also, avoid overusing any type style. For example, putting too many words in boldface dilutes the impact of the special treatment by creating too many focal points in the paragraph.

TABLE 6.4	Typeface Personalities: Serious to Casual to Playful	
Serif Typefaces	**Sans Serif Typefaces**	**Specialty Typefaces (rarely used for routine business communication)**
Bookman Old Style	Arial	**Bauhaus**
Century Schoolbook	Calibri	**Broadway**
Courier	Eras Bold	Harrington
Garamond	Franklin Gothic Book	*Zapfino*
Georgia	Gill Sans	**Magneto**
Times New Roman	Verdana	**STENCIL**

Type size is an important consideration as well. For most printed business messages, use a size of 10 to 12 points for regular text and 12 to 18 points for headings and subheadings (1 point is approximately 1/72 inch). Resist the temptation to reduce type size too much in order to squeeze in extra text or to enlarge it to fill up space. Type that is too small is hard to read, whereas extra-large type looks unprofessional. Be particularly careful with small type online. Small type that looks fine on a medium-resolution screen can be hard to read on both low-resolution screens (because these displays can make letters look jagged or fuzzy) and high-resolution screens (because these monitors reduce the apparent size of the type even further).

REAL-TIME UPDATES

LEARN MORE BY VISITING THIS WEBSITE

See the newest designs from some of the brightest minds in typography

Type design is a fascinating and dynamic field; this portfolio shows dozens of innovative new typefaces. Go to http://real-timeupdates.com/ebc12 and click on Learn More in the Students section.

FORMATTING FORMAL LETTERS AND MEMOS

Formal business letters usually follow certain design conventions, as the letter in Figure 6.2 illustrates. Most business letters are printed on *letterhead stationery*, which includes the company's name, address, and other contact information. The first element to appear after the letterhead is the date, followed by the inside address, which identifies the person receiving the letter. Next is the salutation, usually in the form of *Dear Mr.* or *Ms. Last Name*. The message comes next, followed by the complimentary close, usually *Sincerely* or *Cordially*. And last comes the signature block: space for the signature, followed by the sender's printed name and title. Your company will probably have a standard format to follow for letters, possibly along with a template in Microsoft Word or whatever word processor is standard in the organization. For in-depth information on letter formats, see Appendix A, "Format and Layout of Business Documents."

Like letters, business memos usually follow a preset design. Memos have largely been replaced by electronic media in many companies, but if they are still in use at the firm you join, the company may have a standard format or template for you to use. Most memos begin with a title such as *Memo, Memorandum,* or *Interoffice Correspondence*. Following that are usually four headings: *Date, To, From,* and *Subject*. (*Re:*, short for *Regarding*, is sometimes used instead of *Subject*.) Memos usually don't use a salutation, complimentary close, or signature, although signing your initials next to your name on the *From* line is standard practice in most companies. Bear in mind that memos are often distributed without sealed envelopes, so they are less private than most other message formats.

DESIGNING MESSAGES FOR MOBILE DEVICES

In addition to making your content mobile-friendly using the writing tips in Chapter 4 (see page 109), you can follow these steps to format that content for mobile devices:

- **Think in small chunks.** Remember that mobile users consume information one screen at a time, so try to divide your message into independent, easy-to-consume bites. If readers have to scroll through a dozen screens to piece together your message, they might miss your point or just give up entirely.
- **Make generous use of white space.** White space is always helpful, but it's critical on small screens because readers are trying to get the point of every message as quickly as possible. Keep your paragraphs short (4–6 lines), and separate them with blank lines so the reader's eyes can easily jump from one point to the next.[6]
- **Format simply.** Avoid anything that is likely to get in the way of fast, easy reading, including busy typefaces, complex graphics, and complicated layouts.
- **Consider horizontal and vertical layouts.** Most phones and tablets can automatically rotate their screen content from horizontal to vertical as the user rotates the device. A layout that doesn't work well with the narrow vertical perspective might be acceptable at the wider horizontal perspective.

Compare the two messages in Figure 6.4 on the next page; notice how much more difficult the screen in Figure 6.4a is to read.

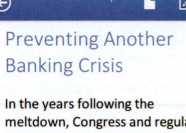

White space between the heading and the body text helps readers perceive the heading as a single block of text.

Generous margins reduce the visual clutter on screen.

The sans serif typeface (right) is easier to read than the serif typeface (left).

Shorter paragraphs simplify reading and allow for more white space breaks between paragraphs.

Figure 6.4   Designing Messages for Mobile Devices
Even simple changes such as revising with shorter paragraphs, choosing cleaner typefaces, and making generous use of white space in and around the text can dramatically improve readability on mobile screens.
Source: MS Office Word 2013, © Microsoft.

Your credibility is affected by your attention to the details of mechanics and form.

The types of details to look for when proofreading include language errors, missing material, design errors, and typographical errors.

MOBILE APP
NounPlus puts a grammar checker, spell checker, and pronunciation guide on your phone, so you're never without tips and advice.

Proofreading Your Message

Proofreading is the quality inspection stage for your documents, your last chance to make sure that your document is ready to carry your message—and your reputation—to the intended audience. Even a small mistake can doom your efforts, so take proofreading seriously.

Look for two types of problems: (1) undetected mistakes from the writing, design, and layout stages and (2) mistakes that crept in during production. For the first category, you can review format and layout guidelines in Appendix A on page 547 and brush up on writing basics with the Handbook of Grammar, Mechanics, and Usage on page 571. The second category can include anything from computer glitches such as missing fonts to broken web links to problems with the ink used in printing. Be particularly vigilant with complex documents and complex production processes that involve multiple colleagues and multiple computers. Strange things can happen as files move from computer to computer, especially when lots of fonts and multimedia elements are involved.

Resist the temptation to treat proofreading as a casual scan up and down the page or screen. Instead, approach it as a methodical procedure in which you look for specific problems that may occur. Use these techniques from professional proofreaders to help ensure high-quality output:

- **Make multiple passes.** Go through the document several times, focusing on a different aspect each time. For instance, look for content errors the first time and layout errors the second time.
- **Use perceptual tricks.** You've probably experienced the frustration of reading over something a dozen times and still missing an obvious error. This happens because your brain has developed a wonderful skill of subconsciously supplying missing

---

CHECKLIST ✔ Proofing Business Messages

A. Look for writing errors.
- Typographical mistakes
- Misspelled words
- Grammatical errors
- Punctuation mistakes

B. Look for missing elements.
- Missing text sections
- Missing exhibits (drawings, tables, photographs, charts, graphs, online images, and so on)
- Missing source notes, copyright notices, or other reference items

C. Look for design, formatting, and programming mistakes.
- Incorrect or inconsistent font selections
- Problems with column sizing, spacing, and alignment
- Incorrect margins
- Incorrect special characters
- Clumsy line and page breaks
- Problems with page numbers
- Problems with page headers and footers
- Lack of adherence to company standards
- Inactive or incorrect links
- Missing files

---

pieces and correcting mistakes when it knows what is *supposed* to be on the page. To keep your brain from tricking you, you need to trick it by changing the way you process the visual information. Try (1) reading each page backward, from the bottom to the top, (2) placing your finger under each word and reading it silently, (3) making a slit in a sheet of paper that reveals only one line of type at a time, and (4) reading the document aloud and pronouncing each word carefully.

- **Double-check high-priority items.** Double-check the spelling of names and the accuracy of dates, addresses, and any number that could cause grief if incorrect (such as telling a potential employer that you'd be happy to work for $5,000 a year when you meant to say $50,000).
- **Give yourself some distance.** If possible, don't proofread immediately after finishing a document; let your mind wander off to new topics and then come back fresh later on.
- **Be vigilant.** Avoid reading large amounts of material in one sitting and try not to proofread when you're tired.
- **Stay focused.** Concentrate on what you're doing. Try to block out distractions and focus as completely as possible on your proofreading task.
- **Review complex electronic documents on paper.** Some people have trouble proofreading webpages, online reports, and other electronic documents on screen. If you have trouble, try to print the materials so you can review them on paper.
- **Take your time.** Quick proofreading is not careful proofreading.

The amount of time you need to spend on proofing depends on the length and complexity of the document and the situation. A typo in an email message to your team may not be a big deal, but a typo in a financial report, a contract, or a medical file certainly could be serious. See "Checklist: Proofing Business Messages" for a handy list of items to review during proofing.

REAL-TIME UPDATES

LEARN MORE BY LISTENING TO THIS PODCAST

Tips for proofing your papers

This advice for class assignments will help you on the job, too. Go to http://real-timeupdates.com/bce7 and click on Learn More in the Students section.

Distributing Your Message

With the production finished, you're ready to distribute your message. As with every other aspect of business communication, your options for distribution multiply with every advance in technology. In some cases, the choice is obvious: Just click the Send button in your email program or the *Publish* button on your blog. In other cases, such as when you have a 100-page report with full-color graphics or a massive multimedia file, you need to plan the distribution carefully so that your message is received by

6 LEARNING OBJECTIVE
Discuss the most important issues to consider when distributing your messages.

everyone who needs it. When choosing a means to distribute messages, consider the following factors:

Consider cost, convenience, time, security, and privacy when choosing a distribution method.

- **Cost.** Cost isn't a concern for most messages, but for lengthy reports or multimedia productions, it may well be. Printing, binding, and delivering reports can be expensive, so weigh the cost versus the benefits. Be sure to consider the nonverbal message you send regarding cost as well. Overnight delivery of a printed report could look responsive in one situation but wasteful in another, for example.
- **Convenience.** How much work is involved for you and your audience? For instance, if you use a file-compression utility to shrink the size of email attachments, make sure your recipients have the means to expand the files on arrival. For extremely large files, consider recordable media such as DVDs or one of the many free or low-cost file-hosting sites now available.
- **Time.** How soon does the message need to reach the audience? Don't waste money on overnight delivery if the recipient won't read the report for a week. And speaking of time, don't mark any messages, printed or electronic, as "urgent" if they aren't truly urgent.
- **Security and privacy.** The convenience offered by electronic communication needs to be weighed against security and privacy concerns. For the most sensitive messages, your company will probably restrict both the people who can receive the messages and the means you can use to distribute them. In addition, most computer users are wary of opening attachments these days. Instead of sending word processor files, you can use Adobe Acrobat or an equivalent product to convert your documents to PDF files (which are more immune to viruses).

MOBILE APP
SignEasy solves the problem of signing digital documents such as contracts; you can sign right on your phone screen.

For more advice on revision, proofreading, and other topics related to this chapter, visit **http://real-timeupdates.com/ebc12** and click on Chapter 6.

ON THE JOB: SOLVING COMMUNICATION DILEMMAS AT JEFFERSON RABB WEB DESIGN

Jefferson Rabb's web business is doing so well that he has hired you to help with a variety of writing and design tasks. Use what you've learned in this chapter about revising messages, designing for readability, and distributing messages to address the following challenges.[7]

1. You received some draft copy for an author website that contains the following rather long sentence:

   > Alexander McCall Smith was born in what is now Zimbabwe and was educated there and in Scotland before becoming a law professor in Scotland and later returning to Africa to help set up a new law school at the University of Botswana.

   Which of these four alternatives does the best job of revising the material to improve its readability without losing any of the original information or introducing any new information?

   a. A native of what is now Zimbabwe, Alexander McCall Smith was educated in what is now Zimbabwe as well as Scotland. He became a law professor in Scotland and later returned to Africa to help set up a law school at the University of Botswana.
   b. Alexander McCall Smith was educated in Zimbabwe and Scotland, where he became a law professor. He

   later returned to Africa to help set up a law school at the University of Botswana.
   c. Returning to Africa to help set up a law school at the University of Botswana must've felt like a homecoming of sorts for Zimbabwe native Alexander McCall Smith, who was educated in both Zimbabwe and Scotland.
   d. Alexander McCall Smith was born in what is now Zimbabwe and was educated there and in Scotland. He became a law professor in Scotland and later returned to Africa to help set up a law school at the University of Botswana.

2. Like many popular authors, Anita Shreve offers guides that help reading groups or book groups explore and discuss her novels. A typical reading guide might contain a dozen or so questions that relate to events or themes from a novel. Groups can use these questions to structure their discussions of a novel. Which of the following navigational link titles would be the most effective to use on Shreve's website?
   a. Guides for Book Groups
   b. Reading Guides
   c. Discuss Shreve's Novels
   d. Explore Anita's Work

3. The following sentence appears on the website for Tom Vanderbilt's *Traffic*, a study of the technical and social

evolution of traffic and the never-ending attempts to making driving less dangerous and more efficient:

> Based on exhaustive research and interviews with driving experts and traffic officials around the globe, *Traffic* gets under the hood of the everyday activity of driving to uncover the surprisingly complex web of physical, psychological, and technical factors that explain how traffic works, why we drive the way we do, and what our driving says about us. [57 words]

Which of the following does the best job of reducing the length and complexity of this sentence without significantly altering its meaning?

a. *Traffic* explores the surprisingly complex web of physical, psychological, and technical factors that explain how traffic works, why we drive the way we do, and what our driving says about us. [31 words]

b. *Traffic* relies on extensive global research to explore the surprisingly complex web of physical, psychological, and technical factors that explain how traffic works, why we drive the way we do, and what our driving says about us. [37 words]

c. How traffic works, why we drive the way we do, and what our driving says about us—these are the questions addressed and answers in the exhaustively researched book *Traffic*. [30 words]

d. *Traffic* gets under the hood of the everyday activity of driving to uncover the surprisingly complex web of physical, psychological, and technical factors that explain how traffic works, why we drive the way we do, and what our driving says about us. [42 words]

4. A number of authors reach out to their reader bases by offering to participate in book group discussions via Skype. If you wanted to get the word out that a new author was available to talk with book groups via Skype, which of the following distribution methods would you choose? (For this exercise, assume that you can choose only one of these.)

a. Posters in book stores

b. A message printed somewhere on the cover of the book

c. A Twitter update from the author

d. An update on the author's Facebook page

Learning Objectives Checkup

Assess your understanding of the principles in this chapter by reading each learning objective and study the accompanying exercises. You can check your responses against the answer key on page 599.

Objective 6.1: Discuss the value of careful revision and describe the tasks involved in evaluating your first drafts and the work of other writers.

1. Which of these is the most important reason you should take care to revise messages before sending them?

a. Revising shows your audience how hard you work.

b. Revising lowers the word count.

c. Revising makes it cheaper to email messages.

d. Revising can usually make your messages more successful.

2. Which of the following is not one of the main tasks involved in completing a business message?

a. Drafting the message

b. Revising the message

c. Producing the message

d. Proofreading the message

Objective 6.2: List four techniques you can use to improve the readability of your messages.

3. Regarding sentence length, the best approach for business messages is to

a. Keep all sentences as short as possible

b. Make most of your sentences long since you will usually have complex information to impart

c. Vary the length of your sentences

d. Aim for an average sentence length of 35 words

4. Regarding paragraph length, the best approach for business messages is to

a. Keep paragraphs short

b. Make most of your paragraphs long since that is standard practice in business writing

c. Make most of your paragraphs one sentence in length

d. Aim for an average paragraph length of 200 words

5. Regarding the use of lists, the best approach for business messages is to

a. Avoid using lists except where absolutely necessary

b. Make sure listed items are in parallel form

c. Use numbered lists rather than bulleted ones

d. Do all of the above

6. Which of the following is not an informative heading?

a. Why We Need a New Distributor

b. Five Challenges Facing Today's Distributors

c. Distributors Are a Better Choice for Us Than Wholesalers

d. Distributor Choices

Objective 6.3: Describe eight steps you can take to improve the clarity of your writing and give four tips on making your writing more concise.

7. Which of the following sentences contains hedging words?

a. It appears that we may have a problem completing the project by May 20.

b. There is a possibility that the project might be done by May 20.

c. It seems that the project could possibly miss its completion date of May 20.

d. All of the above contain hedging words.

8. Which of the following sentences lacks parallelism?

a. Consumers can download stock research, electronically file their tax returns, create a portfolio, or choose from an array of recommended mutual funds.

   b. Consumers can download stock research, can electronically file their tax returns, create a portfolio, or they can choose from an array of recommended mutual funds.

   c. Consumers can download stock research, can electronically file their tax returns, can create a portfolio, or can choose from an array of recommended mutual funds.

   d. Consumers can download stock research, they can electronically file their tax returns, they can create a portfolio, or they can choose from an array of recommended mutual funds.

9. Which of the following sentences does not have a dangling modifier?
   a. Lacking brand recognition, some consumers are wary of using Internet-only banks.
   b. Because Internet-only banks lack brand recognition, some consumers are wary of using them.
   c. Because of a lack of brand recognition, some consumers are wary of using Internet-only banks.
   d. All have dangling modifiers.

10. When editing for conciseness, you should look for
    a. Unnecessary words and phrases
    b. Dangling modifiers
    c. Lack of parallelism
    d. Awkward references

11. Which of the following is not an example of a redundancy?
    a. Visible to the eye
    b. Free gift
    c. Very useful
    d. Repeat again

Objective 6.4: List four principles of effective design and explain the role of major design elements in document readability.

12. A well-designed document
    a. Includes a wide variety of typefaces
    b. Balances the space devoted to text, artwork, and white space
    c. Fills as much of the available space as possible with text and art
    d. Does all of the above

13. Any blank areas in a document are referred to as _____ _____.

14. Type that is justified is
    a. Flush on the left and ragged on the right
    b. Flush on the right and ragged on the left
    c. Flush on both the left and the right
    d. Centered

15. Why is it a good idea to think in small chunks when writing for mobile audiences?
    a. Mobile users consume information one screen at a time.
    b. More than 50 percent of mobile users refuse to scroll past the first screen.
    c. Many smartphones don't offer scrolling.
    d. Graphics are easier to create on mobile devices.

Objective 6.5: Explain the importance of proofreading and give eight tips for successful proofreading.

16. The best time to proofread is
    a. As you are writing
    b. Immediately after you finish the first draft, while the information is still fresh in your mind
    c. A day or so after you finish the first draft
    d. After you distribute the document

17. When proofreading, you should look for errors in
    a. Spelling and punctuation
    b. Grammar and usage
    c. Typography and format
    d. All of the above

Objective 6.6: Discuss the most important issues to consider when distributing your messages.

18. As a general rule, the cost of distributing a business message should be balanced against
    a. The importance and urgency of the message
    b. The length of the message
    c. Your career goals as they relate to the message
    d. The number of recipients

19. Which of the following concerns is the most important to consider when distributing messages through digital media such as email?
    a. The difficulty of reading on screen
    b. Privacy and security
    c. Differences between flat-panel and CRT monitors
    d. The difficulty of keeping email addresses current

Quick Learning Guide

CHAPTER OUTLINE

Revising Your Message: Evaluating the First Draft

Evaluating Your Content, Organization, Style, and Tone

Evaluating, Editing, and Revising the Work of Others

Revising to Improve Readability

Varying Your Sentence Length

Keeping Your Paragraphs Short

Using Lists to Clarify and Emphasize

Adding Headings and Subheadings

Editing for Clarity and Conciseness

Editing for Clarity

Editing for Conciseness

Producing Your Message

Designing for Readability

Formatting Formal Letters and Memos

Designing Messages for Mobile Devices

Proofreading Your Message

Distributing Your Message

LEARNING OBJECTIVES

1 Discuss the value of careful revision, and describe the tasks involved in evaluating your first drafts and the work of other writers. (page 159)

2 List four techniques you can use to improve the readability of your messages. (page 162)

3 Describe eight steps you can take to improve the clarity of your writing, and give four tips on making your writing more concise. (page 166)

4 List four principles of effective design, and explain the role of major design elements in document readability. (page 170)

5 Explain the importance of proofreading, and give eight tips for successful proofreading. (page 174)

6 Discuss the most important issues to consider when distributing your messages. (page 175)

KEY TERMS

descriptive headings Headings that simply identify a topic

heading A brief title that tells readers about the content of the section that follows

informative headings Headings that guide readers to think in a certain way about the topic

sans serif typefaces Typefaces whose letters lack serifs

serif typefaces Typefaces with small crosslines (called *serifs*) at the ends of letter strokes

subheadings Titles that are subordinate to headings, indicating subsections within a major section

type style Any modification that lends contrast or emphasis to type, including boldface, italic, underlining, color, and other highlighting and decorative styles

typeface The physical design of letters, numbers, and other text characters (*font* and *typeface* are often used interchangeably, although strictly speaking, a font is a set of characters in a given typeface)

white space Space (of any color) in a document or screen that doesn't contain any text or artwork

CHECKLIST ✔ Proofing Business Messages

A. Look for writing errors.
- Typographical mistakes
- Misspelled words
- Grammatical errors
- Punctuation mistakes

B. Look for missing elements.
- Missing text sections
- Missing exhibits (drawings, tables, photographs, charts, graphs, online images, and so on)
- Missing source notes, copyright notices, or other reference items

C. Look for design, formatting, and programming mistakes.
- Incorrect or inconsistent font selections
- Problems with column sizing, spacing, and alignment
- Incorrect margins
- Incorrect special characters
- Clumsy line and page breaks
- Problems with page numbers
- Problems with page headers and footers
- Lack of adherence to company standards
- Inactive or incorrect links
- Missing files

CHECKLIST ✔ Revising Business Messages

A. Evaluate content, organization, style, and tone.
- Make sure the information is accurate, relevant, and sufficient.
- Check that all necessary points appear in logical order.
- Verify that you present enough support to make the main idea convincing and compelling.
- Be sure the beginning and ending of the message are effective.
- Make sure you've achieved the right tone for the audience and the situation.

B. Review for readability.
- Consider using a readability index, but be sure to interpret the answer carefully.
- Use a mix of short, medium, and long sentences.
- Keep paragraphs short.

- Use bulleted and numbered lists to emphasize key points.
- Make the document easy to skim with headings and subheadings.

C. Edit for clarity.
- Break up overly long sentences and rewrite hedging sentences.
- Impose parallelism to simplify reading.
- Correct dangling modifiers.
- Reword long noun sequences and replace camouflaged verbs.
- Clarify sentence structure and awkward references.

D. Edit for conciseness.
- Delete unnecessary words and phrases.
- Shorten long words and phrases.
- Eliminate redundancies.
- Rewrite sentences that start with "It is" or "There are."

Apply Your Knowledge

To review chapter content related to each question, refer to the
indicated Learning Objective.

★ **6.1.** How does careful revision reflect the "you" attitude? [LO-1]

6.2. Why should you limit the number of typefaces and type
styles in most business documents? [LO-4]

6.3. Why is white space particularly critical when designing
documents for mobile devices? [LO-4]

★ **6.4.** How can you demonstrate good business sense in the
choices you make regarding message distribution? [LO-6]

Practice Your Skills

Message for Analysis 6.A: Revising to Improve Readability [LO-2]

Analyze the strengths and weaknesses of this message, then
revise it so that it follows the guidelines in Chapters 4 through 6:

As an organization, the North American Personal Motorsports
Marketing Association has committed ourselves to helping our
members—a diverse group comprising of dealers of motorcycles,
all-terrain vehicles, Snowmobiles, and personal watercraft—
achieve their business objectives. Consequently, our organization,
which usually goes under the initials NAPMMA, has the following
aims, goals, and objectives. Firstly, we endeavor to aid or assist
our members in reaching their business objectives. Second,
NAPMMA communicates ("lobbying" in slang terms) with local,
state, and national governmental agencies and leaders on issues
of importance to our members. And lastly, we educate the
motorsports public, that being current motorsports vehicle owners,
and prospective owners of said vehicles, on the safe and enjoyable
operation of they're vehicles.

Message for Analysis 6.B: Designing for Readability [LO-4]

To access this message, visit **http://real-timeupdates.com/ebc12**,
click on Student Assignments, select Chapter 6, Message 6.B.
Download and open the document. Using the various page, paragraph, and font formatting options available in your word processor, modify the formatting of the document so that its visual tone
matches the tone of the message.

Message for Analysis 6.C: Evaluating the Work of Another Writer [LO-1]

To access this message, visit **http://real-timeupdates.com/
ebc12**, click on Student Assignments, select Chapter 6, Message
6.C. Download and open the document. Using your knowledge of
effective writing and the tips on page 162 for evaluating the work
of other writers, evaluate this message. After you set Microsoft

Word to track changes, make any necessary corrections. Insert
comments, as needed, to explain your changes to the author.

Exercises

Each activity is labeled according to the primary skill or skills
you will need to use. To review relevant chapter content, you
can refer to the indicated Learning Objective. In some instances,
supporting information will be found in another chapter, as
indicated.

6.5. **Evaluating the Work of Other Writers [LO-1]** Find
a blog post (at least three paragraphs long) on any business-related topic. Evaluate it using the 10 questions on
page 162. Email your analysis to your instructor, along
with a permalink (a permanent link to this specific post,
rather than to the blog overall) to the blog post.

6.6. **Revising for Readability (Sentence and Paragraph
Length [LO-2])** Rewrite the following paragraph to vary
the length of the sentences and to shorten the paragraph
so it looks more inviting to readers:

Although major league baseball remains popular, more
people are attending minor league baseball games because
they can spend less on admission, snacks, and parking and
still enjoy the excitement of America's pastime. Connecticut,
for example, has three AA minor league teams, including
the New Haven Ravens, who are affiliated with the St. Louis
Cardinals; the Norwich Navigators, who are affiliated with
the New York Yankees; and the New Britain Rock Cats, who
are affiliated with the Minnesota Twins. These teams play in
relatively small stadiums, so fans are close enough to see
and hear everything, from the swing of the bat connecting
with the ball to the thud of the ball landing in the outfielder's
glove. Best of all, the cost of a family outing to see rising
stars play in a local minor league game is just a fraction of
what the family would spend to attend a major league game
in a much larger, more crowded stadium.

6.7. **Revising for Readability (Sentence Length) [LO-2]**
Break the following sentences into shorter ones by adding more periods and revise as needed for smooth flow:

a. The next time you write something, check your average sentence length in a 100-word passage, and if
your sentences average more than 16 to 20 words, see
whether you can break up some of the sentences.

b. Don't do what the village blacksmith did when he
instructed his apprentice as follows: "When I take the
shoe out of the fire, I'll lay it on the anvil, and when
I nod my head, you hit it with the hammer." The
apprentice did just as he was told, and now he's the
village blacksmith.

c. Unfortunately, no gadget will produce excellent writing, but using a yardstick like the Fog Index gives us
some guideposts to follow for making writing easier
to read because its two factors remind us to use short
sentences and simple words.

d. Know the flexibility of the written word and its
power to convey an idea, and know how to make
your words behave so that your readers will understand.

e. Words mean different things to different people, and a word such as *block* may mean city block, butcher block, engine block, auction block, or several other things.

6.8. Editing for Conciseness (Unnecessary Words) [LO-3] Cross out unnecessary words in the following phrases:
  a. Consensus of opinion
  b. New innovations
  c. Long period of time
  d. At a price of $50
  e. Still remains

6.9. Editing for Conciseness (Long Words) [LO-3] Revise the following sentences, using shorter, simpler words:
  a. The antiquated calculator is ineffectual for solving sophisticated problems.
  b. It is imperative that the pay increments be terminated before an inordinate deficit is accumulated.
  c. There was unanimity among the executives that Ms. Jackson's idiosyncrasies were cause for a mandatory meeting with the company's personnel director.
  d. The impending liquidation of the company's assets was cause for jubilation among the company's competitors.
  e. The expectations of the president for a stock dividend were accentuated by the preponderance of evidence that the company was in good financial condition.

6.10. Editing for Conciseness (Lengthy Phrases) [LO-3] Use infinitives as substitutes for the overly long phrases in these sentences:
  a. For living, I require money.
  b. They did not find sufficient evidence for believing in the future.
  c. Bringing about the destruction of a dream is tragic.

6.11. Editing for Conciseness (Lengthy Phrases) [LO-3] Rephrase the following in fewer words:
  a. In the near future
  b. In the event that
  c. In order that
  d. For the purpose of
  e. With regard to
  f. It may be that
  g. In very few cases
  h. With reference to
  i. At the present time
  j. There is no doubt that

6.12. Editing for Conciseness (Lengthy Phrases) [LO-3] Revise to condense these sentences to as few words as possible:
  a. We are of the conviction that writing is important.
  b. In all probability, we're likely to have a price increase.
  c. Our goals include making a determination about that in the near future.
  d. When all is said and done at the conclusion of this experiment, I'd like to summarize the final windup.
  e. After a trial period of three weeks, during which time she worked for a total of 15 full working days, we found her work was sufficiently satisfactory so that we offered her full-time work.

6.13. Editing for Conciseness (Unnecessary Modifiers) [LO-3] Remove all the unnecessary modifiers from these sentences:
  a. Tremendously high pay increases were given to the extraordinarily skilled and extremely conscientious employees.
  b. The union's proposals were highly inflationary, extremely demanding, and exceptionally bold.

6.14. Editing for Clarity (Hedging) [LO-3] Rewrite these sentences so that they no longer contain any hedging:
  a. It would appear that someone apparently entered illegally.
  b. It may be possible that sometime in the near future the situation is likely to improve.
  c. Your report seems to suggest that we might be losing money.
  d. I believe Nancy apparently has somewhat greater influence over employees in the e-marketing department.
  e. It seems as if this letter of resignation means you might be leaving us.

6.15. Editing for Clarity (Indefinite Starters) [LO-3] Rewrite these sentences to eliminate the indefinite starters:
  a. There are several examples here to show that Elaine can't hold a position very long.
  b. It would be greatly appreciated if every employee would make a generous contribution to Mildred Cook's retirement party.
  c. It has been learned in Washington today from generally reliable sources that an important announcement will be made shortly by the White House.
  d. There is a rule that states that we cannot work overtime without permission.
  e. It would be great if you could work late for the next three Saturdays.

6.16. Editing for Clarity (Parallelism) [LO-3] Revise these sentences to present the ideas in parallel form:
  a. Mr. Hill is expected to lecture three days a week, to counsel two days a week, and must write for publication in his spare time.
  b. She knows not only accounting, but she also reads Latin.
  c. Both applicants had families, college degrees, and were in their thirties, with considerable accounting experience but few social connections.
  d. This book was exciting, well written, and held my interest.
  e. Don is both a hard worker and he knows bookkeeping.

6.17. Editing for Clarity (Awkward References) [LO-3] Revise the following sentences to delete the awkward references:
  a. The vice president in charge of sales and the production manager are responsible for the keys to 34A and 35A, respectively.
  b. The keys to 34A and 35A are in executive hands, with the former belonging to the vice president in charge of sales and the latter belonging to the production manager.

c. The keys to 34A and 35A have been given to the production manager, with the aforementioned keys being gold embossed.

d. A laser printer and an inkjet printer were delivered to John and Megan, respectively.

e. The walnut desk is more expensive than the oak desk, the former costing $300 more than the latter.

6.18. Editing for Clarity (Dangling Modifiers) [LO-3] Rewrite these sentences to clarify the dangling modifiers:

a. Full of trash and ripped-up newspapers, we left Dallas on a plane that apparently hadn't been cleaned in days.

b. Lying on the shelf, Ruby found the operations manual.

c. With leaking plumbing and outdated wiring, I don't think we should buy that property.

d. Being cluttered and filthy, Sandy took the whole afternoon to clean up her desk.

e. After proofreading every word, the letter was ready to be signed.

6.19. Editing for Clarity (Noun Sequences) [LO-3] Rewrite the following sentences to eliminate the long strings of nouns:

a. The focus of the meeting was a discussion of the bank interest rate deregulation issue.

b. Following the government task force report recommendations, we are revising our job applicant evaluation procedures.

c. The production department quality assurance program components include employee training, supplier cooperation, and computerized detection equipment.

d. The supermarket warehouse inventory reduction plan will be implemented next month.

e. The State University business school graduate placement program is one of the best in the country.

6.20. Editing for Clarity (Sentence Structure) [LO-3] Rearrange the following sentences to bring the subjects closer to their verbs:

a. Trudy, when she first saw the bull pawing the ground, ran.

b. It was Terri who, according to Ted, who is probably the worst gossip in the office (Tom excepted), mailed the wrong order.

c. William Oberstreet, in his book Investment Capital Reconsidered, writes of the mistakes that bankers through the decades have made.

d. Judy Schimmel, after passing up several sensible investment opportunities, despite the warnings of her friends and family, invested her inheritance in a jojoba plantation.

e. The president of U-Stor-It, which was on the brink of bankruptcy after the warehouse fire, the worst tragedy in the history of the company, prepared a press announcement.

6.21. Editing for Clarity (Camouflaged Verbs) [LO-3] Rewrite each sentence so that the verbs are no longer camouflaged:

a. Adaptation to the new rules was performed easily by the employees.

b. The assessor will make a determination of the tax due.

c. Verification of the identity of the employees must be made daily.

d. The board of directors made a recommendation that Mr. Ronson be assigned to a new division.

6.22. The auditing procedure on the books was performed by the vice president.

6.23. Completing: Designing for Readability; Media Skills: Blogging, [LO-4], Chapter 7 Compare the home pages of Bloomberg (www.bloomberg.com) and MarketWatch (www.marketwatch.com), two websites that cover financial markets. What are your first impressions of these two sites? How do their overall designs compare in terms of information delivery and overall user experience? Choose three pieces of information that a visitor to these sites would be likely to look for, such as a current stock price, news from international markets, and commentary from market experts. Which site makes it easier to find this information? Why? Present your analysis in a post for your class blog.

6.24. Communication Ethics: Making Ethical Choices; Media Skills: Blogging, [LO-3] Chapter 7 The time and energy required for careful revision can often benefit you or your company directly, such as by increasing the probability that website visitors will buy your products. But what about situations in which the quality of your writing and revision work really doesn't stand to benefit you directly? For instance, assume that you are putting a notice on your website, informing the local community about some upcoming construction to your manufacturing plant. The work will disrupt traffic for nearly a year and generate a significant amount of noise and air pollution, but knowing the specific dates and times of various construction activities will allow people to adjust their commutes and other activities to minimize the negative impact on their daily lives. However, your company does not sell products in the local area, so the people affected by all this are not potential customers. Moreover, providing accurate information to the surrounding community and updating it as the project progresses will take time away from your other job responsibilities. Do you have an ethical obligation to keep the local community informed with accurate, up-to-date information? Why or why not?

6.25. Proofreading [LO-5] Proofread the following email message, and revise it to correct any problems you find:

Our final company orrientation of the year will be held on Dec. 20. In preparation for this sesssion, please order 20 copies of the Policy handbook, the confindentiality agreenemt, the employee benefits Manual, please let me know if you anticipate any delays in obtaining these materials.

Expand Your Skills

Critique the Professionals

Identify a company website that in your opinion violates one or more of the principles of good design discussed on pages 170–173. Using whatever medium your instructor requests, write a brief analysis of the site (no more than one page), citing specific elements from the piece and support from the chapter.

Sharpening Your Career Skills Online

Bovée and Thill's Business Communication Web Search, at http://websearch.businesscommunicationnetwork.com, is a unique research tool designed specifically for business communication research. Use the Web Search function to find a website, video, PDF document, podcast, or presentation that offers advice on effective proofreading. Write a brief email message to your instructor, describing the item you found and summarizing the career skills information you learned from it.

Improve Your Grammar, Mechanics, and Usage

The following exercises help you improve your knowledge of and power over English grammar, mechanics, and usage. Turn to the Handbook of Grammar, Mechanics, and Usage at the end of this book and review Section 1.6.1 (Prepositions). Then look at the following 10 items. Underline the preferred choice within each set of parentheses. (Answers to these exercises appear on page 601.)

6.26. Where was your argument (*leading to, leading*)?

6.27. I wish he would get (*off, off of*) the phone.

6.28. U.S. Mercantile must become (*aware, aware of*) and sensitive to its customers' concerns.

6.29. Dr. Namaguchi will be talking (*with, to*) the marketing class, but she has no time for questions.

6.30. Matters like this are decided after thorough discussion (*among, between*) all seven department managers.

6.31. We can't wait (*on, for*) their decision much longer.

6.32. Their computer is similar (*to, with*) ours.

6.33. This model is different (*than, from*) the one we ordered.

6.34. She is active (*in not only, not only in*) a civic group but also in an athletic organization.

6.35. Carolyn told Jorge not to put the used inkjet cartridges (*in, into*) the trash can.

For additional exercises focusing on prepositions, visit MyBComm Lab. Click on Chapter 6; click on Additional Exercises to Improve Your Grammar, Mechanics, and Usage; and then click on 10. Prepositions.

MyBCommLab

Go to the Assignments section of your MyLab to complete these writing exercises.

6.36 Why is it helpful to put your first draft aside for a while before you begin the editing process? [LO-1]

6.37 How do your typeface selections help determine the personality of your documents and messages? [LO-4]

Endnotes

1. Jefferson Rabb website, accessed 21 January 2013, www.jeffersonrabb.com; Joshua Bodwell, "Artful Author Web Sites," *Poets & Writers*, January/February 2011, 79–84; Super Sad True Love Story website, accessed 22 January 2011, http://supersadtruelovestory.com; Beat the Reaper website, accessed 22 January 2011, www.beatthereaper.com.

2. Deborah Gunn, "Looking Good on Paper," *Office Pro*, March 2004, 10–11.

3. Jacci Howard Bear, "Desktop Publishing Rules of Page Layout," About.com, accessed 22 August 2005, www.about.com.

4. Kas Thomas, "The Serif Readability Myth," assertTrue blog, 18 January 2013, asserttrue.blogspot.com; Ole Lund, "Knowledge Construction in Typography: The Case of Legibility Research and the Legibility of Sans Serif Typefaces," doctoral dissertation, University of Reading, October 1999.

5. Jacci Howard Bear, "Desktop Publishing Rules for How Many Fonts to Use," About.com, accessed 22 August 2005, www.about.com.

6. "Mobile Message Mayhem," Verne Ordman & Associates, accessed 12 March 2014, www.businesswriting.biz.

7. The writing samples in this exercise were taken or adapted from the Alexander McCall Smith website, accessed 2 June 2011, www.alexandermccallsmith.com; Anita Shreve website, accessed 2 June 2011, www.anitashreve.com; *Traffic* website, accessed 2 June 2011, http://tomvanderbilt.com/traffic.

Crafting Brief Business Messages

CHAPTER **7** Crafting Messages for Digital Channels

CHAPTER **8** Writing Routine and Positive Messages

CHAPTER **9** Writing Negative Messages

CHAPTER **10** Writing Persuasive Messages

Most of your communication on the job will be through brief messages, from Twitter updates and blog posts to formal letters that might run to several pages. Learning how to write these messages effectively is vital to maintaining productive working relationships with colleagues and customers. Start by adapting what you already know about digital media to the professional challenges of business communication. Then learn specific techniques for crafting routine, positive, negative, and persuasive messages—techniques that will help you in everything from getting a raise to calming an angry customer to promoting your next great idea.

wong yu liang/Fotolia

7

Crafting Messages for Digital Channels

LEARNING OBJECTIVES

After studying this chapter, you will be able to

1 Identify the major digital channels used for brief business messages, and describe the nine compositional modes needed for digital media.

2 Describe the use of social networks in business communication.

3 Explain how companies and business professionals can use information and content sharing websites.

4 Describe the evolving role of email in business communication, and explain how to adapt the three-step writing process to email messages.

5 Describe the business benefits of instant messaging (IM), and identify guidelines for effective IM in the workplace.

6 Describe the use of blogging and microblogging in business communication, and briefly explain how to adapt the three-step process to blogging.

7 Explain how to adapt the three-step writing process for podcasts.

ON THE JOB: COMMUNICATING AT GOPRO

Building a Brand Through Social Engagement

If you've watched a daredevil video on YouTube in the past few years, chances are the video was shot with a GoPro camera. GoPro's digital cameras have captured everything from extreme snowboarders to Felix Baumgartner's epic 24-mile freefall leap from the edge of space. The "adrenaline market" is at the core of the GoPro brand, but the growing population of GoPro users also includes filmmakers, sports and wildlife photographers, oceanographers, atmospheric researchers, and others who need high-quality video footage from a small, rugged, and relatively inexpensive digital camera.

Not surprisingly, for its own business communication needs, GoPro makes extensive use of video. Like many companies, it uses video to showcase new products and provide how-to advice for customers. However, GoPro has gone far beyond what many companies do with video by harnessing the amplifying power of social media. The company has taken user-generated content to the extreme, using a variety of recognition and reward mechanisms to encourage GoPro customers to submit video clips. For example, GoPro runs a nonstop contest that recognizes several customers every day

Viewer interest in extreme sports and other eye-catching events and phenomena has created a huge market for GoPro's video cameras. The company, led by founder and CEO Nick Woodman, has capitalized on this visceral appeal with an extensive social media presence centered around online video.

Eric Millette/Corbis Outline

for the best footage shot on GoPro cameras. These clips are then highlighted on the company's website and all across the major social media platforms, including YouTube, Facebook, Twitter, Google+, and Instagram. In addition, a daily sweepstakes awards one lucky participant with one of every product the company makes, which maintains a high level of interest among people who don't yet own a GoPro camera.

The company's strategy of building a global video community has been a huge success. When Google (which owns YouTube) announced its first-ever monthly ranking of the highest-performing branded channels on YouTube, it determined that GoPro had the most engaged fan base. To measure engagement, Google factors in such variables as the amount of time visitors spending watching videos, the number of repeat visitors, and the number of times people "like" a video or leave a comment. When you consider that virtually every video on GoPro's YouTube channel functions as an advertisement for the company's cameras, you get an idea of the immense promotional power that this high level of engagement represents.

Even if your job doesn't involve snowboarding off cliffs or parachuting from space, GoPro offers a great example of how creative companies can build connections in today's digital, social business environment.[1]

HTTP://GOPRO.COM

Digital Channels for Business Communication

GoPro's choice of social media for customer communication may seem like an obvious move, but the use of social media represents a fundamental shift in business communication. The shift is still taking place, as more consumers adopt social and mobile media and as businesses experiment with the best ways to integrate these media and adapt them to their internal and external communication practices.

Social media such as Facebook are digital media/channel combinations that empower stakeholders as participants in the communication process by allowing them to share content, revise content, respond to content, or contribute new content. For instance, many people now rely heavily on content sharing through social media tools to get information of personal and professional interest. Additionally, many consumers and professionals frequently engage in "content snacking," consuming large numbers of small pieces of information and bypassing larger documents that might require more than a few minutes or even a few seconds to read.[2] Moreover, the amount of content accessed from mobile devices (with the challenges they present in terms of screen size and input mechanisms) continues to rise.[3] Faced with such behavior, communicators need to be more careful than ever to create audience-focused messages and to consider restructuring messages using more *teasers, orientations,* and *summaries* (see pages 188–189).

With all these changes taking place, the field of business communication is a lot more interesting—but also a lot more complicated—than it was just a few years ago. For example, newer and smaller firms have a better opportunity to compete against big companies with big communication budgets because the quality of the message and the credibility of the sender carry more weight in this new environment. Empowered stakeholders can use the reach of social media to help companies that appear to be acting in stakeholders' best interests and harm companies that are not. Social media also have the potential to increase transparency, with more eyes and ears to monitor business activities and to use the crowd's voice to demand accountability and change.

Although social media have reduced the amount of control businesses have over the content and process of communication,[4] today's smart companies are learning how to adapt their communication efforts to this new media landscape and to welcome customers' participation. Social media are also revolutionizing internal communication, breaking down traditional barriers in the organizational hierarchy, promoting the flow of information and ideas, and enabling networks of individuals and organizations to collaborate on a global scale.[5]

Increasingly, employees expect the leaders in their organizations to be active in social media. In one recent study, more than 80 percent of U.S. employees agreed that "CEOs who engage in social media are better equipped than their peers to lead companies in a

1   LEARNING OBJECTIVE
Identify the major digital channels used for brief business messages, and describe the nine compositional modes needed for digital media.

The range of options for short business messages continues to grow with innovations in digital and social media.

Social media reduce a communicator's control over messages.

Web 2.0 world." Moreover, roughly the same percentage are more likely to trust companies whose leadership teams engage with stakeholders via social media, and they would prefer to work for such companies as well.[6]

MEDIA CHOICES FOR BRIEF MESSAGES

Social media are not the only options available for business communication, of course. Individuals and companies have a broad range of options for sending brief messages (from one or two sentences up to several pages long), including the following:

- Social networks
- Information and content sharing sites
- Email
- Instant messaging (IM)
- Text messaging
- Blogging and microblogging
- Podcasting

This chapter covers all of these media, and Chapters 11 and 12 explore two other key media, websites and wikis, which are used for longer messages and documents.

As this list suggests, businesses use many of the same tools you use for personal communication. Generally speaking, companies are quick to jump on any communication platform where consumers are likely to congregate or that promise more-efficient internal or external communication.

Although most of your business communication is likely to be via digital means, don't automatically dismiss the benefits of printed messages. Here are several situations in which you should use a printed message over digital alternatives:

- When you want to make a formal impression
- When you are legally required to provide information in printed form
- When you want to stand out from the flood of digital messages
- When you need a permanent, unchangeable, or secure record

> Even with the widespread use of digital formats, printed memos and letters still play an important role in business communication.

Obviously, if you can't reach a particular audience through digital channels, you'll also need to use a printed message. Appendix A offers guidelines on formatting printed memos and letters.

COMPOSITIONAL MODES FOR DIGITAL MEDIA

As you practice using digital media in this course, focus on the principles of social media communication and the fundamentals of planning, writing, and completing messages, rather than on the specific details of any one medium or system.[7] Fortunately, the basic communication skills required usually transfer from one system to another. You can succeed with written communication in virtually all digital media by using one of nine *compositional modes*:

> Communicating successfully with digital media requires a wide range of writing approaches.

- **Conversations.** IM is a great example of a written medium that mimics spoken conversation. And just as you wouldn't read a report to someone sitting in your office, you wouldn't use conversational modes to exchange large volumes of information or to communicate with more than a few people at once.
- **Comments and critiques.** One of the most powerful aspects of social media is the opportunity for interested parties to express opinions and provide feedback, whether it's leaving comments on a blog post or reviewing products on an e-commerce site. Sharing helpful tips and insightful commentary is also a great way to build your personal brand. To be an effective commenter, focus on short chunks of information that a broad spectrum of other site visitors will find helpful. Rants, insults, jokes, and blatant self-promotion are usually of little benefit to other visitors.

- **Orientations.** The ability to help people find their way through an unfamiliar system or subject is a valuable writing skill and a talent that readers greatly appreciate. Unlike summaries (see next item), orientations don't give away the key points in the collection of information, but rather tell readers where to find those points. Writing effective orientations can be a delicate balancing act because you need to know the material well enough to guide others through it while being able to step back and view it from the inexperienced perspective of a "newbie."

- **Summaries.** At the beginning of an article or webpage, a summary functions as a miniature version of the document, giving readers all the key points while skipping over details. At the end of an article or webpage, a summary functions as a review, reminding readers of the key points they've just read. A series of key points extracted from an article or webpage can also serve as a summary (see the discussion of *tweetables*).

- **Reference materials.** One of the greatest benefits of the Internet is the access it can provide to vast quantities of reference materials—numerical or textual information that people typically don't read in a linear way but rather search through to find particular data points, trends, or other details. One of the challenges of writing reference material is that you can't always know how readers will want to access it. Making the information accessible via search engines is an important step. However, readers don't always know which search terms will yield the best results, so consider an orientation and organize the material in logical ways with clear headings that promote skimming.

- **Narratives.** The storytelling techniques covered in Chapter 4 (see page 119) can be effective in a wide variety of situations, from company histories to product reviews and demonstrations. Narratives work best when they have an intriguing beginning that piques readers' curiosity, a middle section that moves quickly through the challenges that an individual or company faced, and an inspiring or instructive ending that gives readers information they can apply in their own lives and jobs.

- **Teasers.** Teasers intentionally withhold key pieces of information as a way to pull readers or listeners into a story or other document. Teasers are widely used in marketing and sales messages, such as a bit of copy on the outside of an envelope that promises important information on the inside. In digital media, the space limitations and URL linking capabilities of Twitter and other microblogging systems make them a natural tool for the teaser approach. Be sure that the *payoff*, the information a teaser links to, is valuable and legitimate. You'll quickly lose credibility if readers think they are being tricked into clicking through to information they don't really want. (*Tweetables* are Twitter-ready bites of information extracted from a blog post or other messages. They often serve as teasers, although a series of them can make an effective summary as well.)

- **Status updates and announcements.** If you use social media frequently, much of your writing will involve status updates and announcements. However, don't post trivial information that only you are likely to find interesting. Post only those updates that readers will find useful, and include only the information they need (see Figure 7.1 on the next page).

- **Tutorials.** Given the community nature of social media, the purpose of many messages is to share how-to advice. Becoming known as a reliable expert is a great way to build customer loyalty for your company while enhancing your own personal value.

> With Twitter and other super-short messaging systems, the ability to write a compelling *teaser* is an important skill.

CREATING CONTENT FOR SOCIAL MEDIA

No matter what media or compositional mode you are using for a particular message, writing for social media requires a different approach than for traditional media. Whether you're writing a blog or posting a product demonstration video to YouTube, consider these tips for creating successful content for social media:[8]

REAL-TIME UPDATES

LEARN MORE BY READING THIS ARTICLE

Telling compelling stories on social media

Storytelling is an effective business communication strategy, and social media can be the idea platform for it. Go to http://real-timeupdates.com/ebc12 and click on Learn More in the Students section.

Courtesy Fender Musical Instruments Corporation.

Figure 7.1   Compositional Modes: Status Updates and Announcements
Contests, such as this one feature Fender musical equipment, are a popular message form on Facebook and other social media.

Writing for social media requires a different approach than writing for traditional media.

- **Remember that it's a conversation, not a lecture or a sales pitch.** One of the great appeals of social media is the feeling of conversation, of people talking *with* one another instead of one person talking *at* everyone else. As more and more people gain a voice in the marketplace, companies that try to maintain the old "we talk, you listen" mindset are likely to be ignored in the social media landscape.
- **Write informally but not carelessly.** Write as a human being with a unique, personal voice. However, don't take this as a license to get sloppy; no one wants to slog through misspelled words and half-baked sentences to find your message.
- **Create concise, specific, and informative headlines.** Given the importance of headlines in the face of content snacking and information overload, headlines are extremely important in social media. Avoid the temptation to engage in clever wordplay when writing headlines and teasers. This advice applies to all forms of business communication, of course, but it is essential for social media. Readers don't want to spend time figuring out what your witty headlines mean. Search engines won't know what they mean either, so fewer people will find your content.
- **Get involved and stay involved.** Social media make some businesspeople nervous because they don't permit a high level of control over messages. However, don't hide from criticism. Take the opportunity to correct misinformation or explain how mistakes will be fixed.
- **Be transparent and honest.** Honesty is always essential, of course, but the social media environment is unforgiving. Attempts to twist the truth, withhold information, or hide behind a virtual barricade only invite attack in the "public square" of social media.

A momentary lapse of concentration or judgment while using social media can cause tremendous damage to your career.

- **Think before you post!** Because of careless messages, individuals and companies have been sued because of Twitter updates, employees have been fired for Facebook wall postings, vital company secrets have been leaked, and business and personal relationships have been strained. Remember that you share the responsibility of keeping your company's and your customers' data private and secure. Assume that every message you send in any digital medium will be stored forever and might be read by people far beyond your original audience. Ask yourself two questions: First, "Would I say this to my audience face to face?" And second, "Am I comfortable with this message becoming a permanent part of my personal and professional communication history?"

REAL-TIME UPDATES

LEARN MORE BY READING THIS ARTICLE

How social media have changed business communication

Katie Wagner highlights immediacy, access, connection, and research. Go to http://real-timeupdates.com/ebc12 and click on Learn More in the Students section.

OPTIMIZING CONTENT FOR MOBILE DEVICES

Chapters 5 and 6 offer tips on writing and formatting messages for mobile devices. While keeping the limitations of small screens and alternative input methods in mind, look for opportunities to take advantage of mobile-specific capabilities via apps and mobile-friendly websites. Mobile expands your options as a content creator, and it gives your audience members a wider range of more-engaging ways to consume your content:

- **Location-based services.** *Location-based social networking* links the virtual world of online social networking with the physical world of retail stores and other locations. As mobile web use in general continues to grow, location-based networking promises to become an important business communication medium because mobile consumers are a significant economic force—through the purchases they make directly and through their ability to influence other consumers.[9]

> Mobile offers a range of exciting ways to enhance the audience experience.

- **Gamification.** The addition of game-playing aspects to apps and web services, known as *gamification,* can increase audience engagement and encourage repeat use. Examples include Foursquare's "check-in" competitions and Bunchball's Nitro competitions for sales teams.[10]

- **Augmented reality.** Superimposing data on live camera images can help mobile consumers learn about companies and services in the immediate vicinity, for example. Another potential business use is on-the-job training, in which training content is provided as workers are learning or performing various tasks.

REAL-TIME UPDATES

LEARN MORE BY VISITING THIS WEBSITE

Learn from the best social media bloggers in the business

See the 10 blogs rated best by readers of *Social Media Examiner.* Go to http://real-timeupdates.com/ebc12 and click on Learn More in the Students section.

- **Wearable technology.** From virtual-reality goggles to smartwatches to body-movement sensors, wearable technology pushes the radical connectivity of mobile to the next level. Some of these work as auxiliary screens and controls for other mobile devices, but others are meant for independent use. One of the key promises of wearable technology is simplifying and enhancing everyday tasks for consumers and employees alike.[11]

- **Mobile blogging.** Smartphones and tablets are idea for mobile blogs, sometimes referred to as *moblogs.* The mobile capability is great for workers whose jobs keep them on the move and for special-event coverage such as live-blogging trade shows and industry conventions.

- **Mobile podcasting.** Similarly, smartphone-based podcasting tools make it easy to record audio on the go and post finished podcasts to your blog or website.

- **Cloud-based services.** Mobile communication is ideal for cloud-based services—digital services that rely on resources stored in the cloud.

MOBILE APP

Mobile Podcaster lets you record audio podcasts on your mobile devices and instantly post them on your WordPress blog.

Social Networks

Social networks—online services that help people and organizations form connections and share information—have become a major force in both internal and external business communication in recent years. In addition to Facebook, a variety of public and private social networks are used by businesses and professionals. They can be grouped into three categories:

2 LEARNING OBJECTIVE
Describe the use of social networks in business communication.

Business communicators make use of a wide range of specialized and private social networks, in addition to public networks such as Facebook and Google+.

- **Public, general-purpose networks.** Facebook is the largest such network, and Google+ has also attracted many companies and brands. Additionally, regionally focused networks have significant user bases in some countries, such as China's Renren and Kaixin001.[12]
- **Public, specialized networks.** Whereas Facebook and Google+ serve a wide variety of personal and professional needs, other networks focus on a particular function or a particular audience. The most widely known of these is LinkedIn, with its emphasis on career- and sales-related networking. Other networks address the needs of entrepreneurs, small-business owners, specific professions, product enthusiasts, and other narrower audiences.
- **Private networks.** Some companies have built private social networks for internal use. For example, the defense contractor Lockheed Martin created its Unity network, complete with a variety of social media applications, to meet the expectations of younger employees accustomed to social media and to capture the expert knowledge of older employees nearing retirement.[13]

Regardless of the purpose and audience, social networks are most beneficial when all participants give and receive information, advice, support, and introductions—just as in offline social interaction. The following two sections describe how social networks are used in business communication and offer advice on using these platforms successfully.

BUSINESS COMMUNICATION USES OF SOCIAL NETWORKS

With their ability to reach virtually unlimited numbers of people through a variety of digital formats, social networks are a great fit for many business communication needs. Here are some of the key applications of social networks for internal and external business communication:

- **Integrating company workforces.** Just as public networks can bring friends and family together, internal social networks can help companies grow closer, including

---

DIGITAL + SOCIAL + MOBILE: TODAY'S COMMUNICATION ENVIRONMENT

Community Manager: One of the Hottest New Jobs in Business

With the rise in social media over the past few years and its transformative effect on business, *community manager* is one of the hottest new jobs in business. In the narrowest sense, a community manager is the social media interface between a company and its external stakeholders. More broadly, some community managers also plan and manage corporate events and oversee customer support operations. In smaller firms, the community manager might be the sole voice in a company's social media presence (running its Twitter account and Facebook pages, for example). In larger firms, the job often entails supervising a team of people who carry out a broad range of audience-engagement activities.

Not surprisingly, communications skills are essential for community managers. These skills include not only handling the nuts and bolts of using social media effectively but also fostering a sense of community and inspiring people to be passionate about a company and its brands. In addition, community management is a data-intensive job in many companies, with managers expected to make full use of analytical tools to measure the effects of social interaction and to use those answers to plan new initiatives. Community managers also have to be well-versed in their company's product and service offerings.

On a personal level, the job requires high energy, resilience, a thick skin for handling negative comments, and a willingness to be connected far beyond the limits of a 40-hour week. You are "the face of brand," as Adobe's community manager Rachael King describes it, and when major events hit, social managers are expected to respond in real time.

If the attractions and challenges of this job sound appealing to you, be sure to add community manager to the list of career paths you explore as you get closer to graduation.

CAREER APPLICATIONS

1. Would someone with limited work experience but a long personal history of using social media be a good candidate for a community manager position? Why or why not?
2. What are the risks of having a single person be the voice of a company, and how should companies address this risk?

Sources: Don Power, "In Their Own Words: What Community Managers Do Every Day," *SproutSocial*, 7 March 2013, sproutsocial.com; Ryan Lytle, "10 Qualities of an Effective Community Manager," *Mashable*, 27 January 2013, http://mashable.com; Jennifer Grayeb, "The 4 Pillars of Community Management," *Forbes*, 25 December 2013, www.forbes.com; Tim McDonald, "Community Manager: Key to the Future of Business," *Huffington Post*, 27 January 2014, www.huffingtonpost.com.

helping new employees navigate their way through the organization, finding experts, mentors, and other important contacts; encouraging workforces to "gel" after reorganizations or mergers; and overcoming structural barriers in communication channels, bypassing the formal communication system to deliver information where it is needed in a timely fashion.

- **Fostering collaboration.** Networks can play a major role in collaboration by identifying the best people, both inside the company and in other companies, to collaborate on projects; finding pockets of knowledge and expertise within the organization; giving meeting or seminar participants a way to meet before an event and to maintain relationships after an event; accelerating the development of teams by helping members get to know one another and to identify individual areas of expertise; and sharing information throughout the organization.

- **Building communities.** Social networks are a natural tool for bringing together *communities of practice*, people who engage in similar work, and *communities of interest*, people who share enthusiasm for a particular product or activity. Large and geographically dispersed companies can benefit greatly from communities of practice that connect experts who may work in different divisions or different countries. Communities of interest that form around a specific product are sometimes called **brand communities**, and nurturing these communities can be a vital business communication task. A majority of consumers now trust their peers more than any other source of product information, so formal and informal brand communities are becoming an essential information source in consumer buying decisions.[14]

- **Socializing brands and companies.** According to one recent survey of company executives, *socialization* now accounts for more than half of a company or brand's global reputation.[15] **Brand socialization** is a measure of how effectively a company engages with its various online stakeholders in a mutually beneficial exchange of information.

  Socializing a brand is becoming an increasingly important element of marketing and public relations strategies.

- **Understanding target markets.** With hundreds of millions of people expressing themselves via social media, you can be sure that smart companies are listening. When asked about the value of having millions of Facebook fans, Coca-Cola CEO Muhtar Kent replied, "The value is you can talk with them. They tell you things that are important for your business and brands."[16] In addition, a number of tools now exist to gather market intelligence from social media more or less automatically. For example, *sentiment analysis* is an intriguing research technique in which companies track social networks and other media with automated language-analysis software that tries to take the pulse of public opinion and identify influential opinion makers.[17]

  Social networks are vital tools for distributing information as well as gathering information about the business environment.

- **Recruiting employees and business partners.** Companies use social networks to find potential employees, short-term contractors, subject-matter experts, product and service suppliers, and business partners. A key advantage here is that these introductions are made via trusted connections in a professional network. On LinkedIn, for example, members can recommend each other based on current or past business relationships, which helps remove the uncertainty of initiating business relationships with complete strangers.

- **Connecting with sales prospects.** Salespeople on networks such as LinkedIn can use their network connections to identify potential buyers and then to ask for introductions through those shared connections. Sales networking can reduce *cold calling*, telephoning potential customers out of the blue—a practice that few people on either end of the conversation find pleasant.

- **Supporting customers.** Customer service is another one of the fundamental areas of business communication that have been revolutionized by social media. *Social customer service* involves using social networks and other social media tools to give customers a more convenient way to get help from the company and to help each other.

- **Extending the organization.** Social networking is also fueling the growth of *networked organizations*, sometimes known as *virtual organizations*, where companies supplement the talents of their employees with services from one or more external partners, such as a design lab, a manufacturing firm, or a sales and distribution company.

STRATEGIES FOR BUSINESS COMMUNICATION ON SOCIAL NETWORKS

Social networks offer lots of business communication potential, but with those opportunities comes a certain degree of complexity. Moreover, the norms and practices of business social networking continue to evolve. Follow these guidelines to make the most of social networks for both personal branding and company communication:[18]

MOBILE APP
The social media management app Social Oomph lets you monitor multiple social media sites, schedule updates, and perform other time-saving tasks.

- **Choose the best compositional mode for each message, purpose, and network.** As you visit various social networks, take some time to observe the variety of message types you see in different parts of each website. For example, the informal status update mode works well for Facebook Wall posts but would be less effective for company overviews and mission statements.
- **Offer valuable content to members of your online communities.** People don't join social networks to be sales targets, of course. They join looking for connections and information. *Content marketing* is the practice of providing free information that is valuable to community members but that also helps a company build closer ties with current and potential customers.[19]

- **Join existing conversations.** Search for online conversations that are already taking place. Answer questions, solve problems, and respond to rumors and misinformation.
- **Anchor your online presence in your hub.** Although it's important to join those conversations and be visible where your stakeholders are active, it's equally important to anchor your presence at your own central *hub*—a web presence you own and control. This can be a combination of a conventional website, a blog, and a company-sponsored online community, for example.[20] Use the hub to connect the various pieces of your online "self" (as an individual or a company) to make it easier for people to find and follow you. For example, you can link to your blog from your LinkedIn profile or automatically post your blog entries into the Notes tab on your Facebook page.
- **Facilitate community building.** Make it easy for customers and other audiences to connect with the company and with each other. For example, you can use the group feature on Facebook, LinkedIn, and other social networks to create and foster special-interest groups within your networks. Groups are a great way to connect people who are interested in specific topics, such as owners of a particular product (see Figure 7.2).

Product promotion can be done on social networks, but it needs to be done in a low-key, indirect way.

- **Restrict conventional promotional efforts to the right time and right place.** Persuasive communication efforts are still valid for specific communication tasks, such as regular advertising and the product information pages on a website, but efforts to inject blatant "salespeak" into social networking conversations will usually be rejected by the audience.
- **Maintain a consistent personality.** Each social network is a unique environment with particular norms of communication.[21] For example, as a strictly business-oriented network, LinkedIn has a more formal "vibe" than Facebook and Google+, which cater to both consumers and businesses. However, while adapting to the expectations of each network, be sure to maintain a consistent personality across all the networks in which you are active.[22]

See "Writing Promotional Messages for Social Media" in Chapter 10 (pages 302–303) for more tips on writing messages for social networks and other social media.

3 **LEARNING OBJECTIVE**
Explain how companies and business professionals can use information and content sharing websites.

Information and Content Sharing Sites

Social networks allow members to share information and media items as part of the networking experience, but a variety of systems have been designed specifically for sharing content. The field is diverse and still evolving, but the possibilities can be divided into user-generated content sites, content curation sites, and community Q&A sites.

Courtesy Polaris Industries. Google and the Google logo are registered trademarks of Google Inc., used with permission.

Figure 7.2   Community Building via Social Media
Customer-affiliation groups can be an effective way to build stakeholder support for a company and its products. Indian Motorcycles used this Google⁺ post to spur interest in its rider groups.

USER-GENERATED CONTENT SITES

YouTube, Flickr, Yelp, and other **user-generated content (UGC) sites**, in which users rather than website owners contribute most or all of the content, have become serious business tools. On YouTube, for example, companies post everything from product demonstrations and TV commercials to company profiles and technical support explanations.

As with other social media, the keys to effective UGC are making it valuable and making it easy. First, provide content that people want to see and share with colleagues. A video clip that explains how to use a product more effectively will be more popular than a clip that talks about how amazing the company behind the product is. Also, keep videos short, generally no longer than three to five minutes, if possible.[23]

Second, make material easy to find, consume, and share. For example, a *branded channel* on YouTube lets a company organize all its videos in one place, making it easy for visitors to browse the selection or subscribe to get automatic updates of future videos. Sharing features let fans share videos through email or their accounts on Twitter, Facebook, and other platforms.

YouTube and other user-generated content sites are now important business communication channels.

CONTENT CURATION SITES

Newsfeeds from blogs and other online publishers can be a great way to stay on top of developments in any field. However, anyone who has signed up for more than a few RSS feeds has probably experienced the "firehose effect" of getting so many feeds so quickly that it becomes impossible to stay on top of them. Moreover, when a highly active publisher feeds every new article, from the essential to the trivial, the reader is left to sort it all out every day.

Content curation is the process of collecting and presenting information on a particular topic in a way that makes it convenient for target readers.

(continued on page 198)

Business Communicators Innovating with Social Media

Companies in virtually every industry use social media and continue to experiment with new ways to connect with customers and other stakeholders. From offering helpful tips on using products to helping customers meet each other, these companies show the enormous range of possibilities that new media continue to bring to business communication.[14]

Recruiting and Business-Focused Social Networks

Marketo, a developer of digital marketing software, maintains a profile on LinkedIn, as do hundreds of its employees.

Tweetups

A powerful capability of online social media is bringing people with similar interests together offline. *Tweetups*, for example, are in-person meetings planned and organized over Twitter.

Value-Added Content via Social Networks

Thousands of companies are on social networking platforms, but blatantly promotional posts are not always welcome by fans and followers. Instead, companies such as Whole Foods use social networks to share information of interest, such as recipes and nutritional advice.

Value-Added Content via Blogging

One of the best ways to become a valued member of a network is to provide content that is useful to others in the network. The Quizzle personal finance blog offers a steady stream of articles and advice that help people manage their finances.

Value-Added Content via Online Video

Lie-Nielsen Toolworks of Warren, Maine, uses its YouTube channel to offer valuable information on choosing and using premium woodworking tools. By offering sought-after information for both current and potential customers free of charge, these videos help Lie-Nielsen foster relationships with the worldwide woodworking community and solidify its position as one of the leaders in this market. Animal Planet, Best Western, and Taco Bell are among the many other companies that make effective use of branded channels on YouTube.

Employee Recruiting

Zappos is one of the many companies now using Twitter as a recruiting tool. The company's @InsideZappos account gives potential employees an insider's look at the company's offbeat and upbeat culture.

An intriguing alternative to newsfeeds is **content curation**, in which someone with expertise or interest in a particular field collects and republishes material on a particular topic. The authors' Business Communication Headline News (**http://bchn .businesscommunicationnetwork.com**), for instance, was one of the earliest examples of content curation in the field of business communication.

New curation tools, including Pinterest and Scoop.it, make it easy to assemble attractive online magazines or portfolios on specific topics. Although it raises important issues regarding content ownership and message control,[24] curation has the potential to bring the power of community and shared expertise to a lot of different fields; ultimately, it could reshape audience behavior and therefore the practice of business communication.

COMMUNITY Q&A SITES

Community Q&A sites, on which visitors answer questions posted by other visitors, are a contemporary twist on the early ethos of computer networking, which was people helping each other. (Groups of like-minded people connected online long before the World Wide Web was even created.) Community Q&A sites include dedicated customer support communities such as those hosted on Get Satisfaction and public sites such as Quora and Yahoo! Answers.

Community Q&A sites offer great opportunities for building your personal brand.

Responding to questions on Q&A sites can be a great way to build your personal brand, demonstrate your company's commitment to customer service, and counter misinformation about your company and its products. Keep in mind that when you respond to an individual query on a community Q&A site, you are also "responding in advance" to every person in the future who comes to the site with the same question. In other words, you are writing a type of reference material in addition to corresponding with the original questioner, so keep the long time frame and wider audience in mind.

4 LEARNING OBJECTIVE
Describe the evolving role of email in business communication, and explain how to adapt the three-step writing process to email messages.

Email

Email has been an important communication tool for many companies for several decades, and in the beginning it offered a huge advantage in speed and efficiency over the media it usually replaced (printed and faxed messages). Over the years, email began to be used for many communication tasks simply because it was the only widely available digital format for written messages and millions of users were comfortable with it. However, newer tools—such as instant messaging, blogs, microblogs, social networks, and shared workspaces—are taking over specific tasks for which they are better suited.[25] For example, email is not usually the best choice for conversational communication (IM is better) or project management discussions and updates (blogs, wikis, and various purpose-built systems are often preferable).

Email remains a primary format for companies, but better alternatives now exist for many types of communication.

In addition to the widespread availability of better alternatives for many communication purposes, the indiscriminate use of email has lowered its appeal in the eyes of many professionals. In a sense, email is too easy to use—with a couple of mouse clicks you can send low-value messages to multiple recipients or trigger long message chains that become impossible to follow as people chime in along the way. In fact, frustration with email is so high in some companies that managers are making changes to reduce or even eliminate its use for internal communication.[26]

Email can seem a bit "old school" in comparison to social networks and other technologies, but it is still one of the more important business communication media.

However, email still has compelling advantages that will keep it in steady use in many companies. First, email is universal. Anybody with an email address can reach anybody else with an email address, no matter which systems the senders and receivers are on. Second, email is still the best medium for many private, short- to medium-length messages, particularly when the exchange is limited to two people. Unlike with microblogs or IM, for instance, midsize messages are easy to compose and easy to read on email. Third, email's noninstantaneous nature is an advantage when used properly. Email lets senders compose substantial messages in private and on their own schedule, and it lets recipients read those messages at their leisure.

PLANNING EMAIL MESSAGES

The solution to email overload starts in the planning step, by making sure every message has a useful, business-related purpose. Also, be aware that many companies now have formal email policies that specify how employees can use email, including restrictions against using company email service for personal messages, sending confidential information, or sending material that might be deemed objectionable. In addition, many employers now monitor email, either automatically with software programmed to look for sensitive content or manually via security staff actually reading selected email messages. Regardless of formal policies, though, every email user has a responsibility to avoid actions that could cause trouble, from opening virus-infected attachments to sending inappropriate photographs.

Even with fairly short messages, spend a moment or two on the message-planning tasks described in Chapter 4: analyzing the situation, gathering necessary information for your readers, and organizing your message. You'll save time in the long run because you will craft a more effective message on the first attempt. Your readers will get the information they need and won't have to generate follow-up messages asking for clarification or additional information.

> Do your part to stem the flood of email by making sure you don't send unnecessary messages or cc people who don't really need to see particular messages.

WRITING EMAIL MESSAGES

When you approach email writing on the job, recognize that business email is a more formal medium than you are probably accustomed to with email for personal communication (see Figure 7.3 on the next page). The expectations of writing quality for business email are higher than for personal email, and the consequences of bad writing or poor judgment can be much more serious. For example, email messages and other digital documents have the same legal weight as printed documents, and they are often used as evidence in lawsuits and criminal investigations.[27]

> Business email messages are more formal than the email messages you send to family and friends.

The email subject line might seem like a small detail, but it is actually one of the most important parts of an email message because it helps recipients decide which messages to read and when to read them. To capture your audience's attention, make your subject lines informative and compelling. Go beyond simply describing or classifying your message; use the opportunity to build interest with keywords, quotations, directions, or questions.[28] For example, "July sales results" may accurately describe the content of a message, but "July sales results: good news and bad news" is more intriguing. Readers will want to know why some news is good and some is bad.

> A poorly written subject line could lead to a message being deleted or ignored.

In addition, many email programs display the first few words or lines of incoming messages, even before the recipient opens them. In the words of social media public relations expert Steve Rubel, you can "tweetify" the opening lines of your email messages to make them stand out. In other words, choose the first few words carefully to grab your reader's attention.[29] Think of the first sentence as an extension of your subject line.

As a lean medium (see page 112), email can present challenges when you need to express particular emotional nuances, whether positive or negative. For years, users of email (as well as IM and text messaging) have used a variety of *emoticons* to express emotions in casual communication. For example, to express sympathy as a way to take some of the sting out of negative news, one might use a "frowny face," either the :(character string or a graphical emoticon such as or one of the colorful and sometimes animated characters available in some systems.

> Attitudes about emoticons in business communication are changing; you'll have to use your best judgment in every case.

In the past, the use of emoticons was widely regarded as unprofessional and therefore advised against in business communication. Recently, though, an increasing number of professionals seem to be using them, particularly for communication with close colleagues, even as other professionals continue to view them as evidence of lazy or immature writing.[30] In the face of these conflicting perspectives, the best advice is to use caution. Avoid emoticons for nearly all types of external communication and for formal internal communication, and avoid those bright yellow graphical emoticons (and particularly animated emoticons) in all business communication.

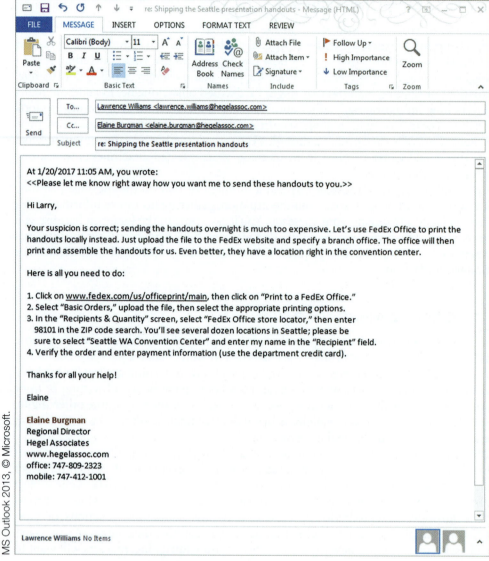

Figure 7.3 **Email for Business Communication**
In this response to an email query from a colleague, Elaine Burgman takes advantage of her email system's features to create an efficient and effective message.

COMPLETING EMAIL MESSAGES

Particularly for important messages, taking a few moments to revise and proofread might save you hours of headaches and damage control. Also, favor simplicity when it comes to producing your email messages. A clean, easily readable font, in black on a white background, is sufficient for nearly all email messages. Take advantage of your email system's ability to include an **email signature**, a small file that automatically includes such items as your full name, title, company, and contact information at the end of your messages.

When you're ready to distribute your message, pause to verify what you're doing before you click on Send. Make sure you've included everyone necessary—and no one else. Did you click on Reply All when you meant to click on only Reply? The difference could be embarrassing or even career threatening. Don't include people in the cc (courtesy copy) or bcc (blind courtesy copy) fields unless you know how these features work. (Everyone who receives the message can see who is on the cc line but not who is on the bcc line.) Also, don't set the message priority to "high" or "urgent" unless your message is truly urgent. And if you intend to include an attachment, be sure that it is indeed attached.

Think twice before clicking on Send. A simple mistake in your content or distribution can cause major headaches.

Will Emoticons Give Your Career a Frowny Face?

Your project team has just been reprimanded by the boss for missing a deadline. Your colleagues left the meeting grumbling about being criticized in public after working nights and weekends, and you fear that morale will slip.

You could craft an inspirational message to soothe the bruised egos and get the team's energy turned around in a positive direction. However, writing such a message could be risky, because world-weary teammates might just brush it off as happytalk and resent you for trying to be a cheerleader.

Alternatively, you could suggest that your colleagues lighten up and stay focused on the ultimate goal of the project. However, you already know that telling grumpy people to cheer up is a surefire way to make most of them even grumpier.

Instead, you opt for a quick bit of gentle sarcasm, designed to help release the negative emotions in a collegial way. When you get back to your desk, you write the following instant message:

Well, let's pick up the pieces of our shattered lives and move on ;-)

The over-the-top phrasing is a subtle way to remind everyone that the criticism wasn't all *that* traumatic, and that winking emoticon tells everyone to lighten up without actually saying so. The apparent sarcasm connects with people who are marinating in their negative emotions, but it's really a pep talk disguised as sarcasm.

Then you worry that the emoticon will seem unprofessional, so you replace it with a simple period:

Well, let's pick up the pieces of our shattered lives and move on.

Oops. That one minor change to make the message more professional turned it into a statement of resigned sadness. You search your keyboard for any acceptable symbol that might help:

Well, let's pick up the pieces of our shattered lives and move on!

Great, now you've managed to sound bitter and demanding at the same time.

Given the difficulty of communicating emotional nuance in lean media such as IM and email, are emoticons really all that bad? The answer depends on the situation, your relationship with your audience, and the company culture. Until emoticons become more widely accepted in business communication, it's wise to err on the side of caution.

CAREER APPLICATIONS

1. As a manager, what reaction would you have to job applicants who use emoticons in their email messages?
2. Are emoticons just a generational difference in perspective, or is there more to the issue? Explain your answer.

To review the tips and techniques for successful email, see Table 7.1 on the next page and "Checklist: Creating Effective Email Messages" below, or click on Chapter 7 at http://real-timeupdates.com/ebc12.

CHECKLIST ✔ CREATING EFFECTIVE EMAIL MESSAGES

A. Planning email messages
- Make sure every email message you send is necessary.
- Don't cc or bcc anyone who doesn't really need to see the message.
- Follow company email policy; understand the restrictions your company places on email usage.
- Practice good email hygiene by not opening suspicious messages, keeping virus protection up to date, and following other company guidelines.
- Follow the chain of command.

B. Writing email messages
- Remember that business email is more formal than personal email.
- Recognize that email messages carry the same legal weight as other business documents.
- Pay attention to the quality of your writing and use correct grammar, spelling, and punctuation.
- Make your subject lines informative by clearly identifying the purpose of your message.
- Make your subject lines compelling by wording them in a way that intrigues your audiences.
- Use the first few words of the email body to catch the reader's attention.

C. Completing email messages
- Revise and proofread carefully to avoid embarrassing mistakes.
- Keep the layout of your messages simple and clean, particularly for mobile recipients.
- Use an email signature file to give recipients your contact information.
- Double-check your recipient list before sending.
- Don't mark messages as "urgent" unless they truly are urgent.

TABLE 7.1 Tips for Effective Email Messages

Tip	Why It's Important
When you request information or action, make it clear what you're asking for, why it's important, and how soon you need it; don't make your reader write back for details.	People will be tempted to ignore your messages if they're not clear about what you want or how soon you want it.
When responding to a request, either paraphrase the request or include enough of the original message to remind the reader what you're replying to.	Some businesspeople get hundreds of email messages a day and may need reminding what your specific response is about.
If possible, avoid sending long, complex messages via email.	Long messages are easier to read as attached reports or web content.
Adjust the level of formality to the message and the audience.	Overly formal messages to colleagues can be perceived as stuffy and distant; overly informal messages to customers or top executives can be perceived as disrespectful.
Activate a signature file, which automatically pastes your contact information into every message you create.	A signature saves you the trouble of retyping vital information and ensures that recipients know how to reach you through other means.
Don't let unread messages pile up in your in-basket.	You'll miss important information and create the impression that you're ignoring other people.
Never type in all caps.	ALL CAPS ARE INTERPRETED AS SCREAMING.
Don't overformat your messages with background colors, multicolored type, unusual fonts, and so on.	Such messages can be difficult and annoying to read on screen.
Remember that messages can be forwarded anywhere and saved forever.	Don't let a moment of anger or poor judgment haunt you for the rest of your career.
Use the "return receipt requested" feature only for the most critical messages.	This feature triggers a message back to you whenever someone receives or opens your message; some consider this an invasion of privacy.
Make sure your computer has up-to-date virus protection.	One of the worst breaches of netiquette is infecting other computers because you haven't bothered to protect your own system.
Pay attention to grammar, spelling, and capitalization.	Some people don't think email needs formal rules, but careless messages make you look unprofessional and can annoy readers.
Use acronyms sparingly.	Shorthand such as IMHO (in my humble opinion) and LOL (laughing out loud) can be useful in informal correspondence with colleagues, but avoid using them in more formal messages.
Be careful with the use of emoticons.	Many people view the use of these symbols as unprofessional.
Assume that recipients may read your messages on small mobile screens.	Email is more difficult to read on small screens, so don't burden recipients with long, complicated messages.

5 **LEARNING OBJECTIVE** Describe the business benefits of instant messaging (IM), and identify guidelines for effective IM in the workplace.

IM is taking the place of email and voicemail for routine communication in many companies.

Phone-based text messaging is being integrated into a variety of digital communication systems.

Instant Messaging and Text Messaging

Computer-based **instant messaging (IM)**, in which users' messages appear on each other's screens instantly, is used extensively for internal and external communication. IM is available in both stand-alone systems and as a function embedded in online meeting systems, collaboration systems, social networks, and other platforms. For conversational exchanges, it's hard to top the advantages of IM, and the technology is replacing both email and voicemail in many situations.[31] Business-grade IM systems offer a range of capabilities, including basic chat, *presence awareness* (the ability to quickly see which people are at their desks and available to IM), remote display of documents, video capabilities, remote control of other computers, automated newsfeeds from blogs and websites, and automated *bot* (derived from the word *robot*) capabilities in which a computer can carry on simple conversations.[32]

Text messaging has a number of applications in business as well, including marketing (alerting customers about new sale prices, for example), customer service (such as airline flight status, package tracking, and appointment reminders), security (for example, authenticating mobile banking transactions), crisis management (such as updating all employees working at a disaster scene), and process monitoring (alerting computer technicians to system failures, for example).[33] As it becomes more tightly integrated with other communication media, text messaging is likely to find even more widespread use in business communication. For instance, texting is now integrated into systems such as Facebook Messages and Gmail, and branded "StarStar numbers" can deliver web-based content such as videos, software apps, and digital coupons to mobile phones.[34]

The following sections focus on IM, but many of the benefits, risks, and guidelines pertain to text messaging as well.

UNDERSTANDING THE BENEFITS AND RISKS OF IM

The benefits of IM include its capability for rapid response to urgent messages, lower cost than phone calls and email, ability to mimic conversation more closely than email, and availability on a wide range of devices.[35] In addition, because it more closely resembles one-on-one conversation, IM doesn't get misused as a one-to-many broadcast method as often as email does.[36]

The potential drawbacks of IM include security problems (computer viruses, network infiltration, and the possibility that sensitive messages might be intercepted by outsiders), the need for *user authentication* (making sure that online correspondents are really who they appear to be), the challenge of logging messages for later review and archiving (a legal requirement in some industries), incompatibility between competing IM systems, and *spim* (unsolicited commercial messages, similar to email spam). Fortunately, with the growth of *enterprise instant messaging (EIM)*, or IM systems designed for large-scale corporate use, many of these problems are being overcome.

> IM offers many benefits:
> - Rapid response
> - Low cost
> - Ability to mimic conversation
> - Wide availability
>
> When using IM, be aware of the potential for constant interruptions and wasted time.

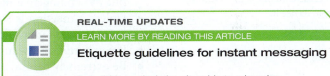

REAL-TIME UPDATES
LEARN MORE BY READING THIS ARTICLE
Etiquette guidelines for instant messaging

As a lean medium, IM is particularly vulnerable to misunderstandings; learn how to avoid them. Go to http://real-timeupdates.com/ebc12 and click on Learn More in the Students section.

ADAPTING THE THREE-STEP PROCESS FOR SUCCESSFUL IM

Although instant messages are often conceived, written, and sent within a matter of seconds, the principles of the three-step process still apply, particularly when communicating with customers and other important audiences:

- **Planning instant messages.** Except for simple exchanges, take a moment to plan IM "conversations" in much the same way you would plan an important oral conversation. A few seconds of planning can help you deliver information in a coherent, complete way that minimizes the number of individual messages required.
- **Writing instant messages.** As with email, the appropriate writing style for business IM is more formal than the style you may be accustomed to with personal IM or text messaging (see Figure 7.4 on the next page). Your company might discourage the use of IM acronyms (such as FWIW for "for what it's worth" or HTH for "hope that helps"), particularly for IM with external audiences.
- **Completing instant messages.** The only task in the completing stage is to send your message. Just quickly scan it before sending, to make sure you don't have any missing or misspelled words and verify that your message is clear and complete.

> Although you don't plan individual instant messages the same way you do longer messages, view important IM exchanges as conversations with specific goals in mind.

To use IM effectively, keep in mind some important behavioral issues when relying on this medium: the potential for constant interruptions, the ease of accidentally mixing personal and business messages, the risk of being out of the loop (if a hot discussion or an impromptu meeting flares up when you're away from your PC or other IM device), and the frustration of being at the mercy of other people's typing abilities.[37]

Regardless of the system you're using, you can make IM more efficient and effective by heeding these tips:[38]

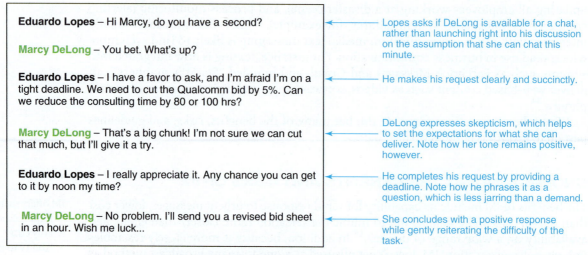

Figure 7.4 **Instant Messaging for Business Communication**
To use IM effectively in the workplace, adopt a casual but still professional tone, particularly when communicating with people outside the organization.

Understand the guidelines for successful business IM before you begin to use it.

- Be courteous; if you don't need an answer instantly, you can avoid interrupting someone by sending an email or other type of message instead.
- Unless a meeting is scheduled or you're expected to be available for other reasons, make yourself unavailable when you need to focus on other work.
- If you're not on a secure system, don't send confidential information using IM.
- Be extremely careful about sending personal messages; they have a tendency to pop up on other people's computers at embarrassing moments.
- Don't use IM for important but impromptu meetings if you can't verify that everyone concerned will be available.
- Don't use IM for lengthy, complex messages.
- Try to avoid carrying on multiple IM conversations at one time, to minimize the chance of sending messages to the wrong people or making one person wait while you tend to another conversation.
- Follow all security guidelines designed to keep your company's information and systems safe from attack.

To review the advice for effective IM in the workplace, see "Checklist: Using IM Productively" or click on Chapter 7 at **http://real-timeupdates.com/ebc12**.

CHECKLIST ✔ **USING IM PRODUCTIVELY**

- Pay attention to security and privacy issues and be sure to follow all company guidelines.
- Treat IM as a professional communication medium, not an informal, personal tool; avoid using IM slang with all but close colleagues.
- Maintain good etiquette, even during simple exchanges.
- Protect your own productivity by making yourself unavailable when you need to focus.
- In most instances, don't use IM for confidential messages, complex messages, or personal messages.

---

6 **LEARNING OBJECTIVE**
Describe the use of blogging and microblogging in business communication, and briefly explain how to adapt the three-step process to blogging.

Blogging and Microblogging

Blogs, online journals that are easier to personalize and update than conventional websites, have become a major force in business communication. Millions of business-oriented blogs are now in operation, and blogs have become an important source of information for consumers and professionals alike.[39] Good business blogs and microblogs pay close attention to several important elements:

- **Communicating with personal style and an authentic voice.** Most business messages designed for large audiences are carefully scripted and written in a "corporate voice" that is impersonal and objective. In contrast, successful business blogs are written by individuals and exhibit their personal style. Audiences relate to this fresh approach and often build closer emotional bonds with the blogger's organization as a result.

- **Delivering new information quickly.** Blogging tools let you post new material as soon as you create it or find it. This feature not only allows you to respond quickly when needed—such as during a corporate crisis—but also lets your audiences know that active communication is taking place. Blogs that don't offer a continuous stream of new and interesting content are quickly ignored in today's online environment.
- **Choosing topics of peak interest to audiences.** Successful blogs cover topics that readers care about.
- **Encouraging audiences to join the conversation.** Not all blogs invite comments, although most do, and many bloggers consider comments to be an essential feature. Blog comments can be a valuable source of news, information, and insights. In addition, the informal nature of blogging seems to make it easier for companies to let their guard down and converse with their audiences. To protect against comments that are not helpful or appropriate, many bloggers review all comments and post only the most helpful or interesting ones.

Writing in a personal, authentic voice is key to attracting and keeping blog readers.

REAL-TIME UPDATES

LEARN MORE BY READING THIS ARTICLE

Ten years later, are business blogs still a good investment?

Mainstream business blogging had been around for about a decade; is it still a good way to connect with audiences? Go to http://real-timeupdates.com/ebc12 and click on Learn More in the Students section.

UNDERSTANDING THE BUSINESS APPLICATIONS OF BLOGGING

Blogs are a potential solution whenever you have a continuing stream of information to share with an online audience—and particularly when you want the audience to have the opportunity to respond. Here are some of the many ways businesses are using blogs for internal and external communication:[40]

- **Anchoring the social media presence.** As noted on page 194, the multiple threads of any social media program should be anchored in a central hub the company or individual owns and controls. Blogs make an ideal social media hub.
- **Project management and team communication.** Using blogs is a good way to keep project teams up to date, particularly when team members are geographically dispersed. For instance, the trip reports that employees file after visiting customers or other external parties can be enhanced vividly with mobile blogs.
- **Company news.** Companies can use blogs to keep employees informed about general business matters, from facility news to benefit updates. Blogs also serve as online community forums, giving everyone in the company a chance to raise questions and voice concerns.
- **Customer support.** Customer support blogs answer questions, offer tips and advice, and inform customers about new products. Also, many companies monitor the *blogosphere* (and *Twittersphere*), looking for complaints and responding with offers to help dissatisfied customers.[41]
- **Public relations and media relations.** Many company employees and executives now share company news with both the general public and journalists via their blogs.
- **Recruiting.** Using a blog is a great way to let potential employees know more about your company, the people who work there, and the nature of the company culture. In the other direction, employers often find and evaluate the blogs and microblogs of prospective employees, making blogging is a great way to build a name for yourself within your industry or profession.
- **Policy and issue discussions.** Executive blogs in particular provide a public forum for discussing legislation, regulations, and other broad issues of interest to an organization.

The business applications of blogs include a wide range of internal and external communication tasks.

- **Crisis communication.** Using blogs is a convenient way to provide up-to-the-minute information during emergencies, correct misinformation, or respond to rumors.
- **Market research.** Blogs can be a clever mechanism for soliciting feedback from customers and experts in the marketplace. In addition to using their own blogs to solicit feedback, today's companies should monitor blogs that are likely to discuss them, their executives, and their products.
- **Brainstorming.** Online brainstorming via blogs offers a way for people to toss around ideas and build on each other's contributions.
- **Employee engagement.** Blogs can enhance communication across all levels of a company, giving lower-level employees a voice that they might not otherwise have and giving senior executives better access to timely information.
- **Customer education.** Blogs are a great way to help current and potential customers understand and use your products and services. This function can improve sales and support productivity as well, by reducing the need for one-on-one communication.
- **Word-of-mouth marketing.** Bloggers often make a point of providing links to other blogs and websites that interest them, giving marketers a great opportunity to have their messages spread by enthusiasts. (Online word-of mouth marketing is often called *viral marketing* in reference to the way biological viruses are transmitted from person to person. However, viral marketing is not really an accurate metaphor. As author Brian Solis puts it, "There is no such thing as viral marketing."[42] Real viruses spread from host to host on their own, whereas word-of-mouth marketing spreads *voluntarily* from person to person. The distinction is critical, because you need to give people a good reason—good content, in other words—to pass along your message.)
- **Influencing traditional media news coverage.** According to social media consultant Tamar Weinberg, "the more prolific bloggers who provide valuable and consistent content are often considered experts in their subject matter" and are often called on when journalists need insights into various topics.[43]
- **Community building.** Blogging is a great way to connect people with similar interests, and popular bloggers often attract a community of readers who connect with one another through the commenting function.

The uses of blogs are limited only by your creativity, so be on the lookout for new ways you can use them to foster positive relationships with colleagues, customers, and other important audiences (see Figure 7.5).

ADAPTING THE THREE-STEP PROCESS FOR SUCCESSFUL BLOGGING

The three-step writing process is easy to adapt to blogging tasks. The planning step is particularly important when you're launching a blog because you're planning an entire communication channel, not just a single message. Pay close attention to your audience, your purpose, and your scope:

- **Audience.** Except with team blogs and other efforts that have an obvious and well-defined audience, defining the target audience for a blog can be challenging. You want an audience large enough to justify the time you'll be investing but narrow enough that you can provide a clear focus for the blog. For instance, if you work for a firm that develops computer games, would you focus your blog on "hardcore" players, the types who spend thousands of dollars on super-fast PCs optimized for video games, or would you broaden the reach to include all video gamers? The decision often comes down to business strategy.
- **Purpose.** A business blog needs to have a business-related purpose that is important to your company and to your chosen audience. Moreover, the purpose has to "have legs"—that is, it needs to be something that can drive the blog's content for months or years—rather than focus on a single event or an issue of only temporary

Blogs are an ideal medium for word-of-mouth marketing, the spread of promotional messages from one audience member to another.

Before you launch a blog, make sure you have a clear understanding of your target audience, the purpose of your blog, and the scope of subjects you plan to cover.

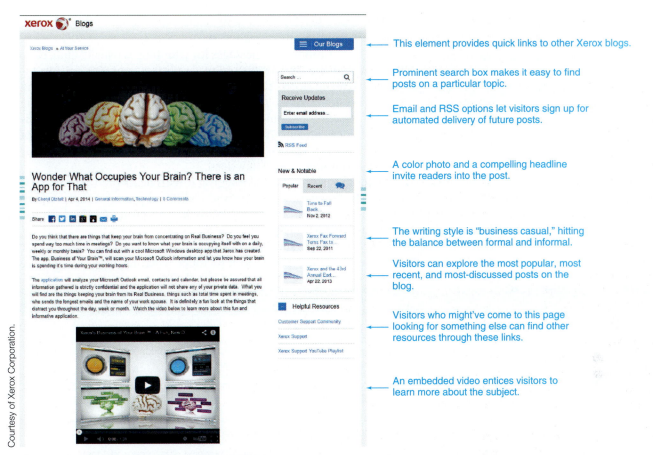

This element provides quick links to other Xerox blogs.

Prominent search box makes it easy to find posts on a particular topic.

Email and RSS options let visitors sign up for automated delivery of future posts.

A color photo and a compelling headline invite readers into the post.

The writing style is "business casual," hitting the balance between formal and informal.

Visitors can explore the most popular, most recent, and most-discussed posts on the blog.

Visitors who might've come to this page looking for something else can find other resources through these links.

An embedded video entices visitors to learn more about the subject.

Courtesy of Xerox Corporation.

Figure 7.5   Business Applications of Blogging
This Xerox blog illustrates the content, writing style, and features that make an effective, reader-friendly company blog.

interest. For instance, if you're a technical expert, you might create a blog to give the audience tips and techniques for using your company's products more effectively—a never-ending subject that's important to both you and your audience. This would be the general purpose of your blog; each posting would have a specific purpose within the context of that general purpose. Finally, if you are not writing an official company blog but rather blogging as an individual employee, make sure you understand your employer's blogging guidelines. IBM, for example, gives its employees 12 specific social computing guidelines, such as identifying their role as IBM employees if they are discussing matters related to the company and respecting intellectual property laws.[44]

- **Scope.** Defining the scope of your blog can be a bit tricky. You want to cover a subject area that is broad enough to offer discussion possibilities for months or years but narrow enough to have an identifiable focus.

After you begin writing your blog, careful planning needs to continue with each message. Unless you're posting to a restricted-access blog, such as an internal blog on a company intranet, you can never be sure who might see your posts. Other bloggers might link to them months or years later.

Use a comfortable, personal writing style. Blog audiences don't want to hear from your company; they want to hear from *you*. Bear in mind, though, that comfortable does not mean careless. Sloppy writing damages your credibility. Successful blog content also needs to be interesting, valuable to readers, and as brief as possible.[45] In addition, although audiences expect you to be knowledgeable in the subject area your blog covers, you don't need to know everything about a topic. If you don't have all the information yourself, provide links to other blogs and websites that supply relevant information. In fact, content curation (see page 195) is one of the most valuable aspects of blogging. Just be sure the content you

Write blog postings in a comfortable—but not careless—style.

REAL-TIME UPDATES

LEARN MORE BY READING THIS INFOGRAPHIC

Grab readers' attention with your blog posts

Follow these tips to make sure your posts get noticed and get read. Go to http://real-timeupdates.com/ebc12 and click on Learn More in the Students section.

share is relevant to your readers and compatible with your communication goals.

Completing messages for your blog is usually quite easy. Evaluate the content and readability of your message, proofread to correct any errors, and post using your blogging system's tools. If you're using any contemporary blogging system, it should offer a *newsfeed* option so that your audience can automatically receive headlines and summaries of new blog posts. Really Simple Syndication (RSS) is the most common type of newsfeed.

Finally, make your material easier to find by **tagging** it with descriptive words. Your readers can then click on these "content labels" to find additional posts on those topics. Tags are usually displayed with each post, and they can also be groups in a *tag cloud* display, which shows all the tags in use on your blog.

Table 7.2 offers a variety of tips for successful blogging, and "Checklist: Blogging for Business" summarizes some of the key points to remember when creating and writing

TABLE 7.2	Tips for Effective Business Blogging
Tip	**Why It's Important**
Don't blog without a clear plan.	Without a clear plan, your blog is likely to wander from topic to topic and fail to build a sense of community with your audience.
Post frequently; the whole point of a blog is fresh material.	If you won't have a constant supply of new information or new links, create a traditional website instead.
Make it about your audience and the issues important to them.	Readers want to know how your blog will help them, entertain them, or give them a chance to communicate with others who have similar interests.
Write in an authentic voice; never create an artificial character who supposedly writes a blog.	Flogs, or fake blogs, violate the spirit of blogging, show disrespect for your audience, and will turn audiences against you as soon as they uncover the truth. Fake blogs used to promote products are now illegal in some countries.
Link generously—but carefully.	Providing interesting links to other blogs and websites is a fundamental aspect of blogging, but make sure the links will be of value to your readers and don't point to inappropriate material.
Keep it brief.	Most online readers don't have the patience to read lengthy reports. Rather than writing long, report-style posts, you can write brief posts that link to in-depth reports.
Don't post anything you wouldn't want the entire world to see.	Future employers, government regulators, competitors, journalists, and community critics are just a few of the people who might eventually see what you've written.
Minimize marketing and sales messages.	Readers want information about them and their needs.
Take time to write compelling, specific headlines for your postings.	Readers usually decide within a couple of seconds whether to read your postings; boring or vague headlines will turn them away instantly.
Pay attention to spelling, grammar, and mechanics.	No matter how smart or experienced you are, poor-quality writing undermines your credibility with intelligent audiences.
Respond to criticism openly and honestly.	Hiding sends the message that you don't have a valid response to the criticism. If your critics are wrong, patiently explain why you think they're wrong. If they are right, explain how you'll fix the situation.
Listen and learn.	If you don't take the time to analyze the comments people leave on your blog or the comments other bloggers make about you, you're missing out on one of the most valuable aspects of blogging.
Respect intellectual property.	Improperly using material you don't own is not only unethical but can be illegal as well.
Be scrupulously honest and careful with facts.	Honesty is an absolute requirement for every ethical business communicator, of course, but you need to be extra careful online because inaccuracies (both intentional and unintentional) are likely to be discovered quickly and shared widely.
If you review products on your blog, disclose any beneficial relationships you have with the companies that make those products.	Bloggers who receive free products or other compensation from companies whose products they write about are now required to disclose the nature of these relationships.

a business blog. For the more information on using blogs in business, visit **http://real-timeupdates.com/ebc12** and click on Chapter 7.

CHECKLIST ✔ **BLOGGING FOR BUSINESS**

- Consider creating a blog or microblog account whenever you have a continuing stream of information to share with an online audience.
- Identify an audience that is broad enough to justify the effort but narrow enough to have common interests.
- Identify a purpose that is comprehensive enough to provide ideas for a continuing stream of posts.
- Consider the scope of your blog carefully; make it broad enough to attract an audience but narrow enough to keep you focused.

- Communicate with a personal style and an authentic voice, but don't write carelessly.
- Deliver new information quickly.
- Choose topics of peak interest to your audience.
- Encourage audiences to join the conversation.
- Consider using Twitter or other microblog updates to alert readers to new posts on your regular blog.

MICROBLOGGING

A **microblog** is a variation on blogging in which messages are sharply restricted to specific character counts. Twitter is the best known of these systems, but many others exist. Some companies have private microblogging systems for internal use only; these systems are sometimes referred to as *enterprise microblogging* or *internal micromessaging*.[46]

Many of the concepts of regular blogging apply to microblogging as well, although the severe length limitations call for a different approach to composition. Microblog messages often involve short summaries or teasers that provide links to more information. In addition, microblogs tend to have a stronger social aspect that makes it easier for writers and readers to forward messages and for communities to form around individual writers.[47]

Like regular blogging, microblogging quickly caught on with business users and is now a mainstream business medium. Microblogs are used for virtually all of the blog applications mentioned on pages 205–206. In addition, microblogs are often used for interacting with customers (see Figure 7.6 on the next page), providing company updates, offering coupons and notice of sales, presenting tips on product usage, sharing relevant and interesting information from experts, announcing headlines of new blog posts, and serving as the *backchannel* in meetings and presentations (see page 465). By following top names in your field, you can customize Twitter as your own real-time news source.[48] Customer service is becoming a popular use for Twitter as well, thanks to its ease, speed, and the option of switching between public tweets and private direct messages as the situation warrants.[49] The social networking aspect of Twitter and other microblogs also makes them good for *crowdsourcing* research questions, asking ones' followers for input or advice.[50] Finally, the ease of *retweeting*, the practice of forwarding messages from other Twitter users, is the microblogging equivalent of sharing other content from other bloggers via content curation.

In addition to its usefulness as a stand-alone system, Twitter is also integrated with other social media systems and a variety of publishing and reading tools and services. Many of these system use the informal Twitter feature known as the *hashtag* (the # symbol followed by a word or phrase), which makes it easy for people to label and search for topics of interest and to monitor ongoing Twitter conversations about particular topics.

MOBILE APP
The mobile app for Twitter helps you stay connected with your followers and the accounts you follow.

The business communication uses of microblogging extend beyond the publication of brief updates.

REAL-TIME UPDATES
LEARN MORE BY READING THIS ARTICLE
Twitter tips for beginners
An experienced user shares tips for getting the most from Twitter. Go to http://real-timeupdates.com/ebc12 and click on Learn More in the Students section.

REAL-TIME UPDATES
LEARN MORE BY READING THIS ARTICLE
Managing multiple Twitter accounts at Walmart
See how Walmart's social media team interacts with followers across seven Twitter accounts. Go to http://real-timeupdates.com/ebc12 and click on Learn More in the Students section.

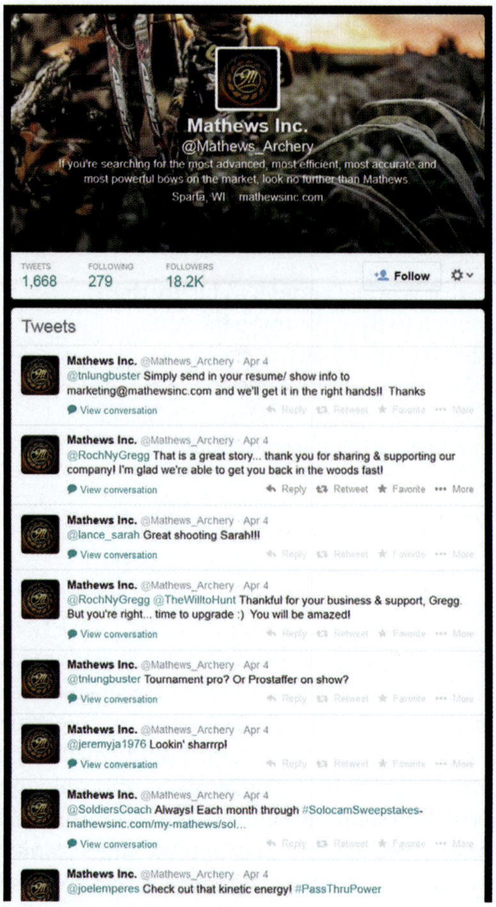

Courtesy of Mathews Archery, Inc.

Figure 7.6   Business Applications of Microblogging
Mathews, a small manufacturer of archery products, uses Twitter to foster relationships with customers and other interested parties. Notice how every tweet in this time line is part of a conversation.

Don't let the speed and simplicity of microblogging lull you into making careless mistakes; every message should support your business communication objectives.

Although microblogs are designed to encourage spontaneous communication, when you're using the medium for business communication, don't just tweet out whatever pops into your head. Make sure messages are part of your overall communication strategy. Twitter followers consider tweets that are entertaining, surprising, informative, or engaging (such as asking followers for advice) as the most valuable. In contrast, the least-valuable tweets tend to be complaints, conversations between the Twitter account owner and a specific follower, and relatively pointless messages such as saying "good morning."[51]

7   LEARNING OBJECTIVE
Explain how to adapt the three-step writing process for podcasts.

Podcasting

Podcasting is the process of recording audio or video files and distributing them online via RSS subscriptions, in the same way that blog posts are automatically fed to subscribers. Podcasting combines the media richness of voice or visual communication with the convenience of portability. Audiences can listen or watch podcasts on a blog or website, or they can download them to phones or portable music players to consume on the go. Particularly with audio podcasts, the hands-off, eyes-off aspect makes them great for listening to while driving or exercising.

Podcasting can be used to deliver a wide range of audio and video messages.

The most obvious use of podcasting is to replace existing audio and video messages, such as one-way teleconferences in which a speaker provides information without expecting to engage in conversation with the listeners. Training is another good use of podcasting; you may have already taken a college course via podcasts. Podcasting is also a great way to offer free previews of seminars and training classes.[52] Many business writers and consultants use podcasting to build their personal brands and to enhance their other product and service offerings. You can find a wide selection on iTunes, many of which are free (go to the Podcasting section and select the Business category).

Although it might not seem obvious at first, the three-step writing process adapts quite nicely to podcasting. First, focus the planning step on analyzing the situation, gathering the information you'll need, and organizing your material. One vital planning step depends on whether you intend to create podcasts for limited use and distribution (such as a weekly audio update to your virtual team) or to create a **podcasting channel** with regular recordings on a consistent theme, designed for a wider public audience. As with planning a blog, if you intend to create a podcasting channel, be sure to think through the range of topics you want to address over time to verify that you have a sustainable purpose. If you bounce from one theme to another, you risk losing your audience.[53] Maintaining a consistent schedule is also important; listeners will stop paying attention if they can't count on regular updates.[54]

As you organize the content for a podcast, pay close attention to previews, transitions, and reviews. These steering devices are especially vital in audio recordings because audio lacks the "street signs" (such as headings) that audiences rely on in print media. Moreover, scanning back and forth to find specific parts of an audio or video message is much more difficult than with textual messages, so you need to do everything possible to make sure your audience successfully receives and interprets your message on the first try.

One of the attractions of podcasting is the conversational, person-to-person feel of the recordings, so unless you need to capture exact wording, speaking from an outline and notes rather than a prepared script is often the best choice. However, no one wants to listen to rambling podcasts that take several minutes to get to the topic or struggle to make a point, so don't try to make up your content on the fly. Effective podcasts, like effective stories, have a clear beginning, middle, and end.

The completing step is where podcasting differs most dramatically from written communication, for the obvious reason that you are recording and distributing audio or video files. Particularly for more formal podcasts, start by revising your script or thinking through your speaking notes before you begin to record. The closer you can get to recording your podcasts in one take, the more productive you'll be.

Most personal computers, smartphones, and other devices now have basic audio recording capability, including built-in microphones, and free editing software such as Audacity is available online (see Figure 7.7 on the next page). These tools can be sufficient for creating informal podcasts for internal use, but to achieve the higher production quality expected in formal or public podcasts, you'll need additional pieces of hardware and software. These can include an audio processor (to filter out extraneous noise and otherwise improve the audio signal), a mixer (to combine multiple audio or video signals), a better microphone, more sophisticated recording and editing software, and perhaps some physical changes in your recording location to improve the acoustics.

Podcasts can be distributed in several ways, including through media stores such as iTunes, by dedicated podcast hosting services, or on a blog with content that supports the podcast channel. If you distribute your podcast on a blog, you can provide additional information and use the commenting feature of the blog to encourage feedback from your audience.[55]

For the latest information on using podcasts in business, visit **http://real-time updates.com/ebc12** and click on Chapter 7.

The three-step process adapts quite well to podcasting.

Steering devices such as transitions, previews, and reviews are vital in podcasts.

Plan your podcast content carefully; editing is more difficult with podcasts than with textual messages.

For basic podcasts, your computer and perhaps even your smartphone might have most of the hardware you already need, and you can download recording software.

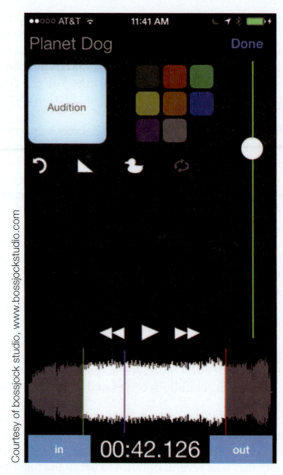

Courtesy of bossjock studio, www.bossjockstudio.com

Figure 7.7 **Mobile Podcasting Tools**
Mobile podcasting apps make it easy to record podcasts on location.

ON THE JOB: SOLVING COMMUNICATION DILEMMAS AT **GOPRO**

You've joined GoPro's community engagement team, and your job involves a variety of communication tasks across multiple channels. Use what you've learned in the course so far to solve these communication dilemmas.

1. You've written a blog post for a competition called "Catch Something Amazing," in which GoPro users can submit "unplanned and unrehearsed" footage of events, performances, or other bits of action they just happen to stumble across while out and about with the GoPro cameras. Which of the following tweets is the best teaser to encourage people to click through to the blog post to read more about the competition?

   a. You've just caught something amazing on camera—don't hoard it; share it!

   b. We're not interested in the same old boring stuff. If you caught something amazing, we want to see it.

   c. Did you catch something amazing with your GoPro? Enter to win $500 worth of equipment accessories.

   d. Enter to win. Competition limited to GoPro users only (any model).

2. One member of the customer engagement team is retiring, and you've been asked to recruit her replacement with someone whose primary responsibility will be blogging. Your plan is to send an email message to everyone in the company, providing a brief reminder of the blog's purpose, describing the writing style you're looking for, and inviting interested writers to submit sample blog entries for evaluation. Which of the following paragraphs is the best way to describe the preferred writing style for the blog? (This message is for employees only; it won't be seen by the public.)

   a. Our best social content connects with thousands of readers because the writing is *engaging* (people want to read and respond), *personal* (readers want to get to know real, live human beings, not a faceless corporation), *honest* (we don't sugar-coat anything or hide from criticism), and *friendly* (our readers want to enjoy the experience).

   b. What kind of writing are we looking for? Well, let me tell you exactly what we need. We need writing that is above all (a) engaging—it makes people *want* to read and become involved in the conversation. Plus, (b), the writing must be *personal*; we don't need anybody to repeat "the company line" here; we want *your unique* thoughts and opinions. However, (c), we, of course (!), need writing that is consistent with GoPro's culture.

  c. You should be able to produce copy that meets the following criteria: Your writing must be engaging, personal, honest, and friendly. Writing that does not meet these criteria, no matter how well written in other respects, will not be accepted for online publication.

  d. I'll be short and to the point: the writing we want for this blog must be engaging, personal, honest, and friendly.

3. Which of the following would be the best subject line for the email message to recruit a new blogger for the customer engagement team?

  a. Opening for a blogger on the customer engagement team
  b. Job opening: customer engagement team
  c. Calling all bloggers
  d. Would you like to join the GoPro social media conversation?

4. Which of the following would be the most effective headline for a Facebook post that announces a new version of the free GoPro Studio software?

  a. The easiest way to edit and share your GoPro videos is now easier than ever
  b. No geek cred? No prob; even you can edit videos with this software!
  c. Creating exciting, pro-quality videos is now as easy as dropping your footage into a GoPro template that's complete with music and special effects.
  d. Forgot those expensive, complicated video editing programs.

Learning Objectives Checkup

Assess your understanding of the principles in this chapter by reading each learning objective and studying the accompanying exercises. You can check your responses against the answer key on page 599.

Objective 7.1: Identify the major digital media used for brief business messages and describe the nine compositional modes needed for digital and social media.

1. How has content sharing through social media changed the information gathering habits of many consumers and professionals?

  a. They frequently "snack" on large numbers of small pieces of information and bypass larger documents that would take more time to read.
  b. Everyone above a certain level in the organization has content readers who "pre-read" documents and messages to select the most important.
  c. All major business decisions now rely on the "hive mind," the collective input of a professional's business network.
  d. Information that doesn't have a catchy teaser is routinely ignored.

2. To express sympathy to the family of one of your employees who recently died in a traffic accident, which of these media would you choose and why?

  a. Facebook post
  b. Printed letter
  c. Email message
  d. Instant message

3. Which of the following is not listed in the chapter as one of the compositional modes for digital media?

  a. Conversations
  b. Redacting

  c. Comments and critiques
  d. Narratives

4. Which of these descriptions best captures the preferred style of writing for social media in business?

  a. Businesslike and message-driven
  b. Unplanned, unrehearsed, and super casual
  c. Conversational, supportive, and engaged
  d. Funny, quirky, and intriguing

Objective 7.2: Describe the use of social networks in business communication.

5. A/an _____ _____ is a group of people united by their interest in and ownership or use of a particular product.

6. Which of these best describes the role of a *hub* in a company's social media strategy?

  a. An open-plan office in which all the company's social media users can congregate in order to ensure a coordinated public presence
  b. The company's Facebook page or its Facebook page and Twitter account
  c. A company-owned web property that serves as the anchor of its online presence
  d. An online brand community

7. _____ _____ is a measure of how effectively a company engages with its various online stakeholders in a mutually beneficial exchange of information.

Objective 7.3: Explain how companies and business professionals can use information and content sharing websites.

8. YouTube, Flickr, and Yelp are examples of

  a. Consumer-only websites
  b. User-generated content sites
  c. Social interactivity blogs
  d. Content exchanges

9. When someone with expertise or interest in a particular field collects and republishes material on a particular topic, the practice is known as
   a. Content curation
   b. Media consolidation
   c. Blog linking
   d. Tagging and pinning

Objective 7.4: Describe the evolving role of email in business communication and explain how to adapt the three-step writing process to email messages.

10. Which of the following is one reason many companies are trying to reduce email usage?
    a. To reduce the number of messages that can be used as legal evidence
    b. To reduce costs, because email hosting has doubled in price in the last decade
    c. To lower the processing demands on company servers
    d. To reduce the number of low-value messages employees have to contend with

11. Which of the following is true of email subject lines?
    a. Only "newbies" bother to use them anymore.
    b. Subject lines should never give away the content of the message because no one will bother to read it if they already know what the message is about.
    c. They can make the difference between a message being read right away, skipped over for later attention, or ignored entirely.
    d. They should always be in all caps to get the audience's attention.

12. Which of the following is the most effective email subject line?
    a. Production line: wiring issues
    b. Wiring errors in production: let's analyze the problem and explore solutions
    c. Wiring errors on the production line MUST STOP NOW!
    d. Careless employees => unhappy customers => fewer customers => fewer employees

13. You work in a customer service department, answering emails from customers. This morning you received an angry message from a customer who has a legitimate complaint about your company's warranty policies. After responding to the message as best you can, which of the following steps should you take?
    a. Forward the message to your immediate supervisor and suggest that the company might want to reconsider its warranty policies.
    b. Forward the message to the CEO and suggest that the company might want to reconsider its warranty policies.
    c. Forward the message to everyone in the department so they are aware of the problem with the warranty policy.
    d. Delete the customer's message; you can't fix the warranty policy.

Objective 7.5: Describe the business benefits of instant messaging (IM) and identify guidelines for effective IM in the workplace.

14. Which of the following reasons helps explain why IM usage is overtaking email in some companies?
    a. People don't have to be so formal when they use IM; it saves time to use acronyms and emoticons and to avoid using capitalization, punctuation, and other time wasters.
    b. IM works better as a broadcast mechanism than email.
    c. IM is faster than email and mimics human conversation better than email, so many people find it a more natural way to communicate.
    d. IM systems let you communicate using different colors of text, which is vital for highlighting key points and conveying nonverbal aspects that are impossible to communicate in email.

15. Which of these statements best describes how the three-step writing process applies to IM?
    a. Because there is no planning step and no completing step in IM, the three-step process does not apply.
    b. The real beauty of IM in the business world is that people don't have to spend so much time composing; they just zap out whatever is on their minds and get back to work.
    c. The three-step process for IM works exactly the same way as it does with letters, memos, and reports. Every message requires audience analysis, information gathering, and outlining.
    d. IM exchanges should be planned the same way conversations are planned to minimize confusion and the number of messages required. And instant messages don't have to be great works of literature, but they do need to be efficient and effective, so some degree of care in writing and revising is important.

16. Which of the following types of messages are most appropriate for IM?
    a. Long, complex messages
    b. Brief conversational messages
    c. Confidential or highly personal messages
    d. All of the above

Objective 7.6: Describe the role of blogging and microblogging in business communication, and briefly explain how to adapt the three-step writing process to blogging.

17. Which of the following is a good strategy for using blogs to promote products and services?
    a. Write in a style that is personal and conversational; minimize direct promotion of your products and services. Focus instead on topics your customers and potential customers find helpful and interesting.
    b. To cut through the noise in the blogosphere, promote your products and services constantly. If you don't, your competitors will drown you out.
    c. Make sure the blog matches all other corporate communications in both style and content; customers get confused when a company communicates in more than one style.
    d. Blogs should never be used for marketing and selling.

18. Which of the following best describes the idea of an "authentic voice" in blogging?
    a. A writing style that is scrupulously precise and free from technical and grammatical errors
    b. The voice of a real, living, breathing human being, communicating to other human beings on a personal level

   c. Writing that is always highly emotional so as to counteract the dehumanizing logic and linear thinking that dominates business today

   d. A detached, professional voice that is careful not to take sides, voice opinions, or otherwise inject elements into the conversation that could disturb or disappoint audiences

19. Which of the following best describes the optimum audience of a blog?

   a. Always the largest audience possible

   b. Only people who are experts in the subject matter so that comments and discussions aren't pulled off track by "newbies" who don't know what they are talking about

   c. An audience large enough to justify the time required to maintain the blog but narrow enough to ensure a clear focus

   d. Whatever audience happens to find the blog on the web

20. Which of the following is *not* a good general purpose for a blog?

   a. Sharing news from the racing circuit, describing how the racers we sponsor are faring and how they use our products

   b. Commenting on economic and social policy decisions that affect the national and international business environment

   c. Explaining to the local community why we've decided not to expand employment at the Nampa facility

   d. Describing the work going on in our research and development labs

21. Which of the following would be a good use of retweeting for an independent consulting engineer who uses Twitter to build relationships with potential clients?

   a. Avoiding retweeting under any circumstances, because it is tantamount to plagiarizing

   b. Retweeting every tweet he or she receives so that clients know how well-rounded and well-read she is

   c. Retweeting fun and interesting messages on nonbusiness topics as a way to build an emotional bond with potential clients

   d. Retweeting selectively, sharing only messages that meet two strict criteria: providing information that followers can use in their work and portraying the consultant as an expert who is up on the latest developments in her field

Objective 7.7: Explain how to adapt the three-step writing process for podcasts.

22. If one of the attractions of podcasting is its spontaneous, conversational feel, why should podcasters take the time to plan their recordings?

   a. Individual podcasts that aren't well thought out can end up being rambling, confusing, and repetitive.

   b. Podcasts are more difficult to edit than textual messages, so it's important to do enough planning to help avoid major mistakes.

   c. If you don't plan ahead, you could run out of ideas and therefore have no reason to continue podcasting.

   d. All of the above are reasons to plan podcasts.

23. A/an ____ ____ is an ongoing series of podcasts on the same general topic.

Quick Learning Guide

CHAPTER OUTLINE

Digital Channels for Business Communication
Media Choices for Brief Messages
Compositional Modes for Digital Media
Creating Content for Social Media
Optimizing Content for Mobile Devices

Social Networks
Business Communication Uses of Social Networks
Strategies for Business Communication on Social Networks

Information and Content Sharing Sites
User-Generated Content Sites
Content Curation Sites
Community Q&A Sites

Email
Planning Email Messages
Writing Email Messages
Completing Email Messages

Instant Messaging and Text Messaging
Understanding the Benefits and Risks of IM
Adapting the Three-Step Process for Successful IM

Blogging and Microblogging
Understanding the Business Applications of Blogging
Adapting the Three-Step Process for Successful Blogging
Microblogging

Podcasting

LEARNING OBJECTIVES

1 Identify the major digital channels used for brief business messages, and describe the nine compositional modes needed for digital media. (page 187)

2 Describe the use of social networks in business communication. (page 191)

3 Explain how companies and business professionals can use information and content sharing websites. (page 194)

4 Describe the evolving role of email in business communication, and explain how to adapt the three-step writing process to email messages. (page 198)

5 Describe the business benefits of instant messaging (IM), and identify guidelines for effective IM in the workplace. (page 202)

6 Describe the use of blogging and microblogging in business communication, and briefly explain how to adapt the three-step process to blogging. (page 204)

7 Explain how to adapt the three-step writing process for podcasts. (page 210)

KEY TERMS

blogs Online journals that are easier to personalize and update than conventional websites

brand communities Communities of interest that form around a specific product

brand socialization A measure of how effectively a company engages with its various online stakeholders in a mutually beneficial exchange of information

community Q&A sites Sites on which visitors answer questions posted by other visitors,

content curation Practice in which someone with expertise or interest in a particular field collects and republishes material on a particular topic

email signature A small file that automatically includes such items as your full name, title, company, and contact information at the end of your messages

instant messaging (IM) Computer-based in which users' messages appear on each other's screens instantly

microblog A variation on blogging in which messages are sharply restricted to specific character counts

podcasting The process of recording audio or video files and distributing them online via RSS subscriptions

podcasting channel Series of podcasts on a consistent theme

social media Digital media-channel combinations that empower stakeholders as participants in the communication process by allowing them to share content, revise content, respond to content, or contribute new content

tagging Assigning descriptive words to social media content to simplify searching

text messaging Transmission of short text-only messages using phones

user-generated content (UGC) sites Sites in which users rather than website owners contribute most or all of the content

CHECKLIST

Using IM Productively

- Pay attention to security and privacy issues and be sure to follow all company guidelines.
- Treat IM as a professional communication medium, not an informal, personal tool; avoid using IM slang with all but close colleagues.
- Maintain good etiquette, even during simple exchanges.
- Protect your own productivity by making yourself unavailable when you need to focus.
- In most instances, don't use IM for confidential messages, complex messages, or personal messages.

CHECKLIST

Blogging for Business

- Consider creating a blog or microblog account whenever you have a continuing stream of information to share with an online audience.
- Identify an audience that is broad enough to justify the effort but narrow enough to have common interests.
- Identify a purpose that is comprehensive enough to provide ideas for a continuing stream of posts.
- Consider the scope of your blog carefully; make it broad enough to attract an audience but narrow enough to keep you focused.

- Communicate with a personal style and an authentic voice, but don't write carelessly.
- Deliver new information quickly.
- Choose topics of peak interest to your audience.
- Encourage audiences to join the conversation.
- Consider using Twitter or other microblog updates to alert readers to new posts on your regular blog.

Apply Your Knowledge

To review chapter content related to each question, refer to the indicated Learning Objective.

⭐ **7.1.** Given the strict limits on length, should all your micro-blogging messages function as teasers that link to more detailed information on a blog or website? Why or why not? [LO-1]

7.2. Can your company stay in control of its messages if it stay off social media? Why or why not? [LO-2]

⭐ **7.3.** Is leveraging your connections on social networks for business purposes ethical? Why or why not? [LO-3]

⭐ **7.4.** If one of the benefits of blogging is the personal, intimate style of writing, is it a good idea to limit your creativity by adhering to conventional rules of grammar, spelling, and mechanics? Why or why not? [LO-6]

7.5. What are some ways the president of a hiking equipment company could use Twitter to engage potential customers without being overtly promotional? [LO-6]

Practice Your Skills

7.6. Message 7.A: Media Skills: IM; Creating a Business-like Tone [LO-5] Review the following IM exchange and explain how the customer service agent could have handled the situation more effectively.

AGENT:	Thanks for contacting Home Exercise Equipment. What's up?
CUSTOMER:	I'm having trouble assembling my home gym.
AGENT:	I hear that a lot! LOL
CUSTOMER:	So is it me or the gym?
AGENT:	Well, let's see <g>. Where are you stuck?
CUSTOMER:	The crossbar that connects the vertical pillars doesn't fit.
AGENT:	What do you mean doesn't fit?
CUSTOMER:	It doesn't fit. It's not long enough to reach across the pillars.
AGENT:	Maybe you assembled the pillars in the wrong place. Or maybe we sent the wrong crossbar.
CUSTOMER:	How do I tell?
AGENT:	The parts aren't labeled so could be tough. Do you have a measuring tape? Tell me how long your crossbar is.

7.7. Message 7.B: Media Skills: Blogging, Creating a Businesslike Tone [LO-6] Read the following blog post and (a) analyze the strengths and weaknesses of each sentence and (b) revise it so that it follows the guidelines in this chapter.

We're DOOMED!!!!!

I was at the Sikorsky plant in Stratford yesterday, just checking to see how things were going with the assembly line retrofit we did for them last year. I think I saw the future, and it ain't pretty. They were demo'ing a prototype robot from Motoman that absolutely blows our stuff out of the water. They

wouldn't let me really see it, but based on the 10-second glimpse I got, it's smaller, faster, and more maneuverable than any of our units. And when I asked about the price, the guy just grinned. And it wasn't the sort of grin designed to make me feel good.

I've been saying for years that we need to pay more attention to size, speed, and maneuverability instead of just relying on our historical strengths of accuracy and payload capacity, and you'd have to be blind not to agree that this experience proves me right. If we can't at least show a design for a better unit within two or three months, Motoman is going to lock up the market and leave us utterly in the dust.

Believe me, being able to say "I told you so" right now is not nearly as satisfying as you might think!!

7.8. Message 7.C: Media Skills: Podcasting [LO-7] To access this podcast exercise, visit **http://real-time updates.com/ebc12**, click on Student Assignments, and select Chapter 7, Message 7.C, and listen to this podcast. Identify at least three ways in which the podcast could be improved, and draft a brief email message you could send to the podcaster with your suggestions for improvement.

Exercises

Each activity is labeled according to the primary skill or skills you will need to use. To review relevant chapter content, you can refer to the indicated Learning Objective. In some instances, supporting information will be found in another chapter, as indicated.

7.9. Collaboration: Working in Teams; Planning: Selecting Media [LO-1], Chapter 2 Working with at least two other students, identify the best medium to use for each of the following messages. For each of these message needs, choose a medium that you think would work effectively and explain your choice. (More than one medium could work in some cases; just be able to support your particular choice.)

   a. A technical support service for people trying to use their digital music players

   b. A message of condolence to the family of an employee who passed away recently

   c. A collection of infographics from a variety of sources on the state of the consumer electronics industry

   d. A series of observations on the state of the industry

   e. A series of messages, questions, and answers surrounding the work of a project team on a confidential company project

7.10. Media Skills: Social Networking [LO-2] Pick a company in any industry that interests you. Imagine you are doing strategic planning for this firm, and identify one of your company's key competitors. (Hint: You can use the free listings on **www.hoovers.com** to find several top competitors for most medium and large companies in the United States.) Now search through social media sources to find three strategically relevant pieces of information about this competitor, such as the hiring of a new executive, the launch of a major new product, or a significant problem of some kind. In a post on your class blog, identify the information you found and the sources you used. (If you can't find useful information, pick another firm or try another industry.)

7.11. Media Skills: Writing Email Subject Lines [LO-4] Using your imagination to make up whatever details you need, revise the following email subject lines to make them more informative:
a. New budget figures
b. Marketing brochure—your opinion
c. Production schedul**e**

7.12. Media Skills: Email [LO-4] The following email message contains numerous errors related to what you've learned about planning and writing business messages. First, list the flaws you find in this version. Then use the following steps to plan and write a better memo.

TO: Felicia August <b_august@evertrust.com>

SUBJECT: Compliance with new break procedure

Some of you may not like the rules about break times; however, we determined that keeping track of employees while they took breaks at times they determined rather than regular breaks at prescribed times was not working as well as we would have liked it to work. The new rules are not going to be an option. If you do not follow the new rules, you could be docked from your pay for hours when you turned up missing, since your direct supervisor will not be able to tell whether you were on a "break" or not and will assume that you have walked away from your job. We cannot be responsible for any errors that result from your inattentiveness to the new rules. I have already heard complaints from some of you and I hope this memo will end this issue once and for all. The decision has already been made.

Starting Monday, January 1, you will all be required to take a regular 15-minute break in the morning and again in the afternoon, and a regular thirty-minute lunch at the times specified by your supervisor, NOT when you think you need a break or when you "get around to it."

There will be no exceptions to this new rule!

Felicia August

Manager

Billing and accounting

First, describe the flaws you discovered in this email message. Next, develop a plan for rewriting the message. Use the following steps to organize your efforts before you begin writing:

- Determine the purpose.
- Identify and analyze your audience.
- Define the main idea.
- Outline the major supporting points.
- Choose between the direct and indirect approaches.

Now rewrite the email message. Don't forget to leave ample time for revision of your own work before you turn it in.

7.13. Media Skills: Blogging [LO-6] The members of the project team of which you are the leader have enthusiastically embraced blogging as a communication medium. Unfortunately, as emotions heat up during the project, some of the blog postings are getting too casual, too personal, and even sloppy. Because your boss and other managers around the company also read this project blog, you don't want the team to look unprofessional in anyone's eyes. Revise the following blog posting so that it communicates in a more businesslike manner while retaining the informal, conversational tone of a blog (be sure to correct any spelling and punctuation mistakes you find as well).

Well, to the profound surprise of absolutely nobody, we are not going to be able meet the June 1 commitment to ship 100 operating tables to Southeast Surgical Supply. (For those of you who have been living in a cave the past six months, we have been fighting to get our hands on enough high-grade chromium steel to meet our production schedule.) Sure enough, we got news, this morning that we will only get enough for 30 tables. Yes, we look lik fools for not being able to follow through on promises we made to the customer, but no, this didn't have to happpen. Six month's ago, purchasing warned us about shrinking supplies and suggested we advance-buy as much as we would need for the next 12 months, or so. We naturally tried to followed their advice, but just as naturally were shot down by the bean counters at corporate who trotted out the policy about never buying more than three months worth of materials in advance. Of course, it'll be us–not the bean counters who'll take the flak when everybody starts asking why revenues are down next quarter and why Southeast is talking to our friends at Crighton Manuf!!! Maybe, some day this company will get its head out of the sand and realize that we need to have some financial flexibility in order to compete.

7.14. Media Skills: Blogging [LO-5] From what you've learned about planning and writing business messages, you should be able to identify numerous errors made by the writer of the following blog post. List them below and then plan and write a better post, following the guidelines given.

Get Ready!

We are hoping to be back at work soon, with everything running smoothly, same production schedule and no late projects or missed deadlines. So you need to clean out your desk, put your stuff in boxes, and clean off the walls. You can put the items you had up on your walls in boxes, also.

We have provided boxes. The move will happen this weekend. We'll be in our new offices when you arrive on Monday.

We will not be responsible for personal belongings during the move.

First, describe the flaws you discovered in this blog post. Next, develop a plan for rewriting the post. Use the following steps to organize your efforts before you begin writing:
- Determine the purpose.
- Identify and analyze your audience.
- Define the main idea.
- Outline the major supporting points.
- Choose between the direct and indirect approaches.

Now rewrite the post. Don't forget to leave ample time for revision of your own work before you turn it in.

7.15. Media Skills: Microblogging [LO-6] Busy knitters can go through a lot of yarn in a hurry, so most keep a sharp eye out for sales. You're on the marketing staff of Knitting-Warehouse, and you like to keep your loyal shoppers up to date with the latest deals. Visit the Knitting-Warehouse website at **www.knitting-warehouse.com**, select any on-sale product that catches your eye, and write a Twitter update that describes the product and the sale. Be sure to include a link back to the website so your Twitter followers can learn more. (Unless you are working on a private Twitter account that is accessible only by your instructor and your classmates, don't actually send this Twitter update. Email it to your instructor instead.)

7.16. Media Skills: Podcasting [LO-7] You've recently begun recording a weekly podcast to share information with your large and far-flung staff. After a month, you ask for feedback from several of your subordinates, and you're disappointed to learn that some people stopped listening to the podcast after the first couple weeks. Someone eventually admits that many staffers feel that the recordings are too long and rambling and that the information they contain isn't valuable enough to justify the time it takes to listen. You aren't pleased, but you want to improve. An assistant transcribes the introduction to last week's podcast so you can review it. You immediately see two problems. Revise the introduction based on what you've learned in this chapter.

So there I am, having lunch with Selma Gill, who just joined and took over the Northeast sales region from Jackson Stroud. In walks our beloved CEO with Selma's old boss at Uni-Plex; turns out they were finalizing a deal to co-brand our products and theirs and to set up a joint distribution program in all four domestic regions. Pretty funny, huh? Selma left Uni-Plex because she wanted sell our products instead, and now she's back selling her old stuff, too. Anyway, try to chat with her when you can; she knows the biz inside and out and probably can offer insight into just about any sales challenge you might be running up against. We'll post more info on the co-brand deal next week; should be a boost for all of us. Other than those two news items, the other big news this week is the change in commission reporting. I'll go into the details in minute, but when you log onto the intranet, you'll now see your sales results split out by product line and industry sector. Hope this helps you see where you're doing well and where you might beef things up a bit. Oh yeah, I almost forgot the most important bit. Speaking of our beloved CEO, Thomas is going to be our guest of honor, so to speak, at the quarterly sales meeting next week and wants an update on how petroleum prices are affecting customer behavior. Each district manager should be ready with a brief report. After I go through the commission reporting scheme, I'll outline what you need to prepare.

Expand Your Skills

Critique the Professionals

Locate the YouTube channel page of any company you find interesting and assess its social networking presence using the criteria for effective communication discussed in this chapter and your own experience using social media. What does this company do well with its YouTube channel? How might it improve? Using whatever medium your instructor requests, write a brief analysis of the company's YouTube presence (no more than one page), citing specific elements from the piece and support from the chapter.

Sharpen Your Career Skills Online

Bovée and Thill's Business Communication Web Search, at **http://websearch.businesscommunicationnetwork.com**, is a unique research tool designed specifically for business communication research. Use the Web Search function to find a website, video, PDF document, podcast, or presentation that offers advice on using social media in business. Write a brief email message to your instructor or a post for your class blog, describing the item that you found and summarizing the career skills information you learned from it.

Improve Your Grammar, Mechanics, and Usage

The following exercises help you improve your knowledge of and power over English grammar, mechanics, and usage. Turn to the Handbook of Grammar, Mechanics, and Usage at the end of this book and review Section 1.6.1 (Prepositions), Section 1.6.2 (Conjunctions), and Section 1.6.3 (Articles and Interjections)text and review Prepositions, Conjunctions, and Articles and Interjections. Then look at the following 10 items and indicate the preferred choice in the following groups of sentences. (Answers to these exercises appear on page 601.)

7.17 a. The response was not only inappropriate but it was also rude.
b. The response was not only inappropriate but also rude.

7.18 a. Be sure to look the spelling up in the dictionary.
b. Be sure to look up the spelling in the dictionary.

7.19 a. We didn't get the contract because our proposal didn't comply with the request for proposals (RFP).
b. We didn't get the contract because our proposals didn't comply to the RFP.

7.20 a. Marissa should of known not to send that email to the CEO.
b. Marissa should have known not to send that email to the CEO.

7.21 a. The Phalanx 1000 has been favorably compared to the Mac iBook.
b. The Phalanx 1000 has been favorably compared with the Mac iBook.

7.22 a. What are you looking for?
b. For what are you looking?

7.23 a. Have you filed an SEC application?
b. Have you filed a SEC application?

7.24 a. The project turned out neither to be easy nor simple.
b. The project turned out to be neither easy nor simple.

7.25 a. If you hire me, you will not regret your decision!
b. If you hire me, you will not regret your decision.

7.26 a. This is truly an historic event.
b. This is truly a historic event.

For additional exercises focusing on conjunctions, articles, and prepositions, visit MyBCommLab. Click on Chapter 7, click on Additional Exercises to Improve Your Grammar, Mechanics, and Usage, and click on 11. Conjunctions, articles, and interjections.

Cases

Website links for selected companies mentioned in cases can be found in the Student Assignments section at **http://real-timeupdates.com/ebc12**.

SOCIAL NETWORKING SKILLS

7.27. Media Skills: Social Networking; Media Skills: Microblogging [LO-2] [LO-6] Foursquare is one of the leading providers of location-based social networking services. Millions of people use Foursquare for social engagement and friendly competition, and many business owners are starting to recognize the marketing potential of having people who are on the move in local areas broadcasting their locations and sharing information about stores, restaurants, clubs, and other merchants.

Your task: Review the information on Foursquare's Merchant Platform at **http://business.foursquare.com**. Now write four brief messages, no more than 140 characters long (including spaces). The first should summarize the benefits to stores, restaurants, and other brick-and-mortar businesses of participating in Foursquare, and the next three messages should convey three compelling points that support that overall benefit statement. If your class is set up with private Twitter accounts, use your private account to send your messages. Otherwise, email your four messages to your instructor or post them on your class blog, as your instructor directs.

SOCIAL NETWORKING SKILLS

7.28. Media Skills: Social Networking; Online Etiquette [LO-2], Chapter 2 Employees who take pride in their work are a practically priceless resource for any business. However, pride can sometimes manifest itself in negative ways when employees come under criticism, and public criticism is a fact of life in social media. Imagine that your company has recently experienced a rash of product quality problems, and these problems have generated some unpleasant and occasionally unfair criticism on a variety of social media sites. Someone even set up a Facebook page specifically to give customers a place to vent their frustrations.

You and your public relations team jumped into action, responding to complaints with offers to provide replacement products and help customers who have been affected by the quality problems. Everything seemed to be going as well as could be expected, when you were checking a few industry blogs one evening and discovered that two engineers in your company's product design lab have been responding to complaints on their own. They identified themselves as company employees and defended their product design, blaming the company's production department and even criticizing several customers for lacking the skills needed to use such a sophisticated product. Within a matter of minutes, you see their harsh comments being retweeted and reposted on multiple sites, only fueling the fire of negative feedback against your firm. Needless to say, you are horrified.

Your task: You manage to reach the engineers by private message and tell them to stop posting messages, but you realize you have a serious training issue on your hands. Write a post for the internal company blog that advises employees on how to respond appropriately when they are representing the company online. Use your imagination to make up any details you need.

SOCIAL NETWORKING SKILLS

7.29. Media Skills: Social Networking [LO-2] Social media can be a great way to, well, socialize during your college years, but employers are increasingly checking up on the online activities of potential hires to avoid bringing in employees who may reflect poorly on the company.

Your task: Team up with another student and review each other's public presence on Facebook, Twitter, Flickr, blogs, and any other website that an employer might check during the interview and recruiting process. Identify any photos, videos, messages, or other material that could raise a red flag when an employer is evaluating a job candidate. Write your teammate an email message that lists any risky material.

EMAIL SKILLS / PORTFOLIO BUILDER

7.30. Media Skills: Email [LO-4] One-quarter of all motor vehicle accidents that involve children under age 12 are side-impact crashes, and these crashes result in higher rates of injuries and fatalities than those with front or rear impacts.

Your task: You work in the consumer information department at Britax, a leading manufacturer of car seats. Your manager has asked you to prepare an email message that can be sent out whenever parents request information about side-impact crashes and the safety features of Britax seats. Start by researching side-impact crashes on the Britax website (**www.britax.com**). Write a three-paragraph message that explains the seriousness of side-impact crashes, describes how injuries and fatalities can be minimized in these crashes, and describes how Britax's car seats are designed to help protect children in side-impact crashes.[56]

EMAIL SKILLS / PORTFOLIO BUILDER

7.31. Media Skills: Email; Message Strategies: Negative Messages, [LO-4], Chapter 9 Many companies operate on the principle that the customer is always right, even when the customer *isn't* right. They take any steps necessary to ensure happy customers, lots of repeat sales, and a positive reputation among potential buyers. Overall, this is a smart and successful approach to business. However, most companies eventually encounter a nightmare customer who drains so much time, energy, and profits that the only sensible option is to refuse the customer's business. For example, the nightmare customer might be someone who constantly berates you and your employees, repeatedly makes outlandish demands for refunds and discounts, or simply requires so much help that you not only lose money on this person but also no longer have enough time to help your other customers. "Firing" a customer is an unpleasant step that should be taken only in the most extreme cases and only after other remedies have been attempted (such as talking with the customer about the problem), but it is sometimes necessary for the well-being of your employees and your company.

Your task: If you are currently working or have held a job in the recent past, imagine that you've encountered just such a customer. If you don't have job experience to call on, imagine that you work in a retail location somewhere around campus or in your neighborhood. Identify the type of behavior this imaginary customer exhibits and the reasons the behavior can no longer be accepted. Write a brief email message to the customer to explain that you will no longer be able to accommodate him or her as a customer. Calmly explain why you have had to reach this difficult decision. Maintain a professional tone and keep your emotions in check.

EMAIL SKILLS / PORTFOLIO BUILDER

7.32. Media Skills: Email; Collaboration: Team Projects, Chapter 2 [LO-2] For the first time in history (aside from special situations such as major wars), more than half of all U.S. adult women now live without a spouse. (In other words, they live alone, with roommates, or as part of an unmarried couple.) Twenty-five percent have never married, and 26 percent are divorced, widowed, or married but living apart from their spouses. In the 1950s and into the 1960s, only 40 percent of women lived without a spouse, but every decade since, the percentage has increased. In your work as a consumer trend specialist for Seymour Powell, a product design firm based in London that specializes in the home, personal, leisure, and transportation sectors, it's your business to recognize and respond to demographic shifts such as this.

Your task: With a small team of classmates, brainstorm possible product opportunities that respond to this trend. In an email message to be sent to the management team at Seymour Powell, list your ideas for new or modified products that might sell well in a society in which more than half of all adult women live without a spouse. For each idea, provide a one-sentence explanation of why you think the product has potential.[57]

EMAIL SKILLS / MOBILE SKILLS

7.33. Media Skills: Email [LO-5] The size limitations of smartphone screens call for a different approach to writing (see page 148) and formatting (see page 173) documents.

Your task: On the website of any company that interests you, find a news release (some companies refer to them as press releases) that announces the launch of a new product. Using Pages or any other writing app at your disposal, revise and format the material in a way that would be effective on smartphone screens.

IM SKILLS

7.34. Media Skills: IM; Compositional Modes: Tutorials [LO-1] [LO-5] High-definition television can be a joy to watch—but, oh, what a pain to buy. The field is cluttered with competing technologies and arcane terminology that is meaningless to most consumers. Moreover, it's nearly impossible to define one technical term without invoking two or three others, leaving consumers swimming in an alphanumeric soup of confusion. As a sales support manager for Crutchfield, a leading online retailer of audio and video systems, you understand the frustration buyers feel; your staff is deluged daily by their questions.

Your task: To help your staff respond quickly to consumers who ask questions via Crutchfield's online IM chat service, you are developing a set of "canned" responses to common questions. When a consumer asks one of these questions, a sales adviser can simply click on the ready-made answer. Research the "Research and DIY" section on the Crutchfield website, then write concise, consumer-friendly definitions of the following terms: *1080p*, *HDMI*, *4K*, and *3D TV*.

BLOGGING SKILLS

7.35. Media Skills: Blogging; Compositional Modes: Tutorials [LO-6] Tumblr has become a popular "short-form" blogging platform by combining the simplicity of Twitter with the ability to share photos and other media easily.

Your task: Write a 300- to 400-word post for your class blog that explains how to set up an account on Tumblr and get involved in the Tumblr community. The help pages on Tumblr are a good place to get more information about the service.

BLOGGING SKILLS

7.36. Media Skills: Blogging [LO-6] Credit card debt can be a crippling financial burden with myriad side effects, from higher insurance rates to more-expensive loans to difficulty getting a job or a promotion. Unfortunately, credit debt is also frighteningly easy to fall into, particularly for young people trying to get started in life with limited cash flow.

Your task: Write a three- to five-paragraph blog post that warns college students about the dangers of credit card debt. Be sure to credit the sources you find in your research.

BLOGGING SKILLS

7.37. Media Skills: Blogging; Compositional Modes: Tutorials [LO-6] Studying abroad for a semester or a year can be a rewarding experience in many ways—improving your language skills, experiencing another culture, making contacts in the international business arena, and building your self-confidence.

Your task: Write a post for your class blog that describes your college's study abroad program and summarizes the steps involved in applying for international study. If your school doesn't offer study-abroad opportunities, base your post on the program offered at another institution in your state.

MICROBLOGGING SKILLS

7.38. Media Skills: Microblogging; Compositional Modes: Summaries [LO-1] [LO-6] A carefully constructed series of tweets can serve as a summary of a blog post, video, or other message or document.

Your task: Find any article, podcast, video, or webpage on a business topic that interests you. Write four to six tweetables that summarize the content of the piece. Restrict the first tweetable to 120 characters to allow for a URL. Email the series to your instructor or publish them on Twitter if your instructor directs. If you quote phrases from the original directly, be sure to put them in quotation marks.

MICROBLOGGING SKILLS

7.39. Media Skills: Microblogging; Compositional Modes: Updates and Announcements [LO-5] JetBlue is known for its innovations in customer service and customer communication, including its pioneering use of Twitter. Nearly two million JetBlue fans and customers follow the company on Twitter to get updates on flight status during weather disruptions, facility upgrades, and other news.[58]

Your task: Write a message of no more than 120 characters that announces the cancellation of all flights into and out of Boston's Logan International from 6:00 a.m. on February 20 to 4:00 p.m. on February 21.

MICROBLOGGING SKILLS

7.40. Media Skills: Microblogging; Compositional Modes: Teasers [LO-1] Twitter updates are a great way to alert people to helpful articles, videos, and other online resources.

Your task: Find an online resource (it can be a website quiz, a YouTube video, a PowerPoint presentation, a newspaper article, or anything else appropriate) that offers some great tips to help college students prepare for job interviews. Write a teaser of no more than 120 characters that hints at the benefits other students can get from this resource. If your class is set up with private Twitter accounts, use your private account to send your message. Otherwise, email it to your instructor. Be sure to include the URL; if you're using a Twitter account, the system should shorten it to 20 characters to keep you within the 140-character limit.

PODCASTING SKILLS / PORTFOLIO BUILDER

7.41. Media Skills: Podcasting [LO-7] While writing the many messages that are part of the job search process, you find yourself wishing you could just talk to some of these companies so your personality could shine through. Well, you've just gotten that opportunity. One of the companies you've applied to has emailed you back, asking you to submit a two-minute podcast

introducing yourself and explaining why you would be a good person to hire.

Your task: Identify a company you'd like to work for after graduation and select a job that would be a good match for your skills and interests. Write a script for a two-minute podcast (two minutes represents roughly 250 words for most speakers). Introduce yourself and the position you're applying for, describe your background, and explain why you think you're a good candidate for the job. Make up any details you need. If your instructor asks you to do so, record the podcast and submit the audio file.

PODCASTING SKILLS

7.42. Media Skills: Podcasting [LO-7] Between this chapter and your own experience as a user of social media, you know enough about social media to offer some insights to other business communicators.

Your task: Write a script for a two- to three-minute podcast (roughly 250 to 400 words) on any social media topic that you find compelling. Be sure to introduce your topic clearly in the introduction and provide helpful transitions along the way. If your instructor asks you to do so, record the podcast and submit the file.

PODCASTING SKILLS / PORTFOLIO BUILDER

7.43. Media Skills: Podcasting; Message Strategies: Marketing and Sales Messages, Chapter 10 [LO-5] With any purchase decision, from a restaurant meal to a college education, recommendations from satisfied customers are often the strongest promotional messages.

Your task: Write a script for a one- to two-minute podcast (roughly 150 to 250 words), explaining why your college or university is a good place to get an education. Your audience is high school juniors and seniors. You can choose to craft a general message, something that would be useful to all prospective students, or you can focus on a specific academic discipline, the athletic program, or some other important aspect of your college experience. Either way, make sure your introductory comments make it clear whether you are offering a general recommendation or a specific recommendation. If your instructor asks you to do so, record the podcast and submit the file electronically.

MyBCommLab

Go to the Assignments section of your MyLab to complete these writing exercises.

7.44. How can businesses make use of social networks such as Facebook for business communication? [LO-2]

7.45. Why does a personal style of writing on blogs and other social media channels help build stronger relationships with audiences? [LO-6]

Endnotes

1. GoPro website, accessed 19 February 2015, www.gopro.com; Garett Sloan, "The 10 Best Brand Channels on YouTube," *Adweek*, 2 April 2014, www.adweek.com; Christopher Ratcliff, "A Look Inside GoPro's Dazzling YouTube Strategy," Econsultancy website, 20 February 2014, http://econsultancy.com; GoPro channel on YouTube, accessed 26 April 2014, www.youtube.com/user/GoProCamera; "YouTube Brand Channel Leaderboard January–March 2014," *Google Think Insights*, 31 March 2014, www.thinkwithgoogle.com; Saya Weissman, "GoPro Might Have the Best Brand Content Around," *Digiday*, 6 February 2014, http://digiday.com; Shorty Industry Awards website, accessed 26 April 2014, http://industry.shortyawards.com; Anderson Cooper, "GoPro's Video Revolution," *60 Minutes*, 10 November 2013, www.cbsnews.com.

2. Angelo Fernando, "Content Snacking—and What You Can Do About It," *Communication World*, January–February 2011, 8–10.

3. Jennifer Van Grove, "Social Networking on Mobile Devices Skyrockets," *Mashable*, 20 October 2011, http://mashable.com.

4. Angelo Fernando, "Social Media Change the Rules," *Communication World*, January–February 2007, 9–10; Geoff Livingston and Brian Solis, *Now Is Gone: A Primer on New Media for Executives and Entrepreneurs* (Laurel, Md.: Bartleby Press, 2007), 60.

5. Don Tapscott and Anthony D. Williams, Wikinomics, *How Mass Collaboration Changes Everything* (London: Portfolio, 2006), 216–217; Dan Schawbel, "Why Social Media Makes It Possible for Gen-Y to Succeed," Personal Branding Blog, 12 December 2007, http://person albrandingblog.wordpress.com.

6. 2012 CEO, Social Media & Leadership Survey, Brandfog, www .brandfog.com.

7. Richard Edelman, "Teaching Social Media: What Skills Do Communicators Need?" in "Engaging the New Influencers; Third Annual Social Media Academic Summit" (white paper), accessed 7 June 2010, www.newmediaacademicsummit.com.

8. Catherine Toole, "My 7 Deadly Sins of Writing for Social Media— Am I Right?" Econsultancy blog, 19 June 2007, www.econsultancy .com; Muhammad Saleem, "How to Write a Social Media Press Release," *Copyblogger*, accessed 16 September 2008, www.copyblogger .com; Melanie McBride, "5 Tips for (Better) Social Media Writing," Melanie McBride Online, 11 June 2008, http://melaniemcbride.net.

9. Samantha Murphy, "Why Mobile Commerce Is on the Rise," *Mashable*, 7 March 2012, http://mashable.com.

10. Christopher Swan, "Gamification: A New Way to Shape Behavior," *Communication World*, May–June 2012, 13–14.

11. "Wearables," AllThingsCK, accessed 6 April 2014, allthingsck.com.

12. Jon Russell, "Why 'Going Global' Makes No Sense for China's Social Networks—for Now," *The Next Web*, 14 May 2012, http://thenextweb.com.

13. Todd Henneman, "At Lockheed Martin, Social Networking Fills Key Workforce Needs While Improving Efficiency and Lowering Costs," *Workforce Management*, March 2010, www.workforce.com.

14. Patrick Hanlon and Josh Hawkins, "Expand Your Brand Community Online," *Advertising Age*, 7 January 2008, 14–15.

15. Todd Wasserman, "What Drives Brand Socialability?" *Mashable*, 12 October 2011.

16. Coca-Cola Facebook page, accessed 4 April 2014, www.facebook .com/cocacola; "Shaking Things Up at Coca-Cola," *Harvard Business Review*, October 2011, 94–99.

17. Alex Wright, "Mining the Web for Feelings, Not Facts," *New York Times*, 23 August 2009, www.nytimes.com.

18. Christian Pieter Hoffmann, "Holding Sway," *Communication World*, November–December 2011, 26–29; Josh Bernoff, "Social Strategy for Exciting (and Not So Exciting) Brands," *Marketing News*, 15 May 2009, 18; Larry Weber, *Marketing to the Social Web* (Hoboken, N.J.: Wiley, 2007), 12–14; David Meerman Scott, *The New Rules of Marketing and PR* (Hoboken, N.J.: Wiley, 2007), 62.

19. Sonia Simone, "What's the Difference Between Content Marketing and Copywriting?" *Copyblogger*, accessed 4 June 2012, www.copyblogger.com.

20. Matt Rhodes, "Build Your Own Community or Go Where People Are? Do Both," FreshNetworks blog, 12 May 2009, www.fresh networks.com.

21. Brian Solis, *Engage!* (Hoboken, N.J.: Wiley, 2010), 13.

22. Zachary Sniderman, "5 Ways to Clean Up Your Social Media Identity," 7 July 2010, *Mashable*, http://mashable.com.

23. Tamar Weinberg, *The New Community Rules: Marketing on the Social Web* (Sebastapol, Calif.: O'Reilly Media, 2009), 288.

24. Rohit Bhargava, "How Curation Could Save the Internet (and Your Brand)," *Communication World*, January–February 2012, 20–23.

25. Reid Goldborough, "More Trends for 2009: What to Expect with Personal Technology," *Public Relations Tactics*, February 2009, 9.

26. Michelle V. Rafter, "If Tim Fry Has His Way, He'll Eradicate Email for Good," *Workforce Management*, 24 April 2012, www.workforce .com.

27. Hilary Potkewitz and Rachel Brown, "Spread of Email Has Altered Communication Habits at Work," *Los Angeles Business Journal*, 18 April 2005, www.findarticles.com; Nancy Flynn, *Instant Messaging Rules* (New York: AMACOM, 2004), 47–54.

28. Mary Munter, Priscilla S. Rogers, and Jone Rymer, "Business Email: Guidelines for Users," *Business Communication Quarterly*, March 2003, 26+; Renee B. Horowitz and Marian G. Barchilon, "Stylistic Guidelines for Email," *IEEE Transactions on Professional Communication* 37, no. 4 (December 1994): 207–212.

29. Steve Rubel, "Tip: Tweetify the Lead of Your Emails," The Steve Rubel Stream blog, 20 July 2010, www.steverubel.com.

30. Judith Newman, "If You're Happy and You Know It, Must I Know, Too?" *New York Times*, 21 October 2011, www.nytimes.com.

31. Michal Lev-Ram, "IBM: Instant Messaging Has Replaced Voicemail," *CNNMoney*, 31 May 2011, http://tech.fortune.cnn.com;

Robert J. Holland, "Connected—More or Less," *Richmond.com*, 8 August 2006, www.richmond.com.

32. Vayusphere website, accessed 22 January 2006, www.vayusphere .com; Christa C. Ayer, "Presence Awareness: Instant Messaging's Killer App," *Mobile Business Advisor*, 1 July 2004, www.highbeam .com; Jefferson Graham, "Instant Messaging Programs Are No Longer Just for Messages," *USA Today*, 20 October 2003, 5D; Todd R. Weiss, "Microsoft Targets Corporate Instant Messaging Customers," *Computerworld*, 18 November 2002, 12; "Banks Adopt Instant Messaging to Create a Global Business Network," *Computer Weekly*, 25 April 2002, 40; Michael D. Osterman, "Instant Messaging in the Enterprise," *Business Communications Review*, January 2003, 59–62; John Pallato, "Instant Messaging Unites Work Groups and Inspires Collaboration," *Internet World*, December 2002, 14.

33. Paul Mah, "Using Text Messaging in Business," Mobile Enterprise blog, 4 February 2008, http://blogs.techrepublic.com/wireless; Paul Kedrosky, "Why We Don't Get the (Text) Message," *Business 2.0*, 2 October 2006, www.business2.com; Dave Carpenter, "Companies Discover Marketing Power of Text Messaging," *Seattle Times*, 25 September 2006, www.seattletimes.com.

34. "About StarStar," Zoove website, accessed 6 June 2012, www .zoove.com.

35. Mark Gibbs, "Racing to Instant Messaging," *NetworkWorld*, 17 February 2003, 74.

36. "Email Is So Five Minutes Ago," *BusinessWeek*, 28 November 2005, www.businessweek.com.

37. Clint Boulton, "IDC: IM Use Is Booming in Business," *InstantMessagingPlanet.com*, 5 October 2005, www.instantmessagingpla net.com; Jenny Goodbody, "Critical Success Factors for Global Virtual Teams," *Strategic Communication Management*, February/March 2005, 18–21; Ann Majchrzak, Arvind Malhotra, Jeffrey Stamps, and Jessica Lipnack, "Can Absence Make a Team Grow Stronger?" *Harvard Business Review*, May 2004, 131–137; Christine Y. Chen, "The IM Invasion," *Fortune*, 26 May 2003, 135–138; Yudhijit Bhattacharjee, "A Swarm of Little Notes," *Time*, 16 September 2002, A3–A8; Mark Bruno, "Taming the Wild Frontiers of Instant Messaging," *Bank Technology News*, December 2002, 30–31; Richard Grigonis, "Enterprise-Strength Instant Messaging," *Convergence.com*, 10–15, accessed 15 March 2003, www.convergence.com.

38. Leo Babauta, "17 Tips to Be Productive with Instant Messaging," *Web Worker Daily*, 14 November 2007, http://webworkerdaily.com; Pallato, "Instant Messaging Unites Work Groups and Inspires Collaboration."

39. "State of the Blogosphere 2011," *Technorati*, 4 November 2011, http://technorati.com.

40. Marcus Sheridan, "5 Reasons Your Business Should Be Blogging," *Social Media Examiner*, 2 December 2011, www.socialmedia examiner.com; Stephen Baker, "The Inside Story on Company Blogs," *BusinessWeek*, 14 February 2006, www.businessweek.com; Jeremy Wright, *Blog Marketing* (New York: McGraw-Hill, 2006), 45–56; Paul Chaney, "Blogs: Beyond the Hype!" 26 May 2005, http://radiantmar ketinggroup.com.

41. Solis, *Engage!*, 314.

42. Solis, Engage!, 86.

43. Weinberg, "The New Community Rules: Marketing on the Social Web," 89.

44. "IBM Social Computing Guidelines," IBM website, accessed 5 June 2012, www.ibm.com.

45. Joel Falconer, "Six Rules for Writing Great Web Content," *Blog News Watch*, 9 November 2007, www.blognewswatch.com.

46. Dion Hinchcliffe, "Twitter on Your Intranet: 17 Microblogging Tools for Business," *ZDNet*, 1 June 2009, www.zdnet.com.

47. Hinchcliffe, "Twitter on Your Intranet: 17 Microblogging Tools for Business."

48. B. L. Ochman, "Why Twitter Is a Better Brand Platform Than Facebook," *Ad Age*, 1 June 2012, http://adage.com.

49. Leon Widrich, "4 Ways to Use Twitter for Customer Service and Support," *Social Media Examiner*, 12 April 2012, www .socialmediaexaminer.com.

50. Paul André, Michael Bernstein, and Kurt Luther, "What Makes a Great Tweet," *Harvard Business Review*, May 2012, 36–37.

51. André et al., "What Makes a Great Tweet."

52. Interview with Cliff Ravenscraft in Michael Stelzner, "Podcasting for Business: What You Need to Know," *Social Media Examiner*, 23 December 2011, www.socialmediaexaminer.com.

53. "Set Up Your Podcast for Success," *FeedForAll* website, accessed 4 October 2006, www.feedforall.com.

54. Nathan Hangen, "4 Steps to Podcasting Success," *Social Media Examiner*, 14 February 2011, www.socialmediaexaminer.com.

55. Shel Holtz, "Ten Guidelines for B2B Podcasts," *Webpronews.com*, 12 October 2005, www.webpronews.com.

56. "Side Impact Protection Revealed," Britax website, accessed 6 June 2012, www.britaxusa.com.

57. Seymour Powell website, accessed 16 January 2007, www.seymourpowell.com; Sam Roberts, "51% of Women Now Living Without a Spouse," *New York Times*, 16 January 2007, www .nytimes.com.

58. JetBlue Twitter page, accessed 19 February 2015, http://twitter.com/ JetBlue.

8

Writing Routine and Positive Messages

LEARNING OBJECTIVES

After studying this chapter, you will be able to

1 Outline an effective strategy for writing routine business requests.

2 Describe three common types of routine requests.

3 Outline an effective strategy for writing routine replies and positive messages.

4 Describe six common types of routine replies and positive messages.

ON THE JOB: COMMUNICATING AT
GET SATISFACTION

Using New Media Concepts to Solve an Age-Old Problem

For about as long as online communication has been possible, frustrated customers have been going online to complain about faulty products, confusing instructions, and poor service. When social media tools appeared, giving even nontechnical consumers a ready voice, the stream of "I need help!" messages turned into a full-time flood. On product review and shopping websites, enthusiast blogs, and various "complaint sites," consumers can vent their frustrations and ask for help when they feel they aren't getting satisfaction from the companies they do business with.

These various websites can occasionally provide answers, but they suffer from four fundamental drawbacks. First, they are randomly scattered all over the Web, so many consumers are never quite sure where to look for help. Second, the right experts from the right companies often aren't involved, meaning that customers often have to rely on each other—which sometimes works but sometimes doesn't. Third, even companies that make a valiant effort to keep their customers satisfied know that everyone can benefit if customers can share ideas, learn from one another, and participate in ongoing conversation.

Get Satisfaction is using social media to help companies that are overwhelmed by support requests and customers who are frustrated by poor service.

lmtmphoto/Alamy

225

Fourth, companies often find that multiple customers have the same routine questions, but communicating with every customer individually can be time-consuming and expensive.

The San Francisco–based company Get Satisfaction is working to address all these issues with social networking technologies designed specifically for community-based customer support. Consumers can post questions or complaints and request notification whenever a response is posted. If someone else has already posted the same complaint, all a visitor needs do is ask to be notified when the issue is resolved, saving time for the people asking and answering questions. Consumers can also suggest ideas for new products and services or improvements to existing offerings.

On the other side of the relationship, employees from companies that sell products and services can register as official representatives to answer questions, solve problems, and solicit feedback. As both knowledgeable consumers and company representatives provide answers and solutions, the responses voted most useful rise to the top, ensuring that visitors always get the most helpful information available. Companies that use Get Satisfaction's services can deploy customer service capabilities in a variety of ways—including via Facebook, Twitter, and their own company blogs—to try to capture as many customer service conversations as possible.

The idea certainly seems to be catching on, with thousands of companies now using Get Satisfaction's "social helpdesk" approach to help millions of customers get satisfaction from the products and services they buy.[1]

HTTP://GETSATISFACTION.COM

1 **LEARNING OBJECTIVE**
Outline an effective strategy for writing routine business requests.

Strategy for Routine Requests

Get Satisfaction (profiled in the chapter-opening On the Job) knows that much of the vital communication between a company and its customers is about routine matters, from product operation hints and technical support to refunds and order glitches. These messages fall into two groups: routine requests, in which you ask for information or action from another party, and a variety of routine and positive messages. Chapter 9 covers messages in which you convey negative information, and Chapter 10 addresses persuasive messages.

Making requests is a routine part of business. In most cases, your audience will be prepared to comply—as long as you're not being unreasonable or asking people to do something they would expect you to do yourself. By applying a clear strategy and tailoring your approach to each situation, you'll be able to generate effective requests quickly.

For routine requests and positive messages
- State the request or main idea
- Give necessary details
- Close with a cordial request for specific action

Like all other business messages, a routine request has three parts: an opening, a body, and a close. Using the direct approach, open with your main idea, which is a clear statement of your request. Use the body to give details and justify your request. Finally, close by requesting specific action.

STATING YOUR REQUEST UP FRONT

With routine requests, you can make your request at the beginning of the message. Of course, getting right to the point should not be interpreted as license to be abrupt or tactless:

Take care that your direct approach doesn't come across as abrupt or tactless.

- **Pay attention to tone.** Instead of demanding action ("Send me the latest version of the budget spreadsheet"), show respect by using words such as *please* and *I would appreciate.*
- **Assume that your audience will comply.** Because the request is routine, you can generally assume that your readers will comply when they clearly understand the reason for your request.
- **Be specific.** State precisely what you want. For example, if you request the latest market data from your research department, be sure to say whether you want a 1-page summary or 100 pages of raw data.

REAL-TIME UPDATES
LEARN MORE BY VISITING THIS WEBSITE

Insight into mobile strategies for routine communication

ClickSoftware's MobileFever blog discusses a range of topics on mobile business communication. Go to http://real-timeupdates .com/ebc12 and click on Learn More in the Students section.

EXPLAINING AND JUSTIFYING YOUR REQUEST

Use the body of your message to explain your request, as needed. Make the explanation a smooth and logical outgrowth of your opening remarks. If complying with the request could

---

CHECKLIST ✔ Writing Routine Requests

A. State your request up front.
- Write in a polite, undemanding, personal tone.
- Use the direct approach because your audience will probably respond favorably to your request.
- Be specific and precise in your request.

B. Explain and justify your request.
- Justify the request or explain its importance.
- Explain any potential benefits of responding.

- Ask the most important questions first.
- Break complex requests into individual questions that are limited to only one topic each.

C. Request specific action in a courteous close.
- Make it easy to comply by including appropriate contact information.
- Express your gratitude.
- Clearly state any important deadlines for the request.

---

benefit the reader, be sure to mention that. If you have multiple requests or questions, ask the most important questions first and deal with only one topic per question. If you have an unusual or complex request, break it down into specific, individual questions so that the reader can address each one separately. This consideration not only shows respect for your audience's time but also gets you a more accurate answer in less time.

> If you have multiple requests or questions, start with the most important one.

REQUESTING SPECIFIC ACTION IN A COURTEOUS CLOSE

Close your message with three important elements: (1) a specific request that includes any relevant deadlines, (2) information about how you can be reached (if it isn't obvious), and (3) an expression of appreciation or goodwill. When you ask readers to perform a specific action, ask for a response by a specific date or time, if appropriate (for example, "Please send the figures by May 5 so that I can return first-quarter results to you before the May 20 conference."). Conclude your message with a sincere thanks. However, don't thank the reader "in advance" for cooperating; many people find that presumptuous. If the reader's reply warrants a word of thanks, send it after you've received the reply. To review, see "Checklist: Writing Routine Requests."

> Close request messages with
> - A request for some specific action
> - Information about how you can be reached
> - An expression of appreciation

Common Examples of Routine Requests

The most common types of routine messages are asking for information or action, asking for recommendations, and making claims and requesting adjustments.

> **2 LEARNING OBJECTIVE**
> Describe three common types of routine requests.

ASKING FOR INFORMATION AND ACTION

Most simple requests can be handled with three message points:

- What you want to know or what you want your readers to do
- Why you're making the request (not required in all cases)
- Why it may be in your readers' interest to help you (not applicable in all cases)

For simple requests, using the direct approach gets the job done with a minimum of fuss. In more complex situations, you may need to provide more extensive reasons and justification for your request. If applicable, point out any benefits to the reader of complying with your request. Naturally, be sure to adapt your request to your audience and the situation (see Figure 8.1 on the next page).

> Routine requests can be handled with simple, straightforward messages, but more complicated requests can require additional justification and explanation.

ASKING FOR RECOMMENDATIONS

The need to inquire about people arises often in business. For example, before extending credit or awarding contracts, jobs, promotions, or scholarships, companies often ask applicants to supply references. Companies ask applicants to list people who can vouch for their ability, skills, integrity, character, and fitness for the job. Before you volunteer someone's name as a reference, ask permission. Some people don't want you to use their

> Always ask for permission before using someone as a reference.

1 Plan → 2 Write → 3 Complete

Analyze the Situation
Verify that the purpose is to request information from company managers.

Gather Information
Gather accurate, complete information about local competitive threats.

Choose Medium and Channel
Email is effective for this internal message, and it allows the attachment of a Word document to collect the information.

Organize the Information
Clarify that the main idea is collecting information that will lead to a better competitive strategy, which will in turn help the various district managers.

Adapt to Your Audience
Show sensitivity to audience needs with a "you"attitude, politeness, positive emphasis, and bias-free language. The writer already has credibility, as manager of the department.

Compose the Message
Maintain a style that is conversational but still business like, using plain English and appropriate voice.

Revise the Message
Evaluate content and review readability; avoid unnecessary details.

Produce the Message
Simple email format is all the design this message needs.

Proofread the Message
Review for errors in layout, spelling, and mechanics.

Distribute the Message
Deliver the message via the company's email system.

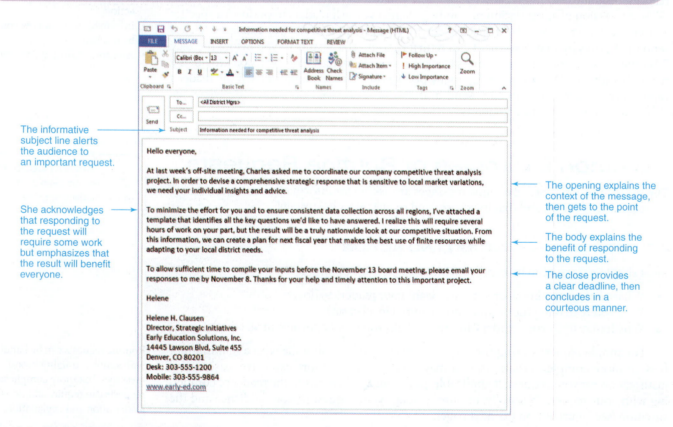

The informative subject line alerts the audience to an important request.

She acknowledges that responding to the request will require some work but emphasizes that the result will benefit everyone.

The opening explains the context of the message, then gets to the point of the request.

The body explains the benefit of responding to the request.

The close provides a clear deadline, then concludes in a courteous manner.

Figure 8.1 Routine Message Requesting Action
In this email request to district managers across the country, Helene Clausen asks them to fill out an attached information collection form. Although the request is not unusual and responding to it is part of the managers' responsibility, Clausen asks for their help in a courteous manner and points out the benefits of responding.
Source: MS Outlook 2013, © Microsoft.

> ### CHECKLIST ✔ Making Claims and Requesting Adjustments
>
> - Maintain a professional tone, even if you're extremely frustrated.
> - Open with a straightforward statement of the problem.
> - Provide specific details in the body.
> - Present facts honestly and clearly.
>
> - Politely summarize the desired action in the closing.
> - Clearly state what you expect as a fair settlement or ask the reader to propose a fair adjustment.
> - Explain the benefits of complying with the request, such as your continued patronage.

names, perhaps because they don't know enough about you to feel comfortable writing a letter or because they or their employers have a policy of not providing recommendations.

Requests for recommendations and references are routine, so you can organize your inquiry using the direct approach. Open your message by clearly stating why the recommendation is required (if it's not for a job, be sure to explain its purpose) and that you would like your reader to write the letter. If you haven't had contact with the person for some time, use the opening to trigger the reader's memory of the relationship you had, the dates of association, and any special events or accomplishments that might bring a clear and favorable picture of you to mind.

Refresh the memory of any potential reference you haven't been in touch with for a while.

Close your message with an expression of appreciation and the full name and address of the person to whom the letter should be sent. When asking for an immediate recommendation, you should also mention the deadline. Always be sure to enclose a stamped, preaddressed envelope as a convenience to the other party. Figure 8.2 on the next page provides an example of a request that follows these guidelines.

REAL-TIME UPDATES

LEARN MORE BY VISITING THIS WEBSITE

Asking for recommendations on LinkedIn

Follow LinkedIn's advice for requesting a recommendation. Go to http://real-timeupdates.com/ebc12 and click on Learn More in the Students section.

MAKING CLAIMS AND REQUESTING ADJUSTMENTS

If you're dissatisfied with a company's product or service, you can opt to make a **claim** (a formal complaint) or request an **adjustment** (a settlement of a claim). In either case, it's important to maintain a professional tone in all your communication, no matter how angry or frustrated you are. Keeping your cool will help you get the situation resolved sooner.

When writing a claim or requesting an adjustment
- *Explain the problem and give details*
- *Provide backup information*
- *Request specific action*

Open with a clear and calm statement of the problem along with your request. In the body, give a complete, specific explanation of the details. Provide any information the recipient needs to verify your complaint. In your close, politely request specific action or convey a sincere desire to find a solution. And, if appropriate, suggest that the business relationship will continue if the problem is solved satisfactorily. Be prepared to back up your claim with invoices, sales receipts, canceled checks, dated correspondence, and any other relevant documents. Send copies and keep the originals for your files.

Be prepared to document any claims you make with a company. Send copies and keep the original documents.

If the remedy is obvious, tell your reader exactly what you expect to be done, such as exchanging incorrectly shipped merchandise for the right item or issuing a refund if the item is out of stock. However, if you're uncertain about the precise nature of the trouble, you could ask the company to assess the situation and then advise you on how the situation could be fixed. Supply your full contact information so that the company can discuss the situation with you, if necessary. Compare the ineffective and effective versions in Figure 8.3 on page 231 for an example of making a claim. To review the tasks involved in making claims and requesting adjustments, see "Checklist: Making Claims and Requesting Adjustments."

Strategy for Routine and Positive Messages

3 LEARNING OBJECTIVE
Outline an effective strategy for writing routine replies and positive messages.

Just as you'll make numerous requests for information and action throughout your career, you'll also respond to similar requests from other people. When you are responding positively to a request, sending routine announcements, or sending a positive or

1 Plan → 2 Write → 3 Complete

Analyze the Situation
Verify that the purpose is to request a recommendation letter from a college professor.

Gather Information
Gather information on classes and dates to help the reader recall you and to clarify the position you seek.

Choose Medium and Channel
The letter format gives this message an appropriate level of formality, although many professors prefer to be contacted by email.

Organize the Information
Messages like this are common and expected, so a direct approach is fine.

Adapt to Your Audience
Show sensitivity to audience needs with a "you" attitude, politeness, positive emphasis, and bias-free language.

Compose the Message
Style is respectful and business like, while still using plain English and appropriate voice.

Revise the Message
Evaluate content and review readability; avoid unnecessary details.

Produce the Message
Simple letter format is all the design this message needs.

Proofread the Message
Review for errors in layout, spelling, and mechanics.

Distribute the Message
Deliver the message via postal mail or email if you have the professor's email address.

1181 Ashport Drive
Tate Springs, TN 38101
March 14, 2017

Professor Lyndon Kenton
School of Business
University of Tennessee, Knoxville
Knoxville, TN 37916

Dear Professor Kenton:

I recently interviewed with Strategic Investments and have been called for a second interview for their Analyst Training Program (ATP). They have requested at least one recommendation from a professor, and I immediately thought of you. May I have a letter of recommendation from you?

> The opening states the purpose of the letter and makes the request, assuming the reader will want to comply with the request.

Tucker includes information near the opening to refresh her professor's memory.

As you may recall, I took BUS 485, Financial Analysis, from you in the fall of 2015. I enjoyed the class and finished the term with an "A." Professor Kenton, your comments on assertiveness and cold-calling impressed me beyond the scope of the actual course material. In fact, taking your course helped me decide on a future as a financial analyst.

My enclosed résumé includes all my relevant work experience and volunteer activities. I would also like to add that I've handled the financial planning for our family since my father passed away several years ago. Although I initially learned by trial and error, I have increasingly applied my business training in deciding what stocks or bonds to trade. This, I believe, has given me a practical edge over others who may be applying for the same job.

> The body refers to the enclosed résumé and mentions experience that could set the applicant apart from other candidates—information the professor could use in writing the recommendation.

She provides a deadline for response and includes information about the person who is expecting the recommendation.

If possible, Ms. Blackmon in Human Resources needs to receive your letter by March 30. For your convenience, I've enclosed a preaddressed, stamped envelope.

> The close mentions the preaddressed, stamped envelope to encourage a timely response.

I appreciate your time and effort in writing this letter of recommendation for me. It will be great to put my education to work, and I'll keep you informed of my progress. Thank you for your consideration in this matter.

Sincerely,

Joanne Tucker

Joanne Tucker

Enclosure

Figure 8.2   Effective Request for a Recommendation

This writer uses a direct approach when asking for a recommendation from a former professor. Note how she takes care to refresh the professor's memory because she took the class a year and a half ago. She also indicates the date by which the letter is needed and points to the enclosure of a stamped, preaddressed envelope.

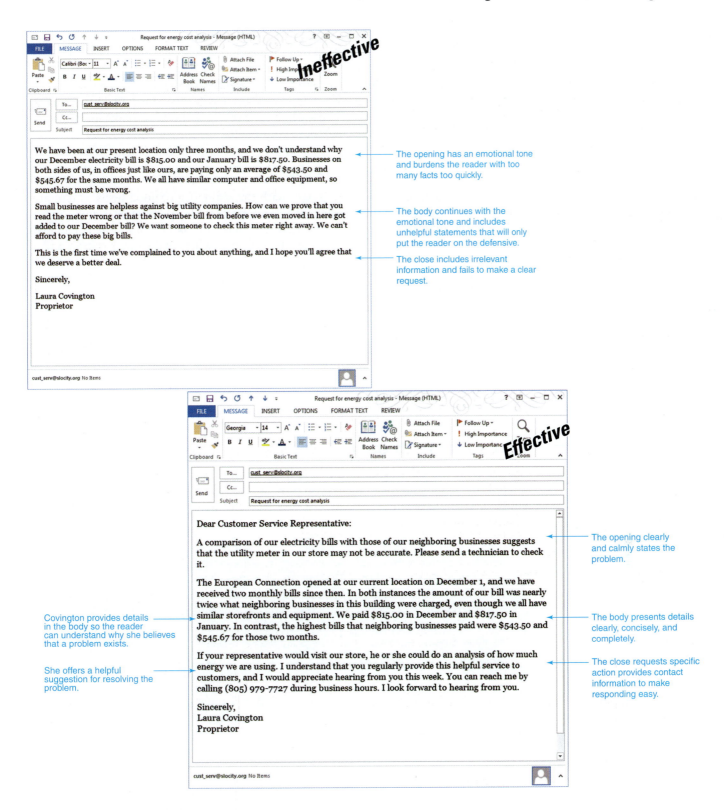

The opening has an emotional tone and burdens the reader with too many facts too quickly.

The body continues with the emotional tone and includes unhelpful statements that will only put the reader on the defensive.

The close includes irrelevant information and fails to make a clear request.

(Ineffective version email)

To... cust_serv@slocity.org
Subject Request for energy cost analysis

We have been at our present location only three months, and we don't understand why our December electricity bill is $815.00 and our January bill is $817.50. Businesses on both sides of us, in offices just like ours, are paying only an average of $543.50 and $545.67 for the same months. We all have similar computer and office equipment, so something must be wrong.

Small businesses are helpless against big utility companies. How can we prove that you read the meter wrong or that the November bill from before we even moved in here got added to our December bill? We want someone to check this meter right away. We can't afford to pay these big bills.

This is the first time we've complained to you about anything, and I hope you'll agree that we deserve a better deal.

Sincerely,

Laura Covington
Proprietor

Covington provides details in the body so the reader can understand why she believes that a problem exists.

She offers a helpful suggestion for resolving the problem.

The opening clearly and calmly states the problem.

The body presents details clearly, concisely, and completely.

The close requests specific action provides contact information to make responding easy.

(Effective version email)

To... cust_serv@slocity.org
Subject Request for energy cost analysis

Dear Customer Service Representative:

A comparison of our electricity bills with those of our neighboring businesses suggests that the utility meter in our store may not be accurate. Please send a technician to check it.

The European Connection opened at our current location on December 1, and we have received two monthly bills since then. In both instances the amount of our bill was nearly twice what neighboring businesses in this building were charged, even though we all have similar storefronts and equipment. We paid $815.00 in December and $817.50 in January. In contrast, the highest bills that neighboring businesses paid were $543.50 and $545.67 for those two months.

If your representative would visit our store, he or she could do an analysis of how much energy we are using. I understand that you regularly provide this helpful service to customers, and I would appreciate hearing from you this week. You can reach me by calling (805) 979-7727 during business hours. I look forward to hearing from you.

Sincerely,
Laura Covington
Proprietor

Figure 8.3 Ineffective and Effective Versions of a Claim
Note the difference in both tone and information content in these two versions. The poor version is emotional and unprofessional, whereas the improved version communicates calmly and clearly.
Source: MS Outlook 2013, © Microsoft.

goodwill message, you have several goals: to communicate the information or the good news, answer all questions, provide all required details, and leave your reader with a good impression of you and your firm.

Readers receiving routine replies and positive messages will generally be interested in what you have to say, so use the direct approach. Place your main idea (the positive reply or the good news) in the opening. Use the body to explain all the relevant details, and close cordially, perhaps highlighting a benefit to your reader.

Use a direct approach for routine replies and positive messages.

STARTING WITH THE MAIN IDEA

With the direct approach, open with a clear and concise expression of the main idea or good news.

By opening routine and positive messages with the main idea or good news, you're preparing your audience for the details that follow. Make your opening clear and concise. Although the following introductory statements make the same point, one is cluttered with unnecessary information that buries the purpose, whereas the other is brief and to the point:

Instead of This

I am pleased to inform you that after careful consideration of a diverse and talented pool of applicants, each of whom did a thorough job of analyzing Trask Horton Pharmaceuticals's training needs, we have selected your bid.

Write This

Trask Horton Pharmaceuticals has accepted your bid to provide public speaking and presentation training to the sales staff.

The best way to write a clear opening is to have a clear idea of what you want to say. Ask yourself, "What is the single most important message I have for the audience?"

PROVIDING NECESSARY DETAILS AND EXPLANATION

Use the body to explain your point completely so that your audience won't be confused or doubtful about your meaning. As you provide the details, maintain the supportive tone established in the opening. This tone is easy to continue when your message is entirely positive, as in this example:

> Your educational background and internship have impressed us, and we believe you would be a valuable addition to Green Valley Properties. As discussed during your interview, your salary will be $4,300 per month, plus benefits. Please plan to meet with our benefits manager, Paula Sanchez, at 8 A.M. on Monday, March 21. She will assist you with all the paperwork necessary to tailor our benefit package to your family situation. She will also arrange various orientation activities to help you acclimate to our company.

Try to embed any negative information in a positive context.

However, if your routine message is mixed and must convey mildly disappointing information, put the negative portion of your message into as favorable a context as possible:

Instead of This

No, we no longer carry the Sportsgirl line of sweaters.

Write This

The new Olympic line has replaced the Sportsgirl sweaters that you asked about. Olympic features a wider range of colors and sizes and more contemporary styling.

In this example, the more complete description is less negative and emphasizes how the recipient can benefit from the change. Be careful, though: You can use negative information in this type of message *only* if you're reasonably sure the audience will respond positively. Otherwise, use the indirect approach (discussed in Chapter 9).

If you are communicating with a customer, you might also want to use the body of your message to assure the person of the wisdom of his or her purchase selection

---

CHECKLIST ✔ Writing Routine Replies and Positive Messages

A. Start with the main idea.
- Be clear and concise.
- Identify the single most important message before you start writing.

B. Provide necessary details and explanation.
- Explain your point completely to eliminate any confusion or lingering doubts.
- Maintain a supportive tone throughout.
- Embed negative statements in positive contexts or balance them with positive alternatives.

- Talk favorably about the choices the customer has made.

C. End with a courteous close.
- Let your readers know you have their personal well-being in mind.
- If further action is required, tell readers how to proceed and encourage them to act promptly.

(without being condescending or self-congratulatory). Using such favorable comments, often known as *resale*, is a good way to build customer relationships. These comments are commonly included in acknowledgments of orders and other routine announcements to customers, and they are most effective when they are short and specific:

> The KitchenAid mixer you ordered is our best-selling model. It should meet your cooking needs for many years.

ENDING WITH A COURTEOUS CLOSE

The close of routine replies and positive messages is usually short and simple because you're leaving things on a neutral or positive note and not usually asking for the reader to do anything. Often, a simple thank you is all you need. However, if follow-up action is required or expected, use the close to identify who will do what and when that action will take place. For a quick reminder of the steps involved in writing routine replies and positive messages, see "Checklist: Writing Routine Replies and Positive Messages."

In the close, make sure audience members understand what to do next and how that action will benefit them (if applicable).

Common Examples of Routine and Positive Messages

4 LEARNING OBJECTIVE Describe six common types of routine replies and positive messages.

Most routine and positive messages fall into six main categories: answers to requests for information and action, grants of claims and requests for adjustment, recommendations, routine information, good-news announcements, and goodwill messages.

ANSWERING REQUESTS FOR INFORMATION AND ACTION

Every professional answers requests for information and action from time to time. If the response is a simple yes or some other straightforward information, the direct approach is appropriate. A prompt, gracious, and thorough response will positively influence how people think about you and the organization you represent.

When you're answering requests and a potential sale is involved, you have three main goals: (1) to respond to the inquiry and answer all questions, (2) to leave your reader with a good impression of you and your firm, and (3) to encourage the future sale.

GRANTING CLAIMS AND REQUESTS FOR ADJUSTMENT

Even the best-run companies make mistakes, and each of these events represents a turning point in your relationship with your customer. If you handle the situation well, your customer is likely to be even more loyal than before because you've proven that you're

Responding to mistakes in a courteous, reader-focused way helps repair important business relationships.

serious about customer satisfaction. However, if a customer believes that you mishandled a complaint, you'll make the situation even worse. Dissatisfied customers often take their business elsewhere without notice and tell numerous friends and colleagues about the negative experience. A transaction that might be worth only a few dollars by itself could cost you many times that amount in lost business. In other words, every mistake is an opportunity to improve a relationship.

Your specific response to a customer complaint depends on your company's policies for resolving such issues and your assessment of whether the company, the customer, or some third party is at fault. In general, take the following steps:

- Acknowledge receipt of the customer's claim or complaint.
- Sympathize with the customer's inconvenience or frustration.
- Take (or assign) personal responsibility for setting matters straight.
- Explain precisely how you have resolved, or plan to resolve, the situation.
- Take steps to repair the relationship.
- Follow up to verify that your response was correct.

In addition to taking these positive steps, maintain a professional demeanor. Don't blame colleagues by name; don't make exaggerated, insincere apologies; don't imply that the customer is at fault; and don't promise more than you can deliver.

To grant a claim when the customer is at fault, try to discourage future mistakes without insulting the customer.

Communication about a claim is a delicate matter when the customer is clearly at fault. If you choose to grant the claim, open with that good news. However, the body needs special attention because you want to discourage similar claims in the future. Close in a courteous manner that expresses your appreciation for the customer's business (see Figure 8.4).

See "Checklist: Granting Claims and Adjustment Requests" to review the tasks involved in these kinds of business messages.

PROVIDING RECOMMENDATIONS AND REFERENCES

Recommendation letters are vulnerable to legal complications, so consult your company's legal department before writing one.

People who need endorsements from employers or colleagues (when applying for a job, for example) often request letters of recommendation. These messages used to be a fairly routine matter, but employment recommendations and references have raised some complex legal issues in recent years. Employees have sued employers and individual managers for providing negative information or refusing to provide letters of recommendation, and employers have sued other employers for failing to disclose negative information about job candidates. Before you write a letter of recommendation for a former employee or provide information in response to another employer's background check, make sure you understand your company's policies. Your company may refuse to provide anything more than dates of employment and other basic details, for example.[2]

CHECKLIST ✔ Granting Claims and Adjustment Requests

A. Responding when your company is at fault.
- Be aware of your company's policies in such cases before you respond.
- For serious situations, refer to the company's crisis management plan.
- Start by acknowledging receipt of the claim or complaint.
- Take or assign personal responsibility for resolving the situation.
- Sympathize with the customer's frustration.
- Explain how you have resolved the situation (or plan to).
- Take steps to repair the customer relationship.
- Verify your response with the customer, and keep the lines of communication open.

B. Responding when the customer is at fault.
- Weigh the cost of complying with or refusing the request.
- If you choose to comply, open with the good news.
- Use the body of the message to respectfully educate the customer about steps needed to avoid a similar outcome in the future.
- Close with an appreciation for the customer's business.

C. Responding when a third party is at fault.
- Evaluate the situation and review your company's policies before responding.
- Avoid placing blame; focus on the solution.
- Regardless of who is responsible for resolving the situation, let the customer know what will happen to resolve the problem.

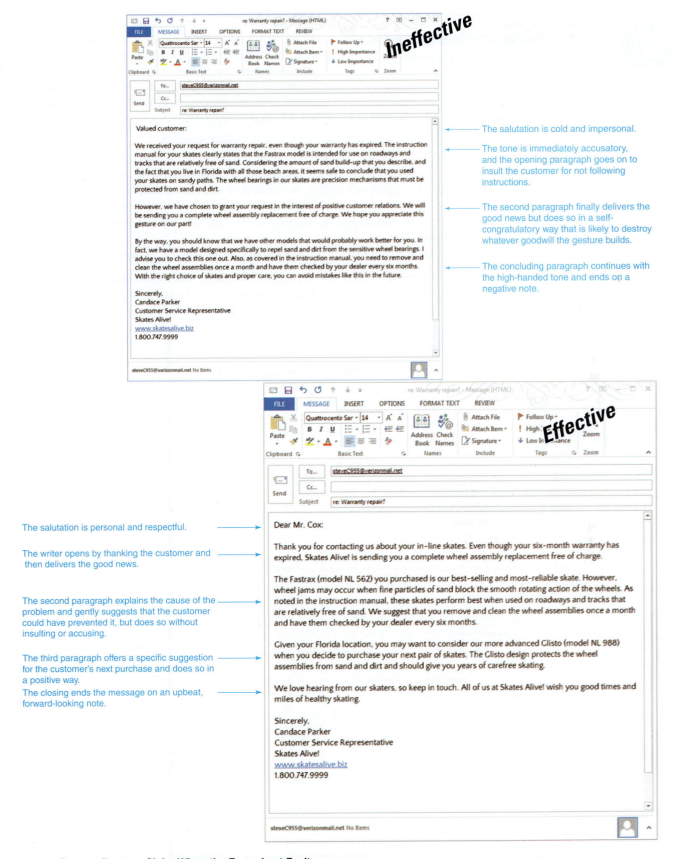

Figure 8.4   Responding to a Claim When the Buyer Is at Fault
Responding to a claim when the buyer is at fault is a positive gesture, so the content and tone of the message need to reflect that. After all, there's no point in fostering a positive relationship through actions but then undermining that through negative communication. Notice how the ineffective version sounds like a crabby parent who gives in to a child's demand but sends a mixed message by being highly critical anyway. The effective version is much more subtle, letting the customer know how to take care of his skates, without blaming or insulting him.
Source: MS Outlook 2013, © Microsoft.

If you decide to write a letter of recommendation or respond to a request for information about a job candidate, your goal is to convince readers that the person being recommended has the characteristics necessary for the job, assignment, or other objective the person is seeking. A successful recommendation letter contains a number of relevant details (see Figure 8.5):

- The candidate's full name
- The position or other objective the candidate is seeking
- The nature of your relationship with the candidate
- Facts and evidence relevant to the candidate and the opportunity
- A comparison of this candidate's potential with that of peers, if available (for example, "Ms. Jonasson consistently ranked in the top 10 percent of our national salesforce.")
- Your overall evaluation of the candidate's suitability for the opportunity

Keep in mind that every time you write a recommendation, you're putting your own reputation on the line. If the person's shortcomings are so pronounced

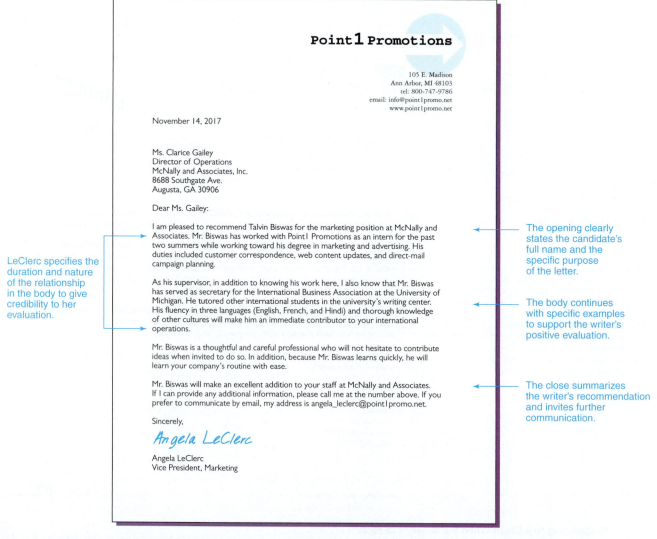

Figure 8.5   Effective Recommendation Letter

This letter clearly states the nature of the writer's relationship to the candidate and provides specific examples to support the writer's endorsements.

Timeline Photos

Back to Album · JetBlue Airways's photos · JetBlue Airways's Page   Previous · Next

JetBlue Airways
Our first flight from Boston to Detroit just landed! We want to hear from those Detroiters in the know. What are your top stops in our newest Blue City? #DepictTheD
10 March

Album: Timeline Photos
Shared with: Public

Open Photo Viewer

Courtesy JetBlue Airways Corporation.

Figure 8.6   Announcing Good News
Encouraging online conversations is an important element of brand socialization. In this Facebook post celebrating its inaugural flight from Boston to Detroit, JetBlue asked residents of Detroit to recommend their favorite places around the city.

that you don't think he or she is a good fit for the job, the only choice is to not write the letter at all. Unless your relationship with the person warrants an explanation, simply suggest that someone else might be in a better position to provide a recommendation.

SHARING ROUTINE INFORMATION

Many messages involve sharing routine information, such as project updates and order status notifications. Use the opening of these routine messages to state the purpose and briefly mention the nature of the information you are providing. Give the necessary details in the body, and end your message with a courteous close.

Most routine communications are neutral, so you don't have to take special steps in anticipation of emotional reactions from readers. However, some routine informative messages may require additional care. For instance, policy statements or procedural changes may be good news for a company, perhaps by saving money. However, it may not be obvious to employees that such savings may make additional employee resources available or even lead to pay raises. In instances in which the reader may not initially view the information positively, use the body of the message to highlight the potential benefits from the reader's perspective. (For situations in which negative news will have a profound effect on the recipients, consider the indirect techniques discussed in Chapter 9.)

> When sharing routine information
> * State the purpose at the beginning and briefly mention the nature of the information you are providing.
> * Provide the necessary details.
> * End with a courteous close.

ANNOUNCING GOOD NEWS

To develop and maintain good relationships, smart companies recognize that it's good business to spread the word about positive developments. Such developments can include opening new facilities, hiring a new executive, introducing new products or services, or sponsoring community events (see Figure 8.6). Because good news is always welcome, use the direct approach.

External good-news announcements are often communicated in a **news release**, also known as a *press release*, a specialized document used to share relevant information with the news media. (News releases are also used to announce negative news, such as plant closings.) In most companies, news releases are usually prepared or at least supervised by

> A news release or press release is a message (usually routine, but not always) designed to share information with the news media, although many are now written with customers and other stakeholders in mind as well.

specially trained writers in the public relations department. The content follows the customary pattern for a positive message: good news followed by details and a positive close. However, traditional news releases have a critical difference: You're not writing directly to the ultimate audience (such as the readers of a newspaper); you're trying to interest an editor or a reporter in a story, and that person will then write the material that is eventually read by the larger audience.

The social media release includes share-ready content that is easy to reuse in blog posts, tweets, and other social media formats.

Until recently, news releases were crafted in a way to provide information to reporters, who would then write their own articles if the subject matter was interesting to their readers. Thanks to the Internet and social media, however, the nature of the news release is changing. Many companies now view it as a general-purpose tool for communicating directly with customers and other audiences, creating *direct-to-consumer news releases*.[3] Many of these are considered *social media releases* because they include social networking links, "Tweetables" (Twitter-ready statements that can be shared on Twitter at the click of a button), and other sharable content.

FOSTERING GOODWILL

Goodwill is the positive feeling that encourages people to maintain a business relationship.

All business messages should be written with an eye toward fostering positive relationships with audiences, but some messages are written specifically to build goodwill. You can use these messages to enhance your relationships with customers, colleagues, and other businesspeople by sending friendly, even unexpected, notes with no direct business purpose (see Figure 8.7). Whether you're thanking an employee for a job well done or congratulating a colleague for a personal or professional achievement, the small effort to send a goodwill message can have a positive and lasting effect on the people around you.

Many routine messages can be adapted to foster goodwill, either by sharing helpful information or providing an element of entertainment.

In addition to creating messages for a specific goodwill reason, you can craft almost any routine message in a way to build goodwill. Two ways to do so are by providing information that your readers might find helpful and by maintaining a positive tone throughout your message.

Sending Congratulations

Taking note of significant events in someone's personal life helps foster the business relationship.

One prime opportunity for sending goodwill messages is to congratulate individuals or companies for significant business achievements. Other reasons for sending congratulations include highlights in people's personal lives, such as weddings, births, graduations,

Figure 8.7 **Goodwill Messages**
Goodwill messages serve a variety of business functions. Fans who follow Steinway on Facebook love great pianos and great piano music. In this post, the company offers its fan community something of value—a playlist of relaxing piano music as a Monday mood booster. The post doesn't attempt to sell anything (the "Buy" link shown in the video capture is for the album itself and isn't part of Steinway's message). It's just a way of fostering goodwill among fellow music lovers.

and success in nonbusiness competitions. You may congratulate business acquaintances on their own achievements or on the accomplishments of a spouse or child. You may also take note of personal events, even if you don't know the reader well. If you're already friendly with the reader, a more personal tone is appropriate.

Sending Messages of Appreciation

An important leadership quality is the ability to recognize the contributions of employees, colleagues, suppliers, and other associates. Your praise does more than just make the person feel good; it encourages further excellence. Moreover, a message of appreciation may become an important part of someone's personnel file. So when you write a message of appreciation, try to specifically mention the person or people you want to praise. The brief message that follows expresses gratitude and reveals the happy result:

An effective message of appreciation documents a person's contributions.

> Thank you and everyone on your team for the heroic efforts you took to bring our servers back up after last Friday's flood. We were able to restore business right on schedule first thing Monday morning. You went far beyond the level of contractual service in restoring our data center within 16 hours. I would especially like to highlight the contribution of networking specialist Julienne Marks, who worked for 12 straight hours to reconnect our Internet service. If I can serve as a reference in your future sales activities, please do not hesitate to ask.

Hearing a sincere thank you can do wonders for morale.[4] Moreover, in today's electronic media environment, a handwritten thank-you note can be a particularly welcome acknowledgment.[5]

REAL-TIME UPDATES

LEARN MORE BY READING THIS ARTICLE

Simple rules for writing effective thank-you notes

These tips are easy to adapt to any business or social occasions in which you need to express appreciation. Go to http://real-timeupdates.com/ebc12 and click on Learn More in the Students section.

Offering Condolences

Condolence letters are brief personal messages written to comfort someone after the death of a loved one. You may have occasion to offer condolences to employees or other business associates (when the person has lost a family member) or to the family of an employee or business associate (when that person has died).

These messages can feel intimidating to write, but they don't need to be. Follow these three principles: short, simple, and sincere. You don't need to produce a work of literary art; the fact that you are writing sends a message that is as meaningful as anything you can say.

Timing and media choice are important considerations with condolence letters. The sooner your message is received, the more comforting it will be, so don't delay. And unless circumstances absolutely leave you no choice, do not use electronic media. A brief, handwritten note on quality stationery is the way to go.

Open a condolence message with a simple expression of sympathy, such as "I am deeply sorry to hear of your loss" or "I am sorry for your loss." How you continue from there depends on the circumstances and your relationships with the deceased and the person to whom you are writing. For example, if you are writing to the husband of a colleague who recently died and you have never met him, you might continue with "Having worked with Janice for more than a decade, I know what a kind and caring person she was." Such a statement accomplishes two goals: explaining why you in particular are writing and letting the recipient know that his loved one was appreciated in the workplace.

The primary purpose of condolence messages is to let the audience know that you and the organization you represent care about the person's loss.

Conversely, if you are writing to a colleague who recently lost a loved one, you might continue with "After meeting Warren at last year's company picnic and hearing your stories about his involvement with your son's soccer league and the many other ways he contributed to his community, I know what a special person he was." Sharing brief and positive memories like this adds meaning and depth to your expression of sympathy.

You can conclude with a simple statement such as "My thoughts are with you during this difficult time." If appropriate for the situation and your relationship, you might also include an offer of assistance. "Please call if there is anything I do for you."

Keep your condolence message focused on the recipient, not on your own emotions, and don't offer "life advice" or trite sayings.

As you decide what to include in the message, keep two points in mind. First, make it a personal expression of sympathy, but don't make the whole message about you and your sense of loss. You might be grieving as well, but unless you, the deceased, and the reader were all personally close, don't say things like "I was so devastated to hear the news about Mollie."

Second, don't offer "life advice," and don't include trite sayings that you may have heard or read. At this point, soon after the loss, the recipient doesn't want your advice, only your sympathy. Also, don't bring religion into the discussion unless you have a close personal relationship with the recipient and religion is already a part of your relationship. Otherwise, you risk offending with unwelcome or inappropriate sentiments.

Condolence letters are the most personal business messages you may ever have to write, so they require the utmost in care and respect for your reader. By keeping the messages simple, short, and sincere, you will be able to achieve the right tone.

To review the tasks involved in writing goodwill messages, see "Checklist: Sending Goodwill Messages." For the latest information on writing routine and positive messages, visit **http://real-timeupdates.com/ebc12**.

CHECKLIST ✔ **Sending Goodwill Messages**

- Be sincere and honest.
- Don't exaggerate or use vague, grandiose language; support positive statements with specific evidence.
- Use congratulatory messages to build goodwill with clients and colleagues.

- Send messages of appreciation to emphasize how much you value the work of others.
- When sending condolence messages, open with a brief statement of sympathy, then adapt your message based on the circumstances and your relationship with the recipient.

ON THE JOB: SOLVING COMMUNICATION DILEMMAS AT **GET SATISFACTION**

After reading the many helpful responses you, as a representative of your company, posted on the Get Satisfaction website, Rahul Sachdev invited you to join the Get Satisfaction team as a customer service specialist; your job is to communicate with the companies that use Get Satisfaction's online services. Take what you've learned in this chapter and put it to good use as you address the following challenges. (Search for a few companies or product names on the Get Satisfaction website at **http://getsatis faction.com** to get a feel for how the system works.)

1. When people are frustrated with a problem and are trying to discuss it via a lean medium such as online postings,

emotions can sometimes boil over. You've been monitoring a conversation between a representative for one of the companies that uses Get Satisfaction and one of its customers. Over the past couple of days, their online conversation has turned into an ugly argument, with accusations of incompetence and even dishonesty flying back and forth. Although the situation doesn't involve Get Satisfaction directly, you think it reflects poorly on your company because the dispute is taking place in full public view on your website—and it certainly isn't doing anybody any good to let this "flame war" keep raging. What is the best way to handle this situation?

a. Email the company representative privately and offer to mediate the dispute.
b. Post a public message offering to mediate the dispute.
c. Post a public message reminding both sides to be civil.
d. Ignore the dispute; it's between the company and its customer.

2. Web-based businesses occasionally suffer from page-loading problems, when a particular web page a visitor requests will not display, even when the rest of a website seems to be working normally. Get Satisfaction recently had a spate of these problems. Which of these is the best way to respond to queries while the company is working to fix the situation?
a. Yes, we've noticed this problem ourselves, but we hope to have everything stabilized soon.
b. We are soooooo sorry! We're working to resolve the situation as soon as possible.
c. Don't you just hate computers sometimes? We're working to resolve the situation as soon as possible.
d. We're having some problems with our host, which seems to be resulting in a lot of these errors. We're working on it now and hope to have everything stabilized soon.

3. Get Satisfaction recently released a new version of its software. Which of the following is the best one-sentence summary of this major milestone?
a. Version 4.0 is a major update that unleashes the full value of customer community to answer questions, solve problems, and collect ideas for developing the next generation of your products and services.
b. Version 4.0 rocks in every way imaginable.
c. Version 4.0 is our best work yet. It clearly shows how far we've come as a company and how much we've learned in the last two years.

d. Version 4.0 is a major update, incorporating multiple new features, expanded customizability, and a vastly improved and simplified user interface.

4. Get Satisfaction recently announced an *enterprise* version of its customer support software that companies can customize as part of their own information systems. The software is available in *beta release* form, a free pre-release version that software companies often release to encourage people to use as a way to see if anything needs to be changed or fixed before the official product is released. Get Satisfaction hasn't yet announced how much the software will cost when it is officially released, so not surprisingly, more than a few interested customers have written questions about the anticipated price. Small business owners in particular want to know if a less-expensive version will be available to small companies. The company is working on a pricing structure that would charge by the volume of usage, meaning that small companies would probably pay less than large companies. Which of the following responses is the most effective response to this question?
a. The pricing structure will be announced when the product is ready for formal release.
b. We can't specify exact pricing yet, because we're still working on those details.
c. We can't specify exact pricing yet, because we're still working on those details. We will make sure that the pricing structure does in fact work both for small companies and large ones, and that if there is a tiered structure, that it scales according to a reliable set of figures/metrics that reflect those size differences.
d. We can't specify exact pricing yet, because we're still working on those details. However, we are trying to figure out a tiered pricing structure that would be fair to both large and small companies.

Learning Objectives Checkup

Assess your understanding of the principles in this chapter by reading each learning objective and studying the accompanying exercises. You can check your responses against the answer key on page 599.

Objective 8.1: Outline an effective strategy for writing routine business requests.

1. When it comes to routine messages, you can
   a. Skip the planning stage
   b. Keep the planning stage brief
   c. Begin by gathering all the information you'll need
   d. Begin by choosing the channel and medium
2. When writing routine messages, you
   a. Can assume that your readers will be interested or neutral
   b. Should open with an "attention getter"

   c. Should use the indirect approach with most audiences
   d. Need not allow much time for revision, production, or proofreading
3. When writing a routine request, the best approach is to begin
   a. With a personal introduction, such as "My name is Lee Marrs, and I am . . ."
   b. With a vague reference to what you are writing about, such as "I have something to ask you."
   c. With a strong demand for action
   d. By politely stating your request
4. What should you do when asking questions in a routine request?
   a. Begin with the least important question and work your way up to the most important question.
   b. Include all possible questions about the topic, even if the list gets long.
   c. Deal with only one topic per question.
   d. Do all of the above.

5. Which of the following should you do when closing a routine request?
   a. Be sure to thank the reader "in advance" for complying with the request.
   b. Ask the reader to respond by a specific and appropriate time.
   c. Ask any remaining questions you have.
   d. Do all of the above.
6. A courteous close contains
   a. A specific request
   b. Information about how you can be reached (if it isn't obvious)
   c. An expression of appreciation or goodwill
   d. All of the above

Objective 8.2: Describe three common types of routine requests.

7. Which of the following would be an inappropriate goal for a routine, simple request?
   a. Explaining what you want to know or what you want the reader to do
   b. Explaining why you're making the request
   c. Explaining how you can use your position in the company to force the reader to comply
   d. Explaining why it may be in your reader's interest to help you
8. Requests for recommendations and references are routine messages, so you can organize your inquiry using the _____ approach.
9. If you are requesting an adjustment from a company but you're not sure what the best solution would be, which of the following tactics would be best?
   a. Ask the company to assess the situation and offer advice on solving the problem.
   b. Don't ask for a solution, because doing so could lead to a suboptimal outcome for you.
   c. Subtly hint that legal action could light a fire under the company.
   d. Demand that the company solve the problem immediately; after all, it's the right thing to do.

Objective 8.3: Outline an effective strategy for writing routine replies and positive messages.

10. If you are making a routine reply to a customer, it's a good idea to
    a. Leave out any negative information
    b. Include resale information to assure the customer of the wisdom of his or her purchase
    c. Leave out sales promotion material, which would be tacky to include
    d. Do all of the above
11. A positive message should open with a clear and concise statement of the _____ _____ or _____ _____.
12. If a message has both positive and negative elements, you should

a. Always start with the bad news to get it out of the way first
b. Write two separate messages; never mix good and bad news
c. Put the bad news in a postscript (p.s.) at the bottom of the letter
d. Try to put the negative news in a positive context

Objective 8.4: Describe six common types of routine replies and positive messages.

13. Which of the following is not among the recommended elements to include in your message if you are responding to a claim or complaint when your company is at fault?
    a. An acknowledgement that you received the customer's claim or complaint
    b. An expression of sympathy for the inconvenience or loss the customer has experienced
    c. An explanation of how you will resolve the situation
    d. Complete contact information for your corporate legal staff
14. If a customer who is clearly at fault requests an adjustment, you should
    a. Ignore the request; the customer is clearly wasting your time
    b. Carefully weigh the cost of complying with the request against the cost of denying it and then decide how to respond based on the overall impact on your company
    c. Always agree to such requests because unhappy customers spread bad publicity about a company
    d. Suggest in a firm but professional tone that the customer take his or her business elsewhere in the future
15. If a third party (such as a shipping company) is at fault when one of your customers makes a claim or requests an adjustment, the best response is to
    a. Follow the terms of whatever customer service agreement your company has with the third party
    b. Explain to the customer that your company is not at fault
    c. Always grant the request; after all, it's your customer, and the customer holds you responsible
    d. Forward the message to the third party as quickly as possible
16. The purpose of goodwill messages is to
    a. Generate sales
    b. Impress others
    c. Make yourself feel better
    d. Enhance relationships with customers, colleagues, and other businesspeople
17. The most effective goodwill messages
    a. Always try to find an "angle" that benefits the sender in addition to the receiver
    b. Avoid details and focus on the emotions of the situation
    c. Are sincere and honest
    d. Do all of the above

Quick Learning Guide

CHAPTER OUTLINE

Strategy for Routine Requests
Stating Your Request Up Front
Explaining and Justifying Your Request
Requesting Specific Action in a Courteous Close

Common Examples of Routine Requests
Asking for Information and Action
Asking for Recommendations
Making Claims and Requesting Adjustments

Strategy for Routine and Positive Messages
Starting with the Main Idea
Providing Necessary Details and Explanation
Ending with a Courteous Close

Common Examples of Routine and Positive Messages
Answering Requests for Information and Action
Granting Claims and Requests for Adjustment
Providing Recommendations and References
Sharing Routine Information
Announcing Good News
Fostering Goodwill

LEARNING OBJECTIVES

1 Outline an effective strategy for writing routine business requests. (page 226)

2 Describe three common types of routine requests. (page 227)

3 Outline an effective strategy for writing routine replies and positive messages. (page 229)

4 Describe six common types of routine replies and positive messages. (page 333)

KEY TERMS

adjustment The settlement of a claim

claim A formal complaint made in response to dissatisfaction over a product or service

condolence letters Brief personal messages written to comfort someone after the death of a loved one

news release Also known as a *press release*, a specialized document traditionally used to share relevant information with the local or national news media; today, many companies issue news releases directly to the public as well

CHECKLIST
Making Claims and Requesting Adjustments

- Maintain a professional tone, even if you're extremely frustrated.
- Open with a straightforward statement of the problem.
- Provide specific details in the body.
- Present facts honestly and clearly.
- Politely summarize the desired action in the closing.

- Clearly state what you expect as a fair settlement or ask the reader to propose a fair adjustment.
- Explain the benefits of complying with the request, such as your continued patronage.

CHECKLIST
Writing Routine Requests

A. State your request up front.
- Write in a polite, undemanding, personal tone.
- Use the direct approach because your audience will probably respond favorably to your request.
- Be specific and precise in your request.

B. Explain and justify your request.
- Justify the request or explain its importance.
- Explain any potential benefits of responding.
- Ask the most important questions first.
- Break complex requests into individual questions that are limited to only one topic each.

C. Request specific action in a courteous close.
- Make it easy to comply by including appropriate contact information.
- Express your gratitude.
- Clearly state any important deadlines for the request.

CHECKLIST
Writing Routine Replies and Positive Messages

A. Start with the main idea.
- Be clear and concise.
- Identify the single most important message before you start writing.

B. Provide necessary details and explanation.
- Explain your point completely to eliminate any confusion or lingering doubts.
- Maintain a supportive tone throughout.

- Embed negative statements in positive contexts or balance them with positive alternatives.
- Talk favorably about the choices the customer has made.

C. End with a courteous close.
- Let your readers know you have their personal well-being in mind.
- If further action is required, tell readers how to proceed and encourage them to act promptly.

CHECKLIST
Sending Goodwill Messages

- Be sincere and honest.
- Don't exaggerate or use vague, grandiose language; support positive statements with specific evidence.
- Use congratulatory messages to build goodwill with clients and colleagues.
- Send messages of appreciation to emphasize how much you value the work of others.
- When sending condolence messages, open with a brief statement of sympathy, then adapt your message based on the circumstances and your relationship with the recipient.

Apply Your Knowledge

To review chapter content related to each question, refer to the indicated Learning Objective.

8.1. You have a complaint against one of your suppliers, but you have no documentation to back it up. Should you request an adjustment anyway? Why or why not? [LO-2]

⭐ **8.2.** The latest issue of a local business newspaper names 10 area executives who have exhibited excellent leadership skills in the past year. You are currently searching for a job, and a friend suggests that you write each executive a congratulatory letter and mention in passing that you are looking for new career opportunities and would appreciate the opportunity for an interview. Is this a smart strategy? Why or why not? [LO-4]

⭐ **8.3.** You've been asked to write a letter of recommendation for an employee who worked for you some years ago. You recall that the employee did an admirable job, but you can't remember any specific information at this point. Should you write the letter anyway? Explain. [LO-4]

8.4 Your company's error cost an important business customer a new client; you know it, and your customer knows it. Do you apologize, or do you refer to the incident in a positive light without admitting any responsibility? Briefly explain. [LO-4]

Practice Your Skills

Messages for Analysis

Read the following messages and then (1) analyze the strengths and weaknesses of each sentence and (2) revise each document so that it follows this chapter's guidelines.

8.5. **Message 8.A: Message Strategies: Routine Requests [LO-2]**

I'm fed up with the mistakes that our current accounting firm makes. I run a small construction company, and I don't have time to double-check every bookkeeping entry and call the accountants a dozen times when they won't return my messages. Please explain how your firm would do a better job than my current accountants. You have a good reputation among homebuilders, but before I consider hiring you to take over my accounting, I need to know that you care about quality work and good customer service.

8.6. **Message 8.B: Message Strategies: Responding to Claims and Requests for Adjustments [LO-4]**

We read your letter, requesting your deposit refund. We couldn't figure out why you hadn't received it, so we talked to our maintenance engineer, as you suggested. He said you had left one of the doors off the hinges in your apartment in order to get a large sofa through the door. He also confirmed that you had paid him $5.00 to replace the door since you had to turn in the U-Haul trailer and were in a big hurry.

This entire situation really was caused by a lack of communication between our housekeeping inspector and the maintenance engineer. All we knew was that the door was off the hinges when it was inspected by Sally Tarnley. You know that our policy states that if anything is wrong with the apartment, we keep the deposit. We had no way of knowing that George just hadn't gotten around to replacing the door.

But we have good news. We approved the deposit refund, which will be mailed to you from our home office in Teaneck, New Jersey. I'm not sure how long that will take, however. If you don't receive the check by the end of next month, give me a call.

Next time, it's really a good idea to stay with your apartment until it's inspected, as stipulated in your lease agreement. That way, you'll be sure to receive your refund when you expect it. Hope you have a good summer.

8.7. **Message 8.C: Message Strategies: Providing Recommendations [LO-4]**

Your letter to Kunitake Ando, president of Sony, was forwarded to me because I am the human resources director. In my job as head of HR, I have access to performance reviews for all of the Sony employees in the United States. This means, of course, that I would be the person best qualified to answer your request for information on Nick Oshinski.

In your letter of the 15th, you asked about Nick Oshinski's employment record with us because he has applied to work for your company. Mr. Oshinski was employed with us from January 5, 2001, until March 1, 2011. During that time, Mr. Oshinski received ratings ranging from 2.5 up to 9.6, with 10 being the top score. As you can see, he must have done better reporting to some managers than to others. In addition, he took all vacation days, which is a bit unusual. Although I did not know Mr. Oshinski personally, I know that our best workers seldom use all the vacation time they earn. I do not know if that applies in this case.

In summary, Nick Oshinski performed his tasks well depending on who managed him.

Exercises

Each activity is labeled according to the primary skill or skills you will need to use. To review relevant chapter content, you can refer to the indicated Learning Objective. In some instances, supporting information will be found in another chapter, as indicated.

Message Strategies: Routine Requests; Revising for Conciseness [LO-1], Chapter 6 Critique the following closing paragraphs. How would you rewrite each to be concise, courteous, and specific?

8.8. I need your response sometime soon so I can order the parts in time for your service appointment. Otherwise, your air-conditioning system may not be in tip-top condition for the start of the summer season.

8.9. Thank you in advance for sending me as much information as you can about your products. I look forward to receiving your package in the very near future.

8.10. To schedule an appointment with one of our knowledgeable mortgage specialists in your area, you can always call our hotline at 1-800-555-8765. This is also the number to call if you have more questions about mortgage rates, closing procedures, or any other aspect of the mortgage process. Remember, we're here to make the home-buying experience as painless as possible.

Message Strategies: Routine Responses; Media Skills: Email [LO-3], Chapter 7 Revise the following short email messages so they are more direct and concise; develop a subject line for each revised message.

8.11. I'm contacting you about your recent email request for technical support on your cable Internet service. Part of the problem we have in tech support is trying to figure out exactly what each customer's specific problem is so that we can troubleshoot quickly and get you back in business as quickly as possible. You may have noticed that in the online support request form, there are a number of fields to enter your type of computer, operating system, memory, and so on. While you did tell us you were experiencing slow download speeds during certain times of the day, you didn't tell us which times specifically, nor did you complete all the fields telling us about your computer. Please return to our support website and resubmit your request, being sure to provide all the necessary information; then we'll be able to help you.

8.12. Thank you for contacting us about the difficulty you had collecting your luggage at Denver International Airport. We are very sorry for the inconvenience this has caused you. As you know, traveling can create problems of this sort regardless of how careful the airline personnel might be. To receive compensation, please send us a detailed list of the items that you lost and complete the following questionnaire. You can email it back to us.

8.13. Sorry it took us so long to get back to you. We were flooded with résumés. Anyway, your résumé made the final 10, and after meeting three hours yesterday, we've decided we'd like to meet with you. What is your schedule like for next week? Can you come in for an interview on June 15 at 3:00 p.m.? Please get back to us by the end of this workweek and let us know if you will be able to attend. As you can imagine, this is our busy season.

8.14. We're letting you know that because we use over a ton of paper a year and because so much of that paper goes into the wastebasket to become so much more environmental waste, starting Monday, we're placing white plastic bins outside the elevators on every floor to recycle that paper and in the process, minimize pollution.

Message Strategies: Routine and Positive Messages; Revising for Conciseness, [LO-3] Chapter 6 Rewrite the following sentences so that they are direct and concise. If necessary, break your answer into two sentences.

8.15. We wanted to invite you to our special 40% off by-invitation-only sale; the sale is taking place on November 9.

8.16. We wanted to let you know that we are giving a tote bag and a voucher for five iTunes downloads with every $50 donation you make to our radio station.

8.17. The director planned to go to the meeting that will be held on Monday at a little before 11 a.m.

8.18. In today's meeting, we were happy to have the opportunity to welcome Paul Eccelson, who reviewed the shopping cart function on our website and offered some great advice; if you have any questions about these new forms, feel free to call him at his office.

8.19. Message Strategies: Responding to Claims and Requests for Adjustments [LO-4] Your company markets a line of automotive accessories for people who like to "tune" their cars for maximum performance. A customer has just written a furious email, claiming that a supercharger he purchased from your website didn't deliver the extra engine power he expected. Your company has a standard refund process to handle situations such as this, and you have the information you need to inform the customer about that. You also have information that could help the customer find a more compatible supercharger from one of your competitors, but the customer's email message is so abusive that you don't feel obligated to help. Is this an appropriate response? Why or why not?

8.20. Message Strategies: Writing Positive Messages; Media Skills: Microblogging, [LO-4] Chapter 7 Locate an online announcement for a new product you find interesting or useful. Read enough about the product to be able to describe it to someone else in your own words and then writer four Twitter tweets: one to introduce the product to your followers and three follow-on tweets that describe three particularly compelling features or benefits of the product.

8.21. Message Strategies: Writing Goodwill Messages [LO-4] Identify someone in your life who has recently accomplished a significant achievement, such as graduating from high school or college, completing a major project, or winning an important professional award. Write a brief congratulatory message using the guidelines presented in the chapter.

Expand Your Skills

Critique the Professionals

Locate an online example of a news release in which a company announces good news, such as a new product, a notable executive hire, an expansion, strong financial results, or an industry award. Analyze the release using the guidance provided in the chapter. In what ways did the writer excel? What aspects of the release could be improved? Does the release provide social media-friendly content and features? Using whatever medium your instructor requests, write a brief analysis of the piece (no more than one page), citing specific elements from the piece and support from the chapter.

Sharpening Your Career Skills Online

Bovée and Thill's Business Communication Web Search, at **http://websearch.businesscommunicationnetwork.com**, is a unique research tool designed specifically for business communication research. Use the Web Search function to find a website, video, PDF document, podcast, or PowerPoint presentation that offers advice on writing goodwill messages such as thank-you notes or congratulatory letters. Write a brief email message to your instructor, describing the item that you found and summarizing the career skills information you learned from it.

Improve Your Grammar, Mechanics, and Usage

The following exercises help you improve your knowledge of and power over English grammar, mechanics, and usage. Turn to the Handbook of Grammar, Mechanics, and Usage at the end of this book and review all of Section 1.7 (Sentences). Then look at the following 10 items. Circle the letter of the preferred choice within each group of sentences. (Answers to these exercises appear on page 601.)

8.22. **a.** Joan Ellingsworth attends every stockholder meeting. Because she is one of the few board members eligible to vote.

   b. Joan Ellingsworth attends every stockholder meeting. She is one of the few board members eligible to vote.

8.23 **a.** The executive director, along with his team members, is working quickly to determine the cause of the problem.

   b. The executive director, along with his team members, are working quickly to determine the cause of the problem.

8.24 **a.** Listening on the extension, details of the embezzlement plot were overheard by the security chief.

   b. Listening on the extension, the chief overheard details of the embezzlement plot.

8.25 **a.** First the human resources department interviewed dozens of people. Then it hired a placement service.

   b. First the human resources department interviewed dozens of people then it hired a placement service.

8.26 **a.** Andrews won the sales contest, however he was able to sign up only two new accounts.

   b. Andrews won the sales contest; however, he was able to sign up only two new accounts.

8.27 **a.** To find the missing file, the whole office was turned inside out.

   b. The whole office was turned inside out to find the missing file.

8.28 **a.** Having finally gotten his transfer, he is taking his assistant right along with him.

   b. Having finally gotten his transfer, his assistant is going right along with him.

8.29 **a.** Irving was recruiting team members for her project, she promised supporters unprecedented bonuses.

   b. Because Irving was recruiting team members for her project, she promised supporters unprecedented bonuses.

8.30 **a.** He left the office unlocked overnight. This was an unconscionable act, considering the high crime rate in this area lately.

   b. He left the office unlocked overnight. An unconscionable act, considering the high crime rate in this area lately.

8.31 **a.** When it comes to safety issues, the abandoned mine, with its collapsing tunnels, are cause for great concern.

   b. When it comes to safety issues, the abandoned mine, with its collapsing tunnels, is cause for great concern.

For additional exercises focusing on sentences, visit MyBCommLab. Click on Chapter 8, click on Additional Exercises to Improve Your Grammar, Mechanics, and Usage, and click on 12. Longer sentences, 13. Sentence fragments, 15. Misplaced modifiers, or 24. Transitional words and phrases.

Cases

Website links for selected companies mentioned in cases can be found in the Student Assignments section at **http://real-time updates.com/ebc12**.

Routine Requests

BLOGGING SKILLS

8.32. Message Strategies: Requesting Information [LO-2] You are writing a book about the advantages and potential pitfalls of using online collaboration systems for virtual team projects. You would like to include several dozen real-life examples from people in a variety of industries. Fortunately, you publish a highly respected blog on the subject, with several thousand regular readers.

Your task: Write a post for your blog that asks readers to submit brief descriptions of their experiences using collaboration tools for team projects. Ask them to email stories of how well a specific system or approach worked for them. Explain that they will receive an autographed copy of the book as thanks and that they will need to sign a release form if their stories are used. In addition, emphasize that you would like to use real names—of people, companies, and software—but you can keep the anecdotes anonymous if readers require. To stay on schedule, you need to have these stories by May 20.

EMAIL SKILLS

8.33. Message Strategies: Requesting a Recommendation [LO-2] One of your colleagues, Katina Vander, was recently promoted to department manager and now serves on the company's strategic planning committee. At its monthly meeting next week, the committee will choose an employee to lead an important market research project that will help define the company's product portfolio for the next five years.

You worked side by side with Vander for five years, so she knows your abilities well and has complimented your business insights on many occasions. You know that because she has only recently been promoted to manager, she needs to build credibility among her peers and will therefore be cautious about making such an important recommendation. On the other hand, making a stellar recommendation for such an important project would show that she has a good eye for talent—an essential leadership trait.

Your task: Write an email message to Vander, telling her that you are definitely interested in leading the project and asking her to put in a good word for you with the committee. Mention four attributes that you believe would serve you well in the role: a dozen years of experience in the industry, an engineering degree that helps you understand the technologies involved in product design, a consistent record of excellent or exceptional ratings in annual employee evaluations, and the three years you spent working in the company's customer support group, which gave you a firsthand look at customer satisfaction and quality issues. Make up any additional details you need to write the message.

EMAIL SKILLS

8.34. Message Strategies: Requesting a Recommendation [LO-2] After five years of work in the human resources department at Cell Genesys (a company that is developing cancer treatment drugs), you were laid off in a round of cost-cutting moves that rippled through the biotech industry in recent years. The good news is that you found stable employment in the grocery distribution industry. The bad news is that in the three years since you left Cell Genesys, you have truly missed working in the exciting biotechnology field and having the opportunity to be a part of something as important as helping people recover from life-threatening diseases. You know careers in biotech are uncertain, but you have a few dollars in the bank now, and you're willing to ride that rollercoaster again.

Your task: Draft an email to Calvin Morris, your old boss at Cell Genesys, reminding him of the time you worked together and asking him to write a letter of recommendation for you.[6]

IM SKILLS

8.35. Message Strategies: Requesting Information [LO-2] Many companies now provide presales and postsales customer support through some form of instant messaging or online chat function. As a consumer looking for information, you'll get better service if you can frame your requests clearly and succinctly.

Your task: Imagine that you need to replace your old laptop computer, but you're not sure whether to go with another laptop or switch to a tablet or perhaps one of the new tablet/laptop hybrids. Think through the various ways you will use this new device, from researching and note-taking during class to watching movies and interacting with friends on social media. Now imagine you're in a chat session with a sales representative from a computer company, and this person has asked how he or she can help you. Draft a message (no more than 100 words) that summarizes your computing and media requirements and asks the representative to recommend the right type of device for you.

TEXT MESSAGING SKILLS

8.36. Message Strategies: Requesting Information [LO-2] The vast Consumer Electronics Show (CES) is the premier promotional event in the industry. More than 150,000 industry insiders from all over the world come to see the exciting new products on display from nearly 1,500 companies—everything from video-game gadgets to Internet-enabled refrigerators with built-in computer screens.[7] You've just stumbled on a video game controller that has a built-in webcam to allow networked gamers to see and hear each other while they play. Your company also makes game controllers, and you're worried that your customers will flock to this new controller-cam. You need to know how much buzz is circulating around the show: Have people seen it? What are they saying about it? Are they excited about it?

Your task: Compose a text message to your colleagues at the show, alerting them to the new controller-cam and asking them to listen for any buzz it might be generating among the attendees at the Las Vegas Convention Center and the several surrounding hotels where the show takes place. Here's the catch: Your text-messaging service limits messages to 160 characters, including spaces and punctuation, so your message can't be any longer than this.

EMAIL SKILLS

8.37. Message Strategies: Requesting an Adjustment [LO-2] Love at first listen is the only way to describe the way you felt when you discovered the music streaming service SongThrong. You enjoy dozens of styles of music, from Afrobeat and Tropicalia to mainstream pop and the occasional blast of industrial metal, and SongThrong has them all for only $9.99 a month. You can explore every genre imaginable, listening to as many tracks as you like for a fixed monthly fee. The service sounded too good to be true—and sadly, it was. The service was so unreliable that you began keeping note of when it was unavailable. Last month, it was down for all or part of 12 days—well over a third of the month. As much as you like it, you've had enough.

Your task: Write an email to support@songthrong.com, requesting a full refund. To get the $9.99 monthly rate, you prepaid for an entire year ($119.88), and you've been a subscriber for two months now. You know the service has been out for at least part of the time on 12 separate days last month, and while you didn't track outages during the first month, you believe it was about the same number of days.

LETTER WRITING SKILLS

8.38. Message Strategies: Requesting an Adjustment [LO-2] As a consumer, you've probably bought something that didn't work right or paid for a service that did not turn out the way you expected. Maybe it was a pair of jeans with a rip in a seam that you didn't find until you got home or a watch that broke a week after you bought it. Or maybe your family hired a lawn service to do some yardwork and no one from the company showed up on the day promised, and when the gardeners finally appeared, they did not do what they'd been hired for but instead did other things that wound up damaging valuable plants.

Your task: Choose an incident from your own experience and write a claim letter, asking for a refund, repair, replacement, or other adjustment. You'll need to include all the details of the transaction, plus your contact address and phone number. If you can't think of such an experience, make up details for an imaginary situation. If your experience is real, you might want to mail the letter. The reply you receive will provide a good test of your claim-writing skills.

EMAIL SKILLS

8.39. Message Strategies: Requesting Action [LO-2] You head up the corporate marketing department for a nationwide chain of clothing stores. The company has decided to launch a new store-within-a-store concept, in which a small section of each store will showcase "business casual" clothing. To ensure a successful launch of this new strategy, you want to get input from the best retailing minds in the company. You also know it's important to get regional insights from around the country, because a merchandising strategy that works in one area might not succeed in another.

Your task: Write an email message to all 87 store managers, asking them to each nominate one person to serve on an advisory team (managers can nominate themselves if they are local market experts). Explain that you want to find people with at least five years of retailing experience, a good understanding of the local business climate, and thorough knowledge of the local retail competition. In addition, the best candidates will be good team players who are comfortable collaborating long distance, using virtual meeting technologies. Also, explain that while you are asking each of the 87 stores to nominate someone, the team will be limited to no more than eight people. You've met many of the store managers, but not all of them, so be sure to introduce yourself at the beginning of the message.

Routine Messages

EMAIL SKILLS

8.40. Message Strategies: Granting Claims [LO-4] Your company sells flower arrangements and gift baskets. Holidays are always a rush, and the overworked staff makes the occasional mistake. Last week, somebody made a big one. As a furious email message from a customer named Anders Ellison explains, he ordered a Valentine's Day bouquet for his wife, but the company sent a bereavement arrangement instead.

Your task: Respond to Ellison's email message, apologizing for the error, promising to refund all costs that Ellison incurred, informing him that the correct arrangement will arrive tomorrow (and he won't be charged anything for it), and offering Ellison his choice of any floral arrangement or gift basket for free on his wife's birthday.

EMAIL SKILLS

8.41. Message Strategies: Granting Claims [LO-4] Like many of the staff at Razer, you are an avid game player. You can therefore sympathize with a customer who got so excited during a hotly contested game that he slammed his Razer Anansi keyboard against his chair in celebration. Razer products are built for serious action, but no keyboard can withstand a blow like that. However, in the interest of building goodwill among the online gaming community, your manager has approved a free replacement. This sort of damage is rare enough that the company isn't worried about unleashing a flood of similar requests.

Your task: Respond to Louis Hapsberg's email request for a replacement, in which he admitted to inflicting some abuse on this keyboard. Explain, tongue in cheek, that the company is "rewarding" him with a free keyboard in honor of his massive gaming win, but gently remind him that even the most robust electronic equipment needs to be used with care.

PODCASTING SKILLS / PORTFOLIO BUILDER

8.42. Message Strategies: Providing Routine Information; Media Skills: Podcasting [LO-4] As a training specialist in Winnebago Industry's human resources department, you're always on the lookout for new ways to help employees learn vital job skills. While watching a production worker page through a training manual while learning how to assemble a new recreational vehicle, you get what seems to be a great idea: Record the assembly instructions as audio files that workers can listen to while performing the necessary steps. With audio instructions, they wouldn't need to keep shifting their eyes between the product and the manual—and constantly losing their place. They could focus on the product and listen for each instruction. Plus, the new system wouldn't cost much at all; any computer can record the audio files, and you'd simply make them available on an intranet site for download into smartphones, tablets, and digital music players.

Your task: You immediately run your new idea past your boss, who has heard about podcasting but doesn't think it has any place in business. He asks you to prove the viability of the idea by recording a demonstration. Choose a process you engage in yourself—anything from replacing the strings on a guitar to sewing a quilt to changing the oil in a car—and write a brief (one page or less) description of the process that could be recorded as an audio file. Think carefully about the limitations of the audio format as a replacement for printed text (for instance, do you need to tell people to pause the audio while they perform a time-consuming task?). If directed by your instructor, record your instructions as a podcast.

BLOGGING SKILLS / PORTFOLIO BUILDER

8.43. Message Strategies: Providing Routine Information [LO-4] You are normally an easygoing manager who gives your employees a lot of leeway in using their own personal communication styles. However, the weekly staff meeting this morning pushed you over the edge. People were interrupting one another, asking questions that had already been answered, sending text messages during presentations, and exhibiting just about every other poor listening habit imaginable.

Your task: Review the advice in Chapter 2 on good listening skills, and then write a post for the internal company blog. Emphasize the importance of effective listening, and list at least five steps your employees can take to become better listeners.

Routine Replies

EMAIL SKILLS

8.44. Message Strategies: Routine Responses [LO-4] As administrative assistant to Walmart's director of marketing, you have just received a request from the company's webmaster to analyze Walmart's website from a consumer's point of view.

Your task: Visit www.walmart.com and browse through the site, considering the language, layout, graphics, and overall ease of use. In particular, look for aspects of the site that might be confusing or frustrating—annoyances that could prompt shoppers to abandon their quests and head to a competitor such as Target or Amazon. Summarize your findings and recommendations in an email message that could be sent to the webmaster.

MICROBLOGGING SKILLS

8.45. Message Strategies: Routine Announcements [LO-4] As a way to give back to the communities in which it does business, your company supports the efforts of the United Way, a global organization that works to improve lives through education, income stability, and healthy living choices.[8] Each year, your company runs a fundraising campaign in which employees are encouraged to donate money to their local United Way agencies, and it also grants employees up to three paid days off to volunteer their time for the United Way. This year, you are in charge of the company's campaign.

Your task: Compose a four-message sequence to be posted on the company's internal microblogging system (a private version of Twitter, essentially). The messages are limited to 200 characters, including spaces and punctuation. The first message will announce the company's annual United Way volunteering and fundraising campaign (make up any details you need), and the other three messages will explain the United Way's efforts in the areas of education, income stability, and healthy living. Visit the United Way to learn more about these three areas.

LETTER WRITING SKILLS / TEAM SKILLS

8.46. Message Strategies: Providing Recommendations [LO-4] As a project manager at Expedia, one of the largest online travel services in the world, you've seen plenty of college interns in action. However, few have impressed you as much as Maxine "Max" Chenault. For one thing, she learned how to navigate the company's content management system virtually overnight and always used it properly, whereas other interns sometimes left things in a hopeless mess. She asked lots of intelligent questions about the business. You've been teaching her blogging and website design principles, and she's picked them up rapidly. Moreover, she is always on time, professional, and eager to assist. Also, she didn't mind doing mundane tasks.

On the downside, Chenault is a popular student. Early on, you often found her busy on the phone planning her many social activities when you needed her help. However, after you had a brief talk with her, this problem vanished.

You'll be sorry to see Chenault leave when she returns to school in the fall, but you're pleased to respond when she asks you for a letter of recommendation. She's not sure where she'll apply for work after graduation or what career path she'll choose, so she asks you to keep the letter fairly general.

Your task: Working with a team of your classmates, discuss what should and should not be in the letter. Prepare an outline based on your discussion and then draft the letter.

SOCIAL NETWORKING SKILLS

8.47. Message Strategies: Writing Routine Informative Messages; Composition Modes: Summarizing [LO-4] As energy costs trend ever upward and more people become attuned to the environmental and geopolitical complexities of petroleum-based energy, interest in solar, wind, and other alternative energy sources continues to grow. In locations with high *insolation*, a measure of cumulative sunlight, solar panels can be cost-effective solutions over the long term. However, the upfront costs are still daunting for most homeowners. To help lower the entry barrier, the Foster City, California–based firm SolarCity now leases solar panels to homeowners for monthly payments that are less than their current electricity bills.[9]

Your task: Visit the Solar City website, click on Residential, and then click SolarLease to read about the leasing program. Next, study SolarCity's presence on Facebook to get a feel for how the company presents itself in a social networking environment. Now assume that you have been assigned the task of writing a brief summary of the SolarLease program that will appear on the Notes tab of SolarCity's Facebook page. In your own language and in 200 words or less, write an introduction to the SolarLease program and email it to your instructor.

Positive Messages

WEB WRITING SKILLS

8.48. Message Strategies: Good News Messages [LO-4] Amateur and professional golfers in search of lower scores want to find clubs that are optimized for their individual swings. This process of *club fitting* has gone decidedly high tech in recent years, with fitters using Doppler radar, motion-capture video, and other tools to evaluate golfers' swing and ball flight characteristics. Hot Stix Golf is a leader in this industry, having fitted more than 200 professionals and thousands of amateurs.[10]

Your task: Imagine that you are the communications director at the Indian Wells Golf Resort in Indian Wells, California. Your operation has just signed a deal with Hot Stix to open a fitting center on site. Write a three-paragraph article that could be posted on the resort website. The first paragraph should announce the news that the Hot Stix center will open in six months, the second should summarize the benefits of club fitting, and the third should offer a brief overview of the services that will be available at the Indian Wells Hot Stix Center. Information on club fitting can be found on the Hot Stix website at www.hotstixgolf.com; make up any additional information you need to complete the article.

BLOGGING SKILLS / PORTFOLIO BUILDER

8.49. Message Strategies: Good-News Messages [LO-4] Most people have heard of the Emmy, Grammy, Oscar, and Tony awards for television, music, movies, and theater performances, but fewer know what the Webby award is all about. Sponsored by the International Academy of Digital Arts and Sciences, the Webbys shine a spotlight on the best in website design, interactive media, and online film and video.[11]

Your task: Visit the Webby Awards website at www.webbyawards.com, click on Winners, and choose one of the companies listed a winner in the Websites or Interactive Advertising categories. Now imagine you are the chief online strategist for this company, and you've just been informed your company won a Webby. Winning this award is a nice validation of the work your team has put in during the last year, and you want to share their success with the entire company. Write a brief post for the internal company blog, describing what the Webby awards are, explaining why they are a significant measure of accomplishment in the online industry, and congratulating the employees in your department who contributed to the successful web effort.

SOCIAL NETWORKING SKILLS

8.50. Message Strategies: Goodwill Messages [LO-4]
As the largest employer in Loganville, your construction company provides jobs, purchasing activity, and tax receipts that make up a vital part of the city's economy. In your role as CEO, however, you realize that the relationship between your company and the community is mutually beneficial, and the company could not survive without the efforts of its employees, the business opportunities offered by a growing marketplace, and the physical and legal infrastructure that the government provides.

The company's dependence on the community was demonstrated in a moving and immediate way last weekend, when a powerful storm pushed the Logan River past flood stage and threatened to inundate your company's office and warehouse facilities. More than 200 volunteers worked alongside your employees through the night to fill and stack sandbags to protect your buildings, and the city council authorized the deployment of heavy equipment and additional staff to help in the emergency effort. As you watched the water rise nearly 10 feet high behind the makeshift dike, you realized that the community came together to save your company.

Your task: Write a post for your company's Facebook page, thanking the citizens and government officials of Loganville for their help in protecting the company's facilities during the storm. Use your creativity to make up any details you need to write a 100- to 200-word message.

LETTER WRITING SKILLS

8.51. Message Strategies: Goodwill Messages [LO-4]
Shari Willison worked as a geologist in your civil engineer firm for 20 years before succumbing to leukemia. With only a few dozen employees, the company has always been a tight-knit group, and you feel like you've lost a good friend in addition to a valued employee.

Your task: Write a letter of condolence to Willison's husband, Arthur, and the couple's teenaged children, Jordan and Amy. You have known all three socially through a variety of company holiday parties and events over the years. Make up any details you need.

MyBCommLab

Go to the Assignments section of your MyLab to complete these writing exercises.

8.52. Should you use the direct or indirect approach for most routine messages? Why? [LO-1]

8.53. Why is it good practice to explain why replying to a request could benefit the reader? [LO-1]

Endnotes

1. Get Satisfaction website, accessed 20 February 2015, http://get satisfaction.com; Dan Fost, "On the Internet, Everyone Can Hear You Complain," *New York Times*, 25 February 2008, www.nytimes.com; Ray Wang, "Executive Profiles: Disruptive Tech Leaders in Social Business—Wendy Lea, Get Satisfaction," *Forbes*, 8 June 2011, www .forbes.com.
2. "How to Write Reference Letters," National Association of Colleges and Employers website, accessed 5 July 2010, www.naceweb.org; "Five (or More) Ways You Can Be Sued for Writing (or Not Writing) Reference Letters," *Fair Employment Practices Guidelines*, July 2006, 1, 3.
3. David Meerman Scott, *The New Rules of Marketing and PR* (Hoboken, N.J.: Wiley, 2007), 62.
4. Pat Cataldo, "Op-Ed: Saying 'Thank You' Can Open More Doors Than You Think," Penn State University Smeal College of Business website, accessed 19 February 2008, www.smeal.psu.edu.

5. Jackie Huba, "Five Must-Haves for Thank-You Notes," Church of the Customer Blog, 16 November 2007, www.churchofthecustomer.com.
6. Tom Abate, "Need to Preserve Cash Generates Wave of Layoffs in Biotech Industry," *San Francisco Chronicle*, 10 February 2003, www.sfgate.com.
7. CES website, accessed 11 June 2012, www.cesweb.org; Darren Murph, "CES 2012 Sets All-Time Records for Attendance, Exhibitors and Claimed Floor Space," *Engadget*, 13 January 2012, www.engadget.com.
8. United Way website, accessed 30 January 2013, www.unitedway.org.
9. SolarCity website, accessed 7 July 2010, www.solarcity.com.
10. Adapted from Hot Stix Golf website, accessed 8 February 2011, www.hotstixgolf.com.
11. The Webby Awards website, accessed 30 January 2013, www.webbyawards.com.

9

Writing Negative Messages

LEARNING OBJECTIVES

After studying this chapter, you will be able to

1 Apply the three-step writing process to negative messages.

2 Explain how to use the direct approach effectively when conveying negative news.

3 Explain how to use the indirect approach effectively when conveying negative news.

4 Explain the importance of maintaining high standards of ethics and etiquette when delivering negative messages.

5 Describe successful strategies for sending negative messages on routine business matters.

6 List the important points to consider when conveying negative organizational news.

7 Describe successful strategies for sending negative employment-related messages.

ON THE JOB: COMMUNICATING AT HAILO

Balancing Logic and Emotion to Take Some of the Sting out of Unpleasant News

No one likes to hear about price increases, whether it's college tuition, your favorite Thai food, or a ride in a taxi. Unfortunately, price increases are a fact of life in business as costs increase or business conditions change.

At the same time, consumers don't like to be kept waiting when they want something. And when that something is a taxi ride to an important meeting or a favorite restaurant, consumers really don't like to wait.

This was the dilemma facing Hailo, a cab-hailing service based in London and now operating in several other major cities around the world. Hailo's business model is based on simplifying the process of getting a taxi. The company connects taxi drivers and passengers through a GPS-enabled smartphone app that lets passengers hail a cab simply by tapping their screens. A driver in the vicinity can choose to make the pickup, and the passenger can then follow the taxi's progress on screen as it approaches.

For the 13,000 of London's 22,000 taxi drivers who have registered with the service, Hailo offers the opportunity to gain more

In an attempt to balance the needs of passengers and taxi drivers during peak periods, the cab-hailing service Hailo announced a higher minimum fare via an email message to registered users.

Paul Thompson Images/Alamy

business without waiting by the curb at busy locations or cruising streets waiting for a people to flag them down. For passengers, Hailo simplifies the process of finding a cab, because drivers come directly to them—no more standing in the street hoping an available taxi will pass by or waiting in line at long taxi ranks.

Hailo's growth suggests that drivers and passengers alike find value in the service. In fact, Hailo was recently tagged as the fastest-growing technology startup in the United Kingdom. As popular as it is, though, there are times when the service doesn't operate to everyone's complete satisfaction. For example, a driver can respond to a Hailo request and on the way to the pickup, pass by several people in the street trying to flag him or her down, only to discover that the Hailo customer just wants to be hauled a few hundred yards down the street to the next club or shop. The result is a double loss for the driver—unpaid time driving to the pickup location and the missed opportunity of potentially higher fares from those would-be customers passed by along the way.

If drivers suspect that a potential passenger will want only a short ride, they are more likely not to respond to the request, because the short ride won't compensate for the time they have to invest. This phenomenon can be troublesome for the system as a whole during peak hours, when more passengers are trying to use it. To keep its app users happy, Hailo wants as many drivers as possible to participate during peak times. To encourage

drivers to pick up more Hailo customers, it guarantees drivers a minimum amount of revenue for every Hailo rider they pick up.

To boost driver participation, Hailo recently decided to increase the minimum fare passengers must pay during certain hours. Such news would be welcome by drivers, of course, but not by those passengers accustomed to using the service for short hops around town.

Hailo announced the change in an email message to its customers, but it didn't just blurt out the news. Instead, it took the indirect approach, which you'll learn to use in this chapter. The email message started with a reader benefit, explaining that in order to increase the availability of cabs, the company was modifying its minimum fares. The message then provided a reminder of how Hailo works—and how it works best if it works well for both drivers and passengers. With that reasoning in place, the message moved on to deliver the unwelcome news about increases in the minimum fare during peak hours. The message ended on a positive note, pointing out that the increase wouldn't affect the majority of customers because most London cab rides already cost more than that amount. The message was a classic example of how to prepare readers, logically and emotionally, before delivering bad news.[1]

WWW.HAILOAPP.COM

1 **LEARNING OBJECTIVE**
Apply the three-step writing process to negative messages.

Using the Three-Step Writing Process for Negative Messages

You may never have to share unwelcome pricing news with customers, as Hailo (profiled in the chapter-opening On the Job) did, but you will have to share unwelcome news at many points in your career. Communicating negative information is a fact of life for all business professionals, whether it's saying no to a request, sharing unpleasant or unwelcome information, or issuing a public apology. With the techniques you'll learn in this chapter, however, you can communicate unwelcome news successfully while minimizing unnecessary stress for everyone involved.

Negative messages can have as many as five goals:
- Give the bad news.
- Ensure acceptance of the bad news.
- Maintain the reader's goodwill.
- Maintain the organization's good image.
- Minimize or eliminate future correspondence on the matter, as appropriate.

Depending on the situation, you can have as many as five distinct goals when communicating negative information: (1) to convey the bad news, (2) to gain acceptance for the bad news, (3) to maintain as much goodwill as possible with your audience, (4) to maintain a good image for your organization, and (5) if appropriate, to reduce or eliminate the need for future correspondence on the matter. Five goals are clearly a lot to accomplish in one message, so careful planning and execution are particularly critical with negative messages.

STEP 1: PLANNING A NEGATIVE MESSAGE

When you need to convey negative news, you can't avoid the fact that your audience does not want to hear what you have to say. To minimize the damage to business relationships and to encourage the acceptance of your message, analyze the situation carefully so you can better understand the context in which the recipient will process your message.

Understanding your readers' concerns helps you be sensitive to their needs while delivering an effective message.

Be sure to consider your purpose thoroughly—whether it's straightforward (such as rejecting a job applicant) or more complicated (such as drafting a negative performance review, in which you not only give the employee feedback on past performance but also help the person develop a plan to improve future performance). With a clear purpose and your audience's needs in mind, identify and gather the information your audience requires in order to understand and accept your message. Negative messages can be intensely personal to the recipient, and in many cases, recipients have a right to expect a thorough explanation of your answer.

Selecting the right medium and channel is also important. For instance, bad news for employees should be delivered in person whenever possible. This helps guard their privacy, demonstrates respect, and gives them an opportunity to ask questions. Doing so isn't always possible or feasible, though, so you will have times when you need to share important negative information through written or electronic media.

Defining your main idea in a negative message is often more complicated than simply saying no. For instance, if you need to respond to a hardworking employee who requested a raise, your message might go beyond saying no to explaining how she can improve her performance by working smarter, not just harder.

Finally, the organization of a negative message requires particular care. One of the most critical planning decisions is choosing whether to use the direct or indirect approach (see Figure 9.1). A negative message using the *direct approach* opens with the bad news, proceeds to the reasons for the situation or the decision, and ends with a positive statement aimed at maintaining a good relationship with the audience. In contrast, the *indirect approach* opens with the reasons behind the bad news before presenting the bad news itself.

To help decide which approach to take in any situation you encounter, ask yourself the following questions:

- **Do you need to get the reader's attention immediately?** If the situation is an emergency, or if someone has ignored repeated messages, the direct approach can help you get attention quickly.
- **Does the recipient prefer a direct style of communication?** Some recipients prefer the direct approach no matter what, so if you know this, go with direct.
- **How important is this news to the reader?** For minor or routine scenarios, the direct approach is nearly always best. However, if the reader has an emotional investment in the situation or the consequences to the reader are considerable, the indirect approach is often better, particularly if the bad news is unexpected.

> When preparing negative messages, choose the medium and channel with care.

> Appropriate organization helps readers accept your negative news.

> You need to consider a variety of factors when choosing between direct and indirect approaches for negative messages.

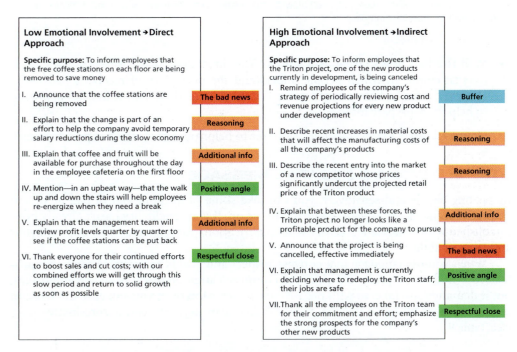

Figure 9.1 **Comparing the Direct and Indirect Approaches for Negative Messages**
The direct and indirect approaches differ in two important ways: the position of the bad news within the sequence of message points and the use of a *buffer* in the indirect approach. ("Using the Indirect Approach for Negative Messages" on page 258 explains the use of a buffer.) Both these messages deal with changes made in response to negative financial developments, but the second example represents a much higher emotional impact for readers, so the indirect approach is called for in that case. Figure 9.2 explains how to choose the right approach for each situation.

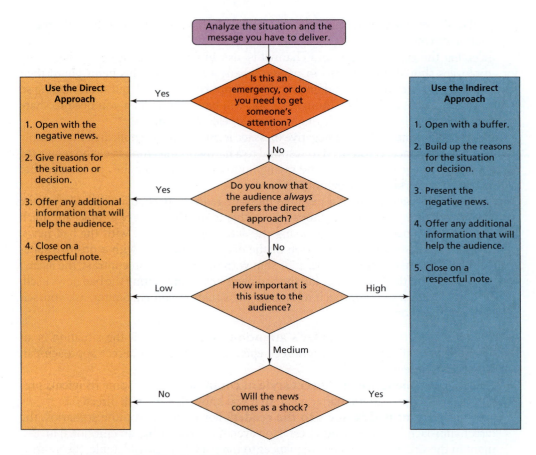

Analyze the situation and the message you have to deliver.

Is this an emergency, or do you need to get someone's attention?

Yes →

Do you know that the audience *always* prefers the direct approach?

Yes →

How important is this issue to the audience?

Low ← | → High

Medium

Will the news comes as a shock?

No ← | → Yes

Use the Direct Approach

1. Open with the negative news.

2. Give reasons for the situation or decision.

3. Offer any additional information that will help the audience.

4. Close on a respectful note.

Use the Indirect Approach

1. Open with a buffer.

2. Build up the reasons for the situation or decision.

3. Present the negative news.

4. Offer any additional information that will help the audience.

5. Close on a respectful note.

Figure 9.2 Choosing the Direct or Indirect Approach
Following this decision tree will help you decide whether the direct or indirect approach is better in a given situation. Of course, use your best judgment as well. Your relationship with the audience could affect your choice of approaches, for example.

- **Will the bad news come as a shock?** The direct approach is fine for many business situations in which people understand the possibility of receiving bad news. However, if the bad news might come as a shock to readers, use the indirect approach to help them prepare for it.

Figure 9.2 offers a convenient decision tree to help you decide which approach to use.

STEP 2: WRITING A NEGATIVE MESSAGE

Writing clearly and sensitively helps take some of the sting out of bad news.

By writing clearly and sensitively, you can take some of the sting out of bad news and help your reader accept the decision and move on. If your credibility hasn't already been established with an audience, clarify your qualifications so recipients won't question your authority or ability.

Protect your audience's pride by using language that conveys respect.

When you use language that conveys respect and avoids an accusing tone, you protect your audience's pride. This kind of communication etiquette is always important, but it demands special care with negative messages. Moreover, you can ease the sense of disappointment by using positive words rather than negative, counterproductive ones (see Table 9.1).

STEP 3: COMPLETING A NEGATIVE MESSAGE

The need for careful attention to detail continues as you complete your message. Revise your content to make sure everything is clear, complete, and concise—bearing in mind that even small flaws are likely to be magnified in readers' minds as they react to the negative news. Produce clean, professional documents and proofread carefully to eliminate

TABLE 9.1   Choosing Positive Words

Examples of Negative Phrasings	Positive Alternatives
Your request *doesn't make any sense.*	Please clarify your request.
The *damage won't be fixed* for a week.	The item will be repaired next week.
Although it wasn't *our fault,* there will be an *unavoidable delay* in your order.	We will process your order as soon as we receive an aluminum shipment from our supplier, which we expect within 10 days.
You are clearly *dissatisfied.*	I recognize that the product did not live up to your expectations.
I was *shocked* to learn that you're *unhappy.*	Thank you for sharing your concerns about your shopping experience.
The enclosed statement is *wrong.*	Please verify the enclosed statement and provide a correct copy.

mistakes. Finally, be sure to deliver messages promptly; withholding or delaying bad news can be unethical, even illegal. See Figure 9.3 on the next page for a message that conveys negative information clearly and concisely.

Using the Direct Approach for Negative Messages

2 LEARNING OBJECTIVE
Explain how to use the direct approach effectively when conveying negative news.

A negative message using the direct approach opens with the bad news, proceeds to the reasons for the situation or the decision, and ends with a positive statement aimed at maintaining a good relationship with the audience. Depending on the circumstances, the message may also offer alternatives or a plan of action to fix the situation under discussion. Stating the bad news at the beginning can have two advantages: It makes a shorter message possible, and it allows the audience to reach the main idea of the message in less time.

Use the direct approach when your negative answer or information will have minimal personal impact.

OPENING WITH A CLEAR STATEMENT OF THE BAD NEWS

No matter what the news is, come right out and say it, but maintain a calm, professional tone that keeps the focus on the news and not on individual failures or other personal factors. Also, if necessary, explain or remind the reader why you're writing.

PROVIDING REASONS AND ADDITIONAL INFORMATION

In most cases, you follow the direct opening with an explanation of why the news is negative. The extent of your explanation depends on the nature of the news and your relationship with the reader. For example, if you want to preserve a long-standing relationship with an important customer, a detailed explanation could well be worth the extra effort such a message would require.

The amount of detail you should provide depends on your relationship with the audience.

However, you will encounter some situations in which explaining negative news is neither appropriate nor helpful, such as when the reasons are confidential, excessively complicated, or irrelevant to the reader. To maintain a cordial working relationship with the reader, you might want to explain why you can't provide the information.

Should you apologize when delivering bad news? The answer isn't quite as simple as one might think, partly because the notion of *apology* is hard to pin down. To some people, it simply means an expression of sympathy that something negative has happened to another person. At the other extreme, it means admitting fault and taking responsibility for specific compensations or corrections to atone for the mistake.

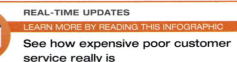

REAL-TIME UPDATES
LEARN MORE BY READING THIS INFOGRAPHIC
See how expensive poor customer service really is
Communication is at the heart of customer service, and poor customer service is the number-one way to drive customers away. Go to http://real-timeupdates.com/ebc12 and click on Learn More in the Students section.

1 Plan → 2 Write → 3 Complete

Analyze the Situation

Verify that the purpose is to decline a request and offer alternatives; audience is likely to be surprised by the refusal.

Gather Information

Determine audience needs and obtain the necessary information.

Select the Right Medium

For formal messages, printed letters on company letterhead are best.

Organize the Information

The main idea is to refuse the request so limit your scope to that; select the indirect approach based on the audience and the situation.

Adapt to Your Audience

Adjust the level of formality based on your degree of familiarity with the audience; maintain a positive relationship by using the "you" attitude, politeness, positive emphasis, and bias-free language.

Compose the Message

Use a conversational but professional style and keep the message brief, clear, and as helpful as possible.

Revise the Message

Evaluate content and review readability to make sure the negative information won't be misinterpreted; make sure your tone stays positive without being artificial.

Produce the Message

Maintain a clean, professional appearance on company letterhead.

Proofread the Message

Review for errors in layout, spelling, and mechanics.

Distribute the Message

Deliver your message using the chosen medium.

The buffer eases the recipient into the message by demonstrating respect and recapping the request.

Kwan suggests an alternative, showing that she cares about the college and has given the matter some thought.

She provides a meaningful reason for the negative response, without apologizing (because the company is not at fault).

Her close emphasizes the importance of the relationship and the company's continuing commitment.

InfoTech

927 Dawson Valley Road, Tulsa, Oklahoma 74151
Voice: (918) 669-4428   Fax: (918) 669-4429
www.infotech.com

March 6, 2017

Dr. Sandra Wofford, President
Whittier Community College
333 Whittier Avenue
Tulsa, OK 74150

Dear Dr. Wofford:

Infotech has been happy to support Whittier Community College in many ways over the years, and we appreciate the opportunities you and your organization provide to so many deserving students. Thank you for considering our grounds for your graduation ceremony on June 3.

We would certainly like to accommodate Whittier as we have in years past, but our companywide sales meetings will be held this year during the weeks of May 29 and June 5. With more than 200 sales representatives and their families from around the world joining us, activities will be taking place throughout our facility.

My assistant, Robert Seagers, suggests you contact the Municipal Botanical Gardens as a possible graduation site. He recommends calling Jerry Kane, director of public relations.

We remain firm in our commitment to you, President Wofford, and to the fine students you represent. Through our internship program, academic research grants, and other initiatives, we will continue to be a strong corporate partner to Whittier College and will support your efforts as you move forward.

Sincerely,

May Yee Kwan

May Yee Kwan
Public Relations Director

lc

Figure 9.3   Effective Letter Declining a Routine Request

In declining a request to use her company's facilities, May Yee Kwan took note of the fact that her company has a long-standing relationship with the college and wants to maintain that positive relationship. Because the news is unexpected based on past experience, she chose an indirect approach to build up to her announcement.

Some experts have advised that a company should never apologize, even when it knows it has made a mistake, because the apology might be taken as a confession of guilt that could be used against the company in a lawsuit. However, several states have laws that specifically prevent expressions of sympathy from being used as evidence of legal liability. In fact, judges, juries, and plaintiffs tend to be more forgiving of companies that express sympathy for wronged parties; moreover, an apology can help repair a company's reputation. Recently, some prosecutors have begun pressing executives to publicly admit guilt and apologize as part of the settlement of criminal cases—unlike the common tactic of paying fines but refusing to admit any wrongdoing.[2]

The best general advice in the event of a serious mistake or accident is to express sympathy immediately and sincerely and offer help if appropriate, without admitting guilt; then seek the advice of your company's lawyers before elaborating. As one survey concluded, "The risks of making an apology are low, and the potential reward is high."[3]

If you do apologize, make it a real apology. Don't say "I'm sorry if anyone was offended" by what you did—this statement implies that you're not sorry at all and that it's the other party's fault for being offended.[4] For example, when Target's information systems were infiltrated in a hacking attack that exposed the personal data of tens of millions of customers, the CEO's apology to customers included the statement, "I know this breach has had a real impact on you, creating a great deal of confusion and frustration."[5] Note that he did not say "*if* this breach caused you any confusion or frustration."

Note that you can also express sympathy with someone's plight without suggesting that you are to blame. For example, if a customer damaged a product through misuse and suffered a financial loss as a result of not being able to use the product, you can say something along the lines of "I'm sorry to hear of your difficulties." This approach demonstrates sensitivity without accepting blame.

> Apologies can have legal ramifications, but refusing to apologize out of fear of admitting guilt can damage a company's relationships with its stakeholders.

REAL-TIME UPDATES

LEARN MORE BY READING THIS ARTICLE

Dissecting the apology letter from Target's CEO

A public relations (PR) consultant evaluates a high-profile apology point by point. Go to **http://real-timeupdates.com/ebc12** and click on Learn More in the Students section.

CLOSING ON A RESPECTFUL NOTE

After you've explained the negative news, close the message in a manner that respects the impact the negative news is likely to have on the recipient. If appropriate, consider offering your readers an alternative solution if you can and if doing so is a good use of your time. Look for opportunities to include positive statements, but avoid creating false hopes or writing in a way that seems to suggest that something negative didn't happen to the recipient. Ending on a false positive can leave readers feeling "disrespected, disregarded, or deceived."[6]

In many situations, an important aspect of a respectful close is describing the actions being taken to avoid similar mistakes in the future. Offering such explanations can underline the sincerity of an apology because doing so signals that the person or organization is serious about not repeating the error.

Using the Indirect Approach for Negative Messages

The indirect approach helps prepare readers for the bad news by presenting the reasons for it first. However, the indirect approach is *not* meant to obscure bad news, delay it, or limit your responsibility. Rather, the purpose of this approach is to ease the blow and help readers accept the situation. When done poorly, the indirect approach can be disrespectful and even unethical. But when done well, it is a good example of audience-oriented communication crafted with attention to ethics and etiquette. Showing consideration for the feelings of others is never dishonest.

> **3 LEARNING OBJECTIVE**
> Explain how to use the indirect approach effectively when conveying negative news.

> Use the indirect approach when some preparation will help your audience accept your bad news.

OPENING WITH A BUFFER

A well-written buffer establishes common ground with the reader.

Messages using the indirect approach open with a **buffer**: a neutral, noncontroversial statement that establishes common ground with the reader (refer to Figure 9.1). A good buffer can express your appreciation for being considered (if you're responding to a request), assure the reader of your attention to the request, or indicate your understanding of the reader's needs. A good buffer also needs to be relevant and sincere.

Poorly written buffers mislead or insult the reader.

In contrast, a poorly written buffer might trivialize the reader's concerns, divert attention from the problem with insincere flattery or irrelevant material, or mislead the reader into thinking your message actually contains good news.

Consider these possible responses to a manager of the order-fulfillment department who requested some temporary staffing help from your department (a request you won't be able to fulfill):

Establishes common ground with the reader and validates the concerns that prompted the original request—without promising a positive answer

> Our department shares your goal of processing orders quickly and efficiently.

Establishes common ground, but in a negative way that downplays the recipient's concerns

> As a result of the last downsizing, every department in the company is running shorthanded.

Potentially misleads the reader into concluding that you will comply with the request

> You folks are doing a great job over there, and I'd love to be able to help out.

Trivializes the reader's concerns by opening with an irrelevant issue

> Those new state labor regulations are driving me crazy over here; how about in your department?

Only the first of these buffers can be considered effective; the other three are likely to damage your relationship with the other manager—and lower his or her opinion of you. Table 9.2 shows several types of effective buffers you could use to tactfully open a negative message.

PROVIDING REASONS AND ADDITIONAL INFORMATION

Phrase your reasons to signal the negative news ahead.

An effective buffer serves as a transition to the next part of your message, in which you build up the explanations and information that will culminate in your negative news. An

TABLE 9.2   Types of Buffers

Buffer Type	Strategy	Example
Agreement	Find a point on which you and the reader share similar views.	We both know how hard it is to make a profit in this industry.
Appreciation	Express sincere thanks for receiving something.	Your check for $127.17 arrived yesterday. Thank you.
Cooperation	Convey your willingness to help in any way you realistically can.	Employee Services is here to assist all associates with their health insurance, retirement planning, and continuing education needs.
Fairness	Assure the reader that you've closely examined and carefully considered the problem, or mention an appropriate action that has already been taken.	For the past week, we have had our bandwidth monitoring tools running around the clock to track your actual upload and download speeds.
Good news	Start with the part of your message that is favorable.	We have credited your account in the amount of $14.95 to cover the cost of return shipping.
Praise	Find an attribute or an achievement to compliment.	The Stratford Group clearly has an impressive record of accomplishment in helping clients resolve financial reporting problems.
Resale	Favorably discuss the product or company related to the subject of the letter.	With their heavy-duty, full-suspension hardware and fine veneers, the desks and file cabinets in our Montclair line have long been popular with value-conscious professionals.
Understanding	Demonstrate that you understand the reader's goals and needs.	So that you can more easily find the printer with the features you need, we are enclosing a brochure that describes all the Epson printers currently available.

ideal explanation section leads readers to your conclusion before you come right out and say it. In other words, the reader has followed your line of reasoning and is ready for the answer. By giving your reasons effectively, as Hailo did in its email message (see page 251), you help maintain focus on the issues at hand and defuse the emotions that always accompany significantly bad news.

Avoid hiding behind company policy to cushion your bad news. If you say, "Company policy forbids our hiring anyone who does not have two years' supervisory experience," you imply that you won't consider anyone on his or her individual merits. Skilled and sympathetic communicators explain company policy (without referring to it as "policy") so that the audience can try to meet the requirements at a later time. Consider this response to an applicant:

> Because these management positions are quite challenging, the human resources department has researched the qualifications needed to succeed in them. The findings show that the two most important qualifications are a bachelor's degree in business administration and two years' supervisory experience.

Shows the reader that the decision is based on a methodical analysis of the company's needs and not on some arbitrary guideline

Establishes the criteria behind the decision and lets the reader know what to expect

This paragraph does a good job of stating reasons for the refusal:

- It provides enough detail to logically support the refusal.
- It implies that the applicant is better off avoiding a program in which he or she might fail.
- It shows that the company's policy is based on experience and careful analysis.
- It doesn't offer an apology for the decision because no one is at fault.
- It avoids negative personal expressions (such as "You do not meet our requirements").

Well-written reasons are
- Detailed
- Tactful
- Individualized
- Unapologetic if no one is at fault
- Positive

Even valid, well-thought-out reasons won't convince every reader in every situation. However, if you've done a good job of laying out your reasoning, you've done everything you can to prepare the reader for the main idea, which is the negative news itself.

CONTINUING WITH A CLEAR STATEMENT OF THE BAD NEWS

After you've thoughtfully and logically established your reasons and readers are prepared to receive the bad news, you can use three techniques to convey the negative information as clearly and as kindly as possible. First, deemphasize the bad news:

- Minimize the space or time devoted to the bad news—without trivializing it or withholding any important information.
- Subordinate bad news in a complex or compound sentence ("My department is already shorthanded, so I'll need all my staff for at least the next two months"). This construction presents the bad news in the middle of the sentence, the point of least emphasis.
- Embed bad news in the middle of a paragraph or use parenthetical expressions ("Our profits, which are down, are only part of the picture").

To handle bad news carefully
- Deemphasize the bad news visually and grammatically.
- Use a conditional statement, if appropriate.
- Tell what you did do, not what you didn't do.

However, keep in mind that it's possible to abuse deemphasis. For instance, if the primary point of your message is that profits are down, it would be inappropriate to marginalize that news by burying it in the middle of a sentence. State the negative news clearly, and then make a smooth transition to any positive news that might balance the story.

Don't disguise bad news when you emphasize the positive.

Second, if appropriate, use a conditional (*if* or *when*) statement to imply that the audience could have received, or might someday receive, a favorable answer ("When you have more managerial experience, you are welcome to reapply"). Such a statement could motivate applicants to improve their qualifications. However, you must avoid any suggestion that you might reverse the decision you've just made and refrain from any phrasing that could give a rejected applicant false hope.

Don't hide behind "company policy" when you deliver bad news; present logical answers instead.

Third, emphasize what you can do or have done rather than what you cannot do. Say "We sell exclusively through retailers, and the one nearest you that carries our merchandise is …" rather than "We are unable to serve you, so please call your nearest dealer." Also, by implying the bad news, you may not need to actually state it, thereby making the bad news less personal ("Our development budget for next year is fully committed to our existing slate of projects"). By focusing on the facts and implying the bad news, you make the impact less personal.

When implying bad news, however, be sure your audience will be able to grasp the entire message—including the bad news. Withholding negative information or over-emphasizing positive information is unethical and unfair to your reader. If an implied message might lead to uncertainty, state your decision in direct terms. Just be sure to avoid overly blunt statements that are likely to cause pain and anger:

Instead of This	Write This
I *must refuse* your request.	I will be out of town on the day you need me.
We *must deny* your application.	The position has been filled.
I *am unable* to grant your request.	Contact us again when you have established …
We *cannot afford to* continue the program.	The program will conclude on May 1.
Much as I would like to attend …	Our budget meeting ends too late for me to attend.
We *must turn down* your extension request.	Please send in your payment by June 14.

CLOSING ON A RESPECTFUL NOTE

A positive close
- Builds goodwill.
- Offers a suggestion for action.
- Provides a look toward the future.

As with the direct approach, the close in the indirect approach offers an opportunity to emphasize your respect for your audience, even though you've just delivered unpleasant news. Express best wishes without ending on a falsely upbeat note. If you can find a positive angle that's meaningful to your audience, by all means consider adding it to your conclusion. However, don't try to pretend that the negative news didn't happen or that it won't affect the reader. Suggest alternative solutions if such information is available and doing so is a good use of your time. If you've asked readers to decide between alternatives or to take some action, make sure that they know what to do, when to do it, and how to do it. Whatever type of conclusion you use, follow these guidelines:

- **Avoid an uncertain conclusion.** If the situation or decision is final, avoid statements such as "I trust our decision is satisfactory," which imply that the matter is open to discussion or negotiation.
- **Manage future correspondence.** Encourage additional communication *only* if you're willing to discuss the situation further. (If you're not, avoid statements such as "If you have further questions, please write.")
- **Express optimism, if appropriate.** If the situation might improve in the future, share that with your readers if it's relevant. However, don't suggest the possibility of a positive change if you don't have insight that it might happen.
- **Be sincere.** Steer clear of clichés that are insincere in view of the bad news. (If you can't help, don't say, "If we can be of any help, please contact us.")

Keep in mind that the close is the last thing audience members have to remember you by. Even though they're disappointed, leave them with the impression that they were treated with respect. For a quick reminder on creating effective negative messages, see "Checklist: Creating Negative Messages."

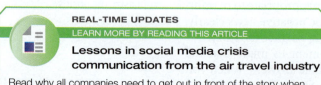

REAL-TIME UPDATES

LEARN MORE BY READING THIS ARTICLE

Lessons in social media crisis communication from the air travel industry

Read why all companies need to get out in front of the story when crisis hits. Go to http://real-timeupdates.com/ebc12 and click on Learn More in the Students section.

CHECKLIST ✔ Creating Negative Messages

A. Choose the better approach.
- Consider using the direct approach when the audience is aware of the possibility of negative news, when the reader is not emotionally involved in the message, when you know that the reader would prefer the bad news first, when you know that firmness is necessary, and when you want to discourage a response.
- Consider using the indirect approach when the news is likely to come as a shock or surprise, when your audience has a high emotional investment in the outcome, and when you want to maintain a good relationship with the audience.

B. For the indirect approach, open with an effective buffer.
- Establish common ground with the audience.
- Validate the request, if you are responding to a request.
- Don't trivialize the reader's concerns.
- Don't mislead the reader into thinking the coming news might be positive.

C. Provide reasons and additional information.
- Explain why the news is negative.
- Adjust the amount of detail to fit the situation and the audience.

- Avoid explanations when the reasons are confidential, excessively complicated, or irrelevant to the reader.
- If appropriate, state how you plan to correct or respond to the negative news.
- Seek the advice of company lawyers if you're unsure what to say.

D. Clearly state the bad news.
- State the bad news as positively as possible, using tactful wording.
- To help protect readers' feelings, deemphasize the bad news by minimizing the space devoted to it, subordinating it, or embedding it.
- If your response might change in the future if circumstances change, explain the conditions to the reader.
- Emphasize what you can do or have done rather than what you can't or won't do.

E. Close on a respectful note.
- Express best wishes without being falsely positive.
- Suggest actions readers might take, if appropriate, and provide them with necessary information.
- Encourage further communication only if you're willing to discuss the situation further.

Maintaining High Standards of Ethics and Etiquette

> **4** LEARNING OBJECTIVE
> Explain the importance of maintaining high standards of ethics and etiquette when delivering negative messages.

All business messages demand attention to ethics and etiquette, of course, but these considerations take on special importance when you are delivering bad news—for several reasons. First, a variety of laws and regulations dictate the content and delivery of many business messages with potentially negative content, such as the release of financial information by a public company. Second, negative messages can have a significant negative impact on the lives of those receiving them. Even if the news is conveyed legally and conscientiously, good ethical practice demands that these situations be approached with care and sensitivity. Third, emotions often run high when negative messages are involved, for both the sender and the receiver. Senders need to manage their own emotions and consider the emotional state of their audiences.

For example, in a message announcing or discussing workforce cutbacks, you have the emotional needs of several stakeholder groups to consider. The employees who lost their jobs are likely to experience fear about their futures and possibly a sense of betrayal. The employees who kept their jobs are likely to feel anxiety about the long-term security of their jobs, the ability of company management to turn things around, and the level of care and respect the company has for its employees. These "survivors" may also feel guilty about keeping their jobs while some colleagues lost theirs. Outside the company, investors, suppliers, and segments of the community affected by the layoffs (such as retailers and homebuilders) will have varying degrees of financial interest in the outcome of the decision. Writing such messages requires careful attention to all these needs, while balancing respect for the departing employees with a positive outlook on the future.

The challenge of sending—and receiving—negative messages can tempt one to delay, downplay, or distort the bad news (see "Practicing Ethical Communication: The Deceptive

PRACTICING ETHICAL COMMUNICATION

The Deceptive Soft Sell

You and your colleagues are nervous. Sales have been declining for months, and you see evidence of budget tightening all over the place—the fruit and pastries have disappeared from the coffee stations, accountants are going over expense reports with magnifying glasses, and managers are slow to replace people who leave the company. Instant messages fly around the office; everyone wants to know if anyone has heard anything about layoffs.

The job market in your area is weak, and you know you might have to sell your house—in one of the weakest housing markets in memory—and move your family out of state to find another position in your field. If your job is eliminated, you're ready to cope with the loss, but you need as much time as possible. You breathe a sigh of relief when the following item from the CEO appears on the company's internal blog:

> With news of workforce adjustments elsewhere in our industry, we realize many of you are concerned about the possibility here.

I'd like to reassure all of you that we remain confident in the company's fundamental business strategy, and the executive team is examining all facets of company operations to ensure our continued financial strength.

The message calms your fears. Should it?

A month later, the CEO announces a layoff of 20 percent of the company's workforce—nearly 700 people.

CAREER APPLICATIONS

1. You're shocked by the news because you felt reassured by the blog posting from last month. In light of what happened, you retrieve a copy of the newsletter and reread the CEO's message. Does it seem ethical now? Why or why not?

2. If you had been in charge of writing this newsletter item and your hands were tied because you couldn't come out and announce the layoffs yet, how would you have rewritten the message?

Soft Sell").[7] However, doing so may be unethical and even illegal. In recent years, numerous companies have been sued by shareholders, consumers, employees, and government regulators for allegedly withholding or delaying negative information in such areas as company finances, environmental hazards, and product safety. In many of these cases, the problem was slow, incomplete, or inaccurate communication between the company and external stakeholders. In others, problems stemmed from a reluctance to send or receive negative news within the organization.

Sharing bad news effectively requires commitment from everyone in the organization.

Effectively sharing bad news within an organization requires commitment from everyone involved. Employees must commit to sending negative messages when necessary and to do so in a timely fashion, even when that is unpleasant or difficult. Conversely, managers must commit to maintaining open communication channels, truly listening when employees have negative information to share and not punishing employees who deliver bad news.

Whistle-blowing is a difficult decision for most employees to make, but it provides a vital element of feedback for managers.

Employees who observe unethical or illegal behavior within their companies and are unable to resolve the problems through normal channels may have no choice but to resort to **whistle-blowing**, expressing their concerns internally through company ethics hotlines—or externally through social media or the news media if they perceive no other options. The decision to "blow the whistle" on one's own employer is rarely easy or without consequences; more than 80 percent of whistleblowers in one survey said they were punished in some way for coming forward with their concerns.[8] Although whistle-blowing is sometimes characterized as "ratting on" colleagues or managers, it has an essential function. According to international business expert Alex MacBeath, "Whistleblowing can be an invaluable way to alert management to poor business practice within the workplace. Often whistleblowing can be the only way that information about issues such as rule breaking, criminal activity, cover-ups, and fraud can be brought to management's attention before serious damage is suffered."[9] Recognizing the value of this feedback, many companies have formal reporting mechanisms that give employees a way to voice ethical and legal concerns to management. Various government bodies have also instituted protections for whistle-blowers, partly in recognition of the role that workers play in food safety and other vital areas.[10]

Sending Negative Messages on Routine Business Matters

5 LEARNING OBJECTIVE
Describe successful strategies for sending negative messages on routine business matters.

Professionals and companies receive a wide variety of requests and cannot respond positively to every single one. In addition, mistakes and unforeseen circumstances can lead to delays and other minor problems that occur in the course of business. Occasionally, companies must send negative messages to suppliers and other parties. Whatever the purpose, crafting routine negative responses and messages quickly and graciously is an important skill for every businessperson.

MAKING NEGATIVE ANNOUNCEMENTS ON ROUTINE BUSINESS MATTERS

On occasion managers need to make unexpected announcements of a negative nature. For example, a company might decide to consolidate its materials purchasing with fewer suppliers and thereby need to tell several firms it will no longer be buying from them. Internally, management may need to announce the elimination of an employee benefit or other changes that employees will view negatively.

Except in the case of minor changes, the indirect approach is usually the better choice. Follow the steps outlined for indirect messages: Open with a buffer that establishes some mutual ground between you and the reader, advance your reasoning, announce the change, and close with as much positive information and sentiment as appropriate under the circumstances.

Negative announcements on routine business matters usually should be handled with the indirect approach because the news is unexpected.

REJECTING SUGGESTIONS AND PROPOSALS

Managers receive a variety of suggestions and proposals, both solicited and unsolicited, from internal and external sources. For an unsolicited proposal from an external source, you may not even need to respond if you don't already have a working relationship with the sender. However, if you need to reject a proposal you solicited, you owe the sender an explanation, and because the news will be unexpected, the indirect approach is better. In general, the closer your working relationship, the more thoughtful and complete you need to be in your response. For example, if you are rejecting a proposal from an employee, explain your reasons fully and carefully so that the employee can understand why the proposal was not accepted and so that you don't damage an important working relationship.

REFUSING ROUTINE REQUESTS

When you are unable to meet a request, your primary communication challenge is to give a clear negative response without generating negative feelings or damaging either your personal reputation or the company's. As simple as such messages may appear to be, they can test your skills as a communicator because you often need to deliver negative information while maintaining a positive relationship with the other party.

When turning down an invitation or a request for a favor, consider your relationship with the reader.

The direct approach works best for most routine negative responses. It not only helps your audience get your answer quickly and move on to other possibilities, but it also helps you save time because messages with the direct approach are often easier to write than those with the indirect approach.

The indirect approach works best when the stakes are high for you or for the receiver, when you or your company has an established relationship with the person making the request, or when you're forced to decline a request that you might have accepted in the past (as was the case in Figure 9.3).

Consider the following points as you develop your routine negative messages:

- Manage your time carefully; focus on the most important relationships and requests.
- If the matter is closed, don't imply that it's still open by using phrases such as "Let me think about it and get back to you" as a way to delay saying no.
- Offer alternative ideas if you can, particularly if the relationship is important.
- Don't imply that other assistance or information might be available if it isn't.

If you aren't in a position to offer additional information or assistance, don't imply that you are.

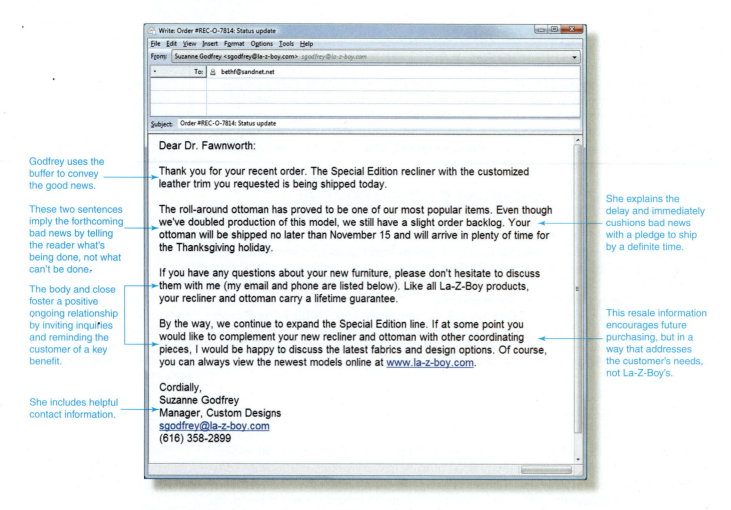

Godfrey uses the buffer to convey the good news.

These two sentences imply the forthcoming bad news by telling the reader what's being done, not what can't be done.

The body and close foster a positive ongoing relationship by inviting inquiries and reminding the customer of a key benefit.

She includes helpful contact information.

She explains the delay and immediately cushions bad news with a pledge to ship by a definite time.

This resale information encourages future purchasing, but in a way that addresses the customer's needs, not La-Z-Boy's.

Figure 9.4 **Effective Negative Message Regarding a Transaction**
This message, which is a combination of good and bad news, uses the indirect approach—with the good news serving as a buffer for the bad news. In this case, the customer wasn't promised delivery by a certain date, so the writer simply informs the customer when to expect the rest of the order. The writer also takes steps to repair the relationship and encourage future business with her firm.

HANDLING BAD NEWS ABOUT TRANSACTIONS

Bad news about transactions is always unwelcome. When you send such messages, you have three goals: (1) modify the customer's expectations, (2) explain how you plan to resolve the situation, and (3) repair whatever damage might have been done to the business relationship.

The specific content and tone of each message can vary widely, depending on the nature of the transaction and your relationship with the customer. Telling an individual consumer that his new sweater will be arriving a week later than you promised is much simpler than telling Toyota that 30,000 transmission parts will be a week late, especially if you know the company will be forced to idle a multimillion-dollar production facility as a result.

If you haven't done anything specific to set the customer's expectations—such as promising delivery within 24 hours—the message simply needs to inform the customer of the situation, with little or no emphasis on apologies action-oriented note (see Figure 9.4).

If you did set the customer's expectations and now find that you can't meet them, your task is more complicated. In addition to resetting those expectations and explaining how you'll resolve the problem, you should include an apology as part of your message. The scope of the apology depends on the magnitude of the mistake. For the customer who

Some negative messages regarding transactions carry significant financial and legal ramifications.

Your approach to bad news about business transactions depends on what you've done previously to set the customer's expectations.

CHECKLIST ✔ Handling Bad News About Transactions

- Reset the customer's expectations regarding the transaction.
- Explain what happened and why, if appropriate.
- Explain how you will resolve the situation.

- Repair any damage done to the business relationship, perhaps offering future discounts, free merchandise, or other considerations.
- Offer a professional, businesslike expression of apology if your organization made a mistake.

---

ordered the sweater, a simple apology followed by a clear statement of when the sweater will arrive would probably be sufficient. For larger business-to-business transactions, the customer may want an explanation of what went wrong to determine whether you'll be able to perform as you promise in the future.

To help repair the damage to the relationship and encourage repeat business, many companies offer discounts on future purchases, free merchandise, or other considerations. However, you don't always have a choice. Business-to-business purchasing contracts often include performance clauses that legally entitle the customer to discounts or other restitution in the event of late delivery. To review the concepts covered in this section, see "Checklist: Handling Bad News About Transactions."

If you've failed to meet expectations that you set for the customer, you should include an element of apology.

REFUSING CLAIMS AND REQUESTS FOR ADJUSTMENT

Customers who make a claim or request an adjustment tend to be emotionally involved, so the indirect approach is usually the better choice when you are denying such a request. Your delicate task is to avoid accepting responsibility for the unfortunate situation and yet avoid blaming or accusing the customer. To steer clear of these pitfalls, pay special attention to the tone of your letter. Demonstrate that you understand and have considered the complaint carefully, and then rationally explain why you are refusing the request. Close on a respectful and action-oriented note (see Figure 9.5 on the next page). And be sure to respond quickly. With so many instantaneous media choices at their disposal, some angry consumers will take their complaints public if they don't hear back from you within a few days or even a few hours.[11]

If you deal with enough customers over a long enough period, chances are you'll get a request that is particularly outrageous. You might even be positive that the person is not telling the truth. However, you need to control your emotions and approach the situation as calmly as possible to avoid saying or writing anything that the recipient might interpret as defamation (see page 27 in Chapter 1). To avoid being accused of defamation, follow these guidelines:

- Avoid any kind of abusive language or terms that could be considered defamatory.
- Provide accurate information and stick to the facts.
- Never let anger or malice motivate your messages.
- Consult your company's legal advisers whenever you think a message might have legal consequences.
- Communicate honestly and make sure you believe what you're saying is true.
- Emphasize a desire for a good relationship in the future.

Keep in mind that nothing positive can come out of antagonizing a customer, even one who has verbally abused you or your colleagues. Reject the claim or request for adjustment in a professional manner and move on to the next challenge. For a brief review of the tasks involved when refusing claims, see "Checklist: Refusing Claims."

MOBILE APP
Pocket Letter Pro includes templates for a variety of letter types to simplify writing business letters on your mobile device.

Use the indirect approach in most cases of refusing a claim.

When refusing a claim
- *Demonstrate your understanding of the complaint.*
- *Explain your refusal.*
- *Suggest alternative action.*

You can help avoid committing defamation by not responding emotionally or abusively.

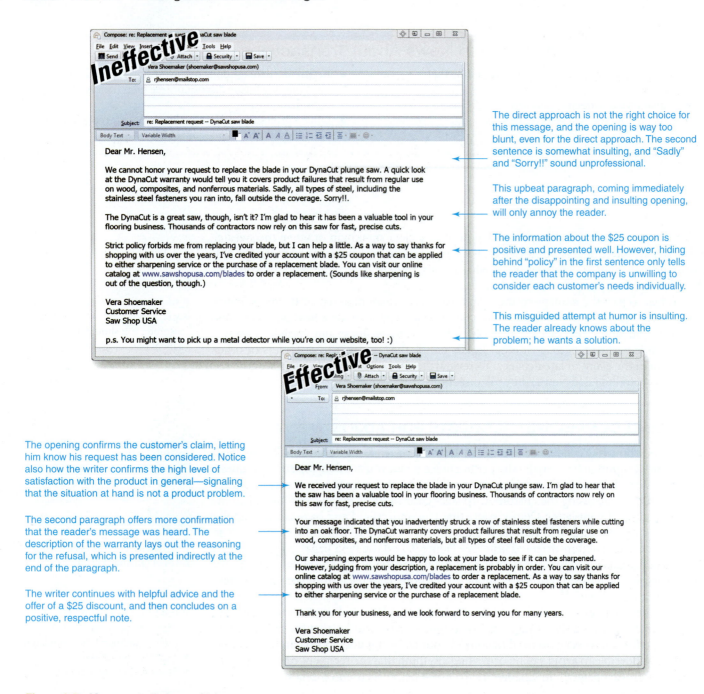

The direct approach is not the right choice for this message, and the opening is way too blunt, even for the direct approach. The second sentence is somewhat insulting, and "Sadly" and "Sorry!!" sound unprofessional.

This upbeat paragraph, coming immediately after the disappointing and insulting opening, will only annoy the reader.

The information about the $25 coupon is positive and presented well. However, hiding behind "policy" in the first sentence only tells the reader that the company is unwilling to consider each customer's needs individually.

This misguided attempt at humor is insulting. The reader already knows about the problem; he wants a solution.

Ineffective

Dear Mr. Hensen,

We cannot honor your request to replace the blade in your DynaCut plunge saw. A quick look at the DynaCut warranty would tell you it covers product failures that result from regular use on wood, composites, and nonferrous materials. Sadly, all types of steel, including the stainless steel fasteners you ran into, fall outside the coverage. Sorry!!.

The DynaCut is a great saw, though, isn't it? I'm glad to hear it has been a valuable tool in your flooring business. Thousands of contractors now rely on this saw for fast, precise cuts.

Strict policy forbids me from replacing your blade, but I can help a little. As a way to say thanks for shopping with us over the years, I've credited your account with a $25 coupon that can be applied to either sharpening service or the purchase of a replacement blade. You can visit our online catalog at www.sawshopusa.com/blades to order a replacement. (Sounds like sharpening is out of the question, though.)

Vera Shoemaker
Customer Service
Saw Shop USA

p.s. You might want to pick up a metal detector while you're on our website, too! :)

The opening confirms the customer's claim, letting him know his request has been considered. Notice also how the writer confirms the high level of satisfaction with the product in general—signaling that the situation at hand is not a product problem.

The second paragraph offers more confirmation that the reader's message was heard. The description of the warranty lays out the reasoning for the refusal, which is presented indirectly at the end of the paragraph.

The writer continues with helpful advice and the offer of a $25 discount, and then concludes on a positive, respectful note.

Effective

Dear Mr. Hensen,

We received your request to replace the blade in your DynaCut plunge saw. I'm glad to hear that the saw has been a valuable tool in your flooring business. Thousands of contractors now rely on this saw for fast, precise cuts.

Your message indicated that you inadvertently struck a row of stainless steel fasteners while cutting into an oak floor. The DynaCut warranty covers product failures that result from regular use on wood, composites, and nonferrous materials, but all types of steel fall outside the coverage.

Our sharpening experts would be happy to look at your blade to see if it can be sharpened. However, judging from your description, a replacement is probably in order. You can visit our online catalog at www.sawshopusa.com/blades to order a replacement. As a way to say thanks for shopping with us over the years, I've credited your account with a $25 coupon that can be applied to either sharpening service or the purchase of a replacement blade.

Thank you for your business, and we look forward to serving you for many years.

Vera Shoemaker
Customer Service
Saw Shop USA

Figure 9.5   Message to Refuse a Claim
Vera Shoemaker diplomatically refuses this customer's request for a new saw blade. Without blaming the customer (even though the customer clearly made a mistake), she points out that the saw blade is not intended to cut steel, so the warranty doesn't cover a replacement in this instance.

CHECKLIST ✔ Refusing Claims

- Use the indirect approach because the reader is expecting or hoping for a positive response.
- Indicate your full understanding of the nature of the complaint.
- Explain why you are refusing the request, without hiding behind company policy.
- Provide an accurate, factual account of the transaction.
- Emphasize ways things should have been handled rather than dwell on the reader's negligence.
- Avoid any appearance of defamation.
- Avoid expressing personal opinions.
- End with a positive, friendly, helpful close.
- Make any suggested action easy for readers to comply with.

Sending Negative Organizational News

6 LEARNING OBJECTIVE
List the important points to consider when conveying negative organizational news.

The messages described in the previous section deal with internal matters or individual interactions with external parties. From time to time, managers must also share negative information with the public at large, and sometimes respond to negative information as well. Most of these scenarios have unique challenges that must be addressed on a case-by-case basis, but the general advice offered here applies to all of them. One key difference among all these messages is whether you have time to plan the announcement. The following section addresses negative messages you do have time to plan for, and "Communicating in a Crisis" later in the chapter offers advice on communication during emergencies.

COMMUNICATING UNDER NORMAL CIRCUMSTANCES

Businesses must at times send a range of negative messages regarding their ongoing operations. As you plan such messages, take extra care to consider all your audiences and their unique needs. Keep in mind that a significant negative event such as a plant closing can affect hundreds or thousands of people in multiple stakeholder groups. Employees need to find new jobs, get training in new skills, or perhaps get emergency financial help. If many of your employees plan to move in search of new jobs, school districts may have to adjust budgets and staffing levels. Your customers need to find new suppliers. Your suppliers may need to find other customers of their own. Government agencies may need to react to everything from a decrease in tax revenues to an influx of people seeking unemployment benefits.

Negative organizational messages to external audiences can require extensive planning.

When making negative announcements, follow these guidelines:

- **Match your approach to the situation.** A modest price increase won't shock most customers, so the direct approach is fine. However, canceling a product that people count on is another matter, so building up to the news via the indirect approach might be better.
- **Consider the unique needs of each group.** As the plant closing example illustrates, various people have different information needs.
- **Give each audience enough time to react as needed.** Negative news often requires readers to make decisions or take action in response, so don't increase their stress by not providing any warning.

Give people as much time as possible to react to negative organizational news.

- **Give yourself enough time to plan and manage a response.** Chances are you're going to be hit with complaints, questions, or product returns after you make your announcement, so make sure you're ready with answers and additional follow-up information.
- **Look for positive angles, but don't exude false optimism.** If eliminating a seldom-used employee benefit means the company can invest more in advertising, by all means promote that positive angle. On the other hand, laying off 10,000 people does not give them "an opportunity to explore new horizons." It's a traumatic event that can affect employees, their families, and their communities for years. The best you may be able to do is to thank people for their past support and wish them well in the future.
- **Seek expert advice if you're not sure.** Many significant negative announcements have important technical, financial, or legal elements that require the expertise of lawyers, accountants, or other specialists.

Ask for legal help and other assistance if you're not sure how to handle a significant negative announcement.

Negative situations will test your skills as a communicator and leader. Inspirational leaders try to seize such opportunities as a chance to reshape or reinvigorate the organization, and they offer encouragement to those around them (see Figure 9.6 on the next page).

MOBILE APP
The Yelp mobile app is an easy way to keep the consumer review site at your fingertips—and to monitor what's being said about your business.

RESPONDING TO NEGATIVE INFORMATION IN A SOCIAL MEDIA ENVIRONMENT

For all the benefits they bring to business, social media and other communication technologies have created a major new challenge: responding to online rumors, false information, and attacks on a company's reputation. Customers who believe they have been treated unfairly like these sites and tools because they can use the public exposure as leverage. Many companies appreciate the feedback, too, and many actively seek out complaints to improve their products and operations.

Responding effectively to rumors and negative information in social media requires continual engagement with stakeholders and careful decision making about which messages should get a response.

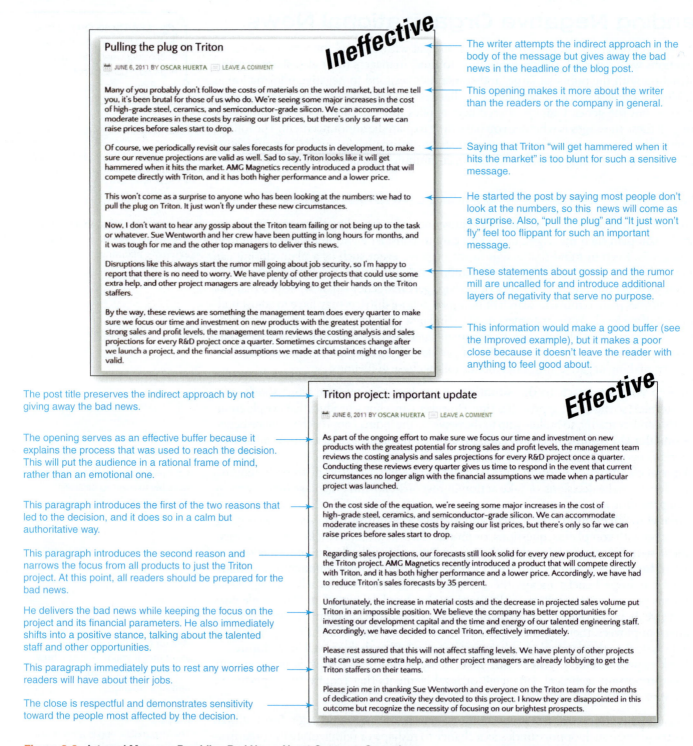

Ineffective

Pulling the plug on Triton

JUNE 6, 2011 BY OSCAR HUERTA   LEAVE A COMMENT

Many of you probably don't follow the costs of materials on the world market, but let me tell you, it's been brutal for those of us who do. We're seeing some major increases in the cost of high-grade steel, ceramics, and semiconductor-grade silicon. We can accommodate moderate increases in these costs by raising our list prices, but there's only so far we can raise prices before sales start to drop.

Of course, we periodically revisit our sales forecasts for products in development, to make sure our revenue projections are valid as well. Sad to say, Triton looks like it will get hammered when it hits the market. AMG Magnetics recently introduced a product that will compete directly with Triton, and it has both higher performance and a lower price.

This won't come as a surprise to anyone who has been looking at the numbers: we had to pull the plug on Triton. It just won't fly under these new circumstances.

Now, I don't want to hear any gossip about the Triton team failing or not being up to the task or whatever. Sue Wentworth and her crew have been putting in long hours for months, and it was tough for me and the other top managers to deliver this news.

Disruptions like this always start the rumor mill going about job security, so I'm happy to report that there is no need to worry. We have plenty of other projects that could use some extra help, and other project managers are already lobbying to get their hands on the Triton staffers.

By the way, these reviews are something the management team does every quarter to make sure we focus our time and investment on new products with the greatest potential for strong sales and profit levels, the management team reviews the costing analysis and sales projections for every R&D project once a quarter. Sometimes circumstances change after we launch a project, and the financial assumptions we made at that point might no longer be valid.

Annotations (right side):

The writer attempts the indirect approach in the body of the message but gives away the bad news in the headline of the blog post.

This opening makes it more about the writer than the readers or the company in general.

Saying that Triton "will get hammered when it hits the market" is too blunt for such a sensitive message.

He started the post by saying most people don't look at the numbers, so this news will come as a surprise. Also, "pull the plug" and "It just won't fly" feel too flippant for such an important message.

These statements about gossip and the rumor mill are uncalled for and introduce additional layers of negativity that serve no purpose.

This information would make a good buffer (see the Improved example), but it makes a poor close because it doesn't leave the reader with anything to feel good about.

Effective

Triton project: important update

JUNE 6, 2011 BY OSCAR HUERTA   LEAVE A COMMENT

As part of the ongoing effort to make sure we focus our time and investment on new products with the greatest potential for strong sales and profit levels, the management team reviews the costing analysis and sales projections for every R&D project once a quarter. Conducting these reviews every quarter gives us time to respond in the event that current circumstances no longer align with the financial assumptions we made when a particular project was launched.

On the cost side of the equation, we're seeing some major increases in the cost of high-grade steel, ceramics, and semiconductor-grade silicon. We can accommodate moderate increases in these costs by raising our list prices, but there's only so far we can raise prices before sales start to drop.

Regarding sales projections, our forecasts still look solid for every new product, except for the Triton project. AMG Magnetics recently introduced a product that will compete directly with Triton, and it has both higher performance and a lower price. Accordingly, we have had to reduce Triton's sales forecasts by 35 percent.

Unfortunately, the increase in material costs and the decrease in projected sales volume put Triton in an impossible position. We believe the company has better opportunities for investing our development capital and the time and energy of our talented engineering staff. Accordingly, we have decided to cancel Triton, effectively immediately.

Please rest assured that this will not affect staffing levels. We have plenty of other projects that can use some extra help, and other project managers are already lobbying to get the Triton staffers on their teams.

Please join me in thanking Sue Wentworth and everyone on the Triton team for the months of dedication and creativity they devoted to this project. I know they are disappointed in this outcome but recognize the necessity of focusing on our brightest prospects.

Annotations (left side):

The post title preserves the indirect approach by not giving away the bad news.

The opening serves as an effective buffer because it explains the process that was used to reach the decision. This will put the audience in a rational frame of mind, rather than an emotional one.

This paragraph introduces the first of the two reasons that led to the decision, and it does so in a calm but authoritative way.

This paragraph introduces the second reason and narrows the focus from all products to just the Triton project. At this point, all readers should be prepared for the bad news.

He delivers the bad news while keeping the focus on the project and its financial parameters. He also immediately shifts into a positive stance, talking about the talented staff and other opportunities.

This paragraph immediately puts to rest any worries other readers will have about their jobs.

The close is respectful and demonstrates sensitivity toward the people most affected by the decision.

Figure 9.6   Internal Message Providing Bad News About Company Operations

The cancelation of a major development project before completion can be a traumatic event for a company's employees. People who worked on the project are likely to feel that all their time and energy were wasted and worry that their jobs are in jeopardy. Employees who didn't work on the project might worry about the company's financial health and the stability of their own jobs. Such messages are therefore prime candidates for the indirect approach. Note how much more effectively the revised version manages the reader's emotions from beginning to end.

However, false rumors and both fair and unfair criticisms can spread around the world in a matter of minutes. Responding to rumors and countering negative information requires an ongoing effort and case-by-case decisions about which messages require a response. Follow these four steps:[12]

- **Engage early, engage often.** Perhaps the most important step in responding to negative information has to be done *before* the negative information appears, and that is to engage with communities of stakeholders as a long-term strategy. Companies that have active, mutually beneficial relationships with customers and other interested parties are less likely to be attacked unfairly online and more likely to survive such attacks if they do occur. In contrast, companies that ignore constituents or jump into "spin doctoring" mode when a negative situation occurs don't have the same credibility as companies that have done the long, hard work of fostering relationships within their physical and online communities.

- **Monitor the conversation.** If people are interested in what your company does, chances are they are blogging, tweeting, podcasting, posting videos, writing on Facebook walls, and otherwise sharing their opinions. Use the available technologies to listen to what people are saying.
- **Evaluate negative messages.** When you encounter negative messages, resist the urge to fire back immediately. Instead, evaluate the source, the tone, and the content of the message—and then choose a response that fits the situation. For example, the Public Affairs Agency of the U.S. Air Force groups senders of negative messages into four categories: "trolls" (those whose only intent is to stir up conflict), "ragers" (those who are just ranting or telling jokes), "the misguided" (those who are spreading incorrect information), and "unhappy customers" (those who have had a negative experience with the Air Force).
- **Respond appropriately.** After you have assessed a negative message, make the appropriate response based on an overall public relations plan. The Air Force, for instance, doesn't respond to trolls or ragers, responds to misguided messages with correct information, and responds to unhappy customers with efforts to rectify the situation and reach a reasonable solution. In addition to replying promptly, make sure your response won't make the situation even worse. For example, taking legal action against critics, even if technically justified, can rally people to their defense and create a public relations nightmare. In some instances, the best response can be to contact a critic privately (through direct messaging on Twitter, for example) to attempt a resolution away from the public forum.

Whatever you do, keep in mind that positive reputations are an important asset and need to be diligently guarded and defended. Everybody has a voice now, and some of those voices don't care to play by the rules of ethical communication.

COMMUNICATING IN A CRISIS

Some of the most critical instances of business communication occur during crises, which can include industrial accidents, crimes or scandals involving company employees, on-site hostage situations, terrorist attacks, information theft, product tampering incidents, and financial calamities. During a crisis, customers, employees, local communities, and others will demand information. In addition, rumors can spread unpredictably and uncontrollably. You can also expect the news media to descend quickly, asking questions of anyone they can find.

The key to successful communication efforts during a crisis is having a **crisis management plan**. In addition to defining operational procedures to deal with the crisis, this plan outlines communication tasks and responsibilities, which can include everything from media contacts to news release templates (see Table 9.3). The plan should clearly specify which people are authorized to speak for the company, provide contact information for all key executives, and include a list of the news outlets and social media tools that will be used to disseminate information.

Anticipation and planning are key to successful communication in a crisis.

Although you can't predict catastrophes, you can prepare for them. Analysis of corporate crises over the past several decades reveals that companies that respond quickly with the information people need tend to fare much better in the long run than those that go into hiding or release inconsistent or incorrect information.[13]

TABLE 9.3   How to Communicate in a Crisis

When a Crisis Hits:

Do	Don't
Prepare for trouble ahead of time by identifying potential problems, appointing and training a response team, and preparing and testing a crisis management plan.	Blame anyone for anything.
Get top management involved immediately.	Speculate in public.
Set up a news center for company representatives and the media that is equipped with phones, computers, and other electronic tools for preparing news releases and online updates. At the news center, take the following steps:	Refuse to answer questions.
	Release information that will violate anyone's right to privacy.
• Issue frequent news updates, and have trained personnel available to respond to questions around the clock.	Use the crisis to pitch products or services.
• Provide complete information packets to the media as soon as possible.	Play favorites with media representatives.
• Prevent conflicting statements, and provide continuity by appointing a single person trained in advance to speak for the company.	
• Tell receptionists and other employees to direct all phone calls to the designated spokesperson in the news center.	
• Provide updates when new information is available via blog postings, Twitter updates, text messaging, Facebook, and other appropriate media.	
Tell the whole story—openly, completely, and honestly. If you are at fault, apologize.	
Demonstrate the company's concern by your statements and your actions.	

7 LEARNING OBJECTIVE
Describe successful strategies for sending negative employment-related messages.

Sending Negative Employment Messages

As a manager, you will find yourself in a variety of situations in which you have to convey bad news to individual employees or potential employees. Recipients often have an emotional stake in your message, so taking the indirect approach is usually advised. In addition, use great care in choosing media for these messages. For instance, email and other written forms let you control the message and avoid personal confrontation, but one-on-one conversations are often viewed as more sensitive and give both sides the opportunity to ask and answer questions.

REFUSING REQUESTS FOR EMPLOYEE REFERENCES AND RECOMMENDATION LETTERS

Managers may get requests for recommendation letters from other employers and from past employees. When sending refusals to prospective employers who have requested information about past employees, your message can be brief and direct:

Implies that company policy prohibits the release of any more information but does provide what information is available

Ends on a positive note

> Our human resources department has authorized me to confirm that Yolanda Johnson worked for Tolson Logistics for three years, from June 2007 to July 2009. Best of luck as you interview applicants.

This message doesn't need to say, "We cannot comply with your request." It simply gives the reader all the information that is allowable.

Refusing an applicant's direct request for a recommendation letter is another matter. Any refusal to cooperate may seem to be a personal slight and a threat to the applicant's future. Diplomacy and preparation help readers accept your refusal:

This message tactfully avoids hurting the reader's feelings because it makes positive comments about the reader's recent activities, implies the refusal, suggests an alternative, and uses a polite close.

Thank you for letting me know about your job opportunity with Coca-Cola. Your internship there and the MBA you've worked so hard to earn should place you in an excellent position to land the marketing job.

Although we do not send out formal recommendations here at PepsiCo, I can certainly send Coca-Cola a confirmation of your employment dates. And if you haven't considered this already, be sure to ask several of your professors to write evaluations of your marketing skills. Best of luck to you in your career.

Uses the indirect approach because the other party is probably expecting a positive response

Announces that the writer cannot comply with the request, without explicitly blaming it on "policy"

Offers to fulfill as much of the request as possible and offers an alternative

Ends on a positive note

REFUSING SOCIAL NETWORKING RECOMMENDATION REQUESTS

Making recommendations in a social networking environment is more complicated than with a traditional recommendation letter because the endorsements you give become part of your online profile. On a network such as LinkedIn, others can see whom you've recommended and what you've written about these people. Much more so than with traditional letters, then, the recommendations you make in a social network become part of your personal brand.[14] Moreover, networks make it easy to find people and request recommendations, so you are likely to get more requests than you would have otherwise—and sometimes from people you don't know well.

Fortunately, social networks give you a bit more flexibility when responding to these requests. You can simply ignore or delete the request—some people make it personal policy to ignore requests from networkers they don't know. Of course, if you do know someone, ignoring a request could create an uncomfortable situation, so you will need to decide each case based on your relationship with the person. Another option is to refrain from making recommendations at all, and just letting people know this policy when they ask. Whatever you decide, remember that it is your choice.[15]

If you choose to make recommendations and want to respond to a request, you can write as much or as little information about the person as you are comfortable sharing. Unlike the situation with an offline recommendation, you don't need to write a complete letter. You can write a briefer statement, even just a single sentence that focuses on one positive aspect.[16] This flexibility allows you to respond positively in those situations in which you have mixed feelings about a person's overall abilities.

Social networks have created new challenges in recommendation requests, but they also offer more flexibility in responding to these requests.

REJECTING JOB APPLICATIONS

Application rejections are routine communications, but saying no is never easy, and recipients are emotionally invested in the decision. Moreover, companies must be aware of the possibility of employment discrimination lawsuits, which have been on the rise in recent years.[17] Of course, having fair and nondiscriminatory hiring practices is essential, but rejections must also be written in a way that doesn't inadvertently suggest any hint of discrimination. Expert opinions differ on the level of information to include in a rejection message, but the safest strategy is to avoid sharing any explanations for the company's decision and to avoid making or implying any promises of future consideration (see Figure 9.7 on the next page):[18]

Poorly written rejection letters tarnish your company's reputation and can even invite legal troubles.

- **Personalize the email message or letter by using the recipient's name.** For example, mail merge makes it easy to insert each recipient's name into a form letter.
- **Open with a courteous expression of appreciation for having applied.** In a sense, this is like the buffer in an indirect message because it gives you an opportunity to begin the conversation without immediately and bluntly telling the reader that his or her application has been rejected.
- **Convey the negative news politely and concisely.** The passive voice is helpful in this situation because it shifts focus away from the people involved and thereby depersonalizes the response. For example, "Your application was not among those selected for an interview" is less blunt than the active phrase "We have rejected your application."

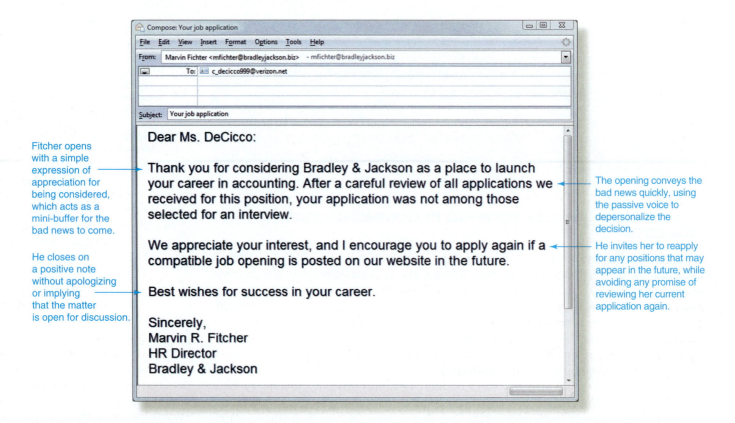

Fitcher opens with a simple expression of appreciation for being considered, which acts as a mini-buffer for the bad news to come.

He closes on a positive note without apologizing or implying that the matter is open for discussion.

The opening conveys the bad news quickly, using the passive voice to depersonalize the decision.

He invites her to reapply for any positions that may appear in the future, while avoiding any promise of reviewing her current application again.

Figure 9.7   Effective Message Rejecting a Job Applicant
This message rejecting a job applicant takes care to avoid making or implying any promises about future opportunities, beyond inviting the person to apply for positions that may appear in the future. Note that this would not be appropriate if the company did not believe the applicant was a good fit for the company in general.

- **Avoid explaining why an applicant was rejected or why other applicants were chosen instead.** Although it was once more common to offer such explanations, and some experts still advocate this approach, the simplest strategy from a legal standpoint is to avoid offering reasons for the decision. Avoiding explanations lowers the possibility that an applicant will perceive discrimination in the hiring decision or be tempted to challenge the reasons given.
- **Don't state or imply that the application will be reviewed at a later date.** Saying that "we will keep your résumé on file for future consideration" can create false hopes for the recipient and leave the company vulnerable to legal complaints if a future hiring decision is made without actually reviewing this candidate's application again. If the candidate might be a good fit for another position in the company in the future, you can suggest he or she reapply if a new job opening is posted.
- **Close with positive wishes for the applicant's career success.** A brief statement such as "We wish you success in your career" is sufficient.

Naturally, you should adjust your tactics to the circumstances. A simple and direct message is fine when someone has only submitted a job application, but rejecting a candidate who has made it at least partway through the interview process requires greater care. Personal contact has already been established through the interview process, so a phone call may be more appropriate.

GIVING NEGATIVE PERFORMANCE REVIEWS

An important goal of any performance evaluation is to give the employee a plan of action for improving his or her performance.

Performance reviews are designed to clarify job requirements, give employees feedback on their performance relative to those requirements, and establish a personal plan of action to ensure continued performance in the future. Performance reviews also help companies set organizational standards and communicate organizational values.[19] In addition, they document evidence of performance in the event that disciplinary action is needed or an employee later disputes management decisions regarding pay or promotions.[20]

The worst possible outcome in an annual review is a negative surprise, such as when an employee has been working toward different goals than the manager expects or has been unknowingly underperforming throughout the year but didn't receive any feedback or improvement coaching along the way.[21] To avoid negative surprises, managers should provide regular feedback and coaching as needed throughout the year if employee performance falls below expectations. In fact, some companies have gone so far as to abandon the traditional performance review altogether. The online retailer Zappos, for example, has replaced annual performance reviews with frequent status reports that give employees feedback on routine job tasks and an annual assessment of how well each employee embodies the company's core values.[22]

> By giving employees clear goals and regular feedback, you can help avoid unpleasant surprises in a performance review.

Regardless of the specific approach a company takes, writing an effective performance review requires careful, objective assessment and a clear statement of how well an employee has done relative to agreed-on goals. If you need to write a review that includes negative information, keep the following points in mind:[23]

- **Document performance problems.** You will need this information in order to write an effective appraisal and to support any decisions that need to be made about pay, promotions, or termination.
- **Evaluate all employees consistently.** Consistency is not only fair but also helps protect the company from claims of discriminatory practices.
- **Write in a calm, objective voice.** The employee is not likely to welcome your negative assessment, but you can manage the emotions of the situation by maintaining professional reserve in your writing.
- **Focus on opportunities for improvement.** This information can serve as the foundation for an improvement plan for the coming year.
- **Keep job descriptions up to date.** If a job evolves over time in response to changes in the business, the employees' current activities may no longer match an outdated job description.

> Negative evaluations should provide careful documentation of performance concerns.

TERMINATING EMPLOYMENT

If an employee's performance cannot be brought up to company standards or if factors such as declining sales cause a reduction in the workforce, a company often has no choice but to terminate employment. As with other negative employment messages, termination is fraught with emotions and legal ramifications, so careful planning, complete documentation, and sensitive writing are essential.

> Carefully word a termination message to avoid creating undue ill will and grounds for legal action.

Termination messages should always be written with input from the company's legal staff, but here are general writing guidelines to bear in mind:[24]

- Clearly present the reasons for this difficult action, whether it is the employee's performance or a business decision unrelated to performance.
- Make sure the reasons are presented in a way that cannot be construed as unfair or discriminatory.
- Follow company policy, contractual requirements, and applicable laws to the letter.
- Avoid personal attacks or insults of any kind.
- Ask another manager to review the letter before issuing it. An objective reviewer who isn't directly involved might spot troublesome wording or faulty reasoning.
- Deliver the termination letter in person if at all possible. Arrange a meeting that will ensure privacy and freedom from interruptions.

Any unplanned termination is clearly a negative outcome for both employer and employee, but careful attention to content and tone in the termination message can help the employee move on gracefully and minimize the misunderstandings and anger that can lead to expensive lawsuits. To review the tasks involved in this type of message, see "Checklist: Writing Negative Employment Messages."

For the latest information on writing negative messages, visit **http://real-timeupdates .com/ebc12** and click on Chapter 9.

CHECKLIST ✔ **Writing Negative Employment Messages**

A. Refusing requests for employee references and recommendations
- Don't feel obligated to write a recommendation letter if you don't feel comfortable doing so.
- Take a diplomatic approach to minimize hurt feelings.
- Compliment the reader's accomplishments.
- Suggest alternatives, if available.
- Use the options available to you on social networks, such as ignoring a request from someone you don't know or writing a recommendation on a single positive attribute.

B. Rejecting job applicants
- If possible, respond to all applications, even if you use only a form message to acknowledge receipt.
- If you use the direct approach, take care to avoid being blunt or cold.
- If you use the indirect approach, don't mislead the reader in your buffer or delay the bad news for more than a sentence or two.
- Avoid explaining why the applicant was rejected.
- Suggest alternatives if possible.

C. Giving negative performance reviews
- Document performance problems throughout the year.
- Evaluate all employees consistently.
- Keep job descriptions up to date as employee responsibilities change.
- Maintain an objective and unbiased tone.
- Use nonjudgmental language.
- Focus on problem resolution.
- Make sure negative feedback is documented and shared with the employee.
- Don't avoid confrontations by withholding negative feedback.
- Ask the employee for a commitment to improve.

D. Terminating employment
- State your reasons accurately and make sure they are objectively verifiable.
- Avoid statements that might expose your company to a wrongful termination lawsuit.
- Consult company lawyers to clarify all terms of the separation.
- Deliver the letter in person if at all possible.
- End the relationship on terms as positive as possible.

ON THE JOB: SOLVING COMMUNICATION DILEMMAS AT **HAILO**

As Hailo expands around the world, it faces the challenges every growing business faces. You recently joined the company as an app development manager in the New York office. Use what you've learned in this chapter to address the following challenges.

1. Another manager stopped by this morning with a request to borrow two of your best employees for a three-week emergency. Under normal conditions, you wouldn't hesitate to help, but your team has its own scheduling challenges to deal with. Plus, this isn't the first time this manager has run into trouble, and you are confident that poor project management is the reason. Which of the following is the most diplomatic way to state your refusal while suggesting that your colleague's management skills need improvement?

a. With the commitments I've made, I won't be able to bail you out this time.

b. I sympathize with the trouble you've gotten yourself into again, I really do, but the commitments I've made on my own projects prevents me from releasing any employees for temporary assignments.

c. The commitments I've made won't allow me to release any staff for temporary assignments. However, would you like to meet to discuss the techniques I've found useful for managing project workloads?

d. Instead of shifting resources around as usual, why don't we meet to discuss some new strategies for staffing and project management?

2. The HR department acts as an internal service provider, helping various departments throughout the company with hiring, benefits, training, and other employment functions. An HR rep is assigned to each division, working with the managers and employees in that department, but reporting to HR managers. As in all other professional relationships, personal aspects can enter the relationship. Even competent professionals can start to rub each other the wrong way at a personal level, which can corrode the business relationship over time. Unfortunately, that has happened with one of your best staff members. Geri Lamb is widely admired for her HR skills, but the general manager of the department where she is assigned has asked you to replace her with a new HR representative. Although you'd prefer to tell Lamb in person, schedule conflicts dictate that you send her an email. Which of these buffers would be the best way to open the message?

a. Your work for the customer support department continues to be first rate, but you never can tell how these things are going to work out, can you?

b. If it were up to me, Geri, I would never deliver a message like this, but the customer support department has asked me to reevaluate the HR staffing assignments.

c. As I've expressed on many occasions, thank you once again for the top-quality work you've done for the customer support department over the years.

d. As you know, Geri, I continually evaluate the HR staffing assignments to make sure the various departments are satisfied with the quality of our work and the overall nature of our relationship with them.

3. Although your project management skills are quite good, you occasionally overlook something or run into unforeseen circumstances. Halfway through the installation of a new applicant tracking system, you realized that you underestimated the complexity of linking this new technology to the company's information systems. You now have the unpleasant task of explaining to your boss that the project will be coming in at least 20 percent over budget and possibly as high as 30 percent over. Which of the following is the best way to begin an email message to your boss?

a. I messed up, big time. The applicant tracking project is going to come in over budget.

b. The applicant tracking project is going to come in at least 20 percent over budget and possibly as much as 30 percent over.

c. I recently discovered that linking the applicant tracking to our existing IT systems was more complicated than anyone realized when I established the budget for this project. As a result of the extra work required to customize the software, the project is going to run 20 to 30 percent over budget.

d. I recently discovered that linking the applicant tracking system to our existing IT systems was more complicated than anyone realized when we established the budget for this project. The fact that there is extra work is not really my fault, per se, since it would've been necessary in any case, but as a result of the extra work required to customize the software, the project is going to run 20 to 30 percent over budget.

4. You've found it easy to say "yes" to recommendation letter requests from former employees who were top performers, and you've learned to say "no" to people who didn't perform so well. The requests you struggle with are from employees in the middle, people who didn't really excel but didn't really cause any trouble, either. You've just received a request from an HR specialist who falls smack in the middle of the middle. Unfortunately, he's applying for a job at a firm that you know places high demands on its employees and generally hires the best of the best. He's a great person, and you'd love to help, but in your heart, you know that if by some chance he does get the job, he probably won't last. Plus, you don't want to get a reputation in the industry for recommending weak candidates. How do you set the stage for the negative news?

a. As your former manager, I'd like to think I can still look out for your best interests, and I'm sorry to say, but based on what I know about the position you're applying for, this might not be the best career move for you at this point.

b. In my view, the responsibility of writing a letter of recommendation goes beyond simply assessing a person's skills; it must consider whether the person is applying for the right job.

c. One of the most important factors I consider when deciding whether to endorse an applicant is whether he or she is pursuing an opportunity that offers a high probability of success.

d. Writing recommendation letters bears a heavy responsibility for the job applicant and the person writing the letter. After all, I have my own reputation to protect, too.

Learning Objectives Checkup

Assess your understanding of the principles in this chapter by reading each learning objective and studying the accompanying exercises. You can check your responses against the answer key on page 599.

Objective 9.1: Apply the three-step writing process to negative messages.

1. Which of the following should be a goal of every negative message?
   a. To convey the bad news clearly
   b. To gain audience acceptance for the news
   c. To maintain as much goodwill as possible with the audience
   d. To maintain a good image for your organization
   e. To reduce or eliminate the need for future correspondence on the matter, if appropriate
   f. None of the above
   g. (a), (c), and (d)
   h. All of the above

2. Which of the following is an effective way to maintain the "you" attitude when crafting negative messages?
   a. Make sure the reader clearly understands that he or she is at fault; after all, recognizing a mistake is the first step toward improvement.
   b. Make it clear that you don't enjoy giving out bad news.
   c. Show respect for the reader by "soft peddling" the negative news, implying it without really coming out and saying it directly.
   d. Show respect for the reader by avoiding negative, accusatory language and emphasizing positives whenever possible.

Objective 9.2: Explain how to use the direct approach effectively when conveying negative news.

3. When using the direct approach with negative messages, you begin with
   a. A buffer
   b. An attention-getter
   c. The bad news
   d. Any of the above

4. An advantage of using the direct approach with negative messages is that it
   a. Saves readers time by helping them reach the main idea more quickly
   b. Eases readers into the message
   c. Is diplomatic
   d. Does all of the above

Objective 9.3: Explain how to use the indirect approach effectively when conveying negative news.

5. When using the indirect approach with negative messages, you begin with
   a. A buffer
   b. An attention-getter
   c. The bad news
   d. Any of the above
6. Which of the following is an advantage of using the indirect approach with negative messages?
   a. Most readers prefer the direct approach for such messages.
   b. It makes a shorter message possible.
   c. It eases the reader into the message.
   d. It does all of the above.
7. The purpose of using the indirect approach is to
   a. Help the writer avoid the unpleasant task of delivering bad news
   b. Help the reader avoid the unpleasant task of receiving bad news
   c. Soften the blow of the bad news for the reader
   d. Reduce the word count in your messages
8. A/an _____ is a neutral, noncontroversial opening statement that establishes common ground with your reader.
9. Which of the following is a good possibility to consider for use in writing a buffer?
   a. Look for subtle opportunities to promote your company and its products.
   b. Assure the reader that your company always follows all applicable laws and regulations.
   c. Indicate your understanding of the reader's situation.
   d. All of the above are useful approaches.

Objective 9.4: Explain the importance of maintaining high standards of ethics and etiquette when delivering negative messages.

10. Which of the following is an important reason to take particular care to maintain ethics and etiquette when crafting negative messages?
    a. In many cases, the communicator needs to adhere to a variety of laws and regulations when delivering negative messages.
    b. Good ethical practice demands care and sensitivity in the content and delivery of negative messages because these messages can have a profoundly negative effect on the people who receive them.
    c. Communicators need to manage their own emotions when crafting and distributing negative messages while at the same time considering the emotional needs of their audiences.
    d. All of the above are important reasons to maintain ethics and etiquette in negative messages.

11. Which of the following is most characteristic of organizational cultures that emphasize open communication?
    a. Managers are willing to listen to bad news from employees, but they understand if employees don't want to deliver bad news.
    b. Managers expect employees to alert them to problems so that corrective action can be taken.
    c. Managers reward employees who deliver bad news with extra vacation time, extra pay, or both.
    d. None of the above are true.

Objective 9.5: Describe successful strategies for sending negative messages on routine business matters.

12. If you need to reject a solicited proposal from an employee, which of the following approaches is best?
    a. Use the indirect approach, but avoid explaining exactly why the proposal does not meet your needs; it's up to the employee to figure that out.
    b. Use the direct approach; rejected proposals are a fact of life of business.
    c. Use the indirect approach, and provide a thoughtful and complete explanation of why the proposal does not meet your needs.
    d. Don't respond at all; doing so will only create an uncomfortable situation for the employee.
13. Which of the following is not a normal goal when sending bad-news messages about transactions?
    a. Modifying the customer's expectations
    b. Explaining how you plan to resolve the situation
    c. Identifying who is responsible for the situation so that the customer understands you are serious about correcting the error
    d. Repair whatever damage might have been done to the business relationship

Objective 9.6: List the important points to consider when conveying negative organizational news.

14. Which of the following best characterizes the nature of crisis management planning?
    a. Good managers should be able to anticipate the specific crisis scenarios their companies might encounter and therefore should be able to plan for every crisis in a specific way.
    b. Faced with everything from terrorism to technological disasters, there's no way for managers to anticipate which crisis might hit any given business, so it's a waste of time to plan a response.
    c. Although you can't anticipate the nature and circumstance of every possible crisis, you can prepare by deciding how to handle such issues as communication with employees and the public.
    d. Only negatively focused managers worry about crisis planning; positive managers keep their organizations moving toward company goals.
15. Continuing advances in communication technology make it
    a. Easier to control rumors through Internet filters and other means
    b. More difficult to control rumors

c. Easier to find the people who start rumors

d. Illegal to spread false rumors about public corporations

Objective 9.7: Describe successful strategies for sending negative employment-related messages.

16. Why do many experts recommend using the indirect approach when rejecting job applicants?

  a. Applicants have a deep emotional investment in the decision.

  b. Laws in most states require the indirect approach.

  c. The indirect approach is easier to write.

  d. The indirect approach is shorter.

17. When explaining why an applicant wasn't chosen for a position, you should

  a. Be specific without being too personal, such as explaining that the position requires specific skills that the applicant doesn't yet possess

  b. Point out the person's shortcomings as that's the honest way and the only way the person knows what he or she need to improve

  c. Be as vague as possible to avoid hurting the person's feelings

  d. Avoid explaining why an applicant wasn't chosen

Quick Learning Guide

CHAPTER OUTLINE

Using the Three-Step Writing Process for Negative Messages

Step 1: Planning a Negative Message

Step 2: Writing a Negative Message

Step 3: Completing a Negative Message

Using the Direct Approach for Negative Messages

Opening with a Clear Statement of the Bad News

Providing Reasons and Additional Information

Closing on a Respectful Note

Using the Indirect Approach for Negative Messages

Opening with a Buffer

Providing Reasons and Additional Information

Continuing with a Clear Statement of the Bad News

Closing on a Respectful Note

Maintaining High Standards of Ethics and Etiquette

Sending Negative Messages on Routine Business Matters

Making Negative Announcements on Routine Business Matters

Rejecting Suggestions and Proposals

Refusing Routine Requests

Handling Bad News About Transactions

Refusing Claims and Requests for Adjustment

Sending Negative Organizational News

Communicating Under Normal Circumstances

Responding to Negative Information in a Social Media Environment

Communicating in a Crisis

Sending Negative Employment Messages

Refusing Requests for Employee References and Recommendation Letters

Refusing Social Networking Recommendation Requests

Rejecting Job Applications

Giving Negative Performance Reviews

Terminating Employment

LEARNING OBJECTIVES

1 Apply the three-step writing process to negative messages. (page 252)

2 Explain how to use the direct approach effectively when conveying negative news. (page 255)

3 Explain how to use the indirect approach effectively when conveying negative news. (page 257)

4 Explain the importance of maintaining high standards of ethics and etiquette when delivering negative messages. (page 261)

5 Describe successful strategies for sending negative messages on routine business matters. (page 263)

6 List the important points to consider when conveying negative organizational news. (page 267)

7 Describe successful strategies for sending negative employment-related messages. (page 270)

KEY TERMS

buffer A neutral, noncontroversial statement that establishes common ground with the reader in an indirect negative message

crisis management plan Plan that defines operational procedures to deal with a crisis, including communication tasks and responsibilities

performance review Employee evaluation procedure giving feedback on performance and guidance for future efforts

whistle-blowing Efforts by employees to report concerns about unethical or illegal behavior

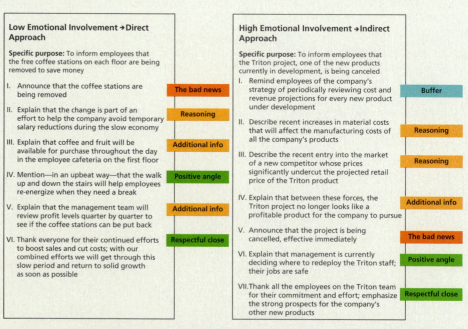

Figure 9.1 Comparing the Direct and Indirect Approaches for Negative Messages

The direct and indirect approaches differ in two important ways: the position of the bad news within the sequence of message points and the use of a *buffer* in the indirect approach. ("Using the Indirect Approach for Negative Messages" on page 258 explains the use of a buffer.) Both these messages deal with changes made in response to negative financial developments, but the second example represents a much higher emotional impact for readers, so the indirect approach is called for in that case. Figure 9.2 explains how to choose the right approach for each situation.

Apply Your Knowledge

To review chapter content related to each question, refer to the indicated Learning Objective.

9.1. Would you choose the direct or indirect approach to announce that a popular employee benefit is being eliminated for cost reasons? Why? [LO-1]

★ **9.2.** Can you express sympathy with someone's negative situation without apologizing for the circumstances? Explain your answer. [LO-2]

9.3. Is intentionally deemphasizing bad news the same as distorting graphs and charts to deemphasize unfavorable data? Why or why not? [LO-3]

9.4. Why is it important to be engaged with stakeholders before trying to use social media during a crisis or other negative scenario? [LO-6]

★ **9.5.** If your social media monitoring efforts pick up a tweet that accuses your customer service staff of lying and claims to have evidence to back it up, how would you respond? [LO-6]

9.6. How would you respond to a LinkedIn network connection who asks for a recommendation when you barely remember working with this person and don't remember whether she was good at her job? [LO-7]

Practice Your Skills

Messages for Analysis

Read the following messages and then (1) analyze the strengths and weaknesses of each sentence and (2) revise each message so that it follows this chapter's guidelines.

9.7. Message 9.A: Sending Negative Organizational News [LO-6]

From: M. Juhasz, Travel & Meeting Services
To: [mailing list]
Subject: Travel

Dear Traveling Executives:

We need you to start using some of the budget suggestions we are going to issue as a separate memorandum. These include using videoconference equipment and web conferencing instead of traveling to meetings, staying in cheaper hotels, arranging flights for cheaper times, and flying from less-convenient but also less-expensive suburban airports.

The company needs to cut travel expenses by fifty percent, just as we've cut costs in all departments of Black & Decker. This means you'll no longer be able to stay in fancy hotels and make last-minute, costly changes to your travel plans.

You'll also be expected to avoid hotel surcharges for phone calls and Internet access. If the hotel you want to stay in

doesn't offer free wireless, go somewhere else. And never, NEVER return a rental car with an empty tank! That causes the rental agency to charge us a premium price for the gas they sell when they fill it up upon your return.

You'll be expected to make these changes in your travel habits immediately.

Sincerely,
M. Juhasz
Travel & Meeting Services

9.8. Message 9.B: Refusing Requests for Claims and Adjustments [LO-5]

I am responding to your letter of about six weeks ago asking for an adjustment on your wireless hub, model WM39Z. We test all our products before they leave the factory; therefore, it could not have been our fault that your hub didn't work.

If you or someone in your office dropped the unit, it might have caused the damage. Or the damage could have been caused by the shipper if he dropped it. If so, you should file a claim with the shipper. At any rate, it wasn't our fault. The parts are already covered by warranty. However, we will provide labor for the repairs for $50, which is less than our cost, since you are a valued customer.

We will have a booth at the upcoming trade show there and hope to see you or someone from your office. We have many new models of hubs, routers, and other computer gear that we're sure you'll want to see. I've enclosed our latest catalog. Hope to see you there.

9.9. Message 9.C: Rejecting Job Applications [LO-7]

I regret to inform you that you were not selected for our summer intern program at Equifax. We had over a thousand résumés and cover letters to go through and simply could not get to them all. We have been asked to notify everyone that we have already selected students for the 25 positions based on those who applied early and were qualified.

We're sure you will be able to find a suitable position for summer work in your field and wish you the best of luck. We deeply regret any inconvenience associated with our reply.

Exercises

Each activity is labeled according to the primary skill or skills you will need to use. To review relevant chapter content, you can refer to the indicated Learning Objective. In some instances, supporting information will be found in another chapter, as indicated.

Planning: Choosing the Direct or Indirect Approach [LO-1]
Select which approach you would use (direct or indirect) for the following negative messages.

9.10. An email message to your boss, informing her that one of your key clients is taking its business to a different accounting firm

9.11. An email message to a customer, informing her that one of the books she ordered over the Internet is temporarily out of stock

9.12. An instant message to a customer, explaining that the DVD recorder he ordered for his new computer is on backorder and that, as a consequence, the shipping of the entire order will be delayed

9.13. A blog post to all employees, notifying them that the company parking lot will be repaved during the first week of June and that the company will provide a shuttle service from a remote parking lot during that period

9.14. A letter from a travel agent to a customer, stating that the airline will not refund her money for the flight she missed but that her tickets are valid for one year

9.15. A form letter from a U.S. airline to a customer, explaining that the company cannot extend the expiration date of the customer's frequent flyer miles even though the customer was living overseas for the past three years and unable to use the miles during that time

9.16. A letter from an insurance company to a policyholder, denying a claim for reimbursement for a special medical procedure that is not covered under the terms of the customer's policy

9.17. A letter from an electronics store, stating that the customer will not be reimbursed for a malfunctioning mobile phone that is still under warranty (because the terms of the warranty do not cover damages to phones that were accidentally dropped from a moving car)

9.18. An announcement to the repairs department, listing parts that are on backorder and will be three weeks late

9.19. **Message Strategies: Refusing Routine Requests [LO-4]** As a customer service supervisor for a mobile phone company, you're in charge of responding to customers' requests for refunds. You've just received an email from a customer who unwittingly ran up a $550 bill for data charges after forgetting to disable his smartphone's WiFi hotspot feature. The customer says it wasn't his fault because he didn't know his roommates were using his phone to get free Internet access. However, you've dealt with this situation before and provided a notice to all customers to be careful about excess data charges resulting from the use of the hotspot capability. Draft a short buffer (one or two sentences) for your email reply, sympathizing with the customer's plight but preparing him for the bad news (that company policy specifically prohibits refunds in such cases).

Etiquette: Communicating with Sensitivity and Tact; Collaboration: Team Projects [LO-4] Working alone, revise the following statements to deemphasize the bad news. Then team up with a classmate and read each other's revisions. Did you both use the same approach in every case? Which approach seems to be most effective for each of the revised statements?

9.20. The airline can't refund your money. The "Conditions" section on the back of your ticket states that there are no refunds for missed flights. Sometimes the airline makes exceptions, but only when life and death are involved. Of course, your ticket is still valid and can be used on a flight to the same destination.

9.21. I'm sorry to tell you, we can't supply the custom decorations you requested. We called every supplier, and none of them can do what you want on such short notice. You can, however, get a standard decorative package on the

same theme in time. I found a supplier that stocks these. Of course, it won't have quite the flair you originally requested.

9.22. We can't refund your money for the malfunctioning MP3 player. You shouldn't have immersed the unit in water while swimming; the users' manual clearly states that the unit is not designed to be used in adverse environments.

9.23. **Communication Ethics [LO-4]** The insurance company where you work is planning to raise all premiums for health-care coverage. Your boss has asked you to read a draft of her letter to customers announcing the new, higher rates. The first two paragraphs discuss some exciting medical advances and the expanded coverage offered by your company. Only in the final paragraph do customers learn that they will have to pay more for coverage starting next year. What are the ethical implications of this draft? What changes would you suggest?

9.24. **Sending Negative Organizational News [LO-6]** Public companies occasionally need to issue news releases to announce or explain downturns in sales, profits, demand, or other business factors. Search the web to locate a company that has issued a press release that recently reported lower earnings or other bad news and access the news release on the firm's website. You can also search for press releases at **www.prnewswire .com** or **www.businesswire.com**. How does the headline relate to the main message of the release? Is the release organized according to the direct or the indirect approach? What does the company do to present the bad news in a favorable light—and does this effort seem sincere and ethical to you?

Expand Your Skills

Critique the Professionals

Locate an example online of a negative-news message from any company. Possible examples include announcements of product recalls, poor financial results, layoffs, and fines or other legal troubles. Analyze the approach the company took; was it the most effective strategy possible? Did the company apologize, if doing so would have been appropriate under the circumstances, and does the apology seem sincere? Does the tone of the message match the seriousness of the situation? Does the message end on a positive note, as appropriate? Using whatever medium your instructor requests, write a brief analysis of the message (no more than one page), citing specific elements from the piece and support from the chapter.

Sharpening Your Career Skills Online

Bovée and Thill's Business Communication Web Search, at **http://websearch.businesscommunicationnetwork.com**, is a unique research tool designed specifically for business communication research. Use the Web Search function to find a website, video, PDF document, podcast, or PowerPoint presentation that offers advice on writing messages that convey negative information. Write a brief email message to your instructor, describing the item you found and summarizing the career skills information you learned from it.

Improve Your Grammar, Mechanics, and Usage

The following exercises help you improve your knowledge of and power over English grammar, mechanics, and usage. Turn to the "Handbook of Grammar, Mechanics, and Usage" at the end of this book and review all of Section 2.6 (Commas). Then look at the following 10 items and indicate the letter of the preferred choice in the following groups of sentences. (Answers to these exercises appear on page 601.)

9.25. **a.** Please send us four cases of filters two cases of wing nuts and a bale of rags.
b. Please send us four cases of filters, two cases of wing nuts and a bale of rags.
c. Please send us four cases of filters, two cases of wing nuts, and a bale of rags.

9.26. **a.** Your analysis, however, does not account for returns.
b. Your analysis however does not account for returns.
c. Your analysis, however does not account for returns.

9.27. **a.** As a matter of fact she has seen the figures.
b. As a matter of fact, she has seen the figures.

9.28. **a.** Before May 7, 1999, they wouldn't have minded.
b. Before May 7, 1999 they wouldn't have minded.

9.29. **a.** Stoneridge Inc. will go public on September 9 2018.
b. Stoneridge, Inc., will go public on September 9, 2018.
c. Stoneridge Inc. will go public on September 9, 2018.

9.30. **a.** "Talk to me" Sandra said "before you change a thing."
b. "Talk to me," Sandra said "before you change a thing."
c. "Talk to me," Sandra said, "before you change a thing."

9.31. **a.** The firm was founded during the long hard recession of the mid-1970s.
b. The firm was founded during the long, hard recession of the mid-1970s.
c. The firm was founded during the long hard, recession of the mid-1970s.

9.32. **a.** You can reach me at this address: 717 Darby St., Scottsdale, AZ 85251.
b. You can reach me at this address: 717 Darby St., Scottsdale AZ 85251.
c. You can reach me at this address: 717 Darby St., Scottsdale, AZ, 85251.

9.33. **a.** Transfer the documents from Fargo, North Dakota to Boise, Idaho.
b. Transfer the documents from Fargo North Dakota, to Boise Idaho.
c. Transfer the documents from Fargo, North Dakota, to Boise, Idaho.

9.34. **a.** Sam O'Neill the designated representative is gone today.
b. Sam O'Neill, the designated representative, is gone today.
c. Sam O'Neill, the designated representative is gone today.

For additional exercises focusing on commas, visit MyBCommLab. Click on Chapter 9, click on Additional Exercises to Improve Your Grammar, Mechanics, and Usage, and then click on 14. Fused sentences and comma splices.

Cases

Website links for selected companies mentioned in cases can be found in the Student Assignments section at **http://real-time updates.com/ebc12**.

Negative Messages on Routine Business Matters

EMAIL SKILLS

9.35. Message Strategies: Rejecting Suggestions and Proposals; Communication Ethics: Making Ethical Choices [LO-5] Knowing how much online product reviews can shape consumer behavior, the other co-founder of your company has just circulated an internal email message with the not-so-subtle hint that everyone in your small startup should pose as happy customers and post glowing reviews of your new product on Amazon and other shopping sites. You're horrified at the idea—not only is this highly unethical, but if (or more likely when) the scheme is exposed, the company's reputation will be severely damaged.

Your task: You would prefer to address this in a private conversation, but because your partner has already pitched the idea to everyone via email, you have no choice but to respond via email as well. You need to act quickly before anyone acts on the suggestion. Write a response, explaining why this is a bad idea and telling employees not to do it. Keep in mind that you are chastising your business partner in front of all your employees. Make up any names or other details you need.

MICROBLOGGING SKILLS

9.36. Message Strategies: Making Routine Negative Announcements [LO-5] Professional musicians do everything they can to keep the show going, particularly for tours that are scheduled months in advance. However, illness and other unforeseeable circumstances can force an act to cancel shows, even after all the tickets have been sold.

Your task: Choose one of you favorite musical acts and assume that you are the tour manager who needs to tell 25,000 fans that an upcoming concert must be canceled because of illness. Ticket holders can apply for a refund at the artist's website or keep their tickets for a future concert date, which will be identified and announced as soon as possible. Write two tweets, one announcing the cancelation and one outlining the options for ticket holders.

Make up any information you need, and send your tweets to your instructor via email (don't actually tweet them!).

EMAIL SKILLS

9.37. Message Strategies: Rejecting Suggestions and Proposals [LO-5]

Walter Joss is one of the best employees in your department, a smart and hard worker with a keen mind for business. His upbeat attitude has helped the entire department get through some rough times recently, and on a personal level, his wise counsel helped you grow into a leadership role when you were promoted to marketing manager several years ago.

You generally welcome Joss's input on the department's operations, and you have implemented several of his ideas to improve the company's marketing efforts. However, the proposal he emailed you yesterday was not his best work, to put it mildly. He proposed that the company dump the advertising agency it has used for a decade and replace it with some new agency you've never heard of. The only reasons he offered were that the agency "had become unresponsive" and that a "smaller agency could meet our needs better." He failed to address any of the other criteria that are used to select advertising agencies, such as costs, creative skills, technical abilities, geographic reach, research capabilities, and media experience.

This is the first you've heard any criticism of the agency, and in fact, their work has helped your company increase sales every year.

Your task: Draft an email message to Joss, rejecting his proposal. (Note that in a real-life setting, you would want to discuss this with Joss in person, rather than through email, but use email for the purposes of this exercise.)

EMAIL SKILLS

9.38. Message Strategies: Making Routine Negative Announcements [LO-5]

You've been proud of many things your gardening tool company has accomplished as it grew from just you working in your basement shop to a nationally known company that employs more than 200 people. However, nothing made you prouder than the company's Helping Our Hometown Grow program, in which employees volunteer on company time to help residents in your city start their own vegetable gardens, using tools donated by the company. Nearly 50 employees participated directly, helping some 500 families supplement their grocery budgets with home-grown produce. Virtually everyone in the company contributed, though, because employees who didn't volunteer to help in the gardens pitched in to cover the work responsibilities of the volunteers.

Sadly, 10 years after you launched the program, you have reached the inescapable conclusion that the company can no longer afford to keep the program going. With consumers around the country still struggling with the after-effects of a deep recession, sales have been dropping for the past three years—even as lower cost competitors step up their presence in the market. To save the program, you would have to lay off several employees, but your employees come first.

Your task: Write an email to the entire company, announcing the cancellation of the program.

TELEPHONE SKILLS

9.39. Message Strategies: Making Routine Negative Announcements [LO-5]

Vail Products of Toledo, Ohio, manufactured a line of beds for use in hospitals and other institutions that have a need to protect patients who might otherwise fall out of bed and injure themselves (including patients with cognitive impairments or patterns of spasms or seizures). These "enclosed bed systems" use a netted canopy to keep patients in bed rather than the traditional method of using physical restraints such as straps or tranquilizing drugs. The intent is humane, but the design is flawed: At least 30 patients have become trapped in the various parts of the mattress and canopy structure, and 8 of them have suffocated.

Working with the U.S. Food and Drug Administration (FDA), Vail issued a recall on the beds, as manufacturers often do in the case of unsafe products. However, the recall is not really a recall. Vail will not be replacing or modifying the beds, nor will it accept returns. Instead, the company is urging institutions to move patients to other beds, if possible. Vail has also sent out revised manuals and warning labels to be placed on the beds. The company also announced that it is ceasing production of enclosed beds.

Your task: A flurry of phone calls from concerned patients, family members, and institutional staff is overwhelming the support staff. As a writer in Vail's corporate communications office, you've been asked to draft a short script to be recorded on the company's phone system. When people call the main number, they'll hear "Press 1 for information regarding the recall of Model 500, Model 1000, and Model 2000 enclosed beds." After they press 1, they'll hear the message you're about to write, explaining that although the action is classified as a recall, Vail will not be accepting returned beds, nor will it replace any of the affected beds. The message should also assure customers that Vail has already sent revised operating manuals and warning labels to every registered owner of the beds in question. The phone system has limited memory, and you've been directed to keep the message to 75 words or less.[25]

MICROBLOGGING SKILLS

9.40. Message Strategies: Making Routine Negative Announcements [LO-5]

JetBlue was one of the first companies to incorporate the Twitter microblogging service into its customer communications, and thousands of fliers and fans now follow the airline's Twittering staff members. Messages include announcements about fare sales (such as limited-time auctions on eBay or special on-site sales at shopping malls), celebrations of company milestones (such as the opening of the carrier's new terminal at New York's JFK airport), schedule updates, and even personalized responses to people who Twitter with questions or complaints about the company.[26]

Your task: Write a Tweet alerting JetBlue customers to the possibility that Hurricane Isaac might disrupt flight schedules from August 13 through August 15. Tell them that decisions about delays and cancellations will be made on a city-by-city basis and will be announced on Twitter and the company's website. The URL will take 20 characters, so you have 120 characters (including spaces) for your message.

BLOGGING SKILLS / PORTFOLIO BUILDER

9.41. Message Strategies: Making Routine Negative Announcements [LO-5]   Marketing specialists usually celebrate when target audiences forward their messages to friends and family—essentially acting as unpaid advertising and sales representatives. In fact, the practice of viral marketing is based on this hope. For one Starbucks regional office, however, viral marketing started to make the company just a bit sick. The office sent employees in the Southeast an email coupon for a free iced drink and invited them to share the coupon with family and friends. To the surprise of virtually no one who understands the nature of online life, the email coupon multiplied rapidly, to the point that Starbucks stores all around the country were quickly overwhelmed with requests for free drinks. The company decided to immediately terminate the free offer, a month ahead of the expiration date on the coupon.[27]

Your task: Write a one-paragraph message that can be posted on the Starbucks website and at individual stores, apologizing for the mix-up and explaining that the offer is no longer valid.

EMAIL SKILLS

9.42. Message Strategies: Refusing Claims and Requests for Adjustment [LO-5]   Your company markets a line of rugged smartphone cases designed to protect the sensitive devices from drops, spills, and other common accidents. Your guarantee states that you will reimburse customers for the cost of a new phone if the case fails to protect it from any of the following: (a) a drop of no more than 6 feet onto any surface; (b) spills of any beverage or common household chemical; (c) being crushed by any object of up to 100 pounds; or (d) being chewed on by dogs, cats, or other common household pets.

Jack Simmons, a rancher from Wyoming, emailed your customer support staff, requesting a reimbursement after he dropped his iPhone in his hog barn and a 900-pound boar crushed it in a single bite.

Your task: Write an email response to the customer, denying his request for a new phone.

PODCASTING SKILLS

9.43. Message Strategies: Negative Announcements on Routine Matters [LO-5]   An employee concierge seemed like a great idea when you added it as an employee benefit last year. The concierge handles a wide variety of personal chores for employees, everything from dropping off dry cleaning to ordering event tickets to sending flowers. Employees love the service, and you know that the time they save can be devoted to work or family activities. Unfortunately, profits are way down, and concierge usage is up—up so far that you'll need to add a second concierge to keep up with the demand. As painful as it will be for everyone, you decide that the company needs to stop offering the service.

Your task: Script a brief podcast, announcing the decision and explaining why it is necessary. Make up any details you need. If your instructor asks you to do so, record your podcast and submit the file.

EMAIL SKILLS / PORTFOLIO BUILDER

9.44. Message Strategies: Negative Announcements on Routine Matters [LO-5]   You can certainly sympathize with employees when they complain about having their email and instant messages monitored, but you're implementing a company policy that all employees agree to abide by when they join the company. Your firm, Webcor Builders of San Mateo, California, is one of the estimated 60 percent of U.S. companies with such monitoring systems in place. More and more companies use these systems (which typically operate by scanning messages for keywords that suggest confidential, illegal, or otherwise inappropriate content) in an attempt to avoid instances of sexual harassment and other problems.

As the chief information officer, the manager in charge of computer systems in the company, you're often the target when employees complain about being monitored. Consequently, you know you're really going to hear it when employees learn that the monitoring program will be expanded to personal blogs as well.

Your task: Write an email message to be distributed to the entire workforce, explaining that the automated monitoring program is about to be expanded to include employees' personal blogs. Explain that, while you sympathize with employee concerns regarding privacy and freedom of speech, it is the management team's responsibility to protect the company's intellectual property and the value of the company name. Therefore, employees' personal blogs will be added to the monitoring system to ensure that employees don't intentionally or accidentally expose company secrets or criticize management in a way that could harm the company.[28]

LETTER WRITING SKILLS

9.45. Message Strategies: Negative Announcements on Routine Matters [LO-5]   Your company, PolicyPlan Insurance Services, is a 120-employee insurance claims processor based in Milwaukee. PolicyPlan has engaged Midwest Sparkleen for interior and exterior cleaning for the past five years. Midwest Sparkleen did exemplary work for the first four years, but after a change of ownership last year, the level of service has plummeted. Offices are no longer cleaned thoroughly, you've had to call the company at least six times to remind them to take care of spills and other messes they're supposed to address routinely, and they've left toxic cleaning chemicals in a public hallway on several occasions. You have spoken with the owner about your concerns twice in the past three months, but his assurances that service would improve have not resulted in any noticeable improvements. When the evening cleaning crew forgot to lock the lobby door last Thursday—leaving your entire facility vulnerable to theft from midnight until 8:00 Friday morning—you decided it was time for a change.

Your task: Write a letter to Jason Allred, owner of Midwest Sparkleen, 4000 South Howell Avenue, Milwaukee, WI, 53207, telling him that PolicyPlan will not be renewing its annual cleaning contract with Midwest Sparkleen when the current contract expires at the end of this month. Cite the examples identified above, and keep the tone of your letter professional.

Negative Organizational News

MICROBLOGGING SKILLS

9.46. Message Strategies: Responding to Rumors [LO-6] Sheila Elliot, a well-known actress, appeared on a national talk show last night and claimed that your company's Smoothstone cookware was responsible for her toddler's learning disability. Elliot claimed that the nonstick surfaces of Smoothstone pots and pans contain a dangerous chemical that affected her child's cognitive development. There's just one problem with her story—well, three problems, actually: (a) your company's cookware line is called Moonstone, not Smoothstone; (b) Moonstone does not contain and never has contained the chemical Elliot mentioned; and (c) the product she is really thinking of was called Smoothfire, which was made by another company and was pulled off the market five years ago.

Thousands of worried parents aren't waiting for the fact checkers, however. They took to the blogosphere and Twittersphere with a vengeance overnight, warning people to throw away anything made by your company (Tatum Housewares). Several television stations have already picked up the Twitter chatter and repeated the rumor. Retailers are already calling your sales staff to cancel orders.

Your task: Write a three-message sequence to be posted on your company's Twitter account, correcting the rumor and conveying the three points outlined above. Each message will include a URL linking to your company's website, so restrict each message to 120 characters, including spaces.

BLOGGING SKILLS

9.47. Message Strategies: Negative Organizational Announcements [LO-6] XtremityPlus is known for its outlandish extreme-sports products, and the Looney Launch is no exception. Fulfilling the dream of every childhood daredevil, the Looney Launch is an aluminum and fiberglass contraption that quickly unfolds to create the ultimate bicycle jump. The product has been selling as fast as you can make it, even though it comes plastered with warning labels proclaiming that its use is inherently dangerous.

As XtremityPlus's CEO, you were nervous about introducing this product, and your fears were just confirmed: You've been notified of the first lawsuit by a parent whose child broke several bones after crash-landing off a Looney Launch.

Your task: Write a post for your internal blog, explaining that the Looney Launch is being removed from the market immediately. Tell your employees to expect some negative reactions from enthusiastic customers and retailers, but explain that (a) the company can't afford the risk of additional lawsuits, and (b) even for XtremityPlus, the Looney Launch pushes the envelope a bit too far. The product is simply too dangerous to sell in good conscience.

BLOGGING SKILLS / PORTFOLIO BUILDER

9.48. Message Strategies: Communicating in a Crisis [LO-6] One of your company's worst nightmares has just come true. EQ Industrial Services (EQIS), based in Wayne, Michigan, operates a number of facilities around the country that dispose of, recycle, and transport hazardous chemical wastes. Last night, explosions and fires broke out at the company's Apex, North Carolina, facility, forcing the evacuation of 17,000 local residents.

Your task: It's now Friday, the day after the fire. Write a brief post for the company's blog, covering the following points:

- A fire broke out at the Apex facility at approximately 10 P.M. Thursday.
- No one was in the facility at the time.
- Because of the diverse nature of the materials stored at the plant, the cause of the fire is not yet known.
- Rumors that the facility stores extremely dangerous chlorine gas and that the fire was spreading to other nearby businesses are not true.
- Special industrial firefighters hired by EQIS have already brought the fire under control.
- Residents in the immediate area were evacuated as a precaution, and they should be able to return to their homes tomorrow, pending permission from local authorities.
- Several dozen residents were admitted to local hospitals with complaints of breathing problems, but most have been released already; about a dozen emergency responders were treated as well.
- At this point (Friday afternoon), tests conducted by the North Carolina State Department of Environment and Natural Resources "had not detected anything out of the ordinary in the air."

Conclude by thanking the local police and fire departments for their assistance and directing readers to EQIS's toll-free hot line for more information.[29]

BLOGGING SKILLS

9.49. Message Strategies: Responding to Rumors and Public Criticism [LO-6] Spreading FUD—fear, uncertainty, and doubt—about other companies is one of the less-honorable ways of dealing with competition in the business world. For example, someone can start a "whisper campaign" in the marketplace, raising fears that a particular company is struggling financially. Customers who don't want to risk future instability in their supply chains might then shift their purchasing away from the company, based on nothing more than the false rumor.

Your task: Find the website of any company that seems interesting. Imagine you are the CEO and the company is the subject of an online rumor about impending bankruptcy. Explore the website to get a basic feel for what the company does. Making up any information you need, write a post for the company's blog, explaining that the bankruptcy rumors are false and that the company is on solid financial ground and plans to keep serving the industry for many years to come. (Be sure to review page 268 for tips.)

SOCIAL NETWORKING SKILLS

9.50. Message Strategies: Responding to Rumors and Public Criticism [LO-6] The consumer reviews on Yelp can be a promotional boon to any local business—provided the reviews are positive, of course. Negative reviews, fair or not, can affect a company's reputation and drive away potential customers.

Fortunately for business owners, sites like Yelp give them the means to respond to reviews, whether they want to apologize for poor service, offer some form of compensation, or correct misinformation in a review.

Your task: Search Yelp for a negative review (one or two stars) on any business in any city. Find a review that has some substance to it, not just a simple, angry rant. Now imagine you are the owner of that business, and write a reply that could be posted via the "Add Owner Comment" feature. Use information you can find on Yelp about the company and fill in any details by using your imagination. Remember that your comment will be visible to everyone who visits Yelp. (Be sure to review page 268 for tips.)

Negative Employment Messages

SOCIAL NETWORKING SKILLS / EMAIL SKILLS

9.51. Message Strategies: Refusing Requests for Recommendations [LO-7]   You're delighted to get a message from an old friend and colleague, Heather Lang. You're delighted right up to the moment you read her request that you write a recommendation about her web design and programming skills for your LinkedIn profile. You would do just about anything for Lang—anything except recommend her web design skills. She is a master programmer whose technical wizardry saved more client projects than you can count, but when it comes to artistic design, Lang simply doesn't have "it." From gaudy color schemes to unreadable type treatment to confusing layouts, her design sense is as weak as her technical acumen is strong.

Your task: First, write a brief email to Lang, explaining that you would be most comfortable highlighting her technical skills because that is where you believe her true strengths lie. Second, write a two-sentence recommendation that you could include in your LinkedIn profile, recommending Lang's technical skills. Make up or research any details you need.

TELEPHONE SKILLS

9.52. Message Strategies: Terminating Employment [LO-7]   As the human resources manager at Alion Science and Technology, a military research firm in McLean, Virginia, you were thrilled when one of the nation's top computer visualization specialists accepted your job offer. Claus Gunnstein's skills would have made a major contribution to Alion's work in designing flight simulators and other systems. Unfortunately, the day after he accepted the offer, Alion received news that a major Pentagon contract had been canceled. In addition to letting several dozen current employees know that the company will be

forced to lay them off, you need to tell Gunnstein that Alion has no choice but to rescind the job offer.

Your task: Outline the points you'll need to make in a telephone call to Gunnstein. Pay special attention to your opening and closing statements. (You'll review your plans for the phone call with Alion's legal staff to make sure everything you say follows employment law guidelines; for now, just focus on the way you'll present the negative news to Gunnstein. Feel free to make up any details you need.)[30]

EMAIL SKILLS

9.53. Message Strategies: Refusing Requests for Recommendations [LO-5]   Well, this is awkward. Daniel Sturgis, who quit last year just as you were planning to fire him for consistently failing to meet agreed-on performance targets, has just emailed you from his new job, asking for a recommendation. He says his new job is awful and he regrets leaving your company. He knows you don't have any openings, but he would be grateful for a recommendation.

Your task: Write an email message to Sturgis, explaining that you will not be able to write him a recommendation. Make up any details you need.

MEMO WRITING SKILLS / PORTFOLIO BUILDER

9.54. Message Strategies: Negative Performance Reviews [LO-7]   Elaine Bridgewater, the former professional golfer you hired to oversee your golf equipment company's relationship with retailers, knows the business inside and out. As a former touring pro, she has unmatched credibility. She also has seemingly boundless energy, solid technical knowledge, and an engaging personal style. Unfortunately, she hasn't been quite as attentive as she needs to be when it comes to communicating with retailers. You've been getting complaints about voicemail messages gone unanswered for days, confusing emails that require two or three rounds of clarification, and reports that are haphazardly thrown together. As valuable as Bridgewater's other skills are, she's going to cost the company sales if this goes on much longer. The retail channel is vital to your company's survival, and she's the employee most involved in this channel.

Your task: Draft a brief (one page maximum) informal performance appraisal and improvement plan for Bridgewater. Be sure to compliment her on the areas in which she excels but don't shy away from highlighting the areas in which she needs to improve, too: punctual response to customer messages; clear writing; and careful revision, production, and proofreading. Use what you've learned in this course so far to supply any additional advice about the importance of these skills.

MyBCommLab

Go to the Assignments section of your MyLab to complete these writing exercises.

9.55. What are the five main goals in delivering bad news? [LO-1]

9.56. What are three techniques for deemphasizing negative news? [LO-3]

Endnotes

1. Email from Hailo dated 29 October 2013; Hailo website, accessed 22 February 2015, www.hailoapp.com; Natasha Lomas, "Hailo Ups Its Minimum Fare in London to £10, Triggers Licensing Complaints," 31 October 2013, TechCrunch, http://techcrunch.com.

2. Ian McDonald, "Marsh Can Do $600 Million, but Apologize?" *Wall Street Journal*, 14 January 2005, C1, C3; Adrienne Carter and Amy Borrus, "What if Companies Fessed Up?" *BusinessWeek*, 24 January 2005, 59–60; Patrick J. Kiger, "The Art of the Apology," *Workforce Management*, October 2004, 57–62.

3. Ameeta Patel and Lamar Reinsch, "Companies Can Apologize: Corporate Apologies and Legal Liability," *Business Communication Quarterly*, March 2003, www.elibrary.com.

4. John Guiniven, "Sorry! An Apology as a Strategic PR Tool," *Public Relations Tactics*, December 2007, 6.

5. "Target Issues Written Apology for Security Breach," NBC Chicago website, 13 January 2014, www.nbcchicago.com.

6. Quinn Warnick, "A Close Textual Analysis of Corporate Layoff Memos," *Business Communication Quarterly*, September 2010, 322–326.

7. "Advice from the Pros on the Best Way to Deliver Bad News," Report on *Customer Relationship Management*, 1 February 2003, www.elibrary.com.

8. Ben Levisohn, "Getting More Workers to Whistle," *BusinessWeek*, 28 January 2008, 18.

9. "Less Than Half of Privately Held Businesses Support Whistleblowing," Grant Thornton website, accessed 13 October 2008, www.internationalbusinessreport.com.

10. Steve Karnowski, "New Food Safety Law Protects Whistleblowers," *Bloomberg Businessweek*, 11 February 2011, www.businessweek.com.

11. Christopher Elliott, "7 Ways Smart Companies Tell Customers 'No,'" *CBS Money Watch*, 7 June 2011, www.cbsnews.com.

12. Micah Solomon, "Mean Tweets: Managing Customer Complaints," CNBC, 22 February 2012, www.cnbc.com; "When Fans Attack: How to Defend a Brand's Reputation Online," Crenshaw Communications blog, 20 May 2010, http://crenshawcomm.com; Leslie Gaines-Ross, "Reputation Warfare," *Harvard Business Review*, December 2010, 70–76; David Meerman Scott, "The US Air Force: Armed with Social Media," WebInkNow blog, 15 December 2008, www.webinknow.com; Matt Rhodes, "How to React If Somebody Writes About Your Brand Online," FreshNetworks blog, 9 January 2009, www.freshnetworks.com; Matt Rhodes, "Social Media as a Crisis Management Tool," Social Media Today blog, 21 December 2009, www.socialmediatoday.com.

13. Courtland L. Bovée, John V. Thill, George P. Dovel, and Marian Burk Wood, *Advertising Excellence* (New York: McGraw-Hill, 1995), 508–509; John Holusha, "Exxon's Public-Relations Problem," *New York Times*, 12 April 1989, D1.

14. Omowale Casselle, "Really, You Want ME to Write YOU a LinkedIn Recommendation," RecruitingBlogs, 22 April 2010, www.recruitingblogs.com.

15. "LinkedIn Profiles to Career Introductions: When You Can't Recommend Your Friend," *Seattle Post-Intelligencer* Personal Finance blog, 16 November 2010, http://blog.seattlepi.com.

16. Neal Schaffer, "How Should I Deal with a LinkedIn Recommendation Request I Don't Want to Give?" Social Web School, 20 January 2010, http://humancapitalleague.com.

17. Dawn Wolf, "Job Applicant Rejection Letter Dos and Donts—Writing an Appropriate 'Dear John' Letter to an Unsuccessful Applicant," 31 May 2009, Employment Blawg.com, www.employmentblawg.com.

18. Wolf, "Job Applicant Rejection Letter Dos and Donts"; "Prohibited Employment Policies/Practices," U.S. Equal Employment Opportunity Commission, accessed 14 July 2010, www.eeoc.gov; Susan M. Heathfield, "Candidate Rejection Letter," About.com, accessed 14 July 2010, http://humanresources.about.com; "Rejection Letters Under Scrutiny: 7 Do's & Don'ts," *Business Management Daily*, 1 April 2009, www.businessmanagementdaily.com.

19. Judi Brownell, "The Performance Appraisal Interviews: A Multipurpose Communication Assignment," *Bulletin of the Association for Business Communication* 57, no. 2 (1994): 11–21.

20. Susan Friedfel, "Protecting Yourself in the Performance Review Process," *Workforce Management*, April 2009, www.workforce.com.

21. Kelly Spors, "Why Performance Reviews Don't Work—And What You Can Do About It," Independent Street blog, *Wall Street Journal*, 21 October 2008, http://blogs.wsj.com.

22. Rita Pyrillis, "Is Your Performance Review Underperforming?" *Workforce Management*, May 2011, 20–22, 24–25.

23. Friedfel, "Protecting Yourself in the Performance Review Process."

24. E. Michelle Bohreer and Todd J. Zucker, "Five Mistakes Managers Make When Terminating Employees," *Texas Lawyer*, 2 May 2006, www.law.com; Deborah Muller, "The Right Things to Do to Avoid Wrongful Termination Claims," *Workforce Management*, October 2008, www.workforce.com; Maria Greco Danaher, "Termination: Telling an Employee," *Workforce Management*, accessed 14 July 2010, www.workforce.com.

25. "FDA Notifies Public That Vail Products, Inc., Issues Nationwide Recall of Enclosed Bed Systems," FDA press release, 30 June 2005, www.fda.gov.

26. Twitter/JetBlue website, accessed 29 October 2008, http://twitter.com/JetBlue.

27. "Viral Effect of Email Promotion," Alka Dwivedi blog, accessed 19 October 2006, www.alkadwivedi.net; Teresa Valdez Klein, "Starbucks Makes a Viral Marketing Misstep," Blog Business Summit website, accessed 19 October 2006, www.blogbusinesssummit.com.

28. Pui-Wing Tam, Erin White, Nick Wingfield, and Kris Maher, "Snooping Email by Software Is Now a Workplace Norm," *Wall Street Journal*, 9 March 2005, B1+.

29. Environmental Quality Company press releases, accessed 27 October 2006, www.eqonline.com; "N.C. Residents to Return After Fire," *Science Daily*, 6 October 2006, www.sciencedaily.com; "Hazardous Waste Plant Fire in N.C. Forces 17,000 to Evacuate," FOXNews.com, 6 October 2006, www.foxnews.com.

30. Alion website, accessed 19 August 2005, www.alionscience.com.

10 Writing Persuasive Messages

LEARNING OBJECTIVES

After studying this chapter, you will be able to

1 Apply the three-step writing process to persuasive messages.

2 Describe an effective strategy for developing persuasive business messages, and identify the three most common categories of persuasive business messages.

3 Describe an effective strategy for developing marketing and sales messages, and explain how to modify your approach when writing promotional messages for social media.

4 Identify steps you can take to avoid ethical lapses in marketing and sales messages.

Building a Business That Fits

Sarah Calhoun was fed up. The rugged work she was doing in her adopted home state of Montana, including clearing trails and peeling logs, was destroying her not-so-rugged clothes. She switched to men's work pants, which were tough enough for the job but didn't fit.

Tired of constantly putting down her tools so she could pull up her misfit britches, Calhoun decided to solve the problem herself. She launched Red Ants Pants with the focus on providing hardwearing pants for hardworking women, meeting the needs of customers whose work makes clothing a matter of practical

Erik Peterson. copyright © Sarah Calhoun.

Sarah Calhoun connects with customers by communicating in a fun, authentic, respectful way.

utility and even on-the-job safety. Red Ants Pants are made from tough, heavy cloth and in both "straight" and "curvy" styles to provide a better fit for more women. In addition, they come in two or three times as many waist/inseam combinations as typical pants, greatly increasing the chance that every woman will find exactly the size she needs.

Why "Red Ants Pants," by the way? In a conversation with a biologist about the social behaviors of ants, she learned that in red ant colonies, females do most of the work. In keeping with the cheeky style she adopted for all her company's communication, she uses the name as a salute to hardworking women everywhere.

Calhoun knew there was a market for her product, but launching a company in the fiercely competitive global clothing industry—and doing so from the tiny town of White Sulphur Springs, Montana, no less—was a huge challenge. However, from the start she has used size and independence to her advantage, making choices that fit her personal values and the needs of her customers. For example, unlike with most clothing brands, she choose to keep production in the United States, rather than offshoring in pursuit of the lowest possible costs.

That spirit of independence extends to her customer communication efforts, demonstrating both the greater flexibility that small companies often have compared to their larger, "more corporate" competitors—and the need to exercise creative brain power over brute-force budget power. Her communication style is more fun and more daring that the typical

corporation would attempt, for example, and it seems to resonate with buyers. How many clothing companies would use photographs (discreetly staged, to be sure) to suggest that hardworking women would rather wear no pants than wear pants that don't fit?

Without a significant marketing budget, Calhoun looks for low-cost, high-visibility ways to reach customers. Her most unusual is hitting the highway in an ant-decorated Airstream travel trailer with her sales manager on trips they call the "Tour de Pants." They invite women to stage in-home gatherings, much like old-school Tupperware parties. Through visiting customers in their homes and hearing stories about women working in what are often male-dominated professions, Calhoun also gains invaluable marketing research insights.

Calhoun's most ambitious communication effort so far has been sponsoring the Red Ants Pants Music Festival, which has attracted such major American artists as Lyle Lovett and Guy Clark. All profits go to the Red Ants Pants Foundation, which she started to "support family farms and ranches, women in business, and rural initiatives."

The combination of meeting customer needs with quality products and a creative marketing effort is paying off. Red Ants Pants now has customers all across the country and around the world, from Europe to Australia, and even women working the research stations in Antarctica.[1]

WWW.REDANTPANTS.COM

1 LEARNING OBJECTIVE
Apply the three-step writing process to persuasive messages.

Using the Three-Step Writing Process for Persuasive Messages

Sarah Calhoun (profiled in the chapter opening On the Job) understands that successful businesses rely on persuasive messages in both internal and external communication. Whether you're trying to convince your boss to open a new office in Europe or encourage potential customers to try your products, you need to call on your abilities of **persuasion**—the attempt to change an audience's attitudes, beliefs, or actions.[2] Because persuasive messages ask audiences to give something of value (money in exchange for a product, for example) or take substantial action (such as changing a corporate policy), they are more challenging to write than routine messages. Successful professionals understand that persuasion is not about trickery or getting people to act against their own best interests; it's about letting audiences know they have choices and presenting your offering in the best possible light.[3]

Persuasion is the attempt to change someone's attitudes, beliefs, or actions.

STEP 1: PLANNING PERSUASIVE MESSAGES

Having a great idea or a great product is not enough; you need to be able to convince others of its merits.

In today's information-saturated business environment, having a great idea or a great product is no longer enough. Every day, untold numbers of good ideas go unnoticed and good products go unsold simply because the messages meant to promote them aren't compelling enough to be heard above the competitive noise. Creating successful persuasive messages in these challenging situations demands careful attention to all four tasks in the planning step, starting with an insightful analysis of your purpose and your audience.

Analyzing the Situation

In defining your purpose, make sure you're clear about what you really hope to achieve. Suppose you want to persuade company executives to support a particular research project. But what does "support" mean? Do you want them to pat you on the back and wish you well? Or do you want them to give you a staff of five researchers and a $1 million annual budget?

The best persuasive messages are closely connected to your audience's desires and interests (see Figure 10.1).[4] Consider these important questions: Who is my audience? What are my audience members' needs? What do I want them to do? How might they resist? Are there alternative positions I need to examine? What does the decision maker consider to be the most important issue? How might the organization's culture influence my strategy?

To understand and categorize audience needs, you can refer to specific information, such as **demographics** (the age, gender, occupation, income, education, and other quantifiable characteristics of the people you're trying to persuade) and **psychographics** (personality, attitudes, lifestyle, and other psychological characteristics). When analyzing your audiences, take into account their cultural expectations and practices so that you don't undermine your persuasive message by using an inappropriate appeal or by organizing your message in a way that seems unfamiliar or uncomfortable to your readers.

If you aim to change someone's attitudes, beliefs, or actions, it is vital to understand his or her **motivation**—the combination of forces that drive people to satisfy their needs. Table 10.1 on the next page lists some of the needs that psychologists have identified or suggested as being important in influencing human motivation. Obviously, the more closely a persuasive message aligns with a recipient's existing motivation, the more effective the message is likely to be. For example, if you try to persuade consumers to purchase a product on the basis of its fashion appeal, that message will connect with consumers who are motivated by a desire to be in fashion, but it probably won't connect with consumers driven more by functional or financial concerns.

Clarifying your purpose is an essential step with persuasive messages.

Demographics include characteristics such as age, gender, occupation, income, and education.

Psychographics include characteristics such as personality, attitudes, and lifestyle.

Motivation is the combination of forces that drive people to satisfy their needs.

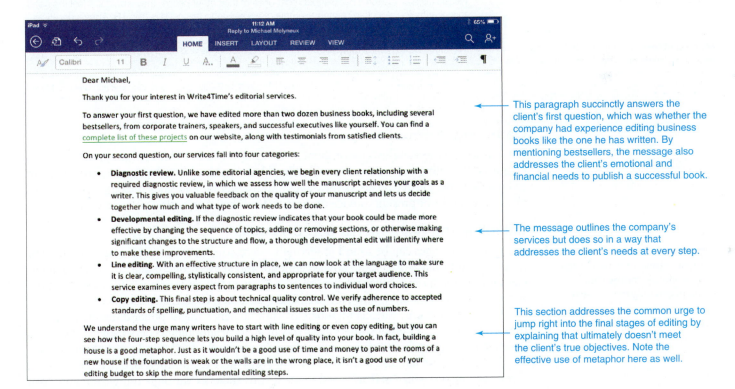

Figure 10.1 Appealing to Audience Needs
This draft of a response to an inquiry about an editorial company's services addresses the writer's concerns about the time, cost, and effectiveness of the company's services.
Source: MS Office Word 2013, © Microsoft.

TABLE 10.1	Human Needs That Influence Motivation
Need	**Implications for Communication**
Basic physiological requirements: The needs for food, water, sleep, oxygen, and other essentials	Everyone has these needs, but the degree of attention an individual gives to them often depends on whether the needs are being met; for instance, an advertisement for sleeping pills will have greater appeal to someone suffering from insomnia than to someone who has no problem sleeping.
Safety and security: The needs for protection from bodily harm, for the safety of loved ones, and for financial security, protection of personal identity, career security, and other assurances	These needs influence both consumer and business decisions in a wide variety of ways; for instance, advertisements for life insurance often encourage parents to think about the financial security of their children and other loved ones.
Affiliation and belonging: The needs for companionship, acceptance, love, popularity, and approval	The need to feel loved, accepted, or popular drives a great deal of human behavior, from the desire to be attractive to potential mates to wearing the clothing style that a particular social group is likely to approve.
Power and control: The need to feel in control of situations or to exert authority over others	You can see many examples appealing to this need in advertisements: *Take control of your life, your finances, your future, your career,* and so on. Many people who lack power want to know how to get it, and people who have power often want others to know they have it.
Achievement: The need to feel a sense of accomplishment—or to be admired by others for accomplishments	This need can involve both *knowing* (when people experience a feeling of accomplishment) and *showing* (when people are able to show others that they've achieved success); advertising for luxury consumer products frequently appeals to this need.
Adventure and distraction: The need for excitement or relief from daily routine	People vary widely in their need for adventure; some crave excitement—even danger—whereas others value calmness and predictability. Some needs for adventure and distraction are met *virtually*, such as through horror movies, thriller novels, etc.
Knowledge, exploration, and understanding: The need to keep learning	For some people, learning is usually a means to an end, a way to fulfill some other need; for others, acquiring new knowledge is the goal.
Aesthetic appreciation: The desire to experience beauty, order, symmetry, etc.	Although this need may seem "noncommercial" at first glance, advertisers appeal to it frequently, from the pleasing shape of a package to the quality of the gemstones in a piece of jewelry.
Self-actualization: The need to "be all that one can be," to reach one's full potential as a human being	Psychologists Kurt Goldstein and Abraham Maslow popularized self-actualization as the desire to make the most of one's potential, and Maslow identified it as one of the higher-level needs in his classic hierarchy; even if people met most or all of their other needs, they would still feel the need to self-actualize. An often-quoted example of appealing to this need is the U.S. Army's one-time advertising slogan "Be all that you can be."
Helping others: The need to believe that one is making a difference in the lives of other people	This need is the central motivation in fundraising messages and other appeals to charity.

Sources: Courtland L. Bovée and John V. Thill, *Business in Action,* 6th ed. (Upper Saddle River, N.J.: Prentice Hall, 2013), 219–232; Saundra K. Ciccarelli and Glenn E. Meyer, *Psychology* (Upper Saddle River, N.J.: Prentice Hall, 2006), 336–346; Abraham H. Maslow, "A Theory of Human Motivation," *Psychological Review* 50 (1943): 370–396.

Gathering Information

Once your situation analysis is complete, you need to gather the information necessary to create a compelling persuasive message. You'll learn more about the types of information to include in persuasive business messages and marketing and sales messages later in this chapter. Chapter 11 presents advice on how to find the information you need.

Selecting the Right Media and Channels

Persuasive messages are often unexpected and sometimes even unwelcome, so choose your medium carefully to maximize the chance of getting through to your audience.

Persuasive messages can be found in virtually every communication format, from instant messages and podcasts to radio advertisements and skywriting. In fact, advertising agencies employ media specialists whose job is to analyze the options available and select the most cost-effective combination for each client and each advertising campaign.

In some situations, various members of your audience might prefer different media for the same message. Some consumers like to do all their car shopping in person, whereas others do most of their car-shopping research online. Some people don't mind promotional emails for products they're interested in; others resent every piece of commercial email they receive. If you can't be sure you can reach most or all of your audience through a single medium, you need to use two or more, such as following up an email campaign with printed letters.

Social media provide some exciting options for persuasive messages, particularly marketing and sales messages. However, as "Writing Promotional Messages for Social Media" on page 302 explains, messages in these media require a unique approach.

Organizing Your Information

The most effective main ideas for persuasive messages have one thing in common: They are about the receiver, not the sender. For instance, if you're trying to convince others to join you in a business venture, explain how it will help them, not how it will help you.

Limiting your scope is vital. If you seem to be wrestling with more than one main idea, you haven't zeroed in on the heart of the matter. If you try to craft a persuasive message without focusing on the one central problem or opportunity your audience truly cares about, you're unlikely to persuade successfully.[5]

Because the nature of persuasion is to convince people to change their attitudes, beliefs, or actions, most persuasive messages use the indirect approach. That means you'll want to explain your reasons and build interest before asking for a decision or for action—or perhaps even before revealing your purpose. In contrast, when you have a close relationship with your audience and the message is welcome or at least neutral, the direct approach can be effective.

> Most persuasive messages use the indirect approach.

For persuasive business messages, the choice between the direct and indirect approaches is also influenced by the extent of your authority, expertise, or power in an organization. For instance, if you are a highly regarded technical expert with years of experience, you might use the direct approach in a message to top executives. In contrast, if you aren't well known and therefore need to rely more on the strength of your message than the power of your reputation, the indirect approach will probably be more successful.

> The choice of approach is influenced by your position (or authority within the organization) relative to your audience's.

STEP 2: WRITING PERSUASIVE MESSAGES

Encourage a positive response to your persuasive messages by (1) using positive and polite language, (2) understanding and respecting cultural differences, (3) being sensitive to organizational cultures, and (4) taking steps to establish your credibility.

> Positive language is an essential feature of persuasive messages.

Positive language usually happens naturally with persuasive messages because you're promoting an idea or product you believe in. However, take care not to inadvertently insult your readers by implying that they've made poor choices in the past and that you're here to save them from their misguided ways.

Be sure to understand cultural expectations as well. For example, a message that seems forthright and direct in a low-context culture might seem brash and intrusive in a high-context culture.

Just as social culture affects the success of a persuasive message, so too does the culture within an organization. For instance, some organizations handle disagreement and conflict indirectly, behind the scenes, whereas others accept and even encourage open discussion and sharing of differing viewpoints.

> Organizational culture can influence persuasion as much as social culture.

Finally, when you are trying to persuade a skeptical or hostile audience, credibility is essential. You must convince people that you know what you're talking about and that you're not trying to mislead them (see "Practicing Ethical Communication: Pushing the Limits of Credibility" on the next page). Use these techniques:

- Use simple language to avoid suspicions of fantastic claims and emotional manipulation.
- Provide objective evidence for the claims and promises you make.
- Identify your sources, especially if your audience already respects those sources.
- Establish common ground by emphasizing beliefs, attitudes, and background experiences you have in common with the audience.
- Be objective and present fair and logical arguments.
- Display your willingness to keep your audience's best interests at heart.
- Persuade with logic, evidence, and compelling narratives, rather than trying to coerce with high-pressure, "hard sell" tactics.
- Whenever possible, try to build your credibility before you present a major proposal or ask for a major decision. That way, audiences don't have to evaluate both you and your message at the same time.[6]

> Audiences often respond unfavorably to over-the-top language, so keep your writing simple and straightforward.

REAL-TIME UPDATES

LEARN MORE BY WATCHING THIS VIDEO

Persuasion skills for every business professional

Persuasion is an essential business skill, no matter what career path you follow. This video offers great tips for understanding, practicing, and applying persuasive skills. Go to http://real-timeupdates.com/ebc12 and click on Learn More in the Students section.

Pushing the Limits of Credibility

As the director of human resources in your company, you're desperate for some help. You want to keep the costs of employee benefits under control while making sure you provide employees with a fair benefits package. However, you don't have time to research all the options for health insurance, wellness programs, retirement plans, family counseling, educational benefits, and everything else, so you decide to hire a consultant. You receive the following message from a consultant interested in working with you:

> I am considered the country's foremost authority on employee health insurance programs. My clients offer universally positive feedback on the programs I've designed for them. They also love how much time I save them—hundreds and hundreds of hours. I am absolutely confident that I can thoroughly

analyze your needs and create a portfolio that realizes every degree of savings possible. I invite you to experience the same level of service that has generated such comments as "Best advice ever!" and "Saved us an unbelievable amount of money."

You'd love to get results like that, but the message almost sounds too good to be true. Is it?

CAREER APPLICATIONS

1. The consultant's message contains at least a dozen instances in which this writer's credibility might be questioned. Identify as many as you can.
2. Explain how you would bolster reader confidence by providing additional or different information.

STEP 3: COMPLETING PERSUASIVE MESSAGES

The pros know from experience that details can make or break a persuasive message, so they're careful not to skimp on this part of the writing process. For instance, advertisers may have a dozen or more people review a message before it's released to the public.

When you evaluate your content, try to judge your argument objectively and try not to overestimate your credibility. If possible, ask an experienced colleague who knows your audience well to review your draft. Make sure your design elements complement, rather than detract from, your persuasive argument. In addition, meticulous proofreading will help you identify any mechanical or spelling errors that would weaken your persuasive potential. Finally, make sure your distribution methods fit your audience's expectations and preferences.

With the three-step model in mind, you're ready to begin composing persuasive messages, starting with *persuasive business messages* (those that try to convince audiences to approve new projects, enter into business partnerships, and so on), followed by *marketing and sales messages* (those that try to convince audiences to consider and then purchase products and services).

Careless production undermines your credibility, so revise and proofread with care.

2 LEARNING OBJECTIVE
Describe an effective strategy for developing persuasive business messages, and identify the three most common categories of persuasive business messages.

Developing Persuasive Business Messages

Your success as a businessperson is closely tied to your ability to encourage others to accept new ideas, change old habits, or act on your recommendations. Unless your career takes you into marketing and sales, most of your persuasive messages will consist of *persuasive business messages*, which are those designed to elicit a preferred response in a nonsales situation.

STRATEGIES FOR PERSUASIVE BUSINESS MESSAGES

Even if you have the power to compel others to do what you want them to do, persuading them is more effective than forcing them. People who are forced into accepting a decision or plan are less motivated to support it and more likely to react negatively than if they're persuaded.[7] Within the context of the three-step process, effective persuasion involves four essential strategies: framing your arguments, balancing emotional and logical appeals, reinforcing your position, and anticipating objections. (Note that all these concepts in this section apply as well to marketing and sales messages, covered later in the chapter.)

Framing Your Arguments

As noted previously, most persuasive messages use the indirect approach. Experts in persuasive communication have developed a number of indirect models for such messages. One of the best known is the **AIDA model**, which organizes messages into four phases (see Figure 10.2):

- **Attention.** Your first objective is to encourage your audience to want to hear about your problem, idea, or new product—whatever your main idea is. Be sure to find some common ground on which to build your case.
- **Interest.** Provide additional details that prompt audience members to imagine how the solution might benefit them.
- **Desire.** Help audience members embrace your idea by explaining how the change will benefit them and answering potential objections.
- **Action.** Suggest the specific action you want your audience to take. Include a deadline, when applicable.

The AIDA model is tailor-made for using the indirect approach, allowing you to save your main idea for the action phase. However, you can also use AIDA for the direct approach, in which case you use your main idea as an attention-getter, build interest with your argument, create desire with your evidence, and reemphasize your main idea in the action phase with the specific action you want your audience to take.

When your AIDA message uses the indirect approach and is delivered by memo or email, keep in mind that your subject line usually catches your reader's eye first. Your challenge is to make it interesting and relevant enough to capture reader attention without revealing your main idea. If you put your request in the subject line, you might get a quick no before you've had a chance to present your arguments:

The AIDA model is a useful approach for many persuasive messages:
- **A**ttention
- **I**nterest
- **D**esire
- **A**ction

The AIDA model is ideal for the indirect approach.

Instead of This	**Write This**
Request for development budget to add automated IM response system	Reducing the cost of customer support inquiries

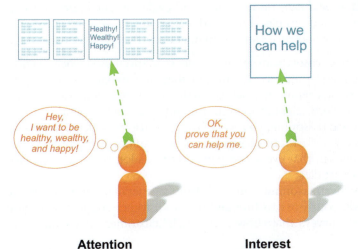

Attention	**Interest**	**Desire**	**Action**
Catch the audience's eyes and ears, then getting people to pay attention to *your* message amid all the other messages clamoring for their attention.	Provide concise information points that "pay off" the promise you made to get their attention as you build a case that you can meet their individual needs.	Move prospects from "I'm interested" to "I want this" by continuing to show how your solution will benefit them and by removing any doubts.	Motivate them to take action, whether that is seeking more information, making a decision in your favor, or making a purchase.

Figure 10.2 **The AIDA Model for Persuasive Messages**
With the AIDA model, you craft one or more messages to move recipients through four stages of attention, interest, desire, and action. The model works well for both persuasive business messages (such as persuading your manager to fund a new project) and marketing and sales messages.

The AIDA approach does have limitations:
- It essentially talks *at* audiences, not *with* them.
- It focuses on one-time events, not long-term relationships.

With either the direct or indirect approach, AIDA and similar models do have limitations. First, AIDA is a unidirectional method that essentially talks *at* audiences, not *with* them. Second, AIDA is built around a single event, such as asking an audience for a decision, rather than on building a mutually beneficial, long-term relationship.[8] AIDA is still a valuable tool for the right purposes, but as you'll read later in the chapter, a conversational approach is more compatible with today's social media.

Balancing Emotional and Logical Appeals

Imagine you're sitting at a control panel with one knob labeled "logic" and another labeled "emotion." As you prepare your persuasive message, you carefully adjust each knob, tuning the message for maximum impact (see Figure 10.3). Too little emotion, and your audience might not care enough to respond. Too much emotion, and your audience might think you are ignoring tough business questions or even being irrational.

REAL-TIME UPDATES

LEARN MORE BY READING THIS ARTICLE

Using stories to persuade

Learn why stories are usually more effective than plain data when it comes to changing minds. Go to http://real-time updates.com/ebc12 and click on Learn More in the Students section.

Generally speaking, persuasive business messages rely more heavily on logical than on emotional appeals because the main idea is usually to save money, increase quality, or improve some other practical, measurable aspect of business. To find the optimum balance, consider four factors: (1) the actions you hope to motivate, (2) your readers' expectations, (3) the degree of resistance you need to overcome, and (4) your position in the formal and informal power structure of the organization.[9]

Emotional appeals attempt to connect with the reader's feelings or sympathies.

Emotional Appeals   As its name implies, an **emotional appeal** calls on audience feelings and sympathies rather than on facts, figures, and rational arguments. For instance, you can make use of the emotion surrounding certain words. The word *freedom* evokes strong feelings, as do words such as *success, prestige, compassion, security,* and *comfort.* Such words can help put your audience members in a positive frame of mind and help them accept your message. However, emotional appeals in business messages aren't usually effective by themselves because the audience wants proof that you can solve a business problem. Even if your audience members reach a conclusion based primarily on emotions, they'll look to you to provide logical support as well.

Logical appeals are based on the reader's notions of reason; these appeals can use analogy, induction, or deduction.

Logical Appeals   A **logical appeal** calls on reasoning and evidence. The basic approach with a logical appeal is to make a claim based on a rational argument, supported by solid evidence. When appealing to your audience's logic, you might use three types of reasoning:

- **Analogy.** With analogy, you reason from specific evidence to specific evidence, in effect "borrowing" from something familiar to explain something unfamiliar. For instance, to convince management to add chat room capability to the company's groupware system, you could explain that it is like a neighborhood community center, only online.
- **Induction.** With inductive reasoning, you work from specific evidence to a general conclusion. To convince your team to change to a new manufacturing process, for example, you could point out that every company that has adopted it has increased profits, so it must be a smart idea.
- **Deduction.** With deductive reasoning, you work from a generalization to a specific conclusion. To persuade your boss to hire additional customer support staff, you might point to industry surveys that show how crucial customer satisfaction is to corporate profits.

Using logical appeals carries with it the ethical responsibility to avoid faulty logic.

Every method of reasoning is vulnerable to misuse, both intentional and unintentional, so verify your rational arguments carefully. For example, in the case of the manufacturing process, are there any other factors that affect the integrity of your reasoning? What if that process works well only for small companies with few products, and your firm is a multinational behemoth with 10,000 products? To guard against faulty logic, follow these guidelines:[10]

- **Avoid hasty generalizations.** Make sure you have plenty of evidence before drawing conclusions.

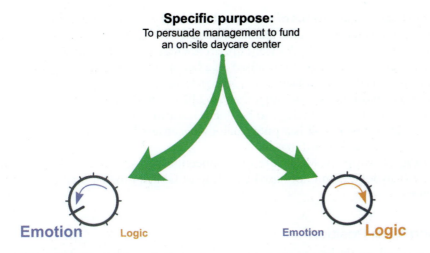

Specific purpose:
To persuade management to fund
an on-site daycare center

Emotion Logic

Emotion Logic

**Proposal to improve employee
satisfaction and work/life balance**

Being separated during the day is stressful
for both parents and children.

Many parents are now working more hours and
second jobs to make ends meet, so the situation
is getting worse.

The extra travel time every morning and evening
to put children in day care adds to the stress and
cost of coming to work.

When parents need to leave work to pick up sick
children from day care or stay home with them,
this often creates an unfair burden on other
employees to pick up the slack.

Knowing that the company cares about them and
their children would boost employee morale.

Therefore, the company should provide an
on-site daycare facility with a separate infirmary
where sick children could stay during the day.

**Proposal to boost productivity
and reduce absenteeism**

Analysis of employee time records shows that
employees with children under the age of 10
take unscheduled days off three times more often
than employees without young children.

Daycare issues are cited as the number one
reason for these unscheduled days off.

In the 98 exit interviews conducted last year,
24 departing employees mentioned the need
to balance family and work commitments as the
primary reason for leaving.

In the last six months, HR has logged 14 complaints
from employees who say they have to take on extra
work when colleagues leave the office to pick up
sick children from day care.

Research shows that on-site day care can improve
productivity by as much as 20 percent—among
parents and nonparents alike.

Therefore, the company should provide an
on-site daycare facility with a separate infirmary
where sick children could stay during the day.

Figure 10.3   Balancing Logical and Emotional Appeals
Whenever you plan a persuasive message, imagine you have a knob that turns from *emotion* at one extreme
to *logic* at the other, letting you adjust the relative proportions of each type of appeal. Compare these two
outlines for a proposal that asks management to fund an on-site daycare center. The version on the left relies
heavily on emotional appeals, whereas the version on the right uses logical appeals (inductive reasoning,
specifically). Through your choice of words, images, and supporting details, you can adjust the emotional-
logical ratio in every message.

- **Avoid circular reasoning.** *Circular reasoning* is a logical fallacy in which you try to
  support your claim by restating it in different words. The statement "We know temporary workers cannot handle this task because temps are unqualified for it" doesn't
  prove anything because the claim and the supporting evidence are essentially identical. It doesn't prove *why* the temps are unqualified.
- **Avoid attacking an opponent.** If your persuasive appeal involves countering a
  competitive appeal made by someone else, make sure you attack the argument your
  opponent is making, not his or her character or qualifications.
- **Avoid oversimplifying a complex issue.** Make sure you present all the factors
  and don't reduce a wide range of choices to a simple "either/or" scenario if that isn't
  the case.

- **Avoid mistaken assumptions of cause and effect.** If you can't isolate the impact of a specific factor, you can't assume that it's the cause of whatever effect you're discussing. You lowered prices, and sales went up. Were lower prices the cause? Maybe, but the sales increase might have been caused by a better advertising campaign, changes in the weather, or some other factor.
- **Avoid faulty analogies.** Be sure that the two objects or situations being compared are similar enough for the analogy to hold. For instance, explaining that an Internet firewall is like a prison wall is a poor analogy because a firewall keeps things out, whereas a prison wall keeps things in.
- **Avoid illogical support.** Make sure the connection between your claim and your support is truly logical and not based on a leap of faith, a missing premise, or irrelevant evidence.

Reinforcing Your Position

After you've worked out the basic elements of your argument, step back and look for ways to strengthen your position. Are all your claims supported by believable evidence? Would a quotation from a recognized expert help make your case?

Choose your words carefully to trigger the desired responses.

Next, examine your language. Can you find more powerful words to convey your message? For example, if your company is in serious financial trouble, talking about *fighting for survival* is a more powerful emotional appeal than talking about *ensuring continued operations*. As with any other powerful tool, though, use vivid language and abstractions carefully and honestly.

In addition to examining individual word choices, consider using metaphors and other figures of speech. If you want to describe a quality-control system as being designed to detect every possible product flaw, you might call it a "spider web" to imply that it catches everything that comes its way. Similarly, anecdotes (brief stories) can help your audience grasp the meaning and importance of your arguments. Instead of just listing the number of times the old laptop computers in your department have failed, you could describe how you lost a sale when your computer broke down during a critical sales presentation.

Beyond specific words and phrases, look for other factors that can reinforce your position. When you're asking for something, your audience members will find it easier to grant your request if they stand to benefit from it as well.

Anticipating Objections

Even powerful persuasive messages can encounter audience resistance.

Even the most compelling ideas and proposals can be expected to encounter some initial resistance. The best way to deal with audience resistance is to anticipate as many objections as you can and address them in your message before your audience can even bring them up. For instance, if you know that your proposal to switch to lower-cost materials will raise concerns about product quality, address this issue head-on in your message. If you wait until people raise the concern after reading your message, they may gravitate toward another firm before you have a chance to address their concerns. By bringing up such potential problems right away, you also demonstrate a broad appreciation of the issue and imply confidence in your message.[11] This anticipation is particularly important in written messages, when you don't have the opportunity to detect and respond to objections on the spot.

If you expect to encounter strong resistance, present all sides of an issue.

To uncover potential audience objections, try to poke holes in your own theories and ideas before your audience does. Then find solutions to the problems you've uncovered. If possible, ask your audience members for their thoughts on the subject before you put together your argument; people are more likely to support solutions they help create.

Keep two things in mind when anticipating objections. First, you don't always have to explicitly discuss a potential objection. You could simply mention that the lower-cost materials have been tested and approved by the quality-control department. Second, if you expect a hostile audience—one biased against your plan from the beginning—present all sides of the story. As you cover each option, explain the pros and cons. You'll gain additional credibility if you present these options before presenting your recommendation or decision.[12]

AVOIDING COMMON MISTAKES IN PERSUASIVE COMMUNICATION

When you believe in a concept or project you are promoting, it's easy to get caught up in your own confidence and enthusiasm and thereby fail to see things from the audience's perspective. When putting together persuasive arguments, avoid these common mistakes (see Figure 10.4 on the next page):[13]

- **Using a hard sell.** Don't push. No one likes being pressured into making a decision, and communicators who take this approach can come across as being more concerned with meeting their own goals than with satisfying the needs of their audiences. In contrast, a "soft sell" is more like a comfortable conversation that uses calm, rational persuasion.

- **Resisting compromise.** Successful persuasion is often a process of give-and-take, particularly in the case of persuasive business messages, where you don't always get everything you asked for in terms of budgets, investments, and other commitments.

- **Relying solely on great arguments.** Great arguments are important, but connecting with your audience on the right emotional level and communicating through vivid language are just as vital. Sometimes a well-crafted story can be even more compelling than dry logic.

- **Assuming that persuasion is a one-shot effort.** Persuasion is often a process, not a one-time event. In many cases, you need to move your audience members along one small step at a time rather than try to convince them to say "yes" in one huge step.

To review the steps involved in developing persuasive messages, refer to "Checklist: Developing Persuasive Messages."

Don't let confidence or enthusiasm lead you to some common mistakes in persuasive communication.

REAL-TIME UPDATES
LEARN MORE BY READING THIS ARTICLE
Fifty tips for being more persuasive

Try these tips when you're crafting persuasive appeals. Go to http://real-timeupdates.com/ebc12 and click on *Learn More* in the Students section.

COMMON EXAMPLES OF PERSUASIVE BUSINESS MESSAGES

Throughout your career, you'll have numerous opportunities to write persuasive messages within your organization, such as reports suggesting more-efficient operating procedures or memos requesting money for new equipment. Similarly, you may produce a variety of persuasive messages for people outside the organization, such as websites

---

CHECKLIST ✔ Developing Persuasive Messages

A. Get your reader's attention.
- Open with an audience benefit, a stimulating question, a problem, or an unexpected statement.
- Establish common ground by mentioning a point on which you and your audience agree.
- Show that you understand the audience's concerns.

B. Build your reader's interest.
- Expand and support your opening claim or promise.
- Emphasize the relevance of your message to your audience.

C. Increase your reader's desire.
- Make audience members want to change by explaining how the change will benefit them.
- Back up your claims with relevant evidence.

D. Motivate your reader to take action.
- Suggest the action you want readers to take.

- Stress the positive results of the action.
- Make the desired action clear and easy.

E. Balance emotional and logical appeals.
- Use emotional appeals to help the audience accept your message.
- Use logical appeals when presenting facts and evidence for complex ideas or recommendations.
- Avoid faulty logic.

F. Reinforce your position.
- Provide additional evidence of the benefits of your proposal and your own credibility in offering it.
- Use abstractions, metaphors, and other figures of speech to bring facts and figures to life.

G. Anticipate objections.
- Anticipate and answer potential objections.
- Present the pros and cons of all options if you anticipate a hostile reaction.

Ineffective

It's time to call the Fast Track program what it truly is—a disaster. Everyone was excited last year when we announced the plan to speed up our development efforts and introduce at least one new product every month. We envisioned rapidly expanding market share and strong revenue growth in all our product lines. What we got instead is a nightmare that is getting worse with every launch.

As a company, we clearly underestimated the resources it would take to market, sell, and support so many new products. We can't hire and train fast enough, and our teams in every department are overwhelmed. Forced to jump from one new product to the next, with no time to focus, the sales and technical specialists can't develop the expertise needed to help buyers before the sale or support them after the sale. As a result, too many customers either buy the wrong product or buy the right product but then can't get knowledgeable help when they need it. We're losing credibility in the market, we're starting to lose sales, and it won't be long before we start losing employees who are fed up with the insanity.

To make matters even worse, some of the recent products were clearly rushed to market before they were ready, with hardware quality problems and buggy software. Returns and warranty costs are skyrocketing.

New products are the lifeblood of the company, to be sure, but there is no point in introducing products that only create enormous support headaches and cost more to support than they generate in profits. We need to put the Fast Track initiative on hold immediately so the entire company can regroup. The R&D lab can devote its time to fixing problems in the recent products, and the rest of us can catch our collective breath and figure out how to meet our sales and support goals with the current product portfolio and our current staffing levels.

The company has clearly staked a lot on this program, so opening by calling it a disaster will only put the reader on the defensive.

Word choices such as *nightmare* and *insanity* give the message an emotional, almost hysterical, tone that detracts from the serious message.

The writer mingles an observation that may be subjective (declining credibility), a hard data point (declining sales), and a prediction (possibility of employee defections).

The claim that recent products were "clearly rushed to market" is unnecessarily inflammatory (because it blames another department) and distracts the reader from the more immediate problems of poor quality.

The first sentence of the last paragraph is insulting to anyone with basic business sense—particularly the president of a company.

Effective

This neutral summary of events serves as an effective buffer for the indirect approach and provides a subtle reminder of the original goals of the program.

This paragraph contains the same information as the poor version, but does so in a calmer way that is less likely to trigger the reader's defense mechanisms and thereby keeps the focus on the facts.

Notice how the writer separates a personal hunch (about the possibility of losing employees) from an observation about the market and a measured data point.

The information about the quality problems is introduced without directing blame.

With the evidence assembled, the writer introduces the main idea of putting the program on hold. The recommendation is a judgment call and a suggestion to a superior, so the hedging clause *I believe* is appropriate.

Everyone was excited last year when we launched the Fast Track program to speed up our development efforts and introduce at least one new product every month. We envisioned rapidly expanding market share and strong revenue growth in all our product lines.

While the R&D lab has met its goal of monthly releases, as a company, we clearly underestimated the resources it would take to market, sell, and support so many new products. We can't hire and train fast enough, and our teams in every department are overwhelmed. The sales and technical specialists haven't had time to develop the expertise needed to help buyers before the sale or support them after the sale. As a result, too many customers either buy the wrong product or buy the right product but then can't get knowledgeable help when they need it.

We're losing credibility in the market, and we're starting to lose sales. If the situation continues, I fear we will being losing employees, too.

In addition, some of the recent products are generating multiple reports of hardware quality problems and buggy software. Returns and warranty costs are climbing at an unprecedented rate.

With costs rising faster than revenues and our people getting overwhelmed, I believe it is time to put the Fast Track initiative on hold until the company can regroup. The hiatus would give R&D time to address the quality problems and give the marketing, sales, and tech support team the chance to re-assess our goals with the current product portfolio and our current staffing levels.

Figure 10.4 Persuasive Argumentation

Imagine you're the marketing manager in a company that decided to speed up its new product launches but did too much too fast and wound up creating chaos. You decide enough is enough and write a memo to the company president advocating that the new program be shut down until the company can regroup—a suggestion you know will meet with resistance. Notice how the ineffective version doesn't quite use the direct approach but comes out swinging, so to speak, and is overly emotional throughout. The effective version builds to its recommendation indirectly, using the same information but in a calm, logical way. Because it sticks to the facts, it is also shorter.

shaping public opinions or letters requesting adjustments that go beyond a supplier's contractual obligations. In addition, some of the routine requests you studied in Chapter 8 can become persuasive messages if you want a nonroutine result or believe that you haven't received fair treatment. Most of these messages can be divided into persuasive requests for action, persuasive presentations of ideas, and persuasive claims and requests for adjustment.

Persuasive Requests for Action

The bulk of your persuasive business messages will involve requests for action. In some cases, your request will be anticipated, so the direct approach is fine. In others, you'll need to introduce your intention indirectly, and the AIDA model or a similar approach is ideal for this purpose (see Figure 10.5 on the next page).

Open with an attention-getting device, and show readers you understand their concerns. Use the interest and desire sections of your message to demonstrate that you have good reason for making such a request and to cover what you know about the situation: the facts and figures, the benefits of helping, and any history or experience that will enhance your appeal. Your goals are (1) to gain credibility (for yourself and your request) and (2) to make your readers believe that helping you will indeed help solve a significant problem. Close with a request for some specific action, and make that course of action as easy to follow as possible to maximize the chances of a positive response.

Most persuasive business messages involve a request for action.

Persuasive Presentations of Ideas

You may encounter situations in which you simply want to change attitudes or beliefs about a particular topic, without asking the audience to decide or do anything—at least not yet. The goal of your first message might be nothing more than convincing your audience to reexamine long-held opinions or admit the possibility of new ways of thinking.

For instance, the World Wide Web Consortium (a global association that defines many of the guidelines and technologies behind the World Wide Web) has launched a campaign called the Web Accessibility Initiative. Although the consortium's ultimate goal is making websites more accessible to people who have disabilities or age-related limitations, a key interim goal is simply making website developers more aware of the need. As part of this effort, the consortium has developed a variety of presentations and documents that highlight the problems many web visitors face.[14]

Sometimes the objective of persuasive messages is simply to encourage people to consider a new idea.

Persuasive Claims and Requests for Adjustments

Most claims and requests for adjustment are routine messages and use the direct approach discussed in Chapter 8. However, consumers and professionals sometimes encounter situations in which they believe they haven't received a fair deal by following normal procedures. These situations require a more persuasive message.

The key ingredients of a good persuasive claim are a complete and specific review of the facts and a confident and positive tone. Keep in mind that you have the right to be satisfied with every transaction. Begin persuasive claims by outlining the problem and continue by reviewing what has been done about it so far, if anything. The recipient might be juggling numerous claims and other demands on his or her attention, so be clear, calm, and complete when presenting your case. Be specific about how you would like to see the situation resolved.

Next, give your reader a good reason for granting your claim. Show how the individual or organization is responsible for the problem, and appeal to your reader's sense of fair play, goodwill, or moral responsibility. Explain how you feel about the problem, but don't get carried away and don't make threats. People generally respond most favorably to requests that are calm and reasonable. Close on a respectful note that reflects how a successful resolution of the situation will repair or maintain a mutually beneficial working relationship.

1 Plan →	**2** Write →	**3** Complete
Analyze the Situation Verify that the purpose is to solve an ongoing problem, so the audience will be receptive. **Gather Information** Determine audience needs and obtain the necessary information on recycling problem areas. **Choose Medium and Channel** Verify that an email message is appropriate for this communication. **Organize the Information** Limit the scope to the main idea, which is to propose a recycling solution; use the indirect approach to lay out the extent of the problem.	**Adapt to Your Audience** Adjust the level of formality based on the degree of familiarity with the audience; maintain a positive relationship by using the "you" attitude, politeness, positive emphasis, and bias-free language. **Compose the Message** Use a conversational but professional style and keep the message brief, clear, and as helpful as possible.	**Revise the Message** Evaluate content and review readability to make sure the information is clear and complete without being overwhelming. **Produce the Message** Emphasize a clean, professional appearance. **Proofread the Message** Review for errors in layout, spelling, and mechanics. **Distribute the Message** Verify that the right file is attached and then deliver the message.

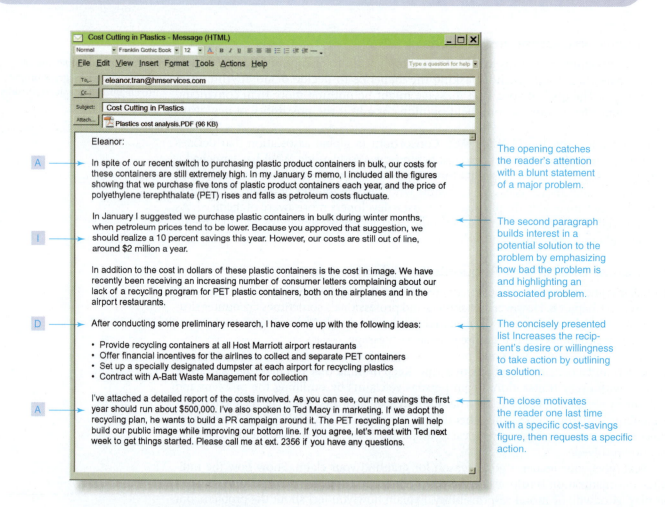

Figure 10.5   Persuasive Message Using the AIDA Model

This message uses the AIDA model in a persuasive message about a program that would try to reduce Host Marriott's annual plastics costs and curtail consumer complaints about the company's recycling record. Note how the writer "sells the problem" before attempting to sell the solution. Few people are interested in hearing about solutions to problems they don't know about or don't believe exist. The interest section introduces an additional, unforeseen problem with plastic product containers.

Source: MS Outlook 2013, © Microsoft.

Developing Marketing and Sales Messages

3 LEARNING OBJECTIVE
Describe an effective strategy for developing marketing and sales messages, and explain how to modify your approach when writing promotional messages for social media.

Marketing and sales messages use the same basic techniques as other persuasive messages, with the added emphasis of encouraging someone to participate in a commercial transaction. Although the terms *marketing message* and *sales message* are often used interchangeably, there is an important difference: **Marketing messages** usher potential buyers through the purchasing process without asking them to make an immediate decision. **Sales messages** take over at that point, encouraging potential buyers to make a purchase decision then and there. Marketing messages focus on such tasks as introducing new brands to the public and encouraging customers to visit websites for more information, whereas sales messages make an explicit request for people to buy a specific product or service. (The text of marketing and sales messages is usually referred to as "copy," by the way.)

Marketing and sales messages use many of the same techniques as persuasive business messages.

Most marketing and sales messages, particularly in larger companies, are created and delivered by professionals with specific training in marketing, advertising, sales, or public relations. However, you may be called on to review the work of these specialists or even to write such messages in smaller companies, and having a good understanding of how these messages work will help you be a more effective manager.

PLANNING MARKETING AND SALES MESSAGES

Everything you've learned about planning messages applies in general to marketing and sales messages, but the planning steps for these messages have some particular aspects to consider as well:

- **Assessing audience needs.** As with every other business message, successful marketing and sales messages start with an understanding of audience needs. Depending on the product and the market, these needs can range from a few functional considerations (such as the size, weight, and finish of office paper) to a complicated mix of emotional and logical issues (all the factors that play into buying a house, for example).

Understanding the purchase decision from the buyer's perspective is a vital step in framing an effective marketing or sales message.

- **Analyzing your competition.** Marketing and sales messages nearly always compete with messages from other companies trying to reach the same audience. When Nike plans a marketing campaign to introduce a new shoe model to current customers, the company knows its audience has also been exposed to messages from Adidas, New Balance, Reebok, and numerous other shoe companies. Finding a unique message in crowded markets can be quite a challenge.

Marketing and sales messages have to compete for the audience's attention.

- **Determining key selling points and benefits.** With some insight into audience needs and the alternatives offered by your competitors, your next step is to decide which features and benefits to highlight. **Selling points** are the most attractive features of a product, whereas **benefits** are the particular advantages purchasers can realize from those features. In other words, selling points focus on what the product does. Benefits focus on what the user experiences or gains. Benefits can be practical, emotional, or a combination of the two. For example, the feature of a thin, flexible sole in a running shoe offers the practical benefit of a more natural feel while running. In contrast, the visual design features of the shoe offer no practical benefits but can offer the emotional benefit of wearing something stylish or unusual.

Selling points focus on the product; benefits focus on the user.

- **Anticipating purchase objections.** Marketing and sales messages usually encounter objections, and as with persuasive business messages, the best way to handle them is to identify these objections up front and address as many as you can. They can range from high price or low quality to a lack of compatibility with existing products or a perceived risk involved with the product. By identifying potential objections up front, you can craft your promotional messages in ways that address those concerns. If price is a likely objection, for instance, you can look for ways to increase the perceived value of the purchase and decrease the perception of high cost. When promoting a home gym, you might say that it costs less than a year's worth of health club dues. Of course, any attempts to minimize perceptions of price or other potential negatives must be done ethically.

Anticipating objections is crucial to effective marketing and sales messages.

WRITING CONVENTIONAL MARKETING AND SALES MESSAGES

Conventional marketing and sales messages are often prepared using the AIDA model or some variation of it. (See the next section on crafting messages for social media.) Here are the key points of using the AIDA model for these messages:

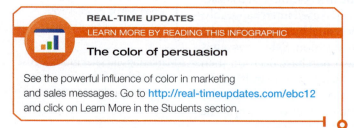

REAL-TIME UPDATES

LEARN MORE BY READING THIS INFOGRAPHIC

The color of persuasion

See the powerful influence of color in marketing and sales messages. Go to http://real-timeupdates.com/ebc12 and click on Learn More in the Students section.

- **Getting the reader's attention.** By looking and listening during any given day, you'll notice the many ways advertisers try to get your attention. For example, a headline might offer an exciting product benefit, a piece of interesting news, an appeal to people's emotions or sense of financial value, or a unique solution to a common problem. Of course, words aren't the only attention-getting devices. Depending on the medium, marketers can use evocative images, music, animation, or video. "Cutting through the clutter" to get the audience's attention is one of the biggest challenges with marketing and sales messages.

To build interest, expand on and support the promises in your attention-getting opening.

- **Building interest.** After catching the reader's or viewer's attention, your next step is to build interest in the product, company, or idea you are promoting. A common technique is to "pay off" the promise made in the headline by explaining how you can deliver those benefits. For example, if the headline offers a way to "Get Fit for $2 a Day," the first paragraph could explain that the home gyms your company sells start at less than $700, which works out to less than $2 a day over the course of a year.

Add details and audience benefits to increase desire for the product or service.

- **Increasing desire.** Now that you've given the audience some initial information to start building their interest, the next step is to boost their desire for the product by expanding on your explanation of how it will benefit them. Think carefully about the sequence of support points and use plenty of subheadings, hyperlinks, video demonstrations, and other devices to help people quickly find the information they need. By keeping the focus on potential customers and their practical and emotional needs, you can layer on information that helps convince people that your product really is the best solution for them. You can also use a variety of techniques to address potential objections and minimize doubts, including testimonials from satisfied users, articles written by industry experts, competitive comparisons, offers of product samples or free demonstrations, independent test results, and money-back guarantees.

After you've generated sufficient interest and desire, you're ready to persuade readers to take the preferred action.

- **Motivating action.** The final step in the AIDA model is persuading the audience to take action, such as encouraging people to pick up the phone to place an order or visit an online app store to download your software. The keys to a successful *call to action* are making it easy and as risk-free as possible. If the process is confusing or time-consuming, you'll lose potential customers.

If you analyze the advertisements you encounter in any medium, you'll see variations on these techniques used again and again.

WRITING PROMOTIONAL MESSAGES FOR SOCIAL MEDIA

The AIDA model and similar approaches have been successful with marketing and sales messages for decades, but in the social media landscape consumers are more apt to look for product information from other consumers, not the companies marketing those products. Consequently, your emphasis should shift to encouraging and participating in online conversations. Follow these guidelines (see Figure 10.6):[15]

MOBILE APP

Talkwalker helps companies monitor social media conversations in real time.

In a social media environment, persuasive efforts require a more conversational, interactive approach.

- **Facilitate community building.** Give customers and other audiences an opportunity to connect with you and one another, such as on your Facebook page or through members-only online forums.
- **Listen at least as much as you talk.** Listening is just as essential for online conversations as it is for in-person conversations.
- **Initiate and respond to conversations within the community.** Through content on your website, blog postings, social network profiles and messages, newsletters, and other tools, make sure you provide the information customers need in order

Courtesy of Fezzari Bicycles. To see more information go to www.fezzari.com. Google and the Google logo are registered trademarks of Google Inc., used with permission.

Figure 10.6   Promotional Messages in Social Media
Persuasive communication on social media often avoids overt promotion and instead tries to engage the target audience, as Fezzari Bicycles did with this post on Google+.

to evaluate your products and services. Use **conversation marketing**, rather than traditional promotion, to initiate and facilitate conversations in your networked community of customers, journalists, bloggers, and other interested parties.

- **Provide information people want.** Whether it's industry-insider news, in-depth technical guides to using your products, or brief answers to questions posted on community Q&A sites, fill the information gaps about your company and its products.

- **Identify and support your champions.** In marketing, *champions* are enthusiastic fans of your company and its products. Champions are so enthusiastic they help spread your message (through their blogs, for instance), defend you against detractors, and help other customers use your products.

- **Be real.** Social media audiences respond positively to companies that are open and conversational about themselves, their products, and subjects of shared interest. In contrast, if a company is serving its stakeholders poorly with shoddy products, bad customer service, or unethical behavior, an attempt to improve its reputation by adopting social media without fixing the underlying problems is likely to fail as soon as audiences see through the superficial attempt to "be social."

- **Integrate conventional marketing and sales strategies at the right time and in the right places.** AIDA and similar approaches are still valid for specific communication tasks, such as conventional advertising and the product promotion pages on your website.

CREATING PROMOTIONAL MESSAGES FOR MOBILE DEVICES

Mobile advertising and mobile commerce (sometimes referred to as *m-commerce*) are two of the hottest developments in marketing communications. Mobile advertising is already a multibillion-dollar business, with nearly 70 percent of those ad dollars spent on Google ads and Facebook.[16] The types of marketing and sales messages created for mobile audiences range from short, simple text ads that appear next to search engine results to mobile-optimized video—the most common form of content marketing in the mobile arena.[17]

Companies are putting so much emphasis on mobile marketing because mobile devices now play such a big role in consumer buying behavior. Smartphone owners tend to use their devices for many shopping-related tasks, from searching for product reviews to finding stores and service businesses, looking for coupons and other promotions, and doing in-store price comparisons. In fact, some 80 percent of smartphone-equipped consumers use their devices to get shopping-related information.[18]

> Promotional messages aimed at mobile audiences need to be short, simple, and easy to respond to.

If you are involved with creating mobile marketing or sales messages, keep two essential points in mind. First, like all mobile messages, promotional messages need to be kept short and simple. Second, the mobile experience needs to be fast and straightforward. Mobile users are often time-constrained, and they will quickly abandon websites that don't load quickly or are confusing to navigate.

Maintaining High Standards of Ethics, Legal Compliance, and Etiquette

4 LEARNING OBJECTIVE
Identify steps you can take to avoid ethical lapses in marketing and sales messages.

The word *persuasion* has negative connotations for some people, especially in a marketing or sales context. However, ethical businesspeople view persuasion as a positive force, aligning their own interests with what is best for their audiences. They influence audience members by providing information and aiding understanding, which allows audiences the freedom to choose.[19] To maintain the highest standards of business ethics, always demonstrate the "you" attitude by showing honest concern for your audience's needs and interests.

> Marketing and sales messages are covered by a wide range of laws and regulations.

As marketing and selling grow increasingly complex, so do the legal ramifications of marketing and sales messages. In the United States, the Federal Trade Commission (www.ftc.gov) has the authority to impose penalties (ranging from cease-and-desist orders to multimillion-dollar fines) on advertisers who violate federal standards for truthful advertising. Other federal agencies have authority over advertising in specific industries, such as transportation and financial services. Individual states have additional laws that may apply. The legal aspects of promotional communication can be quite complex, varying from state to state and from country to country, and most companies require marketing and salespeople to get clearance from company lawyers before sending messages.

Moreover, communicators must stay on top of changing regulations, such as the latest laws governing unsolicited bulk email ("spam"), disclosure requirements for bloggers who review products, privacy, and data security. For example, two ethical concerns that could produce new legislation are *behavioral targeting*, which tracks the online behavior of website visitors and serves up ads based on what they appear to be interested in, and *remarketing*, in which behaviorally targeted ads follow users even as they move on to other websites. Many users consider the practice invasive.[20]

> Marketers have a responsibility to stay up to date on laws and regulations that restrict promotional messages.

For all marketing and sales efforts, pay close attention to the following legal considerations:[21]

- **Marketing and sales messages must be truthful and nondeceptive.** The FTC considers messages to be deceptive if they include statements that are likely to mislead reasonable customers and the statements are an important part of the purchasing decision. Failing to include important information is also considered deceptive.

The FTC also looks at *implied claims*—claims you don't explicitly make but that can be inferred from what you do or don't say.

- **You must back up your claims with evidence.** According to the FTC, offering a money-back guarantee or providing letters from satisfied customers is not enough; you must still be able to support claims for your product with objective evidence such as a survey or scientific study. If you claim that your food product lowers cholesterol, you must have scientific evidence to support that claim.
- **"Bait and switch" advertising is illegal.** Trying to attract buyers by advertising a product that you don't intend to sell—and then trying to sell them another (and usually more expensive) product—is illegal.
- **Marketing messages and websites aimed at children are subject to special rules.** For example, online marketers must obtain consent from parents before collecting personal information about children under age 13.
- **Marketing and sales messages are considered binding contracts in many states.** If you imply or make an offer and then can't fulfill your end of the bargain, you can be sued for breach of contract.
- **In most cases, you can't use a person's name, photograph, or other identity without permission.** Doing so is considered an invasion of privacy. You can use images of people considered to be public figures as long as you don't unfairly imply that they endorse your message.

Meeting your ethical and legal obligations will go a long way toward maintaining good communication etiquette. However, you may still face etiquette decisions within ethical and legal boundaries. For instance, you can produce a marketing campaign that complies with all applicable laws and yet is offensive or insulting to your audience. Taking an audience-centered approach, in which you show respect for your readers and their values, should help you avoid any such etiquette missteps.

Technology also gives communicators new ways to demonstrate sensitivity to user needs. One example is automated RSS newsfeeds from blogs, alerting customers to information in which they've expressed an interest. *Opt-in* email newsletters are another technology that shows the "you" attitude at work. Unlike the unwelcome spam messages that litter email inboxes these days, opt-in messages are sent only to those people who have specifically requested information.

For the latest information on writing persuasive messages, visit **http://real-time updates.com/ebc12** and click on Chapter 10.

ON THE JOB: SOLVING COMMUNICATION DILEMMAS AT **RED ANTS PANTS**

Sarah Calhoun likes your style—your writing style, that is. She hired you to take care of all the company's customer communication efforts, from managing the website to writing an email newsletter. Use what you've learned in this chapter to address these challenges.

1. Red Ants Pants are much tougher than regular jeans, so their higher price is in line with the lasting value they offer customers. However, paying $129 for a pair of pants is a tough decision for many working women. Which of these statements addresses the cost concerns some customers are likely to have while reflecting the tone of company's other communication efforts?

a. What's more annoying than spending money when your work clothes wear out? How about spending it over and over again because you unwisely keep buying clothes that wear out too quickly.

b. Yes, you might pay more to put a pair of Red Ants Pants on your bod, but they'll stay there for a good long time—and not only because they fit better. With tough fabric and expert production, these pants are built to last.

c. We attest to the highest standards of fabric and craftwork, include heavyweight 12-ounce cotton canvas duck with a tight weave.

d. We were raised to believe that if you're not going to do your best, they why even show up? That's why we use the best fabrics and the best production processes.

2. Not many companies have the irreverent self-confidence to present their company history in the form of poetry—and fairly goofy poetry at that. The rhyming couplets in the Our History section of the Red Ants Pants website (under Our Story) do the job quite nicely, but you need a shorter version to use on the company's Facebook page. Which of these paragraphs does the best job of describing the company's founding in the Red Ants Pants communication style?

   a. Sarah Calhoun was tired of pants that didn't fit and didn't last, so she decided to do something about it: Red Ants Pants.

   b. If you've ever cleared a trail, dug a ditch, or repaired a truck, you know how rough these jobs can be on your clothes. If you're of the male persuasion, well lucky you—companies made rugged clothes just for you. But a woman? If you wanted tough clothes, well tough luck. You had a choice between women's pants that weren't up to rugged work or men's pants that didn't fit. After years of working in the wild, Sarah Calhoun decided she wasn't going to stand for this. She launched Red Ants Pants to provide hardworking women with pants that worked just as hard.

   c. Sarah Calhoun had a dream of starting her own company in the rustic wilds of Montana, creating useful, high-value products for hardworking women like herself. This quest for meaning manifested itself in the company you are now visiting in virtual space: Red Ants Pants.

3. Red Ants Pants also sells a handful of books on its website. These are books that Calhoun and her staff admire and that reflect aspects of life in Montana, such as Ivan Doig's classic *This House of Sky*. Which of these sentences would be a good introductory statement for the book page on the website?

   a. We love our Montana home, and these stories will help you understand why.

   b. We'd like to share some of the stories that explain why we love our Montana home.

   c. We present here a variety of stories set in Montana.

   d. Welcome to our tiny online bookstore with a few books about Montana.

4. Sarah Calhoun has been an inspiration to many entrepreneurs and has delivered speeches to a wide variety of audiences. For a reasonable fee, she is available to speak to conferences, civic groups, and other gatherings. Which of these is an effective way to introduce her availability as an inspirational speaker?

   a. Laugh, cry, cheer—and get inspired by Sarah's message of courageously following your dreams.

   b. Sarah Calhoun is available to speak to your group on a variety of topics.

   c. Is your organization tired of the same old speechifying? Sarah Calhoun will stir them up!

   d. Looking for inspiration? You and your people need to hear Sarah?

Learning Objectives Checkup

Assess your understanding of the principles in this chapter by reading each learning objective and studying the accompanying exercises. You can check your responses against the answer key on page 599.

Objective 10.1: Apply the three-step writing process to persuasive messages.

1. Which of the following is an accurate general statement about good ideas in the business world?

   a. Newer employees are not expected to contribute fresh ideas.

   b. Many good ideas pass unnoticed or are misunderstood because they are communicated poorly.

   c. Business leaders always jump on new ideas, even if they are poorly presented.

   d. Good ideas speak for themselves and don't need to be "communicated" in today's social media environment.

2. Why is the indirect approach often used in persuasive messages?

   a. It is more courteous and therefore gives the writer the opportunity to build up goodwill before slipping in the sales pitch.

   b. It takes less time.

   c. It is the traditional way to do persuasive messages and therefore expected.

   d. It lets the writer build audience interest and desire before asking for action or commitment.

3. Which of the following is not a good way to establish credibility with your audience?

   a. Support your argument with clear reasoning and objective evidence.

   b. Identify your sources.

   c. Establish common ground with your readers.

   d. Present only your side of the argument to avoid reminding the audience of alternatives.

Objective 10.2: Describe an effective strategy for developing persuasive business messages and identify the three most common categories of persuasive business messages.

4. The first phase in the AIDA model is to

   a. Do your research

   b. Gain the audience's attention

   c. Analyze the audience

   d. Call for action

5. The body of a message that follows the AIDA model

   a. Captures the audience's attention

   b. Contains the buffer

   c. Generates interest and heightens desire

   d. Calls for action

6. Which of the following is a good way to build desire using the AIDA approach?
   a. Explain how the proposed change will help your audience.
   b. Reduce resistance by addressing objections the audience might have.
   c. Explain complex ideas or products in more detail.
   d. Do all of the above.

7. The final phase of the AIDA method
   a. Provides in-depth information to help generate interest
   b. Reduces resistance by increasing the audience's desire
   c. Calls for action
   d. Captures the audience's attention

8. An argument that is based on human feelings is known as a/an _____ appeal.

9. An argument that is based on facts and reason is known as a/an _____ appeal.

10. The best approach to using emotional appeals is usually to
    a. Use them by themselves
    b. Use them in conjunction with logical appeals
    c. Use them only when the audience is particularly hostile
    d. Avoid them in all business messages

Objective 10.3: Describe an effective strategy for developing marketing and sales messages and explain how to modify your approach when writing promotional messages for social media.

11. Why is it important to anticipate objections when planning and writing persuasive messages?
    a. You are legally required to anticipate audience objections in all marketing messages.
    b. By anticipating potential objections, you have the opportunity to address them in a persuasive manner before the audience settles on a firm no answer.
    c. By anticipating potential objections, you have the opportunity to explain to audience members why they are viewing the situation incorrectly.
    d. By anticipating potential objections, you can explain to the audience all the negative consequences of accepting your message.

12. Prioritizing which features and benefits to write about is
    a. A waste of time because people don't read in sequential order
    b. Important because doing so lets you start with low-priority issues and work your way up to high-priority issues
    c. Important because it helps you focus your message on items and issues that the audience cares about the most
    d. Important because it helps ensure that you remember to talk about every single feature and benefit, no matter how inconsequential

13. How do marketing messages and sales messages differ?
    a. Sales messages use oral media exclusively.
    b. Sales messages are "hard sell," whereas marketing messages are "soft sell."
    c. Marketing messages move audiences toward a purchase decision without actually asking them to make a decision; sales messages ask them to make a decision then and there.
    d. The vast majority of marketing messages are still legal, but most traditional sales messages have been outlawed in both the United States and the European Union.

14. What is the relationship between features and benefits?
    a. They are different words for the same idea.
    b. Features are aspects of an idea or product; benefits are the advantages that readers will realize from those features.
    c. Features tell people how to use a product; benefits tell them how a product differs from the competition.
    d. Features are the primary advantages of a product; benefits are the secondary advantages.

15. Which of the following is the best definition of social commerce?
    a. It encompasses any aspect of buying and selling products and services or supporting customers through the use of social media.
    b. It is another term for group buying or committee buying within corporations.
    c. It encompasses all of the communication traffic on a given social network.
    d. It refers to the communication aspects of marketing and selling, as distinct from the transactional and financial aspects.

16. Which of the following is not a good guideline for using social media in sales and marketing?
    a. Rely on the conventional news media to distribute your messages; frequent outages and too much "chatter" make social networks unreliable.
    b. Identify and support your *champions*, those people who are enthusiastic fans of your company and its products.
    c. Initiate and respond to conversations within the community.
    d. Integrate conventional marketing and sales strategies at the right time and in the right places.

17. What is the likely reaction of mobile shoppers if they encounter e-commerce websites that are slow to load or confusing to navigate?
    a. They will quickly abandon such websites.
    b. They will shift over to their PCs and continue shopping on the websites.
    c. They will file complaints with the website owners' customer service departments.
    d. They will file complaints with the Federal Trade Commission (FTC).

Objective 10.4: Identify steps you can take to avoid ethical lapses in marketing and sales messages.

18. Which of the following steps should you take to make sure your persuasive messages are ethical?
    a. Align your interest with your audience's interests.
    b. Choose words that offer multiple interpretations.
    c. Limit the amount of information you provide to avoid overloading the audience and thereby confusing your readers.
    d. Do all of the above.

19. If it adheres to all applicable federal laws, a marketing or sales message
    a. Is certain to be both legal and ethical
    b. Could still violate some state laws
    c. Could still be unethical
    d. Both b and c

Quick Learning Guide

CHAPTER OUTLINE

Using the Three-Step Writing Process for Persuasive Messages
Step 1: Planning Persuasive Messages
Step 2: Writing Persuasive Messages
Step 3: Completing Persuasive Messages

Developing Persuasive Business Messages
Strategies for Persuasive Business Messages
Avoiding Common Mistakes in Persuasive Communication
Common Examples of Persuasive Business Messages

Developing Marketing and Sales Messages
Planning Marketing and Sales Messages
Writing Conventional Marketing and Sales Messages
Writing Promotional Messages for Social Media
Creating Promotional Messages for Mobile Devices

Maintaining High Standards of Ethics, Legal Compliance, and Etiquette

LEARNING OBJECTIVES

1 Apply the three-step writing process to persuasive messages. (page 288)

2 Describe an effective strategy for developing persuasive business messages, and identify the three most common categories of persuasive business messages. (page 292)

3 Describe an effective strategy for developing marketing and sales messages, and explain how to modify your approach when writing promotional messages for social media. (page 301)

4 Identify steps you can take to avoid ethical lapses in marketing and sales messages. (page 304)

KEY TERMS

AIDA model Message sequence that involves attention, interest, desire, and action

benefits The particular advantages that readers will realize from a product's selling points

conversation marketing Approach in which companies initiate and facilitate conversations in a networked community of customers, journalists, bloggers, and other interested parties

demographics Quantifiable characteristics of a population, including age, gender, occupation, income, and education

emotional appeal Persuasive approach that calls on audience feelings and sympathies rather than facts, figures, and rational arguments

logical appeal Persuasive approach that calls on reasoning and evidence

marketing messages Promotional messages that usher potential buyers through the purchasing process without asking them to make an immediate decision

motivation The combination of forces that drive people to satisfy their needs

persuasion The attempt to change an audience's attitudes, beliefs, or actions

psychographics Psychological characteristics of an audience, including personality, attitudes, and lifestyle

sales messages In contrast to marketing messages, sales messages encourage potential buyers to make a purchase decision then and there

selling points The most attractive features of a product or service

CHECKLIST

Developing Persuasive Messages

A. Get your reader's attention.
- Open with an audience benefit, a stimulating question, a problem, or an unexpected statement.
- Establish common ground by mentioning a point on which you and your audience agree.
- Show that you understand the audience's concerns.

B. Build your reader's interest.
- Expand and support your opening claim or promise.
- Emphasize the relevance of your message to your audience.

C. Increase your reader's desire.
- Make audience members want to change by explaining how the change will benefit them.
- Back up your claims with relevant evidence.

D. Motivate your reader to take action.
- Suggest the action you want readers to take.
- Stress the positive results of the action.
- Make the desired action clear and easy.

E. Balance emotional and logical appeals.
- Use emotional appeals to help the audience accept your message.
- Use logical appeals when presenting facts and evidence for complex ideas or recommendations.
- Avoid faulty logic.

F. Reinforce your position.
- Provide additional evidence of the benefits of your proposal and your own credibility in offering it.
- Use abstractions, metaphors, and other figures of speech to bring facts and figures to life.

G. Anticipate objections.
- Anticipate and answer potential objections.
- Present the pros and cons of all options if you anticipate a hostile reaction.

MyBCommLab

To complete the problems with the ⭐, go to EOC Discussion Questions in the MyLab.

Apply Your Knowledge

To review chapter content related to each question, refer to the indicated Learning Objective.

10.1. Why is it essential to understand your readers' likely motivations before writing a persuasive message? [LO-1]

10.2. Why is it important to present all sides of an argument when writing a persuasive message to a potentially hostile audience? [LO-2]

⭐ **10.3.** Are emotional appeals ethical? Why or why not? [LO-2]

⭐ **10.4.** What is likely to happen if a promotional message starts immediately with a call to action? Why? [LO-3]

Practice Your Skills

Messages for Analysis

For Message 10.A and Message 10.B, read the following documents and then (1) analyze the strengths and weaknesses of each sentence, and (2) revise each document so that it follows this chapter's guidelines.

10.5. Message 10.A: Message Strategies: Persuasive Claims and Requests for Adjustment [LO-2]

Dear TechStar Computing:

I'm writing to you because of my disappointment with my new multimedia PC display. The display part works all right, but the audio volume is set too high and the volume knob doesn't turn it down. It's driving us crazy. The volume knob doesn't seem to be connected to anything but simply spins around. I can't believe you would put out a product like this without testing it first.

I depend on my computer to run my small business and want to know what you are going to do about it. This reminds me of every time I buy electronic equipment from what seems like any company. Something is always wrong. I thought quality was supposed to be important, but I guess not. Anyway, I need this fixed right away. Please tell me what you want me to do.

10.6. Message 10.B: Message Strategies: Sales Messages [LO-3]

We know how awful dining hall food can be, and that's why we've developed the "Mealaweek Club." Once a week, we'll deliver food to your dormitory or apartment. Our meals taste great. We have pizza, buffalo wings, hamburgers and curly fries, veggie roll-ups, and more!

When you sign up for just six months, we will ask what day you want your delivery. We'll ask you to fill out your selection of meals. And the rest is up to us. At "Mealaweek," we deliver! And payment is easy. We accept MasterCard and Visa or a personal check. It will save money especially when compared with eating out.

Just fill out the enclosed card and indicate your method of payment. As soon as we approve your credit or check, we'll begin delivery. Tell all your friends about Mealaweek. We're the best idea since sliced bread!

10.7. Message 10.C: Media Skills: Podcasting [LO-2]

To access this message, visit http://real-timeupdates .com/ebc12, click on Student Assignments, and select Chapter 10, Message 10.C. Listen to this podcast. Identify at least three ways in which the podcast could be more persuasive, and draft a brief email message you could send to the podcaster with your suggestions for improvement.

Exercises

Each activity is labeled according to the primary skill or skills you will need to use. To review relevant chapter content, you can refer to the indicated Learning Objective. In some instances, supporting information will be found in another chapter, as indicated.

Choosing a Message Strategy [LO-1], Chapters 10–11 Now that you've explored routine, positive, negative, and persuasive messages, review the following message scenarios and identify which of the four message strategies would be most appropriate for the situation. Offer a brief justification for your choices. (Depending on the particular circumstances, a scenario might lend itself to more than one type of message; just be sure to offer compelling reasons for your choices.)

10.8. An unsolicited message to your department manager, explaining why you believe the company's experiment with self-managed work teams has not been successful

10.9. An unsolicited message to your department manager, explaining why you believe the company's experiment with self-managed work teams has not been successful and suggesting that one of the more experienced employees (such as yourself) should be promoted to supervisor

10.10. A message to a long-time industrial customer, explaining that a glitch in your accounting system resulted in the customer being overcharged on its last five orders, apologizing for the problem, and assuring the customer that you will refund the overcharged amount immediately

10.11. A news release announcing that your company plans to invite back 50 employees who were laid off earlier in the year

Message Strategies: Persuasive Business Messages; Collaboration: Team Projects [LO-2] With another student, analyze the persuasive email message to Eleanor Tran at Host Marriott (Figure 10.5) by answering the following questions:

10.12. What techniques are used to capture the reader's attention?

10.13. Does the writer use the direct or indirect organizational approach? Why?

10.14. Is the subject line effective? Why or why not?

10.15. Does the writer use an emotional or a logical appeal? Why?

10.16. What reader benefits are included?

10.17. How does the writer establish credibility?

10.18. What tools does the writer use to reinforce his position?

Message Strategies: Persuasive Business Messages, Marketing and Sales Messages: Media Skills: Email [LO-2], [LO-3] Compose effective subject lines for the following persuasive email messages:

10.19. A recommendation was sent by email to your branch manager to install wireless networking throughout the facility. Your primary reason is that management has encouraged more teamwork, but teams often congregate in meeting rooms, the cafeteria, and other places that lack network access—without which they can't do much of the work they are expected to do.

10.20. A message to area residents, soliciting customers for your new business, "Meals à la Car," a carryout dining service that delivers from most of the local restaurants.

10.21. An email message to the company president, asking that employees be allowed to carry over their unused vacation days to the following year. Apparently, many employees canceled their fourth-quarter vacation plans to work on the installation of a new company computer system. Under their current contract, vacation days not used by December 31 can't be carried over to the following year.

10.22. Communication Ethics: Making Ethical Choices [LO-2], [LO-4] Your boss has asked you to post a message on the company's internal blog, urging everyone in your department to donate money to the company's favorite charity, an organization that operates a summer camp for children with physical challenges. You wind up writing a lengthy posting, packed with facts and heartwarming anecdotes about the camp and the children's experiences. When you must work that hard to persuade your audience to take an action such as donating money to a charity, aren't you being manipulative and unethical? Explain.

Message Strategies: Marketing and Sales Messages [LO-3] (Customer Benefits) Determine whether the following sentences focus on features or benefits; rewrite as necessary to focus all the sentences on benefits.

10.23. All-Cook skillets are coated with a durable, patented nonstick surface.

10.24. You can call anyone and talk as long as you like on Saturdays and Sundays with our new FamilyTalk wireless plan.

10.25. With 8-millisecond response time, the Samsung LN-S4095D 40-inch LCD TV delivers fast video action that is smooth and crisp.[22]

10.26. Message Strategies: Marketing and Sales Messages [LO-3] Have you ever wondered why certain websites and blogs appear at the top of the list when you use an online search engine? Or why a site you might expect to find doesn't show up at all? Such questions are at the heart of one of the most important activities in online communication: *search engine optimization* (SEO). (SEO applies to the *natural* or *organic* search results, not the sponsored, paid results you see above, beside, or below the main search results listing.)

SEO is a complex topic that factors in dozens of variables, but even without becoming an expert in SEO, every website owner can work toward improving rankings by focusing on three important areas. First, offer fresh, high-quality, audience-oriented content. Content that doesn't appeal to people won't appeal to search engines, either. Second, use relevant keywords judiciously, particularly in important areas such as the page title that displays at the top of the browser screen. Third, encourage links to your site from other high-quality sites with relevant content. These links from other sites are crucial because they tell the search engines that other people find your content interesting and useful. Not surprisingly, given the importance of links from other sites, the content sharing encouraged by social media has had a huge impact on SEO in recent years.[23]

Locate a website for any company that sells products to consumers and write a new title for the site's homepage (the title that appears at the top of a web browser). Make the title short enough to read quickly while still summarizing what the company offers. Be sure to use one or more keywords that online shoppers would likely use when searching for the types of products the company sells. Next, identify three high-quality websites that would be good ones to link to the site you chose. For instance, if you chose a website that sells automotive parts and supplies, one of the three linking sites could be a popular blog that deals with automotive repair. Or if the site you chose sells golf equipment, you might find a sports website that covers the professional golf tours or one that provides information about golf courses around the world.

Expand Your Skills

Critique the Professionals

Visit the Facebook pages of six companies in several industries. How do the companies make use of their timeline? Do any of the companies use timeline posts to promote their products? Compare the material on the About tabs. Which company has the most compelling information here? How about the use of custom tabs; which company does the best job of using this Facebook feature? Using whatever medium your instructor requests, write a brief analysis of the message (no more than one page), citing specific elements from the piece and support from the chapter.

Sharpening Your Career Skills Online

Bovée and Thill's Business Communication Web Search, at **http://websearch.businesscommunicationnetwork.com**, is a unique research tool designed specifically for business communication research. Use the Web Search function to find a website, video, PDF document, podcast, or PowerPoint presentation that offers advice on writing persuasive messages (either persuasive business messages or marketing and sales messages). Write a brief email message to your instructor, describing the item you found and summarizing the career skills information you learned from it.

Improve Your Grammar, Mechanics, and Usage

The following exercises help you improve your knowledge of and power over English grammar, mechanics, and usage. Turn to the Handbook of Grammar, Mechanics, and Usage at the end of this book and review all of Sections 2.4 (Semicolons) and 2.5 (Colons). Then look at the following 10 items. Indicate the preferred choice in the following groups of sentences. (Answers to these exercises appear on page 601.)

10.27. **a.** This letter looks good; that one doesn't.
   b. This letter looks good: that one doesn't.

10.28. **a.** I want to make one thing clear: None of you will be promoted without teamwork.
   b. I want to make one thing clear; none of you will be promoted without teamwork.
   c. I want to make one thing clear: None of you will be promoted; without teamwork.

10.29. **a.** The Zurich airport has been snowed in, therefore I can't attend the meeting.
   b. The Zurich airport has been snowed in, therefore, I can't attend the meeting.
   c. The Zurich airport has been snowed in; therefore, I can't attend the meeting.

10.30. **a.** His motivation was obvious: to get Meg fired.
   b. His motivation was obvious; to get Meg fired.

10.31. **a.** Only two firms have responded to our survey; J. J. Perkins and Tucker & Tucker.
   b. Only two firms have responded to our survey: J. J. Perkins and Tucker & Tucker.

10.32. **a.** Send a copy to: Nan Kent, CEO, Bob Bache, president, and Dan Brown, CFO.

b. Send a copy to Nan Kent, CEO; Bob Bache, president; and Dan Brown, CFO.
   c. Send a copy to Nan Kent CEO; Bob Bache president; and Dan Brown CFO.

10.33. **a.** You shipped three items on June 7; however, we received only one of them.
   b. You shipped three items on June 7, however; we received only one of them.
   c. You shipped three items on June 7; however we received only one of them.

10.34. **a.** Workers wanted an immediate wage increase: they hadn't had a raise in 10 years.
   b. Workers wanted an immediate wage increase; because they hadn't had a raise in 10 years.
   c. Workers wanted an immediate wage increase; they hadn't had a raise in 10 years.

10.35. **a.** His writing skills are excellent however; he needs to polish his management style.
   b. His writing skills are excellent; however, he needs to polish his management style.
   c. His writing skills are excellent: however he needs to polish his management style.

10.36. **a.** We want to address three issues; efficiency; profitability; and market penetration.
   b. We want to address three issues; efficiency, profitability, and market penetration.
   c. We want to address three issues: efficiency, profitability, and market penetration.

For additional exercises focusing on semicolons and colons, visit MyBCommLab. Click on Chapter 10, click on Additional Exercises to Improve Your Grammar, Mechanics, and Usage, and click on 16. Punctuation A.

Cases

Website links for selected companies mentioned in cases can be found in the Student Assignments section at **http://real-time updates.com/ebc12.**

Persuasive Business Messages
MICROBLOGGING SKILLS

10.37. Message Strategies: Persuasive Business Messages [LO-2] You've been trying for months to convince your boss, company CEO Will Florence, to start using Twitter. You've told him that top executives in numerous industries now use Twitter as a way to connect with customers and other stakeholders without going through the filters and barriers of formal corporate communications, but he doesn't see the value.

Your task: You come up with the brilliant plan to demonstrate Twitter's usefulness using Twitter itself. First, find three executives from three companies who are on Twitter (choose any companies and executives you find interesting). Second, study their tweets to get a feel for the type of information they share. Third, if you don't already have a Twitter account set up for this class, set one up for the purposes of this exercise (you can deactivate later). Fourth, write four tweets to demonstrate the value of executive microblogging: one that summarizes the value of having a company CEO use Twitter and three support tweets, each one summarizing how your three real-life executive role models use Twitter.

BLOGGING SKILLS / TEAM SKILLS

10.38. Message Strategies: Persuasive Business Messages [LO-2] As a strong advocate for the use of social media in business, you are pleased by how quickly people in your company have taken up blogging, wiki writing, and other new-media activities. You are considerably less excited by the style and quality of what you see in the writing of your colleagues. Many seem to have interpreted "authentic and conversational" to mean "anything goes." Several of the Twitter users in the company seem to have abandoned any pretense of grammar and spelling. A few managers have dragged internal disagreements about company strategy out into public view, arguing with each other through comments on various industry-related forums. Product demonstration videos have been posted to the company's YouTube channel virtually unedited, making the whole firm look unpolished and unprofessional. The company CEO has written some blog posts that bash competitors with coarse and even crude language.

You pushed long and hard for greater use of these tools, so you feel a sense of responsibility for this situation. In addition, you are viewed by many in the company as the resident expert on social media, so you have some "expertise authority" on this issue. On the other hand, you are only a first-level manager, with three levels of managers above you, so while you have some "position authority" as well, you can hardly dictate best practices to the managers above you.

Your task: Working with two other students, write a post for the company's internal blog (which is not viewable outside the company), outlining your concerns about these communication practices. Use the examples mentioned previously, and make up any additional details you need. Emphasize that while social media communication is often less formal and more flexible than traditional business communication, it shouldn't be unprofessional. You are thinking of proposing a social media training program for everyone in the company, but for this message you just want to bring attention to the problem.

LETTER WRITING SKILLS

10.39. Message Strategies: Persuasive Business Messages [LO-2]
The coffee shop across the street from your tiny apartment is your haven away from home—great beverages, healthy snacks, free wireless, and an atmosphere that is convivial but not so lively that you can't focus on your homework. It lacks only one thing: some way to print out your homework and other files when you need hard copies. Your college's libraries and computer labs provide printers, but you live three miles from campus, and it's a long walk or an inconvenient bus ride.

Your task: Write a letter to the owner of the coffee shop, encouraging her to set up a printing service to complement the free wireless access. Propose that the service run at break-even prices, just enough to pay for paper, ink cartridges, and the cost of the printer itself. The benefit to the shop would be enticing patrons to spend more time—and, therefore, more of their coffee and tea money—in the shop. You might also mention that you had to take the bus to campus to print this letter, so you bought your afternoon latté somewhere else.

EMAIL SKILLS / PORTFOLIO BUILDER

10.40. Message Strategies: Persuasive Business Messages [LO-2]
As someone who came of age in the "post-email" world of blogs, wikis, social networks, and other Web 2.0 technologies, you were rather disappointed to find your new employer solidly stuck in the age of email. You use email, of course,

but it is only one of the tools in your communication toolbox. From your college years, you have hands-on experience with a wide range of social media tools, having used them to collaborate on school projects, to become involved in your local community, to learn more about various industries and professions, and to research potential employers during your job search. (In fact, without social media, you might never have heard about your current employer in the first place.) Moreover, your use of social media on the job has already paid several important dividends, including finding potential sales contacts at several large companies, connecting with peers in other companies to share ideas for working more efficiently, and learning about some upcoming legislative matters in your state that could profoundly hamper your company's current way of doing business.

You hoped that by setting an example through your own use of social media at work, your new colleagues and company management would quickly adopt these tools as well. However, just the opposite has happened. Waiting in your email in-box this morning was a message from the CEO, announcing that the company is now cutting off access to social networking websites and banning the use of any social media at work. The message says using company time and company computers for socializing is highly inappropriate and might be considered grounds for dismissal in the future if the problem gets out of hand.

Your task: You are stunned by the message. You fight the urge to fire off a hotly worded reply to straighten out the CEO's misperceptions. Instead, you wisely decide to send a message to your immediate superior first, explaining why you believe the new policy should be reversed. Using your boss's favorite medium (email, of course!), write a persuasive message, explaining why Facebook, Twitter, and other social networking technologies are valid—and valuable—business tools. Bolster your argument with examples from other companies and advice from communication experts.

IM SKILLS

10.41. Message Strategies: Requests for Action [LO-2]
At IBM, you're one of the coordinators for the annual Employee Charitable Contributions Campaign. Since 1978, the company has helped employees contribute to more than 2,000 health and human service agencies. These groups may offer child care; treat substance abuse; provide health services; or fight illiteracy, homelessness, and hunger. Some offer disaster relief or care for the elderly. All deserve support. They're carefully screened by IBM, one of the largest corporate contributors of cash, equipment, and people to nonprofit organizations and educational institutions in the United States and around the world. As your literature states, the program "has engaged our employees more fully in the important mission of corporate citizenship."

During the winter holidays, you target agencies that cater to the needs of displaced families, women, and children. It's not difficult to raise enthusiasm. The prospect of helping children enjoy the holidays—children who otherwise might have nothing—usually awakens the spirit of your most distracted workers. But some of them wait until the last minute and then forget.

They have until December 16 to make cash contributions. To make it in time for holiday deliveries, they can also bring in toys, food, and blankets through Tuesday, December 20. They shouldn't have any trouble finding the collection bins; they're everywhere, marked with bright red banners. But some will want to call you with questions or (you hope) to make credit card contributions: 800-658-3899, ext. 3342.

Your task: It's December 14. Write a 75- to 100-word instant message, encouraging last-minute holiday gifts.[24]

EMAIL SKILLS

10.42. Message Strategies: Requests for Action [LO-2]

Managing a new-product launch can be an aggravating experience as you try to coordinate a wide variety of activities and processes while barreling toward a deadline that is often defined more by external factors than a realistic assessment of whether you can actually meet it. You depend on lots of other people to meet their deadlines, and if they fail, you fail. The pressure is enough to push anybody over the edge. Unfortunately, that happened to you last week. After a barrage of bad news from suppliers and the members of the team you lead, you lost your cool in a checkpoint meeting. Shouting at people and accusing them of slacking off was embarrassing enough, but the situation got a hundred times worse this morning when your boss suggested you needed some low-pressure work for a while and removed you as the leader of the launch team.

Your task: Write an email message to your boss, Sunil, requesting to be reinstated as the project team leader. Make up any information you need.

EMAIL SKILLS

10.43. Message Strategies: Requests for Action [LO-2]

You appreciate how important phones are to your company's operations, but the amount of conversational chatter in your work area has gotten so bad that it's hard to concentrate on your work. You desperately need at least a few quiet hours every day to engage in the analytical thinking your job requires.

Your task: Write an email message to the division vice president, Jeri Ross, asking her to designate one of the conference rooms as a quiet-zone work room. It would have WiFi so that employees can stay connected to the corporate network, but it would not have any phone service, either landline or mobile. (Mobile reception is already weak in the conference rooms, but you will propose to equip the room with a mobile signal jammer to ensure that no calls can be made or received.) In addition, conversation of any kind would be strictly forbidden. Make up any details you need.

EMAIL SKILLS / MOBILE SKILLS

10.44. Message Strategies: Requests for Action [LO-2]

Your new company, WorldConnect Language Services, started well and is going strong. However, to expand beyond your Memphis, Tennessee, home market, you need a one-time infusion of cash to open branch offices in other cities around the Southeast. At the Entrepreneur's Lunch Forum you attended yesterday, you learned about several *angels*, as they are called in the investment community—private individuals who invest money in small

companies in exchange for a share of ownership. One such angel, Melinda Sparks, told the audience she is looking for investment opportunities outside of high technology, where angels often invest their money. She also indicated that she looks for entrepreneurs who know their industries and markets well, who are passionate about the value they bring to the marketplace, who are committed to growing their businesses, and who have a solid plan for how they will spend an investor's money. Fortunately, you meet all of her criteria.

Your task: Draft an email message to Sparks, introducing yourself and your business and asking for a meeting at which you can present your business plan in more detail. Explain that your Memphis office was booked to capacity within two months of opening, thanks to the growing number of international business professionals looking for translators and interpreters. You've researched the entire Southeast region and identified at least 10 other cities that could support a language services office such as yours. Making up whatever other information you need, draft a four-paragraph message following the AIDA model, ending with a request for a meeting within the next four weeks. You know Sparks tends to read email on her phone, so craft your message to be mobile friendly.

EMAIL SKILLS

10.45. Message Strategies: Persuasive Claims and Requests for Adjustment [LO-2]

You thought it was strange that no one called you on your new mobile phone, even though you had given your family members, friends, and boss your new number. Two weeks after getting the new phone and agreeing to a $49 monthly fee, you called the service provider, InstantCall, just to see if everything was working. Sure enough, the technician discovered that your incoming calls were being routed to an inactive number. You're glad she found the problem, but then it took the company nearly two more weeks to fix it. When you called to complain about paying for service you didn't receive, the customer service agent suggests you send an email to Judy Hinkley at the company's regional business office to request an adjustment.

Your task: Decide how much of an adjustment you think you deserve under the circumstances and then send an email message to Hinkley to request the adjustment to your account. Write a summary of events in chronological order, supplying exact dates for maximum effectiveness. Make up any information you need, such as problems that the malfunctioning service caused at home or at work.

LETTER WRITING SKILLS

10.46. Message Strategies: Requests for Information [LO-2]

As a motivated, ambitious employee, you naturally care about your performance on the job—and about making sure your performance is being fairly judged and rewarded. Unfortunately, the company has gone through a period of turmoil over the past several years, and you have reported to seven managers during the past five years. One year, your annual performance review was done by someone who had been your boss for only three weeks and knew almost nothing about you or your work.

Last year, your boss was fired the day after he wrote your review, and you can't help but wonder whether you got a fair review from someone in that situation. Overall, you are worried that your career progression and wage increases have been hampered by inconsistent and ill-informed performance reviews.

The company allows employees to keep copies of their reviews, but you haven't been diligent about doing so. You would like to get copies of your last five reviews, but you heard from a colleague that the human resources department will not release copies of past reviews without approval from the managers who wrote them. In your case, however, three of the managers who reviewed you are no longer with the company, and you do not want your current boss to know you are concerned about your reviews.

Your task: Write an email message to the director of human resources, Leon Sandes, requesting copies of your performance reviews over the past five years. Use the information included above and make up any additional details you need.

Marketing and Sales Messages: Conventional Media

LETTER WRITING SKILLS / PORTFOLIO BUILDER

10.47. Message Strategies: Marketing and Sales Messages [LO-3] Like all other states, Kentucky works hard to attract businesses that are considering expanding into the state or relocating entirely from another state. The Kentucky Cabinet for Economic Development is responsible for reaching out to these companies and overseeing the many incentive programs the state offers to new and established businesses.

Your task: As the communication director of the Kentucky Cabinet for Economic Development, you play the lead role in reaching out to companies that want to expand or relocate to Kentucky. Visit www.thinkkentucky.com and read "Top 10 Reasons for Locating or Expanding Your Business in Kentucky" (look under "Why Kentucky"). Identify the major benefits the state uses to promote Kentucky as a great place to locate a business. Summarize these reasons in a one-page form letter that will be sent to business executives throughout the country. Be sure to introduce yourself and your purpose in the letter, and close with a compelling call to action (have them reach you by telephone at 800-626-2930 or by email at econdev@ky.gov). As you plan your letter, try to imagine yourself as the CEO of a company and consider what a complex choice it would be to move to another state.[25]

LETTER WRITING SKILLS / PORTFOLIO BUILDER

10.48. Message Strategies: Marketing and Sales Messages [LO-3] Water polo is an active sport that provides great opportunities for exercise and for learning the collaborative skills involved in teamwork. You can learn more at www.usawaterpolo.org.

Your task: Write a one-page letter to parents of 10- to 14-year-old boys and girls, promoting the health and socialization benefits of water polo and encouraging them to introduce their children to the sport through a local club. Tell them they can learn more about the sport and find a club in their area by visiting the USA Water Polo website.

WEB WRITING SKILLS

10.49. Message Strategies: Marketing and Sales Messages [LO-3] Convincing people to give their music a try is one of the toughest challenges new bands and performers face.

Your task: Imagine you've taken on the job of promoting an amazing new band or performer you just discovered. Choose someone you've heard live or online and write 100 to 200 words of webpage copy describing the music in a way that will convince people to listen to a few online samples.

MOBILE SKILLS / TEAM SKILLS / PORTFOLIO BUILDER

10.50. Message Strategies: Marketing and Sales Messages [LO-3] You never intended to become an inventor, but you saw a way to make something work more easily, so you set to work. You developed a model, found a way to mass-produce it, and set up a small manufacturing studio in your home. You know that other people are going to benefit from your invention. Now all you need to do is reach that market.

Your task: Team up with other students assigned by your instructor and imagine a useful product that you might have invented—perhaps something related to a hobby or sporting activity. List the features and benefits of your imaginary product, and describe how it helps customers. Then write the copy for the first screen of a mobile-friendly website that would introduce and promote this product, using what you've learned in this chapter and making up details as you need them. Using word processing software or another tool if your instructor indicates, format the screen to show how the information would appear on a typical smartphone screen.

PODCASTING SKILLS

10.51. Message Strategies: Marketing and Sales Messages [LO-3] Your new podcast channel, School2Biz, offers advice to business students making the transition from college to career. You provide information on everything from preparing résumés to interviewing to finding a place in the business world and building a successful career. As you expand your audience, you'd eventually like to turn School2Biz into a profitable operation (perhaps by selling advertising time during your podcasts). For now, you're simply offering free advice.

Your task: As your instructor directs, either write a 50-word description of your new podcast or record a 30-second podcast describing the new service. Make up any information you need to describe School2Biz. Be sure to mention who you are and why the information you present is worth listening to.[26]

LETTER WRITING SKILLS / PORTFOLIO BUILDER

10.52. Message Strategies: Marketing and Sales Messages [LO-3] Kelly Services is a large staffing company based in Troy, Michigan. Client firms turn to Kelly to strategically balance their workloads and workforces during peaks and valleys of demand, to handle special projects, and to evaluate employees prior to making a full-time hiring decision. Facing the economic pressures of global competition, many companies now rely on a dynamic combination of permanent employees and temporary contractors hired through service providers such as Kelly. In addition to these staffing services, Kelly offers project services (managing both short- and long-term projects) and outsourcing and consulting services (taking over entire business functions).[27]

Your task: Write a one-page sales letter that would be sent to human resources executives at large U.S.-based corporations describing Kelly's three groups of business services. For current information, visit the Kelly website.

WEB WRITING SKILLS / PORTFOLIO BUILDER

10.53. Message Strategies: Marketing and Sales Messages [LO-3] After a shaky start as the technology matured and advertisers tried to figure out this new medium, online advertising has finally become a significant force in both consumer and business marketing. Companies in a wide variety of industries are shifting some of the ad budgets from traditional media such as TV and magazines to the increasing selection of advertising possibilities online—and more than a few companies now advertise almost exclusively online. That's fine for companies that sell advertising time and space online, but your job involves selling advertising in print magazines that are worried about losing market share to online publishers.

Online advertising has two major advantages that you can't really compete with: interactivity and the ability to precisely target individual audience members. On the other hand, you have several advantages going for you, including the ability to produce high-color photography, the physical presence of print (such as when a magazine sits on a table in a doctor's waiting room), portability, guaranteed circulation numbers, and close reader relationships that go back years or decades.

Your task: You work as an advertising sales specialist for the Time Inc. division of Time Warner, which publishes dozens of magazines around the world. Write a brief persuasive message about the benefits of magazine advertising; the statement will be posted on the individual websites of Time Inc.'s numerous magazines, so you can't narrow in on any single publication. Also, Time Inc. coordinates its print publications with an extensive online presence (including thousands of paid online ads), so you can't bash online advertising, either.[28]

Marketing and Sales Messages: Social Media

WEB WRITING SKILLS

10.54. Message Strategies: Marketing and Sales Messages; Media Skills: Social Networking [LO-3], Chapter 8 Curves is a fitness center franchise that caters to

women who may not feel at home in traditional gyms. With its customer-focused and research-based approach, Curves has become a significant force in the fitness industry and one of the most successful franchise operations in history.[29]

Your task: Read about the company on its website and imagine that you are adapting this material for the company's Facebook page. Write a "Company Overview" (95–100 words) and "Mission" statement (45–50 words).

SOCIAL NETWORKING SKILLS / TEAMWORK SKILLS

10.55. Message Strategies: Marketing and Sales Messages; Media Skills: Social Networking [LO-3], Chapter 8 You chose your college or university based on certain expectations, and you've been enrolled long enough now to have some idea about whether those expectations have been met. In other words, you are something of an expert about the "consumer benefits" your school can offer prospective students.

Your task: In a team of four students, interview six other students who are not taking this business communication course. Try to get a broad sample of demographics and psychographics, including students in a variety of majors and programs. Ask these students (1) why they chose this college or university and (2) whether the experience has met their expectations so far. To ensure the privacy of your respondents, do not record their names with their answers. Each member of the team should then answer these same two questions, so that you have responses from a total of 10 students.

After compiling the responses (you might use Google Docs or a similar collaboration tool so that everyone on the team has easy access to the information), analyze them as a team to look for any recurring "benefit themes." Is it the quality of the education? Research opportunities? Location? The camaraderie of school sporting events? The chance to meet and study with fascinating students from a variety of backgrounds? Identify two or three strong benefits that your college or university can promise—and deliver—to prospective students.

Now nominate one member of the team to draft a short marketing message that could be posted on your school's Facebook page. The message should include a catchy title that makes it clear the message is a student's perspective on why this is a great place to get a college education. When the draft is ready, the other members of the team should review it individually. Finally, meet as a team to complete the message.

MICROBLOGGING SKILLS

10.56. Message Strategies: Marketing and Sales Messages; Media Skills: Microblogging [LO-3], Chapter 8 Effective microblogging messages emphasize clarity and conciseness—and so do effective sales messages.

Your task: Find the website of any product that can be ordered online (any product you find interesting and that is appropriate to use for a class assignment). Adapt the information on the website, using your own words, and write four tweets to promote the product. The first should get your audience's attention (e.g., with an intriguing benefit claim), the second should build audience interest by providing some support for the claim you made in the first message, the third should increase readers' desire to have the product by layering on one or two more buyer benefits, and the fourth should motivate readers to take action to place an order. Your first three tweets can be up to 140 characters, but the fourth should be limited to 120 to accommodate a URL (you don't need to include the URL in your message, however).

If your class is set up with private Twitter accounts, use your private account to send your messages. Otherwise, email your four messages to your instructor or post them on your class blog, as your instructor directs.

MyBCommLab

Go to the Assignments section of your MyLab to complete these writing exercises.

10.57. What role do demographics and psychographics play in audience analysis during the planning of a persuasive message? [LO-1]

10.58. Why do the AIDA model and similar approaches need to be modified when writing persuasive messages in social media? [LO-3]

Endnotes

1. Red Ants Pants website, accessed 8 May 2014, www.redantspants .com; Becky Warren, "Ants on the Pants," *Country Woman*, February–March 2011, www.countrywomanmagazine.com; Dan Testa, "Red Ants Pants: By Working Women, for Working Women," *Flathead Beacon*, 4 March 2010, www.flatheadbeacon.com; Sammi Johnson, "Outdoor Woman: Red Ants Pants," *406 Woman*, April/May 2010, 52–53; Beth Judy, "Fit for Her," *Montana Magazine*, March–April 2010, 14–16; *Montana Quarterly*, Summer 2010, www.redantspants.com; Devan Grote, "Red Ants Pants," *Gettysburg*, Spring 2009, www.redantspants .com.

2. Jay A. Conger, "The Necessary Art of Persuasion," *Harvard Business Review*, May–June 1998, 84–95; Jeanette W. Gilsdorf, "Write Me Your Best Case for … ," *Bulletin of the Association for Business Communication* 54, no. 1 (March 1991): 7–12.

3. "Vital Skill for Today's Managers: Persuading, Not Ordering, Others," *Soundview Executive Book Summaries*, September 1998, 1.

4. Mary Cross, "Aristotle and Business Writing: Why We Need to Teach Persuasion," *Bulletin of the Association for Business Communication* 54, no. 1 (March 1991): 3–6.

5. Stephen Bayley and Roger Mavity, "How to Pitch," *Management Today*, March 2007, 48–53.

6. Robert B. Cialdini, "Harnessing the Science of Persuasion," *BusinessWeek*, 4 December 2007, www.businessweek.com.

7. Wesley Clark, "The Potency of Persuasion," *Fortune*, 12 November 2007, 48; W. H. Weiss, "Using Persuasion Successfully," *Supervision*, October 2006, 13–16.

8. Tom Chandler, "The Copywriter's Best Friend," *The Copywriter Underground blog*, 20 December 2006, http://copywriterunderground .com.

9. Raymond M. Olderman, *10-Minute Guide to Business Communication* (New York: Macmillan Spectrum/Alpha Books, 1997), 57–61.

10. John D. Ramage and John C. Bean, *Writing Arguments: A Rhetoric with Readings*, 3rd ed. (Boston: Allyn & Bacon, 1995), 430–442.

11. Philip Vassallo, "Persuading Powerfully: Tips for Writing Persuasive Documents," *Et Cetera*, Spring 2002, 65–71.

12. Dianna Booher, *Communicate with Confidence* (New York: McGraw-Hill, 1994), 102.

13. Conger, "The Necessary Art of Persuasion."

14. "Social Factors in Developing a Web Accessibility Business Case for Your Organization," W3C website, accessed 4 February 2013, www.w3.org.

15. Tamar Weinberg, *The New Community Rules: Marketing on the Social Web* (Sebastapol, Calif.: O'Reilly Media, 2009), 22; 23–24; 187–191; Larry Weber, *Marketing to the Social Web* (Hoboken, N.J.: Wiley, 2007), 12–14; David Meerman Scott, *The New Rules of Marketing and PR* (Hoboken, N.J.: Wiley, 2007), 62; Paul Gillin, *The New Influencers* (Sanger, Calif.: Quill Driver Books, 2007), 34–35; Jeremy Wright, *Blog Marketing: The Revolutionary Way to Increase Sales, Build Your Brand, and Get Exceptional Results* (New York: McGraw-Hill, 2006), 263–365.

16. Ingrid Lunden, "Global Mobile Ad Spend Jumped 105% in 2013, on Track for $31.5B In 2014 Led by Google, Says eMarketer," *TechCrunch*, 19 March 2014, http://techcrunch.com.

17. Inessa Davydova, "The Rise in Mobile Video," *DigitalSurgeons*, 1 October 2013, www.digitalsurgeons.com.

18. Chris Kelley, "Why You Need a Mobile Website," *V2 Marketing Communications*, 18 June 2013, http://blog.marketingv2.com.

19. Gilsdorf, "Write Me Your Best Case for …"

20. Robert Brady, "The Dark Side of Remarketing," *Clix*, 21 January 2014, www.clixmarketing.com; Miguel Helft and Tanzina Vega, "Retargeting Ads Follow Surfers to Other Sites," *New York Times*, 29 August 2010, www.nytimes.com.

21. "How to Comply with the Children's Online Privacy Protection Rule," U.S. Federal Trade Commission website, accessed 17 July 2010, www.ftc.gov; "Frequently Asked Advertising Questions: A Guide for Small Business," U.S. Federal Trade Commission website, accessed 17 July 2010, www.ftc.gov.

22. Samsung website, accessed 22 October 2006, www.samsung.com.

23. "Webmaster Guidelines," Google, accessed 5 February 2013, www.google.com; Brian Clark, "How to Create Compelling Content That Ranks Well in Search Engines," *Copyblogger*, May 2010, www.copyblogger.com; P. J. Fusco, "How Web 2.0 Affects SEO Strategy," *ClickZ*, 23 May 2007, www.clickz.com.

24. IBM website, accessed 15 January 2004, www.ibm.com; "DAS Faces an Assured Future with IBM," IBM website, accessed 16 January 2004, www.ibm.com; "Sametime," IBM website, accessed 16 January 2004, www.ibm.com.

25. Kentucky Cabinet for Economic Development website, accessed 8 May 2014, www.thinkkentucky.com.

26. Adapted from Podcast Bunker website, accessed 19 July 2010, www.podcastbunker.com.

27. Kelly Services website, accessed 19 July 2010, www.kellyservices .com.

28. Time Inc. website, accessed 8 May 2014, www.timewarner.com.

29. Curves website, accessed 19 July 2010, www.curves.com.

Preparing Reports and Presentations

CHAPTER **11** Planning Reports and Proposals

CHAPTER **12** Writing Reports and Proposals

CHAPTER **13** Completing Reports and Proposals

CHAPTER **14** Designing and Delivering Business Presentations

Reports and presentations offer important opportunities to demonstrate your value to the organization. Depending on the project, you might analyze complex problems, educate audiences, address opportunities in the marketplace, win contracts, or even launch an entire company with the help of a compelling business plan. Adapt what you've learned so far to the particular challenges of long-format messages, including some special touches that can make formal reports stand out from the crowd. Learn how to plan effective presentations, overcome the anxieties that every speaker feels, and respond to questions from the audience. Discover some tips and techniques for succeeding with the Twitter-enabled *backchannel* and with online presentations. Finally, complement your talk with compelling visual materials and learn how to create presentation slides that engage and excite your audience.

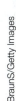

BraunS/Getty Images

11

Planning Reports and Proposals

LEARNING OBJECTIVES

After studying this chapter, you will be able to

1 Adapt the three-step writing process to reports and proposals.

2 Describe an effective process for conducting business research, explain how to evaluate the credibility of an information source, and identify the five ways to use research results.

3 Explain the role of secondary research, and describe the two major categories of online research tools.

4 Explain the role of primary research, and identify the two most common forms of primary research for business communication purposes.

5 Explain how to plan informational reports and website content.

6 Identify the three most common ways to organize analytical reports.

7 Explain how to plan proposals.

ON THE JOB: COMMUNICATING AT
MYCITYWAY

Transforming a Great Idea into a Great Business

Any experienced entrepreneur will tell you there's a big difference between having a great idea for a business and actually building a successful business. Many things have to go right, from creating a compelling product or service to finding the right employees to getting enough money to launch, expand, and sustain operations.

For Archana Patchirajan, Sonpreet Bhatia, and Puneet Mehta, the adventure started with the NYC BigApps competition. This contest is sponsored by the city of New York to encourage entrepreneurs to create better ways for people to use the NYC Data Mine, a huge trove of data created by all the government departments and agencies in the city.

The three partners jumped on the opportunity with NYC Way, a mobile application that helps people "navigate and explore" the city, whether they are residents looking for apartment deals or visitors looking for a great restaurant. One key aspect of the BigApps competition is that entrepreneurs must put their apps online for people to try out. By the time the contest ended, 100,000 people were using NYC Way.

MyCityWay's effective use of a business plan helped secure financing that allowed the company to expand far beyond its initial New York City market.

Patchirajan, Bhatia, and Mehta clearly had a hit product on their hands. The next challenge was to turn it into a thriving business. As with most startups, that meant getting money to expand operations. The competition garnered the new firm, MyCityWay, priceless publicity and a small amount of *seed funding* that let the team set up offices and begin hiring.

Momentum continued to build as they enhanced the product and several hundred thousand more people began using it. After a successful launch in the New York City market, the next step was to conquer the world. That would require a significant infusion of capital, and to attract that, the three founders knew they needed a formal *business plan* to show potential investors why MyCityWay would be a smart place to invest their money.

With their Wall Street backgrounds, Patchirajan, Bhatia, and Mehta understood the fundamentals of business finance, which gave them a good foundation for their plan. They also got smart advice on what today's investors are looking for: short, compelling documents that strike a balance between providing enough

information to be persuasive and providing so much information that potential investors balk at reading it. With so many plans crossing their desks day after day, most venture capitalists and other investors don't have the time to slog through 50 or 60 pages of details to judge whether a company might be worth pursuing as an investment candidate. They want to be captivated in a matter of seconds and persuaded to learn more in a matter of minutes.

MyCityWay clearly found the right balance with its plan, as a second round of funding brought in $1 million in capital and then luxury carmaker BMW invested $5 million as part of its "BMW i" program, which promotes the development of innovative automotive materials and technologies. The company now has apps for more than 70 cities around the world and is well on its way to becoming a global player in the field of mobile information.[1]

WWW.MYCITYWAY.COM

Applying the Three-Step Writing Process to Reports and Proposals

1 LEARNING OBJECTIVE
Adapt the three-step writing process to reports and proposals.

Whether you're sharing your latest great idea with your boss or launching an entirely new company (see the profile of MyCityWay in the chapter opening On the Job), reports will play a vital role in your business career. Reports fall into three basic categories (see Figure 11.1 on the next page):

- **Informational reports** offer data, facts, feedback, and other types of information, without analysis or recommendations.
- **Analytical reports** offer both information and analysis, and they can also include recommendations.
- **Proposals** offer structured persuasion for internal or external audiences.

Reports can be classified as informational reports, analytical reports, and proposals.

The nature of reports varies widely, from one-page trip reports that follow a standard format to detailed business plans and proposals that can run hundreds of pages. No matter what the circumstances, try to view every business report as an opportunity to demonstrate your understanding of your audience's challenges and your ability to contribute to your organization's success.

Reports can be a lot of work, but they also give you the opportunity to demonstrate your grasp of important business issues.

The three-step process you studied in Chapters 4 though 6 and applied to short messages in Chapters 7 through 10 is even more beneficial with reports and proposals because a methodical, efficient approach to planning, writing, and completing is even more valuable with these larger projects. This chapter addresses the planning step, focusing on two major areas that require special attention in long documents: gathering and organizing information. Chapter 12 covers the writing step and also includes advice on creating effective visuals for your reports and proposals. Chapter 13 describes the tasks involved in completing reports and proposals.

ANALYZING THE SITUATION

Reports can be complex, time-consuming projects, so be sure to analyze the situation carefully before you begin to write. Pay special attention to your **statement of purpose**, which explains *why* you are preparing the report and *what* you plan to deliver in the report (see Table 11.1 on the next page).

Define your purpose clearly so you don't waste time with unnecessary rework.

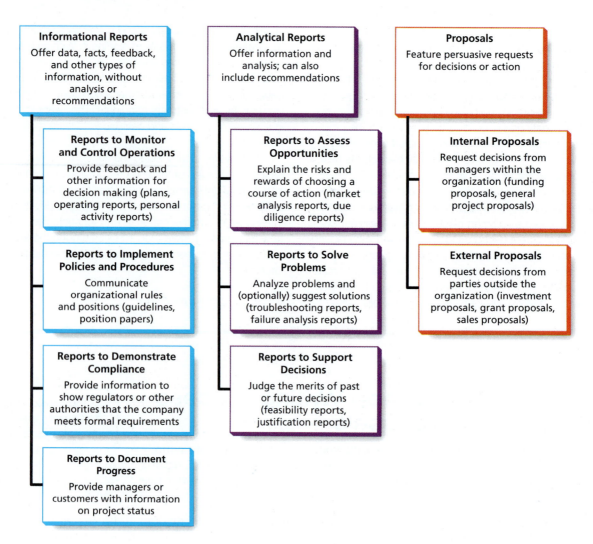

Figure 11.1 **Common Types of Business Reports and Proposals**
You will have the opportunity to read and write many types of reports in your career; here are some of the most common.

The most useful way to phrase a purpose statement is to begin with an infinitive phrase (*to* plus a verb), which helps pin down your general goal (*to inform, to identify, to analyze,* and so on). Consider these examples for informational reports:

- To update clients on the progress of the research project (progress report)
- To develop goals and objectives for the coming year (strategic plan)

TABLE 11.1   Problem Statements Versus Purpose Statements

Problem Statement	Statement of Purpose
Our company's market share is steadily declining.	To explore new ways of promoting and selling our products and to recommend the approaches most likely to stabilize our market share
Our current computer network lacks sufficient bandwidth and cannot be upgraded to meet our future needs.	To analyze various networking options and to recommend the system that will best meet our company's current and future needs
We need $2 million to launch our new product.	To convince investors that our new business would be a sound investment so that we can obtain desired financing
Our current operations are too decentralized and expensive.	To justify the closing of the Newark plant and the transfer of East Coast operations to a single Midwest location in order to save the company money

- To identify customers and explain how the company will serve them (marketing plan)
- To submit monthly sales statistics to management (operating report)
- To summarize what occurred at the annual sales conference (personal activity report)
- To explain building access procedures (policy implementation report)
- To submit required information to the Securities and Exchange Commission (compliance report)

The statement of purpose for an analytical report often needs to be more comprehensive than a statement for an informational report. For example, a report suggesting ways to reduce employee travel and entertainment (T&E) costs might have the following as a statement of purpose:

> … to analyze the T&E [travel and entertainment] budget, evaluate the impact of recent changes in airfares and hotel costs, and suggest ways to tighten management's control over T&E expenses.

If the writer had been assigned an informational report instead, she might have stated her purpose differently:

> To summarize the company's spending on travel and entertainment

You can see from these two examples how much influence the purpose statement has on the scope of your report. Because she was assigned an analytical report rather than an informational report, the writer had to go beyond merely collecting data; she had to draw conclusions and make recommendations. (You can see a full analytical report based on this statement of purpose in Chapter 13.)

When writing a proposal, you must also be guided by a clear statement of purpose to help focus on crafting a persuasive message. Here are several examples:

> To secure $400k of funding in next year's capital budget for a new conveyor system in the warehouse (funding proposal)

> To get management approval to reorganize the North American salesforce (general project proposal)

> To secure $2 million in venture capital funding to complete design and production of the new line of titanium mountain bikes (investment proposal as part of a business plan)

> To convince CommuniCo to purchase a trial subscription to our latest database offering (sales proposal)

In addition to considering your purpose carefully, you will also want to prepare a *work plan* for most reports and proposals in order to make the best use of your time. For simpler reports, the work plan can be an informal list of tasks and a simple schedule. However, if you're preparing a lengthy report, particularly when you're collaborating with others, you'll want to develop a more detailed work plan (see Figure 11.2 on the next page).

The statement of purpose for a proposal should help guide you in developing a persuasive message.

A detailed work plan saves time and often produces more effective reports.

GATHERING INFORMATION

Obtaining the information needed for many reports and proposals requires careful planning, and you may even need to do a separate research project to acquire the data and information you need (see "Supporting Your Messages with Reliable Information" on page 327). To stay on schedule and on budget, be sure to review your statement of purpose and your audience's needs so that you can focus on the most important information needs. Whenever possible, try to reuse or adapt existing information to save time.

Some reports require formal research projects in order to gather all the necessary information.

SELECTING THE BEST COMBINATION OF MEDIA AND CHANNELS

Just as you would for other business messages, choose media and channels for your reports based on the needs of your audience and the practical advantages and disadvantages of the choices available to you. In addition to the general selection criteria discussed in

The best medium for any given report might be anything from a professionally printed and bound document to an online executive dashboard that displays live updates.

The problem statement clearly and succinctly defines the problem the writers intend to address.

This section explains how the researchers will find the data and information they need.

The assignments and schedule section clearly lists responsibilities and due dates.

This paragraph identifies exactly what will be covered by the research and addressed in the final report.

The preliminary outline has enough detail to guide the research and set reader expectations.

STATEMENT OF THE PROBLEM

The rapid growth of our company over the past five years has reduced the sense of community among our staff. People no longer feel like part of an intimate organization that values teamwork.

PURPOSE AND SCOPE OF WORK

The purpose of this study is to determine whether social networking technology such as Facebook and Socialtext would help rebuild a sense of community within the workforce and whether encouraging the use of such tools in the workplace will have any negative consequences. The study will attempt to assess the impact of social networks in other companies in terms of community-building, morale, project communication, and overall productivity.

SOURCES AND METHODS OF DATA COLLECTION

Data collection will start with secondary research, including a review of recently published articles and studies on the use of social networking in business and a review of product information published by technology vendors. Primary research will focus on an employee and management survey to uncover attitudes about social networking tools. We will also collect anecdotal evidence from bloggers and others with experience using networks in the workplace.

PRELIMINARY OUTLINE

The preliminary outline for this study is as follows:
I. What experiences have other companies had with social networks in the workplace?
  A. Do social networks have a demonstrable business benefit?
  B. How do employees benefit from using these tools?
  C. Has network security and information confidentiality been an issue?
II. Is social networking an appropriate solution for our community-building needs?
  A. Is social networking better than other tools and methods for community building?
  B. Are employees already using social networking tools on the job?
  C. Will a company-endorsed system distract employees from essential duties?
  D. Will a company system add to managerial workloads in any way?
III. If we move ahead, should we use a "business-class" network such as Socialtext or a consumer tool such as Facebook?
  A. How do the initial and ongoing costs compare?
  B. Do the additional capabilities of a business-class network justify the higher costs?
IV. How should we implement a social network?
  A. Should we let it grow "organically," with employees choosing their own tools and groups?
  B. Should we make a variety of tools available and let employees improvise on their own?
  C. Should we designate one system as the official company social network and make it a permanent, supported element of the information technology infrastructure?
V. How can we evaluate the success of a new social network?
  A. What are the criteria of success or failure?
  B. What is the best way to measure these criteria?

TASK ASSIGNMENTS AND SCHEDULE

Each phase of this study will be completed by the following dates:

Secondary research: Hank Waters	September 15, 2016
Employee and management survey: Julienne Cho	September 22, 2016
Analysis and synthesis of research: Hank Waters/Julienne Cho	October 6, 2016
Comparison of business and consumer solutions: Julienne Cho	October 13, 2016
Comparison of implementation strategies: Hank Waters	October 13, 2016
Final report: Hank Waters	October 20, 2016

Figure 11.2 **Work Plan for a Report**

A formal work plan such as this is a vital tool for planning and managing complex writing projects. The preliminary outline here helps guide the research; as the writers move forward with the project and begin drafting the report, they may modify the outline to improve the flow or to incorporate new information uncovered during their research.

MOBILE APP

Sage Evolution Executive Dashboard and Databox are two of the executive dashboard apps available for mobile devices.

Chapter 4, consider several points for reports and proposals. First, for many reports and proposals, audiences have specific media requirements, and you might not have a choice. For instance, executives in many corporations now expect to review reports via their in-house intranets, sometimes in conjunction with an *executive dashboard*, a customized online presentation of key operating variables such as revenue, profits, quality, customer satisfaction, and project progress. Executive dashboards are particularly helpful for accessing report content on mobile devices (see Figure 11.3).

Second, consider how your audience wants to provide feedback on your report or proposal, if applicable. Will your readers prefer to write comments on a printed document

Klipfolio, Inc.

Figure 11.3 **Executive Dashboards**

To help managers avoid information overload, many companies now use executive dashboards to present carefully filtered highlights of key performance parameters. Dashboards are essentially super-summarized reports. The latest generation of software and mobile apps make it easy to customize screens to show each manager the specific summaries he or she needs to see.

or to use the commenting and markup features in a word processing program or Adobe Reader? Third, will multiple people need to update the document over time? A wiki could be an ideal choice because it gives everyone easy access to the content. Fourth, bear in mind that your choice of medium and channel also sends a nonverbal message. For instance, a routine sales report dressed up in fancy printed covers or animated multimedia could look like a waste of time and money.

ORGANIZING YOUR INFORMATION

The direct approach is used often for reports because it is efficient and easy to follow. When an audience is likely to be receptive or at least open minded, use the direct approach: Lead with a summary of your key findings, conclusions, recommendations, or proposal, whichever is relevant. This "up-front" arrangement is by far the most popular and convenient for business reports. It saves time and makes the rest of the report easier to follow. For those who have questions or want more information, later parts of the report provide complete findings and supporting details.

However, if the audience is unsure about your credibility or is not ready to accept your main idea without first seeing some reasoning or evidence, the indirect approach is a better choice because it gives you a chance to prove your points and gradually overcome audience reservations. To enable the use of AIDA-style persuasion, unsolicited proposals in particular often use the indirect approach. Bear in mind, though, that the longer the document, the less effective the indirect approach is likely to be.

Both approaches have merit, so businesspeople often combine them, revealing their conclusions and recommendations in stages as they go along rather than putting them all first or last (see Figure 11.4 on the next page).

Use the direct approach for most reports; consider the indirect approach if you haven't established credibility with your readers, or if your main idea will be met with resistance.

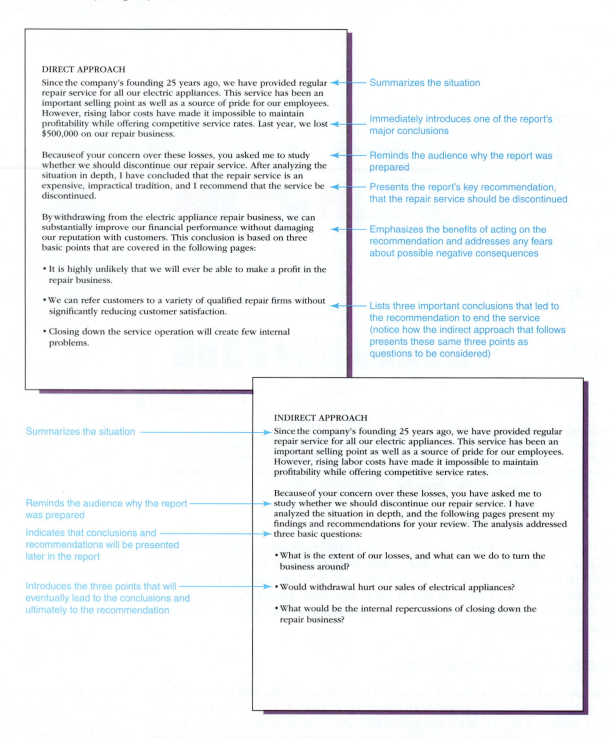

DIRECT APPROACH

Since the company's founding 25 years ago, we have provided regular repair service for all our electric appliances. This service has been an important selling point as well as a source of pride for our employees. However, rising labor costs have made it impossible to maintain profitability while offering competitive service rates. Last year, we lost $500,000 on our repair business. — *Summarizes the situation*

— *Immediately introduces one of the report's major conclusions*

Because of your concern over these losses, you asked me to study whether we should discontinue our repair service. After analyzing the situation in depth, I have concluded that the repair service is an expensive, impractical tradition, and I recommend that the service be discontinued. — *Reminds the audience why the report was prepared*

— *Presents the report's key recommendation, that the repair service should be discontinued*

By withdrawing from the electric appliance repair business, we can substantially improve our financial performance without damaging our reputation with customers. This conclusion is based on three basic points that are covered in the following pages: — *Emphasizes the benefits of acting on the recommendation and addresses any fears about possible negative consequences*

• It is highly unlikely that we will ever be able to make a profit in the repair business.

• We can refer customers to a variety of qualified repair firms without significantly reducing customer satisfaction. — *Lists three important conclusions that led to the recommendation to end the service (notice how the indirect approach that follows presents these same three points as questions to be considered)*

• Closing down the service operation will create few internal problems.

Summarizes the situation —

INDIRECT APPROACH

Since the company's founding 25 years ago, we have provided regular repair service for all our electric appliances. This service has been an important selling point as well as a source of pride for our employees. However, rising labor costs have made it impossible to maintain profitability while offering competitive service rates.

Reminds the audience why the report was prepared →

Indicates that conclusions and recommendations will be presented later in the report →

Because of your concern over these losses, you have asked me to study whether we should discontinue our repair service. I have analyzed the situation in depth, and the following pages present my findings and recommendations for your review. The analysis addressed three basic questions:

Introduces the three points that will eventually lead to the conclusions and ultimately to the recommendation →

• What is the extent of our losses, and what can we do to turn the business around?

• Would withdrawal hurt our sales of electrical appliances?

• What would be the internal repercussions of closing down the repair business?

Figure 11.4   Direct Approach Versus Indirect Approach in an Introduction
In the direct version of this introduction, the writer quickly presents the report's recommendation, followed by the conclusions that led to that recommendation. In the indirect version, the same topics are introduced in the same order, but no conclusions are drawn about them; the conclusions and the ultimate recommendation appear later, in the body of the report.

When you outline your content, use informative ("talking") headings rather than simple descriptive ("topical") headings (see Table 11.2). When in question or summary form, informative headings force you to really think through the content rather than simply identify the general topic area. Using informative headings will not only help you plan more effectively but also facilitate collaborative writing. A heading such as "Industry Characteristics" could mean five different things to the five people on your writing team,

TABLE 11.2   Types of Outline Headings

Descriptive (topical)	Informative (Talking) Outline	
Outline	Question Form	Summary Form

1. Industry Characteristics
 a. Annual sales
 b. Profitability
 c. Growth rate
  i. Sales
  ii. Profit
	1. What is the nature of the industry?
	 a. What are the annual sales?
	 b. Is the industry profitable?
	 c. What is the pattern of growth?
	  i. Sales growth?
	  ii. Profit growth?
		1. Flour milling is a mature industry.
		 a. Market is large.
		 b. Profit margins are narrow.
		 c. Growth is modest.
		  i. Sales growth averages less than 3 percent a year.
		  ii. Profits are flat.

so use a heading that conveys a single, unambiguous meaning, such as "Flour milling is a mature industry."

For a quick review of adapting the three-step process to long reports, refer to "Checklist: Adapting the Three-Step Writing Process to Informational and Analytical Reports." Sections later in this chapter provide specific advice on how to plan informational reports, analytical reports, and proposals.

Supporting Your Messages with Reliable Information

Audiences expect you to support your message with solid research. As you've probably discovered while doing school projects, effective research involves a lot more than simply typing a few terms into a search engine. Save time and get better results by using a clear process:

1. **Plan your research.** A solid plan yields better results in less time.
2. **Locate the data and information you need.** The research plan tells you *what* to look for; your next step is to figure out *where* the data and information are and *how* to access them.
3. **Process the data and information you've located.** The data and information you find probably won't be in a form you can use immediately and will require some

2 LEARNING OBJECTIVE
Describe an effective process for conducting business research, explain how to evaluate the credibility of an information source, and identify the five ways to use research results.

Researching without a plan wastes time and usually produces unsatisfactory results.

CHECKLIST ✔ **Adapting the Three-Step Writing Process to Informational and Analytical Reports**

A. Analyze the situation.
- Clearly define your purpose before you start writing.
- If you need to accomplish several goals in the report, identify all of them in advance.
- Prepare a work plan to guide your efforts.

B. Gather information.
- Determine whether you need to launch a separate research project to collect the necessary information.
- Reuse or adapt existing information whenever possible.

C. Select the right medium.
- Base your decision on audience expectations (or requirements, as the case may be).

- Consider the need for commenting, revising, distributing, and storing.
- Remember that the medium you choose also sends a message.

D. Organize your information.
- Use the direct approach if your audience is receptive.
- Use the indirect approach if your audience is skeptical.
- Use the indirect approach when you don't want to risk coming across as arrogant.
- Combine approaches if doing so will help build support for your primary message.

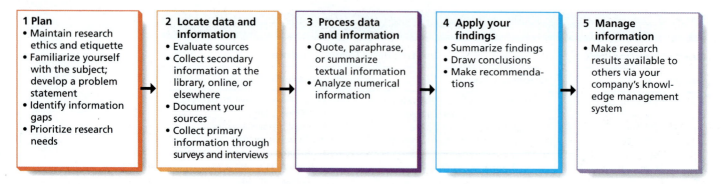

Figure 11.5 **The Research Process**
By following a methodical research process, you can save time and money while uncovering better information.

processing, which might involve anything from statistical analysis to resolving the differences between two or more expert opinions.

4. **Apply your findings.** You can apply your research findings in three ways: summarizing information for someone else's benefit, drawing conclusions based on what you've learned, or developing recommendations.

5. **Manage information efficiently.** Many companies today are trying to maximize the return on the time and money they invest in business research by collecting and sharing research results in a variety of computer-based systems, known generally as **knowledge management (KM)** systems. At the very least, be sure to share your results with any colleagues who may be able to benefit from them.

You can see the sequence of these steps in Figure 11.5; the following sections offer more details, starting with planning your research.

PLANNING YOUR RESEARCH

With so much information online these days, it's tempting just to punch some keywords into a search engine and then grab something from the first screen or two of results. However, this haphazard approach limits your effectiveness and can lead to expensive and embarrassing mistakes.

To maximize your chances of finding useful information and minimize the time you spend looking for it, start by familiarizing yourself with the subject so that you can frame insightful questions. As you explore the general subject area, try to identify basic terminology, significant trends, important conflicts, influential people, and potential sources of information. Next, develop a **problem statement** that will define the purpose of your research. This statement should explicitly define the decision you need to make or the conclusion you need to reach at the end of the process. For example, a retailer might want to know whether consumers are starting to turn away from bottled water because of concerns about cost and the environmental impact of plastic packaging and transportation. The problem statement could be "We need to determine whether we should we reduce the number or variety of bottled water brands carried in our stores."

Before you begin your research project, recognize that research carries some significant ethical responsibilities. To avoid ethical lapses, keep the following points in mind:

- Don't force a specific outcome by skewing your research.
- Respect the privacy of your research participants.
- Document sources and give appropriate credit.
- Respect *intellectual property rights*, the ownership of unique ideas that have commercial value in the marketplace.[2]
- Don't distort information from your sources.
- Don't misrepresent who you are or what you intend to do with the research results.

> The problem statement guides your research by focusing on the decision you need to make or the conclusion you need to reach.

In addition to ethics, research etiquette deserves careful attention. For example, respect the time of anyone who agrees to be interviewed or to be a research participant, and maintain courtesy throughout the interview or research process.

LOCATING DATA AND INFORMATION

The range of sources available to business researchers today can be overwhelming. The good news is that if you have a question about an industry, a company, a market, a new technology, or a financial topic, somebody else has probably already researched the subject. Research done previously for another purpose is considered **secondary research** (covered on pages 332–336) when the results are reused in a new project. This secondary information can be anything from magazine articles to survey results. Don't let the name *secondary* fool you, though. You want to start with secondary research because it might save you considerable time and money. If you can't find existing research that meets your needs, you'll have to engage in **primary research** (covered on pages 337–340), which is new research done specifically for the current project.

Primary research involves collecting information for the first time, specifically for a new project; secondary research involves finding and reusing information others have gathered in previous projects.

EVALUATING SOURCES

No matter where you're searching, it is your responsibility to separate quality information from unreliable junk, so you don't taint your results or damage your reputation. Social media have complicated this challenge by making many new sources of information available. On the positive side, independent sources communicating through blogs, Twitter, wikis, user-generated content sites, and podcasting channels can provide valuable and unique insights, often from experts or insiders whose voices might never be heard otherwise. On the negative side, these nontraditional information sources often lack the editorial boards and fact checkers commonly used in traditional publishing. You cannot assume that the information you find in blogs and other sources is accurate, objective, and current. Answer the following questions about each piece of material:

You have the responsibility to evaluate your sources carefully to avoid embarrassing and potentially damaging mistakes.

- **Does the source have a reputation for honesty and reliability?** Generally speaking, you can feel more comfortable using information from an established source that has a reputation for accuracy. For sources that are new or obscure, your safest bet is to corroborate anything you learn with information from several other sources.
- **Is the source potentially biased?** To interpret an organization's information, you need to know its point of view. For example, information about a particular company can be presented quite differently by a competitor, a union trying to organize the company's workforce, an investment research firm, and an environmental advocacy group. Information from a source with a particular point of view isn't necessarily bad, of course, but knowing this context is always helpful and sometimes essential for interpreting the information correctly.
- **What is the purpose of the material?** For instance, was the material designed to inform others of new research, advance a political position, or promote a product? Was it designed to promote or sell a product? Be sure to distinguish among advertising, advocating, and informing. And don't lower your guard just because an organization has a reassuring name like the American Institute for the Advancement of All Things Good and Wonderful; many innocuously labeled groups advocate a particular line of political, social, or economic thinking.
- **Is the author credible?** Is the author a professional journalist? An industry insider? An informed amateur? Merely someone with an opinion?
- **Where did the source get *its* information?** Try to find out who collected the data, the methods they used, their qualifications, and their professional reputation.
- **Can you verify the material independently?** Verification can uncover biases or mistakes, which is particularly important when the information goes beyond simple facts to include projections, interpretations, and estimates. If you can't verify critical information, let your audience know that.

MOBILE APP
Instapaper's mobile app lets you save web pages and articles to read later—a convenient capability when you're exploring a topic and want to collect potential sources for review.

- **Is the material current?** Make sure you are using the most current information available by checking the publication date of a source. Look for a "posted on" or "updated on" date with online material. If you can't find a date, don't assume the information is current without verifying it against another source.
- **Is the material complete?** Have you accessed the entire document or only a selection from it? If it's a selection, which parts were excluded? Do you need more detail?
- **Are all claims supported with evidence?** Are opinions presented as facts? Does the writer make broad claims, such as "most people believe ..." without citing any surveys to support this?
- **Do the source's claims stand up to logical scrutiny?** Finally, step back and ask whether the information makes sense. If that little voice in your head says that something sounds suspicious, listen!

You probably won't have time to conduct a thorough background check on all your sources, so focus your efforts on the most important or most suspicious pieces of information. And if you can't verify critical facts or figures, be sure to let your readers know that.

USING YOUR RESEARCH RESULTS

After you've collected all the necessary information, the next step is to transform it into the specific content you need. For simple projects, you may be able to drop your material directly into your report, presentation, or other application. However, when you have gathered a significant amount of information or raw data from surveys, you need to process the material before you can use it. This step can involve analyzing numeric data; quoting, paraphrasing, or summarizing textual material; drawing conclusions; and making recommendations.

Analyzing Data

Mean, median, and *mode* provide specific insights into sets of numerical data.

Business research often yields numeric data, but these numbers alone might not provide the insights managers need in order to make good business decisions. Fortunately, even without advanced statistical techniques, you can use simple arithmetic to help extract meaning from sets of research data. Table 11.3 shows several answers you can gain about a collection of numbers, for instance. The **mean** (which is what people are usually referring to when they use the term *average*) is the sum of all the items in the group divided by the number of items in that group. The **median** is the "middle of the road," or the midpoint of a series, with an equal number of items above and below. The **mode** is the number that occurs more often than any other in the sample; it's the best answer to a question such as "What is the usual amount?" Each of the three measures can tell you different things about a set of data.

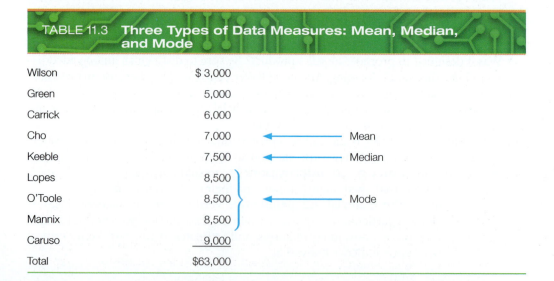

TABLE 11.3　Three Types of Data Measures: Mean, Median, and Mode

Wilson	$ 3,000	
Green	5,000	
Carrick	6,000	
Cho	7,000	← Mean
Keeble	7,500	← Median
Lopes	8,500	
O'Toole	8,500	← Mode
Mannix	8,500	
Caruso	9,000	
Total	$63,000	

Next, look at the data to spot **trends**—definite patterns taking place over time, including growth, decline, and cyclical trends that vary between growth and decline. By examining data over a period of time, you can detect patterns and relationships that help you answer important questions.

Trends suggest directions or patterns in a series of data points.

Statistical measures and trends identify *what* is happening. To understand *why* those things are happening, look at **causation** (the cause-and-effect link between two factors, where one of them causes the other to happen) and **correlation** (the simultaneous change in two variables you're measuring, such as customer satisfaction dropping when product reliability drops). Bear in mind that causation can be easy to assume but difficult to prove. The drop in customer satisfaction might have been caused by a new accounting system that fouled up customer invoices. To prove causation, you need to be able to isolate the suspected cause as the *only* potential source of the change in the measured effect. However, eliminating all but one possible cause isn't always feasible, so you often have to apply careful judgment to correlations. Researchers frequently explore the relationships between subsets of data using a technique called *cross-tabulation*. For instance, if you're trying to figure out why total sales rose or fell, you might look separately at sales data by age, gender, location, and product type.

Causation shows cause-and-effect relationships; *correlation* indicates simultaneous changes in two variables that may not necessarily be causally related.

Quoting, Paraphrasing, and Summarizing Information

You can use textual information from sources in three ways. *Quoting* a source means you reproduce it exactly as you found it, and you either set it off with quotation marks (for shorter passages) or extract it in an indented paragraph (for longer passages). Use direct quotations when the original language will enhance your argument or when rewording the passage would lessen its impact. However, try not to quote sources at great length. Too much quoting creates a choppy patchwork of varying styles and gives the impression that all you've done is piece together the work of other people.

Quoting a source means reproducing the content exactly and indicating who created the information originally.

You can often maximize the impact of secondary material in your own writing by *paraphrasing* it, restating it in your own words and with your own sentence structures.[3] Paraphrasing helps you maintain a consistent tone while using vocabulary familiar to your audience. Of course, you still need to credit the originator of the information, but not with quotation marks or indented paragraphs.

Paraphrasing is expressing someone else's ideas in your own words.

To paraphrase effectively, follow these tips:[4]

- Reread the original passage until you fully understand its meaning and are able to express it in your own words.
- Use language that matches the flow and tone of the rest of your report and that your audience is familiar with.
- Check your version with the original source to verify that you have not altered the meaning.
- Use quotation marks to identify any unique terms or phrases you have borrowed exactly from the source.
- Record the source so that you can give proper credit if you use this material in your report.

Summarizing is similar to paraphrasing but presents the gist of the material in fewer words than the original. An effective summary identifies the main ideas and major support points from your source material but leaves out most details, examples, and other information that is less critical to your audience. Summarizing is not always a simple task, and your audience will judge your ability to separate significant issues from less significant details. Identify the main idea and the key support points, and separate these from details, examples, and other supporting evidence (see Figure 11.6 on the next page).

Summarizing is similar to paraphrasing but distills the content into fewer words.

Of course, all three approaches require careful attention to ethics. When quoting directly, take care not to distort the original intent of the material by quoting selectively or out of context. And never resort to plagiarism.

Drawing Conclusions

A **conclusion** is a logical interpretation of the facts and other information in a report. A sound conclusion is not only logical but flows from the information included in a report,

A conclusion is a logical interpretation of the information at hand.

Original: 116 words

Our facilities costs spiraled out of control last year. The 23 percent jump was far ahead of every other cost category in the company and many times higher than the 4 percent average rise for commercial real estate in the Portland metropolitan area. The rise can be attributed to many factors, but the major factors include repairs (mostly electrical and structural problems at the downtown office), energy (most of our offices are heated by electricity, the price of which has been increasing much faster than for oil or gas), and last but not least, the loss of two sublease tenants whose rent payments made a substantial dent in our cost profile for the past five years.

Analyze the text to find main idea, major supporting points, and details

Main idea → Our facilities costs spiraled out of control last year. The 23 percent jump was far ahead of every other cost category in the company and many times higher than the 4 percent average rise for commercial real estate in the Portland metropolitan area.

Major support points → The rise can be attributed to many factors, but the major factors include repairs (mostly electrical and structural problems at the downtown office), energy (most of our offices are heated by electricity, the price of which has been increasing much faster than for oil or gas), and last but not least, the

Details → loss of two sublease tenants whose rent payments made a substantial dent in our cost profile for the past five years.

45-word summary

Our facilities costs jumped 23 percent last year, far ahead of every other cost category in the company and many times higher than the 4 percent local average. The major factors contributing to the increase are repairs, energy, and the loss of two sublease tenants.

22-word summary

Our facilities costs jumped 23 percent last year, due mainly to rising repair and energy costs and the loss of sublease income.

Figure 11.6 **Summarizing Effectively**
To summarize a section of text, first analyze it to find the main idea, the major support points, and the less-important details. Then assemble the appropriate pieces with additional words and phrases as needed to ensure a smooth flow.

meaning that it should be based on the information included in the report and shouldn't rely on information that isn't in the report. Moreover, if you or the organization you represent have certain biases that influence your conclusion, ethics obligate you to inform the audience accordingly.

Reaching good conclusions based on the evidence at hand is one of the most important skills you can develop in your business career. In fact, the ability to see patterns and possibilities that others can't see is one of the hallmarks of innovative business leaders. Consequently, take your time with this part of the process. Play "devil's advocate," attacking your conclusion as an audience might to make sure it stands up to rigorous scrutiny.

Making Recommendations

A recommendation is a suggested course of action based on what you have concluded about a particular situation.

Whereas a conclusion interprets information, a **recommendation** suggests action—what to do in response to the information. The following example illustrates the difference between a conclusion and a recommendation:

Conclusion	Recommendation
On the basis of its track record and current price, I believe that this company is an attractive buy.	I recommend that we offer to buy the company at a 10 percent premium over the current market value of its stock.

To be credible, recommendations must be based on logical analysis and sound conclusions. They must also be practical and acceptable to the people who have to make your recommendations work. Finally, when making a recommendation, be certain that you have adequately described the steps needed to implement your recommendation.

3 **LEARNING OBJECTIVE**
Explain the role of secondary research, and describe the two major categories of online research tools.

Conducting Secondary Research

Even if you intend to eventually conduct primary research, start with a review of any available secondary research. Inside your company, you might be able to find a variety of reports and other documents that could help. Outside the company, business researchers can choose from a wide range of print and online resources, both in libraries and online. Table 11.4 provides a small sample of the many secondary resources available.

TABLE 11.4   Important Resources for Business Research

COMPANY, INDUSTRY, AND PRODUCT RESOURCES (URLs are provided for online resources)

AnnualReports.com (www.annualreports.com). Free access to annual reports from thousands of public companies.

Brands and Their Companies/Companies and Their Brands. Contains data on several hundred thousand consumer products, manufacturers, importers, marketers, and distributors. Also available as an online database; ask at your library.

CNN/Money (http://money.cnn.com). News, analysis, and financial resources covering companies, industries, and world markets.

D&B Directories. A variety of directories, including America's Corporate Families (ownership connections among companies), Business Rankings (25,000 leading companies), Directory of Service Companies (more than 50,000 companies in the service sector), and Industrial Guide (more than 120,000 manufacturing companies).

Hoover's Handbook of American Business. Profiles of hundreds of influential public and private corporations.

Hoover's Online (www.hoovers.com). Database of millions of companies worldwide, including in-depth coverage of thousands of leading companies around the world. Basic information available free; in-depth information requires a subscription.

Manufacturing & Distribution USA. Data on thousands of companies in the manufacturing, wholesaling, and retailing sectors.

NAICS Codes (www.census.gov/eos/www/naics). North American Industry Classification System.

Reference USA. Concise information on millions of U.S. companies; subscription database.

SEC filings (www.sec.gov/edgar.shtml). SEC filings, including 10Ks, 10Qs, annual reports, and prospectuses for U.S. public firms.

Standard & Poor's Net Advantage. Comprehensive range of directories and databases focusing on publicly traded companies and their industries and markets.

ThomasNet (www.thomasnet.com). Information on thousands of U.S. manufacturers, indexed by company name and product.

RESEARCH DIRECTORIES AND INDEXES

Books in Print. Database indexes millions of books, audio books, and video titles from around the world. Available in print and professional online versions.

Directories in Print. Information on thousands of business and industrial directories.

Encyclopedia of Associations. Index of thousands of associations, listed by broad subject category, specific subject, association, and location. Available as an online database as well.

Reader's Guide to Periodical Literature. Classic index of general-interest magazines, categorized by subject and author; also available in electronic format, including a version with the full text of thousands of articles.

TRADEMARKS AND PATENTS

Official Gazette of the United States Patent and Trademark Office (www.uspto.gov). Weekly publication (one for trademarks and one for patents) providing official record of newly assigned trademarks and patents, product descriptions, and product names.

United States Patent and Trademark Office (www.uspto.gov). Trademark and patent information records.

STATISTICS AND OTHER BUSINESS DATA

Bureau of Economic Analysis (www.bea.gov). Large collection of economic and government data.

Europa—The European Union Online (http://europa.eu). A portal that provides up-to-date coverage of current affairs, legislation, policies, and EU statistics.

FedStats (www.fedstats.gov). Access to a full range of statistics and information from more than 70 U.S. government agencies.

Key Business Ratios (Dun & Bradstreet). Industry, financial, and performance ratios.

Information Please Almanac. Compilation of broad-range statistical data, with strong focus on labor force.

Annual Statement Studies. Industry, financial, and performance ratios published by the Risk Management Association.

Statistical Abstract of the United States (www.census.gov). Annual compendium of U.S. economic, social, political, and industrial statistics.

The World Almanac and Book of Facts. Facts on economic, social, educational, and political events for major countries.

U.S. Bureau of Labor Statistics (www.bls.gov). Extensive national and regional information on labor and business, including employment, industry growth, productivity, the Consumer Price Index (CPI), and the overall U.S. economy.

U.S. Census Bureau (www.census.gov). Demographic data and analysis on consumers and businesses based on census results.

(Continued)

TABLE 11.4 **Continued**

COMMERCIAL DATABASES (Require subscriptions; check with your school library)

ABI/INFORM Trade & Industry. Access to more than 750 periodicals and newsletters that focus on specific trades or industries.

Business Source Premier (Ebsco). Access to a variety of databases on a wide range of disciplines from leading information providers.

ProQuest Dialog. Hundreds of databases that include areas such as business and finance, news and media, medicine, pharmaceuticals, references, social sciences, government and regulation, science and technology, and more.

ProQuest. Thousands of periodicals and newspapers with extensive archives.

HighBeam Research. Thousands of full-text newspaper, magazine, and newswire sources, plus maps and photographs.

Gale Business & Company Resource Center. A comprehensive research tool designed for undergraduate and graduate students, job searchers, and investors; offers a wide variety of information on companies and industries.

LexisNexis. Several thousand databases covering legal, corporate, government, and academic subjects.

FINDING INFORMATION AT A LIBRARY

Libraries offer information and resources you can't find anywhere else—including experienced research librarians.

Public, corporate, and university libraries offer printed sources with information that is not available online and online sources that are available only by subscription. Libraries are also where you'll find one of your most important resources: librarians. Reference librarians are trained in research techniques and can often help you find obscure information you can't find on your own. They can also direct you to the typical library's many sources of business information:

- **Newspapers and periodicals.** Libraries offer access to a wide variety of popular magazines, general business magazines, *trade journals* (which provide information about specific professions and industries), and *academic journals* (which provide research-oriented articles from researchers and educators).
- **Business books.** Although less timely than newspapers, periodicals, and online sources, business books provide comprehensive coverage, in-depth analysis, and broad perspective that often can't be found anywhere else.
- **Directories.** Thousands of directories are published in print and electronic formats in the United States, and many include membership information for all kinds of professions, industries, and special-interest groups.
- **Almanacs and statistical resources.** Almanacs are handy guides to factual and statistical information about countries, politics, the labor force, and so on. One of the most extensive is the *Statistical Abstract of the United States* (available at **www.census .gov**).

Local, state, and federal government agencies publish a huge array of information that is helpful to business researchers.

- **Government publications.** Information on laws, court decisions, tax questions, regulatory issues, and other governmental concerns can often be found in collections of government documents.
- **Online databases.** Databases offer vast collections of computer-searchable information, often in specific areas such as business, law, science, technology, and education. Some of these are available only by institutional subscription, so the library may be your only way to gain access to them. Some libraries offer remote online access to some or all databases; for others, you'll need to visit in person.

FINDING INFORMATION ONLINE

Internet research tools fall into two basic categories: search tools and monitoring tools.

The Internet can be a tremendous source of business information, provided that you know where to look and how to use the tools available. Roughly speaking, the tools fall into two categories: those you can use to actively *search* for existing information and those you can use to *monitor* selected sources for new information. (Some tools can perform both functions.)

Online Search Tools

The most familiar search tools are general-purpose **search engines**, such as Google and Bing, which scan millions of websites to identify individual webpages that contain a specific word or phrase and then attempt to rank the results from most useful to least useful. Search engines have the advantage of scanning millions or billions of individual webpages, and the best engines use powerful ranking algorithms to present the pages that are probably the most relevant to your search request.

For all their ease and power, conventional search engines have three primary shortcomings: (1) no human editors are involved to evaluate the quality or ranking of the search results; (2) various engines use different search techniques, so they often find different material; and (3) search engines can't reach all the content on some websites (this part of the Internet is sometimes called the *hidden Internet* or the *deep Internet*).

A variety of tools are available to overcome the three main weaknesses of general-purpose search engines, and you should consider one or more of them in your business research. First, **web directories**, such as the Open Directory Project at **www.dmoz.org** use human editors to categorize and evaluate websites. A variety of other directories focus on specific media types, such as blogs or podcasts.

Second, **metasearch engines** help overcome the differences among search engines by formatting your search request for multiple search engines, making it easy to find a broader range of results. With a few clicks, you can compare results from multiple search engines to make sure you are getting a broad view of the material.

Third, **online databases** help address the challenge of the hidden Internet by offering access to newspapers, magazines, journals, electronic copies of books, and other resources often not available with standard search engines. Some of these databases offer free access to the public, but others require a subscription (check with your library). Also, a variety of specialized search engines now exist to reach various parts of the hidden Internet.

Online Monitoring Tools

One of the most powerful aspects of online research is the ability to automatically monitor selected sources for new information. The possibilities include subscribing to newsfeeds from blogs and websites, following people on Twitter and other microblogs, setting up alerts on search engines and online databases, and using specialized monitors such as TweetDeck or Hootsuite to track tweets that mention specific companies or other terms.

Exercise some care when setting up monitoring tools, however, because it's easy to get overwhelmed by the flood of information. Remember that you can always go back and search your information sources if you need to gather additional information.

Search Tips

Search engines, web directories, and databases work in different ways, so make sure you understand how to optimize your search and interpret the results. Search engines have evolved to include a variety of features to help you find the information you need, so invest some time to find out how to use them effectively. Major search engines such as Google and Bing have help pages with detailed advice.

To make the best use of any search tool, keep the following points in mind:

- Think before you search. The results you get from a search engine can create the illusion that the Internet is a neatly organized warehouse of all the information in the universe, but the reality is far different. The Internet is an incomplete, unorganized

REAL-TIME UPDATES
LEARN MORE BY WATCHING THIS VIDEO

Step up your search skills

Learn tips and tricks that will make your Google searches better and faster. Go to http://real-timeupdates.com/ebc12 and click on Learn More in the Students section.

General-purpose search engines are tremendously powerful tools, but they do have several shortcomings you need to consider.

"Human-powered search engines" and web directories rely on human editors to evaluate and select content.

REAL-TIME UPDATES
LEARN MORE BY VISITING THIS INTERACTIVE WEBSITE

Use this powerful search tool for easier online searches

Bovée and Thill Web Search is a custom metasearch engine that automatically formats more than 300 types for searches for optimum results. Go to http://real-timeupdates.com/ebc12 and click on Web Search in the navigation bar.

REAL-TIME UPDATES
LEARN MORE BY VISITING THIS WEBSITE

Try these 100 serious search tools

This list is billed as "100 serious tools for academic search," but most are great tools for general business research, too. Go to http://real-timeupdates.com/ebc12 and click on Learn More in the Students section.

Online databases and specialty search engines can help you access parts of the hidden Internet.

The tools available for monitoring online sources for new information can help you track industry trends, consumer sentiment, and other information.

Search tools work in different ways, and you can get unpredictable results if you don't know how each one operates.

Before you begin searching, think about where the information you need might be located, how it might be structured, and what terms might be used to describe it.

hodgepodge of millions of independent websites with information that ranges in value from priceless to worse-than-worthless. After you have identified what you need to know, spend a few moments thinking about where that information might be found, how it might be structured, and what terms various websites might use to describe it.

- Read the instructions and pay attention to the details. A few minutes of learning can save hours of inefficient search time. For example, if you use multiple words in your search phrase, Bing advises you to put the most important words first because word order affects search results.[5]
- Review the search and display options carefully so you don't misinterpret the results; some settings can make a huge difference in the results you see.
- Try variations of your terms, such as *adolescent* and *teenager* or *management* and *managerial*.
- Adjust the scope of your search, if needed. User fewer search terms to find more results; use more search terms to find fewer results.
- Look beyond the first page of results. Don't assume that the highest-ranking results are the best sources for you. For example, materials that haven't been optimized for search engines won't rank as highly (meaning they won't show up in the first few pages of results), but they may be far better for your purposes.

Search technologies continue to evolve rapidly, so look for new ways to find the information you need. Some new tools search specific areas of information (such as Twitter) in better ways, whereas others approach search in new ways. For instance, Yolink (**www .yolink.com**) finds webpages like a regular search engine does but then also searches through documents and webpages that are linked to those first-level results.[6] Pearltrees taps into the "hive mind" by showing links to information that other users have collected on the topics you're interested in.[7]

Other powerful search tools include *desktop search engines* that search all the files on your personal computer, *enterprise search engines* that search all the computers on a company's network, *research and content managers* such as the free Zotero browser extension (**www.zotero.org**), and *social tagging* or *bookmarking sites* such as Reddit (**www.reddit.com**), and media curation sites such as Pinterest (**http://pinterest .com**) and Scoop.it (**www.scoop.it**).

For information on the latest online research tools and techniques, visit **http://real-timeupdates.com/ebc12** and click on Chapter 11.

REAL-TIME UPDATES

LEARN MORE BY VISITING THIS WEBSITE

Learn to use Google more effectively

Google's Inside Search offers the tips and techniques you need to get the best research results in the least amount of time. Go to http://real-timeupdates.com/ebc12 and click on Learn More in the Students section.

DOCUMENTING YOUR SOURCES

Proper documentation of the sources you use is both ethical and an important resource for your readers.

Documenting your sources serves three important functions: It properly and ethically credits the person who created the original material, it shows your audience that you have sufficient support for your message, and it helps readers explore your topic in more detail, if desired.

Be sure to take advantage of source documentation tools whenever you can, to help ensure that you accurately track all your sources. Most word-processing programs can automatically track and number endnotes for you, and you can use the "table of authorities" feature to create a bibliography of all the sources you've used. A wide variety of *citation management* or *reference management* tools are available with popular web browsers.

Appendix B discusses the common methods of documenting sources. Whatever method you choose, documentation is necessary for books, articles, tables, charts, diagrams, song lyrics, scripted dialogue, letters, speeches—anything that you take from someone else, including ideas and information that you've presented through paraphrasing or summarizing. However, you do not have to cite a source for knowledge that's generally known among your readers, such as the fact that Facebook is a large social network or that computers are pervasive in business today.

Research on the Go with Mobile Devices

Smartphones and tablets have opened up new possibilities for collecting information for business reports and other communication purposes. Using built-in capabilities such as audio and video recording, as well as apps made specifically for research, business researchers can collect qualitative and quantitative information in a variety of ways:

- **Mobile surveys.** Tablets with interactive software can replace the clipboards long used by researchers for "mall intercept" surveys and other efforts to collect data from shoppers.
- **Collecting and sharing.** Collaborative apps such as Pearltrees make it easy to collect online information and organize it across multiple devices, then connect with relevant information collected by other users.
- **Note taking.** Evernote, OneNote, and other note-taking apps simplify the process of compiling notes, webpages, photos, and other pieces of research.
- **Sketching.** Sometimes a simple picture is more powerful than words or photos. With touchscreen apps on phones and tablets, researchers can quickly sketch maps, process diagrams, and other visuals on the spot.
- **Audio, photo, and video recording.** Whether it's snapping images of street scenes for a report on potential store locations or recording test subjects using a new product prototype, the audiovisual capabilities of today's mobile devices give researchers a host of new tools.
- **Document scanning.** Scanning apps let researchers record and organize images of documents that can't be removed from their storage locations.
- **Real-time thoughts and impressions.** Asking survey subjects to record information on their mobile devices

while they are observing store displays or making purchase decisions, for example, promises to enhance some classic research methods. With the old methods, shoppers would answer survey questions about the choices they made well after the fact, leaving the accuracy of their answers up to the quality of the memories. With their mobile phones in hand, shoppers who've agreed to participate in research can describe their impressions and decisions on the spot and even take photos of displays that caught their eye.

As more consumers adopt mobile devices and software developers continue to create new research apps, mobile research promises to revolutionize research the same way it was changed business communication in general.

CAREER APPLICATIONS

1. Assume you're about to visit another college where you're applying for the masters' program, and you want to learn as much as you can about the school in the limited time you have available. How could you use your mobile phone to improve your information collection?
2. Mobile research raises some important ethical and legal questions involving privacy. Identify three possible privacy violations that researchers need to guard against.

Sources: Shelly Terrell, "Research on the Go! Effective Research with Mobile Devices," presentation, 7 November 2013, www.slideshare.net; Derek Matisz, "Mobile-Enabled Ethnography: 4 Tips for Using Mobile Devices in Your Research," Vision Critical blog, 24 July 2013, www.visioncritical.com; "Let's Go Shopping: Using Mobile Qualitative Research for Shop-Alongs," 2020Resarch, accessed 9 May 2014, www.2020research.com.

Conducting Primary Research

If secondary research can't provide the information and insights you need, you may need to gather the information yourself with primary research. Two common primary research methods are surveys and interviews. Other important primary techniques are *observations* (including tracking the behavior of website visitors) and *experiments* such as test marketing.

> **4 LEARNING OBJECTIVE**
> Explain the role of primary research, and identify the two most common forms of primary research for business communication purposes.

CONDUCTING SURVEYS

A carefully prepared and conducted survey can provide invaluable insights, but only if it is *reliable* (would produce identical results if repeated under similar conditions) and *valid* (measures what it's supposed to measure). To conduct a survey that generates reliable and valid results, you need to choose research participants carefully and develop an effective set of questions. For important surveys on strategically important topics with lots at stake, you're usually better off hiring a research specialist who knows how to avoid errors during planning, execution, and analysis.

When selecting people to participate in a survey, the most critical task is getting a *representative sample* of the entire population in question. For instance, if you want to know how U.S. consumers feel about something, you can't just survey a few hundred people in

> Surveys and interviews are the most common primary research techniques.
>
> Surveys need to be reliable, valid, and representative in order to be useful.

a shopping mall. Different types of consumers shop at different times of the day and different days of the week, and many consumers do not shop at malls. The online surveys you see on many websites today potentially suffer from the same *sampling bias*: They capture only the opinions of people who visit the sites and want to participate, which might not be a representative sample of the population. A good handbook on survey research will help you select the right people for your survey, including selecting enough people to have a statistically valid survey.[8]

To develop an effective survey questionnaire, start with the information needs you identified at the beginning of the research process. Then break these points into specific questions, choosing an appropriate type of question for each point (see Figure 11.7). The following guidelines will help you produce results that are valid and reliable:[9]

On surveys, provide clear instructions to prevent mistaken answers.

QUESTION TYPE   EXAMPLE

Open-ended   How would you describe the flavor of this ice cream?

Either-or   Do you think this ice cream is too rich?
_____ Yes
_____ No

Multiple choice   Which description best fits the taste of this ice cream?
(Choose only one.)
  a. Delicious
  b. Too fruity
  c. Too sweet
  d. Too intense
  e. Bland
  f. Stale

Scale   Please mark an X on the scale to indicate how you perceive the texture of this ice cream.

Too light   Light   Creamy   Too creamy

Checklist   Which of the following ice cream brands do you recognize?
(Check all that apply.)
_____ Ben & Jerry's
_____ Breyers
_____ Carvel
_____ Dreyer's
_____ Häagen-Dazs

Ranking   Rank these flavors in order of your preference, from 1 (most preferred) to 5 (least preferred):
_____ Vanilla
_____ Cherry
_____ Strawberry
_____ Chocolate
_____ Coconut

Short-answer   In the past 2 weeks, how many times did you buy ice cream in a grocery store? _____

In the past 2 weeks, how many times did you buy ice cream in an ice cream shop? _____

Figure 11.7 **Types of Survey Questions**
For each question you have in your survey, choose the type of question that will elicit the most useful answers.

- Provide clear instructions to make sure people can answer every question correctly.
- Don't ask for information that people can't be expected to remember, such as how many times they went grocery shopping in the past year.
- Keep the questionnaire short and easy to answer; don't expect people to give you more than 10 or 15 minutes of their time.
- Whenever possible, formulate questions that provide answers that are easy to analyze. Numbers and facts are easier to summarize than opinions, for instance.
- Avoid *leading questions* that could bias your survey. If you ask, "Do you prefer that we stay open in the evenings for customer convenience?" you'll no doubt get a "yes." Instead, ask, "What time of day do you normally do your shopping?"
- Avoid ambiguous descriptors such as "often" or "frequently." Such terms mean different things to different people.
- Avoid compound questions such as "Do you read books and magazines?" People who read one but not the other won't know whether to answer yes or no.
- Make the survey *adaptive*. Whether you're surveying people manually or using software, build in ways to adjust the flow of questions in response to each person's answers. This way you can make the best use of each respondent's time and get more useful information.

Online surveys offer a number of advantages, including speed, cost, and the ability to adapt the question set along the way based on a respondent's answers. However, to deliver reliable and valid results, they must be designed and administered as carefully as offline surveys.

> Online surveys are fast and convenient, but in order to produce meaningful data, they must be designed with the same care as offline surveys.

CONDUCTING INTERVIEWS

Getting in-depth information straight from an expert or an individual concerned about an issue can be a great method for collecting primary information. Interviews can dig deeper than the "hands-off" approach of surveys, and skilled interviewers can also watch for non-verbal signals that provide additional insights. Interviews can take a variety of formats, from email exchanges to group discussions.

> Interviews can take place online, over the phone, or in person, and they can involve individuals or groups.

Be aware that the answers you receive in an interview are influenced by the types of questions you ask, by the way you ask them, and by each subject's cultural and language background. Potentially significant factors include the person's race, gender, age, educational level, and social status.[10]

Ask **open-ended questions** (such as "Why do you believe that South America represents a better opportunity than Europe for this product line?") to solicit opinions, insights, and information. Ask **closed questions** to elicit a specific answer, such as yes or no. However, don't use too many closed questions in an interview, or the experience will feel more like a simple survey and won't take full advantage of the interactive interview setting.

> Open-ended questions, which can't be answered with a simple yes or no, can provide deeper insights, opinions, and information.

Think carefully about the sequence of your questions and the subject's potential answers so you can arrange questions in an order that helps uncover layers of information. Also consider providing the other person with a list of questions at least a day or two before the interview, especially if you'd like to quote your subject in writing or if your questions might require your subject to conduct research or think extensively about the answers. If you want to record the interview, ask the person ahead of time and respect his or her wishes.

> Arrange the sequence of questions to help uncover layers of information.

As soon as possible after the interview, take a few moments to write down your thoughts, go over your notes, and organize your material. Look for important themes, helpful facts or statistics, and direct quotes. If you made an audio recording, *transcribe* it (take down word for word what the person said) or take notes from the recording just as you would while listening to someone in person.

Face-to-face interviews give you the opportunity to gauge the reaction to your questions and observe the nonverbal signals that accompany the answers, but interviews can also take place via email and other digital media.

In addition to individual interviews, business researchers can also use a form of group interview known as the **focus group**. In this format, a moderator guides a group through

---

---

a series of discussion questions while the rest of the research team observes through a one-way mirror. The key advantage of focus groups is the opportunity to learn from group dynamics as the various participants bounce ideas and questions off each other. By allowing a group to discuss topics and problems in this manner, the focus group technique can uncover much richer information than a series of individual interviews.[11]

As a reminder of the tasks involved in interviews, see "Checklist: Conducting Effective Information Interviews."

Planning Informational Reports

Informational reports provide the material that employees, managers, and others need in order to make decisions, take action, and respond to dynamic conditions inside and outside the organization. Although these reports come in dozens of particular formats, they can be grouped into four general categories:

Informational reports are used to monitor and control operations, to implement policies and procedures, to demonstrate compliance, and to document progress.

- **Reports to monitor and control operations.** Managers rely on a wide range of reports to see how well their companies are functioning. *Plans* establish expectations and guidelines to direct future action. Some of the most significant of these are *business plans* (see "Creating Successful Business Plans" on page 341). *Operating reports* provide feedback on a wide variety of an organization's functions, including sales, inventories, expenses, shipments, and so on. *Personal activity reports* provide information regarding an individual's experiences during sales calls, industry conferences, market research trips, and so on.
- **Reports to implement policies and procedures.** *Policy reports* range from brief descriptions of business procedures to manuals that run dozens or hundreds of pages. *Position papers*, sometimes called *white papers* or *backgrounders*, outline an organization's official position on issues that affect the company's success.
- **Reports to demonstrate compliance.** Businesses are required to submit a variety of *compliance reports*, from tax returns to reports that describe the proper handling of hazardous materials.
- **Reports to document progress.** Supervisors, investors, and customers frequently expect to be informed of the status of projects and other activities via *progress reports*.

ORGANIZING INFORMATIONAL REPORTS

The messages conveyed by informational reports can range from extremely positive to extremely negative, so the approach you take warrants careful consideration.

In most cases, the direct approach is the best choice for informational reports. However, if the information is both surprising and disappointing, such as a project that is behind schedule or over budget, you might consider using the indirect approach to build up to the bad news. Most informational reports use a **topical organization**, arranging material in one of the following ways:

- **Comparison.** Showing similarities and differences (or advantages and disadvantages) between two or more entities
- **Importance.** Building up from the least important item to the most important (or from most important to the least, if you don't think your audience will read the entire report)

- **Sequence.** Organizing the steps or stages in a process or procedure
- **Chronology.** Organizing a chain of events in order from oldest to newest or vice versa
- **Geography.** Organizing by region, city, state, country, or other geographic unit
- **Category.** Grouping by topical category, such as sales, profit, cost, or investment

Whichever pattern you choose, use it consistently so that readers can easily follow your discussion from start to finish. Bear in mind, however, that in many instances, you might be expected to follow a particular type of organization.

Of course, effective informational reports must also be audience centered, logical, focused, and easy to follow, with generous use of previews and summaries. Your audience expects you to sort out the details and separate major points from minor points.

CREATING SUCCESSFUL BUSINESS PLANS

A **business plan** such as the one written by the founders of MyCityWay is a comprehensive document that describes a company's mission, structure, objectives, and operations. Roughly speaking, business plans can be written during three separate phases of a company's life: (1) before the company is launched, when the founders are defining their vision of what the company will be; (2) when the company is seeking funding, in which case the business plan takes on a persuasive tone to convince outsiders that investing in the firm would be a profitable decision; and (3) after the company is up and running and the business plan serves as a monitor-and-control mechanism to make sure operations are staying on track.

At any stage, a comprehensive business plan forces you to think about personnel, marketing, facilities, suppliers, distribution, and a host of other issues vital to a company's success. The specific elements to include in a business plan can vary based on the situation; here are the sections typically included in a plan written to attract outside investors:[12]

REAL-TIME UPDATES

LEARN MORE BY VISITING THIS WEBSITE

Step-by-step advice for developing a successful business plan

Take advantage of the Small Business Administration's comprehensive guide to preparing a business plan. Go to http://real-time updates.com/ebc12 and click on Learn More in the Students section.

- **Summary.** In one or two paragraphs, summarize your business concept, particularly the *business model*, which defines how the company will generate revenue and produce a profit. The summary must be compelling, catching the investor's attention and giving him or her reasons to keep reading. Describe your product or service and its market potential. Highlight some things about your company and its leaders that will distinguish your firm from the competition. Summarize your financial projections and indicate how much money you will need from investors or lenders and where it will be spent.
- **Mission and objectives.** Explain the purpose of your business and what you hope to accomplish.
- **Company and industry.** Give full background information on the origins and structure of your venture and the characteristics of the industry in which you plan to compete.
- **Products or services.** Concisely describe your products or services, focusing on their unique attributes and their appeal to customers.
- **Market and competition.** Provide data that will persuade investors that you understand your target market and can achieve your sales goals. Be sure to identify the strengths and weaknesses of your competitors.
- **Management.** Summarize the background and qualifications of the key management personnel in your company. Include résumés in an appendix.
- **Marketing strategy.** Provide projections of sales volume and market share; outline a strategy for identifying and reaching potential customers, setting prices, providing customer support, and physically delivering your products or services. Whenever possible, include evidence of customer acceptance, such as advance product orders.

The summary is a critical part of business plan because it has to excite readers about the concept enough to make them want to read more.

- **Design and development plans.** If your product requires design or development, describe the nature and extent of what needs to be done, including costs and possible problems. For new or unusual products, you may want to explain how the product will be manufactured.

- **Operations plan.** Provide information on facilities, equipment, and personnel requirements.

- **Overall schedule.** Forecast important milestones in the company's growth and development, including when you need to be fully staffed and when your products will be ready for the market.

- **Critical risks and problems.** Identify significant negative factors and discuss them honestly.

- **Financial projections and requirements.** Include a detailed budget of start-up and operating costs, as well as projections for income, expenses, and cash flow for the first few years of business. Identify the company's financing needs and potential sources, if appropriate.

- **Exit strategy.** Explain how investors will be able to profit from their investment, such as through a public stock offering, sale of the company, or a buyback of the investors' interest.

Be aware that not all start-up veterans and investors believe in the value of a conventional business plan, at least in a company's early stages. Reasons for the skepticism include the amount of time and energy required to research and write a plan, the reluctance of many target readers to read such lengthy documents, the uncertainty of whether a new product or company idea will even work, and the difficulty of correctly anticipating all the circumstances and obstacles that a young company will encounter. Particularly for companies that are developing new products or new business models before they can launch, some experts recommend that entrepreneurs devote most of their energy to getting a working product or service model in front of potential customers as quickly as possible so they can verify and fine-tune it before proceeding to extensive business planning. Two popular alternatives to conventional business plans are high-level overviews known as the Business Model Canvas and the Lean Canvas. They are essentially one-page business plans that present only the essential ideas that make up an intended business model.[13]

REAL-TIME UPDATES

LEARN MORE BY VISITING THIS WEBSITE

Crafting your "wow" statement

Bill Reichert of Garage Technology Ventures offers advice on capturing an investor's attention in just a matter of seconds. Go to http://real-timeupdates.com/ebc12 and click on Learn More in the Students section.

ORGANIZING WEBSITE CONTENT

Many websites, particularly company websites, function as informational reports, offering sections with information about the company, its history, its products and services, its executive team, and so on. While most of what you've already learned about informational reports applies to website writing, the online experience requires some special considerations and practices.

As you begin to plan a website, start by recognizing the unique nature of online communication:

When planning online reports or other website content, remember that the online reading experience differs from offline reading in several important ways.

- **Web readers are demanding.** If site visitors can't find what they're looking for in a matter of minutes, they'll leave and look elsewhere.[14] Figure 11.8 is an example of a webpage that makes it easy for readers to find information of interest.

- **Reading online can be difficult.** Studies show that reading speeds are about 25 percent slower on a monitor than on paper.[15] Reading from computer screens can also be tiring on the eyes, even to the point of causing headaches, double vision, blurred vision, and other physical problems.[16]

- **The web is a nonlinear, multidimensional medium.** Readers of online material move around in any order they please; there often is no beginning, middle, or end. As a web writer, you need to anticipate the various paths your readers will want to follow and to make sure you provide the right hyperlinks in the right places to help readers explore successfully.

- **Consider a mobile-first strategy.** Many businesses now optimize their websites to be viewed on mobile devices, particularly tablets, rather than larger PC screens. The major changes this involves include simpler navigation, more linear organization of content, and supporting touch interaction.

REAL-TIME UPDATES

LEARN MORE BY VISITING THIS WEBSITE

Effective examples of one-page web design

One Page Love has a large gallery of one-page webs designs. Go to http://real-timeupdates.com/ebc12 and click on Learn More in the Students section.

Business websites often have multiple audiences and multiple communication functions, so planning websites can be a challenge. Professional website designers often use the term **information architecture** to describe the structure and navigational flow of all the parts of a website. In a sense, the information architecture is a three-dimensional outline of the site, showing (1) the vertical hierarchy of pages from the homepage down to the lower level, (2) the horizontal division of pages across the various sections of the site, and (3) the links that tie all these pages together, both internally (between various pages on the site) and externally (between your site and other websites).

On simpler sites with few content categories, the information architecture is fairly straightforward. A recent trend toward *one-page websites*, in which all the content is presented on a single, scrolling page, represents the ultimate in website simplicity. These sites can be particularly good for mobile devices because navigating them requires nothing

The *information architecture* of a website is the equivalent of the outline for a paper report, but it tends to be much more complicated than a simple linear outline.

Courtesy of Zappos.com

Figure 11.8   Reader-Friendly Website Design
This page from Zappos's website shows how to organize content in ways that help readers find desired information quickly. The numbered list on the left side serves as both a high-level overview and a clickable table of contents, and clicking on any item displays a one-sentence summary and a more-detailed description. Readers can quickly explore all 10 values without bouncing around from page to page.

more than simple scrolling action by the user. Companies also use one-page designs for individual sections of a larger website.

However, on large corporate or organizational websites (such as your college or university's website), the architecture can be extremely complex, and it is the information architect's job to make each visitor's experience as simple as possible.

To organize your site effectively, keep the following advice in mind:

- Plan your site structure and navigation before you write.[17]
- Let your readers be in control; give them clearly labeled pathways that let them explore on their own.
- Help online readers scan and absorb information by breaking it into self-contained, easily readable chunks that are linked together logically.

Planning Analytical Reports

6 **LEARNING OBJECTIVE**
Identify the three most common ways to organize analytical reports.

Analytical reports are used to assess opportunities, to solve problems, and to support decisions.

The purpose of analytical reports is to analyze, to understand, or to explain a problem or an opportunity and figure out how it affects the company and how the company should respond. In many cases, you'll also be expected to make a recommendation based on your analysis. As you saw in Figure 11.1, analytical reports fall into three basic categories:

- **Reports to assess opportunities.** Every business opportunity carries some degree of risk and also requires a variety of decisions and actions in order to capitalize on the opportunity. You can use analytical reports to assess risk and required decisions and actions. For instance, *market analysis reports* are used to judge the likelihood of success for new products or sales. *Due diligence reports* examine the financial aspects of a proposed decision, such as acquiring another company.
- **Reports to solve problems.** Managers often ask for *troubleshooting reports* when they need to understand why something isn't working properly and what needs to be done to fix it. A variation, the *failure analysis report*, studies events that happened in the past, with the hope of learning how to avoid similar failures in the future.
- **Reports to support decisions.** *Feasibility reports* are called for when managers need to explore the ramifications of a decision they're about to make, such as switching materials used in a manufacturing process. *Justification reports* explain a decision that has already been made.

Writing analytical reports presents a greater challenge than writing informational reports because you need to use your reasoning abilities and persuasive skills in addition to your writing skills. With analytical reports, you're doing more than simply delivering information: You're also analyzing a problem or an opportunity and presenting your conclusions in a compelling and persuasive manner. Finally, because analytical reports often convince other people to make significant financial and personnel decisions, your reports carry the added responsibility of the consequences of these decisions.

To help define the problem your analytical report will address, answer these questions:

- What needs to be determined?
- Why is this issue important?
- Who is involved in the situation?
- Where is the trouble located?
- How did the situation originate?
- When did it start?

Problem factoring is the process of breaking down a problem into smaller questions to help identify causes and effects.

Not all of these questions apply in every situation, but asking them helps you define the problem being addressed and limits the scope of your discussion.

Also try **problem factoring**, dividing the problem into a series of logical, connected questions that try to identify cause and effect. When you speculate on the cause of a problem, you're forming a **hypothesis**, a potential explanation that needs to be tested. By subdividing a problem and forming hypotheses based on available evidence, you can tackle even the most complex situations.

TABLE 11.5 Common Ways to Structure Analytical Reports

Element	Focus on Conclusions or Recommendations	Focus On Logical Argument	
		Use 2 + 2 = 4 Model	Use Yardstick Model
Reader mindset	Likely to accept	Hostile or skeptical	Hostile or skeptical
Approach	Direct	Indirect	Indirect
Writer credibility	High	Low	Low
Advantages	Readers quickly grasp conclusions or recommendations	Works well when you need to show readers how you built toward an answer by following clear, logical steps	Works well when you have a list of criteria (standards) that must be considered in a decision; alternatives are all measured against same criteria
Drawbacks	Structure can make topic seem too simple	Can make report longer	Readers must agree on criteria; can be lengthy because of the need to address each criteria for every alternative

As with all other business messages, the best organizational structure for each analytical report depends largely on your audience's likely reaction. The three basic structures involve focusing on conclusions, focusing on recommendations, and focusing on logic (see Table 11.5).

FOCUSING ON CONCLUSIONS

When writing for audiences that are likely to accept your conclusions—either because they've asked you to perform an analysis or they trust your judgment—consider using a direct approach that focuses immediately on your conclusions. This structure communicates the main idea quickly, but it presents some risks. Even if audiences trust your judgment, they may have questions about your data or the methods you used. Moreover, starting with the conclusion may create the impression that you have oversimplified the situation. You're generally better off taking the direct approach in a report only when your credibility is high—when your readers trust you and are willing to accept your conclusions (see Figure 11.9 on the next page).

Focusing on conclusions is often the best approach when you're addressing a receptive audience.

FOCUSING ON RECOMMENDATIONS

A slightly different approach is useful when your readers want to know what they ought to do in a given situation (as opposed to what they ought to conclude). Start with the following general outline and adapt it as needed:

When readers want to know what you think they should do, organize your report to focus on recommendations.

1. Establish the need for action in the introduction by briefly describing the problem or opportunity.
2. Introduce the benefit(s) that can be achieved if the recommendation is adopted, along with any potential risks.
3. List the steps (recommendations) required to achieve the benefit, using action verbs for emphasis.
4. Explain each step more fully, giving details on procedures, costs, and benefits; if necessary, also explain how risks can be minimized.
5. Summarize your recommendations.

FOCUSING ON LOGICAL ARGUMENTS

When readers are skeptical or hostile to the conclusion or recommendation you plan to make, use an indirect approach that logically builds toward your conclusion or recommendation. If you guide the audience along a rational path toward the answer, they are more likely to accept it when they encounter it. The two most common logical approaches are known as the *2 + 2 = 4 approach* and the *yardstick approach*.

Logical arguments can follow two basic approaches: 2 + 2 = 4 (adding everything up) and the yardstick method (comparing ideas against a predetermined set of standards).

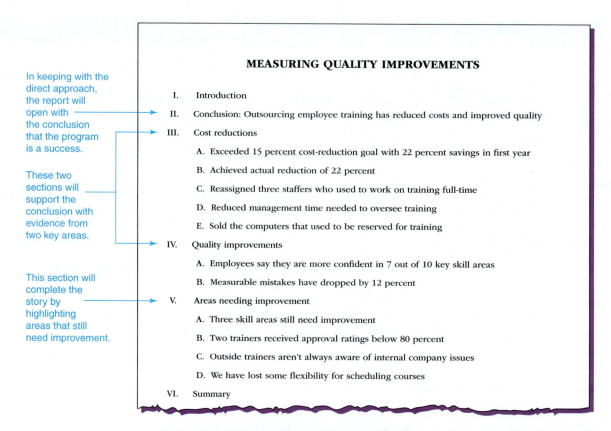

In keeping with the direct approach, the report will open with the conclusion that the program is a success.

These two sections will support the conclusion with evidence from two key areas.

This section will complete the story by highlighting areas that still need improvement.

MEASURING QUALITY IMPROVEMENTS

I.   Introduction

II. Conclusion: Outsourcing employee training has reduced costs and improved quality

III. Cost reductions

    A. Exceeded 15 percent cost-reduction goal with 22 percent savings in first year

    B. Achieved actual reduction of 22 percent

    C. Reassigned three staffers who used to work on training full-time

    D. Reduced management time needed to oversee training

    E. Sold the computers that used to be reserved for training

IV. Quality improvements

    A. Employees say they are more confident in 7 out of 10 key skill areas

    B. Measurable mistakes have dropped by 12 percent

V.   Areas needing improvement

    A. Three skill areas still need improvement

    B. Two trainers received approval ratings below 80 percent

    C. Outside trainers aren't always aware of internal company issues

    D. We have lost some flexibility for scheduling courses

VI. Summary

Figure 11.9   Preliminary Outline of a Research Report Focusing on Conclusions
A year after a bank decided to have an outside firm handle its employee training, an analyst was asked to prepare a report evaluating the results. The analysis shows that the outsourcing experiment was a success, so the report opens with that conclusion but supports it with clear evidence. Readers who accept the conclusion can stop reading, and those who desire more information can continue.

The 2 + 2 = 4 Approach

The **2 + 2 = 4 approach** is so named because it convinces readers of your point of view by demonstrating that everything adds up. The main points in your outline are the main reasons behind your conclusions and recommendations. You support each reason with the evidence you collected during your analysis. With its natural feel and versatility, the 2 + 2 = 4 approach is generally the most persuasive and efficient way to develop an analytical report for skeptical readers, so try this structure first. You'll find that most of your arguments fall naturally into this pattern.

The troubleshooting report shown in Figure 11.10 is built on the main idea that the company should establish separate sales teams for major national accounts rather than continuing to service them through the company's four regional divisions. The writer knew his plan would be controversial because it required a big change in the company's organization and in the way sales representatives are paid. His thinking had to be clear and easy to follow, so he used the 2 + 2 = 4 approach to focus on his reasons.

The Yardstick Approach

The **yardstick approach** is useful when you need to use a number of criteria to decide which option to select from two or more possibilities. With this approach, you begin by discussing the problem or opportunity, and then you list the criteria that will guide the decision. The body of the report then evaluates the alternatives against those criteria. Figure 11.11 on page 349 is an outline of a feasibility report that uses the yardstick approach, listing five criteria to evaluate two alternative courses of action.

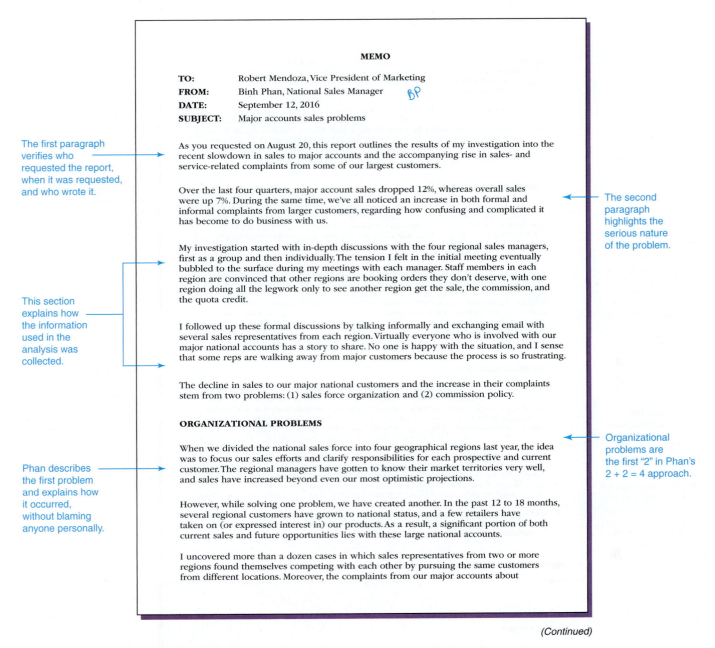

The first paragraph verifies who requested the report, when it was requested, and who wrote it.

This section explains how the information used in the analysis was collected.

Phan describes the first problem and explains how it occurred, without blaming anyone personally.

The second paragraph highlights the serious nature of the problem.

Organizational problems are the first "2" in Phan's 2 + 2 = 4 approach.

MEMO

TO: Robert Mendoza, Vice President of Marketing
FROM: Binh Phan, National Sales Manager   BP
DATE: September 12, 2016
SUBJECT: Major accounts sales problems

As you requested on August 20, this report outlines the results of my investigation into the recent slowdown in sales to major accounts and the accompanying rise in sales- and service-related complaints from some of our largest customers.

Over the last four quarters, major account sales dropped 12%, whereas overall sales were up 7%. During the same time, we've all noticed an increase in both formal and informal complaints from larger customers, regarding how confusing and complicated it has become to do business with us.

My investigation started with in-depth discussions with the four regional sales managers, first as a group and then individually. The tension I felt in the initial meeting eventually bubbled to the surface during my meetings with each manager. Staff members in each region are convinced that other regions are booking orders they don't deserve, with one region doing all the legwork only to see another region get the sale, the commission, and the quota credit.

I followed up these formal discussions by talking informally and exchanging email with several sales representatives from each region. Virtually everyone who is involved with our major national accounts has a story to share. No one is happy with the situation, and I sense that some reps are walking away from major customers because the process is so frustrating.

The decline in sales to our major national customers and the increase in their complaints stem from two problems: (1) sales force organization and (2) commission policy.

ORGANIZATIONAL PROBLEMS

When we divided the national sales force into four geographical regions last year, the idea was to focus our sales efforts and clarify responsibilities for each prospective and current customer. The regional managers have gotten to know their market territories very well, and sales have increased beyond even our most optimistic projections.

However, while solving one problem, we have created another. In the past 12 to 18 months, several regional customers have grown to national status, and a few retailers have taken on (or expressed interest in) our products. As a result, a significant portion of both current sales and future opportunities lies with these large national accounts.

I uncovered more than a dozen cases in which sales representatives from two or more regions found themselves competing with each other by pursuing the same customers from different locations. Moreover, the complaints from our major accounts about

(Continued)

Figure 11.10 Analytical Report Using the 2 + 2 = 4 Approach
To make his argument clear and compelling, this writer used the 2 + 2 = 4 approach.

The yardstick approach has two potential drawbacks. First, your audience needs to agree with the criteria you're using in your analysis. If they don't, they won't agree with the results of the evaluation. If you have any doubt about their agreement, build consensus before you start your report, if possible, or take extra care to explain why the criteria you're using are the best ones in this particular case. Second, the yardstick approach can get a little boring when you have many options to consider or many criteria to compare them against. One way to minimize the repetition is to compare the options in tables and then highlight the most unusual or important aspects of each alternative in the text so that you get the best of both worlds. This approach allows you to compare all the alternatives against the same yardstick while calling attention to the most significant differences among them.

2

overlapping or nonexistent account coverage are a direct result of the regional organization. In some cases, customers aren't sure which of our representatives they're supposed to call with problems and orders. In other cases, no one has been in contact with them for several months.

For example, having retail outlets across the lower tier of the country, AmeriSport received pitches from reps out of our West, South, and East regions. Because our regional offices have a lot of negotiating freedom, the three were offering different prices. But all AmeriSport buying decisions were made at the Tampa headquarters, so all we did was confuse the customer. The irony of the current organization is that we're often giving our weakest selling and support efforts to the largest customers in the country.

COMMISSION PROBLEMS

The regional organization problems are compounded by the way we assign commissions and quota credit. Salespeople in one region can invest a lot of time in pursuing a sale, only to have the customer place the order in another region. So some sales rep in the second region ends up with the commission on a sale that was partly or even entirely earned by someone in the first region. Therefore, sales reps sometimes don't pursue leads in their regions, thinking that a rep in another region will get the commission.

For example, Athletic Express, with outlets in 35 states spread across all four regions, finally got so frustrated with us that the company president called our headquarters. Athletic Express has been trying to place a large order for tennis and golf accessories, but none of our local reps seem interested in paying attention. I spoke with the rep responsible for Nashville, where the company is headquartered, and asked her why she wasn't working the account more actively. Her explanation was that last time she got involved with Athletic Express, the order was actually placed from their L.A. regional office, and she didn't get any commission after more than two weeks of selling time.

RECOMMENDATIONS

Our sales organization should reflect the nature of our customer base. To accomplish that goal, we need a group of reps who are free to pursue accounts across regional borders—and who are compensated fairly for their work. The most sensible answer is to establish a national account group. Any customers whose operations place them in more than one region would automatically be assigned to the national group.

In addition to solving the problem of competing sales efforts, the new structure will also largely eliminate the commission-splitting problem because regional reps will no longer invest time in prospects assigned to the national accounts team. However, we will need to find a fair way to compensate regional reps who are losing long-term customers to the national team. Some of these reps have invested years in developing customer relationships that will continue to yield sales well into the future, and everyone I talked to agrees that reps in these cases should receive some sort of compensation. Such a "transition commission" would also motivate the regional reps to help ensure a smooth transition from one sales group to the other. The exact nature of this compensation would need to be worked out with the various sales managers.

3

SUMMARY

The regional sales organization is effective at the regional and local levels but not at the national level. We should establish a national accounts group to handle sales that cross regional boundaries. Then we'll have one set of reps who are focused on the local and regional levels and another set who are pursuing national accounts.

To compensate regional reps who lose accounts to the national team, we will need to devise some sort of payment to reward them for the years of work invested in such accounts. This can be discussed with the sales managers once the new structure is in place.

Phan brings the first problem to life by complementing the general description with a specific example.

In discussing the second problem, he simplifies the reader's task by maintaining a parallel structure: a general description followed by a specific example.

He explains how his recommendation (a new organizational structure) will solve both problems.

He acknowledges that the recommended solution does create a temporary compensation problem but expresses confidence that a solution to that can be worked out.

Commission problems are the second "2" in Phan's 2 + 2 = 4 approach.

Phan concludes the 2 + 2 = 4 approach: organizational problems + commission problems = the need for a new sales structure.

The summary concisely restates both the problem and the recommended solution.

Figure 11.10 Analytical Report Using the 2 + 2 = 4 Approach (Continued)

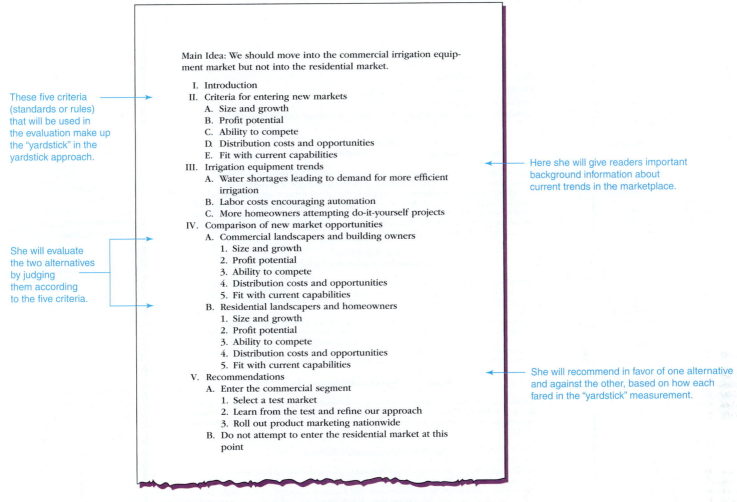

Main Idea: We should move into the commercial irrigation equipment market but not into the residential market.

I. Introduction
II. Criteria for entering new markets
   A. Size and growth
   B. Profit potential
   C. Ability to compete
   D. Distribution costs and opportunities
   E. Fit with current capabilities
III. Irrigation equipment trends
   A. Water shortages leading to demand for more efficient irrigation
   B. Labor costs encouraging automation
   C. More homeowners attempting do-it-yourself projects
IV. Comparison of new market opportunities
   A. Commercial landscapers and building owners
      1. Size and growth
      2. Profit potential
      3. Ability to compete
      4. Distribution costs and opportunities
      5. Fit with current capabilities
   B. Residential landscapers and homeowners
      1. Size and growth
      2. Profit potential
      3. Ability to compete
      4. Distribution costs and opportunities
      5. Fit with current capabilities
V. Recommendations
   A. Enter the commercial segment
      1. Select a test market
      2. Learn from the test and refine our approach
      3. Roll out product marketing nationwide
   B. Do not attempt to enter the residential market at this point

These five criteria (standards or rules) that will be used in the evaluation make up the "yardstick" in the yardstick approach.

She will evaluate the two alternatives by judging them according to the five criteria.

Here she will give readers important background information about current trends in the marketplace.

She will recommend in favor of one alternative and against the other, based on how each fared in the "yardstick" measurement.

Figure 11.11 **Outline of an Analytical Report Using the Yardstick Approach**
This report was drafted by a market analyst for a company that makes irrigation equipment for farms and ranches. The company has been so successful in the agricultural market that it is starting to run out of potential customers. To keep growing, it needs to find another market. Two obvious choices to consider were commercial buildings and residences, but management needed to evaluate both carefully before making a decision.

Planning Proposals

7 **LEARNING OBJECTIVE**
Explain how to plan proposals.

The specific formats for proposals are innumerable, but they can be grouped into two general categories. *Internal proposals* request decisions from managers within the organization, such as proposals to buy new equipment or launch new research projects (see Figure 11.12 on the next page). *External proposals* request decisions from parties outside the organization. Examples of external proposals include *investment proposals*, which request funding from external investors; *grant proposals*, which request funds from government agencies and other sponsoring organizations; and *sales proposals*, which suggest individualized solutions for potential customers and request purchase decisions.

The most significant factor in planning a proposal is whether the recipient has asked you to submit a proposal. *Solicited proposals* are generally prepared at the request of external parties that require a product or a service, but they may also be requested by such internal sources as management or the board of directors. To solicit proposals from potential suppliers, an organization might prepare a formal invitation to bid, called a **request for proposals (RFP)**, which includes instructions that specify exactly the type of work to be performed or products to be delivered, along with budgets, deadlines, and other requirements. Companies then respond by preparing proposals that show how they would meet the requirements spelled out in the RFP. In most cases, organizations that

The best strategy for a proposal depends on whether it is unsolicited or solicited.

A subject line with a compelling promise catches the reader's attention.

"The Solution" explains the proposed solution in enough detail to make it convincing, without burdening the reader with excessive detail.

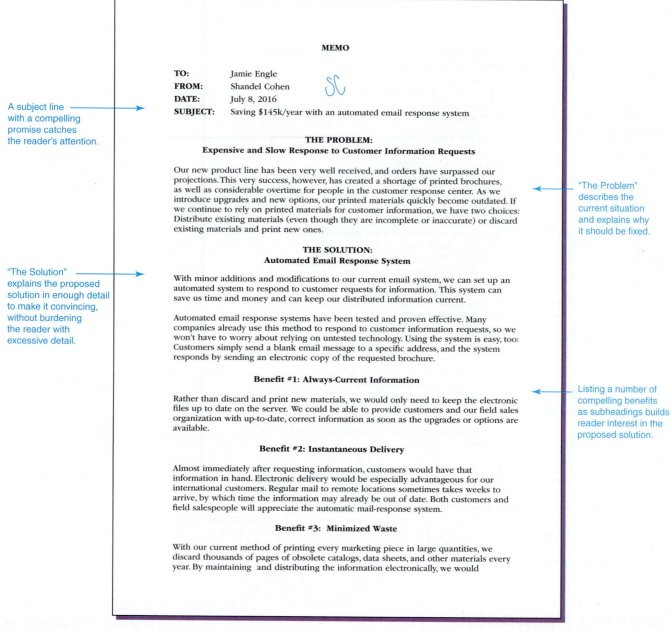

MEMO

TO: Jamie Engle
FROM: Shandel Cohen
DATE: July 8, 2016
SUBJECT: Saving $145k/year with an automated email response system

THE PROBLEM:
Expensive and Slow Response to Customer Information Requests

Our new product line has been very well received, and orders have surpassed our projections. This very success, however, has created a shortage of printed brochures, as well as considerable overtime for people in the customer response center. As we introduce upgrades and new options, our printed materials quickly become outdated. If we continue to rely on printed materials for customer information, we have two choices: Distribute existing materials (even though they are incomplete or inaccurate) or discard existing materials and print new ones.

THE SOLUTION:
Automated Email Response System

With minor additions and modifications to our current email system, we can set up an automated system to respond to customer requests for information. This system can save us time and money and can keep our distributed information current.

Automated email response systems have been tested and proven effective. Many companies already use this method to respond to customer information requests, so we won't have to worry about relying on untested technology. Using the system is easy, too: Customers simply send a blank email message to a specific address, and the system responds by sending an electronic copy of the requested brochure.

Benefit #1: Always-Current Information

Rather than discard and print new materials, we would only need to keep the electronic files up to date on the server. We could be able to provide customers and our field sales organization with up-to-date, correct information as soon as the upgrades or options are available.

Benefit #2: Instantaneous Delivery

Almost immediately after requesting information, customers would have that information in hand. Electronic delivery would be especially advantageous for our international customers. Regular mail to remote locations sometimes takes weeks to arrive, by which time the information may already be out of date. Both customers and field salespeople will appreciate the automatic mail-response system.

Benefit #3: Minimized Waste

With our current method of printing every marketing piece in large quantities, we discard thousands of pages of obsolete catalogs, data sheets, and other materials every year. By maintaining and distributing the information electronically, we would

"The Problem" describes the current situation and explains why it should be fixed.

Listing a number of compelling benefits as subheadings builds reader interest in the proposed solution.

(Continued)

Figure 11.12   Internal Proposal
This internal proposal seeks management's approval to install an automatic mail-response system. The writer lays out the problem concisely, describes her proposed solution, itemizes the four benefits it would provide, and provides a clear analysis of the financial impact.

issue RFPs also provide strict guidelines on what the proposals should include, and you need to follow these guidelines carefully in order to be considered.

Unsolicited proposals offer more flexibility but a completely different sort of challenge than solicited proposals because recipients aren't expecting to receive them. In fact, your audience may not be aware of the problem or opportunity you are addressing, so before you can propose a solution, you might first need to convince your readers that a problem or an opportunity exists. Consequently, using an indirect approach is often a wise choice for unsolicited proposals.

Regardless of its format and structure, a good proposal explains what a project or course of action will involve, how much it will cost, and how the recipient and his or her organization will benefit.

2

eliminate this waste. We would also free up a considerable amount of expensive floor space and shelving that is required for storing printed materials.

Of course, some of our customers may still prefer to receive printed materials, or they may not have access to electronic mail. For these customers, we could simply print copies of the files when we receive such requests. The new Xerox DocuColor printer just installed in the Central Services building would be ideal for printing high-quality materials in small quantities.

Benefit #4: Lower Overtime Costs

In addition to saving both paper and space, we would also realize considerable savings in wages. Because of the increased interest in our new products, we must continue to work overtime or hire new people to meet the demand. An automatic mail response system would eliminate this need, allowing us to deal with fluctuating interest without a fluctuating workforce.

Cost Analysis

The necessary equipment and software costs approximately $15,000. System maintenance and upgrades are estimated at $5,000 per year. However, those costs are offset many times over by the predicted annual savings:

Printing	$100,000
Storage	25,000
Postage	5,000
Wages	20,000
Total	**$150,000**

Based on these figures, the system would save $130,000 the first year and $145,000 every year after that.

CONCLUSION

An automated email response system would yield considerable benefits in both customer satisfaction and operating costs. If you approve, we can have it installed and running in 6 weeks. Please give me a call if you have any questions.

She acknowledges one potential shortcoming with the new approach but provides a convincing solution to that as well.

A detailed breakdown of cost savings provides credible support for the $145k/year claim made in the subject line.

Her conclusion summarizes the benefits and invites further discussion.

Figure 11.13 **Internal Proposal (Continued)**

ON THE JOB: SOLVING COMMUNICATION DILEMMAS AT MYCITYWAY

You recently joined MyCityWay as a market development manager, working on a variety of research, planning, and customer communication projects. Using what you've learned in this chapter about effective research methods and report planning, choose appropriate solutions to these report-writing challenges.

1. MyCityWay faces a problem that bedevils most smartphone app developers: an extremely crowded marketplace. The iTunes app store alone, for example, has more than 4,000 apps in its travel category. You are planning a research project to help identify tactics that MyCityWay could use to stand out from the crowd. Which of the following problem statements would do the best job of guiding this research?
   a. We need to figure out how we can stand out from the crowd.
   b. We need to identify how leading software apps gained the brand recognition they have and whether we could adapt those tactics to our brand.
   c. We need to know if we should we pursue more brand partnerships like the arrangement with BMW.
   d. We need to know if changing our brand name would improve our brand recognition.

2. Your readers appreciate how easy your reports are to read, with their generous use of previews, reviews, and transitions. For a section in the body of a report that describes the range of advertising possibilities in electronic media, which of these is the best review?
   a. As this section has shown, today's new media landscape is full of intriguing, but challenging, choices, from advertising on blogs to advertising in video games.
   b. As this section has shown, today's new media landscape is full of intriguing, but challenging, choices, including product placement in traditional movies and television programs, product placement in and sponsorship of online movies, webcasts, advertising on blogs and in podcasts, advertising in video games, advertising on social networks, stealth marketing and buzz marketing, and music and fashion sponsorships.
   c. As this section has shown, today's new media landscape is full of intriguing, but challenging, choices:
      • Product placement in traditional movies and television programs
      • Product placement in and sponsorship of online movies
      • Webcasts
      • Advertising on blogs and in podcasts
      • Advertising in video games
      • Advertising on social networks
      • Stealth marketing and buzz marketing
      • Music and fashion sponsorships
   d. As this section has shown, today's advertisers have a staggering array of new choices when it comes to connecting with target customers.

3. With several years of experience, you now find routine business reports to be fairly easy. It's usually just a matter of quickly assessing the situation at hand, gathering the information you'll need, and getting to work with organizing and writing. This morning, however, you were given an assignment that is anything but routine. The three founders have asked you to spend the next month on an analytical report that will answer a single question: What's next? They're not asking for a detailed business plan, but rather your advice on the overall direction the company should take over the next five years, after the company has created mobile apps for all the major cities around the world. Should it go after smaller cities next? Should it expand into other lines of businesses? Settle into a "maintain and protect" mode, in which it just keeps its existing products up to date, without attempting to grow? Faced with such an open-ended question, which of the following research and report writing strategies should you use?
   a. Gather all the secondary research you can find on the market for mobile apps of any kind. Study these reports in depth to look for promising opportunities, and then describe the top 10 opportunities in a well-written report.
   b. Design and conduct a consumer survey that is integrated with the MyCityWay app—this way you'll get data directly from the people who use the company's products. Split the survey into two audiences. Ask one group closed-ended questions, in which you identify a number of new product possibilities and ask customers to indicate which ones they would be most likely to buy. Ask the other group open-ended questions about which products the company should develop and which market opportunities it should go after. Compile the results in an analytical report focused on recommendations.
   c. Conduct in-depth individual interviews with MyCityWay's founders, its major investors, and the company's top marketing and technology experts. Ask each person to give candid and complete assessments of the company's strengths and weaknesses as well as the opportunities and threats they see in the marketplace. Spend some time analyzing these in-depth answers and identify a strategic direction that has a good balance of risks and rewards and that is achievable, given the company's capabilities. Explain your analysis and recommendation in a concise report.
   d. Research the history of one hundred of the world's most successful corporations to find out how they grew, and then distill those insights into a "wisdom handbook" that contains the best ideas adopted by the best companies in history.

4. MyCityWay's director of product planning believes a great opportunity exists to convert the company's

consumer-oriented mobile apps to commercial use. For example, real estate agents could use the information to scout out various neighborhoods and help buyers find the locations they'll really like. You've been assigned to write an analytical report on competition in this market segment, with the directive to study the major competitors and assess each one's strengths and weaknesses in preparation for MyCityWay's entry into the market. The report will be distributed to all executives in the company. In the course of your research, however, you conclude that the entire strategy is a mistake, that the competition in the commercial apps market is already too well entrenched and too strong for MyCityWay to make any sort of meaningful progress. You believe the company will waste millions of dollars on the venture and should instead stay focused on the consumer segment. How should you handle this unexpected conclusion?

a. The decision to enter the commercial market has already been made, and it's not your job to question it. Don't mention this conclusion at all in your report.
b. Discuss your concerns with the director of product planning before you write your first draft and don't add this conclusion to your report unless he instructs you do to so.
c. Your conclusion is more important than following your instructions to the letter. Moreover, your discovery is too important to keep from the executive team. Organize your report with the direct approach, opening immediately with conclusion and then offering supporting evidence and reasons.
d. Add your conclusion to the report but organize the report indirectly. Insert your surprising conclusion at the very end of the report, after you've discussed the competitive situation in detail.

Learning Objectives Checkup

Assess your understanding of the principles in this chapter by reading each learning objective and studying the accompanying exercises. You can check your responses against the answer key on page 599.

Objective 11.1: Adapt the three-step writing process to reports and proposals.

1. Why is it particularly important in long reports to clearly identify your purpose before you begin writing?
   a. A clear statement of purpose helps you avoid extensive revisions.
   b. A clear statement of purpose gives you the opportunity to decline projects that don't match your skill set or professional interests.
   c. A clear statement of purpose helps you avoid time-consuming research.
   d. All of the above are important factors.

2. ____ reports focus on the delivery of facts, figures, and other types of information, without making recommendations or proposing new ideas or solutions.

3. ____ reports assess a situation or problem and recommend a course of action in response.

4. ____ present persuasive messages that encourage readers to take a specific course of action.

Objective 11.2: Describe an effective process for conducting business research, explain how to evaluate the credibility of an information source, and identify the five ways to use research results.

5. Which of the following is the appropriate first step in any research project?
   a. Evaluate secondary research to see if you can reuse anything from earlier research projects.
   b. Conduct a preliminary phone survey to measure the extent of the issue you're about to research.
   c. Conduct a thorough statistical analysis of any existing data.
   d. Develop a research plan by familiarizing yourself with the subject, identifying information gaps, and prioritizing research needs.

6. Consider this series of values: 14, 37, 44, 44, 44, 74, 76, 88, 93, 100, and 112.
   a. The mean is 66.
   b. The median is 74.
   c. The mode is 44.
   d. All of the above are correct.

7. Research being conducted for the first time is called ____ research.

8. Research that was conducted for other projects but is being considered for a new project is called ____ research.

9. Why is it important to understand the purpose for which source material was created?
   a. Knowing the purpose helps alert you to any potential biases.
   b. You are required to indicate this purpose in your bibliography.
   c. The purpose tells you whether the material is copyrighted.
   d. The purpose tells you whether you need to pay usage rights.

10. If you uncover critically important information (the sort that could make or break your company) that is from a credible source and appears to be unbiased, well documented, current, and complete but is the only source of this information you can find, how should you handle this situation in your subsequent reporting?
    a. Use it as you would use any other information.
    b. Use it but clearly indicate the source in your report.
    c. Use it but clearly indicate in your report that this is the only source of the information and you weren't able to verify it through a second, independent source.
    d. Don't use it.

11. What is the difference between quoting and paraphrasing?
    a. Quoting is for printed sources; paraphrasing is for electronic sources.
    b. Quoting is legal (as long as appropriate credit is given); paraphrasing is not.
    c. Paraphrasing is just a shorter version of quoting.
    d. Quoting is reproducing someone else's writing exactly as you found it; paraphrasing is expressing someone else's ideas in your own words.

Objective 11.3: Explain the role of secondary research, and describe the two major categories of online research tools.

12. Secondary research is
    a. Generally used before primary research
    b. Generally used after primary research
    c. Generally used at the same time as primary research
    d. Another name for unpaid research

13. Why is it important to fully understand the instructions for using an individual search engine, web directory, database, or other computer-based research tool?
    a. You can be fined if you use these tools improperly.
    b. Most search tools don't return any results if you don't know how to use them.
    c. Using the tool without understanding how it works can produce unpredictable and misleading results.
    d. Today's search tools are so easy to use that you don't need to worry about learning the details.

Objective 11.4: Explain the role of primary research, and identify the two most common forms of primary research for business communication purposes.

14. What does it mean for a survey to be valid?
    a. It works every time.
    b. It returns the data and information the researchers expect it to return.
    c. Meets all ethical and legal criteria in a given industry.
    d. It measures what it was intended to measure.

15. "Why do some consumers refuse to switch to smartphones?" is an example of
    a. An open-ended question

b. A value statement
c. A closed question
d. An in-depth question

Objective 11.5: Explain how to plan informational reports and website content.

16. Which of the following is not a common way to organize informational reports?
    a. Comparison
    b. Section size
    c. Sequence
    d. Chronology

17. The structure and navigational flow of all the parts of a website are commonly referred to as ____ ____ .

Objective 11.6: Identify the three most common ways to organize analytical reports

18. If you have a long history of success in business and are highly regarded by your audience, which two organizing models will probably be sufficient for most reports to this audience?
    a. Focusing on conclusions or focusing on recommendations
    b. Focusing on conclusions and focusing on troubleshooting
    c. Focusing on logic or focusing on analysis
    d. Focusing on reason and focusing on logic

Objective 11.7: Explain how to plan proposals.

19. What is the most significant factor to consider when planning a business proposal?
    a. Whether the recipient prefers printed or electronic media
    b. Whether the proposal is solicited or unsolicited
    c. How many writers will be involved
    d. Whether the audience will be receptive to new ideas

20. RFP stands for
    a. Request for proposals
    b. Reason for proposing
    c. Release form project
    d. Research for proposal

Quick Learning Guide

CHAPTER OUTLINE

Applying the Three-Step Writing Process to Reports and Proposals
Analyzing the Situation
Gathering Information
Selecting the Right Combination of Media and Channels
Organizing Your Information

Supporting Your Messages with Reliable Information
Planning Your Research
Locating Data and Information
Evaluating Sources
Using Your Research Results

Conducting Secondary Research
Finding Information at a Library
Finding Information Online
Documenting Your Sources

Conducting Primary Research
Conducting Surveys
Conducting Interviews

Planning Informational Reports
Organizing Informational Reports
Creating Successful Business Plans
Organizing Website Content

Planning Analytical Reports
Focusing on Conclusions
Focusing on Recommendations
Focusing on Logical Arguments

Planning Proposals

LEARNING OBJECTIVES

1 Adapt the three-step writing process to reports and proposals. (page 321)

2 Describe an effective process for conducting business research, explain how to evaluate the credibility of an information source, and identify the five ways to use research results. (page 327)

3 Explain the role of secondary research, and describe the two major categories of online research tools. (page 332)

4 Explain the role of primary research, and identify the two most common forms of primary research for business communication purposes. (page 337)

5 Explain how to plan informational reports and website content. (page 340)

6 Identify the three most common ways to organize analytical reports. (page 344)

7 Explain how to plan proposals. (page 349)

KEY TERMS

analytical reports Reports that offer both information and analysis; they can also include recommendations

business plan A comprehensive document that describes a company's mission, structure, objectives, and operations

causation The cause-and-effect linkage between two factors, where one of them causes the other to happen

closed questions Questions with a fixed range of possible answers

conclusion A logical interpretation of the facts and other information in a report

correlation The simultaneous change in two variables being measured, without proof of causation

focus group A form of group interview in which a moderator leads participants through a series of questions while a research team hidden behind a one-way mirror listens to their responses and observes their nonverbal behavior.

hypothesis A potential explanation that needs to be tested and verified

information architecture The structure and navigational flow of all the parts of a website

informational reports Reports that offer data, facts, feedback, and other types of information, without analysis or recommendations

knowledge management (KM) Set of technologies, policies, and procedures that let colleagues capture and share information throughout an organization

mean Equal to the sum of all the items in the group divided by the number of items in that group; what people refer to when they use the term *average*

median The midpoint of a series, with an equal number of items above and below

metasearch engines Special search tools that format online searches for multiple search engines simultaneously

mode The number that occurs more often than any other in a sample

online databases Online compilations of newspapers, magazines, journals, and other information sources

open-ended questions Questions without simple, predetermined answers; used to solicit opinions, insights, and information

primary research New research done specifically for the current project

problem factoring Dividing a problem into a series of smaller questions that try to identify cause and effect

problem statement Defines the problem for which a research project will be designed to collect data and information

proposals Reports that combine information delivery and persuasive communication

recommendation A suggested course of action

request for proposals (RFP) A formal invitation to bid on a contract

search engines Online search tools that identify individual webpages containing specific words or phrases you've asked for

secondary research Research done previously for another purpose

statement of purpose Planning statement that defines why you are preparing the report

topical organization Arranging material according to comparisons, importance, sequence, chronology, spatial orientation, geography, or category

trends Repeatable patterns taking place over time

2 + 2 = 4 approach Logical argumentation approach that convinces readers of your point of view by demonstrating how everything "adds up"

web directories Online lists of websites selected by human editors

yardstick approach Logical argumentation approach that uses a number of criteria to evaluate one or more possible solutions

355

Assumptions

- Transfer 5 workers from California to Georgia.
- Hire 45 new workers in Georgia.
- Lay off 75 workers in California.
- Georgia plant would require a total of 150 workers to produce the combined volume of both plants.

a. Which approach (focus on conclusions, recommendations, or logical arguments) will you use to structure your report to the president? Why?

b. Suppose this report were to be circulated to plant managers and supervisors instead. What changes, if any, might you make in your approach?

c. List some conclusions you might draw from the above information to use in your report.

d. Using the structure you selected for your report to the president, draft a final report outline with first- and second-level informative headings.

11.18. Message Strategies: Proposals; Collaboration: Team Projects [LO-7], Chapter 2 Break into small groups and identify an operational problem occurring at your campus that involves either registration, university housing, food services, parking, or library services. Then develop a workable solution to that problem. Finally, develop a list of pertinent facts your team will need to gather to convince the reader that the problem exists and that your solution will work.

11.19. Planning Proposals [LO-7] You're getting ready to launch a new lawn-care business that offers mowing, fertilizing, weeding, and other services. The lawn surrounding a nearby shopping center looks as if it could use better care, so you target that business for your first unsolicited proposal. What questions will you need to answer before you can write a proposal to solve the reader's problem? Be as specific as possible.

Expand Your Skills

Critique the Professionals

Company websites function as multidimensional informational reports, with numerous sections and potentially endless ways for visitors to navigate through all the various pages. Locate the website of a public corporation with a fairly complex website. Imagine you are approaching the site as (a) a potential employee, (b) a potential investor (purchaser of stock), (c) a member of one of the local communities in which this company operates, and (d) a potential customer of the company's products and services. Analyze how easy or difficult it is to find the information that each of these four visitors would typically be looking for. Using whatever medium your instructor requests, write a brief analysis of the information architecture of the website, describing what works well and what doesn't work well.

Sharpening Your Career Skills Online

Bovée and Thill's Business Communication Web Search, at http://websearch.businesscommunicationnetwork.com, is a unique research tool designed specifically for business communication research. Use the Web Search function to find a website, video, PDF document, podcast, or PowerPoint presentation that offers advice on conducting research for business reports. Write a brief email message to your instructor, describing the item that you found and summarizing the career skills information you learned from it.

Improve Your Grammar, Mechanics, and Usage

The following exercises help you improve your knowledge of and power over English grammar, mechanics, and usage. Turn to the Handbook of Grammar, Mechanics, and Usage at the end of this book and review all of Sections 2.1 (Periods), 2.2 (Question Marks), and 2.3 (Exclamation Points). Then indicate the preferred choice in the following groups of sentences. (Answers to these exercises appear on page 601.)

11.20. a. Dr. Eleanor H Hutton has requested information on TaskMasters, Inc.?
  b. Dr. Eleanor H. Hutton has requested information on TaskMasters, Inc.

11.21. a. That qualifies us as a rapidly growing new company, don't you think?
  b. That qualifies us as a rapidly growing new company, don't you think.

11.22. a. Our president is a C.P.A. On your behalf, I asked him why he started the firm.
  b. Our president is a CPA. On your behalf, I asked him why he started the firm.

11.23. a. Contact me at 1358 N. Parsons Ave., Tulsa, OK 74204.
  b. Contact me at 1358 N. Parsons Ave, Tulsa, OK. 74204.

11.24. a. Jeb asked, "Why does he want to know! Maybe he plans to become a competitor."
  b. Jeb asked, "Why does he want to know? Maybe he plans to become a competitor!"

11.25. a. The debt load fluctuates with the movement of the U.S. prime rate.
  b. The debt load fluctuates with the movement of the US prime rate.

11.26. a. Is consumer loyalty extinct? Yes and no!
  b. Is consumer loyalty extinct? Yes and no.

11.27. a. Will you please send us a check today so that we can settle your account.
  b. Will you please send us a check today so that we can settle your account?

11.28. a. Will you be able to speak at the conference, or should we find someone else.
  b. Will you be able to speak at the conference, or should we find someone else?

11.29. a. So I ask you, "When will we admit defeat?" Never!
  b. So I ask you, "When will we admit defeat"? Never!

For additional exercises focusing on periods, question marks, and exclamation points, visit MyBCommLab. Click on Chapter 11, click on Additional Exercises to Improve Your Grammar, Mechanics, and Usage, and click on 17. Punctuation B.

MyBCommLab

Go to the Assignments section of your MyLab to complete these writing exercises

11.30. Can knowing the source of information that you find online unfairly bias you against the information? Explain your answer. [LO-2]

11.31. Why are unsolicited proposals more challenging to write than solicited proposals? [LO-7]

Endnotes

1. MyCityWay website, accessed 28 February 2015, http://mycityway .com; BMW i website, accessed 18 June 2013, www.bmw-i.com; Adam Bluestein and Amy Barrett, "How Business-Plan Competitions Reward Innovation," Inc., 1 July 2010, www.inc.com; Nick Saint, "Mayor Bloomberg Announces First Investment by NYC-Sponsored Venture Fund: MyCityWay," *SAI Business Insider*, 25 May 2010, www .businessinsider.com; Heidi Brown, "How to Write a Winning Business Plan," *Forbes*, 18 June 2010, www.forbes.com; NYC DataMine website, accessed 5 March 2011, www.nyc.gov.

2. Legal-Definitions.com, accessed 17 December 2003, www.legal-definitions.com.

3. Lynn Quitman Troyka, *Simon & Schuster Handbook for Writers*, 6th ed. (Upper Saddle River, N.J.: Simon & Schuster, 2002), 481.

4. "How to Paraphrase Effectively: 6 Steps to Follow," ResearchPaper .com, accessed 26 October 1998, www.researchpaper.com/writing_center/30.html.

5. "Search Effectively," Bing, accessed 23 February 2011, www.bing .com.

6. Christina Warren, "Yolink Helps Web Researchers Search Behind Links," Mashable, 24 July 2010, http://mashable.com.

7. Pearltrees product description, Google Play store, accessed 9 May 2014, http://play.google.com.

8. A. B. Blankenship and George Edward Breen, *State of the Art Marketing Research* (Chicago: NTC Business Books, 1993), 136.

9. Naresh K. Malhotra, *Basic Marketing Research* (Upper Saddle River, N.J.: Prentice-Hall, 2002), 314–317; "How to Design and Conduct a Study," *Credit Union Magazine*, October 1983, 36–46.

10. Sherwyn P. Morreale and Courtland L. Bovée, *Excellence in Public Speaking* (Fort Worth: Harcourt Brace College Publishers, 1998), 177.

11. Blankenship and Breen, *State of the Art Marketing Research*, 225.

12. Brown, "How to Write a Winning Business Plan"; Michael Gerber, "The Business Plan That Always Works," *Her Business*, May/June 2004, 23–25; J. Tol Broome Jr., "How to Write a Business Plan," *Nation's Business*, February 1993, 29–30; Albert Richards, "The Ernst & Young Business Plan Guide," *R & D Management*, April 1995, 253; David Lanchner, "How Chitchat Became a Valuable Business Plan," *Global Finance*, February 1995, 54–56; Marguerita Ashby-Berger, "My Business Plan—And What Really Happened," *Small Business Forum*, Winter 1994–1995, 24–35; Stanley R. Rich and David E. Gumpert, *Business Plans That Win $$$* (New York: Harper & Row, 1985).

13. Strategyzer website, accessed 1 March 2015, www.businessmodel generation.com; Ash Maurya, "Why Lean Canvas vs Business Model Canvas?" Practice Trumps Theory blog, 27 February 2012, http:// practicetrumpstheory.com

14. Jakob Nielsen, "How Users Read on the Web," accessed 11 November 2004, www.useit.com/alertbox/9710a.html.

15. Reid Goldsborough, "Words for the Wise," *Link-Up*, September-October 1999, 25–26.

16. Julie Rohovit, "Computer Eye Strain: The Dilbert Syndrome," Virtual Hospital website, accessed 9 November 2004, www.vh.org.

17. Shel Holtz, *Writing for the Wired World* (San Francisco: International Association of Business Communicators, 1999), 28–29.

18. SXSW website, accessed 1 March 2015, http://sxsw.com; Catherine Holahan and Spencer E. Ante, "SXSW: Where Tech Mingles with Music," *BusinessWeek*, 7 March 2008, www.businessweek .com.

LEARNING OBJECTIVES

After studying this chapter, you will be able to

1 Explain how to adapt to your audiences when writing reports and proposals, and describe the choices involved in drafting report and proposal content.

2 Identify five characteristics of effective writing in online reports, and explain how to adapt your writing approach for wikis.

3 Discuss six principles of graphic design, and identify the most common types of visuals used to present data, information, concepts, and ideas.

4 Explain how to integrate visuals with text effectively and how to verify the quality of your visuals.

ON THE JOB: COMMUNICATING AT
WARBY PARKER

Eyeing a New Way to Sell Eyeglasses

When a company sets out to disrupt an entire industry, it's not surprising that its communication efforts don't follow all the old rules, either.

Much of the worldwide market for eyeglasses is controlled by the Italian company Luxottica, which owns such well-known brands as Ray-Ban and Oakley and manufactures glasses for a host of high-fashion labels, from Dolce & Gabbana to Versace. Luxottica also operates more than 7,000 retail stores, including LensCrafters and Sunglass Hut. If you've ever purchased a pair of prescription glasses or sunglasses, chances are you've done business with Luxottica in one form or another. And business has been very good for Luxottica, earning it some 80 percent of the global market for glasses.

Much of the remaining 20 percent of the market is in the hands of Costco and Walmart, two companies that compete on cost more than fashion. Between high fashion on one hand and low prices on the other, these three giants seem to have wrapped up the market.

Neil Blumenthal and David Gilboa looked at the data and drew a different conclusion, however. They believed an opportunity

Neil Blumenthal and David Gilboa's unconventional ideas behind the eyewear startup Warby Parker is reflected in the company's cheeky communication style.

existed for a company to compete on fashion *and* price. Together with University of Pennsylvania classmates Andrew Hunt and Jeffrey Raider, they crafted a business model that combines fashion-forward designs and a brand image that appeals to younger consumers with the operational efficiency of online commerce. Echoing their unconventional aspirations, they named the company Warby Parker after two characters from the works of the Beat Generation writer Jack Kerouac.

The quest to connect with buyers in a market dominated by a handful of major corporations gives Warby Parker's communication efforts a different look and feel. You won't find supermodels posing on yachts in the company's promotional campaigns. You're more likely to find a blog post about what company employees are reading or a wistful goodbye note to a summer intern heading back to high school.

The company's "annual reports" are a great example of how unconventional thinking can lead to communications that connect with audiences in fresh ways. All U.S. companies that sell stock to the public are required to issue annual reports that disclose a variety of financial details. Most companies expand on these minimum requirements with glossy, persuasive messages about their operations, products, and prospects.

As a privately held company (as of 2015), Warby Parker isn't required to publish an annual report, but it does so anyway—sort of. Its annual reports aren't anything like normal. One year, the report was an online calendar of major, minor, and just plain goofy things that happened around the company, from product launches to a survey about how many pairs of pants employees wear in a typical month. The following year, it was an interactive message generator that created personalized reports for website visitors based on how good or bad *their* year had been.

This tradition-defying approach to communication fits the transparent, social, and conversational style of today's younger consumers. And it helps position Warby Parker as a different kind of company, one more in touch with those customers and their needs and aspirations. The company won't dethrone Luxottica anytime soon, but it has already carved out a nice chunk of the eyewear market and continues to grow as it heads toward a possible initial public offering in the stock market. At that point, it will have to bend to convention just a little, at least enough to meet government reporting requirements, but it will surely maintain an offbeat approach in the rest of its communication efforts.[1]

WWW.WARBYPARKER.COM

Composing Reports and Proposals

Like all successful business communicators, Neil Blumenthal and David Gilboa (profiled in the chapter-opening On the Job) know that the writing stage is where you make your ideas from the planning stage come alive. This chapter builds on the writing techniques and ideas you learned in Chapter 5, focusing on issues that are particularly important when preparing longer message formats, including website and wiki content. In addition, you'll get an introduction to creating effective visuals, which are a vital aspect of many reports and proposals.

As with shorter messages, take a few moments before you start writing to make sure you're ready to adapt your approach to your audience.

> **1 LEARNING OBJECTIVE**
> Explain how to adapt to your audiences when writing reports and proposals, and describe the choices involved in drafting report and proposal content.

ADAPTING TO YOUR AUDIENCE

Successful report writers adapt to their intended audiences by being sensitive to audience needs, building strong relationships with the audience, and controlling style and tone.

Chapter 5 introduced four aspects of audience sensitivity, and all four apply to reports and proposals: adopting the "you" attitude, maintaining a strong sense of etiquette, emphasizing the positive, and using bias-free language. Reports and proposals that are highly technical, complex, or lengthy can put heavy demands on your readers, so the "you" attitude is especially important with these long messages.

Be sure to plan how you will adapt your style and your language to reflect the image of your organization. Many companies have specific guidelines for communicating with public audiences, so be aware of these preferences before you start writing.

If you know your readers reasonably well and your report is likely to meet with their approval, you can adopt a fairly informal tone (as long as that is appropriate in your organization, of course). A more formal tone is appropriate for longer reports, especially those that deal with controversial or complex information. You also need a more formal tone when your report will be sent to other parts of the organization or to outsiders, such as customers, suppliers, or members of the community (see Figure 12.1 on the next page).

Long or complex reports demand a lot from readers, making the "you" attitude especially important.

Many companies have specific guidelines for reports, particularly those intended for external audiences.

Long and somewhat rigorous sentences help give the report its formal tone. For a more consumer-oriented publication, this writing could certainly be simplified.

A less-formal report might've said something along the lines of "Poor diet and physical inactivity are killing U.S. citizens" instead of the more formal (and more precise) "are associated with major causes of morbidity and mortality."

This paragraph mentions the troubling statistic that 15 percent of U.S. households can't afford to meet basic nutritional requirements, but because the report is presenting dietary recommendations and not public policy statements about economics or other issues, the tone is objective and dispassionate.

Eating and physical activity patterns that are focused on consuming fewer calories, making informed food choices, and being physically active can help people attain and maintain a healthy weight, reduce their risk of chronic disease, and promote overall health. The *Dietary Guidelines for Americans, 2010* exemplifies these strategies through recommendations that accommodate the food preferences, cultural traditions, and customs of the many and diverse groups who live in the United States.

By law (Public Law 101-445, Title III, 7 U.S.C. 5301 et seq.), *Dietary Guidelines for Americans* is reviewed, updated if necessary, and published every 5 years. The U.S. Department of Agriculture (USDA) and the U.S. Department of Health and Human Services (HHS) jointly create each edition. *Dietary Guidelines for Americans, 2010* is based on the *Report of the Dietary Guidelines Advisory Committee on the Dietary Guidelines for Americans, 2010* and consideration of Federal agency and public comments.

Dietary Guidelines recommendations traditionally have been intended for healthy Americans ages 2 years and older. However, *Dietary Guidelines for Americans, 2010* is being released at a time of rising concern about the health of the American population. Poor diet and physical inactivity are the most important factors contributing to an epidemic of overweight and obesity affecting men, women, and children in all segments of our society. Even in the absence of overweight, poor diet and physical inactivity are associated with major causes of morbidity and mortality in the United States. Therefore, the *Dietary Guidelines for Americans, 2010* is intended for Americans ages 2 years and older, including those at increased risk of chronic disease.

Dietary Guidelines for Americans, 2010 also recognizes that in recent years nearly 15 percent of American households have been unable to acquire adequate food to meet their needs.[1] This dietary guidance can help them maximize the nutritional content of

1. Nord M, Coleman-Jensen A, Andrews M, Carlson S. Household food security in the United States, 2009. Washington (DC): U.S. Department of Agriculture, Economic Research Service. 2010 Nov. Economic Research Report No. ERR-108. Available from http://www.ers.usda.gov/publications/err108.

viii   DIETARY GUIDELINES FOR AMERICANS, 2010

(Continued)

Figure 12.1   Choosing the Appropriate Tone for a Report
This report excerpt (part of the executive summary of the *Dietary Guidelines for Americans* published by the U.S. Department of Agriculture and the U.S. Department of Health and Human Services) uses a number of techniques to create a formal tone. This is a formal policy document whose intended readers are educators, government regulators, and others charged with using the information to help inform consumers. If the document had been written with consumers in mind, you can imagine how the tone might have been lighter and less formal.

Source: Dietary Guidelines for Americans 2010 published by the U.S. Department of Agriculture and the U.S. Department of Health and Human Services.

Reports destined for audiences outside the United States often require a more formal tone to match the expectations of audiences in many other countries.

Communicating with people in other cultures often calls for more formality, for two reasons. First, the business environment outside the United States tends to be more formal in general, and that formality must be reflected in your communication. Second, the things you do to make a document informal (such as using humor and idiomatic language) often translate poorly from one culture to another, so you risk offending or confusing your readers.

This is an example of a sentence that is precise and uses language appropriate for the purpose of this report. In contrast, a document aimed primarily at consumers might've said "We've converted the latest nutritional insights into recommendations for healthy eating."

their meals. Many other Americans consume less than optimal intake of certain nutrients even though they have adequate resources for a healthy diet. This dietary guidance and nutrition information can help them choose a healthy, nutritionally adequate diet.

The intent of the Dietary Guidelines is to summarize and synthesize knowledge about individual nutrients and food components into an interrelated set of recommendations for healthy eating that can be adopted by the public. Taken together, the Dietary Guidelines recommendations encompass two overarching concepts:

- **Maintain calorie balance over time to achieve and sustain a healthy weight.** People who are most successful at achieving and maintaining a healthy weight do so through continued attention to consuming only enough calories from foods and beverages to meet their needs and by being physically active. To curb the obesity epidemic and improve their health, many Americans must decrease the calories they consume and increase the calories they expend through physical activity.

- **Focus on consuming nutrient-dense foods and beverages.** Americans currently consume too much sodium and too many calories from solid fats, added sugars, and refined grains.[2] These replace nutrient-dense foods and beverages and make it difficult for people to achieve recommended nutrient intake while controlling calorie and sodium intake. A healthy eating pattern limits intake of sodium, solid fats, added sugars, and refined grains and emphasizes nutrient-dense foods and beverages—vegetables, fruits, whole grains, fat-free or low-fat milk and milk products,[3] seafood, lean meats and poultry, eggs, beans and peas, and nuts and seeds.

A basic premise of the Dietary Guidelines is that nutrient needs should be met primarily through consuming foods. In certain cases, fortified foods and dietary supplements may be useful in providing one or more nutrients that otherwise might be consumed in less than recommended amounts. Two eating patterns that embody the Dietary Guidelines are the USDA Food Patterns and their vegetarian adaptations and the DASH (Dietary Approaches to Stop Hypertension) Eating Plan.

A healthy eating pattern needs not only to promote health and help to decrease the risk of chronic diseases, but it also should prevent foodborne illness. Four basic food safety principles (Clean, Separate, Cook, and Chill) work together to reduce the risk of foodborne illnesses. In addition, some foods (such as milks, cheeses, and juices that have not been pasteurized, and undercooked animal foods) pose high risk for foodborne illness and should be avoided.

The information in the *Dietary Guidelines for Americans* is used in developing educational materials and aiding policymakers in designing and carrying out nutrition-related programs, including Federal food, nutrition education, and information programs. In addition, the *Dietary Guidelines for Americans* has the potential to offer authoritative statements as provided for in the Food and Drug Administration Modernization Act (FDAMA).

The following are the *Dietary Guidelines for Americans, 2010* Key Recommendations, listed by the chapter in which they are discussed in detail. These Key Recommendations are the most important in terms of their implications for improving public health.[4] To get the full benefit, individuals should carry out the Dietary Guidelines recommendations in their entirety as part of an overall healthy eating pattern.

In a less-formal report, the authors might've written "One of our basic premises is that nutrient needs should be met primarily through consuming foods" or even "You should meet your nutrient needs by eating food, not by taking supplements." However, to maintain a formal tone, they avoid both first- and second-person usage.

2. Added sugars: Caloric sweeteners that are added to foods during processing, preparation, or consumed separately. Solid fats: Fats with a high content of saturated and/or *trans* fatty acids, which are usually solid at room temperature. Refined grains: Grains and grain products missing the bran, germ, and/or endosperm; any grain product that is not a whole grain.
3. Milk and milk products also can be referred to as dairy products.
4. Information on the type and strength of evidence supporting the Dietary Guidelines recommendations can be found at http://www.nutritionevidencelibrary.gov.

DIETARY GUIDELINES FOR AMERICANS, 2010   ix

Figure 12.1   **Choosing the Appropriate Tone for a Report (Continued)**

DRAFTING REPORT CONTENT

Your credibility and career advancement are on the line with every business report you write, so make sure your content is

- **Accurate.** Double-check your facts and references and check for typos. If an audience ever gets an inkling that your information is shaky, they'll start to view all your work with skepticism.
- **Complete.** Tell your readers what they need to know—no more, no less—and present the information in a way that is geared to their needs.

- **Balanced.** Present all sides of the issue fairly and equitably and include all the essential information, even if some of the information doesn't support your line of reasoning. Omitting relevant information or facts can bias your report.
- **Clear and logical.** Save your readers time by making sure your writing is uncluttered, and proceeds logically from point to point.
- **Documented properly.** If you use primary and secondary sources for your report or proposal, be sure to properly document and give credit to your sources.

Keeping these points in mind will help you draft the most effective introduction, body, and close for your report.

Report Introduction

As with other written business communications, the text of reports and proposals has three main sections: an introduction, a body, and a close. The *introduction* (or *opening*) is the first section in the text of any report or proposal. An effective introduction accomplishes at least four things:

- Puts the report or proposal in a broader context by tying it to a problem or an assignment
- Introduces the subject or purpose of the report or proposal and indicates why the subject is important
- Previews the main ideas and the order in which they'll be covered
- Establishes the tone of the document and the writer's relationship with the audience

The specific elements you should include in an introduction depend on the nature and length of the report, the circumstances under which you're writing the report, and your relationship with the audience. An introduction could contain any or all of the following:

- **Authorization.** When, how, and by whom the report was authorized; who wrote it; and when it was submitted. This material is especially important when you don't accompany the report with a *letter of transmittal* (see Chapter 13).
- **Problem/opportunity/purpose.** The reason the report was written and what is to be accomplished as a result of your having written it.
- **Scope.** What is and what isn't covered in the report. The scope also helps with the critical job of setting the audience's expectations.
- **Background.** Any relevant historical conditions or factors that can help readers grasp the report's message.
- **Sources and methods.** The primary and secondary sources of information used. As appropriate, this section can also explain how the information was collected.
- **Definitions.** Definitions of important terms used in the report. Define any terms that might be unfamiliar to the audience or any terms you use in an unfamiliar way.
- **Limitations.** Factors beyond your control that affect the quality of the report, such as budgets, schedule constraints, or limited access to information or people. However, don't apologize or try to explain away personal shortcomings, such as your own poor planning.
- **Report organization.** The organization of the report. This "road map" helps readers understand what's coming in the report and why.

In a brief report, these topics may be discussed in only a paragraph or two. In a longer formal report, the discussion of these topics may span several pages and constitute a significant section within the report.

Report Body

The report's *body* presents, analyzes, and interprets the information gathered during your investigation and supports the recommendations or conclusions discussed in your document (see Figure 12.2). As with the introduction, the body of your report can require some tough decisions about which elements to include and how much detail to offer. Here again, your decisions depend on many variables, including the needs of your audience. Provide only enough detail in the body to support your conclusions and recommendations.

[Margin notes]

Your introduction needs to put the report in context for the reader, introduce the subject, preview main ideas, and establish the tone of the document.

Carefully select the elements to include in your introduction; strive for a balance between necessary, expected information and brevity.

The body of your report presents, analyzes, and interprets the information you gathered during your investigation.

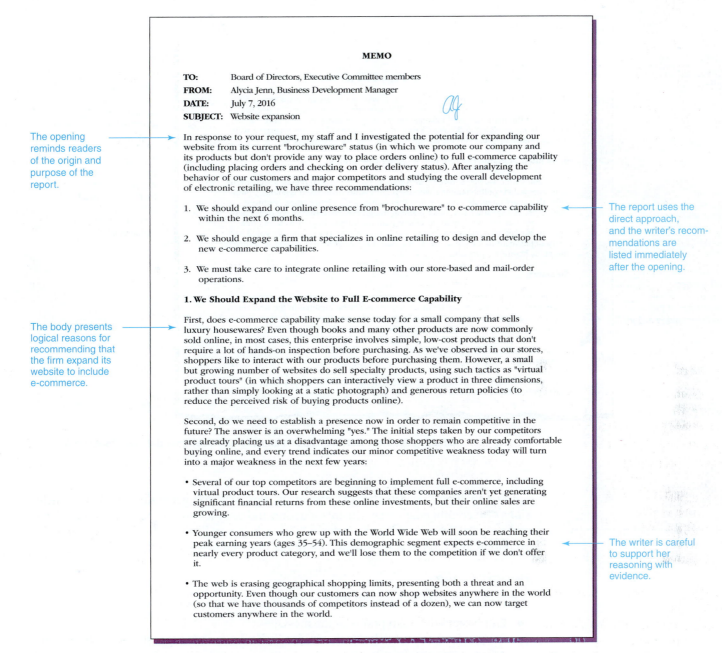

The opening reminds readers of the origin and purpose of the report.

The body presents logical reasons for recommending that the firm expand its website to include e-commerce.

MEMO

TO: Board of Directors, Executive Committee members
FROM: Alycia Jenn, Business Development Manager
DATE: July 7, 2016
SUBJECT: Website expansion

In response to your request, my staff and I investigated the potential for expanding our website from its current "brochureware" status (in which we promote our company and its products but don't provide any way to place orders online) to full e-commerce capability (including placing orders and checking on order delivery status). After analyzing the behavior of our customers and major competitors and studying the overall development of electronic retailing, we have three recommendations:

1. We should expand our online presence from "brochureware" to e-commerce capability within the next 6 months.

2. We should engage a firm that specializes in online retailing to design and develop the new e-commerce capabilities.

3. We must take care to integrate online retailing with our store-based and mail-order operations.

1. We Should Expand the Website to Full E-commerce Capability

First, does e-commerce capability make sense today for a small company that sells luxury housewares? Even though books and many other products are now commonly sold online, in most cases, this enterprise involves simple, low-cost products that don't require a lot of hands-on inspection before purchasing. As we've observed in our stores, shoppers like to interact with our products before purchasing them. However, a small but growing number of websites do sell specialty products, using such tactics as "virtual product tours" (in which shoppers can interactively view a product in three dimensions, rather than simply looking at a static photograph) and generous return policies (to reduce the perceived risk of buying products online).

Second, do we need to establish a presence now in order to remain competitive in the future? The answer is an overwhelming "yes." The initial steps taken by our competitors are already placing us at a disadvantage among those shoppers who are already comfortable buying online, and every trend indicates our minor competitive weakness today will turn into a major weakness in the next few years:

• Several of our top competitors are beginning to implement full e-commerce, including virtual product tours. Our research suggests that these companies aren't yet generating significant financial returns from these online investments, but their online sales are growing.

• Younger consumers who grew up with the World Wide Web will soon be reaching their peak earning years (ages 35–54). This demographic segment expects e-commerce in nearly every product category, and we'll lose them to the competition if we don't offer it.

• The web is erasing geographical shopping limits, presenting both a threat and an opportunity. Even though our customers can now shop websites anywhere in the world (so that we have thousands of competitors instead of a dozen), we can now target customers anywhere in the world.

The report uses the direct approach, and the writer's recommendations are listed immediately after the opening.

The writer is careful to support her reasoning with evidence.

(Continued)

Figure 12.2   Effective Problem-Solving Report Focusing on Recommendations
In this report recommending that her firm expand its website to full e-commerce capability, the writer uses the body of her report to provide enough information to support her argument, without burdening her high-level readership with a lot of tactical details.

The topics commonly covered in a report body include

• Explanations of a problem or opportunity
• Facts, statistical evidence, and trends
• Results of studies or investigations
• Discussion and analyses of potential courses of action
• Advantages, disadvantages, costs, and benefits of a particular course of action
• Procedures or steps in a process
• Methods and approaches
• Criteria for evaluating alternatives and options
• Conclusions and recommendations
• Supporting reasons for conclusions or recommendations

The report body should contain only enough information to convey your message in a convincing fashion; don't overload readers with interesting but unnecessary material.

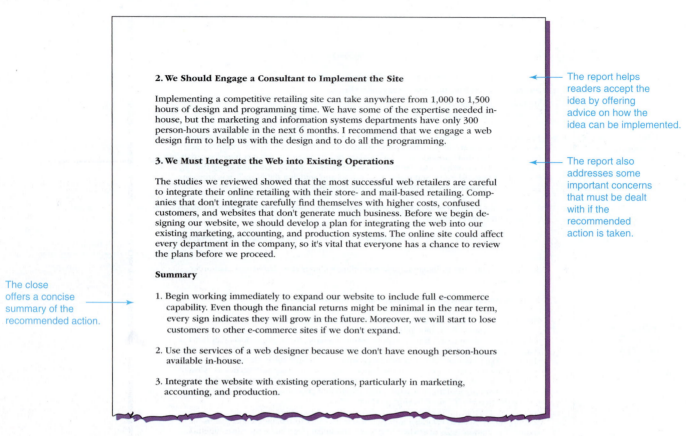

2. We Should Engage a Consultant to Implement the Site

Implementing a competitive retailing site can take anywhere from 1,000 to 1,500 hours of design and programming time. We have some of the expertise needed in-house, but the marketing and information systems departments have only 300 person-hours available in the next 6 months. I recommend that we engage a web design firm to help us with the design and to do all the programming.

3. We Must Integrate the Web into Existing Operations

The studies we reviewed showed that the most successful web retailers are careful to integrate their online retailing with their store- and mail-based retailing. Companies that don't integrate carefully find themselves with higher costs, confused customers, and websites that don't generate much business. Before we begin designing our website, we should develop a plan for integrating the web into our existing marketing, accounting, and production systems. The online site could affect every department in the company, so it's vital that everyone has a chance to review the plans before we proceed.

Summary

1. Begin working immediately to expand our website to include full e-commerce capability. Even though the financial returns might be minimal in the near term, every sign indicates they will grow in the future. Moreover, we will start to lose customers to other e-commerce sites if we don't expand.

2. Use the services of a web designer because we don't have enough person-hours available in-house.

3. Integrate the website with existing operations, particularly in marketing, accounting, and production.

The report helps readers accept the idea by offering advice on how the idea can be implemented.

The report also addresses some important concerns that must be dealt with if the recommended action is taken.

The close offers a concise summary of the recommended action.

Figure 12.2 Effective Problem-Solving Report Focusing on Recommendations (Continued)

For analytical reports that use the direct approach, you generally state your conclusions or recommendations in the introduction and use the body to provide your evidence and support. If you're using the indirect approach, you're likely to use the body to discuss your logic and reserve your conclusions or recommendations until the very end.

Report Close

A report's *close* has three important functions:

- Emphasizes the main points of the message
- Summarizes the benefits to the reader if the document suggests a change or some other course of action
- Brings all the action items together in one place and gives the details about who should do what, when, where, and how

The close might be the only part of your report some readers have time for, so make sure it conveys the full weight of your message.

Research shows that the final section of a report or proposal leaves a lasting impression. The close gives you one last chance to make sure your report says what you intended.[2]

The nature of your close depends on the type of report (informational or analytical) and the approach (direct or indirect).

The content and length of your report close depend on your choice of direct or indirect order, among other variables. If you're using the direct approach, you can end with a summary of key points, listed in the order in which they appear in the report body. If you're using the indirect approach, you can use the close to present your conclusions or recommendations if you didn't end the body with them. Just remember that a conclusion or recommendation isn't the place to introduce new facts; your readers should have all the information they need by the time they reach this point in your report.

If your report is intended to prompt others to action, use the ending to spell out exactly what should happen next and who is responsible for each task. If you'll be taking all the actions yourself, make sure your readers understand this fact so that they know what to expect from you.

In a short report, the close may be only a paragraph or two. However, the close of a long report may have separate sections for conclusions, recommendations, and actions. Having separate sections helps your reader locate this material and focus on each element. Such an arrangement also gives you a final opportunity to emphasize this important content. If you have multiple conclusions, recommendations, or actions, you may want to number and list them as well for easier reference.

For long reports, you may need to divide your close into separate sections for conclusions, recommendations, and actions.

DRAFTING PROPOSAL CONTENT

With proposals, the content for each section is governed by many variables—the most important of which is the source of your proposal. If your proposal is unsolicited, you have some latitude in the scope and organization of content. However, if you are responding to a request for proposals (RFP), you need to follow the instructions in the RFP in every detail. Most RFPs spell out precisely what a proposal must cover and in what order so that all bids will be similar in form and therefore easier to compare.

The general purpose of any proposal is to persuade readers to do something, such as purchase goods or services, fund a project, or implement a program. Thus, your writing approach for a proposal is similar to that used for persuasive messages (see Chapter 10). As with other persuasive messages, the AIDA model of gaining attention, building interest, creating desire, and motivating action is an effective structure. Here are key strategies to strengthen your argument:[3]

Approach proposals the same way you approach persuasive messages.

- Demonstrate your knowledge in terms that are meaningful to the audience.
- Provide concrete information and examples.
- Research the competition so you know what other proposals your audience is likely to read.
- Prove that your proposal is appropriate and feasible for your audience.
- Relate your product, service, or personnel to the reader's exact needs.
- Produce your proposal in a format and medium that meets audience expectations.

In addition, make sure your proposal is letter perfect, inviting, and readable. Readers will prejudge the quality of your products, services, and capabilities by the quality of the proposal you submit.

Proposal Introduction

The introduction of a proposal presents and summarizes the problem or opportunity you want to address, along with your proposed solution. If your proposal is solicited, follow the RFP's instructions about indicating which RFP you're responding to. If your proposal is unsolicited, your introduction should mention any factors that led you to submit your proposal, such as previous conversations you've had with readers. The following topics are commonly covered in a proposal introduction:

- **Background or statement of the problem or opportunity.** Briefly review the reader's situation and establish the need for action. Remember that readers may not perceive a problem or an opportunity the same way you do. In unsolicited proposals in particular, you need to convince them that a problem or an opportunity exists before you can convince them to accept your solution.
- **Solution.** Briefly describe the change you propose and highlight your key selling points and their benefits, showing how your proposal will help readers meet their business objectives.
- **Scope.** State the boundaries of the proposal—what you will and will not do. Sometimes called *delimitations*.
- **Organization.** Orient the reader to the remainder of the proposal and call attention to the major divisions of information.

In an unsolicited proposal, your introduction needs to convince readers that a problem or an opportunity exists.

In short proposals, your discussion of these topics will be brief—perhaps only a sentence or two for each. For long, formal proposals, each topic may warrant separate subheadings and several paragraphs of discussion.

Proposal Body

The proposal's body gives complete details on the proposed solution and specifies what the anticipated results will be. Because a proposal is by definition a persuasive message, your audience expects you to promote your offering in a confident but professional manner.

In addition to providing facts and evidence to support your conclusions, an effective body covers this information:

- **Proposed solution.** Describe what you have to offer: your concept, product, or service (see Figure 12.3). Stress the benefits of your product, service, or investment opportunity that are relevant to your readers' needs and point out any advantages that you have over your competitors.

Readers understand that a proposal is a persuasive message, so they're willing to accommodate a degree of promotional emphasis—as long as it is focused on their needs.

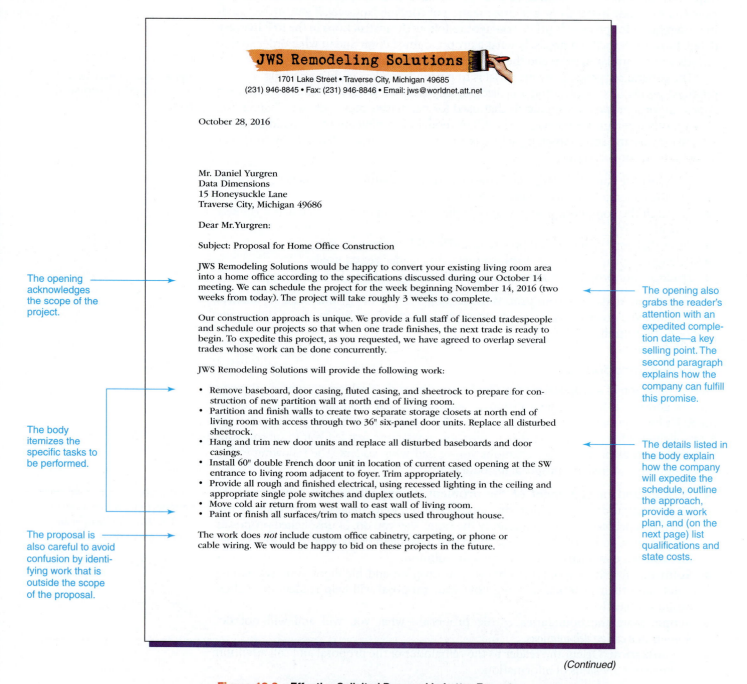

The opening acknowledges the scope of the project.

The body itemizes the specific tasks to be performed.

The proposal is also careful to avoid confusion by identifying work that is outside the scope of the proposal.

The opening also grabs the reader's attention with an expedited completion date—a key selling point. The second paragraph explains how the company can fulfill this promise.

The details listed in the body explain how the company will expedite the schedule, outline the approach, provide a work plan, and (on the next page) list qualifications and state costs.

(Continued)

Figure 12.3 Effective Solicited Proposal in Letter Format
This informal solicited proposal in letter format provides the information the customer needs in order to make a purchase. Note that by signing the proposal and returning it, the customer will enter into a legal contract to pay for the services described.

- **Work plan.** Explain the steps you'll take, the methods or resources you'll use, and the person(s) responsible. For solicited proposals, make sure your dates match those specified in the RFP. Keep in mind that if your proposal is accepted, the work plan is contractually binding, so don't promise more than you can deliver.
- **Statement of qualifications.** Describe your organization's experience, personnel, and facilities—all in relation to reader needs. You can supplement your qualifications by including a list of client references, but get permission ahead of time to use those references.
- **Costs.** Cover pricing, reimbursable expenses, discounts, and other financial concerns.

In an informal proposal, discussion of some or all of these elements may be grouped together and presented in a letter format, such as in Figure 12.3. In a formal proposal, the discussion of these elements can be quite long and thorough. The format may resemble long reports with multiple parts, as Chapter 13 discusses.

The work plan indicates exactly how you will accomplish the solution presented in the proposal.

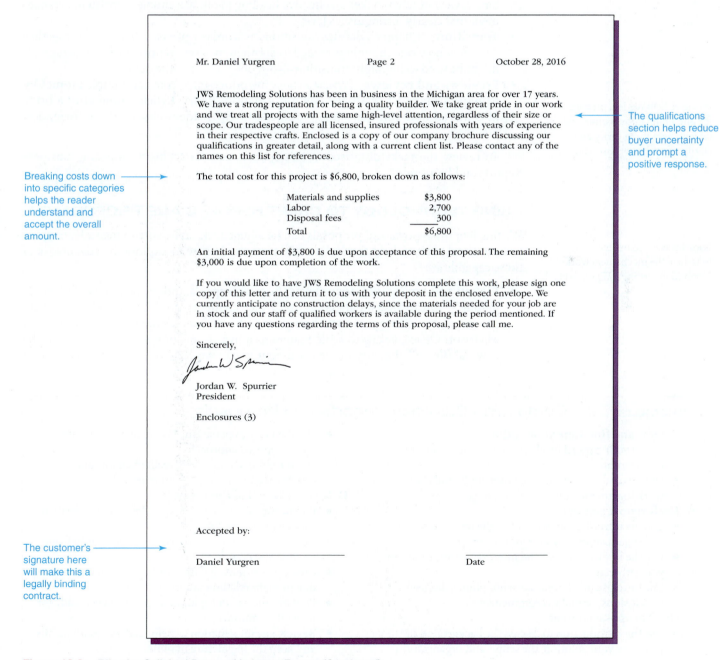

Mr. Daniel Yurgren   Page 2   October 28, 2016

JWS Remodeling Solutions has been in business in the Michigan area for over 17 years. We have a strong reputation for being a quality builder. We take great pride in our work and we treat all projects with the same high-level attention, regardless of their size or scope. Our tradespeople are all licensed, insured professionals with years of experience in their respective crafts. Enclosed is a copy of our company brochure discussing our qualifications in greater detail, along with a current client list. Please contact any of the names on this list for references.

The qualifications section helps reduce buyer uncertainty and prompt a positive response.

The total cost for this project is $6,800, broken down as follows:

Breaking costs down into specific categories helps the reader understand and accept the overall amount.

Materials and supplies	$3,800
Labor	2,700
Disposal fees	300
Total	$6,800

An initial payment of $3,800 is due upon acceptance of this proposal. The remaining $3,000 is due upon completion of the work.

If you would like to have JWS Remodeling Solutions complete this work, please sign one copy of this letter and return it to us with your deposit in the enclosed envelope. We currently anticipate no construction delays, since the materials needed for your job are in stock and our staff of qualified workers is available during the period mentioned. If you have any questions regarding the terms of this proposal, please call me.

Sincerely,

Jordan W. Spurrier
President

Enclosures (3)

The customer's signature here will make this a legally binding contract.

Accepted by:

_____   _____
Daniel Yurgren   Date

Figure 12.3   Effective Solicited Proposal in Letter Format (Continued)

Proposal Close

The close is your last chance to convince the reader of the merits of your proposal, so make especially sure it's clear, compelling, and audience oriented.

The final section of a proposal generally summarizes your key points, emphasizes the benefits readers will get from your solution, and asks for a decision from the reader. The close is your last opportunity to persuade readers to accept your proposal. In both formal and informal proposals, make this section relatively brief, assertive (but not brash or abrupt), and confident.

HELPING REPORT READERS FIND THEIR WAY

Help your audiences navigate through your reports by providing clear directions to key pieces of content.

Today's time-pressed readers want to browse reports and quickly find information of interest. To help them find what they're looking for and stay on track as they navigate through your documents, learn to make good use of headings and links, smooth transitions, and previews and reviews:

- **Headings.** Readers should be able to follow the structure of your document and pick up the key points of your message from the headings and subheadings. (See Chapter 6 for a review of what makes an effective heading.) Follow a simple, consistent arrangement that clearly distinguishes levels.
- **Transitions.** Chapter 5 defines transitions as words or phrases that tie ideas together and show how one thought is related to another. In a long report, an entire paragraph might be used to highlight transitions from one section to the next.
- **Previews and reviews.** *Preview sections* introduce important or complex topics by helping readers get ready for new information. *Review sections* come after a body of material and summarize key points to help readers absorb the information just read.

Previews help readers prepare for upcoming information, and reviews help them verify and clarify what they've just read.

To review the tasks discussed in this section, see "Checklist: Composing Business Reports and Proposals."

USING TECHNOLOGY TO CRAFT REPORTS AND PROPOSALS

Look for ways to use technology to reduce the mechanical work involved in writing long reports.

Writing lengthy reports and proposals can be a huge task, so be sure to take advantage of technological tools to help throughout the process. Be sure to explore the advantages of these capabilities:

- **Linked and embedded documents.** In many reports and proposals, you'll include graphics, spreadsheets, databases, and other elements produced in other software programs. Make sure you know how your software handles the files. For instance, in Microsoft Office, *linking* to a file maintains a live connection to it, so changes in the original file will show up in the document you're working on. However, *embedding* a

---

CHECKLIST ✔ Composing Business Reports and Proposals

A. Review and fine-tune your outline.
- Match your parallel headings to the tone of your report or proposal.
- Understand how the introduction, body, and close work together to convey your message.

B. Draft report content.
- Use the introduction to establish the purpose, scope, and organization of your report or proposal.
- Use the body to present and interpret the information you gathered.
- Use the close to summarize major points, discuss conclusions, or make recommendations.

C. Draft proposal content.
- Use the introduction to discuss the background or problem, your solution, the scope, and organization.

- Use the body to persuasively explain the benefits of your proposed approach.
- Use the close to emphasize reader benefits and summarize the merits of your approach.

D. Help readers find their way.
- Provide headings to improve readability and clarify the framework of your ideas.
- Use hyperlinks online to allow readers to jump from section to section.
- Create transitions that tie together ideas and show how one thought relates to another.
- Preview important topics to help readers get ready for new information.
- Review key information to help readers absorb details and keep the big picture in mind.

file breaks that link, so any subsequent changes made to the original will not automatically appear in the new document.

- **Electronic forms.** For recurring reports such as sales reports and compliance reports, consider creating a document that uses *form tools* such as text boxes (in which users can type new text) and check boxes (which can be used to select from a set of predetermined choices).
- **Electronic documents.** Portable document format (PDF) files have become a universal replacement for printed reports and proposals. Using Adobe Acrobat or similar products, you can quickly convert reports and proposals to PDF files that are easy to share electronically.
- **Multimedia documents.** Video clips, animation, presentation software slides, screencasts (recordings of on-screen activity), and other media elements can enhance the communication and persuasion powers of the written word.
- **Proposal-writing software.** Proposal-writing software can automatically personalize proposals, ensure proper structure (making sure you don't forget any sections, for instance), organize storage of all your boilerplate text, integrate contact information from sales databases, scan RFPs to identify questions (and even assign them to content experts), and fill in preliminary answers to common questions from a centralized knowledge base.[4]

Writing for Websites and Wikis

In addition to stand-alone reports and proposals, you may be asked to write in-depth content for websites or to collaborate on a wiki. The basic principles of report writing apply to both formats, but each has some unique considerations as well.

LEARNING OBJECTIVE
2 Identify five characteristics of effective writing in online reports, and explain how to adapt your writing approach for wikis.

DRAFTING WEBSITE CONTENT

Major sections on websites, particularly those that are fairly static (unlike, say, a blog) function in much the same way as reports. The skills you've developed for report writing adapt easily to this environment, as long as you keep a few points in mind:

- Take special care to build trust with your intended audiences because careful readers can be skeptical of online content. Make sure your content is accurate, current, complete, and authoritative.
- As much as possible, adapt your content for a global audience. Translating content is expensive, so some companies compromise by *localizing* the homepage while keeping the deeper, more detailed content in its original language.
- In an environment that presents many reading challenges, compelling, reader-oriented content is key to success.[5] Wherever you can, use the *inverted pyramid* style, in which you cover the most important information briefly at first and then gradually reveal successive layers of detail—letting readers choose to see those additional layers if they want to (see Figure 12.4 on the next page).
- Present your information in a concise, skimmable format. Effective websites use a variety of means to help readers skim pages quickly, including lists, careful use of color and boldface, informative headings, and helpful summaries that give readers a choice of learning more if they want to.
- Write effective links that serve for both site navigation and content skimming. Above all else, clearly identify where a link will take readers. Don't rely on cute wordplay that obscures the content, and don't force readers to click through and try to figure out where they're going.

COLLABORATING ON WIKIS

Wikis are a great way for teams and other groups to collaborate on writing projects, from brief articles to long reports and reference works. The benefits of wikis are compelling, but they do require a unique approach to writing. To be a valuable wiki contributor, keep these points in mind:[6]

Home Game Ticket Sales

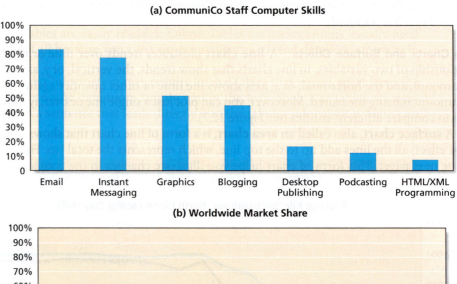

Figure 12.8   Surface Chart
Surface, or area, charts can show a combination of trends over time and the individual contributions of the components of a whole.

something over time. When preparing a surface chart, put the most important segment against the baseline and restrict the number of strata to four or five.

Bar Charts and Pie Charts   A **bar chart**, or *bar graph*, portrays numbers with the height or length of its rectangular bars, making one or more series of numbers easy to read or understand. Bar charts are particularly valuable when you want to show or compare quantities over time. As the charts in Figure 12.9 suggest, bar charts can be used in a variety of ways to convey particular points about the underlying data.

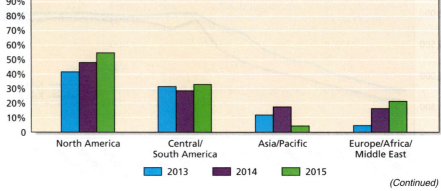

(Continued)

Figure 12.9   Bar Charts
Here are six of the dozens of variations possible with bar charts: singular (12.9a), grouped (12.9b), deviation (12.9c), segmented (12.9d), combination (12.9e), and paired (12.9f).

(c) CommuniCo Stock Price

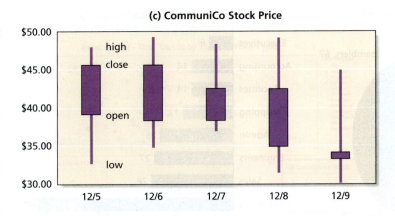

(d) CommuniCo Preferred Communication Media

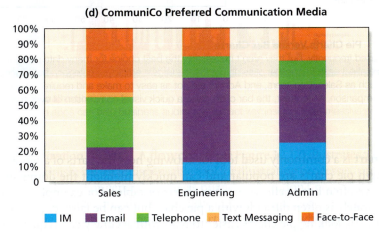

IM ■ Email ■ Telephone ■ Text Messaging ■ Face-to-Face

(e) CommuniCo Employee Training Costs

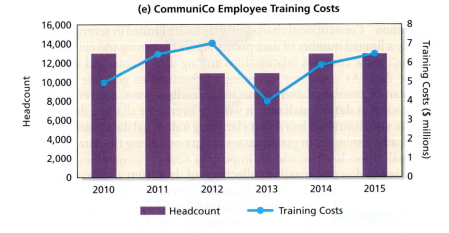

■ Headcount ● Training Costs

(f) Conference Attendance by Gender

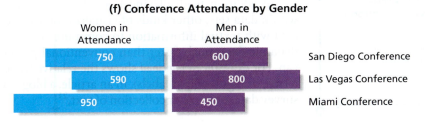

Figure 12.9 **Bar Charts (Continued)**

specific meaning (diamonds are decision points, and rectangles are process steps, for example). If you're communicating with computer programmers and others who are accustomed to formal flowcharting, make sure you use the correct symbols to avoid confusion.

As the name implies, an **organization chart** illustrates the positions, units, or functions of an organization and the way they interrelate. An organization's normal communication channels are almost impossible to describe without the benefit of a chart like the one in Figure 1.4 on page 9.

Maps and Geographic Information Systems Maps can show location, distance, points of interest (such as competitive retail outlets), and geographic distribution of data, such as sales by region or population by state. In addition to presenting facts and figures, maps are useful for showing market territories, distribution routes, and facilities locations.

When combined with databases and aerial or satellite photography in *geographic information systems (GIS)*, maps become extremely powerful visual reporting tools (see Figure 12.13). As one example, retailing specialists can explore the demographic and psychographic makeup of neighborhoods within various driving distances from a particular store location. Using such information, managers can plan everything from new building sites to delivery routes to marketing campaigns.

Drawings, Diagrams, and Photographs The opportunities to use drawings, diagrams, and photographs are virtually endless. Simple drawings can show the network of suppliers in an industry, the flow of funds through a company, or the process for completing the payroll each week. More complex diagrams, including interactive online diagrams, can convey technical topics such as the operation of a machine or repair procedures.

Word processors and presentation software now offer fairly advanced drawing capabilities, but for more precise and professional illustrations, you may need a specialized package such as Adobe Illustrator or SketchUp.

Photographs offer both functional and decorative value, and nothing can top a photograph when you need to show exact appearances. Because audiences expect photographs to show literal visual truths, you must take care when using image-processing tools such as Adobe Photoshop.

Margin notes:

Use maps to represent statistics by geographic area and to show spatial relationships.

Use drawings and diagrams to show how something works or how it is made or used; drawings are sometimes better than photographs because they let you focus on the most important details.

Use photographs for visual appeal and to show exact appearances.

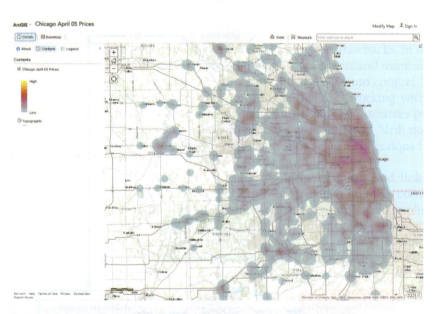

Figure 12.13 **Geographic Information Systems**
Businesses use geographic information systems (GIS) in a variety of ways. By overlaying maps and aerial or satellite imagery with descriptive data (such as this map of gas prices in the Chicago area), companies can use these displays for such purposes as planning sales campaigns, optimizing transportation routing, and selecting retail or production sites.

Source: Copyright © 2013 Esri, DigitalGlobe, GeoEye, i-cubed, USDA, USGS, AEX, Getmapping, Aerogrid, IGN, IGP, swisstopo, and the GIS User Community. All rights reserved.

To use photographs successfully, consider these guidelines:

- **Consider whether a diagram would be more effective than a photograph.** Photographs are often unmatched in their ability to communicate spatial relationships, sizes, shapes, and other physical parameters, but sometimes they communicate too much information. For example, to show how to adjust a specific part of a complicated machine, a photo can be confusing because it shows all the parts within the camera's view. A simplified diagram is often more effective because it allows you to emphasize the specific parts that are relevant to the problem at hand.
- **Learn how to use basic image-processing functions.** For most business reports, websites, and presentations, you won't need to worry about more advanced image-processing functions and special effects. However, you need to know such basic operations such as the difference between resizing (changing the size of an image without removing any parts of it) and cropping (cutting away parts of the image).
- **Make sure the photographs have communication value.** Except for covers, title slides, and other special uses, it's usually best to avoid including photographs simply for decorative value.
- **Be aware of copyrights and model permissions.** Just as with textual information you find online, you can't simply insert online photographs into your documents. Unless they are specifically offered for free, you have to assume that someone owns the photos and is entitled to payment or at least a photo credit. In addition, professional photographers are careful to have any person who poses in photos sign a model release form, which gives the photographer permission to use the person's image.

Infographics   **Infographics** are a special class of diagrams that can convey both data as well as concepts or ideas. In addition, they contain enough visual and textual information to function as independent, stand-alone documents. Broadly speaking, there are two types of infographics: those that are stylized collections of charts or graphs and those that have a structured narrative. The first do not necessarily convey any more information than basic charts and graphs in a conventional report would, but their communication value lies in their ability to catch the audience's attention and the ease with which they can be distributed online. The second type, represented by Figure 12.14 on the next page, go beyond this to take full advantage of the visual medium to tell stories or show interconnected processes. These infographics can be powerful communication tools, even to the point of replacing conventional reports.

Video   From tutorials and product demonstrations to seminars and speeches, online video is now an essential business communication medium. For videos that require the highest production quality, companies usually hire specialists with the necessary skills and equipment. However, for most routine needs, any business communicator with modest equipment and a few basic skills can create effective video. The three-step process adapts easily to video; professionals refer to the three steps as *preproduction*, *production*, and *postproduction*. The Real-Time Updates Learn More item to the right suggests a resource for advice on getting started with digital video.

REAL-TIME UPDATES
LEARN MORE BY VISITING THIS WEBSITE
Ideas for using Instagram for business communication
The Instagram for Business blog discusses ways to use the popular photo-sharing service. Go to http://real-timeupdates.com/ebc12 and click on Learn More in the Students section.

Make sure you have the right to use photographs you find online.

REAL-TIME UPDATES
LEARN MORE BY EXPLORING THIS WEBSITE
Ten tools for creating infographics
These online tools (many are free) offer a variety of ways to create infographics. Go to http://real-timeupdates.com/ebc12 and click on Learn More in the Students section.

MOBILE APP
Videoshop offers a variety of postprocessing tools for enhancing mobile videos right on your phone.

REAL-TIME UPDATES
LEARN MORE BY EXPLORING THIS WEBSITE
Great advice for getting started in digital video
This website offers a wealth of advice on producing quality videos. Go to http://real-timeupdates.com/ebc12 and click on Learn More in the Students section.

Producing and Integrating Visuals

After you have chosen the best visuals to illustrate key points in your report, website, or presentation, it's time to get creative. This section offers advice on creating visuals, integrating them with your text, and verifying the quality of your visual elements.

4   LEARNING OBJECTIVE
Explain how to integrate visuals with text effectively and how to verify the quality of your visuals.

Figure 12.14 **Infographics**
Roughly speaking, infographics can be divided into simple presentations of data and visual narratives such as this example that use the full power of the medium to tell stories or illustrate processes.

CREATING VISUALS

Computers make it easy to create visuals, but they also make it easy to create ineffective, distracting, and even downright ugly visuals. However, by following the basic design principles discussed on pages 373–374, you can create all the basic visuals you need—visuals that are attractive and effective. If possible, have a professional designer set up a *template* for the various types of visuals you and your colleagues need to create. In addition to helping ensure an effective design, using templates saves you the time of making numerous design decisions every time you create a chart or graphic.

Remember that the style and quality of your visuals communicate a subtle message about your relationship with the audience. A simple sketch might be fine for a working meeting but inappropriate for a formal presentation or report. On the other hand, elaborate, full-color visuals may be viewed as extravagant for an informal report but may be entirely appropriate for a message to top management or influential outsiders.

Integrating Visuals with Text

For maximum effectiveness and minimum disruption for the reader, visual elements need to be carefully integrated with the text of your message. In some instances, visual elements are somewhat independent from the text, as in the *sidebars* that occasionally accompany magazine articles. Such images are related to the content of the main story, but they aren't referred to by a specific title or figure number.

For reports and most other business documents, however, visuals are tightly integrated with the text so that readers can move back and forth between text and visuals with as little disruption as possible. Successful integration involves four decisions: maintaining a balance between visuals and text, referring to visuals in the text, placing the visuals in a document, and writing titles and other descriptions.

Balancing Illustrations and Words

Strong visuals enhance the descriptive and persuasive power of your writing, but putting too many visuals into a report can distract your readers. If you're constantly referring to tables, drawings, and other visual elements, the effort to switch back and forth from words to visuals can make it difficult for readers to maintain focus on the thread of your message. The space occupied by visuals can also disrupt the flow of text on the page or screen.

As always, take into account your readers' specific needs. If you're addressing an audience with multiple language backgrounds or widely varying reading skills, you can shift the balance toward more visual elements to help get around any language barriers. The professional experience, education, and training of your audience should influence your approach as well. For instance, statistical plots and mathematical formulas are everyday reading material for quality-control engineers but not for most salespeople or top executives.

Referencing Visuals

Unless a visual element clearly stands on its own, visuals should be referred to by number in the text of your report. Some report writers refer to all visuals as "exhibits" and number them consecutively throughout the report; many others number tables and figures separately (in which case everything that isn't a table is regarded as a figure). In a long report with numbered sections, illustrations may have a double number (separated by a period or a hyphen) representing the section number and the individual illustration number within that section. Whatever scheme you use, make sure it's clear, consistent, and easy to follow.

Help your readers understand the significance of visuals by referring to them before readers encounter them in the document or onscreen. The following examples show how you can make this connection in the text:

> Figure 12.1 summarizes the financial history of the motorcycle division over the past five years, with sales broken into four categories.

> Total sales were steady over this period, but the mix of sales by category changed dramatically (see Figure 12.2).

The underlying reason for the remarkable growth in our sales of youth golf apparel is suggested by Table 1, which shows the growing interest in junior golf around the world.

When describing the data shown in your visuals, be sure to emphasize the main point you are trying to make. Don't make the mistake of simply repeating the data to be shown.

Placing Visuals

Try to position your visuals so that your audience doesn't have to flip back and forth (in printed documents) or scroll (on screen) between the visuals and the text. Ideally, it's best to place each visual within, beside, or immediately after the paragraph it illustrates so that readers can consult the explanation and the visual at the same time. If possible, avoid bunching several visuals in one section of the document. (Bunching is unavoidable in some cases, such as when multiple visuals accompany a single section of text—as in this chapter, for instance.)

Writing Titles, Captions, and Legends

Titles, captions, and legends provide more opportunities to connect your visual and textual messages. A **title** is similar to a subheading, providing a short description that identifies the content and purpose of the visual, along with whatever label and number you're using to refer to the visual. Readers should be able to grasp the point of a visual without digging into the surrounding text. For instance, a title that says simply "Refineries" doesn't say much at all. A **descriptive title** that identifies the topic of the illustration, such as "Relationship Between Petroleum Demand and Refinery Capacity in the United States" provides a better idea of what the chart is all about. An **informative title** tells even more by calling attention to the conclusion that ought to be drawn from the data, such as "Refinery Capacity Declines as Petroleum Demand Continues to Grow."

A **caption** usually offers additional discussion of the visual's content and can be several sentences long, if appropriate. Captions can also alert readers that additional discussion is available in the accompanying text. Titles usually appear above visuals, and captions appear below, but effective designs can place these two elements in other positions. Sometimes titles and captions are combined in a single block of text as well. A **legend** helps readers decode the visual by explaining what various colors, symbols, or other design choices mean.

VERIFYING THE QUALITY OF YOUR VISUALS

Visuals have a particularly strong impact on your readers and on their perceptions of you and your work, so verifying their quality is vital. Ask yourself three questions about every visual element:

- **Is the visual accurate?** Be sure to check visuals for mistakes such as typographical errors, inconsistent color treatment, confusing or undocumented symbols, and misaligned elements. Does each visual deliver your message accurately? For data presentations, particularly if you're producing charts with a spreadsheet, verify any formulas used to generate the numbers and make sure you've selected the right numbers for each chart.
- **Is the visual properly documented?** As with the textual elements in your reports and presentations, visuals based on other people's research, information, and ideas require full citation.
- **Is the visual honest?** As a final precaution, step back and make sure your visuals communicate truthful messages (see "Practicing Ethical Communication: Distorting the Data").

VISUAL MEDIA ON MOBILE DEVICES

Whether it's a training video, an interactive big-data tool, or a GIS system used for onsite analysis, more and more employees need to consume visual media on smartphones and tablets. The constraints of small screens are even more acute with visuals than they are with text, so preparing visual content for mobile users takes careful planning and the

PRACTICING ETHICAL COMMUNICATION

DISTORTING THE DATA

Take a quick look at these three line charts, all of which display the level of impurities found in a particular source of drinking water. Chart (a) suggests that the source has a consistently high level of impurities throughout the year, Chart (b) indicates that the level of impurities jumps up and down throughout the year, and Chart (c) shows an impurity level that is fairly consistent throughout the year—and fairly low.

Here's the catch: All three charts are displaying *exactly the same data.*

Look again at Chart (a). The vertical scale is set from 0 to 120, sufficient to cover the range of variations in the data. However, what if you wanted to persuade an audience that the variations from month to month were quite severe? In Chart (b), the scale is "zoomed in" on 60 to 110, making the variations look much more dramatic. The result could be a stronger emotional impact on the reader, creating the impression that these impurities are out of control.

On the other hand, what if you wanted to create the impression that things were humming along just fine, with low levels of impurities and no wild swings from month to

month? You would follow the example in Chart (c), where the scale is expanded from 0 to 200, which appears to minimize the variations in the data. This graph is visually "calmer," potentially creating the impression that there's really nothing to worry about.

If all three graphs show the same data, is any one of them more honest than the others? The answer to this question depends on your intent and your audience's information needs. For instance, if dramatic swings in the measurement from month to month suggest a problem with the quality of your product or the safety of a process that affects the public, then visually minimizing the swings might well be considered dishonest.

CAREER APPLICATIONS

1. What sort of quick visual impression would such a chart give if the vertical scale is set to 0 to 500? Why?
2. If the acceptable range of impurities in this case is from 60 to 120 parts per million, which of these three charts is the fairest way to present the data? Why?

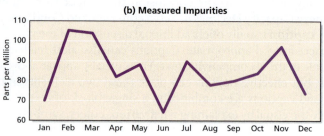

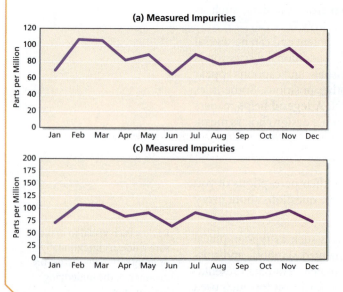

use of display tools designed for mobile devices. With screen space at a premium, think carefully about audience members' needs, including the circumstances in which they'll be using their devices, so you can prioritize and sequence the delivery of information (see Figure 12.15).[22]

For the latest information on report writing and visuals, visit **http://real-time updates.com/ebc12** and select Chapter 12. For a review of the important points to remember when creating visuals, see "Checklist: Creating Effective Visuals" on the next page.

Courtesy of Hipmunk, http://www.hipmunk.com

Figure 12.15 **Visual Displays on Mobile Devices**
Visual displays for mobile audiences need to be clear and simple, as this air travel shopping app from Hipmunk illustrates.

CHECKLIST ✔ **Creating Effective Visuals**

- Emphasize visual consistency to connect parts of a whole and minimize audience confusion.
- Avoid arbitrary changes of color, texture, typeface, position, or scale.
- Highlight contrasting points through color, position, and other design choices.
- Decide whether you want to achieve formal or informal balance.
- Emphasize dominant elements and deemphasize less important pieces in a design.
- Understand and follow (at least most of the time) the visual conventions your audience expects.
- Strive for simplicity and clarity; don't clutter your visuals with meaningless decoration.
- Follow the guidelines for avoiding ethical lapses.

- Carefully consider your message, the nature of your information, and your audience to choose which points to illustrate.
- Select the proper types of graphics for the information at hand and for the objective of the message.
- Be sure the visual contributes to overall understanding of the subject.
- Understand how to use your software tools to maximize effectiveness and efficiency.
- Integrate visuals and text by maintaining a balance between illustrations and words, clearly referring to visuals within the text, and placing visuals carefully.
- Use titles, captions, and legends to help readers understand the meaning and importance of your visuals.
- Verify the quality of your visuals by checking for accuracy, proper documentation, and honesty.

ON THE JOB: SOLVING COMMUNICATION DILEMMAS AT WARBY PARKER

You work as a communication specialist at Warby Parker, and you're currently helping CEO David Gilboa prepare a report about the company. Gilboa characterizes the report as a "public business plan," in that it will discuss the company and its objectives, strategies, and operations, without disclosing the sort of confidential information that a typical business plan includes. The target audience includes potential investors, employees, and business partners. Using the skills you've been practicing in this course, respond to these challenges.

1. To help overcome shoppers' reluctance to buy eyewear online, Warby Parker offers Home Try-On, in which people can order five pairs of frames, keep them for five days at no cost, then decide which pair they would like to order. This gives shoppers lots of time to try on the frames they are considering and get the opinions of family and friends. Which of the following headings would you choose for a section in the report that explains this unique program?
   a. Home Try-On: Making online shopping even better than in-store shopping
   b. Home Try-On: Our tried-and-true way to eliminate the risk of buying eyewear online
   c. Home Try-On: Now you can try on five frames in the comfort of your own home
   d. How we reduce a major perceived risk in the Warby Parker business model

2. Warby Parker is a certified B Corporation, a designation awarded to companies that align their business strategies with social and environmental strategies. In a section on company values, the report draft has the following paragraphs:

   When we set out to serve the eyewear market in a different and better way, we had other, larger goals in mind, too. Sure, we wanted to be a successful and profitable company, but we wanted success to be about more than just profits. We wanted it to be about how we treat each other, how we support our local and global communities, and the footprints we leave on the environment. All of these things define "success" for Warby Parker.

   B Corporations are companies that are committed to something larger than maximizing profits at the expense of everyone and everything else. This designation, which was established and is managed by the not-for-profit B Corporation organization (**www.bcorporation.net**), is granted to companies that meet a rigorous set of standards related to how they are managed, how they treat their workers, how they interact with and impact their communities, and how their business operations affect the environment.

   You want to write a transitional sentence to smooth the flow from the first to the second paragraph. Which of the following sentences and placements is the best choice? (Assume that you'll fine-tune the surrounding text if needed after inserting the new transition.)
   a. At the end of the first paragraph, add this sentence: "The model of success we chose is the *B Corporation*, which is a fresh and broader way of looking at business."
   b. Add the same sentence as in (a), but add it at the beginning of the second paragraph.
   c. At the beginning of the second paragraph, add this sentence: "Entrepreneurs can define success in a lot of different ways."
   d. The flow between the two paragraphs is fine as is; there is no need to add a transition.

3. Fashion is a fast-moving business, and market conditions that are true one month might not be the next month. Which of the following statements would be the best way to express this limitation of the report?
   a. It must be pointed out that the information in this report may become obsolete as market conditions change. This is a function of the dynamic nature of the market and is not an issue with the quality of our research or report writing.
   b. The information contained herein was current as of the time of publication. We cannot guarantee its accuracy in the future.
   c. The dynamic nature of the fashion means that information is likely to change over time. Please accept our apologies for this limitation.
   d. The dynamic nature of the fashion business means that information is likely to change over time. Please check with us for the latest news and insights on the topics covered in this report.

4. To help readers quickly assess the relative contributions of Warby Parker's various product lines to the company's overall revenues, year by year over a 10-year period, which type of visual would be most effective?
   a. Ten pie charts, one per year, showing the breakdown of sales by product line
   b. A table, with the years in columns and the product lines in rows
   c. An area chart
   d. A bar chart

Learning Objectives Checkup

Assess your understanding of the principles in this chapter by reading each learning objective and studying the accompanying exercises. You can check your responses against the answer key on page 599.

Objective 12.1: Explain how to adapt to your audiences when writing reports and proposals, and describe the choices involved in drafting report and proposal content.

1. Why is the "you" attitude particularly important with long or complex reports and proposals?
   a. The "you" attitude takes less time to write, so you'll save considerable time with long documents.
   b. Professionals are accustomed to reading long reports, so they don't require a lot of "hand holding."
   c. People simply don't read reports that don't demonstrate good business etiquette.
   d. The length and complexity of these reports put a heavy demand on readers, making it particularly important to be sensitive to their needs.

2. Which of these sentences has the most formal tone?
   a. We discuss herein the possibility of synergistic development strategies between our firm and U.S. Medical.
   b. This report explores the potential for a strategic partnership with U.S. Medical.
   c. My report is the result of a formal investigation into the possibility of a strategic partnership with U.S. Medical.
   d. In this report, I address the potential for a strategic partnership with U.S. Medical.

3. Which of these does not belong in the body of an informational or analytical report?
   a. An explanation of weaknesses in the report
   b. Facts, statistical evidence, and trends
   c. Conclusions and recommendations
   d. Criteria for evaluating alternatives and options

4. Where would you list action items in a report?
   a. In the opening
   b. In the body
   c. In the close
   d. Action items are never listed in reports.

5. How are audiences likely to react if they spot several errors in your reports?
   a. They'll become skeptical about the quality of all your work.
   b. They'll forgive you and move on without thinking any more about it; everybody makes mistakes.
   c. They'll stop reading your reports.
   d. They'll respect the fact that you don't waste time proofreading.

6. Which of the following is not a recommended strategy for strengthening your proposal argument?
   a. Provide concrete examples of the value of your proposal.
   b. Demonstrate your knowledge.
   c. Identify the amount of time you've invested in the proposal.
   d. Adopt a "you" attitude.

7. If packaging and presentation are only superficial, why are they so important in proposal writing?
   a. Readers tend to prejudge the quality of your products and services based on the quality of your proposal.
   b. They show that you're more than just a "numbers" person—that you can think creatively.
   c. They show the audience that you're willing to invest time and money in getting your proposal accepted.
   d. Attractive documents almost always have high-quality information in them.

8. Which of the following elements is usually *not* part of a proposal's introduction?
   a. Background or statement of the problem
   b. Detailed cost analysis
   c. Organization of the proposal
   d. Scope of the proposal

9. The primary purpose of the body of a proposal is to
   a. List your firm's qualifications for the project in question
   b. Explain why the recipient needs to address a particular problem or opportunity
   c. Communicate your passion for solving the problem or addressing the opportunity
   d. Give complete details on the proposed solution and its anticipated benefits

10. If a proposal is being sent in response to an RFP, how should the body of the proposal address the issue of costs?
    a. It should avoid any mention of costs.
    b. It should provide a total cost figure without wasting the reader's time with a lot of details.
    c. It should follow whatever your company's policy is regarding cost estimates.
    d. It should follow the instructions in the RFP exactly.

Objective 12.2: Identify five characteristics of effective writing in online reports, and explain how to adapt your writing approach for wikis.

11. _____ goes a step beyond translating, making sure web content reflects not only the native language of your readers but also their cultural norms, weights, measures, currency, and other specific elements.

12. Which of the following is the most effectively worded link to a webpage that describes a company's products and services?
    a. <u>Click here</u> to learn more about what we do.
    b. Learn more about <u>our products and services</u>.
    c. <u>Next page</u>
    d. You have problems? <u>We have solutions</u>.

13. Which of the following best summarizes some key advice for wiki collaboration?
    a. Because so many writers can be involved in a wiki, managerial control of content and process is essential.
    b. Personal responsibility is paramount with wikis, so all contributors must safeguard their contributions against unwelcome editing.
    c. Conventional web security measures such as access control should never be used on wikis because they inhibit free collaboration.
    d. Wikis writers need to let go of traditional expectations of authorship, including individual recognition and control.

Objective 12.3: Discuss six principles of graphic design, and identify the most common types of visuals used to present data, information, concepts, and ideas.

14. Why is consistency important in visual design?
    a. It shows the audience that you're not wasting precious time doing artistic designs.
    b. It reduces confusion by eliminating arbitrary changes that force people to relearn your design scheme every time they encounter another visual.
    c. It saves on ink and toner when reports are printed.
    d. It shows the audience that you're serious and businesslike.

15. Which of the following steps could you take to call attention to the most important elements in a visual?
    a. Use a dominant color for the important elements.
    b. Call attention to the important elements in the caption or in the text of your report.
    c. Make the important elements larger.
    d. Do all of the above.

16. Which of the following is a good candidate for illustrating in a report?
    a. Comparison of customer satisfaction ratings of 12 stores across a 12-month period
    b. Percentage of employees who have attended 10 different training courses
    c. Ranking of webpages on a website, from most visited to least visited
    d. All of the above

17. Which of the following is *not* a good reason to use a visual in a report?
    a. To communicate more effectively with multilingual audiences
    b. To help unify the separate parts of a process, an organization, or another entity, such as by using a flowchart to depict the various steps in a process
    c. To simplify access to specific data points, such as by listing them in a quick-reference table
    d. To demonstrate your creative side

18. ____ ____ overcomes several shortcomings of conventional charts and graphs—the inability to show only a limited number of data points before becoming too cluttered to interpret, a limited ability to show complex relationships among data points, and the ability to represent only numeric data.

19. Which of these is a good reason to use a diagram instead of a photograph?
    a. Diagrams are more colorful and aren't limited to colors found in real life.
    b. Diagrams are more realistic than photographs.
    c. Diagrams allow you to control the amount of detail shown to focus reader attention on particular parts of the image.
    d. All of the above are true.

Objective 12.4: Explain how to integrate visuals with text effectively and how to verify the quality of your visuals.

20. Which of the following steps should you take to verify the accuracy of the visuals in your reports?
    a. Make sure that data presentations such as line charts and bar charts accurately portray the data that you intended to show.
    b. Make sure flowcharts and other computer-generated artwork are correct and clear.
    c. Make sure that you've inserted the correct visuals at each place in your report.
    d. Do all of the above.

21. Assume that you have a line chart with a vertical axis scaled from 0 to 100 and data points that vary within a range of roughly 10 to 90. How would you influence audience perceptions if you increased the vertical scale so that it stretched from 0 to 200 instead of 0 to 100?
    a. The scaling change would have no affect on audience perceptions.
    b. The scaling change would maximize the perceived variations in the data.
    c. The scaling change would minimize the perceived variations in the data.
    d. You have no way of predicting in advance how the scaling change would affect perceptions.

Quick Learning Guide

CHAPTER OUTLINE

Composing Reports and Proposals
Adapting to Your Audience
Drafting Report Content
Drafting Proposal Content
Helping Report Readers Find Their Way
Using Technology to Craft Reports and Proposals

Writing for Websites and Wikis
Drafting Website Content
Collaborating on Wikis

Illustrating Your Reports with Effective Visuals
Understanding Visual Design Principles
Understanding the Ethics of Visual Communication
Identifying Points to Illustrate
Selecting the Right Type of Visual

Producing and Integrating Visuals
Creating Visuals
Integrating Visuals with Text
Verifying the Quality of Your Visuals
Visual Media on Mobile Devices

LEARNING OBJECTIVES

1 Explain how to adapt to your audiences when writing reports and proposals, and describe the choices involved in drafting report and proposal content. (page 361)

2 Identify five characteristics of effective writing in online reports, and explain how to adapt your writing approach for wikis. (page 371)

3 Discuss six principles of graphic design, and identify the most common types of visuals used to present data, information, concepts, and ideas. (page 373)

4 Explain how to integrate visuals with text effectively, and how to verify the quality of your visuals. (page 383)

KEY TERMS

area chart Another name for a surface chart

bar chart Chart that portrays quantities by the height or length of its rectangular bars

caption Brief commentary or explanation that accompanies a visual

data visualization A diverse class of displays that can show enormous sets of data in a single visual or show text and other complex information visually

descriptive title Title that simply identifies the topic of an illustration

flowchart Process diagram that illustrates a sequence of events from start to finish

infographics Diagrams that contain enough visual and textual information to function as independent documents

informative title Title that highlights the conclusion to be drawn from the data

legend A "key" that helps readers decode a visual by explaining what various colors, symbols, or other design choices mean

line chart Chart that illustrates trends over time or plots the relationship of two or more variables

organization chart Diagram that illustrates the positions, units, or functions of an organization and their relationships

pie chart Circular chart that shows how the parts of a whole are distributed

surface chart Form of line chart with a cumulative effect; all the lines add up to the top line, which represents the total

table A systematic arrangement of numerical or textual data in columns and rows

title Identifies the content and purpose of a visual

visual literacy The ability (as a sender) to create effective images and (as a receiver) to correctly interpret visual messages

visual symbolism The connotative (as opposed to the denotative, or literal) meaning of visuals

CHECKLIST

Composing Business Reports and Proposals

A. Review and fine-tune your outline.
- Match your parallel headings to the tone of your report or proposal.
- Understand how the introduction, body, and close work together to convey your message.

B. Draft report content.
- Use the introduction to establish the purpose, scope, and organization of your report or proposal.
- Use the body to present and interpret the information you gathered.
- Use the close to summarize major points, discuss conclusions, or make recommendations.

C. Draft proposal content.
- Use the introduction to discuss the background or problem, your solution, the scope, and organization.

- Use the body to persuasively explain the benefits of your proposed approach.
- Use the close to emphasize reader benefits and summarize the merits of your approach.

D. Help readers find their way.
- Provide headings to improve readability and clarify the framework of your ideas.
- Use hyperlinks online to allow readers to jump from section to section.
- Create transitions that tie together ideas and show how one thought relates to another.
- Preview important topics to help readers get ready for new information.
- Review key information to help readers absorb details and keep the big picture in mind.

Apply Your Knowledge

To review chapter content related to each question, refer to the indicated Learning Objective.

⭐ **12.1.** Would "Power to the People" be an effective headline for the section in an analytical report that recommends relaxing a company's strict limits on employee use of social media at work? Why or why not? [LO-1]

⭐ **12.2.** If a company receives a solicited formal proposal outlining the solution to a particular problem, is it ethical for the company to adopt the proposal's recommendations without hiring the firm that submitted the proposal? Why or why not? [LO-1]

12.3. If you wanted to compare average monthly absenteeism for five divisions in your company over the course of a year, which type of visual would you use? Explain your choice. [LO-3]

Practice Your Skills

Messages for Analysis

12.4. **Message 12.A: Revising Web Content with a "You" Attitude [LO-3]** To access this wiki exercise, visit **http://real-timeupdates.com/ebc12**, click on Student Assignments, and select Chapter 12, Message 12.A. Follow the instructions for evaluating the existing content and revising it to make it more reader oriented.

12.5. **Message 12.B: Improving the Effectiveness of a Wiki Article [LO-3]** To access this wiki exercise, go to **http://real-timeupdates.com/ebc12**, click on Student Assignments, and select Chapter 12, Message 12.B. Follow the instructions for evaluating the existing content and revising it to make it clear and concise.

Message 12.C: Improving a Solicited Proposal [LO-1] Read Figure 12.16, a solicited proposal, and then (1) analyze the strengths and weaknesses of this document and (2) revise the document so that it follows this chapter's guidelines.

Exercises

Each activity is labeled according to the primary skill or skills you will need to use. To review relevant chapter content, you can refer to the indicated Learning Objective. In some instances, supporting information will be found in another chapter, as indicated.

12.6. **Adapting to Your Audience [LO-1]** Review the reports shown in Figures 12.1 through 12.3. Give specific examples of how each of these reports establishes a good relationship with the audience. Consider such things as using the "you" attitude, emphasizing the positive,

establishing credibility, being polite, using bias-free language, and projecting a good company or organizational image.

12.7. **Drafting Report Content [LO-1]** You are writing an analytical report on the U.S. sales of your newest product. Of the following topics, identify those that should be covered in the report's introduction, body, and close. Briefly explain your decisions.

  a. Regional breakdowns of sales across the country

  b. Date the product was released in the marketplace

  c. Sales figures from competitors selling similar products worldwide

  d. Predictions of how the struggling U.S. economy will affect sales over the next six months

  e. Method used for obtaining the above predictions

  f. The impact of similar products being sold in the United States by Japanese competitors

  g. Your recommendation as to whether the company should sell this product internationally

  h. Actions that must be completed by year end if the company decides to sell this product internationally

12.8. **Drafting Report Content [LO-1]** Find an article in a business newspaper or journal (in print or online) that recommends a solution to a problem. Identify the problem, the recommended solution(s), and the supporting evidence provided by the author to justify his or her recommendation(s). Did the author cite any formal or informal studies as evidence? What facts or statistics did the author include? Did the author cite any criteria for evaluating possible options? If so, what were they?

12.9. **Drafting Report Content; Communication Ethics: Making Ethical Choices [LO-1], Chapter 1** Your boss has asked you to prepare a feasibility report to determine whether the company should advertise its custom-crafted cabinetry in the weekly neighborhood newspaper. Based on your primary research, you think they should. As you draft the introduction to your report, however, you discover that the survey administered to the neighborhood newspaper subscribers was flawed. Several of the questions were poorly written and misleading. You used the survey results, among other findings, to justify your recommendation. The report is due in three days. What actions might you want to take, if any, before you complete your report?

12.10. **Drafting Online Content [LO-2]** Compare the "About Us" pages on the websites of three companies in same industry. Which page is the most reader-friendly? Which is the worst? What specific elements make each of these pages effective or ineffective?

12.11. **Applying Visual Design Principles [LO-3]** Find a diagram on any company website that explains how one of the company's product works or how a product's features benefit customers. Referring to the visual design principles on pages 373–374, analyze the effectiveness of the diagram's design.

12.12. **Applying Visual Design Principles [LO-3]** From online sources, find three visual presentations of data. Which of the three presents its data most clearly? What design

Memco Construction
187 W. Euclid Avenue, Glenview, IL 60025
www.memco.com
April 19, 2016

Dear Mr. Estes:

PROJECT: IDOT Letting Item #83 Contract No. 79371 DuPage County

Memco Construction proposes to furnish all labor, material, equipment, and supervision to provide Engineered Fill—Class II and IV—for the following unit prices.

Engineered Fill—Class II and IV

Description	Unit	Quantity	Unit Price	Total
Mobilization*	Lump Sum	1	$4,500.00	$4,500.00
Engineered Fill Class II	Cubic Yards	1,267	$33.50	$41,811.00
Engineered Fill Class IV	Cubic Yards	1,394	$38.00	$52,972.00

* Mobilization includes one move-in. Additional move-ins to be billed at $1,100.00 each.

The following items clarify and qualify the scope of our subcontracting work:
1. All forms, earthwork, clearing, etc., to be provided and maintained by others at
no cost to Memco Construction.
2. General Contractor shall provide location for staging, stockpiling material,
equipment, and storage at the job site.
3. Memco Construction shall be paid strictly based upon the amount of material
actually used on the job.
4. All prep work, including geotechnical fabrics, geomembrane liners, etc., to be
done by others at no cost to Memco Construction.
5. Water is to be available at project site at no charge to Memco Construction.
6. Dewatering to be done by others at no cost to Memco Construction.
7. Traffic control setup, devices, maintenance, and flagmen are to be provided by
others at no cost to Memco Construction.
8. Memco Construction LLC may withdraw this bid if we do not receive a written
confirmation that we are the apparent low sub-bidder within 10 days of your
receipt of this proposal.
9. Our F.E.I.N. is 36-4478095.
10. Bond is not included in above prices. Bond is available for an additional
1 percent.

If you have any questions, please contact me at the phone number listed below.

Sincerely

Kris Beiersdorf

Kris Beiersdorf
Memco Construction
187 W. Euclid Avenue, Glenview, IL 60025
Office: (847) 352-9742, ext. 30
Fax: (847) 352-6595
Email: Kbeiersdorf@memco.com

Figure 12.16   Solicited Proposal (for Message 12.C on page 392)

choices promote this level of clarity? What improvements would you make to the other visuals to make them clearer?

12.13. Communication Ethics [LO-3] Using a spreadsheet, create a bar chart or line chart, using data you find online or in a business publication. Alter the horizontal and vertical scales in several ways to produce different displays of the original data. How do the alterations distort the information? How might a reader detect whether a chart's scale has been altered?

12.14. Visual Communication: Choosing the Best Visual [LO-3] You're preparing the annual report for FretCo Guitar Corporation. For each of the following types of information, select an appropriate chart or visual to illustrate the text. Explain your choices.

a. Data on annual sales for the past 20 years

b. Comparison of FretCo sales, product by product (electric guitars, bass guitars, amplifiers, acoustic guitars), for this year and last year

c. Explanation of how a FretCo acoustic guitar is manufactured

d. Explanation of how the FretCo Guitar Corporation markets its guitars

e. Data on sales of FretCo products in each of 12 countries

f. Comparison of FretCo sales figures with sales figures for three competing guitar makers over the past 10 years

12.15. **Presenting Data (Line Charts) [LO-3]** Here are last year's sales figures for the appliance and electronics megastore where you work. Construct a line chart based on these figures to help explain to the store's general manager seasonal variations in each department.

Store Sales in 2016 (in $ thousands)

Month	Home Electronics	Computers	Appliances
January	$68	$39	$36
February	72	34	34
March	75	41	30
April	54	41	28
May	56	42	44
June	49	33	48
July	54	31	43
August	66	58	39
September	62	58	36
October	66	44	33
November	83	48	29
December	91	62	24

12.16. **Visual Communication: Creating Visuals (Maps) [LO-4]** You work for C & S Holdings, a company that operates coin-activated, self-service car washes. Research shows that the farther customers live from a car wash, the less likely they are to visit. You know that 50 percent of customers at each of your car washes live within a 4-mile radius of the location, 65 percent live within 6 miles, 80 percent live within 8 miles, and 90 percent live within 10 miles. C & S's owner wants to open two new car washes in your city and has asked you to prepare a report recommending locations. Using a map of your city (print or online), choose two possible locations for car washes and create a visual depicting the customer base surrounding each location. (Make up whatever population data you need.)

12.17. **Presenting Data (Data Visualization) [LO-3]** Explore several of the data visualization tools available through the Bovée & Thill Data Visualization and Infographics Gateway. (Go to http://real-timeupdates.com/ebc12, click on Learn More and then select Chapter 12. Data Visualization and Infographics Gateway.) Select one that has the potential to help business managers make decisions. Write a post for your class blog, explaining how this tool could assist with decision making. Be sure to include a link to the site where you found it.

12.18. **Presenting Information, Concepts, and Ideas (Photographs) [LO-3]** As directed by your instructor, team up with other students, making sure that at least one of you has a digital camera or phone capable of downloading images to your word-processing software. Find a busy location on campus or in the surrounding neighborhood, someplace with lots of signs, storefronts, pedestrians, and traffic. Scout out two different photo opportunities, one that maximizes the visual impression

of crowding and clutter, and one that minimizes this impression. For the first, assume that you are someone who advocates reducing the crowding and clutter, so you want to show how bad it is. For the second, assume that you are a real estate agent or someone else who is motivated to show people that even though the location offers lots of shopping, entertainment, and other attractions, it's actually a rather calm and quiet neighborhood. Insert the two images in a word-processing document and write a caption for each that emphasizes the two opposite messages just described. Finally, write a brief paragraph, discussing the ethical implications of what you've just done. Have you distorted reality or just presented it in ways that work to your advantage? Have you prevented audiences from gaining the information they would need to make informed decisions?

Expand Your Skills

Critique the Professionals

Download the latest issue of the *International Trade Update* from http://trade.gov. What techniques does the report use to help readers find their way through the document or direct readers to other sources of information? What techniques are used to highlight key points in the document? Are these techniques effective? Using whatever medium your instructor requests, write a brief summary of your analysis.

Sharpening Your Career Skills Online

Bovée and Thill's Business Communication Web Search, at http://websearch.businesscommunicationnetwork.com/, is a unique research tool designed specifically for business communication research. Use the Web Search function to find a website, video, PDF document, podcast, or PowerPoint presentation that offers advice on writing business reports or on creating effective visuals for documents and presentations. Write a brief email message to your instructor, describing the item that you found and summarizing the career skills information you learned from it.

Improve Your Grammar, Mechanics, and Usage

The following exercises help you improve your knowledge of and power over English grammar, mechanics, and usage. Turn to the Handbook of Grammar, Mechanics, and Usage at the end of this book and review all of Sections 2.7 (Dashes) and 2.8 (Hyphens). Then identify the preferred choice in the following groups of sentences. (Answers to these exercises appear on page 601.)

12.19. **a.** Three qualities—speed, accuracy, and reliability are desirable in any applicant.

b. Three qualities—speed, accuracy, and reliability—are desirable in any applicant.

12.20. **a.** A highly placed source explained the top-secret negotiations.

b. A highly-placed source explained the top-secret negotiations.

c. A highly placed source explained the top secret negotiations.

12.21. a. The file on Mary Gaily—yes—we finally found it reveals a history of tardiness.

b. The file on Mary Gaily, yes—we finally found it—reveals a history of tardiness.

c. The file on Mary Gaily—yes, we finally found it—reveals a history of tardiness.

12.22. a. They're selling a well designed machine.

b. They're selling a well-designed machine.

12.23. a. Argentina, Brazil, Mexico—these are the countries we hope to concentrate on.

b. Argentina, Brazil, Mexico—these are the countries—we hope to concentrate on.

12.24. a. Only two sites maybe three—offer the things we need.

b. Only two sites—maybe three—offer the things we need.

12.25. a. How many owner operators are in the industry?

b. How many owner—operators are in the industry?

c. How many owner-operators are in the industry?

12.26. a. Your ever-faithful assistant deserves—without a doubt—a substantial raise.

b. Your ever faithful assistant deserves—without a doubt—a substantial raise.

12.27. a. The charts are well placed—on each page—unlike the running heads and footers.

b. The charts are well-placed on each page—unlike the running heads and footers.

c. The charts are well placed on each page—unlike the running heads and footers.

12.28. a. Your devil-may-care attitude affects everyone in the decision-making process.

b. Your devil may care attitude affects everyone in the decision-making process.

c. Your devil-may-care attitude affects everyone in the decision making process.

For additional exercises focusing on dashes and hyphens, visit MyBcommLab. Click on Chapter 12, click on Additional Exercises to Improve Your Grammar, Mechanics, and Usage, and click on 18. Punctuation C.

Cases

WEB WRITING SKILLS/MOBILE SKILLS/ PORTFOLIO BUILDER

12.29. Message Strategies: Online Content [LO-2] Adapting conventional web content to make it mobile friendly can require rethinking the site's information architecture to simplify navigation and revising the content.

Your task: Choose the website of a company that makes products you find interesting. (Make it a conventional website, not one already optimized for mobile.) Analyze the section of the website that contains information about the company's products and determine the best way to present that material on mobile device screens. Mock up at least two screens showing how you'd reformat the content to make it mobile friendly. Create a brief presentation with "before" and "after" views to show how your redesign would benefit mobile site visitors.

Informational Reports

12.30. Message Strategies: Informational Reports [LO-1], [LO-2] Concern is growing in many youth sports about the negative consequences of existing approaches to player development and competition. The long-term athlete development (LTAD) approach aims to instill methods and mindsets that will make athlete development more successful in the long run while making sports more enjoyable for kids. The American Development Model (ADM) used by USA Hockey is one example of the LATD approach in a specific sport.

Your task: Visit USA Hockey's ADM website at www .admkids.com. Read the material on the Athlete Development page, then write a brief informational report (one to two pages) on the ADM concept, including the rationale behind it and the benefits it offers youth athletes.

12.31. Message Strategies: Informational Reports [LO-1], [LO-2] Anyone contemplating stock market investing is likely to shudder at least a little bit at the market's penchant for taking a tumble now and again.

Your task: Write a brief informational report that contains a chart of one of the major stock market indices (such as the Dow Jones Industrial Average or the S&P 500) over the past 20 years. Pick out four significant drops in the index during this time period and investigate economic or political events that occurred immediately before or during these declines. Briefly describe the events and their likely effect on the stock market.

WIKI SKILLS / TEAM SKILLS

12.32. Message Strategies: Informational Reports; Media Skills: Wiki Writing [LO-1], [LO-2] The use of social networks by employees during work hours remains a controversial topic, with some companies encouraging networking, some at least allowing it, and others prohibiting it.

Your task: Using the free wiki service offered by Zoho (www .zoho.com/wiki/) or a comparable system, collaborate on a report that summarizes the potential advantages and disadvantages of allowing social network usage in the workplace.

WEB WRITING SKILLS / TEAM SKILLS

12.33. Message Strategies: Online Content; Collaboration: Team Projects [LO-2], Chapter 2 If you're like many other college students, your first year was more than you expected: more difficult, more fun, more frustrating, more expensive, more exhausting, more rewarding—more of everything, positive and negative. Oh, the things you know now that you didn't know then!

Your task: With several other students, identify five or six things you wish you would've realized or understood better before you started your first year of college. These can relate to your school life (such as "I didn't realize how much work I would have for my classes" or "I should've asked for help as soon as I got stuck") and your personal and social life ("I wish I would've been more open to meeting people"). Use these items as the foundation of a brief informational report that you could post on a blog that is read by high school students and their families. Your goal with this report is to help the next generation of students make a successful and rewarding transition to college.

WEB WRITING SKILLS

12.34. Message Strategies: Online Content [LO-2] As you probably experienced, trying to keep all the different schools straight in one's mind while researching and applying for colleges can be rather difficult. Applicants and their families would no doubt appreciate a handy summary of your college or university's key points as they relate to the selection and application process.

Your task: Adapt content from your college or university's website to create a one-page "Quick Facts" sheet about your school. Choose the information that you think prospective students and their families would find most useful. (Note that adapting existing content would be acceptable in a real-life scenario like this, because you would be reusing content on behalf of the content owner. Doing so would definitely *not* be acceptable if you were using the content for yourself or for someone other than the original owner.)

Analytical Reports

12.35. Message Strategies: Analytical Reports [LO-1] Mistakes can be wonderful learning opportunities if we're honest with ourselves and receptive to learning from the mistake.

Your task: Identify a mistake you've made—something significant enough to have cost you a lot of money, wasted a lot of time, harmed your health, damaged a relationship, created serious problems at work, prevented you from pursuing what could've been a rewarding opportunity, or otherwise had serious consequences. Now figure out why you made that mistake. Did you let emotions get in the way of clear thinking? Did you make a serious financial blunder because you didn't take the time to understand the consequences of a decision? Were you too cautious? Not cautious enough? Perhaps several factors led to a poor decision.

Write a brief analytical report to your instructor that describes the situation and outlines your analysis of why the failure occurred and how you can avoid making a similar mistake in the future. If you can't think of a significant mistake or failure that you're comfortable sharing with your instructor, write

about a mistake that a friend or family member made (without revealing the person's identify or potentially causing him or her any embarrassment).

EMAIL SKILLS

12.36. Message Strategies: Analytical Reports [LO-1], [LO-2] Your company develops a mobile phone app that helps people get detailed technical information about products while they are shopping. The original plan was to incorporate Quick Reference (QR) codes into the app, so that people could scan QR stickers placed on product displays in retail stores. After decoding the QR code, the app would then pull up information about the product on display. However, you've recently learning about near-field communication, a short-range radio technology that might able to accomplish the same thing in a way that is simpler for consumers to use.

Your task: Research the prospects for QR codes and NFC technology and write a short comparative report. Draw a conclusion about which technology you think will dominate in the coming years.

12.37. Message Strategies: Analytical Reports (Yardstick Approach) [LO-1] Assume you will have time for only one course next term.

Your task: List the pros and cons of each of four or five courses that interest you and use the yardstick approach to settle on the course that is best for you to take at this time. Write your report in memo format and address it to your academic adviser.

LETTER WRITING SKILLS

12.38. Message Strategies: Analytical Reports [LO-1] Visit any restaurant, including your school cafeteria.

Your task: After your visit, write a short letter to the owner or manager, explaining (1) what you did and what you observed, (2) any violations of policy that you observed, and (3) your recommendations for improvement. The first part of your report (what you did and what you observed) will be the longest. Include a description of the premises, inside and out. Tell how long it took for each step in ordering and receiving your meal. Describe the service and food thoroughly. You are interested in both the good and bad aspects of the establishment's décor, service, and food. For the second section (violations of policy), use some common sense. If all the servers but one have their hair covered, you may assume that policy requires hair to be covered; a dirty window or restroom obviously violates policy. The last section (recommendations for improvement) involves professional judgment. What management actions would improve the restaurant?

Proposals

PORTFOLIO BUILDER

12.39. Message Strategies: Proposals [LO-3] Your boss, the national sales manager, insists that all company sales reps continue to carry full-size laptop computers for making presentations to clients and to manage files and communications tasks. In addition to your laptops, you and you colleagues have to carry a bulky printed catalog and a variety product samples—up and down stairs, on and off airplanes, and in and out of your cars. You are desperate to lighten the load, and you think switching from laptops to tablets would help.

Your task: Write an informal proposal, suggesting that the company equip its traveling salespeople with tablets instead of laptops. Making up any information you need, address three questions you know your boss will have. First, can sales reps type at an adequate speed on tablets, without a conventional keyboard? Second, can sales reps make informal "table top" presentations on tablets, they way they can on their laptops? (Currently, sales reps can sit at a conference room table and give a PowerPoint or Prezi presentation to two or three people, without the need for a projector screen.) Third, do tablets have a sufficient selection of business software, from word processing to database management software?

12.40. Message Strategies: Proposals [LO-1] One of the banes of apartment living is those residents who don't care about the condition of their shared surroundings. They might leave trash all over the place, dent walls when they move furniture, spill food and beverages in common areas, destroy window screens, and otherwise degrade living conditions for everyone. Landlords obviously aren't thrilled about this behavior, either, because it raises the costs of cleaning and maintaining the facility.

Your task: Assume that you live in a fairly large apartment building some distance from campus. Write an email proposal that you could send to your landlord, suggesting that fostering a sense of stronger community among residents in your building might help reduce incidents of vandalism and neglect. Propose that the little-used storage area in the basement of the building be converted to a community room, complete with a simple kitchen and a large-screen television. By attending Super Bowl parties and other events there, residents could get to know one another and perhaps forge bonds that would raise the level of shared concern for their living environment. You can't offer any proof of this in advance, of course, but share your belief that a modest investment in this room could pay off long term in lower repair and maintenance costs. Moreover, it would be an attractive feature to entice new residents.

12.41. Message Strategies: Proposals [LO-1] Select a product you are familiar with and imagine that you are the manufacturer trying to get a local retail outlet to carry it. Use the Internet and other resources to gather information about the product.

Your task: Write an unsolicited sales proposal in letter format to the owner (or manager) of the store, proposing that the item be stocked. Use the information you gathered to describe some of the product's features and benefits to the store. Then make up some reasonable figures, highlighting what the item costs, what it can be sold for, and what services your company provides (return of unsold items, free replacement of unsatisfactory items, necessary repairs, and so on).

PORTFOLIO BUILDER

12.42. Message Strategies: Proposals [LO-1] As a sales manager for Air-Trak, one of your responsibilities is writing sales proposals for potential buyers of your company's Air-Trak tracking system. The system uses global positioning system (GPS) technology to track the location of vehicles and other assets. For example, the dispatcher for a trucking company can simply click a map display on a computer screen to find out where all the company's trucks are at that instant. Air-Trak lists the following as benefits of the system:

- Making sure vehicles follow prescribed routes with minimal loitering time
- "Geofencing," in which dispatchers are alerted if vehicles leave a designated area
- Route optimization, in which fleet managers can analyze routes and destinations to find the most time- and fuel-efficient path for each vehicle
- Comparisons between scheduled and actual travel
- Enhanced security to protect both drivers and cargos

Your task: Write a brief proposal in letter format to Doneta Zachs, fleet manager for Midwest Express, 338 S.W. 6th, Des Moines, Iowa, 50321. Introduce your company, explain the benefits of the Air-Trak system, and propose a trial deployment in which you would equip five Midwest Express trucks. For the purposes of this assignment, you don't need to worry about the technical details of the system; focus on promoting the benefits and asking for a decision regarding the test project. (You can learn more about the Air-Trak system at **www.air-trak.com**.)[23]

MyBCommLab

Go to the Assignments section of your MyLab to complete these writing exercises.

12.43. What are the risks of not explaining the purpose of a proposal within the introduction? [LO-1]

12.44. What are some ways a wiki could be used for employee training? [LO-2]

Endnotes

1. Warby Parker website, accessed 2 March 2015, www.warbyparker .com; Jessica Pressler, "20/30 Vision," *New York Magazine*, 11 August 2013, http://nymag.com; Andrew Mascio, "Luxottica: An Unstoppable Machine," *Seeking Alpha*, 29 December 2014, http://seekingalpha.com; Luxottica website, accessed 2 March 2015, www.luxottica.com; Manuela Mesco, "Italian Eyewear Marker Luxottica Profit, Sales Up," *MarketWatch*, 2 March 2015, www.marketwatch.com; Ross Crooks, "12 Lessons from Warby Parker's Annual Report," *Forbes*, 30 January 2014, www.forbes.com; Warby Parker profile, B Corporation website, accessed 3 March 2015, www.bcorporation.net.

2. A. S. C. Ehrenberg, "Report Writing—Six Simple Rules for Better Business Documents," *Admap*, June 1992, 39–42.

3. Philip C. Kolin, *Successful Writing at Work*, 8th ed. (Boston: Houghton Mifflin, 2007), 598–602.

4. Qvidian website, accessed 26 June 2012, www.qvidian.com.

5. "Web Writing: How to Avoid Pitfalls," *Investor Relations Business*, 1 November 1999, 15.

6. "Codex: Guidelines," WordPress website, accessed 16 February 2008, http://wordpress.org; Michael Shanks, "Wiki Guidelines," Traumwerk website, accessed 18 August 2006, http://metamedia .stanford.edu/projects/traumwerk/home; Joe Moxley, MC Morgan, Matt Barton, and Donna Hanak, "For Teachers New to Wikis," *Writing Wiki*, accessed 18 August 2006, http://writingwiki.org; "Wiki Guidelines," Psi, http://psi-im.org.

7. Rachael King, "No Rest for the Wiki," *BusinessWeek*, 12 March 2007, www.businessweek.com.

8. "Codex: Guidelines," WordPress website, accessed 14 February 2008, http://wordpress.org.

9. Alexis Gerard and Bob Goldstein, *Going Visual* (Hoboken, N.J.: Wiley, 2005), 18.

10. Charles Kostelnick and Michael Hassett, *Shaping Information: The Rhetoric of Visual Conventions* (Carbondale, Ill.: Southern Illinois University Press, 2003), 177.

11. Gerard and Goldstein, *Going Visual*, 103–106.

12. Edward R. Tufte, *Visual Explanations: Images and Quantities, Evidence and Narrative* (Cheshire, Conn.: Graphics Press, 1997), 82.

13. Kostelnick and Hassett, *Shaping Information*, 17.

14. Kostelnick and Hassett, *Shaping Information*, 216.

15. Edward R. Tufte, *The Visual Display of Quantitative Information* (Cheshire, Conn.: Graphic Press, 1983), 113.

16. Based in part on Tufte, *Visual Explanations*, 29–37, 53; Paul Martin Lester, *Visual Communication: Images with Messages*, 4th ed. (Belmont, Calif.: Thomson Wadsworth, 2006), 95–105, 194–196.

17. Hoover's Online, accessed 3 December 2008, www.hoovers.com.

18. Stephen Few, "Save the Pies for Dessert," *Visual Business Intelligence Newsletter*, August 2007, www.perceptualedge.com.

19. Maria Popova, "Data Visualization: Stories for the Information Age," *BusinessWeek*, 12 August 2009, www.businessweek.com.

20. "Big Data: What It Is and Why It Matters," SAS website, accessed 25 April 2014, www.sas.com.

21. "Data Visualization: Modern Approaches," *Smashing Magazine* website, 2 August 2007, www.smashingmagazine.com; "7 Things You Should Know About Data Visualization," *Educause Learning Initiative*, accessed 15 March 2008, www.educause.edu; *TagCrowd* website, accessed 15 March 2008, www.tagcrowd.com.

22. "Making Data Visualization Work: 4 Tips to Read Before You Start," Roambi blog, 13 August 2013, ww.roambi.com.

23. Air-Trak website, accessed 2 March 2015, www.air-trak.com.

13

Completing Reports and Proposals

LEARNING OBJECTIVES

After studying this chapter, you will be able to

1 Describe the process of revising formal reports and proposals.

2 Identify the major components of formal reports.

3 Identify the major components of formal proposals.

4 Describe an effective plan for proofreading reports and proposals.

5 Describe the decision process for distributing reports and proposals.

ON THE JOB: COMMUNICATING AT
GARAGE TECHNOLOGY VENTURES

Scanning Business Plans to Find the Next Big Thing

The "garage" is a well-known metaphor in entrepreneurial circles that dates back at least to the founding of the giant technology company Hewlett-Packard, which was literally started in a garage in the late 1930s by Bill Hewlett and Dave Packard. More than just the physical space of a workshop, the garage suggests a mindset, with inspired visionaries working on shoestring budgets in humble surroundings but pouring their hearts and minds into business ideas that can change the world—or at least make a lot of money.

Noted entrepreneur, author, speaker, and investor Guy Kawasaki and his colleagues carry on this tradition with a venture capital firm called, appropriately enough, Garage Technology Ventures. Garage is based in the heart of Silicon Valley: Palo Alto,

ZUMA Press, Inc./Alamy

Guy Kawasaki, one of the founders of the venture capital firm Garage Technology Ventures, advises entrepreneurs to craft concise, compelling summaries of their businesses before pitching their ideas to investors.

California (which also happens to be the current and ancestral home of Hewlett-Packard).

Venture capitalists (VCs) invest in young companies, primarily in high-technology fields, and help them through the early growth stages with an eye toward recouping their investments when the company gets big enough to go public or is sold to another company. The personal finance website Motley Fool and the online music service Pandora are among the many firms in which Garage has invested in recent years.

In the Silicon Valley VC culture, the process of presenting a new company to potential investors usually involves a short presentation, "the pitch," that is supported by the executive summary from a business plan. The entire plan might become part of the conversation later, but in the early stages the executive summary has to carry the load by itself.

After listening to thousands of pitches and reading thousands of business plans, the Garage team has a clear idea of what it takes for entrepreneurs to get the attention—and money—of a VC. Garage advises entrepreneurs to keep their executive summaries under 20 pages and to include nine particular elements, starting with "the grab," a compelling one- or two-sentence statement that gets an investor's attention. Following that are the customer problems the entrepreneurs aim to solve, the solution they propose, and the business opportunity this offering represents. The next three items describe the new company's competitive advantages, its business model (how it will generate revenue), and the key personnel involved in the new venture—including why these are the right people to drive this new company forward. The final two elements are directly about money: "the promise," which is how much investors can expect to earn from their stake in the company, followed by "the ask," which is how much money the new company wants.

This is a lot of information to pack into a relatively short document, but doing so is essential. If investors don't understand the business model or don't think the start-up team has honed in on a real market opportunity, they won't keep listening. Fortunately, entrepreneurs can tap into the expertise of those who have gone before them and use this advice to craft powerful business plans that get noticed.[1]

WWW.GARAGE.COM

Revising Reports and Proposals

1 **LEARNING OBJECTIVE**
Describe the process of revising formal reports and proposals.

Experienced business communicators such as Guy Kawasaki (profiled in the On the Job chapter opener) recognize that the process of writing a report or proposal doesn't end with a first draft. This chapter addresses all four tasks involved in completing longer messages: revising, producing, proofreading, and distributing. Although the tasks covered in this chapter are similar in concept to those you studied for short messages in Chapter 6, the completion stage for reports and proposals can require a lot more work. And as you've probably already experienced while doing school reports, computers, printers, network connections, and other resources have an uncanny knack for going haywire when you're frantic to finish and have no time to spare. When you're completing an important report on the job, try to leave yourself double or even triple the amount of time you think you'll need so that last-minute glitches don't compromise the quality of all your hard work.

Formal reports have a higher degree of polish and production quality, and they often contain elements not found in informal reports.

Most of the discussion in this chapter applies to *formal* reports and proposals, documents that require an extra measure of polish and professionalism and often include packaging elements not used in informal reports and other documents. Few reports and proposals require every component described in this chapter, but be sure to carefully select the elements you want to include in each of your documents.

MOBILE APP

Redbooth's file and content management features help teams manage collaborative report writing.

The revision process is essentially the same for reports as for other business messages, although it may take considerably more time, depending on the length of your document. Evaluate your organization, style, and tone, making sure that you've said what you want to say and that you've said it in the most logical order and in a way that responds to your audience's needs. Then work to improve the report's readability by varying sentence length, keeping paragraphs short, using lists and bullets, adding headings and subheadings, and making generous use of transitions. Keep revising the content until it is clear, concise, and compelling. Figure 13.1 shows an informal solicited proposal that demonstrates these points.

Revising for clarity and conciseness is especially important for online reports because reading online can be difficult.

Tight, efficient writing that is easy to skim is always a plus, but it's especially important for impatient online audiences.[2] Review online report content carefully; strip out all information that doesn't directly meet audience needs, and condense everything else as much as possible. Audiences will gladly return to sites that deliver quality information quickly—and they'll avoid sites that don't.

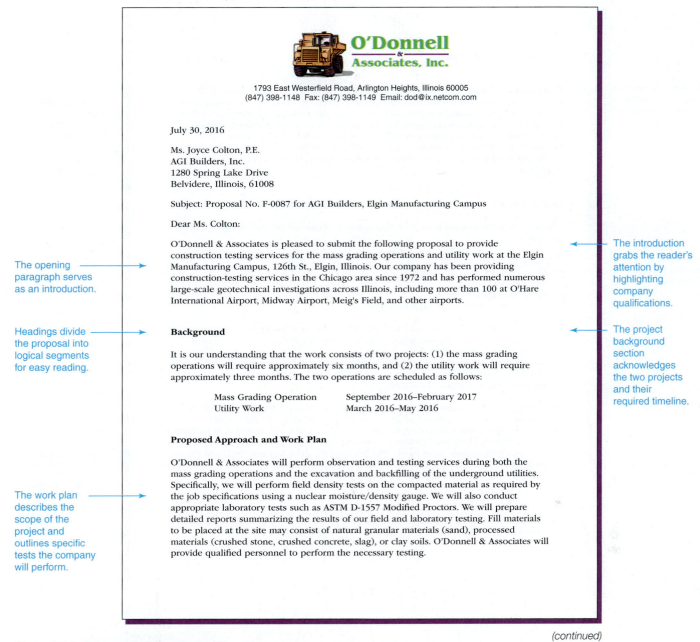

The opening paragraph serves as an introduction.

Headings divide the proposal into logical segments for easy reading.

The work plan describes the scope of the project and outlines specific tests the company will perform.

The introduction grabs the reader's attention by highlighting company qualifications.

The project background section acknowledges the two projects and their required timeline.

(continued)

Figure 13.1 **Informal Solicited Proposal**
This proposal was submitted by a geotechnical engineering firm that conducts a variety of environmental testing services. As you review this document, pay close attention to the specific items addressed in the proposal's introduction, body, and close.

Producing Formal Reports

When you are satisfied with the quality of your text, you're ready to produce your report by incorporating the design elements discussed in Chapter 6. At this point, you should also start to add charts, graphs, and other visuals, as well as any missing text elements, such as previews and reviews.

In some organizations, you'll be able to rely on the help of specialists in design and production, particularly when you are working on important, high-visibility reports. You may also have clerical help available to assist with the mechanical assembly and distribution.

2 **LEARNING OBJECTIVE**
Identify the major components of formal reports.

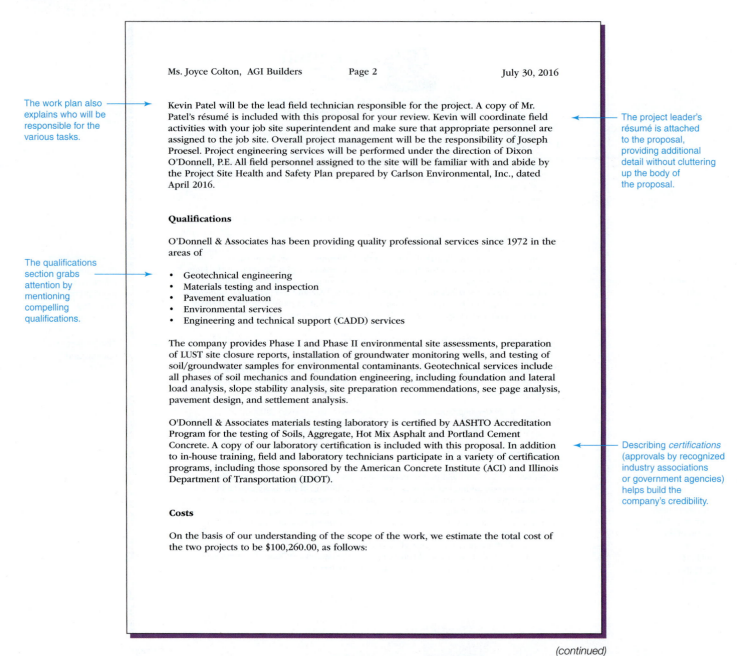

Ms. Joyce Colton, AGI Builders   Page 2   July 30, 2016

The work plan also explains who will be responsible for the various tasks.

Kevin Patel will be the lead field technician responsible for the project. A copy of Mr. Patel's résumé is included with this proposal for your review. Kevin will coordinate field activities with your job site superintendent and make sure that appropriate personnel are assigned to the job site. Overall project management will be the responsibility of Joseph Proesel. Project engineering services will be performed under the direction of Dixon O'Donnell, P.E. All field personnel assigned to the site will be familiar with and abide by the Project Site Health and Safety Plan prepared by Carlson Environmental, Inc., dated April 2016.

The project leader's résumé is attached to the proposal, providing additional detail without cluttering up the body of the proposal.

Qualifications

O'Donnell & Associates has been providing quality professional services since 1972 in the areas of

The qualifications section grabs attention by mentioning compelling qualifications.

- Geotechnical engineering
- Materials testing and inspection
- Pavement evaluation
- Environmental services
- Engineering and technical support (CADD) services

The company provides Phase I and Phase II environmental site assessments, preparation of LUST site closure reports, installation of groundwater monitoring wells, and testing of soil/groundwater samples for environmental contaminants. Geotechnical services include all phases of soil mechanics and foundation engineering, including foundation and lateral load analysis, slope stability analysis, site preparation recommendations, see page analysis, pavement design, and settlement analysis.

O'Donnell & Associates materials testing laboratory is certified by AASHTO Accreditation Program for the testing of Soils, Aggregate, Hot Mix Asphalt and Portland Cement Concrete. A copy of our laboratory certification is included with this proposal. In addition to in-house training, field and laboratory technicians participate in a variety of certification programs, including those sponsored by the American Concrete Institute (ACI) and Illinois Department of Transportation (IDOT).

Describing certifications (approvals by recognized industry associations or government agencies) helps build the company's credibility.

Costs

On the basis of our understanding of the scope of the work, we estimate the total cost of the two projects to be $100,260.00, as follows:

(continued)

Figure 13.1   Informal Solicited Proposal (*Continued*)

In today's leanly staffed companies, you should be prepared to produce formal reports with little or no assistance from design specialists or other professionals.

However, for most reports in many of today's leanly staffed companies, you should count on doing most or all of the production work yourself.

The parts you include in a report depend on the type of report you are writing, its length, your audience's expectations and requirements, and your organization's preferences. See Table 13.1 on page 405 for a summary of the elements to consider including. You can use this table as a handy reference whenever you need to write a report in school or on the job. For an illustration of how the various parts fit together, see "Report Writer's Notebook: Analyzing a Formal Report" starting on page 413.

A component of a formal report may start on a new page, but not always. Keep in mind that inserting page breaks consumes more paper and adds to the bulk of your report. On the other hand, starting a section on a new page helps readers navigate the report and recognize transitions between major sections or features.

If you want a section to stand out, start it on a new page.

When you want a particular section to stand apart, start it on a new page (in the same way that each chapter in this booktext starts on a new page). Most prefatory parts, such as the table of contents, should also be placed on their own pages. However, the various parts

Ms. Joyce Colton, AGI Builders   Page 3   July 30, 2016

Cost Estimates

Cost Estimate: Mass Grading	Units	Rate ($)	Total Cost ($)
Field Inspection			
Labor	1,320 hours	$38.50	$ 50,820.00
Nuclear Moisture Density Meter	132 days	35.00	4,620.00
Vehicle Expense	132 days	45.00	5,940.00
Laboratory Testing			
Proctor Density Tests (ASTM D-1557)	4 tests	130.00	520.00
Engineering/Project Management			
Principal Engineer	16 hours	110.00	1,760.00
Project Manager	20 hours	80.00	1,600.00
Administrative Assistant	12 hours	50.00	600.00
Subtotal			$ 65,860.00

Cost Estimate: Utility Work	Units	Rate ($)	Total Cost ($)
Field Inspection			
Labor	660 hours	$ 38.50	$ 25,410.00
Nuclear Moisture Density Meter	66 days	5.00	2,310.00
Vehicle Expense	66 days	45.00	2,970.00
Laboratory Testing			
Proctor Density Tests (ASTM D-1557)	2 tests	130.00	260.00
Engineering/Project Management			
Principal Engineer	10 hours	110.00	1,100.00
Project Manager	20 hours	80.00	1,600.00
Administrative Assistant	15 hours	50.00	750.00
Subtotal			$ 34,400.00
Total Project Costs			**$100,260.00**

This estimate assumes full-time inspection services. However, our services may also be performed on an as-requested basis, and actual charges will reflect time associated with the project. We have attached our standard fee schedule for your review. Overtime rates are for hours in excess of 8.0 hours per day, before 7:00 a.m., after 5:00 p.m., and on holidays and weekends.

A clear and complete itemization of estimated costs builds confidence in dependability of the project's financial projections.

To give the client some budgetary flexibility, the proposal offers an alternative to the fixed-fee approach—which may lower any resistance to accepting the bid.

(continued)

Figure 13.1   Informal Solicited Proposal (*Continued*)

in the report text are often run together. If your introduction is only a paragraph long, don't bother with a page break before moving into the body of your report. If the introduction runs longer than a page, however, a page break can signal the reader that a major shift is occurring in the flow of the report.

PREFATORY PARTS

Prefatory parts are front-end materials that provide key preliminary information so that readers can decide whether and how to read the report.[3] Many of these parts—such as the table of contents, list of illustrations, and executive summary—are easier to prepare after the text has been completed because they are based on the main text of the report. When your text is complete, you can also use your word-processing software to automatically compile the table of contents and the list of illustrations.

REAL-TIME UPDATES

LEARN MORE BY VISITING THIS WEBSITE

Get practical advice on developing research reports

The Online Writing Lab offers advice on developing all the sections of a typical research report. Go to http://real-timeupdates.com/ebc12 and click on Learn More in the Students section.

Formal reports can contain a variety of prefatory parts, from a cover page to a synopsis or executive summary.

Ms. Joyce Colton, AGI Builders   Page 4   July 30, 2016

Authorization

With a staff of over 30 personnel, including registered professional engineers, resident engineers, geologists, construction inspectors, laboratory technicians, and drillers, we are confident that O'Donnell & Associates is capable of providing the services required for a project of this magnitude.

The brief close emphasizes the bidder's qualifications and asks for a decision.

If you would like our firm to provide the services as outlined in this proposal, please sign this letter and return it to us along with a certified check in the amount of $10,000 (our retainer) by August 14, 2013. Please call me if you have any questions regarding the terms of this proposal or our approach.

The call to action clarifies the steps needed to put the project in motion.

Sincerely,

Dixon O'Donnell

Dixon O'Donnell
Vice President

Enclosures

Accepted for AGI BUILDERS, INC.

By_____   Date _____

The customer's signature will make the proposal a binding contract.

Figure 13.1 **Informal Solicited Proposal (*Continued*)**

Cover

Many companies have standard covers for reports, made of heavy paper and imprinted with the company's name and logo. If your company doesn't have such covers, you can usually find something suitable in a good stationery or office supply store. Look for cover stock that is attractive, convenient, and appropriate to the subject matter.

Covers are typically labeled with the report title, the writer's name (optional), and the submission date (also optional). Think carefully about the title. You want it be concise and compelling while still communicating the essence of the subject matter.

Title Fly and Title Page

The **title fly** is a single sheet of paper with only the title of the report on it. It adds a touch of formality, but it isn't really necessary, and it consumes additional paper. The **title page** includes four blocks of information: (1) the title of the report; (2) the name, title, and

TABLE 13.1 Content Elements to Consider for Reports and Proposals

Reports	Proposals
Introduction: Establish the context, identify the subject, preview main ideas (if using the direct approach), and establish tone and reader relationship.	**Introduction:** Identify the problem you intend to solve or the opportunity you want to pursue.
• **Authorization.** Reiterate who authorized the report, if applicable.	• **Background or statement of the problem.** Briefly review the situation at hand, establish a need for action, and explain how things could be better. In unsolicited proposals, convince readers that a problem or an opportunity exists.
• **Problem/purpose.** Explain the reason for the report's existence and what the report will achieve.	
• **Scope.** Describe what will and won't be covered in the report.	• **Solution.** Briefly describe the change you propose, highlighting your key selling points and their benefits to show how your proposal will solve the reader's problem.
• **Background.** Review historical conditions or factors that led up to the report.	
• **Sources and methods.** Discuss the primary and secondary sources consulted and methods used.	• **Scope.** State the boundaries of the proposal—what you will and will not do.
• **Definitions.** List terms and their definitions, including any terms that might be misinterpreted. Terms may also be defined in the body, explanatory notes, or glossary.	• **Report organization.** Orient the reader to the remainder of the proposal and call attention to the major divisions of thought.
• **Limitations.** Discuss factors beyond your control that affect report quality (but do not use this as an excuse for poor research or a poorly written report).	
• **Report organization.** Identify the topics to be covered and in what order.	
Body: Present relevant information and support your recommendations or conclusions.	**Body:** Give complete details on the proposed solution and describe anticipated results.
• **Explanations.** Give complete details of the problem, project, or idea.	• **Facts and evidence to support your conclusions.** Give complete details of the proposed solution and anticipated results.
• **Facts, statistical evidence, and trends.** Lay out the results of studies or investigations.	
• **Analysis of action.** Discuss potential courses of action.	• **Proposed approach.** Describe your concept, product, or service. Stress reader benefits and emphasize any advantages you have over your competitors.
• **Pros and cons.** Explain advantages, disadvantages, costs, and benefits of a particular course of action.	
• **Procedures.** Outline steps for a process.	• **Work plan.** Describe how you'll accomplish what must be done (unless you're providing a standard, off-the-shelf item). Explain the steps you'll take, their timing, the methods or resources you'll use, and the person(s) responsible. State when work will begin, how it will be divided into stages, when you'll finish, and whether follow-up will be needed.
• **Methods and approaches.** Discuss how you've studied a problem (or gathered evidence) and arrived at your solution (or collected your data).	
• **Criteria.** Describe the benchmarks for evaluating options and alternatives.	
• **Conclusions and recommendations.** Discuss what you believe the evidence reveals and what you propose should be done about it.	• **Statement of qualifications.** Describe your organization's experience, personnel, and facilities—relating it all to readers' needs. Include a list of client references.
• **Support.** Give the reasons behind your conclusions or recommendations.	• **Costs.** Prove that your costs are realistic—break them down so that readers can see the costs of labor, materials, transportation, travel, training, and other categories.
Close: Summarize key points, emphasize benefits of any recommendations, list action items; label as "Summary" or "Conclusions and Recommendations."	**Close:** Summarize key points, emphasize the benefits and advantages of your proposed solution, ask for a decision from the reader.
• **For direct approach.** Summarize key points (except in short reports), listing them in the order in which they appear in the body. Briefly restate your conclusions or recommendations, if appropriate.	• **Review of argument.** Briefly summarize the key points.
	• **Review of reader benefits.** Briefly summarize how your proposal will help the reader.
• **For indirect approach.** If you haven't done so at the end of the body, present your conclusions or recommendations.	• **Review of the merits of your approach.** Briefly summarize why your approach will be more effective than alternatives.
• **For motivating action.** Spell out exactly what should happen next and provide a schedule with specific task assignments.	• **Restatement of qualifications.** For external proposals, briefly reemphasize why you and your firm should do the work.
	• **Request.** Ask for a decision from the reader.

address of the person, group, or organization that authorized the report (if anyone); (3) the name, title, and address of the person, group, or organization that prepared the report; and (4) the date on which the report was submitted. On some title pages, the second block of information is preceded by the words *Prepared for* or *Submitted to,* and the third block of information is preceded by *Prepared by* or *Submitted by.* In some cases, the title page serves as the cover of the report, especially if the report is relatively short and is intended solely for internal use.

Letter of Authorization and Letter of Acceptance

A letter of authorization is a document that instructs you to produce a report; a letter of acceptance is your written agreement to produce the report.

If you received written authorization to prepare a report, you might want to include that **letter of authorization** (or *memo of authorization*) in your report. If you wrote a **letter of acceptance** (or *memo of acceptance*) in response to that communication, accepting the assignment and clarifying any conditions or limitations, you might also include that letter here, in the report's prefatory parts. In general, letters of authorization and acceptance are included in only the most formal reports. However, consider including one or both if a significant amount of time has passed since you started the project or if you do not have a close working relationship with the audience. These pieces help make sure everyone is clear about the report's intent and the approach you took to create it.

Letter of Transmittal

A letter or memo of transmittal introduces your report to your audience.

The **letter of transmittal** (or *memo of transmittal*), a specialized form of a cover letter that is usually positioned right before the table of contents, introduces your report to the audience. This piece says what you would say if you were handing the report directly to the person who authorized it, so the style is often less formal than the rest of the report.

If your readers are likely to be skeptical of or even hostile to something in your report, the letter of transmittal is a good place to acknowledge their concerns and explain how the report addresses the issues they care about. Also, if you need to convey sensitive information to selected audience members, you can opt to include the letter in just those copies.

If you don't include a synopsis, you can summarize the report's content in your letter of transmittal.

Depending on the nature of your report, your letter of transmittal can follow either the direct approach for routine or positive messages described in Chapter 8 or the indirect approach for negative messages described in Chapter 9. Open by introducing the report and summarizing its purpose, with a statement such as "Here is the report you asked me to prepare on . . ." The rest of the introduction includes information about the scope of the report, the methods used to complete the study, limitations, and any special messages you need to convey. If the report does not have a synopsis, the letter of transmittal may summarize the major findings, conclusions, and recommendations.

> **REAL-TIME UPDATES**
> LEARN MORE BY WATCHING THIS PRESENTATION
> **The 10 worst mistakes to make in a business plan**
>
> Entrepreneur Tim Berry tells you what to watch out for. Go to http://real-timeupdates.com/ebc12 and click on Learn More in the Students section.

In the body of the letter, you may also highlight important points or sections of the report, make comments on side issues, give suggestions for follow-up studies, and offer any details that will help readers understand and use the report. You may also want to acknowledge help given by others. The conclusion of the transmittal letter often includes a note of thanks for having been given the report assignment, an expression of willingness to discuss the report, and an offer to assist with future projects.

Table of Contents

The table of contents (often titled simply "Contents") indicates in outline form the coverage, sequence, and relative importance of the information in the report. The headings used in the text of the report are the basis for the table of contents. Depending on the length and complexity of the report, you may need to decide how many levels of headings to show in the contents; it's a trade-off between simplicity and completeness. Contents that show only first-level heads are easy to scan but could frustrate people looking for specific subsections in the report. Conversely, contents that show every level of heading—down to the fourth or fifth level in detailed reports—identify all the sections but can intimidate readers and blur the focus by detracting from your most important message points. Where the detailed table of contents could have dozens or even hundreds of entries, consider including two tables: a high-level table that shows only major headings, followed by a detailed table that includes everything (as this and many other textbooks do). No matter how many levels you include, make sure readers can easily distinguish between them.

Also, take extra care to verify that your table of contents is accurate, consistent, and complete. Even minor errors could damage your credibility if readers turn to a given page and don't find what they expect to see there, or if they find headings that seem similar to those in the table of contents but aren't worded quite the same. To ensure accuracy, construct the table of contents after your report is complete, thoroughly edited, and proofed. This way, the headings and subheadings aren't likely to change or move from page to page. And if at all possible, use the automatic features in your word-processing software to generate the table of contents. Doing so helps improve accuracy by eliminating typing mistakes, and it keeps your table current in the event that you have to repaginate or revise headings late in the process.

To save time and reduce errors, use the table of contents generator in your word-processing software.

If you will be creating a PDF file of the report for digital distribution, you can make life easier for your readers by formatting the entries in the table of contents as clickable links.

List of Illustrations

If you have more than a handful of illustrations in your report, or if you want to call attention to them, include a list of illustrations after the table of contents. For simplicity's sake, some reports refer to all visuals as *illustrations* or *exhibits*. In other reports, as in Moreno's Electrovision report, tables are labeled separately from other types of visuals, which are called *figures*. Regardless of the system you use, be sure to include titles and page numbers.

If you have enough space on a single page, include the list of illustrations directly beneath the table of contents. Otherwise, put this list on the page after the contents page. When tables and figures are numbered separately, they should also be listed separately.

Synopsis or Executive Summary

A **synopsis** is a brief overview (one page or less) of a report's most important points, designed to give readers a quick preview of the contents. It's often included in long informational reports dealing with technical, professional, or academic subjects and can also be called an **abstract**. Because it's a concise representation of an entire report, it may be distributed separately to a wide audience; interested readers can then request a copy of the entire report. A synopsis or an abstract is not a lengthy element, but take your time with it. In a sense, it's an advertisement for the entire report, so you want it to represent the report accurately.

A synopsis is a brief preview of the most important points in your report.

The phrasing of a synopsis can be either informative or descriptive. An *informative synopsis* presents the main points of the report in the order in which they appear in the text. A *descriptive synopsis*, on the other hand, simply tells what the report is about, using only moderately greater detail than the table of contents; the actual findings of the report are omitted. Here are examples of statements from each type:

Informative Synopsis	Descriptive Synopsis
Sales of super-premium ice cream make up 11 percent of the total ice cream market.	This report contains information about super-premium ice cream and its share of the market.

The way you handle a synopsis reflects the approach you use in the text. If you're using the indirect approach in your report, you're better off with a descriptive synopsis because an informative synopsis "gives away the ending" of your report. No matter which type of synopsis you use, be sure to present an accurate picture of the report's contents.[4]

Many report writers prefer to include an **executive summary** instead of a synopsis or an abstract (see Figure 13.2 on the next page). Whereas a synopsis is a "prose table of contents" that outlines the main points of the report, an executive summary is a fully developed "mini" version of the report itself. An executive summary is more comprehensive than a synopsis; it can contain headings, well-developed transitions, and even visual elements. It is usually organized in the same way as the report, using a direct or an indirect approach, depending on the audience's receptivity.

An executive summary is a "mini" version of your report.

Figure 13.2 Executive Summary
This executive summary from a Boeing report on the worldwide air cargo market highlights key facts, figures, and trends using both text and visuals.

Executive summaries are intended for readers who lack the time or motivation to study the complete text. As a general rule, the length of an executive summary should be proportionate to the length of the report. A brief business report may have only a one-page or shorter executive summary. Longer business reports may have a two- or three-page summary. Anything longer, however, might cease to be a summary.[5]

Many reports require neither a synopsis nor an executive summary. Length is usually the determining factor. Most reports of fewer than 10 pages either omit such a preview or combine it with the letter of transmittal. However, if your report is more than 20 or 30 pages long, you'll probably want to include either a synopsis or an executive summary as a convenience for readers. Which one you provide depends on the traditions of your organization.

TEXT OF THE REPORT

> No matter how many separate elements are in a formal report, the heart of the report is still the introduction, body, and close.

The heart of a report consists of three main parts: the introduction, body, and close.

- **Introduction.** A good introduction prepares your readers to follow and comprehend the information that follows. It invites audience members to continue reading by telling them what the report is about, why they should be concerned, and how the report is organized. If your report has a synopsis or an executive summary, minimize redundancy by balancing the introduction with the material in your summary, as Linda Moreno does in her Electrovision report. For example, Moreno's executive summary is fairly detailed, so she keeps her introduction brief.

- **Body.** This section contains information that supports your conclusions and recommendations as well as your analysis, logic, and interpretation of the information. See the body of Linda Moreno's Electrovision report for an example of the types of supporting details commonly included in this section.
- **Close.** The close of your report should summarize your main ideas, highlight your conclusions or recommendations (if any), and list any courses of action that you expect readers to take or that you will be taking yourself. This section may be labeled "Summary" or "Conclusions and Recommendations." In reports that use the direct approach, the close is relatively brief. In contrast, with the indirect approach, you may be using this section to present your conclusions and recommendations for the first time, in which case this section might be fairly extensive.

SUPPLEMENTARY PARTS

Supplementary parts follow the text of the report and provide information for readers who seek more detailed discussion. For online reports, you can put supplements on separate webpages and allow readers to link to them from the main report pages. Supplements are more common in long reports than in short ones, and they typically include appendixes, a bibliography, and an index.

Appendixes

An **appendix** contains materials related to the report but not included in the text because they are too long or perhaps not relevant to everyone in the audience. If your company has an intranet, shared workspaces, or other means of storing and accessing information online, consider putting your detailed supporting evidence there and referring readers to those sources for more detail.

> Use an appendix for materials that are too lengthy or detailed for the body or not directly relevant to all audience members.

The content of report appendixes varies widely, including any sample questionnaires and cover letters, sample forms, computer printouts, statistical formulas, financial statements and spreadsheets, copies of important documents, and multipage illustrations that would break up the flow of text. You might also include a glossary as an appendix or as a separate supplementary part.

If you have multiple categories of supporting material, give each type a separate appendix. An appendix is usually identified with a letter and a short, descriptive title. All appendixes should be mentioned at appropriate places in the text and listed in the table of contents.

Bibliography

To fulfill your ethical and legal obligation to credit other people for their work and to assist readers who want to research your topic further, include a **bibliography**, a list of the secondary sources you consulted when preparing your report. In her Electrovision report, Linda Moreno labeled her bibliography "Works Cited" because she listed only the works that were mentioned in the report. You might call this section "References" if it includes works consulted but not mentioned in your report. Moreno uses the author–date system to format her bibliographic sources. An alternative is to use numbered footnotes (at the bottom of the page) or endnotes (at the end of the report). For more information on citing sources, see Appendix B, "Documentation of Report Sources."

> A bibliography fulfills your ethical obligation to credit your sources, and it allows readers to consult those sources for more information.

In addition to providing a bibliography, some authors prefer to cite references in the report text. Acknowledging your sources in the body of your report demonstrates that you have thoroughly researched your topic. Furthermore, mentioning the names of well-known or important authorities on the subject helps build credibility for your message. Such source references should be handled as smoothly as possible. One approach, especially for internal reports, is simply to mention a source in the text:

> According to Dr. Lewis Morgan of Northwestern Hospital, hip replacement operations account for 7 percent of all surgeries performed on women age 65 and over.

However, if your report will be distributed to outsiders, include additional information on where you obtained the data. You are probably familiar with citation methods suggested by the Modern Language Association (MLA) or the American Psychological Association (APA). *The Chicago Manual of Style* is a reference often used by typesetters and publishers. All these sources encourage the use of in-text citations (inserting the author's last name and a year of publication or a page number directly in the text).

Index

An **index** is an alphabetical list of names and subjects mentioned in a report, along with the pages on which they occur (see the indexes in this book for examples). If you think your readers will need to access specific points of information in a lengthy report, consider including an index that lists all key topics, product names, markets, or important persons—whatever is relevant to your subject matter. As with your table of contents, accuracy in an index is critical. The good news is that you can also use your word-processing software to compile the index. Just be sure to update the index (and any other automatically generated elements, such as the table of contents) right before you produce and distribute your report.

Producing Formal Proposals

3 LEARNING OBJECTIVE Identify the major components of formal proposals.

Proposals addressed to external audiences, including potential customers and investors, are nearly always formal. For smaller projects and situations in which you already have a working relationship with the audience, a proposal can be less formal and skip some of the components described in this section.

Formal proposals contain many of the same components as other formal reports. The difference lies mostly in the text, although a few of the prefatory parts are also different. With the exception of an occasional appendix, most proposals have few supplementary parts. As always, if you're responding to a request for proposals (RFP), follow its specifications to the letter, being sure to include everything it asks for and nothing it doesn't ask for.

Formal proposals must have a high degree of polish and professionalism.

PREFATORY PARTS

The cover, title fly, title page, table of contents, and list of illustrations are handled the same way in a formal proposal as in other formal reports. However, you'll want to handle other prefatory parts a bit differently, such as a copy of the RFP, the synopsis or executive summary, and the letter of transmittal.

Copy of or Reference to the RFP

An RFP may require you to include a copy of the RFP in your prefatory section; be sure to follow its instructions carefully.

RFPs usually have specific instructions for referring to the RFP itself in your proposal because the organizations that issue RFPs need a methodical way to track all their active RFPs and the incoming responses. Some organizations require that you include a copy of the entire RFP in your proposal; others simply want you to refer to the RFP by name or number. Just make sure you follow the instructions in every detail. If the RFP offers no specific instructions, use your best judgment, based on the length of the RFP and whether you received a printed copy or accessed it online.

Synopsis or Executive Summary

Although you may include a synopsis or an executive summary for your reader's convenience when your proposal is quite long, these components are often less useful in a formal proposal than they are in a formal report. If your proposal is unsolicited, your transmittal letter will already have caught the reader's interest, making a synopsis or an executive summary redundant. It may also be less important if your proposal is solicited because the reader is already committed to studying your proposal to find out how you intend to satisfy the terms of a contract. The introduction of a solicited proposal would provide an adequate preview of the contents.

Letter of Transmittal

The way you handle the letter of transmittal depends on whether the proposal is solicited or unsolicited. If the proposal is solicited, approach the letter of transmittal as a positive message, highlighting those aspects of your proposal that may give you a competitive advantage. If the proposal is unsolicited, approach the letter as a persuasive message that must convince the reader you have something worthwhile to offer, something that justifies the time required to read the entire proposal.

TEXT OF THE PROPOSAL

Just as with reports, the text of a proposal is composed of three main parts: the introduction, body, and close. The content and depth of each part depend on whether the proposal is solicited or unsolicited, formal or informal. Here's a brief review:[6]

- **Introduction.** This section presents and summarizes the problem you intend to solve and your solution to that problem, including any benefits the reader will receive from your solution.
- **Body.** This section explains the complete details of the solution: how the job will be done, how it will be broken into tasks, what method will be used to do it (including the required equipment, material, and personnel), when the work will begin and end, how much the entire job will cost (including a detailed breakdown, if required or requested), and why you are qualified.
- **Close.** This section emphasizes the benefits readers will realize from your solution, and it urges readers to act.

Table 13.2 summarizes the production elements to consider including in a formal report or proposal.

TABLE 13.2 Production Elements to Consider for Formal Reports and Proposals

Reports	Proposals
Prefatory elements (before the introduction)	**Prefatory elements** (before the introduction)
• **Cover.** Include a concise title that gives readers the information they need to grasp the purpose and scope of the report. For a formal printed report, choose heavy, high-quality *cover stock*.	• **Cover, title fly, title page.** Same uses as with reports; be sure to follow any instructions in the RFP, if relevant.
• **Title fly.** Some formal reports open with a plain sheet of paper that has only the title of the report on it, although this is certainly not necessary.	• **Copy of or reference to the RFP.** Instead of having a letter of authorization, a solicited proposal should follow the instructions in the RFP. Some will instruct you to include the entire RFP in your proposal; others may want you to simply identify it by a name and tracking number.
• **Title page.** Typically includes the report title, name(s) and title(s) of the writer(s), and date of submission; this information can be put on the cover instead.	• **Synopsis or executive summary.** These components are more common in formal proposals than in reports. In an unsolicited proposal, your letter of transmittal will catch the reader's interest. In a solicited proposal, the introduction will provide an adequate preview of the contents.
• **Letter of authorization.** If you received written authorization to prepare the report, you may want to include that letter or memo in your report.	
• **Letter of transmittal.** "Cover letter" that introduces the report and can include scope, methods, limitations, highlights of the report; offers to provide follow-on information or assistance; and acknowledges help received while preparing the report.	• **Letter of transmittal.** If the proposal is solicited, treat the transmittal letter as a positive message, highlighting those aspects of your proposal that may give you a competitive advantage. If the proposal is unsolicited, the transmittal letter should follow the advice for persuasive messages (see Chapter 10)—the letter must persuade the reader that you have something worthwhile to offer that justifies reading the proposal.
• **Table of contents.** List all section headings and major subheadings to show the location and hierarchy of the information in the report.	
• **List of illustrations.** Consider including if the illustrations are particularly important, and you want to call attention to them.	
• **Synopsis or executive summary.** See discussion on pages 407–408.	
Supplementary elements (after the close)	**Supplementary elements** (after the close)
• **Appendixes.** Additional information related to the report but not included in the main text because it is too lengthy or lacks direct relevance. List appendixes in your table of contents and refer to them as appropriate in the text.	• **Appendixes.** Same uses as with reports; be sure to follow any instructions in the RFP, if relevant.
• **Bibliography.** List the secondary sources you consulted; see Appendix B.	• **Résumés of key players.** For external proposals, résumés can convince readers that you have the talent to achieve the proposal's objectives.
• **Index.** List names, places, and subjects mentioned in the report, along with the pages on which they occur.	

4 LEARNING OBJECTIVE
Describe an effective plan for proofreading reports and proposals.

MOBILE APP
For report writing on the go, LogMeIn lets you access your computer's programs and files from your mobile device.

Ask for proofreading assistance from someone who hasn't been involved in the development of your proposal; he or she might see errors you've been overlooking.

Proofreading Reports and Proposals

After you have assembled all the components of your report or proposal, revised the document's content for clarity and conciseness, and designed the document to ensure readability and a positive impression on your readers, you have essentially produced your document in its final form. Now you need to review it thoroughly one last time, looking for inconsistencies, errors, and missing components. Proofing can catch minor flaws that might diminish your credibility—and major flaws that might damage your career.

Proofreading the text portions of your report is essentially the same as proofreading any other business message—you check for typos, spelling errors, and mistakes in punctuation. However, reports often have elements that may not be included in other messages, so don't forget to proof your visuals thoroughly and make sure they are positioned correctly. If you need specific tips on proofreading documents, look back at Chapter 6 for some reminders on what to look for when proofreading text and how to proofread like a pro.

Whenever possible, arrange for someone with fresh eyes to proofread the report, somebody who hasn't been involved with the text so far. At this point in the process, you are so familiar with the content that your mind will fill in missing words, fix misspelled words, and subconsciously compensate for other flaws, without you even being aware of it. Someone else might see mistakes that you've passed over a dozen times without noticing. An ideal approach is to have two people review it, one who is an expert in the subject matter and one who isn't. The first person can ensure its technical accuracy, and the second can ensure that a wide range of readers will understand it.[7]

5 LEARNING OBJECTIVE
Describe the decision process for distributing reports and proposals.

Using portable document format (PDF) is a common and relatively safe way to distribute reports electronically.

Distributing Reports and Proposals

All the distribution issues explored in Chapter 6 apply to reports and proposals, but pay particular attention to the length and complexity of your documents. For physical distribution, consider spending the few extra dollars for a professional courier or package delivery service, if that will help your document stand apart from the crowd. The online tracking offered by FedEx, UPS, and other services can verify that your document arrived safely. On the other hand, if you've prepared the document for a single person or small group, delivering it in person can be a nice touch. In addition to answering any immediate questions about it, you can promote the results in person—reminding the recipient of the benefits contained in your report or proposal.

For digital distribution, unless your audience specifically requests a word-processor file, provide documents as PDF files. Many people are reluctant to open word-processor files these days, particularly from outsiders, given the greater vulnerability of such files to macro viruses and other contaminations. Moreover, using PDF files lets you control how your document is displayed on your audience's computer, ensuring that your readers see your document as you intended. Review and commenting features in Adobe Acrobat and other systems make PDFs a handy way to gather input from a team of reviewers, too. In addition, making documents available as downloadable PDF files is almost universally expected these days, if only for the sake of convenience.

If your company or client expects you to distribute your reports via a web-based content management system, intranet, or extranet, be sure to upload the correct file(s) to the correct online location. Verify the onscreen display of your report after you've posted it, too; make sure graphics, charts, links, and other elements are in place and operational.

MOBILE APP
Dropbox, MediaFire, and other apps let you store files in the cloud and access or share them from PCs and mobile devices.

(Continued on page 428)

Analyzing a Formal Report

The report presented in the following pages was prepared by Linda Moreno, manager of the cost accounting department at Electrovision, a high-tech company based in Los Gatos, California. Electrovision's main product is optical character recognition equipment, which is used by the U.S. Postal Service for sorting mail. Moreno's job is to help analyze the company's costs. She has this to say about the background of the report:

> For the past three or four years, Electrovision has been on a roll. Our A-12 optical character reader was a real breakthrough, and the post office grabbed up as many as we could make. Our sales and profits kept climbing, and morale was fantastic. Everybody seemed to think that the good times would last forever. Unfortunately, everybody was wrong. When the Postal Service announced that it was postponing all new equipment purchases because of cuts in its budget, we woke up to the fact that we are essentially a one-product company with one customer. At that point, management started scrambling around looking for ways to cut costs until we could diversify our business a bit.
>
> The vice president of operations, Dennis McWilliams, asked me to help identify cost-cutting opportunities in travel and entertainment. On the basis of his personal observations, he felt that Electrovision was overly generous in its travel policies and that we might be able to save a significant amount by controlling these costs more carefully. My investigation confirmed his suspicion.
>
> I was reasonably confident that my report would be well received. I've worked with Dennis for several years and know what he likes: plenty of facts, clearly stated conclusions, and specific recommendations for what should be done next. I also knew that my report would be passed on to other Electrovision executives, so I wanted to create a good impression. I wanted the report to be accurate and thorough, visually appealing, readable, and appropriate in tone.

When writing the analytical report that follows, Moreno based the organization on conclusions and recommendations presented in direct order. The first two sections of the report correspond to Moreno's two main conclusions: that Electrovision's travel and entertainment costs are too high and that cuts are essential. The third section presents recommendations for achieving better control over travel and entertainment expenses. As you review the report, analyze both the mechanical aspects and the way Moreno presents her ideas. Be prepared to discuss the way the various components convey and reinforce the main message.

Masterfile

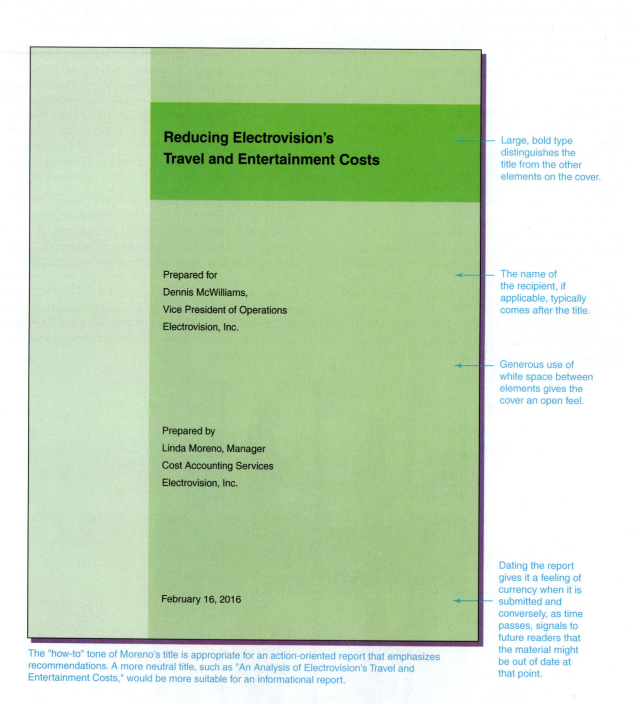

**Reducing Electrovision's
Travel and Entertainment Costs**

Large, bold type distinguishes the title from the other elements on the cover.

Prepared for
Dennis McWilliams,
Vice President of Operations
Electrovision, Inc.

The name of the recipient, if applicable, typically comes after the title.

Generous use of white space between elements gives the cover an open feel.

Prepared by
Linda Moreno, Manager
Cost Accounting Services
Electrovision, Inc.

February 16, 2016

Dating the report gives it a feeling of currency when it is submitted and conversely, as time passes, signals to future readers that the material might be out of date at that point.

The "how-to" tone of Moreno's title is appropriate for an action-oriented report that emphasizes recommendations. A more neutral title, such as "An Analysis of Electrovision's Travel and Entertainment Costs," would be more suitable for an informational report.

The memo format is appropriate for this internal report; the letter format would be used for transmitting an external report.

The tone is conversational yet still businesslike and respectful.

Acknowledging help given by others is good etiquette and a way to foster positive working relationships.

MEMORANDUM

TO:	Dennis McWilliams, Vice President of Operations
FROM:	Linda Moreno, Manager of Cost Accounting Services *LM*
DATE:	February 16, 2016
SUBJECT:	Reducing Electrovision's Travel and Entertainment Costs

Here is the report you requested January 28 on Electrovision's travel and entertainment costs.

Your suspicions were right. We are spending far too much on business travel. Our unwritten policy has been "anything goes," leaving us with no real control over T&E expenses. Although this hands-off approach may have been understandable when Electrovision's profits were high, we can no longer afford the luxury of going first class.

The solutions to the problem seem rather clear. We need to have someone with centralized responsibility for travel and entertainment costs, a clear statement of policy, an effective control system, and a business-oriented travel service that can optimize our travel arrangements. We should also investigate alternatives to travel, such as videoconferencing. Perhaps more important, we need to change our attitude. Instead of viewing travel funds as a bottomless supply of money, all traveling employees need to act as if they were paying the bills themselves.

Getting people to economize is not going to be easy. In the course of researching this issue, I've found that our employees are deeply attached to their generous travel privileges. I think some would almost prefer a cut in pay to a loss in travel status. We'll need a lot of top management involvement to sell people on the need for moderation. One thing is clear: People will be very bitter if we create a two-class system in which top executives get special privileges while the rest of the employees make the sacrifices.

I'm grateful to Mary Lehman and Connie McIllvain for their considerable help in rounding up and sorting through five years' worth of expense reports.

Thanks for giving me the opportunity to work on this assignment. It's been a real education. If you have any questions about the report, please give me a call.

Moreno expects a positive response, so she presents her main conclusion right away.

She closes graciously, with thanks and an offer to discuss the results.

In this report, Moreno decided to write a brief memo of transmittal and include a separate executive summary. Short reports (fewer than 10 pages) often combine the synopsis or executive summary with the memo or letter of transmittal.

The table of contents doesn't include any elements that appear before the "Contents" page.

The headings are worded exactly as they appear in the text.

Moreno lists the figures because they are all significant, and the list is fairly short.

This and other prefatory pages are numbered with Roman numerals.

The table lists only the page number on which a section begins, not the entire range of numbers.

CONTENTS

                                       PAGE

Executive Summary iv

Introduction 1

The High Cost of Travel and Entertainment 1
    $16 Million per Year Spent on Travel and Entertainment 2
    Electrovision's Travel Expenses Exceed National Averages.................... 3
    Spending Has Been Encouraged 3

Growing Impact on the Bottom Line 4
    Lower Profits Underscore the Need for Change 4
    Airfares and Hotel Rates Are Rising 5

Methods for Reducing T&E Costs 5
    Four Ways to Trim Expenses 5
    The Impact of Reforms 8

Conclusions and Recommendations 9

Works Cited 10

LIST OF ILLUSTRATIONS

FIGURES   **PAGE**

1. Airfares and Lodging Account for Over Two-Thirds of
    Electrovision's T&E Budget 2

2. T&E Expenses Continue to Increase
    as a Percentage of Sales 2

3. Electrovision Employees Spend Over Twice as Much as
    the Average Business Traveler 3

TABLE

1. Electrovision Can Trim Travel and Entertainment Costs
    by an Estimated $6 Million per Year 8

iii

Moreno included only first- and second-level headings in her table of contents, even though the report contains third-level headings. She prefers a shorter table of contents that focuses attention on the main divisions of thought. She used informative titles, which are appropriate for a report to a receptive audience.

The executive summary begins by stating the purpose of the report.

Moreno presents the points in the executive summary in the same order as they appear in the report, using subheadings that summarize the content of the main sections of the report.

EXECUTIVE SUMMARY

This report analyzes Electrovision's travel and entertainment (T&E) costs and presents recommendations for reducing those costs.

Travel and Entertainment Costs Are Too High

Travel and entertainment is a large and growing expense category for Electrovision. The company spends over $16 million per year on business travel, and these costs have been increasing by 12 percent annually. Company employees make roughly 3,390 trips each year at an average cost per trip of $4,720. Airfares are the biggest expense, followed by hotels, meals, and rental cars.

The nature of Electrovision's business does require extensive travel, but the company's costs are excessive: Our employees spend more than twice the national average on travel and entertainment. Although the location of the company's facilities may partly explain this discrepancy, the main reason for our high costs is a management style that gives employees little incentive to economize.

Cuts Are Essential

Electrovision management now recognizes the need to gain more control over this element of costs. The company is currently entering a period of declining profits, prompting management to look for every opportunity to reduce spending. At the same time, rising airfares and hotel rates are making T&E expenses more significant.

Electrovision Can Save $6 Million per Year

Fortunately, Electrovision has a number of excellent opportunities for reducing T&E costs. Savings of up to $6 million per year should be achievable, judging by the experience of other companies. A sensible travel-management program can save companies as much as 35 percent a year (Gilligan 39–40), and we should be able to save even more, since we purchase many more business-class tickets than the average. Four steps will help us cut costs:

1. Hire a director of travel and entertainment to assume overall responsibility for T&E spending, policies, and technologies, including the hiring and management of a national travel agency.
2. Educate employees on the need for cost containment, both in avoiding unnecessary travel and reducing costs when travel is necessary.
3. Negotiate preferential rates with travel providers.
4. Implement technological alternatives to travel, such as virtual meetings.

As necessary as these changes are, they will likely hurt morale, at least in the short term. Management will need to make a determined effort to explain the rationale for reduced spending. By exercising moderation in their own travel arrangements, Electrovision executives can set a good example and help other employees accept the changes. On the plus side, using travel alternatives such as web conferencing will reduce the travel burden on many employees and help them balance their business and personal lives.

iv

Her audience is receptive, so the tone in the executive summary is forceful; a more neutral approach would be better for hostile or skeptical readers.

The executive summary uses the same font and paragraph treatment as the text of the report.

The page numbering in the executive summary continues with Roman numerals.

Moreno decided to include an executive summary because her report is aimed at a mixed audience, some of whom are interested in the details of her report and others who just want the "big picture." The executive summary is aimed at the second group, giving them enough information to make a decision without burdening them with the task of reading the entire report.

Her writing style matches the serious nature of the content without sounding distant or stiff. Moreno chose the formal approach because several members of her audience are considerably higher up in the organization, and she did not want to sound too familiar. In addition, her company prefers the impersonal style for formal reports.

A color bar highlights the report title and the first-level headings; a variety of other design treatments are possible as well.

REDUCING ELECTROVISION'S TRAVEL AND ENTERTAINMENT COSTS

INTRODUCTION

Electrovision has always encouraged a significant amount of business travel. To compensate employees for the stress and inconvenience of frequent trips, management has authorized generous travel and entertainment (T&E) allowances. This philosophy has been good for morale, but last year Electrovision spent $16 million on travel and entertainment—$7 million more than it spent on research and development.

This year's T&E costs will affect profits even more, due to increases in airline fares and hotel rates. Also, the company anticipates that profits will be relatively weak for a variety of other reasons. Therefore, Dennis McWilliams, Vice President of Operations, has asked the accounting department to explore ways to reduce the T&E budget.

The introduction opens by establishing the need for action.

The purpose of this report is to analyze T&E expenses, evaluate the effect of recent hotel and airfare increases, and suggest ways to tighten control over T&E costs. The report outlines several steps that could reduce Electrovision's expenses, but the precise financial impact of these measures is difficult to project. The estimates presented here provide a "best guess" view of what Electrovision can expect to save.

In preparing this report, the accounting department analyzed internal expense reports for the past five years to determine how much Electrovision spends on travel and entertainment. These figures were then compared with average statistics compiled by Dow Jones (Publisher of the *Wall Street Journal*) and presented as the Dow Jones Travel Index. We also analyzed trends and suggestions published in a variety of business journal articles to see how other companies are coping with the high cost of business travel.

Moreno mentions her sources and methods to increase credibility and to give readers a complete picture of the study's background.

THE HIGH COST OF TRAVEL AND ENTERTAINMENT

Although many companies view travel and entertainment as an incidental cost of doing business, the dollars add up. At Electrovision the bill for airfares, hotels, rental cars, meals, and entertainment totaled $16 million last year. Our T&E budget has increased by 12 percent per year for the past five years. Compared to the average U.S. business traveler, Electrovision's expenditures are high, largely because of management's generous policy on travel benefits.

A *running footer* that contains the report title and the page number appears on every page.

In her brief introduction, Moreno counts on topic sentences and transitions to indicate that she is discussing the purpose, scope, and limitations of the study.

$16 Million per Year Spent on Travel and Entertainment

Electrovision's annual budget for travel and entertainment is only 8 percent of sales. Because this is a relatively small expense category compared with such things as salaries and Commissions, it is tempting to dismiss T&E costs as insignificant. However, T&E is Electrovision's third-largest controllable expense, directly behind salaries and information systems.

Last year Electrovision personnel made about 3,390 trips at an average cost per trip of $4,720. The typical trip involved a round-trip flight of 3,000 miles, meals, and hotel accommodations for two or three days, and a rental car. Roughly 80 percent of trips were made by 20 percent of the staff—top management and sales personnel traveled most, averaging 18 trips per year.

Figure 1 illustrates how the T&E budget is spent. The largest categories are airfares and lodging, which together account for $7 out of $10 that employees spend on travel and entertainment. This spending breakdown has been relatively steady for the past five years and is consistent with the distribution of expenses experienced by other companies.

Figure 1
Airfares and Lodging Account for Over Two-Thirds of Electrovision's T&E Budget

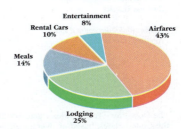

Although the composition of the T&E budget has been consistent, its size has not. As mentioned earlier, these expenditures have increased by about 12 percent per year for the past five years, roughly twice the rate of the company's sales growth (see Figure 2). This rate of growth makes T&E Electrovision's fastest-growing expense item.

Figure 2
T&E Expenses Continue to Increase as a Percentage of Sales

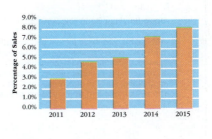

The visual is placed as close as possible to the point it illustrates.

Each visual has a title that clearly indicates what it's about; titles are consistently placed to the left of each visual.

Moreno opens the first main section of the body with a topic sentence that introduces an important fact about the subject of the section. Then she orients the reader to the three major points developed in the section.

Electrovision's Travel Expenses Exceed National Averages

Much of our travel budget is justified. Two major factors contribute to Electrovision's high T&E budget:

- With our headquarters on the West Coast and our major customer on the East Coast, we naturally spend a lot of money on cross-country flights.

- A great deal of travel takes place between our headquarters here on the West Coast and the manufacturing operations in Detroit, Boston, and Dallas. Corporate managers and division personnel make frequent trips to coordinate these disparate operations.

However, even though a good portion of Electrovision's travel budget is justifiable, the company spends considerably more on T&E than the average business traveler (see Figure 3).

Figure 3
Electrovision Employees Spend Over Twice as Much as the Average Business Traveler

Source: *Wall Street Journal* and company records

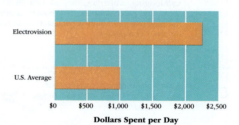

Dollars Spent per Day

The Dow Jones Travel Index calculates the average cost per day of business travel in the United States, based on average airfare, hotel rates, and rental car rates. The average fluctuates weekly as travel companies change their rates, but it has been running at about $1,000 per day for the last year or so. In contrast, Electrovision's average daily expense over the past year has been $2,250—a hefty 125 percent higher than average. This figure is based on the average trip cost of $4,720 listed earlier and an average trip length of 2.1 days.

Spending Has Been Encouraged

Although a variety of factors may contribute to this differential, Electrovision's relatively high T&E costs are at least partially attributable to the company's philosophy and management style. Since many employees do not enjoy business travel, management has tried to make the trips more pleasant by authorizing business-class airfare, luxury hotel accommodations, and full-size rental cars. The sales staff is encouraged to entertain clients at top restaurants and to invite them to cultural and sporting events.

The visuals are numbered consecutively and referred to by their numbers in the text.

Moreno introduces visuals before they appear and indicates what readers should notice about the data.

The chart in Figure 3 is simple but effective; Moreno includes just enough data to make her point. Notice how she is as careful about the appearance of her report as she is about the quality of its content.

A bulleted list makes it easy for readers to identify and distinguish related points.

The cost of these privileges is easy to overlook, given the weakness of Electrovision's system for keeping track of T&E expenses:

- The monthly financial records do not contain a separate category for travel and entertainment; the information is buried under Cost of Goods Sold and under Selling, General, and Administrative Expenses.

- Each department head is given authority to approve any expense report, regardless of how large it may be.

- Receipts are not required for expenditures of less than $100.

- Individuals are allowed to make their own travel arrangements.

- No one is charged with the responsibility for controlling the company's total spending on travel and entertainment.

GROWING IMPACT ON THE BOTTOM LINE

Informative headings focus reader attention on the main points. Such headings are appropriate when a report uses the direct order and is intended for a receptive audience. However, descriptive headings are more effective when a report uses the indirect order and readers are less receptive.

During the past three years, the company's healthy profits have resulted in relatively little pressure to push for tighter controls over all aspects of the business. However, as we all know, the situation is changing. We're projecting flat to declining profits for the next two years, a situation that has prompted all of us to search for ways to cut costs. At the same time, rising airfares and hotel rates have increased the impact of T&E expenses on the company's financial results.

Lower Profits Underscore the Need for Change

The next two years promise to be difficult for Electrovision. After several years of steady increases in spending, the Postal Service is tightening procurement policies for automated mail-handling equipment. Funding for the A-12 optical character reader has been canceled. As a consequence, the marketing department expects sales to drop by 15 percent. Although Electrovision is negotiating several other promising R&D contracts, the marketing department does not foresee any major procurements for the next two to three years.

At the same time, Electrovision is facing cost increases on several fronts. As we have known for several months, the new production facility now under construction in Salt Lake City, Utah, is behind schedule and over budget. Labor contracts in Boston and Dallas will expire within the next six months, and plant managers there anticipate that significant salary and benefits concessions may be necessary to avoid strikes.

Moreover, marketing and advertising costs are expected to increase as we attempt to strengthen these activities to better cope with competitive pressures. Given the expected decline in revenues and increase in costs, the Executive Committee's prediction that profits will fall by 12 percent in the coming fiscal year does not seem overly pessimistic.

Reducing Electrovision's Travel and Entertainment Costs   P a g e **4**

Moreno designed her report to include plenty of white space so even those pages that lack visuals are still attractive and easy to read.

Moreno supports her argument with objective facts and sound reasoning.

Airfares and Hotel Rates Are Rising

Business travelers have grown accustomed to frequent fare wars and discounting in the travel industry in recent years. Excess capacity and aggressive price competition, particularly in the airline business, made travel a relative bargain.

However, that situation has changed as weaker competitors have been forced out and the remaining players have grown stronger and smarter. Airlines and hotels are better at managing inventory and keeping occupancy rates high, which translates into higher costs for Electrovision. Last year saw some of the steepest rate hikes in years. Business airfares (tickets most likely to be purchased by business travelers) jumped more than 40 percent in many markets. The trend is expected to continue, with rates increasing another 5 to 10 percent overall (Phillips 331; "Travel Costs Under Pressure" 30; Dahl B6).

Given the fact that air and hotel costs account for almost 70 percent of our T&E budget, the trend toward higher prices in these two categories will have serious consequences, unless management takes action to control these costs.

METHODS FOR REDUCING T&E COSTS

The recommendations are realistic, noting both the benefits and the risks of taking action.

By implementing a number of reforms, management can expect to reduce Electrovision's T&E budget by as much as 40 percent. This estimate is based on the general assessment made by American Express (Gilligan 39) and on the fact that we have an opportunity to significantly reduce air travel costs by eliminating business-class travel. However, these measures are likely to be unpopular with employees. To gain acceptance for such changes, management will need to sell employees on the need for moderation in T&E allowances.

Four Ways to Trim Expenses

By researching what other companies are doing to curb T&E expenses, the accounting department has identified four prominent opportunities that should enable Electrovision to save about $6 million annually in travel-related costs.

Institute Tighter Spending Controls

A single individual should be appointed director of travel and entertainment to spearhead the effort to gain control of the T&E budget. More than a third of all U.S. companies now employ travel managers ("Businesses Use Savvy Managers" 4). The director should be familiar with the travel industry and should be well versed in both accounting and information technology. The director should also report to the vice president of operations. The director's first priorities should be to establish a written T&E policy and a cost-control system.

Electrovision currently has no written policy on travel and entertainment, a step that is widely recommended by air travel experts (Smith D4). Creating a policy would clarify management's position and serve as a vehicle for communicating the need for moderation.

Moreno creates a forceful tone by using action verbs in the third-level subheadings of this section. This approach is appropriate to the nature of the study and the attitude of the audience. However, in a status-conscious organization, the imperative verbs might sound a bit too presumptuous coming from a junior member of the staff.

At a minimum, the policy should include the following:

- All travel and entertainment should be strictly related to business and should be approved in advance.

- Except under special circumstances to be approved on a case-by-case basis, employees should travel by coach and stay in mid-range business hotels.

- The T&E policy should apply equally to employees at all levels.

To implement the new policy, Electrovision will need to create a system for controlling T&E expenses. Each department should prepare an annual T&E budget as part of its operating plan. These budgets should be presented in detail so that management can evaluate how T&E dollars will be spent and can recommend appropriate cuts. To help management monitor performance relative to these budgets, the director of travel should prepare monthly financial statements showing actual T&E expenditures by department.

The director of travel should also be responsible for retaining a business-oriented travel service that will schedule all employee business trips and look for the best travel deals, particularly in airfares. In addition to centralizing Electrovision's reservation and ticketing activities, the agency will negotiate reduced group rates with hotels and rental car firms. The agency selected should have offices nationwide so that all Electrovision facilities can channel their reservations through the same company. This is particularly important in light of the dizzying array of often wildly different airfares available between some cities. It's not uncommon to find dozens of fares along commonly traveled routes (Rowe 30). In addition, the director can help coordinate travel across the company to secure group discounts whenever possible (Barker 31; Miller B6).

Reduce Unnecessary Travel and Entertainment

One of the easiest ways to reduce expenses is to reduce the amount of traveling and entertaining that occurs. An analysis of last year's expenditures suggests that as much as 30 percent of Electrovision's travel and entertainment is discretionary. The professional staff spent $2.8 million attending seminars and conferences last year. Although these gatherings are undoubtedly beneficial, the company could save money by sending fewer representives to each function and perhaps by eliminating some of the less valuable seminars.

Similarly, Electrovision could economize on trips between headquarters and divisions by reducing the frequency of such visits and by sending fewer people on each trip. Although there is often no substitute for face-to-face meetings, management could try to resolve more internal issues through telephone, electronic, and written communication.

Electrovision can also reduce spending by urging employees to economize. Instead of flying business class, employees can fly coach class or take advantage of discount fares. Rather than ordering a $50 bottle of wine, employees can select a less expensive bottle or dispense with

In addition to making key points easy to find, bulleted lists help break up the text to relieve the reader's eye.

Moreno lists the steps needed to implement her recommendations.

Moreno takes care not to overstep the boundaries of her analysis. For instance, she doesn't analyze the value of the seminars that employees attend every year, so she avoids any absolute statements about reducing travel to seminars.

alcohol entirely. People can book rooms at moderately priced hotels and drive smaller rental cars.

Obtain Lowest Rates from Travel Providers

Apart from urging employees to economize, Electrovision can also save money by searching for the lowest available airfares, hotel rates, and rental car fees. Currently, few employees have the time or knowledge to seek out travel bargains. When they need to travel, they make the most convenient and comfortable arrangements. A professional travel service will be able to obtain lower rates from travel providers.

Judging by the experience of other companies, Electrovision may be able to trim as much
as 30 to 40 percent from the travel budget simply by looking for bargains in airfares and negotiating group rates with hotels and rental car companies. Electrovision should be able to achieve these economies by analyzing its travel patterns, identifying frequently visited locations, and selecting a few hotels that are willing to reduce rates in exchange for quar-
anteed business. At the same time, the company should be able to save up to 40 percent on rental car charges by negotiating a corporate rate.

The possibilities for economizing are promising; however, making the best travel arrangements often requires trade-offs such as the following:

- The best fares might not always be the lowest. Indirect flights are usually cheaper, but they take longer and may end up costing more in lost work time.

- The cheapest tickets often require booking 14 or even 30 days in advance, which is often impossible for us.

- Discount tickets are usually nonrefundable, which is a serious drawback when a trip needs to be canceled at the last minute.

Replace Travel with Technological Alternatives

Online meeting systems such as WebEx and GoTo Meeting offer a compelling alternative to many instances of business travel. With webcam video, application/ screen sharing, and collaboration tools such as virtual whiteboards, they have made great strides toward replicating the in-person meeting experience.

As effective as they can be, though, they shouldn't automatically replace every in-person meeting. When establishing a business relationship, for example, meeting face to face is an important part of building trust and getting past the uncertainties of working with a new partner. Part of the new travel director's job would be to draft guidelines for choosing travel or on-line meeting options.

By pointing out possible difficulties and showing that she has considered all angles, Moreno builds reader confidence in her judgment.

Note how Moreno makes the transition from section to section. The first sentence under the second heading on this page refers to the subject of the previous paragraph and signals a shift in thought.

The Impact of Reforms

By implementing tighter controls, reducing unnecessary expenses, negotiating more favorable rates, and exploring alternatives to travel, Electrovision should be able to reduce its T&E budget significantly. As Table 1 illustrates, the combined savings should be in the neighborhood of $6 million, although the precise figures are somewhat difficult to project.

Table 1
Electrovision Can Trim Travel and Entertainment Costs
by an Estimated $6 Million per Year

SOURCE OF SAVINGS	ESTIMATED SAVINGS
Switching from business-class to coach airfare	$2,300,000
Negotiating preferred hotel rates	940,000
Negotiating preferred rental car rates	460,000
Systematically searching for lower airfares	375,000
Reducing interdivisional travel	675,000
Reducing seminar and conference attendance	1,250,000
TOTAL POTENTIAL SAVINGS	**$6,000,000**

To achieve the economies outlined in the table, Electrovision will incur expenses for hiring a director of travel and for implementing a T&E cost-control system. These costs are projected at $115,000: $105,000 per year in salary and benefits for the new employee and a one-time expense of $10,000 for the cost-control system. The cost of retaining a full-service travel agency is negligible, even with the service fees that many are now passing along from airlines and other service providers.

The measures required to achieve these savings are likely to be unpopular with employees. Electrovision personnel are accustomed to generous T&E allowances, and they are likely to resent having these privileges curtailed. To alleviate their disappointment

- Management should make a determined effort to explain why the changes are necessary.

- The director of corporate communication should be asked to develop a multifaceted campaign that will communicate the importance of curtailing T&E costs.

- Management should set a positive example by adhering strictly to the new policies.

- The limitations should apply equally to employees at all levels in the organization.

An informative title in the table is consistent with the way headings are handled throughout this report, and it is appropriate for a report to a receptive audience.

The in-text reference to the table highlights the key point the reader should get from the table.

Including financial estimates helps management envision the impact of the suggestions, even though the estimated savings are difficult to project accurately.

Note how Moreno calls attention in the first paragraph to items in the following table, without repeating the information in the table.

She uses a descriptive heading for the last section of the text. In informational reports, this section is often called "Summary"; in analytical reports, it is called "Conclusions" or "Conclusions and Recommendations."

Moreno summarizes her conclusions in the first two paragraphs—a good approach because she organized her report around conclusions and recommendations, so readers have already been introduced to them.

CONCLUSIONS AND RECOMMENDATIONS

Electrovision is currently spending $16 million per year on travel and entertainment. Although much of this spending is justified, the company's costs are high relative to competitors' costs, mainly because Electrovision has been generous with its travel benefits.

Electrovision's liberal approach to travel and entertainment was understandable during years of high profitability; however, the company is facing the prospect of declining profits for the next several years. Management is therefore motivated to cut costs in all areas of the business. Reducing T&E spending is particularly important because the bottom-line impact of these costs will increase as airline fares increase.

Electrovision should be able to reduce T&E costs by as much as 40 percent by taking four important steps:

1. *Institute tighter spending controls.* Management should hire a director of travel and entertainment who will assume overall responsibility for T&E activities. Within the next six months, this director should develop a written travel policy, institute a T&E budget and a cost-control system, and retain a professional, business-oriented travel agency that will optimize arrangements with travel providers.

2. *Reduce unnecessary travel and entertainment.* Electrovision should encourage employees to economize on T&E spending. Management can accomplish this by authorizing fewer trips and by urging employees to be more conservative in their spending.

3. *Obtain lowest rates from travel providers.* Electrovision should also focus on obtaining the best rates on airline tickets, hotel rooms, and rental cars. By channeling all arrange-ments through a professional travel agency, the company canoptimize its choices and gain clout in negotiating preferred rates.

4. *Replace some travel with technological alternatives.* Online meeting systems should be adequate for most of our tactical meetings with established clients and for most internal communication as well.

Because these measures may be unpopular with employees, management should make a concerted effort to explain the importance of reducing travel costs. The director of corporate communication should be given responsibility for developing a plan to communicate the need for employee cooperation.

Presenting the recommendations in a list gives each one emphasis.

Moreno doesn't introduce any new facts in this section. In a longer report she might have divided this section into subsections, labeled "Conclusions" and "Recommendations," to distinguish between the two.

WORKS CITED

Barker, Julie. "How to Rein in Group Travel Costs." *Successful Meetings* Feb. 2015: 31. Print.

"Businesses Use Savvy Managers to Keep Travel Costs Down." *Christian Science Monitor* 17 July 2014: 4. Print.

Dahl, Jonathan. "2000: The Year Travel Costs Took Off." *Wall Street Journal* 29 Dec. 2007: B6. Print.

Gilligan, Edward P. "Trimming Your T&E Is Easier Than You Think." *Managing Office Technology* Nov. 2015: 39–40. Print.

Miller, Lisa. "Attention, Airline Ticket Shoppers." *Wall Street Journal* 7 July 2015: B6. Print.

Phillips, Edward H. "Airlines Post Record Traffic." *Aviation Week & Space Technology* 8 Jan. 2016: 331. Print.

"Product Overview: Cisco WebEx Meeting Center," *Webex.com*. Web Ex, n.d. 2 Feb. 2016. Web.

Rowe, Irene Vlitos. "Global Solution for Cutting Travel Costs." *European Business* 12 Oct. 2011: 30. Print.

Smith, Carol. "Rising, Erratic Airfares Make Company Policy Vital." *Los Angeles Times* 2 Nov. 2012: D4. Print.

Solheim, Shelley. "Web Conferencing Made Easy." *eWeek* 22 Aug. 2012: 26. Web.

"Travel Costs Under Pressure." *Purchasing* 15 Feb. 2012: 30. Print.

MLA style lists references alphabetically by the author's last name, and when the author is unknown, by the title of the reference. (See Appendix B for additional details on preparing reference lists.)

Moreno's list of references follows the style recommended in the *MLA Style Manual*. The box below shows how these sources would be cited following American Psychological Association (APA) style.

REFERENCES

Barker, J. (2016, February). How to rein in group travel costs. *Successful Meetings*, p. 31.

Businesses use savvy managers to keep travel costs down. (2014, July 17). *Christian Science Monitor*, p. 4.

Dahl, J. (2007, December 29). 2000: The year travel costs took off. *Wall Street Journal*, p. B6.

Gilligan, E. (2015, November). Trimming your T&E is easier than you think. *Managing Office Technology*, pp. 39–40.

Miller, L. (2015, July 7). Attention, airline ticket shoppers. *Wall Street Journal*, p. B6.

Phillips, E. (2016, January 8). *Aviation Week & Space Technology*, p. 331.

Rowe, I. (2011, October 12). Global solution for cutting travel costs. *European*, p. 30.

Smith, C. (2012, November 2). Rising, erratic airfares make company policy vital. *Los Angeles Times*, D4.

Solheim, S. (2012, August 22). Web conferencing made easy. *eWeek*, p. 26.

Travel costs under pressure. (2012, February 15). *Purchasing*, p. 30.

WebEx.com. (2016). Cisco WebEx Meeting Center. Retrieved from http://www.webex.com/product-overview/index.html

When you've completed your formal report or proposal and sent it off to your audience, your next task is to wait for a response. If you don't hear from your readers within a week or two, you might want to ask politely whether the report arrived. (Some RFPs specify a response time frame. In such a case, *don't* pester the recipient ahead of schedule, or you'll hurt your chances.) In hope of stimulating a response, you might ask a question about the report, such as "How do you think accounting will react to the proposed budget increase?" You might also offer to answer any questions or provide additional information. To review the ideas presented in this chapter, see "Checklist: Producing Formal Reports and Proposals."

CHECKLIST: ✔ Producing Formal Reports and Proposals

A. Prefatory parts
- Use your company's standard report covers, if available.
- Include a concise, descriptive title on the cover.
- Include a title fly only if you want an extra-formal touch.
- On the title page, list (1) report title; (2) name, title, and address of the group or person who authorized the report; (3) name, title, and address of the group or person who prepared the report; and (4) date of submission.
- Include a copy of the letter of authorization, if appropriate.
- If responding to an RFP, follow its instructions for including a copy or referring to the RFP by name or tracking number.
- Include a letter of transmittal that introduces the report.
- Provide a table of contents in outline form, with headings worded exactly as they appear in the body of the report.
- Include a list of illustrations if the report contains a large number of them.
- Include a synopsis (brief summary of the report) or an executive summary (a condensed, "mini" version of the report) for longer reports.

B. Text of the report
- Draft an introduction that prepares the reader for the content that follows.
- Provide information that supports your conclusions, recommendations, or proposals in the body of the report.
- Don't overload the body with unnecessary detail.
- Close with a summary of your main idea.

C. Supplementary parts
- Use appendixes to provide supplementary information or supporting evidence.
- List in a bibliography any secondary sources you used.
- Provide an index if your report contains a large number of terms or ideas and is likely to be consulted over time.

ON THE JOB: SOLVING COMMUNICATION DILEMMAS AT
GARAGE TECHNOLOGY VENTURES

You recently joined Guy Kawasaki and the rest of the team at Garage Technology Ventures in Palo Alto. Your responsibilities include screening executive summaries of business plans submitted by start-up companies seeking financing. Review the criteria discussed in the chapter-opening vignette on pages 399–400 to address the following challenges.

1. You've just received an intriguing executive summary from a start-up company whose technology reduces the cost of providing Internet service by nearly 30 percent, an amount that would spark interest from just about every Internet service provider in the world. The financial projections in the executive summary are realistic—and quite positive. Even if this investment panned out only half as well as the numbers suggest, it would bring in a sizable amount of cash when the company eventually goes public. The patented technological solution is sound, too; you used to work as a network engineer, and these people know what they're doing. There is just one problem: the submission is entirely anonymous. The document describes, in vague terms, four experienced technical and business specialists but without giving their names or their specific work experiences. A note attached to the plan apologizes for the secrecy but says the four principles in the new firm can't reveal themselves until they get financing and can therefore leave their current jobs. What should you do?

   a. Reject the submission without a second thought; you can't invest in them if you don't know who they are.

   b. Pass it on to Kawasaki and the other managing directors for their consideration, like any other promising business plan.

   c. Forward it to another networking company in the Garage portfolio and ask them to explore bringing this technology to market.

   d. Write a message to the email address provided in the plan, stating that Garage might be interested, but only if the people behind the plan are willing to reveal themselves. If they refuse or don't respond, toss out the plan.

2. Review these "grabs" presented in three executive summaries. Discuss their strengths and weaknesses and decide which one of the three you would forward to Kawasaki and the other directors.

   a. **Company A:** Pardon our bullish tone, but this is the best investment opportunity you are likely to see this year. As one of our board members recently said, we are already on track to out-Apple Apple and out-Google Google.

   b. **Company B:** Cooling the huge data centers that power the Internet costs millions of dollars a year and consumes massive amounts of energy. Our low-temperature server technology pays for itself in less than a year by reducing energy bills and extending the life of data center hardware.

   c. **Company C:** Our travel-search website has already proven so popular that last month we had 140,000 site visitors. By the way, we have interest from three other investment firms, so our advice would be to jump on this opportunity!

3. You are finalizing this year's portfolio update report for the company's partners and investors, an important document that summarizes the performance over the last year of all the companies in which Garage has an investment stake. Accuracy and clarity are essential with this document, because the information it contains can lead to significant changes in investment and oversight strategies for the companies in the portfolio. Which of the following proofreading strategies should you use to make sure your report is free of errors?

   a. Take advantage of technology. Double-check the settings in your word-processing software to make sure every checking tool is activated as you type, including the spell checker, grammar checker, and style checker. When you're finished with the first draft, run each of these tools again, just to make sure the computer didn't miss anything.

   b. Recognize that no report, particularly a complex 60-page document with multiple visuals, is going to be free of errors. Include a statement on the title page apologizing for any errors that may still exist in the report. Provide your email address and invite people to send you a message when they find errors.

   c. As soon as you finish typing the first draft, immediately review it for accuracy while the content is still fresh in your mind. After you have done this, you can be reasonably sure that the document is free from errors. If you wait a day or two, you'll start to forget what you've written, thereby lowering your chances of catching errors.

   d. Put the report aside for at least a day and then proofread it carefully. Also, recruit two colleagues to review it for you—one who can review the technical and financial accuracy of the material and one who has a good eye for language and clarity.

4. Looking over past editions of the annual performance report, you see that it has always had the generic main title of "Annual Performance Review," followed by a subtitle that summarizes the overall performance of the companies in the portfolio. Which of the following subtitles would be most effective and most appropriate for this year's report, a year in which half the companies in the portfolio experienced major technical or legal setbacks, and only two met their revenue projections?

   a. A Year We'd Rather Forget

   b. We Can't Continue at This Rate

   c. A Year of Serious Challenges

   d. A Portfolio in Crisis

Learning Objectives Checkup

Assess your understanding of the principles in this chapter by reading each learning objective and studying the accompanying exercises. You can check your responses against the answer key on page 599.

Objective 13.1: Describe the process of revising formal reports and proposals.

1. Which of the following is *not* one of the four major tasks involved in completing business reports and proposals?
   a. Revising the report's organization, style, tone, and readability
   b. Formatting the report
   c. Deciding which visuals to create for the report
   d. Proofreading the report

Objective 13.2: Identify the major components of formal reports.

2. In what situation should you consider including a letter or memo of authorization in a formal report?
   a. If you're getting paid to write the report
   b. If you received written authorization to write the report
   c. If the audience outranks you
   d. If you outrank the audience

3. What is the purpose of including a letter of acceptance in a formal report?
   a. It reminds your audience what you previously agreed to address in the report and why you were assigned to write it.
   b. It makes your report feel more formal and official.
   c. It prevents others from taking credit for your work.
   d. It summarizes the key points of your report for people who are too busy to read the report itself.

4. A letter or memo of _____ is a specialized form of a cover letter that introduces your report to the audience.

5. A/an _____ is a brief overview (usually one page or less) of a report's most important points.

6. A/an _____ _____ is a fully developed "mini" version of the report itself.

7. Which of the following may contain headings, visual aids, and enough information to help busy executives make quick decisions?
   a. An executive summary
   b. A synopsis
   c. Both
   d. Neither

8. Which of the following is *not* a typical supplementary part of a formal report?
   a. Appendixes
   b. Bibliography
   c. Letter of authorization
   d. Index

Objective 13.3: Identify the major components of formal proposals.

9. If you've submitted a proposal that is in response to an RFP, and the RFP doesn't include specific instructions for referring to the RFP, what steps can you take to make sure the recipient understands which RFP you're responding to?

   a. Include the formal title of the RFP (and its reference number, if it has one) as a footnote in the first appendix of your report.
   b. If the RFP is short, include it with the other prefatory parts of your proposal; if the RFP is lengthy, include just the introductory page(s) from it.
   c. Include the entire RFP in the body of your proposal, no matter how long it is.
   d. The RFP was written by someone else, so you can ignore it in your report.

10. How should you handle the letter of transmittal for an unsolicited proposal?
    a. Treat the letter as a routine message; businesspeople get proposals all the time, so they don't expect anything more than a simple announcement that identifies you and your proposal.
    b. Treat the letter as a positive message, highlighting the good news that you have to offer in the proposal.
    c. Treat the letter as a persuasive message, persuading the reader that your report offers information of value.
    d. Don't waste the reader's time with a letter of transmittal; get right to the point with the body of your proposal.

Objective 13.4: Describe an effective plan for proofreading reports and proposals.

11. The following sentence appears in your first draft of a report that analyzes perceived shortcomings in your company's employee health benefits: "Among the many criticisms and concerns expressed by the workforce, at least among the 376 who responded to our online survey (out of 655 active employees), the issues of elder care, health insurance during retirement, and the increased amount that employees are being forced to pay every month as the company's contribution to health insurance coverage has declined over the past two years were identified as the most important." You realize that this 69-word sentence could be shorter, more direct, and more powerful. Which of these revisions is the most effective?
    a. The employees who responded to our online survey (376 out of 655 active employees) identified these three issues: elder care, insurance coverage after they retire, and rising monthly payments.
    b. Elder care, insurance coverage after they retire, and rising monthly payments were the three most important issues identified in our survey of employees regarding their complaints and criticisms of health care benefits. Out of a current active workforce of 655 people, 376 employees completed the online survey. They complained about quite a range of issues, but these three were the most important to them overall.
    c. The top three employee concerns: elder care, insurance coverage after they retire, and increases in the amounts that employees pay every month for health insurance.
    d. Based on responses from 376 employees (out of 655) who responded to an online survey, the top three concerns our employees have regarding their health benefits are elder care, insurance coverage after they retire, and increases in the monthly cost of insurance.

Objective 13.5: Describe the decision process for distributing reports and proposals.

12. Why are PDF files a popular format for distributing reports digitally?
    a. Senders appreciate the ability to maintain control over how their documents appear on the receiving end.
    b. Receivers are often reluctant to open word-processor files.
    c. Most businesspeople expect most reports to be distributed as PDF files.
    d. All of the above are true.

13. What is the best strategy when you've sent a formal proposal in response to an RFP but you haven't heard back within a week or two?

    a. Immediately follow up with the recipient, regardless of the response window specified in the RFP; doing so is a sign that you're hungry for the business.
    b. Never pester a proposal recipient under any circumstances, even if you have to wait months for a response.
    c. Remove the project from your workload planner and get on with something else; if you haven't heard back in a week or two, you're not going to get the contract.
    d. If the response time frame specified in the RFP has passed, follow up with a question related to the content of the proposal or an offer to answer any questions.

Quick Learning Guide

CHAPTER OUTLINE

Revising Reports and Proposals
Producing Formal Reports
  Prefatory Parts
  Text of the Report
  Supplementary Parts
Producing Formal Proposals
  Prefatory Parts
  Text of the Proposal
Proofreading Reports and Proposals
Distributing Reports and Proposals

LEARNING OBJECTIVES

1 Describe the process of revising formal reports and proposals. (page 400)

2 Identify the major components of formal reports. (page 401)

3 Identify the major components of formal proposals. (page 410)

4 Describe an effective plan for proofreading reports and proposals (page 412)

5 Describe the decision process for distributing reports and proposals. (page 412)

KEY TERMS

abstract Name usually given to a synopsis that accompanies long technical, professional, or academic reports

appendix Supplementary section that contains materials related to the report but not included in the text because they are too long or perhaps not relevant to everyone in the audience

bibliography A list of the secondary sources consulted in the preparation of a report

executive summary A complete but summarized version of the report; may contain headings, well-developed transitions, and even visual elements

index An alphabetical list of names and subjects mentioned in a report, along with the pages on which they occur

letter of acceptance Message written in response to a letter of authorization

letter of authorization Written authorization to prepare a report

letter of transmittal A specialized form of cover letter that introduces a report to the audience

synopsis A brief overview (one page or less) of a report's most important points, designed to give readers a quick preview of the contents

title fly A single sheet of paper with only the title of the report on it

title page Page that includes the report title; the name, title, and address of the person or organization that authorized the report (if anyone); the name, title, and address of the person or organization that prepared the report; and the date on which the report was submitted

---

CHECKLIST:

Producing Formal Reports and Proposals

A. Prefatory parts
- Use your company's standard report covers, if available.
- Include a concise, descriptive title on the cover.
- Include a title fly only if you want an extra-formal touch.
- On the title page, list (1) report title; (2) name, title, and address of the group or person who authorized the report; (3) name, title, and address of the group or person who prepared the report; and (4) date of submission.
- Include a copy of the letter of authorization, if appropriate.
- If responding to an RFP, follow its instructions for including a copy or referring to the RFP by name or tracking number.
- Include a letter of transmittal that introduces the report.
- Provide a table of contents in outline form, with headings worded exactly as they appear in the body of the report.
- Include a list of illustrations if the report contains a large number of them.
- Include a synopsis (brief summary of the report) or an executive summary (a condensed, "mini" version of the report) for longer reports.

B. Text of the report
- Draft an introduction that prepares the reader for the content that follows.
- Provide information that supports your conclusions, recommendations, or proposals in the body of the report.
- Don't overload the body with unnecessary detail.
- Close with a summary of your main idea.

C. Supplementary parts
- Use appendixes to provide supplementary information or supporting evidence.
- List in a bibliography any secondary sources you used.
- Provide an index if your report contains a large number of terms or ideas and is likely to be consulted over time.

MyBCommLab

To complete the problems with the ⭐, go to EOC Discussion Questions in the MyLab.

Apply Your Knowledge

To review chapter content related to each question, refer to the indicated Learning Objective.

⭐ **13.1.** Is an executive summary a persuasive message? Explain your answer. [LO-2]

⭐ **13.2.** How would you report on a confidential survey in which employees rated their managers' capabilities? Both employees and managers expect to see the results. Would you give the same report to employees and managers? What components would you include or exclude for each audience? Explain your choices. [LO-2]

13.3. If you were submitting a solicited proposal to build a small shopping center, would you include as references the names and addresses of other clients for whom you recently built similar facilities? Where in the proposal would you include these references? Why? [LO-3]

Practice Your Skills

13.4. Message 13.A: Executive Summaries [LO-2]
To access the document for this exercise, go to http://real-timeupdates.com/ebc12, click on Student Assignments, and select Chapter 13, Message 13.A. Download this PDF file, which is the executive summary of *Dietary Guidelines for Americans*, a publication from the U.S. Center for Nutrition Policy and Promotion. Using the information in this chapter, analyze the executive summary and offer specific suggestions for revising it.

Exercises

Each activity is labeled according to the primary skill or skills you will need to use. To review relevant chapter content, you can refer to the indicated Learning Objective. In some instances, supporting information will be found in another chapter, as indicated.

13.5. Revising for Clarity and Conciseness [LO-1] Revise the following sentence to make it clearer and more direct. Feel free to break it into two sentences, if you prefer.

> This job requires someone with both tact and perseverance, because you don't have authority over other people, but your success depends on getting them to perform certain tasks, and you need to persuade them to perform these tasks and not be afraid to follow up to make sure the tasks get done.

13.6. Producing Formal Reports; Collaboration: Team Projects [LO-2], Chapter 2 You and a classmate are helping Linda Moreno prepare her report on Electrovision's travel and entertainment costs (see "Report Writer's Notebook" on page 413). This time, however, the report is to be informational rather than analytical, so it will not include recommendations. Review the existing report and determine what changes would be needed to make it an informational report. Be as specific as possible. For example, if your team decides the report needs a new title, what title would you use? Now draft a transmittal memo for Moreno to use in conveying this informational report to Dennis McWilliams, Electrovision's vice president of operations.

13.7. Producing Formal Reports [LO-2] You are president of the Friends of the Library, a nonprofit group that raises funds and provides volunteers to support your local library. Every February, you send a report of the previous year's activities and accomplishments to the County Arts Council, which provides an annual grant of $1,000 toward your group's summer reading festival. Now it's February 6, and you've completed your formal report. Here are the highlights:

- Back-to-school book sale raised $2,000.
- Holiday craft fair raised $1,100.
- Promotion and prizes for summer reading festival cost $1,450.
- Materials for children's program featuring local author cost $125.
- New reference databases for library's career center cost $850.
- Bookmarks promoting library's website cost $200.

Write a letter of transmittal to Erica Maki, the council's director. Because she is expecting this report, you can use the direct approach. Be sure to express gratitude for the council's ongoing financial support.

13.8. Producing Formal Reports [LO-2] Government reports vary in purpose and structure. Read through the Department of Education's report "Helping Your Child Become a Reader," available at www2.ed.gov/parents/academic/help/reader/index.html. What is the purpose of this document? Does the title communicate this purpose? What type of report is this, and what is the report's structure? Which prefatory and supplementary parts are included? Now analyze the visuals. What types of visuals are included in this report? Are they all necessary? Are the titles and legends sufficiently informative? How does this report take advantage of the online medium to enhance readability?

13.9. Distributing Reports; Communication Ethics: Resolving Ethical Dilemmas [LO-5], Chapter 1 You submitted what you thought was a masterful report to your boss over three weeks ago. The report analyzes current department productivity and recommends several steps that you think will improve employee output without increasing individual workloads. Brilliant, you thought. But you haven't heard a word from your boss. Did you overstep your boundaries by making recommendations that might imply that she has not been doing a good job? Did you overwhelm her with your ideas? You'd like some feedback. In your last email to her, you asked if she had read your report. So far you've received no reply. Then yesterday, you overheard the company vice president talk about some productivity changes in your department. The changes were ones that you recommended in your report. Now you're worried that your boss submitted your report to senior management and will take full credit for your terrific ideas. What, if anything, should you do? Should you confront your boss about this? Should you ask to meet with the company vice president? Discuss this situation with your teammates and develop a solution to this sticky situation. Present your solution to the class, explaining the rationale behind your decision.

Expand Your Skills

Critique the Professionals

Browse the websites of several companies to find a downloadable PDF file of a report, white paper, company backgrounder, product overview, or other document at least two pages long. Evaluate the design and production quality of this document. Does the layout enhance the message or distract your attention from it? It what ways do design elements convey the company's brand image? Does the document strike you as "under-designed" or "over-designed" for its intended purpose? Using whatever medium your instructor requests, write a brief summary of your analysis. Be sure to include a link to the document.

Sharpening Your Career Skills Online

Bovée and Thill's Business Communication Web Search, at http://websearch.businesscommunicationnetwork.com, is a unique research tool designed specifically for business communication research. Use the Web Search function to find a website, video, PDF document, or PowerPoint presentation that offers advice on producing formal reports and proposals. Write a brief email message to your instructor, describing the item that you found and summarizing the career skills information you learned from it.

Improve Your Grammar, Mechanics, and Usage

The following exercises help you improve your knowledge of and power over English grammar, mechanics, and usage. Turn to the Handbook of Grammar, Mechanics, and Usage at the end of this book and review all of Sections 2.10 (Quotation Marks), 2.11 (Parentheses), and 2.12 (Ellipses). Then look at the following 10 items. Circle the letter of the preferred choice in the following groups of sentences. (Answers to these exercises appear on page 601.)

13.10. **a.** Be sure to read (How to Sell by Listening) in this month's issue of Fortune.

   b. Be sure to read "How to Sell by Listening" in this month's issue of *Fortune*.

   c. Be sure to read "How to Sell by Listening . . ." in this month's issue of *Fortune*.

13.11. **a.** Her response . . . see the attached memo . . . is disturbing.

   b. Her response (see the attached memo) is disturbing.

   c. Her response "see the attached memo" is disturbing.

13.12. **a.** We operate with a skeleton staff during the holidays (December 21 through January 2).

   b. We operate with a skeleton staff during the holidays "December 21 through January 2".

   c. We operate with a skeleton staff during the holidays (December 21 through January 2.)

13.13. **a.** "The SBP's next conference . . ." the bulletin noted, ". . . will be held in Minneapolis."

   b. "The SBP's next conference," the bulletin noted, "will be held in Minneapolis."

   c. "The SBP's next conference," the bulletin noted, "will be held in Minneapolis".

13.14. **a.** The term "up in the air" means "undecided."

   b. The term "up in the air" means *undecided*.

   c. The term *up in the air* means "undecided."

13.15. **a.** Her assistant (the one who just had the baby) won't be back for four weeks.

   b. Her assistant (the one who just had the baby), won't be back for four weeks.

   c. Her assistant . . . the one who just had the baby . . . won't be back for four weeks.

13.16. **a.** "Ask not what your country can do for you," begins a famous John Kennedy quotation.

   b. ". . . Ask not what your country can do for you" begins a famous John Kennedy quotation.

   c. "Ask not what your country can do for you . . ." begins a famous John Kennedy quotation.

13.17. **a.** Do you remember who said, "And away we go?"

   b. Do you remember who said, "And away we go"?

13.18. **a.** Refinements may prove profitable. (More detail about this technology appears in Appendix A).

   c. Refinements may prove profitable. (More detail about this technology appears in Appendix A.)

13.19. **a.** The resignation letter begins, "Since I'll never regain your respect . . . ," and goes on to explain why that's true.

   b. The resignation letter begins, "Since I'll never regain your respect, . . ." and goes on to explain why that's true.

   c. The resignation letter begins, "Since I'll never regain your respect . . ." and goes on to explain why that's true.

For additional exercises focusing on quotation marks, parentheses, and ellipses, visit MyBcommLab. Click on Chapter 13, click on Additional Exercises to Improve Your Grammar, Mechanics, and Usage, and then click on 19. Punctuation D.

Cases

Short Formal Reports Requiring No Additional Research

PORTFOLIO BUILDER

13.20. Message Strategies: Analytical Reports You've been in your new job as human resources director for only a week, and already you have a major personnel crisis on your hands. Some employees in the marketing department got their hands on a confidential salary report, only to learn that, on average, marketing employees earn less than engineering employees. In addition, several top performers in the engineering group make significantly more money than anybody in marketing. The report was passed around the company instantly by email, and now everyone is discussing the situation. You'll deal with the data security issue later; for now, you need to address the dissatisfaction in the marketing group.

Case Table 13.1 lists the salary and employment data you were able to pull from the employee database. You also had the opportunity to interview the engineering and marketing directors to get their opinions on the pay situation; their answers are listed in Case Table 13.2.

Your task: The CEO has asked for a short report, summarizing the data and information you have on engineering and marketing salaries. Feel free to offer your own interpretation of the situation as well (make up any information you need), but keep in mind that as a new manager with almost no experience in the company, your opinion might not have a lot of influence.

PORTFOLIO BUILDER

13.21. Message Strategies: Analytical Reports Spurred on in part by the success of numerous television shows and even entire cable networks devoted to remodeling, homeowners across the country are redecorating and rebuilding like never before. Many people are content with superficial changes, such as new paint or new accessories, but some are more ambitious. These homeowners want to move walls, add rooms, redesign kitchens, convert garages to home theaters—the big stuff.

With many consumer trends, publishers try to create magazines that appeal to carefully identified groups of potential readers and the advertisers who'd like to reach them. The do-it-yourself (DIY) market is already served by numerous magazines, but you see an opportunity in those homeowners who tackle the

CASE TABLE 13.1 Selected Employment Data for Engineers and Marketing Staff

Employment Statistic	Engineering Department	Marketing Department
Average number of years of work experience	18.2	16.3
Average number of years of experience in current profession	17.8	8.6
Average number of years with company	12.4	7.9
Average number of years of college education	6.9	4.8
Average number of years between promotions	6.7	4.3
Salary range	$58–165K	$45–85K
Median salary	$77K	$62K

CASE TABLE 13.2 Summary Statements from Department Director Interviews

Question	Engineering Director	Marketing Director
1. Should engineering and marketing professionals receive roughly similar pay?	In general, yes, but we need to make allowances for the special nature of the engineering profession. In some cases, it's entirely appropriate for an engineer to earn more than a marketing person.	Yes.
2. Why or why not?	Several reasons: (1) Top engineers are extremely hard to find, and we need to offer competitive salaries; (2) the structure of the engineering department doesn't provide as many promotional opportunities, so we can't use promotions as a motivator the way marketing can; (3) many of our engineers have advanced degrees, and nearly all pursue continuing education to stay on top of the technology.	Without marketing, the products the engineers create wouldn't reach customers, and the company wouldn't have any revenue. The two teams make equal contributions to the company's success.
3. If we decide to balance pay between the two departments, how should we do it?	If we do anything to cap or reduce engineering salaries, we'll lose key people to the competition.	If we can't increase payroll immediately to raise marketing salaries, the only fair thing to do is freeze raises in engineering and gradually raise marketing salaries over the next few years.

CASE TABLE 13.3 Rooms Most Frequently Remodeled by DIYers

Room	Percentage of Homeowners Surveyed Who Have Tackled or Plan to Tackle at Least a Partial Remodel
Kitchen	60
Bathroom	48
Home office/study	44
Bedroom	38
Media room/home theater	31
Den/recreation room	28
Living room	27
Dining room	12
Sun room/solarium	8

CASE TABLE 13.4 Average Amount Spent on Remodeling Projects

Estimated Amount	Percentage of Surveyed Homeowners
Under $5K	5
$5–10K	21
$10–20K	39
$20–50K	22
More than $50K	13

CASE TABLE 13.5 Tasks Performed by Homeowner on a Typical Remodeling Project

Task	Percentage of Surveyed Homeowners Who Perform or Plan to Perform Most or All of This Task Themselves
Conceptual design	90
Technical design/architecture	34
Demolition	98
Foundation work	62
Framing	88
Plumbing	91
Electrical	55
Heating/cooling	22
Finish carpentry	85
Tile work	90
Painting	100
Interior design	52

heavy-duty projects. Case Tables 13.3 through 13.5 summarize the results of some preliminary research you asked your company's research staff to conduct.

Your task: You think the data show a real opportunity for a "big projects" DIY magazine, although you'll need more extensive research to confirm the size of the market and refine the editorial direction of the magazine. Prepare a brief analytical report that presents the data you have, identifies the opportunity or opportunities you've found (suggest your own ideas based on the tables), and requests funding from the editorial board to pursue further research.

Short Formal Reports Requiring Additional Research

PORTFOLIO BUILDER

13.22. Message Strategies: Analytical Reports Like any other endeavor that combines hard-nosed factual analysis and creative freethinking, the task of writing business plans generates a range of opinions.

Your task: Find at least six sources of advice on writing successful business plans (focus on start-up businesses that are likely to seek outside investors). Use at least two books, two magazine or journal articles, and two websites or blogs. Analyze the advice you find and identify points where most or all the experts agree and points where they don't agree. Wherever you find points of significant disagreement, identify which opinion you find most convincing and explain why. Summarize your findings in a brief formal report.

TEAM SKILLS / PORTFOLIO BUILDER

13.23. Message Strategies: Analytical Reports Anyone looking at the fragmented 21st-century landscape of media and entertainment options might be surprised to learn that poetry was once a dominant medium for not only creative literary expression but philosophical, political, and even scientific discourse. Alas, such is no longer the case.

Your task: With a team of fellow students, your challenge is to identify opportunities to increase sales of poetry—any kind of poetry, in any medium. The following suggestions may help you get started:

- Research recent bestsellers in the poetry field and try to identify why they have been popular.
- Interview literature professors, professional poets, librarians, publishers, and bookstore personnel.
- Conduct surveys and interviews to find out why consumers don't buy more poetry.
- Attend a few poetry slams or readings and talk to the participants about their poetry buying needs and habits.
- Review professional journals that cover the field of poetry, including *Publishers Weekly* and *Poets & Writers*, from both business and creative standpoints.

Summarize your recommendations in a brief formal report; assume that your target readers are executives in the publishing industry.

13.24. Message Strategies: Analytical Reports After 15 years in the corporate world, you're ready to strike out on your own. Rather than building a business from the ground up, however, you think that buying a franchise is a better idea. Unfortunately, some of the most lucrative franchise opportunities, such as the major fast-food chains, require significant start-up costs—some more than a half-million dollars. Fortunately, you've met several potential investors who seem willing to help you get started in exchange for a share of ownership. Between your own savings and money from these investors, you estimate that you can raise from $350,000 to $600,000, depending on how much ownership share you want to concede to the investors.

You've worked in several functional areas already, including sales and manufacturing, so you have a fairly well-rounded business résumé. You're open to just about any type of business, too, as long as it provides the opportunity to grow; you don't want to be so tied down to the first operation that you can't turn it over to a hired manager and expand into another market.

Your task: To convene a formal meeting with the investor group, you first need to draft a report that outlines the types of franchise opportunities you'd like to pursue. Write a brief report, identifying five franchises you would like to explore further. (Choose five based on your own personal interests and the criteria already identified.) For each possibility, identify the nature of the business, the financial requirements, the level of support the company provides, and a brief statement of why you could run such a business successfully (make up any details you need). Be sure to carefully review the information you find about each franchise company to make sure you can qualify for it. For instance, McDonald's doesn't allow investment partnerships to buy franchises, so you won't be able to start up a McDonald's outlet until you have enough money to do it on your own.

For a quick introduction to franchising, see How Stuff Works (http://money.howstuffworks.com/franchising.htm). You can also learn more about the business of franchising at Franchising.com (www.franchising.com). In addition, many companies that sell franchises, such as Subway, offer additional information on their websites.

PORTFOLIO BUILDER

13.25. Message Strategies: Informational Reports Health-care costs are a pressing concern at every level in the economy, from individual households up through companies of all sizes on up to state and federal governments. Many companies that want to continue offering or to start offering some level of health insurance to their employees are struggling with a cost spiral that seems out of control.

Your task: Identify five ways companies are reducing the cost of providing health-care insurance for their employees (other than eliminating this benefit entirely). Compile your findings in a brief report that includes at least one real-life example for each of the five ways.

PORTFOLIO BUILDER

13.26. Message Strategies: Analytical Reports After several false-starts over the past few years, tablet computers to have finally caught on among business users. In addition to Apple's popular iPad, seemingly every computer company on the planet is looking to get a share of this market.

Your task: Prepare a short analytical report that compares the advantages and disadvantages of tablet computers for traveling salespeople.

Long Formal Reports Requiring No Additional Research

PORTFOLIO BUILDER

13.27. Message Strategies: Informational Reports Your company is the largest private employer in your metropolitan area, and the 43,500 employees in your workforce have a tremendous impact on local traffic. A group of city and county transportation officials recently approached your CEO with a request to explore ways to reduce this impact. The CEO has assigned you the task of analyzing the workforce's transportation habits and attitudes as a first step toward identifying potential solutions. He's willing to consider anything from subsidized bus passes to company-owned shuttle buses to telecommuting, but the decision requires a thorough understanding of employee transportation needs. Case Tables 13.6 through 13.10 summarize data you collected in an employee survey.

Your task: Present the results of your survey in an informational report, using the data provided in Case Tables 13.6 through 13.10.

Long Formal Reports Requiring Additional Research

PORTFOLIO BUILDER

13.28. Message Strategies: Informational Reports The partners in your accounting firm have agreed to invest some

CASE TABLE 13.6   Employee Carpool Habits

Frequency of Use: Carpooling	Portion of Workforce
Every day, every week	10,138 (23%)
Certain days, every week	4,361 (10%)
Randomly	983 (2%)
Never	28,018 (64%)

CASE TABLE 13.7   Use of Public Transportation

Frequency of Use: Public Transportation	Portion of Workforce
Every day, every week	23,556 (54%)
Certain days, every week	2,029 (5%)
Randomly	5,862 (13%)
Never	12,053 (28%)

CASE TABLE 13.8 Effect of Potential Improvements to Public Transportation

Which of the Following Would Encourage You to Use Public Transportation More Frequently (check all that apply)	Portion of Respondents
Increased perceptions of safety	4,932 (28%)
Improved cleanliness	852 (5%)
Reduced commute times	7,285 (41%)
Greater convenience: fewer transfers	3,278 (18%)
Greater convenience: more stops	1,155 (6%)
Lower (or subsidized) fares	5,634 (31%)
Nothing could encourage me to take public transportation	8,294 (46%)

Note: This question was asked of respondents who use public transportation randomly or never, a subgroup that represents 17,915 employees, or 41 percent of the workforce.

CASE TABLE 13.9 Distance Traveled to/from Work

Distance You Travel to Work (one way)	Portion of Workforce
Less than 1 mile	531 (1%)
1–3 miles	6,874 (16%)
4–10 miles	22,951 (53%)
11–20 miles	10,605 (24%)
More than 20 miles	2,539 (6%)

CASE TABLE 13.10 Is Telecommuting an Option?

Does the Nature of Your Work Make Telecommuting a Realistic Option?	Portion of Workforce
Yes, every day	3,460 (8%)
Yes, several days a week	8,521 (20%)
Yes, random days	12,918 (30%)
No	18,601 (43%)

of the company's profits in the stock market. A previous team effort identified two leading companies in each of five different industries:

- Boeing; Lockheed Martin (aerospace, defense)
- Hewlett-Packard; Dell (computers and software)
- Barnes & Noble; Amazon (retailing)
- UPS; FedEx (delivery and logistics)

The partners have already done an in-depth financial analysis of all 10 firms, and they have asked you to look for more qualitative information, such as

- Fundamental philosophical differences in management styles, launch and handling of products and services, marketing of products and services, and approach to e-commerce that sets one rival company apart from the other
- Future challenges each competitor faces
- Important decisions made by the two competitors and how those decisions affected their company
- Fundamental differences in each company's vision of its industry's future (for instance, do they both agree on what consumers want, what products to deliver, and so on?)
- Specific competitive advantages of each rival
- Past challenges each competitor has faced and how each met those challenges
- Strategic moves made by one rival that might affect the other
- Company success stories
- Brief company background information
- Brief comparative statistics, such as annual sales, market share, number of employees, number of stores, types of equipment, number of customers, sources of revenue, and so on

Your task: Select two competitors from the preceding list (or another list provided by your instructor) and write a long formal informational report comparing how the two companies are addressing the topics outlined by the partners. Of course, not every topic will apply to each company, and some will be more important than others—depending on the companies you select. The partners will invest in only one of the two companies in your report. (*Note:* Because these topics require considerable research, your instructor may choose to make this a team project.)

PORTFOLIO BUILDER

13.29. Message Strategies: Analytical Reports As a college student and an active consumer, you may have considered one or more of the following questions at some point in the past few years:

a. What criteria distinguish the top-rated MBA programs in the country? How well do these criteria correspond to the needs and expectations of business? Are the criteria fair for students, employers, and business schools?

b. Which of three companies you might like to work for has the strongest corporate ethics policies?

c. What will the music industry look like in the future? What's next after online stores such as Apple iTunes and digital players such as the iPod?

d. Which industries and job categories are forecast to experience the greatest growth—and therefore the greatest demands for workers—in the next 10 years?

e. What has been the impact of Starbucks's aggressive growth on small, independent coffee shops? On midsized chains or franchises? In the United States or in another country?

f. How large is the "industry" of major college sports? How much do the major football or basketball programs contribute—directly or indirectly—to other parts of a typical university?

g. How much have minor league sports—baseball, hockey, arena football—grown in small- and medium-market cities? What is the local economic impact when these municipalities build stadiums and arenas?

Your task: Answer one of these questions, using secondary research sources for information. Be sure to document your sources in the correct form. Make conclusions and offer recommendations where appropriate.

PORTFOLIO BUILDER

13.30. Message Strategies: Analytical Reports An observer surveying the current consumer electronics landscape and seeing Apple products everywhere might be surprised to learn that during part of the company's history, it was regarded by some as a fairly minor player in the computer industry—and at times a few pundits even wondered whether the company would survive.

Your task: In a two- to three-page report, identify the reasons Apple has been successful and explain how other companies can apply Apple's strategies and tactics to improve their business results.

Formal Proposals

PORTFOLIO BUILDER

13.31. Message Strategies: Proposals Presentations can make or break both careers and businesses. A good presentation can bring in millions of dollars in new sales or fresh investment capital. A bad presentation might cause a number of troubles, from turning away potential customers to upsetting fellow employees to derailing key projects. To help business professionals plan, create, and deliver more effective presentations, you offer a three-day workshop that covers the essentials of good presentations:

- Understanding your audience's needs and expectations
- Formulating your presentation objectives
- Choosing an organizational approach
- Writing openings that catch your audience members' attention
- Creating effective graphics and slides
- Practicing and delivering your presentation
- Leaving a positive impression on your audience
- Avoiding common mistakes with Microsoft PowerPoint
- Making presentations online using webcasting tools
- Handling questions and arguments from the audience
- Overcoming the top 10 worries of public speaking (including How can I overcome stage fright? and I'm not the performing type; can I still give an effective presentation?)

Here is some additional information about the workshop:

- **Workshop benefits:** Students will learn how to prepare better presentations in less time and deliver them more effectively.

- **Who should attend:** Top executives, project managers, employment recruiters, sales professionals, and anyone else who gives important presentations to internal or external audiences.

- **Your qualifications:** 18 years of business experience, including 14 years in sales and 12 years in public speaking. Experience speaking to audiences as large as 5,000 people. More than a dozen speech-related articles published in professional journals. Have conducted successful workshops for nearly 100 companies.

- **Workshop details:** Three-day workshop (9 AM to 3:30 PM) that combines lectures, practice presentations, and both individual and group feedback. Minimum number of students: 6. Maximum number of students per workshop: 12.

- **Pricing:** The cost is $3,500, plus $100 per student. 10 percent discount for additional workshops.

- **Other information:** Each attendee will have the opportunity to give three practice presentations that will last from three to five minutes. Everyone is encouraged to bring PowerPoint files containing slides from actual business presentations. Each attendee will also receive a workbook and a digital video recording of his or her final class presentation. You'll also be available for phone or email coaching for six months after the workshop.

Your task: Identify a company in your local area that might be a good candidate for your services. Learn more about the company by visiting its website so you can personalize your proposal. Using the information listed previously in this exercise, prepare a sales proposal that explains the benefits of your training and what students can expect during the workshop.

PORTFOLIO BUILDER

13.32. Message Strategies: Proposals For years, a controversy has been brewing over the amount of junk food and soft drinks being sold through vending machines in local schools. Schools benefit from revenue-sharing arrangements, but many parents and health experts are concerned about the negative effects of these snacks and beverages. You and your brother have almost a decade of experience running espresso and juice stands in malls and on street corners, and you'd love to find some way to expand your business into schools. After a quick brainstorming session, the two of you craft a plan that makes good business sense while meeting the financial concerns of school administrators and the nutritional concerns of parents and dietitians. Here are the notes from your brainstorming session:

- Set up portable juice bars on school campuses, offering healthy fruit and vegetable drinks along with simple healthy snacks.
- Offer schools 30 percent of profits in exchange for free space and long-term contracts.
- Provide job training opportunities for students (during athletic events, etc.).
- Provide detailed dietary analysis of all products sold.
- Establish a nutritional advisory board composed of parents, students, and at least one certified health professional.
- Assure schools and parents that all products are safe (for example, no stimulant drinks, no dietary supplements, and so on).

- Support local farmers and specialty food preparers by buying locally and giving these vendors the opportunity to test market new products at your stands.

Your task: Based on the ideas listed, draft a formal proposal to the local school board, outlining your plan to offer healthier alternatives to soft drinks and prepackaged snack foods. Invent any details you need to complete your proposal.

PORTFOLIO BUILDER

13.33. Message Strategies: Proposals Seems like everybody in the firm is frustrated. On the one hand, top executives complain about the number of lower-level employees who want promotions but just don't seem to "get it" when it comes to dealing with customers and the public, recognizing when to speak out and when to be quiet, knowing how to push new ideas through the appropriate channels, and performing other essential but difficult-to-teach tasks. On the other hand, ambitious employees who'd like to learn more feel that they have nowhere to turn for career advice from people who've been there. In between, a variety of managers and midlevel executives are overwhelmed by the growing number of mentoring requests they're getting, sometimes from employees they don't even know.

You've been assigned the challenge of proposing a formal mentoring program—and a considerable challenge it is:

- The number of employees who want mentoring relationships far exceeds the number of managers and executives willing and able to be mentors. How will you select people for the program?
- The people most in demand for mentoring also tend to be some of the busiest people in the organization.

- After several years of belt tightening and staff reductions, the entire company feels overworked; few people can imagine adding another recurring task to their seemingly endless to-do lists.
- What's in it for the mentors? Why would they be motivated to help lower-level employees?
- How will you measure success or failure of the mentoring effort?

Your task: Identify potential solutions to the issues (make up any information you need) and draft a proposal to the executive committee for a formal, companywide mentoring program that would match selected employees with successful managers and executives.

PORTFOLIO BUILDER / TEAM SKILLS

13.34. Message Strategies: Proposals Either to create opportunities in a slow job market or to avoid traditional employment altogether, some college graduates create their own jobs as independent freelancers or as entrepreneurs launching new companies.

Your task: Assemble a team of classmates as your instructor directs, then brainstorm all the services you could perform for local businesses. Identify as many services as you can that are related to you and your teammates' colleges majors and career interests, but also include anything you are willing to do to generate revenue. Next, identify a specific company that might have some opportunities for you. Outline and draft a short proposal that describes what your team can do for this company, how the company would benefit from your services, why you're the right people for the job, and how much you propose to charge for your services. Remember that this is an unsolicited proposal, so be sure introduce your proposal accordingly.

MyBCommLab

Go to the Assignments section of your MyLab to complete these writing exercises

13.35. Under what circumstances would you include more than one table of contents in a report? [LO-2]

13.36. If you included a bibliography in your report, would you also need to include in-text citations? Please explain. [LO-2]

Endnotes

1. "Writing a Compelling Executive Summary," *Garage Technology Ventures*, accessed 6 March 2015, www.garage.com; "Getting to Wow!" *Garage Technology Ventures*, accessed 6 March 2015, www.garage.com; Guy Kawasaki website, accessed 23 June 2013, www.guykawasaki .com.
2. John Morkes and Jakob Nielsen, "Concise, Scannable, and Objective: How to Write for the Web," *UseIt.com*, accessed 13 November 2006, www.useit.com.

3. Michael Netzley and Craig Snow, *Guide to Report Writing* (Upper Saddle River, N.J.: Prentice Hall, 2001), 57.
4. Oswald M. T. Ratteray, "Hit the Mark with Better Summaries," *Supervisory Management*, September 1989, 43–45.
5. Netzley and Snow, *Guide to Report Writing*, 43.
6. Alice Reid, "A Practical Guide for Writing Proposals," accessed 31 May 2001, http://members.dca.net/areid/proposal.htm.
7. Toby B. Gooley, "Ocean Shipping: RFPs That Get Results," *Logistics Management*, July 2003, 47–52.

14

Developing and Delivering Business Presentations

LEARNING OBJECTIVES

After studying this chapter, you will be able to

1 Highlight the importance of presentations in your business career, and explain how to adapt the planning step of the three-step process to presentations.

2 Describe the tasks involved in developing a presentation.

3 Describe the six major design and writing tasks required to enhance your presentation with effective visuals.

4 Outline four major tasks involved in completing a presentation.

5 Describe four important aspects of delivering a presentation in today's social media environment.

The Serious Side of the Comedy Business

The business of being funny can be profoundly unfunny these days, particularly for comedians who want to break into movies and television shows. Fewer movies are being made, and the audience for television and online shows is so fragmented that trying to build a fan base is an uphill struggle. Making the situation even worse for comedians, many of whom are writers at heart, is the seemingly unstoppable growth of reality shows, which require neither writers nor actors in any conventional sense.

John Shearer/Getty Images

Talent agent Peter Principato (*right*, with actor Will Arnett) coaches his comedian clients to hone their presentations before pitching movie and TV show ideas to studio executives.

Talent agent Peter Principato knows this landscape as well as anyone, and as he puts it, "There's less and less real estate every year." Studios are increasingly reluctant to "green-light" projects, particularly with the young and not-quite-top-of-the-marquee talent that is the specialty of Principato-Young Entertainment, the Beverly Hills company he cofounded with producer Paul Young. But comedy is in Principato's blood, so he works overtime to make his clients successful, even in this challenging environment.

In the entertainment industry, the road to success often starts with "the pitch," a brief presentation to one or more studio executives by an individual writer, actor, director, or producer or by a team of these people. If the executive is intrigued by the concept, it might be discussed further within the studio, and eventually a decision will be made about funding production.

With so much riding on this brief presentation, you can imagine that it's a high-anxiety event for the presenters, requiring vital communication skills. In fact, the ability to pitch effectively is so important that it has its own slang term: being "good in a room."

Pitches can fall flat for a number of reasons, whether the concept is not a good fit for a particular studio, the idea is so unusual that executives are unwilling to risk investing in it, or the pitch is poorly presented. A presenter may fail by being unable to summarize what a new show or movie idea is all about, by smothering executives in too many details, or by trying too hard to sell the concept.

The pointers Principato gives his clients constitute good advice for presentations in any industry, but they're vital in the entertainment industry. First, come up with a single compelling sentence that describes the show or movie. If presenters can't do this, chances are they haven't thought the idea out well enough, or the idea is so complicated that it would be too risky or too expensive to attempt. This one-line summary is essential for another reason, in that the first studio executive to hear the pitch will usually need to share it with other executives or potential financiers before a decision can be made. A catchy, succinct idea is a lot easier to repeat than a rambling, confused concept.

Second, expand on that one sentence with a single paragraph that builds interest by substantiating the concept and helping the listener envision what the show or movie would be like. Third, for a proposed series, explain how the concept would play out, week by week, by describing several episodes. Fourth, fill in the "big picture," such as by describing how the show would look on screen or by rounding out the main characters.

You've probably noticed how this advice follows the classic AIDA model of getting attention, building interest, increasing desire, and asking for a decision, which is what makes Principato's advice valuable for just about any profession.

The funny business is tough and getting tougher, but Principato is clearly doing something right. Principato-Young continues to expand and attract more of the young comedians who might be box office stars for the next several decades. And his love of comedy and comedians continues to motivate Principato himself. As he describes it, having his job "is like getting to hang out with your favorite band."[1]

WWW.PRINCIPATOYOUNG.COM

1 **LEARNING OBJECTIVE**
Highlight the importance of presentations in your business career, and explain how to adapt the planning step of the three-step process to presentations.

Presentations involve all of your communication skills, from research through nonverbal communication.

Creating a high-quality presentation for an important event can take many days, so be sure to allow enough time.

Planning a Presentation

You might not pitch the next Oscar winner to a studio executive as Peter Principato (profiled in the On the Job chapter opener) hopes to do, but wherever your career takes you, speeches and presentations will offer important opportunities to put all your communication skills on display, including research, planning, writing, visual design, and interpersonal and nonverbal communication. Presentations also let you demonstrate your ability to think on your feet, grasp complex business issues, and handle challenging situations—all attributes that executives look for when searching for talented employees to promote.

Planning presentations is much like planning other business messages: You analyze the situation, gather information, select the best media and channels, and organize the information (see Figure 14.1). Gathering information for presentations is essentially the same as it is for written communication projects. The other three planning tasks have some special applications when it comes to oral presentations; they are covered in the following sections.

On the subject of planning, be aware that preparing a professional-quality business presentation can take a considerable amount of time. Nancy Duarte, whose design firm has years of experience creating presentations for corporations, offers this rule of thumb: For a 1-hour presentation, allow 36 to 90 hours to research, conceive, create, and practice.[2] Not every 1-hour presentation justifies a week or two of preparation, of course, but the important presentations that can make your career or your company certainly can.

ANALYZING THE SITUATION

As with written communications, analyzing the situation involves defining your purpose and developing an audience profile (see Table 14.1). The purpose of most of your presentations will be to inform or to persuade, although you may occasionally need to make a

1 Plan →	**2** Write →	**3** Complete
Analyze the Situation Define your purpose and develop a profile of your audience, including their likely emotional states and language preferences.	**Adapt to Your Audience** Adapt your content, presentation style, and room setup to the audience and the specific situation. Be sensitive to audience needs and expectations with a "you" attitude, politeness, positive emphasis, and bias-free language. Plan to establish your credibility as required.	**Revise the Message** Evaluate your content and speaking notes.
Gather Information Determine audience needs and obtain the information necessary to satisfy those needs.		**Master Your Delivery** Choose your delivery mode and practice your presentation.
Choose Medium and Channel Identify the best combination for the situation, message, and audience, including handouts and other support materials.	**Compose Your Presentation** Outline an attention-getting introduction, body, and close. Prepare supporting visuals and speaking notes.	**Prepare to Speak** Verify facilities and equipment, including online connections and software setups. Hire an interpreter if necessary.
Organize the Information Define your main idea, limit your scope and verify timing, select the direct or indirect approach, and outline your content.		**Overcome Anxiety** Take steps to feel more confident and appear more confident on stage.

Figure 14.1 The Three-Step Process for Developing Business Presentations
Although you rarely "write" a presentation or speech in the sense of composing every word ahead of time, the tasks in the three-step writing process adapt quite well to the challenge of planning, creating, and delivering oral and online presentations.

TABLE 14.1 Analyzing Audiences for Business Presentations

Task	Actions
To determine audience size and composition	• Estimate how many people will attend (in person and online). • Identify what they have in common and how they differ. • Analyze the mix of organizational position, professions, language fluencies, and other demographic factors that could influence your content and delivery choices.
To predict the audience's probable reaction	• Analyze why audience members are attending the presentation. • Determine the audience's general attitude toward the topic: interested, moderately interested, unconcerned, open-minded, or hostile. • Analyze your audience's likely mood when you speak to them. • Find out what kind of supporting information will help the audience accept and respond to your message: technical data, historical information, financial data, demonstrations, samples, and so on. • Consider whether the audience has any biases that might work against you. • Anticipate possible objections or questions.
To gauge the audience's experience	• Analyze whether everybody has the same background and level of understanding. • Determine what the audience already knows about the subject. • Consider whether the audience is familiar with the vocabulary you intend to use. • Analyze what the audience expects from you. • Think about the mix of general concepts and specific details you will need to present.

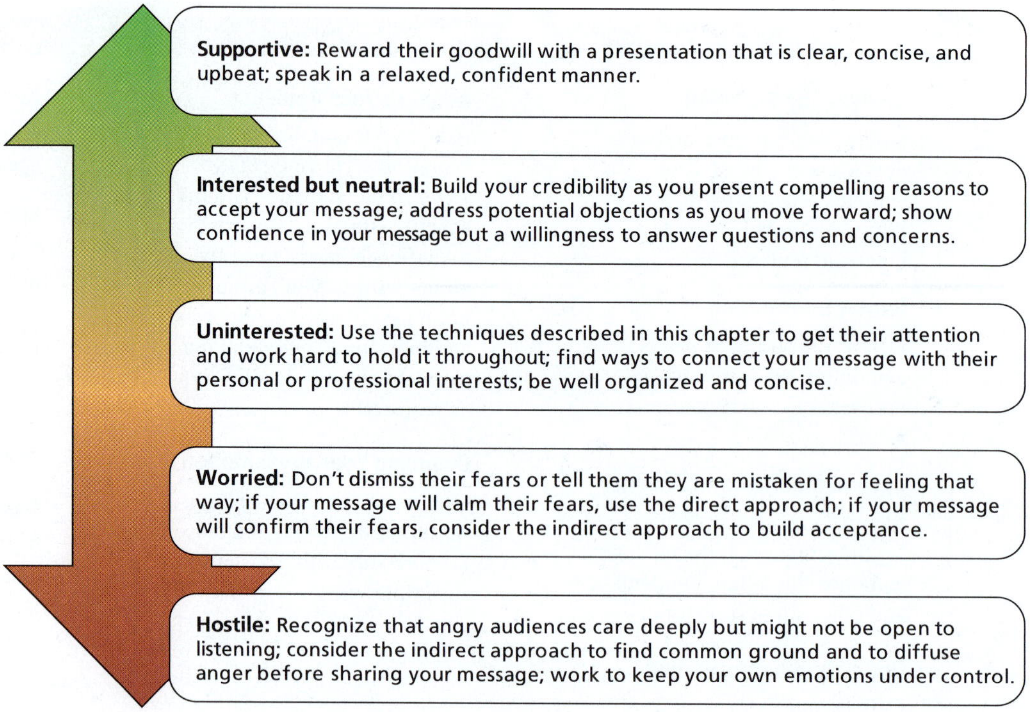

Supportive: Reward their goodwill with a presentation that is clear, concise, and upbeat; speak in a relaxed, confident manner.

Interested but neutral: Build your credibility as you present compelling reasons to accept your message; address potential objections as you move forward; show confidence in your message but a willingness to answer questions and concerns.

Uninterested: Use the techniques described in this chapter to get their attention and work hard to hold it throughout; find ways to connect your message with their personal or professional interests; be well organized and concise.

Worried: Don't dismiss their fears or tell them they are mistaken for feeling that way; if your message will calm their fears, use the direct approach; if your message will confirm their fears, consider the indirect approach to build acceptance.

Hostile: Recognize that angry audiences care deeply but might not be open to listening; consider the indirect approach to find common ground and to diffuse anger before sharing your message; work to keep your own emotions under control.

Figure 14.2 **Planning for Various Audience Mindsets**
Try to assess the emotional state of your audience ahead of time so you can plan your presentation approach accordingly.

Try to learn as much as you can about the setting and circumstances of your presentation, from the size of the audience to seating arrangements.

collaborative presentation, such as when you're leading a problem-solving or brainstorming session.

In addition to following the audience analysis advice in Chapter 4, try to anticipate the likely emotional state of your audience members. Figure 14.2 offers tips for dealing with a variety of audience mindsets.

As you analyze the situation, also consider the circumstances. If some or all of the audience members will be in the same room with you, how will they be seated? Can you control the environment to minimize distractions? What equipment will you need? If some or all of your audience members will be online, how will the meeting system you're using affect their ability to hear and see you and your presentation materials? Such variables can influence not only the style of your presentation but the content itself.

> **REAL-TIME UPDATES**
> LEARN MORE BY WATCHING THIS VIDEO
>
> **Dealing with the difficult four**
>
> Get advice on dealing with four difficult audience members: the Resister, the Expert, the Dominator, and the Rambler. Go to http://real-timeupdates.com/ebc12 and click on "Learn More in the Students section."

SELECTING THE BEST MEDIA AND CHANNELS

For some presentations, you'll be expected to use whatever media and channels your audience, your boss, or the circumstances require. For example, you might be required to use specific presentation software and a conference room's built-in display system or your company's online meeting software.

For other presentations, though, you might be able to choose from an array of presentation modes, from live, in-person presentations to *webcasts* (online presentations that people either view live or download later from the web), screencasts (recordings of activity on computer displays with audio voiceover), or *twebinars* (the use of Twitter as a *backchannel*—see page 465—for real-time conversation during a web-based seminar[3]).

ORGANIZING A PRESENTATION

Linear presentations generally follow a fixed path or from start to finish.

The possibilities for organizing a business presentation fall into two basic categories, *linear* or *nonlinear*. Linear presentations are like printed documents in the sense that they are outlined like conventional messages and follow a predefined flow from start to finish. The linear model is appropriate for speeches, technical and financial presentations, and other presentations in which you want to convey your message point by point or build up to a conclusion following logical steps.

In contrast, a nonlinear presentation doesn't flow in any particularly direction but rather gives the presenter the option to move back and forth between topics and up and down in terms of level of detail. Nonlinear presentations can be useful when you want to be able to show complicated relationships between multiple ideas or elements, to zoom in and out between the "big picture" and specific details, to explore complex visuals, or to have the flexibility to move from topic to topic in any order.

Nonlinear presentation can move back and forth between topics and up and down in levels of detail.

The difference between the two styles can be seen in the type of software typically used to create and deliver a presentation. Microsoft PowerPoint, Apple Keynote, and similar packages use sequences of individual slides, often referred to as a *slide deck*. They don't necessarily need to be presented in a strict linear fashion, because the presenter does have the option of jumping out of the predefined order, but in most presentations using slides the speaker moves from start to finish in that order.

Prezi is the best-known nonlinear presentation software and doesn't use the concept of individual slides. Instead, you start from a main screen, or canvas, which often presents the big-picture overview of your topic (see Figure 14.3). From there, you add individual objects (including blocks of text, photos, or videos) that convey specific information points. When you present, you can zoom in and out, discussing the individual objects and their relationship to the big picture and to each other. You can also establish a narrative flow by defining a path from one object to the next, which also lets people view the presentation on their own[4] (and effectively turns a Prezi presentation into a linear presentation).

Prezi is sometimes viewed as a more dynamic and engaging way to present, and it certainly has that potential. However, keep several points in mind if you have a choice of which approach to take and which software to use. First, match the tool to the task, not the other way around. A detailed technical discussion might need a linear presentation, whereas a free-form brainstorming session might benefit from a nonlinear approach. Second, if they are used well, software features can help you tell your story, but your story

Remember that presentations—using any software or system—are not about flash and dazzle; they are about sharing ideas, information, and emotions with your audience.

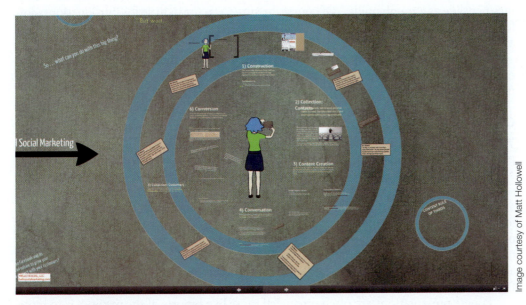

Image courtesy of Matt Hollowell

Figure 14.3 Nonlinear Presentations
Nonlinear presentations, particularly those using the cloud-based Prezi system, give the presenter more freedom in zooming in and out from the big picture to the details and covering topics in any order.

is what matters—not the software. If they are used poorly, software features only get in the way. (Overuse of zooming in Prezi is a good example.[5]) Third, despite their reputation, PowerPoint and other slide programs aren't limited to creating boring, linear flows of bullet points (see "Choosing Structured or Free-Form Slides" on page 454).

Defining Your Main Idea

If you can't express your main idea in a single sentence, you probably haven't defined it clearly enough.

Regardless of which overall approach you take, a successful presentation starts with a clear statement of the main idea you want to share with your audience. Start by composing a one-sentence summary that links your subject and purpose to your audience's frame of reference. Here are some examples:

> Convince management that reorganizing the technical support department will improve customer service and reduce employee turnover.
>
> Convince the board of directors that we should build a new plant in Texas to eliminate manufacturing bottlenecks and improve production quality.
>
> Address employee concerns regarding a new health-care plan by showing how the plan will reduce costs and improve the quality of their care.

Each of these statements puts a particular slant on the subject, one that directly relates to the audience's interests. By focusing on your audience's needs and using the "you" attitude, you help keep their attention and convince them your points are relevant.

Limiting Your Scope

Limiting you scope ensures that your presentation fits the allotted time and your content meets audience needs and expectations.

The only sure way to measure the length of your presentation is to complete a practice run.

Limiting your scope is important with any message, but it's particularly vital with presentations, for two reasons. First, for most presentations, you must work within strict time limits. Second, the longer you speak, the more difficult it is to hold the audience's attention levels, and the more difficult it is for your listeners to retain your key points.[6]

The only sure way to know how much material you can cover in a given time is to practice your presentation after you complete it. If possible, complete a dry run in front of a live audience in order to simulate real-life speaking conditions. As an alternative, if you're using conventional structured slides (see page 454), you can figure on 3 or 4 minutes per slide as a rough guide.[7] Of course, be sure to factor in time for introductions, coffee breaks, demonstrations, question-and-answer sessions, and anything else that takes away from your speaking time.

Approaching time constraints as a creative challenge can actually help you develop more effective presentations. Limitations can force you to focus on the most essential message points that are important to your audience.[8]

Choosing Your Approach

Organize short presentations the same way you would a letter or brief memo; organize long presentations as you would a report or proposal.

With a well-defined main idea to guide you and a clear notion of the scope of your presentation, you can begin to arrange your message. If you have 10 minutes or less, consider organizing your presentation much as you would a letter or other brief message: Use the direct approach if the subject involves routine information or good news, and use the indirect approach if the subject involves bad news or persuasion. Plan your introduction to arouse interest and to give a preview of what's to come. For the body of the presentation, be prepared to explain the who, what, when, where, why, and how of your subject. In the final section, review the points you've made and close with a statement that will help your audience remember the subject of your speech (see Figure 14.4).

Longer presentations are often organized more like reports. If the purpose is to motivate or inform, you'll typically use the direct approach and a structure imposed naturally

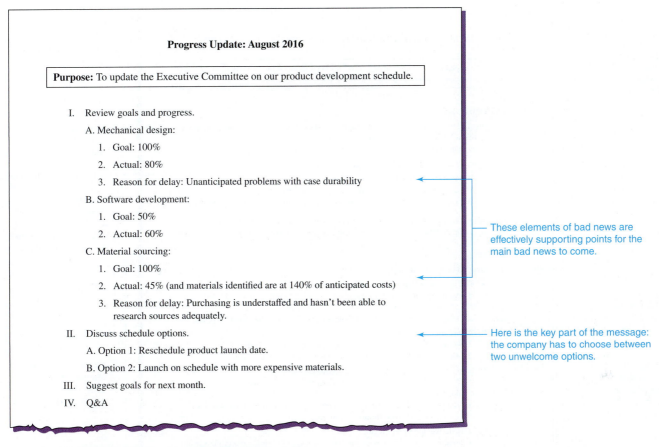

Progress Update: August 2016

Purpose: To update the Executive Committee on our product development schedule.

I.   Review goals and progress.

   A. Mechanical design:

      1. Goal: 100%

      2. Actual: 80%

      3. Reason for delay: Unanticipated problems with case durability

   B. Software development:

      1. Goal: 50%

      2. Actual: 60%

   C. Material sourcing:

      1. Goal: 100%

      2. Actual: 45% (and materials identified are at 140% of anticipated costs)

      3. Reason for delay: Purchasing is understaffed and hasn't been able to research sources adequately.

II. Discuss schedule options.

   A. Option 1: Reschedule product launch date.

   B. Option 2: Launch on schedule with more expensive materials.

III. Suggest goals for next month.

IV. Q&A

These elements of bad news are effectively supporting points for the main bad news to come.

Here is the key part of the message: the company has to choose between two unwelcome options.

Figure 14.4 Effective Outline for a 10-Minute Presentation
Here is an outline of a short presentation that updates management on the status of a key project; the presenter has some bad news to deliver, so she opted for an indirect approach to lay out the reasons for the delay before sharing the news of the schedule slip.

by the subject: comparison, importance, sequence, chronology, geography, or category (as discussed in Chapter 11). If your purpose is to analyze, persuade, or collaborate, organize your material around conclusions and recommendations or around a logical argument. Use the direct approach if the audience is receptive and the indirect approach if you expect resistance.

No matter what the length, look for opportunities to integrate storytelling into the structure of your presentation. The dramatic tension (not knowing what will happen to the "hero") at the heart of effective storytelling is a great way to capture and keep the audience's attention.

Using a storytelling model can be a great way to catch and hold the audience's attention.

Preparing Your Outline

An outline helps you organize your message, and it serves as the foundation for delivering your speech. Prepare your outline in several stages:[9]

In addition to planning your speech, a presentation outline helps you plan your speaking notes.

- State your purpose and main idea, and then use these elements to guide the rest of your planning.
- Organize your major points and subpoints in logical order, expressing each major point as a single, complete sentence.
- Identify major points in the body first, then outline the introduction and close.
- Identify transitions between major points or sections, then write these transitions in full-sentence form.

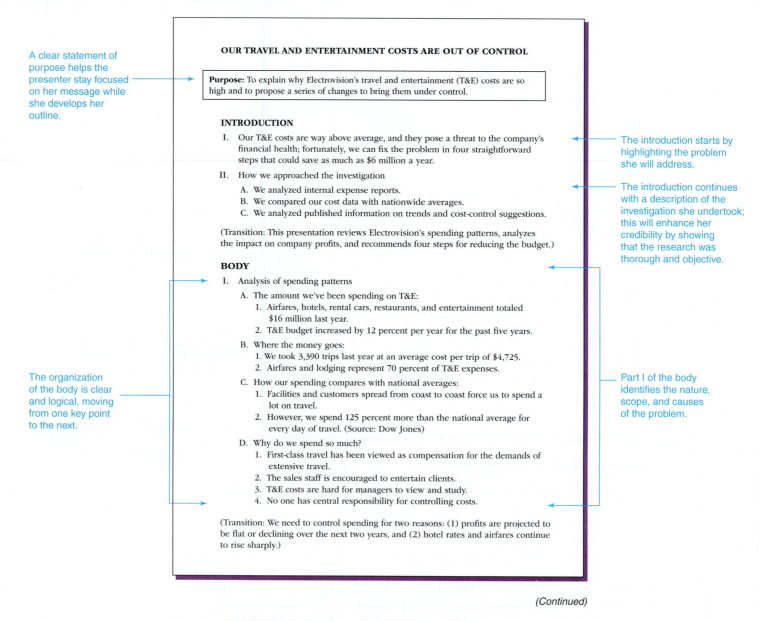

A clear statement of purpose helps the presenter stay focused on her message while she develops her outline.

OUR TRAVEL AND ENTERTAINMENT COSTS ARE OUT OF CONTROL

Purpose: To explain why Electrovision's travel and entertainment (T&E) costs are so high and to propose a series of changes to bring them under control.

INTRODUCTION

I. Our T&E costs are way above average, and they pose a threat to the company's financial health; fortunately, we can fix the problem in four straightforward steps that could save as much as $6 million a year.

II. How we approached the investigation
   A. We analyzed internal expense reports.
   B. We compared our cost data with nationwide averages.
   C. We analyzed published information on trends and cost-control suggestions.

(Transition: This presentation reviews Electrovision's spending patterns, analyzes the impact on company profits, and recommends four steps for reducing the budget.)

BODY

I. Analysis of spending patterns
   A. The amount we've been spending on T&E:
      1. Airfares, hotels, rental cars, restaurants, and entertainment totaled $16 million last year.
      2. T&E budget increased by 12 percent per year for the past five years.
   B. Where the money goes:
      1. We took 3,390 trips last year at an average cost per trip of $4,725.
      2. Airfares and lodging represent 70 percent of T&E expenses.
   C. How our spending compares with national averages:
      1. Facilities and customers spread from coast to coast force us to spend a lot on travel.
      2. However, we spend 125 percent more than the national average for every day of travel. (Source: Dow Jones)
   D. Why do we spend so much?
      1. First-class travel has been viewed as compensation for the demands of extensive travel.
      2. The sales staff is encouraged to entertain clients.
      3. T&E costs are hard for managers to view and study.
      4. No one has central responsibility for controlling costs.

(Transition: We need to control spending for two reasons: (1) profits are projected to be flat or declining over the next two years, and (2) hotel rates and airfares continue to rise sharply.)

The introduction starts by highlighting the problem she will address.

The introduction continues with a description of the investigation she undertook; this will enhance her credibility by showing that the research was thorough and objective.

Part I of the body identifies the nature, scope, and causes of the problem.

The organization of the body is clear and logical, moving from one key point to the next.

(Continued)

Figure 14.5 Effective Outline for a 30-Minute Presentation
This outline clearly identifies the purpose and the distinct points to be made in the introduction, body, and close. Notice also how the speaker has written her major transitions in full-sentence form to be sure she can clearly phrase these critical passages when it's time to speak.

- Prepare your bibliography or source notes; highlight those sources you want to identify by name during your talk.
- Choose a compelling title. Make it brief, action oriented, and focused on what you can do for the audience.[10]

You may find it helpful to create a simpler speaking outline from your planning outline.

Many speakers like to prepare both a detailed *planning outline* (see Figure 14.5) and a simpler *speaking outline* that provides all the cues and reminders they need in order to present their material. To prepare an effective speaking outline, follow these steps:[11]

- Start with the planning outline and then strip away anything you don't plan to say directly to your audience.
- Condense points and transitions to key words or phrases.
- Add delivery cues, such as places where you plan to pause for emphasis or use visuals.
- Arrange your notes on numbered cards or use the notes capability in your presentation software.

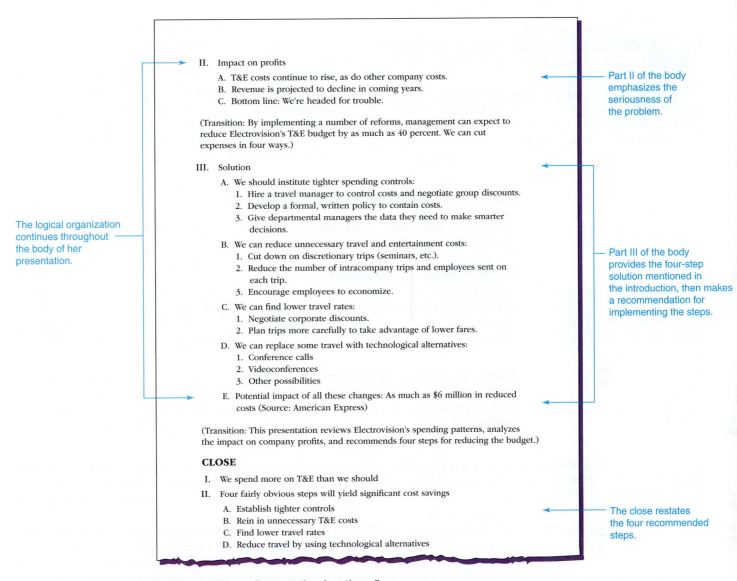

II. Impact on profits

    A. T&E costs continue to rise, as do other company costs.
    B. Revenue is projected to decline in coming years.
    C. Bottom line: We're headed for trouble.

(Transition: By implementing a number of reforms, management can expect to reduce Electrovision's T&E budget by as much as 40 percent. We can cut expenses in four ways.)

III. Solution

    A. We should institute tighter spending controls:
        1. Hire a travel manager to control costs and negotiate group discounts.
        2. Develop a formal, written policy to contain costs.
        3. Give departmental managers the data they need to make smarter decisions.
    B. We can reduce unnecessary travel and entertainment costs:
        1. Cut down on discretionary trips (seminars, etc.).
        2. Reduce the number of intracompany trips and employees sent on each trip.
        3. Encourage employees to economize.
    C. We can find lower travel rates:
        1. Negotiate corporate discounts.
        2. Plan trips more carefully to take advantage of lower fares.
    D. We can replace some travel with technological alternatives:
        1. Conference calls
        2. Videoconferences
        3. Other possibilities
    E. Potential impact of all these changes: As much as $6 million in reduced costs (Source: American Express)

(Transition: This presentation reviews Electrovision's spending patterns, analyzes the impact on company profits, and recommends four steps for reducing the budget.)

CLOSE

I. We spend more on T&E than we should

II. Four fairly obvious steps will yield significant cost savings

    A. Establish tighter controls
    B. Rein in unnecessary T&E costs
    C. Find lower travel rates
    D. Reduce travel by using technological alternatives

The logical organization continues throughout the body of her presentation.

Part II of the body emphasizes the seriousness of the problem.

Part III of the body provides the four-step solution mentioned in the introduction, then makes a recommendation for implementing the steps.

The close restates the four recommended steps.

Figure 14.5 Effective Outline for a 30-Minute Presentation *(continued)*

Developing a Presentation

2 **LEARNING OBJECTIVE** Describe the tasks involved in developing a presentation.

Although you usually don't write out a presentation word for word, you still engage in the writing process—developing your ideas, structuring support points, phrasing your transitions, and so on. Depending on the situation and your personal style, the eventual presentation might follow your initial words closely, or you might express your thoughts in fresh, spontaneous language.

ADAPTING TO YOUR AUDIENCE

The size of your audience, the venue (in person or online), your subject, your purpose, your budget, and the time available for preparation all influence the style of your presentation. If you're speaking to a small group, particularly people you already know, you can use a casual style that encourages audience participation. A small conference room, with your audience seated around a table, may be appropriate. Use simple visuals and invite

Adapting to your audience involves a number of issues, from speaking style to technology choices.

your audience to interject comments. Deliver your remarks in a conversational tone, using notes to jog your memory if necessary.

If you're addressing a large audience or if the event is important, establish a more formal atmosphere. During formal presentations, speakers are often on a stage or platform, standing behind a lectern and using a microphone so that their remarks can be heard throughout the room or captured for broadcasting or webcasting.

CRAFTING PRESENTATION CONTENT

Like written documents, oral presentations are composed of distinct elements: the introduction, the body, and the close.

Presentation Introduction

> An effective introduction arouses interest in your topic, establishes your credibility, and prepares the audience for the body of your presentation.

A good introduction fires up the audience's interest in your topic, establishes your credibility, and prepares your listeners for the information and insights you have to share. That's a lot to accomplish in the first few minutes, so give yourself plenty of time to develop the words and visuals you'll use to get your presentation off to a great start.

Getting Your Audience's Attention   Some subjects are naturally more interesting to some audiences than others. If your presentation involves the health, wealth, or happiness of your listeners, most people will be interested, regardless of how you begin. With other subjects, though, you need to use some imagination to pull people in. Here are seven ways to arouse audience interest:[12]

> Spend some time thinking about the best technique to capture the audience's attention and interest with your opening remarks.

- If it's appropriate for the presentation, encourage your listeners to unite around a meaningful business objective. For example, if the company is struggling and your presentation offers a turnaround solution, you could start by urging your listeners to join together for the common good.
- Open with a brief story that makes a point relevant to your presentation. Be sure to keep it brief and directly on topic so listener attention doesn't start to wander.
- Consider using a prop or some other kind of visual that relates to your main idea. This gives you an opportunity to be clever and creative, as long as it's appropriate for the setting. If your presentation is about how the company's outdated policies keep customer service agents from offering top-quality service, you might walk on stage with yours hands tied together to illustrate employee frustration about having their "hands tied" by rigid policies. To point your listeners in the direction of your main idea, ask a question that your presentation will end up answering. If you're sharing the results of a consumer research project, for instance, you might open with "Why do some consumers reject our products and buy from one of our competitors?"
- Surprise or shock your listeners with an important and relevant statistic or detail, such as "If we could cut product returns in half, we would save enough to give every person in this room a 10-percent raise."
- In the right circumstances, you can open with some appropriate humor that helps endear you to the audience, shows empathy with your listeners, or sheds some light on your subject matter. Humor needs to be approached with great care, however. If you open with a joke that is irrelevant, offensive, or simply not funny, you'll dig yourself into a hole before you even start your presentation.
- Open with a bold and specific promise about how the presentation will help your audience by providing valuable insights, information, or inspiration.

Regardless of which technique you choose, make sure you can give audience members a reason to care and to believe that the time they're about to spend listening to you will be worth their while.[13] The more you can make your opening about your listeners and their concerns, the more likely they will be to lock in your message and stay tuned.

Building Your Credibility   Audiences tend to decide within a few minutes whether you're worth listening to, so establishing your credibility quickly is vital.[14] If you're not a well-known expert or haven't already earned your audience's trust in other situations, you'll need to build credibility in your introduction. If someone else will introduce you, he or she can present your credentials. If you will be introducing yourself, keep your comments brief, but don't be afraid to mention your accomplishments. Your listeners will be curious about your qualifications, so tell them briefly who you are, why you're there, and how they'll benefit from listening to you. You might say something like this:

> I'm Karen Whitney, a market research analyst with Information Resources Corporation. For the past five years, I've specialized in studying high-technology markets. Your director of engineering, John LaBarre, asked me to talk about recent trends in computer-aided design so that you'll have a better idea of how to direct your development efforts.

This speaker establishes credibility by tying her credentials to the purpose of her presentation. By mentioning her company's name, her specialization and position, and the name of the audience's boss, she lets her listeners know immediately that she is qualified to tell them something they need to know.

If someone else will be introducing you, ask this person to present your credentials.

Previewing Your Message   In addition to getting the audience's attention and establishing your credibility, a good introduction gives your audience a preview of what's ahead. Your preview should summarize the main idea of your presentation, identify major supporting points, and indicate the order in which you'll develop those points. By giving listeners the framework of your message, you help them process the information you'll be sharing, Of course, if you're using the indirect approach, you'll have to decide how much of your main idea to give away in the introduction.

Offer a preview to help your audience understand the importance, the structure, and the content of your message.

Presentation Body

The bulk of your presentation is devoted to a discussion of the main points in your outline. No matter what organizational pattern you're using, your goals are to make sure that the organization is clear and that you hold the audience's attention.

Connecting Your Ideas   In written documents, you can show how ideas are related with a variety of design clues: headings, paragraph indentions, white space, and lists. However, with oral communication—particularly when you aren't using visuals for support—you have to rely primarily on spoken words to link various parts and ideas.

For the links between sentences and paragraphs, use one or two transitional words: *therefore, because, in addition, in contrast, moreover, for example, consequently, nevertheless,* or *finally*. To link major sections of a presentation, use complete sentences or paragraphs, such as "Now that we've reviewed the problem, let's take a look at some solutions." Every time you shift topics, be sure to stress the connection between ideas by summarizing what's been said and previewing what's to come. The longer your presentation, the more important your transitions. Your listeners need clear transitions to guide them to the most important points. Furthermore, they'll appreciate brief interim summaries to pick up any ideas they may have missed.

Use transitions to repeat key ideas, particularly in longer presentations.

Holding Your Audience's Attention   A successful introduction will have grabbed your audience's attention; now the body of your presentation needs to hold that attention. Here are a few helpful tips for keeping the audience tuned into your message:

- Keep relating your subject to your audience's needs.
- Anticipate—and answer—likely questions as you move along so people don't get confused or distracted.

REAL-TIME UPDATES

LEARN MORE BY VISITING THIS WEBSITE

The latest tools and trends in presentations

From design trends to new software tools, this blog covers the newest ideas in presentations. Go to http://real-timeupdates.com/ebc12 and click on Learn More in the Students section.

The most important way to hold an audience's attention is to show how your message relates to their individual needs and concerns.

- Use clear, vivid language and throw in some variety; repeating the same words and phrases over and over puts people to sleep.
- Show how your subject is related to ideas that audience members already understand, and give people a way to categorize and remember your points.[15]
- If appropriate, encourage participation by asking for comments or questions.
- Illustrate your ideas with visuals, which enliven your message, help you connect with audience members, and help them remember your message more effectively (see "Enhancing Your Presentation with Effective Visuals," pages 453–460).

Presentation Close

Plan your close carefully so that your audience leaves with a clear summary of your main idea.

The close of a speech or presentation has two critical tasks to accomplish: making sure your listeners leave with the key points from your talk clear in their minds and putting your audience in the appropriate emotional state. For example, if the purpose of your presentation is to warn managers that their out-of-control spending threatens the company's survival, you want them to leave with that message ringing in their ears—and with enough concern for the problem to stimulate changes in their behavior.

When you repeat your main idea in the close, emphasize what you want your audience to do or to think.

Restating Your Main Points   Use the close to succinctly restate your main points, emphasizing what you want your listeners to do or to think. For example, to close a presentation on your company's executive compensation program, you could repeat your specific recommendations and then conclude with a memorable statement to motivate your audience to take action:

> We can all be proud of the way our company has grown. However, if we want to continue that growth, we need to take four steps to ensure that our best people don't start looking for opportunities elsewhere:
>
> - First, increase the overall level of compensation
> - Second, establish a cash bonus program
> - Third, offer a variety of stock-based incentives
> - Fourth, improve our health insurance and pension benefits
>
> By taking these steps, we can ensure that our company retains the management talent it needs to face our industry's largest competitors.

Repetition of key ideas, as long as you don't overdo it, greatly improves the chance that your audience will hear your message in the way you intended.

Plan your final statement carefully so you can end on a strong, positive note.

Ending with Clarity and Confidence   If you've been successful with the introduction and body of your presentation, your listeners now have the information they need, and they're in the right frame of mind to put that information to good use. Now you're ready to end on a strong note that confirms expectations about any actions or decisions that will follow the presentation—and to bolster the audience's confidence in you and your message one final time.

Some presentations require the audience to reach a decision or agree to take specific action, in which case the close should provide a clear wrap-up. If the audience reached agreement on an issue covered in the presentation, briefly review the consensus. If they didn't agree, make the lack of consensus clear by saying something like "We seem to have some fundamental disagreement on this question." Then be ready to suggest a method of resolving the differences.

If you expect any action to occur as a result of your speech, be sure to identify who is responsible for doing what. List the action items and, if possible within the time you have available, establish due dates and assign responsibility for each task.

Being a Team Player

Professionals know that they are contributors to a larger cause, that it's not all about them. Just as in athletics and other team efforts, being a team player in business is something of a balancing act. On the one hand, you need to pay enough attention to your own efforts and skills to make sure you're pulling your own weight. On the other hand, you need to pay attention to the overall team effort to make sure the team succeeds. Remember that if the team fails, you fail, too.

Great team players know how to make those around them more effective, whether it's by lending a hand during crunch time, sharing resources, removing obstacles, making introductions, or offering expertise. In fact, the ability to help others improve their performance is one of the key attributes executives look for when they want to promote people into management.

Being a team player also means showing loyalty to your organization and protecting your employer's reputation—one of the most important assets any company has. Pros don't trash their employers in front of customers or in their personal blogs. When they have a problem, they solve it; they don't share it.

CAREER APPLICATIONS

1. If you prefer to work by yourself, should you take a job in a company that uses a team-based organization structure? Why or why not?
2. You can see plenty of examples of unprofessional business behavior in the news media and in your own consumer and employee experiences. Why should you bother being professional yourself?

Make sure your final remarks are memorable and expressed in a tone that is appropriate to the situation. For example, if your presentation is a persuasive request for project funding, you might emphasize the importance of this project and your team's ability to complete it on schedule and within budget. Expressing confident optimism will send the message that you believe in your ability to perform. Conversely, if your purpose is to alert the audience to a problem or risk, false optimism will undermine your message.

Whatever final message is appropriate, think through your closing remarks carefully before stepping in front of the audience. You don't want to wind up on stage with nothing to say but "Well, I guess that's it."

> Make sure your final remarks are memorable and have the right emotional tone.

Enhancing Your Presentation with Effective Visuals

> **3 LEARNING OBJECTIVE**
> Describe the six major design and writing tasks required to enhance your presentation with effective visuals.

Slides and other visuals can improve the quality and impact of your presentation by creating interest, illustrating points that are difficult to explain in words alone, adding variety, and increasing the audience's ability to absorb and remember information.

You can select from a variety of visuals to enhance presentations. Don't overlook "old-school" technologies such as overhead transparencies, chalkboards, whiteboards, and flipcharts; they can all have value in the right circumstances. However, most business presentation visuals are created using Microsoft PowerPoint, Apple Keynote, or Google Documents for linear presentations and Prezi for nonlinear presentations. Presentations slides and "Prezis" are easy to edit and update; you can add sound, photos, video, and animation; they can be incorporated into online meetings, webcasts, and *webinars* (a common term for web-based seminars); and you can record self-running presentations for trade shows, websites, and other uses.

> Thoughtfully designed visuals create interest, illustrate complex points in your message, add variety, and help the audience absorb and remember information.

> **MOBILE APP**
> With Apple Keynote, you can create and deliver presentations on your iOS mobile devices.

Presentation slides are practically universal in business today, but their widespread use is not always welcome. You may have already heard the expression "death by PowerPoint," which refers to the agonizing experience of sitting through too many poorly conceived and poorly delivered slide shows. In the words of presentation expert and author Garr Reynolds, "most presentations remain mind-numbingly dull, something to be endured by presenter and audience alike."[16]

That's the bad news. The good news is that both linear and nonlinear presentations can provide an experience that is satisfying, and sometimes even enjoyable, for presenter and audience alike. Start with the mindset of *simplicity* (clear ideas presented clearly) and *authenticity* (talking *with* your audience about things they care about, rather than talking at

> Focusing on making your presentations simple and authentic will help you avoid the "death by PowerPoint" stigma that presentations have in the mind of many professionals.

them or trying to be a "performer"), and you'll be well on your way to becoming an effective presenter.

CHOOSING STRUCTURED OR FREE-FORM SLIDES

Structured slides are usually based on templates that give all the slides in a presentation the same general look (which usually involves a lot of bullet points); free-form slides are much less rigid and emphasize visual appeal.

Free-form slides often have far less content per slide than structured designs, which requires many more slides to cover a presentation of equal length.

For linear presentations, the most important design choice you face when creating slides is whether to use conventional, bullet point-intensive **structured slides** or the looser, visually oriented **free-form slides** that many presentation specialists now advocate. Compare the two rows of slides in Figure 14.6. The structured slides in the top row follow the same basic format throughout the presentation. In fact, they're based directly on the templates built into PowerPoint, which tend to feature lots and lots of bullet points.

The free-form slides in the bottom row don't follow a rigid structure. However, free-form designs should not change randomly from one slide to the next. Effectively designed slides should still be unified by design elements such as color and font selections, as can be seen in Figures 14.6 (c) and 14.6 (d). Also, note how Figure 14.6d combines visual and textual messages to convey the point about listening without criticizing. This complementary approach of pictures and words is a highlight of free-form design.

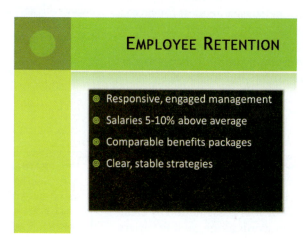

Figure 14.6 (a)

Figure 14.6 (b)

Figure 14.6 (c)

Figure 14.6 (d)

Figure 14.6 **Structured Versus Free-Form Slide Design**
Compare the rigid, predictable design of the two slides in the top row with the more dynamic free-form designs in the bottom row. Although the two free-form slides don't follow the same design structure, they are visually linked by color and font choices. Note that Figure 14.6 (d) is a humorous way of conveying the first bullet point in Figure 14.6 (b).

Advantages and Disadvantages of Structured Slides

Structured slides have the advantage of being easy to create; you simply choose an overall design scheme for the presentation, select a template for a new slide, and start typing. If you're in a schedule crunch, going the structured route might save the day because at least you'll have *something* ready to show. Given the speed and ease of creating them, structured slides can be a more practical choice for routine presentations such as project status updates.

Also, because more information can usually be packed on each slide, carefully designed structured slides can be more effective at conveying complex ideas or sets of interrelated data to the right audiences. For example, if you are talking to a group of executives who must decide where to make budget cuts across the company's eight divisions, at some point in the presentation they will probably want to see summary data for all eight divisions on a single slide for easy comparison. Such a slide would be overcrowded by the usual definition, but this might be the only practical way to get a "big-picture" view of the situation. (The best solution is probably some high-level, summary slides supported by a detailed handout, as "Creating Effective Handouts" on page 461 explains.)

The primary disadvantage of structured design is that mind-numbing effect Garr Reynolds describes caused by text-heavy slides that all look alike. Slide after slide of dense, highly structured bullet points with no visual relief can put an audience to sleep.

Structured slides are often the best choice for project updates and other routine information presentations, particularly if the slides are intended to be used only once.

Advantages and Disadvantages of Free-Form Slides

Free-form slides can overcome the drawbacks of text-heavy structured design. Such slides can fulfill three criteria researchers have identified as important for successful presentations: (1) providing complementary information through both textual and visual means, (2) limiting the amount of information delivered at any one time to prevent cognitive overload, and (3) helping viewers process information by identifying priorities and connections, such as by highlighting the most important data points in a graph.[17] (Of course, well-designed structured slides can also meet these criteria, but the constraints of prebuilt templates make doing so more of a challenge.)

With appropriate imagery, free-form designs can also create a more dynamic and engaging experience for the audience. Given their ability to excite and engage, free-form designs are particularly good for motivational, educational, and persuasive presentations—particularly when the slides will be used multiple times and therefore compensate for the extra time and effort required to create them.

Free-form slides have several potential disadvantages, however. First, effectively designing slides with both visual and textual elements is more creatively demanding and more time-consuming than simply typing text into preformatted templates. The emphasis on visual content also requires more images, which take time to find.

Second, because far less textual information tends to be displayed on screen, the speaker is responsible for conveying more of the content. Ideally, of course, this is how a presentation *should* work, but presenters sometimes find themselves in less-than-ideal circumstances, such as being asked to fill in for a colleague on short notice.

Third, if not handled carefully, the division of information into smaller chunks can make it difficult to present complex subjects in a cohesive, integrated manner. For instance, if you're discussing a business problem that has five interrelated causes, it might be helpful to insert a conventional bullet-point slide as a summary and reminder after discussing each problem on its own.

Well-designed free-form slides help viewers understand, process, and remember the speaker's message.

Free-form slides can require more skill and time to create, and they put more demands on the speaker during the presentation.

DESIGNING EFFECTIVE SLIDES

Despite complaints about "death by PowerPoint," the problem is not with that software itself (or with Apple Keynote or any other presentation program). It is just a tool and, like other tools, can be used well or poorly. Unfortunately, lack of design awareness, inadequate training, schedule pressures, and the instinctive response of doing things the way they've always been done can lead to ineffective slides and lost opportunities to really connect with audiences. And although Prezi is sometimes promoted as the antidote to

Use presentation software wisely to avoid the "death by PowerPoint" stigma that presentations have in the mind of many professionals.

PowerPoint, using Prezi does not guarantee you'll end up with an effective presentation; it, too, can be misused and wind up creating a barrier between the speaker and the audience.

Another reason for ineffective slides is the practice of treating slide sets as standalone documents that can be read on their own, without a presenter. (The emergence of websites such as SlideShare might be contributing to this problem, too, by making it so easy to share slide sets.) These "slideument" hybrids that try to function as both presentation visuals and printed documents don't work well as either: They often have too much information to be effective visuals and too little to be effective reports (in addition to being clumsy to read).

As the section "Creating Effective Handouts" on page 461 explains, the ideal solution is to create an effective slide set and a separate handout document that provides additional details and supporting information. This way, you can optimize each piece to do the job it is really meant to do. An alternative is to use the notes field in your presentation software to include your speaking notes for each slide. Anyone who gets a copy of your slides can at least follow along by reading your notes, although you will probably need to edit and embellish them to make them understandable by others.

However, if creating slideuments is your only option for some reason, be sure to emphasize clarity and simplicity. If you have to add more slides to avoid packing individual slides with too much text, by all means do so. Having a larger number of simpler slides is a better compromise all around than a smaller number of jam-packed slides. Remember that the primary purpose of the slides is supporting your presentation, so make sure your slides work well for that purpose.

> "Slideuments" are hybrids that try to function as both presentations slides and readable documents—and usually fail at both tasks.

> Rather than packing your slides with enough information to make them readable as standalone documents, complement well-designed slides with printed handouts.

REAL-TIME UPDATES

LEARN MORE BY VISITING THIS WEBSITE

Advice and free templates for more-effective slideuments

The free ebook and a pair of PowerPoint templates will help you make more-effective slide-document hybrids. Go to http://real-timeupdates.com/ebc12 and click on Learn More in the Students section.

Designing Slides Around a Key Visual

> Organizing a slide around a key visual can help the audience quickly grasp how ideas are related.

With any type of presentation, it is often helpful to structure specific slides around a key visual that helps organize and explain the points you are trying to make. For example, a pyramid suggests a hierarchical relationship, and a circular flow diagram emphasizes that the final stage in a process loops back to the beginning of the process. Figure 14.7 shows six of the many types of visual designs you can use to organize information on a slide.

Writing Readable Content

> Use slide text sparingly and only to emphasize key points, not to convey your entire message.

One of the most common mistakes beginners make—and one of the chief criticisms leveled at structured slide designs in general—is stuffing slides with too much text. Doing so overloads the audience with too much information too fast, takes attention away from the speaker by forcing people to read more, and requires the presenter to use smaller type.

Effective text slides supplement your words and help the audience follow the flow of ideas (see Figure 14.8 on page 458). Use text to highlight key points, summarize and preview your message, signal major shifts in thought, illustrate concepts, or help create interest in your spoken message.

Creating Charts and Tables for Slides

> Charts and tables for presentations need to be simpler than visuals for printed documents.

Charts and tables for presentations need to be simpler than visuals for printed documents. Detailed images that look fine on the printed page can be too dense and too complicated for presentations. Remember that your audience will view your slides from across the room—not from a foot or two away, as you do while you create them. Keep the level of detail to a minimum, eliminating anything that is not absolutely essential. If necessary, break information into more than one chart or table. It may also be useful to provide detailed versions of charts and tables in a handout.

MOBILE APP

authorSTREAM lets you replay webcasts and other recorded presentations on your mobile device.

Selecting Design Elements

As you create slides, pay close attention to the interaction of color, background and foreground designs, artwork, typefaces, and type styles:

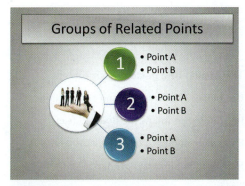

Figure 14.7 (a)

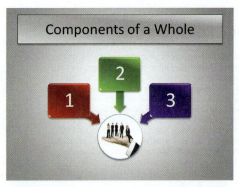

Figure 14.7 (b)

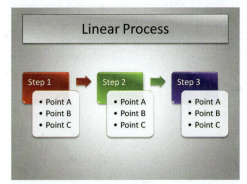

Figure 14.7 (c)

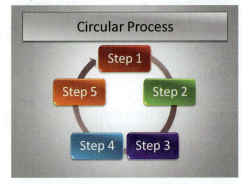

Figure 14.7 (d)

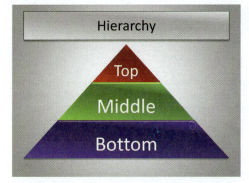

Figure 14.7 (e)

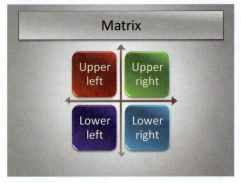

Figure 14.7 (f)

Figure 14.7   Using a Key Visual to Organize Points on a Slide
Simple graphical elements such as these "SmartArt" images in Microsoft PowerPoint make it easy to organize slide content using a key visual. Whether you're trying to convey the relationship of ideas in a hierarchy, a linear process, a circular process, or just about any other configuration, a key visual can work in tandem with your written and spoken messages to help audiences get your message.

- **Color.** Color is a critical design element that can grab attention, emphasize important ideas, create contrast, influence acceptance of your ideas, improve retention, and stimulate a variety of emotions (see Table 14.2 on the next page).[18] Color is powerful, so use it carefully.
- **Background designs and artwork.** All visuals have two layers of design: the *background* and the *foreground*. The background is the equivalent of paper in a printed document, and the elements in the foreground are the essential content of your slides. Make sure the background stays in the background and doesn't distract viewers or compete with the foreground. (Note that many of the template designs in presentation software have backgrounds that are too distracting for serious business use.)
- **Foreground designs and artwork.** The foreground contains the unique text and graphic elements that make up each individual slide. Foreground elements can be

Color is more than just decoration; colors have meanings themselves, based on both cultural experience and the relationships that you established between the colors in your designs.

Make sure the background of your slides stays in the background; it should never get in the way of the informational elements in the foreground.

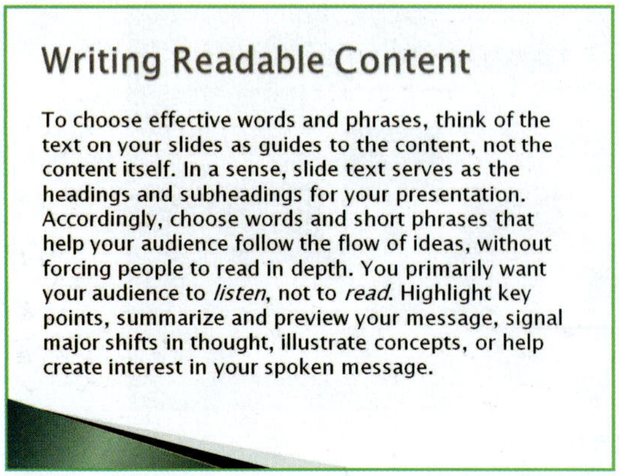

Writing Readable Content

To choose effective words and phrases, think of the text on your slides as guides to the content, not the content itself. In a sense, slide text serves as the headings and subheadings for your presentation. Accordingly, choose words and short phrases that help your audience follow the flow of ideas, without forcing people to read in depth. You primarily want your audience to *listen*, not to *read*. Highlight key points, summarize and preview your message, signal major shifts in thought, illustrate concepts, or help create interest in your spoken message.

Figure 14.8 (a)

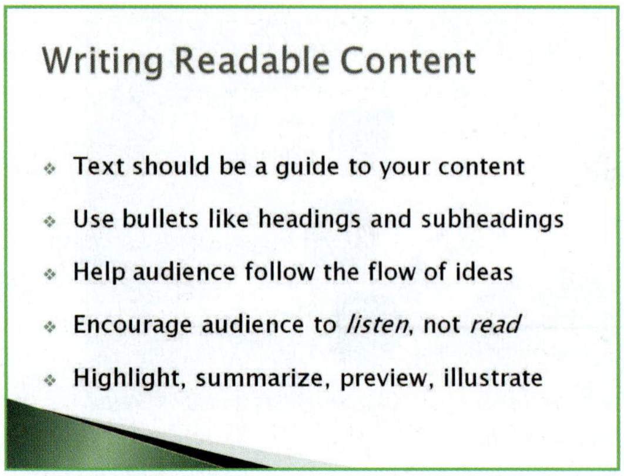

Writing Readable Content

- ❖ Text should be a guide to your content
- ❖ Use bullets like headings and subheadings
- ❖ Help audience follow the flow of ideas
- ❖ Encourage audience to *listen*, not *read*
- ❖ Highlight, summarize, preview, illustrate

Figure 14.8 (b)

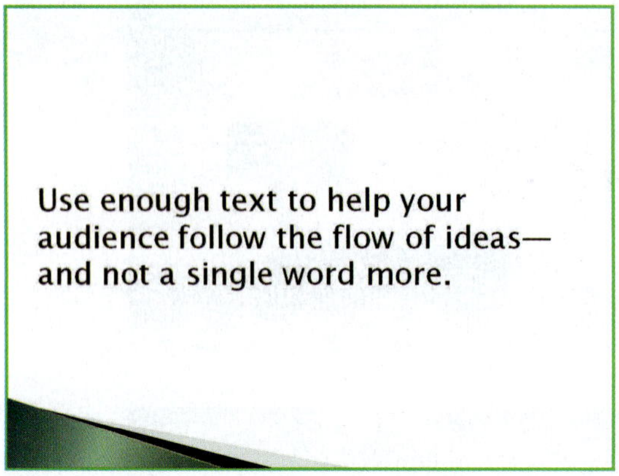

Use enough text to help your audience follow the flow of ideas—and not a single word more.

Figure 14.8 (c)

Just enough

Figure 14.8 (d)

Figure 14.8 Writing Text for Slides
Effective text slides are clear, simple guides that help the audience understand and remember the speaker's message. Notice the progression toward simplicity in these slides: Figure 14.8 (a) is a paragraph that would distract the audience for an extended period of time. Figure 14.8 (b) offers concise, readable bullets, although too many slides in a row in this structured design would become tedious. Figure 14.8 (c) distills the message down to a single thought that is complete on its own but doesn't convey all the information from the original and would need embellishment from the speaker. Figure 14.8 (d) pushes this to the extreme, with only the core piece of the message to serve as an "exclamation point" for the spoken message. Figure 14.8 (c), and especially Figure 14.8 (d), could be even more powerful with a well-chosen visual that illustrates the idea of following the flow.

TABLE 14.2	Color and Emotion	
Color	**Emotional Associations (for U.S. audiences)**	**Best Uses**
Blue	Peaceful, soothing, tranquil, cool, trusting	Background for electronic business presentations (usually dark blue); safe and conservative
White	Neutral, innocent, pure, wise	Font color of choice for most electronic business presentations with a dark background
Yellow	Warm, bright, cheerful, enthusiastic	Text bullets and subheadings with a dark background
Red	Passionate, dangerous, active, painful	For promoting action or stimulating the audience; seldom used as a background ("in the red" specifically refers to financial losses)
Green	Assertive, prosperous, envious, relaxed	Highlight and accent color (green symbolizes money in the United States but not in other countries).

Source: Claudyne Wilder and David Fine, *Point, Click & Wow* (San Francisco: Jossey-Bass Pfeiffer, 1996), 63, 527.

either functional or decorative. *Functional artwork* includes photos, technical drawings, charts, and other visual elements containing information that's part of your message. In contrast, *decorative artwork* simply enhances the look of your slides and should be using sparingly, if at all.

- **Typefaces and type styles.** Type is harder to read on screen than on the printed page, so you need to choose fonts and type styles with care. Sans serif fonts are usually easier to read than serif fonts. Use both uppercase and lowercase letters, with generous space between lines of text, and limit the number of fonts to one or two per slide. Choose font sizes that are easy to read from anywhere in the room, usually between 28 and 36 points, and test them in the room if possible. A clever way to test readability at your computer is to stand back as many feet from the screen as your screen size in inches (17 feet for a 17-inch screen, for example). If the slides are readable at this distance, you're probably in good shape.[19]

Many of the typefaces available on your computer are difficult to read on screen, so they aren't good choices for presentation slides.

REAL-TIME UPDATES
LEARN MORE BY READING THIS ARTICLE
Inspire your presentations with advice from these bloggers

These visual design specialists offer advice and inspiration that can benefit all business presenters. Go to http://real-timeupdates.com/ebc12 and click on Learn More in the Students section.

Maintaining design consistency is critical because audiences start to assign meaning to visual elements beginning with the first slide. For instance, if yellow is used to call attention to the first major point in your presentation, viewers will expect the next occurrence of yellow to also signal an important point. The *slide master* feature makes consistency easy to achieve because it applies consistent design choices to every slide in a presentation.

Design inconsistencies confuse and annoy audiences; don't change colors and other design elements randomly throughout your presentation.

Adding Animation and Multimedia

Today's presentation software offers many options for livening up your slides, including sound, animation, video clips, transition effects, hyperlinks, and zooming. Think about the impact that all these effects will have on your audience, and use only those special effects that support your message.[20]

Functional animation involves motion that is directly related to your message, such as a highlight arrow that moves around the screen to emphasize specific points in a technical diagram. Such animation is also a great way to demonstrate sequences and procedures. In contrast, *decorative animation*, such as having a block of text cartwheel in from off screen or using the zooming and panning capabilities in Prezi in ways that don't enhance audience understanding, needs to be incorporated with great care. These effects don't add any functional value, and they easily distract audiences.

You can animate just about everything in an electronic presentation, but resist the temptation to do so; make sure an animation has a purpose.

Slide transitions control how one slide replaces another, such as having the current slide gently fade out before the next slide fades in. Subtle transitions like this can ease your viewers' gaze from one slide to the next, but many of the transition effects now available are little more than distractions and are best avoided. **Slide builds** control the release of text, graphics, and other elements on individual slides. With builds, you can make key points appear one at a time rather than having all of them appear on a slide at once, thereby making it easier for you and the audience to focus on each new message point.

If you use transitions between slides, make sure they are subtle; they should do nothing more than ease the eye from one slide to the next.

A *hyperlink* instructs your computer to jump to another slide in your presentation, to a website, or to another program entirely. Using hyperlinks is also a great way to build in flexibility so that you can instantly change the flow of your presentation in response to audience feedback.

Hyperlinks let you build flexibility into your presentations.

Multimedia elements offer the ultimate in active presentations. Using audio and video clips can be a great way to complement your textual message. Just be sure to keep these elements brief and relevant, as supporting points for your presentation, not as replacements for it.

INTEGRATING MOBILE DEVICES IN PRESENTATIONS

Smartphones and tablets offer a variety of ways to enhance presentations for presenters as well as audience members (see Figure 14.9 on the next page). For example, you can get around the problem of everyone in the audience having a clear view of the screen with systems that broadcast your slides to tablets and smartphones. In fact, these systems can

MOBILE APP
SlideShark lets you present and share PowerPoint slides with mobile and PC users.

Figure 14.9 Using Mobile Devices in Presentations
A variety of mobile apps and cloud-based systems can free presenters and audiences from the constraints of a conventional conference room.

eliminate a conventional projection system entirely; everyone in the audience can view your slides on their mobile devices. You can also broadcast a live presentation to mobile users anywhere in the world. Each time you advance to a new slide, it is sent to the phone or tablet of everyone who is subscribed to your presentation.[21]

4 **LEARNING OBJECTIVE**
Outline four major tasks involved in completing a presentation.

Completing a Presentation

The completion step for presentations involves a wider range of tasks than most printed documents require. Make sure you allow enough to time to test your presentation slides, verify equipment operation, practice your speech, and create handout materials. With a first draft of your presentation in hand, revise your slides to make sure they are readable, concise, consistent, and fully operational (including transitions, builds, animation, and multimedia). Complete your production efforts by finalizing your slides, creating handouts, choosing your presentation method, and practicing your delivery.

FINALIZING YOUR SLIDES

Electronic presentation software can help you throughout the editing and revision process. For example, the *slide sorter* view (different programs have different names for this feature) lets you see some or all of the slides in your presentation on a single screen. Use this view to add and delete slides, reposition slides, check slides for design consistency, and verify the operation of any effects. Moreover, the slide sorter is a great way to review the flow of your story.[22]

In addition to using content slides, you can help your audience follow the flow of your presentation by creating slides for your title, agenda and program details, and navigation:

- **Title slide(s).** You can make a good first impression with one or two title slides, the equivalent of a report's cover and title page.
- **Agenda and program details.** These slides communicate the agenda for your presentation and any additional information the audience might need, such as hashtags and WiFi log-in information.

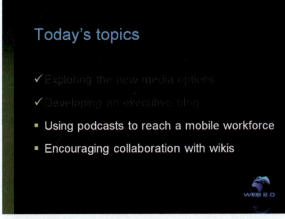

Figure 14.10 (a)

Figure 14.10 (b)

Figure 14.10   **Blueprint Slides**
Here are two ways you can use a *blueprint slide* as a navigational aid to help your audience stay on track with the presentation. Figure 14.10 (a) visually "mutes" and checks off the sections of the presentation that have already been covered. In contrast, Figure 14.10 (b) uses a sliding highlight box to indicate the next section to be covered.

- **Navigation slides.** To tell your audience where you're going and where you've been, you can use a series of **navigation slides**. A simple way to do this is to repeat your agenda slide at the beginning of each major section in your presentation, with the up-coming section highlighted in some way (see Figure 14.10).

Navigation slides help your audience keep track of what you've covered already and what you plan to cover next.

Figure 14.11 on the next page illustrates some of the many options you have for presenting various types of information. Note that although these slides don't follow a rigid structure of text-heavy bullet points, they are unified by the color scheme (silver background and bold color accents) and typeface selections.

CREATING EFFECTIVE HANDOUTS

Handouts—any printed materials you give the audience to supplement your talk—should be considered an integral part of your presentation strategy. Handouts can include detailed charts and tables, case studies, research results, magazine articles, and anything else that supports the main idea of your presentation.

Use handout materials to support the points made in your presentation and to offer the audience additional information on your topic.

Plan your handouts as you develop your presentation so that you use each medium as effectively as possible. Your presentation should paint the big picture, convey and connect major ideas, set the emotional tone, and rouse the audience to action (if that is relevant to your talk). Your handouts can then carry the rest of the information load, providing the supporting details that audience members can consume at their own speed, on their own time. You won't need to worry about stuffing every detail into your slides, because you have the more appropriate medium of printed documents to do that. As Garr Reynolds puts it, "Handouts can set you free."[23]

For a quick review of the key steps in creating effective visuals, see "Checklist: Enhancing Presentations with Visuals." For the latest information on presentation design, visit **http://real-timeupdates.com/ebc12** and click on Chapter 14.

CHOOSING YOUR PRESENTATION METHOD

With all your materials ready, your next step is to decide which method of speaking you want to use. Speaking from notes (rather than from a fully written script) is nearly always the most effective and easiest delivery mode. This approach gives you something to refer to as you progress while still allowing for plenty of eye contact, a natural speaking flow, interaction with the audience, and improvisation in response to audience feedback.

In nearly all instances, speaking from notes (rather than a full script) is the most effective delivery mode.

Left: This introductory slide is a blunt attention-getter, something that would have to be used with caution and only in special circumstances.

Right: This simple math equation gets the point across about how expensive high employee turnover is.

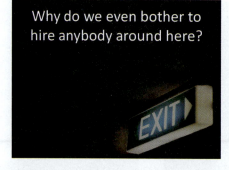

Left: This stylized bar graph sends a stark visual message about how bad the company's turnover really is.

Right: This slide is essentially a bullet list, with three groups of two bullets each. Repeating the photo element from the introductory slide emphasizes the message about employee turnover.

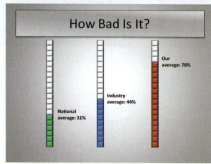

These two *navigation slides* show one way to introduce each of the four subtopics in this particular section. As the highlight moves around the central circle, the audience is reminded of which subtopics have been covered and which subtopic is going to be covered next. And each time it is shown, the message is repeated that all these problems are the "true cost of chaos" in the company's employment practices.

Left: This slide introduces three key points the speaker wants to emphasize in this particular section.

Right: This slide shows a linear flow of ideas, each with bulleted subpoints. This slide could be revealed one section at a time to help the speaker keep the audience's attention focused on a single topic.

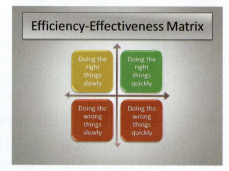

Left: This flowchart packs a lot of information onto one slide, but seeing the sequence of events in one place is essential.

Right: This simple visual highlights the presenter's spoken message about being careful to choose the right tasks to focus on and then completing them quickly.

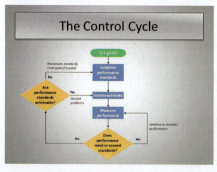

Figure 14.11 **Designing Effective Visuals: Selected Slides**
These slides, from a presentation that addresses a company's high employee turnover rate, illustrate the wide variety of design options for creating effective, appealing slides. (All the slides were created using features in PowerPoint.)

CHECKLIST: ✔ Enhancing Presentations With Visuals

A. Plan your presentation visuals.
- Make sure you and your message, not your visuals, remain the focus of your presentation.
- Follow effective design principles, with an emphasis on simplicity and authenticity.

B. Choose structured or free-form slides.
- Structured slides using bullet-point templates are easy to create, require little design time or skill, and can be completed in a hurry. Best uses: routine, internal presentations
- Free-form slides make it easier to combine textual and visual information, to create a more dynamic and engaging experience, and to maintain a conversational connection with the audience. Best uses: motivational, educational, and persuasive presentations

C. Design effective slides.
- Avoid the temptation to create "slideuments," slides that are so packed with information that they can be read as stand-alone documents.
- Use a key visual to organize related ideas in a clear and meaningful way.
- Write text content that will be readable from everywhere in the room.
- Write short, active, parallel phrases that support, not replace, your spoken message.
- Limit the amount of text so that your audience can focus on listening, not reading.
- Use color to emphasize important ideas, create contrast, isolate visual elements, and convey intended nonverbal signals.
- Limit color to a few compatible choices and use them consistently.

- Make sure your slide background doesn't compete with the foreground.
- Use decorative artwork sparingly and only to support your message.
- Emphasize functional artwork—photos, technical drawings, charts, and other visual elements containing information that is part of your message.
- Choose typefaces that are easy to read on screen; limit the number of typefaces and use them consistently.
- Use slide masters to maintain consistency throughout your presentation.
- Use functional animation when it can support your message.
- Make sure slide transitions are subtle, if used at all.
- Use builds carefully to control the release of information.
- Use hyperlinks and action buttons to add flexibility to your presentation.
- Incorporate multimedia elements that can help engage your audience and deliver your message.

D. Complete slides and support materials.
- Review every slide carefully to ensure accuracy, consistency, and clarity.
- Make sure that all slides are fully operational.
- Use the slide sorter to verify and adjust the sequence of slides, if needed.
- Have a backup plan in case your electronic presentation plan fails.
- Create navigation and support slides.
- Create handouts to complement and support your presentation message.

In contrast, reciting your speech from memory is nearly always a bad idea. Even if you can memorize the entire presentation, you will sound stiff and overly formal because you are "delivering lines," rather than talking to your audience. However, memorizing a quotation, an opening statement, or a few concluding remarks can bolster your confidence and strengthen your delivery.

Reading a speech is necessary in rare instances, such as when delivering legal information, policy statements, or other messages that must be conveyed in an exact manner. However, for all other business presentations, reading is a poor choice because it limits your interaction with the audience and lacks the fresh, dynamic feel of natural talking.

Another important decision at this point is preparing the venue where you will speak. In many instances, you won't have much of a choice, and in some situations, you won't even be able to visit the venue ahead of time. However, if you do have some control over the environment, think carefully about the seating for the audience, your position in the room, and the lighting. For instance, dimming the lights is common practice for many presenters, but dimming them too far can hamper the nonverbal communication between you and your audience and therefore limit opportunities for interaction.[24]

PRACTICING YOUR DELIVERY

Practicing your presentation is essential. Practice boosts your confidence, gives you a more professional demeanor, and lets you verify the operation of your visuals and

The more you practice, the more confidence you'll have in yourself and your material.

equipment. A test audience can tell you if your slides are understandable and whether your delivery is effective. A day or two before you're ready to step on stage for an important talk, make sure you and your presentation are ready:

Make sure you're comfortable with the equipment you'll be expected to use; you don't want to be fumbling with controls while the audience is watching and waiting.

- Can you present your material naturally, without reading your slides?
- Could you still make a compelling and complete presentation if you experience an equipment failure and have to proceed without using your slides at all?
- Is the equipment working, and do you know how to work it?
- Is your timing on track?
- Can you easily pronounce all the words you plan to use?
- Have you anticipated likely questions and objections?

If you're addressing an audience that doesn't speak your language, consider using an interpreter. Send your interpreter a copy of your speech and visuals as far in advance of your presentation as possible. If your audience is likely to include persons with hearing impairments, be sure to team up with a sign-language interpreter as well.

When you deliver a presentation to people from other cultures, you may need to adapt the content of your presentation. It is also important to take into account any cultural differences in appearance, mannerisms, and other customs. Your interpreter or host will be able to suggest appropriate changes for a specific audience or occasion.

Delivering a Presentation

5 LEARNING OBJECTIVE
Describe four important aspects of delivering a presentation in today's social media environment.

It's show time. This section offers practical advice on four important aspects of delivery: overcoming anxiety, handling questions responsively, embracing the backchannel, and giving presentations online.

OVERCOMING ANXIETY

Preparation is the best antidote for anxiety; it gives you confidence that you know your material and that you can recover from any glitches you might encounter.

Even seasoned pros get a little nervous before a big presentation, and that is a good thing. Nervousness is an indication that you care about your audience, your topic, and the occasion. These techniques will help you convert anxiety into positive energy:[25]

- **Stop worrying about being perfect.** Successful speakers focus on making an authentic connection with their listeners, rather than on trying to deliver a note-perfect presentation.
- **Know your subject.** The more familiar you are with your material, the less panic you'll feel.
- **Practice, practice, practice.** The more you rehearse, the more confident you will feel.
- **Visualize success.** Visualize mental images of yourself in front of the audience, feeling confident, prepared, and able to handle any situation that might arise.[26] Remember that your audience wants you to succeed, too.
- **Remember to breathe.** Tension can lead people to breathe in a rapid and shallow fashion, which can create a lightheaded feeling. Breathe slowly and deeply to maintain a sense of calm and confidence.
- **Be ready with your opening line.** Have your first sentence memorized so you don't have to improvise your opening.
- **Be comfortable.** Dress appropriately but as comfortably as possible. Drink plenty of water ahead of time to hydrate your voice (bring a bottle of water with you, too).
- **Take a three-second break if you need to.** If you sense that you're starting to race, pause and arrange your notes or perform some other small task while taking several deep breaths. Then start again at your normal pace.
- **Concentrate on your message and your audience, not on yourself.** When you're busy thinking about your subject and observing your audience's response, you tend to forget your fears.

REAL-TIME UPDATES
LEARN MORE BY READING THIS ARTICLE
Two secrets to presenting like a pro
Read how to build your confidence and stay in the moment. Go to http://real-timeupdates.com/ebc12 and click on Learn More in the Students section.

- **Maintain eye contact with friendly audience members.** Eye contact not only makes you appear sincere, confident, and trustworthy but can give you positive feedback as well.
- **Keep going.** Things usually get better as you move along, with each successful minute giving you more and more confidence.

HANDLING QUESTIONS RESPONSIVELY

Whether you take them during a formal question-and-answer (Q&A) period or as they come up during your presentation, questions are often one of the most important parts of a presentation. They give you a chance to obtain important information, to emphasize your main idea and supporting points, and to build enthusiasm for your point of view. When you're speaking to high-ranking executives in your company, the Q&A period will often consume most of the time allotted for your presentation.[27]

Whether or not you can establish ground rules for questions depends on the audience and the situation. If you're presenting to a small group of upper managers or potential investors, for example, you will probably have no say in the matter: Audience members will likely ask as many questions as they want, whenever they want, to get the information they need. On the other hand, if you are presenting to your peers or a large public audience, establish some guidelines, such as the number of questions allowed per person and the overall time limit for questions.

Don't assume you can handle whatever comes up without some preparation.[28] Learn enough about your audience members to get an idea of their concerns, and think through answers to potential questions.

When people ask questions, pay attention to nonverbal signals to help determine what each person really means. Repeat the question to confirm your understanding and to ensure that the entire audience has heard it. If the question is vague or confusing, ask for clarification; then give a simple, direct answer.

If you are asked a difficult or complex question, avoid the temptation to sidestep it. Offer to meet with the questioner afterward if the issue isn't relevant to the rest of the audience or if giving an adequate answer would take too long. If you don't know the answer, don't pretend you do. Instead, offer to get a complete answer as soon as possible.

Be on guard for audience members who use questions to make impromptu speeches or to take control of your presentation. Without offending anyone, find a way to stay in control. You might admit that you and the questioner have differing opinions and offer to get back to the questioner after you've done more research.[29]

If a question ever puts you on the hot seat, respond honestly but keep your cool. Look the person in the eye, answer the question as well as you can, and keep your emotions under control. Defuse hostility by paraphrasing the question and asking the questioner to confirm that you've understood it correctly. Maintain a businesslike tone of voice and a pleasant expression.[30]

EMBRACING THE BACKCHANNEL

Many business presentations these days involve more than just the conversation between the speaker and his or her audience. Using Twitter and other electronic media, audience members often carry on their own parallel communication during a presentation via the **backchannel**, which presentation expert Cliff Atkinson defines as "a line of communication created by people in an audience to connect with others inside or outside the room, with or without the knowledge of the speaker."[31] Chances are you've participated in a backchannel already, such as when texting with your classmates or live-blogging during a lecture.

The backchannel presents both risks and rewards for business presenters. On the negative side, for example, listeners can research your claims the instant you make them and spread the word quickly if they think your information is shaky. The backchannel also gives contrary audience members more leverage, which can lead to presentations spinning out of control. On the plus side, listeners who are excited about your message can

Don't leave the question-and-answer period to chance: Anticipate potential questions and think through your answers.

If you don't have the complete answer to an important question, offer to provide it after the presentation.

If you ever face hostile questions, respond honestly and directly while keeping your cool.

Twitter and other social media are changing business presentations by making it easy for all audience members to participate in the backchannel.

Resist the urge to ignore or fight the backchannel; instead, learn how to use it to your advantage.

build support for it, expand on it, and spread it to a much larger audience in a matter of seconds. You can also get valuable feedback during and after presentations.[32]

By embracing the backchannel, rather than trying to fight it or ignore it, presenters can use this powerful force to their advantage. Follow these tips to make the backchannel work for you:[33]

- **Integrate social media into the presentation process.** For example, you can create a website for the presentation so that people can access relevant resources during or after the presentation, create a Twitter hashtag that everyone can use when sending tweets, or display the Twitterstream during Q&A so that everyone can see the questions and comments on the backchannel.
- **Monitor and ask for feedback.** Using a free service such as TweetDeck, which organizes tweets by hashtag and other variables, you can monitor comments from people in the audience. To avoid trying to monitor the backchannel while speaking, you can schedule "Twitter breaks," during which you review comments and respond as needed.
- **Review comments point by point to improve your presentation.** After a presentation is over, review comments on audience members' Twitter accounts and blogs to see which parts confused them, which parts excited them, and which parts seemed to have little effect (based on few or no comments).
- **Automatically tweet key points from your presentation while you speak.** Add-ons for presentation software can send out prewritten tweets as you show specific slides during a presentation. By making your key points readily available, you make it easy for listeners to retweet and comment on your presentation.
- **Establish expectations with the audience.** Explain that you welcome audience participation, but to ensure a positive experience for everyone, comments should be civil, relevant, and productive.

GIVING PRESENTATIONS ONLINE

Online presentations give you a way to reach more people in less time, but they require special preparation and skills.

Online presentations offer many benefits, including the opportunity to communicate with a geographically dispersed audience at a fraction of the cost of travel and the ability for a project team or an entire organization to meet at a moment's notice. However, this format also presents some challenges for the presenter, thanks to that layer of technology between you and your audience. Many of those "human moments" that guide and encourage you through an in-person presentation won't travel across the digital divide. For instance, it's often difficult to tell whether audience members are bored or confused, because your view of them is usually confined to small video images (and sometimes not even that).

To ensure successful online presentations, keep the following advice in mind:

- **Consider sending preview study materials ahead of time.** Doing so allows audience members to familiarize themselves with any important background information. Also, by using a free service such as SlideShare, you can distribute your presentation slides to either public or private audiences, and you can record audio narrative to make your presentations function on their own.[34] Some presenters advise against giving out your slides ahead of time, however, because doing so gives away the ending of your presentation, so to speak.
- **Keep your presentation as simple as possible.** Break complicated slides down into multiple slides if necessary, and keep the direction of your discussion clear so that no one gets lost.
- **Ask for feedback frequently.** You won't have as much of the visual feedback that alerts you when audience members are confused, and many online viewers will be reluctant to call attention to themselves by interrupting you to ask for clarification. Setting up a backchannel via Twitter or as part of your online meeting system will help in this regard.
- **Consider the viewing experience from the audience members' point of view.** Will they be able to see what you think they can see? For instance, webcast video

is typically displayed in a small window on-screen, so viewers may miss important details.

- **Allow plenty of time for everyone to get connected and familiar with the screen they're viewing.** Build extra time into your schedule to ensure that everyone is connected and ready to start.

Last but not least, don't get lost in the technology. Use these tools whenever they'll help, but remember that the most important aspect of any presentation is getting the audience to receive, understand, and embrace your message.

For the latest information on online presentations, visit **http://real-timeupdates .com/ebc12** and click on Chapter 14.

ON THE JOB: SOLVING COMMUNICATION DILEMMAS AT
PRINCIPATO-YOUNG ENTERTAINMENT

You share Peter Principato's love of comedy, and now you get to learn from his decades of experience in the business. You've joined Principato-Young as an apprentice talent manager, working side by side with Principato to coach comedians through their careers and to pitch TV and movie ideas to studio executives.

Principato was struck by the rapport you established with Lysette Laria, a new client, and he has asked you to team up with Laria to pitch a new weekly situation comedy she created, tentatively called *You Just Missed Me.* In it she will play a character on the run from the mob who hides in plain sight in various professions—impersonating a new character every week and generally making a mess of every job she steps into.

1. You and Laria know how important an attention-getting opening is when it comes to pitching a new show. You have a meeting with a studio executive next week, and you've brainstormed five possibilities. Which of these should you use?
   a. You don't want to miss *You Just Missed Me!*
   b. *You Just Missed Me* gives comic treatment to a fear that many of us have or can imagine having: being uncovered as a fraud.
   c. Just imagine what it would be like to go to work in disguise every day with the fear that your real identity might be uncovered.
   d. *M.A.S.H., Cheers, Seinfeld, Friends, The Office*—which sitcom is next to join these classics in the pantheon of money-making shows?
   e. Imagine all the trouble you could get into by clumsily faking your way through a new profession every day of your life, all while running from a bunch of bad guys who are as clueless as they are heartless.

2. When Laria first described her show's concept to Principato, he chuckled at the comic possibilities but then went glum when he stopped to consider the cost and complexity of producing a show set in a different location every episode. He knows any studio executive will have the same reservations. How should you and Laria handle this objection in your pitch?

   a. Emphasize that if the show turns out to be as popular as you honestly believe it will be, it will generate high ratings, which will lead to higher advertising rates, which will then pay for the higher production costs.
   b. See if you can identify any other successful shows that have had to use a variety of sets and use them as justification for whatever *You Just Missed Me* is likely to cost.
   c. Explain to the studio executive that you will adapt the episode storylines to fit the studio's existing sets, whatever those are.
   d. Do some research to find out which shows and movies this studio has produced in the past and which of those sets are still available. Then sketch out two or three episodes that could adapt these specific resources to help keep costs down.

3. You've seen Laria perform in comedy clubs a dozen times, and on stage she is witty, chatty, and relaxed. Unfortunately, off stage she is withdrawn and fidgety, giving the impression that she is either terrified to be in someone's presence or so bored she can't wait to leave. Neither impression will help in a pitch meeting where you're trying to sell her as the capable star of a show that will cost millions of dollars to produce. How should you handle the situation?

   a. As awkward as Laria is in one-on-one settings, she will be the star of the show, so she simply has to step up and perform in the pitch meeting. Let her give the presentation and just hope her on-stage persona somehow comes through. Or hope that the studio executive finds her quirky personality appealing somehow.
   b. Send her for some emergency training sessions so that she can become "good in a room." Then let her give the presentation.
   c. You are comfortable giving presentations and actually enjoy meeting with executives, so you should give the presentation yourself. Laria will come along, but only as a prop and proof that she exists, without saying anything beyond simple introductions.

d. You should give the bulk of the presentation but plan it so that Laria can weave in a few of her comedy routines along the way, as though she were on stage. This will show off her talents without draining the life out of the presentation.

4. Principato warned you that some studio executives can be blunt, but that didn't prepare you for the shock you received after you and Laria gave your pitch. The executive sat silently for a long moment and then without even looking at you, asked in a derisive tone, "Seriously? Is that the best you can do?" How should you respond to this hostile question?

a. Respond with confidence, saying, "Yes, it absolutely is the best."

b. Respond with a question, asking the executive if he has specific concerns about the show.

c. Respond with an air of submissive respect, saying, "Well, if you don't like it, I suppose we could tweak the format or come up with something else."

d. Respond with confidence, saying, "Yes, it absolutely is the best, and we're happy to walk out of here and pitch it to another studio."

Learning Objectives Checkup

Assess your understanding of the principles in this chapter by reading each learning objective and studying the accompanying exercises. You can check your responses against the answer key on page 599.

Objective 14.1: Highlight the importance of presentations in your business career, and explain how to adapt the planning step of the three-step process to presentations.

1. _____ presentations are outlined like conventional messages and follow a predefined flow from start to finish; _____ presentations don't flow in any particularly direction but rather give the presenter the option to move back and forth between topics and up and down in terms of level of detail

2. Which of the following is the best way to know how much material you can cover in a given amount of time?
   a. Divide the amount of time you have for your presentation by 20 to figure out how many slides you can show.
   b. Figure on one or two slides per main heading in your planning outline.
   c. For the equivalent of 100 words of written speech, plan to create one slide.
   d. Complete a dry run in front of a live audience after you've developed your speaking notes, slides, and other materials.

3. If you are facing an audience that is apprehensive about what you might have to say in a presentation, which of the following approaches is best?
   a. Even if your presentation will confirm their worst fears, use the direct approach to confront the negative emotions head-on.
   b. If your message will calm their fears, use the direct approach; if your message will confirm their fears, consider the indirect approach to build acceptance.
   c. Ignore the emotional undercurrents and focus on the practical content of your message.
   d. Diffuse the situation with a humorous story that dismisses the audience members' fears.

Objective 14.2: Describe the tasks involved in developing a presentation.

4. Which of the following is the best way to arouse interest in a presentation to a group of fellow employees on the importance of taking ownership of the problem whenever a customer calls in with a complaint?
   a. "If customers leave, so do our jobs."
   b. "Everything we want as employees of this company—from stable jobs to pay raises to promotional opportunities—depends on one thing: satisfied customers."
   c. "How are customers supposed to get their problems solved if we keep passing the buck from one person to the next without ever doing anything?"
   d. "The company's profit margins depend on satisfied customers, and it's up to us to make sure those customers are satisfied."

5. If you suspect that your audience doesn't really care about the topic you plan to discuss, how can you generate interest in your presentation?
   a. Look for ways to help them relate to the information on a personal level, such as helping the company ensure better job security.
   b. Speak louder and, if possible, use lots of sound effects and visual special effects in your presentation.
   c. Show your passion for the material by speaking faster than normal and pacing the room in an excited fashion.
   d. Show that you care about their feelings by saying up front that you don't really care about the topic either, but you've been assigned to talk about it.

6. If you're giving a presentation in a subject area you've researched thoroughly but in which you don't have any hands-on experience (suppose your topic is coordinating a major facility relocation or hiring a tax attorney, for instance), which of these steps should you take to build credibility?
   a. During your introduction, explain that your presentation is the result of research that you've done and briefly explain the extent of the research.
   b. Explain that you don't have any experience in the subject area, but you've done some research.
   c. Emphasize that you know a great deal about the subject matter.
   d. Sidestep the issue of credibility entirely in the introduction and let your knowledge shine through during the body of your presentation.

7. Which of the following would do the best job of holding an audience's attention during a presentation on the growing importance of social networking in corporate

communication? In this particular case, the audience members are all managers of the same company, but they represent a half-dozen countries and speak four different native languages (although they all have basic English skills).

   a. "Social networks are now an important feature in the corporate communication landscape."

   b. "Successful managers around the world now view social networks as an essential tool in their communication efforts."

   c. "Millions of customers and employees are now hip to the latest wave to blow through corporate communication, the clumsily named but nevertheless vital social network."

   d. "I personally get dozens of interesting social networking updates every day, which is solid evidence of how important social networks have become."

8. Your company recently relocated from another state, and the owners are eager to begin building a positive relationship with the local community. You've been asked to speak to employees about volunteering in various community organizations. Which of the following statements does the best job of communicating the owners' wishes while appealing to employees' personal interests?

   a. "Becoming involved in community organizations is a great way for you and your families to meet new people and feel more at home in your new city."

   b. "Becoming involved in community organizations shows our new neighbors that we're an organization of positive, caring people—and it's a great way for you and your families to meet new people and feel more at home in your new city."

   c. "We really owe it to our new community to give back by volunteering."

   d. "The owners feel it is vital for us to become more involved in the community."

9. Which of these techniques is mentioned in the chapter as a way to hold an audience's attention during a presentation?

   a. Speak louder than average.

   b. Tell people that management expects them to pay attention.

   c. Use clear and vivid language.

   d. None of the above.

Objective 14.3: Describe the six major design and writing tasks required to enhance your presentation with effective visuals.

10. Which of the following is an advantage of structured slide designs over free-form designs?

   a. Structured designs are more colorful and therefore keep audience attention better.

   b. People are accustomed to structured designs, so they are more comfortable with them.

   c. Structured slides are generally easier to create than free-form slides.

   d. Structured slides are cheaper.

11. Which of the following is a benefit of organizing a slide around a key visual such as a pyramid or a circular flow diagram?

   a. Slides without key visuals are always boring and repetitive.

   b. The key visual shows how the various ideas are related, making it easier for viewers to grasp your message.

   c. With a key visual to rely on, the speaker doesn't have to know the subject matter quite as thoroughly.

   d. You can use the key visual for every slide, making your presentation more consistent.

12. Which of the following is a problem that results from cramming too much text on a slide?

   a. It forces the audience members to spend more time reading than listening to speaker.

   b. It forces the presenter to use smaller type on the slide.

   c. It overloads the audience with too much information too fast.

   d. All of the above are problems that result from cramming too much text on a slide.

13. Charts and tables used for presentations should be

   a. Simpler than charts and tables used for printed documents.

   b. More complex than charts and tables used for printed documents.

   c. Exactly the same as charts and tables used for printed documents.

14. Slide _____ control how one slide replaces another, whereas slide _____ control how text and graphical elements are revealed on an individual slide.

15. Why is consistent use of colors, typefaces and type treatments, size, and other design elements important in presentations?

   a. Consistency is not important; in fact, it's a sign of a dull presentation.

   b. Consistency shows that you're a smart businessperson who doesn't waste time on trivial details.

   c. Consistency simplifies the viewing and listening process for your audience and enables them to pay closer attention to your message rather than spending time trying to figure out your visuals.

   d. Consistency shows that you're a team player who can follow instructions.

Objective 14.4: Outline four major tasks involved in completing a presentation.

16. How does the completion stage of the three-step writing process differ between reports and presentations?

   a. Completion is exactly the same for reports and presentations.

   b. Presentations are never proofread or tested ahead of time; doing so would destroy the spontaneity of your delivery.

   c. You never revise presentation slides because they're locked in place once you create them.

   d. The completion state for presentations involves a wider range of tasks, including testing your presentation slides, verifying equipment operation, practicing your speech, and creating handout materials.

17. What advice would you give to a novice presenter regarding practicing before a big presentation?

   a. Don't practice; it destroys the spontaneity you need to give an upbeat presentation.

   b. Make multiple practice runs, a half dozen if needed, to make sure you can deliver the material smoothly and confidently.

c. Write out a script and memorize it word for word; you can't risk forgetting any key points.

d. One practice session is adequate; use the extra time to polish your presentation slides instead.

18. What is the best approach to developing handout materials?

a. Create them after you've planned, developed, and tested your presentation so that you can see which points are confusing and could benefit from additional support.

b. Wait until you give the presentation and then ask your viewers what they would like to see in terms of additional information.

c. Always follow the lead of whatever the more experienced presenters in your department do; they've already set audience expectations.

d. Plan your handouts as you plan and create your slides so that you maintain an effective balance between information that you'll cover during the presentation and information that is better suited to a printed handout.

Objective 14.5: Describe four important aspects of delivering a presentation in today's social media environment.

19. Which of the following is an effective way to respond if you feel nervous right before giving a presentation?

a. Think up a short joke to begin your presentation; the audience's laughter will help you relax.

b. Begin your presentation by telling people that you're nervous and asking them to be sympathetic if you make any mistakes.

c. Begin your presentation by telling the audience how much you dislike speaking in public; most of them dislike public speaking, too, so they'll be more sympathetic toward you.

d. Remind yourself that everybody gets nervous and that being nervous simply means you care about doing well; use the nervousness to be more energetic when you begin speaking.

20. Which of these actions should you take when an audience member asks you a question?

a. Observe the questioner's body language and facial expression to help determine what the person really means.

b. Nod your head or show some other sign that you acknowledge the question.

c. Repeat the question to confirm your understanding and to ensure that the entire audience has heard it.

d. Do all of the above.

21. If you receive a question that is important and relevant to the topic you're presenting but you lack the information needed to answer it, which of the following would be the best response?

a. "I'm sorry; I don't know the answer."

b. "You've asked an important question, but I don't have the information needed to answer it properly. I'll research the issue after we're finished here today and then send everyone an email message with the answer."

c. "Let me get back to you on that."

d. "I'd really like to stay focused on the material that I prepared for this presentation."

22. What is the best strategy for using the Twitter-enabled backchannel in a presentation?

a. Build automated Twitter feeds into your presentation slides that send out capsule points as you move through the presentation, but ignore whatever audience members might be doing on Twitter and stay focused on your presentation.

b. Announce up front that the use of Twitter and other messaging tools is forbidden during the presentation; the audience's job is to pay attention to you, the speaker.

c. Embrace the backchannel fully, including building in automated feeds from your presentation, providing a hashtag for everyone to use making it easy to follow tweets related to the presentation, and take occasional Twitter breaks to check for feedback and questions from the audience.

d. Ignore it; you can't stop people from tweeting during a presentation, so you might as well just accept that they are going to do so.

23. Which of the following is a disadvantage of conducting presentations online?

a. The lack of audio communication

b. The inability of most people to participate, since businesses have different Internet connection speeds

c. The inability to use PowerPoint slides online

d. The shortage (or sometimes complete lack) of nonverbal signals such as posture, which can provide vital feedback during a presentation

24. Which of the following is an advantage of online presentations?

a. Lower costs as a result of less travel

b. More opportunities for employees to meet customers in person

c. The ability to multitask during meetings

d. All of the above

Quick Learning Guide

CHAPTER OUTLINE

Planning a Presentation
Analyzing the Situation
Selecting the Right Medium
Organizing A Presentation

Developing a Presentation
Adapting to Your Audience
Crafting Presentation Content

Enhancing Your Presentation with Effective Visuals
Choosing Structured or Free-Form Slides
Designing Effective Slides
Integrating Mobile Devices in Presentations

Completing a Presentation
Finalizing Your Slides
Creating Effective Handouts
Choosing Your Presentation Method
Practicing Your Delivery

Delivering a Presentation
Overcoming Anxiety
Handling Questions Responsively
Embracing the Backchannel
Giving Presentations Online

LEARNING OBJECTIVES

1 Highlight the importance of presentations in your business career, and explain how to adapt the planning step of the three-step process to presentations. (page 442)

2 Describe the tasks involved in developing a presentation. (page 449)

3 Describe the six major design and writing tasks required to enhance your presentation with effective visuals. (page 453)

4 Outline three special tasks involved in completing a presentation. (page 460)

5 Describe four important aspects of delivering a presentation in today's social media environment. (page 464)

KEY TERMS

backchannel A social media conversation that takes place during a presentation, in parallel with the speaker's presentation

free-form slides Presentation slides that are not based on a template, often with each slide having a unique look but unified by typeface, color, and other design choices; tend to be much more visually oriented than structured slides

navigation slides Noncontent slides that tell your audience where you're going and where you've been

slide builds Similar to slide transitions, these effects control the release of text, graphics, and other elements on individual slides

slide transitions Software effects that control how one slide replaces another on-screen

structured slides Presentation slides that follow the same design templates throughout and give all the slides in a presentation the same general look; they emphasize textual information in bullet-point form

---

CHECKLIST: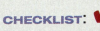

Enhancing Presentations With Visuals

A. Plan your presentation visuals.
- Make sure you and your message, not your visuals, remain the focus of your presentation.
- Follow effective design principles, with an emphasis on simplicity and authenticity.

B. Choose structured or free-form slides.
- Structured slides using bullet-point templates are easy to create, require little design time or skill, and can be completed in a hurry. Best uses: routine, internal presentations
- Free-form slides make it easier to combine textual and visual information, to create a more dynamic and engaging experience, and to maintain a conversational connection with the audience. Best uses: motivational, educational, and persuasive presentations

C. Design effective slides.
- Avoid the temptation to create "slideuments," slides that are so packed with information that they can be read as standalone documents.
- Use a key visual to organize related ideas in a clear and meaningful way.
- Write text content that will be readable from everywhere in the room.
- Write short, active, parallel phrases that support, not replace, your spoken message.
- Limit the amount of text so that your audience can focus on listening, not reading.
- Use color to emphasize important ideas, create contrast, isolate visual elements, and convey intended nonverbal signals.
- Limit color to a few compatible choices and use them consistently.
- Make sure your slide background doesn't compete with the foreground.
- Use decorative artwork sparingly and only to support your message.
- Emphasize functional artwork—photos, technical drawings, charts, and other visual elements containing information that is part of your message.
- Choose typefaces that are easy to read on-screen; limit the number of typefaces and use them consistently.
- Use slide masters to maintain consistency throughout your presentation.
- Use functional animation when it can support your message.
- Make sure slide transitions are subtle, if used at all.
- Use builds carefully to control the release of information.
- Use hyperlinks and action buttons to add flexibility to your presentation.
- Incorporate multimedia elements that can help engage your audience and deliver your message.

D. Complete slides and support materials.
- Review every slide carefully to ensure accuracy, consistency, and clarity.
- Make sure that all slides are fully operational.
- Use the slide sorter to verify and adjust the sequence of slides, if needed.
- Have a backup plan in case your electronic presentation plan fails.
- Create navigation and support slides.
- Create handouts to back up your presentation message.

Apply Your Knowledge

To review chapter content related to each question, refer to the indicated Learning Objective.

14.1. How do linear and nonlinear presentations differ? [LO-1]

14.2. You just gave an in-depth presentation on the company's new marketing programs, intended for the specialists in the marketing department. The marketing manager then asked you to give a shorter version of the presentation to the company's top executives. Generally speaking, how should you modify the scope of your presentation for this new audience? [LO-1]

⭐ **14.3.** Is it ethical to use design elements and special effects to persuade an audience? Why or why not? [LO-3]

⭐ **14.4.** Why is speaking from notes usually the best method of delivery? [LO-4]

Practice Your Skills

Messages for Analysis

14.5. **Message 14.A: Improving a Presentation Slide**
To access this PowerPoint presentation, visit **http://real-timeupdates.com/ebc12**, click on Student Assignments, and select Chapter 14, Message 14.A. Revise the text on these slides to make them more effective for presentation use.

14.6. **Message 14.A: Analyzing Animation**
To access this PowerPoint presentation, visit **http://real-timeupdates.com/ebc12**, click on Student Assignments, and select Chapter 14, Message 14.B. Download and watch the presentation in slide show mode. After you've watched the presentation, identify at least three ways in which various animations, builds, and transitions either enhanced or impeded your understanding of the subject matter.

Exercises

Each activity is labeled according to the primary skill or skills you will need to use. To review relevant chapter content, you can refer to the indicated Learning Objective. In some instances, supporting information will be found in another chapter, as indicated.

14.7. **Presentations: Planning a Presentation [LO-1]** Select one of the following topics, then research and prepare a brief presentation (5–10 minutes) to be given to your class:

a. What I expect to learn in this course

b. Past public speaking experiences: the good, the bad, and the ugly

c. I would be good at teaching _____

d. I am afraid of _____

e. It's easy for me to _____

f. I get angry when _____

g. I am happiest when I _____

h. People would be surprised if they knew that I _____

i. My favorite older person

j. My favorite charity

k. My favorite place

l. My favorite sport

m. My favorite store

n. My favorite television show

o. The town you live in suffers from a great deal of juvenile vandalism. Explain to a group of community members why juvenile recreational facilities should be built instead of a juvenile detention complex.

p. You are speaking to the Humane Society. Support or oppose the use of animals for medical research purposes.

q. You are talking to civic leaders of your community. Try to convince them to build an art gallery.

r. You are speaking to a first-grade class at an elementary school. Explain why they should brush their teeth after meals.

s. You are speaking to a group of traveling salespeople. Convince them that they should wear seat belts while driving.

t. You are speaking to a group of elderly people. Convince them to adopt an exercise program.

u. Energy issues (supply, conservation, alternative sources, national security, global warming, pollution, etc.)

v. Financial issues (banking, investing, family finances, etc.)

w. Government (domestic policy, foreign policy, Social Security taxes, welfare, etc.)

x. Interesting new technologies (virtual reality, geographic information systems, nanotechnology, bioengineering, etc.)

y. Politics (political parties, elections, legislative bodies and legislation, the presidency, etc.)

z. Sports (amateur and professional, baseball, football, golf, hang gliding, hockey, rock climbing, tennis, etc.)

14.8. **Presentations: Planning, Developing, and Delivering [LO-1], [LO-2], [LO-3]** Identify a company whose prospects look bright over the next few years because of highly competitive products, strong leadership, fundamental changes in the market, or any other significant reason. Prepare a five-minute speech, without visuals, explaining why you think this company is going to do well in the near future.

14.9. **Presentations: Developing a Presentation; Collaboration: Team Projects [LO-2], Chapter 2** You've been asked to give an informative 10-minute talk on vacation opportunities in your home state. Draft your introduction, which should last no more than 2 minutes. Then pair up with a classmate and analyze each other's introductions. How well do these two introductions arouse the audience's interest, build credibility, and preview the presentation? Suggest how these introductions might be improved.

14.10. **Presentations: Developing a Presentation [LO-2]** Locate the transcript of a speech, either online or through your school library. A good source *Vital Speeches of the Day*; ask if your library has a subscription to the database.) Many corporate websites also have archives of executives' speeches; look in the "investor relations" section. Examine the introduction and the close of the speech you've chosen and then analyze how these two sections work together to emphasize the main idea. What action does the speaker want the audience to take? Next, identify the transitional sentences or phrases that clarify the speech's structure for the listener, especially those that help the speaker shift between supporting points. Using these transitions as clues, list the main message and supporting points; then indicate how each transitional phrase links the current supporting point to the succeeding one. Prepare a two- to three-minute presentation summarizing your analysis for your class.

14.11. **Presentations: Designing Presentation Visuals [LO-4]** Look through recent issues (print or online) of *Bloomberg Businessweek, Fortune,* or other business publications for articles discussing challenges that a specific company or industry is facing. Using the articles and the guidelines discussed in this chapter, create a short Prezi or three to five slides summarizing these issues.

14.12. **Presentations: Designing Presentation Visuals [LO-4]** Find a business-related slide presentation online and analyze the design. Do you consider it structured or free form? Does the design help the audience understand and remember the message? Why or why not? What improvements would you suggest to the design?

14.13. **Presentations: Mastering Delivery; Nonverbal Communication: Analyzing Nonverbal Signals [LO-5], Chapter 2** Observe and analyze the delivery of a speaker in a school, work, or other setting. What type of delivery did the speaker use? Was this delivery appropriate for the occasion? What nonverbal signals did the speaker use to emphasize key points? Were these signals effective? Which nonverbal signals would you suggest to further enhance the delivery of this oral presentation? Why?

14.14. **Presentations: Delivering a Presentation; Collaboration: Team Projects; Media Skills: Microblogging [LO-5], Chapter 2, Chapter 7** In a team of six students, develop a 10-minute Prezi or slide presentation on any topic that interests you. Nominate one person to give the presentation; the other five will participate via a Twitter backchannel. Create a web page that holds at least one downloadable file that will be discussed during the presentation. Practice using the backchannel, including using a hashtag for the meeting and having the presenter ask for audience feedback during a "Twitter break." Be ready to discuss your experience with the entire class.

Expand Your Skills

Critique the Professionals

Visit the TED website at **www.ted.com/talks** and listen to any presentation that interests you. Compare the speaker's delivery and visual support materials with the concepts presented in this chapter. What works? What doesn't work? Using whatever medium your instructor requests, write a brief summary of your analysis.

Sharpen Your Career Skills Online

Bovée and Thill's Business Communication Web Search, at **http://websearch.businesscommunicationnetwork.com**, is a unique research tool designed specifically for business communication research. Use the Web Search function to find a website, video, PDF document, podcast, or presentation that offers advice on creating and delivering business presentations. Write a brief email message to your instructor or a post for your class blog, describing the item that you found and summarizing the career skills information you learned from it.

Improve Your Grammar, Mechanics, and Usage

The following exercises help you improve your knowledge of and power over English grammar, mechanics, and usage. Turn to the Handbook of Grammar, Mechanics, and Usage at the end of this book and review all of Sections 3.1 (Capitalization), 3.2 (Underscores and Italics), and 3.3 (Abbreviations). Then indicate the preferred choice in the following groups of sentences. (Answers to these exercises appear on page 601.)

14.15. a. Send this report to Mister H. K. Danforth, RR 1, Albany, NY 12885.
b. Send this report to Mister H. K. Danforth, Rural Route 1, Albany, New York 12885.
c. Send this report to Mr. H. K. Danforth, RR 1, Albany, NY 12885.

14.16. a. She received her MBA degree from the University of Michigan.
b. She received her Master of Business Administration degree from the university of Michigan.

14.17. a. Sara O'Rourke (a reporter from The Wall Street Journal) will be here Thursday.
b. Sara O'Rourke (a reporter from The Wall Street Journal) will be here Thursday.
c. Sara O'Rourke (a reporter from the *Wall Street Journal*) will be here Thursday.

14.18. a. The building is located on the corner of Madison and Center streets.
b. The building is located on the corner of Madison and Center Streets.

14.19. a. Call me at 8 a.m. tomorrow morning, PST, and I'll have the information you need.
b. Call me at 8 tomorrow morning, PST, and I'll have the information you need.
c. Call me tomorrow at 8 a.m. PST, and I'll have the information you need.

14.20. a. Whom do you think *Time* magazine will select as its Person of the Year?

b. Whom do you think *Time magazine* will select as its *Person of the Year?*

c. Whom do you think *Time magazine* will select as its Person of the Year?

14.21. a. The art department will begin work on Feb. 2, just one wk. from today.

b. The art department will begin work on February 2, just one week from today.

c. The art department will begin work on Feb. 2, just one week from today.

14.22. a. You are to meet him on friday at the UN building in NYC.

b. You are to meet him on Friday at the UN building in NYC.

c. You are to meet him on Friday at the un building in New York city.

14.23. a. You must help her distinguish between i.e. (which means "that is") and e.g. (which means "for example").

b. You must help her distinguish between i.e. (which means "that is") and *e.g.* (which means "for example").

c. You must help her distinguish between *i.e.* (which means that is) and *e.g.* (which means for example).

14.24. a. We plan to establish a sales office on the West coast.

b. We plan to establish a sales office on the west coast.

c. We plan to establish a sales office on the West Coast.

For additional exercises focusing on mechanics, visit MyBCommLab. Click on Chapter 14, click on Additional Exercises to Improve Your Grammar, Mechanics and Usage, and then click on 20. Capitals or 21. Word division.

Cases

Website links for selected companies mentioned in cases can be found in the Student Assignments section at **http://real-time-updates.com/ebc12**.

PRESENTATION SKILLS / PORTFOLIO BUILDER

14.25. Presentations: Planning a Presentation [LO-1] Pecha-kucha is a style of presentation that might be the ultimate in creative constraint: The speaker is limited to 20 slides, each of which is displayed for exactly 20 seconds before automatically advancing. Pecha-kucha Nights, which are open to the public, are now put on in cities all over the world. Visit **www.pecha-kucha.org** for more information on these events or to view some archived presentations.

Your task: Select one of the subjects from Exercise 14.7 on page 472 and develop a pecha-kucha style presentation with 20 slides, each designed to be displayed for 20 seconds. Use the slide-timing capabilities in your presentation software to control the timing. Make sure you practice before presenting to your class so that you can hit the precise timing requirements.[35]

PRESENTATION SKILLS / SOCIAL NETWORKING SKILLS

14.26. Presentations: Planning a Presentation [LO-1] You know those times when you're craving Thai food or the perfect fruit smoothie, but you don't know where to go? Or when you're out shopping or clubbing and want to let your friends know where you are? Foursquare's location-based services connect you with friends and companies that offer products and services of interest.

Your task: Create a brief presentation explaining the Foursquare concept and its features and benefits. List two Foursquare competitors and give a brief assessment of which of the three you would recommend to your classmates.

PRESENTATION SKILLS

14.27. Planning, Designing, and Creating Presentation Slides [LO-1], [LO-2], [LO-3], [LO-4] Not long ago, snowboarding seemed to be on pace to pass skiing as the country's favorite way to zoom down snowy mountains, but the sport's growth has cooled off in recent years.[36]

Your task: Research and prepare a 10-minute presentation on participation trends in snowboarding and skiing, including explanations for the relative popularity of both sports. Include at least three quotations to emphasize key points in your presentation. Use either structured or free-form slides.

PRESENTATION SKILLS

14.28. Planning, Designing, and Creating Presentation Slides [LO-1], [LO-2], [LO-3], [LO-4] Many companies publish stories of their founding and early years. The computer company Hewlett-Packard (HP), for example, tells the story of how founders Bill Hewlett and Dave Packard started the company in a garage in Palo Alto, California, in 1938, doing anything they could to "bring in a nickel." That garage is now preserved as "the birthplace of Silicon Valley," which helps maintain HP's image as a technology pioneer.[37]

Your task: Choose a company that has been in business for at least two decades and prepare a 10-minute presentation on its history.

PRESENTATION SKILLS / TEAM SKILLS

14.29. Presentations: Planning a Presentation [LO-1] In your job as a business development researcher for a major corporation, you're asked to gather and process information on a wide variety of subjects. Management has gained confidence in your research and analysis skills and would now like you to begin making regular presentations at management retreats and other functions. Topics are likely to include the following:

- Offshoring of U.S. jobs
- Foreign ownership of U.S. firms
- Employment issues involving workers from other countries
- Tax breaks offered by local and state governments to attract new businesses
- Economic impact of environmental regulations

Your task: With a team assigned by your instructor, choose one of the topics from the list and conduct enough research to familiarize yourself with the topic. Identify at least three important issues that anyone involved with this topic should know about. Prepare a 10-minute presentation that introduces the topic, comments on its importance to the U.S. economy, and discusses the issues you've identified. Assume that your audience is a cross-section of business managers who don't have any particular experience in the topic you've chosen.

PRESENTATION SKILLS / PORTFOLIO BUILDER

14.30. Presentations: Designing Presentation Visuals [LO-4] Depending on the sequence your instructor chose for this course, you've probably covered a dozen chapters at this point and learned or improved many valuable skills. Think through your progress and identify five business communication skills that you've either learned for the first time or developed during this course.

Your task: Create a Prezi or slide presentation that describes each of the five skills you've identified. Be sure to explain how each skill could help you in your career. Use any visual style that you feel is appropriate for the assignment.

PRESENTATION SKILLS / MOBILE SKILLS

14.31. Presentations: Designing Presentation Visuals; Mobile Media [LO-4] On SlideShare or any other source, find a business presentation on any topic that interests you.

Your task: Re-create the first five slides in the presentation in a manner that will make them more mobile-friendly. Create as many additional slides as you need.

PRESENTATION SKILLS / TEAM SKILLS

14.32. Planning, Designing, and Creating Presentation Slides; Collaboration: Team Projects [LO-1], [LO-2], [LO-3], [LO-4], Chapter 2 Changing a nation's eating habits is a Herculean task, but the physical and financial health of the United States depends on it. You work for the USDA Center for Nutrition Policy and Promotion (**www.cnpp .usda.gov**), and it's your job to educate people on the dangers of unhealthy eating and the changes they can make to eat more balanced and healthful diets.

Your task: Visit **http://real-timeupdates.com/ebc12**, click on Student Assignments, and download Chapter 14 Case (*Dietary Guidelines for Americans*). With a team assigned by your instructor, develop a 10- to 15-minute presentation that conveys the key points from Chapter 3 of the *Guidelines*, "Food and Food Components to Reduce." The objectives of your presentation are to alert people to the dangers of excessive consumption of the five components discussed in the chapter and to let them know what healthy levels of consumptions are. This chapter has a lot of information, but you don't need to pack it all into your presentation; you can assume that the chapter will be available as a handout to anyone who attends your presentation. Along with your presentation, draft speaking notes that someone outside your team could use to give the presentation. You can use images from the *Guidelines* PDF, the websites of the U.S. Department of Agriculture and the U.S. Department of Health and Human Services, or a nongovernment source such as Creative Commons. Cite all your image sources and make sure you follow the usage and attribution guidelines for any photos you find on nongovernment sites.

MyBCommLab

Go to the Assignments section of your MyLab to complete these writing exercises.

14.33. How can visually oriented free-form slides help keep an audience engaged in a presentation? [LO-3]

14.34. How does embracing the backchannel reflect the "you" attitude? [LO-5]

Endnotes

1. John Bowe, "Funny = Money," *New York Times*, 30 December 2010, www.nytimes.com; Stephanie Palmer Taxy, Good in a Room website, accessed 13 March 2011, www.goodinaroom.com; Mike Fleming, "A Banner Day for Two Former Assistants," *Deadline Hollywood*, 20 January 2011, www.deadline.com.

2. Nancy Duarte, *Slide:ology: The Art and Science of Creating Great Presentations* (Sebastopol, Calif.: O'Reilly Media, 2008), 13.

3. Amber Naslund, "Twebinar: GE's Tweetsquad," 4 August 2009, www.radian6.com/blog.

4. "Get Started with Prezi," *Prezi* website, accessed 2 May 2014, https://prezi.com.

5. Adam Noar, "PowerPoint vs. Prezi: What's the Difference?" Presentation Panda blog, 21 February 2012, http://presentationpanda.com.

6. Carmine Gallo, "How to Deliver a Presentation Under Pressure," *BusinessWeek* online, 18 September 2008, www.businessweek.com.

7. Sarah Lary and Karen Pruente, "Powerless Point: Common PowerPoint Mistakes to Avoid," *Public Relations Tactics*, February 2004, 28.

8. Garr Reynolds, *Presentation Zen: Simple Ideas on Presentation Design and Delivery* (Berkeley, Calif.: New Riders, 2008), 39–42.

9. Sherwyn P. Morreale and Courtland L. Bovée, *Excellence in Public Speaking* (Fort Worth, Tex.: Harcourt Brace College Publishers, 1998), 234–237.

10. John Windsor, "Presenting Smart: Keeping the Goal in Sight," *Presentations*, 6 March 2008, www.presentations.com.

11. Morreale and Bovée, *Excellence in Public Speaking*, 241–243.

12. "12 Most Engaging Presenter Behaviors … to Keep Your Audience Awake," Wilder Presentations, 12 August 2012, www.wilderpresentations.com; Sims Whyeth, "10 Ways Great Speakers Capture People's Attention," *Inc.*, 14 July 2015, www.inc.com; Jacquelyn Smith, "7 Excellent Ways to Start a Presentation and Capture Your Audience's Attention," *Financial Post*, 7 July 2014, http://business.financialpost.com.

13. Carmine Gallo, "Grab Your Audience Fast," *BusinessWeek*, 13 September 2006, 19.

14. Walter Kiechel III, "How to Give a Speech," *Fortune*, 8 June 1987, 180.

15. *Communication and Leadership Program* (Santa Ana, Calif.: Toastmasters International, 1980), 44, 45.

16. Reynolds, *Presentation Zen*, 10.

17. Cliff Atkinson, "The Cognitive Load of PowerPoint: Q&A with Richard E. Mayer," *Sociable Media*, accessed 15 August 2009, www.sociablemedia.com/articles_mayer.htm.

18. "The Power of Color in Presentations," 3M *Meeting Network*, accessed 25 May 2007, www.3rd-force.org/meetingnetwork/readingroom/meetingguide_power_color.html.

19. Duarte, *Slide:ology: The Art and Science of Creating Great Presentations*, 152.

20. Lary and Pruente, "Powerless Point: Common PowerPoint Mistakes to Avoid," 28.

21. Greg Anderson, "Presefy Syncs and Controls Presentations over Your Phone," *Arctic Startup*, 14 March 2013, www.arcticstartup.com; Kanda Software website, accessed 2 May 2014, www.kandasoft.com; Heather Clancy, "Broadcast Your Mobile Presentations to Remote Attendees," *ZDNet*, 27 March 2013, www.zdnet.com.

22. Reynolds, *Presentation Zen*, 85.

23. Reynolds, *Presentation Zen*, 66.

24. Reynolds, *Presentation Zen*, 208.

25. Richard Zeoli, "The Seven Things You Must Know About Public Speaking," *Forbes*, 3 June 2009, www.forbes.com; Morreale and Bovée, *Excellence in Public Speaking*, 24–25.

26. Jennifer Rotondo and Mike Rotondo, Jr., *Presentation Skills for Managers* (New York: McGraw-Hill, 2002), 9.

27. Rick Gilbert, "Presentation Advice for Boardroom Success," *Financial Executive*, September 2005, 12.

28. Rotondo and Rotondo, *Presentation Skills for Managers*, 151.

29. Teresa Brady, "Fielding Abrasive Questions During Presentations," *Supervisory Management*, February 1993, 6.

30. Robert L. Montgomery, "Listening on Your Feet," *The Toastmaster*, July 1987, 14–15.

31. Cliff Atkinson, *The Backchannel* (Berkeley, Calif.: New Riders, 2010), 17.

32. Atkinson, *The Backchannel*, 51, 68–73.

33. Olivia Mitchell, "10 Tools for Presenting with Twitter," Speaking About Presenting blog, 3 November 2009, www.speakingaboutpresenting.com; Atkinson, *The Backchannel*, 51, 68–73, 99.

34. SlideShare website, accessed 2 July 2012, www.slideshare.net.

35. PechaKucha20x20 website, accessed 4 August 2010, www.pecha-kucha.org; Reynolds, *Presentation Zen*, 41.

36. Hugo Martin, "Snowboarding Craze Fades, Skiing Becomes Cool Again," *Seattle Times*, 7 February 2013, http://seattletimes.com.

37. HP website, accessed 11 February 2013, www.hp.com

Writing Employment Messages and Interviewing for Jobs

CHAPTER **15** Building Careers and Writing Résumés

CHAPTER **16** Applying and Interviewing for Employment

The same techniques you use to succeed in your career can also help you launch and manage that career. Understand the employer's perspective on the hiring process so that you can adapt your approach and find the best job in the shortest possible time. Learn the best ways to craft a résumé and the other elements in your job search portfolio. Understand the interviewing process to make sure you're prepared for every stage and every type of interview.

Laflor/Getty Images

Building Careers and Writing Résumés

LEARNING OBJECTIVES

After studying this chapter, you will be able to

1 List eight key steps to finding the ideal opportunity in today's job market.

2 Explain the process of planning your résumé, including how to choose the best résumé organization.

3 Describe the tasks involved in writing your résumé, and list the major sections of a traditional résumé.

4 Characterize the completing step for résumés, including the six most common formats in which you can produce a résumé.

ON THE JOB: COMMUNICATING AT
VMWARE

Software Maker's Early Experiment with Social Media Recruiting Pays Off

Innovative businesspeople are always on the lookout for better ways to work and for any developments in the business environment that can give their companies a competitive edge. Back in 2009, James Malloy, a recruiting manager at VMWare, picked up on the early buzz surrounding *social recruiting* and wanted to know if his company might benefit from the growth of LinkedIn, Facebook, and other social platforms.

Social networking wasn't a new technology at that point, but most companies were still feeling their way through this new world and trying to figure out if or how to use all these new tools. In addition, corporate recruiters already had well-established systems for finding, evaluating, and recruiting new talent, and few companies knew if social media could add value to such a vital business process.

Moreover, even though social media were taking off with consumers and many consumer-oriented companies, VMWare is about as far from the frontlines of consumer activity as a company can get. Its specialty is *virtualization*, a software technique that lets a single computer act like multiple, independent machines. Virtualization is a critical technology behind cloud computing and much of today's information technology (IT)

James Molloy's hunch that social media might benefit VMWare's employee recruiting set off a revolution in how the company finds, evaluates, and recruits top talent.

infrastructure, but it's not exactly the sort of trendy topic that blows up on Twitter or prompts a million "you have to see this" shares on Facebook.

However, Malloy was intrigued by social recruiting and decided to conduct a low-risk experiment on Facebook to see if there was any potential. He set up a page and began posting job openings to it—and the effort caught on quickly as interested candidates found the openings. Importantly, the Facebook presence brought VMWare in touch with talented people that it hadn't been in contact with before.

Technology companies compete fiercely with one another to attract the best software designers and other specialists, so anything that gives recruiters an advantage is going to get attention. Malloy's simple Facebook experiment was so successful that VMWare's top management decided to realign its entire recruiting strategy around social networking.

Recruiting isn't the only aspect of company operations that adopted social media with gusto. The company is social through and through, with hundreds of official social media accounts and groups focused on specific technical or business issues, including nearly a hundred Twitter accounts alone. Four of those Twitter accounts are dedicated to careers and recruiting, including @VMWareU, the account for the VMWare University Recruiting Team. Through this account, the company announces job openings targeted at recent graduates, internship opportunities, and news of interest to potential employees.

The company's social recruiting strategy goes far beyond simple announcements, however. Molloy and his colleagues use these channels to build relationships with potential hires, to share videos and other media that showcase the VMWare corporate culture, and to brand VMWare as an exciting, supportive place to work. The social recruiting effort has been so successful that the company continues to expand it. Moving the forward, it is focusing on expanding its use of mobile recruiting apps and in helping employees become effective "brand advocates" for the company in their own social networks.[1]

WWW.VMWARE.COM

Finding the Ideal Opportunity in Today's Job Market

The social recruiting efforts made by VMWare (profiled in the chapter-opening On the Job) show the importance that top companies place on finding the right employees and the investments these companies are willing to make in both personnel and technology to attract and keep valuable talent. Whether you'll be looking for your first professional job on graduation or you're already in mid-career, you need to put as much thought and care into finding the right job as employers put into finding the right employees.

Identifying and landing a job can be a long and challenging process. Fortunately, the skills you're developing in this course will give you a competitive advantage. This section offers a general job-search strategy with advice that applies to just about any career path you might want to pursue. As you craft your personal strategy, keep these three guidelines in mind:

- **Get organized.** Your job search could last many months and involve multiple contacts with dozens of companies. You need to keep all the details straight to ensure that you don't miss opportunities or make mistakes such as losing someone's email address or forgetting an appointment.
- **Start now and stick to it.** Even if you are a year or more away from graduation, now is not too early to get started with some of the essential research and planning tasks. If you wait until the last minute, you will miss opportunities and you won't be as prepared as other candidates.
- **Look for stepping-stone opportunities.** Particularly in today's tough job market, you might not find the opportunity you're looking for right away. You might need to take a job that doesn't meet your expectations while you keep looking to get on the right track. But view every job as an opportunity to learn workplace skills, observe effective and ineffective business practices, and fine-tune your sense of how you'd like to spend your career.

WRITING THE STORY OF YOU

Writing or updating your résumé is a great opportunity to step back and think about where you've been and where you'd like to go. Do you like the path you're on, or is it time for a change? Are you focused on a particular field, or do you need some time to explore?

1 LEARNING OBJECTIVE
List eight key steps to finding the ideal opportunity in today's job market.

If you haven't already, read the Prologue, "Building a Career with Your Communication Skills," before studying this chapter.

What's your story? Thinking about where you've been and where you want to go will help focus your job search.

My Story

Where I Have Been

- Honor student and all around big shot in high school (but discovered that college is full of big shots!)
- Have worked several part-time jobs; only thing that really appealed to me in any of them was making improvements, making things work better

What experiences from your past give you insight into where you would like to go in the future?

Where I Am Now

- Junior; on track to graduate in 2017
- Enjoy designing creative solutions to challenging problems
- Not a high-end techie in an engineering sense, but I figure most things out eventually
- Not afraid to work hard, whatever it takes to get the job done
- I can tolerate some routine, as long as I have the opportunity to make improvements if needed
- Tend to lead quietly by example, rather than by visibly and vocally taking charge
- Knowing that I do good work is more important than getting approval from others
- I tend not to follow fads and crowds; sometimes I'm ahead of the curve, sometimes I'm behind the curve

Where do you stand now in terms of your education and career, and what do you know about yourself?

Where I Want to Be

- Get an advanced degree; not sure what subject area yet, though
- Haven't really settled on one industry or profession yet; working with systems of any kind is more appealing than any particular profession that I've learned about so far
- Develop my leadership and communication skills to become a more "obvious" leader
- Collaborate with others while still having the freedom to work independently (may be become an independent contractor or consultant at some point?)
- Have the opportunity to work internationally, at least for a few years
- I like the big bucks that corporate executives earn, but I don't want to live in the public eye like that or have to "play the game" to get ahead
- Believe I would be good manager, but not sure I want to spend all my time just managing people
- What to be known as an independent thinker and creative problem solver, as somebody who can analyze tough situations and figure out solutions that others might not consider
- Are there jobs where I could focus on troubleshooting, improving processes, or designing new systems?

What would you like your future to be? What do you like and dislike? What would you like to explore? If you haven't figured everything out yet, that's fine—as long as you've started to think about the future.

Figure 15.1   Writing the Story of You
Writing the "story of you" is a helpful way to think through where you've been in your life and career so far, where you are now, and where you would like to go from here. Remember that this is a private document designed to help you clarify your thoughts and plans, although you probably will find ways to adapt some of what you've written to various job-search documents, including your résumé.

You might find it helpful to think about the "story of you," the things you are passionate about, your skills, your ability to help an organization reach its goals, the path you've been on so far, and the path you want to follow in the future (see Figure 15.1). Think in terms of an image or a theme you'd like to project. Are you academically gifted? An effective leader? A well-rounded professional with wide-ranging talents? A creative problem solver? A technical wizard? Writing your story is a valuable planning exercise that helps you think about where you want to go and how to present yourself to target employers.

LEARNING TO THINK LIKE AN EMPLOYER

Employers judge their recruiting success by quality of hire, *and you can take steps to be—and look like—a high-quality hire.*

When you know your side of the hiring equation a little better, switch sides and look at it from an employer's perspective. To begin with, recognize that companies take risks with every hiring decision—the risk that the person hired won't meet expectations and the risk that a better candidate has slipped through their fingers. Many companies judge the success of their recruiting efforts by *quality of hire*, a measure of how closely new employees meet the company's needs.[2] Given this perspective, what steps can you take to present yourself as the low-risk, high-reward choice?

Of course, your perceived ability to perform the job is an essential part of your potential quality as a new hire. However, hiring managers consider more than just your ability to handle the job. They want to know if you'll be reliable and motivated—if you're somebody who "gets it" when it comes to being a professional in today's workplace. A great way to get inside the heads of corporate recruiters is to "listen in" on their professional conversations by reading periodicals such as *Workforce Management* and blogs such as Fistful of Talent and The HR Capitalist.

Follow the online conversations of professional recruiters to learn what their hot-button issues are.

RESEARCHING INDUSTRIES AND COMPANIES OF INTEREST

Learning more about professions, industries, and individual companies is a vital step in your job search. It also impresses employers, particularly when you go beyond the easily available sources such as a company's own website. "Detailed research, including talking to our customers, is so rare it will almost guarantee you get hired," explains the recruiting manager at Alcon Laboratories.[3]

Table 15.1 lists some of the many websites where you can learn more about companies and find job openings. Start with The Riley Guide, which offers advice for online job searches as well as links to hundreds of specialized websites that post openings in specific industries and professions. Your college's career center placement office probably maintains an up-to-date list as well.

To learn more about contemporary business topics, peruse leading business periodicals and newspapers with significant business sections (in some cases, you may need to go through your library's online databases in order to access back issues).

Employers expect you to be familiar with important developments in their industries, so stay on top of business news.

TABLE 15.1 Selected Job-Search Websites		
Website*	**URL**	**Highlights**
Riley Guide	www.rileyguide.com	Vast collection of links to both general and specialized job sites for every career imaginable; don't miss this one—it could save you hours of searching
TweetMyJobs.com	http://tweetmyjobs.com	The largest Twitter job board, with thousands of channels segmented by geography, job type, and industry
CollegeRecruiter.com	www.collegerecruiter.com	Focused on opportunities for graduates with fewer than three years of work experience
Monster	www.monster.com	One of the most popular job sites, with hundreds of thousands of openings, many from hard-to-find small companies; extensive collection of advice on the job search process
MonsterCollege	http://college.monster.com	Focused on job searches for new college grads; your school's career center site probably links here
CareerBuilder	www.careerbuilder.com	One of the largest job boards; affiliated with more than 150 newspapers around the country
Jobster	www.jobster.com	Uses social networking to link employers with job seekers
USAJOBS	www.usajobs.gov	The official job-search site for the U.S. government, featuring everything from jobs for economists to astronauts to border patrol agents
IMDiversity	www.imdiversity.com	Good resource on diversity in the workplace, with job postings from companies that have made a special commitment to promoting diversity in their workforces
Dice.com	www.dice.com	One of the best sites for high-technology jobs
Net-Temps	www.net-temps.com	Popular site for contractors and freelancers looking for short-term assignments
InternshipPrograms.com	http://internshipprograms.com	Posts listings from companies looking for interns in a wide variety of professions
Simply Hired Indeed	www.simplyhired.com www.indeed.com	Specialized search engines that look for job postings on hundreds of websites worldwide; they find many postings that aren't listed on job board sites such as Monster

**Note:* This list represents only a small fraction of the hundreds of job-posting sites and other resources available online; be sure to check with your college's career center for the latest information.
Sources: Individual websites, all accessed 13 March 2015.

In addition, thousands of bloggers, microbloggers, and podcasters offer news and commentary on the business world. AllTop is another good resource for finding people who write about topics that interest you. In addition to learning more about professions and opportunities, this research will help you get comfortable with the jargon and buzzwords currently in use in a particular field, including essential *keywords* to use in your résumé (see page 491).

Take advantage of job-search apps as well, including those offered by job posting websites and major employers You can use them to learn more about the company as well as specific jobs. See "Job Search Strategies: Maximize Your Mobile" for more tips on using a smartphone in your job search.

MOBILE APP

Indeed.com's mobile app lets you search for jobs and apply from your phone.

TRANSLATING YOUR GENERAL POTENTIAL INTO A SPECIFIC SOLUTION FOR EACH EMPLOYER

An essential task in your job search is presenting your skills and accomplishments in a way that is relevant to the employer's business challenges.

An important aspect of the employer's quality-of-hire challenge is trying to determine how well a candidate's attributes and experience will translate into the demands of a specific position. As a job candidate, customizing your résumé to each job opening is an important step in showing employers that you will be a good fit. As you can see from the sample résumés in Figures 15.4 through 15.6 on pages 494–496, customizing your résumé is not difficult if you have done your research. From your initial contact all the

---

DIGITAL + SOCIAL + MOBILE: TODAY'S COMMUNICATION ENVIRONMENT

Job Search Strategies: Maximize Your Mobile

The mobile business communication revolution is changing the way employers recruit new talent and the way job candidates look for opportunities. Many companies have optimized their careers websites for mobile access, and some have even developed mobile apps that offer everything from background information on what it's like to work there to application forms that you can fill out right on your phone.

However, don't be too quick to abandon a job application or an investigation into an employer just because the firm doesn't have a careers app or a mobile-friendly job site. Creating apps and mobile-friendly websites takes time and money, and many employers are still in the process of optimizing their online career materials for mobile devices. In a recent survey, 40 percent of mobile users said they would abandon a nonmobile job application—a distressingly high number in a slow job market. Don't miss a great opportunity just because an employer hasn't caught up to your mobile habits.

In addition to researching companies and applying for openings, integrating a mobile device into your job search strategy can help with networking and staying on top of your active job applications. For instance, some companies don't wait long after extending an offer; if they don't hear from the top candidate in a short amount of time, they'll move on their next choice. By staying plugged in via your mobile device, you won't let any opportunities pass you by.

Think of ways to use your mobile device to enhance your personal brand and your online portfolio. If you want to work in retail, for example, you could take photos of particularly good or particularly bad merchandising displays and post them with commentary on your social media accounts. Employers doing background research on you will see these

posts and recognize you as a candidate who is invested in his or her career and the industry as a whole. Many of the tools you can use to build your personal brand are available as mobile apps, including blogging platforms, Twitter, Facebook, and LinkedIn.

In addition, dozens of apps are available to help with various aspects of your job search. Résumé-creation apps let you quickly modify your résumé if you come across a good opportunity. Business-card scanning apps make it easy to keep digital copies of business cards, so you'll never lose important contact information. Note-taking apps are a great way to plan for interviews and record your post-interview notes. Use your phone's scheduling capability to make sure you never miss an interviewing or a filing deadline. Polish your interviewing skills with your phone's audio and video recording features or a practice-interview app. If an employer wants to interview you via Cisco Webex or another online meeting system, those apps are available for your phone or tablet as well.

You've been paying a lot for your mobile service—now make that mobile work for you by helping you land a great job.

CAREER APPLICATIONS

1. Would it be a good idea to present your online portfolio on your smartphone during a job interview? Why or why not?
2. Is it wise for applicants to shun a company that doesn't have a mobile-friendly careers website or a career app? Why or why not?

Sources: David Cohen, "Social Recruiting Goes Mobile," AllFacebook blog, 23 December 2013, http://allfacebook.com; Ryan Rancatore, "The 33 Best iPhone Apps For Personal Branding," Personal Branding 101 blog, 27 December 2009, http://personalbranding101.com; Jule Gamache, "The Rise of Mobile Job Search," Come Recommended blog, 12 June 2013, http://comerecommended.com.

way through the interviewing process, in fact, you will have opportunities to impress recruiters by explaining how your general potential translates to the specific needs of the position.

TAKING THE INITIATIVE TO FIND OPPORTUNITIES

When it comes to finding the right opportunities for you, the easiest ways are not always the most productive ways. The major job boards such as Monster and classified services such as Craigslist might have thousands of openings, but thousands of job seekers are looking at and applying for these same openings. Moreover, posting job openings on these sites is often a company's last resort, after it has exhausted other possibilities.

To maximize your chances, take the initiative and go seek opportunities. Identify the companies you want to work for and focus your efforts on them. Get in touch with their human resources departments (or individual managers, if possible), describe what you can offer the company, and ask to be considered if any opportunities come up.[4] Reach out to company representatives on social networks. Your message might appear right when a company is busy looking for someone but hasn't yet advertised the opening to the outside world. And be sure to take advantage of the growing number of career-related mobile apps (see Figure 15.2).

Don't hesitate to contact interesting companies even if they haven't advertised job openings to the public yet; they might be looking for somebody just like you.

Courtesy of Glassdoor.

Figure 15.2 Mobile Job Search Tools
Put your mobile phone or tablet to work in your job search, using some of the many employment apps now available.

BUILDING YOUR NETWORK

Networking is the process of making informal connections with mutually beneficial business contacts. Networking takes place wherever and whenever people talk: at industry functions, at social gatherings, at alumni reunions—and all over the Internet, from LinkedIn and Twitter to Facebook and Google+. In addition to making connections through social media tools, you might get yourself noticed by company recruiters.

Networking is more essential than ever because the vast majority of job openings are never advertised to the general public. To avoid the time and expense of sifting through thousands of applications and the risk of hiring complete strangers, most companies prefer to ask their employees for recommendations first.[5] The more people who know you, the better chance you have of being recommended for one of these hidden job openings.

Start building your network now, before you need it. Your classmates could end up being some of your most valuable contacts, if not right away then possibly later in your career. Then branch out by identifying people with similar interests in your target professions, industries, and companies. Read news sites, blogs, and other online sources. Follow industry leaders on Twitter. You can also follow individual executives at your target companies to learn about their interests and concerns.[6] Be on the lookout for career-oriented *Tweetups*, in which people who've connected on Twitter get together for in-person networking events. Connect with people on LinkedIn and Facebook, particularly in groups dedicated to particular career interests. Depending on the system and the settings on individual users' accounts, you may be able to introduce yourself via public or private messages. Just make sure you are respectful of people, and don't take up much of their time.[7]

Participate in student business organizations, especially those with ties to professional organizations. Visit *trade shows* to learn about various industries and rub shoulders with people who work in those industries.[8] Don't overlook volunteering; you not only meet people but also demonstrate your ability to solve problems, manage projects, and lead others. You can do some good while creating a network for yourself.

Remember that networking is about people helping each other, not just about other people helping you. Pay close attention to networking etiquette: Try to learn something about the people you want to connect with, don't overwhelm others with too many messages or requests, be succinct in all your communication efforts, don't give out other people's names and contact information without their permission to do so, never email your résumé to complete strangers, and remember to say thank you every time someone helps you.[9]

To become a valued network member, you need to be able to help others in some way. You may not have any influential contacts yet, but because you're researching industries and trends as part of your own job search, you probably have valuable information you can share via your online and offline networks. Or you might simply be able to connect one person with another who can help. The more you network, the more valuable you become in your network—and the more valuable your network becomes to you.

Finally, be aware that your online network reflects on who you are in the eyes of potential employers, so exercise some judgment in making connections. Also, many employers now contact people in a candidate's public network for background information, even if the candidate doesn't list those people as references.[10]

SEEKING CAREER COUNSELING

Your college's career center probably offers a wide variety of services, including individual counseling, job fairs, on-campus interviews, and job listings. Counselors can advise on career planning and provide workshops on job search techniques, résumé preparation, job readiness training, interview techniques, self-marketing, and more.[11] You can also find career planning advice online. Many of the websites listed in Table 15.1 offer articles and online tests to help you choose a career path, identify essential skills, and prepare to enter the job market.

AVOIDING MISTAKES

While you're making all these positive moves to show employers you will be a quality hire, take care to avoid the simple blunders that can torpedo a job search, such as not catching

---

Start thinking like a networker now; your classmates could turn out to be some of your most important business contacts.

MOBILE APP
Stay in touch with your professional network with LinkedIn's mobile app.

Networking is a mutual beneficial activity, so look for opportunities to help others in some way.

Don't overlook the many resources available through your college's career center.

Don't let a silly mistake knock you out of contention for a great job.

Striving to Excel

Pros are good at what they do, and they never stop improving. No matter what your job might be at any given time—even if it is far from where you aspire to be—strive to perform at the highest possible level. Not only do you have an ethical obligation to give your employer and your customers your best effort, but excelling at each level in your career is also the best way to keep climbing up to new positions of responsibility. Plus, being good at what you do delivers a sense of satisfaction that is hard to beat.

In many jobs and in many industries, performing at a high level requires a commitment to continuous learning and improvement. The nature of the work often changes as markets and technologies evolve, and expectations of quality tend to increase over time as well. View this constant change as a positive thing, as a way to avoid stagnation and boredom.

Striving to excel can be a challenge when there is a mismatch between the job's requirements and your skills and knowledge. If you are underqualified for a job, you need to identify your weaknesses quickly and come up with a plan to address them. A supportive manager will help you identify these areas and encourage improvement through training or mentoring. Don't wait for a boss to tell you your work is subpar, however. If you know you're floundering, don't wait until you've failed to get help.

If you are overqualified for a job, it's easy to slip into a rut and eventually underperform simply because you aren't being challenged. However, current and future bosses aren't going to judge you on how well you performed relative to your needs and expectations; they're going to judge you on how well you performed relative to job's requirements. Work with your boss to find ways to make your job more challenging if possible, or start looking for a better job if necessary, but be sure to maintain your level of performance until you can bring your responsibilities and talents into closer alignment.

CAREER APPLICATIONS

1. Should you ever try to sell yourself into a job for which you are not yet 100 percent qualified? Explain your answer.
2. Do you agree that you have an ethical obligation to excel at your job? Why or why not?

mistakes in your résumé, misspelling the name of a manager you're writing to, showing up late for an interview, tweeting something unprofessional, failing to complete application forms correctly, asking for information that you can easily find yourself on a company's website, or making any other error that could flag you as someone who is careless or disrespectful. Assume that every employer will conduct an online search on you. Busy recruiters will seize on these errors as a way to narrow the list of candidates they need to spend time on, so don't give them a reason to toss out your résumé.

Planning Your Résumé

Although you will create many messages during your career search, your **résumé**, a structured, written summary of your education, employment background, and job qualifications, will be the most important document in this process. You will be able to use it directly in many instances, adapt it to a variety of uses such an e-portfolio or a social media résumé, and reuse pieces of it in social networking profiles and online application forms. Even if you apply to a company that doesn't want to see résumés from applicants, the process of developing your résumé will prepare you for interviewing and preemployment testing.

Developing a résumé is one of those projects that really benefits from multiple planning, writing, and completing sessions spread out over several days or weeks. You are trying to summarize a complex subject (yourself!) and present a compelling story to strangers in a brief document. Follow the three-step writing process (see Figure 15.3 on the next page) and give yourself plenty of time.

Before you dive into your résumé, be aware that you will find a wide range of opinions about résumés, regarding everything from appropriate length, content, design, distribution methods, and acceptable degrees of creativity to whether it even makes sense to write a traditional résumé in this age of online applications. For example, you may encounter a prospective employer that wants you to tweet your résumé or submit all the links that make up your online presence, rather than submit a conventional résumé.[12] You may run across examples of effective résumés that were produced as infographics, interactive

2 LEARNING OBJECTIVE
Explain the process of planning your résumé, including how to choose the best résumé organization.

1 Plan →	2 Write →	3 Complete
Analyze the Situation Recognize that the purpose of your résumé is to get an interview, not to get a job.	**Adapt to Your Audience** Plan your wording carefully so that you can catch a recruiter's eye within seconds; translate your education and experience into attributes that target employers find valuable.	**Revise the Message** Evaluate content and review readability and then edit and rewrite for conciseness and clarity.
Gather Information Research target industries and companies so that you know what they're looking for in new hires; learn about various jobs and what to expect; learn about the hiring manager, if possible.	**Compose the Message** Write clearly and succinctly, using active, powerful language that is appropriate to the industries and companies you're targeting; use a professional tone in all communications.	**Produce the Message** Use effective design elements and suitable layout for a clean, professional appearance; seamlessly combine text and graphical elements. When printing, use quality paper and a good printer.
Choose Media and Channels Start with a traditional paper résumé and develop scannable, plain text, PDF, and social/online versions, as needed. Consider other formats as supplements.		**Proofread the Message** Review for errors in layout, spelling, and mechanics; mistakes can cost you interview opportunities.
Organize the Information Choose an organizational model that highlights your strengths and downplays your shortcomings; use the chronological approach unless you have a strong reason not to.		**Distribute the Message** Deliver your résumé, carefully following the specific instructions of each employer or job board website.

Figure 15.3 Three-Step Writing Process for Résumés
Following the three-step writing process will help you create a successful résumé in a short time. Remember to pay particular attention to the "you" attitude and presentation quality; your résumé will probably get tossed aside if it doesn't speak to audience needs or if it contains mistakes.

videos, simulated search engine results, puzzles, games, graphic novels—you name it, somebody has probably tried it.

When you hear conflicting advice or see trendy concepts that you might be tempted to try, remember the most important question in business communication: What is the most effective way to adapt your message to the individual needs of each member of your audience? An approach that is wildly successful with one company or in one industry could be a complete disaster in another industry. To forge your own successful path through this maze of information, get inside the heads of the people you are trying to reach—try to think the way they think—and then apply the principles of effective communication you are learning in this course.

ANALYZING YOUR PURPOSE AND AUDIENCE

Planning an effective résumé starts with understanding its true function—as a brief, persuasive business message intended to stimulate an employer's interest in meeting you and learning more about you (see Table 15.2). In other words, the purpose of a résumé is not to get you a job but rather to get you an interview.[13]

As you conduct your research on various professions, industries, companies, and individual managers, you will have a better perspective on your target readers and their information needs. Learn as much as you can about the individuals who may be reading your résumé. Many professionals and managers are bloggers, Twitter users, and LinkedIn members, for example, so you can learn more about them online even if you've never met them. Any bit of information can help you craft a more effective message.

You will see lots of ideas and even some conflicting advice about résumés; use what you know about effective business communication to decide what is right for your résumés.

Once you view your résumé as a persuasive business message, it's easier to decide what should and shouldn't be in it.

Thanks to Twitter, LinkedIn, and other social media, you can often learn valuable details about individual managers in your target employers.

TABLE 15.2   Fallacies and Facts About Résumés

Fallacy	Fact
The purpose of a résumé is to list all your skills and abilities.	The purpose of a résumé is to kindle employer interest and generate an interview.
A good résumé will get you the job you want.	All a résumé can do is get you in the door.
Your résumé will always be read carefully and thoroughly.	In most cases, your résumé needs to make a positive impression within a few seconds; only then will someone read it in detail. Moreover, it will likely be screened by a computer looking for keywords first—and if it doesn't contain the right keywords, a human being may never see it.
The more good information you present about yourself in your résumé, the better, so stuff your résumé with every positive detail.	Recruiters don't need that much information about you at the initial screening stage, and they probably won't read it.

By the way, if employers ask to see your "CV," they're referring to your *curriculum vitae*, the term used instead of *résumé* in academic professions and in many countries outside the United States. Résumés and CVs are essentially the same, although CVs can be much more detailed and include personal information that is not included in a résumé.

REAL-TIME UPDATES

LEARN MORE BY VISITING THIS WEBSITE

Converting your résumé to a CV

If you need to convert your U.S-style résumé to the *curriculum vitae* format used in many other countries (and in many academic positions in the United States), this website will tell you everything you need to know. Go to http://real-timeupdates.com/ebc12 and click on Learn More in the Students section.

GATHERING PERTINENT INFORMATION

If you haven't been building an employment portfolio thus far, you may need to do some research on yourself at this point. Gather all the pertinent personal history you can think of, including all the specific dates, duties, and accomplishments from any previous jobs you've held. Compile all your educational accomplishments, including formal degrees, training certificates, professional and technical certifications, academic awards, and scholarships. Also, gather information about school or volunteer activities that might be relevant to your job search, including offices you have held in any club or professional organization, presentations given, and online or print publications. You probably won't use every piece of information you come up with, but you'll want to have it at your fingertips.

SELECTING THE BEST MEDIA AND CHANNELS

You should expect to produce your résumé in several media and formats. "Producing Your Résumé" on page 497 discusses your options.

ORGANIZING YOUR RÉSUMÉ AROUND YOUR STRENGTHS

Although there are a number of ways to organize a résumé, most are some variation of chronological, functional, or a combination of the two. The right choice depends on your background and your goals.

The Chronological Résumé

In a **chronological résumé**, the work experience section dominates and is placed immediately after your contact information and introductory statement (see Figure 15.6 on page 496 for an example). The chronological approach is the most common way to organize a résumé, and many employers prefer this format because it presents your professional history in a clear, easy-to-follow arrangement.[14] If you're just graduating from college and have limited professional experience, you can vary this chronological approach by putting your educational qualifications before your experience.

Develop your work experience section by listing your jobs in reverse chronological order, beginning with the most recent one and giving more space to the most recent positions you've held. For each job, start by listing the employer's name and location, your

The chronological résumé is the most common approach, but it might not be right for you at this stage in your career.

official job title, and the dates you held the position (write "to present" if you are still in your most recent job). Next, in a short block of text, highlight your accomplishments in a way that is relevant and understandable to your readers. If the general responsibilities of the position are not obvious from the job title, provide a little background to help readers understand what you did.

The Functional Résumé

The functional résumé is often considered by people with limited or spotty employment history, but many employers are suspicious of this format.

A **functional résumé**, sometimes called a *skills résumé*, emphasizes your skills and capabilities, identifying employers and academic experience in subordinate sections. This arrangement stresses individual areas of competence rather than job history. The functional approach has three benefits: (1) Without having to read through job descriptions, employers can get an idea of what you can do for them; (2) you can emphasize previous job experience through the skills you gained in those positions; and (3) you can deemphasize any lengthy unemployment or lack of career progress. However, you should be aware that because the functional résumé can obscure your work history, many employment professionals are suspicious of it.[15] Moreover, it lacks the evidence of job experience that supports your skills claims. If you don't believe the chronological format will work for you, consider the combination résumé instead.

The Combination Résumé

If you don't have a lot of work history to show, consider a combination résumé to highlight your skills while still providing a chronological history of your employment.

A **combination résumé** meshes the skills focus of the functional format with the job history focus of the chronological format. Figures 15.4 (page 494) and 15.5 (page 495) show examples of combination résumés. The chief advantage of this format is that it allows you to highlight your capabilities and education when you don't have a long or steady employment history, without raising concerns that you might be hiding something about your past.

As you look at a number of sample résumés, you'll probably notice many variations on the three basic formats presented here. Study these other options in light of the effective communication principles you've learned in this course and the unique circumstances of your job search. If you find one that seems like the best fit for your unique situation, by all means use it.

ADDRESSING AREAS OF CONCERN

Many people have gaps in their careers or other issues that could be a concern for employers. Here are some common issues and suggestions for handling them in a résumé:[16]

- **Frequent job changes.** If you've had a number of short-term jobs of a similar type, such as independent contracting and temporary assignments, you can group them under a single heading. Also, if past job positions were eliminated as a result of layoffs or mergers, find a subtle way to convey that information (if not in your résumé, then in your cover letter). Reasonable employers understand that many professionals have been forced to job hop by circumstances beyond their control.
- **Gaps in work history.** Mention relevant experience and education you gained during employment gaps, such as volunteer or community work.
- **Inexperience.** Mention related volunteer work and membership in professional groups. List relevant course work and internships.
- **Overqualification.** Tone down your résumé, focusing exclusively on the experience and skills that relate to the position.
- **Long-term employment with one company.** Itemize each position held at the firm to show growth within the organization and increasing responsibilities along the way.
- **Job termination for cause.** Be honest with interviewers and address their concerns with proof, such as recommendations and examples of completed projects.

REAL-TIME UPDATES

LEARN MORE BY READING THIS ARTICLE

Smart strategies to explain gaps in your work history

Get three key pieces of advice if you have been or were out of work for a period of time. Go to http://real-timeupdates.com/ebc12 and click on Learn More in the Students section.

- **Criminal record.** You don't necessarily need to disclose a criminal record or time spent incarcerated on your résumé, but you may be asked about it on job application forms. Laws regarding what employers may ask (and whether they can conduct a criminal background check) vary by state and profession, but if you are asked and the question applies to you, you are legally bound to answer truthfully. Use the interview process to explain any mitigating circumstances and to emphasize your rehabilitation and commitment to being a law-abiding, trustworthy employee.[17]

Writing Your Résumé

With the necessary information and a good plan in hand, you're ready to begin writing. If you feel uncomfortable writing about yourself, you're not alone. Many people, even accomplished writers, can find it difficult to write their own résumés. If you get stuck, imagine you are somebody else, writing a résumé for this person called you. By "being your own client" in this sense, you might find the words and idea flow more easily. You can also find a classmate or friend who is writing a résumé and swap projects for a while. Working on each other's résumés might speed up the process for both of you.

> **3 LEARNING OBJECTIVE**
> Describe the tasks involved in writing your résumé, and list the major sections of a traditional résumé.

> If you're uncomfortable writing your own résumé, you might try to trade with a classmate and write each other's résumé.

KEEPING YOUR RÉSUMÉ HONEST

Estimates vary, but one comprehensive study uncovered lies about work history in more than 40 percent of the résumés tested.[18] And dishonest applicants are getting bolder all the time—going so far as to buy fake diplomas online, pay a computer hacker to insert their names into prestigious universities' graduation records, and sign up for services that offer phony employment verification.[19] "It's becoming common to cheat," observes Professor George Gollin of the University of Illinois, Urbana, mentioning the 200,000 fake college degrees sold every year as one example.[20]

> **REAL-TIME UPDATES**
> LEARN MORE BY WATCHING THIS VIDEO
> **Learn to use LinkedIn's résumé builder**
> See how to build and customize a résumé on LinkedIn and then use it on other social networking sites. Go to http://real-timeupdates .com/ebc12 and click on Learn More in the Students section.

Applicants with integrity know they don't need to stoop to lying. If you are tempted to stretch the truth, bear in mind that professional recruiters have seen all sorts of fraud by job applicants, and frustrated employers are working aggressively to uncover the truth. Nearly all employers do some form of background checking, from contacting references and verifying employment to checking criminal records and sending résumés through verification services.[21] Employers are also beginning to craft certain interview questions specifically to uncover dishonest résumé entries.[22]

More than 90 percent of companies that find lies on résumés refuse to hire the offending applicants, even if that means withdrawing formal job offers.[23] And if you do sneak past these filters and get hired, you'll probably be exposed on the job when you can't live up to your own résumé. Given the networked nature of today's job market, lying on a résumé could haunt you for years—and you could be forced to keep lying throughout your career to hide the misrepresentations on your original résumé.[24]

> Résumé fraud has reached epidemic proportions, but employers are fighting back with more rigorous screening techniques.

> **MOBILE APP**
> Need a simple résumé in a hurry? Resume App Pro and Resume Builder Pro let you build one right on your phone.

ADAPTING YOUR RÉSUMÉ TO YOUR AUDIENCE

The importance of adapting your résumé to your target readers' needs and interests cannot be overstated. In a competitive job market, the more you look like a good fit—a quality hire—the better your chances of securing interviews. Address your readers' business concerns by showing how your capabilities meet the demands and expectations of the position and the organization as a whole.

For example, an in-house public relations (PR) department and an independent PR agency perform many of the same tasks, but the outside agency must also sell its services to multiple clients. Consequently, it needs employees who are skilled at attracting and keeping paying customers, in addition to being skilled at PR. If you are applying for both in-house and agency PR jobs, you need to adapt your résumé for each of these audiences.

> Translate your past accomplishments into a compelling picture of what you can do for employers in the future.

REAL-TIME UPDATES

LEARN MORE BY READING THIS INFOGRAPHIC

See how an applicant tracking system handles your résumé

Once you see how the system works, you'll understand why it's so crucial to customize the wording on your résumé for every job opening. Go to http://real-timeupdates.com/ebc12 and click on Learn More in the Students section.

An essential step in adapting your résumé is using the same terminology as the employer uses to describe job responsibilities and professional accomplishments. In Figures 15.4 through 15.6 starting on page 494, you can see how the sample résumés do this, echoing key terms and phrases from the job postings. With the rise of automated **applicant tracking systems**, which attempt to analyze the content of résumés in order to find good matches with company job descriptions, aligning your language to the employer's will help you get past the keyword filters these systems use to rank incoming résumés.

> Military service and other specialized experiences may need to be "translated" into terms more readily understandable by your target readers.

If you are applying for business positions after military service or moving from one industry to another, you may need to "translate" your experience into the language of your target employers. For instance, military experience can help you develop many skills that are valuable in business, but military terminology can sound like a foreign language to people who aren't familiar with it. Isolate the important general concepts and present them in the business language your target employers use.

COMPOSING YOUR RÉSUMÉ

> Draft your résumé using short, crisp phrases built around strong verbs and nouns.

Write your résumé using a simple and direct style. Use short, crisp phrases instead of whole sentences and focus on what your reader needs to know. Avoid using the word *I*, which can sound both self-involved and repetitive by the time you outline all your skills and accomplishments. Instead, start your phrases with strong action verbs such as these:[25]

accomplished	coordinated	initiated	participated	set up
achieved	created	installed	performed	simplified
administered	demonstrated	introduced	planned	sparked
approved	developed	investigated	presented	streamlined
arranged	directed	launched	proposed	strengthened
assisted	established	maintained	raised	succeeded
assumed	explored	managed	recommended	supervised
budgeted	forecasted	motivated	reduced	systematized
chaired	generated	negotiated	reorganized	targeted
changed	identified	operated	resolved	trained
compiled	implemented	organized	saved	transformed
completed	improved	oversaw	served	upgraded

For example, you might say, "Created a campus organization for students interested in entrepreneurship" or "Managed a fast-food restaurant and four employees." Whenever you can, quantify the results so that your claims don't come across as empty puffery. Don't just say that you're a team player or detail oriented—show that you are by offering concrete proof.[26] Here are some examples of phrasing accomplishments using active statements that show results:

Instead of This	**Write Active Statements That Show Results**
Responsible for developing a new filing system	Developed a new filing system that reduced paperwork by 50 percent
I was in charge of customer complaints and all ordering problems	Handled all customer complaints and resolved all product order discrepancies
I won a trip to Europe for opening the most new customer accounts in my department	Generated the highest number of new customer accounts in my department
Member of special campus task force to resolve student problems with existing cafeteria assignments	Assisted in implementing new campus dining program that balances student wishes with cafeteria capacity

Providing specific supporting evidence is vital, but make sure you don't go overboard with details.[27] Carefully select the most compelling evidence so that your message is clear and immediate.

In addition to clear writing with specific examples, the particular words and phrases used throughout your résumé are critically important. The majority of résumés are now subjected to *keyword searches* in an applicant tracking system or other database, in which a recruiter searches for résumés most likely to match the requirements of a particular job. Résumés that don't closely match the requirements may never be seen by a human reader, so it is essential to use the words and phrases that a recruiter is most likely to search on. (Although most experts used to advise including a separate *keyword summary* as a stand-alone list, the trend nowadays is to incorporate your keywords into your introductory statement and other sections of your résumé.)[28]

Include relevant keywords in your introductory statement, work history, and education sections.

Identifying these keywords requires some research, but you can uncover many of them while you are looking into various industries and companies. In particular, study job descriptions carefully. In contrast to the action verbs that catch a human reader's attention, keywords that catch a computer's attention are usually nouns that describe the specific skills, attributes, and experiences an employer is looking for in a candidate. Keywords can include the business and technical terms associated with a specific profession, industry-specific jargon, names or types of products or systems used in a profession, job titles, and college degrees.[29]

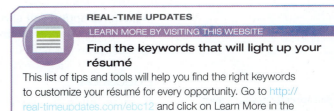

REAL-TIME UPDATES

LEARN MORE BY VISITING THIS WEBSITE

Find the keywords that will light up your résumé

This list of tips and tools will help you find the right keywords to customize your résumé for every opportunity. Go to http://real-timeupdates.com/ebc12 and click on Learn More in the Students section.

Name and Contact Information

Your name and contact information constitute the heading of your résumé; include the following:

- Name
- Address (both permanent and temporary, if you're likely to move during the job-search process)
- Email address
- Phone number(s)
- The URL of your personal webpage, e-portfolio, or social media résumé (if you have one)

Be sure to provide complete and accurate contact information; mistakes in this section of the résumé are surprisingly common.

If the only email address you have is through your current employer, get a free personal email address from one of the many services that offer them. It's not fair to your current employer to use company resources for a job search, and doing so sends a bad signal to potential employers. Also, if your personal email address is anything like precious.princess@something.com or PsychoDawg@something.com, get a new email address for your business correspondence.

Use a professional-sounding email address for business correspondence, such as firstname .lastname@something.com).

Introductory Statement

Of all the parts of a résumé, the brief introductory statement that follows your name and contact information probably generates the most disagreement. You can put one of three things here:[30]

You can choose to open with a career objective, a qualifications summary, or a career summary.

- **Career objective.** A career objective identifies either a specific job you want to land or a general career track you would like to pursue. Some experts advise against including a career objective because it can categorize you so narrowly that you miss out on interesting opportunities, and it is essentially about fulfilling your desires, not about meeting the employer's needs. In the past, most résumés included a career objective, but in recent years more job seekers are using a qualifications summary or a career summary. However, if you have little or no work experience in your target profession, a career objective might be your best option. If you do opt for an objective, word it in a way that relates your qualifications to employer needs.
- **Qualifications summary.** A qualifications summary offers a brief view of your key qualifications. The goal is to let a reader know within a few seconds what you

If you have a reasonably focused skill set but don't yet have a long career history, a qualifications summary is probably the best type of introductory statement for you.

can deliver. You can title this section generically as "Qualifications Summary" or "Summary of Qualifications," or, if you have one dominant qualification, you can use that as the title. Consider using a qualifications summary if you have one or more important qualifications but don't yet have a long career history. Also, if you haven't been working long but your college education has given you a dominant professional "theme," such as multimedia design or statistical analysis, you can craft a qualifications summary that highlights your educational preparedness.

- **Career summary.** A career summary offers a brief recap of your career with the goal of presenting increasing levels of responsibility and performance (see Figure 15.6 on page 496 for an example). A career summary can be particularly useful for managers who have demonstrated the ability to manage increasingly larger and more complicated business operations—a key consideration when companies look to hire upper-level executives.

Whichever option you choose, make sure it includes many of the essential keywords you identified in your research—and adapt these words and phrases to each job opportunity as needed.

Education

If you are early in your career, your education is probably your strongest selling point.

If you're still in college or have recently graduated, education is probably your strongest selling point. Present your educational background in depth, choosing facts that support your professional theme. Give this section a heading such as "Education," "Technical Training," or "Academic Preparation," as appropriate. Then, starting with the most recent, list the name and location of each school you have attended, the month and year of your graduation (say "anticipated graduation: ____" if you haven't graduated yet), your major and minor fields of study, significant skills and abilities you've developed in your course work, and the degrees or certificates you've earned. Fine-tune your message by listing courses that are most relevant to each job opening, and indicate any scholarships, awards, or academic honors you've received.

The education section should also include relevant training sponsored by business or government organizations. Mention high school or military training only if the associated achievements are pertinent to your career goals.

Whether you list your grade point average depends on the job you want and the quality of your grades. If you don't show your GPA on your résumé—and there's no rule saying you have to—be prepared to answer questions about it during the interview process because many employers will assume that your GPA is not spectacular if you didn't list it on your résumé. If you choose to show a grade point average, be sure to mention the scale, especially if it isn't a four-point scale. If your grades are better within your major than in other courses, you can also list your GPA as "Major GPA" and include only those courses within your major.

Work Experience, Skills, and Accomplishments

When you describe past job responsibilities, identify the skills and knowledge that you can apply to a future job.

This section can be called "Work Experience," "Professional Experience," or "Work and Volunteer Experience," if you have limited work experience and want to bolster that with volunteer experience. Like the education section, the work experience section should focus on your overall theme in a way that shows how your past can contribute to an employer's future. Use keywords to call attention to the skills you've developed on the job and to your ability to handle responsibility. Emphasize what you accomplished in each position, not just the generic responsibilities of the job.

List your jobs in reverse chronological order, starting with the most recent. Include military service and any internships and part-time or temporary jobs related to your career objective. Include the name and location of the employer, and if readers are unlikely to recognize the organization, briefly describe what it does. When you want to keep the name of your current employer confidential, you can identify the firm by industry only ("a large video game developer"). If an organization's name or location has changed since you worked there, state the current name and location and include the old information preceded by "formerly . . ." Before or after each job listing, state your job title and give the years you worked in the job; use the phrase "to present" to denote current employment. Indicate whether a job was part time.

Devote the most space to the jobs that are most recent or most closely related to your target position. If you were personally responsible for something significant, be sure to mention it. Facts about your skills and accomplishments are the most important information you can give a prospective employer, so quantify them whenever possible.

One helpful exercise is to write a 30-second "commercial" for each major skill you want to highlight. The commercial should offer proof that you really do possess the skill. For your résumé, distill the commercials down to brief phrases; you can use the more detailed proof statements in cover letters and as answers to interview questions.[31]

If you have a number of part-time, temporary, or entry-level jobs that don't relate to your career objective, you have to use your best judgment when it comes to including or excluding them. Too many minor and irrelevant work details can clutter your résumé, particularly if you've been in the professional workforce for a few years. However, if you don't have a long employment history, including these jobs shows your ability and willingness to keep working.

> Devote the most space to jobs that are related to your target position.

Activities and Achievements

This optional section can be used to highlight activities and achievements outside of a work or educational context—but only if they make you a more attractive job candidate. For example, traveling, studying, or working abroad and fluency in multiple languages could weigh heavily in your favor with employers who do business internationally.

Because many employers are involved in their local communities, they tend to look positively on applicants who are active and concerned members of their communities as well. Consider including community service activities that suggest leadership, teamwork, communication skills, technical aptitude, or other valuable attributes.

You should generally avoid indicating membership or significant activity in religious or political organizations (unless, of course, you're applying to such an organization) because doing so might raise concerns for people with differing beliefs or affiliations. However, if you want to highlight skills you developed while involved with such a group, you can refer to it generically as a "not-for-profit organization."

Finally, if you have little or no job experience and not much to discuss outside of your education, indicating involvement in athletics or other organized student activities lets employers know that you don't spend all your free time hanging around your apartment playing video games. Also consider mentioning publications, projects, and other accomplishments that required relevant business skills.

> Include personal accomplishments only if they suggest special skills or qualities that are relevant to the jobs you're seeking.

Personal Data and References

In nearly all instances, your résumé should not include any personal data beyond the information described in the previous sections. When applying to U.S. companies, never include any of the following: physical characteristics, age, gender, marital status, sexual orientation, religious or political affiliations, race, national origin, salary history, reasons for leaving jobs, names of previous supervisors, names of references, Social Security number, or student ID number.

However, be aware that standards can vary in other countries. For example, some international employers might require you to include your citizenship, nationality, or marital status.[32]

The availability of references is assumed, so you don't need to put "References available upon request" at the end of your résumé. However, be sure to have a list of several references ready when you begin applying for jobs. Prepare your reference sheet with your name and contact information at the top. For a finished look, use the same design and layout you use for your résumé. Then list three or four people who have agreed to serve as references. Include each person's name, job title, organization, address, telephone number, email address (if the reference prefers to be contacted by email), and the nature of your relationship.

Figures 15.4 through 15.6 show how a job applicant can put these guidelines to work in three job-search scenarios.

> When applying to U.S. companies, your résumé should not include any personal data such as age, marital status, physical description, or Social Security number.

> Prepare a list of references but don't include them on your résumé.

The Scenario

You are about to graduate and have found a job opening that is in your chosen field. You don't have any experience in this field, but the courses you've taken in pursuit of your degree have given you a solid academic foundation for this position.

The Opportunity

The job opening is for an associate market analyst with Living Social, the rapidly growing advertising and social commerce service that describes itself as "the online source for discovering valuable local experiences." (A market analyst researches markets to find potentially profitable business opportunities.)

The Communication Challenge

You don't have directly relevant experience as a market analyst, and you might be competing against people who do. Your education is your strongest selling point, so you need to show how your coursework relates to the position.

Don't let your lack of experience hold you back; the job posting makes it clear that this is an entry-level position. For example, the first bullet point in the job description says "Become an expert in market data . . .," and the required skills and experience section says that "Up to 2 years of experience with similar research and analysis is preferred." The important clues here are *become* (the company doesn't expect you to be an expert already) and *preferred* (experience would be great if you have it, but it's not required).

Keywords and Key Phrases

You study the job posting and highlight the following elements:

1. Working in a team environment
2. Research, including identifying trendy new businesses
3. Analyzing data using Microsoft Excel
4. Managing projects
5. Collaborating with technical experts and sales staff
6. Creating new tools to help maximize revenue and minimize risks
7. Bachelor's degree is required
8. Natural curiosity and desire to learn
9. Detail oriented
10. Hands-on experience with social media

Emma Gomes
(847) 555–2153
emma.gomes@mailsystem.net
emmawrites.blogspot.com

Address:
860 North 8th Street, Terre Haute, IN 47809

Permanent Address:
993 Church Street, Barrington, IL 60010

Summary of Qualifications

- In-depth academic preparation in marketing analysis techniques
- Intermediate skills with a variety of analytical tools, including Microsoft Excel and Google Analytics
- Front-line experience with consumers and business owners
- Multiple research and communication projects involving the business applications of social media

Education

B.S. in Marketing (Marketing Management Track), Indiana State University, Terre Haute, IN, anticipated graduation: May 2014

Program coursework

- 45 credits of core business courses, including Business Information Tools, Business Statistics, Principles of Accounting, and Business Finance
- 27 credits of marketing and business management courses, including Buyer Behavior, Marketing Research, Product and Pricing Strategy, and seminars in e-commerce and social media

Special projects

- "Handcrafting a Global Marketplace: The Etsy Phenomenon," in-depth analysis of how Etsy transformed the market for handmade craft items by bringing e-commerce capabilities to individual craftspeople
- "Hybrid Communication Platforms for Small Businesses," team service project for five small businesses in Terre Haute, recommending best practices for combining traditional and social-media methods of customer engagement and providing a customized measurement spreadsheet for each company

Work and Volunteer Experience

Independent math tutor, 2009-present. Assist students with a variety of math courses at the elementary, junior high, and high school level; all clients have achieved combined test and homework score improvements of at least one full letter grade, with an average improvement of 38 percent

Volunteer, LeafSpring Food Bank, Terre Haute, IN (weekends during college terms, 2012–present). Stock food and supply pantries; prepare emergency baskets for new clients; assist director with public relations activities, including website updates and social media news releases.

Customer care agent, Owings Ford, Barrington, IL (summers, 2011–2013). Assisted the service and sales managers of this locally owned car dealership with a variety of customer-service tasks; scheduled service appointments; designed and implemented improvements to service-center waiting room to increase guest comfort; convinced dealership owners to begin using Twitter and Facebook to interact with current and potential customers.

Professional Engagement

- Collegiate member, American Marketing Association; helped establish the AMA Collegiate Chapter at Indiana State
- Participated in AMA International Collegiate Case Competition, 2011-2012

Awards

- Dean's List: 2012, 2013
- Forward Youth award, Barrington Chamber of Commerce, 2010

Gomes includes phone and email contacts, along with a blog that features academic-oriented writing.

Using a *summary of qualifications* for her opening statement lets her target the résumé and highlight her most compelling attributes.

Her education is a much stronger selling point than her work experience, so she goes into some detail—carefully selecting course names and project descriptions to echo the language of the job description.

She adjusts the descriptions and accomplishments of each role to highlight the aspects of her work and volunteer experience that are relevant to the position.

The final sections highlight activities and awards that reflect her interest in marketing and her desire to improve her skills.

Notice how Gomes adapts her résumé to "mirror" the keywords and phrases from the job posting:

1. Offers concrete evidence of teamwork (rather than just calling herself a "team player," for example)
2. Emphasizes research skills and experience in multiple instances
3. Calls out Microsoft Excel, as well as Google Analytics, a key online tool for measuring activity on websites
4. Indicates the ability to plan and carry out projects, even if she doesn't have formal project management experience
5. Indicates some experience working in a supportive or collaborative role with technical experts and sales specialists (the content of the work doesn't translate to the new job, but the concept does)
6. Suggests the ability to work with new analytical tools
7. Displays her B.S. degree prominently
8. Demonstrates a desire to learn and to expand her skills
9. Tracking the progress of her tutoring clients is strong evidence of a detail-oriented worker—not to mention someone who cares about results and the quality of her work
10. Lists business-oriented experience with Facebook, Twitter, and other social media

Figure 15.4 Crafting Your Résumé, Scenario 1: Positioning Yourself for an Ideal Opportunity
Even for an ideal job-search scenario, where your academic and professional experiences and interests closely match the parameters of the job opening, you still need to adapt your résumé content carefully to "echo" the specific language of the job description.[42]

Emma Gomes
(847) 555–2153
emma.gomes@mailsystem.net
emmawrites.blogspot.com

Address:
860 North 8th Street, Terre Haute, IN 47809

Permanent Address:
993 Church Street, Barrington, IL 60010

Summary of Qualifications

- ⑧ • Front-line customer service experience with consumers and business owners
- • Strong business sense based on work experience and academic preparation
- ⑥ • Intermediate skills with a variety of software tools, including Microsoft Excel and Google Analytics
- ⑩ • Record of quality work in both business and academic settings

Education

B.S. in Marketing (Marketing Management Track), Indiana State University, Terre Haute, IN, expected graduation May 2014

Program coursework

- ⑥ • 45 credits of core business courses, including Business Information Tools, Business Statistics, Principles of Accounting, and Business Finance
- ① • 27 credits of marketing and marketing management courses, including Marketing Fundamentals, Buyer Behavior, Marketing Research, Retail Strategies and seminars in e–commerce and social media

Special projects

- ① ② • "Handcrafting a Global Marketplace: The Etsy Phenomenon," in-depth analysis of how the Etsy e-commerce platform helps craftspeople and artisans become more successful merchants
- ① ② ⑨ • "Hybrid Communication Platforms for Small Businesses," team service project for five small businesses in Terre Haute, recommending best practices for combining traditional and social–media methods of customer engagement and providing a customized measurement spreadsheet for each company

Work and Volunteer Experience

- ③ ④ ⑩ **Independent math tutor, 2009-present.** Assist students with a variety of math courses at the elementary, junior high, and high school level; all clients have achieved combined test and homework score improvements of at least one full letter grade, with an average improvement of 38 percent

- ② **Volunteer, LeafSpring Food Bank, Terre Haute, IN (weekends during college terms, 2012–present).** Stock food and supply pantries; prepare emergency baskets for new clients; assist director with public relations activities, including website updates and social media news releases.

- ⑧ ⑤ **Customer care agent, Owings Ford, Barrington, IL (summers, 2011–2013).** Assisted the service and sales managers of this locally owned car dealership with a variety of customer-service tasks; scheduled service appointments; designed and implemented improvements to service-center waiting room to increase guest comfort; convinced dealership owners to begin using Twitter and Facebook to interact with current and potential customers.

Professional Engagement

- ⑦ • Collegiate member, American Marketing Association; helped establish the AMA Collegiate Chapter at Indiana State
- • Participated in AMA International Collegiate Case Competition, 2011-2012

Awards

- ③ ④ ⑩ • Dean's List: 2012, 2013
- ① • Forward Youth award, Barrington Chamber of Commerce, 2010

Gomes modified her summary of qualifications to increase emphasis on customer service.

She adjusts the selection of highlighted courses to reflect the retail and e-commerce aspects of this particular job opening.

She adjusts the wording of this Etsy project description to closely mirror what Amazon is—an e-commerce platform serving a multitude of independent merchants.

She provides more detail regarding her customer support experience.

The final sections are still relevant to this job opening, so she leaves them unchanged.

Notice how Gomes adapts her résumé to "mirror" the keywords and phrases from the job posting:

① Suggests strong awareness of the needs of various businesses

② Examples of experience with written business communication; she can demonstrate oral communication skills during phone, video, or in-person interviews

③ Results-oriented approach to tutoring business suggests high degree of professionalism, as do the two awards

④ The ability to work successfully as an independent tutor while attending high school and college is strong evidence of self-motivation and good time management

⑤ Indicates ability to understand problems and design solutions

⑥ Suggests the ability to work with a variety of software tools

⑦ Demonstrates a desire to learn and to expand her skills

⑧ Highlights customer service experience

⑨ Offers concrete evidence of teamwork (rather than just calling herself a "team player," for example)

⑩ Tracking the progress of her tutoring clients is strong evidence of someone who cares about results and the quality of her work; Dean's List awards also suggest quality of work; record of working while attending high school and college suggests strong productivity

Figure 15.5   Crafting Your Résumé, Scenario 2: Repositioning Yourself for Available Opportunities
If you can't find an ideal job opening, you'll need to adjust your plans and adapt your résumé to the openings that are available. Look for opportunities that meet your near-term financial needs while giving you the chance to expand your skill set so that you'll be even more prepared when an ideal opportunity does come along.[43]

The Scenario

Moving forward from Figures 15.4 and 15.5, let's assume you have worked in both those positions, first for two years as a seller support associate at Amazon and then for almost three years an associate market analyst at Living Social. You believe you are now ready for a bigger challenge, and the question is how to adapt your résumé for a higher-level position now that you have some experience in your chosen field. (Some of the details from the earlier résumés have been modified to accommodate this example.)

The Opportunity

The job opening is for a senior strategy analyst for Nordstrom. The position is similar in concept to the position at Living Social, but at a higher level and with more responsibility.

The Communication Challenge

This job is an important step up; a senior strategy analyst is expected to conduct in-depth financial analysis of business opportunities and make recommendations regarding strategy changes, merchandising partnerships with other companies, and important decisions.

You worked with a wide variety of retailers in your Amazon and Living Social jobs, including a number of fashion retailers, but you haven't worked directly in fashion retailing yourself.

Bottom line: You can bring a good set of skills to this position, but your financial analysis skills and retailing insights might not be readily apparent, so you'll need to play those up.

Keywords and Key Phrases

You study the job posting and highlight the following elements:

1. Provide research and analysis to guide major business strategy decisions
2. Communicate across business units and departments within Nordstrom
3. Familiar with retail analytics
4. Knowledge of fashion retailing
5. Qualitative and quantitative analysis
6. Project management
7. Strong communication skills
8. Bachelor's required; MBA preferred
9. Advanced skills in financial and statistical modeling
10. Proficient in PowerPoint and Excel

Emma Gomes
(847) 555–2153
emma.gomes@mailsystem.net
Twitter: www.twitter.com/emmagomes
1605 Queen Anne Avenue North, Seattle, WA 98109

Market and Strategy Analyst

- Five years of experience in local and online retailing, with three years of focus on market opportunity analysis
- Strong business sense developed through more than 60 marketing programs across a range of retail sectors, including hospitality, entertainment, and fashion
- Recognized by senior management for ability to make sound judgment calls in situations with incomplete or conflicting data
- Adept at coordinating research projects and marketing initiatives across organizational boundaries and balancing the interests of multiple stakeholders
- Advanced skills with leading analysis and communication tools, including Excel, PowerPoint, and Google Analytics

Professional Experience

Associate Market Analyst, LivingSocial, Seattle, WA (July 2011-present). Analyzed assigned markets for such factors as consumer demand, merchandising opportunities, and seller performance; designed, launched, and managed marketing initiatives in 27 retailing categories, including fashions and accessories; met or exceeded profit targets on 90 percent of all marketing initiatives; appointed team lead/trainer in recognition of strong quantitative and qualitative analysis skills; utilized both established and emerging social media tools and helped business partners use these communication platforms to increase consumer engagement in local markets.

Seller support associate, Amazon, Seattle, WA (July 2009–June 2011). Worked with more than 300 product vendors, including many in the fashion and accessories sectors, to assure profitable retailing activities on the Amazon e-commerce platform; resolved vendor issues related to e-commerce operations, pricing, and consumer communication; anticipated potential vendor challenges and assisted in the development of more than a dozen new selling tools that improved vendor profitability while reducing Amazon's vendor support costs by nearly 15 percent.

Education

Evening MBA program, University of Washington, Seattle, WA; anticipated graduation: May 2015. Broad-based program combining financial reporting, marketing strategy, competitive strategy, and supply chain management with individual emphasis on quantitative methods, financial analysis, and marketing decision models.

B.S. in Marketing (Marketing Management Track), Indiana State University, Terre Haute, IN, May 2009. Comprehensive coursework in business fundamentals, accounting and finance, marketing fundamentals, retailing, and consumer communications.

Professional Engagement

- Member, American Marketing Association
- Member, International Social Media Association
- Active in National Retail Federation and Retail Advertising & Marketing Association

Awards

- Living Social Top Ten Deals (monthly employee achievement award for designing the most profitable couponing deals); awarded seven times, 2011—2013
- Social Commerce Network's Social Commerce Innovators: 30 Under 30; 2012

Gomes stays with a summary of qualifications as her opening statement but gives it a new title to reflect her experience and to focus on her career path as a market analyst.

Work experience is now her key selling point, so she shifts to a conventional chronological résumé that puts employment ahead of education. She also removes the part-time jobs she had during high school and college.

She updates the Education section with a listing for the MBA program she has started (selecting points of emphasis relevant to the job opening) and reduces the amount of detail about her undergraduate degree.

She updates the Professional Engagement and Awards section with timely and relevant information.

Notice how Gomes adapts her résumé to "mirror" the keywords and phrases from the job posting:

1. Highlights her experience in market and business analysis and her continuing education in this area
2. Mentions skill at coordinating cross-functional projects
3. Lists experiences that relate to the collection and analysis of retail data
4. Emphasizes the work she has done with fashion-related retailing and retailing in general
5. Identifies experience and education that relates to quantitative and qualitative analysis (this point overlaps #1 and #3 to a degree)
6. Mentions project management experience
7. Lists areas that suggest effective communication skills
8. Lists education, with emphasis on coursework that relates most directly to the job posting
9. Mentions work experience and educational background related to these topics
10. Includes these programs in the list of software tools she uses

---

Figure 15.6 **Crafting Your Résumé, Scenario 3: Positioning Yourself for More Responsibility**
When you have a few years of experience under your belt, your résumé strategy should shift to emphasize work history and accomplishments. Here is how Emma Gomes might reshape her résumé if she had held the two jobs described in Figures 15.4 and 15.5 and is now ready for a bigger challenge.[44]

Completing Your Résumé

4 **LEARNING OBJECTIVE**
Characterize the completing step for résumés, including the six most common formats in which you can produce a résumé.

Completing your résumé involves revising it for optimum quality, producing it in the various forms and media you'll need, and proofreading it for any errors before distributing it or publishing it online.

REVISING YOUR RÉSUMÉ

Revising your résumé for clarity and conciseness is essential. Recruiters and hiring managers want to find key pieces of information about you, including your top skills, your current job, and your education, in a matter of seconds. Many are overwhelmed with résumés, and if they have to work to find or decode this information, chances are they'll toss yours aside and move on to the next one in the pile. Remember the fundamental purpose of the résumé—to get you an interview, not to get you a job. Weed out details and irrelevant information until your résumé is tight, clear, and focused.

> Revise your résumé until it is as short and clear as possible.

The ideal length of your résumé depends on the depth of your experience and the level of the positions for which you are applying. As a general guideline, if you have fewer than five years of professional experience, keep your conventional résumé to one page. For online résumé formats, you can always provide links to additional information. If you have more experience and are applying for a higher-level position, you may need to prepare a somewhat longer résumé.[33] For highly technical positions, longer résumés are often the norm as well because the qualifications for such jobs can require more description.

> If your employment history is brief, keep your résumé to one page.

PRODUCING YOUR RÉSUMÉ

No matter how many media and formats you eventually choose for producing your résumé, a clean, professional-looking design is a must. Recruiters and hiring managers typically skim your essential information in a matter of seconds, and anything that distracts or delays them will work against you.

> Effective résumé designs are clear, clean, and professional.

Choosing a Design Strategy for Your Résumé

You'll find a wide range of résumé designs in use today, from text-only examples that follow a conventional layout to full-color infographics with unique designs. As with every type of business message, keep your audience, your goals, and your resources in mind. Don't choose a style just because it seems trendy or flashy or different. For example, you can find a lot of eye-catching infographic résumés online, but many of those are created by graphic designers applying for visual jobs in advertising, fashion, web design, and other areas in which graphic design skills are a must. In other words, the intended audience expects an applicant to have design skills, and the résumé is a good opportunity to demonstrate those. In contrast, a colorful, graphically intense résumé might just look odd to recruiters in finance, engineering, or other professions.

> Don't pick a résumé style just because it's trendy or different; make sure it works for your specific needs.

The sample résumés in Figures 15.4 through 15.6 use a classic, conservative design that will serve you well for most business opportunities. Notice how they feature simplicity, an easy-to-read layout, effective use of white space, and clear typefaces. Recruiters can pick out the key pieces of information in a matter of seconds.

> With any résumé design, make sure that readers can find essential information in a matter of seconds.

You can certainly enhance your résumé beyond this style, but do so carefully and always with an eye on what will help the reader. Make subheadings easy to find and easy to read. Avoid big blocks of text, and use lists to itemize your most important qualifications. Color is not necessary by any means, but if you add color, make it subtle and sophisticated. Above all, don't make the reader work to find the key points of story. Your résumé should be a high-efficiency information-delivery system, not a treasure hunt.

Depending on the companies you apply to, you might want to produce your résumé in as many as six formats (all are explained in the following sections):

> Be prepared to produce versions of your résumé in multiple formats.

- Printed traditional résumé
- Printed scannable résumé

- Electronic plain-text file
- Microsoft Word file
- Online résumé
- PDF file

Unfortunately, no single format or medium will work for all situations, and employer expectations continue to change as technology evolves. Find out what each employer or job posting website expects, and provide your résumé in that specific format.

Considering Photos, Videos, Presentations, and Infographics

As you produce your résumé in various formats, you will encounter the question of whether to include a photograph of yourself on or with your résumé. For print or electronic documents that you will be submitting to employers or job websites, the safest advice is to avoid photos. The reason is that seeing visual cues of the age, ethnicity, and gender of candidates early in the selection process exposes employers to complaints of discriminatory hiring practices. In fact, some employers won't even look at résumés that include photos, and some applicant tracking systems automatically discard résumés with any extra files.[34] However, photographs are acceptable and expected for social media résumés and other online formats where you are not actively submitting a résumé to an employer.

In addition to the six main résumé formats, some applicants create PowerPoint or Prezi presentations, videos, or infographics to supplement a conventional résumé. Two key advantages of a presentation supplement are flexibility and multimedia capabilities. For instance, you can present a menu of choices on the opening screen and allow viewers to click through to sections of interest. (Note that most of the things you can accomplish with a presentation can be done with an online résumé, which is probably more convenient for most readers.)

A video résumé can be a compelling supplement as well, but be aware that some employment law experts advise employers not to view videos, at least not until after candidates have been evaluated solely on their credentials. The reason for this caution is the same as with photographs. In addition, videos are more cumbersome to evaluate than paper or electronic résumés, and some recruiters refuse to watch them.[35] However, not all companies share this concern over videos, so you'll have to research their individual preferences. In fact, the online retailer Zappos encourages applicant videos and provides a way to upload videos on its job application webpage.[36]

An infographic résumé attempts to convey a person's career development and skill set graphically through a visual metaphor such as a timeline or subway map or as a poster with array of individual elements. A well-designed infographic could be an intriguing element of the job-search package for candidates in certain situations and professions because it can definitely stand out from traditional résumés and can show a high level of skill in visual communication. However, infographics are likely to be incompatible with most applicant tracking systems and with the screening habits of most recruiters, so while you might stand out with an infographic, you might also get tossed out if you try to use an infographic in place of a conventional résumé. In virtually every situation, an infographic should complement a conventional résumé, not replace it. In addition, successful infographics require skills in graphical design, and if you lack those skills, you'll need to hire a designer.

Producing a Traditional Printed Résumé

Even though most of your application activity will take place online, having a copy of a conventional printed résumé is important for taking to job fairs, interviews, and other events. Many interviewers expect you to bring a printed résumé to the interview, even if you applied online. The résumé can serve as a note-taking form or discussion guide, and it is tangible evidence of your attention to professionalism and detail.[37] When printing a résumé, choose a heavier, higher-quality paper designed specifically for résumés and other important documents. White or slightly off-white is the best color choice. Avoid papers with borders or backgrounds.

Do not include or enclose a photo in résumés that you send to employers or post on job websites.

Use high-quality paper when printing your résumé.

Printing a Scannable Résumé

You might encounter a company that prefers *scannable résumés*, a type of printed résumé that is specially formatted to be compatible with optical scanning systems that convert printed documents to electronic text. These systems were quite common just a few years ago, but their use appears to be declining rapidly as more employers prefer email delivery or website application forms.[38] A scannable résumé differs from the traditional format in two major ways: It should always include a keyword summary, and it should be formatted in a simpler fashion that avoids underlining, special characters, and other elements that can confuse the scanning system. If you need to produce a scannable résumé, search online for "formatting a scannable résumé" to get detailed instructions.

Some employers still prefer résumés in scannable format, but most now want electronic submissions.

Creating a Plain-Text File of Your Résumé

A *plain-text file* (sometimes known as an ASCII text file) is an electronic version of your résumé that has no font formatting, no bullet symbols, no colors, no lines or boxes, and no other special formatting. The plain-text version can be used in two ways. First, you can include it in the body of an email message, for employers who want email delivery but don't want file attachments. Second, you can copy and paste the sections into the application forms on an employer's website.

A plain-text version of your résumé is simply a computer file without any of the formatting that you typically apply using word-processing software.

A plain-text version is easy to create with your word processor. Start with the file you used to create your résumé, use the "Save As" choice to save it as "plain text" or whichever similarly labeled option your software has, and verify the result by using a basic text editor (such as Microsoft Notepad). If necessary, reformat the page manually, moving text and inserting space as needed. For simplicity's sake, left-justify all your headings rather than trying to center them manually.

Make sure you verify the plain-text file that you create with your word processor; it might need a few manual adjustments using a text editor such as NotePad.

Creating a Word File of Your Résumé

In some cases, an employer or job-posting website will want you to upload a Microsoft Word file or attach it to an email message. (Although there are certainly other word-processing software programs available, Microsoft Word is the de facto standard in business these days.) This method of transferring information preserves the design and layout of your résumé and saves you the trouble of creating a plain-text version. However, before you submit a Word file to anyone, make sure your computer is free of viruses. Infecting a potential employer's computer will not make a good first impression.

Some employers and websites want your résumé in Microsoft Word format; make sure your computer is thoroughly scanned for viruses first, however.

Creating a PDF Version of Your Résumé

Creating a PDF file is a simple procedure, but you need the right software. Adobe Acrobat (not the free Adobe Reader) is the best-known program, but many others are available, including some free versions. You can also use Adobe's online service to create PDFs without buying software. The advantages of creating PDFs are that you preserve the formatting of your résumé (unlike pasting plain text into an email message), and you create a file type that is less vulnerable to viruses than word-processer files.

Creating an Online or Social Media Résumé

A variety of online résumé formats, variously referred to as *e-portfolios, interactive résumés,* or *social media résumés,* provide the opportunity to create a dynamic, multimedia presentation of your qualifications. You can expand on the information contained in your basic résumé with links to projects, publications, screencasts, online videos, course lists, blogs, social networking profiles, and other elements that give employers a more complete picture of who you are and what you can offer.

You have many options for creating an online résumé, from college-hosted e-portfolios to multimedia résumés on commercials websites.

You have a number of options for hosting an online résumé. Start with your college's career center; many such centers offer hosting for e-portfolios, for example, where you can showcase your academic achievements. You can also chose one of the commercial résumé hosting services, such as LinkedIn, VisualCV, and Gozaik. In addition to being free (for basic services, at least), these sites provide easy-to-use tools for creating your online profile. You can also use them to peruse examples of various résumés, from students just about to enter the workforce full-time all the way up to corporate CEOs.

Regardless of the approach you take to creating an online résumé, keep these helpful tips in mind:

- **Remember that your online presence is a career-management tool.** The way you are portrayed online can work for you or against you, and it's up to you to create a positive impression.
- **Take advantage of social networking.** Use whatever tools are available to direct people to your online résumé, such as including your URL in your Twitter profile.
- **During the application process, don't expect or ask employers to retrieve a résumé from a website.** Submit your résumé using whatever method and medium each employer prefers. If employers then want to know more about you, they will likely do a web search on you and find your site, or you can refer them to your site in your résumé or application materials.

PROOFREADING YOUR RÉSUMÉ

Your résumé can't be "pretty good" or "almost perfect"—it needs to be *perfect*, so proofread it thoroughly and ask several other people to verify it, too.

Employers view your résumé as a concrete example of your attention to quality and detail. Your résumé doesn't need to be good or pretty good—it needs to be *perfect*. Although it may not seem fair, just one or two errors in a job application package are enough to doom a candidate's chances.[39]

REAL-TIME UPDATES

LEARN MORE BY READING THIS ARTICLE

Don't let these mistakes cost you an interview

Make sure you don't commit these nine costly blunders. Go to http://real-timeupdates.com/ebc12 and click on Learn More in the Students section.

Your résumé is one of the most important documents you'll ever write, so don't rush or cut corners when it comes to proofreading. Check all headings and lists for clarity and parallelism, and be sure your grammar, spelling, and punctuation are correct. Double-check all dates, phone numbers, email addresses, and other essential data. Ask at least three other people to read it, too. As the creator of the material, you could stare at a mistake for weeks and not see it.

DISTRIBUTING YOUR RÉSUMÉ

When distributing your résumé, pay close attention to the specific instructions provided by every employer, job website, or other recipient.

How you distribute your résumé depends on the number of employers you target and their preferences for receiving résumés. Employers usually list their requirements on their websites, so verify this information and follow it carefully. Beyond that, here are some general distribution tips:

- **Mailing printed résumés.** Take some care with the packaging. Spend a few extra cents to mail these documents in a flat 9 × 12 envelope, or better yet, use a Priority Mail flat-rate envelope, which gives you a sturdy cardboard mailer and faster delivery for just a few more dollars.
- **Emailing your résumé.** Some employers want applicants to include the text of their résumés in the body of an email message; others prefer an attached Microsoft Word or PDF file. If you have a reference number or a job ad number, include it in the subject line of your email message.
- **Submitting your résumé to an employer's website.** Many employers, including most large companies, now prefer or require applicants to submit their résumés online. In some instances, you will be asked to upload a complete file. In others, you will need to copy and paste sections of your résumé into individual boxes in an online application form.
- **Posting your résumé on job websites.** You can post your résumé on general-purpose job websites such as Monster and CareerBuilder, on more specialized websites such as Jobster or Jobfox, or with staffing services such as Volt. Roughly 100,000 job boards are now online, so you'll need to spend some time looking for sites that specialize in your target industries, regions, or professions.[40] Before you upload your résumé to any site, however, learn about its privacy protection. Some sites allow you

---

CHECKLIST ✔ Writing an Effective Résumé

A. Plan your résumé.
- Analyze your purpose and audience carefully to make sure your message meets employers' needs.
- Gather pertinent information about your target companies.
- Select the required media types by researching the preferences of each employer.
- Organize your résumé around your strengths, choosing the chronological, functional, or combination structure. (Be careful about using the functional structure.)

B. Write your résumé.
- Keep your résumé honest.
- Adapt your résumé to your audience to highlight the qualifications each employer is looking for.
- Choose a career objective, qualifications summary, or career summary as your introductory statement—and make it concise, concrete, and reader-focused.

- Use powerful language to convey your name and contact information, introductory statement, education, work experience, skills, work or school accomplishments, and activities and achievements.

C. Complete your résumé.
- Revise your résumé until it is clear, concise, compelling—and perfect.
- Produce your résumé in all the formats you might need: traditional printed résumé, scannable, plain-text file, Microsoft Word file, PDF, or online.
- Proofread your résumé to make sure it is absolutely perfect.
- Distribute your résumé using the means that each employer prefers.

---

to specify levels of confidentiality, such as letting employers search your qualifications without seeing your personal contact information or preventing your current employer from seeing your résumé. Don't post your résumé to any website that doesn't give you the option of restricting the display of your contact information. Only employers that are registered clients of the service should be able to see your contact information.[41]

Don't post a résumé on any public website unless you understand its privacy and security policies.

For a quick summary of the steps to take when planning, writing, and completing your résumé, refer to "Checklist: Writing an Effective Résumé." For the latest information on résumé writing and distribution, visit http://real-timeupdates.com/ebc12 and click on Chapter 15.

ON THE JOB: SOLVING COMMUNICATION DILEMMAS AT VMWARE

You work as a recruiter in the human resources department at VMWare, where part of your responsibility involves using the applicant tracking system to identify promising job candidates. Solve these challenges by using what you've learned about presenting oneself effectively on a résumé.

1. You've learned to pay close attention to the introductory statement on résumés in order to match applicants' interests with appropriate job openings. You've selected four résumés for an accountant position. Which of the following is the most compelling statement for this position?
   a. Career objective: An entry-level financial position in a large company
   b. Qualifications summary: Proven track record of using accounting and financial talent and business savvy in shepherding companies toward explosive growth

   c. Qualifications summary: Solid academic grounding in business administration with experience in cash management and basic accounting procedures
   d. Career objective: To learn all I can about accounting in an exciting environment with a company whose reputation is as outstanding as VMWare's.

2. Of the education sections included in the résumés, which of the following is the most effective?
   a. **Morehouse College, Atlanta, GA, 2009–2013.** Received BA degree with a major in Business Administration and a minor in Finance. Graduated with a 3.65 grade point average. Played varsity football and basketball. Worked 15 hours per week in the library. Coordinated the local student chapter of the American Management Association. Member of Alpha Phi Alpha social fraternity.

b. **I attended Wayne State University in Detroit, Michigan, for two years and then transferred to the University of Michigan at Ann Arbor, where I completed my studies.** My major was economics, but I also took many business management courses, including employee motivation, small business administration, history of business start-ups, and organizational behavior. I selected courses based on the professors' reputation for excellence, and I received mostly A's and B's. Unlike many college students, I viewed the acquisition of knowledge—rather than career preparation—as my primary goal. I believe I have received a well-rounded education that has prepared me to approach management situations as problem-solving exercises.

c. **University of Connecticut, Storrs, Connecticut. Graduated with a BA degree in 2013.** Majored in Physical Education. Minored in Business Administration. Graduated with a 2.85 average.

d. **North Texas State University and University of Texas at Tyler.** Received BA and MBA degrees. I majored in business as an undergraduate and concentrated in financial management during my MBA program. Received a special $2,500 scholarship offered by Rotary international recognizing academic achievement in business courses. I also won the MEGA award in 2012. Dean's List.

3. Which of the résumés does the best job of portraying each candidate's work experience?

a. **McDonald's, Peoria, IL, 2009–2010. Part-time cook.** Worked 15 hours per week while attending high school. Prepared all menu items. Received employee-of-the-month award for outstanding work habits.
   University Grill, Ames, IA, 2011–2015. Part-time cook. Worked 20 hours per week while attending college. Prepared hot and cold sandwiches. Helped manager purchase ingredients. Trained new kitchen workers. Prepared work schedules for kitchen staff.

b. Although I have never held a full-time job, I have worked part-time and during summer vacations throughout my high school and college years. During my freshman and sophomore years in high school, I bagged groceries at the A&P store three afternoons a week, where I was generally acknowledged as one of the hardest-working employees. During my junior and senior years, I worked at the YMCA as an after-school counselor for elementary school children. I know I made a positive difference in their lives because I still get letters from some of them. During summer vacations while I was in college, I did construction work for a local homebuilder. The job paid well, and I also learned a lot about carpentry. I also worked part-time in college in the student cafeteria.

c. **Macy's Department Store, Sherman Oaks, CA, Summers, 2011–2014. Sales Consultant, Furniture Department.** Interacted with a diverse group of customers while endeavoring to satisfy their individual needs and make their shopping experience efficient and enjoyable. Under the direction of the sales manager, prepared employee schedules and completed departmental reports. Demonstrated computer skills and attention to detail while assisting with inventory management, working the cash register, and handling a variety of special orders and customer requests. Received the CEO Award (for best monthly sales performance) three times.

d. **Athens, GA, Civilian Member of Public Safety Committee, January–December 2015.**
   - Organized and promoted a lecture series on vacation safety and home security for the residents of Athens, GA; recruited and trained seven committee members to help plan and produce the lectures; persuaded local businesses to finance the program; designed, printed, and distributed flyers; wrote and distributed press releases; attracted an average of 120 people to each of three lectures
   - Developed a questionnaire to determine local residents' home security needs; directed the efforts of 10 volunteers working on the survey; prepared written report for city council and delivered oral summary of findings at town meeting; helped persuade city to fund new home security program
   - Initiated the Business Security Forum as an annual meeting at which local business leaders could meet to discuss safety and security issues; created promotional flyers for the first forum; convinced 19 business owners to fund a business security survey; arranged press coverage of the first forum

4. While you are analyzing four résumés suggested by your applicant tracking system, a fellow employee hands you the following résumé and says this person would be great for the opening in accounting. What action will you take?

a. Definitely recommend that VMWare take a look at this outstanding candidate.

b. Reject the application. He doesn't give enough information about when he attended college, what he majored in, or where he has worked.

c. Review the candidate's web-based e-portfolio, in which he has posted many of his school projects. If the assessment contains the missing information and the candidate sounds promising, recommend him for a closer look. If vital information is still missing, send the candidate an email requesting additional information. Make the decision once you receive all necessary information.

d. Consider the candidate's qualifications relative to those of other applicants. Recommend him if you cannot find three or four other applicants with more directly relevant qualifications.

Darius Jaidee
809 N. Perkins Rd, Stillwater, OK 74075
Phone: (405) 369-0098
Email: dariusj@okstate.edu

Career Objective: To build a successful career in financial management

Summary of Qualifications: As a student at the University of Oklahoma, Stillwater, completed a wide variety of assignments that demonstrate skills related to accounting and management. For example:

Planning skills: As president of the university's foreign affairs forum, organized six lectures and workshops featuring 36 speakers from 16 foreign countries within a nine-month period. Identified and recruited the speakers, handled their travel arrangements, and scheduled the facilities.

Communication skills: Wrote more than 25 essays and term papers on various academic topics, including at least 10 dealing with business and finance. As a senior, wrote a 20-page analysis of financial trends in the petroleum industry, interviewing five high-ranking executives in accounting and finance positions at ConocoPhillip's refinery in Ponca City, Oklahoma, and company headquarters in Houston, Texas.

Accounting and computer skills: Competent in all areas of Microsoft Office, including Excel spreadsheets and Access databases. Assisted with bookkeeping activities in parents' small business, including the conversion from paper-based to computer-based accounting (Peachtree software). Have taken courses in accounting, financial planning, database design, web design, and computer networking.

For more information, including employment history, please access my e-portfolio at http://dariusjaidee.com.

Learning Objectives Checkup

Assess your understanding of the principles in this chapter by reading each learning objective and studying the accompanying exercises. You can check your responses against the answer key on page 599.

Objective 15.1: List eight key steps to finding the ideal opportunity in today's job market.

1. How does writing the "story of you" help you plan your job search and craft your résumé?
   a. It helps you focus your résumé on your needs, rather than on the employer's.
   b. It helps you think about where you want to go and how to present yourself to target employers.
   c. It allows you to avoid writing a traditional structured résumé.
   d. It helps you plan the speech you should make at the beginning of every job interview.

2. ____ ____ ____ is a measure of how closely new employees meet a company's needs.

3. What is the first step that employers usually take when they need to find candidates to interview for a job opening?
   a. They search online for personal websites and e-portfolios that might contain information about potential candidates.
   b. They look inside the company for likely candidates.
   c. They post job openings on job boards such as Monster.com and CareerBuilder.com.
   d. They run ads in the local newspaper.

4. Which of these most accurately characterizes the respective approaches that employers use to find new employees and employees use to find new opportunities?
   a. Employers and employees look in the same places, in the same general sequence.
   b. The respective approaches of employers and employees are essentially opposite, with employers starting inside the firm and gradually moving toward help wanted ads as a last resort and employees starting with help wanted ads and moving in the other direction.
   c. Because websites are the only places that employers now communicate news of job openings, the web is the only place employees should look.
   d. The approaches of employees and employers have nothing in common.

5. Which of the following best describes the process of networking as it applies to your career?
   a. Making sure you are plugged into the online scene so that you don't miss out on any new Internet developments
   b. Making informal connections with a broad sphere of mutually beneficial business contacts
   c. Asking as many people as possible to alert you to interesting job opportunities
   d. Making sure you get to know everyone in your company shortly after accepting a new position

6. If you don't yet have significant work experience but still want to become a valued network member, which of the following tactics should you consider?
   a. Limit your networking to people whose work experience is similar to yours so that you can share similar information.
   b. Create a convenient, foldable, business-card-size version of your résumé that you can give to everyone you meet so they don't have to carry a full-size copy of your résumé.
   c. Avoid networking until you have enough work experience to be able to offer insider tips on the job market in your industry.
   d. Research recent trends in the business world in order to have interesting and useful information at your fingertips whenever you encounter people in your network.

Objective 15.2: Explain the process of planning your résumé, including how to choose the best résumé organization.

7. A/an ____ résumé highlights employment experience, listing jobs in reverse order from most recent to earliest.

8. A/an ____ résumé focuses on a person's particular skills and competencies, without itemizing his or her job history.

9. A/an ____ résumé uses elements of both the chronological and functional formats.

10. Which of the following is an advantage of the chronological résumé?
    a. It helps employers easily locate necessary information.
    b. It highlights your professional growth and career progress.
    c. It emphasizes continuity and stability in your employment background.
    d. It performs all of these communication functions.

11. Why are many employers suspicious of the functional résumé?
    a. It allows applicants to hide or downplay lengthy periods of unemployment or a lack of career progress.
    b. It doesn't scan into computer databases as effectively as other résumé formats.
    c. It doesn't provide any information about education.
    d. It encourages applicants to include accomplishments that were the result of teamwork rather than individual efforts.

12. Which of the following is a disadvantage of the combination résumé?
    a. It is impossible to convert to scannable format.
    b. It tends to be longer than other formats and can be repetitious.
    c. It doesn't work for people who have extensive job experience.
    d. The combination résumé has no disadvantages.

Objective 15.3: Describe the tasks involved in writing your résumé and list the major sections of a traditional résumé.

13. Which of the following sections should be included in any résumé, regardless of the format you've chosen?
    a. Contact information, education, and work experience
    b. Contact information, education, and personal references
    c. Personal data, contact information, and education
    d. Education, personal references, and career objectives

14. Why do some experts recommend against using a career objective as the introductory statement on your résumé?
    a. It can limit your possibilities as a candidate, particularly if you want to be considered for a variety of positions.

b. It shows that you're selfish and thinking only about your own success.

c. It shows that you're unrealistic because no one can plan a career that might last for 40 or 50 years.

d. It helps focus you as a candidate in the minds of potential employers.

15. How does a qualifications summary differ from a career summary?

a. They are identical.

b. A qualifications summary offers a brief view of your most important skills and attributes, whereas a career summary is a recap of your career progress.

c. No one uses a qualifications summary anymore, whereas a career summary is still popular.

d. The career summary is best for recent graduates, whereas the qualifications summary is best for people with a decade or two of experience.

16. Which should come first on your résumé, your education or your work experience?

a. Education should come first.

b. Work experience should come first.

c. It depends on which is more meaningful to an employer, given where you are in your career at this moment.

d. The best résumés today use a two-column format in which education and work experience are listed side by side.

17. How much personal data should you put on a résumé aimed at U.S. employers?

a. You should list your age, marital status, and physical handicaps that might require special accommodation.

b. You should list your age, marital status, a general assessment of your health (without mentioning any specific problems), and religious affiliation.

c. You should not list any personal data on your résumé.

d. You should not list anything related to health or nationality, but you should list age, gender, and salary history (assuming you've had at least one full-time job).

Objective 15.4: Characterize the completing step for résumés, including the six most common formats in which you can produce a résumé.

18. Which of the following best describes the level of quality you should achieve when producing your résumé?

a. With the advent of email and social networking, most companies are much more relaxed about grammar, spelling, and other old-school concerns, so don't sweat the details.

b. The typical recruiter in a major corporation sees so many résumés on any given day that most errors pass by unnoticed.

c. Your résumé needs to be perfect.

d. Your résumé should reflect your work habits, so if you're more of a strategic thinker and don't worry about insignificant details, make sure your résumé reflects that.

19. Most résumés are now subjected to _____ _____ in an applicant tracking system or other database, in which a recruiter looks for résumés most likely to match the requirements of a particular job.

20. A/an _____ _____ version of your résumé has the same content as a traditional résumé but has had all the formatting removed so that it can be easily emailed or copied into online forms.

21. Which of these is a significant advantage of an online résumé?

a. You can expand on the information contained in your basic résumé with links to projects, publications, screencasts, online videos, course lists, social networking profiles, and other elements.

b. You can build up your résumé over time and don't have to worry about having every little detail in place when you launch your job search.

c. You can use lots of color.

d. You can use the flexibility of the web to provide extensive details on your life history

Quick Learning Guide

CHAPTER OUTLINE

Finding the Ideal Opportunity in Today's Job Market
- Writing the Story of You
- Learning to Think Like an Employer
- Researching Industries and Companies of Interest
- Translating Your General Potential into a Specific Solution for Each Employer
- Taking the Initiative to Find Opportunities
- Building Your Network
- Seeking Career Counseling
- Avoiding Mistakes

Planning a Résumé
- Analyzing Your Purpose and Audience
- Gathering Pertinent Information
- Selecting the Best Media
- Organizing Your Résumé Around Your Strengths
- Addressing Areas of Concern

Writing a Résumé
- Keeping Your Résumé Honest
- Adapting Your Résumé to Your Audience
- Composing Your Résumé

Completing Your Résumé
- Revising Your Résumé
- Producing Your Résumé
- Proofreading Your Résumé
- Distributing Your Résumé

LEARNING OBJECTIVES

1 List eight key steps to finding the ideal opportunity in today's job market. (page 479)

2 Explain the process of planning your résumé, including how to choose the best résumé organization. (page 485)

3 Describe the tasks involved in writing your résumé, and list the major sections of a traditional résumé. (page 489)

4 Characterize the completing step for résumés, including the six most common formats in which you can produce a résumé. (page 497)

KEY TERMS

applicant tracking systems Computer systems that capture and store incoming résumés and help recruiters find good prtospects for current openings

chronological résumé The most common résumé format; it emphasizes work experience, with past jobs shown in reverse chronological order

combination résumé Format that includes the best features of the chronological and functional approaches

functional résumé Format that emphasizes your skills and capabilities while identifying employers and academic experience in subordinate sections; many recruiters view this format with suspicion

networking The process of making connections with mutually beneficial business contacts

résumé A structured, written summary of a person's education, employment background, and job qualifications

---

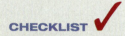

CHECKLIST ✔
Writing an Effective Résumé

A. Plan your résumé.
- Analyze your purpose and audience carefully to make sure your message meets employers' needs.
- Gather pertinent information about your target companies.
- Select the required media types by researching the preferences of each employer.
- Organize your résumé around your strengths, choosing the chronological, functional, or combination structure. (Be careful about using the functional structure.)

B. Write your résumé.
- Keep your résumé honest.
- Adapt your résumé to your audience to highlight the qualifications each employer is looking for.
- Choose a career objective, qualifications summary, or career summary as your introductory statement—and make it concise, concrete, and reader-focused.

- Use powerful language to convey your name and contact information, introductory statement, education, work experience, skills, work or school accomplishments, and activities and achievements.

C. Complete your résumé.
- Revise your résumé until it is clear, concise, compelling—and perfect.
- Produce your résumé in all the formats you might need: traditional printed résumé, scannable, plain-text file, Microsoft Word file, PDF, or online.
- Proofread your résumé to make sure it is absolutely perfect.
- Distribute your résumé using the means that each employer prefers.

Apply Your Knowledge

To review chapter content related to each question, refer to the indicated Learning Objective.

⭐ **15.1.** How can you "think like an employer" if you have no professional business experience? [LO-1]

15.2. If you were a team leader at a summer camp for children with special needs, should you include this in your employment history if you are applying for work that is unrelated? Explain your answer. [LO-3]

15.3. Can you use a qualifications summary if you don't yet have extensive professional experience in your desired career? Why or why not? [LO-3]

⭐ **15.4.** Some people don't have a clear career path when they enter the job market. If you're in this situation, how would your uncertainty affect the way you write your résumé? [LO-3]

⭐ **15.5.** Between your sophomore and junior years, you quit school for a year to earn the money to finish college. You worked as a loan-processing assistant in a finance company, checking references on loan applications, typing, and filing. Your manager made a lot of the fact that he had never attended college. He seemed to resent you for pursuing your education, but he never criticized your work, so you thought you were doing okay. After you'd been working there for six months, he fired you, saying that you'd failed to be thorough enough in your credit checks. You were actually glad to leave, and you found another job right away at a bank, doing similar duties. Now that you've graduated from college, you're writing your résumé. Will you include the finance company job in your work history? Explain. [LO-3]

Practice Your Skills

Message for Analysis

Read the following résumé information and then (1) analyze the strengths or weaknesses of the information and (2) revise the résumé so that it follows the guidelines presented in this chapter.

15.6. Message 15.A: Writing a Résumé [LO-3]

Sylvia Manchester
765 Belle Fleur Blvd.
New Orleans, LA 70113
(504) 312-9504
smanchester@rcnmail.com

Personal: Single, excellent health, 5'7", 136 lbs.; hobbies include cooking, dancing, and reading.

Job Objective: To obtain a responsible position in marketing or sales with a good company.

Education: BA degree in biology, University of Louisiana, 1998. Graduated with a 3.0 average. Member of the varsity cheerleading squad. President of Panhellenic League. Homecoming queen.

Work Experience

Fisher Scientific Instruments, 2014 to now, field sales representative. Responsible for calling on customers and explaining the features of Fisher's line of laboratory instruments. Also responsible for writing sales letters, attending trade shows, and preparing weekly sales reports.

Fisher Scientific Instruments, 2011–2013, customer service representative. Was responsible for handling incoming phone calls from customers who had questions about delivery, quality, or operation of Fisher's line of laboratory instruments. Also handled miscellaneous correspondence with customers.

Medical Electronics, Inc., 2008–2011, administrative assistant to the vice president of marketing. In addition to handling typical secretarial chores for the vice president of marketing, I was in charge of compiling the monthly sales reports, using figures provided by members of the field sales force. I also was given responsibility for doing various market research activities.

New Orleans Convention and Visitors Bureau, 2005–2008, summers, tour guide. During the summers of my college years, I led tours of New Orleans for tourists visiting the city. My duties included greeting conventioneers and their spouses at hotels, explaining the history and features of the city during an all-day sightseeing tour, and answering questions about New Orleans and its attractions. During my fourth summer with the bureau, I was asked to help train the new tour guides. I prepared a handbook that provided interesting facts about the various tourist attractions, as well as answers to the most commonly asked tourist questions. The Bureau was so impressed with the handbook they had it printed up so that it could be given as a gift to visitors.

University of Louisiana, 2005–2008, part-time clerk in admissions office. While I was a student in college, I worked 15 hours a week in the admissions office. My duties included filing, processing applications, and handling correspondence with high school students and administrators.

Exercises

Each activity is labeled according to the primary skill or skills you will need to use. To review relevant chapter content, you can refer to the indicated Learning Objective. In some instances, supporting information will be found in another chapter, as indicated.

15.7. Career Management: Researching Career Opportunities [LO-1]   Based on the preferences you identified in your career self-assessment (see page xlv in the Prologue) and the academic, professional, and personal qualities you have to offer, perform an online search for a career that matches your interests (starting with the websites listed in Table 15.1). Draft a brief report for your instructor, indicating how the career you select and the job openings you find match your strengths and preferences.

Message Strategies: Writing a Résumé; Collaboration: Team Projects [LO-3], Chapter 2 Working with another student, change the following statements to make them more effective for a résumé by using action verbs.

15.8. Have some experience with database design.

15.9. Assigned to a project to analyze the cost accounting methods for a large manufacturer.

15.10. I was part of a team that developed a new inventory control system.

15.11. Am responsible for preparing the quarterly department budget.

15.12. Was a manager of a department with seven employees working for me.

15.13. Was responsible for developing a spreadsheet to analyze monthly sales by department.

15.14. Put in place a new program for ordering supplies.

15.15. **Message Strategies: Writing a Résumé; Communication Ethics: Resolving Ethical Dilemmas, [LO-3] Chapter 1** Assume that you achieved all the tasks shown in Exercises 15.8 through 15.14 not as an individual employee but as part of a work team. In your résumé, must you mention other team members? Explain your answer.

15.16. **Completing a Résumé [LO-4]** Using your revised version of the résumé in Message for Analysis 15.A, create a plain-text file that Sylvia Manchester could use to include in email messages.

15.17. **Completing a Résumé [LO-4]** Imagine you are applying for work in a field that involves speaking in front of an audience, such as sales, consulting, management, or training. Using material you created for any of the exercises or cases in Chapter 14, record a two- to three-minute video demonstration of your speaking and presentation skills. Record yourself speaking to an audience, if one can be arranged.

Expand Your Skills

Critique the Professionals

Locate an example of an online résumé (a sample or an actual résumé). Analyze the résumé following the guidelines presented in this chapter. Using whatever medium your instructor requests, write a brief analysis (no more than one page) of the résumé's strengths and weaknesses, citing specific elements from the résumé and support from the chapter. If you are analyzing a real résumé, do not include any personally identifiable data, such as the person's name, email address, or phone number, in your report.

Sharpen Your Career Skills Online

Bovée and Thill's Business Communication Web Search, at http://websearch.businesscommunicationnetwork.com, is a unique research tool designed specifically for business communication research. Use the Web Search function to find a website, video, PDF document, podcast, or presentation that offers advice on creating effective online résumés. Write a brief email message to your instructor or a post for your class blog, describing the item that you found and summarizing the career skills information you learned from it.

Improve Your Grammar, Mechanics, and Usage

The following exercises help you improve your knowledge of and power over English grammar, mechanics, and usage. Turn to the "Handbook of Grammar, Mechanics, and Usage" at the end of this book and review all of Sections 4.1 (Frequently Confused Words), 4.2 (Frequently Misused Words), and 4.3 (Frequently Misspelled Words). Then review the following items and indicate the preferred choice within each set of parentheses. (Answers to these exercises appear on page 601.)

15.18. Everyone (*accept, except*) Barbara King has registered for the company competition.

15.19. We need to find a new security (*device, devise*).

15.20. The Jennings are (*loath, loathe*) to admit that they are wrong.

15.21. That decision lies with the director, (*who's whose*) in charge of this department.

15.22. In this department, we see (*a lot, alot*) of mistakes like that.

15.23. In my (*judgement, judgment*), you'll need to redo the cover.

15.24. He decided to reveal the information, (*irregardless, regardless*) of the consequences.

15.25. Why not go along when it is so easy to (*accomodate, accommodate*) his demands?

15.26. When you say that, do you mean to (*infer, imply*) that I'm being unfair?

15.27. All we have to do is try (*and, to*) get along with him for a few more days.

For additional exercises focusing on frequently confused, misused, or misspelled words, visit MyBCommLab. Click on Chapter 15, click on Additional Exercises to Improve Your Grammar, Mechanics, and Usage, and then click on 21. Frequently confused words, 22. Frequently misused words, or 23. Frequently misspelled words.

Cases

Website links for selected companies mentioned in cases can be found in the Student Assignments section at http://real-time updates.com/ebc12.

CAREER SKILLS/EMAIL SKILLS

15.28. Career Planning: Researching Career Opportunities [LO-1] Knowing the jargon and "hot button" issues in a par-ticular profession or industry can give you a big advantage when it comes to writing your résumé and participating in job interviews. You can fine-tune your résumé for both human readers and applicant tracking systems, sound more confident and informed in interviews, and present yourself as a professional-class individual with an inquiring mind.

Your task: Imagine a specific job category in a company that has an informative, comprehensive website (to facilitate the research you'll need to do). This doesn't have to be a current job opening, but a position you know exists or is likely to exist in this company, such as a business systems analyst at Apple or a brand manager at Unilever.

Explore the company's website and other online sources to find the following: (1) a brief description of what this job entails, with enough detail that you could describe it to a fellow student; (2) some of the terminology used in the profession or industry, both formal terms that might serve as keywords on your résumé and informal terms and phrases that insiders are likely to use in publications and conversations; (3) an ongoing online conversation among people in this profession, such as a LinkedIn Group, a popular industry or professional blog that seems to get quite a few comments, or an industry or professional publication that attracts a lot of comments; and (4) at least one significant issue that will affect people in this profession or companies in this industry over the next few years. For example, if your chosen profession involves accounting in a publicly traded corporation, upcoming changes in international financial reporting standards would be a significant issue. Similarly, for a company in the consumer electronics industry, the recycling and disposal of e-waste is an issue. Write a brief email message summarizing your findings and explaining how you could use this information on your résumé and during job interviews.

CAREER SKILLS/EMAIL SKILLS

15.29. Career Management: Researching Career Opportunities [LO-1] Perhaps you won't be able to land your ultimate dream job right out of college, but that doesn't mean you shouldn't start planning right now to make that dream come true.

Your task: Using online job search tools, find a job that sounds just about perfect for you, even if you're not yet qualified for it. It might even be something that would take 10 or 20 years to reach. Don't settle for something that's not quite right—find a job that is so "you" and so exciting that you would jump out of bed every morning, eager to go to work (such jobs really do exist!). Start with the job description you found online and then supplement it with additional research so that you get a good picture of what this job and career path are all about. Compile a list of all the qualifications you would need in order to have a reasonable chance of landing such a job. Now compare this list with your current résumé. Write a brief email message to your instructor that identifies all the areas in which you would need to improve your skills, work experience, education, and other qualifications in order to land your dream job.

CAREER SKILLS/TEAM SKILLS

15.30. Planning a Résumé [LO-2] If you haven't begun your professional career yet or you are pursuing a career change, the employment history section on your résumé can sometimes be a challenge to write. A brainstorming session with your wise and creative classmates could help.

Your task: In a team assigned by your instructor, help each other evaluate your employment histories and figure out the best way to present your work backgrounds on a résumé. First, each member of the team should compile his or her work history, including freelance projects and volunteer work if relevant, and share this information with the team. After allowing some time for everyone to review each other's information, meet as a team (in person if you can, or online otherwise). Discuss each person's history, pointing out strong spots and weak spots, and then brainstorm the best way to present each person's employment history.

Note: If there are aspects of your employment history you would rather not share with your teammates, substitute a reasonably similar experience of the same duration.

CAREER SKILLS/TEAM SKILLS

15.31. Writing a Résumé [LO-3] The introductory statement of a résumé requires some careful thought, both in deciding which of the three types of introductory statement (see page 491) to use and what information to include in it. Getting another person's perspective on this communication challenge can be helpful. In this activity, in fact, someone else is going to write your introductory statement for you, and you will return the favor.

Your task: Pair off with a classmate. Provide each other with the basic facts about your qualifications, work history, education, and career objectives. Then meet in person or online for an informal interview, in which you ask each other questions to flesh out the information you have on each other. Assume that each of you has chosen to use a qualifications summary for your résumé. Now write each other's qualifications summary and then trade them for review. As you read what your partner wrote about you, ask yourself if this feels true to what you believe about yourself and your career aspirations. Do you think it introduces you effectively to potential employers? What might you change about it?

PRESENTATION SKILLS/PORTFOLIO BUILDER

15.32. Message Strategies: Completing a Résumé [LO-4] Creating presentations and other multimedia supplements can be a great way to expand on the brief overview that a résumé provides.

Your task: Starting with any version of a résumé you've created for yourself, create a PowerPoint presentation that expands on your résumé information to give potential employers a more complete picture of what you can contribute. Include samples of your work, testimonials from current or past employers and colleagues, videos of speeches you've made, and anything else that tells the story of the professional "you." If you have a specific job or type of job in mind, focus your presentation on that. Otherwise, present a more general picture that shows why you would be a great employee for any company to consider. Be sure to review the information from Chapter 14 about creating professional-quality presentations.

CAREER SKILLS/VIDEO SKILLS

15.33. Message Strategies: Completing a Résumé [LO-4] In the right circumstances, brief videos can be an effective complement to a traditional job-search communication package.

Your task: Find a job opening that interests you (something you are at least partially qualified for at this stage of your career) and produce a two-minute video profile of yourself, highlighting the skills mentioned in the job description. For tips on producing effective video, visit **www.indie-film-making.com**.

Endnotes

1. Ladan Nikravan, "Socially Exceptional Recruiting," *Talent Management*, 6 March 2015, www.talentmgt.com; VMWare website, accessed 13 March 2015, www.vmware.com; VMWare Careers profile on LinkedIn, accessed 12 March 2015, www.linkedin.com/company/vmware/careers; VMWare University Twitter account, accessed 13 March 2015, https://twitter.com/vmwareu; VMWare Community portal, accessed 13 March 2015, https://communities.vmware.com; James Molloy profile on LinkedIn, accessed 13 March 2015, www.linkedin.com/in/jmolloy.

2. Courtland L. Bovée and John V. Thill, *Business in Action*, 5th ed. (Boston: Pearson Prentice Hall, 2011), 241–242.

3. Anne Fisher, "How to Get Hired by a 'Best' Company," *Fortune*, 4 February 2008, 96.

4. Eve Tahmincioglu, "Revamping Your Job-Search Strategy," *MSNBC.com*, 28 February 2010, www.msnbc.com.

5. Jessica Dickler, "The Hidden Job Market," *CNNMoney.com*, 10 June 2009, http://money.cnn.com.

6. Tara Weiss, "Twitter to Find a Job," *Forbes*, 7 April 2009, www.forbes.com.

7. Miriam Saltpeter, "Using Facebook Groups for Job Hunting," Keppie Careers blog, 13 November 2008, www.keppiecareers.com.

8. Anne Fisher, "Greener Pastures in a New Field," *Fortune*, 26 January 2004, 48.

9. Liz Ryan, "Etiquette for Online Outreach," Yahoo! Hotjobs website, accessed 26 March 2008, http://hotjobs.yahoo.com.

10. Eve Tahmincioglu, "Employers Digging Deep on Prospective Workers," *MSNBC.com*, 26 October 2009, www.msnbc.com.

11. Career and Employment Services, Danville Area Community College website, accessed 23 March 2008, www.dacc.edu/career; Career Counseling, Sarah Lawrence College website, accessed 23 March 2008, www.slc.edu/occ/index.php; Cheryl L. Noll, "Collaborating with the Career Planning and Placement Center in the Job-Search Project," *Business Communication Quarterly* 58, no. 3 (1995): 53–55.

12. Rachel Emma Silverman, "No More Résumés, Say Some Firms," *Wall Street Journal*, 24 January 2012, http://online.wsj.com.

13. Randall S. Hansen and Katharine Hansen, "What Résumé Format Is Best for You?" QuintCareers.com, accessed 7 August 2010, www.quintcareers.com.

14. Hansen and Hansen, "What Résumé Format Is Best for You?"

15. Katharine Hansen, "Should You Consider a Functional Format for Your Resume?" QuintCareers.com, accessed 7 August 2010, www.quintcareers.com.

16. Kim Isaacs, "Resume Dilemma: Criminal Record," Monster.com, accessed 23 May 2006, www.monster.com; Kim Isaacs, "Resume Dilemma: Employment Gaps and Job-Hopping," Monster.com, accessed 23 May 2006, www.monster.com; Susan Vaughn, "Answer the Hard Questions Before Asked," *Los Angeles Times*, 29 July 2001, W1–W2.

17. John Steven Niznik, "Landing a Job with a Criminal Record," *About.com*, accessed 12 December 2006, http://jobsearchtech.about.com.

18. "How to Ferret Out Instances of Résumé Padding and Fraud," *Compensation & Benefits for Law Offices*, June 2006, 1.

19. "Resume Fraud Gets Slicker and Easier," *CNN.com*, accessed 11 March 2004, www.cnn.com.

20. "Resume Fraud Still Major Problem HR Needs to Address," *HR Focus*, July 2012, 13–15.

21. Cari Tuna and Keith J. Winstein, "Economy Promises to Fuel Résumé Fraud," *Wall Street Journal*, 17 November 2008, http://online.wsj.com; Lisa Takeuchi Cullen, "Getting Wise to Lies," *Time*, 1 May 2006, 59; "Resume Fraud Gets Slicker and Easier"; Employment Research Services website, accessed 18 March 2004, www.erscheck.com.

22. "How to Ferret Out Instances of Résumé Padding and Fraud."

23. Jacqueline Durett, "Redoing Your Résumé? Leave Off the Lies," *Training*, December 2006, 9; "Employers Turn Their Fire on Untruthful CVs," *Supply Management*, 23 June 2005, 13.

24. Cynthia E. Conn, "Integrating Writing Skills and Ethics Training in Business Communication Pedagogy: A Résumé Case Study Exemplar," *Business Communication Quarterly*, June 2008, 138–151; Marilyn Moats Kennedy, "Don't Get Burned by Résumé Inflation," *Marketing News*, 15 April 2007, 37–38.

25. Rockport Institute, "How to Write a Masterpiece of a Résumé," accessed 9 August 2010, www.rockportinstitute.com.

26. Lora Morsch, "25 Words That Hurt Your Resume," *CNN.com*, 20 January 2006, www.cnn.com.

27. Liz Ryan, "The Reengineered Résumé," *BusinessWeek*, 3 December 2007, SC12.

28. Katharine Hansen, "Tapping the Power of Keywords to Enhance Your Resume's Effectiveness," QuintCareers.com, accessed 7 August 2010, www.quintcareers.com.

29. Hansen, "Tapping the Power of Keywords to Enhance Your Resume's Effectiveness."

30. Anthony Balderrama, "Resume Blunders That Will Keep You from Getting Hired," *CNN.com*, 19 March 2008, www.cnn.com; Michelle Dumas, "5 Resume Writing Myths," Distinctive Documents blog, 17 July 2007, http://blog.distinctiveweb.com; Kim Isaacs, "Resume Dilemma: Recent Graduate," Monster.com, accessed 26 March 2008, http://career-advice.monster.com.

31. Karl L. Smart, "Articulating Skills in the Job Search," *Business Communication Quarterly* 67, no. 2 (June 2004): 198–205.

32. "When to Include Personal Data," ResumeEdge.com, accessed 25 March 2008, www.resumeedge.com.

33. "Résumé Length: What It Should Be and Why It Matters to Recruiters," *HR Focus*, June 2007, 9.

34. John Hazard, "Resume Tips: No Pictures, Please and No PDFs," Career-Line.com, 26 May 2009, www.career-line.com; "25 Things You Should Never Include on a Resume," HR World website 18 December 2007, www.hrworld.com.

35. John Sullivan, "Résumés: Paper, Please," *Workforce Management*, 22 October 2007, 50; "Video Résumés Offer Both Pros and Cons During Recruiting," *HR Focus*, July 2007, 8.

36. Jobs page, Zappos website, accessed 24 March 2011, http://about .zappos.com/jobs.

37. Rachel Louise Ensign, "Is the Paper Résumé Dead?" *Wall Street Journal*, 24 January 2012, http://online.wsj.com.

38. Nancy M. Schullery, Linda Ickes, and Stephen E. Schullery, "Employer Preferences for Résumés and Cover Letters," *Business Communication Quarterly*, June 2009, 163–176.

39. "10 Reasons Why You Are Not Getting Any Interviews," *Miami Times*, 7–13 November 2007, 6D.

40. Deborah Silver, "Niche Sites Gain Monster-Sized Following," *Workforce Management*, March 2011, 10–11.

41. "Protect Yourself from Identity Theft When Hunting for a Job Online," *Office Pro*, May 2007, 6.

42. Job description keywords and key phrases quoted or adapted in part from "Associate Market Analyst" job opening posted on LivingSocial website, accessed 9 July 2012, http://corporate.livingsocial.com.

43. Job description keywords and key phrases quoted or adapted in part from "Seller Support Associate" job opening posted on Amazon website, accessed 12 July 2012, https://us-amazon.icims.com/jobs.

44. Job description keywords and key phrases quoted or adapted in part from "Senior Strategy Analyst" job opening posted on Nordstrom website, accessed 17 July 2012, http://careers .nordstrom.com.

Applying and Interviewing for Employment

LEARNING OBJECTIVES

After studying this chapter, you will be able to

1 Explain the purposes of application letters and describe how to apply the AIDA organizational approach to them.

2 Describe the typical sequence of job interviews, the major types of interviews, and the attributes employers look for during an interview.

3 List six tasks you need to complete to prepare for a successful job interview.

4 Explain how to succeed in all three stages of an interview.

5 Identify the most common employment messages that follow an interview and explain when you would use each one.

ON THE JOB: COMMUNICATING AT
ZAPPOS

Unconventional Approaches to Finding Unconventional Employees

When a company communicates its core values with the help of a cartoon amphibian named Core Values Frog, you can guess the company doesn't quite fit the stuffy corporate stereotype. While it is passionately serious about customer satisfaction and employee engagement, the Las Vegas–based online shoe and clothing retailer Zappos doesn't take itself too seriously. In fact, one of the 10 values the frog promotes is "Create fun and a little weirdness."

Fun and a little weirdness can make a workplace more enjoyable, but CEO Tony Hsieh's commitment to employees runs

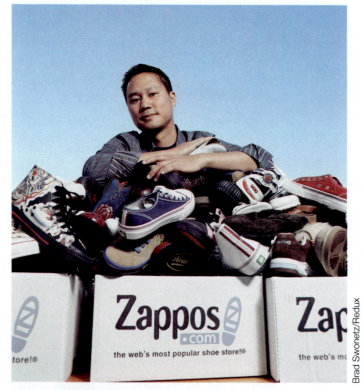

Brad Swonetz/Redux

Zappos CEO Tony Hsieh makes sure the company's interviewing process finds the candidates who are compatible with an offbeat customer- and colleague-focused culture.

much deeper than that. The company makes frequent reference to "the Zappos Family," and it embraces the ideals of taking care of one another and enjoying time spent together. These activities can range from parades in the workplace and other goofy events to the Wishez program, in which employees can ask one another to fulfill personal wishes, from lighthearted desires such as getting backstage access at concerts to serious matters such as getting help during tough financial times.

To find employees who will thrive in and protect the unconventional Zappos culture, the company takes an unorthodox path when it comes to recruiting and interviewing. For example, in stark contrast to the companies that refuse to look at videos as part of job application packages, Zappos encourages applicants to send videos of themselves. And in perhaps its boldest recruiting move yet, the company no longer posts job openings. Instead, it now requires would-be employees to join a customized social network called Inside Zappos. The network lets candidates learn more about what it's like to work at Zappos, and it lets the company learn more about the candidates—including how they interact with other people.

The Zappos interviewing process is designed to find passionate, free-thinking candidates who fit the culture, from the offbeat antics to the serious commitment to customers and fellow employees. Some of the questions interviewees can expect to encounter include "What was the best mistake you made on the job?" and "On a scale of 1 to 10, how weird are you?"

Speaking of offbeat interviews, the company recently screened software engineering candidates using 30-minute coding challenges, in which the first programmer to solve the problem was "fast-tracked to Vegas" for the next round of interviews. Coding contests are not all that unusual for recruiting programmers, but it's unlikely that many feature an open bar, as the Zappos competition did.

A strong customer- and employee-focused culture, a strong commitment to maintaining that culture, and a recruiting strategy that finds the right people for that culture—this relentless focus on doing business the Zappos way keeps paying off. The company continues to grow and to be ranked as one of the best places to work in the United States.[1]

WWW.ZAPPOS.COM

Submitting Your Résumé

Your résumé (see Chapter 15) is the centerpiece of your job search package, but it needs support from several other employment messages, including application letters, job-inquiry letters, application forms, and follow-up notes.

1   LEARNING OBJECTIVE
Explain the purposes of application letters and describe how to apply the AIDA organizational approach to them.

WRITING APPLICATION LETTERS

Whenever you mail, email, hand-deliver, or upload your résumé, you should include an **application letter**, also known as a *cover letter*, to let readers know what you're sending, why you're sending it, and how they can benefit from reading it. (Even though this message is often not a printed letter anymore, many professionals still refer to it as a letter.) Take the same care with your application letter that you took with your résumé. A poorly written application letter can prompt employers to skip over your résumé, even if you are a good fit for a job.[2] Staffing specialist Abby Kohut calls the application letter "a writing-skills evaluation in disguise" and emphasizes that even a single error can get you bounced from contention.[3]

Always accompany your résumé with an application letter (printed or email) that motivates the recipient to read the résumé.

The best approach for an application letter depends on whether you are applying for an identified job opening or are *prospecting*—taking the initiative to write to companies even though they haven't announced a job opening that is right for you.[4] In many ways, the difference between the two is like the difference between solicited and unsolicited proposals (see page 349). Figure 16.1 on the next page shows an application message written in response to a posted job opening. The writer knows exactly what qualifications the organization is seeking and can "echo" those attributes back in his letter.

As with proposals, the best approach for an application letter depends on whether your application is solicited or unsolicited.

Writing a prospecting letter is more challenging because you don't have the clear target you have with a solicited letter, and the message is unexpected. You will need to do more research to identify the qualities that a company would probably seek for the position you hope to occupy (see Figure 16.2 on page 515). Also, search for news items that involve the company, its customers, the profession, or the individual manager to whom you are writing. Using this information in your application letter helps you establish common ground with your reader—and it shows that you are tuned in to what is going on in the industry.

MOBILE APP
The CareerBuilder app lets you search and apply for jobs from your phone or tablet.

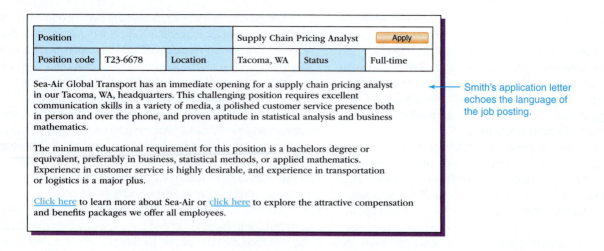

Smith's application letter echoes the language of the job posting.

Position			Supply Chain Pricing Analyst		Apply
Position code	T23-6678	Location	Tacoma, WA	Status	Full-time

Sea-Air Global Transport has an immediate opening for a supply chain pricing analyst in our Tacoma, WA, headquarters. This challenging position requires excellent communication skills in a variety of media, a polished customer service presence both in person and over the phone, and proven aptitude in statistical analysis and business mathematics.

The minimum educational requirement for this position is a bachelors degree or equivalent, preferably in business, statistical methods, or applied mathematics. Experience in customer service is highly desirable, and experience in transportation or logistics is a major plus.

Click here to learn more about Sea-Air or click here to explore the attractive compensation and benefits packages we offer all employees.

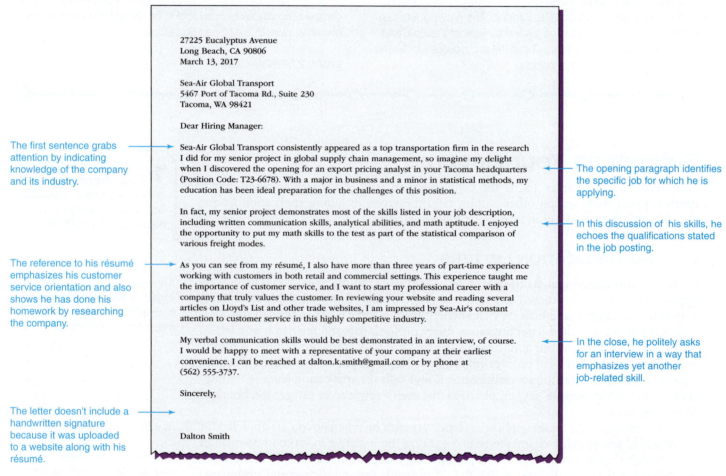

The first sentence grabs attention by indicating knowledge of the company and its industry.

The reference to his résumé emphasizes his customer service orientation and also shows he has done his homework by researching the company.

The letter doesn't include a handwritten signature because it was uploaded to a website along with his résumé.

27225 Eucalyptus Avenue
Long Beach, CA 90806
March 13, 2017

Sea-Air Global Transport
5467 Port of Tacoma Rd., Suite 230
Tacoma, WA 98421

Dear Hiring Manager:

Sea-Air Global Transport consistently appeared as a top transportation firm in the research I did for my senior project in global supply chain management, so imagine my delight when I discovered the opening for an export pricing analyst in your Tacoma headquarters (Position Code: T23-6678). With a major in business and a minor in statistical methods, my education has been ideal preparation for the challenges of this position.

In fact, my senior project demonstrates most of the skills listed in your job description, including written communication skills, analytical abilities, and math aptitude. I enjoyed the opportunity to put my math skills to the test as part of the statistical comparison of various freight modes.

As you can see from my résumé, I also have more than three years of part-time experience working with customers in both retail and commercial settings. This experience taught me the importance of customer service, and I want to start my professional career with a company that truly values the customer. In reviewing your website and reading several articles on Lloyd's List and other trade websites, I am impressed by Sea-Air's constant attention to customer service in this highly competitive industry.

My verbal communication skills would be best demonstrated in an interview, of course. I would be happy to meet with a representative of your company at their earliest convenience. I can be reached at dalton.k.smith@gmail.com or by phone at (562) 555-3737.

Sincerely,

Dalton Smith

The opening paragraph identifies the specific job for which he is applying.

In this discussion of his skills, he echoes the qualifications stated in the job posting.

In the close, he politely asks for an interview in a way that emphasizes yet another job-related skill.

Figure 16.1 Solicited Application Message
In this response to an online job posting, Dalton Smith highlights his qualifications while mirroring the requirements specified in the posting. Following the AIDA model, he grabs attention immediately by letting the reader know he is familiar with the company and the global transportation business.

For either type of letter, follow these tips to be more effective:[5]

- Resist the temptation to stand out with gimmicky application letters; impress with knowledge and professionalism instead.
- If the name of an individual manager is findable, address your letter to that person. (And if it is findable, make sure you find it, because other applicants will.) Search LinkedIn, the company's website, industry directories, Twitter, and anything else

Ineffective

457 Mountain View Rd.
Clear Lake, IA 50428
June 16, 2017

Ms. Patricia Downing, Store Manager
Walmart
840 South Oak
Iowa Falls, IA 50126

Dear Ms. Downing:

Do you have any openings for people who want to move into store management? I am really looking for an opportunity to get a job like yours, even if it takes starting at a low level and working my way up.

Allow me to list some highlights from my enclosed résumé. First, I have a BA degree in retailing, which included such key courses as retailing, marketing, management, and business information systems. Second, I have worked as a clerk and as an assistant manager in a large department store. Third, I have experience in the customer-facing aspect of retailing, as well as operations, marketing, and personnel supervision.

Successful retailing is about more than systems and procedures. It is also about anticipating customer needs, fostering positive relationships with the community, and delivering the type of service that keeps customers coming back. Retailers that fail in any of these areas are doomed to decline in today's hypercompetitive sales environment. I am the sort of forward-thinking, customer-focused leader who can help you avoid this fate.

I will call you next Wednesday at 2:00 to explain why I would make a great addition to your team.

Sincerely,

Glenda Johns

Glenda Johns
Enclosure

> The writer commits three major mistakes in the first paragraph: asking a question that she could answer herself by visiting the company's website, failing to demonstrate any knowledge of the company, and making the message all about her.

> This paragraph merely repeats information from the enclosed résumé, which wastes the reader's time and wastes the opportunity for the writer to present a more complete picture of herself.

> Johns attempts to show that she understands retailing, but this paragraph comes across as an arrogant lecture. The tone is particularly inappropriate, given that she is writing to the store's top manager.

> The call to action is overly aggressive, and it presumes that the reader will be available and willing to take a phone call from a complete stranger about a job opening that might not even exist.

Effective

457 Mountain View Rd.
Clear Lake, IA 50428
June 16, 2017

Ms. Patricia Downing, Store Manager
Walmart
840 South Oak
Iowa Falls, IA 50126

Dear Ms. Downing:

Even with its world-class supply chain, admired brand name, and competitive prices, Walmart obviously would not be the success it is without enthusiastic, service-driven associates and managers. If you have or foresee an opening for such a professional, someone eager to learn the Walmart way and eventually move into a management position, please consider me for the opportunity.

As an associate or management trainee, I can bring a passion for retailing and the perspective I've gained through academic preparation and four years of experience. (Please refer to my enclosed résumé for more information.)

Working as a clerk and then as an assistant manager in a large department store taught me how to anticipate customer needs, create effective merchandising, and deliver service that keeps customers coming back. Moreover, my recent BA degree in retailing, which encompassed such courses as retailing concepts, marketing fundamentals, management, and business information systems, prepared me with in-depth awareness of contemporary retailing issues and strategies.

I understand Walmart prefers to promote its managers from within, and I would be pleased to start out with an entry-level position until I gain the necessary experience. Could we have a brief conversation about the possibilities of joining your team? I am available by phone at 641-747-2222 or email at glendajohns@mailnet.com.

Sincerely,

Glenda Johns

Glenda Johns
Enclosure

> Johns gets the reader's attention by demonstrating good awareness of the company and the type of people it hires, presents herself as just such a professional, and then asks to be considered for any relevant job openings.

> Johns uses the body of her letter to expand on the information presented in her résumé, rather than simply repeating that information.

> The close builds the reader's interest by demonstrating knowledge of the company's policy regarding promotion.

> The call to action is respectful, and it makes a response easy for the reader by providing both phone and email contact information.

Figure 16.2   Unsolicited Application Letter: Poor and Improved
Demonstrating knowledge of the employer's needs and presenting your qualifications accordingly are essential steps in an unsolicited application letter.

you can think of to locate an appropriate name. Ask the people in your network if they know a name. If you can't find a name, addressing your letter to "Dear Hiring Manager" is perfectly acceptable.

- Clearly identify the opportunity you are applying for or expressing interest in.
- Show that you understand the company and its marketplace.
- Never volunteer salary history or requirements unless an employer has asked for this information.
- Keep it short—no more than three or four brief paragraphs. Remember that all you are trying to do at this point is move the conversation forward one step.
- Show some personality, while maintaining a business-appropriate tone. The letter gives you the opportunity to balance the facts-only tone of your résumé.
- Project confidence without being arrogant.
- Don't just repeat information from your résumé; use the conversational tone of the letter to convey additional professional and personal qualities and your reasons for wanting this particular job.

Because application letters are persuasive messages, the AIDA approach you learned in Chapter 10 is ideal, as the following sections explain.

Getting Attention

> *The opening paragraph of your application letter needs to clearly convey the reason you're writing and give the recipient a compelling reason to keep reading.*

The opening paragraph of your application letter must accomplish two essential tasks: (1) explaining why you are writing and (2) giving the recipient a reason to keep reading by demonstrating that you have some immediate potential for meeting the company's needs. Consider this opening:

> With the recent slowdown in corporate purchasing, I can certainly appreciate the challenge of new fleet sales in this business environment. With my high energy level and 16 months of new-car sales experience, I believe I can produce the results you listed as vital in the job posting on your website.

This applicant does a smooth job of echoing the company's stated needs while highlighting his personal qualifications and providing evidence that he understands the broader market. He balances his relative lack of experience with enthusiasm and knowledge of the industry. Table 16.1 suggests some other ways you can spark interest and grab attention in your opening paragraph.

Building Interest and Increasing Desire

> *Use the middle section of your application letter to expand on your opening and present a more complete picture of your strengths.*

The middle section of your letter presents your strongest selling points in terms of their potential benefit to the organization, thereby building interest in you and creating a desire to interview you. Be specific and back up your assertions with convincing evidence:

> **Poor:** I completed three college courses in business communication, earning an A in each course, and have worked for the past year at Imperial Construction.
>
> **Improved:** Using the skills gained from three semesters of college training in business communication, I developed a collection system for Imperial Construction that reduced annual bad-debt losses by 25 percent.

In a solicited letter, be sure to discuss each major requirement listed in the job posting. If you are deficient in any of these requirements, stress other solid selling points to help strengthen your overall presentation. Don't restrict your message to just core job duties, either. Also highlight personal characteristics that apply to the targeted position, such as your ability to work hard or handle responsibility:

TABLE 16.1   Tips for Getting Attention in Application Letters

Tip	Example
Unsolicited Application Letters	
Show how your strongest skills will benefit the organization.	If you need a regional sales specialist who consistently meets sales targets while fostering strong customer relationships, please consider my qualifications.
Describe your understanding of the job's requirements and show how well your qualifications fit them.	Your annual report stated that improving manufacturing efficiency is one of the company's top priorities for next year. Through my postgraduate research in systems engineering and consulting work for several companies in the industry, I've developed reliable methods for quickly identifying ways to cut production time while reducing resource use.
Mention the name of a person known to and highly regarded by the reader.	When Janice McHugh of your franchise sales division spoke to our business communication class last week, she said you often need promising new marketing graduates at this time of year.
Refer to publicized company activities, achievements, changes, or new procedures.	Today's issue of the *Detroit News* reports that you may need the expertise of computer programmers versed in robotics when your Lansing tire plant automates this spring.
Use a question to demonstrate your understanding of the organization's needs.	Can your fast-growing market research division use an interviewer with two years of field survey experience, a B.A. in public relations, and a real desire to succeed? If so, please consider me for the position.
Use a catchphrase opening if the job requires ingenuity and imagination.	*Haut monde*—whether referring to French, Italian, or Arab clients, it still means "high society." As an interior designer for your Beverly Hills showroom, not only could I serve and sell to your distinguished clientele, but I could also do it in all these languages. I speak, read, and write them fluently.
Solicited Application Letters	
Identify where you discovered the job opening; describe what you have to offer.	Your job posting on Monster.com for a cruise-line social director caught my eye. My eight years of experience as a social director in the travel industry would equip me to serve your new Caribbean cruise division well.

> While attending college full-time, I worked part-time during the school year and up to 60 hours a week each summer in order to be totally self-supporting while in college. I can offer your organization the same level of effort and perseverance.

Mention your salary requirements only if the organization has asked you to state them. If you don't know the salary appropriate for the position and someone with your qualifications, you can find typical salary ranges at the Bureau of Labor Statistics website, **www.bls.gov**, or a number of commercial websites. If you do state a target salary, tie it to the value you would offer:

> Don't bring up salary in your application letter unless the recipient has asked you to include your salary requirements.

> For the past two years, I have been helping a company similar to yours organize its database marketing efforts. I would therefore like to receive a salary in the same range (the mid-60s) for helping your company set up a more efficient customer database.

Toward the end of this section, refer the reader to your résumé by citing a specific fact or general point covered there:

> As you can see in the attached résumé, I've been working part-time with a local publisher since my sophomore year. During that time, I've used client interactions as an opportunity to build strong customer service skills.

Motivating Action

In the final paragraph of your application letter, respectfully ask for specific action and make it easy for the reader to respond.

The final paragraph of your application letter has two important functions: to ask the reader for a specific action (usually an interview) and to facilitate a reply. Offer to come to the employer's office at a convenient time or, if the firm is some distance away, to meet with its nearest representative or arrange a telephone or Skype interview. Include your email address and phone number, as well as the best times to reach you:

> After you have reviewed my qualifications, could we discuss the possibility of putting my marketing skills to work for your company? I am available at (360) 555-7845 from 2 p.m. to 10 p.m. Monday to Friday or by email at john.wagner462@gmail.com.

After editing and proofreading your application letter, give it a final quality check by referring to "Checklist: Writing Application Letters." Then send it along with your résumé promptly, especially if you are responding to an advertisement or online job posting.

FOLLOWING UP AFTER SUBMITTING A RÉSUMÉ

Think creatively about a follow-up letter; show that you've continued to add to your skills or that you've learned more about the company or the industry.

Deciding if, when, and how to follow up after submitting your résumé and application letter is one of the trickiest parts of a job search. First and foremost, keep in mind that employers continue to evaluate your communication efforts and professionalism during this phase, so don't say or do anything to leave a negative impression. Second, adhere to whatever instructions the employer has provided. If a job posting says "no calls," for example, don't call. Third, if the job posting lists a *close date*, don't call or write before then, because the company is still collecting applications and will not have made a decision about inviting people for interviews. Wait a week or so after the close date. If no close date is given and you have no other information to suggest a timeline, you can generally contact the company starting a week or two after submitting your résumé.[6]

When you follow up by email or telephone, you can share an additional piece of information that links your qualifications to the position (keep an eye out for late-breaking news about the company, too) and ask a question about the hiring process as a way to gather some information about your status. Good questions to ask include:[7]

- Has a hiring decision been made yet?
- Can you tell me what to expect next in terms of the hiring process?
- What is the company's timeframe for filling this position?
- Could I follow up in another week if you haven't had the chance to contact me yet?
- Can I provide any additional information regarding my qualifications for the position?

Whatever the circumstances, a follow-up message can demonstrate that you're sincerely interested in working for the organization, persistent in pursuing your goals, and committed to upgrading your skills.

CHECKLIST ✔ **Writing Application Letters**

- Take the same care with your application letter that you took with your résumé.
- If you are *prospecting* using an unsolicited message, do deep research to identify the qualities the company likely wants.
- For solicited messages in response to a posted job opening, word your message in a way that echoes the qualifications listed in the posting.
- Open the letter by capturing the reader's attention in a businesslike way.
- Use specific language to clearly state your interests and objectives.

- Build interest and desire in your potential contribution by presenting your key qualifications for the job.
- Link your education, experience, and personal qualities to the job requirements.
- Outline salary requirements only if the organization has requested that you provide them.
- Request an interview at a time and place that is convenient for the reader.
- Make it easy to comply with your request by providing your complete contact information and good times to reach you.
- Adapt your style for cultural variations, if required.

If you don't land a job at your dream company on the first attempt, don't give up. You can apply again if a new opening appears, or you can send an updated résumé with a new unsolicited application letter that describes how you have gained additional experience, taken a relevant course, or otherwise improved your skill set. Many leading employers take note of applicants who came close but didn't quite make it and may extend offers when positions open up in the future.[8]

REAL-TIME UPDATES

LEARN MORE BY VISITING THIS INTERACTIVE WEBSITE

Prepare for your next interview with these Pinterest pins

The Pinterest pinboard maintained by St. Edward's University offers dozens of helpful resources. Go to http://real-timeupdates.com/ebc12 and click on Learn More in the Students section.

Understanding the Interviewing Process

An **employment interview** is a meeting during which both you and the prospective employer ask questions and exchange information. The employer's objective is to find the best talent to fill available job openings, and your objective is to find the right match for your goals and capabilities.

As you get ready to begin interviewing, keep two vital points in mind. First, recognize that the process takes time. Start your preparation and research early; the best job offers usually go to the best-prepared candidates. Second, don't limit your options by looking at only a few companies. By exploring a wide range of firms and positions, you might uncover great opportunities that you would not have found otherwise. You'll increase the odds of getting more job offers, too.

2 LEARNING OBJECTIVE Describe the typical sequence of job interviews, the major types of interviews, and the attributes employers look for during an interview.

Start preparing early for your interviews—and be sure to consider a wide range of options.

THE TYPICAL SEQUENCE OF INTERVIEWS

Most employers interview an applicant multiple times before deciding to make a job offer. At the most selective companies, you might have a dozen or more individual interviews across several stages.[9] Depending on the company and the position, the process may stretch out over many weeks, or it may be completed in a matter of days.[10]

Employers start with the *screening stage*, in which they filter out applicants who are unqualified or otherwise not a good fit for the position. Screening can take place on your school's campus, at company offices, via telephone (including Skype or another Internet-based phone service), or through a computer-based screening system. Time is limited in screening interviews, so keep your answers short while providing a few key points that confirm your fit for the position. If your screening interview will take place by phone, try to schedule it for a time when you can be focused and free from interruptions.[11]

The next stage of interviews, the *selection stage*, helps the organization identify the top candidates from all those who qualify. During these interviews, show keen interest in the job, relate your skills and experience to the organization's needs, listen attentively, and ask questions that show you've done your research.

If the interviewers agree that you're a good candidate, you may receive a job offer, either on the spot or a few days later by phone, mail, or email. In other instances, you may be invited back for a final evaluation, often by a higher-ranking executive. The objective of the *final stage* is often to sell you on the advantages of joining the organization.

MOBILE APP Add the Skype mobile app to your phone to be ready for video interviews.

During the screening stage of interviews, use the limited time available to confirm your fit for the position.

During the selection stage, continue to show how your skills and attributes can help the company.

During the final stage, the interviewer may try to sell you on working for the firm.

COMMON TYPES OF INTERVIEWS

Be prepared to encounter a variety of interviewing approaches. These can be distinguished by the way they are structured, the number of people involved, and the purpose of the interview.

Structured Versus Unstructured Interviews

In a **structured interview**, the interviewer (or a computer program) asks a series of questions in a predetermined order. Structured interviews help employers identify candidates who don't meet basic job criteria, and they allow the interview team to compare answers from multiple candidates.[12]

A structured interview follows a set sequence of questions, allowing the interview team to compare answers from all candidates.

In an open-ended interview, the interviewer adapts the line of questioning based on your responses and questions.

In contrast, in an **open-ended interview**, the interviewer adapts his or her line of questioning based on the answers you give and any questions you ask. Even though it may feel like a conversation, remember that it's still an interview, so keep your answers focused and professional.

Panel and Group Interviews

In a panel interview, you meet with several interviewers at once; in a group interview, you and several other candidates meet with one or more interviewers at once.

Although one-on-one interviews are the most common format, some employers use panel or group interviews as well. In a **panel interview**, you meet with several interviewers at once.[13] Try to make a connection with each person on the panel, and keep in mind that each person has a different perspective, so tailor your responses accordingly.[14] For example, an upper-level manager is likely to be interested in your overall business sense and strategic perspective, whereas a potential colleague might be more interested in your technical skills and ability to work in a team. In a **group interview**, one or more interviewers meet with several candidates simultaneously. A key purpose of a group interview is to observe how the candidates interact.[15] Group interviews can be tricky because you want to stand out while coming across as a supportive team player. Be sure to treat your fellow candidates with respect, while looking for opportunities to demonstrate the depth of knowledge you have about the company and its needs.

Behavioral, Situational, Working, and Stress Interviews

In a behavioral interview, you are asked to describe how you handled situations from your past.

Interviewing techniques also vary based on the types of questions you are asked. Perhaps the most common type of interview these days is the **behavioral interview**, in which you are asked to relate specific incidents and experiences from your past.[16] In contrast to generic questions that can often be answered with "canned" responses, behavioral questions require candidates to use their own experiences and attributes to craft answers. Studies show that behavioral interviewing is a much better predictor of success on the job than traditional interview questions.[17] To prepare for a behavioral interview, review your work or college experiences to recall several instances in which you demonstrated an important job-related attribute or dealt with a challenge such as uncooperative team members or heavy workloads. Get ready with responses that quickly summarize the situation, the actions you took, and the outcome of those actions.[18]

In situational interviews, you're asked to explain how you would handle various hypothetical situations.

A **situational interview** is similar to a behavioral interview except that the questions focus on how you would handle various hypothetical situations on the job. The situations will likely relate closely to the job you're applying for, so the more you know about the position, the better prepared you'll be.

In a working interview, you perform actual work-related tasks.

A **working interview** is the most realistic type of interview: You actually perform a job-related activity during the interview. You may be asked to lead a brainstorming session, solve a business problem, engage in role playing, or even make a presentation.[19]

Stress interviews help recruiters see how you handle yourself under pressure.

The most unnerving type of interview is the **stress interview**, during which you might be asked questions designed to unsettle you or might be subjected to long periods of silence, criticism, interruptions, and or even hostile reactions by the interviewer. The theory behind this approach is that you'll reveal how well you handle stressful situations, although some experts find the technique of dubious value.[20] If you find yourself in a stress interview, recognize what is happening and collect your thoughts for a few seconds before you respond.

You might encounter two or more types of interview questions within a single interview, so stay alert and try to understand the type of question you're facing before you answer each one.

INTERVIEW MEDIA

Expect to use a variety of media when you interview, from in-person conversations to virtual meetings.

Expect to be interviewed through a variety of media. Employers trying to cut travel costs and the demands on staff time now interview candidates via telephone, email, instant messaging, virtual online systems, and videoconferencing, in addition to traditional face-to-face meetings.

Treat a telephone interview as seriously as you would an in-person interview.

To succeed at a telephone interview, make sure you treat it as seriously as an in-person interview. Be prepared with a copy of all the materials you have sent to the employer, including your résumé and any correspondence. In addition, prepare some note cards with key message points you'd like to make and questions you'd like to ask. And remember that you won't be able to use a pleasant smile, a firm handshake, and other nonverbal signals to create a good impression. A positive, alert tone of voice is therefore vital.[21]

Email and IM are also sometimes used in the screening stage. Although you have almost no opportunity to send and receive nonverbal signals with these formats, you do have the major advantage of being able to review and edit each response before you send it. Maintain a professional style in your responses, and be sure to ask questions that demonstrate your knowledge of the company and the position.[22]

When interviewing via email or IM, be sure to take a moment to review your responses before sending them.

Many employers use video technology for both live and recorded interviews. For instance, Zappos uses video interviews on Skype to select the top two or three finalists for each position and then invites those candidates for in-person interviews.[23] Recruiters can also use mobile apps for interviews. With recorded video interviews, an online system asks a set of questions and records the respondent's answers. Recruiters then watch the videos as part of the screening process.[24] Prepare for a video interview as you

REAL-TIME UPDATES
LEARN MORE BY WATCHING THIS VIDEO
Video interviewing on Skype

Watch this video for essential tips on preparing for and participating in an online video interview. Go to http://real-timeupdates.com/ebc12 and click on Learn More in the Students section.

would for an in-person interview—including dressing and grooming—and take the extra steps needed to become familiar with the equipment and the process. If you're interviewing from home, arrange your space so that the webcam doesn't pick up anything distracting or embarrassing in the background. During any video interview, remember to sit up straight and focus on the camera.

In a video interview, speak to the camera as though you are addressing the interviewer in person.

Online interviews can range from simple structured questionnaires and tests to sophisticated job simulations that are similar to working interviews (see Figure 16.3). These simulations help identify good candidates, give applicants an idea of what the job is like, and reduce the risk of employment discrimination lawsuits because they closely mimic actual job skills.[25]

Computer-based virtual interviews range from simple structured interviews to realistic job simulations to meetings in virtual worlds.

WHAT EMPLOYERS LOOK FOR IN AN INTERVIEW

Interviews give employers the chance to go beyond the basic data of your résumé to get to know you and to answer two essential questions. The first is whether you can handle the responsibilities of the position. Naturally, the more you know about the demands of the position, and the more you've thought about how your skills match those demands, the better you'll be able to respond.

Suitability for a specific job is judged on the basis of such factors as
- *Academic preparation*
- *Work experience*
- *Job-related personality traits*

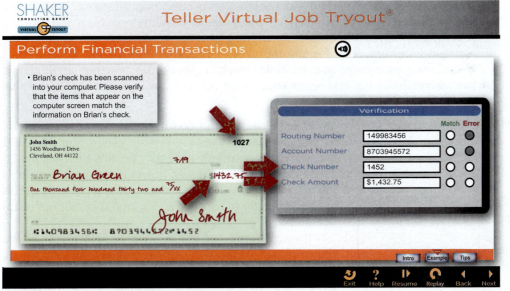

Figure 16.3   Job Task Simulations
Computer-based job simulations are an increasingly popular approach to testing job-related skills.

Compatibility with an organizational culture and a position is judged on such factors as personal background, attitudes, and communication style.

The second essential question is whether you will be a good fit with the organization and the target position. All good employers want people who are confident, dedicated, positive, curious, courteous, ethical, and willing to commit to something larger than their own individual goals. Companies also look for fit with their individual cultures. Just like people, companies have different "personalities." Some are intense; others are more laid back. Some emphasize teamwork; others expect employees to forge their own way and even to compete with one another. Expectations also vary from job to job within a company and from industry to industry. An outgoing personality is essential for sales but less so for research, for instance.

PREEMPLOYMENT TESTING AND BACKGROUND CHECKS

Preemployment tests attempt to provide objective, quantitative information about a candidate's skills, attitudes, and habits.

In an effort to improve the predictability of the selection process, many employers now conduct a variety of preemployment evaluations and investigations. Here are types of assessments you are likely to encounter during your job search:[26]

- **Integrity tests.** Integrity tests attempt to measure how truthful and trustworthy a candidate is likely to be.
- **Personality tests.** Personality tests are designed to gauge such aspects as attitudes toward work, interests, managerial potential, dependability, commitment, and motivation.
- **Cognitive tests.** Cognitive tests measure a variety of attributes involved in acquiring, processing, analyzing, using, and remembering information. Typical tests involve reading comprehension, mathematics, problem solving, and decision making.
- **Language proficiency.** You may be asked to take a reading or writing test.
- **Job knowledge and job skills tests.** These assessments measure the knowledge and skills required to succeed in a particular position. An accounting candidate, for example, might be tested on accounting principles and legal matters (knowledge) and asked to create a simple balance sheet or income statement (skills).
- **Substance tests.** A majority of companies perform some level of drug and alcohol testing. Many employers believe such testing is necessary to maintain workplace safety, ensure productivity, and protect companies from lawsuits, but others view it as an invasion of employee privacy.
- **Background checks.** In addition to testing, most companies conduct some sort of background check, including reviewing your credit record, checking to see whether you have a criminal history, and verifying your education. Moreover, you should assume that every employer will conduct a general online search on you. To help prevent a background check from tripping you up, verify that your college transcripts are current, look for any mistakes or outdated information in your credit record, plug your name into multiple search engines to see whether anything embarrassing shows up, and scour your social network profiles and connections for potential problems.

Preemployment assessments are a complex and controversial aspect of workforce recruiting. For instance, even though personality testing is widely used, some research suggests that commonly used tests are not a reliable predictor of job success.[27] However, expect to see more innovation in this area and greater use of testing in general in the future as companies try to reduce the risks and costs of poor hiring decisions.

If you're concerned about any preemployment test, ask the employer for more information or ask your college career center for advice. You can also get more information from the Equal Employment Opportunity Commission, at **www.eeoc.gov**.

REAL-TIME UPDATES

LEARN MORE BY LISTENING TO THIS PODCAST

Expert tips for successful phone interviews

Recruiting experts offer invaluable advice on nailing a phone interview. Go to http://real-timeupdates.com/ebc12 and click on Learn More in the Students section.

Preparing for a Job Interview

Now that you're armed with insights into the interviewing and assessment process, you're ready to begin preparing for your interviews. Preparation will help you feel more confident and perform better under pressure, and preparation starts with learning about the organization.

3 LEARNING OBJECTIVE
List six tasks you need to complete to prepare for a successful job interview.

LEARNING ABOUT THE ORGANIZATION AND YOUR INTERVIEWERS

Employers expect serious candidates to demonstrate an understanding of the company's operations, its markets, and its strategic and tactical challenges.[28] You've already done some initial research to identify companies of interest, but when you're invited to an interview, it's time to dig a little deeper (see Table 16.2). Making this effort demonstrates your interest in the company, and it identifies you as a business professional who knows the importance of investigation and analysis.

In addition to learning about the company and the job opening, try to find out as much as you can about the managers who will be interviewing you, if you can get their names. Search LinkedIn in particular. It's also perfectly acceptable to ask your contact at the company for the names and titles of the people who will be interviewing you.[29] Think about ways to use whatever information you find during your interview. For example, if an interviewer lists membership in a particular professional organization, you might ask whether the organization is a good forum for people to learn about vital issues in the profession or industry. This question gives the interviewer an opportunity to talk about his

Interviewers expect you to know some basic information about the company and its industry.

TABLE 16.2   Investigating an Organization and a Job Opportunity

Where to Look and What You Can Learn

- **Company website, blogs, and social media accounts:** Overall information about the company, including key executives, products and services, locations and divisions, employee benefits, job descriptions
- **Competitors' websites, blogs, and social media accounts:** Similar information from competitors, including the strengths these companies claim to have
- **Industry-related websites and blogs:** Objective analysis and criticism of the company, its products, its reputation, and its management
- **Marketing materials (print and online):** The company's marketing strategy and customer communication style
- **Company publications (print and online):** Key events, stories about employees, new products
- **Your social network contacts:** Names and job titles of potential contacts within a company
- **Periodicals (newspapers and trade journals, both print and online):** In-depth stories about the company and its strategies, products, successes, and failures; you may find profiles of top executives
- **Career center at your college:** Often provides a wide array of information about companies that hire graduates
- **Current and former employees:** Insights into the work environment

Points to Learn About the Organization

- Full name
- Location (headquarters and divisions, branches, subsidiaries, or other units)
- Ownership (public or private; whether it is owned by another company)
- Brief history
- Products and services
- Industry position (whether the company is a leader or a minor player; whether it is an innovator or more of a follower)
- Key financial points (such as stock price and trends, if a public company)
- Growth prospects (whether the company is investing in its future through research and development; whether it is in a thriving industry)

Points to Learn About the Position

- Title
- Functions and responsibilities
- Qualifications and expectations
- Possible career paths
- Salary range
- Travel expectations and opportunities
- Relocation expectations and opportunities

REAL-TIME UPDATES

LEARN MORE BY READING THIS ARTICLE

The ultimate interview preparation checklist

Prepare for your next interview by following this advice. Go to http://real-timeupdates.com/ebc12 and click on Learn More in the Students section.

or her own interests and experiences for a moment, which builds rapport and might reveal vital insights into the career path you are considering. Just make sure your questions are sincere and not uncomfortably personal.

THINKING AHEAD ABOUT QUESTIONS

Planning ahead for the interviewer's questions will help you handle them more confidently and successfully. In addition, you will want to prepare insightful questions of your own.

Planning for the Employer's Questions

You can expect to face a number of common questions in your interviews, so be sure to prepare for them.

Many general interview questions are "stock" queries you can expect to hear again and again during your interviews. Get ready to face these six at the very least:

- **What is the hardest decision you've ever had to make?** Be prepared with a good example (that isn't too personal), explaining why the decision was difficult, how you made the choice you made, and what you learned from the experience.
- **What is your greatest weakness?** This question seems to be a favorite of some interviewers, although it probably rarely yields useful information. One good strategy is to mention a skill or attribute you haven't had the opportunity to develop yet but would like to in your next position.[30] Another option is to discuss a past shortcoming you took steps to correct.
- **Where do you want to be five years from now?** This question tests (1) whether you're merely using this job as a stopover until something better comes along and (2) whether you've given thought to your long-term goals. Your answer should reflect your desire to contribute to the employer's long-term goals, not just your own goals. Whether this question often yields useful information is also a matter of debate, but be prepared to answer it.[31]
- **What didn't you like about previous jobs you've held?** Answer this one carefully: The interviewer is trying to predict whether you'll be an unhappy or difficult employee.[32] Describe something that you didn't like in a way that puts you in a positive light, such as having limited opportunities to apply your skills or education. Avoid making negative comments about former employers or colleagues.
- **Tell me something about yourself.** One good strategy is to briefly share the "story of you" (see page 479)—quickly summarizing where you have been and where you would like to go—in a way that aligns your interests with the company's. Alternatively, you can focus on a specific skill you know is valuable to the company, share something business-relevant that you are passionate about, or offer a short summary of what colleagues or customers think about you.[33] Whatever tactic you choose, this is not the time to be shy or indecisive, so be ready with a confident, memorable answer.
- **How do you spend your free time?** This question can pop up late in an interview, after the interviewer has covered the major work-related questions and wants to get a better idea of what sort of person you are.[34] Prepare an answer that is honest and that puts you in a positive light, without revealing more than you are comfortable revealing or suggesting that you might not fit in the corporate culture. Sports, hobbies, reading, spending time with family, and volunteer work are all "safe" answers.

REAL-TIME UPDATES

LEARN MORE BY READING THIS ARTICLE

Prepare your answers to these tough interview questions

Use this advice to getting ready for five questions you're likely to encounter. Go to http://real-timeupdates.com/ebc12 and click on Learn More in the Students section.

Continue your preparation by planning a brief answer to each question in Table 16.3.

As you prepare answers, look for ways to frame your responses as brief stories (30 to 90 seconds) rather than simple

Look for ways to frame your responses as brief stories rather than as dry facts or statements.

declarative answers.[35] Cohesive stories tend to stick in the listener's mind more effectively than disconnected facts and statements.

TABLE 16.3 Twenty-Five Common Interview Questions

Questions About College

1. What courses in college did you like most? Least? Why?
2. Do you think your extracurricular activities in college were worth the time you spent on them? Why or why not?
3. When did you choose your college major? Did you ever change your major? If so, why?
4. Do you feel you did the best scholastic work you are capable of?
5. How has your college education prepared you for this position?

Questions About Employers and Jobs

6. Why did you leave your last job?
7. Why did you apply for this job opening?
8. Why did you choose your particular field of work?
9. What are the disadvantages of your chosen field?
10. What do you know about our company?
11. What do you think about how this industry operates today?
12. Why do you think you would like this particular type of job?

Questions About Work Experiences and Expectations

13. What was your biggest failure?
14. Describe an experience in which you learned from one of your mistakes.
15. What motivates you? Why?
16. What do you think determines a person's progress in a good organization?
17. Are you a leader or a follower?
18. What have you done that shows initiative and willingness to work?
19. Why should I hire you?

Questions About Work Habits

20. Do you prefer working with others or by yourself?
21. What type of boss do you prefer?
22. Have you ever had any difficulty getting along with colleagues or supervisors? With instructors? With other students?
23. What would you do if you were given an unrealistic deadline for a task or project?
24. How do you feel about overtime work?
25. How do you handle stress or pressure on the job?

Sources: Alison Green, "The 10 Most Common Job Interview Questions," *U.S. News & World Report*, 24 January 2011, http://money.usnews.com; "Most Common Interview Questions," Glassdoor blog, 29 December 2011, www.glassdoor.com; *The Northwestern Endicott Report* (Evanston, Ill.: Northwestern University Placement Center).

Planning Questions of Your Own

Remember that an interview is a two-way conversation: The questions you ask are just as important as the answers you provide. By asking insightful questions, you can demonstrate your understanding of the organization, steer the discussion into areas that allow you to present your qualifications to best advantage, and verify for yourself whether this is a good opportunity. Plus, interviewers expect you to ask questions and look negatively on candidates who don't have any questions to ask. For good questions that you might use as a starting point, see Table 16.4 on the next page.

> Preparing questions of your own helps you understand the company and the position, and it sends an important signal that you are truly interested.

BOOSTING YOUR CONFIDENCE

Interviewing is stressful for everyone, so some nervousness is natural. However, you can take steps to feel more confident. Start by reminding yourself that you have value to offer the employer, and the employer already thinks highly enough of you to invite you to an interview.

 If some aspect of your appearance or background makes you uneasy, correct it if possible or offset it by emphasizing positive traits such as warmth, wit, intelligence, or charm. Instead of dwelling on your weaknesses, focus on your strengths. Instead of worrying about how you will perform in the interview, focus on how you can help the organization succeed. As with public speaking, the more prepared you are, the more confident you'll be.

> The best way to build your confidence is to prepare thoroughly and address shortcomings as best you can. In other words, take action.

TABLE 16.4 Ten Questions to Consider Asking an Interviewer

Question	Reason for Asking
1. What are the job's major responsibilities?	A vague answer could mean that the responsibilities have not been clearly defined, which is almost guaranteed to cause frustration if you take the job.
2. What qualities do you want in the person who fills this position?	This will help you go beyond the job description to understand what the company really wants.
3. How do you measure success for someone in this position?	A vague or incomplete answer could mean that the expectations you will face are unrealistic or ill defined.
4. What is the first problem that needs the attention of the person you hire?	Not only will this help you prepare, but it can also signal whether you're about to jump into a problematic situation.
5. Would relocation be required now or in the future?	If you're not willing to move often or at all, you need to know those expectations now.
6. Why is this job now vacant?	If the previous employee got promoted, that's a good sign. If the person quit, that might not be such a good sign.
7. What makes your organization different from others in the industry?	The answer will help you assess whether the company has a clear strategy to succeed in its industry and whether top managers communicate this to lower-level employees.
8. How would you define your organization's managerial philosophy?	You want to know whether the managerial philosophy is consistent with your own working values.
9. What is a typical workday like for you?	The interviewer's response can give you clues about daily life at the company.
10. What are the next steps in the selection process? What's the best way to follow up with you?	Knowing where the company is in the hiring process will give you clues about following up after the interview and possibly give you hints about where you stand.

Sources: Heather Huhman, "5 Must-Ask Questions at Job Interviews," Glassdoor blog, 7 February 2012, www.glassdoor.com; Joe Conklin, "Turning the Tables: Six Questions to Ask Your Interviewer," *Quality Progress,* November 2007, 55; Andrea N. Browne, "Keeping the Momentum at the Interview; Ask Questions, Do Your Research, and Be a Team Player," *Washington Post,* 29 July 2007, K1.

POLISHING YOUR INTERVIEW STYLE

Staging mock interviews with a friend is one good way to hone your style.

Competence and confidence are the foundation of your interviewing style, and you can enhance them by giving the interviewer an impression of poise, good manners, and good judgment. You can develop a smooth style by staging mock interviews with a friend or using an interview simulator on your phone or tablet (see Figure 16.4). Record these mock interviews so you can evaluate yourself. Your college's career center may have computer-based systems for practicing interviews as well.

After each practice session, look for opportunities to improve. Have your mock interview partner critique your performance, or critique yourself if you're able to record your practice interviews, using the list of warning signs shown in Table 16.5 on page 528. Pay close attention to the length of your planned answers as well. Interviewers want you to give complete answers, but they don't want you to take up valuable time or test their patience by chatting about minor or irrelevant details.[36]

Evaluate the length and clarity of your answers, your nonverbal behavior, and the quality of your voice.

In addition to reviewing your answers, evaluate your nonverbal behavior, including your posture, eye contact, facial expressions, and hand gestures and movements. Do you come across as alert and upbeat or passive and withdrawn? Pay close attention to your speaking voice as well. If you tend to speak in a monotone, for instance, practice speaking in a livelier style, with more inflection and emphasis. And watch out for "filler words" such as *uh* and *um.* Many people start sentences with a filler without being conscious of doing so. Train yourself to pause silently for a moment instead as you gather your thoughts and plan what to say.

PRESENTING A PROFESSIONAL IMAGE

Dress conservatively and be well groomed for every interview.

Clothing and grooming are important elements of preparation because they reveal something about a candidate's personality, professionalism, and ability to sense the unspoken

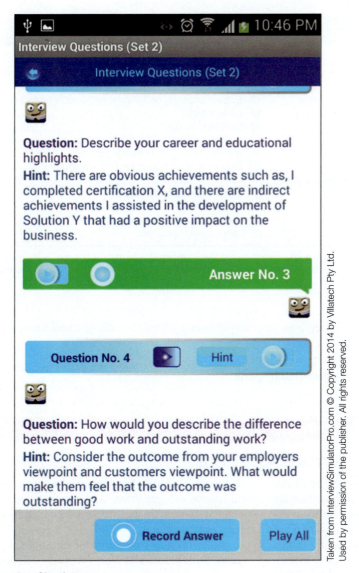

Figure 16.4 Interview Simulators
A number of mobile apps are available to help you practice and polish your interviewing skills.

"rules" of a situation. Your research into various industries and professions should give you insight into expectations for business attire. If you're not sure what to wear, ask someone who works in the same industry or even visit the company at the end of the day and see what employees are wearing as they leave the office. You don't need to spend a fortune on interview clothes, but your clothes must be clean, pressed, and appropriate. The following look will serve you well in most interview situations:[37]

- Neat, "adult" hairstyle
- For more formal environments, a conservative business suit (for women, that means no exposed midriffs, short skirts, or plunging necklines) in a dark solid color or a subtle pattern such as pinstripes; white shirt and understated tie for men; coordinated blouse for women
- For less formal environments, smart-looking "business casual," including a pressed shirt or blouse and nice slacks or a skirt
- Limited jewelry (men, especially, should wear very little jewelry)
- No visible piercings other than one or two earrings (for women only)
- No visible tattoos
- Stylish but professional-looking shoes (no extreme high heels or casual shoes)
- Clean hands and nicely trimmed fingernails

TABLE 16.5 Warning Signs: 25 Attributes Interviewers Don't Like to See

1. Poor personal appearance
2. Overbearing, overaggressive, or conceited demeanor; a "superiority complex"; a know-it-all attitude
3. Inability to express ideas clearly; poor voice, diction, or grammar
4. Lack of knowledge or experience
5. Poor preparation for the interview
6. Lack of interest in the job
7. Lack of planning for career; lack of purpose or goals
8. Lack of enthusiasm; passive and indifferent demeanor
9. Lack of confidence and poise; appearance of being nervous and ill at ease
10. Insufficient evidence of achievement
11. Failure to participate in extracurricular activities
12. Overemphasis on money; interest only in the best offer
13. Poor scholastic record
14. Unwillingness to start at the bottom; expecting too much too soon
15. Tendency to make excuses
16. Evasive answers; hedging on unfavorable factors in record
17. Lack of tact
18. Lack of maturity
19. Lack of courtesy and common sense, including answering mobile phones, texting, or chewing gum during the interview
20. Being critical of past or present employers
21. Lack of social skills
22. Marked dislike for schoolwork
23. Lack of vitality
24. Failure to look interviewer in the eye
25. Limp, weak handshake

Sources: Donna Fuscaldo, "Seven Deadly Interview Sins," Glassdoor blog, 4 April 2012, www.glassdoor.com; "Employers Reveal Outrageous and Common Mistakes Candidates Made in Job Interviews, According to New CareerBuilder Survey," CareerBuilder.com, 12 January 2011, www.careerbuilder.com; *The Northwestern Endicott Report* (Evanston, Ill.: Northwestern University Placement Center).

- Little or no perfume or cologne (some people are allergic and many people are put off by strong smells)
- Subtle makeup (for women)
- Exemplary personal hygiene

COMMUNICATING ACROSS CULTURES

Successfully Interviewing Across Borders

Interviewing for a job in another country can be one of the most exciting steps in your career. To succeed, you need to pay close attention to the important elements of the interviewing process, including personal appearance, an awareness of what interviewers are really trying to learn about you, and things you should learn about the organization you're hoping to join.

Some countries and cultures place a much higher importance on dress and personal grooming than many employees in the United States are accustomed to; moreover, expectations of personal appearance can vary dramatically from country to country. Ask people who've been to the country before and observe local businesspeople when you arrive. Many people interpret inappropriate dress as more than a simple fashion mistake; they view it as an inability or unwillingness to understand another culture. Even if you are interviewing via Skype, as is often the case in the early rounds, make sure your on-screen appearance is appropriate.

For instance, business image consultant Ashley Rothschild points out that you could get away with wearing a boldly colored suit in Italy but probably not in Japan. Business professionals tend to dress formally in Italy, but as a worldwide fashion leader, the country has a broad definition of what is appropriate business attire.

Smart recruiters always analyze both nonverbal signals and verbal messages to judge whether an applicant truly has the qualities necessary for a job. In international employment situations, you'll probably be under even closer scrutiny. Recruiters abroad will want to know if you really have what it takes to succeed in unfamiliar social settings, how your family will handle the transition, and whether you can adapt your personal work style and habits enough to blend in with the hiring organization.

Remember to ask plenty of questions and do your research, both before and after the interview. Some employees view overseas postings as grand adventures, only to collide headfirst with the reality of what it's like to live and work in a completely different culture. For instance, if you've grown accustomed to the independent work style you enjoy in your current job or in school, could you handle a more structured work environment with a hierarchical chain of command? Make sure to get a sense of the culture both within the company and within its social community before you commit to a job in another country.

CAREER APPLICATIONS

1. Explain how you could find out what is appropriate dress for a job interview in South Africa.
2. Would it be appropriate to ask an interviewer to describe the culture in his or her country? Explain your answer.

Sources: Sharon Ann Holgate, "Gaining an Edge in Overseas Interviews," *Science Careers*, 4 August 2014; http://sciencecareers.sciencemag.org; Jean-Marc Hachey, "Interviewing for an International Job," excerpt from *The Canadian Guide to Working and Living Overseas*, 3rd ed., accessed 23 February 2004, www.workingoverseas.com; Rebecca Falkoff, "Dress to Impress the World: International Business Fashion," Monster.com, accessed 23 February 2004, www.monster.com; Mary Ellen Slater, "Navigating the Details of Landing an Overseas Job," *Washington Post*, 11 November 2002, E4.

An interview is not the place to express your individuality or to let your inner rebel run wild. Send a clear signal that you understand the business world and know how to adapt to it. You won't be taken seriously otherwise.

If you want to be taken seriously, dress and act seriously.

REAL-TIME UPDATES

LEARN MORE BY WATCHING THIS PRESENTATION

Simple tips for a professional interview look

Not sure how to get the right look? Follow this advice. Go to http://real-timeupdates.com/ebc12 and click on Learn More in the Students section.

BEING READY WHEN YOU ARRIVE

When you go to your interview, take a small notebook, a pen, a list of the questions you want to ask, several copies of your résumé (protected in a folder), an outline of what you have learned about the organization, and any past correspondence about the position. You may also want to take a small calendar, a transcript of your college grades, a list of references, and a portfolio containing samples of your work, performance reviews, and certificates of achievement.[38] Think carefully if you plan to use a tablet computer or any other device for note taking or reference during an interview. You don't want to waste any of the interviewer's time fumbling with it. Also, turn off your mobile phone; in a recent survey of hiring professionals, answering calls or texting while in an interview was identified as the most common mistake job candidates make during their interviews.[39]

Be ready to go the minute you arrive at the interviewing site; don't fumble around for your résumé or your list of questions.

Be sure you know when and where the interview will be held. The worst way to start any interview is to be late. Verify the route and time required to get there, even if that means traveling there ahead of time. Plan to arrive early, but don't approach the reception desk until 5 minutes or so before your appointed time.[40] Chances are the interviewer won't be ready to receive you until the scheduled time.

If you have to wait for the interviewer, use this time to review the key messages about yourself you want to get across in the interview. Conduct yourself professionally while waiting. Show respect for everyone you encounter, and avoid chewing gum, eating, or drinking. Anything you do or say at this stage may get back to the interviewer, so make sure your best qualities show from the moment you enter the premises. To review the steps for planning a successful interview, see "Checklist: Planning for a Successful Job Interview."

Interviewing for Success

At this point, you have a good sense of the overall process and know how to prepare for your interviews. The next step is to get familiar with the three stages of every interview: the warm-up, the question-and-answer session, and the close.

4 LEARNING OBJECTIVE
Explain how to succeed in all three stages of an interview.

CHECKLIST ✔ Planning for a Successful Job Interview

- Learn about the organization, including its operations, markets, and challenges.
- Learn as much as you can about the people who will be interviewing you, if you can find their names.
- Plan for the employer's questions, including questions about tough decisions you've made, your perceived shortcomings, what you didn't like about previous jobs, and your career plans.
- Plan questions of your own to find out whether this is really the job and the organization for you and to show that you've done your research.
- Bolster your confidence by removing as many sources of apprehension as you can.

- Polish your interview style by staging mock interviews.
- Present a professional appearance with appropriate dress and grooming.
- Be ready when you arrive and bring along a pen, paper, a list of questions, copies of your résumé, an outline of your research on the company, and any correspondence you've had regarding the position.
- Double-check the location and time of the interview and map out the route beforehand.
- Relax and be flexible; the schedule and interview arrangements may change when you arrive.

THE WARM-UP

Of the three stages, the warm-up is the most important, even though it may account for only a small fraction of the time you spend in the interview. Studies suggest that many interviewers make up their minds within the first 20 seconds of contact with a candidate.[41] Don't let your guard down if the interviewer engages in what feels like small talk; these exchanges are every bit as important as structured questions.

Body language is crucial at this point. Stand or sit up straight, maintain regular but natural eye contact, and don't fidget. When the interviewer extends a hand, respond with a firm but not overpowering handshake. Repeat the interviewer's name when you're introduced ("It's a pleasure to meet you, Ms. Litton"). Wait until you're asked to be seated or the interviewer has taken a seat. Let the interviewer start the discussion, and be ready to answer one or two substantial questions right away. The following are some common openers:[42]

- Why do you want to work here?
- What do you know about us?
- Tell me a little about yourself.

THE QUESTION-AND-ANSWER STAGE

Questions and answers usually consume the greatest part of the interview. Depending on the type of interview, the interviewer will likely ask about your qualifications, discuss some of the points mentioned in your résumé, and ask about how you have handled particular situations in the past or would handle them in the future. You'll also be asking questions of your own.

Answering and Asking Questions

Let the interviewer lead the conversation and never answer a question before he or she has finished asking it. Not only is this type of interruption rude, but the last few words of the question might alter how you respond. As much as possible, avoid one-word yes-or-no answers. Use the opportunity to expand on a positive response or explain a negative response. If you're asked a difficult question or the offbeat questions that companies such as Zappos and Google are known to use, pause before responding. Think through the implications of the question. For instance, the recruiter may know that you can't answer a question and only wants to know how you'll respond under pressure or whether you can construct a logical approach to solving a problem.

Whenever you're asked if you have any questions, or whenever doing so naturally fits the flow of the conversation, ask a question from the list you've prepared. Probe for what the company is looking for in its new employees so that you can show how you meet the firm's needs. Also try to zero in on any reservations the interviewer might have about you so that you can dispel them.

Listening to the Interviewer

Paying attention when the interviewer speaks can be as important as giving good answers or asking good questions. Review the tips on listening offered in Chapter 2. The interviewer's facial expressions, eye movements, gestures, and posture may tell you the real meaning of what is being said. Be especially aware of how your answers are received. Does the interviewer nod in agreement or smile to show approval? If so, you're making progress. If not, you might want to introduce another topic or modify your approach.

Handling Potentially Discriminatory Questions

A variety of federal, state, and local laws prohibit employment discrimination on the basis of race, ethnicity, gender, age (at least if you're between 40 and 70), marital status, religion, national origin, or disability. Interview questions designed to elicit information on these topics are potentially illegal.[43] Table 16.6 compares some specific questions that employers are and are not allowed to ask during an employment interview.

The first minute of the interview is crucial, so stay alert and be on your best business behavior.

Recognize that you could face substantial questions as soon as your interview starts, so make sure you are prepared and ready to go.

Listen carefully to questions before you answer.

Paying attention to both verbal and nonverbal messages can help you turn the question-and-answer stage to your advantage.

TABLE 16.6 Acceptable Versus Potentially Discriminatory Interview Questions

Interviewers May Ask This . . .	But Not This
What is your name?	What was your maiden name?
Are you over 18?	When were you born?
Did you graduate from high school?	When did you graduate from high school?
[No questions about race are allowed.]	What is your race?
Can you perform [specific tasks]?	Do you have physical or mental disabilities?
	Do you have a drug or alcohol problem?
	Are you taking any prescription drugs?
Would you be able to meet the job's requirement to frequently work weekends?	Would working on weekends conflict with your religion?
Do you have the legal right to work in the United States?	What country are you a citizen of?
Have you ever been convicted of a felony?	Have you ever been arrested?
This job requires that you speak Spanish. Do you?	What language did you speak in your home when you were growing up?

Sources: Dave Johnson, "Illegal Job Interview Questions," *CBS Money Watch*, 27 February 2012, www.cbsnews.com; "5 Illegal Interview Questions and How to Dodge Them," *Forbes*, 20 April 2012, www.forbes.com; Deanna G. Kucler, "Interview Questions: Legal or Illegal?" *Workforce Management*, accessed 28 September 2005, www.workforce.com.

If an interviewer asks a potentially unlawful question, consider your options carefully before you respond. You can answer the question as it was asked, you can ask tactfully whether the question might be prohibited, you can simply refuse to answer it, or you can try to answer "the question behind the question."[44] For example, if an interviewer inappropriately asks whether you are married or have strong family ties in the area, he or she might be trying to figure out if you're willing to travel or relocate—both of which are acceptable questions. Only you can decide which is the right choice based on the situation.

Even if you do answer the question as it was asked, think hard before accepting a job offer from this company if you have alternatives. Was the off-limits question possibly accidental (it happens) and therefore not really a major concern? If you think it was intentional, would you want to work for an organization that condones illegal or discriminatory questions or that doesn't train its employees to avoid them?

If you believe an interviewer's questions to be unreasonable, unrelated to the job, or an attempt to discriminate, you have the option of filing a complaint with the U.S. Equal Employment Opportunity Commission or with the agency in your state that regulates fair employment practices.

> Federal, state, and local laws prohibit employment discrimination based on a variety of factors, and well-trained interviewers know to avoid questions that could be used to discriminate in the hiring process.
>
> Think about how you might respond if you were asked a potentially unlawful question.

THE CLOSE

Like the warm-up, the end of the interview is more important than its brief duration would indicate. These last few minutes are your final opportunity to emphasize your value to the organization and to correct any misconceptions the interviewer might have. Be aware that many interviewers will ask whether you have any more questions at this point, so save one or two from your list.

REAL-TIME UPDATES
LEARN MORE BY WATCHING THIS VIDEO

Stay calm by pressing your "panic reset button"

Learn how to reset your emotions if you feel like you're starting to panic in a job interview. Go to http://real-timeupdates.com/ebc12 and click on Learn More in the Students section.

Concluding Gracefully

You can usually tell when the interviewer is trying to conclude the session. He or she may ask whether you have any more questions, check the time, summarize the discussion, or simply tell you that the allotted time for the interview is up. When you get the signal, be sure to thank the interviewer for the opportunity and express your interest in the

> Conclude an interview with courtesy and enthusiasm.

REAL-TIME UPDATES

LEARN MORE BY EXPLORING THIS INTERACTIVE WEBSITE

How much are you worth?

Find real-life salary ranges for a wide range of jobs. Go to http://real-timeupdates.com/ebc12 and click on Learn More in the Students section.

organization. If you can do so comfortably, try to pin down what will happen next, but don't press for an immediate decision.

If this is your second or third visit to the organization, the interview may end with an offer of employment. If you have other offers or need time to think about this offer, it's perfectly acceptable to thank the interviewer for the offer and ask for some time to consider it. If no job offer is made, the interview team may not have reached a decision yet, but you may tactfully ask when you can expect to know the decision.

Discussing Salary

Research salary ranges in your job, industry, and geographic region before you try to negotiate salary.

If you receive an offer during the interview, you'll naturally want to discuss salary. However, let the interviewer raise the subject. If asked your salary requirements during the interview or on a job application, you can say that your requirements are open or negotiable or that you would expect a competitive compensation package.[45]

How far you can negotiate depends on several factors, including market demand for your skills, the strength of the job market, the company's compensation policies, the company's financial health, and any other job offers you may be considering. Remember that you're negotiating a business deal, not asking for personal favors, so focus on the unique value you can bring to the job. The more information you have, the stronger your position will be.

Negotiating benefits may be one way to get more value from an employment package.

If salary isn't negotiable, look at the overall compensation and benefits package. You may find flexibility in a signing bonus, profit sharing, retirement benefits, health coverage, vacation time, and other valuable elements.[46]

To review the important tips for successful interviews, see "Checklist: Making a Positive Impression in Job Interviews."

INTERVIEW NOTES

Keeping a careful record of your job interviews is essential.

Maintain a notebook or simple database with information about each company, interviewers' answers to your questions, contact information for each interviewer, the status of follow-up communication, and upcoming interview appointments. Carefully organized

---

CHECKLIST ✔ Making a Positive Impression in Job Interviews

A. Be ready to make a positive impression in the warm-up stage.
- Be alert from the moment you arrive; even initial small talk is part of the interviewing process.
- Greet the interviewer by name, with a smile and direct eye contact.
- Offer a firm (not crushing) handshake if the interviewer extends a hand.
- Take a seat only after the interviewer invites you to sit or has taken his or her own seat.
- Listen for clues about what the interviewer is trying to get you to reveal about yourself and your qualifications.
- Exhibit positive body language, including standing up straight, walking with purpose, and sitting up straight.

B. Convey your value to the organization during the question-and-answer stage.
- Let the interviewer lead the conversation.
- Never answer a question before the interviewer finishes asking it.
- Listen carefully to the interviewer and watch for nonverbal signals.
- Don't limit yourself to simple yes-or-no answers; expand on the answer to show your knowledge of the company (but don't ramble on).
- If you encounter a potentially discriminatory question, decide how you want to respond before you say anything.
- When you have the opportunity, ask questions from the list you've prepared; remember that interviewers expect you to ask questions.

C. Close on a strong note.
- Watch and listen for signs that the interview is about to end.
- Quickly evaluate how well you've done and correct any misperceptions the interviewer might have.
- If you receive an offer and aren't ready to decide, it's entirely appropriate to ask for time to think about it.
- Don't bring up salary but be prepared to discuss it if the interviewer raises the subject.
- End with a warm smile and a handshake and thank the interviewer for meeting with you.

notes will help you decide which company is the right fit for you when it comes time to choose from among the job offers you receive.

For the latest information on interviewing strategies, visit http://real-timeupdates .com/ebc12 and click on Chapter 16.

Following Up After the Interview

5 LEARNING OBJECTIVE
Identify the most common employment messages that follow an interview and explain when you would use each one.

Staying in contact with a prospective employer after an interview shows that you really want the job and are determined to get it. Doing so also gives you another chance to demonstrate your communication skills and sense of business etiquette. Following up brings your name to the interviewer's attention once again and reminds him or her that you're actively looking and waiting for the decision.

Any time you hear from a company during the application or interview process, be sure to respond quickly. Companies flooded with résumés may move on to another candidate if they don't hear back from you within 24 hours.[47]

FOLLOW-UP MESSAGE

Send a follow-up message within two days of the interview, even if you feel you have little chance of getting the job. These messages are often referred to as "thank-you notes," but they give you an important opportunity to go beyond merely expressing your appreciation. You can use the message to reinforce the reasons you are a good choice for the position, modify any answers you gave during the interview if you realize you made a mistake or have changed your mind, and respond to any negatives that might have arisen in the interview (see Figure 16.5 on the next page).[48] Email is usually acceptable for follow-up messages, unless the interviewer has asked you to use other media.

A follow-up message after an interview is more than a professional courtesy; it's another chance to promote yourself to an employer.

MESSAGE OF INQUIRY

If you're not advised of the interviewer's decision by the promised date or within two weeks, you might make an inquiry. A message of inquiry (which can be handled by email if the interviewer has given you his or her email address) is particularly appropriate if you've received a job offer from a second firm and don't want to accept it before you have an answer from the first. The following message illustrates the general model for a direct request:

Use the model for a direct request when you write an inquiry about a hiring decision.

When we talked on April 7 about the fashion coordinator position in your Park Avenue showroom, you indicated that a decision would be made by May 1. I am still enthusiastic about the position and eager to know what conclusion you've reached.

Identifies the position and introduces the main idea

To complicate matters, another firm has now offered me a position and has asked that I reply within the next two weeks.

Places the reason for the request second

Because your company seems to offer a greater challenge, I would appreciate knowing about your decision by Thursday, May 12. If you need more information before then, please let me know.

Makes a courteous request for specific action last, while clearly stating a preference for this organization

REQUEST FOR A TIME EXTENSION

If you receive a job offer while other interviews are still pending, you can ask the employer for a time extension. Open with a strong statement of your continued interest in the job, ask for more time to consider the offer, provide specific reasons for the request, and assure the reader that you will respond by a specific date (see Figure 16.6 on page 535).

LETTER OF ACCEPTANCE

When you receive a job offer you want to accept, reply within five days. Begin by accepting the position and expressing thanks. Identify the job you're accepting. In the next paragraph, cover any necessary details. Conclude by saying that you look forward to reporting

Use the model for positive messages when you write a letter of acceptance.

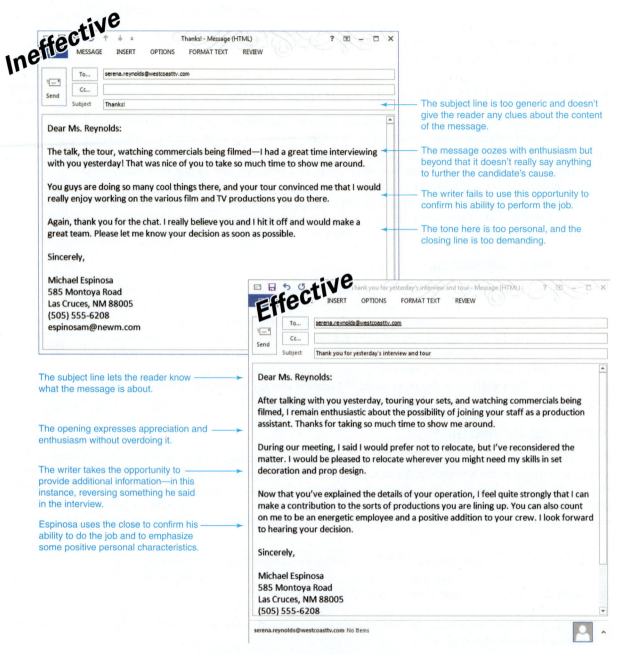

Ineffective

Thanks! - Message (HTML)

MESSAGE INSERT OPTIONS FORMAT TEXT REVIEW

To... serena.reynolds@westcoasttv.com

Cc...

Subject Thanks!

Dear Ms. Reynolds:

The talk, the tour, watching commercials being filmed—I had a great time interviewing with you yesterday! That was nice of you to take so much time to show me around.

You guys are doing so many cool things there, and your tour convinced me that I would really enjoy working on the various film and TV productions you do there.

Again, thank you for the chat. I really believe you and I hit it off and would make a great team. Please let me know your decision as soon as possible.

Sincerely,

Michael Espinosa
585 Montoya Road
Las Cruces, NM 88005
(505) 555-6208
espinosam@newm.com

The subject line is too generic and doesn't give the reader any clues about the content of the message.

The message oozes with enthusiasm but beyond that it doesn't really say anything to further the candidate's cause.

The writer fails to use this opportunity to confirm his ability to perform the job.

The tone here is too personal, and the closing line is too demanding.

Effective

...thank you for yesterday's interview and tour - Message (HTML)

INSERT OPTIONS FORMAT TEXT REVIEW

To... serena.reynolds@westcoasttv.com

Cc...

Subject Thank you for yesterday's interview and tour

Dear Ms. Reynolds:

After talking with you yesterday, touring your sets, and watching commercials being filmed, I remain enthusiastic about the possibility of joining your staff as a production assistant. Thanks for taking so much time to show me around.

During our meeting, I said I would prefer not to relocate, but I've reconsidered the matter. I would be pleased to relocate wherever you might need my skills in set decoration and prop design.

Now that you've explained the details of your operation, I feel quite strongly that I can make a contribution to the sorts of productions you are lining up. You can also count on me to be an energetic employee and a positive addition to your crew. I look forward to hearing your decision.

Sincerely,

Michael Espinosa
585 Montoya Road
Las Cruces, NM 88005
(505) 555-6208

serena.reynolds@westcoasttv.com No Items

The subject line lets the reader know what the message is about.

The opening expresses appreciation and enthusiasm without overdoing it.

The writer takes the opportunity to provide additional information—in this instance, reversing something he said in the interview.

Espinosa uses the close to confirm his ability to do the job and to emphasize some positive personal characteristics.

Figure 16.5 **Follow-Up Message: Ineffective and Effective**
Use the follow-up message after an interview to express continued interest in the opportunity, to correct or expand on any information you provided in the interview, and to thank the interviewer for his or her time.
Source: MS Outlook 2013, © Microsoft.

for work. As always, a positive letter should convey your enthusiasm and eagerness to cooperate:

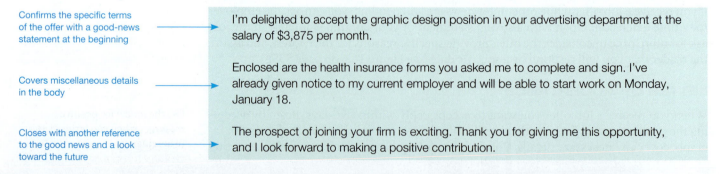

Confirms the specific terms of the offer with a good-news statement at the beginning

I'm delighted to accept the graphic design position in your advertising department at the salary of $3,875 per month.

Covers miscellaneous details in the body

Enclosed are the health insurance forms you asked me to complete and sign. I've already given notice to my current employer and will be able to start work on Monday, January 18.

Closes with another reference to the good news and a look toward the future

The prospect of joining your firm is exciting. Thank you for giving me this opportunity, and I look forward to making a positive contribution.

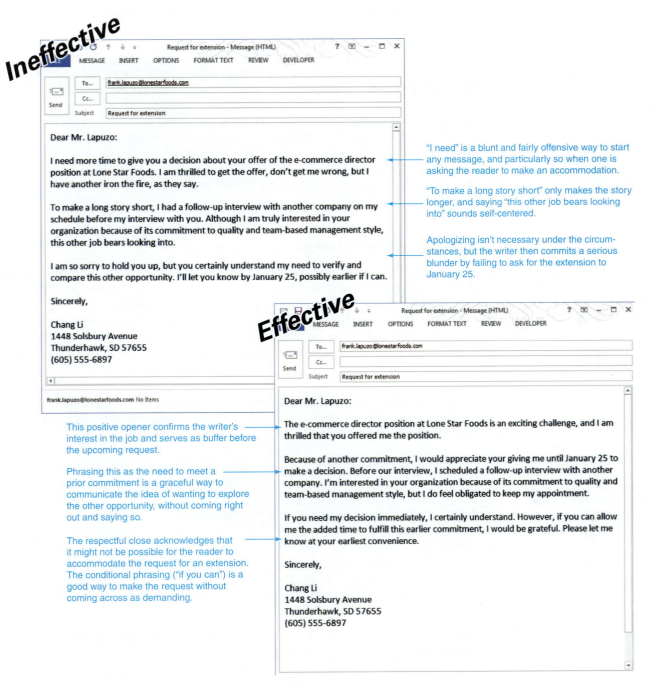

Ineffective

Effective

Figure 16.6   Request for a Time Extension: Ineffective and Effective
Needing more time to decide on a job offer is not uncommon, particularly for candidates with desirable credentials. However, make the request in a respectful and subtle way. The reader understands you are comparing opportunities and looking for the best offer, so you don't need to belabor this point.
Source: MS Outlook 2013, © Microsoft.

Be aware that a job offer and a written acceptance of that offer can constitute a legally binding contract, for both you and the employer. Before you send an acceptance letter, be sure you want the job.

Written acceptance of a job offer can be considered a legally binding contract.

LETTER DECLINING A JOB OFFER

After all your interviews, you may find that you need to write a letter declining a job offer. Use the techniques for negative messages (see Chapter 9): Open warmly, state the reasons for refusing the offer, decline the offer explicitly, and close on a pleasant note that

If you decide to decline a job offer, do so tactfully, using the model for negative messages.

expresses gratitude. By taking the time to write a sincere, tactful letter, you leave the door open for future contact:

Uses a buffer in the opening paragraph

> Thank you for your hospitality during my interview at your Durham facility last month. I'm flattered that you would offer me the computer analyst position that we talked about.

Precedes the bad news with tactfully phrased reasons for the applicant's unfavorable decision

> I was fortunate to receive two job offers during my search. Because my desire to work abroad can more readily be satisfied by another company, I have accepted that job offer.

Lets the reader down gently with a sincere and cordial ending

> I deeply appreciate the time you spent talking with me. Thank you again for your consideration and kindness.

LETTER OF RESIGNATION

Letters of resignation should always be written in a gracious and professional style that avoids criticism of your employer or your colleagues.

If you get a job offer while employed, you can maintain good relations with your current employer by writing a thoughtful letter of resignation to your immediate supervisor. Follow the advice for negative messages and make the letter sound positive, regardless of how you feel. Say something favorable about the organization, the people you work with, or what you've learned on the job. Then state your intention to leave and give the date of your last day on the job. Be sure you give your current employer at least two weeks' notice.

Uses an appreciative opening to serve as a buffer

> My sincere thanks to you and to all the other Emblem Corporation employees for helping me learn so much about serving the public these past two years. You have given me untold help and encouragement.

States reasons before the bad news itself, using tactful phrasing to help keep the relationship friendly, should the writer later want letters of recommendation

> You may recall that when you first interviewed me, my goal was to become a customer relations supervisor. Because that opportunity has been offered to me by another organization, I am submitting my resignation. I will miss my friends and colleagues at Emblem, but I want to take advantage of this opportunity.

Discusses necessary details in an extra paragraph

> I would like to terminate my work here two weeks from today (June 13) but can arrange to work an additional week if you want me to train a replacement.

Tempers any disappointment with a cordial close

> My sincere thanks and best wishes to all of you.

To verify the content and style of your follow-up messages, consult the tips in "Checklist: Writing Follow-Up Messages."

CHECKLIST ✔ Writing Follow-Up Messages

A. Thank-you messages
- Write a brief thank-you letter within two days of the interview.
- Acknowledge the interviewer's time and courtesy.
- Restate the specific job you're applying for.
- Express your enthusiasm about the organization and the job.
- Add any new facts that may help your chances.
- Politely ask for a decision.

B. Messages of inquiry
- If you haven't heard from the interviewer by the promised date, write a brief message of inquiry.
- Use the direct approach: main idea, necessary details, specific request.

C. Requests for a time extension
- Request an extension if you have pending interviews and need time to decide about an offer.
- Open on a friendly note.

- Explain why you need more time and express continued interest in the company.
- In the close, promise a quick decision if your request is denied and ask for a confirmation if your request is granted.

D. Letters of acceptance
- Send this message within five days of receiving the offer.
- State clearly that you accept the offer, identify the job you're accepting, and confirm vital details such as salary and start date.
- Make sure you want the job; an acceptance letter can be treated as a legally binding contract.

E. Letters declining a job offer
- Use the indirect approach for negative messages.
- Open on a warm and appreciative note and then explain why you are refusing the offer.
- End on a sincere, positive note.

F. Letters of resignation
- Send a letter of resignation to your current employer as soon as possible.
- Begin with an appreciative buffer.
- In the middle section, state your reasons for leaving and actually state that you are resigning.
- Close cordially.

ON THE JOB: SOLVING COMMUNICATION DILEMMAS AT ZAPPOS

You recently joined the recruiting team at Zappos' headquarters in Las Vegas. You're looking to hire experienced customer support specialists who remain calm when things get chaotic and who are comfortable communicating in the Zappos style with a diverse range of customers. Using what you know about job applications and interviewing, address these challenges. (To learn more about working at Zappos, you can visit https://jobs.zappos.com/)

1. The first step for someone hoping to get a job at Zappos is to become an "Insider" by joining the Inside Zappos social network. Because written communication skills are such an important part of the job, you pay close attention to how people present themselves in their networking profiles. Based on the following opening paragraphs, which of these four candidates has done the best job of capturing your attention and interest?
   a. With 4.5 years of customer service experience, solid performance reviews, and a firm commitment to excellence in customer service, I trust I don't sound overconfident when I say that I posses the qualities a fine organization such as Zappos needs to help achieve its goals and objectives.
   b. You do wacky. I do wacky. Let's make this happen.
   c. Given your reputation for hiring coolest cats in town, the big question is why the heck don't I work there yet? I'm driven, way smarter than average, and would feel right at home in Vegas, baby!
   d. In addition to being an enthusiastic Zappos customer, I am also a customer service professional myself. A brilliant idea came to me last week while I was having yet another satisfying interaction with your customer support crew: I want to be part of the team that can create such positive experiences for customers.

2. You like to put applicants at ease right away, so you usually start interviews by asking an offbeat question to break the tension while also prompting the candidate to reveal something about his or her personality and knowledge. Which of these questions would you choose to start an interview?
   a. Who is the most ridiculously demanding customer you ever encountered?
   b. If we gave you a jetpack to fly all over town surprising customers with product deliveries, would you take the job?
   c. Ever have one of those days when life seems like one endless job interview?
   d. So . . . buying that weekly lottery ticket still hasn't worked out, eh?

3. Zappos likes employees who can think on their feet, even when faced with outlandish questions and circumstances. Which of these questions would you use to judge a candidate's ability to grasp a problem and begin developing a solution?
   a. You're a scientist with the Environmental Protection Agency, specializing in toxic waste from electronic products. You're testifying before a congressional committee, and a senator wants to know how many mobile phone batteries will be thrown away in the next 10 years. Without access to any additional information, how would you start to construct an estimate of this number?
   b. Guess how old I am.
   c. Why do telephone numbers in movies and TV shows always start with 555?
   d. How would you explain the concept of a human family to a creature from another planet?

4. At the end of each interview, you make a point to ask candidates if they have any questions for you. Which of the following responses impresses you the most?

  a. No, thanks. I think I'm all set. You've done a wonderful job of answering whatever questions I might've come in with.

  b. Oh, I don't need to take any more of your time. I'm a pretty good independent thinker. If I have any questions, I'll just look you up online when I get back to home.

  c. Absolutely. Can you give me the inside scoop? Is this fun Zappos family environment stuff for real or just a show to impress people on the outside?

  d. Yes, thanks, I do. Now that Amazon has acquired Zappos, do you think there will be opportunities to spread the Zappos spirit through the entire Amazon operation? Or is there a risk that the Zappos spirit might be lost now that it's part of a much larger company?

Learning Objectives Checkup

Assess your understanding of the principles in this chapter by reading each learning objective and studying the accompanying exercises. You can check your responses against the answer key on page 599.

Objective 16.1: Explain the purposes of application letters and describe how to apply the AIDA organizational approach to them.

1. What is the primary reason for sending an application letter?
  a. To encourage the reader to look at your résumé
  b. To ask for a job
  c. To itemize your qualifications
  d. To ask for an application form

2. Why are unsolicited application letters more challenging to write than solicited application letters?
  a. Nobody wants to receive unsolicited application letters.
  b. With an unsolicited letter, you have to do the research to identify the qualities the company would likely be looking for and convince someone to consider you for a job that might not even be open yet.
  c. Solicited application letters are shorter, making it more likely than recruiters will bother to read them.
  d. Unsolicited letters do not lend themselves to the AIDA model.

3. Which of the following is a good technique to gain attention in the opening paragraph of any application letter?
  a. Make sure you "jump off the page" with an eye-catching design.
  b. Explain how you have some immediate potential to meet the company's needs.
  c. Invoke a sense of dramatic mystery by withholding either the job you are applying for or some key facts about yourself.
  d. Go deep; structure your letter more along the lines of a comprehensive informational report.

4. What are the two vital functions of the final paragraph of an application letter?
  a. To ask the reader for an interview (or other appropriate action) and to express how happy would you be to work for the company
  b. To ask the reader for an interview (or other appropriate action) and to make it easy for the reader to reply
  c. To ask the reader for an interview (or other appropriate action) and to state your salary expectations

  d. To encourage the reader to read your résumé and to highlight at least three key points from your résumé

Objective 16.2: Describe the typical sequence of job interviews, the major types of interviews, and the attributes employers look for during an interview.

5. Which of these interview stages happens first?
  a. The selection stage
  b. The screening stage
  c. The filtering stage
  d. The sorting stage

6. A/an _____ interview, often used in the screening stage, features a series of prepared questions in a set order.

7. How does a behavioral interview differ from a situational interview?
  a. A behavioral interview asks you to relate incidents and experiences from your past, whereas a situational interview puts you in actual work situations and asks you to perform some task, such as leading a brainstorming session.
  b. They are essentially the same thing, although behavioral interviews are generally conducted by computer rather than a live interviewer.
  c. A situational interview asks you to relate incidents and experiences from your past, whereas a behavioral interview asks how you would respond to various hypothetical situations in the future.
  d. A behavioral interview asks you to relate incidents and experiences from your past, whereas a situational interview asks how you would respond to various hypothetical situations in the future.

8. What are the two most important factors employers look for during interviews?
  a. Fit with the organization and motivation
  b. Motivation and ability to perform the job
  c. Motivation and years of experience
  d. Ability to perform the job and compatibility with the organization

9. Which of the following preemployment tests might you encounter while applying for jobs?
  a. Integrity tests
  b. Substance tests
  c. Personality tests
  d. All of the above

Objective 16.3: List six tasks you need to complete to prepare for a successful job interview.

10. If an interviewer asks you to describe your biggest weakness, which of the following is a good strategy for your response?
    a. The interviewer is just trying to rattle you, so what you say is less important than staying cool and calm while you say it.
    b. Frame your response in terms of skills you plan to develop in the future, specifically a skill that will benefit the company.
    c. Respectfully explain to the interviewer that the question is illegal.
    d. Explain that you don't have any major weaknesses.

11. What is the best strategy for asking questions of your own during an interview?
    a. Try to ask all of them at the beginning of the interview so that you don't run out of time.
    b. Wait until after the interview and then email your questions to the interviewer.
    c. Try to work your questions in naturally throughout the course of the interview.
    d. Wait until the interviewer asks if you have any questions.

12. If you believe that you have a particular disadvantage related to some aspect of your appearance, interviewing skills, job skills, or work experience, how should you handle the situation when preparing for an interview?
    a. Plan to make a joke about your weakness early in the interview; this will break the tension and allow you to focus on the interviewer's questions.
    b. Compensate by focusing on your strengths, both while you're preparing and during the interview.
    c. Correct the perceived shortcoming if possible; if not, focus on your positive attributes.
    d. Ignore the situation; there's nothing you can do about a weakness at this point.

13. If you're not sure what style of clothing to wear to a particular interview and you're not able to ask someone at the company for advice, what should you do?
    a. Dress in a fairly conservative style; it's better to be a little too dressy than too casual.
    b. Dress as you would like to dress on the job.
    c. Dress in an eye-catching style that will make a lasting impression on the interviewer.
    d. Arrive early with several different changes of clothes; try to see what people there are wearing, then find a place to change into whichever outfit you have that most closely matches.

Objective 16.4: Explain how to succeed in all three stages of an interview.

14. Studies show that many interviewers, particularly those with poor training, make up their minds about candidates
    a. In the first 20 seconds of the interview
    b. In the final 20 seconds of the interview
    c. On the basis of the résumé
    d. On the basis of the cover letter

15. Which of the following is an advisable response to an interviewer who asks you about your marital status, how many children you have, and what their ages are?
    a. Answer the questions; it is perfectly within the interviewer's right to ask you such personal questions, even if they are not directly related to the job you are applying for.
    b. Tell the interviewer that such questions are illegal and threaten to sue for invasion of privacy.
    c. Sidestep the questions by asking if the interviewer has some specific concerns about your commitment to the job, your willingness to travel, or some other factor.
    d. If you want the job, refuse to answer the questions but promise that you won't report the illegal questioning to the EEOC.

16. What should you do if the interviewer tells you the salary for the job being offered?
    a. Always take whatever the company offers.
    b. Respond with a figure higher than what is offered.
    c. Respond with a figure lower than what is offered.
    d. Ask if there is any room to negotiate on salary.

Objective 16.5: Identify the most common employment messages that follow an interview and explain when you would use each one.

17. After a job interview, you should send a follow-up message
    a. Within two days after the interview
    b. Only if you think you got the job
    c. That follows the AIDA organizational model
    d. That does all of the above

18. A letter declining a job offer should follow
    a. The direct approach
    b. The AIDA model
    c. A negative news approach
    d. The polite plan

Exercises

Each activity is labeled according to the primary skill or skills you will need to use. To review relevant chapter content, you can refer to the indicated Learning Objective. In some instances, supporting information will be found in another chapter, as indicated.

16.10. **Career Management: Preparing for Interviews [LO-3]** Google yourself, Bing yourself, scour your social networking profiles, review your Twitter messages, and explore every other possible online source you can think of that might have something about you. If you find anything potentially embarrassing, remove it if possible. Write a summary of your search-and-destroy mission (you can skip any embarrassing details in your report to your instructor!).

Career Management: Researching Target Employers [LO-3] Select a medium or large company (one that you can easily find information on) where you might like to work. Use Internet sources to gather some preliminary research on the company; don't limit your search to the company's own website.

16.11. What did you learn about this organization that would help you during an interview there?

16.12. What Internet sources did you use to obtain this information?

16.13. Armed with this information, what aspects of your background do you think might appeal to this company's recruiters?

16.14. Based on what you've learned about this company's culture, what aspects of your personality should you try to highlight during an interview?

16.15. **Career Management: Interviewing; Collaboration: Team Projects [LO-4], Chapter 2** Divide the class into two groups. Half the class will be recruiters for a large chain of national department stores, looking to fill manager trainee positions (there are 16 openings). The other half of the class will be candidates for the jobs. The company is specifically looking for candidates who demonstrate these three qualities: initiative, dependability, and willingness to assume responsibility.

- Have each recruiter select and interview an applicant for 10 minutes.
- Have all the recruiters discuss how they assessed the applicant in each of the three desired qualities. What questions did they ask or what did they use as an indicator to determine whether the candidate possessed the quality?
- Have all the applicants discuss what they said to convince the recruiters that they possessed each of these qualities.

16.16. **Career Management: Interviewing [LO-3]** Write a short email to your instructor, discussing what you believe are your greatest strengths and weaknesses from an employment perspective. Next, explain how these strengths and weaknesses would be viewed by interviewers evaluating your qualifications.

16.17. **Career Management: Interviewing [LO-3]** Prepare written answers to 10 of the questions listed in Table 16.3.

Message Strategies: Employment Messages, Communication Ethics: Resolving Ethical Dilemmas [LO-5], Chapter 1 You have decided to accept a new position with a competitor of your company. Write a letter of resignation to your supervisor, announcing your decision.

16.18. Will you notify your employer that you are joining a competing firm? Explain.

16.19. Will you use the direct or the indirect approach? Explain.

16.20. Will you send your letter by email, send it by regular mail, or place it on your supervisor's desk?

Expand Your Skills

Critique the Professionals

Find an online video of a business professional being interviewed by a journalist. Using whatever medium your instructor requests, write a brief assessment (no more than one page) of the professional's performance and any tips that you picked up that could you use in job interviews.

Sharpen Your Career Skills Online

Bovée and Thill's Business Communication Web Search, at http://websearch.businesscommunicationnetwork.com, is a unique research tool designed specifically for business communication research. Use the Web Search function to find a website, video, PDF document, podcast, or presentation that offers advice on successful interviewing techniques. Write a brief email message to your instructor or a post for your class blog, describing the item that you found and summarizing the career skills information you learned from it.

Improve Your Grammar, Mechanics, and Usage

The following exercises help you improve your knowledge of and power over English grammar, mechanics, and usage. Turn to the Handbook of Grammar, Mechanics, and Usage at the end of this book and review all of Section 3.4 (Numbers). Then look at the following items and indicate the preferred choice in each group of sentences. (Answers to these exercises appear on page 601.)

16.21. **a.** We need to hire one office manager, four bookkeepers, and 12 clerk-typists.
   b. We need to hire one office manager, four bookkeepers, and twelve clerk-typists.
   c. We need to hire 1 office manager, 4 bookkeepers, and 12 clerk-typists.

16.22. **a.** The market for this product is nearly 6 million people in our region alone.
   b. The market for this product is nearly six million people in our region alone.
   c. The market for this product is nearly 6,000,000 million people in our region alone.

16.23. **a.** Make sure that all 1,835 pages are on my desk no later than 9:00 a.m.

b. Make sure that all 1835 pages are on my desk no later than nine o'clock in the morning.

c. Make sure that all 1,835 pages are on my desk no later than nine o'clock a.m.

16.24. a. Our deadline is 4/7, but we won't be ready before 4/11.

b. Our deadline is April 7, but we won't be ready before April 11.

c. Our deadline is 4/7, but we won't be ready before April 11.

16.25. a. 95 percent of our customers are men.

b. Ninety-five percent of our customers are men.

c. Of our customers, ninety-five percent are men.

16.26. a. More than half the U.S. population is female.

b. More than ½ the U.S. population is female.

c. More than one-half the U.S. population is female.

16.27. a. Last year, I wrote 20 15-page reports, and Michelle wrote 24 three-page reports.

b. Last year, I wrote 20 fifteen-page reports, and Michelle wrote 24 three-page reports.

c. Last year, I wrote twenty 15-page reports, and Michelle wrote 24 three-page reports.

16.28. a. Our blinds should measure 38 inches wide by 64 and one-half inches long by 7/16 inches deep.

b. Our blinds should measure 38 inches wide by 64-1/2 inches long by 7/16 inches deep.

c. Our blinds should measure 38 inches wide by 64-1/2″ long by 7/16 inches deep.

16.29. a. Deliver the couch to 783 Fountain Rd., Suite 3, Procter Valley, CA 92074.

b. Deliver the couch to 783 Fountain Rd., Suite three, Procter Valley, CA 92074.

c. Deliver the couch to seven eighty-three Fountain Rd., Suite three, Procter Valley, CA 92074.

16.30. a. Here are the corrected figures: 42.7% agree, 23.25% disagree, 34% are undecided, and the error is 0.05%.

b. Here are the corrected figures: 42.7% agree, 23.25% disagree, 34.0% are undecided, and the error is .05%.

c. Here are the corrected figures: 42.70% agree, 23.25% disagree, 34.00% are undecided, and the error is 0.05%.

For an overall review of your grammar, mechanics, and usage skills, visit MyBCommLab. Click on Chapter 16, click on Additional Exercises to Improve Your Grammar, Mechanics, and Usage, and then click on 25. Grammar and usage.

Cases

Website links for selected companies mentioned in cases can be found in the Student Assignments section at **http://realtimeupdates.com/ebc12**.

Application Messages

VIDEO SKILLS

16.31. Media Skills: Video; Message Strategies: Employment Messages [LO-1], Chapter 7 With its encouragement of video applications and abandonment of traditional job postings, Zappos might be starting a mini-trend toward a new style of employment application.

Your task: Identify a company where you would like to work and assume that it encourages candidates to submit video introductions. Plan, record, and produce a short video (no longer than three minutes) that you might submit to this employer. Don't worry too much about fancy production quality, but make sure your content and presentation match the company's style and brand image. For example, a fun and goofy video would be great for Zappos but not for many other companies.

EMAIL SKILLS

16.32. Message Strategies: Employment Messages [LO-1] Use one of the websites listed in Table 16.1 on page 517 to find a job opening in your target profession. If you haven't narrowed down to one career field yet, choose a business job for which you will have at least some qualifications at the time of your graduation.

Your task: Write an email message that would serve as your application letter if you were to apply for this job. Base your message on your actual qualifications for the position, and be sure to "echo" the requirements listed in the job description. Include the job description in your email message when you submit it to your instructor.

MICROBLOGGING SKILLS

16.33. Message Strategies: Employment Messages [LO-1] If you want to know whether job candidates can express themselves clearly on Twitter, why not test them as part of the application process? That's exactly what the Minneapolis advertising agency Campbell Mithun does. Rather than having them using conventional application methods, the company asks intern candidates to tweet their applications in 13 messages.[49]

Your task: Find a job opening on Twitter by searching on any of the following hashtags: #hiring, #joblisting, or #nowhiring.[50] Next, write an "application letter" composed of 13 individual tweets (140 characters maximum). If your class is set up with private Twitter accounts, go ahead and send the tweets. Otherwise, email them to your instructor or post them on your class blog, as your instructor indicates.

EMAIL SKILLS

16.34. Message Strategies: Employment Messages [LO-1] Finding job openings that align perfectly with your professional interests is wonderful, but it doesn't always happen. Sometimes you have to widen your search and go after whatever opportunities happen to be available. Even when the opportunity is not ideal, however, you still need to approach the employer with enthusiasm and a focused, audience-centric message.

Your task: Find a job opening for which you will be qualified when you graduate (or close to being qualified, for the purposes of this activity), but make it one that is outside your primary field of interest. Write an email application letter for this opening, making a compelling case that you are the right candidate for this job.

Interviewing

BLOGGING SKILLS/TEAM SKILLS

16.35. Career Management: Researching Target Employers [LO-3] Research is a critical element of the job search process. With information in hand, you increase the chance of finding the right opportunity (and avoiding bad choices), and you impress interviewers in multiple ways by demonstrating initiative, curiosity, research and analysis skills, an appreciation for the complex challenges of running a business, and willingness to work to achieve results.

Your task: With a small team of classmates, use online job listings to identify an intriguing job opening that at least one member of the team would seriously consider pursuing as graduation approaches. (You'll find it helpful if the career is related to at least one team member's college major or on-the-job experience so that the team can benefit from some knowledge of the profession in question.) Next, research the company, its competitors, its markets, and this specific position to identify five questions that would (1) help the team member decide if this is a good opportunity and (2) show an interviewer that you've really done your homework. Go beyond the basic and obvious questions to identify current, specific, and complex issues that only deep research can uncover. For example, is the company facing significant technical, financial, legal, or regulatory challenges that threaten its ability to grow or perhaps even survive in the long term? Or is the market evolving in a way that positions this particular company for dramatic growth? In a post for your class blog, list your five questions, identify how you uncovered the issue, and explain why each is significant.

TEAM SKILLS

16.36. Career Management: Interviewing [LO-4] Interviewing is a skill that can be improved through observation and practice.

Your task: You and all other members of your class are to write letters of application for an entry-level or management-trainee position that requires an engaging personality and intelligence but a minimum of specialized education or experience. Sign your letter with a fictitious name that conceals your identity. Next, polish (or create) a résumé that accurately identifies you and your educational and professional accomplishments.

Now, three members of the class who volunteer as interviewers divide up all the anonymously written application letters. Then each interviewer selects a candidate who seems the most convincing in his or her letter. At this time, the selected candidates identify themselves and give the interviewers their résumés.

Each interviewer then interviews his or her chosen candidate in front of the class, seeking to understand how the items on the résumé qualify the candidate for the job. At the end of the interviews, the class decides who gets the job and discusses why this candidate was successful. Afterward, retrieve your letter, sign it with the right name, and submit it to the instructor for credit.

TEAM SKILLS

16.37. Career Management: Interviewing [LO-4] Select a company in an industry in which you might like to work and then identify an interesting position within the company. Study the company and prepare for an interview with that company.

Your task: Working with a classmate, take turns interviewing each other for your chosen positions. Interviewers should take notes during the interview. When the interview is complete, critique each other's performance. (Interviewers should critique how well candidates prepared for the interview and answered the questions; interviewees should critique the quality of the questions asked.) Write a follow-up letter thanking your interviewer and submit the letter to your instructor.

Following Up After an Interview

LETTER WRITING SKILLS

16.38. Message Strategies: Employment Messages [LO-5] Because of a mix-up in your job application scheduling, you accidentally applied for your third-choice job before going after the one you really wanted. What you want to do is work in retail marketing with the upscale department store Neiman Marcus in Dallas; what you have been offered is a job with Longhorn Leather and Lumber, 65 miles away in the small town of Commerce, Texas.

You review your notes. Your Longhorn interview was three weeks ago with the human resources manager, R. P. Bronson, who has just written to offer you the position. The store's address is 27 Sam Rayburn Drive, Commerce, TX 75428. Mr. Bronson notes that he can hold the position open for 10 days. You have an interview scheduled with Neiman Marcus next week, but it is unlikely that you will know the store's decision within this 10-day period.

Your task: Write to Mr. Bronson, requesting a reasonable delay in your consideration of his job offer.

LETTER WRITING SKILLS/EMAIL SKILLS

16.39. Message Strategies: Employment Messages [LO-5] Fortunately for you, your interview with Neiman Marcus (see the previous case) went well, and you've just received a job offer from the company.

Your task: Write a letter to R. P. Bronson at Longhorn Leather and Lumber, declining his job offer, and write an email message to Clarissa Bartle at Neiman Marcus, accepting her job offer. Make up any information you need when accepting the Neiman Marcus offer.

LETTER WRITING SKILLS

16.40. Message Strategies: Employment Messages (Letters of Resignation) [LO-5] Leaving a job is rarely stress free, but it's particularly difficult when you are parting ways with a mentor who played an important role in advancing your career. A half-dozen years into your career, you have benefited greatly from the advice, encouragement, and professional connections offered by your mentor, who also happens to be your current boss. She seemed to believe in your potential from the beginning and went out of her way on numerous occasions to help you. You returned the favor by becoming a stellar employee who has made important contributions to the success of the department your boss leads.

Unfortunately, you find yourself at a caree impasse. You believe you are ready to move into a management position, but your company is not growing enough to create many opportunities.

Worse yet, you joined the firm during a period of rapid expansion, so there are many eager and qualified internal candidates at your career level interested in the few managerial jobs that do become available. You fear it may be years before you get the chance to move up in the company. Through your online networking activities, you found an opportunity with a firm in another industry and have decided to pursue it.

Your task: You have a close relationship with your boss, so you will announce your intention to leave the company in a private, one-on-one conversation. However, you also recognize the need to write a formal letter of resignation, which you will hand to your boss during this meeting. This letter is addressed to your boss, but as formal business correspondence that will become part of your personnel file, it should not be a "personal" letter. Making up whatever details you need, write a brief letter of resignation.

MyBCommLab

Go to the Assignments section of your MyLab to complete these writing exercises.

16.41. How can you prepare for a situational or behavioral interview if you have no experience with the job for which you are interviewing? [LO-2]

16.42. Why are the questions you ask during an interview as important as the answers you give to the interviewer's questions? [LO-3]

Endnotes

1. Zappos Inside Zappos page, accessed 8 August 2014, https://jobs .zappos.com; Blair Hanley Frank, "Zappos Ditches Job Posts, Replaces Them with a Social Network," *GeekWire*, 27 May 2014, www .geekwire.com. "Wishez Is Live," Zappos Family blog, 17 November 2010, http://blogs.zappos.com; Tony Hsieh, "Amazon & Zappos, 1 Year Later," Zappos CEO & COO blog, 22 July 2010, http://blogs .zappos.com; Todd Raphael, "7 Interview Questions from Zappos," Todd Raphael's World of Talent blog, 22 July 2010, http://community .ere.net; Jeffrey M. O'Brien, "Zappos Knows How to Kick It," *Fortune*, 22 January 2009, http://about.zappos.com/ press-center; "Zappos Family Seattle Coding Challenge and Tech Tweet Up," Zappos Family blog, 22 March 2011, http://blogs.zappos.com.
2. Matthew Rothenberg, "Manuscript vs. Machine," The Ladders, 15 December 2009, www.theladders.com; Joann Lublin, "Cover Letters Get You in the Door, So Be Sure Not to Dash Them Off," *Wall Street Journal*, 6 April 2004, B1.
3. Lisa Vaas, "How to Write a Great Cover Letter," The Ladders, 20 November 2009, www.theladders.com.
4. Allison Doyle, "Introduction to Cover Letters," *About.com*, accessed 13 August 2010, http://jobsearch.about.com.
5. Alison Green, "Are You Making These 8 Mistakes on Your Cover Letter?" *U.S. News & World Report*, 18 July 2012, http://money.usnews .com; Doyle, "Introduction to Cover Letters"; Vaas, "How to Write a Great Cover Letter"; Toni Logan, "The Perfect Cover Story," *Kinko's Impress* 2 (2000): 32, 34.

6. Lisa Vaas, "How to Follow Up a Résumé Submission," The Ladders, 9 August 2010, www.theladders.com.
7. Alison Doyle, "How to Follow Up After Submitting a Resume," *About.com*, accessed 13 August 2010, http://jobsearch.about.com; Vaas, "How to Follow Up a Résumé Submission."
8. Anne Fisher, "How to Get Hired by a 'Best' Company," *Fortune*, 4 February 2008, 96.
9. Fisher, "How to Get Hired by a 'Best' Company."
10. Sarah E. Needleman, "Speed Interviewing Grows as Skills Shortage Looms; Strategy May Help Lock in Top Picks; Some Drawbacks," *Wall Street Journal*, 6 November 2007, B15.
11. Scott Beagrie, "How to Handle a Telephone Job Interview," *Personnel Today*, 26 June 2007, 29.
12. John Olmstead, "Predict Future Success with Structured Interviews," *Nursing Management*, March 2007, 52–53.
13. Anne Fisher, "How to Get Hired by a 'Best' Company," *Fortune*, 4 February 2008, 96.
14. Erinn R. Johnson, "Pressure Sessions," *Black Enterprise*, October 2007, 72.
15. "What's a Group Interview?" About.com Tech Careers, accessed 5 April 2008, http://jobsearchtech.about.com.
16. Fisher, "How to Get Hired by a 'Best' Company."
17. Katherine Hansen, "Behavioral Job Interviewing Strategies for Job-Seekers," QuintCareers.com, accessed 13 August 2010, www .quintcareers.com.

18. Hansen, "Behavioral Job Interviewing Strategies for Job-Seekers."

19. Chris Pentilla, "Testing the Waters," *Entrepreneur*, January 2004, www.entrepreneur.com; Terry McKenna, "Behavior-Based Interviewing," *National Petroleum News*, January 2004, 16; Nancy K. Austin, "Goodbye Gimmicks," *Incentive*, May 1996, 241.

20. William Poundstone, "Beware the Interview Inquisition," *Harvard Business Review*, May 2003, 18.

21. Peter Vogt, "Mastering the Phone Interview," Monster.com, accessed 13 December 2006, www.monster.com; Nina Segal, "The Global Interview: Tips for Successful, Unconventional Interview Techniques," Monster.com, accessed 13 December 2006, www.monster.com.

22. Segal, "The Global Interview."

23. Barbara Kiviat, "How Skype Is Changing the Job Interview," *Time*, 20 October 2009, accessed 13 August 2010, www.time.com.

24. HireVue website, accessed 4 April 2008, www.hirevue.com; in2View website, accessed 4 April 2008, www.in2view.biz; Victoria Reitz, "Interview Without Leaving Home," *Machine Design*, 1 April 2004, 66.

25. Gina Ruiz, "Job Candidate Assessment Tests Go Virtual," *Workforce Management*, January 2008, www.workforce.com; Connie Winkler, "Job Tryouts Go Virtual," *HR Magazine*, September 2006, 131–134.

26. U.S. Equal Employment Opportunity Commission, "Employment Test and Selection Procedures," EEOC website, accessed 24 July 2012, www.eeoc.gov; Jonathan Katz, "Rethinking Drug Testing," *Industry Week*, March 2010, 16–18; Ashley Shadday, "Assessments 101: An Introduction to Candidate Testing," *Workforce Management*, January 2010, www.workforce.com; Dino di Mattia, "Testing Methods and Effectiveness of Tests," *Supervision*, August 2005, 4–5; David W. Arnold and John W. Jones, "Who the Devil's Applying Now?" *Security Management*, March 2002, 85–88; Matthew J. Heller, "Digging Deeper," *Workforce Management*, 3 March 2008, 35–39.

27. Frederick P. Morgeson, Michael A. Campion, Robert L. Dipboye, John R. Hollenbeck, Kevin Murphy, and Neil Schmitt, "Are We Getting Fooled Again? Coming to Terms with Limitations in the Use of Personality Tests in Personnel Selection," *Personnel Psychology* 60, no. 4 (Winter 2007): 1029–1049.

28. Austin, "Goodbye Gimmicks."

29. Hannah Morgan, "The Ultimate Interview Prep Checklist," *U.S. News & World Report*, 23 April 2014, http://money.usnews.com.

30. Rachel Zupek, "How to Answer 10 Tough Interview Questions," *CNN.com*, 4 March 2009, www.cnn.com; Barbara Safani, "How to Answer Tough Interview Questions Authentically," The Ladders, 5 December 2009, www.theladders.com.

31. Nick Corcodilos, "How to Answer a Misguided Interview Question," *Seattle Times*, 30 March 2008, www.seattletimes.com.

32. Katherine Spencer Lee, "Tackling Tough Interview Questions," *Certification Magazine*, May 2005, 35.

33. Scott Ginsberg, "10 Good Ways to 'Tell Me About Yourself,'" The Ladders, 26 June 2010, www.theladders.com.

34. Richard A. Moran, "The Number One Interview Trap Question," *Business Insider*, 23 April 2014, www.businessinsider.com.

35. Joe Turner, "An Interview Strategy: Telling Stories," Yahoo! HotJobs, accessed 5 April 2008, http://hotjobs.yahoo.com.

36. "A Word of Caution for Chatty Job Candidates," *Public Relations Tactics*, January 2008, 4.

37. Randall S. Hansen, "When Job-Hunting: Dress for Success," QuintCareers.com, accessed 5 April 2008, www.quintcareers.com; Alison Doyle, "Dressing for Success," *About.com*, accessed 5 April 2008, http://jobsearch.about.com.

38. William S. Frank, "Job Interview: Pre-Flight Checklist," *The Career Advisor*, accessed 28 September 2005, http://careerplanning.about.com.

39. "Employers Reveal Outrageous and Common Mistakes Candidates Made in Job Interviews, According to New CareerBuilder Survey," CareerBuilder.com, accessed 24 March 2011, www.careerbuilder.com.

40. Alison Green, "10 Surefire Ways to Annoy a Hiring Manager," *U.S. News & World Report*, accessed 24 July 2012, http://money.usnews.com.

41. T. Shawn Taylor, "Most Managers Have No Idea How to Hire the Right Person for the Job," *Chicago Tribune*, 23 July 2002, www.ebsco.com.

42. "10 Minutes to Impress," *Journal of Accountancy*, July 2007, 13.

43. Steven Mitchell Sack, "The Working Woman's Legal Survival Guide: Testing," *FindLaw.com*, accessed 22 February 2004, www.findlaw.com.

44. Todd Anten, "How to Handle Illegal Interview Questions," Yahoo! HotJobs, accessed 7 August 2009, http://hotjobs.yahoo.com.

45. "Negotiating Salary: An Introduction," *InformationWeek*, accessed 22 February 2004, www.informationweek.com.

46. "Negotiating Salary."

47. Lisa Vaas, "Resume, Meet Technology: Making Your Resume Format Machine-Friendly," The Ladders, accessed 13 August 2010, www.theladders.com.

48. Alison Green, "How a Thank-You Note Can Boost Your Job Chances," *U.S. News & World Report*, 27 June 2012, http://money.usnews.com; Joan S. Lublin, "Notes to Interviewers Should Go Beyond a Simple Thank You," *Wall Street Journal*, 5 February 2008, B1.

49. Tiffany Hsu, "Extreme Interviewing: Odd Quizzes, Weird Mixers, Improve Pitches. Can You Get Past the Hiring Gatekeepers?" *Los Angeles Times*, 19 February 2012, B1.

50. From Ritika Trikha, "The Best Tips for Tweeting Your Way to a Job," *U.S. News & World Report*, 24 July 2012, http://money.usnews.com.

Format and Layout of Business Documents

The format and layout of business documents vary from country to country. In addition, many organizations develop their own variations of standard styles, adapting documents to the types of messages they send and the kinds of audiences they communicate with. The formats described here are the most common approaches used in U.S. business correspondence, but be sure to follow whatever practices are expected at your company.

First Impressions

Your documents tell readers a lot about you and about your company's professionalism. So all your documents must look neat, present a professional image, and be easy to read. Your audience's first impression of a document comes from the quality of its paper, the way it is customized, and its general appearance.

PAPER

To give a quality impression, businesspeople consider carefully the paper they use. Several aspects of paper contribute to the overall impression:

- **Weight.** Paper quality is judged by the weight of four reams (each a 500-sheet package) of letter-size paper. The weight most commonly used by U.S. business organizations is 20-pound paper, but 16- and 24-pound versions are also used.
- **Cotton content.** Paper quality is also judged by the percentage of cotton in the paper. Cotton doesn't yellow over time the way wood pulp does, plus it's both strong and soft. For letters and outside reports, use paper with a 25 percent cotton content. For memos and other internal documents, you can use a lighter-weight paper with lower cotton content. Airmail-weight paper may save money for international correspondence, but make sure it isn't too flimsy.[1]
- **Size.** In the United States, the standard paper size for business documents is 8½ by 11 inches. Standard legal documents are 8½ by 14 inches. Executives sometimes have heavier 7-by-10-inch paper on hand (with matching envelopes) for personal messages such as congratulations.[2] They may also have a box of note cards imprinted with their initials and a box of plain folded notes for condolences or for acknowledging formal invitations.

- **Color.** White is the standard color for business purposes, although neutral colors such as gray and ivory are sometimes used. Memos can be produced on pastel-colored paper to distinguish them from external correspondence. In addition, memos are sometimes produced on various colors of paper for routing to separate departments. Light-colored papers are appropriate, but bright or dark colors make reading difficult and may appear too frivolous.

CUSTOMIZATION

For letters to outsiders, U.S. businesses commonly use letterhead stationery, which may be either professionally printed or designed in-house using word-processing templates and graphics. Letterhead typically contains the company name, logo, address, telephone and fax numbers, general email address, website URL, and possibly one or more social media URLs.

In the United States, businesses always use letterhead for the first page of a letter. Successive pages are usually plain sheets of paper that match the letterhead in color and quality. Some companies use a specially printed second-page letterhead that bears only the company's name.

APPEARANCE

Nearly all business documents are produced using an inkjet or laser printer; make sure to use a clean, high-quality printer. Certain documents, however, should be handwritten (such as a short informal memo or a note of condolence). Be sure to handwrite, print, or type the envelope to match the document. However, even a letter on the best-quality paper with the best-designed letterhead may look unprofessional if it's poorly produced. So pay close attention to all the factors affecting appearance, including the following:

- **Margins.** Business letters typically use 1-inch margins at the top, bottom, and sides of the page, although these parameters are sometimes adjusted to accommodate letterhead elements.
- **Line length.** Lines are rarely justified, because the resulting text looks too formal and can be difficult to read.
- **Character spacing.** Use proper spacing between characters and after punctuation. For example, U.S. conventions include leaving one space after commas, semicolons, colons, and sentence-ending periods. Each letter in a person's initials is followed by a period and a

single space. However, abbreviations such as U.S.A. or MBA may or may not have periods, but they never have internal spaces.

- **Special symbols.** Take advantage of the many special symbols available with your computer's selection of fonts. In addition, see if your company has a style guide for documents, which may include particular symbols you are expected to use.
- **Corrections.** Messy corrections are unacceptable in business documents. If you notice an error after printing a document with your word processor, correct the mistake and reprint. (With informal memos to members of your own team or department, the occasional small correction in pen or pencil is acceptable, but never in formal documents.)

Letters

All business letters have certain elements in common. Several of these elements appear in every letter; others appear only when desirable or appropriate. In addition, these letter parts are usually arranged in one of three basic formats.

STANDARD LETTER PARTS

The letter in Figure A.1 shows the placement of standard letter parts. The writer of this business letter had no letterhead available but correctly included a heading. All business letters typically include these seven elements.

Heading

The elements of the letterhead make up the heading of a letter in most cases. If letterhead stationery is not available, the heading includes a return address (but no name) and starts 13 lines from the top of the page, which leaves a 2-inch top margin.

Date

If you're using letterhead, place the date at least one blank line beneath the lowest part of the letterhead. Without letterhead, place the date immediately below the return address. The standard method of writing the date in the United States uses the full name of the month (no abbreviations), followed by the day (in numerals, without *st, nd, rd,* or *th*), a comma, and then the year: July 31, 2017 (7/31/2017). Many

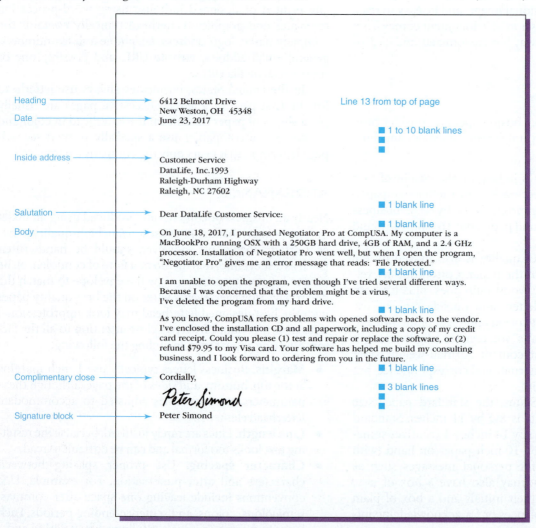

Figure A.1 Standard Letter Parts

TABLE A.1	Common Date Forms	
Convention	**Order**	**Examples**
U.S. standard	Month day year	July 31, 2017
		7/31/2017
		7-31-2017
Japan	Year month day	17/07/31
Europe (most countries)	Day month year	31 July 2017
		31/07/17
		31.07.17
International (ISO) format	Year month day	2017-07-31

other countries use other formats (see Table A.1), which can create confusion in international correspondence. To avoid misinterpretation in such cases, spell out the month.[3]

Inside Address

The inside address identifies the recipient of the letter. For U.S. correspondence, begin the inside address at least one line below the date. Precede the addressee's name with a courtesy title, such as *Dr., Mr.,* or *Ms.* The accepted courtesy title for women in business is *Ms.,* although a woman known to prefer the title *Miss* or *Mrs.* is always accommodated. If you don't know whether a person is a man or a woman (and you have no way of finding out), omit the courtesy title. For example, *Terry Smith* could be either a man or a woman. The first line of the inside address would be just *Terry Smith,* and the salutation would be *Dear Terry Smith.* The same is true if you know only a person's initials, as in *S. J. Adams.*

Spell out and capitalize titles that precede a person's name, such as *Professor* or *General* (see Table A.2 on the next page for the proper forms of address). The person's organizational title, such as *Director,* may be included on this first line (if it is short) or on the line below; the name of a department may follow. In addresses and signature lines, don't forget to capitalize any professional title that follows a person's name:

Mr. Ray Johnson, Dean
Ms. Patricia T. Higgins
Assistant Vice President

However, professional titles not appearing in an address or signature line are capitalized only when they directly precede the name:

President Kenneth Johanson will deliver the speech.
Maria Morales, president of ABC Enterprises, will deliver the speech.
The Honorable Helen Masters, senator from Arizona, will deliver the speech.

If the name of a specific person is unavailable, you may address the letter to the department or to a specific position within the department. Also, be sure to spell out company names in full, unless the company itself uses abbreviations in its official name.

Other address information includes the treatment of buildings, house numbers, and compass directions (see Table A.3 on page 551). The following example shows all the information that may be included in the inside address and its proper order for U.S. correspondence:

Ms. Linda Coolidge, Vice President
Corporate Planning Department
Midwest Airlines
Kowalski Building, Suite 21-A
7279 Bristol Ave.
Toledo, OH 43617

Canadian addresses are similar, except that the name of the province is usually spelled out:

Dr. H. C. Armstrong
Research and Development
Commonwealth Mining Consortium
The Chelton Building, Suite 301
585 Second St. SW
Calgary, Alberta T2P 2P5

The order and layout of address information vary from country to country. So when addressing correspondence for other countries, carefully follow the format and information that appear in the company's letterhead. However, when you're sending mail from the United States, be sure that the name of the destination country appears on the last line of the address in capital letters. Use the English version of the country name so that your mail is routed from the United States to the right country. Then, to be sure your mail is routed correctly within the destination country, use the foreign spelling of the city name (using the characters and diacritical marks that would be commonly used in

TABLE A.2   Forms of Address

Person	In Address	In Salutation
Personal Titles		
Man	Mr. [first & last name]	Dear Mr. [last name]:
Woman*	Ms. [first & last name]	Dear Ms. [last name]:
Two men (or more)	Mr. [first & last name] and Mr. [first & last name]	Dear Mr. [last name] and Mr. [last name] or Messrs. [last name] and [last name]:
Two women (or more)	Ms. [first & last name] and Ms. [first & last name]	Dear Ms. [last name] and Ms. [last name] or Mses. [last name] and [last name]:
One woman and one man	Ms. [first & last name] and Mr. [first & last name]	Dear Ms. [last name] and Mr. [last name]:
Couple (married with same last name)	Mr. [husband's first name] and Mrs. [wife's first name] [couple's last name]	Dear Mr. and Mrs. [last name]:
Couple (married with different last names)	Mr. [first & last name of husband] Ms. [first & last name of wife]	Dear Mr. [husband's last name] and Ms. [wife's last name]:
Couple (married professionals with same title and same last name)	[title in plural form] [husband's first name] and [wife's first name] [couple's last name]	Dear [title in plural form] [last name]:
Couple (married professionals with different titles and same last name)	[title] [first & last name of husband] and [title] [first & last name of wife]	Dear [title] and [title] [last name]:
Professional Titles		
President of a college or university	[title] [first & last name], President	Dear [title] [last name]:
Dean of a school or college	Dean [first & last name] or Dr., Mr., or Ms. [first & last name], Dean of [title]	Dear Dean [last name]: or Dear Dr., Mr., or Ms. [last name]:
Professor	Professor or Dr. [first & last name]	Dear Professor or Dr. [last name]:
Physician	[first & last name], M.D.	Dear Dr. [last name]:
Lawyer	Mr. or Ms. [first & last name], Attorney at Law	Dear Mr. or Ms. [last name]:
Military personnel	[full rank, first & last name, abbreviation of service designation] (add *Retired* if applicable)	Dear [rank] [last name]:
Company or corporation	[name of organization]	Ladies and Gentlemen: or Gentlemen and Ladies:
Governmental Titles		
President of the United States	The President	Dear Mr. or Madam President:
Senator of the United States	The Honorable [first & last name]	Dear Senator [last name]:
Cabinet member	The Honorable [first & last name]	Dear Mr. or Madam Secretary:
Attorney General	The Honorable [first & last name]	Dear Mr. or Madam Attorney General:
Mayor	The Honorable [first & last name], Mayor of [name of city]	Dear Mayor [last name]:
Judge	The Honorable [first & last name]	Dear Judge [last name]:

*Use *Mrs.* or *Miss* only if the recipient has specifically requested that you use one of these titles; otherwise *always* use *Ms.* in business correspondence. Also, never refer to a married woman by her husband's name (e.g., Mrs. Robert Washington) unless she specifically requests that you do so.

the region). For example, the following address uses *Köln* instead of *Cologne*:

H. R. Veith, Director   Addressee
Eisfieren Glaswerk   Company name
Blaubachstrasse 13   Street address
Postfach 10 80 07   Post office road
D-5000 Köln I   District, city
GERMANY   Country

Be sure to use organizational titles correctly when addressing international correspondence. Job designations vary around the world. In England, for example, a managing director is often what a U.S. company would call its chief executive officer or president, and a British deputy is the equivalent of a vice president. In France, responsibilities are assigned to individuals without regard to title or organizational structure, and in China the title *project manager* has meaning, but the title *sales manager* may not.

TABLE A.3 | Inside Address Information

Description	Example
Capitalize building names.	Empire State Building
Capitalize locations within buildings (apartments, suites, rooms).	Suite 1073
Use numerals for all house or building numbers, except the number one.	One Trinity Lane; 637 Adams Ave., Apt. 7
Spell out compass directions that fall within a street address.	1074 West Connover St.
Abbreviate compass directions that follow the street address.	783 Main St., N.E., Apt. 27

In addition, be aware that businesspeople in some countries sign correspondence without their names typed below.

In Germany, for example, the belief is that employees represent the company, so it's inappropriate to emphasize personal names.[4]

REAL-TIME UPDATES
LEARN MORE BY VISITING THIS WEBSITE

Addressing international correspondence

The Universal Postal Union offers examples for most countries around the world. Go to http://real-timeupdates.com/ebc12 and click on Learn More in the Students section.

Salutation

In the salutation of your letter, follow the style of the first line of the inside address. If the first line is a person's name, the salutation is *Dear Mr.* or *Ms. Name*. The formality of the salutation depends on your relationship with the addressee. If in conversation you would say "Mary," your letter's salutation should be *Dear Mary*, followed by a colon. Otherwise, include the courtesy title and last name, followed by a colon. Presuming to write *Dear Lewis* instead of *Dear Professor Chang* demonstrates a disrespectful familiarity that the recipient will probably resent.

If the first line of the inside address is a position title such as *Director of Personnel*, then use *Dear Director*. If the addressee is unknown, use a polite description, such as *Dear Alumnus, Dear SPCA Supporter*, or *Dear Voter*. If the first line is plural (a department or company), then use *Ladies and Gentlemen* (look again at Table A.2). When you do not know whether you're writing to an individual or a group (for example, when writing a reference or a letter of recommendation), use *To whom it may concern*.

In the United States some letter writers use a "salutopening" on the salutation line. A salutopening omits *Dear* but includes the first few words of the opening paragraph along with the recipient's name. After this line, the sentence continues a double space below as part of the body of the letter, as in these examples:

Thank you, Mr. Brown, for your prompt payment of your bill.	Salutopening
Your payment of $88.13 was received on January 24, 2016.	Body

Whether your salutation is informal or formal, be especially careful that names are spelled correctly. A misspelled name is glaring evidence of carelessness, and it belies the personal interest you're trying to express.

Body

The body of the letter is your message. Almost all letters are single-spaced, with one blank line before and after the salutation or salutopening, between paragraphs, and before the complimentary close. The body may include indented lists, entire paragraphs indented for emphasis, and even subheadings. If it does, all similar elements should be treated in the same way. Your department or company may select a format to use for all letters.

Complimentary Close

The complimentary close begins on the second line below the body of the letter. Alternatives for wording are available, but currently the trend seems to be toward using one-word closes, such as *Sincerely* and *Cordially*. In any case, the complimentary close reflects the relationship between you and the person you're writing to. Avoid cute closes, such as *Yours for bigger profits*. If your audience doesn't know you well, your sense of humor may be misunderstood.

Signature Block

Leave three blank lines for a written signature below the complimentary close, and then include the sender's name (unless it appears in the letterhead). The person's title may appear on the same line as the name or on the line below:

Cordially,

Raymond Dunnigan
Director of Personnel

Your letterhead indicates that you're representing your company. However, if your letter is on plain paper or runs to a second page, you may want to emphasize that you're speaking legally for the company. The accepted way of doing that is to place the company's name in capital letters, a double space below the complimentary close, and then include the sender's name and title four lines below that:

> Sincerely,
> WENTWORTH INDUSTRIES
>
>
> Helen B. Taylor
> President

If your name could be taken for either a man's or a woman's, a courtesy title indicating gender should be included, with or without parentheses. Also, women who prefer a particular courtesy title should include it:

> Mrs. Nancy Winters
> (Ms.) Juana Flores
> Ms. Pat Li
> (Mr.) Jamie Saunders

ADDITIONAL LETTER PARTS

Letters vary greatly in subject matter and thus in the identifying information they need and the format they adopt. The letter in Figure A.2 shows how these additional parts should be arranged. The following elements may be used in any combination, depending on the requirements of the particular letter:

- **Addressee notation.** Letters that have a restricted readership or that must be handled in a special way should include such addressee notations as *PERSONAL, CONFIDENTIAL,* or *PLEASE FORWARD.* This sort of notation appears a double space above the inside address, in all-capital letters.
- **Attention line.** Although not commonly used today, an attention line can be used if you know only the last name of the person you're writing to. It can also direct a letter to a position title or department. Place the attention line on the first line of the inside address and put the company name on the second.[5] Match the address on the envelope with the style of the inside address. An attention line may take any of the following forms or variants of them:

> Attention Dr. McHenry
> Attention Director of Marketing
> Attention Marketing Department

- **Subject line.** The subject line tells recipients at a glance what the letter is about (and indicates where to file the letter for future reference). It usually appears below the salutation, either against the left margin, indented (as a paragraph in the body), or centered. It can be placed above the salutation or at the very top of the page, and

it can be underscored. Some businesses omit the word *Subject*, and some organizations replace it with *Re:* or *In re:* (meaning "concerning" or "in the matter of"). The subject line may take a variety of forms, including the following:

> Subject: RainMaster Sprinklers
> Re: About your February 2, 2017, order
> In re: FALL 2017 SALES MEETING
> Reference Order No. 27920

- **Second-page heading.** Use a second-page heading whenever an additional page is required. Some companies have second-page letterhead (with the company name and address on one line and in a smaller typeface). The heading bears the name (person or organization) from the first line of the inside address, the page number, the date, and perhaps a reference number. Leave two blank lines before the body. Make sure that at least two lines of a continued paragraph appear on the first and second pages. Never allow the closing lines to appear alone on a continued page. Precede the complimentary close or signature lines with at least two lines of the body. Also, don't hyphenate the last word on a page. All the following are acceptable forms for second-page headings:

> Ms. Melissa Baker
> May 10, 2016
> Page 2
> Ms. Melissa Baker, May 10, 2017, Page 2
> Ms. Melissa Baker-2-May 10, 2017

- **Company name.** If you include the company's name in the signature block, put it a double space below the complimentary close. You usually include the company's name in the signature block only when the writer is serving as the company's official spokesperson or when letterhead has not been used.
- **Reference initials.** When businesspeople keyboard their own letters, reference initials are unnecessary, so they are becoming rare. When one person dictates a letter and another person produces it, reference initials show who helped prepare it. Place initials at the left margin, a double space below the signature block. When the signature block includes the writer's name, use only the preparer's initials. If the signature block includes only the department, use both sets of initials, usually in one of the following forms: *RSR/sm, RSR:sm,* or *RSR:SM* (writer/preparer). When the writer and the signer are different people, at least the file copy should bear both their initials as well as the typist's: *JFS/RSR/sm* (signer/writer/preparer).
- **Enclosure notation.** Enclosure notations appear at the bottom of a letter, one or two lines below the

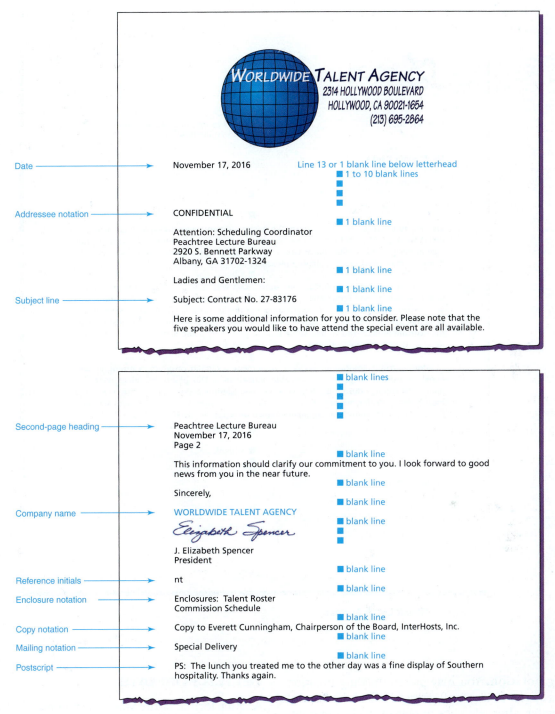

Figure A.2 Additional Letter Parts

reference initials. Some common forms include the following:

Enclosure
Enclosures (2)
Enclosures: Résumé
        Photograph
        Brochure

- **Copy notation.** Copy notations may follow reference initials or enclosure notations. They indicate who's receiving a *courtesy copy* (*cc*). Recipients are listed in order of rank or (rank being equal) in alphabetical order. Among the forms used are the following:

cc: David Wentworth, Vice President
Copy to Hans Vogel
748 Chesterton Road
Snohomish, WA 98290

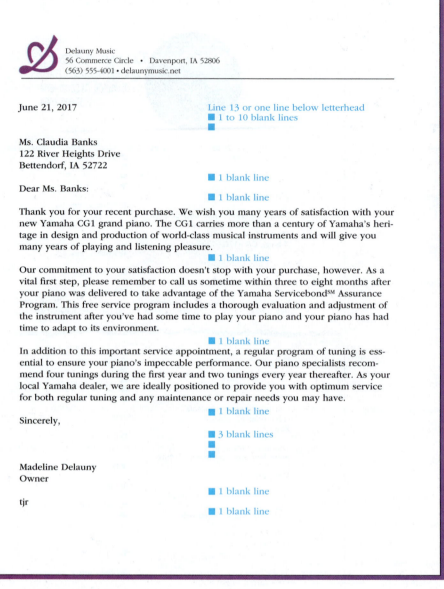

Figure A.3 **Block Letter Format**

- **Mailing notation.** You may place a mailing notation (such as *Special Delivery* or *Registered Mail*) at the bottom of the letter, after reference initials or enclosure notations (whichever is last) and before copy notations. Or you may place it at the top of the letter, either above the inside address on the left side or just below the date on the right side. For greater visibility, mailing notations may appear in capital letters.
- **Postscript.** A postscript is presented as an afterthought to the letter, a message that requires emphasis, or a personal note. It is usually the last thing on any letter and may be preceded by *P.S.*, *PS.*, *PS:*, or nothing at all. A second afterthought would be designated *P.P.S.* (post postscript).

LETTER FORMATS

A letter format is the way of arranging all the basic letter parts. Sometimes a company adopts a certain format as its policy; sometimes the individual letter writer or preparer is allowed to choose the most appropriate format. In the United States, three major letter formats are commonly used:

- **Block format.** Each letter part begins at the left margin. The main advantage is quick and efficient preparation (see Figure A.3).
- **Modified block format.** Same as block format, except that the date, complimentary close, and signature block start near the center of the page (see Figure A.4). The modified block format does permit indentions as

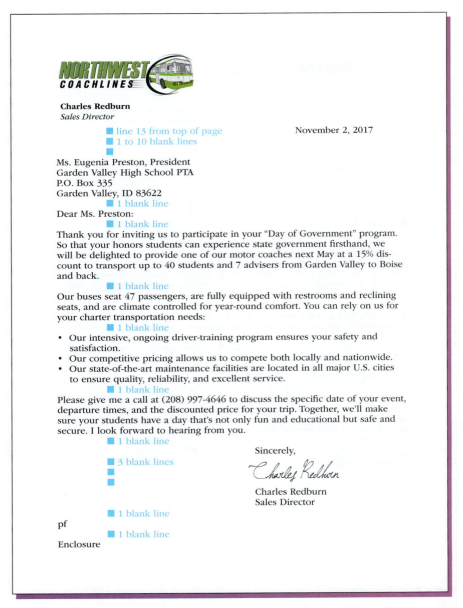

Figure A.4   **Modified Block Letter Format**

an option. This format mixes preparation speed with traditional placement of some letter parts. It also looks more balanced on the page than the block format does. (Note: The address and contact information in the left margin of this letter is part of this company's particular stationery design; other designs put this information at the top or bottom of the page.)

- **Simplified format.** Instead of using a salutation, this format often weaves the reader's name into the first line or two of the body and often includes a subject line in capital letters (see Figure A.5 on the next page). This format does not include a complimentary close, so your signature appears immediately below the body text. Because certain letter parts are eliminated, some line spacing is changed.

These three formats differ in the way paragraphs are indented, in the way letter parts are placed, and in some punctuation. However, the elements are always separated by at least one blank line, and the printed name is always separated from the line above by at least three blank lines to allow space for a signature. If paragraphs are indented, the indention is normally five spaces. The most common formats for intercultural business letters are the block style and the modified block style.

In addition to these three letter formats, letters may also be classified according to their style of punctuation. *Standard,* or *mixed, punctuation* uses a colon after the salutation (a comma if the letter is social or personal) and a comma after the complimentary close. *Open punctuation*

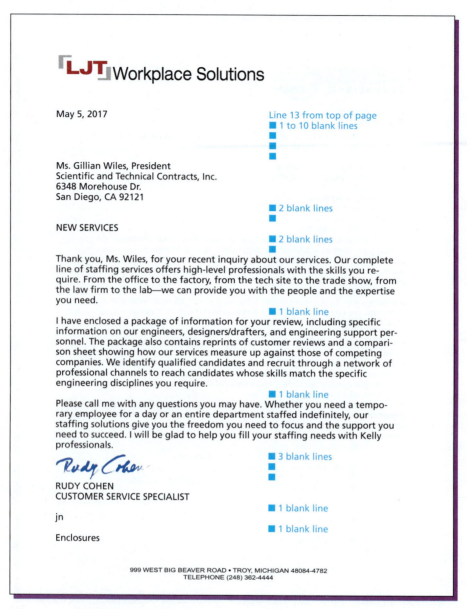

Figure A.5 **Simplified Letter Format**

uses no colon or comma after the salutation or the complimentary close. Although the most popular style in business communication is mixed punctuation, either style of punctuation may be used with block or modified block letter formats. Because the simplified letter format has no salutation or complimentary close, the style of punctuation is irrelevant.

Envelopes

For a first impression, the quality of the envelope is just as important as the quality of the stationery. Letterhead and envelopes should be of the same paper stock, have the same color ink, and be imprinted with the same address and logo. Most envelopes used by U.S. businesses are No. 10 envelopes (9 ½ inches long), which are sized for an 8 ½-by-11-inch piece of paper folded in thirds. Some occasions call for a smaller, No. 6 ¾, envelope or for envelopes proportioned to fit special stationery. Figure A.6 shows the two most common sizes.

ADDRESSING THE ENVELOPE

No matter what size the envelope, the address is always single-spaced with all lines aligned on the left. The address on the envelope is in the same style as the inside address and presents the same information. The order to follow is from the smallest division to the largest:

1. Name and title of recipient
2. Name of department or subgroup

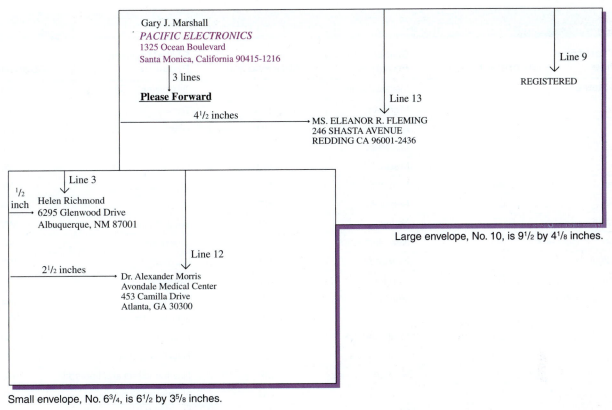

Gary J. Marshall
PACIFIC ELECTRONICS
1325 Ocean Boulevard
Santa Monica, California 90415-1216

↓ 3 lines

Please Forward

4½ inches →

Line 13 ↓

MS. ELEANOR R. FLEMING
246 SHASTA AVENUE
REDDING CA 96001-2436

Line 9 ↓

REGISTERED

Large envelope, No. 10, is 9½ by 4⅛ inches.

Line 3 ↓

½ inch →   Helen Richmond
6295 Glenwood Drive
Albuquerque, NM 87001

2½ inches →

Line 12 ↓

Dr. Alexander Morris
Avondale Medical Center
453 Camilla Drive
Atlanta, GA 30300

Small envelope, No. 6¾, is 6½ by 3⅝ inches.

Figure A.6   **Prescribed Envelope Format**

3. Name of organization
4. Name of building
5. Street address and suite number, or post office box number
6. City, state, or province, and zip code or postal code
7. Name of country (if the letter is being sent abroad)

Because the U.S. Postal Service uses optical scanners to sort mail, envelopes for quantity mailings, in particular, should be addressed in the prescribed format. Everything is in capital letters, no punctuation is included, and all mailing instructions of interest to the post office are placed above the address area (see Figure A.6). Canada Post requires a similar format, except that only the city is all in capitals, and the postal code is placed on the line below the name of the city. The post office scanners read addresses from the bottom up, so if a letter is to be sent to a post office box rather than to a street address, the street address should appear on the line above the box number. Figure A.6 also shows the proper spacing for addresses and return addresses.

The U.S. Postal Service and the Canada Post Corporation have published lists of two-letter mailing abbreviations for states, provinces, and territories (see Table A.4 on the next page). Postal authorities prefer no punctuation with these abbreviations. Quantity mailings should always follow post office requirements. For other letters, a reasonable compromise is to use traditional punctuation, uppercase and lowercase letters for names and street addresses, but two-letter state or province abbreviations, as shown here:

Mr. Kevin Kennedy
2107 E. Packer Dr.
Amarillo, TX 79108

Canadian postal codes are alphanumeric, with a three-character "area code" and a three-character "local code" separated by a single space (K2P 5A5). Zip and postal codes should be separated from state and province names by one space. Canadian postal codes may be treated the same or may be positioned alone on the bottom line of the address all by itself.

FOLDING TO FIT

The way a letter is folded also contributes to the recipient's overall impression of your organization's professionalism. When sending a standard-size piece of paper in a No. 10 envelope, fold it in thirds, with the bottom folded up first and the top folded down over it (see Figure A.7 on the next page); the open end should be at the top of the envelope and facing out. Fit smaller stationery neatly into the appropriate envelope simply by folding it in half or in thirds. When sending a standard-size letterhead in a No. 6 ¾ envelope, fold it in half from top to bottom and then in thirds from side to side.

TABLE A.4 Two-Letter Mailing Abbreviations for the United States and Canada

State/Territory/Province	Abbreviation	State/Territory/Province	Abbreviation	State/Territory/Province	Abbreviation
United States		Massachusetts	MA	Tennessee	TN
Alabama	AL	Michigan	MI	Texas	TX
Alaska	AK	Minnesota	MN	Utah	UT
American Samoa	AS	Mississippi	MS	Vermont	VT
Arizona	AZ	Missouri	MO	Virginia	VA
Arkansas	AR	Montana	MT	Virgin Islands	VI
California	CA	Nebraska	NE	Washington	WA
Canal Zone	CZ	Nevada	NV	West Virginia	WV
Colorado	CO	New Hampshire	NH	Wisconsin	WI
Connecticut	CT	New Jersey	NJ	Wyoming	WY
Delaware	DE	New Mexico	NM	**Canada**	
District of Columbia	DC	Maryland	MD	Alberta	AB
Florida	FL	New York	NY	British Columbia	BC
Georgia	GA	North Carolina	NC	Manitoba	MB
Guam	GU	North Dakota	ND	New Brunswick	NB
Hawaii	HI	Northern Mariana	MP	Newfoundland and Labrador	NL
Idaho	ID	Ohio	OH	Northwest Territories	NT
Illinois	IL	Oklahoma	OK	Nova Scotia	NS
Indiana	IN	Oregon	OR	Nunavut	NU
Iowa	IA	Pennsylvania	PA	Ontario	ON
Kansas	KS	Puerto Rico	PR	Prince Edward Island	PE
Kentucky	KY	Rhode Island	RI	Quebec	QC
Louisiana	LA	South Carolina	SC	Saskatchewan	SK
Maine	ME	South Dakota	SD	Yukon Territory	YT

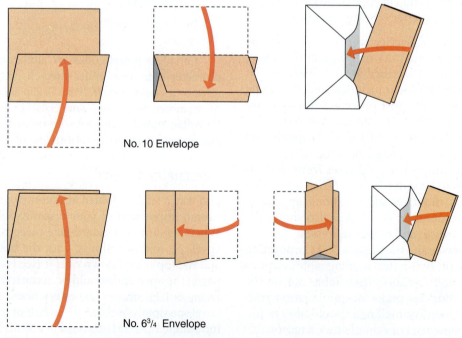

No. 10 Envelope

No. 6³/₄ Envelope

Figure A.7 **Folding Standard-Size Letterhead**

INTERNATIONAL MAIL

Postal service differs from country to country, so it's always a good idea to investigate the quality and availability of various services before sending messages and packages internationally. Also, compare the services offered by delivery companies such as UPS and FedEx to find the best rates and options for each destination and type of shipment. No matter which service you choose, be aware that international mail requires more planning than domestic mail. For example, for anything beyond simple letters, you generally need to prepare *customs forms* and possibly other documents, depending on the country of destination and the type of shipment. You are responsible for following the laws of the United States and any countries to which you send mail and packages.

The U.S. Postal Service currently offers four classes of international delivery, listed here from the fastest (and most expensive) to the slowest (and least expensive):

- **Global Express Guaranteed** is the fastest option. This service, offered in conjunction with FedEx, provides delivery in one to three business days to more than 190 countries and territories.
- **Express Mail International** guarantees delivery in three to five business days to a limited number of countries, including Australia, China, Hong Kong, Japan, and South Korea.
- **Priority Mail International** offers delivery guarantees of 6 to 10 business days to more than 190 countries and territories.
- **First Class Mail International** is an economical way to send correspondence and packages weighing up to four pounds to virtually any destination worldwide.

To prepare your mail for international delivery, follow the instructions provided at the U.S. Postal Service website. There you'll find complete information on the international services available through the USPS, along with advice on addressing and packaging mail, completing customs forms, and calculating postage rates and fees. The *International Mail Manual*, also available on this website, offers the latest information and regulations for both outbound and inbound international mail. For instance, you can click on individual country names to see current information about restricted or prohibited items and materials, required customs forms, and rates for various classes of service.[6] Various countries have specific and often extensive lists of items that may not be sent by mail at all or that must be sent using particular postal service options.

Memos

Electronic media have replaced most internal printed memos in many companies, but you may have occasion to send printed memos from time to time. These can be simple announcements or messages, or they can be short reports using the memo format.

On your document, include a title such as MEMO or INTEROFFICE CORRESPONDENCE (all in capitals) centered at the top of the page or aligned with the left margin. Also at the top, include the words *To, From, Date,* and *Subject*–followed by the appropriate information–with a blank line between as shown here:

MEMO

TO:
FROM:
DATE:
SUBJECT:

Sometimes the heading is organized like this:

MEMO

| TO: | FROM: |
| DATE: | SUBJECT: |

The following guidelines will help you effectively format specific memo elements:

- **Addressees.** When sending a memo to a long list of people, include the notation *See distribution list* or *See below* in the *To* position at the top; then list the names at the end of the memo. Arrange this list alphabetically, except when high-ranking officials deserve more prominent placement. You can also address memos to groups of people—*All Sales Representatives, Production Group, New Product Team.*
- **Courtesy titles.** You need not use courtesy titles anywhere in a memo; first initials and last names, first names, or even initials alone are often sufficient. However, use a courtesy title if you would use one in a face-to-face encounter with the person.
- **Subject line.** The subject line of a memo helps busy colleagues quickly find out what your memo is about, so take care to make it concise and compelling.
- **Body.** Start the body of the memo on the second or third line below the heading. Like the body of a letter, it's usually single-spaced with blank lines between paragraphs. Indenting paragraphs is optional. Handle lists, important passages, and subheadings as you do in letters.
- **Second page.** If the memo carries over to a second page, head the second page just as you head the second page of a letter.
- **Writer's initials.** Unlike a letter, a memo doesn't require a complimentary close or a signature, because your name is already prominent at the top. However, you may initial the memo–either beside the name appearing at the top of the memo or at the bottom of the memo.

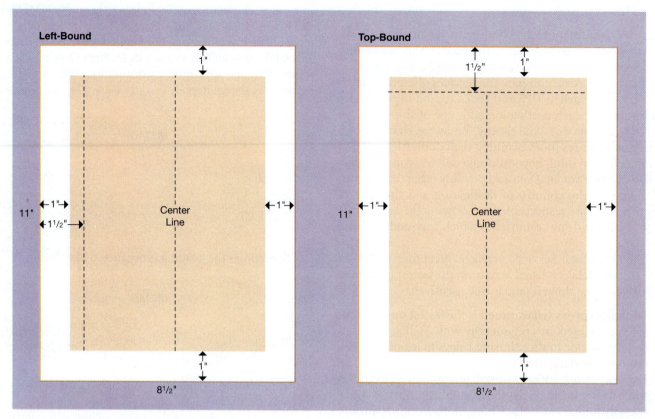

Figure A.8 **Margins for Formal Reports**

- **Other elements.** Treat elements such as reference initials and copy notations just as you would in a letter. One difference between letters and memos is that while letters use the term *enclosure* to refer to other pieces included with the letter, memos usually use the word *attachment.*

Memos may be delivered by hand, by the post office (when the recipient works at a different location), or through interoffice mail. Interoffice mail may require the use of special reusable envelopes that have spaces for the recipient's name and department or room number; the name of the previous recipient is simply crossed out. If a regular envelope is used, the words *Interoffice Mail* appear where the stamp normally goes, so that it won't accidentally be stamped and mailed with the rest of the office correspondence.

Informal, routine, or brief reports for distribution within a company are often presented in memo form. Don't include report parts such as a table of contents and appendixes, but write the body of the memo report just as carefully as you'd write a formal report.

Reports

Enhance the effectiveness of your reports by paying careful attention to their appearance and layout. Follow whatever guidelines your organization prefers, always being neat and

consistent throughout. If it's up to you to decide formatting questions, the following conventions may help you decide how to handle margins, headings, and page numbers.

MARGINS

All margins on a report page should be at least 1 inch wide. The top, left, and right margins are usually the same, but the bottom margins can be 1 ½ times deeper. Some special pages also have deeper top margins. Set top margins as deep as 2 inches for pages that contain major titles: prefatory parts (such as the table of contents or the executive summary), supplementary parts (such as the reference notes or bibliography), and textual parts (such as the first page of the text or the first page of each chapter).

If you're going to bind your report at the left or at the top, add half an inch to the margin on the bound edge (see Figure A.8): The space taken by the binding on left-bound reports makes the center point of the text a quarter-inch to the right of the center of the paper. Be sure to center headings between the margins, not between the edges of the paper.

HEADINGS

If you don't have a template supplied by your employer, choose a design for headings and subheadings that clearly distinguishes the various levels in the hierarchy. The first-level headings should be the most prominent, on down to the lowest-level subheading.

PAGE NUMBERS

Every page in a report is counted; however, not all pages show numbers. The first page of the report, normally the title page, is unnumbered. All other pages in the prefatory section are numbered with a lowercase roman numeral, beginning with *ii* and continuing with *iii, iv, v,* and so on.

Start numbering again with arabic numerals (1, 2, and so on) starting at the first page of the body.

You have many options for placing and formatting the page numbers, although these choices are usually made for you in a template. If you're not using a standard company template, position the page number where it is easy to see as the reader flips through the report. If the report will be stapled or otherwise bound along the left side, for instance, the best place for the page number is the upper right or lower right corner.

Endnotes

1. Mary A. De Vries, *Internationally Yours* (Boston: Houghton Mifflin, 1994), 9.

2. Patricia A. Dreyfus, "Paper That's Letter Perfect," *Money,* May 1985, 184.

3. Linda Driskill, *Business and Managerial Communication: New Perspectives* (Orlando, Fla.: Harcourt Brace Jovanovich, 1992), 470.

4. Lennie Copeland and Lewis Griggs, *Going International: How to Make Friends and Deal Effectively in the Global Marketplace,* 2nd ed. (New York: Random House, 1985), 24–27.

5. De Vries, *Internationally Yours,* 8.

6. U.S. Postal Service, *International Mail Manual,* Issue 34, 14 May 2007, www.usps.gov.

By providing information about your sources, you improve your own credibility as well as the credibility of the facts and opinions you present. Documentation gives readers the means for checking your findings and pursuing the subject further. Also, documenting your report is the accepted way to give credit to the people whose work you have drawn from.

What style should you use to document your report? Experts recommend various forms, depending on your field or discipline. Moreover, your employer or client may use a form different from those the experts suggest. Don't let this discrepancy confuse you. If your employer specifies a form, use it; the standardized form is easier for colleagues to understand. However, if the choice of form is left to you, adopt one of the styles described here. Whatever style you choose, be consistent within any given report, using the same order, punctuation, and format from one reference citation or bibliography entry to the next.

A wide variety of style manuals provide detailed information on documentation. These publications explain the three most commonly used styles:

- American Psychological Association, *Publication Manual of the American Psychological Association*, 6th ed. (Washington, D.C.: American Psychological Association, 2009). Details the author-date system, which is preferred in the social sciences and often in the natural sciences as well.
- *The Chicago Manual of Style*, 16th ed. (Chicago: University of Chicago Press, 2010). Often referred to only as "*Chicago*" and widely used in the publishing industry; provides detailed treatment of source documentation and many other aspects of document preparation.
- Joseph Gibaldi, *MLA Style Manual and Guide to Scholarly Publishing*, 3rd ed. (New York: Modern Language Association, 2008). Serves as the basis for the note and bibliography style used in much academic writing and is recommended in many college textbooks on writing term papers; provides a lot of examples in the humanities.

For more information on these three guides, visit **http://real-timeupdates.com/ebc12** and click on Appendix B. Although many schemes have been proposed for organizing the information in source notes, all of them break the information into parts: (1) information about the author (name), (2) information about the work (title, edition, volume number), (3) information about the publication (place, publisher), (4) information about the date, and (5) information on relevant page ranges.

The following sections summarize the major conventions for documenting sources in three styles: *The Chicago Manual of Style* (Chicago), the *Publication Manual of the American Psychological Association* (APA), and the *MLA Style Manual* (MLA).

Chicago Humanities Style

The Chicago Manual of Style recommends two types of documentation systems. The *documentary-note*, or *humanities*, style gives bibliographic citations in notes—either footnotes (when printed at the bottom of a page) or endnotes (when printed at the end of the report). The humanities system is often used in literature, history, and the arts. The other system recommended by *Chicago* is the *author-date* system, which cites the author's last name and the date of publication in the text, usually in parentheses, reserving full documentation for the reference list (or bibliography). For the purpose of comparing styles, this section concentrates on the humanities system, which is described in detail in *Chicago*.

IN-TEXT CITATION—*CHICAGO* HUMANITIES STYLE

To document report sources in text, the humanities system relies on superscripts—arabic numerals placed just above the line of type at the end of the reference:

> Toward the end of his speech, Myers sounded a note of caution, saying that even though the economy is expected to grow, it could easily slow a bit.[10]

The superscript lets the reader know how to look for source information in either a footnote or an endnote (see Figure B.1 on the next page). Some readers prefer footnotes so that they can simply glance at the bottom of the page for information. Others prefer endnotes so that they can read the text without a clutter of notes on the page. Also, endnotes relieve the writer from worrying about how long each note will be and how much space it will take away from the page. Both footnotes and endnotes are handled automatically by today's word processing software.

For the reader's convenience, you can use footnotes for *content notes* (which may supplement your main text with asides about a particular issue or event, provide a

Notes

Journal article with volume and issue numbers
1. Jonathan Clifton, "Beyond Taxonomies of Influence," *Journal of Business Communication* 46, no. 1 (2009): 57–79.

Brochure
2. BestTemp Staffing Services, *An Employer's Guide to Staffing Services*, 2d ed. (Denver: BestTemp Information Center, 2016), 31.

Newspaper article, no author
3. "Might Be Harder Than It Looks," *Los Angeles Times*, 30 January 2015, sec. A, p. 22.

Annual report
4. The Walt Disney Company, *2015 Annual Report* (Burbank, Calif.: The Walt Disney Company, 2016), 48.

Magazine article
5. Kerry A. Dolan, "A Whole New Crop" *Forbes*, 2 June 2013, 72–75.

Television broadcast
6. Daniel Han, "Trade Wars Heating Up Around the Globe," *CNN Headline News* (Atlanta: CNN, 5 March 2013).

Internet, World Wide Web
7. "Intel—Company Capsule," Hoover's Online [cited 19 June 2011], 3 screens; available from www.hoovers.com/intel/-ID_13787-/free-co-factsheet.xhtml.

Book, component parts
8. Sonja Kuntz, "Moving Beyond Benefits," in *Our Changing Workforce*, ed. Randolf Jacobson (New York: Citadel Press, 2001), 213–27.

Unpublished dissertation or thesis
9. George H. Morales, "The Economic Pressures on Industrialized Nations in a Global Economy" (Ph.D. diss., University of San Diego, 2001), 32–47.

Paper presented at a meeting
10. Charles Myers, "HMOs in Today's Environment" (paper presented at the Conference on Medical Insurance Solutions, Chicago, Ill., August 2001), 16–17.

Online magazine article
11. Leo Babauta, "17 Tips to Be Productive with Instant Messaging," in *Web Worker Daily* [online] (San Francisco, 2011 [updated 14 November 2012; cited 14 February 2016]); available from http://webworkerdaily.com.

Interview
12. Georgia Stainer, general manager, Day Cable and Communications, interview by author, Topeka, Kan., 2 March 2011.

Newspaper article, one author
13. Evelyn Standish, "Global Market Crushes OPEC's Delicate Balance of Interests," *Wall Street Journal*, 19 January 2016, sec. A, p. 1.

Book, two authors
14. Miriam Toller and Jay Fielding, *Global Business for Smaller Companies* (Rocklin, Calif.: Prima Publishing, 2001), 102–3.

Government publication
15. U.S. Department of Defense, *Stretching Research Dollars: Survival Advice for Universities and Government Labs* (Washington, D.C.: GPO, 2002), 126.

Figure B.1   Sample Endnotes—*Chicago* Humanities Style
(Note: This is a collection of sample entries, not a page from an actual report.)

cross-reference to another section of your report, or direct the reader to a related source). Then you can use endnotes for *source notes* (which document direct quotations, paraphrased passages, and visual aids). Consider which type of note is most common in your report, and then choose whether to present these notes all as endnotes or all as footnotes. Regardless of the method you choose for referencing textual information in your report, notes for visual aids (both content notes and source notes) are placed on the same page as the visual.

BIBLIOGRAPHY—*CHICAGO* HUMANITIES STYLE

The humanities system may or may not be accompanied by a bibliography (because the notes give all the necessary bibliographic information). However, endnotes are arranged in order of appearance in the text, so an alphabetical bibliography can be valuable to your readers. The bibliography may be titled *Bibliography, Reference List, Sources, Works Cited* (if you include only those sources you actually cited in your report), or *Works Consulted* (if you include uncited sources as well). This list of sources may also serve as a reading list for those who want to pursue the subject of your report further, so you may want to annotate each entry—that is, comment on the subject matter and viewpoint of the source, as well as on its usefulness to readers. Annotations may be written in either complete or incomplete sentences. A bibliography may also be more manageable if you subdivide it into categories (a classified bibliography), either by type of reference (such as books, articles, and unpublished material) or by subject matter (such as government regulation, market

Bibliography

Online magazine article
Babauta, Leo. "17 Tips to Be Productive with Instant Messaging," In *Web Worker Daily* [online], San Francisco, 2011 [updated 14 November 2012, cited 14 February 2016]. Available from http://webworkerdaily.com.

Brochure
BestTemp Staffing Services. *An Employer's Guide to Staffing Services.* 2d ed. Denver: BestTemp Information Center, 2016.

Journal article with volume and issue numbers
Clifton, Jonathan. "Beyond Taxonomies of Influence." *Journal of Business Communication* 46, no. 1 (2009): 57–79.

Magazine article
Dolan, Kerry A. "A Whole New Crop," *Forbes*, 2 June 2013, 72–75.

Television broadcast
Han, Daniel. "Trade Wars Heating Up Around the Globe." *CNN Headline News*. Atlanta: CNN, 5 March 2013.

Internet, World Wide Web
"Intel—Company Capsule." *Hoover's Online* [cited 19 June 2015]. 3 screens; Available from www.hoovers.com/intel/-ID_13787-/free-co-factsheet.xhtml.

Book, component parts
Kuntz, Sonja. "Moving Beyond Benefits." In *Our Changing Workforce*, edited by Randolf Jacobson. New York: Citadel Press, 2001.

Newspaper article, no author
"Might Be Harder Than It Looks." *Los Angeles Times*, 30 January 2015, sec. A, p. 22.

Unpublished dissertation or thesis
Morales, George H. "The Economic Pressures on Industrialized Nations in a Global Economy." Ph.D. diss., University of San Diego, 2001.

Paper presented at a meeting
Myers, Charles. "HMOs in Today's Environment." Paper presented at the Conference on Medical Insurance Solutions, Chicago, Ill., August 2001.

Interview
Stainer, Georgia, general manager, Day Cable and Communications. Interview by author. Topeka, Kan., 2 March 2011.

Newspaper article, one author
Standish, Evelyn. "Global Market Crushes OPEC's Delicate Balance of Interests." *Wall Street Journal*, 19 January 2016, sec. A, p. 1.

Book, two authors
Toller, Miriam, and Jay Fielding. *Global Business for Smaller Companies.* Rocklin, Calif.: Prima Publishing, 2001.

Government publication
U.S. Department of Defense. *Stretching Research Dollars: Survival Advice for Universities and Government Labs.* Washington, D.C.: GPO, 2002.

Annual report
The Walt Disney Company, *2015 Annual Report*, Burbank, Calif.: The Walt Disney Company, 2016.

Figure B.2 Sample Bibliography—*Chicago* Humanities Style
(Note: This is a collection of sample entries, not a page from an actual report.)

forces, and so on). Following are the major conventions for developing a bibliography according to *Chicago* style (see Figure B.2):

- Exclude any page numbers that may be cited in source notes, except for journals, periodicals, and newspapers.
- Alphabetize entries by the last name of the lead author (listing last name first). The names of second and succeeding authors are listed in normal order. Entries without an author name are alphabetized by the first important word in the title.
- Format entries as hanging indents (indent second and succeeding lines three to five spaces).
- Arrange entries in the following general order: (1) author name, (2) title information, (3) publication information, (4) date, (5) periodical page range.

- Use quotation marks around the titles of articles from magazines, newspapers, and journals. Capitalize the first and last words, as well as all other important words (except prepositions, articles, and coordinating conjunctions).
- Use italics to set off the names of books, newspapers, journals, and other complete publications. Capitalize the first and last words, as well as all other important words.
- For journal articles, include the volume number and the issue number (if necessary). Include the year of publication inside parentheses and follow with a colon and the page range of the article: *Journal of Business Communication* 46, no. 1 (2009): 57–79. (In this source, the volume is 46, the number is 1, and the page range is 57–79.)
- Use brackets to identify all electronic references: [Online database] or [CD-ROM].

- Explain how electronic references can be reached if it's not obvious from the URL.
- Give the citation date for online references: Cited 23 August 2016.

APA Style

The American Psychological Association (APA) recommends the author-date system of documentation, which is popular in the physical, natural, and social sciences. When using this system, you simply insert the author's last name and the year of publication within parentheses following the text discussion of the material cited. Include a page number if you use a direct quotation. This approach briefly identifies the source so that readers can locate complete information in the alphabetical reference list at the end of the report. The author-date system is both brief and clear, saving readers time and effort.

IN-TEXT CITATION—APA STYLE

To document report sources in text using APA style, insert the author's surname and the date of publication at the end of a statement. Enclose this information in parentheses. If the author's name is referred to in the text itself, then the name can be omitted from parenthetical material.

> Some experts recommend both translation and back-translation when dealing with any non-English-speaking culture (Clifton, 2013).
>
> Toller and Fielding (2015) make a strong case for small companies succeeding in global business.

Personal communications and interviews conducted by the author would not be listed in the reference list at all. Such citations would appear in the text only.

> Increasing the role of cable companies is high on the list of Georgia Stainer, general manager at Day Cable and Communications (personal communication, March 2, 2015).

LIST OF REFERENCES—APA STYLE

For APA style, list only those works actually cited in the text (so you would not include works for background or for further reading). Following are the major conventions for developing a reference list according to APA style (see Figure B.3):

- Format entries as hanging indents.
- List all author names in reversed order (last name first), and use only initials for the first and middle names.

- Arrange entries in the following general order: (1) author name, (2) date, (3) title information, (4) publication information, (5) periodical page range.
- Follow the author name with the date of publication in parentheses.
- List titles of articles from magazines, newspapers, and journals without underlines or quotation marks. Capitalize only the first word of the title, any proper nouns, and the first word to follow an internal colon.
- Italicize titles of books, capitalizing only the first word, any proper nouns, and the first word to follow a colon.
- Italicize titles of magazines, newspapers, journals, and other complete publications. Capitalize all the important words in the title.
- For journal articles, include the volume number (in italics) and, if necessary, the issue number (in parentheses). Finally, include the page range of the article: *Journal of Business Communication, 46*(1), 57–79. (In this example, the volume is 46, the number is 1, and the page range is 57–79.)
- Include personal communications (such as letters, memos, email, and conversations) only in text, not in reference lists.
- Electronic references include author, date of publication, title of article, name of publication (if one), volume, and the URL.
- For electronic references, indicate the actual year of publication.
- For web pages with extremely long URLs, use your best judgment to determine which URL from the site to use. For example, rather than giving the URL of a specific news release with a long URL, you can provide the URL of the "Media relations" webpage.
- APA citation guidelines for social media are still evolving. For the latest information, visit the APA Style Blog.
- For online journals or periodicals that assign a digital object identifier (DOI), include that instead of a conventional URL. If no DOI is available, include the URL of the publication's home page.

MLA Style

The style recommended by the Modern Language Association of America is used widely in the humanities, especially in the study of language and literature. Like APA style, MLA style uses brief parenthetical citations in the text. However, instead of including author name and year, MLA citations include author name and page reference.

IN-TEXT CITATION—MLA STYLE

To document report sources in text using MLA style, insert the author's last name and a page reference inside parentheses following the cited material: (Matthews 63). If the author's name is mentioned in the text reference, the name can be omitted from the parenthetical citation: (63). The citation indicates that the reference came from page 63 of

References

Online magazine article	Babauta, L. (2007, November 14). 17 tips to be productive with instant messaging. *Web Worker Daily*. Retrieved from http://webworkerdaily.com
Brochure	BestTemp Staffing Services. (2016). *An employer's guide to staffing services* (2nd ed.) [Brochure]. Denver, CO: BestTemp Information Center.
Journal article with volume and issue numbers	Clifton, J. (2009). Beyond taxonomies of influence. *Journal of Business Communication, 46*(1), 57.
Magazine article	Dolan, K. A. (2013, June 2). A whole new crop. *Forbes*, 72–75.
Television broadcast	Han, D. (2013, March 5). Trade wars heating up around the globe. *CNN Headline News* [Television broadcast]. Atlanta, GA: CNN.
Internet, World Wide Web	Hoover's Online. (2011). *Intel—company capsule*. Retrieved from http://www.hoovers.com/intel/-ID_13787-/free-co-factsheet.xhtml
Book, component parts	Kuntz, S. (2001). Moving beyond benefits. In Randolph Jacobson (Ed.), *Our changing workforce* (pp. 213–227). New York, NY: Citadel Press.
Newspaper article, no author	Might be harder than it looks. (2015, January 30). *Los Angeles Times*, p. A22.
Unpublished dissertation or thesis	Morales, G. H. (2001). *The economic pressures on industrialized nations in a global economy*. Unpublished doctoral dissertation, University of San Diego.
Paper presented at a meeting	Myers, C. (2001, August). *HMOs in today's environment*. Paper presented at the Conference on Medical Insurance Solutions, Chicago, IL.
Interview	*Cited in text only, not in the list of references.*
Newspaper article, one author	Standish, E. (2016, January 19). Global market crushes OPEC's delicate balance of interests. *Wall Street Journal*, p. A1.
Book, two authors	Toller, M., & Fielding, J. (2001). *Global business for smaller companies*. Rocklin, CA: Prima Publishing.
Government publication	U.S. Department of Defense. (2002). *Stretching research dollars: Survival advice for universities and government labs*. Washington, DC: U.S. Government Printing Office.
Annual report	The Walt Disney Company. (2016). *2015 Annual report*, Burbank, CA: The Walt Disney Company.

Figure B.3   Sample References—APA Style
(Note: This is a collection of sample references, not a page from an actual report. Also, it is single-spaced as is the norm for business reports; APA references are double-spaced in academic reports.)

a work by Matthews. With the author's name, readers can find complete publication information in the alphabetically arranged list of works cited that comes at the end of the report.

> Some experts recommend both translation and back-translation when dealing with any non-English-speaking culture (Clifton 57).
>
> Toller and Fielding make a strong case for small companies succeeding in global business (102–03).

LIST OF WORKS CITED—MLA STYLE

The *MLA Style Manual* recommends preparing the list of works cited first so that you will know what information to give in the parenthetical citation (for example, whether to add a short title if you're citing more than one work by the same author, or whether to give an initial or first name if you're citing two authors who have the same last name). The list of works cited appears at the end of your report, contains all the works that you cite in your text, and lists them in alphabetical order. Following are the major conventions for developing a reference list according to MLA style (see Figure B.4 on the next page):

- Format entries as hanging indents.
- Arrange entries in the following general order: (1) author name, (2) title information, (3) publication information, (4) date, (5) periodical page range.
- List the lead author's name in reverse order (last name first), using either full first names or initials. List second and succeeding author names in normal order.
- Use quotation marks around the titles of articles from magazines, newspapers, and journals. Capitalize all important words.

Works Cited

Online magazine article	Babauta, Leo. "17 Tips to Be Productive with Instant Messaging," *Web Worker Daily* 14 Nov. 2012. 14 Feb. 2016. http://webworkerdaily.com
Brochure	BestTemp Staffing Services. *An Employer's Guide to Staffing Services.* 2d ed. Denver: BestTemp Information Center, 2016.
Journal article with volume and issue numbers	Clifton, Jonathan. "Beyond Taxonomies of Influence." *Journal of Business Communication* 46, 1 (2009): 57–79.
Magazine article	Dolan, Kerry A. "A Whole New Crop" *Forbes*, 2 June 2013: 72–75.
Television broadcast	Han, Daniel. "Trade Wars Heating Up Around the Globe." *CNN Headline News*. CNN, Atlanta. 5 Mar. 2013.
Internet, World Wide Web	"Intel—Company Capsule." *Hoover's Online*. 2011. Hoover's Company Information. 19 June 2011 http://www.hoovers.com/intel/-ID_13787/free-co-factsheet.xhtml
Book, component parts	Kuntz, Sonja. "Moving Beyond Benefits." *Our Changing Workforce*. Ed. Randolf Jacobson. New York: Citadel Press, 2001. 213–27.
Newspaper article, no author	"Might Be Harder Than It Looks." *Los Angeles Times,* 30 Jan. 2013: A22.
Unpublished dissertation or thesis	Morales, George H. "The Economic Pressures on Industrialized Nations in a Global Economy." Diss. U of San Diego, 2001.
Paper presented at a meeting	Myers, Charles. "HMOs in Today's Environment." Conference on Medical Insurance Solutions. Chicago. 13 Aug. 2001.
Interview	Stainer, Georgia, general manager, Day Cable and Communications. Telephone interview. 2 Mar. 2011.
Newspaper article, one author	Standish, Evelyn. "Global Market Crushes OPEC's Delicate Balance of Interests." *Wall Street Journal,* 19 Jan. 2016: A1.
Book, two authors	Toller, Miriam, and Jay Fielding. *Global Business for Smaller Companies*. Rocklin, CA: Prima Publishing, 2001.
Government publication	United States. Department of Defense. *Stretching Research Dollars: Survival Advice for Universities and Government Labs.* Washington: GPO, 2002.
Annual report	The Walt Disney Company, *2015 Annual Report*. Burbank, Calif.: The Walt Disney Company, 2016.

Figure B.4   Sample Works Cited—MLA Style
(Note: This is a collection of sample references, not a page from an actual report. Also, it is single-spaced as is the norm for business reports; MLA works cited are double-spaced in academic reports.)

- Italicize the names of books, newspapers, journals, and other complete publications, capitalizing all main words in the title.
- For journal articles, include the volume number and the issue number (if necessary). Include the year of publication inside parentheses and follow with a colon and the page range of the article: *Journal of Business Communication* 46, 1 (2009): 57. (In this source, the volume is 46, the number is 1, and the page is 57.)
- Electronic sources are less fixed than print sources, and they may not be readily accessible to readers. So citations for electronic sources must provide more information. Always try to be as comprehensive as possible, citing whatever information is available (however, see the note about extremely long URLs).
- The date for electronic sources should contain both the date assigned in the source (if no date is shown,

write "n.d." instead) and the date accessed by the researcher.
- The URL for electronic sources must be as accurate and complete as possible, from access-mode identifier (such as http or ftp) to all relevant directory and file names. If the URL is extremely long, however, use the URL of the website's home page or the URL of the site's search page if you used the site's search function to find the article. The *MLA Style Manual* no longer requires writers to include URLs for materials retrieved online. However, follow whatever guidelines your instructor gives you in this regard.
- MLA style requires you to indicate the medium of publication. For most sources, this will be "Web" or "Print," but you may also cite "CD-ROM" and other media, as appropriate.

C Correction Symbols

Instructors often use these short, easy-to-remember correction symbols and abbreviations when evaluating students' writing. You can use them as well to understand your instructor's suggestions and to revise and proofread your own letters, memos, and reports. Refer to the Handbook of Grammar, Mechanics, and Usage (pp. 571–598) for further information.

Content and Style

Acc	Accuracy. Check to be sure information is correct.
ACE	Avoid copying examples.
ACP	Avoid copying problems.
Adp	Adapt. Tailor message to reader.
App	Follow proper organization approach. (Refer to Chapter 4.)
Assign	Assignment. Review instructions for assignment.
AV	Active verb. Substitute active for passive.
Awk	Awkward phrasing. Rewrite.
BC	Be consistent.
BMS	Be more sincere.
Chop	Choppy sentences. Use longer sentences and more transitional phrases.
Con	Condense. Use fewer words.
CT	Conversational tone. Avoid using overly formal language.
Depers	Depersonalize. Avoid attributing credit or blame to any individual or group.
Dev	Develop. Provide greater detail.
Dir	Direct. Use direct approach; get to the point.
Emph	Emphasize. Develop this point more fully.
EW	Explanation weak. Check logic; provide more proof.
Fl	Flattery. Avoid compliments that are insincere.
FS	Figure of speech. Find a more accurate expression.
GNF	Good news first. Use direct order.
GRF	Give reasons first. Use indirect order.
GW	Goodwill. Put more emphasis on expressions of goodwill.
H/E	Honesty/ethics. Revise statement to reflect good business practices.
Imp	Imply. Avoid being direct.
Inc	Incomplete. Develop further.
Jar	Jargon. Use less specialized language.
Log	Logic. Check development of argument.
Neg	Negative. Use more positive approach or expression.
Obv	Obvious. Do not state point in such detail.
OC	Overconfident. Adopt humbler language.
OM	Omission.
Org	Organization. Strengthen outline.
OS	Off the subject. Close with point on main subject.
Par	Parallel. Use same structure.
Pom	Pompous. Rephrase in down-to-earth terms.
PV	Point of view. Make statement from reader's perspective rather than your own.
RB	Reader benefit. Explain what reader stands to gain.
Red	Redundant. Reduce number of times this point is made.
Ref	Reference. Cite source of information.
Rep	Repetitive. Provide different expression.
RS	Resale. Reassure reader that he or she has made a good choice.
SA	Service attitude. Put more emphasis on helping reader.
Sin	Sincerity. Avoid sounding glib or uncaring.

SL	Stereotyped language. Focus on individual's characteristics instead of on false generalizations.
Spec	Specific. Provide more specific statement.
SPM	Sales promotion material. Tell reader about related goods or services.
Stet	Let stand in original form.
Sub	Subordinate. Make this point less important.
SX	Sexist. Avoid language that contributes to gender stereotypes.
Tone	Tone needs improvement.
Trans	Transition. Show connection between points.

UAE	Use action ending. Close by stating what reader should do next.
UAS	Use appropriate salutation.
UAV	Use active voice.
Unc	Unclear. Rewrite to clarify meaning.
UPV	Use passive voice.
USS	Use shorter sentences.
V	Variety. Use different expression or sentence pattern.
W	Wordy. Eliminate unnecessary words.
WC	Word choice. Find a more appropriate word.
YA	"You" attitude. Rewrite to emphasize reader's needs.

Grammar, Mechanics, and Usage

Ab	Abbreviation. Avoid abbreviations in most cases; use correct abbreviation.
Adj	Adjective. Use adjective instead.
Adv	Adverb. Use adverb instead.
Agr	Agreement. Make subject and verb or noun and pronoun agree.
Ap	Appearance. Improve appearance.
Apos	Apostrophe. Check use of apostrophe.
Art	Article. Use correct article.
BC	Be consistent.
Cap	Capitalize.
Case	Use cases correctly.
CoAdj	Coordinate adjective. Insert comma between coordinate adjectives; delete comma between adjective and compound noun.
CS	Comma splice. Use period or semicolon to separate clauses.
DM	Dangling modifier. Rewrite so that modifier clearly relates to subject of sentence.
Exp	Expletive. Avoid expletive beginnings, such as it is, there are, there is, this is, and these are.
F	Format. Improve layout of document.
Frag	Fragment. Rewrite as complete sentence.
Gram	Grammar. Correct grammatical error.
HCA	Hyphenate compound adjective.
lc	Lowercase. Do not use capital letter.

M	Margins. Improve frame around document.
MM	Misplaced modifier. Place modifier close to word it modifies.
NRC	Nonrestrictive clause (or phrase). Separate from rest of sentence with commas.
P	Punctuation. Use correct punctuation.
Par	Parallel. Use same structure.
PH	Place higher. Move document up on page.
PL	Place lower. Move document down on page.
Prep	Preposition. Use correct preposition.
RC	Restrictive clause (or phrase). Remove commas that separate clause from rest of sentence.
RO	Run-on sentence. Separate two sentences with comma and coordinating conjunction or with semicolon.
SC	Series comma. Add comma before *and*.
SI	Split infinitive. Do not separate *to* from rest of verb.
Sp	Spelling error. Consult dictionary.
S-V	Subject-verb pair. Do not separate with comma.
Syl	Syllabification. Divide word between syllables.
WD	Word division. Check dictionary for proper end-of-line hyphenation.
WW	Wrong word. Replace with another word.

Proofreading Marks

Symbol	Meaning	Symbol Used in Context	Corrected Copy
═══	Align horizontally	meaningful result	meaningful result
‖	Align vertically	1. Power cable 2. Keyboard	1. Power cable 2. Keyboard
bf	Boldface	Recommendations (bf)	**Recommendations**
≡	Capitalize	Pepsico, Inc.	PepsiCo, Inc.
⊐⊏	Center	⊐Awards Banquet⊏	Awards Banquet
⌒	Close up space	self- confidence	self-confidence
ℓ	Delete	harrassment and abuse	harassment
ds	Double-space	text in first line text in second line (ds)	text in first line text in second line
∧	Insert	turquoise shirts	turquoise and white shirts
∨	Insert apostrophe	our teams goals	our team's goals
∧	Insert comma	a, b and c	a, b, and c
⸗	Insert hyphen	third quarter sales	third-quarter sales
⊙	Insert period	Harrigan et al	Harrigan et al.
∨ ∨	Insert quotation marks	This team isn't cooperating.	This "team" isn't cooperating.
#	Insert space	real estate testcase	real estate test case
ital	Italics	Quarterly Report (ital)	*Quarterly Report*
/	Lowercase	TULSA, South of here	Tulsa, south of here
⌊ ⌋	Move down	Sincerely,	Sincerely,
⊏	Move left	Attention: ⊏Security	Attention: Security
⊐	Move right	February 2, 2015	February 2, 2015
⌐¬	Move up	THIRD-QUARTER SALES	THIRD-QUARTER SALES
STET	Restore	staff talked openly and frankly STET	staff talked openly
⸟	Run lines together	Manager, Distribution	Manager, Distribution
ss	Single space	text in first line text in second line	text in first line text in second line
⬭	Spell out	COD	cash on delivery
sp	Spell out	(sp) Assn. of Biochem. Engrs.	Association of Biochemical Engineers
⌐⌐	Start new line	Marla Fenton, Manager, Distribution	Marla Fenton, Manager, Distribution
¶	Start new paragraph	¶The solution is easy to determine but difficult to implement in a competitive environment like the one we now face.	The solution is easy to determine but difficult to implement in a competitive environment like the one we now face.
∿	Transpose	airy, light, casual tone	light, airy, casual tone

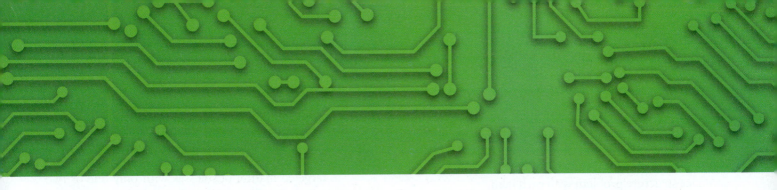

Handbook of Grammar, Mechanics, and Usage

The rules of grammar, mechanics, and usage provide the guidance every professional needs in order to communicate successfully with colleagues, customers, and other audiences. Understanding and following these rules helps you in two important ways. First, the rules determine how meaning is encoded and decoded in the communication process. If you don't encode your messages using the same rules your readers or listeners use to decode them, chances are your audiences will not extract your intended meaning from your messages. Without a firm grasp of the basics of grammar, mechanics, and usage, you risk being misunderstood, damaging your company's image, losing money for your company, and possibly even losing your job. In other words, if you want to get your point across, you need to follow the rules of grammar, mechanics, and usage. Second, apart from transferring meaning successfully, following the rules tells your audience that you respect the conventions and expectations of the business community.

You can think of *grammar* as the agreed-on structure of a language, the way that individual words are formed and the manner in which those words are then combined to form meaningful sentences. *Mechanics* are style and formatting issues such as capitalization, spelling, and the use of numbers and symbols. *Usage* involves the accepted and expected way in which specific words are used by a particular community of people—in this case, the community of businesspeople who use English. This handbook can help you improve your knowledge and awareness in all three areas. It is divided into the following sections:

- **Diagnostic Test of English Skills.** Testing your current knowledge of grammar, mechanics, and usage helps you find out where your strengths and weaknesses lie. This test offers 50 items taken from the topics included in this handbook.
- **Assessment of English Skills.** After completing the diagnostic test, use the assessment form to highlight the areas you most need to review.
- **Essentials of Grammar, Mechanics, and Usage.** This section helps you quickly review the basics. You can study the things you've probably already learned but may have forgotten about grammar, punctuation, mechanics (including capitalization, abbreviation, number style, and word division), and vocabulary (including frequently confused words, frequently misused words, frequently misspelled words, and transitional words and phrases). Use this essential review not only to study and improve your English skills but also as a reference for any questions you may have during this course.

Diagnostic Test of English Skills

Use this test to determine whether you need more practice with grammar, punctuation, mechanics, or vocabulary. When you've answered all the questions, ask your instructor for an answer sheet so that you can score the test. On the Assessment of English Skills form (page 573), record the number of questions you answered incorrectly in each section.

The following choices apply to items 1–5. Write in each blank the letter of the choice that best describes the part of speech that is underlined.

A. noun
B. pronoun
C. verb
D. adjective
E. adverb
F. preposition
G. conjunction
H. article

_____ 1. The new branch location will be decided <u>by</u> next week.
_____ 2. We must hire only <u>qualified</u>, ambitious graduates.
_____ 3. After their <u>presentation</u>, I was still undecided.
_____ 4. See <u>me</u> after the meeting.
_____ 5. Margaret, pressed for time, turned in <u>unusually</u> sloppy work.

In the blanks for items 6–15, write the letter of the word or phrase that best completes each sentence.

_____ 6. (A. Russ's, B. Russ') laptop was stolen last week.
_____ 7. Speaking only for (A. me, B. myself), I think the new policy is discriminatory.
_____ 8. Of the five candidates we interviewed yesterday, (A. who, B. whom) do you believe is the best choice?
_____ 9. India has increased (A. it's, B. its) imports of corn and rice.
_____10. Anyone who wants to be (A. their, B. his or her) own boss should think about owning a franchise.
_____11. If the IT department can't (A. lie, B. lay) the fiber-optic cable by March 1, the plant will not open on schedule.
_____12. Starbucks (A. is, B. are) opening five new stores in San Diego in the next year.
_____13. The number of women-owned small businesses (A. has, B. have) increased sharply in the past two decades.

571

_____ **14.** Greg and Bernyce worked (A. good, B. well) together.

_____ **15.** They distributed the supplies (A. among, B. between) the six staff members.

The following choices apply to items 16–20. Write in each blank the letter of the choice that best describes the sentence structure problem with each item.

A. sentence fragment
B. comma splice
C. misplaced modifier
D. fused sentence
E. lack of parallelism
F. unclear antecedent

_____ **16.** The number of employees who took the buyout offer was much higher than expected, now the entire company is understaffed.

_____ **17.** The leader in Internet-only banking.

_____ **18.** Diamond doesn't actually sell financial products rather it acts as an intermediary.

_____ **19.** Helen's proposal is for not only the present but also for the future.

_____ **20.** When purchasing luxury products, quality is more important than price for consumers.

For items 21–30, circle the letter of the preferred choice in each of the following groups of sentences.

21. A. What do you think of the ad slogan "Have it your way?"
B. What do you think of the ad slogan "Have it your way"?

22. A. Send copies to Jackie Cross, Uniline, Brad Nardi, Peale & Associates, and Tom Griesbaum, MatchMakers.
B. Send copies to Jackie Cross, Uniline; Brad Nardi, Peale & Associates; and Tom Griesbaum, MatchMakers.

23. A. They've recorded 22 complaints since yesterday, all of them from long-time employees.
B. They've recorded 22 complaints since yesterday; all of them from long-time employees.

24. A. We are looking for two qualities in applicants: experience with computers and an interest in people.
B. We are looking for two qualities in applicants; experience with computers and an interest in people.

25. A. At the Center for the Blind the clients we serve have lost vision, due to a wide variety of causes.
B. At the Center for the Blind, the clients we serve have lost vision due to a wide variety of causes.

26. A. Replace your standard light bulbs with new, compact fluorescent bulbs.
B. Replace your standard light bulbs with new, compact, fluorescent bulbs.
C. Replace your standard light bulbs with new compact fluorescent bulbs.

27. A. Blue Cross of California may have changed its name to Anthem Blue Cross but the company still has the same commitment to California.
B. Blue Cross of California may have changed its name to Anthem Blue Cross, but the company still has the same commitment to California.

28. A. Only eight banks in this country—maybe nine can handle transactions of this magnitude.
B. Only eight banks in this country—maybe nine—can handle transactions of this magnitude.

29. A. Instead of focusing on high-growth companies, we targeted mature businesses with only one or two people handling the decision making.
B. Instead of focusing on high growth companies, we targeted mature businesses with only one or two people handling the decision-making.

30. A. According to board president Damian Cabaza "having a crisis communication plan is a high priority."
B. According to board president Damian Cabaza, "Having a crisis communication plan is a high priority."

For items 31–40, select the best choice from among those provided.

31. A. At her previous employer, Mary-Anne worked in Marketing Communications and Human Resources.
B. At her previous employer, Mary-Anne worked in marketing communications and human resources.

32. A. By fall, we'll have a dozen locations between the Mississippi and Missouri rivers.
B. By Fall, we'll have a dozen locations between the Mississippi and Missouri Rivers.

33. A. The Board applauded President Donlan upon her reelection for a fifth term.
B. The board applauded president Donlan upon her reelection for a fifth term.
C. The board applauded President Donlan upon her reelection for a fifth term.

34. A. If you want to travel to France, you need to be au courant with the business practices.
B. If you want to travel to France, you need to be "au courant" with the business practices.

35. A. As the company's CEO, Thomas Spurgeon handles all dealings with the FDA.
B. As the company's C.E.O., Thomas Spurgeon handles all dealings with the F.D.A.

36. A. The maximum speed limit in most states is 65 mph.
B. The maximum speed limit in most states is 65 m.p.h.

37. A. Sales of graphic novels increased nine percent between 2008 and 2009.
B. Sales of graphic novels increased 9 percent between 2008 and 2009.

38. A. Our store is open daily from nine a.m. to seven p.m.
B. Our store is open daily from 9:00 a.m. to 7:00 p.m.

39. A. The organizing meeting is scheduled for July 27, and the event will be held in January 2017.
B. The organizing meeting is scheduled for July 27th, and the event will be held in January, 2017.

40. A. We need six desks, eight file cabinets, and 12 trashcans.
B. We need 6 desks, 8 file cabinets, and 12 trashcans.

For items 41–50, write in each blank the letter of the word that best completes each sentence.

_____ **41.** Will having a degree (A. affect, B. effect) my chances for promotion?

_____ **42.** Try not to (A. loose, B. lose) this key; we will charge you a fee to replace it.

_____ **43.** I don't want to discuss my (A. personal, B. personnel) problems in front of anyone.

_____ **44.** Let us help you choose the right tie to (A. complement, B. compliment) your look.

_____ **45.** The repairman's whistling (A. aggravated, B. irritated) all of us in accounting.

_____ **46.** The bank agreed to (A. loan, B. lend) the Smiths $20,000 for their start-up.

_____ **47.** The credit card company is (A. liable, B. likely) to increase your interest rate if you miss a payment.

_____ **48.** The airline tries to (A. accommodate, B. accomodate) disabled passengers.

_____ **49.** Every company needs a policy regarding sexual (A. harrassment, B. harassment).

_____ **50.** Use your best (A. judgment, B. judgement) in selecting a service provider.

Assessment of English Skills

In the space provided, record the number of questions you answered incorrectly.

Questions	Skills Area	Number of Incorrect Answers
1–5	Parts of speech	_____
6–15	Usage	_____
16–20	Sentence structure	_____
21–30	Punctuation	_____
31–40	Mechanics	_____
41–50	Vocabulary	_____

If you had more than two incorrect answers in any of the skills areas, focus on those areas in the appropriate sections of this handbook.

Essentials of Grammar, Mechanics, and Usage

The following sentence looks innocent, but is it really?

> We sell tuxedos as well as rent.

You sell tuxedos, but it's highly unlikely that you sell rent—which is what this sentence says. Whatever you're selling, some people will ignore your message because of a blunder like this. The following sentence has a similar problem:

> Vice President Eldon Neale told his chief engineer that he would no longer be with Avix, Inc., as of June 30.

Is Eldon or the engineer leaving? No matter which side the facts are on, the sentence can be read the other way. Now look at this sentence:

> The year before we budgeted more for advertising sales were up.

Confused? Perhaps this is what the writer meant:

> The year before, we budgeted more for advertising. Sales were up.

Or maybe the writer meant this:

> The year before we budgeted more for advertising, sales were up.

These examples show that even short, simple sentences can be misunderstood because of errors on the part of the writer. As you've learned in numerous courses over your schooling, an English sentence consists of the parts of speech being combined with punctuation, mechanics, and vocabulary to convey meaning. Making a point of brushing up on your grammar, punctuation, mechanics, and vocabulary skills will help ensure that you create clear, effective business messages.

1.0 Grammar

Grammar is the study of how words come together to form sentences. Categorized by meaning, form, and function, English words fall into various parts of speech: nouns, pronouns, verbs, adjectives, adverbs, prepositions, conjunctions, articles, and interjections. You will communicate more clearly if you understand how each of these parts of speech operates in a sentence.

1.1 NOUNS

A **noun** names a person, a place, a thing, or an idea. Anything you can see or detect with one of your senses has a noun to name it. Some things you can't see or sense are also nouns—ions, for example, or space. So are things that exist as ideas, such as accuracy and height. (You can see that something is accurate or that a building is tall, but you can't see the idea of accuracy or the idea of height.) These names for ideas are known as **abstract nouns**. The simplest nouns are the names of things you can see or touch: *car, building, cloud, brick*; these are termed **concrete nouns**. A few nouns, such as *algorithm, software*, and *code*, are difficult to categorize as either abstract or concrete but can reasonably be considered concrete even though they don't have a physical presence.

1.1.1 Proper Nouns and Common Nouns

So far, all the examples of nouns have been **common nouns**, referring to general classes of things. The word *building* refers to a whole class of structures. Common nouns such as *building* are not capitalized.

If you want to talk about one particular building, however, you might refer to the Glazier Building. The name is capitalized, indicating that *Glazier Building* is a **proper noun**.

Here are three sets of common and proper nouns for comparison:

Common	Proper
city	Kansas City
company	Blaisden Company
store	Books Galore

1.1.2 Nouns as Subject and Object

Nouns may be used in sentences as subjects or objects. That is, the person, place, thing, or idea that is being or doing (subject) is represented by a noun. So is the person, place, idea, or thing that is being acted on (object). In the following sentence, the nouns are underlined:

The web designer created the homepage.

The web designer (subject) is acting in a way that affects the home page (object). The following sentence is more complicated:

The installer delivered the carpet to the customer.

Installer is the subject. *Carpet* is the object of the main part of the sentence (acted on by the installer), and *customer* is the object of the phrase *to the customer*. Nevertheless, both *carpet* and *customer* are objects.

1.1.3 Plural Nouns

Nouns can be either singular or plural. The usual way to make a plural noun is to add *s* or *es* to the singular form of the word:

Singular	Plural
file	files
tax	taxes
cargo	cargoes

Many nouns have other ways of forming the plural. Some plurals involve a change in a vowel (*mouse/mice, goose/geese, woman/women*), the addition of *en* or *ren* (*ox/oxen, child/children*), the change from *y* to *ies* (*city/cities, specialty/specialties*), or the change from *f* to *v* (*knife/knives, half/halves*; some exceptions: *fifes, roofs*). Some words of Latin origin offer a choice of plurals (*phenomena/phenomenons, indexes/indices, appendixes/appendices*). It's always a good idea to consult a dictionary if you are unsure of the correct or preferred plural spelling of a word.

The plurals of compound nouns are usually formed by adding *s* or *es* to the main word of the compound (*fathers-in-law, editors-in-chief, attorneys-at-law*).

Some nouns are the same whether singular or plural (*sleep, deer, moose*). Some nouns are plural in form but singular in use (*ethics, measles*). Some nouns are used in the plural only (*scissors, trousers*).

Letters, numbers, and words used as words are sometimes made plural by adding an apostrophe and an *s* (*A's, Ph.D.'s, I's*). However, if no confusion would be created by leaving off the apostrophe, it is common practice to just add the *s* (*1990s, RFPs, DVDs*).

1.1.4 Possessive Nouns

A noun becomes possessive when it's used to show the ownership of something. Then you add *'s* to the word:

the man's car	the woman's apartment

However, ownership does not need to be legal:

the secretary's desk	the company's assets

Also, ownership may be nothing more than an automatic association:

a day's work	the job's prestige

An exception to the rule about adding *'s* to make a noun possessive occurs when the word is singular and already has two "s" sounds at the end. In cases like the following, an apostrophe is all that's needed:

crisis' dimensions	Mr. Moses' application

When the noun has only one "s" sound at the end, however, retain the *'s*:

Chris's book	Carolyn Nuss's office

With compound (hyphenated) nouns, add *'s* to the last word:

Compound Noun	Possessive Noun
mother-in-law	mother-in-law's
mayor-elect	mayor-elect's

To form the possessive of plural nouns, just begin by following the same rule as with singular nouns: add *'s*. However, if the plural noun already ends in an *s* (as most do), drop the one you've added, leaving only the apostrophe:

the clients' complaints	employees' benefits

To denote joint possession by two or more proper nouns, add the *'s* to the last name only (*Moody, Nation, and Smith's* ad agency). To denote individual possession by two or more persons, add an *'s* to each proper noun (*Moody's, Nation's,* and *Smith's* ad agencies).

1.1.5 Collective Nouns

Collective nouns encompass a group of people or objects: *crowd, jury, committee, team, audience, family, couple, herd, class.* They are often treated as singular nouns. (For more on collective nouns, see Section 1.3.4, Subject-Verb Agreement.)

1.2 PRONOUNS

A **pronoun** is a word that stands for a noun; it saves repeating the noun:

> Employees have some choice of weeks for vacation, but *they* must notify the HR office of *their* preference by March 1.

The pronouns *they* and *their* stand in for the noun *employees.* The noun that a pronoun stands for is called the **antecedent** of the pronoun; *employees* is the antecedent of *they* and *their.*

When the antecedent is plural, the pronoun that stands in for it has to be plural; *they* and *their* are plural pronouns because *employees* is plural. Likewise, when the antecedent is singular, the pronoun has to be singular:

> We thought the contract had expired, but we soon learned that *it* had not.

1.2.1 Multiple Antecedents

Sometimes a pronoun has a double (or even a triple) antecedent:

> Kathryn Boettcher and Luis Gutierrez went beyond *their* sales quotas for January.

If taken alone, *Kathryn Boettcher* is a singular antecedent. So is *Luis Gutierrez.* However, when together they are the plural antecedent of a pronoun, so the pronoun has to be plural. Thus the pronoun is *their* instead of *her* or *his.*

1.2.2 Unclear Antecedents

In some sentences the pronoun's antecedent is unclear:

> Sandy Wright sent Jane Brougham *her* production figures for the previous year. *She* thought they were too low.

To which person does the pronoun *her* refer? Someone who knew Sandy and Jane and knew their business relationship might be able to figure out the antecedent for *her.* Even with such an advantage, however, a reader might receive the wrong meaning. Also, it would be nearly impossible for any reader to know which name is the antecedent of *she.*

The best way to clarify an ambiguous pronoun is usually to rewrite the sentence, repeating nouns when needed for clarity:

> Sandy Wright sent her production figures for the previous year to Jane Brougham. Jane thought they were too low.

The noun needs to be repeated only when the antecedent is unclear.

1.2.3 Pronoun Classes

Personal pronouns consist of *I, you, we/us, he/him, she/her, it,* and *they/them.*

Compound personal pronouns are created by adding *self* or *selves* to simple personal pronouns: *myself, ourselves, yourself, yourselves, himself, herself, itself, themselves.* Compound personal pronouns are used either *intensively,* to emphasize the identity of the noun or pronoun (I *myself* have seen the demonstration), or *reflexively,* to indicate that the subject is the receiver of his or her own action (I promised *myself* I'd finish by noon). Compound personal pronouns are used incorrectly if they appear in a sentence without their antecedent:

> Walter, Virginia, and *I* (not *myself*) are the top salespeople. You need to tell *her* (not *herself*) about the mixup.

Relative pronouns refer to nouns (or groups of words used as nouns) in the main clause and are used to introduce clauses:

> Purina is the brand *that* most dog owners purchase.

The relative pronouns are *which, who, whom, whose,* and *what.* Other words used as relative pronouns include *that, whoever, whomever, whatever,* and *whichever.*

Interrogative pronouns are those used for asking questions: *who, whom, whose, which,* and *what.*

Demonstrative pronouns point out particular persons, places, or things:

> *That* is my desk.   *This* can't be correct.

The demonstrative pronouns are *this, these, that,* and *those.*

Indefinite pronouns refer to persons or things not specifically identified. They include *anyone, someone, everyone, everybody, somebody, either, neither, one, none, all, both, each, another, any, many,* and similar words.

1.2.4 Case of Pronouns

The case of a pronoun tells whether it's acting or acted upon:

> *She* sells an average of five packages each week.

In this sentence, *she* is doing the selling. Because *she* is acting, *she* is said to be in the **nominative case.** Now consider what happens when the pronoun is acted upon:

> After six months, Ms. Browning promoted *her.*

In this sentence, the pronoun *her* is acted upon and is thus said to be in the **objective case.**

Contrast the nominative and objective pronouns in this list:

Nominative	Objective
I	me
we	us
he	him
she	her
they	them
who	whom
whoever	whomever

Objective pronouns may be used as either the object of a verb (such as *promoted*) or the object of a preposition (such as *with*):

Rob worked with *them* until the order was filled.

In this example, *them* is the object of the preposition *with* because Rob acted upon—worked with—them. Here's a sentence with three pronouns, the first one nominative, the second the object of a verb, and the third the object of a preposition:

He paid *us* as soon as the check came from *them*.

He is nominative; *us* is objective because it's the object of the verb *paid*; *them* is objective because it's the object of the preposition *from*.

Every writer sometimes wonders whether to use *who* or *whom*:

(*Who, Whom*) will you hire?

Because this sentence is a question, it's difficult to see that *whom* is the object of the verb *hire*. You can figure out which pronoun to use if you rearrange the question and temporarily try *she* and *her* in place of *who* and *whom*: "Will you hire *she*?" or "Will you hire *her*?" *Her* and *whom* are both objective, so the correct choice is "Whom will you hire?" Here's a different example:

(*Who, Whom*) logged so much travel time?

Turning the question into a statement, you get:

He logged so much travel time.

Therefore, the correct statement is:

Who logged so much travel time?

1.2.5 Possessive Pronouns

Possessive pronouns work like possessive nouns—they show ownership or automatic association:

her job	their preferences
his account	its equipment

However, possessive pronouns are different from possessive nouns in the way they are written. Possessive pronouns never have an apostrophe:

Possessive Noun	Possessive Pronoun
the woman's estate	her estate
Roger Franklin's plans	his plans
the shareholders' feelings	their feelings
the vacuum cleaner's attachments	its attachments

The word *its* is the possessive of *it*. Like all other possessive pronouns, *its* has no apostrophe. Some people confuse *its* with *it's*, the contraction of *it is*. (Contractions are discussed in Section 2.9, Apostrophes.)

1.2.6 Pronoun-Antecedent Agreement

Like nouns, pronouns can be singular or plural. Pronouns must agree in number with their antecedents—a singular antecedent requires a singular pronoun:

The president of the board tendered *his* resignation.

Multiple antecedents require a plural pronoun:

The members of the board tendered *their* resignations.

A pronoun referring to singular antecedents connected by *or* or *nor* should be singular:

Neither Sean nor Terry made *his* quota.

But a pronoun referring to a plural and a singular antecedent connected by *or* or *nor* should be plural:

Neither Sean nor the twins made *their* quotas.

Formal English prefers the nominative case after the linking verb *to be*:

It is *I*.   That is *he*.

However, for general usage it's perfectly acceptable to use the more natural "It's me" and "That's him."

1.3 VERBS

A **verb** describes an action or acts as a link between a subject and words that define or describe that subject:

They all *quit* in disgust.
Working conditions *were* substandard.

The English language is full of **action verbs**. Here are a few you'll often run across in the business world:

verify	perform	fulfill
hire	succeed	send
leave	improve	receive
accept	develop	pay

You could undoubtedly list many more.

The most common **linking verbs** are all the forms of *to be*: I *am, was,* or *will be*; you *are, were,* or *will be*. Other words that can serve as linking verbs include *seem, become, appear, prove, look, remain, feel, taste, smell, sound, resemble, turn,* and *grow*:

> It *seemed* a good plan at the time.
> She *sounds* impressive at a meeting.
> The time *grows* near for us to make a decision.

These verbs link what comes before them in the sentence with what comes after; no action is involved. (See Section 1.7.5 for a fuller discussion of linking verbs.)

An **auxiliary verb** is one that helps another verb and is used for showing tense, voice, and so on. A verb with its helpers is called a **verb phrase**. Verbs used as auxiliaries include *do, did, have, may, can, must, shall, might, could, would,* and *should*.

1.3.1 Verb Tenses

English has three simple verb tenses: present, past, and future.

Present:	Our branches in Hawaii *stock* other items.
Past:	We *stocked* Purquil pens for a short time.
Future:	Rotex Tire Stores *will stock* your line of tires when you begin a program of effective national advertising.

With most verbs (the regular ones), the past tense ends in *ed*, and the future tense always has *will* or *shall* in front of it. But the present tense is more complex, depending on the subject:

	First Person	Second Person	Third Person
Singular	I stock	you stock	he/she/it stocks
Plural	we stock	you stock	they stock

The basic form, *stock*, takes an additional *s* when *he, she,* or *it* precedes it. (See Section 1.3.4 for more on subject–verb agreement.)

In addition to the three simple tenses, the three **perfect tenses** are created by adding forms of the auxiliary verb *have*. The present perfect tense uses the past participle

(regularly the past tense) of the main verb, *stocked,* and adds the present-tense *have* or *has* to the front of it:

> (I, we, you, they) *have stocked*.
> (He, she, it) *has stocked*.

The past perfect tense uses the past participle of the main verb, *stocked,* and adds the past-tense *had* to the front of it:

> (I, you, he, she, it, we, they) *had stocked*.

The future perfect tense also uses the past participle of the main verb, *stocked,* but adds the future-tense *will have*:

> (I, you, he, she, it, we, they) *will have stocked*.

Verbs should be kept in the same tense when the actions occur at the same time:

> When the payroll checks *came in,* everyone *showed up* for work.
> We *have found* that everyone *has pitched* in to help.

When the actions occur at different times, you may change tense accordingly:

> The shipment *came* last Wednesday, so if another one *comes* in today, please return it.
> The new employee *had been* ill at ease, but now she *has become* a full-fledged member of the team.

1.3.2 Irregular Verbs

Many verbs don't follow some of the standard patterns for verb tenses. The most irregular of these verbs is *to be*:

Tense	Singular	Plural
Present:	I *am*	we *are*
	you *are*	you *are*
	he, she, it *is*	they *are*
Past:	I *was*	we *were*
	you *were*	you *were*
	he, she, it *was*	they *were*

The future tense of *to be* is formed in the same way that the future tense of a regular verb is formed.

The perfect tenses of *to be* are also formed as they would be for a regular verb, except that the past participle is a special form, *been,* instead of just the past tense:

Present perfect:	you have been
Past perfect:	you had been
Future perfect:	you will have been

Here's a sampling of other irregular verbs:

Present	Past	Past Participle
begin	began	begun
shrink	shrank	shrunk
know	knew	known
rise	rose	risen
become	became	become
go	went	gone
do	did	done

Dictionaries list the various forms of other irregular verbs.

1.3.3 Transitive and Intransitive Verbs

Many people are confused by three particular sets of verbs:

lie/lay	sit/set	rise/raise

Using these verbs correctly is much easier when you learn the difference between transitive and intransitive verbs.

Transitive verbs require a receiver; they "transfer" their action to an object. **Intransitive verbs** do not have a receiver for their action. Some intransitive verbs are complete in themselves and need no help from other words (prices *dropped*; we *won*). Other intransitive words must be "completed" by a noun or adjective called a **complement**. Complements occur with linking verbs.

Here are some sample uses of transitive and intransitive verbs:

Intransitive	Transitive
We should include in our new offices a place to *lie* down for a nap.	The workers will be here on Monday to *lay* new carpeting.
Even the way an interviewee *sits* is important.	That crate is full of stemware, so *set* it down carefully.
Salaries at Compu-Link, Inc., *rise* swiftly.	They *raise* their level of production every year.

The workers *lay* carpeting, you *set down* the crate, they *raise* production; each action is transferred to something. In the intransitive sentences, a person *lies* down, an interviewee *sits*, and salaries *rise* without affecting anything else. Intransitive sentences are complete with only a subject and a verb; transitive sentences are not complete unless they also include an object; or something to transfer the action to.

Tenses are a confusing element of the *lie/lay* problem:

Present	Past	Past Participle
I *lie*	I *lay*	I *have lain*
I *lay* (something down)	I *laid* (something down)	I *have laid* (something down)

The past tense of *lie* and the present tense of *lay* look and sound alike, even though they're different verbs.

1.3.4 Subject-Verb Agreement

Whether regular or irregular, every verb must agree with its subject, both in person (first, second, or third) and in number (single or plural).

	First Person	Second Person	Third Person
Singular	I *am*	you *are*	he/she/it *is*
	I *write*	you *write*	he/she/it *writes*
Plural	we *are*	you *are*	they *are*
	we *write*	you *write*	they *write*

In a simple sentence, making a verb agree with its subject is a straightforward task:

> Hector Ruiz *is* a strong competitor. (third-person singular)
> We *write* to you every month. (first-person plural)

Confusion sometimes arises when sentences are a bit more complicated. For example, be sure to avoid agreement problems when words come between the subject and verb. In the following examples, the verb appears in italics, and its subject is underlined:

> The <u>analysis</u> of existing documents *takes* a full week.

Even though *documents* is a plural, the verb is in the singular form. That's because the subject of the sentence is *analysis*, a singular noun. The phrase *of existing documents* can be disregarded. Here is another example:

> The <u>answers</u> for this exercise *are* in the study guide.

Take away the phrase *for this exercise* and you are left with the plural subject *answers*. Therefore, the verb takes the plural form.

Verb agreement is also complicated when the subject is a collective noun or pronoun or when the subject may be considered either singular or plural. In such cases, you often have to analyze the surrounding sentence to determine which verb form to use:

> The <u>staff</u> *is* quartered in the warehouse.
> The <u>staff</u> *are* at their desks in the warehouse.
> The <u>computers</u> and the staff *are* in the warehouse.
> Neither the staff nor the <u>computers</u> *are* in the warehouse.
> <u>Every</u> computer *is* in the warehouse.
> Many a <u>computer</u> *is* in the warehouse.

Did you notice that words such as *every* use the singular verb form? In addition, when an *either/or* or a *neither/nor* phrase combines singular and plural nouns, the verb takes the form that matches the noun closest to it.

In the business world, some subjects require extra attention. Company names, for example, are considered singular and therefore take a singular verb in most cases—even if they contain plural words:

> Stater Brothers *offers* convenient grocery shopping.

In addition, quantities are sometimes considered singular and sometimes plural. If a quantity refers to a total amount, it takes a singular verb; if a quantity refers to individual, countable units, it takes a plural verb:

> Three hours *is* a long time.
> The eight dollars we collected for the fund *are* tacked on the bulletin board.

Fractions may also be singular or plural, depending on the noun that accompanies them:

> One-third of the warehouse *is* devoted to this product line.
> One-third of the products *are* defective.

To decide whether to use a singular or plural verb with subjects such as *number* and *variety*, follow this simple rule: If the subject is preceded by *a*, use a plural verb:

> *A* number of products *are* being displayed at the trade show.

If the subject is preceded by *the*, use a singular verb:

> *The* variety of products on display *is* mind-boggling.

For a related discussion, see Section 1.7.1, Longer Sentences.

1.3.5 Voice of Verbs

Verbs have two voices, active and passive. When the subject comes first, the verb is in **active voice**; when the object comes first, the verb is in **passive voice**:

> **Active:**   The buyer *paid* a large amount.
> **Passive:** A large amount *was paid* by the buyer.

The passive voice uses a form of the verb *to be*, which adds words to a sentence. In the example, the passive-voice sentence uses eight words, whereas the active-voice sentence uses only six to say the same thing. The words *was* and *by* are unnecessary to convey the meaning of the sentence. In fact, extra words usually clog meaning. So be sure to opt for the active voice when you have a choice.

At times, however, you have no choice:

> Several items *have been taken*, but so far we don't know who took them.

The passive voice becomes necessary when you don't know (or don't want to say) who performed the action; the active voice is bolder and more direct.

1.3.6 Mood of Verbs

Verbs can express one of three moods: indicative, imperative, or subjunctive. The **indicative mood** is used to make a statement or to ask a question:

> The secretary mailed a letter to each supplier.
> Did the secretary mail a letter to each supplier?

Use the **imperative mood** when you wish to command or request:

> Please mail a letter to each supplier.

With the imperative mood, the subject is the understood *you*.

The **subjunctive mood** is used to express doubt or a wish or a condition contrary to fact:

> If I *were* you, I wouldn't send that email.

The subjunctive is also used to express a suggestion or a request:

> I asked that Rosario *be* [not *is*] present at the meeting.

1.3.7 Verbals

Verbals are verbs that are modified to function as other parts of speech. They include infinitives, gerunds, and participles.

Infinitives are formed by placing a *to* in front of the verb (*to go*, *to purchase*, *to work*). They function as nouns. Although many of us were taught that it is "incorrect" to split an infinitive—that is, to place an adverb between the *to* and the verb—that rule is not a hard and fast one. In some cases, the adverb is best placed in the middle of the infinitive to avoid awkward constructions or ambiguous meaning:

> Production of steel is expected to *moderately exceed* domestic use.

Gerunds are verbals formed by adding *ing* to a verb (*going*, *having*, *working*). Like infinitives, they function as nouns. Gerunds and gerund phrases take a singular verb:

> *Borrowing* from banks *is* preferable to getting venture capital.

Participles are verb forms used as adjectives. The present participle ends in *ing* and generally describes action going on at the same time as other action:

> *Checking* the schedule, the contractor was pleased with progress on the project.

The **past participle** is usually the same form as the past tense and generally indicates completed action:

> When *completed*, the project will occupy six city blocks.

The **perfect participle** is formed by adding *having* to the past participle:

> *Having completed* the project, the contractor submitted his last invoice.

1.4 ADJECTIVES

An **adjective** modifies (tells something about) a noun or pronoun. Each of the following phrases says more about the noun or pronoun than the noun or pronoun would say alone:

> an *efficient* staff   a *heavy* price
>
> *brisk* trade   *light* web traffic

Adjectives modify nouns more often than they modify pronouns. When adjectives do modify pronouns, however, the sentence usually has a linking verb:

> They were *attentive*.   It looked *appropriate*.
>
> He seems *interested*.   You are *skillful*.

1.4.1 Types of Adjectives

Adjectives serve a variety of purposes. **Descriptive adjectives** express some quality belonging to the modified item (*tall, successful, green*). **Limiting** or **definitive adjectives**, on the other hand, point out the modified item or limit its meaning without expressing a quality. Types include:

- Numeral adjectives (*one, fifty, second*)
- Articles (*a, an, the*)
- Pronominal adjectives: pronouns used as adjectives (*his desk, each* employee)
- Demonstrative adjectives: *this, these, that, those* (*these* tires, *that* invoice)

Proper adjectives are derived from proper nouns:

> *Chinese* customs   *Orwellian* overtones

Predicate adjectives complete the meaning of the predicate and are introduced by linking verbs:

> The location is *perfect*.   Prices are *high*.

1.4.2 Comparative Degree

Most adjectives can take three forms: simple, comparative, and superlative. The simple form modifies a single noun or pronoun. Use the comparative form when comparing two items. When comparing three or more items, use the superlative form:

Simple	Comparative	Superlative
hard	harder	hardest
safe	safer	safest
dry	drier	driest

The comparative form adds *er* to the simple form, and the superlative form adds *est*. (The *y* at the end of a word changes to *i* before the *er* or *est* is added.)

A small number of adjectives are irregular, including these:

Simple	Comparative	Superlative
good	better	best
bad	worse	worst
little	less	least

When the simple form of an adjective has two or more syllables, you usually add *more* to form the comparative and *most* to form the superlative:

Simple	Comparative	Superlative
useful	more useful	most useful
exhausting	more exhausting	most exhausting
expensive	more expensive	most expensive

The most common exceptions are two-syllable adjectives that end in *y*:

Simple	Comparative	Superlative
happy	happier	happiest
costly	costlier	costliest

If you choose this option, change the *y* to *i* and tack *er* or *est* onto the end.

Some adjectives cannot be used to make comparisons because they themselves indicate the extreme. For example, if something is perfect, nothing can be more perfect. If something is unique or ultimate, nothing can be more unique or more ultimate.

1.4.3 Hyphenated Adjectives

Many adjectives used in the business world are actually combinations of words: *up-to-date* report, *last-minute* effort, *fifth-floor* suite, *well-built* engine. As you can see, they are hyphenated when they come before the noun they modify. However, when such word combinations come after the noun they modify, they are not hyphenated. In the following example, the adjectives appear in italics and the nouns they modify are underlined:

> The <u>report</u> is *up to date* <u>because</u> of our team's *last-minute* <u>efforts</u>.

Hyphens are not used when part of the combination is a word ending in *ly* (because that word is usually not an adjective). Hyphens are also omitted from word combinations that are used so frequently that readers are used to seeing the words together:

> We live in a *rapidly shrinking* world.
> Our *highly motivated* employees will be well paid.
> Please consider renewing your *credit card* account.
> Send those figures to our *data processing* department.
> Our new intern is a *high school* student.

1.5 ADVERBS

An **adverb** modifies a verb, an adjective, or another adverb:

Modifying a verb:	Our marketing department works *efficiently*.
Modifying an adjective:	She was not dependable, although she was *highly* intelligent.
Modifying another adverb:	When signing new clients, he moved *extremely* cautiously.

An adverb can be a single word (*clearly*), a phrase (*very clearly*), or a clause (*because it was clear*).

1.5.1 Types of Adverbs

Simple adverbs are simple modifiers:

> The door opened *automatically*.
> The order arrived *yesterday*.
> Top companies were *there*.

Interrogative adverbs ask a question:

> *Where* have you been?

Conjunctive adverbs connect clauses:

> The boardroom isn't available for the meeting; *however*, the conference room should be clear.
> We met all our sales goals for April; *therefore*, all sales reps will get a bonus.

Words frequently used as conjunctive adverbs include *however, nevertheless, therefore, similarly, thus,* and *meanwhile*.

Negative adverbs include *not, never, seldom, rarely, scarcely, hardly,* and similar words. Negative adverbs are powerful words and therefore do not need any help in conveying a negative thought. Avoid using double negatives like these:

> I don't want no mistakes.
> (Correct: "I don't want any mistakes," or "I want no mistakes.")
> They couldn't hardly read the report.
> (Correct: "They could hardly read the report," or "They couldn't read the report.")
> They scarcely noticed neither one.
> (Correct: "They scarcely noticed either one," or "They noticed neither one.")

1.5.2 Adverb-Adjective Confusion

Many adverbs are adjectives turned into adverbs by adding *ly: highly, extremely, officially, closely, really.* In addition, many words can be adjectives or adverbs, depending on their usage in a particular sentence:

The *early* bird gets the worm. [adjective]	We arrived *early*. [adverb]
It was a *hard* decision. [adjective]	He hit the wall *hard*. [adverb]

Because of this situation, some adverbs are difficult to distinguish from adjectives. For example, in the following sentences, is the underlined word an adverb or an adjective?

> They worked <u>well</u>.
> The baby is <u>well</u>.

In the first sentence, *well* is an adverb modifying the verb *worked*. In the second sentence, *well* is an adjective modifying the noun *baby*. You may find it helpful to remember that a *linking verb* (such as *is* in "The baby is well") connects an adjective to the noun it modifies. In contrast, an *action verb* is modified by an adverb:

Adjective	**Adverb**
He is a *good* worker. (What kind of worker is he?)	He works *well*. (How does he work?)
It is a *real* computer. (What kind of computer is it?)	It *really* is a computer. (To what extent is it a computer?)
The traffic is *slow*. (What quality does the have?)	The traffic moves *slowly*. (How does the traffic move?)
This food tastes *bad* without salt. (What quality does the food have?)	This food *badly* needs salt. (How much is it needed?)

1.5.3 Comparative Degree

Like adjectives, adverbs can be used to compare items. Generally, the basic adverb is combined with *more* or *most,* just as long adjectives are. However, some adverbs have one-word comparative forms:

One Item	Two Items	Three Items
quickly	more quickly	most quickly
sincerely	less sincerely	least sincerely
fast	faster	fastest
well	better	best

1.6 OTHER PARTS OF SPEECH

Nouns, pronouns, verbs, adjectives, and adverbs carry most of the meaning in a sentence. Four other parts of speech link them together in sentences: prepositions, conjunctions, articles, and interjections.

1.6.1 Prepositions

A **preposition** is a word or group of words that describes a relationship between other words in a sentence. A simple preposition is made up of one word: *of, in, by, above, below*. A *compound preposition* is made up of two prepositions: *out of, from among, except for, because of*.

A **prepositional phrase** is a group of words introduced by a preposition that functions as an adjective (an adjectival phrase) or as an adverb (adverbial phrase) by telling more about a pronoun, noun, or verb:

> The shipment will be here *by next Friday*.
> Put the mail *in the out-bin*.

Prepositional phrases should be placed as close as possible to the element they are modifying:

> Shopping *on the Internet* can be confusing for the uninitiated. (*not* Shopping can be confusing for the uninitiated *on the Internet*.)

Some prepositions are closely linked with a verb. When using phrases such as *look up* and *wipe out*, keep them intact and do not insert anything between the verb and the preposition.

You may have been told that it is unacceptable to put a preposition at the end of a sentence. However, that is not a hard-and-fast rule, and trying to follow it can sometimes be a challenge. You can end a sentence with a preposition as along as the sentence sounds natural and as long as rewording the sentence would create awkward wording:

> I couldn't tell what they were interested in.
> What did she attribute it to?
> What are you looking for?

Avoid using unnecessary prepositions. In the following examples, the prepositions in parentheses should be omitted:

> All (of) the staff members were present.
> I almost fell off (of) my chair with surprise.

> Where was Mr. Steuben going (to)?
> They couldn't help (from) wondering.

The opposite problem is failing to include a preposition when you should. Consider these two sentences:

> Sales were over $100,000 for Linda and Bill.
> Sales were over $100,000 for Linda and for Bill.

The first sentence indicates that Linda and Bill had combined sales over $100,000; the second, that Linda and Bill each had sales over $100,000, for a combined total in excess of $200,000. The preposition *for* is critical here.

When the same preposition can be used for two or more words in a sentence without affecting the meaning, only the last preposition is required:

> We are familiar (with) and satisfied with your company's products.

But when different prepositions are normally used with the words, all the prepositions must be included:

> We are familiar with and interested in your company's products.

Some prepositions have come to be used in a particular way with certain other parts of speech. Here is a partial list of some prepositions that have come to be used with certain words:

according to	independent of
agree to (a proposal)	inferior to
agree with (a person)	plan to
buy from	prefer to
capable of	prior to
comply with	reason with
conform to	responsible for
differ from (things)	similar to
differ with (person)	talk to (without interaction)
different from	talk with (with interaction)
get from (receive)	wait for (person or thing)
get off (dismount)	wait on (like a waiter)

If you are unsure of the correct idiomatic expression, check a dictionary.

Some verb-preposition idioms vary depending on the situation: You agree *to* a proposal but *with* a person, *on* a price, or *in* principle. You argue *about* something, *with* a person, and *for* or *against* a proposition. You compare one item *to* another to show their similarities; you compare one item *with* another to show differences.

Here are some other examples of preposition usage that have given writers trouble:

among/between: *Among* is used to refer to three or more (Circulate the memo *among* the staff); *between* is used to refer to two (Put the copy machine *between* Judy and Dan).

as if/like: *As if* is used before a clause (It seems *as if* we should be doing something); *like* is used before a noun or pronoun (He seems *like* a nice guy).

have/of: *Have* is a verb used in verb phrases (They should *have* checked first); *of* is a preposition and is never used in such cases.

in/into: *In* is used to refer to a static position (The file is *in* the cabinet); *into* is used to refer to movement toward a position (Put the file *into* the cabinet).

1.6.2 Conjunctions

Conjunctions connect the parts of a sentence: words, phrases, and clauses. A **coordinating conjunction** connects two words, phrases, or clauses of equal rank. The simple coordinating conjunctions include *and, but, or, nor, for, yet,* and *so*. **Correlative conjunctions** are coordinating conjunctions used in pairs: *both/and, either/or, neither/nor, not only/ but also*. Constructions with correlative conjunctions should be parallel, with the same part of speech following each element of the conjunction:

> The purchase was *not only* expensive *but also* unnecessary.
>
> The purchase *not only* was expensive *but also was* unnecessary.

Conjunctive adverbs are adverbs used to connect or show relationships between clauses. They include *however, nevertheless, consequently, moreover,* and *as a result*.

A **subordinate conjunction** connects two clauses of unequal rank; it joins a dependent (subordinate) clause to the independent clause on which it depends (for more on dependent and independent clauses, see Section 1.7.1). Subordinate conjunctions include *as, if, because, although, while, before, since, that, until, unless, when, where,* and *whether*.

1.6.3 Articles and Interjections

Only three **articles** exist in English: *the, a,* and *an*. These words are used, like adjectives, to specify which item you are talking about. *The* is called the *definite article* because it indicates a specific noun; *a* and *an* are called the *indefinite articles* because they are less specific about what they are referring to.

If a word begins with a vowel (soft) sound, use *an*; otherwise, use *a*. It's *a history*, not *an history, a hypothesis,* not *an hypothesis*. Use *an* with an "h" word only if it is a soft "h," as in *honor* and *hour*. Use *an* with words that are pronounced with a soft vowel sound even if they are spelled beginning with a consonant (usually in the case of abbreviations): *an SEC application, an MP3 file*. Use *a* with words that begin with vowels if they are pronounced with a hard sound: *a university, a Usenet account*.

Repeat an article if adjectives modify different nouns: *The red house and the white house are mine*. Do not repeat an article if all adjectives modify the same noun: *The red and white house is mine*.

Interjections are words that express no solid information, only emotion:

> Wow!   Well, well!
> Oh, no!   Good!

Such purely emotional language has its place in private life and advertising copy, but it only weakens the effect of most business writing.

1.7 SENTENCES

Sentences are constructed with the major building blocks, the parts of speech. Take, for example, this simple two-word sentence:

> Money talks.

It consists of a noun (*money*) and a verb (*talks*). When used in this way, the noun works as the first requirement for a sentence, the **subject**, and the verb works as the second requirement, the **predicate**. Without a subject (who or what does something) and a predicate (the doing of it), you have merely a collection of words, not a sentence.

1.7.1 Longer Sentences

More complicated sentences have more complicated subjects and predicates, but they still have a simple subject and a predicate verb. In the following examples, the subject is underlined once, the predicate verb twice:

> <u>Marex</u> and <u>Contron</u> <u>enjoy</u> higher earnings each quarter.

Marex [and] *Contron* do something; *enjoy* is what they do.

> My <u>interview</u>, coming minutes after my freeway accident, <u>did</u> not <u>impress</u> or <u>move</u> anyone.

Interview is what did something. What did it do? It *did* [not] *impress* [or] *move*.

> In terms of usable space, a steel <u>warehouse</u>, with its extremely long span of roof unsupported by pillars, <u>makes</u> more sense.

Warehouse is what *makes*.

These three sentences demonstrate several things. First, in all three sentences, the simple subject and predicate verb are the "bare bones" of the sentence, the parts that carry the core idea of the sentence. When trying to find the subject and predicate verb, disregard all prepositional phrases, modifiers, conjunctions, and articles.

Second, in the third sentence, the verb is singular (*makes*) because the subject is singular (*warehouse*). Even though the plural noun *pillars* is closer to the verb, *warehouse* is the subject. So *warehouse* determines whether the verb is singular or plural. Subject and predicate must agree.

Third, the subject in the first sentence is compound (*Marex* [and] *Contron*). A compound subject, when connected by *and*, requires a plural verb (*enjoy*). Also, the second sentence shows how compound predicates can occur (*did* [not] *impress* [or] *move*).

Fourth, the second sentence incorporates a group of words—*coming minutes after my freeway accident*—containing a form of a verb (*coming*) and a noun (*accident*). Yet, this group of words is not a complete sentence for two reasons:

- **Not all nouns are subjects:** *Accident* is not the subject of *coming*.
- **Not all verbs are predicates:** A verb that ends in *ing* can never be the predicate of a sentence (unless preceded by a form of *to be*, as in *was coming*).

Because they don't contain a subject and a predicate, the words *coming minutes after my freeway accident* (called a **phrase**) can't be written as a sentence. That is, the phrase cannot stand alone; it cannot begin with a capital letter and end with a period. So a phrase must always be just one part of a sentence.

Sometimes a sentence incorporates two or more groups of words that do contain a subject and a predicate; these word groups are called **clauses**:

> My interview, because it came minutes after my freeway accident, did not impress or move anyone.

The **independent clause** is the portion of the sentence that could stand alone without revision:

> My *interview* did not impress or move anyone.

The other part of the sentence could stand alone only by removing *because*:

> (because) It came minutes after my freeway accident.

This part of the sentence is known as a **dependent clause**; although it has a subject and a predicate (just as an independent clause does), it's linked to the main part of the sentence by a word (*because*) showing its dependence.

In summary, the two types of clauses—dependent and independent—both have a subject and a predicate. Dependent clauses, however, do not bear the main meaning of the sentence and are therefore linked to an independent clause. Nor can phrases stand alone, because they lack both a subject and a predicate. Only independent clauses can be written as sentences without revision.

1.7.2 Types of Sentences

Sentences come in four main types, depending on the extent to which they contain clauses. A **simple sentence** has one subject and one predicate; in short, it has one main independent clause:

> Boeing is the world's largest aerospace company.

A **compound sentence** consists of two independent clauses connected by a coordinating conjunction (*and, or, but,* etc.) or a semicolon:

> Airbus outsold Boeing for several years, but Boeing has recently regained the lead.

A **complex sentence** consists of an independent clause and one or more dependent clauses:

> Boeing is betting [independent clause] that airlines will begin using moderately smaller planes to fly passengers between smaller cities [dependent clause introduced by *that*].

A **compound-complex sentence** has two main clauses, at least one of which contains a subordinate (dependent clause):

> Boeing is betting [independent clause] that airlines will begin using moderately smaller planes to fly passengers between smaller cities [dependent clause], and it anticipates that new airports will be developed to meet passenger needs [independent clause].

1.7.3 Sentence Fragments

An incomplete sentence (a phrase or a dependent clause) that is written as though it were a complete sentence is called a **fragment**. Consider the following sentence fragments:

> Marilyn Sanders, having had pilferage problems in her store for the past year. Refuses to accept the results of our investigation.

This serious error can easily be corrected by putting the two fragments together:

> Marilyn Sanders, having had pilferage problems in her store for the past year, refuses to accept the results of our investigation.

The actual details of a situation will determine the best way for you to remedy a fragment problem.

The ban on fragments has one exception. Some advertising copy contains sentence fragments, written knowingly to convey a certain rhythm. However, advertising is the only area of business in which fragments are acceptable.

1.7.4 Fused Sentences and Comma Splices

Just as there can be too little in a group of words to make it a sentence, there can also be too much:

> All our mail is run through a postage meter every afternoon someone picks it up.

This example contains two sentences, not one, but the two have been blended so that it's hard to tell where one ends and the next begins. Is the mail run through a meter every afternoon? If so, the sentences should read:

> All our mail is run through a postage meter every afternoon. Someone picks it up.

Perhaps the mail is run through a meter at some other time (morning, for example) and is picked up every afternoon:

> All our mail is run through a postage meter. Every afternoon someone picks it up.

The order of words is the same in all three cases; sentence division makes all the difference. Either of the last two cases is grammatically correct. The choice depends on the facts of the situation.

Sometimes these so-called **fused sentences** have a more obvious point of separation:

> Several large orders arrived within a few days of one another, too many came in for us to process by the end of the month.

Here, the comma has been put between two independent clauses in an attempt to link them. When a lowly comma separates two complete sentences, the result is called a **comma splice**. A comma splice can be remedied in one of three ways:

- **Replace the comma with a period and capitalize the next word:** "...one another. Too many..."
- **Replace the comma with a semicolon and do not capitalize the next word:** "...one another; too many..." This remedy works only when the two sentences have closely related meanings.
- **Change one of the sentences so that it becomes a phrase or a dependent clause.** This remedy often produces the best writing, but it takes more work.

The third alternative can be carried out in several ways. One is to begin the sentence with a subordinating conjunction:

> Whenever several large orders arrived within a few days of one another, too many came in for us to process by the end of the month.

Another way is to remove part of the subject or the predicate verb from one of the independent clauses, thereby creating a phrase:

> Several large orders arrived within a few days of one another, too many for us to process by the end of the month.

Finally, you can change one of the predicate verbs to its *ing* form:

> Several large orders arrived within a few days of one another, too many coming in for us to process by the end of the month.

In many cases, simply adding a coordinating conjunction can separate fused sentences or remedy a comma splice:

> You can fire them, or you can make better use of their abilities.
> Margaret drew up the designs, and Matt carried them out.
> We will have three strong months, but after that sales will taper off.

Be careful with coordinating conjunctions: Use them only to join simple sentences that express similar ideas.

Also, because they say relatively little about the relationship between the two clauses they join, avoid using coordinating conjunctions too often: *and* is merely an addition sign; *but* is just a turn signal; *or* only points to an alternative. Subordinating conjunctions such as *because* and *whenever* tell the reader a lot more.

1.7.5 Sentences with Linking Verbs

Linking verbs were discussed briefly in the section on verbs (Section 1.3). Here, you can see more fully the way they function in a sentence. The following is a model of any sentence with a linking verb:

> A *(verb)* B.

Although words such as *seems* and *feels* can also be linking verbs, let's assume that the verb is a form of *to be*:

> A *is* B.

In such a sentence, A and B are always nouns, pronouns, or adjectives. When one is a noun and the other is a pronoun, or when both are nouns, the sentence says that one is the same as the other:

> She is president.
> Rachel is president.
> She is forceful.

Recall from Section 1.3.3 that the noun or adjective that follows the linking verb is called a *complement*. When it is a noun or noun phrase, the complement is called a *predicate nominative*, when the complement is an adjective, it is referred to as a *predicate adjective*.

1.7.6 Misplaced Modifiers

The position of a modifier in a sentence is important. The movement of *only* changes the meaning in the following sentences:

> Only we are obliged to supply those items specified in your contract.

> We are obliged only to supply those items specified in your contract.
>
> We are obliged to supply only those items specified in your contract.
>
> We are obliged to supply those items specified only in your contract.

In any particular set of circumstances, only one of those sentences would be accurate. The others would very likely cause problems. To prevent misunderstanding, place such modifiers as close as possible to the noun or verb they modify.

For similar reasons, whole phrases that are modifiers must be placed near the right noun or verb. Mistakes in placement create ludicrous meanings:

> Antia Information Systems bought new computer chairs for the programmers with more comfortable seats.

The anatomy of programmers is not normally a concern of business writers. Obviously, the comfort of the chairs was the issue:

> Antia Information Systems bought programmers the new computer chairs with more comfortable seats.

Here is another example:

> I asked him to file all the letters in the cabinet that had been answered.

In this ridiculous sentence, the cabinet has been answered, even though no cabinet in history is known to have asked a question. *That had been answered* is too far from *letters* and too close to *cabinet*. Here's an improvement:

> I asked him to file in the cabinet all the letters that had been answered.

The term **dangling modifier** is often used to refer to a clause or phrase that because of its position in the sentence seems to modify a word that it is not meant to modify. For instance:

> Lying motionless, co-workers rushed to Barry's aid.

Readers expect an introductory phrase to modify the subject of the main clause. But in this case it wasn't the *co-workers* who were lying motionless but rather *Barry* who was in this situation. Like this example, most instances of dangling modifiers occur at the beginning of sentences. The source of some danglers is a passive construction:

> To find the needed information, the whole book had to be read.

In such cases, switching to the active voice can usually remedy the problem:

> To find the needed information, you will need to read the whole book.

1.7.7 Parallelism

Two or more sentence elements that have the same relation to another element should be in the same form. Otherwise, the reader is forced to work harder to understand the meaning of the sentence. When a series consists of phrases or clauses, the same part of speech (preposition, gerund, etc.) should introduce them. Do not mix infinitives with participles or adjectives with nouns. Here are some examples of nonparallel elements:

> Andersen is hiring managers, programmers, and people who work in accounting. [nouns not parallel]
>
> Andersen earns income by auditing, consulting, and by bookkeeping. [prepositional phrases not parallel]
>
> Andersen's goals are to win new clients, keeping old clients happy, and finding new enterprises. [infinitive mixed with gerunds]

2.0 Punctuation

On the highway, signs tell you when to slow down or stop, where to turn, and when to merge. In similar fashion, punctuation helps readers negotiate your prose. The proper use of punctuation keeps readers from losing track of your meaning.

2.1 PERIODS

Use a period (1) to end any sentence that is not a question, (2) with certain abbreviations, and (3) between dollars and cents in an amount of money.

2.2 QUESTION MARKS

Use a question mark after any direct question that requests an answer:

> Are you planning to enclose a check, or shall we bill you?

Don't use a question mark with commands phrased as questions for the sake of politeness:

> Will you send us a check today.

A question mark should precede quotation marks, parentheses, and brackets if it is part of the quoted or parenthetical material; otherwise, it should follow:

> This issue of *Inc.* has an article titled "What's Your Entrepreneurial IQ?"

> Have you read the article "Five Principles of Guerrilla Marketing"?

Do not use the question mark with indirect questions or with requests:

> Mr. Antonelli asked whether anyone had seen Nathalia lately.

Do not use a comma or a period with a question mark; the question mark takes the place of these punctuation marks.

2.3 EXCLAMATION POINTS

Use exclamation points after highly emotional language. Because business writing almost never calls for emotional language, you will seldom use exclamation points.

2.4 SEMICOLONS

Semicolons have three main uses. One is to separate two closely related independent clauses:

> The outline for the report is due within a week; the report itself is due at the end of the month.

A semicolon should also be used instead of a comma when the items in a series have commas within them:

> Our previous meetings were on November 11, 2014; February 20, 2015; and April 28, 2016.

Finally, a semicolon should be used to separate independent clauses when the second one begins with a conjunctive adverb such as *however, therefore,* or *nevertheless* or a phrase such as *for example* or *in that case:*

> Our supplier has been out of part D712 for 10 weeks; however, we have found another source that can ship the part right away.
> His test scores were quite low; on the other hand, he has a lot of relevant experience.

Section 4.4 provides more information on using transitional words and phrases.

Semicolons should always be placed outside parentheses:

> Events Northwest has the contract for this year's convention (August 23–28); we haven't awarded the contract for next year yet.

2.5 COLONS

Use a colon after the salutation in a business letter. You should also use a colon at the end of a sentence or phrase introducing a list or (sometimes) a quotation:

> Our study included the three most critical problems: insufficient capital, incompetent management, and inappropriate location.

A colon should not be used when the list, quotation, or idea is a direct object of the verb or preposition. This rule applies whether the list is set off or run in:

> We are able to supply
>   staples
>   wood screws
>   nails
>   toggle bolts
> This shipment includes 9 DVDs, 12 CDs, and 4 USB flash drives.

Another way you can use a colon is to separate the main clause and another sentence element when the second explains, illustrates, or amplifies the first:

> Management was unprepared for the union representatives' demands: this fact alone accounts for their arguing well into the night.

However, in contemporary usage, such clauses are frequently separated by a semicolon.

Like semicolons, colons should always be placed outside parentheses:

> He has an expensive list of new demands (none of which is covered in the purchase agreement): new carpeting, network cabling, and a new security system.

2.6 COMMAS

Commas have many uses; the most common is to separate items in a series:

> He took the job, learned it well, worked hard, and succeeded.
> Put paper, pencils, and paper clips on the requisition list.

Company style may dictate omitting the final comma in a series. However, if you have a choice, use the final comma; it's often necessary to prevent misunderstanding.

A second place to use a comma is between independent clauses that are joined by a coordinating conjunction (*and, but,* or *or*):

> She spoke to the sales staff, and he spoke to the production staff.
> I was advised to proceed, and I did.

A third use for the comma is to separate a dependent clause at the beginning of a sentence from an independent clause:

> Because of our lead in the market, we may be able to risk introducing a new product.

However, a dependent clause at the end of a sentence is separated from the independent clause by a comma only when the dependent clause is unnecessary to the main meaning of the sentence:

> We may be able to introduce a new product, although it may involve some risk.

A fourth use for the comma is after an introductory phrase or word:

> Starting with this amount of capital, we can survive in the red for one year.
>
> Through more careful planning, we may be able to serve more people.
>
> Yes, you may proceed as originally planned.

However, with short introductory prepositional phrases and some one-syllable words (such as *hence* and *thus*), the comma is often omitted:

> Before January 1 we must complete the inventory.
>
> Thus we may not need to hire anyone.
>
> In July we will complete the move to Tulsa.

Fifth, paired commas are used to set off nonrestrictive clauses and phrases. A **restrictive clause** is one that cannot be omitted without altering the meaning of the main clause, whereas a **nonrestrictive clause** can be:

> The *Time* magazine website, which is produced by Steve Conley, has won several design awards. [nonrestrictive: the material set off by commas could be omitted]
>
> The website that is produced by Steve Conley has won several design awards. [restrictive: no commas are used before and after *that is produced by Steve Conley* because this information is necessary to the meaning of the sentence—it specifies which website]

A sixth use for commas is to set off appositive words and phrases. (An **appositive** has the same meaning as the word it is in apposition to.) Like nonrestrictive clauses, appositives can be dropped without changing or obscuring the meaning of the sentence:

> Conley, a freelance designer, also produces the websites for several nonprofit corporations.

Seventh, commas are used between adjectives modifying the same noun (coordinate adjectives):

> She left Monday for a long, difficult recruiting trip.

To test the appropriateness of such a comma, try reversing the order of the adjectives: *a difficult, long recruiting trip.* If the order cannot be reversed, leave out the comma (*a good old friend* isn't the same as an *old good friend*). A comma should not be used when one of the adjectives is part of the noun. Compare these two phrases:

> a distinguished, well-known figure
>
> a distinguished public figure

The adjective-noun combination of *public* and *figure* has been used together so often that it has come to be considered a single thing: *public figure.* So no comma is required.

Eighth, commas are used both before and after the year in sentences that include month, day, and year:

> It will be sent by December 15, 2017, from our Cincinnati plant.

Some companies use the European style: 15 December 2017. No commas should be used in that case. Nor is a comma needed when only the month and year are present (December 2017).

Ninth, commas are used to set off a variety of parenthetical words and phrases within sentences, including state names, dates, abbreviations, transitional expressions, and contrasted elements:

> They were, in fact, prepared to submit a bid.
>
> Habermacher, Inc., went public in 1999.
>
> Our goal was increased profits, not increased market share.
>
> Service, then, is our main concern.
>
> The factory was completed in Chattanooga, Tennessee, just three weeks ago.
>
> Joanne Dubiik, M.D., has applied for a loan from First Savings.
>
> I started work here on March 1, 2003, and soon received my first promotion.

Tenth, a comma is used to separate a quotation from the rest of the sentence:

> Your warranty reads, "These conditions remain in effect for one year from date of purchase."

However, the comma is left out when the quotation as a whole is built into the structure of the sentence:

> He hurried off with an angry "Look where you're going."

Finally, a comma should be used whenever it's needed to avoid confusion or an unintended meaning. Compare the following:

> Ever since they have planned new ventures more carefully.
> Ever since, they have planned new ventures more carefully.

2.7 DASHES

Use dashes to surround a comment that is a sudden turn in thought:

> Membership in the IBSA—it's expensive but worth it—may be obtained by applying to our New York office.

A dash can also be used to emphasize a parenthetical word or phrase:

> Third-quarter profits—in excess of $2 million—are up sharply.

Finally, use dashes to set off a phrase that contains commas:

> All our offices—Milwaukee, New Orleans, and Phoenix—have sent representatives.

Don't confuse a dash with a hyphen. A dash separates and emphasizes words, phrases, and clauses more strongly than commas or parentheses can; a hyphen ties two words so tightly that they almost become one word.

When using a computer, use the em dash symbol. When typing a dash in email, type two hyphens with no space before, between, or after.

A second type of dash, the en dash, can be produced with computer word processing and page-layout programs. This kind of dash is shorter than the regular dash and longer than a hyphen. It is reserved almost exclusively for indicating "to" or "through" with numbers such as dates and pages: *2015–2016, pages 30–44.*

2.8 HYPHENS

Hyphens are mainly used in three ways. The first is to separate the parts of compound words beginning with such prefixes as *self-, ex-, quasi-,* and *all-*:

self-assured	quasi-official
ex-wife	all-important

However, do not use hyphens in words that have prefixes such as *pro, anti, non, re, pre, un, inter,* and *extra*:

prolabor	nonunion
antifascist	interdepartmental

Exceptions occur when (1) the prefix occurs before a proper noun or (2) the vowel at the end of the prefix is the same as the first letter of the root word:

pro-Republican	anti-American
anti-inflammatory	extra-atmospheric

When in doubt, consult your dictionary.

Hyphens are used in some types of spelled-out numbers. For instance, they are used to separate the parts of a spelled-out number from *twenty-one* to *ninety-nine* and for spelled-out fractions: *two-thirds, one-sixth* (although some style guides say not to hyphenate fractions used as nouns).

Certain compound nouns are formed by using hyphens: *secretary-treasurer, city-state.* Check your dictionary for compounds you're unsure about.

Hyphens are also used in some compound adjectives, which are adjectives made up of two or more words. Specifically, you should use hyphens in compound adjectives that come before the noun:

> an interest-bearing account   well-informed executives

However, you need not hyphenate when the adjective follows a linking verb:

> This account is interest bearing.
> Their executives are well informed.

You can shorten sentences that list similar hyphenated words by dropping the common part from all but the last word:

> Check the costs of first-, second-, and third-class postage.

Finally, hyphens may be used to divide words at the end of a typed line. Such hyphenation is best avoided, but when you have to divide words at the end of a line, do so correctly (see Section 3.5). Dictionaries show how words are divided into syllables.

2.9 APOSTROPHES

Use an apostrophe in the possessive form of noun (but not in a pronoun):

> On his desk was a reply to Bette *Ainsley's* application for the *manager's* position.

Apostrophes are also used in place of the missing letter(s) of a contraction:

Whole Words	Contraction
we will	we'll
do not	don't
they are	they're

2.10 QUOTATION MARKS

Use quotation marks to surround words that are repeated exactly as they were said or written:

> The collection letter ended by saying, "This is your third and final notice."

Remember: (1) When the quoted material is a complete sentence, the first word is capitalized. (2) The final comma or period goes inside the closing quotation marks.

Quotation marks are also used to set off the title of a newspaper story, magazine article, or book chapter:

> You should read "Legal Aspects of the Collection Letter" in *Today's Credit*.

Quotation marks may also be used to indicate special treatment for words or phrases, such as terms that you're using in an unusual or ironic way:

> Our management "team" spends more time squabbling than working to solve company problems.

When you are defining a word, put the definition in quotation marks:

> The abbreviation *etc.* means "and so forth."

When using quotation marks, take care to insert the closing marks as well as the opening ones.

Although periods and commas go inside any quotation marks, colons and semicolons generally go outside them. A question mark goes inside the quotation marks only if the quotation is a question:

> All that day we wondered, "Is he with us?"

If the quotation is not a question but the entire sentence is, the question mark goes outside:

> What did she mean by "You will hear from me"?

For quotes within quotes, use single quotation marks within double:

> Bonnie Schulman fired up the project team by saying, "We've all heard the doubts that this team can meet the goals outlined in '2015: The Strategic Imperative,' but I have total confidence in your ability and commitment."

Otherwise, do not use single quotation marks for anything, including titles of works—that's British style.

2.11 PARENTHESES AND BRACKETS

Use parentheses to surround comments that are entirely incidental or to supply additional information:

> Our figures do not match yours, although (if my calculations are correct) they are closer than we thought.
> Sally Wagner (no relation to our own John Wagner) was just promoted to general manager of the Detroit office.

Parentheses are used in legal documents to surround figures in arabic numerals that follow the same amount in words:

> Remittance will be One Thousand Two Hundred Dollars ($1,200).

Be careful to put punctuation marks (period, comma, and so on) outside the parentheses unless they are part of the statement in parentheses. And keep in mind that parentheses have both an opening and a closing mark; both should always be used, even when setting off listed items within text: (*1*), not *1*).

Brackets are used for notation, comment, explanation, or correction within quoted material:

> When asked for a reason, Jackson said, "The dismissal was a carefully considered decision, with input from every member [of the board of directors]."

Brackets are also used for parenthetical material that falls within parentheses:

> Drucker's magnum opus (*Management: Tasks, Responsibilities, Practices* [Harper & Row, 1979]) has influenced generations of entrepreneurs.

2.12 ELLIPSES

Use ellipsis points, or three evenly spaced periods, to indicate that material has been left out of a direct quotation. Use them only in direct quotations and only at the point where material was left out. In the following example, the first sentence is quoted in the second:

> The Dow Jones Industrial Average fell 276.39 points, or 2.6%, during the week to 10292.31.
> According to the *Wall Street Journal*, "The Dow Jones Industrial Average fell 276.39 points . . . to 10,292.31."

The number of dots in ellipses is not optional; always use three. Occasionally, the points of an ellipsis come at the end of a sentence, where they seem to grow a fourth dot. Don't be fooled: One of the dots is a period. Ellipsis points should always be preceded and followed by a space.

Avoid using ellipses to represent a pause in your writing; use a dash for that purpose:

> At first we had planned to leave for the conference on Wednesday—but then we changed our minds. [not *on Wednesday . . . but then*]

3.0 Mechanics

The most obvious and least tolerable mistakes that a business writer makes are probably those related to grammar and punctuation. However, a number of small details, known as writing mechanics, demonstrate the writer's polish and reflect on the company's professionalism.

When it comes to mechanics, also called *style*, many of the "rules" are not hard and fast. Publications and organizations vary in their preferred styles for capitalization, abbreviations, numbers, italics, and so on. Here, we'll try to differentiate between practices that are generally accepted and those that can vary. When you are writing materials for a specific company or organization, find out the preferred style (such as *The Chicago Manual of Style* or *Webster's Style Manual*). Otherwise, choose a respected style guide. The key to style is consistency: If you spell out the word *percent* in one part of a document, don't use the percent sign in a similar context elsewhere in the same document.

3.1 CAPITALIZATION

With capitalization, you can follow either an "up" style (when in doubt, capitalize: *Federal Government, Board of Directors*) or a "down" style (when in doubt, use lowercase: *federal government, board of directors*). The trend over the last few decades has been toward the down style. Your best bet is to get a good style manual and consult it when you have a capitalization question. Following are some rules that most style guides agree on.

Capital letters are used at the beginning of certain word groups:

- Complete sentence: Before hanging up, he said, "We'll meet here on Wednesday at noon."
- Formal statement following a colon: She has a favorite motto: Where there's a will, there's a way.
- Phrase used as sentence: Absolutely not!
- Quoted sentence embedded in another sentence: Scott said, "Nobody was here during lunch hour except me."
- List of items set off from text:

> Three preliminary steps are involved:
>   Design review
>   Budgeting
>   Scheduling

Capitalize proper adjectives and proper nouns (the names of particular persons, places, and things):

> Darrell Greene lived in a Victorian mansion.
> We sent Ms. Larson an application form, informing her that not all applicants are interviewed.
> Let's consider opening a branch in the West, perhaps at the west end of Tucson, Arizona.

> As office buildings go, the Kinney Building is a pleasant setting for TDG Office Equipment.
> We are going to have to cancel our plans for hiring French and German sales reps.

Larson's name is capitalized because she is a particular applicant, whereas the general term *applicant* is left uncapitalized. Likewise, *West* is capitalized when it refers to a particular place but not when it means a direction. In the same way, *office* and *building* are not capitalized when they are general terms (common nouns), but they are capitalized when they are part of the title of a particular office or building (proper nouns). Some proper adjectives are lowercased when they are part of terms that have come into common use, such as *french fries* and *roman numerals.*

Titles within families or companies as well as professional titles may also be capitalized:

> I turned down Uncle David when he offered me a job.
> I wouldn't be comfortable working for one of my relatives.
> We've never had a president quite like President Sweeney.

People's titles are capitalized when they are used in addressing a person, especially in a formal context. They are not usually capitalized, however, when they are used merely to identify the person:

> Address the letter to Chairperson Anna Palmer.
> I wish to thank Chairperson Anna Palmer for her assistance.
> Anna Palmer, chairperson of the board, took the podium.

Also capitalize titles if they are used by themselves in addressing a person:

> Thank you, Doctor, for your donation.

Always capitalize the first word of the salutation and complimentary close of a letter:

> *Dear* Mr. Andrews: *Yours* very truly,

The names of organizations are capitalized, of course; so are the official names of their departments and divisions. However, do not use capitals when referring in general terms to a department or division, especially one in another organization:

> Route this memo to Personnel.
> Larry Tien was transferred to the Microchip Division.
> Will you be enrolled in the Psychology Department?
> Someone from the personnel department at EnerTech stopped by the booth.

Capitalization is unnecessary when using a word like *company, corporation,* or *university* alone:

> The corporation plans to issue 50,000 shares of common stock.

Likewise, the names of specific products are capitalized, although the names of general product types are not:

> Apple Inc.　　　　　　Xerox machine
> Tide laundry detergent

When it comes to government terminology, here are some guides to capitalization: (1) Lowercase *federal* unless it is part of an agency name; (2) capitalize names of courts, departments, bureaus, offices, and agencies but lowercase such references as *the bureau* and *the department* when the full name is not used; (3) lowercase the titles of government officers unless they precede a specific person's name: *the secretary of state, the senator, the ambassador, the governor, and the mayor* but *Mayor Gonzalez* (Note: style guides vary on whether to capitalize *president* when referring to the president of the United States without including the person's name); (4) capitalize the names of laws and acts: *the Sherman Antitrust Act, the Civil Rights Act;* (5) capitalize the names of political parties but lowercase the word *party: Democratic party, Libertarian party.*

When writing about two or more geographic features of the same type, it is now accepted practice to capitalize the common noun in addition to the proper nouns, regardless of word order:

> Lakes Ontario and Huron
> Allegheny and Monongahela Rivers
> Corson and Ravenna Avenues

The names of languages, races, and ethnic groups are capitalized: Japanese, Caucasian, Hispanic. But racial terms that denote only skin color are not capitalized: black, white.

When referring to the titles of books, articles, magazines, newspapers, reports, movies, and so on, you should capitalize the first and last words and all nouns, pronouns, adjectives, verbs, and adverbs, and capitalize prepositions and conjunctions with five letters or more. Except for the first and last words, do not capitalize articles:

> *Economics During the Great War*
>
> "An Investigation into the Market for Long-Distance Services"
>
> "What Successes Are Made Of"

When *the* is part of the official name of a newspaper or magazine, it should be treated this way too:

> *The Wall Street Journal*

Style guides vary in their recommendations regarding capitalization of hyphenated words in titles. A general guide is to capitalize the second word in a temporary compound (a compound that is hyphenated for grammatical reasons and not spelling reasons), such as *Law-Abiding Citizen,* but to lowercase the word if the term is always hyphenated, such as *Son-in-law*).

References to specific pages, paragraphs, lines, and the like are not capitalized: *page 73, line 3.* However, in most other numbered or lettered references, the identifying term is capitalized:

> Chapter 4　　　　Serial No. 382-2203　　　　Item B-11

Finally, the names of academic degrees are capitalized when they follow a person's name but are not capitalized when used in a general sense:

> I received a bachelor of science degree.
> Thomas Whitelaw, Doctor of Philosophy, will attend.

Similarly, general courses of study are not capitalized, but the names of specific classes are:

> She studied accounting as an undergraduate.
> She is enrolled in Accounting 201.

3.2 UNDERSCORES AND ITALICS

Usually a line typed underneath a word or phrase either provides emphasis or indicates the title of a book, magazine, or newspaper. If possible, use italics instead of an underscore. Italics (or underlining) should also be used for defining terms and for discussing words as words:

> In this report, *net sales* refers to after-tax sales dollars.

Also use italics to set off foreign words, unless the words have become a common part of English:

> Top Shelf is considered the *sine qua non* of comic book publishers.
> Chris uses a laissez-faire [no italic] management style.

3.3 ABBREVIATIONS

Abbreviations are used heavily in tables, charts, lists, and forms. They're used sparingly in prose. Here are some abbreviation situations to watch for:

- In most cases do not use periods with acronyms (words formed from the initial letter or letters of parts of a term): *CEO, CD-ROM, DOS, YWCA, FDA;* but *Ph.D., M.A., M. D.*
- Use periods with abbreviations such as *Mr., Ms., Sr., Jr., a.m., p.m., B.C.,* and *A.D.*
- The trend is away from using periods with such units of measure as *mph, mm,* and *lb.*

- Use periods with such Latin abbreviations as *e.g., i.e., et al.,* and *etc.* However, style guides recommend that you avoid using these Latin forms and instead use their English equivalents (*for example, that is, and others,* and *and so on,* respectively). If you must use these abbreviations, such as in parenthetical expressions or footnotes, do not put them in italics.
- Some companies have abbreviations as part of their names (*&, Co., Inc., Ltd.*). When you refer to such firms by name, be sure to double-check the preferred spelling, including spacing: *AT&T; Barnes & Noble; Carson Pirie Scott & Company; PepsiCo; Kate Spade, Inc.; National Data Corporation; Siemens Corp.; Glaxo Wellcome PLC; US Airways; U.S. Business Reporter.*
- Most style guides recommend that you spell out *United States* as a noun and reserve *U.S.* as an adjective preceding the noun modified.

One way to handle an abbreviation that you want to use throughout a document is to spell it out the first time you use it, follow it with the abbreviation in parentheses, and then use the abbreviation in the remainder of the document.

3.4 NUMBERS

Numbers may be correctly handled many ways in business writing, so follow company style. In the absence of a set style, however, generally spell out all numbers from one to nine and use arabic numerals for the rest.

There are some exceptions to this general rule. For example, never begin a sentence with a numeral:

> Twenty of us produced 641 units per week in the first 12 weeks of the year.

Use numerals for the numbers one through nine if they're in the same list as larger numbers:

> Our weekly quota rose from 9 to 15 to 27.

Use numerals for percentages, time of day (except with o'clock), dates, and (in general) dollar amounts:

> Our division is responsible for 7 percent of total sales.
> The meeting is scheduled for 8:30 a.m. on August 2.
> Add $3 for postage and handling.

When using numerals for time, be consistent: It should be *between 10:00 a.m. and 4:30 p.m.,* not *between 10 a.m. and 4:30 p.m.* Expressions such as *4:00 o'clock* and *7 a.m. in the morning* are redundant.

Use a comma in numbers expressing thousands (1,257), unless your company specifies another style. When dealing with numbers in the millions and billions, combine words and figures: *7.3 million, 2 billion.*

When writing dollar amounts, use a decimal point only if cents are included. In lists of two or more dollar amounts, use the decimal point either for all or for none:

> He sent two checks, one for $67.92 and one for $90.00.

When two numbers fall next to each other in a sentence, use figures for the number that is largest, most difficult to spell, or part of a physical measurement; use words for the other:

> I have learned to manage a classroom of 30 twelve-year-olds.
> She won a bonus for selling 24 thirty-volume sets.
> You'll need twenty 3-inch bolts.

In addresses, all street numbers except One are in numerals. So are suite and room numbers and zip codes. For street names that are numbered, practice varies so widely that you should use the form specified on an organization's letterhead or in a reliable directory. All the following examples are correct:

> One Fifth Avenue   297 Ninth Street
> 1839 44th Street   11026 West 78 Place

Telephone numbers are always expressed in numerals. Parentheses may separate the area code from the rest of the number, but a slash or a hyphen may be used instead, especially if the entire phone number is enclosed in parentheses:

> 382-8329   (602/382-8329)   602-382-8329

Percentages are always expressed in numerals. The word *percent* is used in most cases, but % may be used in tables, forms, and statistical writing

Ages are usually expressed in words—except when a parenthetical reference to age follows someone's name:

> Mrs. Margaret Sanderson is seventy-two.
> Mrs. Margaret Sanderson, 72, swims daily.

Also, ages expressed in years and months are treated like physical measurements that combine two units of measure: *5 years, 6 months.*

Physical measurements such as distance, weight, and volume are also often expressed in numerals: *9 kilometers, 5 feet 3 inches, 7 pounds 10 ounces.*

Decimal numbers are always written in numerals. In most cases, add a zero to the left of the decimal point if the number is less than one and does not already start with a zero:

> 1.38   .07   0.2

In a series of related decimal numbers with at least one number greater than one, make sure that all numbers smaller than one have a zero to the left of the decimal point: 1.20, 0.21, 0.09.

Simple fractions are written in words, but more complicated fractions are expressed in figures or, if easier to read, in figures and words:

two-thirds	9/32	2 hundredths

When typing ordinal numbers, such as *3rd edition* or *21st century*, your word processing program may automatically make the letters *rd* (or *st*, *th*, or *nd*) into a superscript. Do yourself a favor and turn that formatting function off in your "Preferences," as superscripts should not be used in regular prose or even in bibliographies.

3.5 WORD DIVISION

In general, avoid dividing words at the end of lines. When you must do so, follow these rules:

- Don't divide one-syllable words (such as *since*, *walked*, and *thought*), abbreviations (*mgr.*), contractions (*isn't*), or numbers expressed in numerals (*117,500*).
- Divide words between syllables, as specified in a dictionary or word-division manual.
- Make sure that at least three letters of the divided words are moved to the second line: *sin-cerely* instead of *sincere-ly*.
- Do not end a page or more than three consecutive lines with hyphens.
- Leave syllables consisting of a single vowel at the end of the first line (*impedi-ment* instead of *imped-iment*), except when the single vowel is part of a suffix such as *-able*, *-ible*, *-ical*, or *-ity* (*re-spons-ible* instead of *re-sponsi-ble*).
- Divide between double letters (*tomor-row*), except when the root word ends in double letters (*call-ing* instead of *cal-ling*).
- Wherever possible, divide hyphenated words at the hyphen only: instead of *anti-inde-pendence*, use *anti-independence*.
- Whenever possible, do not break URLs or email addresses. If you have to break a long URL or email address, do not insert a hyphen at the end of the first line.

4.0 Vocabulary

Using the right word in the right place is a crucial skill in business communication. However, many pitfalls await the unwary.

4.1 FREQUENTLY CONFUSED WORDS

Because the following sets of words sound similar, be careful not to use one when you mean to use the other:

Word	Meaning
accede	to comply with
exceed	to go beyond

Word	Meaning
accept	to take
except	to exclude
access	admittance
excess	too much
advice	suggestion
advise	to suggest
affect	to influence
effect	the result
allot	to distribute
a lot	much or many
all ready	completely prepared
already	completed earlier
born	given birth to
borne	carried
capital	money; chief city
capitol	a government building
cite	to quote
sight	a view
site	a location
complement	complete amount; to go well with
compliment	expression of esteem; to flatter
corespondent	party in a divorce suit
correspondent	letter writer
council	a panel of people
counsel	advice; a lawyer
defer	to put off until later
differ	to be different
device	a mechanism
devise	to plan
die	to stop living; a tool
dye	to color
discreet	careful
discrete	separate
envelop	to surround
envelope	a covering for a letter
forth	forward
fourth	number four
holey	full of holes
holy	sacred
wholly	completely
human	of people
humane	kindly
incidence	frequency
incidents	events
instance	example
instants	moments
interstate	between states

Word	Meaning
intrastate	within a state
its	indicates possession
it's	contracted form of it is
later	afterward
latter	the second of two
lead	a metal; to guide
led	guided
lean	to rest at an angle
lien	a claim
levee	embankment
levy	tax
loath	reluctant
loathe	to hate
loose	free; not tight
lose	to mislay
material	substance
materiel	equipment
miner	mineworker
minor	underage person
moral	virtuous; a lesson
morale	sense of well-being
ordinance	law
ordnance	weapons
overdo	to do in excess
overdue	past due
peace	lack of conflict
piece	a fragment
pedal	a foot lever
peddle	to sell
persecute	to torment
prosecute	to sue
personal	private
personnel	employees
precedence	priority
precedents	previous events
principal	sum of money; chief; main
principle	general rule
rap	to knock
wrap	to cover
residence	home
residents	inhabitants
right	correct
rite	ceremony
write	to form words on a surface
role	a part to play
roll	to tumble; a list
root	part of a plant

Word	Meaning
rout	to defeat
route	a traveler's way
shear	to cut
sheer	thin, steep
stationary	immovable
stationery	paper
than	as compared with
then	at that time
their	belonging to them
there	in that place
they're	they are
to	a preposition
too	excessively; also
two	the number
waive	to set aside
wave	a swell of water; a gesture
weather	atmospheric conditions
whether	if
who's	contraction of "who is" or "who has"
whose	possessive form of who

In the preceding list, only enough of each word's meaning is given to help you distinguish between the words in each group. Several meanings are left out entirely. For more complete definitions, consult a dictionary.

4.2 FREQUENTLY MISUSED WORDS

The following words tend to be misused for reasons other than their sound. Reference books (including the *Random House College Dictionary*, revised edition; Follett's *Modern American Usage*; and Fowler's *Modern English Usage*) can help you with similar questions of usage:

a lot: When the writer means "many," *a lot* is always two separate words, never one.

aggravate/irritate: *Aggravate* means "to make things worse." Sitting in the smoke-filled room *aggravated* his sinus condition. *Irritate* means "to annoy." Her constant questions *irritated* [not *aggravated*] me.

anticipate/expect: *Anticipate* means "to prepare for": Macy's *anticipated* increased demand for athletic shoes in spring by ordering in November. In formal usage, it is incorrect to use *anticipate* for *expect*: I *expected* (not *anticipated*) a better response to our presentation than we actually got.

compose/comprise: The whole comprises the parts:

The company's distribution division *comprises* four departments.

The following usage is incorrect:

> The company's distribution division *is comprised of* four departments.

In that construction, *is composed of* or *consists of* would be preferable. It might be helpful to think of *comprise* as meaning "encompasses" or "contains."

continual/continuous: *Continual* refers to ongoing actions that have breaks:

> Her *continual* complaining will accomplish little in the long run.

Continuous refers to ongoing actions without interruptions or breaks:

> A *continuous* stream of paper came out of the fax machine.

convince/persuade: One is *convinced* of a fact or that something is true; one is *persuaded* by someone else to do something. The use of *to* with *convince* is unidiomatic—you don't convince someone to do something, you persuade them to do it.

correspond with: Use this phrase when you are talking about exchanging letters. Use *correspond to* when you mean "similar to." Use either *correspond with* or *correspond to* when you mean "relate to."

dilemma/problem: Technically, a *dilemma* is a situation in which one must choose between two undesirable alternatives. It shouldn't be used when no choice is actually involved.

disinterested: This word means "fair, unbiased, having no favorites, impartial." If you mean "bored" or "not interested," use *uninterested.*

etc.: This abbreviated form of the Latin phrase *et cetera* means "and so on" or "and so forth," so it is never correct to write *and etc.* The current tendency among business writers is to use English rather than Latin.

flaunt/flout: To *flaunt* is to be ostentatious or boastful; to *flout* is to mock or scoff at.

impact: Avoid using *impact* as a verb when *influence* or *affect* is meant.

imply/infer: Both refer to hints. Their great difference lies in who is acting. The writer *implies,* the reader *infers,* sees between the lines.

its/their: Use *its* to indicate possession by a singular entity such as a company, not *their.* "HP released its quarterly results" is correct; "HP released their quarterly results" is not.

lay: This word is a transitive verb. Never use it for the intransitive *lie.* (See Section 1.3.3.)

lend/loan: *Lend* is a verb; *loan* is a noun. Usage such as "Can you loan me $5?" is therefore incorrect.

less/fewer: Use *less* for uncountable quantities (such as amounts of water, air, sugar, and oil). Use *fewer* for countable quantities (such as numbers of jars, saws, words, page, and humans). The same distinction applies to *much* and *little* (uncountable) versus *many* and *few* (countable).

liable/likely: *Liable* means "responsible for": I will hold you *liable* if this deal doesn't go through. It is incorrect to use *liable* for "possible": Anything is *likely* (not *liable*) to happen.

literally: *Literally* means "actually" or "precisely"; it is often misused to mean "almost" or "virtually." It is usually best left out entirely or replaced with *figuratively.*

many/much: See *less/fewer.*

regardless: The *less* suffix is the negative part. No word needs two negative parts, so don't add *ir* (a negative prefix) to the beginning. There is no such word as *irregardless.*

try: Always follow with *to,* never *and.*

verbal: People in the business community who are careful with language frown on those who use *verbal* to mean "spoken" or "oral." Many others do say "verbal agreement." Strictly speaking, *verbal* means "of words" and therefore includes both spoken and written words. Follow company usage in this matter.

4.3 FREQUENTLY MISSPELLED WORDS

All of us, even the world's best spellers, sometimes have to check a dictionary for the spelling of some words. People who have never memorized the spelling of commonly used words must look up so many that they grow exasperated and give up on spelling words correctly.

Don't expect perfection and don't surrender. If you can memorize the spelling of just the words listed here, you'll need the dictionary far less often and you'll write with more confidence:

absence	asphalt
absorption	assistant
accessible	asterisk
accommodate	auditor
accumulate	
achieve	bankruptcy
advantageous	believable
affiliated	brilliant
analyze	bulletin
apparent	
appropriate	calendar
argument	campaign
	category

ceiling
changeable
clientele
collateral
committee
comparative
competitor
concede
congratulations
connoisseur
consensus
convenient
convertible
corroborate
criticism

definitely
description
desirable
dilemma
disappear
disappoint
disbursement
discrepancy
dissatisfied
dissipate

eligible
embarrassing
endorsement
exaggerate
exceed
exhaust
existence
extraordinary

fallacy
familiar
flexible
fluctuation
forty

gesture
grievous

haphazard
harassment
holiday

illegible
immigrant
incidentally
indelible
independent
indispensable
insistent
intermediary
irresistible

jewelry
judgment
judicial

labeling
legitimate
leisure
license
litigation

maintenance
mathematics
mediocre
minimum

necessary
negligence
negotiable
newsstand
noticeable

occurrence
omission

parallel
pastime
peaceable
permanent
perseverance
persistent
personnel
persuade
possesses
precede
predictable
preferred
privilege
procedure

proceed
pronunciation
psychology
pursue

questionnaire

receive
recommend
repetition
rescind
rhythmical
ridiculous

salable
secretary
seize
separate
sincerely

succeed
suddenness
superintendent
supersede
surprise

tangible
tariff
technique
tenant
truly

unanimous
until

vacillate
vacuum
vicious

4.4 TRANSITIONAL WORDS AND PHRASES

The following sentences don't communicate as well as they could because they lack a transitional word or phrase:

Production delays are inevitable. Our current lag time in filling orders is one month.

A semicolon between the two sentences would signal a close relationship between their meanings, but it wouldn't even hint at what that relationship is. Here are the sentences again, now linked by means of a semicolon, with a space for a transitional word or phrase:

Production delays are inevitable; ____, our current lag time in filling orders is one month.

Now read the sentence with *nevertheless* in the blank space. Then try *therefore, incidentally, in fact,* and *at any rate* in the blank. Each substitution changes the meaning of the sentence.

Here are some transitional words (conjunctive adverbs) that will help you write more clearly:

accordingly	furthermore	moreover
anyway	however	otherwise
consequently	incidentally	still
finally	likewise	therefore
	meanwhile	

The following transitional phrases are used in the same way:

as a result	in other words
for example	in the second place
in fact	on the other hand
	to the contrary

When one of these words or phrases joins two independent clauses, it should be preceded by a semicolon and followed by a comma:

The consultant recommended a complete reorganization; moreover, she suggested that we drop several products.

Answer Keys

CHAPTER 1

1. b
2. b
3. c
4. d
5. d
6. b
7. a
8. a
9. a
10. sense, select, perceive
11. d
12. a
13. b
14. information, people
15. a
16. c
17. d
18. dilemma, lapse

CHAPTER 2

1. d
2. d
3. constructive
4. d
5. a
6. a
7. b
8. parliamentary
9. virtual
10. telepresence
11. decode
12. c
13. d
14. a
15. d
16. d
17. c
18. a
19. a

CHAPTER 3

1. d
2. d
3. b
4. b
5. c
6. d
7. ethnocentrism

8. stereotyping
9. d
10. a
11. c
12. b
13. nonverbal
14. a
15. d
16. a
17. b
18. b

CHAPTER 4

1. b
2. c
3. a
4. general purpose
5. b
6. a
7. c
8. c
9. d
10. d
11. digital, nondigital
12. d
13. a
14. b
15. d
16. direct
17. indirect
18. a
19. a

CHAPTER 5

1. a
2. d
3. d
4. b
5. c
6. c
7. passive
8. active
9. b
10. b
11. c
12. a
13. a
14. c
15. c
16. examples

17. differences, similarities
18. a
19. b
20. inverted pyramid
21. c

CHAPTER 6

1. d
2. a
3. c
4. a
5. b
6. c
7. d
8. b
9. b
10. a
11. c
12. b
13. white space
14. c
15. a
16. c
17. d
18. a
19. b

CHAPTER 7

1. a
2. b
3. b
4. c
5. brand community
6. c
7. brand socialization
8. b
9. a
10. d
11. c
12. b
13. a
14. c
15. d
16. b
17. a
18. b
19. c
20. c
21. d
22. d
23. podcast channel

CHAPTER 8

1. b
2. a
3. d
4. c
5. b
6. d
7. c
8. direct
9. a
10. b
11. good news *or* positive news
12. d
13. d
14. b
15. a
16. d
17. c

CHAPTER 9

1. h
2. d
3. c
4. a
5. a
6. c
7. c
8. buffer
9. c
10. d
11. b
12. c
13. c
14. c
15. b
16. a
17. d

CHAPTER 10

1. b
2. d
3. d
4. b
5. c
6. d
7. c
8. emotional
9. logical
10. b
11. b
12. c
13. c
14. b
15. a
16. a
17. a
18. a
19. d

CHAPTER 11

1. a
2. informational

3. analytical
4. proposals
5. d
6. d
7. primary
8. secondary
9. a
10. c
11. d
12. a
13. c
14. d
15. a
16. b
17. information architecture
18. a
19. b
20. a

CHAPTER 12

1. d
2. b
3. a
4. c
5. a
6. c
7. a
8. b
9. d
10. d
11. localizing
12. b
13. d
14. b
15. d
16. d
17. d
18. data visualization
19. c
20. d
21. c

CHAPTER 13

1. c
2. b
3. a
4. transmittal
5. synopsis
6. executive summary
7. a
8. c
9. b
10. c
11. d
12. d
13. d

CHAPTER 14

1. linear, nonlinear
2. d
3. b
4. b

5. a
6. a
7. b
8. b
9. c
10. c
11. b
12. d
13. a
14. transitions, builds
15. c
16. d
17. b
18. d
19. d
20. d
21. b
22. c
23. d.
24. a

CHAPTER 15

1. b
2. quality of hire
3. b
4. b
5. b
6. d
7. chronological
8. functional
9. combination
10. d
11. a
12. b
13. a
14. a
15. b
16. c
17. c
18. c
19. keyword searches
20. plain text
21. a

CHAPTER 16

1. a
2. b
3. b
4. b
5. b
6. structured
7. d
8. d
9. d
10. b
11. c
12. c
13. a
14. a
15. c
16. d
17. a
18. c

ANSWER KEY FOR "IMPROVE YOUR GRAMMAR, MECHANICS, AND USAGE" EXERCISES

CHAPTER 1

1.19. boss's (1.1.4)
1.20. sheep (1.1.3)
1.21. 1990s (1.1.3)
1.22. Joneses, stopwatches (1.1.3)
1.23. attorneys (1.1.3)
1.24. copies (1.1.3)
1.25. employees' (1.1.4)
1.26. sons-in-law, businesses (1.1.3, 1.1.4)
1.27. parentheses (1.1.3)
1.28. Ness's, week's (1.1.4)

CHAPTER 2

2.16. its (1.2.5)
2.17. their (1.2.5)
2.18. its (1.2.5)
2.19. their (1.2.1)
2.20. his or her (1.2.3)
2.21. his or her (1.2.3)
2.22. a, them (1.2.3, 1.2.4)
2.23. Who (1.2.4)
2.24. whom (1.2.4)
2.25. its (1.2.5)

CHAPTER 3

3.13. b (1.3.1)
3.14. b (1.3.1)
3.15. a (1.3.1)
3.16. b (1.3.5)
3.17. a (1.3.5)
3.18. a (1.3.4)
3.19. b (1.3.4)
3.20. b (1.3.4)
3.21. a (1.3.4)
3.22. b (1.3.4)

CHAPTER 4

4.16. greater (1.4.1)
4.17. perfect (1.4.1)
4.18. most interesting (1.4.1)
4.19. hardest (1.4.1)
4.20. highly placed, last-ditch (1.4.2)
4.21. top-secret (1.4.2)
4.22. 30.year-old (1.4.2)
4.23. all-out, no-holds-barred struggle (1.4)
4.24. tiny metal (1.4)
4.25. usual cheerful, prompt service (1.4)

CHAPTER 5

5.85. good (1.5)
5.86. surely (1.5)
5.87. sick (1.5)
5.88. well (1.5)
5.89. good (1.5)
5.90. faster (1.5.2)
5.91. better (1.5.2)
5.92. any (1.5.1)
5.93. ever (1.5.1)
5.94. can, any (1.5.1)

CHAPTER 6

6.26. leading (1.6.1)
6.27. off (1.6.1)
6.28. aware of (1.6.1)
6.29. to (1.6.1)
6.30. among (1.6.1)
6.31. for (1.6.1)
6.32. to (1.6.1)
6.33. from (1.6.1)
6.34. not only in (1.6.1)
6.35. into (1.6.1)

CHAPTER 7

7.17. b (1.6.2)
7.18. b (1.6.1)
7.19. a (1.6.1)
7.20. b (1.6.1)
7.21. b (1.6.1)
7.22. a (1.6.1)
7.23. a (1.6.3)
7.24. b (1.6.2)
7.25. b (1.6.3)
7.26. b (1.6.3)

CHAPTER 8

8.22. b (1.7.3)
8.23. a (1.7.2)
8.24. b (1.7.6)
8.25. a (1.7.4)
8.26. b (1.7.4)
8.27. b (1.7.6)
8.28. a (1.7.6)
8.29. b (1.7.4)
8.30. a (1.7.3)
8.31. b (1.7.2)

CHAPTER 9

9.25. c (2.6)
9.26. a (2.6)
9.27. b (2.6)
9.28. a (2.6)
9.29. b (2.6)
9.30. c (2.6)
9.31. b (2.6)
9.32. a (2.6)
9.33. c (2.6)
9.34. b (2.6)

CHAPTER 10

10.27. a (2.4)
10.28. a (2.5)
10.29. c (2.4)
10.30. a (2.5)
10.31. b (2.5)
10.32. b (2.4)
10.33. a (2.4)
10.34. c (2.4)
10.35. b (2.4)
10.36. c (2.5)

CHAPTER 11

11.20. b (2.1)
11.21. a (2.2)
11.22. b (2.1)
11.23. a (2.1)
11.24. b (2.2, 2.3)
11.25. a (2.1)
11.26. b (2.2, 2.1)
11.27. a (2.2)
11.28. b (2.2)
11.29. a (2.2, 2.3)

CHAPTER 12

12.19. b (2.7)
12.20. a (2.8)
12.21. c (2.7)
12.22. b (2.8)
12.23. a (2.7)
12.24. b (2.7)
12.25. c (2.8)
12.26. a (2.8, 2.7)
12.27. c (2.8, 2.7)
12.28. a (2.8)

CHAPTER 13

13.10. b (2.10)
13.11. b (2.11)
13.12. a (2.11)
13.13. b (2.10)
13.14. c (2.10)
13.15. a (2.11)
13.16. c (2.10, 2.12)
13.17. b (2.10)
13.18. b (2.11)
13.19. c (2.10, 2.12)

CHAPTER 14

14.15. c (3.1, 3.3)
14.16. a (3.1, 3.3)
14.17. c (3.2)
14.18. a (3.1)
14.19. c (3.3)
14.20. a (3.1, 3.2)
14.21. b (3.1, 3.3)
14.22. b (3.1, 3.3)
14.23. a (3.2)
14.24. c (3.1)

CHAPTER 15

15.18. except (4.1)
15.19. device (4.1)
15.20. loath (4.1)
15.21. who's (4.1)
15.22. a lot (4.2)
15.23. judgment (4.3)
15.24. regardless (4.2)

15.25. accommodate (4.3)
15.26. imply (4.2)
15.27. to (4.2)

CHAPTER 16

16.21. c (3.4)
16.22. a (3.4)

16.23. a (3.4)
16.24. b (3.4)
16.25. b (3.4)
16.26. a (3.4)
16.27. b (3.4)
16.28. b (3.4)
16.29. a (3.4)
16.30. c (3.4)

Brand, Organization, Name, and Website Index

A

Adobe Acrobat. See Subject Index
Adobe Illustrator, 382
Adobe Photoshop, 382
Aetna, 269
Air-Trak, 397
Al-Taee, Mohammed, xlvii
Alcon Laboratories, 481
AllTop, 482
American Institute of Certified Public
    Accountants, 139
American Psychological Association
    (APA), 410, 427
Apple, 110, 439
Apple Keynote, 445, 453
Archer Daniels Midland, 132
Arnett, Will, 441
Atkinson, Cliff, 465
Audacity, 211
AuthorStream app, 456
Autodesk AREA, 23

B

Badgeville, 19
Behance, xlvi
Berry, Tim, 406
Bhatia, Sonpreet, 320
Blue Man Group, 42
Blumenthal, Neil, 360
BMW, 321
Boeing, 408
Bovée & Thill, 22
Boynton, Andy, 40
Brown, Dan, 158
Bunchball, 19, 191
Burns, Ursula, 132
Business Communication Headline
    News, 198

C

C&S Holdings*, 394
Calhoun, Sarah, 287–288, 305
Campbell Mithun, 543
CareerBuilder, 481, 500, 513
CD Baby, 129
Cell Genesys, 247
Cemex, 36–37, 59
Cisco, 33

Cisco Webex, 482
City Sourced app, 293
Click Software, 226
Coca-Cola, 193
CollegeRecruiter.com, 481
Consumer Electronics Show, 247
Craigslist, xlv
Creative Commons, 136, 137
Crutchfield, 221
Cube Rules, xlvii
Curves, 315

D

Databox app, 324
Delany Music*, 160, 161
Dice.com, 481
Diversity Now app, 69
DiversityWorking.com, 70
Dolce & Gabbana, 360
Dragon Dictation app, 138
Dropbox app, 428
Duarte, Nancy, 442, 445

E

Electronic Frontier Foundation, 27
Electrovision*, 413
EQ Industrial Services, 284
Ernst & Young, 69
Evernote app, 103, 337
Expedia, 249
EY, 68–69, 89

F

Facebook. See Subject Index
FedEx, 559
Fender Guitar, 190
Fezzari Bicycles, 303
Fisher, Bill, 40
Foursquare, 19, 23, 191, 220
Fraley, Gregg, 133
Freedcamp app, 41

G

Gamification Wiki, 19
Garage Technology Ventures, 342,
    399–400, 429
Garcia, Gilberto, 37

Genius Scan app, 170
Get Satisfaction, 198, 225–226, 240
Gibaldi, Joseph, 562
Gilboa, David, 360, 388
Glover, Ron, 78
Goldstein, Kurt, 290
Gollin, George, 489
Google. See Subject Index
Google+, 192, 194, 303, 484
Google Translate, 94
GoPro, 186–187, 212
Gozaik, 499
Gruber, Peter, 450

H

H&R Block, 98–99, 120
Hailo, 251–252, 274
Harley-Davidson, 108
Heath, Chip, 119
Heath, Dan, 119
Hewlett, Bill, 399, 474
Hewlett-Packard (HP), 399, 474–475
Hightail app, 232
Hillenbrand, Laura, 158
Hipmunk, 387
Hot Stix Golf, 249
Hsieh, Tony, 512, 537
Hunt, Andrew, 361

I

IBM, 78, 206, 312
Ignite, 145
IMDiversity, 481
Indeed.com, 481, 482
Indian Motorcycle, 195
Indian Wells Golf Resort, 249
InfoTech*, 256
InnoCentive, 21
Instagram, 383
Instapaper app, 329
International Academy of Digital Arts
    and Sciences, 249
International Federation of Red Cross, 373
InternshipPrograms.com, 481
Iron to Iron, 171
Israel, Shel, 98
iTranslate app, 81
iTunes, 211

*Indicates a fictional company used in examples or exercises.

J

Jefferson Rabb Web Design, 158–159, 176
JetBlue, 2–3, 28, 222, 237
Jibber Jobber, xlvii
Jobfox, 500
Jobster, 481, 500
Johnstone, Morgan, 2
JWS Remodeling Solutions*, 368–369

K

K&J Brick*, 93
Kaixin001, 192, 195
Kawasaki, Guy, 399, 429
Kelly Services, 314–315
Kent, Muhtar, 193
Kentucky Cabinet for Economic
       Development, 314
Knitting Warehouse, 218
Kohut, Abby, 513

L

Lahiri, Jhumpa, 158
LensCrafters, 360
Lettr app, 239
Lie-Nielsen Toolworks, 197
LinkedIn. See Subject Index
Locale app, 58
Lockheed Martin, 192
LogMeIn app, 412
Looney Launch, 284
Lopez, Maribel, 15
Luxottica, 360

M

MacNeil, Natalie, 127–128, 150
Malloy, James, 478–479
Marketo, 196
Maslow, Abraham, 290
Matthews, 210
MediaFire app, 428
Mehta, Puneet, 320
Mele, Nico, 17
Merck, 69
Microsoft Notepad, 499
Microsoft Office, 20, 370
Microsoft Outlook, 21
Microsoft PowerPoint. See PowerPoint in
       Subject Index
Microsoft Word, 499
Mobile Marketing Association, 304
Mobile Podcaster app, 191
MobileFever, 226
Modern Language Association (MLA), 410,
       427, 562, 565–567
Monster.com, 481, 500
MonsterCollege, 481
Moreno, Linda, 413
Motley Fool, 21l, 399, 400
MyCityWay, 320–321, 352

N

Nelson Norman Group, 148
Net-Temps, 481
Nike, 301
Nitro, 19, 191
Nixon, Gord, 70
Note Taker HD, 15
Notebook app, 103
NounPlus app, 174

O

O'Donnell & Associates*, 401
Oakley, 360
One Note app, 337
One Page Love, 343
Online Writing Lab, 403

P

Packard, Dave, 399, 474
Pages app, 144
Pandora, 400
Patchirajan, Archana, 320
Pearltrees, 336, 337
Personal Branding Blog, xlv
Pfizer, 43
Photoshop, 382
Pinterest, 4, 22, 198, 336, 519
PlayStation, 372
Pocket app, 18
Pocket Letter Pro app, 265
Point1 Promotions*, 236
PolicyPlan Insurance Services, 283
Prezi, 445, 453, 455–456
Principato, Peter, 441, 442, 467
Principato-Young Entertainment,
       441–442, 467
ProAudioLand, 190
PRSA Ethics app, 26

Q

Quizzle, 197
Quora, 198

R

Rabb, Jefferson, 58–159, 176
Raider, Jeffrey, 361
Ray-Ban, 360
Razer, 248
Red Ants Pants, 287–288, 305
Red Cross, 373
Redbooth app, 400
Reddit, 336
Reichert, Bill, 342
Renren, 192
Reputation Mechanics, 19
Reynolds, Garr, 453, 461
Riley Guide, 481
Rothschild, Ashley, 528
Royal Bank of Canada, 70

S

Sachdev, Rahul, 240
Sage Evolution Dashboard
       app, 324
Schoendorf, Joe, 15
Schwabel, Dan, 64
Scoop.It, 22, 198, 336
Second Life, 98
Segway, 23
Shaker Consulting Group, 521
She Takes on the World, 127–128, 150
Shift, 37
Shreve, Anita, 158
Shteyngart, Gary, 158
SimplyHired.com, 481
SketchUp, 382
Skype, 521
Skype app, 519
SlideShare, 456, 466, 473
SlideShark app, 459
Smith, Michael, 24
Social Media Examiner, 191
Social Oomph app, 194
Solar City, 249
Solis, Brian, 206
SongThrong.com, 247
Sony, 372
South by Southwest, 356
Steinway, 238
Sunglass Hut, 360
SunStar Sports, 25, 26

T

Target, 257
TED, 473
Tobak, Steve, 119
Tuckman, Bruce, 40
Tufte, Edward R., 374
Turtledove, Robert, 120
Twaronite, Karen, 69, 89
TweetBeep, 335
TweetDeck, 335, 466
TweetMyJobs.com, 481
Twitter. See Subject Index

U

United Way, 249
Unity network, 192
Uno Noteband, 16
UPS, 559
USA Hockey, 395
USA Water Polo, 314
USAJOBS, 481

V

Vail Products, 282
Vargas, Lauren, 269
Versace, 360
Videoshop app, 383

VisualCV, 499
VMWare, 478–479, 501
Volt, 500

W

Wagner, Katie, 191
Walmart, 209, 248–249
Warby Parker, 360–361, 388
Webby Awards, 249
Webcor Builders, 283
WebEx Mobil app, 48
Weinberg, Tamar, 206

WhatsApp app, 19, 111
Whole Foods, 196
Wikipedia, 42
Winnebago Industry, 248
Woertz, Patricia, 132
WordPress, 372
WorldLingo, 88
Worldwide Web Consortium, 299

X

Xerox Corporation, 22, 132, 206
XtremityPlus*, 284

Y

Yahoo! Answers, 198
Yelp app, 267
Yolink, 336
Young, Paul, 442
YouTube. See Subject Index

Z

Zappos, 43, 197, 343, 498, 512–513, 521, 537
ZOHO, 22, 395
Zotero, 336

Subject Index

A

a lot, 595
a/an, 583
abbreviations, 592–593
    punctuation with, 547–548
    for states, 557, 558
abstract, in reports, 407, 432
abstract words, 140, 153, 573
abusive language, 265
academic degrees, 592
academic journals, as resources, 334
acceptance letters, 406, 533–535
accountability, professionalism and, 134
accuracy
    of information, 104, 363
    of visuals, 385
achievement, congratulating people on, 238–239
achievement need, 290
achievements section, on résumés, 493
Acrobat. See Adobe Acrobat
acronyms, 592
    in email messages, 202
    in instant messages, 203
action, persuasive requests for, 299, 300
action items, in oral presentations, 452
action phase, of AIDA model, 293, 299, 302, 518
action plan, in reports, 366
action verbs, 577
    in reports, 422
    on résumés, 490
active listening, 41, 50, 62
active voice, 137, 138, 153, 579
address, proper forms of, 549, 550
addressee notation, 552
addresses
    for envelopes, 556–557
    for international correspondence, 84
    style for, 593
adjectives, 580–588
    coordinate, 588
    placement of, 166, 167
    predicate, 580, 585
adjustments, 229, 243
    granting, 233–234, 235
    persuasive requests for, 299
    refusing, 265, 265
    requesting, 229, 231

Adobe Acrobat
    commenting in, 412
    for reports and proposals, 371
    for résumés, 499
adventure and distraction needs, 290
adverbs, 581–582
    conjunctive, 581, 583, 587, 597
    placement of, 166, 167
advertising
    deceptive, 27
    of job openings, 483
    media specialists for, 290
    online, 304
    social media and, 194, 304
    truth in, 304–305
aesthetic appreciation, need for, 290
affiliation and belonging needs, 290
age bias, 131, 132
age differences, culture and, 76
agenda
    for meetings, 45, 46
    in oral presentations, 460
agendas, hidden, 38
aggravate/irritate, 595
agreement
    pronoun-antecedent, 576
    subject-verb, 578, 583–584
AIDA plan, 293–294, 308
    for entertainment pitches, 442
    for job application letters, 516–518
    for persuasive requests, 299, 300
    for proposals, 325, 367
    for sales messages, 302
alcohol testing, 522
almanacs, 334
American Development Model (ADM), 395
among/between, 582
analogies, faulty, 296
analogy, arguing by, 294
analytical reports, 321, 322, 355
    checklist for, 327
    direct approach for, 345, 366
    example of, 413–427
    indirect approach for, 345–347, 366
    memo format for, 365–366
    organization of, 345–348
    planning, 344–349
    purpose of, 344
    statement of purpose for, 323

2 + 2 approach to, 346, 347–348
    types of, 344
    yardstick approach to, 346, 349
Android devices, 110
anecdotes, 296
animation, in slide shows, 459
announcements
    company, 267
    negative, 263
    in social media, 189
antecedents, 575, 576
anticipate/expect, 595
anxiety, speech, 464–465
APA style, 427, 565, 566
apologies, 255, 257
    to customers, 234, 264–265
apostrophes, 589
    for plurals, 574
    with possessives, 574, 576
appeals, emotional versus logical, 294–296
appearance
    in job interviews, 525, 526–528
    as nonverbal communication, 53, 54–55
appendixes, in reports, 409
applicant tracking systems, 22, 490, 506
application letters, 513–518, 545
appositives, 588
appreciation, messages of, 239
area chart, 377, 391
arguments
    logical, 294
    persuasive, 5
Arial font, 172
articles, definite versus indefinite, 583
as if/like, 583
ASCII text, 499
"ask," the, 400
assistive technologies, 78
attachments, 176
    résumés as, 499
attacks, personal, 57, 295
attention
    audience's, 450
    during meetings, 49
    in job interviews, 530
    listening and, 51
    to nonverbal cues, 54

attention line, 552
attention phase, of AIDA model, 293, 299, 302, 516
attention-getters, 299, 302
    for job application letters, 516, 517
    for oral presentations, 450
attitudes, changing, 299
audience
    adapting to, 128–132
    analyzing, 101–103
    arousing interest of, 450
    building relationship with, 132–134
    for business blogs, 206
    composition of, 101, 102, 443
    decoding of messages by, 12–13
    emotional versus logical appeals to, 294–296
    expectations of, 12, 103
    feedback from, 112
    geographic distribution of, 101
    holding attention of, 451–452
    hostile, 291, 296, 443, 465
    information needs of, 103
    input from, 103
    level of understanding of, 103, 443
    media preferences of, 112
    mindsets of, 444
    needs of, 132, 289, 290, 301
    offending, 130
    for online content, 342
    for online presentations, 466–467
    for oral presentations, 442, 443, 444
    for persuasive messages, 289, 290
    in social media, 14
    primary, 101
    probable reaction of, 103, 115, 345, 443
    questions from, 465
    for reports, 361
    response of, 13
    for résumés, 486–487
    size of, 101, 443, 449–450
    skeptical, 345
audience-centered approach, 8–9, 31, 128–129
    in negative messages, 257–258
    for résumés, 489–490
    for sales messages, 305
audience profile, 101–103
audio equipment, 211
audio recording, 337
augmented reality, 191
author-date system, 409, 562
authority, reference to, 117
authorization
    letter of, 406
    of reports, 364
auxiliary verbs, 577
awkward references, 166, 168

B

B Corporation, 388
Baby Boomers, 76, 77

back-translation, 88
backchannels, 209, 444, 465, 471
background checks, by employers, 489
backgrounders, 340
bad news
    communicating, 130
    deemphasizing, 259
    opening with, 255
    see also negative messages
bad/badly, 581
bait and switch, 305
balance
    as design element, 170, 374
    in reports, 364
    between visuals and text, 384
bandwidth, for mobile devices, 109, 110
bar charts, 378, 379, 391
barcodes, 111
bcc (blind courtesy copy), 200
behavioral interviews, 520, 540
behavioral targeting, 304
beliefs, implicit, 73
benefits
    to audience, 130, 301
    employment, 532
bias-free language, 131–132, 153
biases
    of audience, 12
    cultural, 73, 78
    of sources, 329
bibliography
    APA style for, 565, 566
    Chicago style for, 563–564
    MLA style for, 566–567
    for reports, 409, 427, 432
big data, 21, 380
Bing, 335
blaming, 137, 234
    of customers, 265
    in negative messages, 257
block format, for letters, 554, 555
blogosphere, 205
blogs/blogging, 188, 204, 216
    business, 204–209, 482
    checklist for, 209
    combining with podcasts, 211
    company, 22
    by employees, 19
    legal aspects of, 27
    personal style in, 205
    as research source, 329
    as social media hub, 205
    three-step process for, 206–207
    tips for, 208
    topics for, 205
    value-added content via, 197
blueprint slides, 461
body
    of claims requests, 229
    of condolence messages, 239–240
    of job application letters, 516–517
    of job interviews, 530–531

    of memos, 559
    of messages, 115
    of negative messages, 255–257, 258–260
    of oral presentations, 451–452
    of persuasive messages, 293, 299
    of positive messages, 232–233
    of proposals, 368–369, 405, 411
    of reports, 364–366, 405, 409
    of routine requests, 226–227
    of sales messages, 303
body art, 56
body language, 52
    in job interviews, 526
boldface type, 172
bookmarking sites, 336
bots, 202
brackets, 590
bragging, 136
brainstorming, 113–114
    using blogs for, 206
    in teams, 39
brand, personal, xlvii–xlviii
brand communities, 193, 216
brand socialization, 193, 216
branded channels, 22, 195
brevity, in international correspondence, 84
broadcasting mindset, 13–14
buffers, 258, 264, 278
builds, in slide shows, 459
bulleted lists, 164
    in reports, 421, 423
    on slides, 454, 458
Bureau of Labor Statistics, 517
business books, 334
business card scanning, 482
business communication, effect of mobile technology on, 17–18
business cultures, adapting to, 78–79
business model, 341
Business Model Canvas, 342
business news, keeping up with, 481
business partners, finding via social networks, 193
business plans, 340, 341–342
business reports. See reports
business-to-business communications, 265
buzzwords, 140, 141

C

cab-hailing service, 251–252
call to action, 303
Canada, 70, 81
Canada Post, 557, 558
Canadian addresses, 549
capital letters
    in email, 202
    on slides, 459
capitalization, 591–599
captions, 385, 391
career, communication skills and, 3–4
career counseling, 484
career objective, on résumés, 491

career planning, xli–xlviii
career self-assessment, xlv
career summary, on résumés, 491–492
case, of pronouns, 575–576
categories, report organization based
  on, 341
causation, 331, 355
  correlation and, 296
cause and effect, 119, 296, 375
  as way to develop paragraphs, 147
cc (courtesy copy) function, 200, 553
cell phones. See mobile phones
cellular versus mobile, 110
cement business, 36–37
centered type, 171
CEOs, use of social media by, 187–188
chalkboards, 453
champions, product, 19, 303
change, resistance to, 40–41
channels (communication), 10, 12, 31
  breakdowns in, 11
  for negative messages, 253
  for oral presentations, 444
  for persuasive messages, 290
  for résumés, 487
  selecting, 106–112
  see also media/medium
character spacing, 547
chartjunk, 374
charts. See bar charts; line charts
check boxes, 371
checklists
  for adapting the three-step writing
    process to reports, 327
  for blogging, 209
  for composing business reports and
    proposals, 370
  for conducting interviews, 340
  for creating email messages, 201
  for creating visuals, 387
  for creating negative messages, 261
  for developing persuasive messages, 297
  for enhancing presentations with
    visuals, 463
  for granting claims and adjustments
    requests, 234
  for handling bad news about
    transactions, 265
  for improving intercultural
    communication skills, 89
  for improving meeting productivity, 47
  for improving nonverbal communication
    skills, 54
  for job interviews, 529, 532
  for making claims and requesting
    adjustments, 229
  for overcoming barriers to effective
    listening, 52
  for planning stage, 120
  for podcasts, 212
  for producing formal reports and
    proposals, 428

for proofreading, 175
for refusing claims, 266
for revising business messages, 168
for sending goodwill messages, 240
for using IM productively, 204
for writing application letters, 518
for writing follow-up messages, 536
for writing negative employment
  messages, 274
for writing résumés, 501
for writing routine replies and positive
  messages, 233
for writing routine requests, 227
for writing stage, 150
Chicago Manual of Style, 410, 562, 591
children, marketing to, 305
China/Chinese, 73, 71, 550
  correspondence with, 83, 84, 85, 86
chronological résumés, 487–488, 496, 506
chronology, report organization
  based on, 341
circular reasoning, 295
citation management, 336
citations, 409
  APA style for, 565
  Chicago style for, 562–563
  MLA style for, 565–566
claims, 229, 243
  checklist for, 229
  granting, 233–234, 235, 299
  implied, 305
  making, 229, 231
  persuasive, 299
  refusing, 265, 265
clarity, editing for, 166–168
classification, as way to develop paragraphs,
  147
clauses, 142, 143, 584
  parallelism in, 165
  restrictive and nonrestrictive, 588
  see also dependent clauses; independent
    clauses
clichés, 136, 140, 141
close
  of claims requests, 229
  complimentary, 173, 551, 591
  of condolence messages, 240
  importance of, 162
  of job application letters, 518
  of job interviews, 531–532
  of meetings, 46
  of messages, 115
  of negative messages, 257, 260, 265
  of oral presentations, 452–453
  of persuasive messages, 293, 299
  of positive messages, 233
  of reports, 366, 405, 409
  of routine requests, 227
  of proposals, 370, 411, 405
  of sales messages, 303
close date, for job postings, 518
closed questions, 339, 355

clothing
  for job interviews, 527–528
  as nonverbal communication, 53
  work, 55
clothing styles, cultural differences in, 81
cloud-based services, 191
cloud computing, 42, 43
codes of ethics, 26, 31
cold calling, 193
collaboration
  defined, 37, 62
  using mobile devices, 43, 44
  as purpose of message, 101, 113
  use of social networks for, 193
  technology for, 21
  web-based, 48–49
collaborative apps, 337
collaborative platforms, 21, 42
  Cemex's use of, 36–37
collaborative writing, 41–42
collective nouns, 575, 578
college career center, xlv, 481,
  484, 499
colons, 587
  for introducing lists, 164
  in salutations, 551
color, on slides, 457, 458
combination résumés, 488, 506
comma splices, 585
commas, 587–589
commenting
  in Acrobat, 412
  on blogs, 22, 205
  online, 58, 188
committees, 37, 62
common nouns, 574
communication
  defined, 3, 31
  effective, 5, 6
  ethical, 24–27, 31
  external, 134
  flow of, 8
  unified, 43
  see also intercultural communication;
    nonverbal communication
communication barriers, 11, 31
communication process, 9–14
  culture and, 71
communication skills
  expected by employers, 7–8
  intercultural, 79–89
  value of, xliii, 3–4
communication style
  American, 79
  credibility and, 133
  cultural differences in, 82–83
  gender and, 76
communication technologies, cultural
  differences and, 75
communities of interest, 193
communities of practice,
  42, 193

community building, 302
  using blogs for, 206
  with social networks, 193, 194
community managers, 192
community Q&A, sites, 23, 198, 216
companies
  information about, 333
  negative news about, 267–270
  researching, 481–482, 523–524
company culture, 76
company documents, as source
  of information, 103
company image, projecting, 134
company names, 579
company news, using blogs for, 205
company policy
  hiding behind, 259
  for recommendation letters, 236
comparative degree
  of adjectives, 580
  of adverbs, 581–582
comparison, report organization
  based on, 340
comparison/contrast, as way to develop
  paragraphs, 147
compatibility, technical, 12
competition, analyzing, 301
complaint sites, 225–226
complaints, customer, 229, 231,
  267–269, 299
complement, of linking verb, 578, 585
completing stage, 99, 100, 159–176
  for business blogs, 208
  for email messages, 200
  for instant messages, 203
  for negative messages, 254–255
  for oral presentations, 460–464
  for persuasive messages, 292, 299, 300
  for podcasts, 211
  for reports and proposals, 400–427
  for résumés, 497–501
  for routine and positive messages,
    226–227, 228
complex sentences, 142, 144, 153, 584
compliance reports, 340
complimentary close, 173, 551, 591
compose/comprise, 595
compositional modes
  for digital media, 188–189
  for social networks, 194
compound-complex sentences, 142,
  153, 584
compound nouns, 574
compound sentences, 142, 143, 584
compound subjects, 583
compound words, 589
compromise, 40, 297
computer screens, legibility of, 342
computers, symbols on, 548
conciseness, 5
  editing for, 168, 169
conclusions, 331–332, 355

focusing on, 345, 346
  placement of, 366
  in reports, 325, 409, 426
concrete words, 140, 153, 573
condolence messages, 239–240
confidence, 8, 133
  in job interviews, 525
  in oral presentations, 452
confidentiality
  of instant messages, 204
  on job boards, 501
conflict, in teams, 39, 40
conformity, to group norms, 38
congratulations, 238–239
conjunctions, 142, 143, 146, 583, 585, 588
conjunctive adverbs, 581, 583, 587, 597
connectivity
  with mobile devices, 109
  radical, 17
connotation, 140, 153, 373
consensus, 452
consistency, as design element, 170, 374, 459
constructive feedback, 44–45, 62
consumers. See customers
content curation, 22, 195, 198, 216, 208
content listening, 49, 62
content management systems, 42, 62, 412
content managers, 336
content marketing, 194
content notes, 562–563
content of messages, evaluating, 159
content sharing, 22, 187, 188
content-sharing sites, 194–198
content snacking, 187
context, cultural, 73–74, 92
context awareness, 111
continual/continuous, 596
contractions, 589
contractors, independent, 3
contracts, 27, 31
  sales messages as, 305
contrast, as design principle, 374
conventions, in design, 374
conversation marketing, 302–303, 308
conversational tone, 135–136, 190
conversations, 106
  via digital media, 188
  intercultural, 86, 88
  listening in, 50
convince/persuade, 596
coordinate adjectives, 588
coordinating conjunctions, 583, 585, 588
copy notation, 553
copyright, 24, 31
  of photographs, 384
corporate blogs, 22
corporate culture, xliv
corporations, financial reporting by, 27
correction symbols, 568–59
corrections, on business documents, 548
correlation, 296, 331, 355
correlative conjunctions, 583

correspond with, 596
correspondence, international, 83–86, 87,
  549–551
courtesy, in business messages, 130, 234
courtesy copy (cc), 553
courtesy titles, 549, 550, 552
cover, for reports, 404, 414
cover letter
  for reports, 406
  for résumés, 513–518
credentials, to establish credibility, 133
credibility
  in analytic reports, 345
  of business blogs, 207
  establishing, 132–133, 153, 255, 291
  grammar errors and, 138
  in oral presentations, 451
  with persuasive messages, 291
  proofreading and, 174
  of sources, 329
credits, for photos, 384
criminal record, résumés and, 489
crisis communication, 269, 270
  using blogs for, 206
crisis management, 203, 269, 278
critical listening, 50, 62
critical thinking, 8
criticism
  giving, 44–45, 130
  online, 267–269
  in performance reviews, 273
  responding to, 190
cross-functional teams, 37
cross-tabulation, 331
crowdsourcing, xlv, 21, 209
cultural competency, 71–73, 92
cultural context, 73–74, 92
cultural differences, 69, 73–74
  in attitudes about work, 74
  in attitudes toward aging, 76
  in audience needs, 289
  business and, 78–79, 81
  in decision making, 73–74
  gender and, 76
  in negotiation 74
  in nonverbal communication, 75–76
  in personal pronoun use, 129
  persuasive messages and, 291
  in problem solving, 74
  religion and, 77
  in social behavior, 74–75
  when meeting new people, 57see also
    intercultural communication
cultural pluralism, 73, 92
culture
  decoding and, 12–13
  defined, 71, 92
  ethics and, 74
  formality of reports and, 362
  influences of, 71
  job interviews and, 528
  law and, 74

culture (*continued*)
learning of, 71–72
nonverbal communication and, 53
oral communication and, 86, 88
oral presentations and, 464
studying another, 79–80
U.S., 79
visuals and, 373
see also intercultural communication
curation, content, 195, 198
curriculum vitae (CV), 487
customer education, using blogs for, 206
customer satisfaction, 234
customer service, 255
text messaging for, 203
customer support, 225–226
using blogs for, 205
via social networking, 193
customer support communities, 198
customers
communicating with, 233–234, 235
communities of, 23
complaints from, 225–226, 229, 231, 299
denying claims by, 265, 265
interacting with via social networks, 193
needs of, 301
negative messages to, 264–265
online rumors by, 268–269
social media and, 2–3
customs forms, 559

D
dangling modifiers, 166, 167, 586
dashes, 589
data, 138
data
analyzing, 330
distortion of, 24, 386
using visuals to present, 375, 377–380
data usage, with mobile devices, 109
data visualization, 21, 380, 381, 391
databases
commercial, 334
company, 103
electronic, 334
online, 335
dates
for international correspondence, 84
format for, 548–549
deception
in advertising, 27
in sales messages, 304
decimal numbers, 593
decision making
cultural differences in, 73–74
mobile devices and, 17, 110
in teams, 37
decision-making meetings, 45
decoding, 10, 12–13, 31, 50, 71
decorative animation, 459
decorative art, for slides, 459
deductive reasoning, 294

deep Internet, 335
defamation, 27, 31, 265
definitions, in report introduction, 364
definitive adjectives, 580
delimitations, 367
delivery, of oral presentations, 464–467
delivery companies, 559
delivery cues, in speaking outline, 448
demographics, 289, 308
demonstrative pronouns, 575
denotation, 140, 153
dependability, professionalism and, 7, 134
dependent clauses, 142, 144, 143, 583, 584, 588, 591
description, as type of detail, 117
descriptive headings, 165, 176, 326, 327, 421
descriptive synopsis, 407
descriptive titles, for visuals, 385, 391
design
of documents, 170–173
principles of, 170, 373–374
proofing of, 174
of résumés, 497–498
of slides, 455–460
desire phase, of AIDA plan, 293, 299, 302, 516
desktop search engines, 336
destructive feedback, 44, 62
detail
as design element, 170
in reports, 364
types of, 117
diagrams, 108, 382, 383
Dietary Guidelines for Americans, 362–363, 475
digital channels
for business communication, 186–211
for oral media, 106, 107
for visual media, 108–109
for written media, 107, 108
digital information fluency, 7
digital media, compositional modes for, 188–189
dilemma/problem, 596
dining etiquette, 57
diplomacy, in business messages, 130
direct approach, 115, 123
for analytical reports, 345
for claims/adjustment requests, 229
for good-news messages, 237
for informational reports, 340
for letter of transmittal, 406
for negative messages, 253–254, 255–257, 263
for oral presentations, 446–447
for persuasive messages, 291, 293, 299
for refusing requests, 263
for replying to requests, 233
for reports, 325, 326, 366
for routine messages, 226, 227
direct-to-consumer news releases, 238
directness, culture and, 82
directories, as resources, 333, 334

disabilities, 78
disability bias, 131, 132
discovery techniques, 104
discrimination, employment, 271, 498, 530–531
disinterested, 596
distractions, 11, 19, 51
distribution
of messages, 175–176
of reports and proposals, 412, 428
diversity
defined, 69, 92
language, 71, 72
in workforce, 70
documentation
of sources, 336, 364, 562–567
of visuals, 385
documents
distribution of, 412, 428
embedded, 370–371
formatting of, 547–561
multimedia, 371
production of, 170–174
security of, 176
double negatives, 581
downward communication, 8
drawings, 382
drug testing, 522
due diligence reports, 344

E
e-portfolio, xlvi, 499, 500
economic systems, 81
economy, job search and, xlii
editing, of others' work, 162
education section, on résumés, 492
either/or, 578
electronic databases, 334
electronic forms, 371
electronic presentations, 453–460
ellipses, 590
em-dash, 589
email, 108, 188
advantages of, 198
as business communication medium, 198–202
bulk, 304
company policy for, 199
for interviews, 339
for job interview follow-up, 533, 534
for job interviews, 521
for responding to customer claims, 235
indiscriminate use of, 198
opt-in, 305
email address, personal, 491
email messages
checklist for, 201
company monitoring of, 199
distributing, 200
etiquette of, 58
formality of, 199
formatting of, 200, 202

legal aspects of, 199
planning of, 199
producing, 200
subject lines for, 199
three-step process for, 199–201
tips for, 202
typeface for, 200
writing of, 199
"tweetifying" opening lines for, 199
email newsletters, 305
email signature, 200, 216
embedded documents, 370–371
emoticons, 112, 199, 201, 202
emotional appeals, 294, 308
emotional intelligence, 9
emotions
color and, 457, 458
employee termination and, 273
in negative messages, 265
empathic listening, 50, 62
empathy, 12
emphasis
as design principle, 374
in sentences, 143–144
type styles for, 172
employees
attitudes toward social media, 187
blogging by, 19
body art and, 56
communication skills of, 7–8
email messages of, 199
ethics codes for, 26
functional IQ of, 19
inappropriate social networking by, 19
involvement in company decision making, 37
negative information for, 267
performance reviews of, 272–273
podcasts for, 211
religious practices of, 77
social network use of, 192
stresses on, 18
termination of, 273
use of mobile devices by, 17, 109, 110–111
virtual communities for, 42
whistleblowing by, 262
see also workforce
employers
use of applicant tracking systems by, 490
attributes sought in job candidates by, 522
background checks by, 489
ethical policies of, 26
expectations of, 7–8
job interviews by, 519–522
job recruiting by, 193, 479–481, 512–513
performance reviews by, 272–273
preemployment testing by, 522
recommendations from, 234
refusing recommendation requests from, 270–271

refusing to provide recommendations, 236
researching potential, 481–482
view of job market, xlii
employment
changing nature of, 3
legal aspects of, 27
negative messages about, 270–273
employment discrimination, 271
employment gaps, 488
employment interviews. See job interviews
employment messages
application letters, 513–518
résumés, 485–501
employment portfolio, xlvi–xlvii, 487
en-dash, 589
enclosure notation, 552–553
encoding, 10, 31, 71
endnotes, 409, 562, 563
endorsements, to establish credibility, 133
England, 550
English, plain, 136–137
English language, 81
enterprise IM systems, 21
enterprise instant messaging (EIM), 203
enterprise microblogging, 209
enterprise search engines, 336
enterprise systems, 42
entrepreneurs, 399–400
envelopes, 556–559
Equal Employment Opportunity Commission (EEOC), 522
equality, as American value, 79
errors, finding, 174
etc., 596
ethical aspects
of job interview questions, 531
of visuals, 374–375, 385, 386
ethical dilemmas, 25, 31
ethical lapses, 25, 31, 374–375
ethics audits, 26, 31
ethics, 105, 24, 31
codes of, 26, 33
in conducting research, 328
culture and, 74, 81
of using euphemisms, 131
of negative messages, 261–262
of persuasive message, 291
of quoting from sources, 331
of sales messages, 304–305
of storytelling approach, 119
ethnic bias, 131, 132
ethnocentrism, 72–73, 92
etiquette
business, 54–58
in business messages, 129–130
in conducting research, 329
cultural differences in, 75
defined, 9, 31
of follow-up messages, 533
for instant messaging, 204
for job application follow-up, 519
for negative messages, 255

in negative messages, 260
of networking, 484
online, 57–58
of sales messages, 305
in social settings, 57
workplace, 54–57
euphemisms, 130, 153
European Union, 27
evidence
for claims, 296
in outlining, 117
exaggeration, 375
example, as type of detail, 117
example/sample, 596
excel, striving to, 485
exclamation marks, 583, 587
executive dashboard, 324, 325
executive summary, 362, 407–408, 419, 432
for mobile messages, 148
in proposals, 410
exit strategy, 342
expectations
of audience, 103
of employers, 7–8
experience, shared, 13
experimental research, 337
expertise, credibility and, 133
experts, interviewing, 339
exports, 70
Express Mail International, 559
eye behavior, 52, 51

eye contact, 54
cultural differences in, 76
listening and, 51
in job interviews, 526
in oral presentations, 465

F

face-to-face communication, 24, 106, 112
face-to-face interviews, 339
Facebook
business use of, 191, 192
Coca-Cola use of, 193
for commenting, 58
for community building, 194
H&R Block use of, 98
Harley-Davidson on, 108
JetBlue on, 2
for job networking, 482, 484
legal aspects of, 190
recruiting via, 479
Steinway on, 238
messages on, 203
VMWare on, 478–479
facial expressions, 52, 76
facts, 5
double-checking, 363
sources for, 332–336
as type of detail, 117
failure analysis reports, 344
fair play, 40

faith-based employee groups, 77
fallacies, logical, 294–295
familiarity, emphasizing, 12
favors, declining, 263
feasibility reports, 344
features, of products, 301
Federal Trade Commission (FTC), 24, 27, 304, 305
feedback
    from audience, 130, 465–466
    in communication process, 10, 11, 31
    constructive, 44–45
    consumer, 267–269
    destructive, 44
    giving, 44–45
    in intercultural conversations, 88
    in listening process, 50
    media choice and, 112
    with oral media, 106
    in performance reviews, 273
    on reports and proposals, 324–325
    in social media, 188
figures, as type of detail, 117
file-hosting sites, 176
files, sending, 176
filters, communication, 11
financial reporting, 27
First Class Mail International, 559
first draft, 138, 159–162
first impressions
    of business documents, 547
    in job interviews, 530
flaunt/flout, 596
Flesch-Kincaid Grade Level index, 162
flipcharts, 453
flogs, 27, 208
flowcharts, 381–382, 391
focus groups, 339–340, 355
follow-up messages, after job interviews, 533–536
following up, on job application letters, 518–519
fonts, 172
    for slides, 459
    symbols in, 548
    see also type
food preferences, cultural differences in, 81
footers, 418
footnotes, 409, 562
foreign words, 592
forgetting, 50
form tools, 371
formal communication network, 8, 31
formality
    cultural differences in, 76
    of email messages, 202
    of instant messages, 203
    medium and, 112
    of oral presentations, 449–450
    of printed documents, 188
    of reports and proposals, 361–362, 400

of social media, 190
    of tone, 135, 161
formatting, of business documents, 173, 547–561
forms, electronic, 371
fractions, 579, 589, 594
franchising, 438
free-form slides, 454–455, 471
free writing, 104, 123
French, 82
functional animation, 459
functional résumés, 488, 506
fused sentences, 584–585
future orientation, 75

G

GAAP, 139
gamification, 19, 191
gaming technologies, 23
gender bias, 131, 132
gender differences, culture and, 76
general purpose, 101, 123
generalizations, hasty, 294
Generation X, 76, 77
Generation Y, 76, 77
generational differences, 76, 77
geofencing, 111
geographic information systems, 382
geography, report organization based on, 341
Germany, 82, 551
gerunds, 579
gestures, 52
    culture and, 75
    in job interviews, 526
Global Express Guaranteed, 559
globalization, 69–70, 80–81
Gmail, 203
goals, career, xliv
Golden Rule, 78
good news
    announcing, 237–238
    opening with, 232
goodwill messages, 238–240
Google
    diversity at, 78
    as search engine, 335
    YouTube and, 187
Google Documents, 453
Google Inside Search, 336
Google+, company use of, 187, 192, 195
government
    consumer information and, 27
    job websites for, 481
government publications, 334
government regulations, 304, 340
government terminology, 592
grade point average (GPA), on résumés, 492
grammar, 573, 580–586
    importance of, 138–139
grant proposals, 349

grapevine, 8
graphics, designing, 374
graphs, 377–379
see also charts
greetings, cultural differences in, 75
grooming
    for job interviews, 526–527
    for workplace, 55
group dynamics, 38–41, 62
group interviews, 520, 540
group norms, 38
groups
    development of, 39–40
    writing in, 41–42
    see also teams
groupthink, 38, 62
groupware, 42
guilt, admitting, 257

H

hairstyle, for job interviews, 527
hand gestures, 75
handouts, 456, 461
handshake, 57, 75
handwritten messages, 239, 547
hard-sell approach, 291
hashtags, 209
have/of, 583
headings, 165, 176
    informative versus descriptive, 326–327
    for mobile messages, 148
    in reports 370, 418, 421, 560–561
    in table of contents, 406, 416
    typefaces for, 172
headlines
    for blogs, 208
    for social media, 190
hearing, 50
hedging sentences, 166, 167
helping others, 290
Helvetica, 172
hidden agendas, 38, 62
high-context cultures, 73–74, 92
hiring, 512–513
    discrimination in, 498
    preemployment testing and, 522
hiring process, 479–481
honesty, 25, 105
    in business blogs, 208
    credibility and, 132
    in intercultural communication, 74
    with negative messages, 131
    on résumés, 489
    in social media, 190
    of sources, 329
    testing for, 522
    in visuals, 385
horizontal communication, 8
hostility, in audience, 291, 296, 443, 465
hub, for social networking, 194, 205
humanities style, 562–568

humor
    during business meals, 57
    in business messages, 136
    in intercultural communication, 78, 85, 362
    in oral presentations, 450
hyperbole, 133
hyperlinks, 342
    in online reports, 371
    in reports, 370–371
    in slide shows, 459
hyphenated adjectives, 580
hyphenated nouns, 574
hyphenation, justified type and, 171
hyphens, 589–597
    for word division, 594
hypothesis, 344, 355

I

ideas, generating, 104, 113–114
idiomatic phrases, 85, 88, 582
illustration
    as type of detail, 117
    as way to develop paragraphs, 147
illustrations, list of, 407, 416
IM. See instant messaging
image processing, 382, 383
immigration, 70
impact, 596
imperative mood, 579
implicit beliefs, 73
imply/infer, 596
importance, report organization
    based on, 340
in/into, 583
inclusiveness, culture and, 75
indefinite pronouns, 575
independent clauses, 142, 583, 584, 587, 588, 598
independent contractors, xli
index, for report, 410
indicative mood, 579
indirect approach, 115, 123
    for analytical reports, 345–347
    for informational reports, 340
    for letter of transmittal, 406
    for negative announcements, 263
    for negative employment messages, 270–271
    for negative messages, 253–254, 257–260, 263
    for negative news about transactions, 264
    for oral presentations, 446, 447
    for persuasive messages, 291, 293
    for refusing requests, 263
    for report synopses, 407
    for reports, 325, 326, 366
individualism, 79
inductive reasoning, 294
industries, information about, 333
infinitive phrase, for statement
    of purpose, 322

infinitives, 168, 169, 579
infographic résumés, 498
infographics, 384
informal communication network, 8, 31
information
    accuracy of, 104, 363
    completeness of, 363
    currency of, 330
    ethical, 105
    gathering, 103–105, 290, 327–332
    intentional omission of, 24
    organization of, 112–118
    pertinence of, 105
    practical, 5
    remembering, 51–52
    requesting, 227
    retrieving from memory, 13
    security and privacy of, 24
    transparency of, 24
    verification of, 329
    withholding, 105
information architecture, 343–344, 355
information overload, 18, 31
information requests, replying to, 233
information technology paradox, 18
informational meetings, 45
informational reports, 321, 322, 355
    checklist for, 327
    direct approach for, 340
    organizing, 340–341
    planning of, 340–344
    statement of purpose for, 323
    types of, 340
    website content as, 342–344
informative headings, 165, 176, 326, 327, 421, 425
informative synopsis, 407
informative titles, for visuals, 385, 391
informing, as purpose of message, 101, 113
initials, on memos, 559
inquiry messages, 533
inside address, 173, 549–551
instant messaging (IM), 21, 188, 202–204, 216
    business benefits of, 203
    casual tone of, 135
    checklist for, 204
    drawbacks of, 203
    etiquette of, 58
    for job interviews, 521
    for meetings, 48
    security of, 203
    three-step process for, 203
    tips for using, 204
    workplace use of, 203
integrity tests, 522
intellectual property, 27, 31, 328
intelligence
    emotional, 9
    practical, 76
interactive media, 112
interactive résumés, 499

interactivity
    social media and, 14
    with mobile devices, 18
intercultural communication, 69, 92
    challenges of, 70–71
    checklist for, 88
    components of, 80
    oral, 86, 88
    see also cultural differences; culture
interest phase, of AIDA plan, 293, 299, 302, 516
interjections, 583
international correspondence, 83–86, 87, 549–551
international mail, 559
International Mail Manual, 559
Internet
    for collaborative writing, 42–44
    for conducting surveys, 339
    distribution of reports via, 412
    evaluating resources on, 329
    finding information on, 334–336
    for job networking, 484
    hidden, 335
    job boards on, 481
    meetings on, 48–49
    posting résumés to, 499, 500
    see also websites
interoffice mail, 559–560
interpreters, 88, 464
interrogative adverbs, 581
interrogative pronouns, 575
interrupting, 51
interview simulators, 526, 527
interviews
    checklist for, 340
    research, 339–340
    see also job interviews
intimacy, in business messages, 136
intranet, 42
intransitive verbs, 578
introducing people, to each other, 57
introducing yourself, 57
introduction
    direct versus indirect approach for, 326
    for oral presentations, 450–451
    for proposals, 367, 411
    for reports, 364, 408, 418
    see also opening
introductory phrases, 586
inverted pyramid style, 148, 371
investment proposals, 349
iOS devices, 110
irregular verbs, 577–578
It is, 168, 169
italic type, 172592
Italy, 528

J

Japan, 57, 71, 83, 528
jargon, 85, 142

job applicants/candidates
  qualities employers seek in, xlii–xliv, 521
  interviewing of, 519–531
  networking by, 484
  personality of, 522
  recommendation requests from, 227, 229, 230
  refusing recommendation requests from, 270–271
  rejecting, 271–272
  responding to requests for recommendations from, 234, 236
  testing of, 522
job application letters, 513–518
  AIDA plan for, 516–518
  checklist for, 518
  follow-ups to, 518–519
job boards, 481
  posting résumés on, 500
job changes, frequent, 488
job descriptions, 27, 273
job interviews, 519–531
  appearance in, 525, 526–528
  arrival for, 529
  candidate's questions in, 525, 526
  checklists for, 529, 532
  close of, 531–532
  confidence in, 525
  discriminatory questions in, 530–531
  following up after, 533–536
  international, 528
  interviewer's questions in, 524, 525
  media for, 520–521
  note taking after, 532–533
  practicing for, 526
  preparing for, 523–529
  question-and-answer stage of, 530–531
  sequence of, 519
  simulators for, 526, 527
  stages of, 529–532
  things to take to, 529
  types of, 519–520
  warm-up in, 530
job market, xli, xlii, 481–482
job offer, 519, 532
  accepting, 533–535
  declining, 535–536
job recruiters, 22, 512–513
job search, xliv–xlviii, 479–485
  apps for, xlviii
  blunders in, 484–485
  see also job interviews; résumés
job simulations, 521, 526, 527
jobs skills tests, 522
journalistic approach, 104, 114, 123
justification, of type, 170–171, 547
justification reports, 344

K

keyboards, for mobile devices, 109
keyword searches, for résumés, 491

keyword summary, on résumés, 491, 492, 499
keywords, 310
knowledge and understanding needs, 290
knowledge management system, 103, 328

L

labor force. See workforce
language
  abusive, 265
  bias-free, 131–132
  concise, 5
  euphemistic, 130
  obsolete, 136
  plain, 136–137
  pompous, 136
  see also words
language differences, 12–13
language proficiency tests, 522
languages
  spoken in U.S., 71, 72
  studying, 80–81
Latin abbreviations, 593
lay/lie, 596
layout, of slides, 456–459
leadership, in meetings, 45–46
leading, of type, 172
leading questions, 339
Lean Canvas, 342
legal aspects
  of apologizing, 257
  of business communication, 27–28
  of inappropriate employee web use, 19
  of job interviews, 530–531
  of job offer acceptance, 535
  of letters to customers, 265
  of messages in social media, 190
  of negative messages, 261–262
  of preemployment testing, 522
  of recommendation letters, 234
  of rejection letters, 271
  of résumés, 489
  of sales messages, 304
  of termination letters, 273
legal systems, 74
legends, for visuals, 385, 391
legibility, of type, 172
lend/loan, 596
less/fewer, 596
letterhead stationery, 173, 547, 548, 550
letters, 106, 123
  acceptance, 406, 432, 533–535
  additional parts for, 552–554
  application, 513–518
  of authorization, 406, 432
  condolence, 239–240
  declining a request, 256
  declining job offer, 535–536
  folding of, 557, 558
  follow-up, 518–519
  formats for, 173, 554–556
  international, 83–86, 549–551

  recommendation, 234, 236
  rejection, 271–272
  requesting recommendation, 227, 229, 230
  resignation, 536
  standard parts for, 548–552
  termination, 273
  transmittal, 406, 411, 415, 432
Lewis model, 74
liable/likely, 596
libel, 27
library, finding information at, 334
Library of Congress, 209
lie/lay, 578
lifestream, xlvi
lifetime employment, xlii
line charts, 377–378, 391
line length, 547
line spacing, 547
linear organization, 148
linear presentations, 445–446, 454–455
lines of command, 8
LinkedIn, 192
  for community building, 194
  for employee recruiting, 193
  for finding business partners, 193
  for job networking, 484
  recommendations on, 229, 271
  résumé builder on, 489
  résumés on, 499
linking, 371
  in business blogs, 208
linking verbs, 577, 585, 589
list of illustrations, 407, 416
listening
  active, 41
  barriers to, 51
  checklist for, 52
  defensive, 51
  effective, 50, 51
  in intercultural communication, 88
  in job interviews, 530
  nonverbal communication and, 54
  in online conversations, 302
  process of, 50
  selective, 51
  types of, 49–50
  value of, 49
listening skills, 49–52
lists, 164
  capitalization with, 591
  in reports, 421, 423
  in résumés, 497
literally, 596
localizing, of web content, 371
location-aware content, 17
location-based social networking, 191
logic
  flaws in, 294
  in reports, 345–347, 364
logical appeals, 294–296, 308
London, taxis in, 251

long-term athletic development (LTAD), 395
long-term memory, 13, 51–52
lose-lose outcomes, 40
low-context cultures, 73–74, 92
loyalty, to employer, 453
-*ly* adverbs, 581
lying
    nonverbal cues to, 54
    on résumés, 489

M

m-commerce, 304
mailing abbreviations, 557, 558
mailing notation, 554
main idea, 113–114, 312
    defining, 113
    for negative messages, 253
    in oral presentations, 446, 447
    in outlining, 116
    for persuasive messages, 291
    in routine messages, 232
    of positive messages, 232
major points
    in oral presentations, 447
    in outlining, 116–117
manipulation, in sales messages, 304
manners, 75
many/much, 596
maps, 382
margins, 170, 547
    for reports, 560
market analysis reports, 344
market research, using blogs for, 206
marketing
    to children, 305
    conversation, 302–303
    legal aspects of, 27
    text messaging for, 203
marketing intelligence, gathering, 193
marketing messages, 301–304, 308
    in digital media, 189
    for mobile devices, 304
marketing strategy, 341
meals, business, 57
mean, 330, 355
meaning
    denotative versus connotative, 140, 373
    understanding of, 12–13
measurements, 593–594
mechanics, 573, 591–594
media/medium, 10, 11, 31
    audience preferences for, 112
    in communication process, 10, 12
    costs of, 112
    formality and, 112
    for negative messages, 253
    oral, 106, 107
    for oral presentations, 444
    for persuasive messages, 290
    for reports, 323–327
    for résumés, 487
    selecting, 106–112

urgency and, 112
    visual, 107, 108
    written, 106–107, 108
    see also specific media
media curation sites, 336
    see also content curation
media news coverage, bloggers as source
        for, 206
media relations, using blogs for, 205
media richness, 112
media specialists, 290
median, 330, 355
medium/channel combinations, 106–108
meeting people, 57
meetings, 45–49
    checklist for, 47
    conducting, 45–46
    formal, 47
    minutes of, 47
    online, 45
    participation in, 46
    preparing for, 45
    purpose of, 45
    selecting participants for, 45
    technology for, 48–49
    types of, 45
    virtual, 48–49
    web-based, 20
memorization, 51, 463
memory, 13, 50, 51–52
memos, 106, 123
    of acceptance, 406
    distribution of, 560
    format for, 173, 559–560
    reports as, 365-366
    of transmittal, 406, 415
mentoring, 76
message(s)
    of appreciation, 239
    in communication process, 10–11, 12
    competing, 11
    composing, 138–147
    of condolence, 239–240
    of congratulations, 238–239
    decoding of, 10, 12–13
    defined, 10, 31
    delivery of, 10, 12
    distribution of, 175–176
    employment, 485–501, 513–518
    encoding of, 10
    ethical, 105
    filtering of, 18
    follow-up, 533–536
    formality of, 112
    goodwill, 238–240
    informative, 237
    of inquiry, 533
    length of, 114–115
    marketing, 301–304
    negative, 252–274
    organization of, 161
    positive, 229, 232–233

producing, 170–174
proofreading of, 174–175
purpose of, 101, 113
retention of, 13
revising, 159–169
sales, 301–304
scope of, 114–115
tact in, 130
timing of, 101
topic of, 113
types of detail in, 117
unnecessary, 18
urgent, 18
whether worth sending, 101
see also negative messages; persuasive
    messages; routine messages;
    three-step process
metaphors, 296
metasearch engines, 335, 355
microblogs/microblogging, 23, 188, 189,
    209–210, 216
see also Twitter
micromessaging, internal, 209
Microsoft PowerPoint. See PowerPoint
military service, on résumés, 490
millennials, 77
mind mapping, 114
minorities, 70
minutes, of meetings, 47, 62
misquoting, 24
mission statement, 341
mistakes, finding, 174
misunderstanding, listening and, 51
MLA style, 427, 565–566
*MLA Style Manual and Guide to Scholarly
    Publishing*, 562
mobile apps, 15, 20
    AuthorStream, 456
    business, 20
    City Sourced, 293
    Databox, 324
    Diversity Now, 69
    Dragon Dictation, 138
    Dropbox, 412
    Evernote, 103, 337
    Freedcamp, 41
    Genius Scan, 170
    Hightail, 232
    Instapaper, 329
    iTranslate, 81
    for job search, xlviii, 482, 483
    Lettr, 239
    Locale, 58
    LogMein, 412
    MediaFire, 412
    Mobile Podcaster, 191
    Notebook, 103
    NounPlus, 174
    One Note, 337
    Pages, 144
    Pocket Letter Pro, 265
    Pocket, 18

mobile apps (*continued*)
PRSA Ethics, 26
Redbooth, 400
for résumés, 482
Sage Evolution Dashboard, 324
Skype, 519
SlideShark, 459
Social Oomph, 194
Videoshop, 383
WebEx Mobil, 48
WhatsApp, 19, 111
Yelp, 267
mobile communication
as a communication platform, 15–16
as a disruptive technology, 15
effect on business communication, 16–18
mobile devices
business uses of, 110–111
for collaboration, 43, 44
designing messages for, 173, 174
executive dashboard on, 324, 325
job recruiting via, xlviii
for job search, 482, 483
during meetings, 46
optimizing content for, 191
for presentations, 459–460
promotional messages for, 304
for research, 337
unique challenges of, 109
visual media on, 385, 387
writing messages for, 148, 149
mobile-first strategy, 16, 343
mobile phones, 15–18
use during job interviews, 529
in workplace, 56
see also smartphones
mobile technology, 15–18
mobile VoIP, 20
moblogs, 191
mode, 330, 355
model release forms, 384
modifiers, 580–582
double, 169
dangling, 166, 167
misplaced, 585–586
placement of, 166, 167, 582
monitor/control reports, 340
monitoring tools, online, 335
monotone
in interviews, 526
in phone calls, 56
mood, of verbs, 579
motivation, of audience, 13, 289, 290
MTV generation, 77
multimedia documents, 371
multimedia presentations, 459
multimedia résumés, 498, 499
multitasking, 11, 17
etiquette of, 58

N

narration, as type of detail, 117
narratives, in digital media, 189
navigation
of online reports, 371
of websites, 343–344
navigational slides, 460, 461, 462
near-field communication (NFC), 111
needs, of audience, 132, 289, 290, 301
negative adverbs, 581
negative information
hiding, 375
in positive messages, 232
withholding, 260
negative messages, 130
buffers in, 258
checklists for, 261
completing, 254–255
declining job offer, 535–536
direct approach for, 253–254, 255–257, 263
about employment, 270–273
goals of, 252
indirect approach for, 253–254, 257–260, 263
of resignation, 536
about organizations, 267–270
organizing, 253–254
planning, 252–253
refusing claims, 265, 265
refusing requests, 263
three-step process for, 252–257
about transactions, 264–265
writing, 254
negotiation, cultural differences in, 74
neither/nor, 578
nervousness
in job interviews, 525
in presentations, 464–465
Net Generation, 77
netiquette, 202
networked organizations, 193
networking, for job hunters, 482, 506

see also social networking

networks, communication, 8
news releases, 237–238, 243, 269
newsfeeds, 305, 335
for business blogs, 208
newsletters, email, 305
newspapers, as resources, 334
noise, as communication barrier, 11, 12
nominative pronouns, 575–576
nonlinear presentations, 445–446, 455
nonrestrictive clauses, 588
nonverbal communication, 52–54, 62
checklist for, 54
cultural differences in, 75–76
culture and, 53
in job interviews, 526, 528
norms, 38, 62
cultural, 72
group, 38

note cards, for oral presentations, 448
note taking, apps for, 337, 482
notes, speaking from, 461
noun sequences, long, 166, 167
nouns, 573–586
numbers
in international communication, 84–85
misrepresenting, 24
style for, 593

O

objections
anticipating, 296, 301
handling, 41
objective pronouns, 575–576
objectivity
credibility and, 132
in persuasive messages, 291
observational research, 337
obsolete phrases, 136
occupations, researching, xliv
office technology, 20
one-page websites, 343–344
online databases, 335, 355
Open Directory Project, 335
open-ended interviews, 520, 540
open-ended questions, 339, 355
opening
of claims requests, 229
of condolence messages, 239
importance of, 162
of job application letters, 516
of job interviews, 530
of messages, 115
of negative messages, 255, 258
of oral presentations, 450
of persuasive messages, 293, 299
of positive messages, 232
of proposals, 405
of reports, 364, 405
of routine messages, 232
of routine requests, 226
of sales messages, 302
openness, culture and, 75
operating reports, 340
operations plan, 342
opinion polls, 339
opinions, 5
in online communications, 57
opt-in email, 305
optimism, 8
false, 267, 456
in negative messages, 260
oral media, 106, 107
feedback in, 130
oral presentations, 442–467
audience analysis for, 442, 443, 444
being introduced for, 451
choosing method for, 461, 463
completing, 460–464
concluding, 465
creating slides for, 454–460

delivery of, 464–467
direct versus indirect approach for, 446
editing, 460
formality of, 449–450
length of, 446
memorizing, 463
organizing, 445–449
outlines for, 447–448
planning of, 442–448
practicing, 446, 463–464
preparing for, 464
purpose of, 442, 444
question period in, 465
three-step process for, 442, 443
writing, 449–453
ordinal numbers, 594
organization charts, 382, 391
for outlining, 116
organization (of messages), 112–118
evaluating, 161
good, 112–113
of negative messages, 253–254
of persuasive messages, 291
of reports, 325–327
organizational culture, 291
organizations, communication within, 8
orientations, writing, 189
outline/outlining, 115–116, 326–327
for analytical report, 345, 349
for oral presentations, 447–448
preliminary, 346
over-the-top (OTT) application, 111
overhead transparencies, 453
oversimplification, 295, 375

P

page numbering, in reports, 414, 416, 417,
    418, 561
panel interviews, 520, 540
panic reset button, 531
paper
    for business documents, 547
    for envelopes, 556
    for résumés, 498
paragraphs, 144–147
    developing, 147
    length of, 163–164
    in letter formats, 555
    for mobile messages, 148, 173
parallelism, 165, 583, 586
    with conjunctions, 583
    visual, 374
paraphrasing, 331
    when listening, 51
parentheses, 590
parliamentary procedure, 46, 62
participative management, 37, 62
participles, 579–580
passive voice, 137, 138, 153, 271, 579
passwords, creating, 58
past participle, 578
patents, 333

payoff, for teasers, 189
PDF format, 371
    for reports, 412
    for résumés, 499
pecha-kucha, 474
percentages, 593
perception, 12, 31, 51
perfect participle, 580
performance
    striving to excel and, 485
    in teams, 38
performance reviews, 252, 272–273, 278
periodicals, as resources, 334
periods, 586
see also abbreviations
personal activity reports, 340
personal appearance
    as nonverbal communication, 53
    in workplace, 54–55
personal attacks, online, 57
personal brand, xlvii–xlix, 482
personal data, on résumés, 493
personal pronouns, 575
    in active versus passive voice, 137
    on résumés, 490
personal space, 53, 75, 79
personality tests, 522
persuasion, 288, 308
    as purpose of message, 101, 113
    negative connotations of, 304
persuasive arguments, 5
persuasive messages, 130, 288–305
    AIDA model for, 293–294
    checklist for, 297
    common mistakes in, 297
    common types of, 297–300
    developing, 292–297
    direct approach for, 291, 293, 299
    ethics of, 304–305
    indirect approach for, 291, 293
    organization of, 291
    proposals as, 367
    in social media, 194, 302–303
    three-step process for, 288–292
phablet, 111
phone networks, 110
phone skills, 56–57
    for job interviews, 520–521
phones. See smartphones; text messaging
photographs, 108, 382–383
    from mobile devices, 337
    permission to use, 305
phrases, 142, 584
    parallelism in, 165
    transitional, 146, 597–598
    wordy, 168, 169
pie charts, 380, 391
piercings, 56
pitch, 400, 442
plagiarism, 24
plain language, 136–137
plain text, for résumés, 499

planning outline, 448–449
planning stage, 99–119
    for analytical reports, 344–349
    for business blogs, 206–207
    checklist for, 119
    for email messages, 199
    for informational reports, 340–344
    for instant messages, 203
    for interviews, 339
    for meetings, 45
    for negative messages, 252–253
    for oral presentations, 442–448
    for persuasive messages, 288–291,
        299, 300
    for podcasts, 211
    for proposals, 349–351
    for reports and proposals, 321–351
    for research, 327, 328
    for résumés, 485–489
    for routine and positive messages,
        226–227, 228
plans, 340
plural nouns, 574, 578
podcasting channels, 211, 216
podcasts/podcasting, 22, 188, 210–211, 216
    business uses of, 211
    checklist for, 212
    creating, 211
    distributing, 211
    mobile apps for, 191, 212
    as research source, 329
    video, 210
policy discussions, via blogs, 205
policy reports, 340
policy statements, 237
politeness, 75
political systems, 81
pompous language, 136
portfolio. See employment portfolio
position papers, 340
positive approach, 8, 130–131, 254,
    255, 291
positive messages
    checklist for, 233
    granting claims, 233–234, 235
    providing recommendations, 234, 236
possessive nouns, 574, 589
possessive pronouns, 576
postal codes, 557, 558
postscript, in letters, 554
posture, 52, 76
power and control needs, 290
PowerPoint, 453, 456
    "death by," 453, 455
    mobile version of, 17
    for résumés, 498
    see also slides
preaching, 136
predicate, 142, 166, 167, 583, 584
predicate adjectives, 580, 585
predicate nominative, 585
preemployment testing, 522

prefatory parts
  numbering of, 561
  for proposals, 410–411
  for reports, 403–408, 411, 414–418
prefixes, hyphenation of, 589
prejudice, 132
prepositional phrases, 166, 167, 582, 588
prepositions, 582–583
presence awareness, 202
presentation software, 453
presentation visuals, 453–460
  checklist for, 463
  completing, 460–464
  see also slides
presentations
  electronic, 453–460
  linear versus nonlinear, 445–446,
    454–455
  using mobile devices for, 459–460
  online, 466–467
  see also oral presentations
press releases, 237–238
previews
  in oral presentations, 451
  in podcasts, 211
  in reports, 364, 370
primary research, 329, 337–340, 355
print media, 106, 107, 108, 188
Priority Mail International, 559
privacy
  as American value, 79
  of information, 24
  invasion of, 305
  media choice and, 112
  of messages, 176
  mobile devices and, 17
  of online messages, 58
  of research participants, 328
  preemployment testing and, 522
  social media and, 190
problem, defining, 344
problem factoring, 344, 355
problem solving
  cultural differences in, 74
  mobile devices and, 17
problem-solving reports, 344, 365–366
problem-solving teams, 37, 39, 62
problem/solution, as way to develop
    paragraphs, 147
problem statement, 322, 328, 355
  in proposals, 367, 405
process monitoring, text messaging for, 203
product champions, 19, 23
product review sites, 225
product reviews, by bloggers, 27, 208
production, of messages, 170–174
productivity
  mobile devices and, 17
  in teams, 38
  technology and, 19
products
  benefits of, 301

capitalization of, 592
claims for, 305
features of, 301
information about, 333
professional titles, 591
professionalism, xliii, 5, 7, 8, 31
  accountability and, 134
  being team player and, 453
  dependability and, 134
  striving to excel and, 485
progress reports, 340
project management
  using blogs, 205
  using mobile devices, 111
promotional communication, 27, 194, 304
pronouns, 575–576
  cultural differences and, 129
  personal, 128–129
  relative, 169
proofreading, 174–175
  checklist for, 175
  of persuasive messages, 292
  of reports and proposals, 412
proofreading symbols, 160, 570
proper adjectives, 580, 591
proper nouns, 574, 591
property, intellectual, 328
proposal writing, software for, 371
proposals, 106, 321, 322, 355
  AIDA plan for, 367
  body of, 405
  checklists for, 370, 428
  close of, 405
  components of, 410–411
  drafting content for, 367–370
  examples of, 350–351, 368–369, 401–404
  internal versus external, 349
  opening of, 405
  planning of, 349–351
  prefatory parts for, 405
  proofreading of, 412
  rejecting, 263
  revision of, 400
  solicited, 349
  statement of purpose for, 323
  three-step process for, 321
  types of, 349
  unsolicited, 325
  using technology for, 370–371
  work plan for, 323, 324
prospecting, for jobs, 513
provinces, abbreviations for, 558
psychographics, 289, 308
public opinion, tracking, 193
public relations, using blogs for, 205
public relations department, 238
public speaking. See oral presentations
*Publication Manual of the American Psychological
    Association*, 562
punctuality, 79
punctuation, 586–590
  letter format and, 555–556

open, 555–556
spacing and, 547–548
purpose
  of analytical reports, 344
  of business blogs, 206–207
  defining, 101
  general, 101, 113
  of meetings, 45
  of negative messages, 252
  of oral presentations, 442, 444
  of persuasive messages, 289
  of podcasts, 211
  of proposals, 367
  of reports and proposals, 321–323, 364
  of research, 328
  statement of, 321–323, 355
  of visuals, 375
  specific, 101, 113

Q

qualifications, in proposals, 369, 405
quality of hire, 480–481
question-and-answer chain, 114
question-and-answer period, 465
question marks, 586
questionnaires, 338–339
questions
  discriminatory, 530–531
  in job interviews, 524, 525
  in request letters, 227
  for research interviews, 339
  for surveys, 338
quick response (QR) codes, 111
quotation marks, 590
quotations, 588
quoting, from sources, 331

R

racial bias, 131, 132
radical connectivity, 17
Radio Generation, 77
raise/rise, 578
Re:, 552
readability
  designing for, 170–173
  of reports, 400
  revising for, 162–165
  of text slides, 456, 458
readability indexes, 162
reality, augmented, 191
reasoning
  in analytical reports, 345–347
  circular, 295
  in logical appeals, 294
receiver, of message, 3, 10, 11, 12, 50
  see also audience
recommendations, 332, 355
  focusing on, 345
  placement of, 366
  providing, 234, 236
  refusing requests for, 236, 270–271
  report based on, 365–366

in reports, 325, 409, 426
requesting, 227, 229, 230
from research, 332
recruiting, 512–513
using blogs, 205
using mobile devices, 111
social, 478–479
using social media, 193, 197
redundancy, 168, 169
reference initials, 552
reference librarians, 334
reference management, 336
reference materials, for digital media, 189
references
for résumés, 493
refusing requests for, 270–271
requesting, 227
References list, 409, 427, 563, 564
regardless, 596
rehearsal, of oral presentations, 464
rejection letters, 271–272
relative pronouns, 575
reliability
of sources, 329
of surveys, 337
religion
cultural differences in, 77
respect for, 79
religious beliefs, 81
religious symbolism, in body art, 56
remarketing, 304
remote workforce management, 111
"Reply All," 58, 200
reports, 106, 321
amount of detail to include in, 364
binding of, 560
body of, 405, 409
checklists for, 370, 428
close of, 366, 405, 409
completing stage for, 400–428
components of, 403–410
composing, 361–373
cover for, 404, 414
distributing, 176, 412, 428
documentation of, 562–567
drafting content for, 363–367
feedback on, 428
formality of, 361–362, 400
format for, 560–561
integrating visuals into, 384
length of, 321, 366, 408
online, 371, 400
opening of, 405
organizing, 325–327
page breaks in, 402
prefatory parts for, 403–408, 411, 414–418
producing, 401–410
proofreading of, 412
revision of, 400
statement of purpose for, 321–323
supplementary parts of, 409–410, 411

three-step process for, 321
types of, 322, 340
using technology for, 370–371
work plan for, 323, 324
see also analytical reports; informational reports
request for proposals (RFP), 349, 355, 367, 371, 410
requests
declining, 256
making, 226–233
persuasive, 299, 300
refusing, 264, 263
see also routine requests
resale information, 233, 258
research
conducting, 327–332
drawing conclusions from, 331–332
ethical aspects of, 328
innovative technologies for, 336
using mobile devices, 337
planning, 327, 328
of potential employers, 481–482
primary, 329, 337–340
purpose of, 328
using results of, 330–332
secondary, 329, 332–336
summarizing results of, 330
research managers, 336
resignation, letters of, 536
resistance, overcoming, 40–41, 296
resources, business, 332–336
respect, in intercultural communication, 74, 78
restrictive clauses, 588
résumés, 485–501, 506
activities/achievements section on, 493
adapting to audience, 489–491
apps for creating, 482
as attachments, 500
career objective on, 491
checklist for, 501
chronological, 487–488, 496
combination, 488, 494, 495
contact information on, 491
content of, 490–493
cover letters for, 513–518
customizing, 482–483
deception on, 489
distributing, 500–501
education section on, 492
emailing, 499, 500
fallacies about, 487
formats for, 497–498, 499–500
functional, 488
including photo with, 498
infographic, 498
introductory statement on, 491
length of, 497
mailing, 500
media for, 487
mistakes on, 500
multimedia, 499

online, 497, 499–500
organization of, 487–489
paper for, 499
personal data on, 493
plain text file for, 499
planning, 485–489
PowerPoint, 498
producing, 497–500
proofreading, 500
purpose of, 486, 487
red flags in, 488–489
sample, 494–496
scannable, 499
social media, 499–500
three-step process for, 485, 486
trendy, 486
video, 498
work experience on, 492
writing, 489–493
retweeting, 209
review sections, in reports, 370
reviews, in podcasts, 211
revision, 159–169
checklist for, 168
of others' work, 162
RFP. See request for proposals
Roberts Rules of Order, 46
roles
culture and, 74–75
in teams, 38–39
routine messages, 226–239
announcing good news, 237–238
asking for information or action, 227, 228
checklist for, 233
of congratulations, 238–239
direct approach for, 226, 227
of goodwill, 238–240
making claims, 229, 231
making requests, 226–233
requesting adjustments, 229, 231
requesting recommendation, 227, 229, 230
sharing information, 237
three-step process for, 226–227, 228
routine requests, 226–233
checklist for, 227
replying to, 233–240
RSS feeds, 195, 208
rumor mill, 8
rumors, online, 268–289

S

safety and security needs, 290
salary requirements
in application letters, 516, 517
in job interviews, 532
sales messages, 301–304, 308
AIDA model for, 302
in digital media, 189
legal aspects of, 304
for mobile devices, 304

sales proposals, 349
sales prospects, 193
salutations, 173, 551, 591
salutopening, 551
samples, representative, 337–338
sampling bias, 338
sandbox, in wikis, 372
sans serif typefaces, 172, 176, 459
saving face, 76
scannable résumés, 499
scanners, for business cards, 482
scanning apps, 337
scope
    of business blogs, 207
    of messages, 114–115, 123
    for oral presentations, 446
    of persuasive messages, 291
    of proposals, 367
    of reports, 364
screen size, of mobile devices, 109
screencasts, 195, 444
screening interviews, 519
search engine optimization (SEO), 310
search engines, 310, 335, 355
    job, 481
search tips, for online research, 335–336
second-page heading, in letters, 552
secondary research, 329, 332–336, 355
security
    of information, 24
    of instant messages, 203
    media choice and, 112
    of messages, 176
    mobile devices and, 17
    social media and, 190
    text messaging for, 203
selection interviews, 519
selective listening, 51, 62
selective perception, 12, 31
self-actualization, 290
self-confidence, in public speaking, 464–465
self-oriented roles, 38–39, 62
selling points, 301, 308
    in job application letters, 516
semicolons, 142, 585, 587, 598
sender, of message, 3, 10, 12
seniority, culture and, 76
sensory memory, 13
sentence fragments, 584
sentences, 142–144
    grammar of, 583–586
    length of, 163
    overly long, 166–167
    parallelism in, 165
    parenthetical words or phrases in, 588
    preposition at end of, 582
    spacing after, 547
    topic, 144–145
    types of, 142
sentiment analysis, 193
sequence, report organization based on, 341
series, comma with, 587

serif fonts, 459
serif typefaces, 172, 176
sexual harassment, inappropriate web
    use and, 19
shared workspaces, 20, 42, 43, 62
short-term memory, 13, 51
sidebars, 384
sign language interpreters, 464
signature block, 173, 551–552, 552
signature file, for emails, 202
simple sentences, 142, 153, 578, 584
simplicity
    as design principle, 170, 374
    in designing slides, 459
    in presentation design, 453–454
simulators, for job interviews, 521
sincerity
    in condolence messages, 239
    credibility and, 133
    in negative messages, 257, 260
sit/set, 578
situation, analyzing, 100–103
situational interviews, 520, 540
sketching
    as discovery technique, 104
    with touchscreen apps, 337
skills, assessing one's, xliv, xlv
skills résumé, 488
skimming
    aids to, 163
    of reports, 400
    of websites, 371
slander, 27
slang, 85
slide builds, 459, 471
slide deck, 445
slide master, 459
slide shows, 453–460
slide sorter view, 460
slide transitions, 459, 471
slides
    artwork for, 459
    background designs for, 457
    checklist for, 463
    creating, 454–460
    design elements for, 456–459
    free-form, 454–455
    key visuals for, 456, 457
    layout of, 456–459
    navigational, 460, 461, 462
    readability of, 459
    structured, 454–455
    templates for, 459
    text, 455, 456, 458
slideuments, 456
Small Business Administration, 341
SmartArt, in PowerPoint, 457
smartphones, 15–16, 20
    for blogging, 191
    challenges of, 109
    composing messages for, 148
    presentations on, 459–460

shopping use of, 304
    see also mobile technology
smartwatches, 191
social behavior, cultural differences in,
    74–75
social communication model, 13–14, 31
social customer service, 193
social customs, cultural differences in, 81
social intranet, 42
social media, 14, 31
    for brief messages, 188
    creating content for, 189–191
    defined, 187, 216
    employee misuse of, 19
    etiquette for, 58
    Get Satisfaction's use of, 225–226
    GoPro's use of, 186–187
    H&R Block use of, 98–99
    handling rumors in, 268–269
    headlines in, 190
    informality of, 190
    innovations for business communica-
        tion, 196–197
    JetBlue's use of, 2–3
    for job search networking, 484
    maintaining consistent personality
        in, 194
    mobile communication and, 16
    for news releases, 238
    oral presentations and, 466
    for persuasive messages, 290
    for presentations, 465
    promotional messages for, 302–303
    responding to negative information in,
        267–269
    as source of stress, 167
    VMWare use of, 479
social media release, 238, 237
social media résumés, 499–500
social network sites
    distributing résumés via, 499
    embarrassing information on, xlvii
    job search and, 484
social networking technologies, 42–43, 62
social networks/networking, 23, 188,
    191–194, 216
    business communication uses of, 42,
        192–194
    for customer interaction, 225–226
    employment background checks
        and, 522
    location-based, 191
    personal brand and, xlviii
    private, 192
    refusing recommendations requests
        from, 271
    value-added content via, 196
social recruiting, 478–479
socialization, brand, 193
solicited application letters, 513, 514,
    516, 540
solicited proposals, 349, 367, 368–369, 411

source notes, 563
sources
    bibliography of, 409
    citing, 291
    documenting, 336, 364, 562–567
    evaluating, 329
spacing, of type, 172
spam, 304
spam filters, 11
speaking
    in intercultural communication, 88
    rate of, 51
speaking notes, 461
    for podcasts, 211
speaking outline, 448
special effects, in slide shows, 459
specific purpose, 101, 123
speech analytics software, 20
speech anxiety, 464–465
speech recognition, 20
speech synthesis, 20
speeches. See oral presentations
spelling, 596–597
spim, 203
stage fright, 464–465
stakeholders, 5, 31
    online communication by, 267–269
    social media and, 187
states, abbreviations for, 557, 558
stationery, letterhead, 173, 547,
        548, 550
Statistical Abstract of the United States, 334
statistics
    analyzing, 331
    misleading, 24
    resources for, 333
status, culture and, 74–75
status updates, in social media, 189
stealth marketing, 24
stereotyping, 73, 92, 132
story of you, xlvii, 479–481, 524
storyteller's tour, 114
storytelling approach, 119
    in digital media, 189
    in oral presentations, 447
stress interviews, 520, 540
structured interviews, 519, 540
structured slides, 454–455, 471
style, 134, 153
    for business blogs, 205, 207–208
    controlling, 134–137
    evaluating, 161
    for executive summary, 408
    for reports and proposals, 361
    for résumés, 491
    mechanics of, 591
    sentence, 143–144
style manuals, 562
subheadings, 145, 165, 176
    in reports, 370
    in résumés, 497
    typefaces for, 172

subject, of sentence, 142, 166, 167, 583
subject line
    attention-getting, 293
    for email messages, 118, 199
    in letters, 552
    for memos, 559
    for mobile messages, 148
subject-verb agreement, 578, 583–584
subjunctive mood, 579
subordinate conjunctions, 583, 583
substance abuse testing, 522
success
    attitudes about, 74
    visualizing, 464
suggestions, rejecting, 263
summarizing
    of research, 330, 331
    from sources, 331, 332
summary
    in digital media, 189
    of qualifications, on résumés, 491–492
summary, in reports, 409
superlative degree, 580
superscripts
    for footnotes, 562
    for ordinal numbers, 594
supplementary parts
    for proposals, 411
    for reports, 409–410, 411
surface chart, 377–378, 391
surveys, 337–339
    mobile, 337
    online, 339
Sweden, 82
symbolism, visual, 373
symbols, in word processors, 548
sympathy, in making apologies, 257
sympathy messages, 239–240
synopsis
    in proposals, 410
    in reports, 407, 432

T
table of contents, 406–407, 416
tables, 376–377, 391
    in reports, 425
    for slides, 456
    standard parts of, 377
tablets, 20
    for blogging, 191
    presentations on, 459–460
    unique challenges of, 109
    see also mobile devices
tact
    in business messages, 130
    in condolence messages, 239
    in negative messages, 265
    in responding to claims, 234
tag cloud, 208, 380
tagging, 208, 216
tagging sites, 336
talent management systems, 22

target markets, 193
targeting, behavioral, 304
task forces, 37, 62
task-oriented roles, 39, 62
tattoos, 56
team-maintenance roles, 39, 62
team player, 7, 453
team skills, xliii
teams,
    advantages of, 37–38
    blogging as communication medium
        for, 205
    communication in, 37–41
    conflict in, 39, 40
    cultural differences and, 70
    defined, 37, 62
    developing via social networking, 193
    disadvantages of, 38
    effective, 38
    evolution of, 39–40
    use of mobile devices by, 111
    problem-solving, 37
    roles in, 38–39
    use of social networks by, 42–43
    types of, 37
    working online, 20
teasers, in digital media, 189, 209
technology
    for business communication, 18–24
    for collaborative writing, 42–44
    keeping in perspective, 18
    for presentations, 465
    for producing reports, 370–371
    using productively, 18–19
    see also mobile devices
telecommuting, 17
teleconferences, 48, 210–211
telephone etiquette, 56–57
telephone interviews, 520–521
telepresence, 20, 48, 49
templates
    for slides, 454, 456, 457
    for visuals, 384
    for wikis, 372
temporary workers, xlii
tense, of verbs, 577, 578
termination, for cause, 488
termination letters, 273
testing, preemployment, 522
text boxes, 371
text messaging, 17, 188, 202, 216
    business uses of, 202–203
    casual tone of, 135
    see also instant messaging
text tables, 376
thank-you messages, 239, 533
There are, 168, 169
thinking, styles of, 13
three-step process, 99–100
    allotting time for, 100
    for business blogs, 206–207
    for email messages, 199–201

three-step process (*continued*)
    for instant messaging, 203
    for negative messages, 252–255, 255–257
    for oral presentations, 442, 443
    for persuasive messages, 288–292, 299, 300
    for podcasts, 211
    for proposals, 321
    for recommendation requests, 229, 230
    for reports, 321
    for résumés, 485, 486
    for routine and positive messages, 226–227, 228
    for routine requests, 226–227, 228
    see also completing stage; planning stage; writing stage
time, concepts of, 75, 79
time allotment, for writing, 100
time and space, as nonverbal communication, 53
time extension, request for, 533, 535
time limits, for oral presentations, 446
time management, xliii
Times New Roman, 172
title fly, 404–405, 414, 432
title page, 404–405, 414, 432
title slides, 460, 461
titles
    capitalization of, 592
    for oral presentations, 448
    professional, 549, 550
    for visuals, 385, 391
tolerance, in intercultural communication, 78
tone, 134, 153
    for blogs, 205
    of claims letters, 229
    of condolences, 239
    controlling, 135–136
    conversational, 135–136
    evaluating, 161
    formality of, 135
    for instant messages, 204
    for negative messages, 255, 265, 265
    objective, 137
    in oral presentations, 452
    of positive messages, 232
    for reports and proposals, 361
    for routine requests, 226
topic, of message, 113, 123
topic sentence, 144–145, 153
topical organization, 340, 355
touching, 53, 75
touchscreens, 109
touchscreen apps, 337
trade journals, as resources, 334
trade shows, for networking, 484
trademarks, 333
traditionalists, 77
training
    using mobile devices, 110
    using podcasts, 211

transactions, bad news about, 264–265
transitions, 146–147, 153, 597–598
    in international correspondents, 84
    list of, 146
    in oral presentations, 447, 451
    in podcasts, 211
    in reports, 370, 424
    in slide shows, 459
transitive verbs, 578
translation, of web content, 371
translation apps, 80, 81, 88
translation software, 88
translators, 88
transmittal
    letter of, 364, 406, 415
    memo of, 406, 415
transparency
    of information, 24, 31
    requirements for, 27
    social media and, 187, 190
travel, advice on, 80
travel industry, 260
trends, 331, 355
    visuals showing, 377
troubleshooting reports, 344, 346
trust, in teams, 38
try and, 596
tutorials, in social media, 189
twebinars, 444
Tweetables, 189, 238, 466
Tweetups, 196, 484
Twitter, 23, 209–210
    backchannels on, 444, 465–466
    H&R Block use of, 98
    job boards via, 481
    for job networking, 484
    legal aspects of, 190
    monitoring tools for, 335
    teasers in, 189
    Toyota's use of, 2–3
    Zappos' use of, 197
Twittersphere, 205
Twitterstream, 466
2 + 2 approach, 346, 347–348, 355
type
    justified, 170–171
    for slides, 459
    for websites, 173
type size, 173
    for slides, 459
type styles, 172, 176
typefaces, 172, 176
    for résumés, 497
typographical errors, 174
typography, 172–173

U
underlining, 172, 592
unemployment, xlii
unified communication, 43
United Kingdom, 81
Universal Postal Union, 551

unsolicited application letters, 513, 515, 540
unsolicited proposals, 350, 367, 411
uppercase letters, 172
upward communication, 8
urgency, of messages, 18, 200
U.S. Air Force, 269
U.S. Department of Agriculture, 362
U.S. Department of Health and Human Services, 362
U.S. Postal Service, 557, 558
usage, 138, 573, 595–596
USDA Center for Nutrition Policy and Promotion, 475
user authentication, with IM, 203
user-generated content, 23, 195, 216

V
validity, of surveys, 337
value-added content, 196–197
values, cultural differences in, 79, 81
venture capitalists, 399
verb phrases, 577
verb-preposition idioms, 582
verbal, 596
verbals, 579
verbs, 576–580
    action, 490
    camouflaged, 166, 167
    linking, 577, 585, 589
    voice of, 137, 138
video, 384
    business uses of, 195
    online, 22
    in slide shows, 459
    value-added content via, 197
    see also YouTube
video interviews, 521
video podcasts, 210
video recording, 337
video résumés, 498
videoconferences, 20, 48–49
viral marketing, using blogs for, 206
virtual communities, 42
virtual meetings, 48–49, 62
virtual office, 42
virtual online interviews, 521
virtual organizations, xli, 193
virtualization, 478–479
virus protection, 57, 202
vision, reading online content and, 342
visual aids, 117
visual literacy, 373, 391
visual media, 107, 108
visual symbolism, 373, 391
visualization, 464
visuals
    audience needs and, 384
    benefits of, 453
    for concepts and ideas, 380–383
    creating, 384
    designing, 373–374
    distortion of, 24, 374–375

effective, 373–387
integrating into text, 384
numbering of, 420
placement of, 385, 419
for presenting data, 375, 377–380
producing, 383–387
proofing, 385
purpose of, 375
referring to, 384, 420
titles for, 419
types of, 375–383
when to use, 375, 376
see also presentation visuals; specific types of visuals
Vital Speeches of the Day, 473
vocabulary, 594–597
vocal characteristics
in job interviews, 526
as nonverbal communication, 52
voice, of verbs, 137, 138, 579
voice recognition, of smartphones, 109
voicemail, 56–57
volunteering, as means of networking, 484

W

"walk-arounds," 106
want ads, responding to, 514
wardrobe, business, 55
warm-up, in job interviews, 530
wearable technologies, 16, 191
web accessibility, 78
Web Accessibility Initiative, 299
web directories, 335, 355
web-based meetings, 20, 48–49
webcasts, 444, 453
webinars, 453
webpages, search engines and, 335
websites
careers, 482
collaborative writing for, 42
content for, 342–344
designing for mobile viewing, 16
for employment portfolios, xlvi
for global audience, 371
job, 481
mobile-friendly, 191
one-page, 343–344
organization of, 344
posting résumés to, 499, 500
as research source, 329
writing for, 371
see also Internet

Webster's Style Manual, 591
well/good, 581
whistleblowing, 262, 278
white papers, 340
white space, 170, 176
in mobile messages, 173
on résumés, 497
whiteboards, 453
wikis, 21, 42, 62, 325
benefits of, 42
collaborating on, 371–372
creating new, 372
purpose of, 372
as research source, 329
revising, 372
win-win strategy, 40
women, in workforce, 76
word choice, 140–142
in international correspondence, 83–84
in logical arguments, 296
word division, 594
word processing
to create table of contents, 407
for résumés, 499
source documentation tools in, 336
word-of-mouth marketing, 206
words
abstract, 140, 573
concrete, 140, 573
correct use of, 138–139
denotative versus connotative, 140
effective, 140, 141
familiar, 140, 141
frequently confused, 594–595
frequently misspelled, 596–597
frequently misused, 595–596
long, 168, 169
positive, 255
powerful, 296
strong versus weak, 140, 141
transitional, 146, 597–598
unnecessary, 168, 169
work, attitudes about, 74
work experience, on résumés, 487–488, 492
work plan, 323, 324, 369, 405
work products, xlvi
workflow, 42
Workforce Management, 482
workforce, xli, xlii
diversity in, 70
integrating with social networks, 192–193
women in, 76, 131

working interviews, 520, 540
workplace
changing, xli–xlii
etiquette in, 54–57
religion in, 77
Works Cited, 409, 427, 563, 567
Works Consulted, 563
workspaces, shared, 20, 42, 43
Writer's Handbook, The, 143
writing, collaborative, 41–42
writing process. See three-step process
writing stage, of three-step process, 99, 100, 127–149
for business blogs, 207–208
checklist for, 150
for email messages, 199
for instant messages, 203–204
for mobile messages, 148, 149
for negative messages, 254
for oral presentations, 449–453
for persuasive messages, 291, 299, 300
for podcasts, 211
for reports and proposals, 361–373
for résumés, 489–493
for routine and positive messages, 226–227, 228
written media, 106–107, 108

X

xenophobia, 72–73, 92

Y

yardstick approach, 346, 349, 355
you, when not to use, 128
"you" attitude, 8–9, 31, 128–129
in job application letters, 516
passive voice and, 137
plain language and, 136
in reports, 361
in sales messages, 304–305
YouTube, 22
business uses of, 195
Google channel on, 78
GoPro use of, 186
H&R Block channel on, 98
Lie-Nielsen Toolworks use of, 197

Z

Zip codes, 557